Recommended citation   Tucker, G. M. and Heath, M. F. (1994) *Birds in Europe: their conservation status*. Cambridge, U.K.: BirdLife International (BirdLife Conservation Series no. 3).

© 1994 BirdLife International

Distributed in the Americas by Smithsonian Institution Press, Washington, DC

ISBN 1 56098 527 5

Series editor   Duncan Brooks
Design   CBA (Cambridge) and Duncan Brooks
Assistant editor   Mike Evans
Layout, text preparation and indexing   Duncan Brooks, Michelle Hines, Regina Pfaff

Text set in Times (9/11 pt) and Optima

Imageset by Spire Origination (Norwich)
Printed and bound in Great Britain by Page Bros (Norwich) Ltd

Cover illustration   Red-backed Shrike *Lanius collurio,* by Norman Arlott.

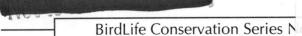

BirdLife Conservation Series N

BI   PE
Their Conservation Status

compiled by
Graham M. Tucker and Melanie F. Heath
with L. Tomiałojć and R. F. A. Grimmett

Maps by Caroline M. Socha and Melanie F. Heath

sponsored by
Royal Society for the Protection of Birds

with additional support from

Vogelbescherming
Nederland

Schweizer Vogelschutz

Swedish Environmental
Protection Agency

Naturvårdsverket

BirdLife®
INTERNATIONAL

BIRDS IN EUROPE: THEIR CONSERVATION STATUS

■

PROJECT STEERING COMMITTEE
M. Avery   O. Biber   R. Fuller   A. Gammell (Chairman)
E. de Juana   T. Larsson   F. Saris   J. van Vessem   T. Wesolowski

■

Data contributions compiled in collaboration with the
European Ornithological Atlas Committee

by

ALBANIA

B. Hallman and F. Lamani

ANDORRA

Associació per a la Defensa de la Natura,
J. Argelich, A. Clamens, J. Crozier,
M.-J. Dubourg, A. Matschke
and M. Pilkington

AUSTRIA

A. Ranner,
with contributions from K. Bauer,
H.-M. Berg, M. Dvorak, A. Gamauf, A. Grüll,
R. Kilzer, A. Landmann, H. Lauermann,
C. Medicus, P. Sackl, O. Samwald,
N. Winding and T. Zuna-Kratky

BELARUS

V. V. Ivanovsky, A. V. Kozulin,
M. E. Nikiforov, I. E. Samusenko,
A. K. Tishechkin and B. V. Yaminsky

BELGIUM

A. Anselin,
with contributions from K. Devos, J. P. Jacob,
P. Meire and J. van Vessem

BULGARIA

P. Iankov,
with contributions from T. Michev,
L. Profirov, B. Ivanov, V. Pomakov,
B. Milchev (Bulgarian Society for the
Protection of Birds)

CROATIA

G. Susic and D. Radovic,
with contributions from T. Mikuska
and J. Mikuska

CYPRUS

M. Charalambides
(Cyprus Ornithological Society)

CZECH REPUBLIC

K. Štastný and V. Bejcek,
with contributions from K. Hudec and J. Hora

DENMARK

M. F. Munk,
with contributions from K. Biledgaard,
F. P. Jensen, H. E. Jørgensen, J. Madsen,
U. G. Sørensen and R. Christensen

FAROE ISLANDS

S. Sørensen

GREENLAND

D. Boertmann,
with contributions from K. Kampp
and K. Falk

ESTONIA

V. Lilleleht,
with contributions from T. Kastepõld,
A. Kuresoo, E. Leibak, A. Leito, A. Leivits,
L. Luigujoe, E. Mägi, T. Randla, O. Renno,
E.Tammur, E. Viht and H. Vilbaste

FINLAND

P. Koskimies,
with contributions from E. Lammi,
M. Mikkola, J. Södersved and R. A. Väisänen

FRANCE

G. Rocamora (Ligue pour la Protection des
Oiseaux), with contributions from
D. Yeatman-Berthelot and
the Société Ornithologique de France

GERMANY
G. Rheinwald,
with contributions from M. Flade, J. Melter,
J. Mooij and
Dachverband Deutscher Avifaunisten

GREECE
G. Catsadorakis and B. Hallman,
with contributions from S. Bourdakis,
S. Csirouhakis, K. Economidis,
V. Hatzirvassanis, M. Malakou, P. Mollat and
K. Poirazidis

HUNGARY
Z. Waliczky,
with contributions from J. Bagyura,
A. Bankovics, L. Haraszthy, L. Holnár,
Z. Kalotás, F. Markus, L. Molnár, E. Schmidt
and T. Szép

ICELAND
Æ. Petersen and O. K. Nielsen,
with contributions from J. Ó. Hilmarsson

REPUBLIC OF IRELAND
E. Callaghan, J. Coveney,
D. W. Gibbons and O. Mearne

ITALY
G. Tallone, M. Gustin, M. Lambertini,
E. Meschini and P. Brichetti,
with contributions from M. Fraissinet

LATVIA
M. Strazds and J. Priedniks
(breeding data),
and G. Vaverinš, J. Priednieks and M. Strazds
(winter data),
with contributions from J. Bauga,
J. Baumanis, M. Bergmanis, U. Bergmanis,
P. Blums, M. Janaus, J. Kazubiernis,
M. Krcilis, J. Lipsbergs, A. Mednis,
A. Petrinš, A. Stipniece and J. Viksne

LIECHTENSTEIN
G. Willi

LITHUANIA
P. Mierauskas,
with contributions from R. R. Budrys,
E. Drobelis, G. Grazulevicius, E. Greimas,
V. Jusys, P. Kurlavicius, G. Margis,
G. Matiukas, S. Paltanavicius, V. Pareigis,
A. Pranaitis, L. Raudonikis and S. Sinkevicius

LUXEMBOURG
D. Crowther and J. Weiss,
with contributions from E. Melchior

MALTA
J. Sultana,
with contributions from
the Research Committee of the
Malta Ornithological Society

MOLDOVA
I. Ganea and N. Zubcov

NETHERLANDS
F. Hustings and J. F. Bekhuis (SOVON)

NORWAY
J. O. Gjershaug, P. G. Thingstad
and S. Eldoy,
with contributions from T. Axelsen,
I. Byrkjedal, A. O. Folkestad, A. Heggland,
J. A. Kålås, V. Ree, J. Sandvik
and G. Bangjord

SVALBARD
V. Bakken

POLAND
M. Gromadzki, P. Chylarecki and A. Sikora,
with contributions from J. Bednorz,
R. Czeraszkiewicz, A. Dombrowski,
W. Górski, A. Jermaczek, A. Sikora,
J. Slupek, A. Staszewski, T. Stawarczyk,
L. Tomialojc, Z. Wojciechowski
and J. Wójciak

PORTUGAL
R. Rufino and R. Neves,
with contributions from P. Catry,
J. C. Farinha, L. Palma, M. Pimenta,
M. Pinto, A. M. Teixeira,
M. de Lourdes Santarém and L. Reino

AZORES

F. M. Medeiros and L. Monteiro

MADEIRA

F. Zino

ROMANIA

D. Munteanu

RUSSIA

V. G. Krivenko, V. O. Avdanin, V. E. Flint,
V. M. Galushin, A. N. Golovkin,
A. S. Koriakin, Y. N. Mineev, E. S. Ravkin
and V. G. Vinogradov,
with contributions from V. P. Belik,
V. T. Butiev, A. V. Filchagov,
A. L. Mischenko, V. Y. Semashko
and P. S. Tomkovich

SLOVAKIA

B. Murin, A. Darolová and Š. Danko,
with contributions from M. Balla, M. Bohuš,
J. Chavko, M. Fulín, S. Harvancík,
P. Kanuch, D. Karaska, P. Karc, D. Kerestúr,
L. Kocian, M. Kornan, J. Kornan, A. Krištín,
R. Kropil, L. Mošanský, S. Pacenovský,
Š. Pcola, P. Pjencák, R. Potocny, P. Rác,
J. Salaj, J. Sládek, J. Somogyi, A. Štollmann,
K. Takác, A. Tirinda, A. Trnka, I. Turcek
and P. Zach

SLOVENIA

I. Geister and A. Sovinc,
with contributions from A. Bibic, F. Bracko,
J. Gregori, T. Jancar, F. Janzekovic,
M. Perušek, B. Štumberger, P. Trontelj
and M. Vogrin

SPAIN

F. J. Purroy, A. Onrubia and J. L. Robles

CANARY ISLANDS

J. J. Naranjo Pérez (breeding data),
K. W. Emmerson and J. A. Lorenzo
(winter data)

SWEDEN

L. Risberg

SWITZERLAND

O. Biber,
with contributions from L. Schifferli
and H. Schmid

TURKEY

S. Baris, J. C. Eames, I. Green, M. Kasparek,
G. Magnin, R. P. Martins, R. F. Porter,
G. Sarigül, G. M. Tucker and M. Yarar,
with contributions from V. van den Berk
and G. Kirwan

UKRAINE

I. M. Gorban,
with contributions from T. B. Ardamatskaya,
V. T. Afanasyev, I. Y. Vergeles,
V. V. Vetrov, M. A. Voinstvensky,
V. I. Gulay, V. N. Grishchenko,
N. L. Klestov, M. P. Knysh, A. I. Koshelev,
V. I. Lysenko, G. N. Molodan, V. D. Siohin,
I. V. Skilsky and I. I. Chernichko

UNITED KINGDOM

R. W. Hudson and D. W. Gibbons,
with contributions from J. H. Marchant,
R. E. Green, G. Williams and A. J. del Nevo

GIBRALTAR

C. Perez and J. Cortes,
with contributions from P. Acolina, R. Attrill,
K. Bensusan, M. Caruana, G. Durante,
J. C. Finlayson, A. Fortuna, E. F. J. Garcia,
H. van Gils, S. T. Holliday, T. Jesty, E. Lamb,
J. Licudi, J. Mead, M. Mosquera, E. Olivares,
D. Price, D. Ramos, N. Ramos, Sir Derek
Reffel, P. Rocca, R. Rutherford, J. Saez,
A. Sheldon and T. Walsh

GUERNSEY

B. Wells, with contributions from J. Medland

ISLE OF MAN

J. P. Cullen

JERSEY

G. Young,
with contributions from J. M. Allan,
I. Buxton, D. Buxton, M. Dryden,
D. and F. Le Sueur, R. Long, M. L. Long,
N. Milton, A. R. Paintin and S. J. Tonge

CONTENTS

FOREWORD

by Jean-Pierre Ribaut
Head of Environment Conservation and Management Division
Council of Europe, Strasbourg

ALTHOUGH it is increasingly accepted that biological diversity is in decline on a worldwide scale, the significance of this loss for future generations continues to be underestimated. While this decline is most striking and of greatest concern in the tropics, it is in the countryside of Europe that many of us are experiencing it firsthand.

Forty years ago, I was able to observe the four species of shrike *Lanius* spp., in the countryside 15 km west of Lausanne in Switzerland. Today, three of them have completely disappeared from this region, and only the Red-backed Shrike is still breeding, although in much smaller numbers. Although the green areas and hedgerows are still there, they have changed and no longer provide suitable habitat. If the shrikes have largely gone, what other fauna and flora will also have disappeared?

For the first time, this study brings together data on all of Europe's birds, from over 400 contributors across the continent, to present a comprehensive picture of their conservation status. The study provides detailed information on distribution, populations and trends, ecology and threats for those species which have an Unfavourable Conservation Status (nearly 40% of the total European avifauna). All the shrikes are included, but many other species, which will be well-known to the citizens of Europe, are also shown to be in decline across the continent. Most importantly, the study points to actions which need to be taken to reverse the downward trends, which will be of benefit not only to birds, but to our entire natural heritage.

Over the past decades, administrations and decision-makers have become increasingly aware of, and are taking steps to address, our conservation problems. The number of nature reserves and national parks has increased considerably, legislation has been improved, and locally extinct species have been reintroduced. The increase in the European Peregrine population, and the current scheme to reintroduce the Lammergeier to the Alps, are testimony to this. Achievements such as these should not be forgotten, since they show man can act to reverse downward population trends.

It is, however, our whole approach to economic development (for example in agriculture, regional planning, land redistribution and wetland drainage) that is responsible for the decline of biological diversity in Europe— and to remedy this situation we need to go much further than establishing protected areas and reintroducing locally extinct species. The conservation of biodiversity needs to be fully integrated into all spheres of economic activity.

Having always attached the highest importance to the work of non-governmental organizations, especially in the context of the Convention on the Conservation of European Wildlife and Natural Habitats (the Bern Convention), the Council of Europe warmly congratulates BirdLife International for this fundamental contribution to the preservation of our biological diversity.

Council of Europe
Conseil de l'Europe

7

FOREWORD

by Christoph Imboden,
Director-General of BirdLife International

THIS BOOK has significant implications for conservation in Europe, and elsewhere. It highlights, and provides data for, an important dimension of biodiversity conservation which is all too often overlooked in the international context.

In today's biodiversity debate, much focus is being given to the problem of rare and endangered species, and they are indeed a sign of acute threat to global species diversity and often deserve our most urgent attention. However, threatened species, those that have already fallen below a critical level, present by no means the full story. The distribution and abundance of species are manifestations of biodiversity complementary to the number of species itself. Many species, while not yet threatened with worldwide extinction, are declining locally or regionally, and are thus undergoing a reduction of their distribution and/or abundance.

This study, the result of four years of data collection and analysis by BirdLife International, its large network of experts throughout Europe, and a number of collaborating organizations, provides some hard evidence of the extent and seriousness of bird species decline in Europe: 25% of the 514 regularly occurring species on the continent have undergone substantial population reductions during the past 20 years.

As birds are generally good environmental indicators we must assume that the picture provided by the birds also reflects what is happening to many other life-forms—a picture that depicts an enormous ongoing degradation of biodiversity in Europe, in relation to both species' distribution and abundance. And all this has been happening during two decades of unprecedented conservation aware-ness in Europe, when governments and conservation NGOs had been active on a wide range of issues, when national and European conservation legislation had become stronger and stricter, when financial resources for conservation from the private and public sector had grown substantially, and when programmes for the reintroduction of vanished species and the restoration of habitats had become regular practice in many parts of Europe.

The conclusion is inevitable: our conservation measures are still largely ineffective, especially in the long term. The reasons for this failure are largely the same as those responsible for our inability to resolve, in a lasting manner, most of our environmental problems, namely man's overwhelming preference for 'technological' solutions, which normally address the *symptoms* only, rather than coming to terms with the real issues of the underlying *causes*. To deal with the latter is much more difficult, because it requires changes in economic and social policy which, ultimately, might affect our personal behaviour and accustomed lifestyles.

In Europe, during the past 20 years, vast sums have been spent on the reintroduction of the White-tailed Eagle to areas from which it had disappeared and where it will require continuing intensive management programmes. At the same time, however, we have failed to stop the decline of the Skylark and many other common and widespread farmland birds, a decline which, as this book shows, is reaching alarming proportions in many parts of the continent. The difference is that the decline of these species cannot be halted by means of a spectacular reintroduction programme, a technological approach, but can only be meaningfully addressed at the level of the underlying causes, namely through a fundamental reappraisal of European farming and land-use policies.

It has been recognized for a while, in Europe and elsewhere, that conservation of bio-diversity needs an integrated approach on three levels: (1) protection of species from persecution and over-exploitation, (2) protection and management of sites for conservation purposes, and (3) conservation-sensitive management of the wider environment. However, what this study underlines is that conservation strategies are still giving vastly inadequate weight to the third point.

The population trends of birds in Europe, especially those inhabiting intensively managed ecosystems, indicate that most of our land-use practices are unsustainable in relation to biodiversity. Agriculture is probably responsible for the biggest effect, especially the monolithic Common Agricultural Policy of the European Union, paying for agricultural 'improvements' that leave the loss of biological capital out of the sums.

Although protected areas are needed, it is, however, not sufficient to create a network of such areas, nor is it adequate merely to add to them larger, but still defined, areas where non-intensive management regimes are achieved through subsidies and other incentives (e.g. schemes of the Environmentally Sensitive Area type). What will ultimately make the difference is how we use the large bulk of the remainder of the land. Policies of any kind for these areas have to ensure that important biological characteristics are being maintained—and enhanced wherever possible.

Nothing short of a holistic approach will stem, let alone reverse, the biodiversity decline in Europe. We must cover the continent in an 'Eco-Blanket' (Imboden 1994), in which *all* parts of the landscape, including urban and other heavily developed areas, should be assigned a defined function in the service of biodiversity conservation.

Why does the message of this book matter so much? Biodiversity loss is not something that happens only in tropical forests—it also occurs, on a large scale, in areas of the world with lower levels of biodiversity. Although not as final as the global extinction of a species, the disappearance of species locally has a large impact on the quality of life for many people—more than the vanishing of a species on the far side of the globe. *Birds in Europe* is about our *personal* environment.

ACKNOWLEDGEMENTS

THIS REVIEW is based on the huge amount of work carried out by several thousands of ornithologists throughout Europe over the last few decades. Without their expertise and commitment this study would not have been possible. Therefore, although it is not feasible to thank everyone personally we wish to dedicate this book to all those who have contributed to bird censusing or monitoring in Europe, and, through these activities, significantly furthered bird conservation.

We particularly wish to thank the national data compilers and contributors (listed at the start of the book)—and the numerous organizations which they represent or with which they are associated—all of whom enthusiastically and diligently collated and synthesized the ornithological information which was available in order to provide the data-sets used for this review. The collection of data was carried out in collaboration with the European Ornithological Atlas project and we are grateful to the European Ornithological Atlas Committee for their cooperation and assistance with this. We are especially indebted to Johan Bekhuis who provided data from the atlas project and helped to establish the joint data collection process. We also thank Mike Blair, Jeremy Greenwood, Goetz Rheinwald and Ward Hagemeijer, all of the European Bird Census Council European Ornithological Atlas Working Group, for their assistance and their advice. Paul Rose of the International Waterfowl and Wetlands Research Bureau (IWRB) helped with data collation through providing helpful comments on the waterfowl data and furnishing new information.

We are very grateful to Alistair Gammell of the Royal Society for the Protection of Birds (RSPB) who arranged for the financing of the project, provided considerable motivation for its completion and chaired the project's steering committee; other members of the committee—Mark Avery, Olivier Biber, Rob Fuller, Eduardo de Juana, Torsten Larsson, Frank Saris, Janine van Vessem and Tomasz Wesolowski—provided invaluable advice and assistance throughout. We also thank Jan Wattel and Eduard Osieck for their constructive comments on draft criteria for identifying Species of European Conservation Concern.

We are of course indebted to the following authors of species texts, all of whom provided their time and expertise for the project, freely and enthusiastically: N. J. Aebischer, Per Angelstam, Bernardo Arroyo, Philip Bacon, Wolfgang Baumgart, Jan H. Beekman, Victor Belik, Jean-Pierre Biber, Eric Bignal, Manuel José Biscoito, Nieves de Borbón, Michael Brinch Pedersen, Emma Brindley, Michael Brooke, Kees Camphuysen, Francisco J. Cantos, Guillermo Delgado Castro, Melis Charalambides, Nigel A. Clark, Alain Crivelli, Stefan Danko, Nick Davidson, Anatoly V. Davygora, J. Carles Dolz, José A. Donázar, Euan Dunn, Andrzej Dyrcz, Arni Einarsson, Jan Ekman, Mats O. G. Eriksson, Mario Díaz Esteban, Brian Etheridge, José Fernández-Palacios, Alv Ottar Folkestad, Tony Fox, Bjørn Frantzen, Hilary Fry, Vladimir Galushin, Luis M. González, Paul Goriup, Andy Green, Adam Gretton, Heinz Hafner, Ben Hallmann, Mike Harris, Joachim Hellmich, Borja Heredia, Rafael Heredia, Miguel A. Hernández, Andrew Hoodless, Guy Jarry, Hans Jerrentrup, Alan Johnson, Eduardo de Juana, Paul E. Jönsson, Yves Kayser, Guido Keijl, Peter de Knijff, Ulf Kolmodin, Alexander I. Koshelev, Pertti Koskimies, Vitaly G. Krivenko, Harald Kutzenberger, Marco Lambertini, Karsten Laursen, Peter Lindberg, Juan Antonio Lorenzo, Vladimir Loskot, Jesper Madsen, Juan Manrique, Loïc Marion, Chris Mead, Heimo Mikkola, Vladimir V. Morozov, Valery N. Moseikin, Joaquin Muñoz-Cobo, Manuel Máñez, Adrian del Nevo, Juan J. Oñate, Eduard Osieck, Christian Perennou, Ævar Petersen, Stefan Pihl, Richard Porter, Roald L. Potapov, G.R. Potts, Hartwig Prange, Piotr Profus, Derek Ratcliffe, Eileen Rees, Lennart Risberg, Gérard Rocamora, Felipe Rodríguez, Paul Rose, Rui Rufino, Otto Samwald, Holger Schulz, Colin Shawyer, Cor Smit, Manuel Soler, Ron Summers, Carlos Sunyer, Francisco Suárez, Peter Südbeck, Alejandro Sánchez, Mark Tasker, Angela Turner, Glen Tyler, Carlos Urdiales, José P. Veiga, V. G. Vinogradov, Javier Viñuela, Jeff Watson, Peter Weber, Michael Wink, Johanna E. Winkelman, Miguel Yanes, Francis Zino and Paul Alexander Zino. Late changes to the conservation status of some species meant that text which had already been prepared for them could, sadly, not be included in the book; such accounts were written by Paul Donald, Andrzej Dyrcz, Vladimir Flint, Pertti Koskimies, Robert Moss, Ævar Petersen, Roald L. Potapov, Carlos Sunyer, Javier Viñuela and Victor

Zubakin. We also thank Euan Dunn for the difficult but excellent job that he made of summarizing the population data for all SPEC category 4 species.

The following reviewers provided invaluable comments on species texts and additional help with the checking of data: Vladimir Anufriev, Bernardo Arroyo, Cristina Barros, Albert Beintema, Vincent van den Berk, Colin Bibby, Olivier Biber, Belén Calvo, Guillem-Manel Chacón i Cabàs, Melis Charalambides, Jens Christensen, Alexey Estafjev, Vladimir Galushin, Murray Grant, Rhys Green, Ward Hagemeijer, Borja Heredia, David Hill, Graham Hirons, Janet Hunter, Petar Iankov, Eduardo de Juana, Alan Knox, Norbert Lefranc, Roy Leigh, Gernant Magnin, Aurélio Martín, Bernd-U. Meyburg, Heimo Mikkola, Alexander Mischenko, Luis Monteiro, Miguel Angel Neveso, Olafur Nielsen, Dries Van Nieuwenhuyse, Tycho Anker-Nilssen, César San Segundo Ontin, Debbie Pain, Francisco Purroy, Goetz Rheinwald, Hans-Ulrich Rissner, Gérard Rocamora, Konyhás Sándor, Derek Scott, Cor Smit, Roland Staav, Karl-Birger Strann, Carlos Sunyer, Mark Tasker, Pavel Tomkovich, Zoltán Waliczky, Johanna E. Winkelman and Francis Zino. Additional material and assistance with the preparation of species texts was provided by Jean-Pierre Biber, Jeff Black, Przcmek Chylarecki, Martina Eiseltova, Keith Emmerson, Vincente Garza, Andy Green, Nathalie Hecker, Eduardo de Juana, Vladimir Loskot, Gernant Magnin, Aurélio Martín, Hans Meltofte, Mai Munk, Dave Pepler, Goetz Rheinwald and Marcus Walsh. Assistance with species text translations was given by D. B. Chaban, Eugene Potapov and Mike Wilson.

Gary Allport, Mark Cocker, Jonathan Eames and Ian Hepburn made data available to the project and founded the principles used to develop the criteria for identifying Species of European Conservation Concern in an earlier project for the UN Economic Commission for Europe, funded by the governments of Finland, the Netherlands and Norway. This project which provided a foundation for the current study benefited greatly from the advice of Gerard Boere, Steinar Eldøy, Torsten Larsson, Esko Jaakkola and Michael Kokine.

Many staff at the Secretariat of BirdLife International in Cambridge have given considerable assistance to this project. We particularly thank Colin Bibby, Nigel Collar and Christoph Imboden for advice at all stages and for comments on draft manuscripts, Mike Crosby for invaluable assistance with the development of the European Bird Database, Henk van Dijkhuizen for computer programming and Alison Stattersfield for guidance on the reference database system. We are particularly grateful to Caroline Socha who, despite numerous technical problems, patiently and in good humour took on the lead role in producing the maps, a process which involved far more work than was originally envisaged. We also thank Joel Smith of the World Conservation Monitoring Centre and Stephen Hawkins of Adept Scientific Micro Systems for guidance on Atlas-GIS and Adrian Long for comments and advice on the development of the maps.

We are highly indebted to the publications team at BirdLife. We especially thank Duncan Brooks for his essential role in managing the book's production and for his selfless dedication to the project which included the sacrifice of evenings and weekends without number, skilfully cutting to length and editing the text and designing much of the layout, as well as overcoming endless problems with importation of the graphics files. Regina Pfaff patiently and meticulously incorporated editorial changes into the entire manuscript and provided invaluable help with the checking, editing and layout of references. Mike Evans provided considerable assistance with the editing of texts and with proof reading, and Will Duckworth also helped with editing of species texts. Layout of species texts and production of figures (other than maps) was carried out by Michelle Hines. Nicola Wiles and James Lowen provided extremely helpful assistance with the completion of the manuscript whilst working as volunteers for BirdLife International. The translations of the book's summary were produced with great care by Isabel Salís, James Lowen, Susanne Müller and Gérard Rocamora. The cover was designed by Clive Bennett and the illustration of the Red-backed Shrike was specifically painted for the publication by Norman Arlott.

Invaluable secretarial assistance was provided by Johanna Barnes, Beverley Childs and Carol Kemp, all of whom suffered greatly at the fax machine (and in other ways) but always persevered. Virtually all the data for the project were entered onto the database by Anne Hunter, and Irene Hughes carried out most of the original typing of references. Much support and encouragement were given in many further ways by all our colleagues at BirdLife International, among whom we thank Gary Allport, Jonathan Eames, Georgina Green, Borja Heredia, Miriam Langeveld, Jenny Loughlin, Carlos Martín-Novella, Margaret Parnwell, Tobias Salathé, Leslie Stanton, Zoltán Waliczky and David Wege for their substantial help and guidance. We also thank John O'Sullivan and Laurence Rose at the RSPB, and David Hill, for their assistance.

We would like to acknowledge the support given by many friends and relatives over the four years of work on this book. Graham Tucker wishes particularly to thank Claire Johnson for her patience and continued encouragement despite the numerous late nights and weekends of work, and Melanie Heath thanks Adrian Long for his unwavering support and understanding throughout the duration of the project.

Lastly, we thank of course the sponsoring organizations whose financial support enabled the project to be carried out. In particular, we are indebted to the Royal Society for the Protection of Birds as the main sponsors, but we are also very grateful for the significant additional contributions from Vogelbescherming Nederland, Schweizer Vogelschutz and the Swedish Environmental Protection Agency.

SUMMARY

THIS BOOK is the first review of the conservation status of all birds in Europe. The geographical scope is continent-wide, and includes Greenland, the islands of the Azores, Madeira and the Canaries, Russia to the Ural mountains, the Caucasus and the whole of Turkey. The aim was to identify species which are in need of conservation measures (Species of European Conservation Concern, SPECs) in order that action might be targeted towards them.

• National population data were collected, in collaboration with the European Ornithological Atlas project, through a combined network of over 400 national data compilers and contributors. Breeding population size and trend data were gathered for all species in all countries, and winter population data were also collected where available, mainly for waterbirds. The resulting database of approximately 50,000 records was then used as the basis for a quantitative assessment of each species' conservation status.

• Criteria were developed to identify Species of European Conservation Concern according to their global and European status, and to the proportion of their total population that occurs in Europe. The SPECs are divided into the following four categories.

SPEC Category 1 Species occurring in Europe which are of global conservation concern because their status on a world-wide basis is classified as Globally Threatened, Conservation Dependent or Data Deficient.

SPEC Category 2 Species whose global populations are concentrated in Europe and which have an Unfavourable Conservation Status in Europe.

SPEC Category 3 Species whose global populations are not concentrated in Europe, but which have an Unfavourable Conservation Status in Europe.

SPEC Category 4 Species whose global populations are concentrated in Europe, but which have a Favourable Conservation Status in Europe.

Species are considered to be concentrated in Europe if more than 50% of their global breeding or wintering population occurs in Europe. Species have an Unfavourable Conservation Status if their European populations are small and non-marginal, or are substantially declining, or are highly localized.

• The analysis reveals that 195 species (38% of the European avifauna) have an Unfavourable Conservation Status. Of these, 24 species are SPEC category 1, 41 are SPEC category 2 and 130 are SPEC category 3. A further 83 species have a Favourable Conservation Status but are concentrated in Europe and are therefore SPEC category 4.

• This published review presents individual species accounts, written by experts, for all SPECs with an Unfavourable Conservation Status (categories 1–3). These include comprehensive tables and maps of national population data and summarize each species' European population status, its ecology (including habitat use), the threats facing it and the required conservation measures. Brief species accounts are given for SPECs in category 4.

• Farmland habitats hold nearly 60% of all SPECs with an Unfavourable Conservation Status, the largest number in any habitat. Of next-most importance are wetlands, followed by forest habitats. Marine, heathland, moorland, tundra and mountain habitats also hold significant numbers of SPECs with an Unfavourable Conservation Status.

• The majority of SPECs that have an Unfavourable Conservation Status qualify because of substantial declines in their European populations. As many of these species are, or once were, common and widely distributed, the enormous scale of the problem becomes apparent.

• Most population declines are believed to be linked to changes in land-use and land management, with agricultural intensification the most common threat, affecting some 42% of SPECs with declining populations. Wetland loss and degradation, disturbance of birds, afforestation, intensification of forestry, forest loss, the abandonment of agriculture, and pollution are other factors related to land-use which are also affecting large numbers of species. Hunting and persecution are further frequent causes of population decline, affecting 31% of declining SPECs.

• The overall message from this review is starkly clear: the numbers, range and overall diversity of European birds are under considerable threat from widespread environmental change, largely as a result of the growing intensity of land-use over the continent. Furthermore, since birds act as good environmental indicators, these conclusions have serious implications regarding the health of the European environment in general.

• In the short term, targeted conservation action is needed for bird species classified as SPECs. Measures to date, which have mainly focused on site conservation and species protection, must be reinforced. From now on, much greater emphasis must be given to incorporating environmental considerations into the management of the wider countryside.

• A European bird conservation strategy with the following three components must be developed and implemented by all concerned agencies:

1. Protection of species from persecution and over-exploitation through the strengthening and effective enforcement of species-protection laws, and the development of hunting management plans

and regulations that ensure sustainable use of species.

2. Conservation of sites through the full protection of all those classified as Important Bird Areas, and the development and implementation of management plans for them.

3. Conservation in the wider environment through tighter regulation of pollution and the integration of environmental objectives into all land-use policies, especially those relating to agriculture, fisheries, forestry and water management.

• Given the scale of the problem, it is clear that nothing less than a massive and urgent response will be adequate if we wish to maintain Europe's rich and abundant birdlife.

ZUSAMMENFASSUNG

DAS VORLIEGENDE WERK ist ein erstmalig durchgeführter Überblick über den Naturschutzstatus aller Vögel Europas. Der behandelte geographische Bereich umfaßt den gesamten Kontinent, einschließlich Grönlands, der Azoren, Madeiras und der Kanarischen Inseln, Rußlands bis zum Uralgebirge, des Kaukasus und der gesamten Türkei. Ziel dieser Übersicht ist es, Vogelarten zu identifizieren, für die Naturschutzmaßnahmen ergriffen werden müssen (Arten, für die der europäische Naturschutz zuständig ist), damit gezielte Aktionen für diese Arten durchgeführt werden können.

• In Zusammenarbeit mit dem Projekt für den Europäischen Ornithologischen Atlas wurden durch ein Verbindungsnetz von über 400 nationalen Mitarbeitern, die Daten sammelten oder beitrugen, Informationen über die nationalen Vogelpopulationen zusammengetragen. Die Daten über die Größe und Veränderung der Brutpopulationen bzw. Brutbereiche wurden für alle Arten in allen Ländern gesammelt. Hauptsächlich für Wasservögel wurden, sofern sie zugänglich waren, auch Daten über Winterpopulationen ermittelt. Die auf diese Weise erarbeitete Datenbank von 50.000 Aufzeichnungen wurde dann als Basis für eine quantitavive Beurteilung des Naturschutzstatus' jeder Art verwendet.

• Es wurden unterschiedliche Kriterien zur Identifikation von Arten, für die der europäische Naturschutz zuständig ist, entwickelt. Diese Kriterien beziehen sich auf den weltweiten Status der Arten, ihren europäischen Status und den Anteil ihrer Gesamtpopulation in Europa. Die Arten, für die der europäische Naturschutz zuständig ist (Species of European Conservation Concern, im folgenden auch SPECs), werden in die diese vier Kategorien eingeteilt:

SPEC-Kategorie 1 In Europa vorkommende Arten, für die weltweite Naturschutzmaßnahmen ergriffen werden müssen, weil ihr Status auf einer weltweiten Basis als 'global bedroht', 'naturschutzabhängig' oder 'unzureichend durch Daten dokumentiert' klassifiziert ist.

SPEC-Kategorie 2 Arten, deren globale Populationen konzentriert in Europa vorkommen, die jedoch in Europa einen ungünstigen Naturschutzstatus haben.

SPEC-Kategorie 3 Arten, deren globale Populationen sich nicht auf Europa konzentrieren und die in Europa einen ungünstigen Naturschutzstatus haben.

SPEC-Kategorie 4 Arten, deren globale Populationen sich auf Europa konzentrieren und die einen günstigen Naturschutzstatus in Europa haben.

• Arten werden dann als konzentriert in Europa vorkommend eingestuft, wenn mehr als 60% ihrer globalen Brut- oder Winterpopulationen in Europa beheimatet sind. Einen ungünstigen Naturschutzstatus haben Arten dann, wenn ihre europäischen Populationen klein sind und nicht nur in Randbereichen Europas vorkommen, in beträchtlichem Ausmaß abnehmen oder lokal äußerst begrenzt vorkommen.

• Aus der Analyse geht hervor, daß 195 Arten (38% des europäischen Vogelbestandes) einen ungünstigen Naturschutzstatus aufweisen. Davon gehören 24 Arten zur SPEC-Kategorie 1, 41 zur SPEC-Kategorie 2 und 130 zur SPEC-Kategorie 3. Weitere 83 Arten haben einen günstigen Naturschutzstatus, treten jedoch konzentriert in Europa auf und sind daher SPEC-Kategorie 4 zuzuordnen.

• Diese von Experten verfaßte Studie präsentiert eine individuelle Darstellung jeder Art mit ungünstigem Naturschutzstatus (Kategorien 1–3). Dabei werden ausführliche Tabellen und Karten mit Daten über die in den einzelnen Nationen vorkommenden Populationen verwendet und Angaben zum europäischen Populationsstatus jeder Art, ihrer Ökologie (einschließlich der Habitatsbedingungen), den Bedrohungen, denen sie ausgesetzt sind, und den erforderlichen Naturschutzmaßnahmen gemacht. Auch die Kategorie 4 angehörenden SPECs werden kurz aufgeführt.

• Fast 50% aller SPECs, für die ein ungünstiger Naturschutzstatus vorliegt, also die größte überhaupt in jeglichem Habitatstyp vorkommende Anzahl, lebt in Habitaten, die in landwirtschaftlich genutzten Gebieten angesiedelt sind. Der zweitwichtigste Habitatstyp sind Feuchtgebiete, gefolgt von Waldhabitaten. In Seegebiets-, Moor-, Tundra- und Gebirgshabitaten kommt ebenfalls eine bedeutende Anzahl von SPECs mit einem ungünstigen Naturschutzstatus vor.

• Die meisten Arten mit ungünstigem Naturschutzstatus werden als solche eingestuft, weil ihre europäischen Populationen zu einem beträchtlichen Ausmaß reduziert sind. Da viele dieser Arten früher oder heutzutage häufig oder weit verbreitet vorkamen bzw. vorkommen, wird der beträchtliche Umfang dieses Problems deutlich.

• Vermutlich ist der größte Anteil des Rückgangs von Populationen auf Veränderungen innerhalb der Landnutzung und -verwaltung zurückzuführen. Dabei ist die Intensivierung der Landwirtschaft die häufigste Bedrohung; sie betrifft 42% der SPECs, deren Populationen abnehmen. Verlust und Verschlechterung der Feuchtgebiete, die Störung der Vögel, Aufforstung, Intensivierung der Forstwirtschaft,

Waldverlust, der Rückgang landwirtschaftlich genutzter Flächen und die Umweltverschmutzung sind andere mit der Landnutzung verbundene Faktoren, die ebenfalls eine große Anzahl von Arten betreffen. Weitere häufige Gründe für den Rückgang der Populationen sind Jagd und Verfolgung, die 31% der abnehmenden SPECs betreffen.

• Die Gesamtaussage der vorliegenden Bestandsaufnahme ist eindeutig: Die Anzahl, der Verbreitungsbereich und die gesamte Artenvielfalt der Vögel Europas sind ernsthaft bedroht. Dieses ist auf weitreichende Umweltveränderungen zurückzuführen, die mit der wachsenden Intensität der Landnutzung im gesamten Kontinent verbunden sind. Weiterhin implizieren diese Schlußfolgerungen Aussagen über das Ausmaß der Schädigung der Umwelt Europas im allgemeinen, da Vögel als gute Indikatoren für den Zustand der Umwelt zu betrachten sind.

• Kurzfristig sind gezielte Maßnahmen für die als SPECs klassifizierten Vogelarten notwendig. Die bisher ergriffenen Maßnahmen, die sich hauptsächlich auf den Schutz von Gebieten und Arten konzentrieren, müssen verstärkt werden. Zukünftig muß ein größerer Schwerpunkt auf die Integration von Gesichtspunkten des Umweltschutzes in die überregionale Verwaltung der Landschaft gelegt werden.

• Eine die folgenden drei Komponenten enthaltende europäische Vogelschutzstrategie muß entwickelt und von allen zuständigen Behörden umgesetzt werden:

1. Schutz der Vogelarten vor Verfolgung und Ausbeutung durch die Vermehrung und effektive Verschärfung von Artenschutzgesetzen und die Entwicklung von Jagdverwaltungsplänen und Verordnungen, die die ökologisch vertretbare Nutzung der Arten absichern.

2. Erhaltung von Brutgebieten durch den vollen Schutz aller als wichtige Vogelgebiete (Important Bird Areas) klassifizierten Regionen und die Entwicklung und Durchführung von Managementplänen für solche Gebiete.

3. Strengere Vorschriften für den regional übergreifenden Umweltschutz und die Integration von Anliegen des Umweltschutzes in jegliche auf die Landnutzung bezogenen politischen Maßnahmen, insbesondere die Landwirtschaft, Fischerei, Forstwirtschaft und Gewässerverwaltung betreffenden Pläne.

• In Anbetracht des Ausmaßes des Problembereichs ist es offensichtlich, daß nur eine unmittelbare und massive Reaktion angemessen ist, wenn die reiche und vielfältige Vogelwelt Europas erhalten bleiben soll.

RÉSUMÉ

CE LIVRE est le premier à faire le bilan du statut de conservation de tous les oiseaux d'Europe. L'étendue géographique englobe l'ensemble du continent y compris le Groenland, les îles des Açores, de Madère et des Canaries, la Russie jusqu'aux monts Oural, le Caucase et la Turquie entière. L'objectif était d'identifier les espèces méritant une attention particulière en matière de conservation (Species of European Conservation Concern, ou SPECs), pour que l'on puisse mettre à exécution des plans d'action en leur faveur à travers des mesures appropriées.

• Les données concernant les effectifs dans chaque pays ont été rassemblées, en collaboration avec l'Atlas Ornithologique Européen, par un réseau de plus de 400 collaborateurs et compilateurs de données à l'échelon national. Les données concernant les effectifs nicheurs et les tendances d'évolution ont été rassemblées pour toutes les espèces dans chaque pays, ainsi que les données concernant les hivernants partout où elles étaient disponibles, principalement pour les oiseaux aquatiques. Cette base de données d'environ 50,000 éléments a ensuite été utilisée pour évaluer quantitativement le statut de conservation de chaque espèce.

• Des critères ont été défini pour identifier les espèces méritant une attention particulière en matière de conservation en fonction de leur statut mondial et européen, et selon le pourcentage de leur effectif total qui se trouve en Europe. Les SPECs sont divisés en quatres catégories.

SPEC Catégorie 1 Les espèces présente en Europe et méritant une attention particulière de conservation à l'échelon mondial, parce que leur statut mondial les place dans la classification: Menacée à l'échelle mondiale, Dépendente de moyens de conservation ou Insuffisament connue.

SPEC Catégorie 2 Les espèces dont la population mondiale est concentrée en Europe, et qui ont un statut de conservation Défavorable en Europe.

SPEC Catégorie 3 Les espèces dont la population mondiale n'est pas concentrée en Europe, mais qui ont un statut de conservation Défavorable en Europe.

SPEC Catégorie 4 Les espèces dont la population mondiale est concentrée en Europe, mais qui ont un statut de conservation Favorable en Europe.

On considère que la population d'une espèce est concentrée en Europe si plus de 50% des effectifs mondiaux nicheurs ou hivernants se trouvent en Europe. Une espèce a un statut de conservation Défavorable si ses effectifs européens sont faibles (sauf s'il s'agit d'une population marginale en limite de son aire de répartition) ou bien si sa population est en diminution considérable ou a une distribution localisée.

• L'étude révèle que 195 espèces (38% de l'avifaune européene) ont un statut de conservation Défavorable, dont 24 espèces sont des SPEC catégorie 1, 41 des SPEC catégorie 2, et 130 des SPEC catégorie 3. 83 autres espèces ont un statut de conservation Favorable tout en ayant des effectifs concentrés en Europe, et sont donc des SPEC catégorie 4.

• Cet ouvrage présente des textes individuels écrit par des spécialistes pour chacune des SPECs qui ont un statut de conservation Défavorable (catégories 1 à 3). Chaque texte résume le statut de la population d'une espèce, son écologie (y compris son utilisation de l'habitat), les nuisances qui la menacent, et les moyens de conservation dont elle a besoin. Le récit est accompagné par un tableau et une carte détaillée qui indiquent les données sur les effectifs et les évolutions de chaque pays. Un récit plus court est donné pour chaque espèce de SPEC catégorie 4.

• Les milieux agricoles possèdent presque 60% de tous les SPECs qui ont un statut de conservation Défavorable, et sont donc prépondérants comparés à tous les autres types d'habitats. Le deuxième habitat par ordre d'importance du nombre de SPEC correspond aux zones humides, et le troisième, aux forêts. Les milieux marins, les landes, la toundra et les zones de montagne possèdent aussi des pourcentages considérables de SPECs qui ont un statut de conservation Défavorable.

• La plupart des SPECs à statut de conservation Défavorable sont identifiées comme telles parce que leurs effectifs européens sont en baisse considérable. La plupart de ces espèces étaient ou sont encore communes, avec une vaste aire de distribution, ce qui met en évidence l'échelle gigantesque de ce problème.

• On pense que la plupart des déclins sont liés aux changements dans l'utilisation du sol et les types de gestion. L'intensification de l'agriculture est la principale cause de régression, touchant environ 42% des SPECs dont les effectifs sont en baisse. La disparition et la dégradation des zones humides, les dérangements, le boisement, l'intensification de la sylviculture, la destruction des forêts, l'abandon de l'agriculture, et la pollution sont les autres facteurs, liés à l'utilisation du sol, qui entraînent des conséquences graves pour beaucoup d'espèces. La chasse et les diverses formes des persécution sont également des facteurs supplémentaires, touchant 31% des SPECs dont la population est en baisse.

• Le message principal de ce rapport est bien évident: les effectifs, l'aire de répartition et la diversité générale des oiseaux européens sont considérablement affectés par ces changements à grande échelle de l'environnement, principalement à cause de l'intensification de l'utilisation du sol sur l'ensemble du continent. En outre, pusique les oiseaux sont de bons bio-indicateurs, ces conclusions ont de sérieuses implications sur la santé de l'environnement européen en général.

• Dans l'immédiat, on a besoin de mesures de conservation ciblées en faveur des espèces classées en SPEC. Les mesures prises jusqu'au présent, principalement concentrées sur la préservation de certaines espèces et de certaines sites, doivent être renforcées. Désormais, il faut attacher plus d'importance à l'incorporation des considérations environnementales à l'exploitation de nos campagnes.

• Une stratégie européene pour la conservation des oiseaux, doit être développée et mise en pratique par l'ensemble des organismes concernés. Celle-ci doit être axée sur les trois orientations suivantes:

1. La protection des espèces contre la persécution et la surexploitation, en renforcant et en appliquant de façon effictive les lois de protection des espèces; le développement des plans de gestion cynégétiques; et des règlements qui garantissent l'utilisation durable des espèces.

2. La conservation des sites par la protection complète de ceux identifiés comme Zones Importantes pour la Conservation des Oiseaux (Important Bird Areas) ainsi que le développement et la réalisation de plans de gestion pour ces sites.

3. La conservation de l'environnement à une vaste échelle par des réglementations plus sévères de l'utilisation du sol, surtout celles qui concernent l'agriculture, la pêche, la sylviculture et l'exploitation du réseau hydrologique.

• Etant donnée l'échelle du problème, il est évident que seule une réaction massive et immédiate sera suffisante si nous désirons maintenir une avifaune riche et abondant en Europe.

RESUMEN

ESTA OBRA es la primera revisión del estado de conservación de todas las aves européas. El ámbito geográfico abarca todo el continente, incluyendo Groenlandia, los archipiélagos de Azores, Madeira y Canarias, Rusia hasta los Urales, el Caúcaso y Turquía.

• Su finalidad es identificar aquellas especies que necesitan medidas de conservación (Species of European Conservation Concern, SPECs) para poder llevar a cabo acciones específicas que contribuyan a mejorar su estatus.

• Los datos nacionales sobre tamaño de población fueron reunidos en colaboración con el European Ornithological Atlas, a traves de una red de más de 400 colaboradores. Se reunió información sobre tamaño de la población reproductora y tendencia poblacional para todas las especies en todos los países, y también sobre población invernal cuando fué posible, principalmente para aves acuáticas. La base de datos resultante, de aproximadamente 50,000 registros, se utilizó como base para el análisis cuantitativo del estado de conservación de cada especie.

• Se desarrollaron criterios para identificar Species of European Conservation Concern de acuerdo con su estatus global y européo, y teniendo en cuenta la proporción de la población total existente en Europa. Los SPECs se dividen en las siguientes categorías.

SPEC Categoría 1   Especies presentes en Europa que son motivo de preocupación a nivel mundial, porque están consideradas como Globalmente Amenazadas, Dependientes de Conservación o Sin Suficientes Datos.

SPEC Categoría 2   Especies que están presentes principalmente en Europa y que tienen un Estado de Conservación Desfavorable en Europa.

SPEC Categoría 3   Especies cuyas poblaciones no están concentradas en Europa pero tienen un Estado de Conservación Desfavorable en Europa.

SPEC Categoría 4   Especies que están presentes principalmente en Europa pero tienen un Estado de Conservación Favorable en Europa.

Una especie se considera como presente principalmente en Europa cuando más del 50% de su población reproductora o de su población invernante se localiza en Europa. Una especie tiene un Estado de Conservación Desfavorable si su población européa es pequeña y no marginal, si está claramente en declive, o si está muy localizada.

• El análisis demuestra que 195 especies (el 38% de la avifauna européa) tienen un Estado de Conservación Desfavorable. De estas, 24 especies pertenecen a la SPEC Categoría 1, 41 a la SPEC Categoría 2 y 130 a la SPEC Categoría 3. Además, 83 especies tienen un Estado de Conservación Favorable, pero como se localizan principalmente en Europa se incluyen en la SPEC Categoría 4.

• Esta revisión incluye un texto, escrito por un experto, para cada una de las SPECs con un Estado de Conservación Desfavorable (Categorías 1 al 3). Estos textos incluyen tablas y mapas con los datos de población en cada país, y resumen para cada una de las especies su estatus poblacional, ecología (uso del hábitat), amenazas y las medidas de conservación requeridas. Para cada una de las SPECs Categoría 4 se incluye un breve texto.

• Los hábitats agrícolas acogen casi un 60% de las especies con un Estado de Conservación Desfavorable, más que cualquier otro. A continuación vienen las zonas húmedas y despues los bosques. Los hábitats marinos, matorrales, landas, tundra y montaña también incluyen un importante número de SPECs con un Estado de Conservación Desfavorable.

• La mayoría de SPECs que tienen un Estado de Conservación Desfavorable lo son debido a los importantes declives en sus poblaciones européas. Puesto que muchas de estas especies son, o fueron en el pasado, comunes o ampliamente distribuidas, la magnitud del problema salta a la vista.

• La mayoría de los declives poblacionales se creé que están relacionados con cambios en los usos del suelo y el manejo de los hábitats, siendo la intensificación agrícola la amenaza mas común, afectando alrededor del 42% de las especies cuya poblacíon está en declive. La pérdida y degradación de zonas húmedas, molestias, reforestación, intensificación de actividades forestales, pérdida de bosques, abandono de la agricultura y contaminación son otros factores relacionados con los usos del suelo que están afectando a un gran número de especies. La caza y la captura ilegal son también causas frecuentes del declive de las poblaciones, afectando al 31% de las SPECs que están en declive.

• El mensaje principal de esta revisión es claro: el número, distribución y diversidad de las aves européas está amenazado por cambios medioambientales generalizados, principalmente como resultado de una creciente intensificación de los usos del suelo en todo el continente. Mas aún, al ser las aves buenos indicadores medioambientales, estas conclusiones son una llamada de atención sobre el estado general de salud del continente européo.

• A corto plazo, es necesario emprender acciones inmediatas de conservación para las SPECs. Las medidas tomadas hasta el momento, que se han centrado principalmente en la conservación de áreas y en la protección de especies, deben ser reforzadas. A partir de ahora, debe hacerse mayor énfasis en la incorporación de criterios medioambientales en el manejo de la naturaleza en general.

• Las agencias implicadas deben desarrollar y poner en práctica una estrategia para la conservación de las aves européas que tenga en cuenta los siguientes aspectos:

1. Prevenir la persecución y sobre-explotación de especies a traves del reforzamiento y efectivo cumplimiento de las leyes de protección de especies y del desarrollo de planes cinegéticos y normativas que aseguren una utilización sostenible.

2. Conservación de los enclaves prioritarios a traves de la total protección de todas las Areas Importantes para las Aves y del desarrollo y aplicación de planes de manejo para cada una de ellas.

3. Conservación general del medio ambiente mediante una regulación más estricta de la contaminación y mediante la integración de objetivos medioambientales en las políticas de desarrollo, especialmente aquellas relacionadas con la agricultura, la pesca, las actividades forestales y el manejo del agua.

• Dada la escala del problema, es evidente que sólo una respuesta masiva y urgente será adecuada si deseamos mantener la riqueza y diversidad ornitológicas de Europa.

INTRODUCTION

THE EXTENT of natural post-glacial climax vegetation of Europe has been considerably reduced by human activities over the last 10,000 years. Most of our forests have been felled and either replanted and managed, or replaced by agriculture. Similarly, most natural wetlands have been drained or highly modified. These changes have had profound effects on the European flora and fauna, probably increasing its overall diversity initially (Hampicke 1978) through the creation of a wide variety of semi-natural habitats such as secondary forest, heathland, grassland, cultivation and human settlement, but at the expense of primary habitats and their species. By the twentieth century, large areas of natural habitat could only be found in northern Europe and in some mountainous regions.

The particularly rapid technological advances and economic development of the twentieth century have brought about further profound changes in the European environment. Agricultural expansion, for example, has been a major cause of the loss of remaining natural habitats and rich semi-natural habitats such as wetlands and heathlands (Baldock 1990), while on farmland itself widespread intensification has steadily degraded habitats through drainage and irrigation, increased use of pesticides and fertilizers, overgrazing, crop specialization and loss of features such as trees, hedgerows and ponds (e.g. Jenkins 1984, O'Connor and Shrubb 1986, Beintema 1988, Fésüs et al. 1990–1991, Fuller et al. 1991, Goriup et al. 1991, de Juana et al. 1993). Similarly, forestry expansion and intensification, fisheries, urbanization, industrialization and increasing recreational demands have all been damaging through habitat loss, degradation and pollution (e.g. Hölzinger 1987, IUCN 1990, 1991, Lloyd et al. 1991, Bernes 1993).

It has been apparent for some time that these habitat changes have been accompanied by a widespread decline in bird populations and diversity. To address this, a long-term strategy is ultimately needed which is based on sustainable use of the environment, as outlined for example in Caring for the Earth

(IUCN/UNEP/WWF 1991) and the Global Biodiversity Strategy (WRI/IUCN/UNEP 1992). Meanwhile, in the shorter term, targeted measures are urgently needed to address the highest bird conservation priorities. BirdLife International has therefore undertaken a comprehensive review of the conservation status of all birds in Europe through the documentation and analysis of current knowledge on species populations and trends. This book presents the results of that review, and for the first time provides a full picture of what is happening to Europe's avifauna.

THE NEED FOR A EUROPE-WIDE REVIEW OF THE CONSERVATION STATUS OF BIRDS

Our principal conservation objective must be the avoidance of global extinction, followed by the maintenance of existing avian populations and distributions, and hence diversity. To achieve this efficiently it is therefore necessary to identify those species that are threatened at global, supra-national and national levels.

Although lists of nationally threatened species have already been produced for many countries, purely national conservation aims and thus species selection criteria often differ from those which are appropriate to a European scale. However, with the information provided here, national priorities can be put into a continental framework. If national conservation priorities are to contribute to the conservation of continental and global biodiversity then such an international framework is needed. This approach has, to date, been difficult because of a lack of data, although national Red Data Books for birds in the United Kingdom (Batten et al. 1990) and the Netherlands (Osieck and Hustings 1994) have taken account of the international context by listing species for which the country holds a high proportion of the regional (north-west European) population.

This review of population status has allowed the

international importance of all species to be assessed on a continental scale and for all countries. It will enable the overall European population trends of species to be taken into account in assessing national conservation priorities. In practice most conservation actions must still be implemented at the national level, but national actions should ideally take account of the European overview, whereby nationally threatened species are given higher priority if they are also of European conservation concern and particularly if the national population comprises a high proportion of that in Europe as a whole.

Supra-national and Europe-wide lists of species judged to be of high conservation concern already exist, for example Annex I of the European Union (EU) Directive and Resolution on the Conservation of Wild Birds (Wild Birds Directive) and Appendix II of the Bern Convention on the Conservation of European Wildlife and Natural Habitats. However, the former only covers part of Europe while the latter covers most European species and does not distinguish those species in need of special conservation measures. Furthermore, the present study provides the opportunity to evaluate and update these previous lists on the basis of a Europe-wide systematic evaluation of available data.

TOWARDS A EUROPEAN BIRD CONSERVATION STRATEGY

As well as informing decision-makers and executants at national and supra-national levels of the status of Europe's birds, this review is also essential to guide the actions that need to be taken for their conservation through the development of a comprehensive bird conservation strategy that incorporates the following three essential elements.

- Protection of species from persecution and over-exploitation.

- Conservation of sites by establishing protected areas and preserving or managing them according to the needs of their flora and fauna.

- Conservation of the wider environment by regulation of activities that modify habitats and landscapes, and by controlling pollution of air, soil and water.

Species protection

Clearly, protection of all species from persecution and over-exploitation is a prerequisite for species conservation. Although many birds are protected by national laws and international conventions and directives (see Box 1), illegal persecution and hunting still continue (e.g. Génsbøl 1987, Magnin 1991, Cadbury 1992, McCulloch et al. 1992). Further-

more, of those birds that are legally hunted none has an adequate hunting management plan that ensures sustainable use. Thus the results of this review will help to identify and justify requirements for improved legal protection of species and the development of management plans.

Site protection

The publication by BirdLife International (known at the time as the International Council for Bird Preservation) and the International Waterfowl and Wetlands Research Bureau of *Important Bird Areas in Europe* (Grimmett and Jones 1989) represented a major contribution towards bird conservation in Europe. For the first time individual sites in each European country were evaluated in a standard way, and a continent-wide network of sites was identified that, if protected, would safeguard a significant proportion of the European populations of many species.

Among other functions, the Important Bird Areas (IBA) inventory aims to guide the implementation of national conservation strategies through the promotion and development of national protected-area programmes. It is also intended to assist the conservation activities of international governmental organizations and to promote the implementation of global agreements and regional measures (see Box 1). The results of the present review will therefore be used to provide further guidance to governments on measures needed to conserve sites for threatened and declining species and their habitats under international agreements, in particular the Bonn Convention on the Conservation of Migratory Species of Wild Animals, the Bern Convention, the Ramsar Convention on Wetlands of International Importance and the EU Wild Birds Directive.

Conservation of the wider environment

Even when protected and managed for conservation (as nature reserves, for example) sites are not independent of the wider environments which surround them; amongst other factors they may be susceptible to fluctuations in water regimes and in nutrient inputs, and to air and water pollution. A further important limitation to the conservation of species by site protection is that many species have dispersed distributions throughout their annual cycle. Although many sites will hold substantial numbers of such species, only a small proportion of their populations can be covered by a protected-area network. Furthermore, of the species that do congregate at some point in the year, and therefore may potentially benefit from site protection, many are dispersed at other times. Thus, although most ducks, geese and waders congregate in winter, they are widely dispersed during the breeding season. Conversely, most gulls, terns

Box 1. International conservation initiatives in Europe (adapted and expanded from IUCN Commission on National Parks and Protected Areas 1994).

Title	Secretariat/focal point	Aims
• GLOBAL		
World Conservation Strategy, and the subsequent Strategy for Sustainable Living (Caring for the Earth)	IUCN/UNEP/WWF	To provide a strategic conservation framework and practical guidance to all nations to (1) maintain essential ecological processes and life support systems; (2) preserve genetic diversity; and (3) ensure the sustainable utilization of species and ecosystems
Convention on Biological Diversity	Permanent secretariat to be established in 1994	The conservation of biological diversity, the sustainable use of its components and the fair and equitable sharing of the benefits arising out of the utilization of genetic resources
Convention on Wetlands of International Importance Especially as Waterfowl Habitat (Ramsar Convention)	Ramsar Convention Bureau, Gland	To ensure the conservation of wetlands, especially those of international importance, by fostering wise use, international cooperation and reserve creation (among other means)
Convention on the Conservation of Migratory Species of Wild Animals (Bonn Convention)	Bonn Convention Secretariat, Bonn	To provide a framework for the conservation of migratory species and their habitats by means of, as appropriate, strict protection and the conclusion of international Agreements
Agreement on the Conservation of African–Eurasian Migratory Waterbirds (under Bonn Convention)	Bonn Convention Secretariat, Bonn	The conservation of African–Eurasian migratory waterbirds through coordinated measures to restore species to a favourable conservation status or to maintain them in such a status
Convention concerning the Protection of the World Cultural and Natural Heritage (World Heritage Convention)	UNESCO, Paris	To protect cultural and natural heritage of outstanding universal value through, among other things, the listing of World Heritage Sites
UNESCO's Man and Biosphere Programme	UNESCO, Paris	To develop within the natural and social sciences a basis for the rational use and conservation of the resources of the biosphere, through such measures as the creation of a worldwide network of Biosphere Reserves
• PAN-EUROPEAN		
Convention on the Conservation of European Wildlife and Natural Habitats (Bern Convention)	Council of Europe, Strasbourg	To maintain populations of wild flora and fauna with particular emphasis on endangered and vulnerable species, including migratory species
European Network of Biogenetic Reserves	Council of Europe, Strasbourg	To conserve representative examples of Europe's habitats, biocenoses and ecosystems through a network of biogenetic reserves
IUCN Action Plan for Protected Areas in Europe	IUCN, Gland	To ensure an adequate, effective and well managed network of protected areas in Europe
European Ecological Network (EECONET)	Ministry of Agriculture, Netherlands	To develop a Europe-wide ecological network for the conservation of nature
Environment Programme for Europe	UN Economic Commission for Europe, EU, UNEP, IUCN, etc.	To prepare the intergovernmental environmental programme for Europe.
European Nature Conservation Year (ENCY) 1995	Council of Europe, Strasbourg	To develop a public awareness campaign in 1995 on 'conservation outside protected areas'

(cont.)

Box 1 (cont.)

Title	Secretariat/focal point	Aims
● *EUROPEAN UNION*		
Fifth Environmental Action Programme (1992)	European Commission DG XI, Brussels	The EU's programme of policy and action on environment and sustainable development
Directive and Resolution of the Council of the European Community on the Conservation of Wild Birds (Wild Birds Directive)	European Commission DG XI, Brussels	To protect wild birds and their habitats, e.g. through the designation of Special Protection Areas (SPAs)
CORINE	European Environmental Agency, Copenhagen	To develop a database for nature conservation in the EU, now being extended to other parts of Europe
Directive on the Conservation of Natural Habitats and of Wild Fauna and Flora (Habitats Directive)	European Commission DG XI, Brussels	To conserve fauna, flora and natural and semi-natural habitats of importance in the EU, including through the designation of the Natura 2000 network of Special Areas for Conservation (SACs)
● *CENTRAL AND EASTERN EUROPE*		
Ecological Bricks for our Common House of Europe	Initiative: Ecological Bricks, c/o European Ecological Movement, Global Challenges Network, Munich	To promote the establishment of 18 trans-boundary protected areas
Environmental Action Programme for Central and Eastern Europe (1993–1995)	Task Force established by Ministers with EU, OECD, World Bank, European Bank for Reconstruction and Development, etc.	To promote environmental protection measures in central and eastern Europe
Green Lungs of Europe (1993)	Inst. of Sustainable Development, Warsaw	Based on Poland's experience, to create sustainable development zones in Belarus, Estonia, Latvia, Lithuania, Poland, Russia and Ukraine
● *BALTIC SEA*		
Helsinki Convention (1974, 1992)	Helsinki Convention Secretariat, Helsinki	To protect the Baltic marine environment against all forms of pollution
The Baltic Sea Joint Comprehensive Environmental Action Programme (under Helsinki Convention)	Helsinki Commission (HELCOM)	To improve the quality of the Baltic environment, by (e.g.) the designation of marine and coastal protected areas
● *BLACK SEA*		
Black Sea Action Plan (BSAP)	UNEP, UNDP, World Bank and others	Environmental protection programme for the Black Sea
Bucharest Convention on the Protection of the Black Sea against Pollution, 1992	UNEP/UNDP	To protect the Black Sea against pollution
● *NORTH SEA*		
Convention for the Protection of the Marine Environment of the North East Atlantic	Oslo-Paris-Commission, London	To prevent pollution of the north-east Atlantic
Ministerial Conference on the North Sea	Ministry of Environment, Denmark	To protect the North Sea ecosystem

(cont.)

Box 1 (cont.)

Title	Secretariat/focal point	Aims
• *MEDITERRANEAN*		
Convention for the Protection of the Mediterranean Sea against Pollution (Barcelona Convention)	UNEP	To protect the Mediterranean Sea against pollution
Mediterranean Action Plan (under Barcelona Convention)	UNEP-Europe, Geneva (Regional Activity Centres in Athens, Valbonne, Tunis, Malta and Split	To improve the quality of the Mediterranean environment implementing the Barcelona Convention, 1976, e.g. through a protocol on Specially Protected Areas
MedSPA (under Barcelona Convention)	UNEP/Barcelona Convention Secretariat	To provide special protection for endangered Mediterranean species and habitats vital for their conservation
MED-PAN	European Investment Bank/World Bank	To strengthen links between managers of protected areas
MedWet	European Commission DG XI, Brussels	To conserve Mediterranean wetlands
Mediterranean Technical Assistance Programme (METAP)	World Bank/European Investment Bank	2nd Phase of European Programme for the Mediterranean, to reverse present environmental degradation
Nicosia Charter (1990)	European Commission, Brussels	To provide closer cooperation on sustainable development in the Euro-Mediterranean region, including nature conservation
• *ARCTIC*		
Arctic Initiative	Working Group on the Conservation of Arctic Flora and Fauna	To prepare a common Arctic Environmental Protection Strategy in order to promote protection and conservation of the Arctic's most important sites, habitats and species
Nordic Arctic Conference	c/o Nordic Council of Ministers	Environmental protection of the Arctic region
• *OTHER INTERNATIONAL PROJECTS*		
Alpine Convention (1991)	c/o Commission Internationale pour la Protection des Alpes (CIPRA), Vaduz	To conserve Alpine ecosystems
Danube River Basin Global Environment Facility (GEF) Programme (1991)	World Bank	Environmental protection for the Danube River
Danube Delta Biodiversity GEF Project	World Bank	To protect the Danube Delta ecosystems
Agreement on the Protection of the Rhine against chemical pollution	International Commission for the Protection of the Rhine (ICPRP)	To protect the Rhine from chemical pollution
Ministerial Declaration on the Sixth Trilateral Governmental Conference on the Protection of the Wadden Sea	The Common Wadden Sea Secretariat, Wilhelmshaven	To coordinate the conservation of the Wadden Sea

and auks are highly concentrated when nesting, but are dispersed when feeding, migrating and in winter.

Vital though site protection is, it is clear that we need to complement this with environmental measures that are effective on a wider scale if we are to maintain the distribution and abundance of Europe's birds. We must ensure the wise management of our European environment as a whole through the integration of conservation objectives into all aspects of land-use policy and activity.

To tackle this issue, the Dispersed Species Project was launched by BirdLife International in September 1990, with the aim of developing wide-scale habitat conservation measures for species that are in need of conservation action. By identifying species of conservation concern, this review represents the first phase of the project, and the data used here were initially collected as part of that work. The second phase is now in progress and aims to draw up a habitat conservation strategy for birds in Europe. This is urgently required as important land-use policy decisions with major environmental implications are presently, and frequently, being made without adequate input from conservationists. Furthermore, where conservation initiatives are being formulated to tackle wide-scale environmental problems, as for example through the recently introduced EU Agri-environment Regulation (EC Reg. 2078/92), they need to be carefully targeted, with habitat management prescriptions for the highest-priority species, if the opportunities are to be used to greatest benefit. In the absence of advice from conservationists there is the danger that broad environmental prescriptions will become vague and ineffective, or even potentially damaging to threatened species.

Such a conservation strategy, of species and site protection and wide-scale habitat measures for species conservation objectives, is practical and allows targeting of measures to identifiable priorities, a requirement that is essential when conservation resources are as limited as at present. It also allows the identification and quantification of threats and so the justification for actions that may be costly in economic terms. In turn, it provides a baseline against which to monitor the success of these actions.

Because birds are components of biodiversity and ecosystems, the identification of patterns of decline and their causes can indicate broad areas of environmental concern. Indeed, as birds are probably better researched and monitored than any other group of animals or plants, they are well placed to indicate the overall health of our environment (Peakall and Boyd 1987, Furness et al. 1993). Thus the status of birds can reveal habitat loss and modification and indicate its likely impact on other species and groups. Birds have also been shown to be good indicators of a variety of other environmental conditions, such as the impact of pesticides (Hardy et al. 1987), water quality (Eriksson 1987, Ormerod and Tyler 1993), the marine environment (Furness 1987, Montevecchi 1993) and the condition of forests (Helle and Järvinen 1986, Welsh 1987, Angelstam and Mikusinski 1994). By setting priorities based on evidence from birds we therefore also make an important contribution to the conservation of biological diversity and the environment in general (ICBP 1992, Thirgood and Heath 1994). Furthermore, birds as 'flagships' for conservation can be effective in gaining public support for the less tangible goals of maintaining biological diversity and functional ecosystems

Clearly, in view of the apparent rapid and widespread loss and degradation of European habitats, this review is urgently needed to provide a comprehensive assessment of the effects of environmental changes on Europe's avifauna. The results will be used to justify and target actions for birds, the implementation of which will benefit all the flora and fauna of Europe.

DATA COLLECTION

IN ORDER to assess the conservation status of Europe's birds reliably and comprehensively, it has been necessary to obtain detailed population information on all species, in each European country, for both breeding and mid-winter populations. To do this, we have collaborated widely with ornithologists throughout Europe, utilizing the BirdLife International network in conjunction with the European Ornithological Atlas project (see Box 1). Data were collated primarily by distributing questionnaires to national compilers (listed at the front of the book) in 39 countries and an additional 10 autonomous regions, who in turn distributed them where possible to appropriate experts, monitoring organizations and regional contributors. These data are thus based ultimately on the very considerable amount of fieldwork carried out by many thousands of mostly amateur ornithologists over many years. This review has therefore only been possible through that massive input of effort and dedication, the result of which is a comprehensive conservation assessment that would not be possible for any other class of plants or animals.

The project covered the whole of Europe, including the Azores, Madeira, the Canary Islands, European Russia (i.e. east to the Ural mountains), Armenia, Azerbaijan and Georgia, and also included the whole of Turkey and Greenland (see Figure 1 on p. 36). The European part of Kazakhstan was not covered. However, as a result of the political instability in the Caucasus region and parts of the former Yugoslavia, no data were obtained by questionnaires for Armenia, Azerbaijan, Georgia, Bosnia and Herzogovina, Yugoslavia and the Former Yugoslav Republic of Macedonia. For consistency, although population data from these countries may be given in the species texts if known to the authors, they are not included in population tables or maps in this book, nor taken into account in the assessment of species' conservation status unless indicated in Appendix 1 (p. 470).

Data on the following factors were collected from each country for both breeding and wintering populations of all bird species.
- Population size.
- Population trend (over the period 1970–1990).
- Range trend (over the period 1970–1990).

Box 1. The European Ornithological Atlas.

In 1985 the European Ornithological Atlas Committee (EOAC) started a project to produce an atlas of breeding birds in Europe. Recording forms were supplied to national organizers in order to collect quantitative data on the breeding distribution and abundance of species on a 50 × 50 km grid scale. Additionally, a questionnaire was distributed in 1989 to collect supplementary information for the atlas on population sizes and trends, habitat preferences and other miscellaneous data for each breeding species in every European country.

In 1990, when the EOAC questionnaire was already in use, BirdLife International started its Dispersed Species Project, the first phase of which aimed to assess the conservation status of all birds in Europe with a view to identifying those in urgent need of conservation action. This required data on national population sizes and trends. To avoid duplication of effort and to ensure consistency between the data-sets, BirdLife International and EOAC decided to combine their questionnaires into a single cooperative project. Having computerized the data so far obtained by EOAC, BirdLife used its European network, in collaboration with the European Atlas contributors, to update existing data, to obtain data from countries that had not so far contributed, and to obtain the midwinter population data and other additional information required for the Dispersed Species Project. The combined data-set therefore forms the basis of this review and will also be used by the European Atlas Working Group of the European Bird Census Council (EBCC), which superseded the EOAC, in *The EBCC Atlas of Breeding Birds in Europe: their distribution and abundance* (Hagemeijer and Blair in prep.).

In addition, the reference sources used to evaluate population sizes and trends were recorded. Each estimate will often have involved the consultation of more than one literature source as well as the incorporation of such unpublished survey data as may have been available. Derivation of figures may also have involved interpretation and extrapolation by the national compiler and personal consultation with other experts. Data verification codes were provided by the suppliers of the information to indicate the accuracy and reliability of the population size and trend data (Box 2).

Because the purpose of this review was to assess the overall European population status of each species, assessments of trends in national population size and range were made according to broad categories only (Box 2). Although it would have been ideal to obtain actual percentage change figures over the 1970–1990 period, this would only have been possible for the few countries with long-established and reliable monitoring schemes.

Full details of the data questionnaires and instructions are given in Appendix 5 (p. 511). All data from completed questionnaires were used to create the BirdLife International/EBCC European Bird Database of some 50,000 records. These data on population sizes and trends, together with their verification codes, formed the basis of the quantitative assessment of the conservation status of each species, as described in the next chapter. After entry into the database, all data were printed out and returned to national com-

> **Box 2. Codes for trends and data quality, as used in the questionnaires.**
>
> **Trends** in population size and range over the period 1970–1990 were recorded according to the following categories.
> +2 Large increase of at least 50%.
> +1 Small increase of 20–49%.
> 0 Stable, or change of less than 20%.
> −1 Small decrease of 20–49%.
> −2 Large decrease of at least 50%.
> F Fluctuating with changes of at least 20%, but no clear trend.
> N New breeder within the period.
> X Gone extinct within the period.
>
> **Verification codes** (data quality) for population size, and for data on trends in population size and range, were as follows.
> 1 Species poorly known, with no quantitative data available.
> 2 Species generally well known, but only poor or incomplete quantitative data available.
> 3 Reliable quantitative data (e.g. atlas survey or monitoring data, etc.) are available for the whole period and region in question.

pilers for checking. Further data checks were also made during the course of writing the species texts that form the bulk of this book and while producing the status maps which accompany them. Any data queries raised by the authors of species texts were referred back to national compilers for comment and approval before amendment.

ASSESSMENT OF CONSERVATION STATUS
Defining Species of European Conservation Concern

THE AIM of this assessment is to identify species that are of conservation concern on a European scale. These birds are termed Species of European Conservation Concern (SPECs) and are divided into four categories (Box 1) depending on their global conservation status, their European Threat Status and the proportion of their world population in Europe (Figure 1). Species are considered to have an Unfavourable Conservation Status if their European Threat Status is Localized, Declining, Rare, Vulnerable, Endangered or Insufficiently Known in Europe according to the criteria summarized in Box 2 and described in full in Box 3 (see Box 4 for definition and explanation of terms).

DATA ANALYSIS

Calculation of population changes
The assessment of European Threat Status is based on the minimum European population size and the percentage of the total European population which is in countries where populations have declined. These

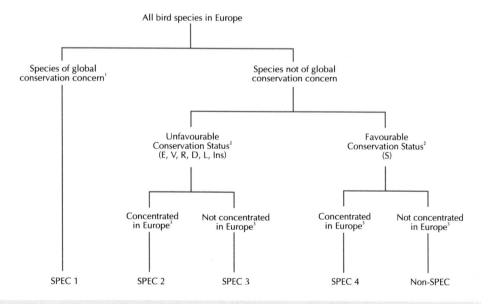

Figure 1. The classification of Species of European Conservation Concern (SPECs).

[1] Species listed as Globally Threatened, Conservation Dependent or Data Deficient by Collar *et al.* (1994).
[2] Determined by European Threat Status:
   E Endangered   V Vulnerable   R Rare   D Declining   L Localized   Ins Insufficiently Known   S Secure
   A European Threat Status category is also assigned to SPEC 1 species but these species are not dependent on this for their SPEC classification.
[3] Concentrated in Europe: species with more than 50% of their global population or range lying within Europe.

Box 1. Species of European Conservation Concern (SPECs).

Category 1 Species of global conservation concern because they are classified as Globally Threatened, Conservation Dependent or Data Deficient in *Birds to Watch 2: the World List of Threatened Birds* (Collar *et al.* 1994).

Category 2 Species whose global populations are concentrated in Europe (i.e. more than 50% of their global population or range in Europe) and which have an Unfavourable Conservation Status in Europe (see Box 4).

Category 3 Species whose global populations are not concentrated in Europe, but which have an Unfavourable Conservation Status in Europe.

Category 4 Species whose global populations are concentrated in Europe (i.e. species with more than 50% of their global population or range in Europe) but which have a Favourable Conservation Status in Europe (see Box 4).

criteria have therefore had to take into consideration the quality and availability of information on European bird populations, and calculations are thus based on categories of population trend rather than on precise figures. Likewise, to take account of the broad ranges involved in most estimates of population size, calculation of proportions in decline are performed using both population minima and maxima, and, as a precautionary measure, the higher proportion is used in the assessment of a species' European Threat Status (see Box 5 for a worked example).

Due to these data limitations it is impossible to use an exact measure of population decline in each country to calculate the rate of a species' decline in Europe as a whole. Consequently, a species that has, for example, 45% of its population in countries where it has declined by 20–49% could feasibly have

a higher overall rate of decline than a species that has 70% of its population in countries where it has declined by 20–49%.

Because the area of each species' range is known only poorly in most countries (except where recent comprehensive atlas studies have been carried out), assessments of the decline in range are based on the percentage of the European population (rather than range) occurring in countries where range has declined. Inevitably therefore, range declines in large populations are given greater weight than those in marginal parts of the range.

Despite the use of flexible and easily applied criteria, data limitations sometimes mean that it is prudent to allocate European Threat Status categories only provisionally. This has been the case when more than 50% of the European population (according to *both* the minima and maxima of the country populations) have:

- population size data that are poor (verification code 1) or of unknown quality, *or*
- population or range trend data that are poor or of unknown quality, or missing (see Box 5).

These assessments are made on the basis of breeding season data unless a species qualifies on winter data. Assessment of overall population trends solely on the basis of the quantitative data which are available (i.e. restricting the analysis for a species to countries with verification code 2 or 3) would introduce regional biases and therefore be invalid. Bird populations in east and south-east Europe, for example, are particularly poorly known, largely due to the lower number of ornithologists in these regions. Clearly, the population trends in these areas may often be different from those in other parts of Europe.

Box 2. Summary of European Threat Status criteria and categories.

Criteria: European population size/trend	<250 pairs	<2,500 pairs	<10,000 pairs	>10,000 pairs
Large decline	ENDANGERED	ENDANGERED	ENDANGERED	VULNERABLE
Moderate decline	ENDANGERED	ENDANGERED	VULNERABLE	DECLINING
No decline	ENDANGERED	VULNERABLE	RARE	SECURE

In addition, species that have more than 10,000 pairs in Europe are categorized as **LOCALIZED** if more than 90% of the population occurs at 10 sites or fewer. See Boxes 3 and 4 for full details of criteria.

Notes
- Winter population criteria use flyway population levels of less than 1,000, 10,000 and 40,000 individuals as respective equivalents to the figures of 250, 2,500 and 10,000 pairs used above for breeding populations.

- Due to inadequate data for most species, declines in winter populations are only considered for Anatidae, Haematopodidae, Charadriidae and Scolopacidae.

Box 3. Classification of European Threat Status.

All population size thresholds refer to minimum population estimates.

Insufficiently Known Suspected to be Localized, Declining, Rare, Vulnerable or Endangered (as below), but insufficient information is available to attribute a European Threat Status, even provisionally.

Remaining categories are ranked here in ascending order of threat.

Secure Population more than 10,000 breeding pairs or 40,000 wintering birds, and neither in moderate or large decline nor Localized. Secure species have a Favourable Conservation Status.

Localized Population more than 10,000 breeding pairs or 40,000 wintering birds, and neither in moderate nor in large decline, but with more than 90% of the population occurring at 10 or fewer sites (Important Bird Areas), as listed in Grimmett and Jones (1989).

Declining Population in moderate decline (see Box 4) and population more than 10,000 breeding pairs or 40,000 wintering individuals.

Rare Population neither in moderate nor in large decline but fewer than 10,000 breeding pairs and not marginal to a larger non-European population; or European wintering population and entire flyway population less than 40,000 birds and therefore at risk due to the susceptibility of small populations to:
– break-up of social structure;
– loss of genetic diversity;
– large-scale population fluctuations and chance events;
– existing or potential exploitation, persecution, disturbance and interference by man.

Vulnerable Any of the following.
• Population in large decline (see Box 4) and of more than 10,000 breeding pairs or 40,000 wintering individuals.
• Population in moderate decline *and* population fewer than 10,000 breeding pairs and not marginal to a larger non-European population or European wintering and entire flyway population fewer than 40,000 birds.
• Population neither in moderate nor in large decline but fewer than 2,500 breeding pairs and not marginal to a larger non-European population; or European wintering and entire flyway population fewer than 10,000 birds and therefore at risk due to the susceptibility of small populations to the factors described under 'Rare' above.

Endangered Any of the following.
• Population in large decline *and* population fewer than 10,000 breeding pairs and not marginal to a larger non-European population or European wintering and entire flyway population fewer than 40,000 birds.
• Population in moderate decline *and* population fewer than 2,500 breeding pairs and not marginal to a larger non-European population or European wintering and entire flyway population fewer than 10,000 birds.
• Population neither in moderate nor in large decline but fewer than 250 breeding pairs and not marginal to a larger non-European population; or European wintering and entire flyway population fewer than 1,000 birds and therefore at risk due to the susceptibility of small populations to factors described above.

Box 4. Definitions of terms used in the criteria.

Concentrated in Europe More than 50% of the species' breeding or wintering population or range occurs in Europe, according to range maps in Cramp et al. (1977–1993) or Harrison (1982) or to global population estimates where available.

Conservation Dependent A species which does not qualify as Globally Threatened but is the focus of a continuing conservation programme, the cessation of which would result in the species qualifying as Globally Threatened (Collar et al. 1994).

Data Deficient A species for which there is inadequate information to make a direct or indirect assessment of its risk of global extinction (Collar et al. 1994).

Favourable Conservation Status The European Threat Status is classed as Secure (see Box 3).

Large decline Applied to a breeding or wintering population which has declined in size or range by at least 20% in at least 66% of the population or by at least 50% in at least 25% of the population between 1970 and 1990, and where the total size of populations that declined is greater than the total size of populations that increased. Only wintering populations of waterbirds of the families Anatidae, Haematopodidae, Charadriidae and Scolopacidae are considered because these are typically the only species which have well monitored winter populations.

Marginal population European populations that are considered to have adequate potential for repopulation from large non-European populations (the combined total of which is 10,000 pairs or more) and which are therefore not at risk from small population size.

Moderate decline Applied to a breeding or wintering population which has declined in size or range by at least 20% in 33–65% of the population or by at least 50% in 12–24% of the population between 1970 and 1990, and where the total size of populations that declined is greater than the total size of populations that increased. See also 'Large decline' (above) for restriction on species covered.

Unfavourable Conservation Status The European Threat Status is classed as Endangered, Vulnerable, Rare, Declining, Localized or Insufficiently Known (see Box 3).

Box 5. Example calculation of population trend parameters and European Threat Status.

Red-throated Diver *Gavia stellata*. Population data are as follows (for an explanation of data tables, see p. 34).

	Breeding population			Breeding
	Size (pairs)	Year	Trend	range trend
Denmark				
Faroe Islands	10–15	81	(–1)	(–1)
Greenland	(5,000–30,000)	—	(0)	(0)
Finland	**800–1,000**	92	–1	**0**
Iceland	1,000–2,000	—	(0)	(0)
Rep. of Ireland	10–10	88–91	0	0
Norway	2,000–5,000	90	–1	**+1**
Svalbard	100–1,000	—	(0)	0
Russia	50,000–100,000	80–90	–1	0
Sweden	1,000–1,500	87	–1	0
United Kingdom	**1,400–1,400**	88–91	**+1**	**+1**
Total (approx.)	61,000–140,000			

Trends	+2 Large increase	+1 Small increase	0 Stable	X Extinct
(1970–1990)	–2 Large decrease	–1 Small decrease	F Fluctuating	N New breeder
Data quality	**Bold:** reliable quantitative data	Normal type: incomplete quantitative data		
	Bracketed figures: no quantitative data	* Data quality not provided		

1. Population size
- Minimum total European population >10,000 pairs.

	Population minima	Population maxima
2. Calculation of population size decline (see Box 4)		
Total of populations which have declined in size by >20% (–2 or –1 in table)	53,810	107,515
Total of populations which have increased in size by >20% (+2 or –1)	1,400	1,400
■ Thus, population size declines are greater than increases.		
Total of populations with unknown size trends	0	0
Percentage of population (with known trends) which have declined in size by >20%	88%	77%
Total of populations which have declined in size by >50%	0	0
Percentage of population (with known trends) that declined in size by >50%	0%	0%

3. Calculation of breeding range decline

Total of populations which have declined in range by >20%	10	15
Total of populations which have increased in range by >20%	3,400	6,400

■ Thus, breeding range declines are less than increases.
Therefore range has not declined and no further calculations are necessary.

4. Assessment of data quality (see p. 26)

Total of populations with no quantitative data for population size, or	5,000	30,000
data quality not provided	=8%	=21%
Total of populations with no quantitative data for population size trend, or	6,110	33,105
data quality not provided	=10%	=23%
Total of populations with no quantitative data for population range trend, or	6,010	32,015
data quality not provided	=10%	=23%

Summary of population status
- Population >10,000 pairs.
- Large decline in population size (i.e. population declined by >20% in >66% of its population and total of populations that declined is greater than total of populations that increased).
- No decline in range.
- <50% of population size and trend data are poor or missing.

Thus, European Threat Status is **VULNERABLE** (and not provisional).

Integration of breeding and wintering population data

For selected well-monitored waterbirds the identification of SPECs and the assessment of European Threat Status is carried out separately on breeding and on wintering populations. SPEC and European Threat Status categories are allocated according to breeding population data if these categories indicate an equal or higher degree of threat than those based on winter populations. This is because winter populations may well be inadequately monitored and declines may be obscured by variable emigration from Europe and by influxes of migrants from outside the region. Consequently, conservation measures should cover the whole year for such species when they winter in significant numbers in Europe.

It would often be inappropriate to apply a higher SPEC category to breeding populations where this is based on winter populations, as breeding and wintering populations may differ considerably in both size and origin. Conservation measures for breeding populations could be misplaced for such birds, especially where breeding populations are apparently secure. In such circumstances, therefore, SPEC and European Threat Status categories are given for both breeding and winter populations. If a species only qualifies as a SPEC according to winter data then this is indicated.

USE AND INTERPRETATION OF THE CRITERIA AND CATEGORIES

In general, conservation importance should be allocated according to SPEC category (i.e. highest importance given to the conservation of species of global concern, category 1) and the urgency for action should take into account the species' Euro-

pean Threat Status. However, the SPEC category and European Threat Status alone do not necessarily indicate the importance of, or urgency for, conservation actions at the national level. Assessment of these should also take into account the proportion of the global and European populations in the country, the species' national population status, the potential for successful action, its costs, the species' potential as a 'flagship' to promote conservation, the effects of action on other species, and other logistical, political and strategic considerations.

Therefore absence of a species from the SPEC list or its allocation to a low European Threat Status does not automatically justify its exclusion from national conservation actions or from regional European programmes (e.g. within the European Union), as the maintenance of regional European and national bird diversities and population levels is highly desirable. On the other hand, recognition as a Species of European Conservation Concern should be seen as additional justification for such conservation measures.

DATA PRESENTATION

DATA COLLECTED during this review form the the main part of this book, which presents concise accounts for every Species of European Conservation Concern, bringing together important information on each species' conservation status. Full species accounts are given in the first section, for species with an Unfavourable Conservation Status, i.e. SPEC categories 1, 2 and 3. In the second section, shorter accounts are given for species that have a Favourable Conservation Status but which have their global population or range concentrated in Europe, i.e. SPEC category 4.

SPECIES OF EUROPEAN CONSERVATION CONCERN, CATEGORIES 1–3

The main section of this book presents species accounts for each of the 195 Species of European Conservation Concern that have an Unfavourable Conservation Status (SPEC categories 1–3). The writing of these texts has depended heavily on the voluntary contributions of a network of over 120 ornithological experts from 30 countries throughout Europe. Additionally, since many of the species have wide distributions, some accounts have been reviewed independently in order to add viewpoints from different geographical parts of the species' European range.

Species accounts are presented in the taxonomic sequence of Voous (1977), and English names largely follow *The birds of the western Palearctic* (Cramp *et al.* 1977–1994) with the exception of those classified as Globally Threatened, Conservation Dependent, Data Deficient and Near Threatened by Collar *et al.* (1994) which follow the names used in that work. New species recognized by Sibley and Monroe (1990, 1993) use the names adopted by those authors. Each account header summarizes the status of the species (see Box 1), giving SPEC and European Threat Status categories, and the criteria for its qualification as a SPEC of Unfavourable Conservation Status (see Figure 1 and Boxes 1–4 on pp. 27–29 for an explanation of the categories and criteria). All species in this section qualify for inclusion on their unfavour-

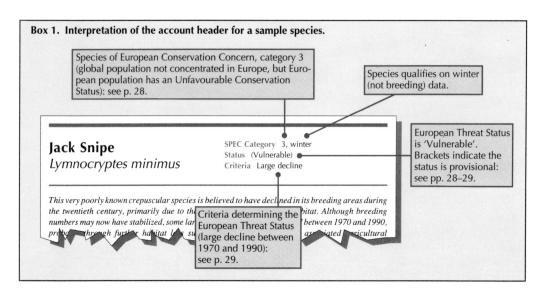

Box 1. Interpretation of the account header for a sample species.

Species of European Conservation Concern, category 3 (global population not concentrated in Europe, but European population has an Unfavourable Conservation Status): see p. 28.

Species qualifies on winter (not breeding) data.

Jack Snipe
Lymnocryptes minimus

SPEC Category 3, winter
Status (Vulnerable)
Criteria Large decline

European Threat Status is 'Vulnerable'. Brackets indicate the status is provisional: see pp. 28–29.

This very poorly known crepuscular species is believed to have declined in its breeding areas during the twentieth century, primarily due to the [...] *bitat. Although breeding numbers may now have stabilized, some lar* [...] *between 1970 and 1990,* [...] *through further habitat l* [...] *su* [...] *iated* [...] *ricultural*

Criteria determining the European Threat Status (large decline between 1970 and 1990): see p. 29.

able *breeding* status, unless the SPEC Category and Status in the header indicate otherwise.

Each species account contains a general summary followed by sections on 'Distribution and population trends', 'Ecology', 'Threats' and 'Conservation measures'. Details of all references cited are presented at the end of the book ('Text References', p. 551).

Distribution and population trends

The broad distribution of the species in Europe is summarized, including the approximate proportion of the global range lying within the region where this is known. Important populations within Europe are emphasized and the quality of available data is discussed. The population trends are described for the 1970–1990 period with, where possible, broader discussion of longer term trends, and emphasis on countries or regions where trends are most significant. The text is largely based on data collated during this review and should be read in conjunction with the accompanying map and population table (see below). For species classified as Localized (see p. 29), important breeding or wintering sites (as appropriate) are listed in a second table (see below).

Ecology

Habitats important for the species throughout its European range are described, with distinctions made, where appropriate, between feeding and nesting requirements, and breeding and wintering habitats. Special attention is given to habitats occupied in countries with important populations. Other aspects of the biology such as general dietary requirements and also population ecology including flocking and migratory status may also be mentioned. The text is a summary of points pertinent to the species' conservation requirements, supporting other sections in the account; it is not a detailed account of the species' ecology.

Threats

Factors considered to be responsible for the species' decline or vulnerability are described. An indication of the relative importance of each threat is given, and where possible the impact of the threat throughout the species' range addressed. Emphasis is given to threats in countries where declines have been greatest or where populations are largest. Demonstrated threats are distinguished from generally claimed threats but in many cases, although probably valid, it is impossible to conclude that claimed threats are definitely affecting the population dynamics of a species. Threats to a species which are limited to its wintering grounds outside Europe are generally considered beyond the remit of this book.

Conservation measures

This section includes recommendations for action, as well as describing measures already being carried out. Species, site and wide-scale habitat conservation measures are addressed where applicable, with emphasis on core population requirements. For example, information on the species' inclusion within protected areas is given, with emphasis on the concentration of birds in Important Bird Areas (Grimmett and Jones 1989), and suitable policy mechanisms that could be used to implement broad habitat management measures are identified. If appropriate, the need for further population monitoring is considered, as are the types of research which are required to determine the reasons for declines or to safeguard existing populations. It is stressed that this section is a brief summary of general conservation measures and does not aspire to fully address the conservation needs of the species.

Tables

A data table, generated directly from the BirdLife International/EBCC European Bird Database, accompanies each species account and presents those data gathered during this review that have been used to assess each species' conservation status (see 'Data Collection', pp. 25–26). The table also provides full details of the data which are presented in the map and which are summarized in the 'Distribution and population trends' section of the account.

Population sizes and trends, and range trends, are listed by country, together with indications of the quality of the data; all of which relate to the 1970–1990 period. Since data quality varies greatly, these codes should be examined closely when interpreting the table. Indeed, *we advise caution in the use of individual population or trend figures that are based on poor, non-quantitative data* (i.e. shown by figures within brackets: see Box 2). When used in combination with other European estimates such data are extremely useful indicators of broad population size and change, but individually they may be subject to significant error. The range for the total European population size of a species, given to two significant figures, should also be regarded only as a guideline estimate (except where comprehensively based on high-quality data) due to the considerable margin of error which is sometimes involved. Only minimum totals are presented for winter data in order to avoid double-counting of birds moving between countries. For guidance on the use of the table and an explanation of codes, see Box 2. Data were not collected by questionnaire for bird populations in Yugoslavia, Bosnia and Herzegovina, Former Yugoslav Republic of Macedonia, Armenia, Georgia and Azerbaijan, and tables (and maps) there-

Box 2. Interpretation of data table.

	Breeding population			Breeding
	Size (pairs)	Year	Trend	range trend
Belarus	(0–5)	90	N	N
Belgium	2–3	—	F	1
Bulgaria	500–5,000	—	(0)	0
Croatia	690–1,000	91	–1*	–1*
Czech Republic	**300–370**	—	**+2**	**0**
France	**4,143–4,143**	89	**+1**	**0**

Breeding population size   The minimum and maximum figures for breeding population size; normally in pairs, but occasionally in individuals, as indicated. All numbers are rounded to two significant figures. 'P' indicates that the species is present but that no other information is available.

Winter population size   The minimum and maximum mid-winter population size; in individuals.

Year   The year(s) to which the population size estimate refers, when based on a survey. If no year is given the population estimate refers to 1992–1993, the period of data collation for this project.

Trend   The overall population trend for the 1970–1990 period:

+2   Large increase of at least 50%
+1   Small increase of 20–49%
 0   Stable, with overall change less than 20%
–1   Small decrease of 20–49%
–2   Large decrease of at least 50%
 F   Fluctuating with changes of at least 20%, but no clear trend
 N   New breeder within period
 X   Gone extinct within period
 —   No trend data

Breeding range trend/Winter range trend   The overall range trend for the 1970–1990 period (the same categories apply as for population trends).

Data quality   Reliability and accuracy of the data are shown by allocation to one of four categories, indicated as follows.

Bold: reliable quantitative data (e.g. atlas, survey or monitoring data) are available for the whole period and region in question (verification code 3: see p. 26).
Normal type: generally well known, but only poor or incomplete quantitative data available (verification code 2).
Bracketed figures: poorly known, no quantitative data available (verification code 1).
* Data quality unknown (no verification code provided).

Nation states are listed alphabetically. Greenland, Svalbard, Faroe Islands, Isle of Man, Guernsey, Jersey, Gibraltar, Azores, Madeira and Canary Islands are listed under their respective nation states. Figures for the Isle of Man, Guernsey and Jersey are included within the United Kingdom totals where indicated in the tables; where there is no such indication (as often for Guernsey and Jersey) the figures are additional to those given for the United Kingdom.

fore do not include data for these countries even when they are mentioned in the text.

The data were collated largely via a network of national compilers (see p. 25), and citation details of the literature sources used are given at the end of the book (see p. 514).

For species whose European Threat Status is defined as Localized, a second table lists the top ten sites according to *Important Bird Areas in Europe* (Grimmett and Jones 1989), for breeding or mid-winter populations as appropriate. The conservation of sites is an important component of any conservation strategy and is of particular significance for Localized species.

Map

Almost every species account is accompanied by a map presenting the population sizes and trends of the species in each European country or autonomous region. These maps present a broad impression of the status of the species in Europe, allowing rapid identification of key countries in which the species occurs and the trends of the population in every country between 1970 and 1990. Patterns in distribution and trend may be easily assessed and compared. The accompanying population table should be consulted for more precise data on numbers and trends and for information on data quality.

The maps are based on data from the European Bird Database, analysed and mapped using a geographical information system software package (Atlas GIS). As with the tables, information is presented for breeding populations unless the species is qualifying on winter data only. See Box 3 for details.

A standard base-map of Europe of the Lambert projection has been used, and in maps for species occurring in the Canary Islands, Azores, Madeira or Svalbard an appropriate inset is included (Figure 1).

Box 3. Interpretation of maps.

A symbol is placed in each country where the species occurs: the *shape and colour* of the symbol represent the population trend and the *height* of the symbol corresponds to population size. Position of the symbol does not relate to the species' distribution within the country.

Symbol shape/colour Population trends for the 1970–1990 period, as presented in the accompanying data table for each species, are grouped into four categories represented by four symbol types:

Symbol type		Equivalent code in data table
Increasing	⬆	Increase of 20% or more (+1, +2) or new breeder (N).
Stable	▮	Stable, i.e. change less than 20% (0), or fluctuating, i.e. changes of 20% or more but no clear trend (F).
Decreasing	⬇	Decrease of 20% or more (-1, -2).
Unknown	☐	No trend data available.

Populations that have gone extinct during the 1970–1990 period are not shown.

A SAMPLE MAP:
EAGLE OWL *BUBO BUBO*

Symbol size Each symbol-type may occur in up to four different sizes. *The overall height of the symbol corresponds to a population size or to a range of population sizes.* The bottom legend on each map gives vertical lines showing the symbol heights which correspond to different population sizes. Note that symbol area is *not* directly proportional to population size.

In order to assign each national population to one of the size categories a number of calculations were made. Firstly for each country the geometric mean of minimum and maximum population sizes was calculated, in order to standardize values logarithmically. For each species, geometric means were ranged in Atlas GIS using an 'optimal ranging' method, placing the values in groups, and allowing maximum distance between groups and minimum distance within groups. These groups may cover a range of values or be a single value.

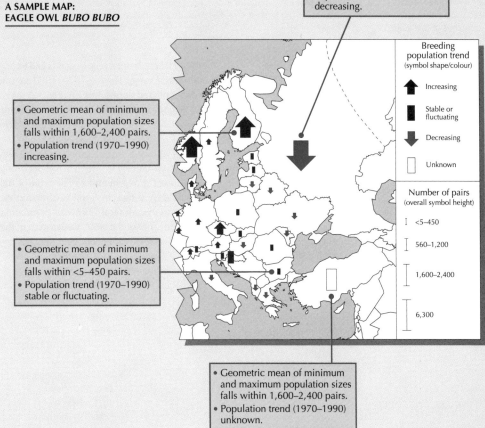

• Geometric mean of minimum and maximum population size is 6,300 pairs.
• Population trend (1970–1990) decreasing.

• Geometric mean of minimum and maximum population sizes falls within 1,600–2,400 pairs.
• Population trend (1970–1990) increasing.

• Geometric mean of minimum and maximum population sizes falls within <5–450 pairs.
• Population trend (1970–1990) stable or fluctuating.

• Geometric mean of minimum and maximum population sizes falls within 1,600–2,400 pairs.
• Population trend (1970–1990) unknown.

Breeding population trend (symbol shape/colour)

⬆ Increasing

▮ Stable or fluctuating

⬇ Decreasing

☐ Unknown

Number of pairs (overall symbol height)

I <5–450

560–1,200

1,600–2,400

6,300

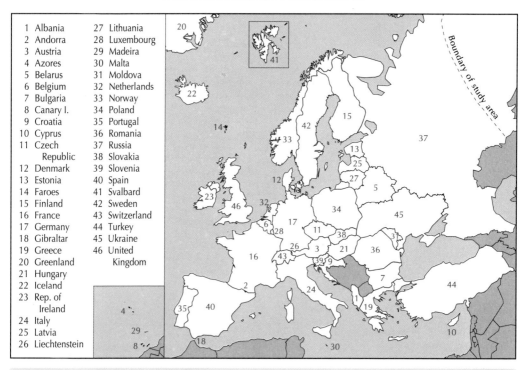

1 Albania	27 Lithuania		
2 Andorra	28 Luxembourg		
3 Austria	29 Madeira		
4 Azores	30 Malta		
5 Belarus	31 Moldova		
6 Belgium	32 Netherlands		
7 Bulgaria	33 Norway		
8 Canary I.	34 Poland		
9 Croatia	35 Portugal		
10 Cyprus	36 Romania		
11 Czech	37 Russia		
Republic	38 Slovakia		
12 Denmark	39 Slovenia		
13 Estonia	40 Spain		
14 Faroes	41 Svalbard		
15 Finland	42 Sweden		
16 France	43 Switzerland		
17 Germany	44 Turkey		
18 Gibraltar	45 Ukraine		
19 Greece	46 United		
20 Greenland	Kingdom		
21 Hungary			
22 Iceland			
23 Rep. of			
Ireland			
24 Italy			
25 Latvia			
26 Liechtenstein			

Figure 1. The geopolitical units for which data are presented in this review (data for Guernsey, Jersey and the Isle of Man were collected separately from that for the United Kingdom but are not shown in the maps, although they are provided in the tables).

As with the tables, no data are shown for bird populations in Yugoslavia, Bosnia and Herzegovina, Former Yugoslav Republic of Macedonia, Armenia, Georgia and Azerbaijan, and maps are therefore not presented for species which occur only in these regions.

SPECIES OF EUROPEAN CONSERVATION CONCERN, CATEGORY 4

Short accounts (p. 439) are presented for this group of species, i.e. those that have a Favourable Conservation Status but which are concentrated in Europe (see p. 28 for criteria). The texts describe distribu-

tion, migratory status, habitat requirements and trends in population and range for the 1970–1990 period based on data collated during this review.

A table accompanying most accounts presents data for population size and trend, and for range trend, in countries which hold more than 5% of the total European numbers (upper group in table) and for any additional countries which have declining populations (lower group in table). The total of the populations held by these two groups of countries, together with the overall total European population size is given at the foot of the table. Codes used in the tables follow those which accompany species accounts for SPEC categories 1–3 (see Box 2).

OVERVIEW OF RESULTS

THIS REVIEW reveals that of the 514 species regularly occurring in Europe, 278 qualify as being Species of European Conservation Concern (Figure 1, and see Appendix 1, p. 470, for a summary of the conservation status of all birds). Twenty-four of these (Table 1) are of global conservation concern (SPEC category 1) and are clearly of highest conservation importance, requiring stringent conservation measures wherever they occur regularly. This is particularly important in cases where Europe holds large proportions, or all, of their world populations, and especially when they are also highly threatened. Such species include Zino's Petrel *Pterodroma madeira* and Spanish Imperial Eagle *Aquila adalberti*.

In total, 195 of the 278 species have an Unfavourable Conservation Status (SPEC categories 1–3) be-

cause their populations are either declining, or are small and non-marginal, or are highly localized in Europe (Table 2). These species comprise approximately 38% of Europe's avifauna.

A further 83 species fall into SPEC category 4 because, although they have a Favourable Conservation Status, the majority of their breeding or midwinter populations are in Europe. Although their European populations are not currently at risk, Europe has a special responsibility for these species and should take measures to safeguard and monitor their numbers. Such species would immediately qualify for SPEC category 2 if their conservation status were to become unfavourable, and in some cases they could quickly become Globally Threatened, especially where their populations or ranges are small. Furthermore, 23 of the SPEC category 4 species (28%) are only provisionally regarded as secure, for example Little Crake *Porzana parva*, Ruff *Philomachus pugnax* and Nightingale *Luscinia megarhynchos*, and should therefore be subject to particular scrutiny.

Of those species with an Unfavourable Conservation Status, 33 species are considered to be Endangered in Europe (Tables 2–3) and are thus particularly in need of urgent conservation actions, or the continuation of conservation programmes where these are already in place. Also of particular concern is the high proportion of European species that are subject to a substantial decline, and indeed, 101 species qualify as having an Unfavourable Conservation Status on this criterion alone (39 have shown moderate declines and therefore qualify as Declining, while 62 have shown large declines and are classed as Vulnerable). More alarming still, however, is the fact that the total number of substantially declining species (those showing moderate or large declines), including those that qualify on other threat criteria, amounts to 129, or 25% of all European species, and 86 of these have shown large declines (Table 4).

Nineteen species are classed as Rare and, although these species may not be declining, they are

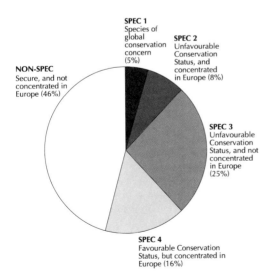

Figure 1. The proportion of European species within each category of Species of European Conservation Concern (SPEC). Altogether there are 514 species which occur regularly in Europe (see Appendix 1, p. 470, for a detailed listing).

Table 1. The European status of species of global conservation concern.

	Threat status		Proportion in Europe [3]	Minimum population in Europe (pairs)	% in decline [4]	% in rapid decline [5]
	Global [1]	Europe [2]				
Fea's Petrel *Pterodroma feae*	VU	E	ooo	150	0	0
Zino's Petrel *Pterodroma madeira*	CR	E	◆	20	?	?
Dalmatian Pelican *Pelecanus crispus*	VU	V	oo	960	19	6
Lesser White-fronted Goose *Anser erythropus*	VU	V	oo	1,000	3	0
Red-breasted Goose *Branta ruficollis* (w)	VU	L ᵂ	◆	76,000 ⁱⁿᵈ	0	0
Marbled Teal *Marmaronetta angustirostris*	VU	E	oo	200	100	100
Ferruginous Duck *Aythya nyroca*	VU	V	oooo	11,000	82	2
Steller's Eider *Polysticta stelleri* (w)	VU	L ᵂ	?	14,000 ⁱⁿᵈ	0	0
White-headed Duck *Oxyura leucocephala*	VU	E	oo	210	0	0
Greater Spotted Eagle *Aquila clanga*	VU	E	ooo	860	98	1
Imperial Eagle *Aquila heliaca*	VU	E	ooo	320	86	13
Spanish Imperial Eagle *Aquila adalberti*	VU	E	◆	150	0	0
Lesser Kestrel *Falco naumanni*	VU	(V)	ooo	10,000	99	73
Corncrake *Crex crex*	VU	V	ooo	92,000	99	56
Great Bustard *Otis tarda*	VU	D	oooo	26,000 ⁱⁿᵈ	61	5
Sociable Plover *Chettusia gregaria*	VU	E	oo	1,000	100	0
Slender-billed Curlew *Numenius tenuirostris*	CR	— [6]	—	—	—	—
Audouin's Gull *Larus audouinii*	CD	L	ooooo	13,000	0	0
Long-toed Pigeon *Columba trocaz*	CD	V	◆	3,500 ⁱⁿᵈ	0	0
Dark-tailed Laurel Pigeon *Columba bollii*	VU	V	◆	1,700 ⁱⁿᵈ	0	0
White-tailed Laurel Pigeon *Columba junoniae*	VU	V	◆	1,200 ⁱⁿᵈ	0	0
Aquatic Warbler *Acrocephalus paludicola*	VU	E	◆	3,700	69	1
Blue Chaffinch *Fringilla teydea*	CD	V	◆	1,000	0	0
Scottish Crossbill *Loxia scotica*	DD	Ins	◆	300	?	?

(w) Data refer to wintering populations in Europe (other data are breeding populations).

ⁱⁿᵈ Population figures refer to individuals.

[1] CR Critical, VU Vulnerable, CD Conservation Dependent, DD Data Deficient (Collar *et al.* 1994). Species listed as Critical or Vulnerable are considered to be Globally Threatened.

[2] E Endangered, V Vulnerable, R Rare, D Declining, L Localized, Ins Insufficiently Known. ᵂ indicates that the category relates to winter populations. Parentheses indicate that the European Threat Status is provisional.

[3] Proportion of the global range (or population where known) within Europe:

◆	Endemic to Europe	ooo	26–50%
ooooo	76–99%	oo	6–25%
oooo	51–75%	o	<5%

[4] Percentage of the European population which is in countries where population size has declined by >20% during 1970–1990.

[5] Percentage of the European population which is in countries where population size has declined by >50% during 1970–1990.

[6] No European Threat Status is given as the species is only a passage migrant in the region.

NB Two further European species listed as Globally Threatened by Collar and Andrew (1988) no longer occur in the region: Canary Islands Oystercatcher *Haematopus meadewaldoi* is now acknowledged to be globally extinct and the wild population of Northern Bald Ibis *Geronticus eremita* has recently become extinct in Europe (Collar *et al.* 1994).

Table 2. The European Threat Status of SPECs with an Unfavourable Conservation Status (i.e. SPECs 1–3).

European Threat Status	SPEC category			Total
	1	2	3	
Endangered	9	2	22	33
Vulnerable	9	20	54	83
Rare	0	5	14	19
Declining	1	9	29	39
Localized	3	4 [1]	9 [2]	16
Insufficiently Known	1	1	2	4
No status	1	0	0	1
Total	24	41	130	195

[1] This includes one species with SPEC category 4 (breeding population), but which is category 2 in winter.
[2] This includes one species with SPEC category 4 (breeding population), but which is category 3 in winter.

Table 3. Population size, and percentage of population in decline, for species with an 'Endangered' European Threat Status. Species of global conservation concern (SPEC category 1) are indicated in bold. Data refer to breeding populations in Europe.

	SPEC category	Minimum population in Europe (pairs)	% in decline [1]	% in rapid decline [2]
Fea's Petrel *Pterodroma feae*	1	150	0	0
Zino's Petrel *Pterodroma madeira*	1	20	?	?
Spoonbill *Platalea leucorodia*	2	5,200	77	34
Marbled Teal *Marmaronetta angustirostris*	1	200	100	100
Barrow's Goldeneye *Bucephala islandica*	3	200	0	0
White-headed Duck *Oxyura leucocephala*	1	210	0	0
Lammergeier *Gypaetus barbatus*	3	200	6	0
Egyptian Vulture *Neophron percnopterus*	3	2,800	98	2
Pallid Harrier *Circus macrourus*	3	1,000	100	1
Long-legged Buzzard *Buteo rufinus*	3	2,000	81	0
Greater Spotted Eagle *Aquila clanga*	1	860	98	1
Imperial Eagle *Aquila heliaca*	1	320	86	13
Spanish Imperial Eagle *Aquila adalberti*	1	150	0	0
Bonnelli's Eagle *Hieraaetus fasciatus*	3	820	94	0
Lanner *Falco biarmicus*	3	200	84	0
Saker *Falco cherrug*	3	370	80	8
Barbary Partridge *Alectoris barbara*	3	3,700	99	0
Andalusian Hemipode *Turnix sylvatica*	3	5	100	100
Crested Coot *Fulica cristata*	3	10	0	0
Houbara Bustard *Chlamydotis undulata*	3	200	?	?
Collared Pratincole *Glareola pratincola*	3	6,700	75	5
Greater Sand Plover *Charadrius leschenaultii*	3	100	?	?
Spur-winged Plover *Hoplopterus spinosus*	3	1,000	97	0
Sociable Plover *Chettusia gregaria*	1	1,000	100	0
Ivory Gull *Pagophila eburnea*	3	1,300	100	0
Gull-billed Tern *Gelochelidon nilotica*	3	6,800	95	0
Caspian Tern *Sterna caspia*	3	4,800	97	0
Roseate Tern *Sterna dougallii*	3	1,600	71	9
Pin-tailed Sandgrouse *Pterocles alchata*	3	6,700	100	98
Black Wheatear *Oenanthe leucura*	3	4,100	100	0
Aquatic Warbler *Acrocephalus paludicola*	1	3,700	69	1
Semi-collared Flycatcher *Ficedula semitorquata*	2	2,500	67	0
Great Rosefinch *Carpodacus rubicilla*	3	500	100	0

[1] Percentage of the European population which is in countries where population size has declined by >20% during 1970–1990.
[2] Percentage of the European population which is in countries where population size has declined by >50% during 1970–1990.

at some risk due to their susceptibility to the effects of population fluctuations, natural catastrophes, existing or potential exploitation, persecution, disturbance or other forms of human interference. Isolated and particularly small or fragmented populations may also be subject to the detrimental effects of loss of genetic diversity and disruptions to social behaviour or may simply be prone to extinction through the cumulative effects of chance demographic events (Soulé 1986, 1987, Pimm 1991).

Sixteen species are classed as Localized and are therefore susceptible because of their dependence on a small number of sites (Table 5). Consequently, although these species may not currently be affected by detrimental environmental changes, they are dependent on the protection and appropriate management of their key sites, including those mentioned in this review and others listed in *Important Bird Areas in Europe* (Grimmett and Jones 1989). This is par-

ticularly important for species whose populations at the global level are concentrated in Europe, such as Storm Petrel *Hydrobates pelagicus*, Gannet *Sula bassana* and especially the globally threatened Red-breasted Goose *Branta ruficollis*, as virtually the entire world population of the species congregates in Europe in winter.

The four species classed as Insufficiently Known (Caucasian Black Grouse *Tetrao mlokosiewiczi*, Caspian Snowcock *Tetraogallus caspius*, Güldenstädt's Redstart *Phoenicurus erythrogaster* and Scottish Crossbill *Loxia scotica*) require studies to assess their population sizes and trends and, in the case of Scottish Crossbill, its taxonomic status. However, in the meantime, conservation measures should be taken as appropriate according to the precautionary principle that the benefit of doubt over a species' status should rest with the species until proven otherwise.

Table 4. SPECs which have shown large declines in population size during 1970–1990. A large decline is shown by a population which has declined by at least 20% in at least 66% of its population or by at least 50% in at least 25% of its population, and the proportion of the population that declined is greater than the proportion that increased. Species of global conservation concern (SPEC category 1) are indicated in bold. For an explanation of European Threat Status codes see Table 1 (p. 38).

	SPEC category	European Threat Status	% in decline [1]	% in rapid decline [2]
European breeding populations				
Red-throated Diver *Gavia stellata*	3	V	88	0
Black-throated Diver *Gavia arctica*	3	V	96	0
Cory's Shearwater *Calonectris diomedea*	2	(V)	76	29
Bittern *Botaurus stellaris*	3	(V)	79	3
Little Bittern *Ixobrychus minutus*	3	(V)	92	7
Squacco Heron *Ardeola ralloides*	3	V	66	5
Purple Heron *Ardea purpurea*	3	V	99	4
White Stork *Ciconia ciconia*	2	V	52	38
Spoonbill *Platalea leucorodia*	2	E	77	34
Gadwall *Anas strepera*	3	V	79	1
Pintail *Anas acuta*	3	V	99	0
Garganey *Anas querquedula*	3	V	96	0
Marbled Teal *Marmaronetta angustirostris*	**1**	**E**	**100**	**100**
Ferruginous Duck *Aythya nyroca*	**1**	**V**	**82**	**2**
Black Kite *Milvus migrans*	3	V	73	1
Egyptian Vulture *Neophron percnopterus*	3	E	98	2
Hen Harrier *Circus cyaneus*	3	V	70	1
Pallid Harrier *Circus macrourus*	3	E	100	1
Long-legged Buzzard *Buteo rufinus*	3	(E)	81	0
Greater Spotted Eagle *Aquila clanga*	**1**	**E**	**98**	**1**
Steppe Eagle *Aquila rapax*	3	V	100	0
Imperial Eagle *Aquila heliaca*	**1**	**E**	**86**	**13**
Bonelli's Eagle *Hieraaetus fasciatus*	3	E	94	0
Lesser Kestrel *Falco naumanni*	**1**	**(V)**	**99**	**73**
Red-footed Falcon *Falco vespertinus*	3	V	100	93
Lanner *Falco biarmicus*	3	(E)	84	0
Saker *Falco cherrug*	3	E	72	12
Black Grouse *Tetrao tetrix*	3	V	69	51
Chukar *Alectoris chukar*	3	V	100	0
Rock Partridge *Alectoris graeca*	2	V	84	1
Red-legged Partridge *Alectoris rufa*	2	V	96	0
Barbary Partridge *Alectoris barbara*	3	E	99	0
Black Francolin *Francolinus francolinus*	3	V	100	0
Partridge *Perdix perdix*	3	V	99	37
Quail *Coturnix coturnix*	3	V	64	50
Andalusian Hemipode *Turnix sylvatica*	3	E	100	100
Corncrake *Crex crex*	**1**	**V**	**99**	**56**
Crane *Grus grus*	3	V	72	0
Little Bustard *Tetrax tetrax*	2	V	80	6
Stone Curlew *Burhinus oedicnemus*	3	V	74	1
Cream-coloured Courser *Cursorius cursor*	3	V	100	100
Collared Pratincole *Glareola pratincola*	3	E	75	5
Caspian Plover *Charadrius asiaticus*	3	(V)	100	100
Spur-winged Plover *Hoplopterus spinosus*	3	(E)	97	0
Sociable Plover *Chettusia gregaria*	**1**	**E**	**100**	**0**
Broad-billed Sandpiper *Limicola falcinellus*	3	(V)	75	0
Great Snipe *Gallinago media*	2	(V)	96	96
Black-tailed Godwit *Limosa limosa*	2	V	92	0
Ivory Gull *Pagophila eburnea*	3	(E)	100	0
Gull-billed Tern *Gelochelidon nilotica*	3	(E)	95	0
Caspian Tern *Sterna caspia*	3	(E)	97	0
Roseate Tern *Sterna dougallii*	3	E	71	9
Puffin *Fratercula arctica*	2	V	49	41
Black-bellied Sandgrouse *Pterocles orientalis*	3	V	100	99
Pin-tailed Sandgrouse *Pterocles alchata*	3	E	100	98
Eagle Owl *Bubo bubo*	3	V	65	57
Short-eared Owl *Asio flammeus*	3	(V)	77	74
Dupont's Lark *Chersophilus duponti*	3	V	100	0

cont.

Table 4 (cont.)

	SPEC category	European Threat Status	% in decline [1]	% in rapid decline [2]
Black Lark *Melanocorypha yeltoniensis*	3	(V)	100	0
Short-toed Lark *Calandrella brachydactyla*	3	V	90	0
Lesser Short-toed Lark *Calandrella rufescens*	3	V	72	0
Thekla Lark *Galerida theklae*	3	V	99	0
Woodlark *Lullula arborea*	2	V	75	0
Skylark *Alauda arvensis*	3	V	69	19
Tawny Pipit *Anthus campestris*	3	V	86	0
Redstart *Phoenicurus phoenicurus*	2	V	83	20
Black-eared Wheatear *Oenanthe hispanica*	2	V	88	0
Black Wheatear *Oenanthe leucura*	3	E	100	0
Blue Rock Thrush *Monticola solitarius*	3	(V)	71	0
Aquatic Warbler *Acrocephalus paludicola*	**1**	**E**	**69**	**1**
Olivaceous Warbler *Hippolais pallida*	3	(V)	82	0
Dartford Warbler *Sylvia undata*	2	V	93	0
Orphean Warbler *Sylvia hortensis*	3	V	94	1
Semi-collared Flycatcher *Ficedula semitorquata*	2	(E)	67	0
Woodchat Shrike *Lanius senator*	2	V	93	0
Masked Shrike *Lanius nubicus*	2	(V)	98	0
Chough *Pyrrhocorax pyrrhocorax*	3	V	92	6
Great Rosefinch *Carpodacus rubicilla*	3	(E)	100	0
Rock Bunting *Emberiza cia*	3	V	88	0
Ortolan Bunting *Emberiza hortulana*	2	(V)	49	41
Black-headed Bunting *Emberiza melanocephala*	2	(V)	81	0
European wintering populations [3]				
Pintail *Anas acuta* [4]	3	V	53	28
Marbled Teal *Marmaronetta angustirostris* [4]	1	E	100	100
Ferruginous Duck *Aythya nyroca* [4]	**1**	**V**	**92**	**79**
Dunlin *Calidris alpina*	3[w]	V [w]	92	26
Jack Snipe *Lymnocryptes minimus*	3[w]	(V) [w]	95	0
Woodcock *Scolopax rusticola*	3[w]	V [w]	86	83

[1] Percentage of the European population which is in countries where population size has declined by >20% during 1970–1990.

[2] Percentage of the European population which is in countries where population size has declined by >50% during 1970–1990.

[3] Only well-monitored species are considered (see p. 30).

[4] Qualifies also on declines in breeding population.

	SPEC category	Season [1]
Manx Shearwater *Puffinus puffinus*	2	B
White-faced Storm-petrel *Pelagodroma marina*	3	B
Storm Petrel *Hydrobates pelagicus*	2	B
Leach's Storm-petrel *Oceanodroma leucorhoa*	3	B
Gannet *Sula bassana*	2	B
Greater Flamingo *Phoenicopterus ruber*	3	B
Bewick's Swan *Cygnus columbianus*	3 [w]	W
Barnacle Goose *Branta leucopsis*	4/2	W
Red-breasted Goose *Branta ruficollis*	**1**	**W**
Scaup *Aythya marila*	3 [w]	W
Steller's Eider *Polysticta stelleri*	**1**	**W**
Velvet Scoter *Melanitta fusca*	3 [w]	W
Avocet *Recurvirostra avosetta*	4/3	W
Knot *Calidris canutus*	3 [w]	W
Bar-tailed Godwit *Limosa lapponica*	3 [w]	W
Audouin's Gull *Larus audouinii*	**1**	**B**

Table 5. Species that qualify as SPECs on the basis of localized populations only. Species of global conservation concern (SPEC category 1) are shown in bold.

[w] SPEC category relates to winter populations. For SPEC categories given as (e.g.) '4/2', the first number is the SPEC category relating to the breeding population, the second relates to the winter population.

[1] Season at which the species is localized: B breeding, W winter.

NB The wintering population of Brent Goose *Branta bernicla* is also localized but this species also qualifies as having an Unfavourable Conservation Status through its small breeding population.

PATTERNS OF DISTRIBUTION OF SPECS

The numbers of SPECs breeding in each country are given in Table 6 and listed in Appendix 2. Figure 2 summarizes those with an Unfavourable Conservation Status (SPEC categories 1–3). Although this simple analysis does not take into account the proportions of each species' European population in each country it does indicate broad levels of responsibility for the conservation of SPECs. Most impor-

tantly, all countries have SPECs and therefore all have responsibilities for the conservation of these species. It shows the particularly high importance of a number of individual countries, for example Russia, which holds within the European sector of its territory 195 breeding SPECs, 133 of which have an Unfavourable Conservation Status, and 11 of which are species of global conservation concern present in significant numbers. In addition, Red-breasted Goose

Table 6. The numbers of SPECs breeding in each country covered by this review.

	SPEC category			Subtotal SPECs 1–3	SPEC 4	Total	Country specific [1]
	1	2	3				
Albania	3	18	61	82	53	135	0
Andorra	0	9	22	31	35	66	0
Austria	3	14	43	60	54	114	0
Belarus	3	13	52	68	52	120	0
Belgium	1	10	34	45	49	94	0
Bulgaria	5	21	62	88	52	140	0
Croatia	4	19	55	78	52	130	0
Cyprus	2	10	22	34	12	46	2
Czech Republic	3	12	44	59	52	111	0
Denmark	1	11	38	50	52	102	0
Faroe Islands	0	7	8	15	20	35	0
Greenland	0	2	11	13	11	24	0
Estonia	1	13	45	59	51	110	0
Finland	3	9	50	62	52	114	0
France	3	26	69	98	61	159	1
Germany	4	12	52	68	60	128	0
Greece	5	25	65	95	52	147	0
Hungary	5	15	52	72	51	123	0
Iceland	0	7	16	23	18	41	1
Republic of Ireland	1	11	22	34	33	67	0
Italy	4	23	55	82	54	136	0
Latvia	3	12	44	59	50	109	0
Liechtenstein	1	2	18	21	36	57	0
Lithuania	3	12	43	58	47	105	0
Luxembourg	1	5	24	30	37	67	0
Malta	0	3	5	8	7	15	0
Moldova	6	13	46	65	40	105	0
Netherlands	2	11	40	53	47	100	0
Norway	2	14	42	58	50	108	0
Svalbard	0	2	5	7	6	13	0
Poland	4	14	54	73	56	128	0
Portugal	2	16	59	77	40	117	0
Azores	0	2	7	9	8	17	0
Madeira	3	3	12	18	10	28	3
Romania	7	19	65	91	52	143	0
Russia	12	23	98	133	62	195	6
Slovakia	4	15	49	68	51	119	0
Slovenia	3	11	38	52	52	104	0
Spain	8	22	76	106	53	159	4
Canary Islands	3	5	21	29	15	44	6
Sweden	2	11	49	62	55	117	0
Switzerland	2	9	38	50	51	101	0
Turkey	9	23	80	112	52	164	0
Ukraine	8	19	72	99	54	153	0
United Kingdom	2	15	38	55	54	109	1
Gibraltar	1	2	9	12	11	23	0
Guernsey	0	4	8	12	23	35	0
Isle of Man	1	7	16	24	28	52	0
Jersey	0	3	9	12	27	39	0

[1] The number of species that are confined to that country within Europe.

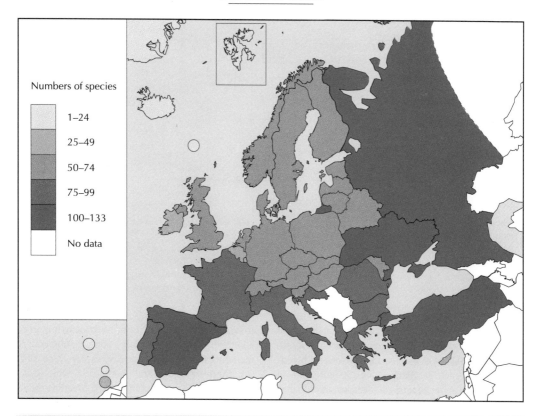

Figure 2. Numbers of Species of European Conservation Concern with an Unfavourable Conservation Status (SPEC categories 1–3) breeding in each European country.

and Slender-billed Curlew *Numenius tenuirostris* (which breed in Asiatic Russia) occur on passage and Steller's Eider *Polysticta stelleri* winters (and also breeds, though in trivial numbers). Obviously the large number of SPECs in European Russia is due partly to the great size of the region and the associated high diversity of habitats, including tundra, boreal and temperate forests, mountains, steppe, deserts, numerous wetlands and marine habitats of the Arctic, Baltic, Black and Caspian Seas. Furthermore, being at the eastern edge of Europe, the region holds a number of SPECs which have predominantly Asian ranges but which occur marginally in European Russia, such as Caspian Plover *Charadrius asiaticus*, Sociable Plover *Chettusia gregaria*, Black Lark *Melanocorypha yeltoniensis* and Black-throated Accentor *Prunella atrogularis*.

Other countries with more than 50% of all SPECs (i.e. 140 or more) breeding within them are Turkey, France, Spain, Ukraine, Greece, Romania and Bulgaria. Although low numbers of SPECs occur on the Canary Islands and Madeira archipelago, these islands are of considerable importance for their SPEC category 1 species, several of which are endemic to them (Zino's Petrel, Long-toed Pigeon *Columba*

trocaz, Dark-tailed Laurel Pigeon *C. bollii*, White-tailed Laurel Pigeon *C. junoniae* and Blue Chaffinch *Fringilla teydea*). Cyprus has two endemic species (Cyprus Pied Wheatear *Oenanthe cypriaca* and Cyprus Warbler *Sylvia melanothorax*), France one (Corsican Nuthatch *Sitta whiteheadi*), and the United Kingdom one (Scottish Crossbill).

Using information from the species accounts of this review, and other data collected at BirdLife International during the Dispersed Species Project, it has been possible to analyse habitat use by SPECs. Figure 3 shows the number of SPECs with an Unfavourable Conservation Status that use each habitat at some point in their annual cycle. Clearly, lowland farmland is the most frequently utilized habitat, being used by some 116 species, approximately 60% of all category 1–3 SPECs. A substantial number of these are highly dependent on this particular habitat, including seven of global conservation concern (Table 7). This reflects both the great extent of this habitat—which comprises c.50% of Europe's land surface outside the former U.S.S.R. and c.70% of the European Union (Anon. 1992b)—and its diversity. For example, particularly important agricultural habitats and their SPECs include: low-intensity hay meadows

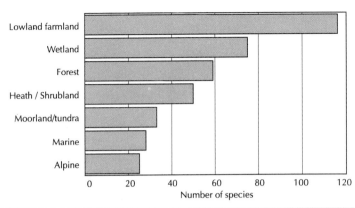

Figure 3. The number of Species of European Conservation Concern with an Unfavourable Conservation Status (SPEC categories 1–3) that use each habitat type at some point in their annual cycle.

Lowland farmland includes intensive farmland, dry grassland and pseudo-steppe, wet grassland, perennial crops and pastoral woodland (e.g. Spanish dehesas).

Wetland includes inland and coastal tidal wetlands.

Forest includes natural and semi-natural forests and woodlands and artificial plantations.

Heath/shrubland includes Atlantic heath below 300 m and Mediterranean shrubland, e.g. maquis and garigue.

Marine includes all coastal and offshore waters within European territorial limits.

Alpine includes all habitats above the tree-line (even if lowered by man through tree-clearance, fire or grazing).

for the Corncrake *Crex crex*; traditional hand-cut sedge meadows for the Aquatic Warbler *Acrocephalus paludicola*; wet grazing marshes for breeding waders such as Black-tailed Godwit *Limosa limosa*; diverse mixed farmland landscapes with permanent pastures, arable cultivations and hedges for the Partridge *Perdix perdix*, Red-backed Shrike *Lanius collurio* and Ortolan Bunting *Emberiza hortulana*; and dry grasslands and extensive dry cereal cultivations of southern, central and eastern parts of Europe for Pallid Harrier *Circus macrourus*, Great Bustard *Otis tarda*, Sociable Plover and Pin-tailed Sandgrouse *Pterocles alchata*. It also obviously reflects the widespread intensification of farming practices that has produced ecological changes detrimental to these habitats and to many of the species which occupy them, as detailed in the individual species accounts of this review (see also Figure 4).

Both wetlands and forests also hold a large number of species with an Unfavourable Conservation Status, many of which are highly dependent on these habitats in Europe (Table 7). Again, the large number of SPECs using these habitats reflects their size and diversity, and the widespread threats that are affecting them. A substantial proportion of wetland SPECs occur only at a few highly important sites (e.g. Table 5) and are thus particularly vulnerable.

Although marine, heath, moorland, tundra and alpine habitats do not hold a large number of SPECs, this in part reflects the relatively limited species richness of the specialized bird communities of these habitats. In fact, a high proportion of species in these communities have an Unfavourable Conservation Status, indicating that these habitats are also subject to widespread habitat changes. Marine habitats hold a number of species of global conservation concern including Fea's Petrel *Pterodroma feae*, Zino's Petrel, Steller's Eider and Audouin's Gull *Larus audouinii*, whilst tundra is the sole breeding habitat of the globally threatened Lesser White-fronted Goose *Anser erythropus*. Mountain habitats are of particular importance to two mountain specialists that are Endangered in Europe: Lammergeier *Gypaetus barbatus* and Great Rosefinch *Carpodacus rubicilla*.

THREATS TO SPECS

The threats affecting SPECs with substantially declining populations are summarized in Figure 4. They closely match the distribution of SPECs across habitat-types, with the most frequently reported one being agricultural intensification, affecting some 42% of declining SPECs. This broad threat, however, covers a range of specific threats, one being the irrigation of dry grasslands and cereals and their subsequent conversion to dense, fast-growing heavily fertilized and pesticide-treated crops. Such changes are particularly important in Spain, where 10,000 km² of land was brought under new irrigation between 1970 and 1989 and a further 10,000–14,000 km² is to be irrigated according to the National Hydrological Plan (Egdell 1993). Consequently, a high proportion of European steppe species, such as the Little Bustard *Tetrax tetrax*, Great Bustard, Black-bellied Sandgrouse *Pterocles orientalis*, Pin-tailed Sandgrouse and Stone Curlew *Burhinus oedicnemus*, are threatened by these projects. Conversely, in northwest Europe, the lowering of water-tables on wet

Table 7. Species with particularly important breeding and/or wintering populations on lowland farmland, wetland and forest habitats. Species of global conservation concern (SPEC category 1) are shown in bold. For an explanation of European Threat Status codes see Table 1 (p. 38). Habitat types are described in Figure 3.

	SPEC category	European Threat Status		SPEC category	European Threat Status
Lowland farmland			Greater Flamingo *Phoenicopterus ruber*	3	L
Lesser White-fronted Goose			Brent Goose *Branta bernicla*	3	V
Anser erythropus	1	**V**	**Red-breasted Goose *Branta ruficollis***	1 ʷ	**L** ʷ
Red-breasted Goose *Branta ruficollis*	1	**L** ʷ	Ruddy Shelduck *Tadorna ferruginea*	3	V
Pallid Harrier *Circus macrourus*	3	E	**Ferruginous Duck *Aythya nyroca***	1	**V**
Long-legged Buzzard *Buteo rufinus*	3	(E)	Harlequin Duck		
Steppe Eagle *Aquila rapax*	3	V	*Histrionicus histrionicus*	3	V
Imperial Eagle *Aquila heliaca*	1	**E**	Smew *Mergus albellus*	3	V
Lesser Kestrel *Falco naumanni*	1	**(V)**	**White-headed Duck**		
Saker *Falco cherrug*	3	E	*Oxyura leucocephala*	1	**E**
Red-legged Partridge *Alectoris rufa*	2	V	Osprey *Pandion haliaetus*	3	R
Partridge *Perdix perdix*	3	V	Baillon's Crake *Porzana pusilla*	3	R
Quail *Coturnix coturnix*	3	V	Purple Gallinule *Porphyrio porphyrio*	3	R
Little Bustard *Tetrax tetrax*	2	V	Avocet *Recurvirostra avosetta*	4/3 ʷ	L ʷ
Houbara Bustard *Chlamydotis undulata*	3	(E)	Kentish Plover		
Great Bustard *Otis tarda*	1	**D**	*Charadrius alexandrinus*	3	D
Stone Curlew *Burhinus oedicnemus*	3	V	Greater Sand Plover		
Cream-coloured Courser			*Charadrius leschenaultii*	3	E
Cursorius cursor	3	V	Spur-winged Plover		
Black-winged Pratincole			*Hoplopterus spinosus*	3	(E)
Glareola nordmanni	3	R	Knot *Calidris canutus*	3 ʷ	L ʷ
Greater Sand Plover			Dunlin *Calidris alpina*	3 ʷ	V ʷ
Charadrius leschenaultii	3	E	Bar-tailed Godwit *Limosa lapponica*	3 ʷ	L ʷ
Caspian Plover *Charadrius asiaticus*	3	(V)	Curlew *Numenius arquata*	3 ʷ	D ʷ
Sociable Plover *Chettusia gregaria*	1	**E**	Redshank *Tringa totanus*	2	D
Great Snipe *Gallinago media*	2	(V)	**Audouin's Gull *Larus audouinii***	1	**L**
Black-tailed Godwit *Limosa limosa*	2	V	Caspian Tern *Sterna caspia*	3	(E)
Black-bellied Sandgrouse			Sandwich Tern *Sterna sandvicensis*	2	D
Pterocles orientalis	3	V	Roseate Tern *Sterna dougallii*	3	E
Pin-tailed Sandgrouse *Pterocles alchata*	3	E	Little Tern *Sterna albifrons*	3	D
Turtle Dove *Streptopelia turtur*	3	D	Whiskered Tern *Chlidonias hybridus*	3	D
Barn Owl *Tyto alba*	3	D	Black Tern *Chlidonias niger*	3	D
Little Owl *Athene noctua*	3	D	Kingfisher *Alcedo atthis*	3	D
Dupont's Lark *Chersophilus duponti*	3	V			
Black Lark *Melanocorypha yeltoniensis*	3	(V)	***Forest habitats***		
Lesser Short-toed Lark			Smew *Mergus albellus*	3	V
Calandrella rufescens	3	V	Lesser Spotted Eagle *Aquila pomarina*	3	R
Crested Lark *Galerida cristata*	3	(D)	**Greater Spotted Eagle *Aquila clanga***	1	**E**
Skylark *Alauda arvensis*	3	V	Woodcock *Scolopax rusticola*	3 ʷ	V ʷ
Swallow *Hirundo rustica*	3	D	**Long-toed Pigeon *Columba trocaz***	1	**V**
Aquatic Warbler	·		**Dark-tailed Laurel Pigeon**		
Acrocephalus paludicola	1	**E**	*Columba bollii*	1	**V**
Red-backed Shrike *Lanius collurio*	3	(D)	**White-tailed Laurel Pigeon**		
Lesser Grey Shrike *Lanius minor*	2	(D)	*Columba junoniae*	1	**V**
Woodchat Shrike *Lanius senator*	2	V	Wryneck *Jynx torquilla*	3	D
Trumpeter Finch *Bucanetes githagineus*	3	R	Grey-headed Woodpecker *Picus canus*	3	D
Ortolan Bunting *Emberiza hortulana*	2	(V)	Green Woodpecker *Picus viridis*	2	D
			Three-toed Woodpecker		
Wetlands			*Picoides tridactylus*	3	D
Black-throated Diver *Gavia arctica*	3	V	Woodlark *Lullula arborea*	2	V
White Pelican *Pelecanus onocrotalus*	3	R	Redstart *Phoenicurus phoenicurus*	2	V
Dalmatian Pelican *Pelecanus crispus*	1	**V**	Semi-collared Flycatcher		
Bittern *Botaurus stellaris*	3	(V)	*Ficedula semitorquata*	2	(E)
Little Bittern *Ixobrychus minutus*	3	(V)	Corsican Nuthatch *Sitta whiteheadi*	2	V
Squacco Heron *Ardeola ralloides*	3	V	Siberian Jay *Perisoreus infaustus*	3	(D)
Purple Heron *Ardea purpurea*	3	V	**Blue Chaffinch *Fringilla teydea***	1	**V**
Spoonbill *Platalea leucorodia*	2	E	**Scottish Crossbill *Loxia scotica***	1	**Ins**

ʷ Indicates that the SPEC category and European Threat Status relates to winter populations. For SPEC categories given as, for example, '4/2', the first number is the SPEC category relating to the breeding population, while the second number relates to the winter population.

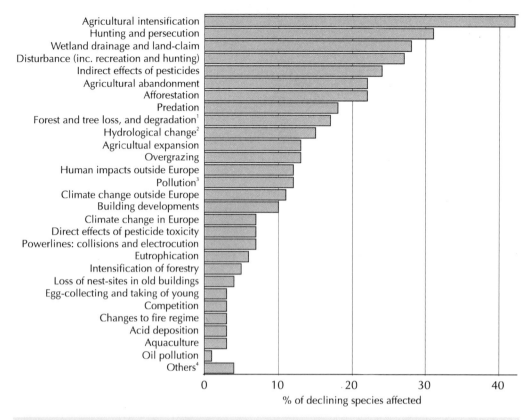

Figure 4. Threats to Species of European Conservation Concern which have substantially declining European populations (i.e. showing moderate or large declines). Threats are only included if they are thought to have contributed to declines in a species' European population over the period 1970–1990.

[1] Clear-cutting, unmanaged cutting, burning, grazing, loss of trees from orchards, farmland copses and hedgerows, etc.

[2] Damming of rivers, water abstraction, flood control, canalization, etc.

[3] Other than acid deposition, oil spills, pesticides and eutrophication.

[4] Includes destruction of haystacks, hybridization, plant disease, drowning in fishing nets and overfishing (each affected only one species).

grasslands, followed by re-seeding, fertilizer applications and high stocking levels, have caused substantial declines to waders such as the Black-tailed Godwit and Redshank *Tringa totanus*, and to some extent to the White Stork *Ciconia ciconia*.

The loss of hay meadows has been widespread across the temperate regions of Europe, often due to their conversion to intensive silage crops, to the detriment of the Quail *Coturnix coturnix*, Corncrake and Barn Owl *Tyto alba*. Perhaps the most widespread change has been the intensification of arable farmland through high inorganic fertilizer inputs, crop specialization and increased field size. High pesticide use often follows such changes, which result in monocultures of tall, dense crops with reduced numbers of invertebrates and wild plants and fewer adjoining hedgerows, trees and ditches. As a consequence, nesting opportunities, food resources

and overall habitat diversity have all decreased. Such factors are probably the major cause of the declines in farmland species such as the Kestrel *Falco tinnunculus*, Partridge, Turtle Dove *Streptopelia turtur* and Skylark *Alauda arvensis*. Pesticide use alone affects 24% of declining SPECs through indirect effects on food supplies, whilst direct toxic effects threaten 7%.

In contrast, agricultural abandonment is also frequently given as a cause of decline and occurs as an indirect effect of agricultural intensification because marginal land becomes less profitable to farm. Lammergeiers and Griffon Vultures *Gyps fulvus*, for example, are highly dependent on sheep and cattle carrion, and consequently on the continuation of extensive pastoral farming and transhumance practices in mountain areas. Low-intensity grazing is also necessary to maintain suitable vegetation structures for many steppe species such as Little Bustard and Great Bustard.

Hunting and persecution form the second most commonly listed threat in Figure 4. However, although there is often insufficient information to assess its effects on populations it is probably less damaging than changes in land-use, which are subdivided into many types of threat. Nevertheless, hunting is probably a significant contributory cause of decline in a number of game species, such as Chukar *Alectoris chukar*, Red-legged Partridge *A. rufa*, Barbary Partridge *A. barbara* and Black Francolin *Francolinus francolinus*. The illegal persecution of raptors is also still occurring and reported as a threat to a number of species, including the Egyptian Vulture *Neophron percnopterus* and Bonnelli's Eagle *Hieraaetus fasciatus* (both Endangered in Europe), and even the Imperial Eagle *Aquila heliaca* (which is Globally Threatened). Large numbers of passerines are also still illegally trapped or shot, including shrikes *Lanius*, Ortolan Bunting and Black-headed Bunting *Emberiza melanocephala*. It is evident that excessive or illegal hunting is particularly common in countries of southern and east Europe that border the Mediterranean, especially where large numbers of migrants congregate, a pattern that was also noted by Woldhek (1980) and McCulloch *et al.* (1992).

Wetland drainage is also a common threat, affecting 28% of all declining SPECs, including Marbled Teal *Marmaronetta angustirostris* and Ferruginous Duck *Aythya nyroca* (both classified as Globally Threatened). It has affected several wetlands of major importance in eastern Europe, including the Danube delta in Romania (IUCN 1992) and the Russian Volga delta (Finlayson 1992a). Wetland drainage has also been particularly prevalent in the Mediterranean region where extensive wetland drainage has damaged many Important Bird Areas such as the Evros delta (HOS 1992) and the Nestos delta (Vassilakis and Vassilakopoulou 1993) in Greece, and the Menderes delta, Sultan marshes and Eregli marshes in Turkey (Kasparek 1985, Brinkman *et al.* 1990, Kiliç and Kasparek 1990).

Disturbance by humans is also felt to be affecting many species and probably occurs in most habitat-types through recreational activities including hunting, and activities connected to land-use such as farming, forestry and fishing.

Afforestation is a widespread threat to a number of habitat-types, but particularly moorland and tundra, where species such as Red-throated Diver *Gavia stellata*, Hen Harrier *Circus cyaneus*, Wood Sandpiper *Tringa glareola* and Short-eared Owl *Asio flammeus* are threatened by such practices, although Hen Harrier and Short-eared Owl may benefit temporarily in the early stages. Other species and habitats frequently affected by afforestation include Nightjar *Caprimulgus europaeus* and Tawny Pipit *Anthus campestris* on heathlands, Rock Thrush *Monticola saxatilis* and Dartford Warbler *Sylvia undata* on Mediterranean maquis and garigue, and Stone Curlew and numerous lark species on the dry steppes.

Although the threats identified in this review are most often based on correlations, and the existence of causal links has not normally been proven, they should nevertheless be treated as real contributory causes of the declines of species' populations until contrary evidence is established. Where there is a significant element of doubt, the benefit of that doubt should rest with the environment since the diagnosis of the cause of population decline is frequently a difficult and time-consuming process (see, for example, Green and Hirons 1991). Waiting for studies to prove threats may lead to delays in taking remedial action, sometimes at considerable future cost. Accurate diagnoses of the causes of population declines are ultimately needed, but, to ensure that necessary measures are taken for threatened species, a need for further research should not be used as an excuse for delaying conservation action; in such cases measures should be taken on the best available information. Measures should, however, be designed to contribute to our understanding of the causes of decline and should at the very least be monitored with a view to assessing their effectiveness.

GEOGRAPHICAL PATTERNS OF POPULATION DECLINE

Many of the species accounts indicate clear regional differences in population trends. Gadwall *Anas strepera* and Sandwich Tern *Sterna sandvicensis*, for example, have declined in the east of their ranges but increased in much of the west. In contrast, species such as Skylark and Lesser Grey Shrike *Lanius minor* have decreased considerably in the west of their ranges but not in the east. To explore this further a full analysis of population trends has been carried out using two separate data-sets; one for the central and east European countries (CEEC) and one for western Europe, i.e. countries that are either in the European Union or are covered by the European Free Trade Agreement (EFTA) plus additional countries within the region. This allows comparison between two regions subject to different past economic and political systems. It may also provide an indication of future trends in bird populations. This analysis showed that 23 species declined in more than 33% of their CEEC population but in less than 33% of their western populations. However, 47 species showed declines in more than 33% of their western population but not in their CEEC population. This greater number of declines in western Europe may reflect some differences in monitoring coverage, as inadequately monitored species are often assumed to be stable. However, it is more likely to reflect the finding from this review that many of the declines are due to the intensification of land-use in the region over the last 20–30 years. For each of these species these relationships were tested statistically, where sample sizes were adequate, by comparing the proportion of countries in the CEEC and western Europe that showed population declines (Table 8)—though because most species occurred in only a few countries sample sizes were usually too small for statistical tests. Most individual comparisons were not statistically significant, but some species were found to have significant differences in the proportion of countries in the CEEC and western countries which showed declines.

The same analysis was also carried out for species that, although not qualifying as SPECs, may never-

theless be declining in substantial parts of their European range. Only an additional 14 species were found to be declining in more than 33% of their population in the CEEC and not in western Europe, whereas 33 species declined by the same amount in western Europe and not the CEEC. Although, as above, comparisons of those species with adequate sample sizes showed that nearly all individual relationships were not statistically significant (Table 9), the greater number of declines in western Europe again probably reflects the intensive land-use in the region. Declines of White-backed Woodpecker *Dendrocopos leucotos* in the region, for example, are believed to have been the result of intensive forestry practices (Aulén 1988). Similarly, declines in the Lapwing *Vanellus vanellus* reflect the intensification of agriculture (O'Connor and Shrubb 1986, Hudson *et al.* 1994). Although not currently at risk on a European scale, species that show such large regional population declines should be considered for conservation actions where they are declining.

Table 8. SPECs with more than 33% of their population declining in either west European or central and east European countries (CEEC), as defined below, and which occur in sufficient countries for statistical comparison[1].

	SPEC category	European Threat Status	% population declining in:		% of countries declining in:		Significance[2]
			West	CEEC	West	CEEC	
SPECs with >33% of their CEEC populations declining but <33% of their west European populations declining							
White Stork *Ciconia ciconia*	2	V	22	37	40	50	NS
Black Kite *Milvus migrans*	3	V	6	98	23	67	*
Hen Harrier *Circus cyaneus*	3	V	5	97	23	67	*
Quail *Coturnix coturnix*	3	V	15	97	39	81	**
Eagle Owl *Bubo bubo*	3	V	23	84	31	44	NS
Short-eared Owl *Asio flammeus*	3	(V)	1	99	8	69	**
Grey-headed Woodpecker *Picus canus*	3	D	6	41	56	31	NS
SPECs with >33% of their west European populations declining but <33% of their CEEC populations declining							
Turtle Dove *Streptopelia turtur*	3	D	95	18	58	50	NS
Little Owl *Athene noctua*	3	D	81	17	80	47	NS
Nightjar *Caprimulgus europaeus*	2	(D)	96	14	72	56	NS
Kingfisher *Alcedo atthis*	3	D	82	12	28	37	NS
Crested Lark *Galerida cristata*	3	(D)	94	8	75	50	NS
Woodlark *Lullula arborea*	2	V	82	22	59	47	*
Skylark *Alauda arvensis*	3	V	99	8	82	27	**
Sand Martin *Riparia riparia*	3	D	76	9	53	12	**
Tawny Pipit *Anthus campestris*	3	V	95	3	75	27	NS
Stonechat *Saxicola torquata*	3	(D)	78	0	40	0	*
Great Grey Shrike *Lanius excubitor*	3	D	93	3	54	60	NS
Ortolan Bunting *Emberiza hortulana*	2	(V)	57	17	77	53	NS

West European countries: Andorra, Austria, Belgium, Cyprus, Denmark, Faroe Islands, Finland, France, Gibraltar, Greece, Greenland, Guernsey, Iceland, Republic of Ireland, Isle of Man, Italy, Jersey, Liechtenstein, Luxembourg, Malta, Netherlands, Norway, Portugal, Spain, Svalbard, Sweden, Switzerland and United Kingdom.

CEEC: Albania, Belarus, Bulgaria, Croatia, Czech Republic, Estonia, Hungary, Latvia, Lithuania, Moldova, Poland, Romania, Russia, Slovakia, Slovenia and Ukraine (Bosnia and Herzegovina, Yugoslavia and Former Yugoslav Republic of Macedonia were not included in the study).

Germany, Turkey, Canary Islands, Azores and Madeira were not included in the analysis. Species with less than 100 pairs in either region are excluded, and populations with unknown trends are excluded from calculations of percentages in decline.

[1] χ^2-tests were carried out where all expected values were greater than one and no more than 1 expected value was less than 5.

[2] Statistical significance of differences in proportion of countries with declining populations according to the χ^2-test: NS not significant, * significant at $P<0.05$, ** significant at $P<0.001$.

Table 9. Species with more than 33% of their populations declining in either central and east European countries (CEEC) or in west European countries, but which do not qualify as SPEC 1–3 on overall European population decline, and which occur in sufficient countries for statistical comparison[1]. Country groupings are as given in Table 8.

	% population declining in:		% of countries declining in:		Signifi-cance [2]
	West	CEEC	West	CEEC	
Non-SPECs with >33% of their CEEC populations declining but <33% of their west European populations declining					
Water Rail *Rallus aquaticus*	32	34	39	50	*
Stock Dove *Columba oenas*	20	50	33	69	*
Hoopoe *Upupa epops*	13	38	50	75	NS
Corn Bunting *Miliaria calandra*	25	45	67	57	NS
Non-SPECs with >33% of their west European populations declining but <33% of their CEEC populations declining					
Red Kite *Milvus milvus*	67	17	25	58	NS
Goshawk *Accipiter gentilis*	44	4	28	40	NS
Spotted Crake *Porzana porzana*	68	26	42	50	NS
Lapwing *Vanellus vanellus*	66	4	50	50	NS
Snipe *Gallinago gallinago*	34	2	58	50	NS
Cuckoo *Cuculus canorus*	38	5	48	19	NS
White-backed Woodpecker *Dendrocopos leucotos*	69	4	55	27	NS
Lesser Spotted Woodpecker *Dendrocopos minor*	61	13	44	37	NS
Whinchat *Saxicola rubetra*	54	1	63	13	**
Sedge Warbler *Acrocephalus schoenobaenus*	39	1	44	13	NS
Great Reed Warbler *Acrocephalus arundinaceus*	70	3	61	27	NS
Whitethroat *Sylvia communis*	65	2	57	19	*

[1] χ^2-tests were carried out where all expected values were greater than one and no more than 1 expected value was less than 5.
[2] Statistical significance of differences in proportion of countries with declining populations according to the χ^2-test: NS not significant, * significant at $P<0.05$, ** significant at $P<0.001$.

Preventive measures should also be taken elsewhere as a much more widespread decline in bird populations might be expected if similar intensive land-use practices are adopted in the CEEC region without environmental considerations.

While many species in Europe have undergone significant population declines, some species have increased (Table 10). Some of these increases, as well as some declines, may be due to natural ecological changes and population fluctuations, but many increasing species have probably benefited from human activities and associated changes in the environment, such as the increases in food supply for the Fulmar *Fulmarus glacialis* through discards from fishing vessels. Most encouragingly, species such as White Pelican *Pelecanus onocrotalus*, White-tailed Eagle *Haliaeetus albicilla* and Spanish Imperial Eagle (although still regarded as SPECs because of their small populations) have increased, almost certainly as a result of increased protection and conservation programmes.

FUTURE REQUIREMENTS FOR RESEARCH AND MONITORING

For some species in some countries available data are insufficient to assess population size and trends reliably. This fact was taken into account in this review through the measures described in the chapters on 'Data Collection' (p. 25) and 'Assessment of Conservation Status' (p. 27). In the long term, however, the adequate censusing and monitoring of all species in all countries is essential to improve the reliability and accuracy of assessments of conservation status. Indeed it should be the responsibility of all governments to ensure that the effects of land-use activities on the environment, including its biodiversity, are adequately monitored (as, for example, stipulated in Article 7 of the Convention on Biological Diversity).

We hope that this study will further the growth of bird monitoring throughout Europe and contribute to the development of a European bird monitoring strategy by:

• demonstrating the value of monitoring studies and the urgent need for better information;

• publishing current data, thereby stimulating the provision of corrections and new data (see Appendix 5);

• guiding monitoring efforts to priority species and regions.

Ultimately we need to monitor all species (whether directly or indirectly), but current limitations on financial resources and, particularly, on the number of fieldworkers, necessitate the selection of priorities

49

Table 10. Species which showed large increases in their European breeding populations during 1970–1990 (large increase defined as an increase of at least 20% in at least 66% of its population, or of at least 50% in at least 25% of its population). Figures are percentages of the European population which are in countries where numbers have increased by >20% and >50%. Species of global conservation concern (SPEC category 1) are shown in bold. Introduced species are not included.

	% increased by:			% increased by:	
	>20%	>50%		>20%	>50%
Great Crested Grebe *Podiceps cristatus*	90	20	Avocet *Recurvirostra avosetta*	74	45
Black-necked Grebe *Podiceps nigricollis*	80	0	Little Ringed Plover *Charadrius dubius*	86	0
Fulmar *Fulmarus glacialis*	95	1	Red-wattled Plover *Hoplopterus indicus*	100	0
Gannet *Sula bassana*	89	8	Marsh Sandpiper *Tringa stagnatilis*	100	0
Cormorant *Phalacrocorax carbo*	96	49	Great Black-headed Gull *Larus ichthyaetus*	100	0
Pygmy Cormorant *Phalacrocorax pygmeus*	51	49	Mediterranean Gull *Larus melanocephalus*	99	99
White Pelican *Pelecanus onocrotalus*	91	0	Little Gull *Larus minutus*	35	35
Dalmatian Pelican *Pelecanus crispus*	**78**	**0**	Sabine's Gull *Larus sabini*	100	100
Cattle Egret *Bubulcus ibis*	100	78	Black-headed Gull *Larus ridibundus*	69	52
Little Egret *Egretta garzetta*	50	35	Slender-billed Gull *Larus genei*	99	1
Great White Egret *Egretta alba*	96	0	**Audouin's Gull *Larus audouinii***	**95**	**95**
Grey Heron *Ardea cinerea*	71	32	Lesser Black-backed Gull *Larus fuscus*	77	36
Black Stork *Ciconia nigra*	66	7	Herring Gull *Larus argentatus*	46	31
Greater Flamingo *Phoenicopterus ruber*	34	34	Glaucous Gull *Larus hyperboreus*	71	71
Whooper Swan *Cygnus cygnus*	77	19	White-winged Black Tern		
Pink-footed Goose *Anser brachyrhynchus*	100	86	*Chlidonias leucopterus*	68	0
Greylag Goose *Anser anser*	99	76	Razorbill *Alca torda*	87	2
Barnacle Goose *Branta leucopsis*	100	16	Stock Dove *Columba oenas*	61	58
Shelduck *Tadorna tadorna*	58	32	Rufous Turtle Dove *Streptopelia orientalis*	100	0
Eider *Somateria mollissima*	96	17	Great Spotted Cuckoo *Clamator glandarius*	99	0
Harlequin Duck *Histrionicus histrionicus*	91	0	Eagle Owl *Bubo bubo*	55	26
Goldeneye *Bucephala clangula*	80	60	White-rumped Swift *Apus caffer*	100	0
White-headed Duck *Oxyura leucocephala*	**36**	**26**	Syrian Woodpecker *Dendrocopos syriacus*	82	2
Black-winged Kite *Elanus caeruleus*	100	0	Red-rumped Swallow *Hirundo daurica*	83	67
White-tailed Eagle *Haliaeetus albicilla*	92	65	Cetti's Warbler *Cettia cetti*	87	0
Griffon Vulture *Gyps fulvus*	90	90	Paddyfield Warbler *Acrocephalus agricola*	91	0
Cinereous Vulture *Aegypius monachus*	96	0	Melodious Warbler *Hippolais polyglotta*	27	27
Marsh Harrier *Circus aeruginosus*	85	7	Cyprus Warbler *Sylvia melanothorax*	100	0
Montagu's Harrier *Circus pygargus*	78	1	Penduline Tit *Remiz pendulinus*	67	18
Goshawk *Accipiter gentilis*	78	66	Magpie *Pica pica*	70	28
Sparrowhawk *Accipiter nisus*	86	19	Rook *Corvus frugilegus*	88	28
Buzzard *Buteo buteo*	68	0	Carrion Crow *Corvus corone*	79	26
Spanish Imperial Eagle *Aquila adalberti*	**100**	**0**	Raven *Corvus corax*	83	18
Saker *Falco cherrug*	33	33	Spotless Starling *Sturnus unicolor*	93	0
Little Crake *Porzana parva*	82	0	Dead Sea Sparrow *Passer moabiticus*	100	0
Purple Gallinule *Porphyrio porphyrio*	97	0	Citril Finch *Serinus citrinella*	95	0
Demoiselle Crane *Anthropoides virgo*	100	0	Greenfinch *Carduelis chloris*	69	1
Oystercatcher *Haematopus ostralegus*	79	34	Red-headed Bunting *Emberiza bruniceps*	100	0

for study. The data collected for this review have been used to identify the major gaps in our knowledge of bird populations (Appendix 3, p. 502). However, other factors that should be taken into account when prioritizing species for national censuses and long-term monitoring include the following.

- A species' overall conservation status in Europe and the importance of its population in a European and global context.

- The need to assess the results of particular conservation actions.

- The potential of a species as a wider environmental indicator.

- The extent to which a species is representative of particular habitats.

- The ease of studying a species.

Clearly, the targeting of population monitoring and census studies is a complex and important subject which needs Europe-wide cooperation and which would therefore benefit from the development of a European bird monitoring strategy.

CONCLUSIONS AND RECOMMENDATIONS

THIS REVIEW presents clear evidence that the European avifauna has changed fundamentally over the past 20 years, largely as a result of the increasing intensity of land-use over the continent. The fact that many declining species are, or once were, common and widespread demonstrates the scale of the problem. Substantial policy changes are required if we are to arrest further declines and impoverishment of the European avifauna and maintain the region's biodiversity as a whole.

As a first step, the results of this review should be incorporated into the existing instruments for conservation (see Introduction, Box 1, pp. 21–23). In particular the Annexes of the EU Wild Birds Directive and the Appendices of the Bern and Bonn Conventions should be extended to take appropriate account of the status of all Species of European Conservation Concern (see Appendix 4, p. 505). Also, national legislation and conservation strategies based on national lists of threatened species (i.e. 'Red Data' lists) should take into account SPEC categories and the proportion of the global and European population that occurs within the country (see Appendix 2, p. 480). Such an approach is being applied in the United Kingdom, where the new Red Data list will incorporate each species' SPEC category and the international importance of the UK population as criteria (Avery et al. 1994).

Although the species are dealt with individually in this review, a species-by-species approach to their conservation is not recommended. Instead, the three combined elements—species protection, site protection and conservation of the wider environment—should form the framework for generic conservation actions that are applied wherever possible to species groups, communities or habitats.

SPECIES PROTECTION

Hunting and illegal persecution are listed as probable contributory causes to declines in 42 species.

Therefore:

- Existing protection laws need to be strengthened and enforced for these species.

- Working on the precautionary principle, regulations for legally hunted species should be based on species-management plans that ensure sustainable use, irrespective of the species' conservation status.

- It should be required that hunting is proved to be sustainable, rather than the reverse. Thus, where management plans do not exist and where hunting is believed to be a likely cause of a species' Unfavourable Conservation Status, tighter controls should be implemented until sustainable use can be assured.

SITE PROTECTION

The publication of *Important Bird Areas in Europe* (Grimmett and Jones 1989) listed a network of sites that should be protected. In practice, however, legislative protection of them has often been poor. In the European Union, for example, where all IBAs should qualify as Special Protection Areas (SPAs) under the Wild Birds Directive (Directive 79/409/EEC), only 28% of the area of IBAs had been designated as SPAs up to 31 May 1994 (CEC 1994) and only three countries had designated more than 50% (Figure 1). Improved protection of IBAs is needed, together with implementation of appropriate management plans. Thus a strategy for protected areas such as that currently being proposed by IUCN Commission on National Parks and Protected Areas (1994) should be urgently and effectively implemented, with priorities for birds taking into account the results of this review. BirdLife International is shortly to update the IBA inventory, and this review will help also to guide that process.

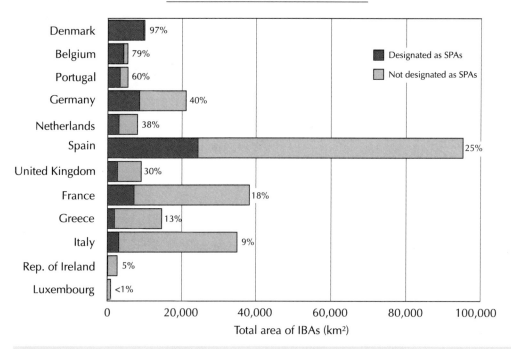

Figure 1. The extent of Important Bird Areas in EU countries and their designation as Special Protection Areas (SPAs) under the EU Wild Birds Directive (areas designated under Article 4 of Directive 79/409/EEC on the Conservation of Wild Birds, as of 31 May 1994: CEC 1994). Percentages shown are the proportions of the total IBA areas which have been designated. The area of SPAs in Germany includes a total of 86 km² that has been classified for nature conservation values other than its importance for birds.

CONSERVATION OF THE WIDER ENVIRONMENT

It is apparent from this review that conservation of Europe's wider environment is vital, but has been particularly inadequate thus far. The substantial declines of many widespread and common species are clear evidence of this, especially in highly man-modified habitats such as farmland. Such habitats and their birds cannot be effectively conserved by traditional site-acquisition or site-protection measures. Conservation objectives must be integrated into *all* policies governing land-use activities. This can be achieved in part by regulations or, since many land-uses are subsidized, through linking such financial support to environmental needs. Therefore:

- tighter and more effective enforcement of regulations is needed to reduce pollution;

- planning regulations and environmental impact assessments should be used more widely to minimize impacts from new developments;

- regulations governing water management, forestry, agriculture and fisheries must be expanded and strengthened to avoid environmental damage from existing activities;

- financial support policies should always incorporate environmental objectives.

For example, agricultural policies such as cross-compliance (under which farmers receive higher rates of financial support if they observe optional environmental restrictions, e.g. on stock density) should be developed to reduce harmful farming practices. Measures under the Agri-environment Regulation (EC Reg. 2078/92) provide considerable potential for positive conservation actions within the European Union, and have been proposed in many of the individual species accounts within this review. Schemes developed under this regulation can provide financial support to farmers who wish to follow environmentally beneficial farming practices. The regulation should therefore be used to maintain agricultural systems of high conservation value, for example low-intensity grazing in important habitats such as wet grasslands, steppes, mountains and pastoral woodlands. Indeed, in Castilla y León (Spain) management agreements developed by the Spanish Ornithological Society (SEO–BirdLife) in collaboration with farming unions and the regional administration have demonstrated the potential for maintaining appropriate farming systems for steppic species (such as the Great Bustard *Otis tarda*) on potentially 16,000 km² of low-intensity agricultural land (Naveso 1992a,b, Naveso and Groves-Raines 1992). Such schemes not only benefit birds but also other wildlife and help to address issues of broad concern including agricultural over-production and rural depopulation.

To identify further the conservation requirements of Species of European Conservation Concern in the wider environment, BirdLife International is developing a series of strategic habitat action plans, focusing on bird conservation priorities, to guide wide-scale actions such as those outlined above. The implementation of these action plans will be a high priority for the conservation of bird species dispersed throughout the wider environment of Europe.

These measures of species protection, site protection and conservation of the wider environment need to be carefully targeted, taking into account the conservation status of species as assessed in this review. Given the current pace of bird population declines and the scale of threats described here, the implementation of even such a targeted strategy may be difficult and costly—but it is essential.

SPECIES OF EUROPEAN CONSERVATION CONCERN, CATEGORIES 1–3

**Species with an Unfavourable Conservation Status
because their European populations are
small and non-marginal, declining, or localized**

Red-throated Diver
Gavia stellata

SPEC Category 3
Status Vulnerable
Criteria Large decline

There has been a decline in large parts of the European breeding range following the loss of breeding sites due to drainage and disturbance from recreational activities. In areas exposed to airborne acidifying pollutants, the decline of fish stocks and increased exposure to mercury are also thought to be significant problems. Protection of breeding sites against drainage and disturbance, reductions in pollutants and (where appropriate) the liming of acidified foraging lakes are suggested conservation measures.

■ Distribution and population trends

The Red-throated Diver's breeding range extends over the boreal and Arctic zones of Europe, Asia and North America. In Europe (which includes less than a quarter of the global range) the breeding area extends from Greenland, across north-west Europe and Fennoscandia, to eastern Europe. Greenland, Norway and Russia each hold a substantial part of the total European breeding population (see table, map).

The species is migratory, with European populations wintering mainly in ice-free marine and coastal waters off Scandinavia and north-west Europe. Small numbers also winter in freshwater lakes and reservoirs in central and south-east Europe.

Between 1970 and 1990 numbers declined over a considerable part of the breeding range (see table, map), with the countries affected accounting for up to almost 90% of the population; in south-west Sweden this can be traced back at least to the 1960s (Eriksson *et al.* 1988, SOF 1990). The breeding population in the United Kingdom, however, is believed to be increasing (Marchant *et al.* 1990, see table).

■ Ecology

Breeding sites are mainly small, oligotrophic freshwater lakes, and the nest is usually just an open scrape on the bank, close to the water's edge. Birds feed almost entirely on fish, of which breeding lakes are often naturally devoid, the chicks then being fed on fish brought by the parents from larger lakes, rivers or the sea. In Sweden, breeding birds have been known to fly 7–8 km to forage (Eriksson *et al.* 1990).

The main winter habitat is open sea, often far from land.

■ Threats

The loss and deterioration of habitat, and disturbance at breeding sites, are the major threats which the species is now facing (e.g. Haga 1980, Pakarinen and Järvinen 1984). Land drainage for forestry is an important cause of the loss of breeding sites (e.g. in Sweden: Eriksson *et al.* 1988), and the disturbance which can result from recreational activities such as fishing has been highlighted as a problem in some regions (e.g. in Scotland: Bundy 1976, Gomersall 1986).

In Fennoscandia the decline of fish stocks in foraging lakes exposed to airborne acidifying pollutants is a threat (Eriksson *et al.* 1988, Eriksson 1994). Coregonid and cyprinid fish (primarily *Rutilus rutilus*) up to 20 cm long are the most common prey delivered to chicks (Eriksson *et al.* 1990), and these are particularly susceptible to low pH. Mercury levels in fish also increase in acidified lakes (Håkanson 1980): in south-west Sweden some fish suitable for chicks were found to have mercury at apparently dangerous levels (Eriksson *et al.* 1992). Furthermore, Eriksson *et al.* (1992) found levels of mercury in eggs sufficient for reproductive impairment to be expected.

In marine winter habitats, the potential risk posed by exposure to oil pollution needs to be evaluated.

| | Breeding population | | | Breeding |
	Size (pairs)	Year	Trend	range trend
Denmark				
Faroe Islands	10–15	81	(–1)	(–1)
Greenland	(5,000–30,000)	—	(0)	(0)
Finland	**800–1,000**	92	–1	**0**
Iceland	1,000–2,000	—	(0)	(0)
Rep. of Ireland	10–10	88–91	0	0
Norway	2,000–5,000	90	–1	**+1**
Svalbard	100–1,000	—	(0)	0
Russia	50,000–100,000	80–90	–1	0
Sweden	1,000–1,500	87	–1	0
United Kingdom	**1,400–1,400**	88–91	+1	**+1**
Total (approx.)	61,000–140,000			

Trends   +2 Large increase   +1 Small increase   0 Stable   X Extinct
(1970–1990)   –2 Large decrease   –1 Small decrease   F Fluctuating   N New breeder
Data quality   **Bold**: reliable quantitative data   Normal type: incomplete quantitative data
Bracketed figures: no quantitative data   * Data quality not provided

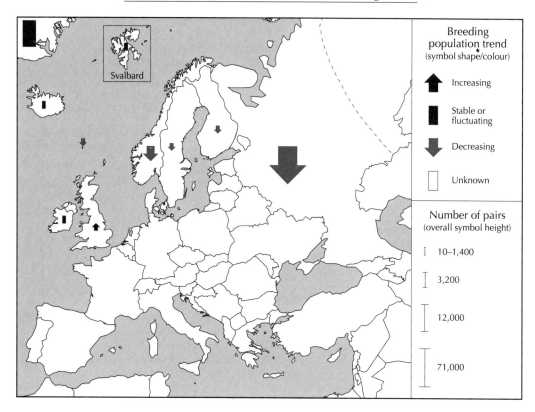

■ Conservation measures

Clearly, breeding lakes and the wetlands surrounding them should not be drained, and where breeding or foraging lakes are subject to high levels of disturbance the regulation of recreational activities should be considered. Liming of acidified foraging lakes may help to restore fish stocks and reduce mercury contamination, but a reduction in acidifying pollutants is likely to be the only long-term solution to this problem.

Population size and reproductive success are monitored on a voluntary basis in parts of the breeding range, but further coordination of these activities could improve data on trends.

MATS O. G. ERIKSSON

Black-throated Diver
Gavia arctica

SPEC Category 3
Status Vulnerable
Criteria Large decline

There has been a recent decline in several European countries. Threats at breeding lakes include disturbance by recreational activities and fluctuation of water-levels. At lakes exposed to acid rain, the decline of fish stocks and increased exposure to mercury are additional problems. Where relevant, measures to limit recreational activities and regulate water-levels should be considered.

■ Distribution and population trends

The Black-throated Diver (excluding *G. pacifica*, generally treated as a separate species) breeds in the boreal and Arctic zones of Eurasia. Roughly a fifth of the world breeding range lies within Europe, extending from Scotland, Fennoscandia and the Baltic states eastwards across the northern half of Russia. Russia holds over 80% of the European breeding population, and Norway, Sweden and Finland also support large numbers.

The species winters in marine and coastal ice-free waters in Scandinavia, north-west, central and south-east Europe, and in freshwater lakes in central and south-east Europe.

During 1970–1990 the European range remained stable, but declines in breeding population size have been suggested for several countries, including Norway, Finland and Russia (see table, map).

| | Breeding population | | | Breeding |
	Size (pairs)	Year	Trend	range trend
Belarus	**15–30**	90	F	F
Estonia	1–10	—	0	0
Finland	**7,000–9,000**	92	–1	**0**
Latvia	**5–10**	—	–1	F
Lithuania	**5–7**	85–88	(–1)	(0)
Norway	5,000–10,000	90	–1	**0**
Russia	100,000–200,000	80–90	–1	0
Sweden	5,000–10,000	87	**0**	**0**
United Kingdom	**150–160**	85–91	**0**	**0**
Total (approx.)	120,000–230,000			

Trends (1970–1990) +2 Large increase +1 Small increase 0 Stable X Extinct
−2 Large decrease −1 Small decrease F Fluctuating N New breeder
Data quality **Bold**: reliable quantitative data Normal type: incomplete quantitative data
Bracketed figures: no quantitative data * Data quality not provided

■ Ecology

The main breeding habitat is medium to large oligotrophic freshwater lakes. Nest-sites close to the waterline are required, and thus lakes with small islands are preferred. Fish are the predominant food, though selection of lakes for feeding is dependent on water clarity as much as prey abundance (Eriksson 1985, Eriksson and Sundberg 1991). The chicks are sometimes fed with prey brought in from other lakes.

The winter habitat is generally open, shallow seas, often far from land.

■ Threats

There are a number of inter-related threats whose relative importance is difficult to evaluate, as is the precise effect that these are having on population levels. Studies in Fennoscandia and the United Kingdom have demonstrated a low reproductive rate, perhaps insufficient to compensate for adult mortality (Nilsson 1977, Andersson *et al*. 1980, Campbell and Talbot 1987, Eriksson 1987a, Pakarinen 1989, Mudge and Talbot 1993). The species has a long lifespan, so it may be some time before any reduction in reproductive success is manifested in population decline.

Predation at breeding lakes is a major threat, as is disturbance from recreational activities; disturbance often facilitates predation by forcing incubating birds to leave their eggs exposed (Götmark *et al*. 1989, 1990). Nests may also be lost through fluctuations in water-levels, as in lakes dammed for power generation (e.g. Götmark *et al*. 1989).

The Fennoscandian population is faced with declining fish stocks in lakes acidified by airborne pollutants. However, this may be compensated for by increases in water clarity and the abundance of alternative food sources such as aquatic insects (Eriksson 1994). Eggs laid at acidified lakes in south-west Sweden have been found to have high levels of mercury (Eriksson *et al*. 1992).

The risk from oil pollution at sea in winter needs to be evaluated. Large aggregations such as those in the eastern North Sea in winter may be particularly vulnerable (M. L. Tasker *in litt.*).

■ Conservation measures

Recreational activities should be controlled at lakes important for breeding and foraging birds so as to minimize disturbance. Water-level regulation schemes at breeding sites should also be adjusted to suit habitat demands: from the break-up of ice until July, a rise of only a few centimetres and a maximum

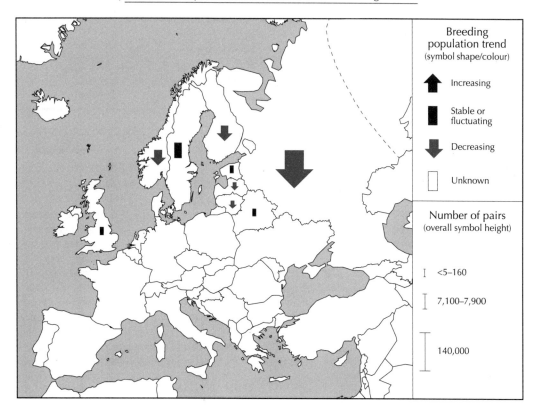

Breeding population trend (symbol shape/colour)

Increasing

Stable or fluctuating

Decreasing

Unknown

Number of pairs (overall symbol height)

<5–160

7,100–7,900

140,000

drop of 30 cm can be accepted. Liming of acidified lakes in order to restore fish stocks could be beneficial, though it may also increase water turbidity and so impair foraging.

Population size and reproductive success have been monitored on a voluntary basis in parts of the breeding range, but improved coordination of these activities could produce better data. Additionally, important wintering areas at sea need to be identified.

MATS O. G. ERIKSSON

Fea's Petrel
Pterodroma feae

SPEC Category 1
Status Endangered
Criteria <250 pairs

This globally threatened species has a known population in Europe of only 150–200 pairs, confined to the island of Bugio in the Madeira archipelago. Although its numbers are probably now stable it has probably declined considerably within historical times and is currently believed to be threatened by loss of habitat and the recent population explosion of Yellow-legged Gull.

■ Distribution and population trends

Within Europe, Fea's Petrel breeds only on Bugio, the southernmost of the Deserta Islands situated to the south-east of Madeira, though a single bird was recently caught in the Azores (Bibby and del Nevo 1992) where Bourne (1965) had suggested the species might occur. There is evidence, based on the recovery of subfossil bones (H. Pieper pers. comm.), that the species once bred on Deserta Grande, the largest of the Deserta Islands. Outside Europe it breeds on several of the Cape Verde Islands (Bannerman and Bannerman 1968), but little is known of its status there or indeed whether the population intermixes with that breeding on Bugio.

On Bugio the population has probably remained fairly stable during recent times, although with increasing study the size of estimates has risen and presently stands at 150–200 breeding pairs. Work on the species has concentrated on the plateau of southern Bugio where the majority of the birds (c.90%) are thought to breed (Jouanin *et al.* 1969, Zino and Zino 1986, authors' own data).

It is very likely that the species was formerly more numerous, and the resources provided by the seas in and around the archipelago of Madeira could theoretically support thousands of pairs of *Pterodroma* petrels. Because of the species' small world population it is listed as Globally Threatened (Collar *et al.* 1994).

	Breeding population			Breeding
	Size (pairs)	Year	Trend	range trend
Portugal Madeira	150–200	91	0	0
Total (approx.)	150–200			

Trends — +2 Large increase +1 Small increase 0 Stable X Extinct
(1970–1990) — −2 Large decrease −1 Small decrease F Fluctuating N New breeder
Data quality — **Bold**: reliable quantitative data Normal type: incomplete quantitative data Bracketed figures: no quantitative data * Data quality not provided

■ Ecology

The southern plateau of Bugio, situated at 350 m altitude, has a sparse covering of vegetation which is heavily cropped by goats and rabbits *Oryctolagus cuniculus*; its southern part has a good covering of grass, while the northern part is dominated by *Mesembryanthemum*, thistles and nettles. In summer the area is totally parched, with neither water nor shelter from the scorching sun. It is essential that earth is available into which the birds can burrow for nesting, and the vegetation cover on the southern plateau is valuable in binding together and retaining the spoil against erosion. The northern plateau of Bugio is more extensive than that in the south, but it is also more arid and has much less vegetation—which may be the reason why so few nests are found in this otherwise apparently ideal area, only 2 km from the main breeding plateau.

Fea's Petrel spends much of its life at sea, and birds come ashore only in order to breed. The food includes plankton, squid and surface crustaceans. Current studies will soon provide more detailed information about the biometrics, breeding biology, diet and other important aspects of this bird and its ecology.

■ Threats

The main threat to the species, limiting its population size and distribution, is probably the continuing loss of breeding habitat. The sparse vegetation is severely cropped by rabbits and goats, and the island suffers considerable erosion from wind and rain. Furthermore, rabbits have been shown to cause considerable disturbance to the breeding burrows of *Pterodroma* species elsewhere (e.g. New Zealand) by invading and modifying burrows (M. J. Imber pers. comm.). This puts considerable stress on breeding pairs and results in the abandonment of breeding sites. Although this potential threat has not been studied on Bugio, rabbits are abundant on the island and are known to enter and modify the burrows of Fea's Petrels.

In the past, man has represented a serious threat, since fishermen formerly took juveniles to eat (Zino and Zino 1986), but recent legislation has rectified this situation and the threat has greatly diminished. A

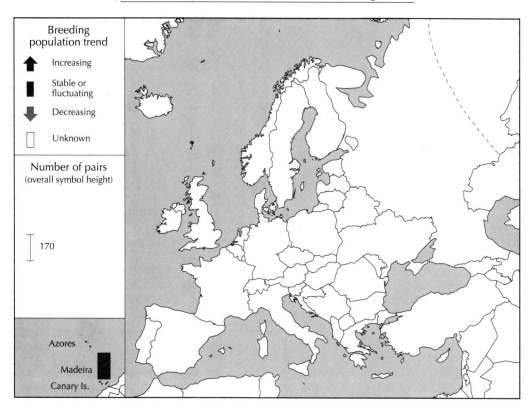

Breeding population trend

↑ Increasing

▮ Stable or fluctuating

↓ Decreasing

☐ Unknown

Number of pairs
(overall symbol height)

⊺ 170

Azores

Madeira

Canary Is.

population explosion of Yellow-legged Gulls *Larus cachinnans* has taken place over the last 10–15 years (Zino and Biscoito in press), and there is concern that they kill many Fea's Petrels (Zino and Zino 1986).

The birds are likely to be affected by many variables at sea such as pollution and the availability of food, but almost nothing is known of these factors. Recently a dying bird was found to have filaments of nylon in its gizzard (F. Zino own data).

▮ Conservation measures

Bugio is part of the Reserva Natural das Desertas, which is also designated as a Special Protection Area in accordance with the EU Wild Birds Directive. Conservation of the habitat of Fea's Petrel is a complex problem, since any attempt to remove rab-

bits and goats from an island of this size, and with such irregular and precipitous terrain, would be extremely difficult and expensive. However, selective culling followed by the establishment of exclusion zones should be considered to protect the areas which have the highest concentrations of breeding Fea's Petrels. In some areas, supporting dry walls could be put up to slow down the rate of erosion and the loss of topsoil. A feasibility study for the eradication of goats and rabbits from the Desertas is currently being prepared by Wildlife Management International Ltd.

Research should be carried out to assess the impact of Yellow-legged Gull predation on the colonies, and if necessary gull numbers should be controlled.

FRANCIS ZINO, MANUEL JOSÉ BISCOITO AND
PAUL ALEXANDER ZINO

Zino's Petrel
Pterodroma madeira

SPEC Category 1
Status Endangered
Criteria <250 pairs

Zino's Petrel is a globally threatened species endemic to the island of Madeira where it has a critically small population of some 20–30 pairs. It is currently threatened by the loss of nesting habitat caused by overgrazing and by predation from black rats and feral cats. The Freira Conservation Project, set up in 1986, is taking action to control the rat and cat population and to monitor breeding success.

■ Distribution and population trends

Zino's Petrel breeds only in a small area of the central mountain massif on Madeira. It was first discovered in 1903, and was thought then to be the same species as Fea's Petrel *P. feae*, which nests on Bugio in the Deserta Islands some 50 km away (Schmitz 1905).

Birds are seen in the Madeiran waters during the breeding season but none have been recorded at other times of the year (Zino and Zino 1986), and indeed the movements of the species outside the breeding season are completely unknown. To date there have been no returns of ringed birds.

It is difficult to estimate the total population of the species, but the current consensus of opinion is that there are 20–30 nesting pairs in the known breeding areas (see table). It is doubtful whether other breeding sites exist. The species has always been rare in modern times, though fossil evidence suggests it was once more widespread. Trends for the 1970–1990 period are unknown (see table, map) but numbers have declined since 1990 (see Threats).

The species is listed as Globally Threatened by Collar *et al.* (1994) because of its extremely small world population size.

	Breeding population			Breeding
	Size (pairs)	Year	Trend	range trend
Portugal Madeira	**20–30**	91	—	**0**
Total (approx.)	20–30			

Trends	+2 Large increase	+1 Small increase	0 Stable	X Extinct
(1970–1990)	–2 Large decrease	–1 Small decrease	F Fluctuating	N New breeder
Data quality	**Bold**: reliable quantitative data	Normal type: incomplete quantitative data		
	Bracketed figures: no quantitative data	* Data quality not provided		

■ Ecology

At sea, birds are seen no closer than about 3–5 km to the shores of Madeira during the day, coming to land only at night. The breeding areas are ledges at 1,600 m altitude in the central mountain massif, which are still rich in endemic flora because of their inaccessibility to goats. It is essential that there is sufficient

earth on the ledges to allow the birds to burrow and to make their nests.

The diet of the two *Pterodroma* species found in the Madeira archipelago is thought to be similar. Material regurgitated has included the remains of small fish, squid and crustaceans, but to date there are insufficient data available to specify the diet.

■ Threats

Heavy grazing by goats and sheep, and the soil erosion which has resulted from it, have caused large reductions in the availability of habitat suitable for the construction of nest burrows. In the past, human predation affected Zino's Petrel when shepherds took nestlings to eat, but this was rare due to the difficulty of reaching the nests (F. Zino pers. obs.). Collectors now pose a much more significant threat, as the egg specimens for both *Pterodroma madeira* and *P. feae* have been stolen from the Funchal Municipal Museum's collection (G. E. Maul pers. comm.) and at least three adult birds and seven eggs have been taken from the colony itself (Zino and Zino 1986).

Feral cats *Felis* and black rats *Rattus rattus* are found throughout the island, as they have been for a very long time. They have presumably long been a serious threat to Zino's Petrel, and remain so (Zino and Zino 1986, Zino and Biscoito 1994). Eggs are eaten and juveniles killed, and in 1991 feral cats killed at least ten adults, possibly breeding birds, on one of the ledges (Zino 1992).

Spending most of its time at sea, Zino's Petrel could be affected there by many factors such as pollution and variation in food availability.

■ Conservation measures

Maintenance of the habitat of Zino's Petrel is essential for its survival. The main breeding area is privately owned land and every encouragement should be given to the local Government of Madeira to purchase it for the Parque Natural da Madeira, then

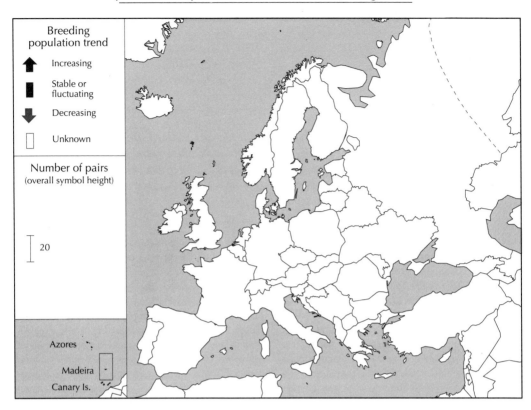

Breeding
population trend

▲ Increasing

■ Stable or
fluctuating

▼ Decreasing

☐ Unknown

Number of pairs
(overall symbol height)

⊥ 20

Azores
Madeira
Canary Is.

to fence it off and remove all sheep and goats.

The Freira Conservation Project (using an alternative common name of the species) was set up in 1986. It makes use of outside helpers but is now administered in Madeira by the BirdLife International representative in conjunction with the Museo Municipal do Funchal and the Park Natural da Madeira. Funding is currently provided by Zeneca in Lisbon, and formerly by Zeneca Public Health in the United Kingdom who still supply all the project's rodenticide at no charge. The project has done a great deal towards the study of this rare bird, as well as protecting it from the black rat and from feral cats. Cordons of specially designed boxes containing the rodenticide Klerat have been placed in rings around the breeding ledges and have certainly restricted the rat population and allowed the birds to breed (Buckle and Zino 1989). Feral cats remain, however, a serious concern: trapping in the immediate vicinity of the ledges has so far caught four animals, and this technique may be the only workable solution to the problem. Unfortunately, even though the area is regularly patrolled by wardens, the project has suffered from the repeated theft of both rat and cat traps.

FRANCIS ZINO, MANUEL JOSÉ BISCOITO AND
PAUL ALEXANDER ZINO

Bulwer's Petrel
Bulweria bulwerii

SPEC Category 3
Status Vulnerable
Criteria Moderate decline, <10,000 pairs

Bulwer's Petrel is found in both the Pacific and Atlantic Oceans. Within Europe it is quite rare with the Madeira archipelago holding the majority of the population, plus smaller but declining numbers on the Canary Islands and Azores. The species is heavily predated by the increasing population of Yellow-legged Gulls. The continued protection of the breeding areas and control of the Yellow-legged Gull population are of the utmost importance.

■ Distribution and population trends

Bulwer's Petrel, a species of both the Pacific and Atlantic Oceans, is quite rare within Europe, totalling 7,500–10,500 pairs (Zino and Biscoito 1994). The archipelago of Madeira (including the Selvagens and Desertas islands) holds the majority of the population (6,000–8,000 pairs), and smaller numbers are present also in the Canary Islands and the Azores (see table, map). Together, these three islands groups comprise over half of the Atlantic population, the remainder breeding in the Cape Verde Islands (Bannerman and Bannerman 1968). Birds are seen flying singly many miles from shore and are observed regularly between Madeira and the Canaries.

The species is migratory, leaving the North Atlantic in winter and returning in early April. The majority of birds apparently move south-westwards into the tropical Atlantic (Cramp and Simmons 1977).

Although there are few data available as this is a difficult bird to study, it seems that the population on Madeira is stable and that numbers on the Canary Islands and Azores appear to be declining (see table, map).

	Breeding population			Breeding
	Size (pairs)	Year	Trend	range trend
Portugal				
Azores	(500–1,000)	—	(–1)	(0)
Madeira	6,000–8,000	91	0	**0**
Spain				
Canary islands	**1,000–1,000**	87	(–2)	(–1)
Total (approx.)	7,500–10,500			

Trends	+2 Large increase	+1 Small increase	0 Stable	X Extinct
(1970-1990)	–2 Large decrease	–1 Small decrease	F Fluctuating	N New breeder
Data quality	**Bold**: reliable quantitative data	Normal type: incomplete quantitative data		
	Bracketed figures: no quantitative data	* Data quality not provided		

■ Ecology

Bulwer's Petrel is a pelagic seabird feeding on the surface off squid, plankton and small fish. In a study of the waters around the Selvagens, Mougin (1989) found that there appeared to be plenty of suitable food available for the species.

Rough nests are made in burrows, which may be excavated in the ground or may already exist as crevices in walls or rocks. Such sites are plentiful in the Madeira archipelago, Canaries and Azores, and the species sometimes uses the same burrows as White-faced Storm-petrel *Pelagodroma marina* and Little Shearwater *Puffinus assimilis*. A single egg is laid in late May or early June and incubated for about 42 days. The young fledge in mid-September after about 62 days in the nest, and by late September almost all birds have moved into the south Atlantic where they winter (Jouanin *et al.* 1979, Zino and Biscoito 1994).

■ Threats

Since the Important Bird Areas (IBAs) of the Selvagens (IBA 012, 013) and the Desertas (IBA 010, 011) were declared Nature Reserves in 1971 and 1990 respectively, the prospects for this petrel have improved enormously through control on human predation. Both these sites have always been free of rats, but there is, however, heavy predation by Yellow-legged Gulls *Larus cachinnans* which have recently undergone a population explosion. Gulls can be observed patrolling the shores at dusk to catch incoming birds.

On the inhabited islands of Madeira, Porto Santo and the Canary Island archipelago the situation is worse, since Bulwer's Petrel almost certainly suffers from predation by rats and, to a lesser extent, by humans.

■ Conservation measures

The necessary conservation legislation exists for protection of this species (Annex I of the EU Wild Birds Directive and Appendix II of the Bern Convention). Many of the breeding sites are already within legally protected nature reserves, and human predation has been largely contained. There is, however, an urgent need to monitor the impact of Yellow-legged Gulls on the species in the Madeira archipelago

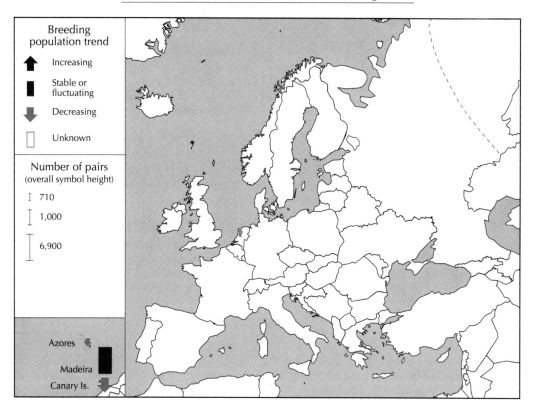

so that management can react. Effective reduction of rat predation on Madeira and Porto Santo is considered impossible at present.

Further research needs to be carried out on this species, especially in the Azores where little is known about the bird, and in the archipelagos of Madeira and the Canaries where more accurate counts are needed in order to monitor the breeding population.

FRANCIS ZINO, MANUEL JOSÉ BISCOITO AND
PAUL ALEXANDER ZINO

Cory's Shearwater
Calonectris diomedea

SPEC Category 2
Status (Vulnerable)
Criteria Large decline

Although numerous, the species has declined, sometimes considerably, in a substantial number of colonies. Introduced predators, human disturbance and continuing exploitation are probably the main threats. Full protection with wardening of major colonies, enforcement of legislation to end human exploitation, and public awareness campaigns to reduce disturbance are therefore needed, together with monitoring to assess trends and conservation action.

■ Distribution and population trends

Cory's Shearwater comprises three well defined sub-species: *C. d. diomedea* nesting on the Balearic Islands and east to the Adriatic and Aegean Seas; *C. d. borealis* breeding off the Iberian peninsula, and especially in the Madeira archipelago, Canary Islands and Azores, and *C. d. edwardsi* on the Cape Verde Islands (Warham 1990). With the exception of several thousands of Cory's Shearwaters on the Cape Verde Islands (de Naurois 1969), several hundreds or thousands in Algeria and 20,000–25,000 pairs in Tunisia (Thibault 1993), Europe holds the entire world population of the species.

The Azores probably holds the largest population (see table, map), which was previously thought by Le Grand *et al.* (1984) to be at least half a million pairs, but recent fieldwork suggests this to have been a substantial overestimate (L. Monteiro *in litt.*; see table, map). Significant populations also exist in the Madeiran archipelago (Portugal), the Canary Islands, the Chafarinas and Balearic Islands (Spain), Malta, Kos island (Greece) and Sicily (Italy). Cory's Shearwaters are also regularly observed off the Turkish coast and may well breed in the region.

The species is difficult to census at some sites, and as a consequence population trends are poorly known, though there have been declines in three-

	Breeding population			Breeding range trend
	Size (pairs)	Year	Trend	
Croatia	1,000–5,000 *	—	0*	0*
France	**810–1,060**	85	0	**0**
Greece	(5,000–5,000)	—	0	(0)
Italy	18,000–20,000	82	(0)	(0)
Malta	8,000–10,000	—	–1	0
Portugal	**150–250**	89	**0**	**0**
Azores	50,000–100,000	—	·(–1)	(0)
Madeira	16,500–25,000	91	**–2**	**0**
Spain	14,000–17,000	—	+1	+1
Canary Islands	**30,000–30,000**	87	(–2)	(–1)
Total (approx.)	140,000–210,000			

Trends (1970–1990)   +2 Large increase   +1 Small increase   0 Stable   X Extinct
  –2 Large decrease   –1 Small decrease   F Fluctuating   N New breeder
Data quality   **Bold:** reliable quantitative data   Normal type: incomplete quantitative data
Bracketed figures: no quantitative data   * Data quality not provided

quarters of the population, including particularly large reductions in the important Canary Islands and Madeiran archipelago populations (although numbers in the Desertas and Selvagens have recently increased). Some increases have been recorded in protected areas in Spain (de Juana 1984) and the Azores (A. J. del Nevo own data).

C. d. diomedea and *C. d. borealis* are trans-Equatorial migrants, with birds of the nominate race moving south to the Benguela current during the northern winter and *C. d. borealis* concentrating off South America and the eastern seaboard of the United States (Mougin *et al.* 1988, Warham 1990). Some birds remain close to breeding colonies during winter. Movements of *C. d. edwardsi* are poorly understood (Cramp and Simmons 1977).

■ Ecology

All races breed colonially during the northern summer, sometimes in large, dense concentrations but more often in widely scattered groups. Nests are amongst rock crevices, recesses or burrows (Cramp and Simmons 1977). Nest-sites and breeding partners are generally retained from year to year, with both sexes sharing incubation and chick-rearing.

Clumsy and vulnerable on land, birds generally congregate offshore, forming large rafts which disperse to nesting colonies soon after nightfall. The behaviour in the Selvagens is unique, as birds here come ashore in daylight (F. Zino *in litt.* 1994). The species forages during the day and night, often in large concentrations capitalizing on prey driven to the surface by predatory fish and sea mammals (A. J. del Nevo own data). The birds feed largely on fish, cephalopods and crustaceans by flying close to the surface and either plunge-diving or picking food from the water (Cramp and Simmons 1977, F. Zino *in litt.* 1994).

■ Threats

Introduced predators, particularly cats, dogs, rats and mustelid species, have caused breeding failure at

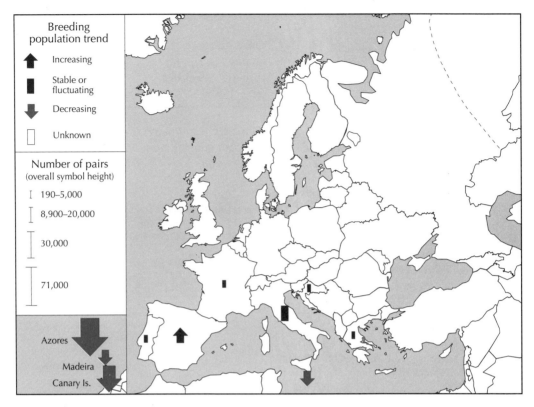

Breeding population trend

Increasing

Stable or fluctuating

Decreasing

Unknown

Number of pairs
(overall symbol height)

190–5,000

8,900–20,000

30,000

71,000

Azores

Madeira

Canary Is.

some colonies and/or movement to inaccessible holes in steep cliffs (for example on the Azores) (A. J. del Nevo own data). On islands near Marseilles the breeding success of *C. d. diomedea* has declined through interference by rabbits *Oryctolagus cuniculus* (O. Fernandez in Warham 1990).

The taking of eggs, chicks and adults by man still occurs at several colonies, e.g. Malta, Azores, island of Madeira and Porto Seguro (F. Zino *in litt.* 1994). In the Madeiran archipelago and the Azores chicks and adults are taken to produce oil, as bait for fishing, and for human consumption, although this problem is now being effectively tackled in Madeira (F. Zino pers. comm., A. J. del Nevo own data).

Disturbance by local people and tourists may be detrimental at some Mediterranean colonies (James 1984, de Juana 1984). Coastal building projects have caused some habitat loss in several Mediterranean colonies (Croxall *et al.* 1984).

■ Conservation measures

Appropriate implementation of the EU Wild Birds Directive and the Bern Convention with respect to key sites (particularly within the Azores, but also on the island of Madeira, Porto Santo and the Canaries) is necessary.

Site protection (including the removal of introduced predators) through wardening and associated education programmes towards conservation goals should be instituted or maintained at a number of Important Bird Areas (IBAs: see Grimmett and Jones 1989). These are, in the Azores, the Coast of Flores (IBA 001), Coast of Corvo (IBA 002), Baixo (IBA 003), Praia (IBA 004) and Ilhéu da Vila do Porto, Santa Maria (IBA 005); in the Madeiran archipelago, Cima (IBA 008), Baixo and Ferro (IBA 009), Bugio (IBA 010), Chão and Deserta Grande (IBA 011) and Selvagem Grande (IBA 012); in Greece, Kyra-Panaghia/Ghioura/Piperi/Skantzoura islands of the northern Sporades (IBA 107); in Italy, Archipelago Maddalena (IBA 108) and north-east coast and islands of Sardinia (IBA 125); in Malta, Ta'Cenc cliffs (IBA 001); and in Spain, the Chafarinas islands (IBA 270) and the north coast of Menorca (IBA 287). The National Park and Biosphere Reserve on Zembra island (Tunisia) should receive full international legislative support. Enforcement of appropriate legislation should be enacted to cease human exploitation, particularly in the Azores, Malta and the Madeiran archipelago.

Population and productivity monitoring should be initiated or maintained at a number of representative colonies in the Azores, Madeira (ongoing in the Selvagens since 1963) and the Chafarinas and north Sporades islands to assess population trends and conservation action.

ADRIAN DEL NEVO

Manx Shearwater
Puffinus puffinus

SPEC Category 2
Status (Localized)
Criteria Localized

Numbers of this burrow-nesting seabird, breeding mostly on offshore islands, appear stable. However, the major part of the population is concentrated at a few sites, the largest colonies all being in north-west Europe. It is vital that island colonies remain free of such land predators as cats and rats.

■ Distribution and population trends

The Manx Shearwater is largely restricted as a breeding bird to the coastal regions of the north-east Atlantic. Less than one percent of the population breeds outside this region, in recently established colonies in North America (Lloyd *et al*. 1991). The Bermuda population became extinct about 1905 (Bourne 1957). Manx Shearwaters come to European waters to breed and are present in force at their colonies from mid-March until early October. They winter off the coasts of South America, mainly off south-east Brazil (Brooke 1990).

Some 300,000 pairs breed in Europe, most being concentrated at a few sites (see Important Bird Area table), with United Kingdom colonies holding about three-quarters of this total (see population table, map). There are also significant colonies in the Republic of Ireland and rather less important ones in Iceland and the Faroes; by comparison, the colonies of France and certain Macaronesian islands are small.

Detailed censuses are difficult because the species normally makes visits to its colonies by night and because it nests in burrows, often at sites shared with burrow-nesting Puffins *Fratercula arctica* and rabbits *Oryctolagus cuniculus*. However, adequate

Important Bird Areas The top ten IBAs for breeding Manx Shearwaters in Europe, together holding over 90% of the total European population.

Faroe Islands	001	Mykines and Mykineshólmur
	004	Eysturoy
	014	Sandoy
	016	Skúvoy
Rep. of Ireland	064	Blasket Islands
	065	Puffin Island
	067	The Skelligs: Great Skellig and Little Skellig
United Kingdom	025	Rum
	215	Bardsey Island and Aberdaron Coast
	219	Skokholm and Skomer

censuses have been undertaken at the key British colonies, and the overall population size is therefore moderately well known. During the twentieth century the Welsh colonies may have grown while some Shetland and Hebridean colonies (but not that on Rum) may have dwindled (Brooke 1990). In more recent years there is evidence of falling numbers in the Azores and the Canary Islands while the French population has grown and small new colonies have become established in the Channel Islands. However, the larger colonies have shown no detectable changes over the past 20 years. Data presented in Gibbons *et al*. (1993) suggest a minor range contraction in Britain over the 1970–1990 period due to the loss of a few small colonies, though because of methodological problems this change is not thought to be significant (D. W. Gibbons pers. comm. 1994).

■ Ecology

Burrow-nesting Manx Shearwaters are not agile on land and require nesting sites secure from terrestrial predators. In practice this means they mostly nest on predator-free offshore islands. Less than one percent of the population nests on mainland cliffs. The majority of Manx Shearwaters nest in burrows dug in soil, but rock debris also appears to be an acceptable substrate.

Studies at sea off Britain and Ireland show that Manx Shearwaters occur largely over the continental

	Breeding population			Breeding
	Size (pairs)	Year	Trend	range trend
Denmark				
Faroe Islands	(15,000–30,000)	81	(0)	(0)
France	**100–150**	91	+2	0
Iceland	7,000–10,000	91	(0)	0
Rep. of Ireland	29,000–49,000	85–87	0	0
Portugal				
Azores	P	—	—	—
Madeira	300–500	91	0	**0**
Spain				
Canary Islands	(200–500)	87	(–2)	(–2)
United Kingdom	220,000–250,000	85–87	(0)	**0**
Guernsey	**25–35**	86–89	N	N
Isle of Man [1]	0–12	—	0	0*
Total (approx.)	**270,000–340,000**			

Trends	+2 Large increase	+1 Small increase	0 Stable	X Extinct
(1970–1990)	–2 Large decrease	–1 Small decrease	F Fluctuating	N New breeder
Data quality	**Bold:** reliable quantitative data	Normal type: incomplete quantitative data		
	Bracketed figures: no quantitative data	* Data quality not provided		
[1] Population figures are included within United Kingdom totals			P Present	

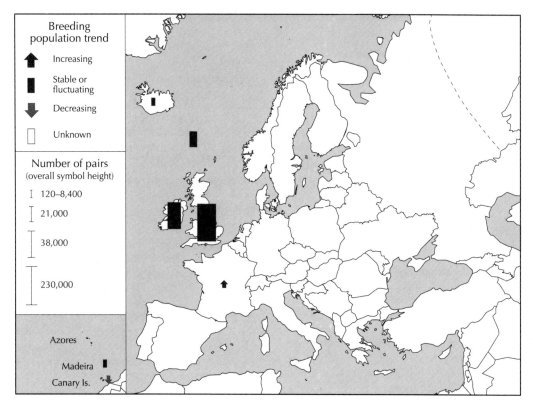

Breeding population trend

- ⬆ Increasing
- ■ Stable or fluctuating
- ⬇ Decreasing
- ☐ Unknown

Number of pairs (overall symbol height)

- 120–8,400
- 21,000
- 38,000
- 230,000

Azores
Madeira
Canary Is.

shelf, and often in relatively nearshore areas (Webb *et al*. 1990). Two main areas of occurrence, in the southern and western Irish Sea and the inshore areas of the Sea of Hebrides, are presumably linked to the two largest breeding areas. The birds mostly feed on fish of the herring family (Clupeidae), but little is known of the interactions between fish populations, shearwater populations and human fisheries.

■ Threats

Given that Manx Shearwater numbers appear stable, the species is not imminently threatened. Predation by gulls *Larus* spp. accounts for under 10% of adult shearwater mortality (Brooke 1990), but the concentration of the major part of the species' population at a few sites makes it vulnerable, especially to rats *Rattus* spp. which have previously devastated certain colonies (e.g. the Calf of Man in the Irish Sea).

Although heavy metals, organochlorine chemicals and plastic pellets have been detected in Manx Shearwaters, there is no evidence of adverse effects of these forms of pollution on populations (Brooke 1990).

Manx Shearwaters have not yet been involved in a serious oil pollution incident, but their habit of forming large rafts on the sea, both in feeding areas and near colonies, might put them at risk should a serious spill occur in one of these areas.

■ Conservation measures

It is imperative that the most important Manx Shearwater colonies remain rat-free. These are the islands of Skokholm and Skomer off the coast of south-west Wales (United Kingdom, Important Bird Area 219) and Puffin Island off the south-west coast of the Republic of Ireland (IBA 065). This need should be promulgated among local boatmen, day visitors, etc.

The important montane colony on Rum (United Kingdom IBA 025) is visited by rats after the main breeding season, but Thompson's (1987) study (summarized in Lloyd *et al*. 1991) concluded that this was not detrimental to the population.

Long-term population monitoring should be continued at those colonies where it is already under way, and needs to be expanded to cover other colonies, particularly in the Republic of Ireland. Tissue samples should also be regularly checked for levels of organochlorines and heavy metals.

M. DE L. BROOKE AND MARK TASKER

Little Shearwater
Puffinus assimilis

SPEC Category 3
Status Vulnerable
Criteria Moderate decline, <10,000 pairs

The Little Shearwater breeds in small numbers on the archipelagos of Madeira, the Azores and the Canary Islands. Although the populations on the Madeiran islands are probably stable, those on the Azores and Canaries have declined in recent decades. Birds are killed by rats in the Canaries, and it is essential that the main breeding sites in Madeira and the Azores remain rat-free.

■ Distribution and population trends

The Little Shearwater has a fragmented distribution in all three major oceans, with the biggest part of this range lying in the southern hemisphere (Harrison 1983). The endemic European race of the Little Shearwater, *baroli*, breeds in the archipelagos of Madeira, the Canaries and the Azores, but has a small total population of only 2,700–3,900 pairs (see table, map).

Over 60% (1,800–2,500 pairs) of the European population breeds in the Madeira archipelago, where numbers are probably stable (see table, map). This includes an estimated 300 pairs (Zino and Biscoito in press) on the Desertas, with the remainder on the Selvagens (Jensen 1981) and small numbers on Porto Santo and its islets and at Ponta de São Lourenço on the island of Madeira. On Selvagem Grande birds are seen onshore long after the breeding season.

In the Canary Islands, the population has declined rapidly over the period 1970–1990 (see table, map).

The first known breeding record in the Azores was at Ferraria on São Miguel in 1953 (Bannerman and Bannerman 1966), but rats are now present at that site and the Little Shearwater seems to be extinct there (Le Grand *et al*. 1984). The major colonies now known are on islets off Graciosa and Santa Maria. In the Azores, as well as in Madeira, birds are seen at the colonies outside the breeding season, though in much smaller numbers than when nesting (L. Monteiro *in litt*. 1993).

■ Ecology

The species breeds in rocky ground, caves, cliffs or stone walls; the rough nest is generally a tunnel in soft soil, a hole between rocks or lies beneath fallen boulders. While some nests are easily accessible others are very deep. The species also utilizes old tunnels of other Procellariidae and Hydrobatidae including Bulwer's Petrel *Bulweria bulwerii* (Zino and Biscoito in press). There appears to be no lack of ideal nesting habitat for these birds.

Unlike other Palearctic shearwaters, Little Shearwater seems to be largely confined to the waters close to the breeding islands and visits the nesting sites outside the breeding period.

The species is difficult to study and little is known of its biology, partly because it is a winter breeder. Birds on Selvagem Grande lay eggs in January and February, and the chicks fledge in May and June (Mougin *et al*. 1992). The species does not flock and is not easy to observe at sea. Stomach content analysis of *P. a. boydi* in the Cape Verde Islands suggests that the diet probably comprises mostly fish and cephalopods (Bourne 1955).

■ Threats

As a winter breeder the Little Shearwater suffers less from human predation and disturbance than do other shearwaters. Also, within the Madeira archipelago the majority nest in rat-free nature reserves, and most of the current breeding sites in the Azores are also free of rats. However, rats probably do kill Little Shearwaters in the Canaries as well as in some areas of Madeira, and in the Azores rats seem to be a major factor in determining the distribution of the species. Yellow-legged Gulls *Larus cachinnans* also take the occasional bird, though they would appear to prefer the smaller petrels. On Ilheu Chão, in the Desertas, fresh remains of Little Shearwater have been found, apparently killed by Short-eared Owls *Asio flammeus* which were present on the island as migrants at the time.

	Breeding population			Breeding
	Size (pairs)	Year	Trend	range trend
Portugal				
Azores	(500–1,000)	—	(–1)	(0)
Madeira	1,800–2,500	91	**0**	**0**
Spain				
Canary Islands	**400–400**	87	(–2)	(–2)
Total (approx.)	2,700–3,900			

Trends   +2 Large increase   +1 Small increase   0 Stable   X Extinct
(1970–1990) –2 Large decrease   –1 Small decrease   F Fluctuating   N New breeder
Data quality **Bold**: reliable quantitative data   Normal type: incomplete quantitative data
Bracketed figures: no quantitative data   * Data quality not provided

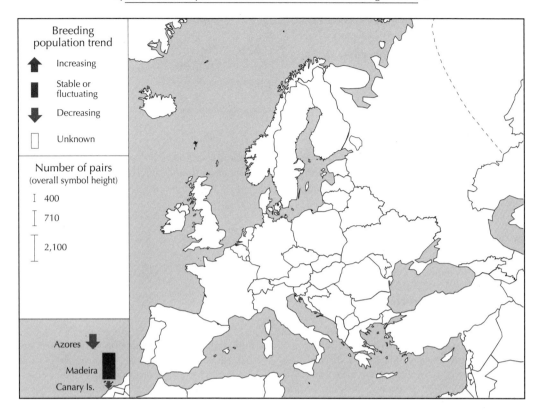

Breeding population trend

↑ Increasing

■ Stable or fluctuating

↓ Decreasing

□ Unknown

Number of pairs
(overall symbol height)

Ⅰ 400

Ⅰ 710

Ⅰ 2,100

Azores ↓

Madeira ■

Canary Is. ↓

■ Conservation measures

The Little Shearwater appears to be a dispersed breeder on the Canaries and Azores and thus difficult to protect. In the Madeira archipelago the species is well protected, since most birds breed within Strict Nature Reserves. It is of vital importance, however, that these reserves remain rat-free, something which can only be achieved by constant vigilance during the transport of materials to the islands.

As the species spends a substantial part of its lifecycle at sea, it is presumably susceptible to marine pollution, and every effort must be made to reduce marine pollutants.

Research into the causes of the decline in the Canaries are urgently needed. Studies with marked nests and ringed birds are in progress on Selvagem Grande to establish basic data on breeding biology (egg-laying, incubation and fledging periods, etc.), and work on distribution, population status and habitat selection is underway in the Azores.

FRANCIS ZINO, MANUEL JOSÉ BISCOITO AND
PAUL ALEXANDER ZINO

White-faced Storm-petrel
Pelagodroma marina

SPEC Category 3
Status Localized
Criteria Localized

The principal population of the White-faced Storm-petrel in Europe breeds in just two colonies, on the Selvagens (Salvage Islands) of the Madeiran archipelago. Although the Selvagens are protected as a nature reserve, the species is susceptible to predation by Yellow-legged Gulls and to vegetation degradation by rabbits on Selvagem Grande. Furthermore, many potentially important aspects of its ecology are currently poorly understood.

■ Distribution and population trends

In Europe this species (subspecies *P. m. hypoleuca*) nests in large numbers only on the Selvagens of Portugal, in the volcanic archipelago of Madeira, where it was first reported in 1895 by Ogilvie Grant (1896). Recently a small population was found on the Canary Islands, estimated at no more than 10 pairs (Martín *et al*. 1989), and occasionally birds are seen at sea off Madeira, but this is unusual (see population table, map). Elsewhere in the North Atlantic the subspecies *P. m. eadesi* breeds on the Cape Verde Islands.

The breeding population of the Selvagens is divided into two main colonies: c.9,000 pairs on Selvagem Grande (Important Bird Area 012) and c.10,000 pairs on Selvagem Pequena and Ilhéu de Fora (IBA 013; see IBA table). On Selvagem Grande the birds nest mostly on Chão dos Caramujos and close to Pico dos Tornozelos, where the soil is suitable for their burrows. The species is found throughout the islands of Selvagem Pequena and Ilhéu de Fora.

It would appear that the European population is stable (see population table).

	Breeding population			Breeding
	Size (pairs)	Year	Trend	range trend
Portugal				
Madeira	16,000–20,000	91	0	**0**
Spain				
Canary Islands	**10–10**	87	(N)	(0)
Total (approx.)	16,000–20,000			

Trends	+2 Large increase	+1 Small increase	0 Stable	X Extinct
(1970–1990)	–2 Large decrease	–1 Small decrease	F Fluctuating	N New breeder
Data quality	**Bold**: reliable quantitative data	Normal type: incomplete quantitative data		
	Bracketed figures: no quantitative data	* Data quality not provided		

■ Ecology

The species breeds in winter, nesting in sandy soil where birds excavate long burrows. The breeding grounds on the Selvagens have a good covering of vegetation, mostly of ice-plants *Mesembryanthemum cristallinum*, the roots of which stabilize the very

Important Bird Areas The major IBAs for breeding White-faced Petrels in Europe, together holding over 90% of the total European population.

Madeira	
012	Selvagem Grande, Selvagens
013	Selvagem Pequena and Ilhéu de Forna, Selvagens

sandy soil. Breeding conditions for the petrel are ideal on Selvagem Pequena and Ilhéu de Fora as there are no herbivores on the islands and the vegetation is in a naturally pristine state. However, Selvagem Grande has introduced rabbits *Oryctolagus cuniculus* which cause considerable damage to the flora.

The White-faced Storm-petrel comes ashore only to breed, from early January until early September (Jouanin and Roux 1965, Jensen 1981). There are many factors which have potential to affect the species, but which are currently poorly understood, notably food availability and the effects of marine pollution. Almost nothing is known about the feeding ecology; the species feeds on the surface and on small prey items, but no study of the diet seems to have been undertaken.

■ Threats

Although the threats to this petrel have greatly diminished in recent times the species remains susceptible in Europe due to its concentration at just two sites. In the past, visitors walking over the breeding grounds during the breeding season caused considerable damage but this is now prohibited. In 1971 the Selvagens were designated a Strict Nature Reserve and landing on the islands is now prohibited.

The main threat to the birds is heavy predation by Yellow-legged Gulls *Larus cachinnans*, which have increased in numbers from about 20 individuals on Selvagem Grande in 1963 to about 100 at the present time, the birds having profited from the advent of motorized fishing boats and consequent supply of offal. The islands are near to each other and the gulls are thus able to move easily between them. There

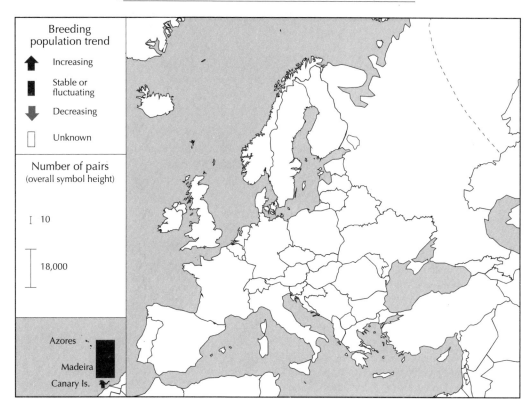

Breeding
population trend

▲ Increasing

■ Stable or
fluctuating

▼ Decreasing

☐ Unknown

Number of pairs
(overall symbol height)

10

18,000

Azores

Madeira

Canary Is.

have been occasional influxes of migratory Short-eared Owls *Asio flammeus*, and these have also been observed to kill some birds of the colony on Selvagem Grande (F. Zino pers. obs.).

■ Conservation measures

Since the designation of the Selvagens as a Strict Nature Reserve, the White-faced Storm-petrel has been given considerable protection. The Parque Natural da Madeira on Selvagem Grande now has permanent wardens, further improving the situation, and a warden's camp has been set up on Selvagem Pequena from April/May to October, so providing additional protection and preventing any human destruction of birds or their habitat during the time when visitors pass the islands. During the remainder of the year the weather is too unstable for this camp to be occupied, but fishermen tend not to visit the island in winter in any case.

On Selvagem Grande grazing rabbits may affect the vegetation which is a very important component of the petrel's breeding environment, and eradication or control of rabbit numbers is therefore being considered. There are, however, fears that this may lead to an unwelcome spread of the introduced plant *Nicotinea glauca*.

Research should be carried out to assess the effects on the colonies of predation by Yellow-legged Gulls, and gull numbers should be controlled if necessary. While every effort is taken to dispose carefully of the warden's rubbish (on which Yellow-legged Gulls scavenge), it is impossible to control fishermen who clean their fish at sea and dump offal overboard, and consequently ornithologists on the islands believe that culling may be necessary.

In the longer term, accurate monitoring of the colonies is necessary to establish reliable population trends, and further research is required to assess the feeding ecology of the species and the effects on it of fishing and marine pollution.

FRANCIS ZINO, MANUEL JOSÉ BISCOITO AND
PAUL ALEXANDER ZINO

Storm Petrel
Hydrobates pelagicus

SPEC Category 2
Status (Localized)
Criteria Localized

As a breeding species, this seabird is virtually endemic to Europe, where it is relatively common in the north-west but rare in the Mediterranean. Both its population size and status are poorly known. The greatest threat is from mammalian predators introduced to breeding islands, as the majority of the population is confined to a few such sites. Measures are required to minimize the possibility of such introductions.

■ Distribution and population trends

There may be small numbers breeding in Morocco but otherwise the entire world population nests in Europe at a small number of sites (see table of Important Bird Areas). The breeding range incorporates European countries with an Atlantic or Mediterranean coastline, but excludes the North Sea and Baltic.

The difficulties of censusing a species that nests in burrows on small offshore islands, emerging only at night, means that little is known of its population size or trends. Declines have been noted at some colonies, however (Lloyd *et al.* 1991), especially in southern parts of its range (see population table, map). The largest populations are in the Faroes, Iceland, Republic of Ireland and United Kingdom, with the total of birds breeding in these countries probably amounting to 90% of the world population. However, it is highly likely that colonies remain to be found, and the range may be even more extensive.

Storm Petrels migrate south to spend the winter at sea off western and southern Africa.

Important Bird Areas The top ten IBAs for breeding Storm Petrels in Europe, together holding over 90% of the total European population.

Faroe Islands	001	Mykines and Mykineshólmur
	009	Fugloy
	010	Svínoy
	011	Nólsoy
	014	Sandoy
	016	Skuvoy
	017	Stóra Dímun
Iceland	006	Vestmannaeyjar
Rep. of Ireland	030	Inishglora and Inishkeeragh
	064	Blasket Islands

■ Ecology

Storm Petrels require breeding islands free of mammalian predators, particularly rats and cats. Nests are placed either in burrows, in rock crevices or under boulders.

At sea to the west of Britain, birds are found widely over the continental shelf (including the edge) in areas influenced by Atlantic water (Webb *et al.* 1990). The smaller numbers that occur in the North Sea are most common in the north-west, in the North Atlantic inflow (Tasker *et al.* 1987). Birds tend to be out of sight of land by day, but are probably much closer inshore at night. They feed on surface-living crustaceans, small fish and other similar foods, and some scavenge pieces of offal from behind fishing vessels (Cramp and Simmons 1977). Concentrations of food in the marine environment, such as those produced by hydrological fronts, provide important feeding areas (Webb *et al.* 1990).

■ Threats

The major threat is the accidental introduction of mammalian predators to breeding sites, the Storm Petrel being highly susceptible to such predation as the majority of its population is concentrated in relatively few sites. This is particularly the case in southern Europe and in the Mediterranean where breeding populations are small and confined to just a

	Breeding population			Breeding
	Size (pairs)	Year	Trend	range trend
Denmark				
Faroe Islands	(150,000–400,000)	—	(0)	(0)
France	400–600	85	–1	(0)
Greece	(10–30)	—	(0)	(0)
Iceland	50,000–100,000	91	(0)	0
Rep. of Ireland	50,000–100,000	1980s	0	0
Italy	(1,500–2,000)	86	(0)	(0)
Malta	5,000–3,000	—	–1	0
Norway	(1,000–10,000)	90	—	—
Spain	1,700–2,000	—	–1	–1
Canary Islands	**1,000**–?	87	(–2)	(–2)
United Kingdom	(20,000–150,000)	1980s	(0)	**0**
Guernsey	**0–100**	86–89	**–2**	**0**
Isle of Man [1]	(0–50)	—	0	0*
Total (approx.)	280,000–770,000			

Trends   +2 Large increase   +1 Small increase   0 Stable   X Extinct
(1970–1990)   –2 Large decrease   –1 Small decrease   F Fluctuating   N New breeder
Data quality   **Bold**: reliable quantitative data   Normal type: incomplete quantitative data
   Bracketed figures: no quantitative data   * Data quality not provided
[1] Population figures are included within United Kingdom totals

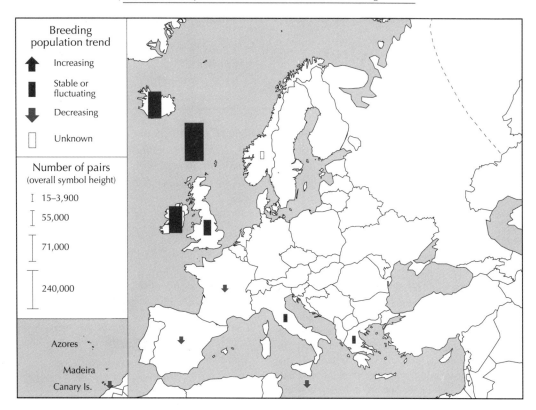

few islands. In some areas, the increases in numbers of large gulls appear to have increased the rate of predation on Storm Petrels (Harvey 1983). Such increases in numbers of gulls may be attributable to human activities such as increased food supplies at rubbish tips or at trawlers, so Storm Petrel population levels may be impacted indirectly by the activities of man.

It is not known if human activities can threaten feeding opportunities for Storm Petrels and there have been no systematic studies of the effects of pollutants on the species.

■ Conservation measures

It is most important to ensure that rats, cats and other alien mammals are kept off those breeding islands presently free of these predators. This requires deliberate policy and action, which does not appear to have been taken in many cases. Some islands, especially those known to hold Storm Petrels in the past, would benefit from predator removal.

At present, the lack of a good method for measuring population size or trends is a serious inhibition to improving the nature conservation status of Storm Petrels and this warrants further research.

MARK TASKER

Leach's Storm-petrel
Oceanodroma leucorhoa

SPEC Category 3
Status (Localized)
Criteria Localized

The population size and ecology are poorly known. Within Europe there are only a few colonies, all on remote islands close to oceanic feeding grounds. Nearly all of these colonies are free of mammalian predators and it is essential that they remain so. Being highly concentrated at a few breeding sites, the species is particularly susceptible to introduced predators.

■ Distribution and population trends

Very little is known of the population size of Leach's Storm-petrel. As a small oceanic seabird, breeding in burrows on offshore islands and present over land only by night, it is very difficult to census. The majority of the world population of 7–9 million pairs nests in Alaska, and in the North Atlantic most nest in North America. Iceland holds the largest population in Europe, and there are also large numbers in the United Kingdom. The southernmost colony in Europe is located in the Republic of Ireland and the northernmost is in Norway (see population table, map). Within Europe the species is highly concentrated at a small number of sites (see Important Bird Area table).

The difficulties involved in carrying out censuses mean that population trends are very poorly known. It is thought that the populations in Iceland and the United Kingdom are stable and that numbers in the Faroes are increasing slightly (see population table, map).

Leach's Storm-petrels are migratory, and spend the winter at sea in the tropics.

Important Bird Areas The top ten IBAs for breeding Leach's Storm-petrels in Europe, together holding over 90% of the total European population.

Faroe Islands	001	Mykines and Mykineshólmur
Iceland	006	Vestmannaeyjar
Norway	025	Røst
Rep. of Ireland	013	Rathlin O'Birne
	026	Stags of Broadhaven
United Kingdom	001	North Rona and Sula Sgeir
	002	Flannan Isles
	003	St Kilda
	039	Ramna Stacks and Gruney
	042	Foula

The food comprises planktonic crustaceans, such as euphausiids and copepods, and other small marine animals. They probably feed mostly near oceanic hydrological features that concentrate these items, such as the upwellings which often occur near the edge of continental shelves. To the west of Britain, most birds are found over or beyond the edge of the continental shelf by day (Webb *et al.* 1990). These birds probably originate from United Kingdom colonies. The feeding grounds of other populations are not known, as there have been no similar studies around Iceland.

■ Threats

By far the greatest threat to Leach's Storm-petrel is the introduction by man of rats or cats to its colonies. Most introductions to European islands occurred before there were written records, so no good information exists on the extent of any impact, though Buckley and Buckley (1984) have recorded decreases in eastern North America due to such introductions. Disturbance by tourists, military bombing and research workers, and the destruction of nesting habitat by heavy grazing animals, are also listed as negative factors by these authors. There have been no systematic studies of hazards to Leach's Storm-petrel from pollutants.

	Breeding population			Breeding
	Size (pairs)	Year	Trend	range trend
Denmark				
Faroe Islands	300–700	—	(+1)	(0)
Iceland	80,000–150,000	91	(0)	0
Rep. of Ireland	200–1,000	88–91	—	0
Norway	(100–1,000)	90	—	—
United Kingdom	(10,000–100,000)	88–91	(0)	**0**
Total (approx.)	91,000–250,000			

Trends	+2 Large increase	+1 Small increase	0 Stable	X Extinct
(1970–1990)	–2 Large decrease	–1 Small decrease	F Fluctuating	N New breeder
Data quality	**Bold**: reliable quantitative data	Normal type: incomplete quantitative data		
	Bracketed figures: no quantitative data	* Data quality not provided		

■ Ecology

Throughout their European range, Leach's Storm-petrels require oceanic islands free of mammalian predators for breeding. They nest in earth burrows in well-drained soil, or under boulders. The burrows can tolerate the weight of light grazing animals such as rabbits or Soay sheep.

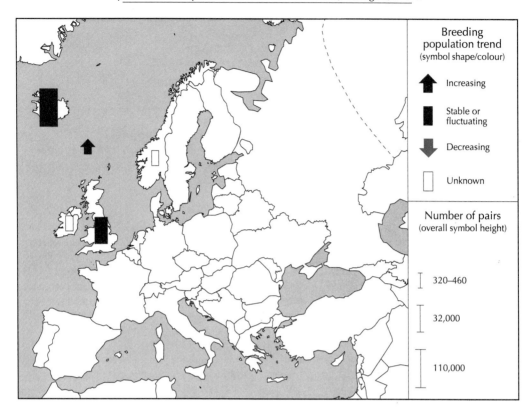

■ Conservation measures

The species is fully protected in EU countries. The main breeding sites are Important Bird Areas (see IBA table), and all breeding sites require strict protection against introduction of mammalian predators. However, the necessary preventive measures do not appear to have been adequately applied so far in Europe. Such predators should be removed from those islands with (probably remnant) populations of Leach's Storm-petrel. Most colonies in Europe are relatively inaccessible, and consequently do not suffer excessive disturbance by tourists or research workers.

So little is known of the species at sea that conservation measures cannot be suggested there, other than the need for further research into its offshore feeding ecology.

MARK TASKER

Madeiran Storm-petrel
Oceanodroma castro

SPEC Category 3
Status Vulnerable
Criteria Moderate decline, <10,000 pairs

The highly pelagic Madeiran Storm-petrel is poorly known, with few data available on population sizes and trends. The population is, however, believed to be small, and is declining on the Azores. Predation is the main threat, by rats in the Azores, and from an increasing Yellow-legged Gull population in the Madeira archipelago.

■ Distribution and population trends

Madeiran Storm-Petrel has a worldwide distribution, nesting on Ascension Island and St Helena in the Atlantic, and in the Pacific on Galápagos, Hawaii and off eastern Japan. Within European waters the species breeds in the Madeira archipelago (Bannerman and Bannerman 1965), on Tenerife in the Canary Islands (Martín 1987), in the Azores (L. Monteiro, A. J. del Nevo and C. J. Bibby in prep.) and off mainland Portugal (see table, map). The species is difficult to separate at sea from similar petrels such as Leach's Storm-petrel *Oceanodroma leucorhoa* and its marine range is little known, though there is no evidence of true migration (Cramp and Simmons 1977).

For the islands of the Desertas and Selvagens of the Madeira archipelago, estimates have been made of over 1,000 breeding pairs in each island group (Zino and Biscoito in press.). The species was first found breeding on the Canaries on the Anagu Rocks off Tenerife in 1983 (Martín *et al.* 1984) and now has an estimated population of 300 pairs (see table). The population in the Azores is also poorly known, but is probably concentrated on the islets of Graciosa and Santa Maria. The species also nests, in small numbers, on the Berlengas and the Farilhões off mainland Portugal (Teixeira and Moore 1983).

There are few data on population trends, though numbers are probably mostly stable or increasing, but may be declining on the Azores (see table, map).

■ Ecology

The majority of nests are in rock piles or old walls. On Selvagem Grande, Madeiran Storm-petrels may occupy nests normally used by White-faced Storm-petrels *Pelagodroma marina* (Mougin 1988), and on Bugio they have been found in December in nests which had been occupied by Cory's Shearwater *Calonectris diomedea* (Zino and Biscoito in press). There is thus no lack of suitable nesting sites.

In the Madeira archipelago eggs have been found in all months of the year and it is even possible that there are two main breeding populations nesting at different times of year. In the Azores the breeding pattern varies between islands: on Graciosa the birds breed throughout the year, while on Santa Maria there are breeding records only in August (L. Monteiro, A. del Nevo and C. J. Bibby in prep.).

The species is highly pelagic and is usually found far from land except in the breeding season when birds come ashore to nest.

Little is known of the diet, but it is thought to comprise largely crustaceans, squid, fish, oily scraps and refuse taken from the surface of the sea (Cramp and Simmons 1977).

■ Threats

The main threats to the Madeiran Storm-petrel are rats *Rattus* and Yellow-legged Gulls *Larus cachinnans*. In the Azores, all principal islands and offshore islets are infested with rats and predation from this source is considerable (L. Monteiro, B. Zonfrillo pers. comm.). In the Madeira archipelago Yellow-legged Gulls kill birds coming ashore at night, and the gulls' pellets bear proof of their success (F. J. A. Zino pers. obs.), so the rapidly increasing populations of these gulls at breeding sites are cause for concern. The principal breeding islands of the Madeira archipelago are free of rats, but some breeding probably occurs on Madeira itself where rats are abundant and predation thus presumably occurs.

The increasing amount of surface pollution at sea, especially the occurrence of small items of floating

	Breeding population			Breeding
	Size (pairs)	Year	Trend	range trend
Portugal	50–50	89	0	**0**
Azores	(1,000–2,000)	—	(–1)	(0)
Madeira	2,000–2,500	91	0	**0**
Spain				
Canary Islands	**300–300**	87	(N)	(N)
Total (approx.)	3,300–4,900			

Trends (1970–1990)   +2 Large increase   +1 Small increase   0 Stable   X Extinct
  –2 Large decrease   –1 Small decrease   F Fluctuating   N New breeder
Data quality   **Bold**: reliable quantitative data   Normal type: incomplete quantitative data
Bracketed figures: no quantitative data   * Data quality not provided

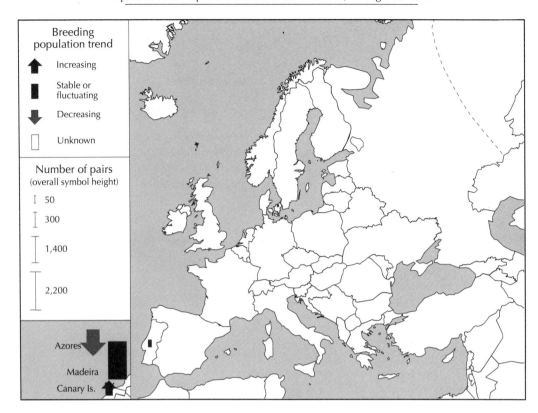

Breeding
population trend

▲ Increasing

■ Stable or
fluctuating

▼ Decreasing

☐ Unknown

Number of pairs
(overall symbol height)

50

300

1,400

2,200

Azores

Madeira

Canary Is.

plastic, is almost certainly a danger to these small petrels.

■ Conservation measures

The principal breeding sites—the Desertas and Selvagens of the Madeira archipelago and the Berlengas off Portugal—are Strict Nature Reserves, managed for the benefit of all fauna and flora. Where they occur, rats are a serious problem and extremely difficult to control; a reduction in the dumping of rubbish, which might be brought about through public education, is of prime importance. Long-term monitoring is needed to explore the impact of Yellow-legged Gull populations, and their numbers should be controlled if necessary.

Clearly, the problem of marine pollution is global and must be addressed for a multitude of reasons, of which the damage it can cause to seabirds is just one. There is also a need for long-term monitoring of Madeiran Storm-petrel numbers.

FRANCIS ZINO, MANUEL JOSÉ BISCOITO AND
PAUL ALEXANDER ZINO

Gannet
Sula bassana

SPEC Category 2
Status Localized
Criteria Localized

Most of the world population nests in Europe, much of it remaining in European waters throughout the year. The European range has expanded in the past 50 years, and colonies have increased in size. However, although there are presently no major threats to the population, except for potential man-induced changes in food supply, the species is susceptible as large numbers of birds are concentrated at few sites.

■ Distribution and population trends

Over three-quarters of the world population of this colonial seabird breeds in Europe. Its North Atlantic breeding range extends from northern Norway to France and west to Iceland; there are further colonies in North America. Many adults are present in northern waters through the winter but most move south after breeding to winter in waters between the Bay of Biscay and western Africa, with some entering the Mediterranean (Nelson 1978). On average, immatures migrate further south than adults and for a longer part of the winter.

The European breeding population, which must be one of the best known and counted of any bird species, was estimated to be about 223,500 pairs by Lloyd *et al*. (1991) and about 230,000 by this review, due to more recent data from France and Norway (see population table). Approximately 70% of the population breeds in the United Kingdom, with over 10% in both Iceland and the Republic of Ireland (see map). Over 90% of birds are concentrated at 10 sites (see Important Bird Area table).

Between 1970 and 1990 numbers in all countries were stable or showed an increase (see population table). The average rise was about 2% per year during 1969–1985, but with substantial variation between colonies, the smallest and newest increas-

Important Bird Areas The top ten IBAs for breeding Gannets in Europe, together holding over 90% of the total European population.

France	051	Les Sept-Iles
Iceland	006	Vestmannaeyjar
	016	Eldey
Rep. of Ireland	067	The Skelligs: Great Skellig and Little Skellig
United Kingdom	001	North Rona and Sula Sgeir
	003	St Kilda
	035	Hermaness and Saxa Vord
	103	Ailsa Craig
	125	Forth Islands
	220	Grassholm

ing most rapidly (Lloyd *et al*. 1991). This population growth has been under way since the first counts at around the start of the twentieth century (Gurney 1913), but recently the rate appears to have slowed.

■ Ecology

Gannets require breeding cliffs or islands safe from mammalian predators (including man), and ledges on cliffs need to be wide enough to accommodate the large nest. Most foraging is done over continental shelf seas, few birds being seen over deep ocean (Webb *et al*. 1990). The species has a wide foraging range, for example c.120 km around North Sea colonies (Tasker *et al*. 1985), and takes a wide variety of shoaling marine fish, and cephalopods. It will forage at trawlers, taking even the largest discarded fish and frequently stealing from other seabirds present (Hudson and Furness 1989).

■ Threats

There seems to be no major threats at present. Indeed, part of the increase in numbers may have resulted from a cessation of human persecution over most of the range. Colonies are, however, concentrated at a small number of sites making them susceptible to oiling or other local catastrophes. Toxic chemicals have been found in relatively high con-

	Breeding population			Breeding
	Size (pairs)	Year	Trend	range trend
Denmark				
Faroe Islands	2,000–2,000	—	0	0
France	**8,800–9,700**	92	+2	0
Germany	1–1	—	N	N
Iceland	**25,000–25,000**	84–85	+1	0
Rep. of Ireland	**25,000–25,000**	84–90	0	+2
Norway	**3,500–4,000**	90	+2	+1
United Kingdom	**160,000–160,000**	84–91	+1	+1
Guernsey	**4,000–5,000**	86–89	+1	0
Total (approx.)	230,000–230,000			

Trends +2 Large increase +1 Small increase 0 Stable X Extinct
(1970–1990) −2 Large decrease −1 Small decrease F Fluctuating N New breeder
Data quality **Bold**: reliable quantitative data Normal type: incomplete quantitative data
Bracketed figures: no quantitative data * Data quality not provided

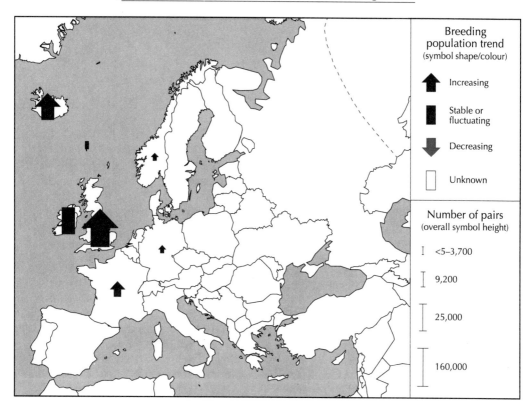

Breeding population trend
(symbol shape/colour)

Increasing

Stable or fluctuating

Decreasing

Unknown

Number of pairs
(overall symbol height)

<5–3,700

9,200

25,000

160,000

centrations in Gannets and their eggs around the United Kingdom (Parslow and Jefferies 1977), but this seems to have had no obvious adverse effect on the population, though, in the western Atlantic a reduction in DDT and dieldrin residues in eggs did coincide with an improvement in breeding performance (Chapdelaine *et al*. 1987). A large oil spill near a major colony while Gannets were resident could have disastrous results. The risks of this happening are higher than for some species due to the location of some colonies near major shipping lanes.

■ Conservation measures

Gannets benefit from full legal protection under national legislation in all EU states and Norway. Some harvesting of chicks and eggs continues in Iceland, the Faroes and on Sula Sgeir off Scotland, though this does not appear to be adversely affecting the populations. Nearly all colonies are Important Bird Areas (IBAs; see IBA table), either for the Gannets themselves or for associated populations of other seabirds, and most such IBAs have received legislative protection. Food sources may be affected by fishery policy, and any cessation in discarding of fish from trawlers could affect food supply, though Gannets are less likely than many other seabirds to suffer from the loss of this food.

Monitoring of numbers should continue on about a ten-year cycle. Monitoring of breeding success, which has been occurring in Britain and Ireland, is valuable as an early warning of any problems, and this could usefully be extended to cover the whole breeding range. If fishery discard practice changes, further research should be carried out to determine its effect on seabird populations.

The routeing of oil tankers further away from large colonies could help in reducing the risk of impact from spills.

MARK TASKER

Pygmy Cormorant
Phalacrocorax pygmeus

SPEC Category 2
Status Vulnerable
Criteria Moderate decline, <10,000 pairs

The species is rare in Europe where it is restricted to the south-east of the region. Numbers have also declined during the twentieth century due to habitat loss and direct persecution, although recently some populations may have begun to stabilize. The species and its main breeding colonies urgently require legislative protection, and natural freshwater habitats need to be maintained and restored.

■ Distribution and population trends

The breeding range extends from Albania and Yugoslavia (Vojvodina), east to central Asia, north to the northern coasts of the Black, Caspian and Aral Seas, and south to the marshes of southern Iraq. More than half the global breeding population is probably within Europe (Rose and Scott 1994), where most colonies are concentrated at a few sites in the south-east. The Danube delta holds about 60% of the European population. Relatively high numbers also breed in Turkey, while in Russia, Moldova, Ukraine, Bulgaria, Albania and Greece smaller numbers are reported (see table, map). The species is extinct in most of the Mediterranean basin, while in central Europe it breeds rarely and irregularly (Bezzel 1985, Bauer and Glutz von Blotzheim 1987). It should be noted that there are no data for Yugoslavia (Serbia, Montenegro) and the breeding population along the Danube in Vojvodina is missing from the data presented here; large numbers were also reported to occur at Lake Skadar, Albania (Important Bird Area 043: see Grimmett and Jones 1989), well in excess of the breeding population given for Albania (see table). Also, this review does not cover Azerbaijan, where 1,400–2,000 pairs were reported at Kirov Bay on the Caspian Sea (IBA 077).

Birds from northern colonies are mainly migratory, while those in the south are largely resident.

	Breeding population			Breeding
	Size (pairs)	Year	Trend	range trend
Albania	100–400	64	–2	(–2)
Bulgaria	90–150	—	0	0
Greece	**300–450**	—	0	0
Hungary	**3–3**	91	N*	0*
Moldova	**200–500**	90	N	0
Romania	4,000–4,000	89	–1	0
Russia	150–250	84–88	+1	+1
Slovakia	1–3 *	92	N*	N*
Turkey	1,500–1,500	—	+2	+2
Ukraine	10–30	76	–1	–1
Total (approx.)	6,400–7,300			

Trends	+2 Large increase	+1 Small increase	0 Stable	X Extinct
(1970–1990)	–2 Large decrease	–1 Small decrease	F Fluctuating	N New breeder
Data quality	**Bold:** reliable quantitative data	Normal type: incomplete quantitative data		
	Bracketed figures: no quantitative data	* Data quality not provided		

Most birds winter in the east Mediterranean region, chiefly along the coasts of the Adriatic and Aegean, as well as in the Middle East.

Most of south-east Europe has seen a steady decline during the twentieth century, with some dramatic local losses, although overall trends have been partially obscured by irregular fluctuations. In the Danube delta in Romania, 8,000 pairs were estimated in the early 1960s, but only 4,000 pairs in 1991 (Anon. 1992a) (see table). This population appears to have stabilized as an increase has been noted since 1990, possibly due to increased stocks of smaller fish species due to eutrophication. In recent decades there have been other indications that some populations have stabilized, while in Turkey large population increases have occurred, though numbers have also continued to decline in Albania and Ukraine (see table). In total, up to 65% of the European population declined during 1970–1990.

Although formerly classified as Globally Threatened (Collar and Andrew 1988), the species is currently listed as Near Threatened (Collar *et al.* 1994).

■ Ecology

Pygmy Cormorants prefer inland water-bodies with luxuriant, emergent, fringing vegetation, including natural lakes, fish-ponds, canals and oxbows. They may, however, also occur along sea coasts, especially outside the breeding season (Dementiev and Gladkov 1951, Cramp and Simmons 1977).

Birds generally breed in small, mixed-species colonies with herons, ibises, spoonbills and other cormorant species, although they sometimes form quite large single-species colonies or even breed solitarily. Nests are placed low in trees or thick reedbeds (Cramp and Simmons 1977).

Foraging is normally done in small groups or singly, in shallow water. Small fish are the main food.

■ Threats

The decline of the Danube population is due to both habitat loss and direct persecution. Large-scale habitat transformation through the drainage of large

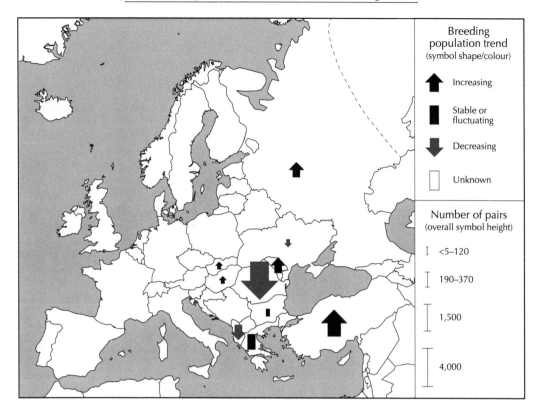

Breeding population trend
(symbol shape/colour)

- Increasing
- Stable or fluctuating
- Decreasing
- Unknown

Number of pairs
(overall symbol height)

- <5–120
- 190–370
- 1,500
- 4,000

wetlands has also resulted in the loss of the best feeding areas. Virtually all the wetlands along the lower course of the Danube, for example, were drained in the middle of the twentieth century (c.100,000 ha), and 20% of the Danube delta was drained during 1980–1990. In the Danube delta Pygmy Cormorants have been treated as pests by the fish-farming industry since the 1970s (along with other fish-eating species), and 280–300 'guards' are employed at fish-ponds to shoot such birds.

■ Conservation measures

Legislation is needed to halt the shooting of Pygmy Cormorants at fish-ponds, both along the Danube and elsewhere, and the Danube Delta Biosphere Reserve (IBA 001) should be gazetted as a National Park (500,000 ha) in law. Adequate legal protecion should also be given to following major breeding colonies, which together with the Danube Delta hold the majority of the European population: Kirov Bay, Azerbaijan (IBA 077); in Greece Lake Kerkini (IBA 012), Lakes Mikri Prespa and Megali Prespa (IBA 032); and in Turkey, Manyas Gölü (Kus Gölü) including Bandirma Kus Cenneti Milli Parki (IBA 006), Eregli Marshes (IBA 023), Hotamis Marshes including Bataklik Gölü (IBA 024) and Sultan Marshes (IBA 030). The status of populations in Lake Skadar on the Yugoslavia–Albania border (Yugoslavia IBA 043/ Albania IBA 001) should be re-assessed and appropriate protection given to the site.

For ecological and long-term economic reasons, the policy of creating intensive fish-farming industries in formerly natural water-bodies should be reconsidered: the long-term costs of ecological damage caused by such activities (through habitat destruction and pollution) are not currently considered, and the fish-ponds in the Danube delta have been sited in formerly ideal Pygmy Cormorant breeding and feeding habitat. There is very little conflict between this species and non-intensive fisheries. Improved protection and restoration of its natural wetland habitat, chiefly in the lower Danube, combined with less intensive reed exploitation, are also required to secure the existence of the species within Europe.

PETER WEBER

White Pelican
Pelecanus onocrotalus

SPEC Category 3
Status Rare
Criteria <10,000 pairs

The European population underwent a considerable decline during the twentieth century, mainly because of wetland drainage. Although now stable, its population is only approximately 4,000 breeding pairs and these birds are concentrated at only a few sites. Like the Dalmatian Pelican, all breeding colonies need protection and measures should be taken to manage the habitat for the species and reduce mortality on breeding, passage and wintering grounds.

■ Distribution and population trends

The White Pelican is a species widely distributed through eastern Europe, Asia and Africa. Two geographically separated populations have been distinguished by Crivelli and Schreiber (1984), one breeding in eastern Europe and Asia and the other in Africa. The Palearctic population is migratory. The Asian part of this population winters largely in the Indus delta but the wintering grounds of the European population are still unknown (Crivelli *et al.* 1991a).

Half of the Palearctic population breeds in Europe (Crivelli 1994), but this totals only around 4,000 pairs, concentrated at fewer than 10 sites. Breeding colonies are located in Greece, Romania, Russia, Turkey and the Caucasus–Caspian Sea area. The largest colony, which represents approximately 70% of the European population, is located in the Danube Delta in Romania (Important Bird Area 001).

The European population has declined sharply since the beginning of the twentieth century, with decreases in total numbers, breeding range and in the number of sites occupied. However, between 1970 and 1990 the population more or less stabilized, with some breeding colonies expanding slightly (e.g. in Romania and the Caucasus–Caspian Sea area) and others contracting (e.g. in Greece and Turkey) (see table, map)—though no quantitative data on trends are available for several colonies. In Greece reliable data are available only for the last 10 years, and for

several colonies in Turkey there are no figures on trends, although a comparison with data from 20–30 years ago indicate a real decline.

■ Ecology

The White Pelican breeds in the most remote of inland wetlands, mainly in deltas and on lakes and, more rarely, on reservoirs. The birds nest on the ground, either within large reedbeds (e.g. in Romania) or on rocky or bare earth islands (e.g. in the Caucasus–Caspian Sea area), always in total isolation from the mainland in order to avoid mammalian predators.

The diet is strictly fish, and feeding takes place almost entirely in groups in shallow waters. Birds quite often fly long distances (sometimes exceeding 100 km) to forage because of the frequent lack of shallow-water feeding areas close to the nesting sites.

■ Threats

Previously, the White Pelican was threatened by the drainage for agriculture of wetlands supporting suitable breeding and feeding grounds, as well as by the destruction of breeding colonies by fishermen. Although drainage has now more or less stopped, water extraction for irrigation continues and has caused temporary and permanent loss of wetlands used by pelicans.

Additional threats such as shooting, collisions with electric powerlines and persecution (due to perceived competition with commercial fisheries) occur during migration and in the winter quarters (Crivelli *et al.* 1988b, 1991b). The destruction of breeding colonies, however, has decreased. Contamination from pesticides, heavy-metal pollution and disturbance by birdwatchers and photographers also threaten some birds.

All the above threats apply also to the Dalmatian Pelican *P. crispus*, which is classified as Globally Threatened (Collar *et al.* 1994).

	Breeding population			Breeding
	Size (pairs)	Year	Trend	range trend
Greece	**50–50**	90–93	–1	**0**
Romania	**3,000–3,500**	89–93	**+1**	**0**
Russia	**100–350**	—	+1ˉ	0
Turkey	250–400	—	–1ˉ	0
Total (approx.)	3,400–4,300			

Trends (1970–1990)   +2 Large increase   +1 Small increase   0 Stable   X Extinct
–2 Large decrease   –1 Small decrease   F Fluctuating   N New breeder
Data quality   **Bold**: reliable quantitative data   Normal type: incomplete quantitative data
Bracketed figures: no quantitative data   * Data quality not provided

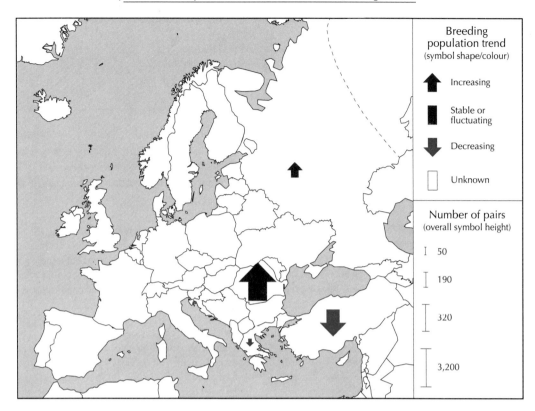

■ Conservation measures

A third of the breeding sites of the White Pelican in Europe are currently unprotected, including Eregli Sazligi (Important Bird Area 023) and Seyfe Gölü (IBA 029) in Turkey, and Manych-Gudilo Lake (IBA 060) in Russia. Clearly, the full protection of all White Pelican breeding colonies is essential.

Conservation measures needed at important sites are habitat management, shooting bans, and a reduction in the mortality caused by electric powerlines (which could be attained by attaching markers, moving or burying the lines). Awareness campaigns directed at hunters, fish-farmers and local people in the vicinity of important sites are also required.

It is essential that the wintering sites used by the European breeding population are discovered and researched, and this work should be initiated as soon as possible in order that an effective conservation strategy may be compiled.

Many of these proposed conservation measures are also applicable to the Dalmatian Pelican.

ALAIN CRIVELLI

Dalmatian Pelican
Pelecanus crispus

SPEC Category 1
Status Vulnerable
Criteria <2,500 pairs

This globally threatened species has declined dramatically since the nineteenth century, principally through the loss of wetlands due to drainage. It is now extremely rare in Europe, but can be considered stable overall, with colonies locally expanding or shrinking. All breeding sites should be protected and measures taken to maintain the species' required habitat and reduce mortality at breeding, passage and wintering sites.

■ Distribution and population trends

Nearly 20% of the total world population of Dalmatian Pelican breeds in Europe, and half of this number occurs in the Caucasus–Caspian Sea area (Rose and Scott 1994, Krivenko *et al.* in press) with other populations in Albania, Greece, Bulgaria, Romania, Ukraine and Turkey (see table, map). Although not included in this review, Yugoslavia (Montenegro) is also known to hold 10–20 pairs (A. J. Crivelli *in litt.* 1993). The species disperses in winter with birds occurring then mainly in Albania, Greece, Turkey, the western coast of the Caspian Sea and Iran.

The number of Dalmatian Pelican breeding sites began to decline dramatically in the middle of the nineteenth century, due primarily to the drainage of a large number of wetlands which supported breeding colonies (Crivelli *et al.* 1991a). The status of the species worsened during the twentieth century, with continuing declines noted over the 1970–1990 period for Albania and Turkey (see table) and Yugoslavia (Montenegro) (A. J. Crivelli *in litt.* 1993), while populations in Greece, Romania, Bulgaria, Ukraine and the Caucasus–Caspian Sea area have fluctuated or increased.

A sharp decrease in the number of wintering birds has also been observed between the 1960s–1970s and the second half of the 1980s (Crivelli *et al.* 1991b); no figures are available for the early 1980s. In Greece, wintering numbers were stable between 1970 and 1990 (A. J. Crivelli, H. Jerrentrup and Naziridis unpubl. data).

Although partially recovering, the Dalmatian Pelican is listed as Globally Threatened by Collar *et al.* (1994), on the basis of its small world population and the continuing threats to it.

■ Ecology

The Dalmatian Pelican breeds at inland and coastal wetlands (Crivelli 1987). Nests are located on floating islands in reedbeds and on bare earth islands, totally isolated from the mainland in order to avoid mammalian predators. In some areas, e.g. Greece and Turkey, birds have accepted artificial nesting sites (Crivelli *et al.* 1991a).

The Dalmatian Pelican eats almost nothing but fish, feeding in either deep or shallow water in wetlands around the breeding colony. The diet depends almost entirely on the relative abundance of fish prey species on the feeding grounds, on their spatial and temporal distribution, and to a lesser extent on the behaviour of the prey. Preferred species are cyprinids in freshwater wetlands, and eels, mullet, gobies and shrimps in brackish waters. Birds prefer to winter in deltas where they can easily find adequate night roosts and abundant stocks of fish (Crivelli 1987, Crivelli *et al.* 1991a).

■ Threats

The Dalmatian Pelican is particularly vulnerable because its small European population is concentrated at only a few sites.

Like the White Pelican *P. onocrotalus*, the Dalmatian Pelican was threatened by the drainage of wetlands for agricultural purposes, together with the destruction of breeding colonies by fishermen. Drainage has now decreased considerably but water extraction for irrigation continues to threaten the wetlands which the pelicans use. As with the White Pelican, the destruction of breeding colonies has, however, decreased.

| | Breeding population | | | Breeding |
	Size (pairs)	Year	Trend	range trend
Albania	**40–70**	90–93	–2	–2
Bulgaria	**70–90**	90–93	F	0
Greece	**200–260**	90–93	+1	0
Romania	**140–140**	89	+1	+1
Russia	**400–450**	90–93	+1	0
Turkey	**100–150**	—	–1	0
Ukraine	6–14 *	—	N	N
Total (approx.)	**960–1,200**			

Trends   +2 Large increase   +1 Small increase   0 Stable   X Extinct
(1970–1990)   –2 Large decrease   –1 Small decrease   F Fluctuating   N New breeder
Data quality   **Bold**: reliable quantitative data   Normal type: incomplete quantitative data
Bracketed figures: no quantitative data   * Data quality not provided

Shooting, collisions with electric powerlines and persecution due to competition with commercial fisheries occur during migration and on the wintering grounds, and are additional threats to pelicans (Crivelli *et al.* 1988b, 1991b). Contamination by pesticides and heavy metal residues, and disturbance by birdwatchers and photographers, also threaten the Dalmatian Pelican locally (Crivelli *et al.* 1989). At Lake Mikri Prespa in Greece, the thickness of eggs collected in 1984–1986 had been reduced by 12–20% due to contamination with DDE (see Crivelli *et al.* 1989).

■ Conservation measures

The full protection of all Dalmatian Pelican breeding colonies is essential to ensure that the species maintains adequate reproductive success. Unfortunately, however, only 40% of the breeding sites of the species in Europe are currently protected, as follows: Lake Manych Nature Reserve (Russia, Important Bird Area 060), Danube Delta Biosphere Reserve (Romania, IBA 001), Srebarna Nature Reserve (Bulgaria, IBA 008), Lake Skadar National Park in Montenegro (Yugoslavia, IBA 043), Lake Mikri Prespa National Park (Greece, IBA 032), Lake Manyas National Park (Turkey, IBA 006) and Menderes National Park (Turkey, IBA 040).

Necessary conservation measures include habitat management directed towards the needs of the species, public awareness campaigns, shooting bans and a reduction in the mortality caused by impact with electric powerlines at important sites (e.g. through burying or moving the lines, or attaching conspicuous markers to them).

Monitoring and scientific research should be continued, particularly in the fields of population dynamics, the exchange of individuals between colonies, and the ecology of birds in the winter quarters and the threats which they face there.

ALAIN CRIVELLI

Bittern
Botaurus stellaris

SPEC Category 3
Status (Vulnerable)
Criteria Large decline

Breeding numbers have declined recently in most European countries, attributed to decreases in habitat quality and availability. Appropriate water management, control of phosphate, nitrate and heavy metal pollution, and promotion of environmentally sensitive, traditional methods of reedbed management are required to secure Bittern populations.

■ Distribution and population trends

The world range of the Bittern extends right across the Palearctic region, in Europe as far north as southern Fennoscandia, and there is also an isolated population in southern Africa (Hancock and Elliot 1978). Approximately three-quarters of the European population is found in Russia and the Ukraine, and in north-west Europe only the Netherlands and France hold substantial numbers (see table, map).

Within Europe, the northern and eastern populations are migratory, but those in the west are more sedentary (Cramp and Simmons 1977), movements generally being associated with harsh winter weather. Birds from eastern and northern Europe

winter in western Europe and North Africa, alongside resident populations in those regions.

The Bittern is known to have declined considerably in Europe in both population size and range during the early 1900s (Cramp and Simmons 1977). This trend has continued, and half of the European countries with breeding populations experienced a decline between 1970 and 1990 (see table, map). The countries with the largest populations tend to have only poor information on population trends, but many of those countries with good census data report continuing decreases in population size.

■ Ecology

The Bittern is most often found in marshes with extensive stands of reeds *Phragmites*, but will breed in marshes dominated by reedmace *Typha* and bulrush *Scirpus lacustris* (Hancock and Elliot 1978), and in eastern Europe also among dense growths of willow *Salix* with some reeds (Dementiev and Gladkov 1951a). Males are polygynous and generally take no part in the rearing of the young (Percy 1951). The nest is a shallow platform of reed stems within the reedbed, normally at water-level. Occasionally, several nests may be found close to each other within the territory of one calling male (Zimmermann 1931, Percy 1951).

Live prey is captured within the cover of vegetation, and consists mainly of fish and amphibians, though aquatic invertebrates are taken regularly and may form a substantial part of the diet. Birds and small mammals are also eaten occasionally (Voisin 1991).

■ Threats

Local extinctions of the species in western Europe during the nineteenth century were probably due to hunting pressure (Turner 1924), but the recent decline has been caused by a reduction in availability and quality of large *Phragmites*-dominated swamps and other marshes. Much of this land has been lost to drainage, but the abandonment of traditional management and uses of reed areas has also caused

	Breeding population			Breeding
	Size (pairs)	Year	Trend	range trend
Albania	1–10	64	–1	(–1)
Austria	(100–150)	—	(F)	0
Belarus	950–1,200	90	(0)	0
Belgium	2–13	81–90	–1	–1
Bulgaria	(10–50)	—	(–1)	(0)
Croatia	(30–50)	—	–1*	–1*
Czech Republic	**20–30**	—	–1	–1
Denmark	**57–76**	91	+2	(0)
Estonia	200–300	—	+1	0
Finland	**100–150**	92	+2	+1
France	300–350	90	–1	–1
Germany	400–600	—	–2	0
Hungary	400–500	—	0	0
Italy	20–30	—	(–1)	(–1)
Latvia	200–300	—	(0)	(0)
Lithuania	200–250	85–88	(0)	(0)
Moldova	**150–200**	90	–1	–1
Netherlands	150–275	89–91	–2	–2
Poland	1,100–1,400	—	0	0
Portugal	(1–5)	89	—	—
Romania	(500–2,000)	—	(–1)	0
Russia	(10,000–30,000)	—	(–1)	(0)
Slovakia	50–150	—	–1	–1
Slovenia	(5–10)	—	(0)	(0)
Spain	25–25	—	–2	–2
Sweden	200–300	87	**0**	**0**
Turkey	(30–500)	—	(–1)	0
Ukraine	**4,000–4,300**	88	**0**	**0**
United Kingdom	**16–16**	88–91	**–2**	**–2**
Total (approx.)	19,000–43,000			

Trends (1970–1990) +2 Large increase +1 Small increase 0 Stable X Extinct –2 Large decrease –1 Small decrease F Fluctuating N New breeder
Data quality **Bold**: reliable quantitative data Normal type: incomplete quantitative data Bracketed figures: no quantitative data * Data quality not provided

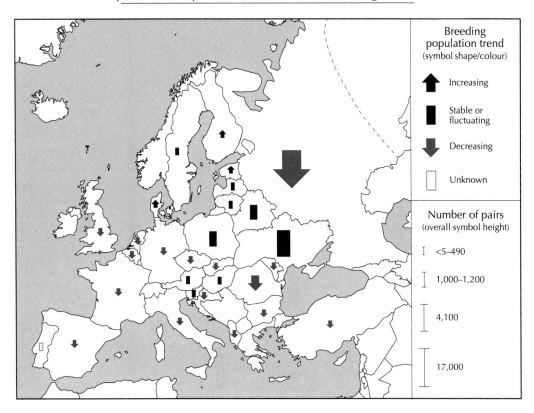

degradation of suitable sites. Elsewhere, conversely, the intensification of reed harvesting has also reduced habitat suitability.

Water pollution, especially eutrophication caused by runoff from domestic or agricultural sources, has also reduced reedbed viability and has disturbed ecological balances in fish populations within reedbed sites (George 1992). Consequently, this has reduced the availability of habitat through the loss of reedbeds as well as the quality and abundance of food within them. In addition Bitterns in recent decades have been exposed to several potentially damaging pollutants such as organochlorine pesticides, PCBs and mercury, and the birds accumulate some of these at high levels (Newton *et al*. 1994). Other threats include shooting of autumn migrant and wintering birds in central and eastern Europe, and disturbance by anglers, water-sports and other human activities (Hölzinger 1987).

■ Conservation measures

Bitterns require extensive networks of reeds and swamps to maintain good populations. Retaining traditional but environmentally sensitive management of reedbeds is therefore important for this bird, but the restoration and creation of suitable habitat is also necessary where this has become scarce or fragmented and degraded.

Effective protection of breeding sites must include conservation and, where necessary, treatment of water supplies. Some wetlands occupied by Bitterns may require the creation of no-disturbance zones as protection from recreational activity, and pressure should be applied to stop illegal hunting (Hölzinger 1987).

Further censuses and monitoring of the European Bittern population are required. Recent investigations in the United Kingdom have shown that care must be taken in interpreting counts of singing males, but techniques for recognizing the voices of individual birds do allow the accurate evaluation of populations (McGregor and Byle 1992, Gilbert *et al*. in press).

GLEN TYLER

Little Bittern
Ixobrychus minutus

SPEC Category 3
Status (Vulnerable)
Criteria Large decline

The European population is declining strongly in size and range, particularly in north-west and central Europe. It is thought that this decline is due largely to drought in its African passage and wintering quarters, rather than to habitat loss or pollution in the European breeding areas.

■ Distribution and population trends

The Little Bittern is a widespread species occurring in the Palearctic, Afrotropical and Australasian regions, with less than a quarter of the global population breeding in Europe. The European population winters principally in eastern Africa from Sudan and Ethiopia west to the Congo and south to South Africa (Hancock and Kushlan 1984, Cramp and Simmons 1977).

The largest European populations are in central, east and south-east Europe, with particularly important numbers in Russia, Romania, Ukraine, Hungary and Turkey (see table, map). However, censuses have been conducted in only a few countries, and data from countries with large populations are mostly poor and qualitative (see table).

	Breeding population			Breeding
	Size (pairs)	Year	Trend	range trend
Albania	100–300	64	–1	(–1)
Austria	(100–150)	—	(–2)	(–2)
Belarus	100–300	90	–2	0
Belgium	2–10	81–90	–1	0
Bulgaria	(200–2,000)	—	(0)	(0)
Croatia	1,000–2,000	—	–1	0
Czech Republic	**50–90**	—	**–2**	–1
Denmark	0–1	87	N	0
France	200–300	90	–2	–1
Germany	100–200	—	–2	–1
Greece	600–700	—	(–1)	(0)
Hungary	3,500–6,000	—	–1	–1
Italy	(1,000–2,000)	—	(–1)	(–1)
Latvia	(10–30)	—	(–2)	(–2)
Lithuania	40–50	85–88	–1	–1
Luxembourg	**0–1**	88	**–1**	–1
Moldova	**1,000–2,000**	90	**–1**	**–1**
Netherlands	**10–20**	89–91	**–2**	**–2**
Poland	400–700	—	–1	–1
Portugal	500–1,000	89	(0)	+1
Romania	(10,000–20,000)	—	(–1)	**0**
Russia	(10,000–50,000)	—	(–1)	(0)
Slovakia	200–400	—	–2	–2
Slovenia	20–50	—	–2	–1
Spain	1,900–2,300	—	–2	–2
Switzerland	**40–60**	77–79	**F**	0
Turkey	1,000–10,000	—	(–1)	(0)
Ukraine	5,000–6,000	88	0	0
Total (approx.)	37,000–110,000			

Trends	+2 Large increase	+1 Small increase	0 Stable	X Extinct	
(1970–1990)	–2 Large decrease	–1 Small decrease	F Fluctuating	N New breeder	
Data quality	**Bold**: reliable quantitative data	Normal type: incomplete quantitative data			
	Bracketed figures: no quantitative data	* Data quality not provided			

A major decline in the population size and range of the species is thought to have occurred over the 1970–1990 period in nearly all countries except Portugal, Ukraine, Bulgaria, Switzerland and Denmark, affecting up to 90% of the total European population. Decreases have been particularly common in north-west and central Europe and in several countries populations have declined by more than 50%; this includes France, where censuses indicate declines exceeding 80% (Duhautois 1984b). A decrease in range size is also evident in most countries where breeding occurs.

■ Ecology

The Little Bittern occurs mainly in freshwater habitats in lowland areas, including reedbeds and other dense vegetation along rivers, fringes of lakes, marshes, and small ponds, preferably with trees such as willows *Salix*. It is a solitary species, and does not require large breeding or feeding areas (Cramp and Simmons 1977). The diet is composed mostly of insects, and secondarily small fish, amphibians and shrimps.

■ Threats

The decline of the European population seems largely to have occurred since 1970 and cannot be attributed to habitat destruction or pollution in the breeding areas alone. Indeed, the Little Bittern is normally tolerant of man, but the species has disappeared even from some extensive wetland areas despite their protection. It is therefore thought that the substantial overall fall in European numbers is due to high mortality of birds during migration or when wintering in Africa (Marion 1993). During migration the Little Bittern crosses the Mediterranean and Sahara in a single flight (Cramp and Simmons 1977). However, the drought in the Sahara during the 1970s and in East Africa in recent years has caused desertification and the loss of wetlands normally used as staging areas, thus extending the length of the trans-Saharan crossing. Similar dramatic declines in European breeding populations of other trans-Saharan migrants, such as Purple Heron *Ardea*

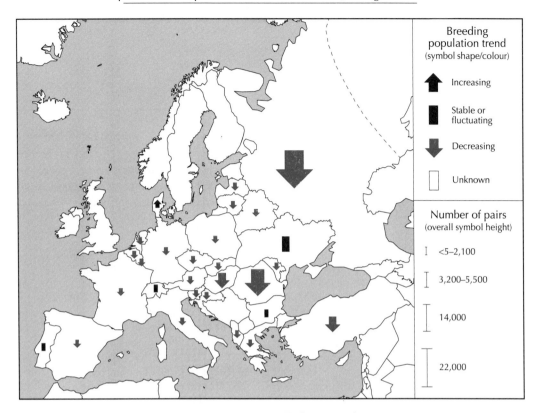

purpurea (Cave 1981), Redstart *Phoenicurus phoenicurus* and Whitethroat *Sylvia communis* (Sharrock 1976) have also been attributed to periods of drought in Africa.

Declines that are explicable by conditions within Europe have occurred in Belgium, where the population decline began in the 1960s and was assumed to be caused by pollution and drainage of wetlands (Lippens and Wille 1972), and at a few localities in the Netherlands and Brittany (France) where building construction has disturbed nesting habitat (Marion 1993).

Conservation measures

Given the likely causes of the Little Bittern's decline, no conservation action on the European breeding grounds seems likely to reverse it. Furthermore, the restoration of former population levels will be very slow even if favourable wintering conditions occur over several years. Nevertheless, wider-scale habitat conservation measures in Europe should be taken, such as the maintenance of reedy fringes to rivers and ditches, to ensure that sufficient habitat exists for the species should conditions in Africa again become more favourable for it.

LOÏC MARION

Night Heron
Nycticorax nycticorax

SPEC Category   3
Status   Declining
Criteria   Moderate decline

The Night Heron is declining in substantial parts of its European range, particularly where it is dependent on the remaining areas of natural and semi-natural wetlands. Although currently secure where the species depends on artificial wetlands resulting from rice cultivation, these populations are susceptible to changes in rice-farming practices. Thus, the species requires the conservation of all its breeding habitats, and, as a migrant, a network of wetlands along its migratory route and within its wintering quarters.

■ Distribution and population trends

The Night Heron is a cosmopolitan species with an estimated 50,000–70,000 pairs in Europe. However, although the species is numerous in total, the birds are patchily distributed across the continent, in the south-west, centre, south-east and east. The largest populations occur in Italy and Russia, and these together comprise about half of the European total (see table, map). The majority of Night Herons nesting in Europe are migratory and winter in tropical Africa.

Between 1970 and 1990, declines were recorded in countries which together hold over 40% of the European population; these included the substantial populations in Russia, Romania, Spain, Moldova, Greece and Turkey (see table, map). However, pre-

cise data are available for only a few of the eastern breeding areas, including the Russian Volga Delta where the population is estimated to be 3,000–4,000 pairs, and is believed to have been stable over the past 10 years (N. Gavrilov pers. comm.). A severe decline of 40–50% is reported to have taken place for the Danube Delta between 1974–1975 and 1987–1989, and just 3,100 pairs were recorded in 1986 (Green 1992, D. Munteanu pers. comm.).

The Spanish population is considered to be vulnerable, having undergone a substantial decrease over the past 10 years (Fernandez-Alcazar and Fernandez-Cruz 1991; see table, map). In contrast, numbers in Italy have increased overall during 1970–1990 (see table) but also showed some fluctuations: 17,000 pairs were censused in 1981 (Fasola *et al.* 1981) compared with 14,000 in 1986, 22,000 in 1990, 18,000 in 1991, 17,000 in 1992 and most recently 18,000 in 1993 (M. Fasola pers. comm.), although these figures are based on extrapolations and should be treated with caution.

■ Ecology

When nesting, Night Herons are markedly arboreal, breeding mostly in deciduous trees near extensive freshwater areas, although also utilizing coniferous woods, thickets of tamarisk *Tamarix*, areas with shrubs and, where woody growth is absent, *Phragmites* reedbeds (Hafner 1980, Hafner and Fasola 1992a). Breeding Night Herons require security, and colonies are often surrounded by water, or are located in high trees.

The birds need freshwater feeding areas, which vary between different regions from rice-fields, which are the major habitat in Italy, to marshes, meanders and undisturbed river edges. Freshwater fish and amphibians are the main items taken as food. Outside the breeding season, the species is nocturnal, hiding during the day in dense foliage and venturing out at sunset to forage.

	Breeding population			Breeding
	Size (pairs)	Year	Trend	range trend
Albania	50–200	64	0	(–1)
Austria	12–16	89–90	–2	–1
Belarus	(0–5)	90	N	N
Belgium	2–3	—	F	1
Bulgaria	500–5,000	—	(0)	0
Croatia	690–1,000	91	0	0
Czech Republic	**300–370**	—	+2	0
France	**4,143–4,143**	89	+1	0
Germany	20–30	—	(0)	0
Greece	500–600	86	–1	(0)
Hungary	4,000–4,800	—	0	0
Italy	**19,000–21,000**	91	+1	+1
Moldova	**3,500–5,000**	85	–1	–1
Netherlands	0–3	89–91	–2	–1
Poland	**50–60**	—	0	0
Portugal	**200–300**	91	F	–1
Romania	**3,000–7,000**	—	–1	+1
Russia	**9,000–11,000**	—	–1	(0)
Slovakia	100–300	—	0	0
Slovenia	(5–10)	—	(0)	(0)
Spain	**1,480–2,210**	89–90	–1	–1
Turkey	1,000–3,000	—	(–1)	(0)
Ukraine	**3,645–5,000**	86	F	F
Total (approx.)	51,000–71,000			

Trends   +2 Large increase   +1 Small increase   0 Stable   X Extinct
(1970–1990)   –2 Large decrease   –1 Small decrease   F Fluctuating   N New breeder
Data quality   **Bold**: reliable quantitative data   Normal type: incomplete quantitative data
Bracketed figures: no quantitative data   * Data quality not provided

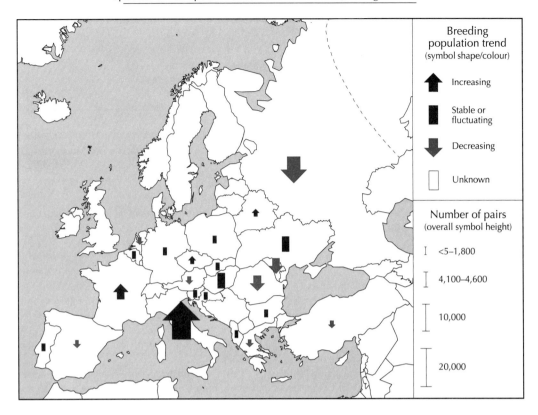

Breeding
population trend
(symbol shape/colour)

Increasing

Stable or
fluctuating

Decreasing

Unknown

Number of pairs
(overall symbol height)

<5–1,800

4,100–4,600

10,000

20,000

Threats

Loss and degradation of natural, semi-natural and artificial freshwater wetland habitats, and of breeding sites, are the most obvious threats throughout the European range of the species. Both breeding and feeding sites suffer from drainage, overgrazing and wood-cutting, particularly in the Mediterranean countries (Hafner and Fasola 1992b), as well as high levels of disturbance from tourists and from watersports.

The 1,300 km² of rice-fields in northern Italy sustain almost half of the Italian breeding population (Fasola 1986), but there is a concern that in the future these areas may be managed more efficiently in order to minimize the amount of irrigation required to farm them (M. Fasola pers. comm.). There is also concern that 'dry' rice-cultivation techniques (at present only experimental and carried out on small-scale) may be agriculturally improved and increasingly used. Such extensive land-use changes as these would have a dramatic impact on the population of Night Herons, since there are few alternative feeding sites left for the birds in the area.

Conservation measures

The maintenance of the European population will depend on the conservation of both the existing breeding areas and an adequate network of wetlands along the species' migration routes and in its African wintering areas.

In particular, because of the importance of the population in northern Italy, the highest priority must be the maintenance of suitable management systems of rice-farming. This will involve an assessment of the impact of changing management regimes on wildlife compared with the socio-economic implications. Reduction of the levels of human disturbance, particularly during the egg-laying and incubation periods, is also needed at some sites.

Further census work and monitoring are necessary to clarify the status of the population in some parts of central and eastern Europe, especially in Russia and Bulgaria.

HEINZ HAFNER

Squacco Heron
Ardeola ralloides

SPEC Category 3
Status Vulnerable
Criteria Large decline

Since the 1970s, in most of the more easterly breeding areas of Europe, numbers have seriously declined due to losses in freshwater habitat. It is therefore necessary that extensive freshwater areas, rich in amphibians and fish, are conserved.

■ Distribution and population trends

The Squacco Heron has a scattered distribution across southern Europe and through south-west Asia to the Aral Sea region, as well as in the Afrotropics and (in small numbers) North Africa. Less than half the world range lies within Europe, with Russia, Romania and Turkey holding more than three-quarters of European breeding-bird numbers (see table, map). Of these countries Russia is undoubtedly the most important, with an estimated population of up to 6,000 pairs in Europe; the entire country's population is estimated at 28,000 pairs (Krivenko 1991a). Eurasian birds are migratory, wintering mainly in the northern tropics of Africa (Cramp and Simmons 1977).

While the population size in Russia as a whole is subject to fluctuations, a serious decline has taken place since the 1970s in some of the eastern breeding areas, including Croatia (Mikuska 1992), Greece (Crivelli *et al.* 1988a), the Russian Volga delta (Gavrilov pers. comm.) and in Bulgaria, Romania, Turkey and the Ukraine (see table, map). Overall, up to two-thirds of the European population occurs in countries which recorded declines during the 1970–1990 period.

■ Ecology

Nesting is in mixed colonies with other waterbird species, generally near water in dense stands of trees and bushes, or, in the absence of these, in reeds. Fundamental requirements for nesting are security, lack of disturbance, secure nest support, shelter against the weather, and materials for nest construction. Many colonies appear to be protected by a combination of water, dense undergrowth and the height of the nests which can be as much as 20 m in the complete absence of water or undergrowth (Hafner 1977).

Permanent freshwater marshes are preferred for feeding, but in Italy and Spain where much of this habitat has been drained, birds mainly use rice-fields and adjacent irrigation systems. Frogs are a preferred prey, with freshwater fish and insects also taken (Hafner *et al.* 1982).

■ Threats

The greatest threat is the loss and deterioration of freshwater feeding habitat. An analysis of 30 mixed heron colonies throughout the Mediterranean region revealed an 800 ha threshold for the area of feeding habitat, below which only very small colonies exist (Hafner and Fasola 1992b). Rice-fields used for foraging in Spain and Italy are susceptible to changes in agricultural practice; more efficient irrigation methods could reduce prey populations.

In Europe and North Africa suitable breeding woodlands within the range of potential feeding sites have become increasingly rare and vulnerable; colonies are frequently forced to move because of habitat degradation through, for example, wood-cutting, burning to create pasture, and overgrazing.

Drought in the Sahel also appears to affect the survival of birds on passage and wintering there, so affecting breeding populations in subsequent years (den Held 1981, Hafner and Wallace 1988).

■ Conservation measures

The maintenance of all suitable feeding areas, including environmentally sensitive management of rice-fields, is essential. Efforts should also be made

	Breeding population			Breeding
	Size (pairs)	Year	Trend	range trend
Albania	200–400	64	–1	(–1)
Bulgaria	300–500	—	–1	–1
Croatia	182–200	91	–2	0
France	**105–140**	92	**0**	**0**
Greece	**200–377**	86	–2	0
Hungary	**200–300**	—	–1	–1
Italy	**250–500**	81	0	(0)
Moldova	**50–80**	90	**0**	–1
Portugal	**1–10**	89	F	F
Romania	1,500–2,500	—	–1	0
Russia	**5,500–6,000**	—	F	(0)
Slovakia	1–10	—	F	0
Spain	**380–822**	89–90	+1	+1
Turkey	3,000–10,000	—	(–1)	(0)
Ukraine	200–290	86	–2	–2
Total (approx.)	12,000–22,000			

Trends	+2 Large increase	+1 Small increase	0 Stable	X Extinct
(1970–1990)	–2 Large decrease	–1 Small decrease	F Fluctuating	N New breeder
Data quality	**Bold**: reliable quantitative data	Normal type: incomplete quantitative data		
	Bracketed figures: no quantitative data	* Data quality not provided		

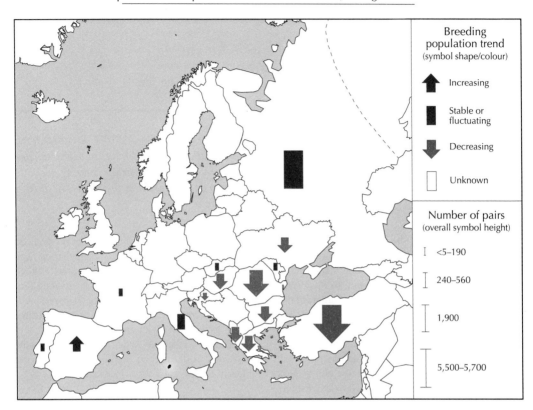

to maintain, manage, and, where necessary, restore or create potential breeding habitat. Small areas of wood can host large colonies of herons and restoration programmes should be considered in key areas, including the Ebro delta (Spain, Important Bird Area 202), Axios delta (Greece, IBA 019) and Göksu delta (Turkey, IBA 052).

HEINZ HAFNER

Purple Heron
Ardea purpurea

SPEC Category 3
Status Vulnerable
Criteria Large decline

The Purple Heron has declined over much of Europe, due largely to the loss and degradation of habitat and possibly to climatic changes causing drought conditions in its winter quarters, at least in West Africa. Action should be taken to protect and to apply appropriate management to freshwater marshlands throughout the range, and to better understand the problems the bird is facing on its wintering grounds.

■ Distribution and population trends

Less than a quarter of the world breeding range of Purple Heron lies within Europe, extending from the Netherlands and Poland in the north, to Spain and Italy in the south and to Turkey and the borders of the Caspian Sea in the east. European Purple Herons are migratory with most birds moving to sub-Saharan Africa, although small numbers winter in southern Europe and Arabia (Cramp and Simmons 1977).

European countries supporting large numbers of breeding pairs are France, Spain, Hungary, Romania, Turkey, Russia and Ukraine (see table, map). A decline was noted in the major part of the Purple Heron's European breeding population between 1970 and 1990. The Dutch population, for example, declined from between 500 and 600 pairs in 1981 to 210 pairs in 1991 (van der Koij 1992). A decline was also well documented in France, particularly in the

Camargue, where the breeding population declined from an average of 1,230 pairs over the period from 1981 to 1990, to 712 in 1992 (Duhautois 1984a). However, data from the new French breeding bird atlas (Yeatman-Berthelot and Jarry in press) indicates that there has been some redistribution of the French population, with increases in central and western regions that may in fact offset declines in the south. Also of particular significance are the declines in Russia and Turkey (see table, map).

■ Ecology

Purple Herons are confined to freshwater marshes, particularly reeds *Phragmites*. Nests are usually built in stands of mature reed which must be inundated throughout the breeding season, since drying out causes nest desertion (Moser 1984). Permanent freshwater marshes are the most typically favoured feeding habitat, although the small canals and ditches which form part of the rice-field irrigation systems in the Camargue, in northern Italy and in the Ebro delta of Spain are also used as these contain high densities of fish and amphibians (Ruiz 1985, Fasola 1986).

Extensive areas of reedbeds and feeding areas are required if a population of Purple Herons is to be supported. In the Camargue, Moser (1984) showed that in reedbeds of less than 30–40 ha population size was limited by the surface area of reedbed available. In addition, an analysis of the feeding habitat requirements of breeding Ardeidae in the Mediterranean region reveals a threshold of 8 km² of freshwater feeding area, below which only very small breeding heron populations can exist (Hafner and Fasola 1992a).

■ Threats

Permanent freshwater marshes are rapidly declining in extent (Jones and Hughes in press), and their destruction and deterioration are probably the major cause of the decline of the Purple Heron in some European countries (Moser 1983).

	Breeding population			Breeding
	Size (pairs)	Year	Trend	range trend
Albania	10–50	87	–1	(–1)
Austria	**60–80**	91	**–2**	**–1**
Bulgaria	50–100	—	–2	–2
Croatia	34–100	91	–2	–2
Czech Republic	**5–25**	—	**–1**	**0**
France	**2,741–2,741**	83	**–1**	**0**
Germany	20–40	—	0	0
Greece	105–140	86	0	–1
Hungary	800–1,000	—	–1	–1
Italy	**350–700**	81	**–1**	**–1**
Moldova	**100–150**	90	**–1**	**–1**
Netherlands	**210–285**	85	**–2**	**–2**
Poland	1–2 *	—	—	—
Portugal	100–500	91	F	F
Romania	800–1,200	—	(–1)	**–1**
Russia	40,000–90,000	—	–1	(0)
Slovakia	40–70	—	0	0
Spain	1,000–1,200	—	–2	–2
Switzerland	**0–5**	86–91	**–2**	**0**
Turkey	2,000–5,000	—	(–1)	(0)
Ukraine	733–1,000	86	**–2**	**–2**
Total (approx.)	49,000–100,000			

Trends +2 Large increase   +1 Small increase   0 Stable   X Extinct
(1970–1990) –2 Large decrease   –1 Small decrease   F Fluctuating   N New breeder
Data quality **Bold**: reliable quantitative data   Normal type: incomplete quantitative data
Bracketed figures: no quantitative data   * Data quality not provided

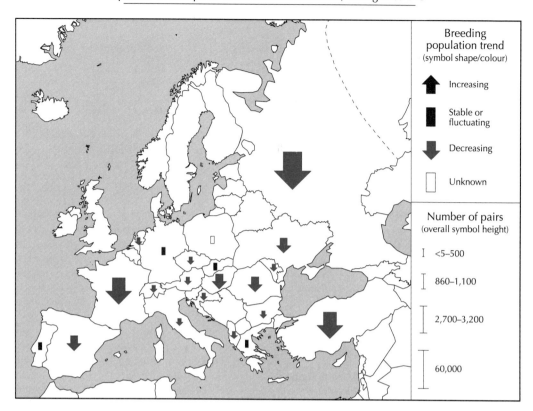

Purple Herons are extremely sensitive to disturbance, particularly when establishing themselves, and consequently some otherwise suitable sites may be rendered unacceptable for breeding (Moser 1984). Reed-cutting or burning removes nest material (dead reeds of the previous season) and therefore prevents nesting unless undamaged areas remain (Moser 1984).

At least in western Europe the species' decline may be related to drought conditions on the wintering grounds in tropical West Africa (den Held 1981, Cavé 1983). Den Held (1981) found that population changes of Purple Heron in the Netherlands for the period from 1961 to 1979 were highly correlated with the annual amount of rainfall in West Africa.

■ Conservation measures

The maintenance throughout Europe of extensive freshwater marshes and reedbeds, rich in fish and amphibians, is essential for the conservation of the breeding populations of Purple Heron. These habitats have become extremely vulnerable in Europe, and in many areas reedbeds are over-exploited. Throughout the Mediterranean basin the Purple Heron's distribution is now extremely patchy as a result of the small number of suitable reedbeds which remain in the region (Hafner and Fasola 1992b). Conservation organizations could take action by acquiring and managing reedbeds.

Steps urgently need to be taken to achieve a better understanding of the ecological requirements of Purple Herons during their migration and in the wintering areas. Data are particularly required to ascertain the most important habitats used outside the breeding season and also the factors which affect the use of these habitats and the birds' survival.

YVES KAYSER

Black Stork
Ciconia nigra

SPEC Category   3
Status   Rare
Criteria   <10,000 pairs

This species, rare and dispersed in Europe, is threatened particularly by the loss of breeding sites and the degradation of forest and wetland feeding areas, also by human disturbance and by hunting in winter. Appropriate forestry management, including the creation of water-bodies within forested areas, is the most appropriate conservation measure.

■ Distribution and population trends

The Black Stork breeds across Eurasia and in southern Africa, with almost half of its global range in Europe, where it is rare and dispersed. A number of birds from Iberia and south-east Europe are resident, but otherwise the entire European population migrates to sub-Saharan Africa.

The current breeding strongholds lie in Poland, Latvia, Belarus, Russia and Turkey, which together hold over two-thirds of the European total (see table, map).

In western and central Europe numbers began to fall in the second half of the nineteenth century and this continued locally until the 1950s. The species became extinct in Belgium, Denmark and Sweden, and declined dramatically in most other countries.

Numbers have since increased in central Europe, Black Storks having repopulated many sites and spread into France and Germany (Cramp and Simmons 1977, Sackl 1985, Bauer and Glutz von Blotzheim 1987, AMBE 1992). Increases are reported for the 1970–1990 period from Spain, most of central Europe and parts of eastern Europe (Golovatsh *et al*. 1990, Lebedeva 1990, Boettcher-Streim 1992, San Segundo 1993, Strazds 1993), but declines continued in Portugal, Lithuania, Croatia, Albania and Greece (see table, map). Population size and trends in Russia are uncertain; it is believed that the species has declined sharply between 1960–1980 (Borodin 1984, Boettcher-Streim 1992), but has recently shown possible signs of stabilization (see table).

■ Ecology

The Black Stork requires 50–150 km² of suitable breeding and feeding habitat per breeding pair (Schröder and Burmeister 1974, Dornbusch 1992). Lowland moist forests and mixed and dry coniferous woods are preferred for breeding, with nearby marshland, damp meadows, streams and fish-ponds for feeding. The species also breeds in mountainous regions up to 1,300 m (Bauer and Glutz von Blotzheim 1987, Hancock *et al*. 1992, Petrov *et al*. 1993). Recently many pairs have bred close to human settlements (Strazds *et al*. 1990, Tomialojc 1990). Large, mature trees are usually selected for nesting, but some mountain populations nest on rock faces (Cramp and Simmons 1977, Ferrero and Roman 1987). Birds often re-use the same nest-site (Schröder and Burmeister 1974, Strazds *et al*. 1990).

Breeding adults feed within 6–15 km of the nest (Dornbusch 1992), principally on fish, amphibians, other small vertebrates and some larger invertebrates (Cramp and Simmons 1977).

■ Threats

Destruction and degradation of forests is the major problem. In Russia the rapid development of farming and industry and over-exploitation of forests have seriously reduced the extent of suitable habitat.

*	Breeding population			Breeding range trend
	Size (pairs)	Year	Trend	
Albania	1–5	92	–1	(–1)
Austria	90–100	—	+2	+2
Belarus	**950–1,300**	90	+1	0
Belgium	7–14	81–90	N	N
Bulgaria	**150–170**	—	+1	+1
Croatia	(200–300)	—	(–1)	(0)
Czech Republic	**200–300**	—	+2	+2
Denmark	**1–1**	91	N	0
Estonia	150–200	—	+2	0
France	**6–11**	90	N	N
Germany	**126–130**	—	+1	+1
Greece	30–40	—	–1	(0)
Hungary	150–200	—	+1	+1
Latvia	**900–1,300**	91	+1	0
Lithuania	300–400	85–88	(–1)	0
Luxembourg	1–2	—	+1	+1
Moldova	**3–8**	89	+1	–1
Poland	950–1,100	—	+1	0
Portugal	30–50	89	–1	–1
Romania	(40–100)	—	(0)	(0)
Russia	(1,000–5,000)	—	(0)	(0)
Slovakia	300–400	—	+1	+1
Slovenia	10–15	—	+2	+2
Spain	**200–220**	—	+1	+1
Turkey	(500–2,000)	—	—	(0)
Ukraine	**250–300**	—	0	–1
Total (approx.)	6,500–19,000			

Trends   +2 Large increase   +1 Small increase   0 Stable   X Extinct
(1970–1990)   –2 Large decrease   –1 Small decrease   F Fluctuating   N New breeder
Data quality   **Bold**: reliable quantitative data   Normal type: incomplete quantitative data
Bracketed figures: no quantitative data   * Data quality not provided

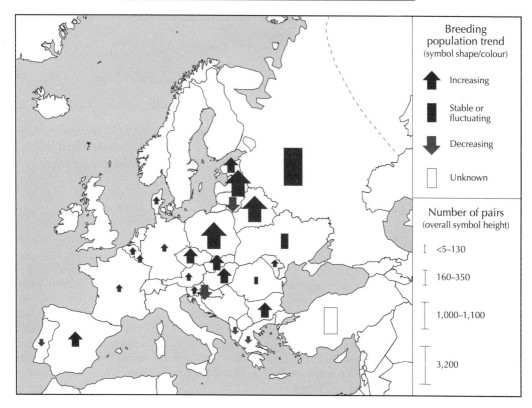

A World Bank loan to Poland which would be repaid with timber is under negotiation; many Black Stork breeding sites would be lost.

The loss of wetlands through agricultural intensification has caused changes in the hydrology of forested areas, which is thought to have impacted on Black Stork populations. Disturbance at breeding sites can have serious effects on nesting success, mostly due to human interference (C. San Segundo Ontin pers. comm.).

After breeding, many birds are killed by illegal hunting in southern Europe and Africa (Boettcher-Streim 1992). Hunting has declined in Spain recently (González and Merino 1988), but birds of the eastern population are still shot on migration (Abuladze 1993), and Spanish-ringed birds found recently in Mali were all shot. Other possible threats include collision with powerlines, and prey contamination by pesticides (Boettcher-Streim 1992, Hancock et al. 1992).

■ Conservation measures

Conservation of breeding and feeding habitat, such as slow-flowing rivers and streams within wooded areas, is important. In many countries, the creation of small reserves, nest protection zones and a positive attitude towards the species among foresters has almost completely eliminated the felling of nesting trees (Nottorf 1978, Strazds et al. 1990, Kurzynski and Zajac 1993).

The recovery of the beaver Castor fiber in some Latvian and Polish forests seems to have restored suitable Black Stork feeding habitat, as the construction of dams by beavers increases the amount of marshy ground (Strazds et al. 1990). The establishment of shallow artificial pools to improve food resources for storks and the construction of nests has also helped to increase nesting success and expand the species' range out of eastern Europe, although artificial nest programmes are not always successful (Nottorf 1978, Ivanovsky and Samusenko 1990, Boettcher-Streim 1992). The effects of reservoir construction and of conversion of wetlands to rice cultivation need to be established.

Noisy machinery should be prohibited near occupied nests (e.g. within 500 m in Poland, 1 km in Spain) during the breeding season, and there should be no human presence within 100 m (C. San Segundo Ontin pers. comm.). Even outside the breeding season, clear-felling should be prevented within about 200 m of nests (Kurzynski and Zajac 1993), and there should be no permanent activity within 3 km.

The hunting of this species during migration and in the winter quarters must be stopped, and a network of safe stopover sites maintained. More data are needed on wintering localities and the threats there.

PIOTR PROFUS

White Stork
Ciconia ciconia

SPEC Category 2
Status Vulnerable
Criteria Large decline

There has been a major decline through the twentieth century, particularly in western Europe, mainly due to habitat loss and alteration through agricultural intensification, and climatic change in the African winter quarters. Urgent measures must be taken to protect and restore extensively managed lowland grasslands.

■ Distribution and population trends

About 90% of the world range of the White Stork lies in Europe, where it is widespread. The remaining birds nest in north-west Africa and south-west and central Asia, with a few also in South Africa.

Practically all European birds winter in the Afrotropics. Those nesting east of a migratory divide running from the Netherlands through Germany to Bavaria head south-east to eastern and southern Africa, while those west of the divide winter in West Africa between Senegal and Chad (Schüz 1953).

Most White Storks breed in central and eastern Europe, with up to half the world population in Poland, Belarus, Ukraine and Russia (e.g. Rheinwald

et al. 1989; see table, map). Turkey also holds large numbers.

The White Stork has declined in Europe throughout the twentieth century. Censuses from 1934 indicate estimated losses of 90% in some countries up to 1984 (Rheinwald 1989). The heaviest declines, which continued between 1970 and 1990 (see table), occurred in Denmark, Netherlands and Belgium, where the species is now almost extinct (Veroman 1987, Rheinwald 1989), and in Sweden, where it last bred in 1954 (Cramp and Simmons 1977). Large declines were also recorded in France from the beginning of the 1960s (Lestan 1992, Schierer 1992), although an increase was noted between 1970 and 1990 due to the release of captive-bred birds which are often resident during the winter (see table, map).

Declines over this period also occurred in many central, east and south-east European countries, including the large populations in Lithuania, Romania, Bulgaria, Ukraine and Turkey (see table, map). However, in Turkey, a comparison of census work of White Stork populations over the last 30 years at three coastal areas, Büyük Menderes valley, Göksu Delta and Kizilirmak Delta, (c.600 pairs total) indicate no such decline, indeed locally numbers increased (V. van den Berk *in litt.*). In Estonia, Latvia and Russia some increases were recorded. The large population in Spain also increased, while numbers in Portugal fluctuated during the period; recent data (received just before publication) suggest that the Spanish population in 1993 was c.14,000 pairs (Schulz in press). Overall, however, up to about half the European population declined during 1970–1990, nearly 40% of the population being in countries which showed rapid declines.

■ Ecology

In south-west Europe the main habitat is dry grassland where high densities of grasshoppers, small mammals and similar prey occur. Populations elsewhere in Europe prefer natural or extensively managed lowland wet grassland or cultivated farmland, preferably with ponds or streams. Highest breeding

	Breeding population			Breeding
	Size (pairs)	Year	Trend	range trend
Albania	100–200	64	–2	(–1)
Austria	**308–308**	92	–1	0
Belarus	**10,500–13,000**	89	0	0
Belgium	**1–1**	90	F	1
Bulgaria	**5,000–5,200**	—	–1	–1
Croatia	1,000–1,200 *	—	–1*	–1*
Czech Republic	**594–689**	—	0	0
Denmark	**9–9**	91	–2	–1
Estonia	2,000–2,000	—	+2	0
France	**120–138**	92	+2	+1
Germany	**3,335–3,371**	84	–2	–1
Greece	2,000–2,500	—	–1	(0)
Hungary	**5,000–5,000**	89	0	0
Italy	**1–10**	91	+2	+2
Latvia	**6,000–7,000**	84	+1	0
Lithuania	**4,000–5,000**	85–88	(–1)	(0)
Moldova	**250–650**	88	0	0
Netherlands	**0–4**	89–91	–2	–2
Poland	**30,500–30,500**	—	0	0
Portugal	**1,000–2,000**	91	F	–1
Romania	4,000–6,000	—	–1	–1
Russia	3,500–4,000	—	+1	(+1)
Slovakia	**1,025–1,080**	—	–1	0
Slovenia	**190–200**	79	–2	+1
Spain	**7,901–7,901**	90	+1	+1
Switzerland	**120–153**	71–74	+2	+1
Turkey	15,000–35,000	—	–2	0
Ukraine	**12,000–18,000**	88	–2	–1
Total (approx.)	120,000–150,000			

Trends (1970–1990) +2 Large increase +1 Small increase 0 Stable X Extinct
  –2 Large decrease –1 Small decrease F Fluctuating N New breeder
Data quality **Bold**: reliable quantitative data Normal type: incomplete quantitative data
  Bracketed figures: no quantitative data * Data quality not provided

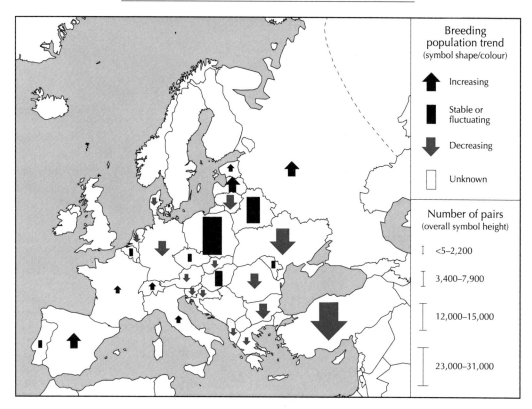

densities are in areas which are regularly flooded, as this provides abundant prey, especially amphibians (Schneider 1988).

Nests are placed mainly on houses, but there are also large colonies on trees or rocks.

■ Threats

The declines are attributed in many countries largely to destruction and deterioration of breeding habitat (Schulz 1988, 1989, Goriup and Schulz 1991). The White Stork's food resources have suffered greatly: this has come about particularly in north-west Europe through the drainage of wet grasslands and other wetlands since the beginning of the twentieth century, and in south-west Europe through the cultivation of grasslands and heavy use of pesticides since the Second World War. Dramatic increases have been recorded in the mortality of both adults and juveniles (G. Rheinwald *in litt.*), but this may be due at least partly to conditions in the winter quarters. Birds wintering in West Africa appear to have been severely affected by long-term reductions in rainfall there, and this may be the main cause of decline in populations wintering in that region; east European birds have probably suffered less in this way. Locust control programmes seem to have significantly reduced food supplies all across Africa (Dallinga and Schoenmakers 1989). Recent studies suggest that hunting pressure during migration is probably not a major contributor to the decline, though it may be significant in West Africa (Schulz 1988, Thauront and Duquet 1992).

In Europe, collision with, and electrocution by, powerlines is a serious threat (Fiedler and Wissner 1980).

■ Conservation measures

Extensive habitat conservation and restoration are required. In north-west Europe, remaining lowland wet grasslands and wetlands must be strictly protected, and, where possible, intensively farmed former wetlands must be restored through re-establishing higher water-levels, periodic flooding and less intensive agriculture. This can only be achieved on the wide scale needed by cooperation between government agricultural agencies and conservation bodies.

In eastern Europe, immediate measures are needed to prevent habitat destruction through the protection of the largest riverine wetlands and lowland wet grasslands. The recent political and economic developments in this region may otherwise lead to declines such as already seen in western Europe.

A reduction in the use of pesticides in breeding, passage and wintering areas would generally improve the situation for the White Stork through the increased food availability that would result.

HOLGER SCHULZ

Glossy Ibis
Plegadis falcinellus

SPEC Category 3
Status Declining
Criteria Moderate decline

During the twentieth century Glossy Ibises have disappeared from a large part of their former European breeding range and numbers have continued to decline in recent decades due to the destruction and degradation of wetlands and to local hunting. A return to non-intensive management of riverine wetlands, the creation of an international network of wetland nature reserves and stricter regulations on hunting of the species are required.

■ Distribution and population trends

The Glossy Ibis has a wide global distribution, though within Europe it is largely restricted to the south-east and east (Dementiev and Gladkov 1951b, Cramp and Simmons 1977). Over 90% of the European population breeds in Russia, Ukraine, Romania and Turkey, mainly along the coasts of the Black and Caspian Seas (see table, map). Smaller numbers breed in Bulgaria, Albania and Greece, and a few pairs breed in each of Moldova, Hungary, Spain, France and Italy.

European birds winter in the eastern Mediterranean or in Africa. However, some birds, especially immatures, may disperse over large distances and such individuals have sporadically occurred over much of Europe (Bauer and Glutz von Blotzheim 1987).

The Glossy Ibis has low site-fidelity, breeding in large numbers in a location in one year and often being absent the next (Bezzel 1985, Cramp and Simmons 1977, Bauer and Glutz von Blotzheim 1987). Despite this behaviour, however, there is reasonable knowledge of its distribution and trends. During the last hundred years a considerable range contraction has been documented, being most severe during recent decades (Bauer and Glutz von Blotzheim 1987, Michev 1990, Weber and Munteanu 1994). Numbers have declined throughout Europe, sometimes sharply (Bauer and Glutz von Blotzheim 1987, Anon. 1992a; see table). In the Russian Volga Delta 8,780 individuals bred in 1934, and 12,620 in 1935, but by 1951 the population had declined to 704 pairs and just one pair in 1959 (Dementiev and Gladkov 1951b, Cramp and Simmons 1977); no more-recent data are available for this site. Over the 1970 to 1990 period the population fluctuated in Russia, but elsewhere mostly declined (totalling up to almost 60% of the population), including large declines of over 50% in the important Romanian and Turkish populations (see table).

■ Ecology

Glossy Ibis breeding colonies typically comprise a few to several thousand pairs, usually mixed with herons, egrets, Rook *Corvus frugilegus* and Pygmy Cormorant *Phalacrocorax pygmeus*. The nests are generally located low down in willow *Salix* bushes, but also rarely in well developed beds of reed *Phragmites*, either among the reeds or in trees within them (Dementiev and Gladkov 1951b, Dolgushin 1960).

Birds may feed tens of kilometres from the breeding colonies, showing a preference for successional vegetation zones with luxuriant emergent aquatic growth at water edges, such as flooded meadows alongside rivers, freshwater reservoirs and lagoons. Less important sites are shallow fish-ponds or rice-fields with scattered reeds. Outside the breeding season, the species also occurs in coastal habitats. In winter it remains gregarious, occurring in flocks and roosting communally.

The Glossy Ibis feeds exclusively on animal prey, mainly insects and their larvae, water snails, leeches and worms. The tadpoles of amphibians may be an important temporary food source (Dolgushin 1960),

	Breeding population			Breeding
	Size (pairs)	Year	Trend	range trend
Albania	100–300	64	–1	(–1)
Bulgaria	200–500	—	–1	–1
France	**0–3**	91	N	N
Greece	**50–70**	86	–1	–1
Hungary	**10–10**	91	F*	0*
Italy	1–12	—	+1	+1
Moldova	1–5	89	–1	–1
Romania	**1,000–1,800**	—	–2	0
Russia	**6,500–8,000**	—	F	0
Spain	1–4	—	–2	–2
Turkey	500–1,400	—	–2	0
Ukraine	5,500–7,000	78	–1	–1
Total (approx.)	14,000–19,000			

Trends +2 Large increase +1 Small increase 0 Stable X Extinct
(1970–1990) –2 Large decrease –1 Small decrease F Fluctuating N New breeder
Data quality **Bold**: reliable quantitative data Normal type: incomplete quantitative data
Bracketed figures: no quantitative data * Data quality not provided

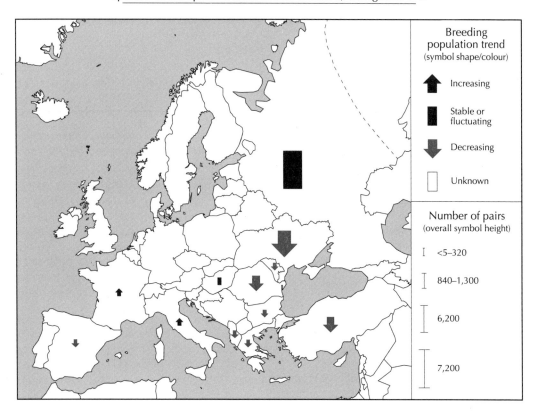

though small fish are taken only exceptionally (Bauer and Glutz von Blotzheim 1987).

▨ Threats

The declines in breeding range and population levels which started in the twentieth century, becoming accentuated by the 1950s and steepening further between 1970 and 1990, were mostly due to the large-scale and systematic drainage of wetlands and to the spread and intensification of agriculture in the lower reaches of river valleys, depriving birds of their main breeding and feeding sites. Also, some wetlands have been turned into fish-ponds and many previously open river valleys have been afforested.

Locally intense hunting pressure may be having detrimental effects on some Glossy Ibis populations, especially in the lower Danube river area and at the Danube Delta, and the species is also sensitive to human presence and disturbance, especially at nesting sites.

▨ Conservation measures

The strict protection of colonies and the general conservation of remaining wetlands, including a return to non-intensive use of water-edge habitats, are necessary. The establishment of an international network of protected wetlands, as proposed under the African–Eurasian Migratory Waterbirds Agreement of the Bonn Convention, may provide such an opportunity if implemented. In addition, the restoration of riverine forest and shallow-water habitats in the Danube Delta Biosphere Reserve should be pursued to completion, given the destruction previously wreaked by channel excavation and dam construction.

Hunting of the species, especially in the lower Danube river area, should be strictly regulated and subject to a sustainable management programme.

PETER WEBER

Spoonbill
Platalea leucorodia

SPEC Category 2
Status   Endangered
Criteria   Large decline, <10,000 pairs

This rare species is declining in more than two-thirds of its population, although it has recently increased in western Europe. Many colonies in south-east and eastern Europe are insufficiently protected, and human impact on feeding habitats is extensive. Breeding sites require strict protection, together with the maintenance of feeding habitats near colonies, along migration routes and in the winter quarters.

■ Distribution and population trends

Half to three-quarters of the global Spoonbill population breeds in Europe, mainly at scattered sites in the Netherlands and Spain and from Hungary and Greece east to the Caspian. Birds from north-west and south-west Europe winter mainly in western Africa; those from south-east Europe winter in the Mediterranean and the northern tropics of Africa, and east European and Turkish birds appear to move to north-east Africa, the Middle East and India.

The European population totals 5,000–9,000 pairs. Russia and possibly Turkey each support a third, while Spain, Netherlands, Hungary and Ukraine hold 5–10% each (see table, map). Although not covered by this review, the species is also known to breed in Yugoslavia (Serbia). New breeding sites have recently been found in Slovakia, Italy (1989), France (1981) and Portugal. Population sizes are generally well known except for Turkey and Ukraine where estimates are less precise.

The Dutch/Spanish population increased from 670 to at least 1,100 birds during 1963–1990, Dutch numbers now being much the same as in the 1920s (van der Hut *et al.* 1992). In central Europe the population in Hungary has increased by two to three times (cf. Müller 1984), while in Austria, although there was no breeding during 1970–1990, 10–15 pairs bred in 1992–1994.

In contrast, declines have occurred in much of south-east Europe this century, including Romania (400 pairs in 1909, 250 by 1940, and fluctuating between 20 and 240 during 1953–1963: Cramp and Simmons 1977) and the lower Volga in Russia (2,500 pairs in the early 1950s declining to 500 by 1980: Borodin 1984). During 1970–1990 declines continued in these and most other east and south-east European countries, including Russia, Ukraine and Turkey (see table, map). Overall, during 1970–1990 European numbers fell by up to a third, with over two-thirds of the population affected.

■ Ecology

The Spoonbill inhabits shallow wetlands, typically deltas, flood-plains or extensive marshes. Colonies of tens to hundreds of pairs nest in extensive reedbeds or on islands, generally secure from disturbance and ground predators. Birds feed in open water up to 30 cm deep by sweeping the bill from side to side for small fish and invertebrates (Cramp and Simmons 1977). As a tactile forager, concentrations of prey are required, so birds may fly up to 25 km to feed.

■ Threats

The main causes of decline in south-east Europe are loss of nesting sites and foraging habitat due to drainage, deterioration and disturbance of wetlands. At Neusiedlersee in Austria early declines were attributed mainly to disturbance through egg-collecting and reed-burning, and the decline after 1970 (with no breeding after 1989) coincided with drainage of foraging pools (Müller 1984). In the Ukraine and Russia, harvesting and burning of reed, and natural vegetation succession, reduce the suitability of the habitat (Borodin 1984), and the Volga delta is

	Breeding population			Breeding
	Size (pairs)	Year	Trend	range trend
Albania	10–100	64	–1	(–1)
Bulgaria	50–70	—	–1	–1
Croatia	**100–150**	92	+1	0*
Czech Republic	**0–5**	91	F	F
France	**5–7**	90	N	N
Greece	**113–172**	86	–1	–1
Hungary	**600–750**	—	+1	+1
Italy	**2–10**	89	N	N
Moldova	**10–20**	89	–1	–1
Netherlands	**400–530**	89–91	+2	+1
Portugal	**1–5**	91	N	N
Romania	**120–120**	89	–2	–1
Russia	**2,300–2,800**	—	–1	0
Slovakia	**1–10**	91	N	N
Spain	**675–675**	—	0	0
Turkey	500–3,000	—	–2	0
Ukraine	300–800	86	–1	–1
Total (approx.)	5,200–9,200			

Trends	+2 Large increase +1 Small increase	0 Stable X Extinct
(1970–1990)	–2 Large decrease –1 Small decrease	F Fluctuating N New breeder
Data quality	**Bold**: reliable quantitative data Normal type: incomplete quantitative data	
	Bracketed figures: no quantitative data * Data quality not provided	

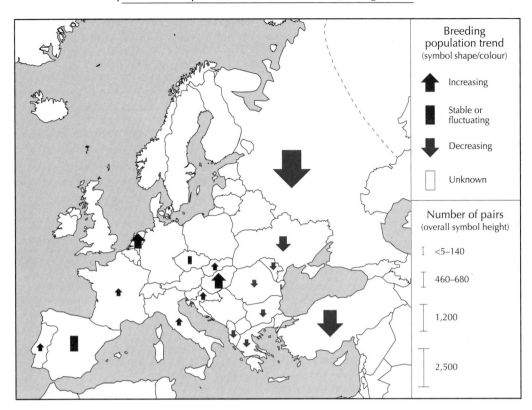

also seriously threatened by pollution and disruption of water-flow (Finlayson 1992a). Declines in Greece have been ascribed to the disappearance of feeding grounds (Grimmett and Jones 1989). Prey abundance, which may be more important for this species than for many fish-eating birds, can be affected by (e.g.) pollution, flood control and water diversion.

On migration and in winter Spoonbills depend largely on coastal wetlands, which are under widespread pressure from land-claim, pollution, aquaculture and disturbance. Only a few of the French and Spanish stopover sites are considered secure (Poorter 1990).

■ **Conservation measures**

The species requires year-round protection. Although legally protected in most if not all European countries, it requires further protection in Africa and Asia, which could be promoted through the proposed African–Eurasian Migratory Waterbirds Agreement under the Bonn Convention. Strict site protection is urgently needed for colonies, and the maintenance or restoration of feeding areas is also essential. In Hungary the species may have benefited from the increase in number of fish-ponds; spring drainage of these ponds increases the extent of feeding habitat (Z. Waliczky pers. comm.).

In most countries 80–100% of breeding sites fall within Important Bird Areas (IBAs). These include,

in the Netherlands, Oostvaardersplassen (IBA 031); in Spain, Ría de Huelva (IBA 246) and Marismas del Guadalquivir (IBA 247); in Hungary, Hortobágy (IBA 016) and Csaj-to (IBA 027); in Romania and Ukraine, the Danube Delta (Romania IBA 001, Ukraine IBA 027); in Turkey, Manyas Gölü (IBA 006) and Eregli Sazligi (IBA 023); and, in Russia, the Volga delta (IBA 086). Site management should be particularly directed to the maintenance of natural water-level fluctuations as this is crucial for both nesting (Müller 1983) and foraging (Bancroft 1989). The Ramsar and Bonn Conventions, and the Wild Birds Directive within the EU, are appropriate international instruments for setting up a network of protected areas along the Spoonbill's migration routes. All sites holding more than 1% of the population concerned qualify for such a network but, unfortunately, detailed measures cannot be prescribed as the distribution of the population outside the breeding season is poorly known. However, one staging area in Croatia, Kopacki rit (IBA 014), which was damaged during the war in 1991, and two in Sicily (Italy), Stagnone di Marsala (IBA 135) and Stagnone di Vendicari (IBA 139), one of which is under serious threat from aquaculture development, are known to be of great importance for migrating central European Spoonbills and are clearly a high priority for protection.

EDUARD OSIECK

Greater Flamingo
Phoenicopterus ruber

SPEC Category 3
Status Localized
Criteria Localized

Breeding occurs in the Mediterranean region, with the largest concentrations normally in France, Spain and Turkey. Although breeding success has recently been good, and populations have not declined, the species is susceptible because of the restricted number of suitable wetland breeding sites. These and the surrounding feeding areas, which may be up to 150 km away, must be conserved, especially those threatened by drainage linked to development for tourism.

■ Distribution and population trends

The Greater Flamingo has a scattered world distribution, including northern, eastern and southern Africa, south-west Asia, the West Indies and Galápagos, as well as Europe, and a total world population of about 900,000 individuals (Rose and Scott 1994).

In Europe the species is confined to the Mediterranean region. Breeding is often irregular and numbers fluctuate greatly from one season to another as there are regular movements between Europe, Africa and Asia. The species is localized, being dependent on a small number of wetland sites (see Important Bird Area table). There is some evidence that one or more of a group of sites is used according to their suitability ferom year to year (Johnson 1989a). The species' range tends to contract during years of drought and extends in wet years which may give rise to breeding at additional sites in Spain, Tunisia and Egypt. Breeding is intermittent in Egypt at El Malaha (Goodman and Meininger 1989) where it was rediscovered nesting in 1970 (Mendelssohn 1975b). The largest European breeding concentrations are found in Spain (Andalucía and wetlands along the Mediterranean coast), Mediterranean France and Turkey (see IBA table, map). One of the most regularly occupied sites in the world is the breeding colony in the Camargue at the Etang du Fangassier, southern France (IBA 130), in industrial saltpans. A new colony was established in Italy in 1993, and substantial numbers occur, but do not breed, in Portugal, Greece (Thrace, see below) and Cyprus.

Important Bird Areas The top ten IBAs for breeding Greater Flamingos in Europe, together holding over 90% of the total European population.

France	130	Camargue
Italy	124*	Stagno di Molentargius, Cagliari
Spain	247*	Marismas del Guadalquivir
	267	Lagunas de Fuente de Piedra
Turkey	023*	Eregli Sazligi
	025*	Karapinar Ovasi
	029*	Seyfe Gölü
	030*	Sultansazligi (Sultan Marshes)
	032	Tuz Gölü
	036*	Çamalti Tuzlasi

* irregularly used site

In the period 1991–1993 an average of 18,000 pairs bred in Europe (outside Turkey) but with marked fluctuations in countries over this period (see population table, map). This is the same as the average population during the preceding 12 years. However, between 1970 and 1990 numbers in France and Spain fluctuated between 3,500 and 27,430 breeding pairs and exceeded 20,000 pairs on seven occasions, when southern Europe may have held as much as a quarter of the world's breeding population (A. Johnson own data). Some individuals are sedentary while others reveal a complex pattern of movements in relation to season and hydrological factors (Johnson 1989a), making any accurate overall assessment of population size, distribution and trends very difficult. The numbers of breeding birds and of chicks raised in both France and Spain are monitored annually and showed an increase in France for the 1970–1990 period (see population table, map). According to the IWRB mid-January census numbers, wintering in France during the same period also increased.

Although there is no evidence of any change in numbers of flamingos present in the eastern Mediterranean, the range has extended recently to wetlands in north-east Greece where the species now occurs regularly throughout the year and where egg-laying was recorded in 1992 (G. Handrinos pers. comm.).

	Breeding population			Breeding
	Size (pairs)	Year	Trend	range trend
France	**12,500–17,000**	91–93	+2	0
Spain	**400–10,500**	91–93	F	0
Italy	**1,600–1,600**	93	N	N
Turkey	**14,000–18,000**	93	F	0
Total (approx.)	28,000–47,000			

Trends	+2 Large increase	+1 Small increase	0 Stable	X Extinct
(1970–1990)	–2 Large decrease	–1 Small decrease	F Fluctuating	N New breeder
Data quality	**Bold**: reliable quantitative data	Normal type: incomplete quantitative data		
	Bracketed figures: no quantitative data	* Data quality not provided		

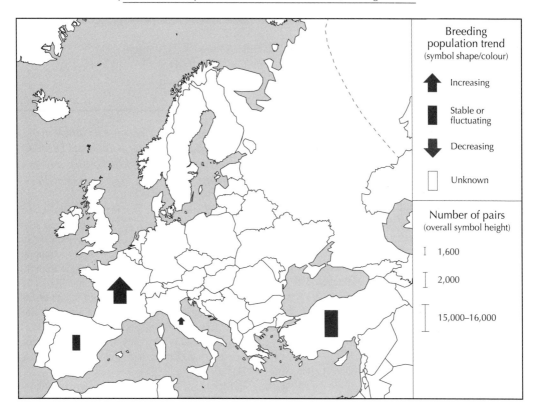

Breeding population trend (symbol shape/colour)

Increasing

Stable or fluctuating

Decreasing

Unknown

Number of pairs (overall symbol height)

1,600

2,000

15,000–16,000

■ Ecology

Flamingos frequent shallow brackish and saltwater lagoons where they filter-feed on aquatic invertebrates, their eggs and larvae, e.g. brine shrimp *Artemia salina*, midge larvae (Chironomidae) and tubificid worms (Jenkin 1957, Johnson 1983). At times they occur in freshwater marshes and even in rice-fields where they may take freshly sown grain. Most colonies number several thousand pairs and are established in traditional extensive wetland sites, free from human disturbance and secure from terrestrial predators (especially fox *Vulpes vulpes*) and with a sufficient supply of food. When local resources are insufficient the species often feeds away from the nesting site; in Spain, for example, flamingos breeding at Fuente de Piedra fly 140 km to feed in the Marismas del Guadalquivir when the nesting lagoon dries out in late spring (Johnson 1989b, Rendon *et al.* 1991a,b).

During breeding, flamingos make mounds of sand or mud on which they lay their single egg, and over a period of years this causes site erosion.

■ Threats

The loss of wetlands through drainage linked to tourist developments constitutes the greatest threat to the Greater Flamingo in the Mediterranean at present. The lagoons used by the species are shallow and many are situated along the Mediterranean coast where urban pressures are greatest. Of the 100 Ramsar Sites in the Mediterranean, only 16 are not threatened (Hollis 1992). Hunting is also a problem.

■ Conservation measures

Conservation of all wetlands used by Greater Flamingos for feeding and breeding, both north and south of the Mediterranean, is vital for the maintenance of the species in Europe. This includes artificial water-bodies (salinas) and temporary salt lakes which may become dry and hold no birds for a number of years. There are few islands suitable for nesting, although the loss of such places has been partly counteracted by the provision of specially created sites which are used by flamingos in both the Camargue (France, Important Bird Area 130) and at Fuente de Piedra (Spain, IBA 267) (Johnson 1982, 1991, 1992, Rendon *et al.* 1991). The breeding sites should be closely monitored to ensure the continuation of appropriate habitat management techniques for the species.

ALAN JOHNSON

Bewick's Swan
Cygnus columbianus

SPEC Category 3, winter
Status Localized
Criteria Localized

Although its numbers have increased slowly, Bewick's Swan is susceptible because it gathers at only a few sites outside the breeding season. Much of its traditional aquatic winter habitat has been lost, and it increasingly uses arable fields and wet pastures, sometimes conflicting with farming interests. Major breeding, moulting and staging areas in Russia are threatened by oil and gas extraction.

■ Distribution and population trends

Bewick's Swans breed in the tundra of the north Russian Palearctic, between the Chukotka Sea and Kanin peninsula. Some 25,000–30,000 birds breed east of the Lena delta (in Asiatic Russia), wintering in eastern Asia (Kondratiev 1991, Mineyev 1991). The western population, which is possibly discrete, breeds largely west of the Urals and winters in north-west Europe; it totalled 16,000–17,000 birds in the 1980s (Dirksen and Beekman 1991, Mineyev 1991), but may now be larger.

Birds concentrate at a small number of sites on migration and in winter. Up to 90% of the wintering population uses about 10 or fewer sites, with the United Kingdom, Republic of Ireland and Netherlands particularly important (see Important Bird Area table). Stopover sites in the Baltic countries, especially Estonia, harbour large numbers in spring, e.g. Matsalu Bay (13,500 birds) and Peipsi Lake (4,000 birds), while 15,000 birds were recently counted in

autumn in Korovinskaya Bay in the Pechora delta of Russia (Rees *et al.* in press). Other important stopovers include, in the Netherlands, Lauwersmeer (Important Bird Area 011, max. 6,500 birds in autumn), Lake Veluwemeer (IBA 032, max. 6,800 in autumn), Noordoostpolder-West (IBA 029, max. 3,000 in autumn), Eempolders (max. 3,500) and the delta area of Walcheren (which includes Veerse Meer, Oosterschelde, Krammer-Volkerak and the Zeeland Isles; max. 3,000), and in Germany, the lower and middle Elbe river (8,000 in spring: Dirksen and Beekman 1991).

European winter numbers have risen overall, but 1970–1990 mid-winter counts suggest variable national trends (see population table, map). Increases were recorded in the United Kingdom, especially in the latter part of the period, following several good breeding seasons, while numbers fluctuated in the Netherlands, and fell in the Republic of Ireland.

	Winter population			Winter
	Size (individuals)	Year	Trend	range trend
Austria	**1–6**	—	N	N
Belgium	**95–250**	85–91	+1	0
Bulgaria	**0–20**	77–89	+1	+1
Czech Republic	0–3 *	—	—	—
Denmark	427–427 *	—	—	—
Estonia	**0–10**	—	0	0
France	**88–88**	84	+1	**0**
Germany	**100–1,500**	86–90	**0**	—
Greece	0–10 *	87–91	—	—
Rep. of Ireland	**2,000–2,500**	—	–1	—
Latvia	**0–10**	89	F	F
Lithuania	5–10	90	+1	—
Netherlands	**3,000–10,000**	79–83	**F**	**0**
Poland	0–80 *	—	—	—
Romania	0–4	—	F	0
Russia	(0–100)	—	(F)	(0)
Slovakia	(0–2)	—	—	—
Spain	**0–2**	—	F*	—
Switzerland	**0–6**	81–91	**0**	**F**
Ukraine	**30–50**	88	+1	+1
United Kingdom	**6,600–6,600**	88	+1	+1
Isle of Man	**5–5**	89	**0**	0*
Total (min., approx.)	12,000			

Trends +2 Large increase +1 Small increase 0 Stable X Extinct
(1970–1990) –2 Large decrease –1 Small decrease F Fluctuating N New breeder
Data quality **Bold:** reliable quantitative data Normal type: incomplete quantitative data
Bracketed figures: no quantitative data * Data quality not provided

Important Bird Areas The top ten IBAs for wintering Bewick's Swans in Europe, together holding over 90% of the total European wintering population.

Netherlands	027	De Wieden and De Weeribben
	029	Noordoostpolder-West
	032	Veluwemeer, Harderbroek and Kievitslanden
	044	Waal and Rijn: Spijk–Nijmegen–Arnhem (including Oude Rijnstrangen and Ooijpolders)
	051	Veerse Meer
	067	Ijssel: Westervoor–Zwolle
Rep. of Ireland	082	Thew Cull/Killag
	086	Wexford Harbour and Slobs
United Kingdom	162	Nene Washes
	163	Ouse Washes

■ Ecology

Preferred breeding habitat is sedge–grass and moss–lichen tundra with numerous small lakes. Moulting and post-breeding flocks gather in shallow bays with abundant aquatic vegetation around the Barents Sea.

Traditional winter habitat of lakes, marshes and flooded pastures has decreased or become unsuitable through eutrophication, and birds increasingly use arable fields and wet pastures (Beekman *et al.* 1991).

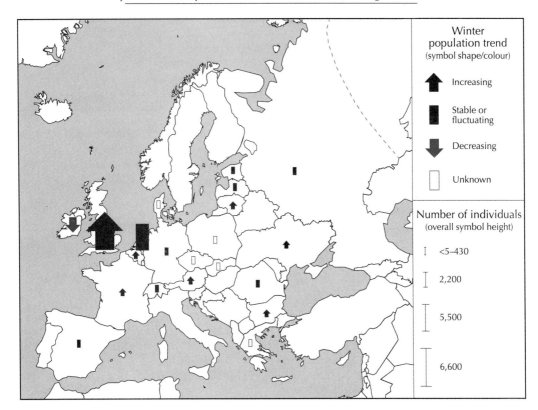

Winter
population trend
(symbol shape/colour)

Increasing

Stable or
fluctuating

Decreasing

Unknown

Number of individuals
(overall symbol height)

<5–430

2,200

5,500

6,600

■ Threats

Eutrophication and drainage have reduced the extent of traditional winter habitat and of Baltic staging sites, and further drainage of safe wetland roosts would be a problem. Private land ownership in the Baltic republics may exacerbate conflicts between farmers and birds, particularly as the legal status of Bewick's Swan is not yet clarified. Conflicts could also occur in western Europe if the swans use agricultural land increasingly. Currently 6,000 birds use the Ouse Washes (United Kingdom) and most farmers in this area are happy for the swans to clean up root-crop fields after the harvest—though this situation could deteriorate if the swans spent more time on winter cereals. Compensation is paid in some countries.

In the breeding grounds, planned oil and gas extraction, especially near Varandei on the Medinski Zavorot peninsula and nearby Khaipudyrskaya Bay, pose a serious threat to habitat in the Bolshezemelskaya Tundra (Nenetski Autonomous District). Further west in the Malozemelskaya Tundra (Nenetski Autonomous District), the Pechora delta, surrounding bays (including Korovinskaya Bay) and the Russkiy Zavorot peninsula are also currently under pressure because concessions have been given for fossil-fuel drilling. This may be a serious problem not only during breeding but also while birds are moulting and fattening prior to autumn migration.

Although legally protected everywhere from hunting, some 40% of Bewick's Swans X-rayed in the United Kingdom had gun-shot in their tissues (Rees *et al.* 1990), and 7% of adult deaths were attributed to hunting (Brown *et al.* 1992). In some countries birds may be accidentally shot during culls of Mute Swans *C. olor*. Collisions with powerlines account for about 20% of deaths.

■ Conservation measures

Critical sites in western Europe, especially safe roosts, need further protection. Water quality of large, shallow water-bodies is an important issue, and management programmes for restoring aquatic ecosystems are currently underway in the Netherlands, allowing birds access to more of their traditional (and natural) food. Where conflicts with agriculture occur, wider compensation payments for winter-crop damage would also improve wintering prospects, as would tighter enforcement of existing hunting laws.

Urgent wide-scale protection of habitat is needed throughout the breeding range, where virtually no reserves exist, to safeguard nesting areas and concentration sites used by moulting and passage birds.

Environmental impact assessments of proposed oil, gas and industrial developments on the Russian tundra, by independent international organizations, are urgently recommended.

Jan H. Beekman, Eileen Rees and Philip Bacon

Lesser White-fronted Goose
Anser erythropus

SPEC Category 1
Status Vulnerable
Criteria <2,500 pairs

Numbers of this globally threatened species have declined drastically during the second half of the twentieth century, and in Fennoscandia no more than 50 breeding pairs now remain. The causes of the decline are uncertain, but probably relate to habitat changes on the wintering grounds. The wintering areas used by the Fennoscandian population are not currently known.

■ Distribution and population trends

The Lesser White-fronted Goose breeds in a belt from northern Fennoscandia and northern Russia to eastern Siberia. Within Europe, Russia holds the majority of the breeding population, and small numbers are also found in Norway, Finland and Sweden (see table, map).

The wintering grounds were once the steppes of central and eastern Europe and south-west Asia, but now that these regions are largely cultivated the wintering areas are poorly known. Autumn staging areas are found in Hungary (Important Bird Area 016 Hortobágy), and occasionally small flocks are encountered in Romania (IBA 001 Danube Delta) and Greece (IBA 001 Evros Delta, IBA 003 Lake Mitrikou, IBA 004 Lake Vistonis and Lakes of Thrace, IBA 012 Lake Kerkini) (Grimmett and Jones 1989, Handrinos 1991, Munteanu *et al.* 1991). Major wintering areas are found in Azerbaijan (077 Kirov Bay, Caspian Sea), though it is thought that these birds mainly come from breeding grounds outside Europe in northern Siberia (Vinogradov 1990, Madsen *et al.* 1993). In western Europe single Lesser White-fronted Geese occasionally occur within wintering flocks of other goose species.

Drastic reductions in population size and range have been recorded in Fennoscandia and northern Russia since the middle of the twentieth century (Norderhaug and Norderhaug 1984, Vinogradov 1990), and this is reflected in the Hungarian autumn staging areas where considerable reductions in numbers have been recorded (Sterbetz 1982). Declines

continued through the 1970–1990 period (although the large Russian population is believed to have been stable), so that by the early 1990s no more than about 50 pairs bred in Fennoscandia, with the Swedish wild population regarded as almost extinct (von Essen 1993, Øien and Aarvak 1993, J. Markkola pers. comm.; see table, map).

Numbers have declined substantially during the twentieth century to the extent that the species is now classified as Globally Threatened (Collar *et al.* 1994).

■ Ecology

The Lesser White-fronted Goose breeds in the low-Arctic tundra zone, primarily nesting in habitat dominated by dwarf birch *Betula nana* and foraging in sedge marshes around lakes. Originally the species wintered on the steppes of central and south-east Europe (Sterbetz 1968), but, since the transformation of much of this biotope, including most of the species' wintering habitat, into agricultural land, its main feeding habitat within Europe has become farmland.

■ Threats

The reasons behind the Lesser White-fronted Goose's dramatic population decline are not known. It has probably been caused primarily by deleterious factors on the wintering grounds, such as deterioration of feeding conditions through the transformation of steppes to cultivated land, and overexploitation through unsustainable hunting.

On the breeding grounds conditions are more stable, but increasing tourism and angling may cause disturbance in some areas, and habitat loss through the creation of reservoirs for hydroelectric power schemes, as well as a northward spread of the red fox *Vulpes vulpes* may also have played a part in the Lesser White-fronted Goose's decline. In addition, spring staging areas in Finland, consisting of cattle-grazed fields and hay fields, no longer receive management conducive to producing acceptable habitat.

	Breeding population			Breeding
	Size (pairs)	Year	Trend	range trend
Finland	15–20	92	(–1)	**0**
Norway	30–50	90	–1	–1
Russia	1,000–2,500	—	0	0
Sweden	1–5	87	–1	–1
Total (approx.)	1,000–2,600			

Trends	+2 Large increase	+1 Small increase	0 Stable	X Extinct
(1970-1990)	–2 Large decrease	–1 Small decrease	F Fluctuating	N New breeder

Data quality **Bold**: reliable quantitative data   Normal type: incomplete quantitative data   Bracketed figures: no quantitative data   * Data quality not provided

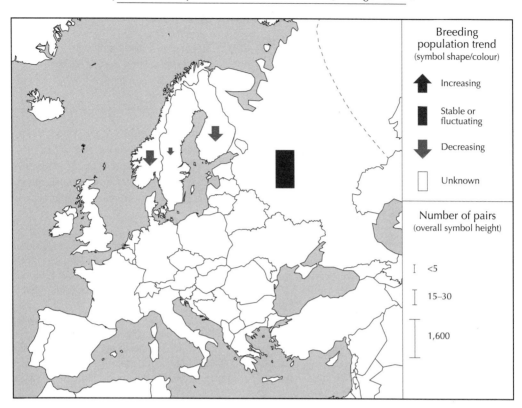

■ Conservation measures

In order to prepare a conservation plan for the Lesser White-fronted Goose there is an urgent need for further information on the location of staging and wintering grounds, the ecological requirements of the species and threats to the populations. On the breeding grounds, measures should be taken to minimize disturbance pressures and to prevent further habitat loss and degradation. Spring staging areas should be managed (where necessary) by reintroduction of hay-cutting and cattle-grazing to meet the needs of the geese.

In Sweden a reintroduction scheme has been in operation since the early 1980s, using Barnacle Geese *Branta leucopsis* to foster broods of Lesser White-front goslings. The intention is to change the migration routes of the Lesser White-fronted Goose population from the original south-easterly direction to a south-west movement, towards wintering grounds in the Netherlands, where the birds are better safeguarded (von Essen 1991, 1993). So far there has been only one (assumed) pair nesting, although a group of about 50 birds is now wintering in the Netherlands; the birds do remain, however, relatively tame (von Essen 1993). In Finland a re-stocking project has been operating since 1988, although no effects have been observed so far (J. Markkola pers. comm.).

JESPER MADSEN

Barnacle Goose
Branta leucopsis

SPEC Category 4, breeding; 2, winter
Status Secure, breeding; Localized, winter
Criteria Localized, winter

The Barnacle Goose is restricted to Europe where three discrete populations breed: in north-east Greenland, Svalbard, and northern Russia and the Baltic. All three populations winter in Scotland, Ireland and the Netherlands, and are susceptible because they concentrate at a small number of sites. These sites therefore require protection, but, as the species feeds primarily on pastures during winter, there are potential conflicts with agricultural interests. Schemes to alleviate these problems are thus also required.

■ Distribution and population trends

There are three populations of Barnacle Goose in the world, all of which breed and winter in Europe, with very little interchange of individuals taking place between them. The north-east Greenland population winters in western Scotland and Ireland, stopping over on spring migration in Iceland; the population breeding in Svalbard winters on the Solway Firth in south-west Scotland (United Kingdom, Important Bird Area 133), stopping over in spring in Helgeland in Norway; and the north Russian population winters in the Netherlands and stops over in spring in Germany, Sweden and Estonia. Since the 1970s some of the birds wintering in the Netherlands have started to breed on islands in the Baltic (Larsson *et al.* 1988).

The north-east Greenland population has increased from approximately 14,000 individuals in the 1960s to 25,000–32,000 in the 1980s (Ogilvie 1983), and the Svalbard population increased from less than 1,000 birds in the 1950s to approximately 13,000 in 1993 (Owen 1984, Wildfowl and Wetlands Trust 1994 unpubl.). The entire Russian population increased from approximately 50,000 birds in the 1970s to 120,000–130,000 in the late 1980s (Ebbinge 1982 and unpubl.). Since 1971 a colony has devel-oped rapidly on the islands of Gotland and Öland in the Baltic, and this numbered approximately 1,000 breeding pairs in 1988 (Larsson *et al.* 1988 and unpubl.). Colonies have also become established in Estonia.

In winter the species is concentrated at a few sites (see population table, Important Bird Area table, map). Increasing numbers stop over in Denmark (3,000–9,000 birds: Jörgensen *et al.* 1994), and a maximum of 66,000 did so in Germany in spring 1988 (Prokosch 1991).

Important Bird Areas The top ten IBAs for wintering Barnacle Geese in Europe, together holding over 90% of the total European wintering population.

Netherlands	001	Waddenzee
	008	Schiermonnikoog
	010	Groningen buitendijks
	017	Oudegnaasterbrekken, Fluessen, Groote Gaastmeer and Morra
	019	Steile Bank, Mokkebank and Sondeler Leyen
	022	Sneekermeer and Terkaplester Poelen
	023	Oude Venen and De Deelen
	047	Haringvliet and Hollands Diep (including Oudeland van Strijen)
United Kingdom	093	Islay: Loch Gruinart
	133	Upper Solway Flats and Marshes

■ Ecology

In the Arctic the Barnacle Goose nests on islets free from Arctic foxes *Alopex lagopus* or on steep cliffs inland, and forages on a variety of tundra plant species (Prop *et al.* 1984). The young are raised amongst vegetation along the fringes of ponds or rivers. In the Baltic the geese nest on low islets.

Barnacle Geese roost in winter on sheltered coasts and feed mainly on cultivated grasslands in the vicinity of the roost (Percival 1991). In spring they shift from cultivated grasslands onto saltmarshes (Prins and Ydenberg 1985), but in the Baltic, Nor-

	Winter population			Winter
	Size (individuals)	Year	Trend	range trend
Austria	**0–1**	—	F	F
Belgium	**10–100**	85–91	F	0
Denmark	**0–2,000**	91	+2	—
Finland	**0–10**	92	N	N
France	**5–20**	89	0	0
Germany	**22,300–22,300**	93	+1	—
Rep. of Ireland	**7,000–8,000**	—	0	—
Netherlands	**50,000–120,000**	79–89	+2	+1
Romania	(0–1)	—	(0)	(0)
Spain	**0–3**	—	F	—
United Kingdom	**33,000–33,000**	88	+1	0
Isle of Man	0–1	—	0	0*
Total (min., approx.) 110,000				

Trends   +2 Large increase   +1 Small increase   0 Stable   X Extinct
(1970–1990) –2 Large decrease   –1 Small decrease   F Fluctuating   N New breeder
Data quality **Bold**: reliable quantitative data   Normal type: incomplete quantitative data
Bracketed figures: no quantitative data   * Data quality not provided

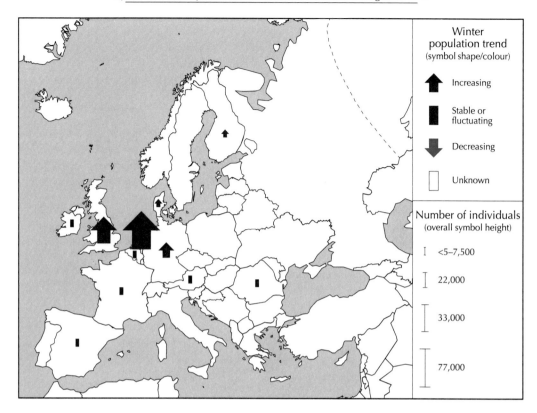

Winter population trend (symbol shape/colour)

Increasing

Stable or fluctuating

Decreasing

Unknown

Number of individuals (overall symbol height)

<5–7,500

22,000

33,000

77,000

way and Iceland agricultural fields are now becoming increasingly important as feeding areas at this season.

■ Threats

With the exception of Greenland, the Barnacle Goose is protected throughout its range, though the species' utilization of pastures during winter has led to conflicts with agriculture in many areas. On Islay in Scotland in the 1980s licences were granted to kill Barnacle Geese in order to alleviate the agricultural damage being caused and to prevent further increases in numbers, and between 447 and 956 were killed annually (J. Brodie in Owen and Pienkowski 1991). In Ireland and Norway feeding conditions have deteriorated on the traditional islands used by the geese due to a reduction in grazing by livestock and the consequent growth of vegetation beyond suitable levels for cropping by the geese (D. Cabot unpubl., Black *et al*. 1991).

In eastern Greenland, Jameson Land, the largest known moulting site, has been threatened by the proposed exploitation of oil resources (Madsen 1984), but these activities have recently been cancelled.

■ Conservation measures

In the Solway Firth and on Islay in Scotland, refuges have been established to create undisturbed and managed feeding areas for the geese (Owen and Pienkowski 1991), and on the Norwegian staging grounds vegetation management is deployed to improve feeding conditions. On Islay, management agreements are now offered to farmers to support sympathetic management for geese, removing the need to shoot under licence to avoid goose damage to crops. The regular re-seeding and fertilizing of grasslands greatly increases the number of geese that can be supported during the winter (Percival 1993), and this may be a means by which feeding conditions can be improved on refuge areas.

JESPER MADSEN

Brent Goose
Branta bernicla

SPEC Category 3
Status Vulnerable
Criteria <2,500 pairs; Localized, winter

Within Europe the Brent Goose is a rare breeder, confined to Greenland, Svalbard and Russia; the Svalbard population is small and isolated, and thus particularly susceptible to threats. All three populations winter in north-west Europe in discrete locations where they feed mainly in the intertidal zone and are thus threatened by pollution, recreation and development pressures. The species feeds increasingly in farmland areas, where it does cause damage.

■ Distribution and population trends

Within Europe Brent Geese breed mainly in north-east Greenland and Svalbard with small numbers also in Russia (see population table, map). In winter three discrete populations occur on the coasts of north-west Europe: the Dark-bellied Brent Goose *B. b. bernicla* of Siberia, wintering primarily in England and France, and concentrating in spring in the Dutch, German and Danish Wadden Sea; the Canadian/north Greenland population of Light-bellied Brent Goose *B. b. hrota* wintering in Ireland and stopping over in Iceland in spring; and the Svalbard Light-bellied Brent Goose which winters in Denmark and north-east England and stops over in Denmark in spring. Important wintering sites are given in the Important Bird Area table.

Dark-bellied Brent Geese, of which only a tiny proportion breeds in European Russia, have increased from about 40,000 birds in the 1960s to 200,000–300,000 in the early 1990s (Ebbinge 1991, Summers and Underhill 1991, IWRB Goose Research Group unpubl.). During the same period the Canadian/Greenland population of Light-bellied Brent Goose increased from 8,000–13,000 to 18,000–24,000 birds (Madsen 1991); the north-east Greenland segment probably does not exceed 1,000 birds (Hjort *et al.* 1987). Numbers in Svalbard increased from 2,000 birds in the 1960s to 4,000–5,000 in the early 1990s, but this remains one of the smallest goose populations in the world (Madsen 1991 and unpubl.).

Important Bird Areas The top ten IBAs for wintering Brent Geese in Europe, together holding over 90% of the total European wintering population.

France	063	Golfe du Morbihan, marais de Suscinio et Ile de Meaban
	068	Anse du Fiers d'Ars-en-Ré
	070	Ile d'Oléron, marais de Brouage et la Gripperie Saint Symphorien
	086	Bassin d'Arcachon et Banc d'Arguin
Netherlands	001	Waddenzee
United Kingdom	164	The Wash
	176	Blackwater, Colne and Dengie
	178	Foulness and Maplin Sands
	196	Chichester and Langstone Harbours
	252	Strangford Lough and islands

■ Ecology

Breeding occurs in the high Arctic, in colonies on islets or solitarily on mainland coasts. Birds forage in grass and sedge vegetation along coasts and river deltas. Nesting success from year to year (in Svalbard at least) depends strongly on the level of predation pressure from Arctic foxes *Alopex lagopus* and polar bears *Ursus maritimus* (Madsen *et al.* 1989, 1992) and on the time of snow-melt.

In autumn and winter, Brent Geese feed primarily on algae and *Zostera* spp. growing on intertidal mudflats and in spring on saltmarsh vegetation (e.g. O'Briain and Healy 1991). However, following the population increases which have taken place, Dark-bellied Brent Geese in particular also frequently graze on cultivated grassland and winter cereal fields in coastal regions (Charman 1979).

■ Threats

During the summer Brent Geese are in remote areas where they are not severely threatened by human activities, though the Svalbard breeding population remains susceptible due to its small size. Furthermore, this and other populations of the species are under some threat on their wintering grounds and staging areas, as the intertidal zone is under consid-

	Breeding population			Breeding
	Size (pairs)	Year	Trend	range trend
Denmark				
Greenland	100–300	85	(0)	(0)
Norway				
Svalbard	**1,000–1,000**	82–86	0	0
Russia	(10–100)	—	F	F
Total (approx.)	1,100–1,400			

Trends   +2 Large increase   +1 Small increase   0 Stable   X Extinct
(1970-1990)   –2 Large decrease   –1 Small decrease   F Fluctuating   N New breeder
Data quality **Bold**: reliable quantitative data   Normal type: incomplete quantitative data
              Bracketed figures: no quantitative data   * Data quality not provided

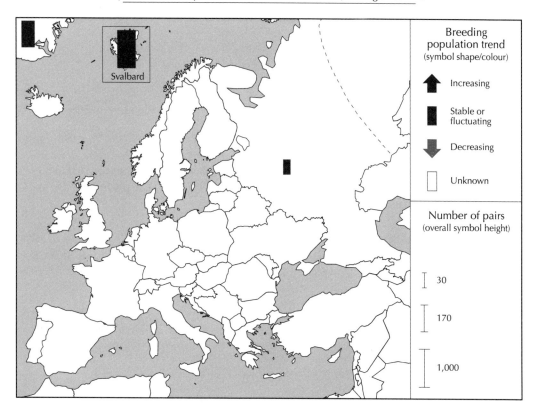

Breeding
population trend
(symbol shape/colour)

Increasing

Stable or
fluctuating

Decreasing

Unknown

Number of pairs
(overall symbol height)

30

170

1,000

erable pressure generally from development activities, pollution (such as that which leads to eutrophication) and recreational activities. In several areas, the lack of management of saltmarshes has reduced the extent of areas suitable for geese to feed on (Clausen 1991). This is a major threat to the Svalbard breeding population, together with the disappearance of *Zostera* due to eutrophication and heavy disturbance from hunting.

The habit of feeding on agricultural areas inland has led to conflicts with farming interests in the Netherlands, Germany, and especially in the United Kingdom where geese are shot under licence to prevent damage to crops in spring (Owen 1992).

■ Conservation measures

To prevent conflicts with agriculture, alternative feeding sites for Brent Geese have been established in England and the Netherlands (Oostenbrugge *et al.* 1992, Owen 1992). Compensation is paid to farmers in the Netherlands suffering damage from geese, and in the German Wadden Sea farmers are subsidized to accept the foraging geese.

In Denmark the improved management of saltmarshes is necessary to improve feeding conditions for the vulnerable Svalbard breeding population of the Light-bellied Brent Goose.

In some countries where Dark-bellied Brent Geese winter, hunters are calling for a resumption of shooting which has not been allowed since 1972. In the event of hunting re-starting, over-exploitation and undesirable disturbance to natural habitats must be avoided. An international management plan, including policies on shooting and crop damage, should be agreed before shooting is resumed in individual countries.

JESPER MADSEN

Red-breasted Goose
Branta ruficollis

SPEC Category 1, winter
Status Localized
Criteria Localized

The world population of the Red-breasted Goose winters almost entirely in Romania and Bulgaria, where about 75,000 individuals were estimated to be present in the early 1990s. This winter population concentrates at only three or four roosts, and relies on the surrounding winter cereal fields for foraging. Consequently, the species is highly vulnerable to changes in land-use and to disturbance on its wintering areas, and is globally threatened.

■ Distribution and population trends

Red-breasted Geese breed in northern Siberia to the east of the Urals. They occur on passage and in winter in Europe, with autumn staging areas along the Ukrainian Black Sea coast (Danube delta and associated lagoons), and almost the entire world population winters along the Black Sea coasts of Romania (Danube delta and associated lagoons to the south) and Bulgaria (Lake Durankulak and Lake Shapla, both on the northern coast) (see population table, Important Bird Area table, map). The geese shift between the Romanian and Bulgarian sites, probably depending on weather conditions. Small flocks occur occasionally on passage or as vagrants in north-east Greece (Handrinos 1991) and in other parts of Europe.

In the 1980s the world population, based on counts in the wintering areas, was estimated at approximately 35,000 individuals (Madsen 1991). One of the most comprehensive surveys ever, in winter 1992/3, estimated the world population at 74,000–75,000, given simultaneous peak counts in Romania and Bulgaria of 14,650 and 59,206 respectively (J. Black *in litt.*, J. Madsen *in litt.*). Rather than a true population increase, it is likely that this upward trend reflects a shift of birds to Bulgaria and Romania from wintering grounds further to the east, outside Europe. This is supported by the observed decreases

in the population in the west Caspian area, where large numbers formerly wintered: up to 60,000 birds were recorded in the Caspian region in the 1950s compared with just 1,000–2,000 since 1968 (Cramp and Simmons 1977).

Although probably stable in population size, the species is classified as Globally Threatened due to its extreme concentration in winter (Collar *et al*. 1994).

Important Bird Areas The major IBAs for wintering Red-breasted Geese in Europe, together holding over 90% of the total European wintering population.

Azerbaijan	077	Kirov Bay, Caspian Sea
Bulgaria	006	Shabla-Ezeretz complex
	009	Lake Durankulak
	017	Cape Kaliakra
Greece	001	Delta Evrou (Evros Delta)
Romania	001	Delta Dunarii (Danube Delta) and Razelm-Sinoie complex
Russia	060	Eastern Manych, Ozero (Lake) Manych-Gudilo (irregularly used site)
Ukraine	052	Yagorlystski and Tendra Bays

■ Ecology

During winter Red-breasted Geese roost together with large concentrations of White-fronted Geese *Anser albifrons* in lagoons or lakes along the Black Sea coast. These flocks feed during the day on surrounding farmland habitat, principally away from human habitation in large, winter-wheat fields on flat ground, which may be located up to 40 km inland from the roosts (Vangeluwe and Stassin 1991, Sutherland and Crockford 1993). The geese graze the green parts of the vegetation. Habitat requirements at the migratory staging posts are not known.

■ Threats

The fact that the majority of the world population of the Red-breasted Goose concentrates at three or four roosting sites in Bulgaria and Romania during winter

	Winter population			Winter
	Size (individuals)	Year	Trend	range trend
Austria	**0–3**	—	F	F
Bulgaria	**59,206–59,206**	92/93	+2	+1
Germany	(1–8)	—	(+1)	—
Greece	**0–116**	87–91	0	0
Netherlands	**5–25**	79–83	F	0
Romania	**14,650–14,650**	92/93	+1	+1
Slovakia	(0–2)	—	—	—
Ukraine	**2,600–3,000**	80	F	F
Total (min., approx.)	76,000			

Trends	+2 Large increase	+1 Small increase	0 Stable	X Extinct
(1970–1990)	–2 Large decrease	–1 Small decrease	F Fluctuating	N New breeder
Data quality	**Bold:** reliable quantitative data	Normal type: incomplete quantitative data		
	Bracketed figures: no quantitative data	* Data quality not provided		

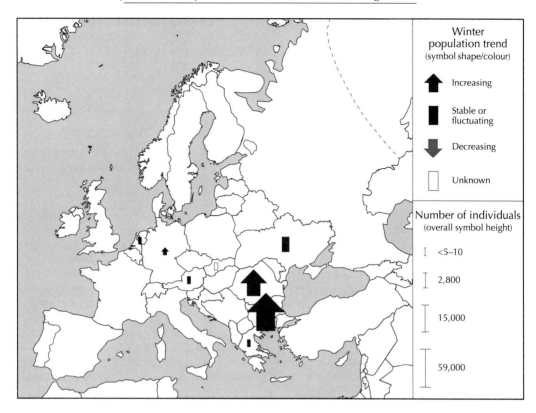

makes the species vulnerable to disturbance and habitat degradation (see Important Bird Area table). Despite being fully protected in both countries, illegal hunting occurs, especially during the morning roost flights (Black and Madsen 1993). Furthermore, since the political changes in these countries, disturbance from shooting at the roosts has become an increasing problem, partly because hunters tend not to respect fences and regulations and partly because of an increase in hunting-tourism from western countries to these areas.

Agricultural policies are likely to change in Bulgaria and Romania towards the establishment of smaller privatized farm units, together perhaps with changes to the types of crops grown which may be unfavourable for Red-breasted Geese. At present, such changes are not regarded as a severe problem in either country (Munteanu 1992), but they may in-

crease. Indeed, the westward shift of the wintering population is thought to be the result of adverse land-use changes in the Caspian Sea area, from cereal crops to vineyards (Collar and Andrew 1988).

■ Conservation measures

It is necessary, especially in Bulgaria, to regulate hunting at the roosts so that they are not disturbed. In view of the potential changes in land-use practices, any policies or plans that may influence land-use in the Dobrogea region of Romania and in Bulgaria should ensure the maintenance of suitable winter feeding habitat for Red-breasted Geese.

The reasons behind the recent shift in winter distribution need to be investigated, and information should be collected on the current conditions at the staging areas in the Ukraine.

JESPER MADSEN

Ruddy Shelduck
Tadorna ferruginea

SPEC Category 3
Status Vulnerable
Criteria Large decline

Following a previous long-term decline of this rather scarce duck of south-east Europe, the breeding population has probably declined further in recent years. The most likely causes are widespread wetland loss and degradation. Broad measures for wetland conservation are therefore necessary together with the strict protection of key wintering sites.

■ Distribution and population trends

The European Ruddy Shelduck population is restricted to the south-east of the region. The majority of the global population lies further east, breeding in the forest-steppe and steppe regions of central Asia and wintering in southern Asia (Rogacheva 1992). Nomadism predominates in the fragments of its range which lie within North Africa and, to a lesser extent, in Europe (Vielliard 1970).

The North African population, which once wintered regularly in Spain, is now stable but no longer migrates northwards to Europe. Consequently, the only European population is in the Black Sea region, concentrated around a largely nomadic population in Turkey which recent fieldwork suggests is in the order of 4,000–8,000 pairs (see table, map).

Although major decreases in breeding population size and range were recorded during the early part of the twentieth century in Bulgaria, Romania and the western parts of the former U.S.S.R. (Dementiev and Gladkov 1952, Cramp and Simmons 1977), recent trends between 1970 and 1990 do not show a consistent pattern. Increases were observed in Bulgaria and Russia, but further declines were recorded in Ukraine and Romania, with decreases of over 50% in the latter. The Turkish population is not monitored during the breeding season, but is thought to have undergone a recent and rapid decline on the basis of data from mid-winter counts. Turkish breeding birds

are mainly resident though dispersive and, although added to by some southwards dispersal from other Black Sea countries, winter trends in Turkey probably mainly reflect breeding trends there.

Monval and Pirot (1989) gave a mean annual figure of 3,960 birds counted in Turkey in winters between 1985/6 and 1987/8. The counts used to produce this figure come from the International Waterfowl Census. They show a rapid decline: 4,019 in 1985/6, 4,808 in 1986/7, 3,064 in 1987/8, 1,643 in 1988/9, 1,357 in 1989/90, 2,845 in 1991/2 and 711 in 1992/3. Accompanying the decline in national totals of Ruddy Shelduck is a comparable decline at the four most important known wintering sites (Tuz Gölü, Tuzla Gölü, Karapinar Ovasi and the Eregli marshes) which held a combined total of only 65 birds when last surveyed in 1990. The current European breeding population of at least 6,000 pairs is, however, still consistent with the previous estimate of 20,000 wintering birds by Monval and Pirot (1989) in the 1980s. This suggests either that the wintering population was previously underestimated or that the recorded decline is only apparent and due to the birds wintering in a more dispersed fashion throughout Turkey. Indeed, there have been slightly increased numbers at regularly counted but traditionally less-preferred wintering sites, and this is consistent with the nomadic and rather opportunistic behaviour of the species. The only alternatives are a shift of wintering grounds towards eastern Turkey or an increased proportion joining migratory birds breeding in Asia and wintering in the Middle East—but for these possibilities there is no evidence.

Clearly, given the rapid nature of the fall in recorded numbers, and the lack of clear evidence to the contrary, it should be assumed that a real decline has taken place.

■ Ecology

The Ruddy Shelduck breeds and winters in association with shallow, sparsely vegetated marshes and lakes in semi-arid regions. Shallow, brackish waterbodies are preferred, with vegetation-free areas for

	Breeding population			Breeding
	Size (pairs)	Year	Trend	range trend
Albania	(0–10)	80	—	—
Bulgaria	50–150	—	+1	+1
Greece	10–40	—	−1	−1
Moldova	3–8	88	—	−1
Romania	(5–10)	—	**−2**	(−1)
Russia	1,900–2,900	—	+1	+1
Turkey	4,000–8,000	—	−1	0
Ukraine	125–180	84	−1	−1
Total (approx.)	6,100–11,000			

Trends	+2 Large increase	+1 Small increase	0 Stable	X Extinct
(1970–1990)	−2 Large decrease	−1 Small decrease	F Fluctuating	N New breeder
Data quality	**Bold**: reliable quantitative data	Normal type: incomplete quantitative data		
	Bracketed figures: no quantitative data	* Data quality not provided		

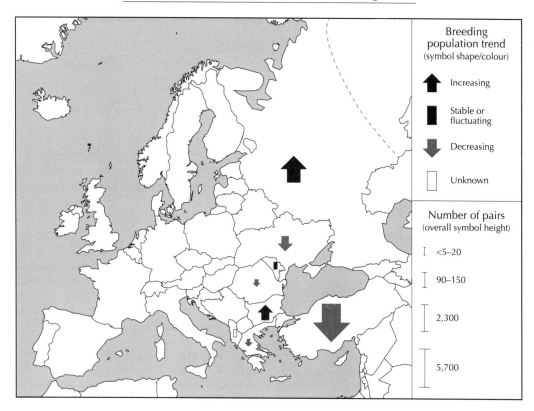

Breeding
population trend
(symbol shape/colour)

Increasing

Stable or
fluctuating

Decreasing

Unknown

Number of pairs
(overall symbol height)

<5–20

90–150

2,300

5,700

feeding; unlike many Anatidae, breeding sites at high altitudes are readily accepted (Cramp and Simmons 1977). The species also depends much less on water-bodies for resting and feeding than do other Anatidae, with individuals often being found a considerable distance from water in the breeding season.

The species is omnivorous, feeding frequently on land, where plant material is the predominant food, but insects (especially locusts) and other invertebrates are also commonly taken (Dementiev and Gladkov 1952, Cramp and Simmons 1977).

Flocking behaviour is variable, depending on climatic conditions. Severe winter weather can lead to altitudinal migration (Vielliard 1970) and consequently to high concentrations of birds in lowland regions surrounding the areas normally occupied.

■ Threats

Key wetland habitat for Ruddy Shelducks is often temporary or has variable water-levels (Vielliard 1970). Thus the wide-scale drainage of shallow marshes and lakes in the semi-arid regions of southeast Europe, particularly the semi-permanent wetlands, has almost certainly led to the long-term range retraction and recent population declines of this species. In Turkey this has been particularly pronounced at the key central Anatolian wintering sites, which have all lost concentrations of Ruddy Shelduck in winter; these have no protected status, suffer much hunting, and are threatened by overgrazing, increasing salt extraction and most importantly by a decreasing water-supply as a result of upstream irrigation systems (van den Berk *et al.* 1985, EPFT 1989).

■ Conservation measures

In Europe there are currently no conservation initiatives for this species, and its nomadic habits limit the effectiveness of continuing site-based protection schemes. Protective measures are, however, required for the key central Anatolian wintering sites mentioned above. Broader legislation to prevent further habitat loss around the Black Sea is hampered by political instability and the need for economic growth and development in the region. Within Asia, conservation measures have halted and possibly reversed the range retraction (Rogacheva 1992), and wintering numbers show no signs of decrease. Details of these measures need to be researched and, if possible, applied urgently in Europe where the situation is distinctly less favourable.

PAUL ROSE

Gadwall
Anas strepera

SPEC Category 3
Status Vulnerable
Criteria Large decline

There is currently a decline in Russia, where most European breeding birds occur, due largely to wetland loss and human disturbance. As a migratory species, the Gadwall requires the maintenance of suitable habitat, primarily through the wise use of wetlands, both in its breeding grounds and throughout its flyways. Reductions in disturbance are also necessary, particularly in important breeding areas and where birds congregate in winter.

■ Distribution and population trends

The extensive breeding range of the Gadwall stretches throughout the temperate Palearctic and Nearctic. In the Palearctic, it nests mainly from the steppes of western and central Russia east to Lake Baykal. It has a patchy distribution throughout Europe, as a result of a westward expansion commencing early in the nineteenth century when the species reached as far west as Iceland (Faber 1822).

	Breeding population			Breeding range trend
	Size (pairs)	Year	Trend	
Albania	(0–5)	64	—	—
Austria	70–90	87–88	0	0
Belarus	100–200	90	0	0
Belgium	**200–235**	90	+1	+1
Bulgaria	30–100	—	0	0
Croatia	3–5 *	—	0*	0*
Czech Republic	**1,500–3,000**	—	+1	0
Denmark	**182–182**	89	+1	(+1)
Estonia	(200–500)	—	(+2)	+1
Finland	**70–130**	92	+2	+2
France	**1,000–1,200**	82	–1	+1
Germany	8,000–8,000	85	0	**0**
Greece	20–50	—	(0)	(–1)
Hungary	100–200	—	+1	0
Iceland	200–300	75–89	F	0
Rep. of Ireland	15–15	90	+2	+1
Italy	20–50	84	(N)	(N)
Latvia	100–300	—	+2	+2
Lithuania	(10–100)	85–88	(0)	(0)
Moldova	**500–800**	89	–1	–1
Netherlands	**1,600–2,400**	79	+2	+2
Norway	0–10	90	F	+1
Poland	1,200–1,700	—	+1	0
Portugal	**200–300**	91	+2	+1
Romania	(2,000–5,000)	—	(–1)	(0)
Russia	55,000–85,000	—	–1	F
Slovakia	50–80	—	(F)	0
Spain	650–1,120	—	+1	+1
Sweden	**300–500**	87	+1	+1
Switzerland	**1–14**	86–91	+1	0
Turkey	500–5,000	—	(0)	0
Ukraine	**700–800**	83	–2	–2
United Kingdom	**790–790**	90	+1	+2
Total (approx.)	75,000–120,000			

Trends (1970–1990): +2 Large increase +1 Small increase 0 Stable –1 Small decrease –2 Large decrease F Fluctuating X Extinct N New breeder
Data quality: **Bold**: reliable quantitative data Normal type: incomplete quantitative data Bracketed figures: no quantitative data * Data quality not provided

Probably almost three-quarters of the European breeding population occurs in Russia, where, although it has shown large fluctuations related to weather conditions (Dementiev and Gladkov 1952), it has consistently declined during 1970–1990 (see table, map). During the same period the breeding range expanded northwards in Russia, although this does not compensate for the overall decline. Numbers also fell in the Ukraine (by over 50%), Moldova and probably in Romania (see table, map). At the same time breeding populations have increased in most other countries throughout much of northern, western and central Europe (Rutshke 1989; see table, map), primarily through an increase in suitable lowland eutrophic waters, such as reservoirs and flooded gravel pits. This expansion is relatively small, however, and does not compensate for declines further east, especially in Russia.

The north-west European wintering population of some 25,000 birds, including resident birds and those breeding in northern Germany, Poland, southern Sweden and west-central Russia, has shown a dramatic increase since the 1970s (Cramp and Simmons 1977, Monval and Pirot 1989, Rose and Scott 1994), reflecting increases in breeding populations in the region. Winter data from the Black Sea and Mediterranean regions, which together hold some 75,000 birds and include breeders from central Europe, the Balkans and south-central Russia, suggest that these populations are probably stable. However, current numbers in the eastern Mediterranean are substantially lower than in the 1970s (Monval and Pirot 1989).

■ Ecology

The Gadwall is mainly a continental, mid-latitude species of open lowland terrain, which has recently colonized more oceanic climatic regions. It forages almost exclusively on the green parts of plants, particularly emergent and submergent macrophytes (Cramp and Simmons 1977). It relies on the con-

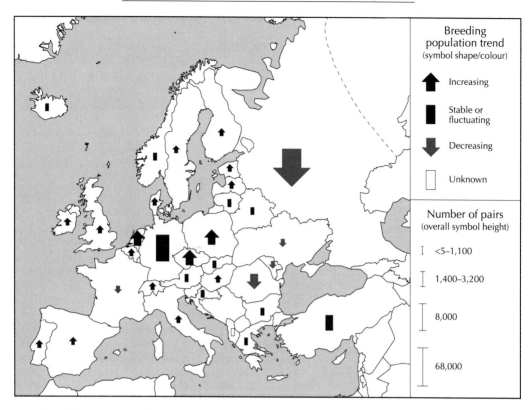

Breeding population trend (symbol shape/colour)

- Increasing
- Stable or fluctuating
- Decreasing
- Unknown

Number of pairs (overall symbol height)

- <5–1,100
- 1,400–3,200
- 8,000
- 68,000

sumption of large amounts of relatively poor quality forage (Mayhew 1988), and is therefore susceptible to disturbance and tends to be restricted to areas where the biomass of food plants is high, predominantly in eutrophic or hypereutrophic waters.

Much of the expansion of breeding and wintering numbers in the United Kingdom has occurred on gravel pits and reservoirs (Fox 1988, Fox and Salmon 1989) where this dabbling duck steals food from Coots *Fulica atra* which bring macrophytes up from deeper water normally inaccessible to the Gadwall. Such a relationship has been reported from France and Spain also, where the species forages in brackish lagoons, predominantly on *Potamogeton pectinatus* (e.g. Amat and Soriguer 1984).

■ Threats

The major threats are disturbance, and loss and modification of habitat. In Russia habitat loss is predominantly the result of wetland drainage and flooding of large river valleys for reservoirs. Shallow eutrophic waters across Europe are greatly threatened by continued eutrophication through increased nitrate and phosphate inputs and, in northern waters, groundwater acidification. Shallow waters are most vulnerable to hydrological modification and land-use change. Increasing desertification of habitats in central Russia is also thought to contribute to the Gadwall's decline there.

Increasing human disturbance at wetlands is also believed to be a cause of the decline in Russia. Indeed, the species' high representation on reserves in the United Kingdom underlines its sensitivity to disturbance; the low-quality diet necessitates prolonged periods of undisturbed foraging.

The impact of hunting on European birds has not been assessed.

■ Conservation measures

Conservation of the species' wetland breeding habitats is clearly essential and a priority in eastern Europe. Wise use of wetlands in this area should be promoted to reduce pressures on this population. Measures should also be taken to avoid further eutrophication of nutrient-rich waters, detrimental hydrological changes to shallow wetlands and human disturbance at regularly visited but important breeding areas.

Because Gadwalls are vulnerable to disturbance, the provision of refuges is important, particularly where the species congregates in winter. Also, its shallow water habitats are amongst the first to freeze in hard weather, and the establishment of a network of refuges at sites known to be important during severe winters therefore remains a priority.

TONY FOX AND V. G. VINOGRADOV

Pintail
Anas acuta

SPEC Category 3
Status Vulnerable
Criteria Large decline

Over 90% of the European population declined slowly but steadily during 1970–1990, due primarily to wetland loss and degradation both on its breeding and wintering grounds. Conservation and restoration of wetlands, as well as reduction of hunting pressure, is necessary. Further censuses and monitoring of breeding and wintering populations are needed.

■ Distribution and population trends

The Pintail has a circumboreal distribution across Eurasia and North America. Roughly a tenth of its population breeds in Europe of which over 90% is in European Russia, mainly at 60–70°N. Other breeding strongholds are in Fennoscandia and Iceland (see table), with other breeding areas scattered across north-west and central Europe, the Hungarian basin, southern Russia and Turkey. The European population size is uncertain due to serious methodological problems with censusing (Rutschke 1989).

The species is migratory, with about 1 million individuals (from Europe and Africa) wintering in tropical Africa, especially in the Senegal, Inner Niger and Lake Chad basins (Perennou 1991). Most of the remainder (300,000 birds), winter in the Mediterra-

nean region, mainly Spain, Greece and Turkey with appreciable numbers in the northern Black Sea (Monval and Pirot 1989). Lower numbers (70,000 individuals) winter in north-west Europe.

Breeding numbers have shown an overall long-term decline, and the range has contracted in central Europe. In the early nineteenth century the species was fairly widespread across the German–Polish–Lithuanian lowlands but is now rare (Rutschke 1989, Tomialojc 1990, see table, map), and breeding numbers appear to have decreased in many European countries, most importantly in southern and central Russia (Krivenko 1984) and Finland (see table, map).

In winter the Pintail is highly concentrated, facilitating relatively complete counts. Although the north-west European wintering population has fluctuated, it appears to have been stable from 1967 to 1986, though recent data suggest decreasing annual peaks at some key sites (P. Rose pers. comm.). Within the Mediterranean wintering grounds Pintail have been well counted in the west but very poorly so in the east. The west Mediterranean wintering population showed a clear increase from 1969 to 1973 followed by a steady decline (averaging 15% per year) until 1982 after which marked peaks in some years have prevented assessments of trends (Monval and Pirot 1989). In the east Mediterranean the poorer data suggest that declines in winter totals have probably been even more pronounced (P. Rose pers. comm.).

■ Ecology

The extensive open areas used for breeding include tundra, treeless river valleys and large fens, and wetlands in the steppe and forest zones. Highest densities occur in the forest-tundra ecotone where Pintails can be very numerous (Dementiev and Gladkov 1952). Periodically inundated grasslands around larger water-bodies are clearly preferred. Nests, generally placed in clumps of tall grass or other vegetation, are scattered widely, except on islets where loose colonies may form (Rutschke 1989).

Birds feed omnivorously in shallow water; animal food predominates on the breeding grounds while

| | Breeding population | | | Breeding |
	Size (pairs)	Year	Trend	range trend
Austria	1–3	82–89	–1	–1
Belarus	70–150	90	F	0
Bulgaria	10–20	—	0	0
Czech Republic	**0–5**	—	F	F
Denmark	**200–250**	88	(–1)	(–1)
Faroe Islands	(0–1)	81	(F)	(F)
Estonia	200–300	—	–1	0
Finland	20,000–30,000	92	–1	**0**
France	5–10	89	0	0
Germany	20–60	—	0	**0**
Hungary	30–50	—	0	0
Iceland	500–500	—	F	0
Latvia	0–50	—	0	F
Lithuania	(1–5)	85–88	(–1)	(–1)
Netherlands	35–65 *	89–91	F	0
Norway	200–1,000	90	0	**0**
Poland	40–60	—	–2	0
Romania	0–3	—	(F)	(0)
Russia	150,000–300,000	—	–1	0
Slovakia	0–10	—	F	F*
Spain	10–50	—	F	F
Sweden	700–2,000	87	0	0
Switzerland	**0–1**	86–91	N	N
Turkey	(500–1,000)	—	—	—
Ukraine	150–280	82	**-2**	**–1**
United Kingdom	**30–40**	88–91	**0**	**0**
Total (approx.)	170,000–340,000			

Trends   +2 Large increase   +1 Small increase   0 Stable   X Extinct
(1970–1990)   –2 Large decrease   –1 Small decrease   F Fluctuating N New breeder
Data quality **Bold:** reliable quantitative data   Normal type: incomplete quantitative data
              Bracketed figures: no quantitative data   * Data quality not provided

122

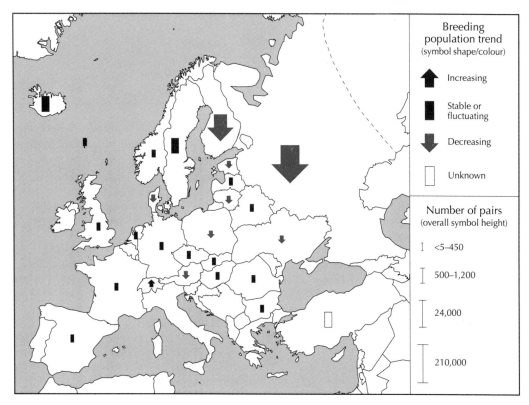

Breeding population trend
(symbol shape/colour)

Increasing

Stable or fluctuating

Decreasing

Unknown

Number of pairs
(overall symbol height)

<5–450

500–1,200

24,000

210,000

plant material is more important in winter (Cramp and Simmons 1977). Outside the breeding season Pintails form large flocks at coastal lagoons, deltas, estuaries or large inland lakes.

■ Threats

Drainage of wetlands, transformation into reservoirs and lowering of the groundwater-table have caused widespread loss of breeding habitat in Russia and appear to be the major threats there (Krivenko 1984), as probably in many other countries (Rutschke 1989).

An additional threat may be excessive hunting, chiefly in France, Russia and south-east Europe. The total European bag is at least c.220,000 per year (Hepburn 1984), while the entire West African/European wintering population is only c.1,400,000 birds.

Falls in Mediterranean wintering numbers also result almost certainly from recent large-scale wetland loss and degradation there (Hollis 1992). The intense human pressure around wintering sites in north-west Europe is a further potential threat that should be monitored closely, since Pintail rely on very few important wintering sites. The concentration of birds in winter at a few major tropical African wetlands also renders them vulnerable to threats such as recurring droughts which reduce available habitat and lead to increased human pressure on that remaining. Currently, there are plans to divert part of the Niger water from the Inner Niger delta, where up to 400,000

Pintail winter (Hughes and Hughes 1992). Irrigation schemes on rivers feeding the Hadejia–Nguru wetlands in northern Nigeria are far more advanced (Hollis *et al*. 1993). Although shelved at present, the last and largest of these schemes at Kafin Zaki, if completed, would drastically affect the wintering habitat of Pintail and (e.g.) Garganey *A. querquedula*.

■ Conservation measures

The maintenance of extensive wetlands throughout Europe is vital to conserve the breeding habitats, especially in the Russian taiga. In the south-western part the range, habitat restoration through the recreation of natural river flood cycles is required. It may also be necessary to reduce hunting pressure.

Conservation of the major wintering wetlands in the Mediterranean and Africa is also essential and requires their wise multiple-use by local communities. Within Europe the continued conservation of key wintering areas must be ensured, including Akyatan Gölü in Turkey and Anse de l'Aiguillon, Golfe du Morbihan (Important Bird Area 063) and Basin de Arcachon (IBA 086) in France.

Further monitoring of both wintering and breeding numbers is required in all areas, but particularly in the east Mediterranean and Russia.

CHRISTIAN PERENNOU, PAUL ROSE
AND LUDWIK TOMIALOJC

Garganey
Anas querquedula

SPEC Category 3
Status Vulnerable
Criteria Large decline

Although numerous, the Garganey has recently declined widely due to wetland drainage and degradation on the breeding grounds and (possibly) the winter quarters. Maintenance of extensive wetlands throughout the European range is vital, especially in the Russian taiga. A reduction in hunting, and more research and monitoring on breeding and wintering grounds, are also necessary.

■ Distribution and population trends

The breeding grounds extend right across Eurasia, and in Europe from the northern coasts of the Adriatic, Black and Caspian Seas to the southern White Sea. The size of the breeding population east of the Urals is unknown but ringing data (Roux *et al.* 1979), although old and incomplete, suggest that the majority of the world population may breed outside Europe. European birds are concentrated in middle (temperate) latitudes (Dementiev and Gladkov 1952,

	Breeding population			Breeding range trend
	Size (pairs)	Year	Trend	
Albania	0–10	92	–1	(–1)
Austria	60–70	87–88	–1	0
Belarus	25,000–36,000	90	0	**0**
Belgium	**70–105**	90	–1	–1
Bulgaria	40–50	—	0	0
Croatia	600–800 *	—	0*	0*
Czech Republic	100–180	—	–2	–1
Denmark	**91–107**	89	(–1)	(0)
Estonia	2,000–2,000	—	–1	0
Finland	**2,000–5,000**	92	F	**0**
France	230–500	92	–2	F
Germany	4,000–4,000	85	–1	**0**
Greece	0–10	—	(0)	(0)
Hungary	1,200–1,500	—	0	0
Rep. of Ireland	0–1	88–91	0	0
Italy	200–300	84	(0)	(0)
Latvia	1,000–2,000	—	–1	–1
Lithuania	3,000–5,000	85–88	(–1)	(–1)
Luxembourg	**0–1**	—	**–1**	–1
Moldova	**300–500**	89	**0**	–1
Netherlands	**1,000–1,900**	89–91	–2	–2
Norway	10–100	90	F	+1
Poland	2,500–4,000	—	–1	0
Portugal	(1–5)	89	—	—
Romania	(2,000–8,000)	—	(–1)	–1
Russia	570,000–960,000	—	–1	0
Slovakia	100–200	—	–1	–1
Slovenia	10–20	—	F	F
Spain	100–130	—	F	F
Sweden	300–500	87	–1	**0**
Switzerland	**0–2**	86–91	**F**	**0**
Turkey	(500–1,000)	—	—	—
Ukraine	26,000–29,000	88	–1	–1
United Kingdom	**40–100**	88–89	**F**	**0**
Total (approx.)	640,000–1,100,000			

Trends (1970-1990) +2 Large increase +1 Small increase 0 Stable X Extinct
−2 Large decrease −1 Small decrease F Fluctuating N New breeder
Data quality **Bold**: reliable quantitative data Normal type: incomplete quantitative data
Bracketed figures: no quantitative data * Data quality not provided

Rutschke 1989) with Russia holding about 90% of the European total, though large numbers also occur in Belarus and Ukraine (see table, map).

The species is totally migratory, wintering mainly in freshwater wetlands in tropical Africa, with only marginal numbers wintering in southern Europe. Between 1.5 and 2 million birds winter in West Africa where they concentrate in the Senegal, Inner Niger and Lake Chad basins (Perennou 1991).

For a century or so, in spite of several climate-dependent fluctuations (Bauer and Glutz von Blotzheim 1968, Ptushenko and Inozemtsev 1968), the total European population size remained high and fairly stable. Later, however, a decline first noted in central and western Europe spread over most of the continent and between 1970 and 1990 affected populations in 18 countries (see table, map), including those with large populations such as Russia, Ukraine and Romania (Krivenko 1984; see table). Comparisons of the number of breeding pairs in western Europe between 1970 and the present day suggest that numbers have fallen from 12,000–22,500 breeding pairs in the 1970s (Rutschke 1989) to less than 8,000 (see table).

■ Ecology

Garganeys breed in open lowland areas including steppe, forest-steppe, extensive wetlands and farmland, settling around lakes sheltered with vegetation, as well as in wide deforested river valleys or among extensive fens. They avoid water-bodies in taiga and in mountainous and peatbog areas (Dementiev and Gladkov 1952). For centuries the species was numerous in extensively managed wet meadows among farmland or surrounding fish-breeding ponds, but many of these sites are now too dry. The Garganey is fairly tolerant of human presence and rather wide-ranging in its selection of nest-sites and food; although omnivorous, animal material forms most of its food (Cramp and Simmons 1977).

The species is widely dispersed on its breeding grounds but highly concentrated in the African winter quarters (Perennou 1991).

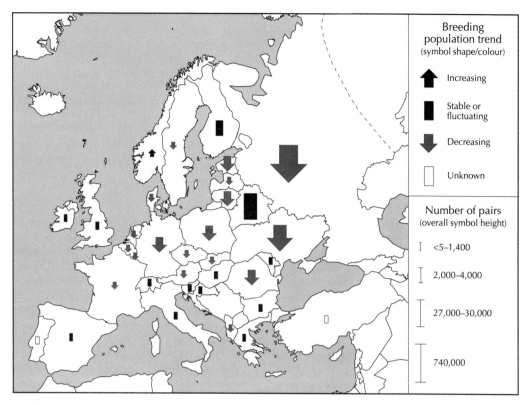

■ Threats

Increasing aridization of the climate in the centre of Europe and subsequent lowering of the water-table, drainage of wetlands, and transformation of wetlands to dammed reservoirs (chiefly in central and southeast Europe) have resulted in widespread loss or deterioration of breeding habitat (Krivenko 1984, Rutschke 1989).

Over half a million Garganey are shot in Europe each year (Rutschke 1989), but especially high numbers are taken in France, southern Russia, Ukraine and Poland, e.g. constituting up to 30% of the duck bag in the Dniepr valley (Dementiev and Gladkov 1952, Rutschke 1989).

Destruction of nests during early mowing of meadows and increasing human disturbance by tourists and anglers also affect the species (Hölzinger 1987). Additionally, Garganey are subject to lead poisoning (Hölzinger 1987) and, during hot summers, botulism (Reichholf 1983).

The concentration of birds during winter at a few major tropical African wetlands renders them vulnerable to potential threats such as recurring droughts which reduce the extent of available wetland habitat and which lead to increased human pressure on those remaining. Currently there are plans to divert part of the Niger river's water from the Inner Niger delta (where up to 1 million Garganey winter) (Hughes and Hughes 1992). Irrigation schemes on rivers feeding the Hadejia–Nguru wetlands in northern Nigeria are far more advanced (Hollis *et al.* 1993). Although shelved at present, the last and largest of these schemes at Kafin Zaki, if completed, would drastically affect the wintering habitat of the Garganey and other western Palearctic breeding populations of ducks, such as Pintail *A. acuta* and Ferruginous Duck *Aythya nyroca*.

■ Conservation measures

The maintenance of extensive wetlands throughout Europe is vital to conserve the Garganey on its breeding grounds. Wetlands important for breeding, migrating or wintering birds should be conserved under the Ramsar and Bonn Conventions, and wetland drainage and intensive grassland management must be restricted. Additionally, hunting pressure should be reduced, especially in Russia and France.

Conservation measures for major wintering wetlands in Africa are also of paramount importance. Action to ensure the wise multiple-use of wetlands by local communities is essential to ensure that they maintain their value to wildlife.

Further data on both breeding and wintering distribution and numbers are required in order to monitor trends adequately.

LUDWIK TOMIALOJC, CHRISTIAN PERENNOU
AND PAUL ROSE

Marbled Teal
Marmaronetta angustirostris

SPEC Category 1
Status Endangered
Criteria Large decline, <250 pairs

This globally threatened species has a very small European population, having undergone marked and continuing declines (with some range reduction) in the twentieth century due to habitat loss and possibly hunting. Habitat protection is urgently required, together with habitat restoration and research into the habitat requirements.

■ Distribution and population trends

About 5–10% of the world population of Marbled Teal breeds in Europe, with important concentrations in Spain, Turkey and Azerbaijan, and small numbers in Armenia and possibly Russia (Green 1993; see table, map). In winter, most European birds migrate south to North Africa and southern Asia, but important numbers often winter in Spain (up to 500 birds: L. García pers. comm. 1992).

In Spain, breeding numbers have declined by over 90% since 1900 (Valverde 1964, Amat 1982, Navarro Medina and Robledano Aymerich 1992). Numbers fluctuated between 50 and 200 pairs between 1988 and 1992 in Andalucía (Mañez 1991, Green 1993), with 3–30 pairs at four sites in Valencia (Dolz García *et al*. 1991).

In Turkey, there are an estimated 150–250 breeding pairs at c.12 sites, with a decline of over 65% in the last 25 years (Green 1993). Azerbaijan has five breeding sites with 70–200 pairs (M. V. Patrekeev *in litt*. 1992), and there are 2–15 pairs in Armenia (Adamyan 1989). The range in Azerbaijan has contracted during the twentieth century and numbers are probably still declining there.

Various small populations have become extinct: the Canary Islands (last bred 1915), France (1926), Former Yugoslav Republic of Macedonia (1937), Greece (Crete, 1925), Cyprus (1914) and the Volga delta (before 1950). Breeding probably also occurred in Italy and Hungary in the 1890s (Green 1993).

Due to the continued declines in Europe and predicted declines in south-west Asia through wetland destruction, the species is listed as Globally Threatened by Collar *et al*. (1994).

■ Ecology

Breeding is typically in shallow, fresh to brackish, eutrophic lakes and other wetlands with extensive emergent and submerged vegetation. Such sites are often very small (e.g. oxbows, ponds), but in disturbed areas larger wetlands are preferred. Nesting is usually in dense reedbeds but in Spain it also occurs in clumps of saltmarsh vegetation (e.g. *Salicornia*, *Sarcocornia* and *Arthrocnemon*). Many permanent sites are important, but breeding also occurs in temporary sites that are dry in some years.

The species often winters on wetlands without emergent vegetation, appearing to prefer recently flooded, seasonal wetlands (Green 1993).

■ Threats

Habitat loss and degradation are probably the major cause of decline. In Spain, breeding habitat has been drastically reduced during the twentieth century (Navarro Medina and Robledano Aymerich 1992, Castroviejo 1993). Valencian sites are threatened by organic pollution and a proposed motorway (Green 1993). Even in the protected part of the Marismas del Guadalquivir there has been a profound loss of Marbled Teal breeding habitat, particularly due to the diversion of two of the three streams feeding the National Park and lowering of the water-table by aquifer extraction for agriculture and tourism. This has drastically reduced the extent and duration of seasonal marshes fed by surface water and of aquifer-fed lagoons. Siltation, overgrazing and ecological change following the introduction of American crayfish are further serious problems (Castroviejo 1993). In Turkey, extensive drainage of breeding habitat has occurred in the Çukurova delta, Göksu delta and elsewhere, including the loss of the Aynaz swamp area which was an important breeding site and held over 1,200 birds in winter 1967 (Aukes *et al*. 1988). There are proposals to drain seasonal wetlands at the Göksu delta which are important for brood rearing (V. van den Berk *in litt*. 1992). Breeding sites in Azerbaijan are also currently affected by drainage (M. V. Patrekeev *in litt*. 1992).

	Breeding population			Breeding
	Size (pairs)	Year	Trend	range trend
Spain	50–230	—	–2	–2
Turkey	150–250	—	–2	—
Total (approx.)	200–480			

Trends (1970–1990) +2 Large increase +1 Small increase 0 Stable X Extinct
−2 Large decrease −1 Small decrease F Fluctuating N New breeder
Data quality **Bold**: reliable quantitative data Normal type: incomplete quantitative data
Bracketed figures: no quantitative data * Data quality not provided

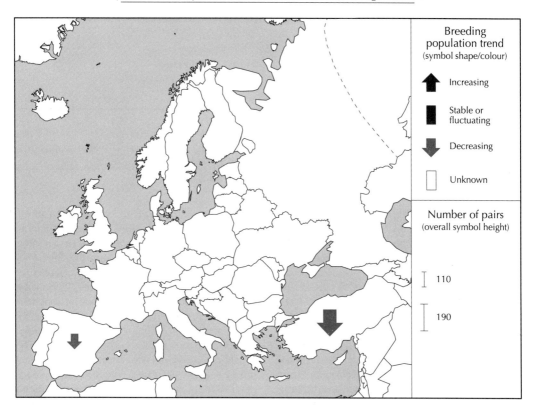

Breeding
population trend
(symbol shape/colour)

Increasing

Stable or
fluctuating

Decreasing

Unknown

Number of pairs
(overall symbol height)

110

190

Hunting is a serious threat. It has probably contributed to the decline in Turkey (e.g. Gürpinar and Wilkinson 1970), and in Spain 74 birds were shot at two sites in Valencia in the winter of 1981/2 alone (J. D. Navarro Medina *in litt.* 1992). Birds are also regularly shot in Azerbaijan, where poaching is intense (M. V. Patrekeev *in litt.* 1992). In Andalucía, mortality from nets used for trapping crayfish is a serious problem (Asensio 1991).

■ Conservation measures

Habitat protection at major breeding sites is of prime importance, and existing protection status and hunting bans should be rigorously enforced in Important Bird Areas (IBAs): in Azerbaijan, at Lake Akgyel (IBA 076) and Kirov Bay on the Caspian Sea (IBA 077), and in Spain at Embalse del Hondo (IBA 215) and Salinas de Santa Pola (IBA 216). In Spain, habitat restoration is required in Valencia and at the Marismas del Guadalquivir (IBA 247), and protection of the southern part of Brazo del Este and Las

Cantaritas (Marismas del Guadalquivir) is an urgent need. In Turkey, protection is required for Eregli Sazligi (IBA 023), Hotamis Sazligi (IBA 024), Çukurova delta (IBA 050), Göksu delta (IBA 052) and Van Sazligi (IBA 077). Drainage or water-diversion schemes should not be designed around any of these sites or within their watersheds until their potential impact has been properly assessed. At the Göksu delta, drainage of marshes must be stopped, especially in the areas east and west of the main river mouth, and clean water should be provided from the river to the polluted Akgöl wetland (DHKD 1992). Hunting needs to be controlled at the Çukurova delta and the impact of pesticide input to Akyatan Gölü should be studied.

The Marbled Teal's ecology is not well known, and research is required into habitat requirements to assess management priorities.

ANDY GREEN

Red-crested Pochard
Netta rufina

SPEC Category   3
Status   Declining
Criteria   Moderate decline

Following earlier expansions, the Red-crested Pochard has declined in Europe between 1970 and 1990, especially in the Russian and Romanian strongholds, largely through the drainage of wetlands. Important wetland sites require protection under the Ramsar Convention, and in some cases habitat management to provide suitable nesting conditions.

■ Distribution and population trends

The Red-crested Pochard's breeding range encompasses the steppe and desert zones extending from the Mediterranean to Mongolia. Within Europe, the strongholds of the species lie in southern Russia, Spain, Romania and Turkey (Dementiev and Gladkov 1952, Mayaud 1966, Cramp and Simmons 1977; see table, map). The species is a short-distance migrant, wintering in two main areas in the western Palearctic: the western Mediterranean, centred around Spain and the Camargue in southern France, and the Black Sea, especially the Danube Delta (Romania). Previous estimates put the western winter population at 20,000 birds (Monval and Pirot 1989) and the Black Sea winter populations at 50,000 birds (Rüger *et al.* 1986). It also occurs in small numbers on inland waters of central Europe (Rutschke 1989).

Red-crested Pochards colonized much of the present European range during the second half of the nineteenth and early twentieth centuries as a result of a shift in breeding grounds from the continental areas of western Asia and population increases since the 1830s (Dementiev and Gladkov 1952). These changes corresponded with a period of long-term climatic warming and aridization (Shnitnikov 1957) which resulted in changes to wetland vegetation beneficial to the species (Krivenko 1991b). This expansion proceeded in cycles of 30–45 years, interrupted by some decreases, with the most rapid expansions at the start of the twentieth century, during the 1930s, and especially during the 1960s (Timmerman 1962, Mayaud 1966, Hauri 1973, Krivenko 1991b).

Population increases and range expansions continued in Spain, Portugal, Switzerland, Austria, Poland, Slovakia and Moldova during the 1970–1990 period (see table, map), but this by no means compensated for the simultaneous decline in the larger populations, particularly in Russia and Romania. The main European Russian breeding grounds in the Volga Delta and Kuban river valley (Azov Sea) held a maximum of c.9,000 breeding pairs in 1973, 6,000 pairs in 1979, and only 4,000 pairs in the early 1990s. Numbers also declined during the 1980s in the Netherlands, France, Italy, Albania and Ukraine (excluding the eastern Sivash region) (Krivenko 1991b, Lysenko 1992; see table, map). Trends in the Turkish population are unknown.

Winter counts suggest that west Mediterranean populations have been stable overall since the late 1960s, while the large east Mediterranean population has declined (Monval and Pirot 1989).

■ Ecology

The main breeding habitats of Red-crested Pochard include large river deltas and medium-sized to large eutrophic lowland lakes, which are normally fringed with reeds. It also uses brackish lakes, estuaries and other coastal areas overgrown with reedbeds. Breeding takes place most frequently on islets covered

	Breeding population			Breeding range trend
	Size (pairs)	Year	Trend	
Albania	10–20	92	–1	(–1)
Austria	20–25	84–88	+1	+1
Bulgaria	10–20	—	0	0
Croatia	**2–5**	—	N	N
Czech Republic	**160–180**	—	0	+1
Denmark	**1–1**	89	0*	—
France	(270–310)	90	–1	**0**
Germany	60–260	—	0	**0**
Greece	0–5	—	(0)	(0)
Hungary	60–70	—	N*	—
Italy	20–30	84	(–1)	(–1)
Moldova	**70–100**	89	+1	–1
Netherlands	**10–25**	91	–2	–1
Poland	30–40	—	N	+1
Portugal	**10–50**	91	+1	+1
Romania	(1,000–3,000)	—	–1	0
Russia	5,500–9,000	—	–1	0
Slovakia	10–30	—	+1	+1
Spain	5,400–8,600	—	+1	+1
Switzerland	**20–40**	86–91	+1	+1
Turkey	(1,000–5,000)	—	—	—
Ukraine	40–80	82	–1	–1
United Kingdom	**50–50**	88–91	(0)	+2
Total (approx.)	14,000–27,000			

Trends	+2 Large increase	+1 Small increase	0 Stable	X Extinct
(1970–1990)	–2 Large decrease	–1 Small decrease	F Fluctuating	N New breeder

Data quality   **Bold**: reliable quantitative data   Normal type: incomplete quantitative data   Bracketed figures: no quantitative data   * Data quality not provided

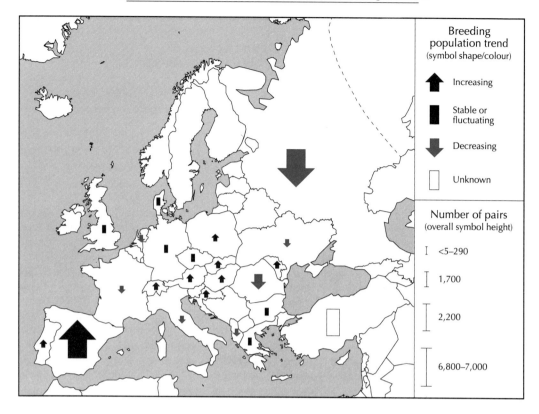

with grass, bushes or reeds. Old broken reeds that form rafts are important for nesting, although in western Europe nesting is known also to occur on water-bodies without reedbeds, but nests are then always located close to the shore line.

The species winters mainly in coastal or inland waters (Cramp and Simmons 1977), open or fringed with reedbeds, and with well-developed, submerged vegetation. Diet mostly comprises waterplants; *Chara*, *Ceratophyllum* and *Zostera* are preferred.

■ Threats

Over a large part of the breeding range, wetland drainage is the major threat, and is especially intensive in the Kuban river valley, where large areas have been transformed into rice-fields (Krivenko 1991b).

In the Volga Delta region, recent climatic change to cooler and wetter conditions, beginning in 1979, has caused a sharp raising of water-levels and consequently a reduction in the extent of reedbeds. Such conditions result in the loss of breeding sites, since old and broken rafts are often destroyed and remaining scattered reedbeds do not protect the nests effectively against wave action during windy days,

resulting in increased mortality from flooded clutches.

■ Conservation measures

Action is urgently required to protect the Russian and Ukrainian breeding grounds. Wetland areas in the Kuban delta and the lower Danube, as well as eastern Sivash, should be protected under the Ramsar Convention. In the Volga Delta, habitat management may also be needed to ensure the availability of suitable nest-sites that are not prone to flooding, perhaps through the creation of reed-rafts or firm islets as artificial sites.

A strategy and action plan to conserve the wetlands of the lower Volga has recently been developed (Finlayson 1992b), advocating the need to conserve the existing wetlands and prevent further degradation, together with the recovery and restoration of wetland sites previously lost. The report recommends that attitudes and awareness need to be improved, the network of protected areas developed, sustainable use of wetland resources adopted, land-use and water pollution reduced, and integrated management of natural and human needs of the area addressed.

Vitaly G. Krivenko

129

Ferruginous Duck
Aythya nyroca

SPEC Category   1
Status   Vulnerable
Criteria   Large decline

The globally threatened Ferruginous Duck has undergone a long-term, but recently massive population decline, particularly in the former European U.S.S.R., due mainly to the drainage of steppe wetlands. It is essential that the remaining wetlands which are important are conserved and the reduction and strict control of hunting would be beneficial.

■ Distribution and population trends

The breeding range of the Ferruginous Duck comprises the steppe, desert and southern forest zones of Eurasia, extending from the Mediterranean basin to central China (Y. A. Isakov in Dementiev and Gladkov 1952, Cramp and Simmons 1977). Although the total population size is poorly known, it is estimated that roughly half of its global breeding range is within Europe, largely concentrated in the southeast (Dementiev and Gladkov 1952, Rutschke 1989) with strongholds in Romania, Ukraine, Turkey, Moldova, Hungary and southern Russia (Lysenko 1992, see table). Numbers in Turkey are little known, although a WIWO survey in 1992 found over 100 breeding pairs in the Kizilirmak delta, suggesting a large Turkish population.

The Ferruginous Duck winters mostly in the coastal zones of the Caspian, Black, Azov and Mediterranean Seas (Cramp and Simmons 1977, Rutschke

	Breeding population			Breeding
	Size (pairs)	Year	Trend	range trend
Albania	100–300	92	–1	(–1)
Austria	(50–200)	—	–1	–1
Belarus	(50–75)	90	–2	**0**
Bulgaria	50–150	—	–1	–1
Croatia	200–300 *	—	0*	0*
Czech Republic	**1–1**	85–89	**–2**	**–2**
Germany	**20–100**	—	(–1)	0
Greece	300–400	—	(0)	(+1)
Hungary	1,200–1,600	—	0	0
Italy	25–50	84	(–1)	–1
Lithuania	(10–100)	85–88	(0)	(0)
Moldova	**1,000–1,300**	89	**–1**	–1
Netherlands	0–1	79	F	F
Poland	400–500	—	–1	–1
Romania	6,000–15,000	—	–1	**–1**
Russia	(500–1,500)	—	–2	–1
Slovakia	20–40	—	–1	0
Slovenia	5–15	—	–2	–2
Spain	1–10	—	**–2**	**–2**
Switzerland	**0–1**	91	N	N
Turkey	(1,000–3,000)	—	—	—
Ukraine	**3,500–5,000**	—	**–2**	**–1**
Total (approx.)	11,000–25,000			

Trends +2 Large increase +1 Small increase 0 Stable X Extinct
(1970–1990) –2 Large decrease –1 Small decrease F Fluctuating N New breeder
Data quality **Bold**: reliable quantitative data   Normal type: incomplete quantitative data
Bracketed figures: no quantitative data   * Data quality not provided

1989). A significant part of the population (7,000–10,000 individuals) winters in tropical Africa, especially in Mali, Chad and Nigeria (Perennou 1991).

The Ferruginous Duck has severely declined in population size and range in Europe. During the late 1960s the total population of the former U.S.S.R. was estimated at 75,000 pairs: 65,000 in the Dniestr–Dniepr region of Ukraine and Moldova and 10,000 in the Kuban valley, Russia) (Cramp and Simmons 1977). However, by the early 1980s, just 12,000–14,000 pairs were estimated in the European part of the former U.S.S.R., falling further to c.6,000 pairs by the early 1990s (see table).

In the Kuban river delta, a former main breeding site, summer numbers also declined between 1971 and the 1980s from 15,000 to 1,500 individuals (V. Krivenko own data). During the 1970s numbers also declined sharply in the Ukraine (Lysenko 1992).

After 1980 some stabilization occurred in parts of Russia and Ukraine and some slight local increases were reported (Chernobay 1986, Lysenko 1992).

As well as the major declines in Russia and Ukraine, breeding populations showed large declines in Belarus, Slovenia and Spain, and declines occurred in most other countries (see table, map). Winter numbers also declined between 1970 and 1990, especially in the Black Sea region. In January 1967 18,000 were counted in the northern Black Sea (Rüger *et al.* 1986) but only up to 1,500 between 1979 and 1988 (Ardamatskaya and Sabinevsky 1990). Data from Africa are insufficient to calculate population trends.

On the basis of the species' apparently rapid decline in Europe and Asia (Rose and Scott 1994) the species is now listed as Globally Threatened (Collar *et al.* 1994).

■ Ecology

The main breeding habitats are large river deltas, fresh, brackish and alkaline lakes among lowlands and oxbows within large river valleys, all characterized by a mosaic of emergent vegetation, diverse submerged plants and a rich fauna. Water-bodies fringed with dense reedbeds are preferred, especially

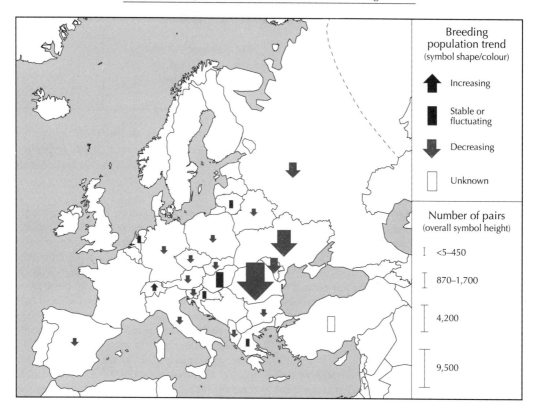

when the latter are interspersed with patches of open water.

The species is rather tolerant of man and utilizes a fairly wide range of nest-sites and food. Nests are located close to the water's edge, often in dense clumps of vegetation. Although omnivorous, mainly plant material is taken (Cramp and Simmons 1977), chiefly soft parts of leaves or roots of waterplants.

Birds winter mainly in coastal or large inland freshwater and brackish water-bodies, open or fringed with reedbeds and rich in submerged vegetation.

◼ Threats

The main threat to this species is the widespread destruction of wetland through most of its range. Wetland drainage is thought to have eliminated many of the western populations (Madge and Burn 1988) and caused the loss of the species' optimal breeding sites in eastern Europe. In Spain much suitable habitat has been lost, for example at Doñana, where the species is now practically extinct. During this century Greece has lost more than 60% of its wetlands due to drainage (G. Handrinos in Finlayson *et al.* 1992), most being prime habitat for the species. Increasing aridization of the climate in the centre of Europe may also have caused widespread loss and deterioration of wetlands (Krivenko 1991b).

High numbers were once shot in southern Russia and Kazakhstan (Dementiev and Gladkov 1952) but

it is now more rarely hunted. In Greece and Italy the species is protected but is still shot due either to misidentification or ignorance of the law, and this is a serious problem at the local level, e.g. at the Evros delta (Rutschke 1989).

Birds wintering in tropical African wetlands are vulnerable to potential threats such as recurring droughts which reduce the extent of available habitat and lead to an increased human pressure on the remaining areas.

◼ Conservation measures

As a rather dispersed breeding species the Ferruginous Duck requires the broad conservation of large areas of steppe wetlands in eastern Europe. Measures are required to discourage drainage of these lakes for agriculture. Wetlands that are important for breeding, migrating or wintering should be designated and protected under the Ramsar or Bonn Conventions, and be subject to the principles of wise use.

Given the crash in the population of the species and lack of knowledge on the effects of hunting, all hunting of the species should be brought under strict control, with bag limits and shortened seasons, to ensure that exploitation is sustainable.

VITALY G. KRIVENKO, V. G. VINOGRADOV, ANDY GREEN AND CHRISTIAN PERENNOU

Scaup
Aythya marila

SPEC Category 3, winter
Status Localized
Criteria Localized

In winter the majority of European Scaup are concentrated in a few areas, making them susceptible to oil pollution and disturbance by hunting. Such threats need to be minimized, important concentration areas at sea identified, and further research initiated to establish the nomadic habits of the species in winter.

■ **Distribution and population trends**

The European breeding range of this circumpolar species extends from Russia, which has c.80–90% of the European breeding population, through Estonia and Fennoscandia to Iceland, and south to c.55°N. Birds winter in coastal habitats in the western part of the Baltic, along the coast of Netherlands, Denmark, France and the United Kingdom, and around the Black Sea (see population table, map). Small numbers also occur in the interior of Europe and in the Mediterranean.

In winter it is estimated that over 90% of the European population is concentrated at fewer than ten sites, but data available for the sites considered most important (see Important Bird Area table) are from a period of severe winters (S. Pihl pers. comm.). More recently, there has been a redistribution of birds with sites such as Wismar Bucht, Greiffswalder Bodden, Darsser Boddenkette and Rügen, Strelasund in Germany and the western part of the Gulf of Gdansk and Stettin Lagoon in Poland, all regularly holding more than 5,000 Scaup. The species seems to be nomadic in winter and numbers consequently fluctuate widely in most parts of its range. The winter population estimate in north-west Europe has recently increased from 150,000 to 310,000 birds (Laursen 1989, Laursen *et al.* 1992), probably due almost exclusively to improved surveys.

Increases have been noted in the IJsselmeer (Important Bird Area 030) in the Netherlands (van Eerden and Zijlstra 1986), along the German Baltic coast (Struwe and Nehls 1992) and along the Polish coast (Meissner and Kosakiewicz 1992), while decreases have been reported from Denmark (Laursen *et al.* in prep.) and eastern Scotland (Salmon 1988).

Important breeding populations are fluctuating in Russia and Iceland, while numbers are decreasing in Estonia and Finland and stable in Sweden (EBD 1994).

■ **Ecology**

Breeding is always close to water, in tundra and wooded tundra, in upland zones (in Scandinavia) and along the Baltic coasts (Cramp and Simmons 1977). On migration the species is mainly recorded in coastal areas in large flocks, sometimes of tens of thousands of birds. It winters also in dense flocks in coastal waters, lagoons and coastal lakes. In freshwater habitats it is often associated with Pochard *Aythya ferina* and Tufted Duck *A. fuligula*.

Scaup wintering in north European seas feed at night (Nilsson 1969, Kirby *et al.* 1993, Laursen *et al.* in prep.), while those in the south feed during the day (Cramp and Simmons 1977). The diet is dominated by molluscs, but also includes dead fish and grain (Madsen 1954). The birds feed by diving, preferring water 6–12 m deep, but frequently reaching 30 m

	Winter population			Winter
	Size (individuals)	Year	Trend	range trend
Austria	**11–11**	91	F	0
Belgium	**20–90**	85–91	F	0
Bulgaria	**0–100**	77–89	0	0
Denmark	**13,000–39,000**	87–91	—	—
Faroe Islands	(0–20)	92	(0)	(0)
Estonia	(50–500)	—	0	0
Finland	10–100	92	0	0
France	**1,583–1,583**	90	+2	0
Germany	**30,000–55,000**	82	(0)	—
Greece	**5–50**	87–91	0	0
Hungary	**22–22**	91	F*	—
Iceland	50–150	—	F	0
Rep. of Ireland	(2,500–3,000)	—	—	—
Italy	(100–2,020)	—	F	0
Lithuania	30–40	89	+1	—
Netherlands	70,000–130,000	79–88	F	0
Norway	1,000–1,000 *	—	—	—
Poland	1,500–60,000 *	—	—	—
Portugal	(1–10)	91	(0)	(0)
Romania	1,000–300	—	0	0
Slovakia	10–100	—	0	0
Slovenia	0–35	—	F	0
Spain	**0–56**	—	F	—
Sweden	**3,000–5,000**	89	0	0
Switzerland	**25–140**	81–91	F	0
Ukraine	50–100	88	+1	+1
United Kingdom	**6,000–8,000**	88	−1	0
Isle of Man	**0–1**	—	0	0*
Total (min., approx.) 130,000				

Trends   +2 Large increase   +1 Small increase   0 Stable   X Extinct
(1970–1990) −2 Large decrease   −1 Small decrease   F Fluctuating N New breeder
Data quality **Bold**: reliable quantitative data   Normal type: incomplete quantitative data
Bracketed figures: no quantitative data   * Data quality not provided

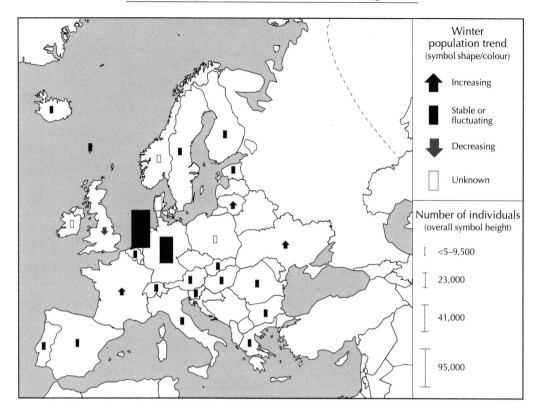

Important Bird Areas The top ten IBAs for wintering Scaup in Europe, together holding over 90% of the total European wintering population.

Denmark	002	Albourg Bugt (northern part)
	012	Løgstør Bredning
	047	Lillebælt
	058	Flensborg Fjord and Nybøl Nor
	063	Sydfynske ø-hav
	105	Kalø and Ebeltoft Vig (including Hjelm and Begtrup Røn)
Germany	007	Küste der Probstei
	021	Neustädter Bucht
Netherlands	001	Waddenzee
	030	IJsselmeer

(Madsen 1954, Cramp and Simmons 1977). In the IJsselmeer the increasing number of birds predominantly feed on the newly colonized stock of zebra mussel *Dreissena polymorpha* (van Eerden and Zijlstra 1986). The population wintering in eastern Scotland feed on waste grain expelled from distilleries via sewage outfalls and have seriously declined due to the introduction of modern sewage systems (Campbell 1984).

■ Threats

Oil pollution is likely to be the main threat, as large winter flocks of Scaup concentrate in the western Baltic, particularly in Danish waters where oil tankers pass daily through narrow straits. Damaging effects to date have, however, been limited (Joensen

1972, Joensen and Hansen 1977).

Hunting of Scaup is legal in seven EU countries (Denmark, France, Germany, Greece, Netherlands, United Kingdom (Northern Ireland) and the Republic of Ireland) and c.8,000 are shot annually (Bertelsen and Simonsen 1986). Disturbance from hunting may also be a problem, though its effect is currently unquantified.

Modernization of sewage systems is known to have had local impacts (Campbell 1984), and commercial exploitation of mussels may also be a problem in some areas.

■ Conservation measures

The Scaup requires large areas of breeding habitat in northern Europe, and the maintenance of suitable conditions in its highly localized north-west European wintering grounds. Efforts should also be made to reduce the risks to which populations are exposed in winter. Important Bird Areas at sea should therefore be identified, and habitats and sites defined and protected. Implementation of stricter regulations on oil exploitation and transportation is also required and there should be restrictions on hunting. Further research is needed on the effects of disturbance from hunting and the reasons for the nomadic habits of the species outside the breeding season.

STEFAN PIHL AND KARSTEN LAURSEN

133

Steller's Eider
Polysticta stelleri

SPEC Category   1, winter
Status   Localized
Criteria   Localized

Within Europe, the Steller's Eider is concentrated in winter along the Barents Sea coastline of northern Norway and Russia. Wintering numbers appear to be increasing but the species remains vulnerable to oil spills and to accidental trapping in gill-nets, and is globally threatened.

■ Distribution and population trends

Steller's Eider breeds along the Arctic coast of Alaska and the eastern half of Siberia, including the Taymyr peninsula of north-central Siberia, where birds were recently discovered nesting. There have been only two recent records of breeding within Europe, both in Russia: in 1987 at a lake near Seven Islands by the Murmansk coast (Y. Krasnov pers. comm.), and in 1991 in Kandalakshskaya bay on the White Sea (Bianki 1992). Small numbers of non-breeding birds are, however, found in summer along the west coast of Novaya Zemlya (Frantzen and Henriksen 1992, Nygård *et al.* in prep., B. Frantzen pers. comm.).

Most birds winter in the northern Pacific, but the main European areas for both non-breeders in summer and for wintering birds are the Varangerfjord in northern Norway (Important Bird Area 003) and the Murmansk coast of north-east Russia which together hold more than two-thirds of the Steller's Eiders in Europe (see Important Bird Area table). In February 1993 small flocks of Steller's Eider were seen in open water among sea ice around Vaygach Island, near Novaya Zemlya (B. Bergflødt pers. comm.). The winter population in the Varangerfjord has been counted only since 1980 and numbers have been stable during this period (see population table, map). Recent counts found approximately 15,000 Steller's Eiders around the coast of the Kola peninsula in March 1994 (T. Nygård pers. comm.) which probably means that there are a maximum of 20,000 birds

wintering in Russia, thus exceeding the totals given in the tables and map of this review. The species is increasingly found in all countries around the Baltic Sea (Nygård *et al.* in prep.), with large numbers wintering in Estonia, especially at Soaremaa Island in Vilsandi State Nature Reserve (Important Bird Area 007).

It should be noted that the wintering population of Steller's Eiders in Alaska has declined significantly (Kertell 1991) and the species is therefore now regarded as Globally Threatened (Collar *et al.* 1994).

■ Ecology

Both wintering and summering birds in the Varangerfjord and along the Murmansk coast occur in flocks of varying size, mostly 10–100 individuals, in sheltered and shallow bays on the outer coast. They are seldom seen in smaller fjords. The largest flocks are in fishing harbours during the capelin *Mallotus villosus* fishery in March–April; indeed dense flocks of up to 3,000 individuals are known from Vadsø in the Varangerfjord (Frantzen 1985) and these installations probably provide an important food source. Local movements are often evident (Frantzen and Henriksen 1992).

■ Threats

In the Varangerfjord the main threats are oil spills and the danger of birds being trapped in fishing nets. A minor oil spill in January 1973 in Vadsø harbour killed 2,500 ducks, many of which were Steller's Eiders (Grastveit 1975). In March 1979 a small spill killed about 20,000 seabirds in the Varangerfjord, mostly auks, but also ducks and again including Steller's Eiders (Barrett 1979). The species is affected by offshore oil spills as well as those in harbours.

In the lumpsucker *Cyclopterus lumpus* fishery, nets are placed in shallow water, close to the shore, where both Steller's Eiders and Eiders *Somateria mollissima* often feed and subsequently drown when they are caught in the nets. No hard figures or even estimates of the total number of birds drowned dur-

	Winter population			Winter
	Size (individuals)	Year	Trend	range trend
Denmark	(5–25)	—	(N)	(N)
Estonia	**1,500–5,000**	—	+2	+1
Finland	**100–500**	92	+2	+2
Latvia	5–500 *	—	—	—
Lithuania	**200–400**	89	0	—
Norway	8,000–15,000	—	0*	0*
Poland	0–80 *	—	—	—
Russia	4,000–10,000 *	—	—	—
Sweden	100–500	89	+2	0
Total (min., approx.)	14,000			

Trends	+2 Large increase	+1 Small increase	0 Stable	X Extinct
(1970–1990)	–2 Large decrease	–1 Small decrease	F Fluctuating	N New breeder
Data quality	**Bold**: reliable quantitative data Normal type: incomplete quantitative data			
	Bracketed figures: no quantitative data * Data quality not provided			

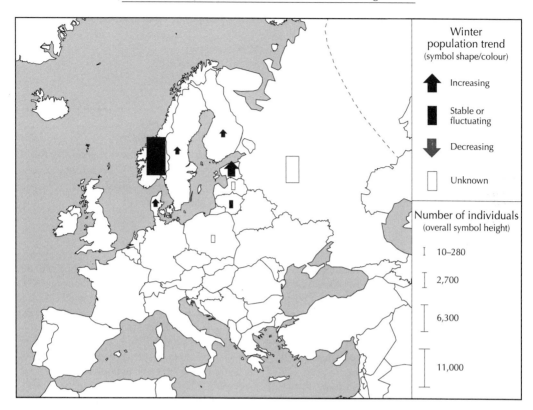

ing each fishing season are available, but there is reason to believe that these losses may be significant, at least in some areas (Frantzen and Henriksen 1992). Fishermen report that birds are caught mostly at the beginning of the season, and they are sold to taxidermists.

Steller's Eider is no longer a legal game species in Europe. Illegal hunting does, however, take place in Norway, and one person has been convicted for this offence in the last two years, though such killing is unlikely to be a significant threat.

▉ Conservation measures

It is essential to prevent oil spills in harbours, both from land-based tanks and from boats and ships, and wildlife officers at the office of the Governor of Finnmark already carry out regular checks on the oil installations. The lumpsucker fishery should be limited to the summer season; during 1994 a new style of net is being tested which should catch fewer birds.

Site protection is difficult, as most of the important areas are harbours. Although parts of the Varanger coast are already protected, two areas of importance for the species, Vadsøya and Store Ekkerøy could easily be made nature reserves by the extension of existing protected areas. Other sites of importance should be considered for protection (Frantzen and Henriksen 1992).

In 1992 the Finnmark County Government office initiated a monitoring programme for Steller's Eider in the Varangerfjord involving several censuses per winter. Counts had been conducted by volunteers in previous years, but these were on the basis of a single count per year. Ornithologists from Russia and Norway are trying to establish joint research projects on Steller's Eiders within the framework of the environmental treaty between the two countries. Steller's Eider is listed on the 'responsibility list' in the Norwegian Red Data List of endangered birds for 1992 (Størkersen 1992).

BJØRN FRANTZEN

Harlequin Duck
Histrionicus histrionicus

SPEC Category 3
Status Vulnerable
Criteria <2,500 pairs

The total European population of Harlequin Duck, in Iceland and Greenland, may be as low as 2,200 pairs. Numbers have increased along the River Laxá in Iceland, although population trends elsewhere are poorly known. In Iceland, the species seems most vulnerable to habitat loss through the manipulation of rivers for hydroelectric schemes, food competition through the release of salmonid fish into the rivers, and possibly predation by American mink.

■ Distribution and population trends

Within Europe the Harlequin Duck breeds and winters only in Iceland and Greenland, though it is also found in Labrador, eastern Siberia, Alaska and western Canada (see table, map). The population in Iceland is thought to be between 2,000 and 3,000 pairs (Gardarsson 1975), although it has not been properly censused and the exact size is consequently uncertain. Numbers in Greenland are even less well known.

In Iceland the Harlequin Duck is widely distributed, breeding wherever there are suitable rivers and streams (Gudmundsson 1971), and densities in the 1968–1971 period ranged from 0.2 to c.7 pairs per km (Bengtson 1972). The River Laxá (Important Bird Area 046), draining Lake Mývatn, holds the highest breeding density. In its upper stretches a population of c.50 males was found during 1965–1975 but this number rose steadily to c.250 in 1992 (Gardarsson 1979, Gardarsson and Einarsson in press and unpubl.). However, part of this increase may be explained by a shift of the population along the river, as numbers downstream have declined. Unfortunately, no comparable data are available from other rivers in Iceland.

The population in Greenland is believed to be stable, although it is very poorly known.

	Breeding population			Breeding
	Size (pairs)	Year	Trend	range trend
Denmark				
Greenland	(200–500)	—	(0)	(0)
Iceland	2,000–3,000	75–89	+1	0
Total (approx.)	2,200–3,500			

Trends   +2 Large increase   +1 Small increase   0 Stable   X Extinct
(1970–1990)   –2 Large decrease   –1 Small decrease   F Fluctuating   N New breeder
Data quality   **Bold**: reliable quantitative data   Normal type: incomplete quantitative data
Bracketed figures: no quantitative data   * Data quality not provided

■ Ecology

In summer (May–September) the breeding Harlequin Duck is a river specialist, being observed only exceptionally on lakes and rarely seen flying over-land. The highest densities occur at lake outlets, where there is a relative abundance of blackfly *Simulium vittatum* larvae, a favoured food resource (Bengtson and Ulfstrand 1971, Gudmundsson 1971).

The species most often breeds on small islands in rivers, where the nest is usually concealed in dense vegetation. On the River Laxá breeding pairs loaf on sand spits, rocks and riverbanks in small groups, with an unpaired male often accompanying a breeding pair. Loafing sites tend to be close to rapids used for feeding. The birds seem to have high site fidelity (Bengtson 1972, Kuchel 1977) but they do not defend the feeding areas. In June the males migrate to the sea where they moult.

In the winter Harlequin Ducks occur in small flocks scattered on exposed rocky seashores where they feed on intertidal and subtidal invertebrates.

■ Threats

There are three main factors which may threaten Icelandic Harlequin Duck populations. Firstly, hydroelectric schemes which involve the diversion and silting up of rivers: one colony may have been lost through diversion of the River Thorisos (Gudmundsson 1971), and in 1973 a planned scheme was cancelled which would have affected the populations on the Rivers Laxá and Svartá (Jónsson 1987). Secondly, the large-scale release of Atlantic salmon *Salmo salar* and brown trout *S. trutta* practised in many Icelandic rivers: for example, the proposed release of salmon in the upper reaches of the Laxá will probably increase competition for blackfly larvae and pupae, the duck's main food (Einarsson 1991). Thirdly, the introduction and subsequent escape of American mink *Mustela vison* in the 1930s (Petersen and Skírnisson 1980) may have reduced the number of viable nest-sites (due to their accessibility) along many rivers, although the actual effect has not been studied.

Also, dredging for minerals in Lake Mývatn may affect blooms of planktonic algae which form an

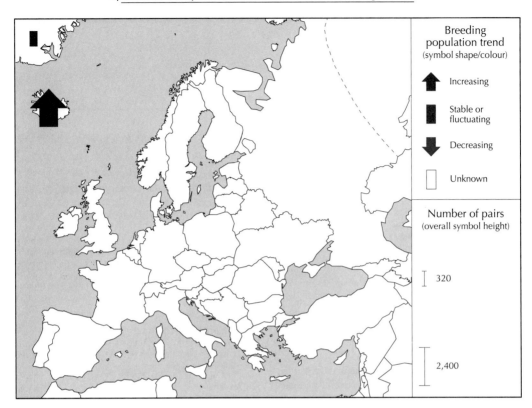

	Breeding population trend
	(symbol shape/colour)

Increasing

Stable or fluctuating

Decreasing

Unknown

Number of pairs
(overall symbol height)

320

2,400

important food (Committee of Experts for Lake Mývatn Research 1991). No potential or other threats to the Greenland population have been identified.

■ Conservation measures

In Iceland and Greenland the species is totally protected from hunting and egg-collecting. The Icelandic core area, River Laxá, is partly protected by law and is also an Important Bird Area (IBA 046) and a Ramsar Site. Other rivers which hold relatively high numbers of breeding pairs should be identified and protected from developments which might destroy feeding and breeding habitats.

A study of the effect of American mink predation on Harlequin Duck populations is also needed.

ARNI EINARSSON

Velvet Scoter
Melanitta fusca

SPEC Category   3, winter
Status   Localized
Criteria   Localized

The wintering and breeding populations of Velvet Scoter are largely stable. In winter the birds are mainly concentrated in five key areas in the Baltic Sea and are therefore particularly susceptible to oil pollution incidents. The species is also vulnerable to hunting, commercial mussel fisheries and exploitation of oil and gravel. Careful management and control of these human activities at key sites is thus necessary.

■ Distribution and population trends

Only a small proportion of the Velvet Scoter's global breeding range is in Europe, where it mainly extends from northern Russia through Finland and Estonia to Scandinavia. Very small, isolated populations also occur in Turkey and the Caucasus (Cramp and Simmons 1977). Russia is the European stronghold with more than three-quarters of the breeding population, which appears to be stable (EBD 1994). Decreases in population size in Finland and Estonia have been reported (EBD 1994), but overall figures for the size and trends of the breeding population are uncertain.

The species is migratory and congregates in winter almost exclusively in marine habitats, with recent counts suggesting a north-west European total of about one million birds (Durinck *et al*. 1994). Small populations winter in the North Sea, along the Atlantic coast south to Spain, in the north-west Mediterranean, in the Black Sea and more rarely in freshwater lakes in central Europe (Cramp and Simmons 1977, EBD 1994). However, the majority are highly concentrated in the Baltic Sea, including the Kattegat (Laursen 1989) and additional important wintering grounds recently located along the southern coast of the Baltic Sea including the Pommerche Bucht (Germany and Poland), the Polish coast, Kursiu Spit (Lithuania) and Riga Bay (Latvia and Estonia) (Durinck *et al*. 1992, 1994, Svazas and Pareigis 1992). Recent surveys have estimated the Baltic wintering populations to be 930,000 birds (Durinck *et al*. 1994).

Because most birds are offshore, and because most important sea areas cross national boundaries, it is difficult to ascribe winter numbers to individual countries. National population totals and maps are therefore not presented here, but instead figures for the most important sea areas are given (see table.)

Trends are not well known for wintering populations but numbers are believed to be mostly stable or fluctuating (EBD 1994).

Sea areas in the Baltic Sea holding important numbers of Velvet Scoter in winter. These population estimates, from Durinck *et al*. (1994), are based on mild winters from 1988 to 1993 and distributions may change in more severe weather.

Sea area	No. of birds
Pommerche Bucht	357,000
Gulf of Riga and Irbe Strait	342,000
North-west Kattegat	82,000
Polish shallow coastal waters	54,000
Lithuania-Kursieu Spit	33,000

■ Ecology

The Velvet Scoter occupies a wide range of breeding habitats: across the continental interior it occurs at middle to high altitudes, in taiga zones and wooded tundra close to fresh water; and in Scandinavia it breeds in alpine areas and coastal zones, on wooded islands and on skerries. On migration it is frequently recorded on inland waters.

Birds winter in marine areas, primarily along exposed shores or offshore, often in large mixed-species flocks of thousands of birds with Common Scoters *M. nigra*. It is sometimes found in estuaries or inlets with mussel beds (Cramp and Simmons 1977).

The Velvet Scoter feeds on molluscs, crustaceans, echinoderms and annelids, and additionally in fresh water on insects, small fish, seeds and submerged vegetation. The birds feed by surface-swimming or diving, preferring water depths of 6–12 m, but frequently diving to 30 m (Madsen 1954, Cramp and Simmons 1977).

■ Threats

Oil pollution is the main identified threat and is exacerbated by the species' concentrations in specific sea areas in winter. Large flocks of Velvet Scoter concentrate in the Baltic, particularly in Danish waters, where supertankers pass daily, and would thus be highly vulnerable to any oil pollution incident. During a large oil spill in March 1972 in the

Danish Kattegat aerial surveys indicated that about 30,000 diving ducks were contaminated by oil including 7,200 Velvet Scoters; it was assumed that all contaminated birds died (Joensen and Hansen 1977). In Lithuania it is planned to construct an oil refinery and harbour facilities some kilometres offshore of Kursiu Spit in an area where up to 40,000 Velvet Scoters assemble in spring (Svazas 1992). Oil pollution is also considered a major threat in British waters (Stroud *et al*. 1990).

Hunting of Velvet Scoter is permitted in Denmark, Germany and France, and a total of about 3,000 birds is shot annually (Bertelsen and Simonsen 1986). Hunting on a serious scale has further been reported from the breeding grounds (Cramp and Simmons 1977).

Additionally, commercial exploitation of mussel beds and other invertebrate resources is considered a threat to Velvet Scoters in the United Kingdom (Stroud *et al*. 1990), but there do not appear to be any mussel fisheries in areas of Velvet Scoter concentration in the Baltic. Disturbance in the main wintering areas (e.g. by planes or ships) does not seem to be a problem.

■ Conservation measures

The Velvet Scoter requires large areas of suitable habitat in northern Europe for breeding, and the protection of its marine habitats in its wintering areas in north-west and eastern Europe. Less than a third of the species' European wintering population occurs within currently recognized Important Bird Areas (IBAs) (Grimmett and Jones 1989). However, IBAs for seabirds at sea are proposed, including the five key areas listed here for this species (see table; Durinck *et al*. 1994), and these should receive protection from oil pollution and from damaging fisheries. Several of the sites are proposed Marine Protected Areas under the Helsinki Convention network. Additionally further studies on the ecology, distribution and density of this species in the Baltic Sea are required (Durinck *et al*. 1992, Pihl and Laursen 1993). The Velvet Scoter would also benefit from further wide-scale restrictive legislation on oil exploitation and transportation, including the prohibition of dumping of bunker oil and the cleaning of tanks in international waters.

Proper regulation of hunting and the commercial use of hunted birds should also be implemented within a management strategy to ensure sustainable exploitation.

KARSTEN LAURSEN AND STEFAN PIHL

Barrow's Goldeneye
Bucephala islandica

SPEC Category 3
Status Endangered
Criteria <250 pairs

The small and isolated European population of Barrow's Goldeneye is confined to Iceland, where 85–90% of birds breed at Lake Mývatn and on the River Laxá. The population is dependent for food on aquatic insects and is consequently threatened by planned introductions of Atlantic salmon into the River Laxá and by sediment dredging which is now in progress at Lake Mývatn.

■ Distribution and population trends

Barrow's Goldeneye has a discontinuous global distribution. Its main breeding range is in north-west North America, mainly in British Columbia (70,000–186,000 birds) and Alaska (45,000 birds) (Palmer 1976, Savard 1986). These birds winter largely on the Pacific coast of North America. In addition, c.2,500 birds winter on the American east coast (Reed and Bourget 1977) and these have been assigned to a hypothetical breeding population in Labrador (Todd 1963).

Within Europe the species is confined to Iceland, although there was a single breeding record from Greenland during the nineteenth century (Salomonsen 1950–1951). The Icelandic population is well studied and totals c.2,000 birds (Gardarsson 1978), with c.400–800 individuals breeding annually, these being confined mostly to the Lake Mývatn–River Laxá area in the north-east of the country (Gardarsson 1978, 1979).

The Icelandic population is essentially resident, but records of vagrants in Greenland and anomalies in census data suggest that some movements occur between Greenland or Labrador and Iceland but these have not been confirmed (Gardarsson 1978). Numbers in Iceland are relatively stable, although in 1989–1990 between 40% and 50% of the population disappeared following a marked reduction in the food supply. In 1989 emigration was observed coinciding with unusually high mortality of adult birds (Gardarsson and Einarsson in press).

Barrow's Goldeneye winters mainly on ice-free fresh water in the breeding area but small numbers winter on other partly ice-free fresh waters, mostly within the volcanic zone of Iceland (Gardarsson 1978). No coastal wintering grounds have been found in Iceland.

■ Ecology

Barrow's Goldeneye is a hole-nesting, highly territorial duck which in Iceland prefers relatively productive lakes and rivers. Outside the breeding season the birds are mainly gregarious. Pair formation takes place in early winter, and prior to and during egg-laying and early incubation the males defend territories on open water along the shore. Nest-sites are mostly in natural holes in the surrounding lava fields, and, although such holes are highly abundant, nesting has been encouraged by the erection of nest-boxes on farmhouses at the edge of the breeding area. Territories are abandoned before the young hatch, but many females establish brood territories soon after hatching. Broods tend to amalgamate in the main nursery areas (Bengtson 1971, Einarsson 1988).

The food is mainly benthic invertebrates, and the outlet of Lake Mývatn, which has an exceptionally high density of blackfly *Simulium vittatum* larvae, is a very important area (Einarsson 1988, 1990). It supports the highest density of territorial pairs in spring, and most females bring their young there soon after hatching.

■ Threats

The main potential threats are hydroelectric schemes, dredging in Lake Mývatn, and the introduction of Atlantic salmon *Salmo salar* in the River Laxá. A planned hydroelectric scheme was abandoned in 1973 and alteration of the river flow or lake level is now prohibited (Jónsson 1987). Dredging for diatomite extraction is currently being carried out in Lake Mývatn and this may affect blooms of planktonic algae in the lake which form an important food resource for blackfly larvae in the River Laxá (Committee of Experts for Lake Mývatn Research 1991). The planned introduction of Atlantic salmon in the upper reaches of the River Laxá will probably increase competition for blackfly larvae and pupae, the

| | Breeding population | | | Breeding |
	Size (pairs)	Year	Trend	range trend
Iceland	**200–400**	75–89	F	0
Total (approx.)	200–400			

Trends	+2 Large increase	+1 Small increase	0 Stable	X Extinct
(1970–1990)	–2 Large decrease	–1 Small decrease	F Fluctuating	N New breeder

Data quality **Bold:** reliable quantitative data   Normal type: incomplete quantitative data
Bracketed figures: no quantitative data   * Data quality not provided

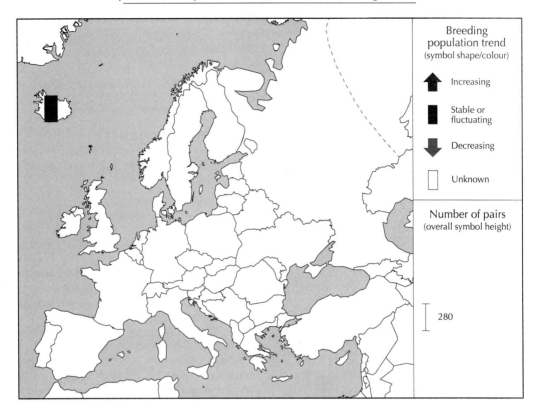

Legend text within the figure:

Breeding
population trend
(symbol shape/colour)

Increasing

Stable or
fluctuating

Decreasing

Unknown

Number of pairs
(overall symbol height)

280

main food source for Barrow's Goldeneye (Einarsson 1991).

Although egg-collection for domestic consumption occurs, 4–5 eggs are normally left in each nest according to both tradition and law (Gudmundsson 1979).

■ Conservation measures

Shooting of Barrow's Goldeneye in Iceland is prohibited by the Bird Preservation Act (no. 33/1966),

and the main breeding and wintering areas fall within the Mývatn–Laxá nature reserve, which is a Ramsar Site. Because of conservation concerns, sediment dredging in Lake Mývatn will not be continued beyond 2010.

ARNI EINARSSON

Smew
Mergus albellus

SPEC Category 3
Status Vulnerable
Criteria Large decline

This dispersed Palearctic breeding species has declined in population and range size during the last two centuries due to habitat loss or degradation and mink predation. Although its population now seems stable, range contractions are believed to have continued in the south . The conservation of forested river valleys and mink control measures are necessary.

■ Distribution and population trends

The Smew's breeding range comprises the boreal and forest-tundra zones of Eurasia, extending from Norway to the Sea of Okhotsk and north to Kamchatka. In European Russia its range extends northwards to the southern edges of the tundra and south to 59°N in the subzone of mixed forests between Narv lake, Ilmen lake, Rybinskoye reservoirs and the upper basin of the Kama river (Dementiev and Gladkov 1952, Cramp and Simmons 1977). About a tenth of the global population breeds in Europe, of which c.80–90% is in European Russia and the remainder in Fennoscandia and Belarus (see table, map).

Smew are short-distance migrants, with a wintering range embracing inland and coastal regions of western Europe, mostly southern parts of the North and Baltic Seas, and also the Black, Azov and Caspian Seas (Rutschke 1989). The species typically winters inland on small ice-free rivers and large ice-free lakes. The winter population has been estimated to be about 15,000 birds in north-west Europe, concentrated largely in the Netherlands (Rüger *et al.* 1986). Isakov (1970) reported up to 57,000 birds wintering in the Black Sea alone, while Atkinson-Willes (1976) estimated numbers for whole Black–Mediterranean Seas region as 65,000 birds and Monval and Pirot (1989) give 50,000 birds for the same region. The size of the population wintering in inland Russia is not known.

A marked fall in breeding numbers undoubtedly occurred during the second half of the nineteenth and first two-thirds of the twentieth centuries, in three main waves. First, during the 1870s and 1880s a sharp decline occurred in the mixed forest subzone due to deforestation, chiefly in river valleys. Second, during the 1920s and 1930s Smew populations in the boreal zone declined due to the widespread felling of forests, again chiefly alongside rivers, as these are used to transport the timber. Latterly, from the 1950s to the early 1970s numbers dropped due to the construction of a network of huge dammed reservoirs, together with mass deforestation and the transformation of river valleys to agriculture in the subzones of mixed and broadleaved forests, which made most Ukrainian and south-Russian rivers unsuitable for use as breeding areas (Lysenko 1992, Krivenko *et al.* 1991).

During the 1970–1990 period all isolated breeding sites in southern Russia and the Ural river valley disappeared (Isakov in Dementiev and Gladkov 1952, Stepanian 1990; see table, map). This represents more than a 20% contraction in the species' range during this period but it affected mainly marginal populations constituting perhaps only 1% of the total population. Since the beginning of the 1970s there have been no marked changes reported in population size and breeding range in the boreal zone, although ncreases were recorded in Finland, and in Belarus the species was a new breeder during that period.

■ Ecology

The breeding grounds of Smew occur in two main habitat-types: oxbow lakes, surrounded by forested tributaries in the lowlands, with a preference for medium-sized river valleys; and oligotrophic lakes and rivers again with nearby forest in mountain or submountain regions such as the Urals and Fennoscandia. Small groves or single trees are ignored by the species. During the breeding season the diet comprises fish and benthic invertebrates.

In the western part of Europe the species winters in inland waters while in the east of the region birds largely winter at sea.

	Breeding population			Breeding
	Size (pairs)	Year	Trend	range trend
Belarus	**40–50**	90	N	N
Finland	1,000–2,000	92	+1	+1
Norway	**10–20**	90	0	0
Russia	7,000–15,000	—	F	–1
Sweden	75–150	87	**0**	0
Total (approx.)	8,100–17,000			

Trends +2 Large increase +1 Small increase 0 Stable X Extinct
(1970–1990) –2 Large decrease –1 Small decrease F Fluctuating N New breeder
Data quality **Bold**: reliable quantitative data Normal type: incomplete quantitative data
Bracketed figures: no quantitative data * Data quality not provided

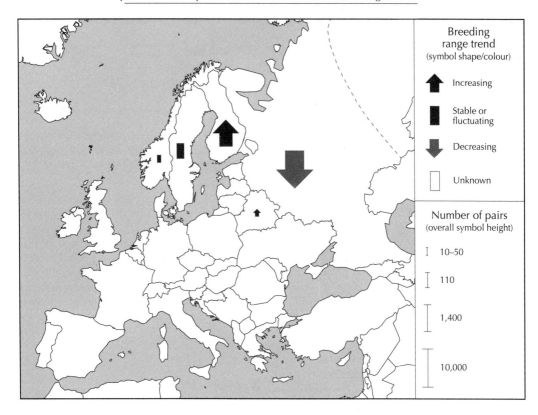

Breeding
range trend
(symbol shape/colour)

Increasing

Stable or
fluctuating

Decreasing

Unknown

Number of pairs
(overall symbol height)

10–50

110

1,400

10,000

■ Threats

Smew breeding habitat has been subject to several threats across the range of the species, including deforestation of river valleys through logging, conversion to agriculture, and destruction due to river canalization. The cutting of timber in riverine forests and its transportation along the waterways was one of the main threats prior to the 1970s. This continues but no longer has such a serious impact on the species. The most destructive factor is now predation by American mink *Mustela vison* (V. G. Vinogradov own data). Since their introduction in the 1930s numbers have increased dramatically, exerting serious pressure on populations of Smew and of Goldeneye *Bucephala clangula* (Bragin 1981).

Marine pollution with oil products and pesticides may also have a negative impact on Smew, although there is no evidence of this yet. Also acid rain pollutes breeding lakes in the western part of the breeding range and may affect Smew.

■ Conservation measures

The main measures should include the strict conservation of mature riverine forests, as well as the rigorous control of the abundance of American mink. However, it is expected that the weakening application of the nature protection law in Russia, combined with the deteriorating economy, may increase the hunting pressure on American mink (for the fur trade) and reduce the population of this predator.

The provision of large nest-boxes (as for the Goldeneye) at some lakes or rivers where only young forests remain may have a positive effect (Cramp and Simmons 1977). The prevention of marine and freshwater pollution is also important.

V. G. VINOGRADOV

White-headed Duck
Oxyura leucocephala

SPEC Category 1
Status Endangered
Criteria <250 pairs

This globally threatened species has become extinct in several European countries during the twentieth century. Numbers are now increasing in Spain and Russia and appear stable in Turkey, but hybridization with the introduced and rapidly increasing Ruddy Duck is now a very serious threat.

■ Distribution and population trends

The White-headed Duck is restricted to the west Palearctic and western Asia. It is mainly migratory, with over three-quarters of the world population wintering in Europe, but most of these birds breed further east in Russia and Kazakhstan. The European breeding range has contracted drastically during the twentieth century following the extinctions by 1976 of small breeding populations in Corsica, Italy, Yugoslavia (Vojvodina), Hungary and Albania (Green and Anstey 1992). Breeding now occurs only in Spain, Russia and Turkey (see table, map) and occasionally in Romania, e.g. in 1986 (D. Ilhes *in litt.* 1991).

Spanish birds are resident and their numbers have increased steadily since coming close to extinction in the late 1970s, with only 22 individuals counted in 1977 (Torres *et al.* 1986). The highest recent count is 786 birds in January 1992 (Agencia de Medio Ambiente *in litt.* 1992), but only 528 could be located in August 1993, the time of severe drought in Andalucía. Overall, there are likely at present to be 50–100 Spanish breeding 'pairs' (the species is polygamous).

Turkey holds a resident population formerly estimated at 150–200 pairs (Green and Moorhouse 1989), but more likely to be 200–250 as Kirwan (in press) suggests about 150 pairs in the central plateau alone. Numbers there increase greatly in winter when migrants arrive, with the main wintering concentration at Burdur Gölü (Important Bird Area 047). Winter counts have fluctuated with no clear trend since 1970, but in January 1993 only 3,576 were found, of which 3,101 were at Burdur Gölü (Green *et al.* 1993)

compared with previous estimates of up to 11,000 birds. It is therefore possible that the Turkish wintering population is in decline.

There has been a slight increase since 1970 in counts of the small breeding population of European Russia (see table, map), although there were drastic declines earlier in the twentieth century (Krivenko 1990). Recent counts probably represent previously undiscovered numbers rather than a genuine increase.

The species is classed as Globally Threatened by Collar *et al.* (1994).

■ Ecology

The White-headed Duck in Europe breeds principally in small, shallow, fresh to brackish wetlands, permanent or temporary, with abundant submerged vegetation and extensive reedbeds. In Turkey and Russia the major breeding sites are marsh areas that freeze in winter, and large winter concentrations form on larger, brackish to saline wetlands which often lack emergent vegetation (Anstey 1989).

■ Threats

The main causes of the decline in range have been wetland drainage and hunting. In Spain, 60% of Andalusian lagoons have been drained this century (Agencia de Medio Ambiente *in litt.* 1991), but the remaining sites are now well protected. The former small populations in central Europe found on small wetlands were particularly vulnerable to hunting, and 8–10 birds were shot annually in Sardinia between 1945 and 1962 (Anstey 1989). Hunting was probably a key factor leading to extinction in Italy, while removal of hunting pressure has played a key role in the Spanish recovery (Amat and Raya 1989). The key winter concentration at Burdur Gölü is still heavily hunted (Green *et al.* 1993).

Many important sites currently face significant threats, including, in Turkey, Burdur Gölü (planned construction of 160 factories and an international airport on the shore, all without Environmental Impact Assessment), Hotamis Marshes (IBA 024, reed-burning and a planned reservoir), Eregli Marshes

	Breeding population			Breeding
	Size (pairs)	Year	Trend	range trend
Russia	10–40	—	+1	F
Spain	50–100	—	**+2**	+2
Turkey	150–250	—	0	0
Total (approx.)	210–390			

Trends +2 Large increase +1 Small increase 0 Stable X Extinct
(1970–1990) –2 Large decrease –1 Small decrease F Fluctuating N New breeder
Data quality **Bold:** reliable quantitative data Normal type: incomplete quantitative data
Bracketed figures: no quantitative data * Data quality not provided

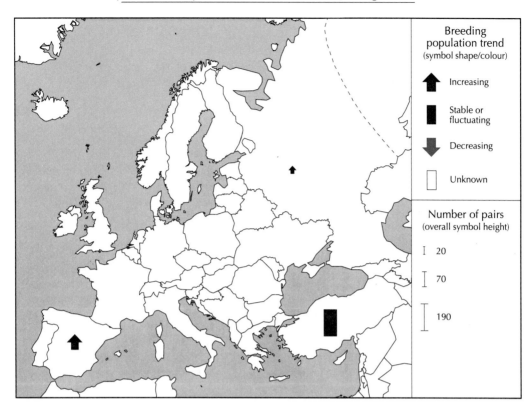

Breeding
population trend
(symbol shape/colour)

Increasing

Stable or
fluctuating

Decreasing

Unknown

Number of pairs
(overall symbol height)

20

70

190

(IBA 023, reed-burning and falling water-levels) and Kulu Gölü (IBA 026, irrigation schemes and hunting). At Burdur Gölü the factories (mainly textiles) are expected to discharge untreated waste directly into the lake (Green *et al*. 1993).

The greatest threat, however, now comes from hybridization and competition with the Ruddy Duck *O. jamaicensis* which was introduced from North America into the United Kingdom in the 1950s and is now spreading rapidly (Hudson 1976). Ruddy Ducks have already been recorded in 14 European countries (Hughes 1991, U.K. Ruddy Duck Working Group 1993) and Morocco. Since Ruddy Ducks arrived in Spain, being first seen in Andalucía in 1986, events have moved at a frightening speed. Breeding was first recorded in 1991, and two hybrids were shot the same year (ICONA 1993). Since then hybridization has increased rapidly, and 34 hybrids and 16 pure Ruddy Ducks had been shot at White-headed Duck sites by the end of 1993 (compiled from lists provided by AMA and ICONA). The hybrids are fully fertile, and a number of second generation birds have already been collected in Spain (Urdiales and Pereira 1994). Of the last seven birds shot from September 1993 onwards, six were young birds bred in 1993, showing that current intensive control efforts in Spain are not sufficient to prevent hybridization (C. Raya pers. comm. 1993).

■ Conservation measures

The highest priority for action must be to prevent the Ruddy Duck from becoming fully established on the European continent. Failure to address this problem would probably result in the extinction of White-headed Duck over the twenty-first century.

Spanish birds form major concentrations in the larger sites such as Laguna de Medina (IBA 252) and are protected there, but most important sites elsewhere still require adequate protection. These include, in Turkey, Kizilirmak Delta (IBA 015), Eregli Marshes, Hotamis Marshes, Kulu Gölü, Burdur Gölü, Çukurova (IBA 050), Yarisli Gölü (IBA 057), Bendimahi Deltasi (IBA 067), Sodali Göl (IBA 076) and Van Marshes (IBA 077), as well as Porto Lagos and Limni Vistonis (IBA 004) in Greece, and Ozero Aggyol (IBA 076) in Azerbaijan. A management plan is required to overcome significant pollution, siltation and water-extraction problems at Burdur Gölü (Salathé and Yarar 1992). Illegal hunting is a problem at many sites, including Burdur Gölü (Green *et al*. 1993) and at Lake Aggel in Azerbaijan (M. V. Patrekeev *in litt*. 1992), and needs to be controlled.

ANDY GREEN

Black-winged Kite
Elanus caeruleus

SPEC Category 3
Status Vulnerable
Criteria <2,500 pairs

The European breeding range of the Black-winged Kite expanded between 1970 and 1990, mostly because of increases in suitable breeding habitat. However, the species remains rare in Europe and its breeding habitat is now subject to pressures from the intensification of agriculture, the abandonment of less productive areas, and the destruction of evergreen oakwoods. The maintenance of non-intensive agricultural practices is necessary to maintain the present population levels.

■ Distribution and population trends

The Black-winged Kite is distributed widely and commonly as a breeding species in southern Asia and in Africa, but it occurs only marginally in Europe. The European population is estimated to number 1,100–2,000 pairs, which constitutes a very small proportion of the total world population. Within Europe the species is concentrated in Iberia (de Juana 1989c, Rufino 1989; see table, map) where it is mostly resident, although there are some movements within the breeding range.

The species' European breeding range is expanding (Palma 1985, de Juana 1989c). Large areas of Spain were colonized from the mid-1960s onwards, and more recently breeding has also been recorded along the Atlantic coast of France (Guyot 1990). According to Carbajo Molinero and Ferrero Cantisán (1985), the expansion in Spain is the result of the opening up of closed oak *Quercus* woodland during the 1950s and 1960s (and the planting of cereals as a ground-layer crop), and the removal of the understorey in most of the remnant oak woodland, both in Spain and in Portugal (Palma 1985).

Breeding numbers have increased as a result of this range expansion and also apparently within the former range. Although the extent of the species' European breeding range is well known, there are no quantitative data from detailed censuses, and population numbers are mostly based on estimates by experts.

| | Breeding population | | | Breeding |
	Size (pairs)	Year	Trend	range trend
France	**1–2**	90	N	N
Portugal	100–1,000	89	+1	+1
Spain	1,000–1,000	—	+1	+1
Total (approx.)	1,100–2,000			

Trends   +2 Large increase   +1 Small increase   0 Stable   X Extinct
(1970–1990) –2 Large decrease   –1 Small decrease   F Fluctuating   N New breeder
Data quality **Bold:** reliable quantitative data   Normal type: incomplete quantitative data
Bracketed figures: no quantitative data   * Data quality not provided

■ Ecology

The preferred breeding habitat of the Black-winged Kite over most of its European range is dehesas or montados, which are associations of evergreen or deciduous open oak woodland with cereal fields and pastures, maintained by low-intensity silvo-pastoral farming systems. At the north-western edge of its range the species also occupies a mosaic of habitats comprising small pine woods, cereal fields and pastures. Additional habitats utilized outside the breeding season include open areas such as wheat, rice and corn stubble and fallows (Carbajo Molinero and Ferrero Cantisán 1985), both inland and close to estuaries.

Black-winged Kites feed mostly on small mammals but are known also to take small passerine birds and insects (Cramp and Simmons 1980, Carbajo Molinero and Ferrero Cantisán 1985).

■ Threats

Although the range of the Black-winged Kite is currently expanding, the species remains rare in Europe and is therefore particularly susceptible to any loss of breeding habitat. Agricultural intensification, through the introduction of new crops and irrigation, combined with a lack of regeneration in, and the continued complete destruction of, woods dominated by holm oak *Qercus ilex* and cork oak *Q. suber* are all affecting the species. In some areas, important habitats which were created 20 or 30 years ago, and which resulted in the expansion of the species' range, are now undergoing such changes. However, the impact of these changes is not fully understood, since it appears that although the breeding habitat will be reduced, the availability of winter habitat will increase, thus possibly reducing winter mortality rates. Conversely, abandonment of agriculture in less productive areas may also reduce suitable habitat for Black-winged Kites.

Direct persecution by hunters and gamekeepers is

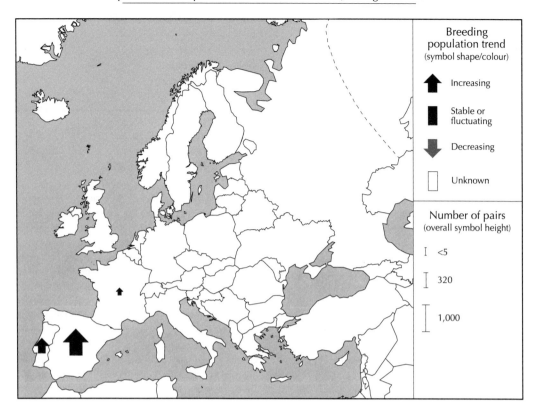

Breeding
population trend
(symbol shape/colour)

Increasing

Stable or
fluctuating

Decreasing

Unknown

Number of pairs
(overall symbol height)

<5

320

1,000

an additional factor which results in losses locally
(L. Palma pers. comm.).

Conservation measures

Although approximately 20–30% of the European
breeding population of Black-winged Kite lies within
Important Bird Areas in Portugal and Spain, there is
no single site which holds significant breeding numbers and the species is generally widely dispersed.
Wide-scale habitat conservation measures are therefore required, including restrictions on both the continuing adoption of intensive agricultural practices
and on large-scale set-aside schemes (carried out
under EC Regulation 1765/92), together with promotion of the natural regeneration of evergreen oaks.
Management agreements within the Agri-environment Regulation (EC Reg. 2078/92) of the EU Common Agricultural Policy may help to maintain
low-intensity agriculture, including the dehesas and
montados, but large-scale set-aside schemes may
have a negative impact on the population.

More research is needed in order to understand
the reasons for the recent range expansion. Furthermore, detailed information on habitat requirements,
breeding numbers and population trends is required.

RUI RUFINO

Black Kite
Milvus migrans

SPEC Category 3
Status Vulnerable
Criteria Large decline

The Black Kite population in Europe has seen a substantial decline during the twentieth century, especially in the east. Human persecution, poisoning and pesticide contamination, and changes in land-use practices and in the disposal of refuse and carrion are the main threats.

■ Distribution and population trends

Black Kites are widely distributed across temperate, subtropical and tropical areas of the Old World and Australasia. The European range extends from Portugal to the Urals (excluding northern latitudes, the Mediterranean and Atlantic Islands), but the numbers involved comprise only a small proportion of the global population (Brown and Amadon 1968). European birds winter south of the Sahara in tropical Africa (Cramp and Simmons 1980); western birds migrate mainly through Gibraltar, but some also use the Messina Strait (Italy), while eastern populations migrate via the Bosporus (Turkey) and Sinai (Egypt).

The main strongholds in western Europe are in Spain and France, although important numbers also occur in Germany and Switzerland (see table, map). The species seems to have declined considerably during the last century and until the 1960s, almost disappearing from Fennoscandia (Cramp and Simmons 1980). Although western populations were largely stable or increased between 1970 and 1990, numbers in Portugal continued to decrease. Rapid local population fluctuations have been observed in Germany, Finland and Spain, but reasons for these are poorly known (e.g. Fiuczynski and Wendland 1968, Bergman 1977, Viñuela 1992).

The eastern population's main numbers are in Russia, with important populations also in Poland, Belarus, Ukraine, Croatia, Romania, Greece and Turkey. From 1970 to 1990 the species declined in most eastern countries, including Russia (Galushin 1991a), stable or increasing populations being reported only from Poland, Croatia, Czech Republic and Hungary.

■ Ecology

The Black Kite inhabits lowland areas or mountain valleys, often near watercourses and lakes, which provide important fish prey. It is also often associated with areas where livestock-rearing occurs extensively. The Black Kite is a highly adaptable species and an opportunistic feeder, hunting over open areas and taking small-sized prey, especially young, injured or sick individuals, insects and small items of carrion. Carrion plays an important part in the distribution of the species, birds often being associated with rubbish dumps, towns and slaughterhouses (Newton 1979), and during migration they tend to concentrate in large numbers over refuse tips.

Black Kites are among the most social of raptor species, often breeding in loose colonies, and also feeding and roosting gregariously (Newton 1979). Both deciduous and coniferous trees are used for nesting, and the nest may be built using a large proportion of human refuse (Cramp and Simmons 1980).

	Breeding population			Breeding
	Size (pairs)	Year	Trend	range trend
Albania	(0–10)	85	—	(–1)
Austria	50–60	—	0	0
Belarus	500–650	90	–1	0
Belgium	4–8	81–90	+1	+1
Bulgaria	40–60	—	–1	–1
Croatia	400–500 *	—	0*	0*
Czech Republic	**70–90**	—	**+2**	+1
Estonia	1–5	—	–1	(–1)
Finland	10–15	92	–1	0
France	**5,800–8,000**	82	+1	**0**
Germany	5,000–7,000	—	0	**0**
Greece	10–30	—	(–1)	(0)
Hungary	**160–160**	91	0	0
Italy	(700–1,000)	—	(0)	(0)
Latvia	20–50	—	(–1)	(–1)
Liechtenstein	**3–4**	—	0	**0**
Lithuania	0–100	85–88	–1	–1
Luxembourg	5–10	—	+1	+1
Moldova	**40–60**	89	–1	–1
Netherlands	**0–1**	79	N	N
Poland	500–700	—	0	0
Portugal	400–1,100	89	–1	(0)
Romania	100–300	—	–1	–1
Russia	50,000–70,000	—	–1	–1
Slovakia	50–60	—	–2	–1
Slovenia	(1–5)	—	(N)	N
Spain	9,000–9,000	—	0	0
Sweden	0–5	87	**0**	**0**
Switzerland	1,000–1,250	69	F	0
Turkey	(100–1,000)	—	(–1)	(0)
Ukraine	**650–700**	88	**–2**	**–2**
Total (approx.)	75,000–100,000			

Trends: +2 Large increase +1 Small increase 0 Stable X Extinct
(1970–1990) –2 Large decrease –1 Small decrease F Fluctuating N New breeder
Data quality: **Bold**: reliable quantitative data Normal type: incomplete quantitative data Bracketed figures: no quantitative data * Data quality not provided

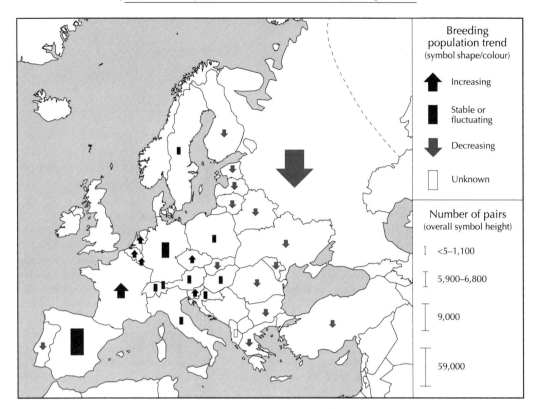

Breeding
population trend
(symbol shape/colour)

↑ Increasing

■ Stable or fluctuating

↓ Decreasing

□ Unknown

Number of pairs
(overall symbol height)

I <5–1,100

I 5,900–6,800

I 9,000

I 59,000

Threats

The main threats are those related to the bird's carrion-feeding habits, in particular its vulnerability to poisoning and pesticide contamination (e.g. Mendelssohn 1972, Chiavetta 1977, Spierenburg *et al.* 1990). Fish mortality due to water pollution may have favoured the species in some areas (Bijleveld 1974), but there may also be a negative effect from the contaminants. Other threats include shooting (e.g. Schifferli 1967, Chiavetta 1977), and collision with and electrocution by powerlines (Ferrer *et al.* 1991).

Negative impacts on the species are likely to follow from recent moves away from traditional methods of disposal of rubbish and of carcasses or refuse from abattoirs, where offal was formerly available in quantity, towards more hygienic methods.

Changes in land-use, especially those related to the intensification of livestock-rearing, may affect the species through reductions in the density of livestock carcasses left lying in the fields, in the density of dung-eating insect prey (scarabaeid beetles), and in the density of scattered trees which provide shade and food for stock, as well as through increasing disturbance by farm machinery.

In Russia, reproductive success is affected by disturbance in spring, at the beginning of the breeding season, from toursists and fishermen invading small forest areas along rivers and lakes (Galushin 1982).

Conservation measures

As with other raptors, the maintenance of large areas of suitable feeding habitat is essential for this species. Within the EU countries, management agreements developed under the Agri-environment Regulation (EC Reg. 2078/92) of the Common Agricultural Policy could help achieve this by the maintenance of traditional livestock-grazing in the main breeding and wintering areas. The preservation of wetlands and riparian forests would also favour the species, at least locally, and its habit of gathering in loose colonies may facilitate the protection of small, but important, nesting areas.

The illegal use of poison baits must be prevented by increased vigilance and by enforcement of existing laws. Where necessary, particularly dangerous electric powerlines should be either modified or relocated.

Further studies are needed to identify the major threats and to accurately monitor the population size of the species.

JAVIER VIÑUELA AND CARLOS SUNYER

White-tailed Eagle
Haliaeetus albicilla

SPEC Category 3
Status Rare
Criteria <10,000 pairs

Although most of the European population has started to recover from a critical level following persecution and environmental poisoning the species remains rare overall. The main conservation measures required are protection of nest-sites, reduction of agro-chemical contamination, the banning of poisoned bait and the prevention of illegal shooting and nest-robbing.

■ Distribution and population trends

The White-tailed Eagle is widely, but sparsely, distributed across the Palearctic and south-west Greenland. The population of Europe (including Greenland) now constitutes c.3,500 breeding pairs (see table). Strongholds are in Norway and Russia, although south-west Greenland, Sweden, Poland and Germany also hold important numbers (see map). European adults are mostly resident, though immatures are partially migratory.

Until the early nineteenth century the White-tailed Eagle was fairly common in many parts of Europe, including the Balkan countries, Mediterranean region, Denmark, Scotland and Ireland (Cramp and Simmons 1980, Fischer 1984). During the nineteenth and first half of the twentieth centuries num-

bers decreased dramatically (Bijleveld 1974), with many populations lost in western Europe and estimated numbers reaching their lowest levels (120–150 pairs) in central Europe in the 1960s (Glutz von Blotzheim *et al.* 1971). In the Nordic countries the population was estimated at c.480–500 pairs in the 1960s and 1970s (Willgohs 1961, Stjernberg 1981, Helander and Gärdehag 1989). New information indicates that the population was partly underestimated, but during the 1970s and 1980s it increased again in Norway, the Baltic countries and parts of central Europe. However, due to former underestimates and insufficient knowledge of parts of the range it is difficult to calculate the real magnitude of the increase, although the stock has doubled in some regions since the 1970s. Declines continue to be observed in Romania, the Balkan countries and Turkey (see table).

■ Ecology

Although always associated with wetlands and coasts, the White-tailed Eagle occurs in a wide variety of habitats, including the rocky coasts of the North Atlantic, the Baltic and Mediterranean coasts, lakes of the tundra, forest and steppe zones, large river valleys, estuaries and lowland marshlands (Fischer 1984). Its nesting sites are diverse but tall trees are preferred when available; otherwise nesting is on cliff ledges, the ground (in tundra, coastal heaths and dunes) or exceptionally among reeds (Willgohs 1961, Fischer 1984).

Territory size can vary considerably, depending mainly on the length of shoreline or area of wetland contained within it. In densely populated areas of Norway there can be up to one pair per 15 km of seashore (more commonly one per 20 km) or 2–5 km between pairs. In most of the range, however, pairs are considerably further apart. The diet is mostly fish but also marine and other waterbirds. To a large extent White-tailed Eagles are scavengers, feeding on everything from large mammal carcasses to dead seabirds, dead fish, and offal from fisheries and fish farms.

	Breeding population			Breeding
	Size (pairs)	Year	Trend	range trend
Albania	(1–5)	—	–2	(–2)
Belarus	**40–50**	90	**0**	**0**
Bulgaria	2–5	—	–2	–2
Croatia	**40–50**	91	**0**	**0**
Czech Republic	**7–10**	—	**+2**	**+2**
Denmark				
Greenland	**147–176**	89	**0**	**0**
Estonia	**35–40**	90	**+1**	**0**
Finland	**80–80**	92	**+2**	**+1**
Germany	**140–150**	—	**0**	**0**
Greece	**1–3**	—	**–1**	**–1**
Hungary	**37–37**	91	**+2**	**+1**
Iceland	**35–40**	83–91	**+1**	**+1**
Latvia	**8–15**	91	**+1**	**+1**
Lithuania	**4–6**	85–88	**+1**	**+1**
Norway	**1,500–1,500**	90	**+2**	**+1**
Poland	**180–240**	—	**+1**	**+1**
Romania	15–20	—	–1	–1
Russia	900–1,100	—	+1	+1
Slovenia	(1–1)	—	(0)	(0)
Sweden	**100–150**	87	**+1**	**0**
Turkey	10–30	—	–2	–1
Ukraine	**40–45**	91	**+1**	**0**
United Kingdom	**8–8**	88–91	**+2**	**+2**
Total (approx.)	3,300–3,800			

Trends +2 Large increase +1 Small increase 0 Stable X Extinct
(1970–1990) –2 Large decrease –1 Small decrease F Fluctuating N New breeder
Data quality **Bold**: reliable quantitative data Normal type: incomplete quantitative data
Bracketed figures: no quantitative data * Data quality not provided

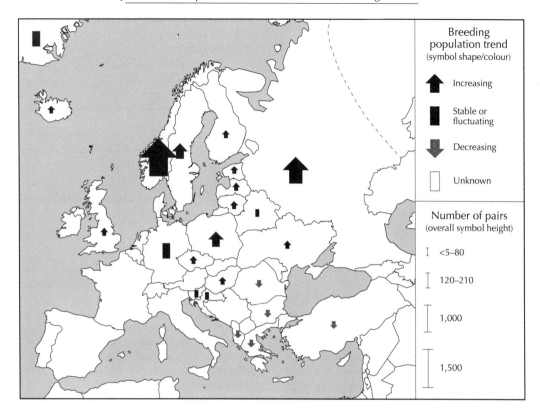

Threats

The population has been reduced over the centuries through shooting, poisoning and nest-robbing, and these actions continue in several countries (Fischer 1984, Love 1983, Bijleveld 1974). Loss and degradation of wetlands and increasing human disturbance also continue, and modern forestry also contributes to reduce the availability of suitable habitat.

Like other raptors the species is highly susceptible to environmental pollution: the accumulation of mercury and of organochlorine and other pesticide residues led to reduced breeding success between 1950 and 1980 (Helander 1977, 1983, Newton 1979, Fischer 1984, Oehme 1987).

Conservation measures

Measures to give further help to the recovery of the species include the prevention of habitat loss from modern forestry and from human developments encroaching on nesting and hunting areas. Nests need also to be protected from human disturbance, and action should be taken against illegal shooting, the robbing of nests, and use of poisoned bait for predators. In parts of the range it may be necessary to provide uncontaminated winter food to improve survival of immatures and to improve reproduction rates for local breeders. Occasionally there may be benefit in reintroduction programmes (Helander 1977, 1983, Newton 1979, Fischer 1984).

LUDWIK TOMIALOJC AND ALV OTTAR FOLKESTAD

Lammergeier
Gypaetus barbatus

SPEC Category 3
Status Endangered
Criteria <250 pairs

The Lammergeier is a very rare European species. It has undergone severe declines during the twentieth century and has become extinct in much of south-east and central Europe. Remaining birds should be protected from habitat loss, shooting, disturbance and indirect poisoning which threaten their existence. The long-term survival of the species is dependent on the maintenance of extensive pastoral farming in mountain regions. Supplementary feeding has also proved successful in increasing the numbers of birds in otherwise suitable habitats.

■ Distribution and population trends

The Lammergeier is widely distributed in mountainous regions of Eurasia and Africa, with a small proportion of its global range in Europe, where it breeds in France, Spain, Russia, Georgia, Armenia, Azerbaijan, Greece and Turkey. Over half the European numbers occur in Turkey and there are 30–40 pairs in the Caucasus, most of them in Georgia. The species is rare in Russia and its status in Albania is uncertain and needs further investigation (see table, map). The species is resident throughout its range.

The population has suffered very severe declines during the nineteenth and twentieth centuries in Europe, having disappeared from Germany in 1855, Switzerland in 1884, Bosnia and Herzegovina in 1893, Austria in 1906, Italy in 1913, Romania in 1935, former Czechoslovakia in 1942, Yugoslavia (Serbia, Montenegro) in 1956, Bulgaria in 1966 and Former Yugoslav Republic of Macedonia in 1990 (Bijleveld 1974, Vasic *et al.* 1985, Grubac 1991). This decline continued during 1970–1990 in Greece and Albania. However, the species is locally stable, or decreasing only slightly in Russia (Galushin 1991b), stable in Turkey and France, and increasing in the Spanish Pyrenees where the numbers of breeding pairs increased from 40 in 1986 to 42 in 1991 (Heredia 1991b; see table, map).

	Breeding population			Breeding
	Size (pairs)	Year	Trend	range trend
Albania	(0–5)	68	–1	0*
France	**25–25**	90	**0**	**0**
Greece	**12–18**	—	–1	0
Russia	20–40	—	0	0
Spain	**42–47**	91	**+2**	**+2**
Turkey	(100–500)	—	(0)	(0)
Total (approx.)	200–640			

Trends +2 Large increase +1 Small increase 0 Stable X Extinct
(1970–1990) –2 Large decrease –1 Small decrease F Fluctuating N New breeder
Data quality **Bold:** reliable quantitative data Normal type: incomplete quantitative data
Bracketed figures: no quantitative data * Data quality not provided

■ Ecology

The Lammergeier inhabits mountainous areas where wild ungulates still occur and/or where extensive pastoral farming persists. Birds forage over extensive areas often remote from the nest-site, feeding on dead animals, mainly domestic ungulates, chamois *Rupicapra rupicapra* and marmots *Marmota marmota*, but also on migratory birds such as Woodpigeons *Columba palumbus* (Hiraldo *et al.* 1979, Heredia 1991d).

Nests are placed in small caves or on cliff ledges in December or January and young hatch in February or March. Birds rear only a single chick which fledges in June, and the post-fledging dependence period lasts until the beginning of a new breeding cycle in November. The young then disperse across large areas (910–10,290 km^2) (Heredia 1991c), returning sporadically to their birth place. Survival rates seem to be very high in the Pyrenees (Heredia 1991c, Sunyer 1992). Cooperative polyandry has been observed in Corsica and in Spain: in the Pyrenees, at least six polyandrous trios have been recorded, all consisting of a female and two males (Heredia and Donázar 1990). Trios had similar reproductive success to that of the pairs which formerly occupied the same territories and also to that of neighbouring pairs. The existence of polyandry may have important implications for the conservation of Lammergeier populations (Heredia and Donázar 1990).

■ Threats

The extinction of the species from many countries during the twentieth century is thought to have resulted from direct persecution by man (due to an unsubstantiated belief that the species takes lambs and other small animals) and the wide use of different kinds of poisons to eliminate vermin.

Today, loss of habitat as a result of human development, shooting and indirect poisoning are prob-

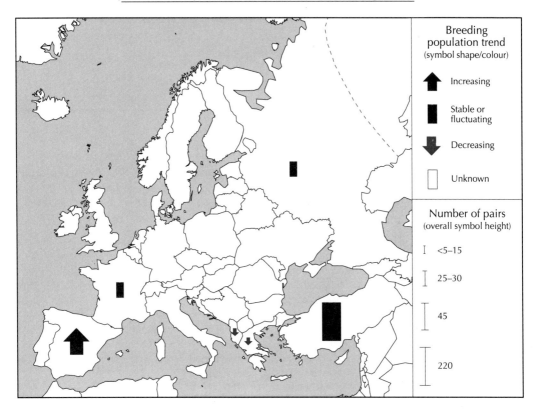

Breeding
population trend
(symbol shape/colour)

Increasing

Stable or
fluctuating

Decreasing

Unknown

Number of pairs
(overall symbol height)

<5–15

25–30

45

220

ably the major threats in Turkey and Greece (Hallmann 1985). In Corsica and Crete, food resources may be scarce or unavailable, and increasing human pressure, together with the effects of isolation could be affecting these small populations (Fasce *et al.* 1989). In the Pyrenees the main threats are habitat alterations related to the opening of new roads and tracks, and human disturbance caused by tourists, hunters, climbers, parachuters and photographers (Heredia 1991a). Illegal shooting and egg robbing by collectors also occasionally occurs.

A decline in the number of cattle due to the abandonment of extensive pastoral farming and new regulations banning traditional methods of carcass disposal (which involved leaving them in the open for scavengers) could cause serious problems in the near future (Heredia 1991d, Terrasse 1991).

■ Conservation measures

In Spain, a conservation plan coordinated by the Instituto para la Conservación de la Naturaleza (ICONA) is being implemented in the regions of Navarra, Aragón and Cataluña to monitor the Lammergier populations, supplement feeding, warden specific nest-sites and carry out applied re-

search. Lammergiers respond very well to artificial feeding and will readily visit feeding stations, especially if the extremities of goats and sheep are provided and if the site is remote and undisturbed; up to 17 different individuals have been recorded during a single day at a specific site (Heredia 1991e). Indeed, the feeding stations have proved to be very effective in increasing the number of breeding pairs locally, in evaluating the size of the non-breeding populations, and in monitoring the movements of marked birds. Nonetheless, feeding stations should be regarded as a temporary measure, albeit a rather prolonged one, and their use should not detract from the urgent need to maintain extensive pastoral farming and traditional methods of carcass disposal. Support for such extensive pastoral farming systems could be provided within Spain, France and Greece through measures under the EU Agri-environment Regulation (EC Reg. 2078/92).

In Navarra, a Recovery Plan for the species has been approved by law, and separate Recovery Plans are also being prepared in Aragón and Cataluña.

A project is underway to reintroduce the species to the Alps in France, Switzerland and Austria by releasing birds bred in European zoos.

BORJA HEREDIA AND RAFAEL HEREDIA

Egyptian Vulture
Neophron percnopterus

SPEC Category 3
Status Endangered
Criteria Large decline, <10,000 pairs

The small European population of the Egyptian Vulture has suffered a decline during the twentieth century. This decline continues throughout most of the species' European range, including Spain and Turkey which hold a major part of the region's population. The main threats are direct persecution and poisoning, and efforts should be made to reinforce legislation and to increase environmental awareness in order that these harmful activities be stopped.

■ Distribution and population trends

Between a quarter and a half of the global breeding range of the Egyptian Vulture lies within Europe, where the species occurs throughout the Mediterranean region from Portugal to Turkey, encompassing some of the Mediterranean and Macaronesian islands (see table, map). Spain and Turkey together hold more than three-quarters of the total European breeding numbers, although the exact population size in the latter country is only poorly known. Most populations are migratory, moving south to winter mainly in the Sahel zone of Africa, but the birds of southern Spain, Menorca, and the Canary Islands are resident.

The Egyptian Vulture population has experienced severe declines throughout its range in Europe during the twentieth century (Elosegi 1989). In Spain, the population trend has paralleled the poor fortunes of other scavenging species, with probably the greatest rate of decline occurring during the 1950s and 1960s when direct persecution was encouraged and rewarded. Declines have continued during the period from 1970 to 1990 in most countries, including

Spain (Perea *et al.* 1990), although numbers in some of the most densely populated areas, such as in Navarra, have remained stable (Fernández 1991). The exact population trends which have taken place in Turkey are very poorly known, but surveys do suggest that Egyptian Vultures there have suffered a recent and very strong decline in their numbers (R. Hartasánchez pers. comm.). In total over 90% of the population occurs in countries where declines were observed.

■ Ecology

The species forages over open areas such as steppes, savannas and river banks (Cramp and Simmons 1980, Ceballos and Donázar 1988, 1990) where it feeds mainly on carcasses of small and medium-sized animals, livestock carrion and garbage (Cramp and Simmons 1980, Donázar and Ceballos 1988, Bergier and Cheylan 1989).

The Egyptian Vulture nests in cliffs or crags in preference to trees but the habitat which surrounds such nesting sites can vary considerably (Cramp and Simmons 1980, Perea *et al.* 1990). For example, the densest populations include those occupying arid areas of the Ebro valley and the cool middle altitudes of the western Pyrenees and Iberian mountains (Perea *et al.* 1990).

■ Threats

The direct persecution of the Egyptian Vulture through hunting and poisoning has been the main reason for its decline in Europe (Bijleveld 1974). The incidence of these factors has recently diminished but poisoning does still occur in some parts of Spain, France and Greece (Handrinos and Demetropoulos 1983, Bergier 1985, Perea *et al.* 1990) and it is widespread in Turkey (Hartasánchez *et al.* pers. comm.). Furthermore, the illegal hunting of birds on migration continues in Provence (France), Malta and Greece (Handrinos 1985a, Elosegi 1989, Portelli 1992).

	Breeding population			Breeding
	Size (pairs)	Year	Trend	range trend
Albania	50–100	—	0*	(–1)
Bulgaria	**100–150**	70–91	–1	–1
France	**60–70**	92	0	0
Greece	150–200	—	–1	–1
Italy	**20–30**	89	–2	–2
Moldova	**1–3**	90	–1	0
Portugal	**30–60**	90	–1	–1
Romania	2–6	—	0	0
Russia	40–60	—	–1	–1
Spain	**1,324–1,373**	88	–1	–1
Canary Islands	**30–36**	87–88	–2	–2
Turkey	(1,000–5,000)	—	(–1)	(–1)
Ukraine	1–2	86	–2	–2
Total (approx.)	2,800–7,100			

Trends (1970–1990) +2 Large increase +1 Small increase 0 Stable X Extinct
–2 Large decrease –1 Small decrease F Fluctuating N New breeder
Data quality **Bold**: reliable quantitative data Normal type: incomplete quantitative data
Bracketed figures: no quantitative data * Data quality not provided

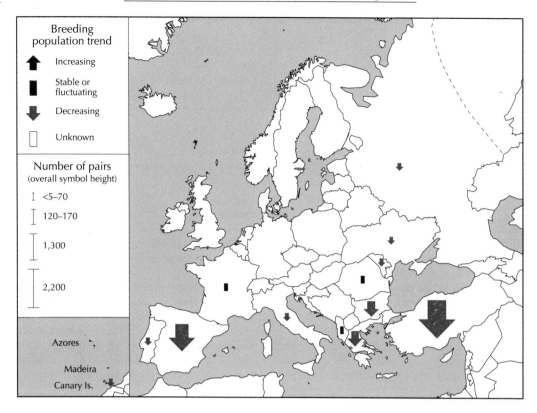

Egyptian Vultures are notably tolerant in the face of incidental, unintentional human disturbance. Generally the density of human populations is low in the vicinity of the important nesting areas in northern Spain (Ceballos and Donázar 1989), but the abandonment of nesting sites has been recorded at some small cliffs in the middle Ebro valley in northern Spain (J. L. Tella pers. comm.), probably due to direct persecution.

Lack of food is not a constraint for the majority of the birds in Spain and France since the species is adaptable and able to exploit a variety of food resources (Bergier and Cheylan 1989, Ceballos and Donázar 1989, Perea et al. 1990). Thus, improvements in animal husbandry and different regimes for the disposal of offal are not considered to pose a threat in Spain, and the national populations elsewhere in Europe are so reduced that such considerations would be of less importance than would the other threats which are outlined above.

■ Conservation measures

The maintenance of the Egyptian Vulture population of Europe requires the cessation of direct persecution of this species on migratory flyways, where birds are still shot every year. Additionally, the poisoning of birds should be prohibited, especially in Turkey and in the regions of Spain where the practice is still common. In order to achieve these requirements, the reinforcement of legislation and a greater emphasis on environmental education are necessary. It is also essential that food resources (as provided by abattoirs and rubbish dumps) near large roosts are maintained (Ceballos and Donázar 1990).

JOSÉ A. DONÁZAR

Griffon Vulture
Gyps fulvus

SPEC Category 3
Status Rare
Criteria <10,000 pairs

Following a marked and continuous decline, the Griffon Vulture's European population is currently recovering. However, the species is still quite rare and is suffering from indirect poisoning. The eradication of this practice and the maintenance and promotion of non-intensive livestock systems are necessary to ensure a widespread recovery.

■ Distribution and population trends

Between a quarter and half of the global range of the Griffon Vulture lies within Europe, where it breeds in the south-west and south-east of the region in countries bordering the Mediterranean (see map). The proportion of the global population which Europe supports is not clear as so few survey data are known from the Asiatic countries. The species' European stronghold is Spain, which supports over three-quarters of the total numbers in Europe (see table). The species is mainly resident, but some birds (mainly juveniles) migrate, moving across the Straits of Gibraltar and the Bosporus into Africa (probably south of the Sahara) and Arabia (Bernís 1983, Elósegui 1989).

A decline in the Griffon Vulture in Europe began as early as the second half of the nineteenth century and resulted in marked reductions both in numbers and in the extent of the breeding range (Bijleveld 1974, Cramp and Simmons 1980). This was due mainly to changes in the abundance and composition of the food supply and also to high mortality caused by the use of poisoned bait to eliminate mammalian predators of livestock. The decline was mostly reversed between 1970 and 1990 (see table, map) due to a decrease in pesticide use and to the advent of more positive attitudes towards the environment. The important population in Spain almost doubled between 1979 and 1989 (Arroyo *et al.* 1990a), and numbers in France are also increasing (Elósegui 1989). A French reintroduction project has also been successful in enlarging the breeding area (Bonnet *et al.* 1990). In some other countries, however, including Portugal (Palma 1985), Italy (Schenk *et al.* 1987) and Greece (Handrinos 1985b), the species is currently considered to be in slight decline (see table, map). The large population in Turkey is also suspected to be declining due to poisoning, but few data are available.

■ Ecology

Griffon Vultures inhabit a wide variety of open areas with few or no trees, in plains, mountains or upland plateaus. They avoid forested regions and areas where vegetation cover inhibits the search for food.

The species normally breeds colonially (although solitary nesting sometimes occurs) on cliffs (rarely in trees), mainly in mountainous regions but also by the sea. In Spain, Griffon Vultures breed at altitudes of 50–2,000 m but the average is about 760 m (Arroyo *et al.* 1990a). The species is largely dependent on domestic livestock carrion for food, though the presence of cliffs is more important in determining the nesting density than is the availability of food (Donázar *et al.* 1985).

■ Threats

The dependence of the Griffon Vulture on carrion and its gregarious behaviour mean that the use of poison to eliminate predators such as red foxes *Vulpes vulpes*, wolves *Canis lupus* and Asiatic jackals *C. aureus* presents a major threat to the species. Poisoning is forbidden in European countries (with the possible exception of Turkey), but is still practised, although on a smaller scale than in the past. In Spain, for example, the laying of poisoned bait is much reduced as a practice but it is still a major cause of Griffon Vulture mortality locally (e.g. 115 individuals found poisoned between 1979 and 1989:

	Breeding population			Breeding
	Size (pairs)	Year	Trend	range trend
Albania	50–200	—	-2	(-2)
Austria	0–1	—	F	F
Bulgaria	**2–10**	70–91	+2	+1
Croatia	50–100 *	—	—	—
Cyprus	10–20	—	-1	0
France	**216–219**	90	+2	+2
Greece	400–500	—	-1	0
Italy	20–30	87	-2	-1
Portugal	**100–150**	90	-1	-1
Russia	250–350	—	0	0
Spain	**8,074–8,074**	89	+2	+2
Turkey	(100–1,000)	—	-1	-1
Ukraine	1–4	86	-2	-2
Total (approx.)	9,300–11,000			

Trends	+2 Large increase	+1 Small increase	0 Stable	X Extinct
(1970–1990)	-2 Large decrease	-1 Small decrease	F Fluctuating	N New breeder
Data quality	**Bold:** reliable quantitative data	Normal type: incomplete quantitative data		
	Bracketed figures: no quantitative data	* Data quality not provided		

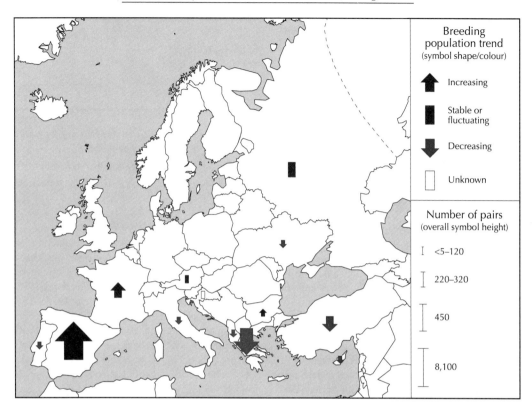

Arroyo *et al*. 1990a). Poisoning is currently an important threat also in the former Yugoslavia (Marinkovi *et al*. 1985) and in Greece (Handrinos 1985b).

Changes in the methods of raising domestic livestock and improvements in veterinary care have reduced the availability of the Griffon Vulture's food. However, given the current size of the Griffon Vulture population, which has been greatly reduced over a long period of time, current food availability does not present a significant problem, at least in France (Leconte 1985), Spain (Donázar and Fernandez 1990) and Italy (Schenk *et al*. 1987). Nevertheless, widespread abandonment of extensive pastoral farming systems could reduce carrion availability to inadequate levels, especially if combined with changes in regulations concerning the disposal of carcasses from extensive stock-rearing farms.

■ Conservation measures
Eradication of the use of poison is the major action required to conserve this species, as shown in Spain where practical measures stopping the use of poisons are leading to recovery (Arroyo *et al*. 1990a).

The maintenance and promotion of non-intensive livestock management systems such as pastoralism are essential to ensure the Griffon Vulture's food supply. In many countries the carcasses of livestock are buried or burnt, and it is therefore necessary to equate these legal regulations with the species' requirements. In fact, feeding stations are a cheap means of eliminating carcasses and are effective in maintaining vulture populations when food shortage is the limiting factor (Mundy 1985).

Since large areas of open habitat are required for foraging, afforestation projects taking in large and continuous areas should be avoided, especially within the feeding ranges of large colonies.

BERNARDO ARROYO

Cinereous Vulture
Aegypius monachus

SPEC Category 3
Status Vulnerable
Criteria <2,500 pairs

There has been a marked decline and range contraction, with extinctions in several central and south-east European countries. Numbers continue to decrease in most countries with the exception of the European stronghold, Spain, where a recovery is underway. The use of poisoned baits and habitat degradation are the main threats and require a ban on the unregulated use of poisons, and the protection of nesting territories.

■ Distribution and population trends

The Cinereous Vulture has an extensive range which stretches across Eurasia to eastern China. In Europe, only Spain still holds appreciable numbers, distributed in the south and central provinces and on Mallorca (Balearic Islands). The species is sedentary with local movements. Elsewhere in Europe, the species breeds in Greece, Former Yugoslav Republic of Macedonia (1–2 pairs in River Crna and Demir Kapya: Grubac 1991), Turkey (small numbers in all regions, but most common on the central plateau and in the east: Beaman and Porter 1985), Ukraine (Crimea) and Russia (see table, map). A. V. Abuladze (*in litt.* 1993) reports 15 pairs in Armenia in 1984, 55–60 pairs in Azerbaijan, and 17–19 pairs in 1988–1991 in Georgia. In Bulgaria birds are regularly seen feeding, and a pair nested in 1993 for the first time since 1982 (Iankov *et al.* 1992, P. Iankov pers. comm).

In Europe the species has suffered a marked decline and a reduction in range, disappearing from many countries and regions, including Portugal, northern and eastern Spain, France, Italy, Austria, Czech Republic, Slovakia, Poland, Hungary, Romania, Cyprus, Croatia, Bosnia and Herzegovina, Albania, Moldova, Crete and most of Greece (Bijleveld 1974). In its remaining European range, declines continued between 1970 and 1990 in Russia, Ukraine and Greece, while trends in Turkey remain unknown (see table, map).

In Spain, Cinereous Vultures were very common in past centuries, occurring north to the Pyrenees

	Breeding population			Breeding
	Size (pairs)	Year	Trend	range trend
Greece	10–14	—	–1	0
Russia	30–50	—	–1	0
Spain	**900–1,000**	92	+2	+1
Turkey	(100–500)	—	—	—
Ukraine	6–6	90	–2	–2
Total (approx.)	1,000–1,500			

Trends   +2 Large increase   +1 Small increase   0 Stable   X Extinct
(1970–1990) –2 Large decrease   –1 Small decrease   F Fluctuating   N New breeder
Data quality **Bold**: reliable quantitative data   Normal type: incomplete quantitative data
             Bracketed figures: no quantitative data   * Data quality not provided

(Terrasse 1989). However, a major range contraction in the twentieth century involved extinctions in the north and east of the country, and severe decreases occurred between 1940 and 1970, with a minimum of 200 pairs remaining between 1966 and 1972 (Bernís 1966, Garzón 1974b, Hiraldo 1974). The population recovered slowly in the 1980s, with 370 pairs in 17 colonies in 1982, 774 pairs in 1990 (González *et al.* 1986, González 1990) and 900–1,000 pairs in 1992 (L. M. González own data). The most spectacular recovery was in Extremadura, where 86 pairs in 1972 became 451 in 1992, and this increase continues. Numbers are monitored annually within the main protected areas (Jiménez 1990, Oria and Caballero 1992b, Sánchez and Rodríguez 1992, SECONA 1992) and there have been four national censuses (Bernís 1966, Garzón 1974b, Hiraldo 1974, González *et al.* 1986, González 1990).

In Mallorca, there were probably hundreds of individuals at the start of the twentieth century (Tewes 1992), but only 40–50 birds in 1975 when monitoring started (Mayol 1977), declining to 19 by 1983. This figure was stable until 1989, but a recovery program, which included the release of 35 captive-bred birds, mainly from 1984 to 1992, produced a rapid increase to 59 birds in 1991 (Tewes 1992).

In the Evros area of Greece numbers rose gradually from about 26 birds in 1985 to 50–56 in 1993. In Olympos, the population collapsed in 1989 when at least five birds were poisoned (Hallman 1993).

Although formerly listed as Globally Threatened (Collar and Andrew 1988), the global status of the Cinereous Vulture is now listed as Near Threatened (Collar *et al.* 1994), on the basis of its partial recovery in Europe and evidence that suggests a larger world population than previously appreciated.

■ Ecology

The species is best known in Spain, where it nests mainly in evergreen oaks *Quercus* in mountainous areas at 300–1,400 m. Loose colonies occur, with nests 30 m to 2 km or more apart (Hiraldo 1983).

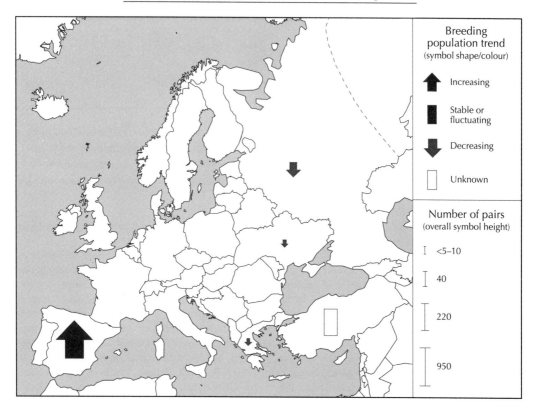

In the mountains and plains surrounding the nesting areas Cinereous Vultures feed on the carrion of medium-sized ungulates such as sheep, goats and deer (Cervidae) and rabbits *Oryctolagus* (Hiraldo 1976). In Spain there is a correlation between the distribution and relative abundance of the Cinereous Vulture and cattle. From 1940 to 1980 cattle numbers declined by 74% and cattle density fell from 80 to 42 per km² (de Juana and de Juana 1984). Nevertheless, the increase in the last decade of fallow deer *Dama dama*, roe deer *Capreolus capreolus* and wild boar *Sus scrofa* within the Cinereous Vulture's range has resulted in an increased use of these as food sources.

■ Threats

The most serious threat is poisoning from poisoned baits to control foxes *Vulpes vulpes*, wolves *Canis lupus*, bears *Ursus arctos*, etc., which is widespread in south-east Europe (e.g. Former Yugoslav Republic of Macedonia, Greece, Bulgaria, Turkey) and often permitted or encouraged by the authorities (Bijleveld 1974, B. Heredia pers. comm.).

Habitat loss and alteration is a significant threat. In Spain, between 1960 and 1980 there were many cases where breeding colonies were abandoned after nesting trees were surrounded by *Eucalyptus* or when the typical Mediterranean scrubland was removed between the trees (Garzón 1974b, Hiraldo 1974).

Disturbance of nest-sites, predominantly through forest exploitation such as the creation of forest tracks or clearance of woodland, is another serious problem, which can result in breeding failure (Garzón 1974b, Hiraldo 1974). Planned infrastructural and hydrological development in Spain and Greece, often with EU financial support, continues to threaten nesting and feeding habitat of Cinereous Vultures through flooding and an increase in disturbance.

■ Conservation measures

Unregulated poisoning of predators should be prohibited throughout the Cinereous Vulture's range, and campaigns are required to publicize the risks to carrion-feeding birds and to advise on alternative methods of predator control when this is essential.

All nesting sites, with priority given to the larger colonies, should be included in protected areas, with strict enforcement where appropriate. It is important for the Cinereous Vulture that large areas are maintained which contain livestock and a broad diversity of prey (game, rabbits, etc.), for example through extensive pastoral agriculture. Forest management plans should consider nesting requirements of the species, as in central Spain. Monitoring of the Spanish population should continue, and surveys and research on the status and conservation problems in other areas, particularly Turkey, should be promoted.

LUIS M. GONZÁLEZ

Short-toed Eagle
Circaetus gallicus

SPEC Category 3
Status Rare
Criteria <10,000 pairs

The Short-toed Eagle has suffered a steep decline in numbers and range in Europe and is now rare and still decreasing in several countries due to changes in agriculture and land-use or to direct persecution. Nesting and feeding habitats should be conserved through the encouragement of traditional low-intensity grazing and agriculture, changes in woodland management and the education of hunters.

■ Distribution and population trends

The breeding distribution of Short-toed Eagle covers extensive areas of south-west and south-east Europe, North Africa, the Middle East and Asia. The European breeding population is estimated to be between 5,900 and 14,000 pairs, mostly concentrated in the Mediterranean region. Spain, southern France and Turkey probably support about 60% of the total, although Italy, Greece and Croatia also have large populations (see table, map). The species is rarer towards the east, in Poland, Slovakia, Hungary, Romania and Bulgaria. Distribution is also restricted in the CIS, although Russia and Belarus together hold over a thousand pairs (V. Ivanovsky pers. comm.; see table, map). It is also scarce in the Baltic countries although nesting more or less regularly.

The species is migratory, wintering south of the Sahara, although a few individuals are regularly recorded wintering in southern Europe and North Africa.

Short-toed Eagles are now absent or only accidental on the Mediterranean islands, and absent from Denmark, Netherlands, Belgium, Germany, Switzerland and Austria. It disappeared from most of these countries during the last hundred years, during which time it suffered a marked decline in numbers and range all over Europe (Géroudet 1965, Génsbøl 1988). Numbers also declined between 1970 and 1990 in Poland, Lithuania, Moldova, Italy, Romania and Ukraine (see table, map), but most of the larger populations are considered stable. In France the species is currently showing certain stability after a long period of decline, having disappeared from several regions during the nineteenth century (Thiollay 1968a, Barbraud and Barbraud in press).

■ Ecology

Short-toed Eagles feed almost exclusively on reptiles, particularly snakes, and thus rely on habitats with traditional agriculture or extensive grazing where these prey animals are abundant, such as open, dry shrublands, rocky Mediterranean habitats (garigue), stony pastures, uncultivated land or open areas with copses (bocage) and hedges (Thiollay 1968a, Cramp and Simmons 1980, Amores and Franco 1981, Petreti 1988). In the eastern part of its range this small eagle is found in steppe areas sometimes mixed with forest.

Nesting is generally in high trees, preferably conifers or forests of evergreen oaks *Quercus*, and thus requires areas of mature woods alternating with open habitats in plains, hills or low mountains. The female lays a single egg and sexual maturity is not reached until 3–4 years old (Newton 1979).

■ Threats

A reduction in the extent of suitable hunting habitat through changes in agriculture and land-use is a major factor limiting the abundance and distribution of the·species. The expansion of modern farming

| | Breeding population | | | Breeding |
	Size (pairs)	Year	Trend	range trend
Albania	(50–100)	—	0*	—
Andorra	3–5	91	0	–1
Belarus	200–500	90	0	0
Bulgaria	50–100	—	0	0
Croatia	400–500 *	—	0*	0*
Estonia	1–5	—	0	0
France	**770–1,100**	82	(0)	0
Greece	300–500	—	0	0
Hungary	**40–50**	91	0	0
Italy	200–400	85	(–1)	(–1)
Latvia	5–12	—	F	F
Lithuania	(1–2)	85–88	(–1)	(–1)
Moldova	1–2	88	–1	0
Poland	10–20	—	–1	–1
Portugal	100–300	89	+1	+1
Romania	30–100	—	–1	**0**
Russia	1,000–3,000	—	0	0
Slovakia	20–30	—	0	0
Slovenia	(10–15)	—	(0)	(0)
Spain	1,700–2,100	—	0	0
Turkey	(1,000–5,000)	—	—	—
Ukraine	30–40	88	–1	–1
Total (approx.)	5,900–14,000			

Trends   +2 Large increase   +1 Small increase   0 Stable   X Extinct
(1970–1990)   –2 Large decrease   –1 Small decrease   F Fluctuating   N New breeder
Data quality   **Bold**: reliable quantitative data   Normal type: incomplete quantitative data
Bracketed figures: no quantitative data   * Data quality not provided

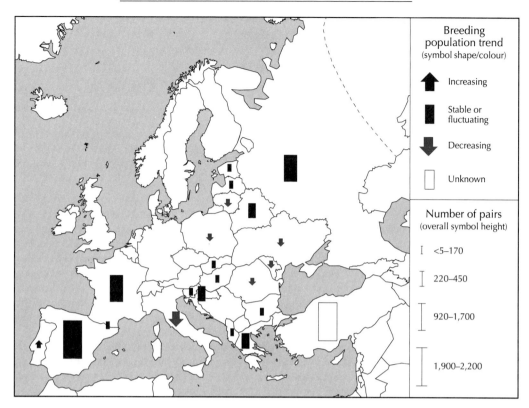

Breeding population trend
(symbol shape/colour)

- Increasing
- Stable or fluctuating
- Decreasing
- Unknown

Number of pairs
(overall symbol height)

- <5–170
- 220–450
- 920–1,700
- 1,900–2,200

practices, involving increases in the cultivation of monocultures, hedge destruction, the use of pesticides, and the abandonment of traditional farmland and subsequent afforestation, have led to a reduction in snake populations.

Other significant problems include forest fires and the construction of roads through forests which result in the fragmentation of the species' nesting habitat and cause excessive disturbance (FIR/UNAO 1984, de Juana 1989c).

The Short-toed Eagle has suffered greatly from shooting and nest destruction (Thiollay 1968a, Cramp and Simmons 1980). Although it is now protected by law in almost all countries within its range, due to its low reproductive potential the species remains susceptible to continuing illegal persecution during migration in many European countries such as Italy and Malta (Petreti and Petreti 1980). Like other raptors the species also suffers from electrocution by powerlines (Sériot and Rocamora 1992, Ferrer *et al.* 1993).

■ Conservation measures

Wide-scale habitat management is required for the species and should include the maintenance of low-intensity farmland, including the preservation of hedges, and a reduction in pesticide use in regions which host important populations of Short-toed Eagles. Such measures may be implemented and finan-

cially supported in the EU through Zonal Programmes developed under the Agri-environment Regulation (EC Reg. 2078/92) of the Common Agricultural Policy.

The appropriate management of woodlands to maintain sufficient densities of old trees, the prevention of fires, control of access and limitation of road construction are necessary to conserve nesting habitats. Important conservation measures identified in Italy, for example, are the conversion of 50% of the existing evergreen oak woodlands into mature forest and a reduction of the October–March wood-harvesting period (Petreti and Petreti 1980).

Education campaigns aimed at hunting organizations should be undertaken to limit the impact of illegal shooting, and flagging, moving or burying of electric powerlines should also be considered as a priority action to be undertaken in areas important for this raptor.

Without effective conservation of both nest-sites and feeding habitats the Short-toed Eagle might soon become extinct in several countries such as Poland which now have only relict populations (Krol 1983).

The monitoring of this and other raptor species needs to be maintained and improved in many countries, particularly in Turkey where it is necessary to obtain accurate population size and trend estimates.

GÉRARD ROCAMORA

161

Hen Harrier
Circus cyaneus

SPEC Category 3
Status Vulnerable
Criteria Large decline

Both the population size and range of the Hen Harrier are declining over much of Europe. This is due to the widespread loss and degradation of breeding habitat, and to intensive persecution by some gamekeepers. Extensive areas of heather moorland, steppe and semi-natural grasslands should be conserved, and the scale of illegal killing must be substantially reduced.

■ Distribution and population trends

The Hen Harrier is a widespread Holarctic species, with less than a third of its global range lying within Europe. Birds breed in suitable habitat throughout north-west Europe, central Fennoscandia and eastern Europe to the Urals. The northern and eastern populations are wholly migratory, wintering throughout central and southern Europe, though only a few birds cross the Mediterranean into North Africa or reach the Middle East (Cramp and Simmons 1980).

Russia holds about two-thirds of the European breeding population, and there are also large numbers in the United Kingdom, Sweden, Finland and France (see table, map).

Numbers fell dramatically during the late nineteenth and early twentieth centuries throughout western and central Europe. The British population later

recovered from this, but those of, for instance, Germany and Poland did not (Glutz von Blotzheim *et al.* 1971, Tomialojc 1990). Between 1970 and 1990 declines in population size were recorded in nearly half the countries within the Hen Harrier's European breeding range, including Russia, most other countries of eastern Europe, Germany, Republic of Ireland, Spain and Portugal (see table, map). In only three countries have increases been recorded. Furthermore, in over a third of the countries where the species currently breeds, including Russia, a contraction in range size has been noted; this trend was particularly marked in Portugal and Latvia.

■ Ecology

At all times of the year the Hen Harrier inhabits dry or damp open terrain with low vegetation, but it generally avoids rocky or mountainous country and stands of mature woodland (Cramp and Simmons 1980).

The species breeds in low, dense vegetation primarily on steppe, open taiga, moorland and river valley meadows but also even on forest bogs (e.g. Dementiev and Gladkov 1951c). There are important regional variations in the habitat used for breeding, including coastal sand-dunes in the Netherlands (SOVON 1988), fields of cereals and other crops in central and northern Spain (B. Arroya pers. comm.) and young conifer plantations in Britain and Ireland (Watson 1977).

The diet consists of a wide range of small mammals (particularly voles *Microtus*, young rabbits *Oryctolagus cuniculus* and hares *Lepus*), the young of nidifugous birds and young and adult songbirds (Cramp and Simmons 1980).

■ Threats

The widespread loss of breeding habitat and the occurrence of localized persecution are considered to be the major causes of the Hen Harrier's population decline. Steppe and other natural and semi-natural grasslands are threatened by increasing cultivation and are being degraded through drainage,

	Breeding population			Breeding
	Size (pairs)	Year	Trend	range trend
Belarus	300–500	90	F	0
Belgium	0–6	81–90	0	0
Czech Republic	**50–80**	—	**0**	**0**
Denmark	**0–2**	88	**0**	**0**
Estonia	200–300	—	–1	(–1)
Finland	**2,000–4,000**	92	F	F
France	**2,500–3,600**	82	+1	+1
Germany	80–110	85	–2	0
Rep. of Ireland	40–60	—	–1	–1
Latvia	10–20	—	–2	–2
Lithuania	(1–2)	85–88	(–1)	(–1)
Luxembourg	**0–1**	—	**0**	0
Moldova	**4–8**	89	–1	**0**
Netherlands	**80–120**	89–91	+1	+2
Norway	10–100	90	F	F
Poland	50–100	—	**0**	0
Portugal	1–25	91	–2	–2
Russia	15,000–20,000	—	–1	–1
Spain	300–400	—	–1	–1
Sweden	1,000–2,000	87	0	0
Ukraine	(10–15)	88	–2	–1
United Kingdom	670–670	88–89	0	+1
Isle of Man [1]	**40–62**	90	N	0*
Total (approx.)	22,000–32,000			

Trends (1970-1990) +2 Large increase +1 Small increase 0 Stable X Extinct –2 Large decrease –1 Small decrease F Fluctuating N New breeder
Data quality **Bold**: reliable quantitative data Normal type: incomplete quantitative data Bracketed figures: no quantitative data * Data quality not provided
[1] Population figures are included within United Kingdom totals

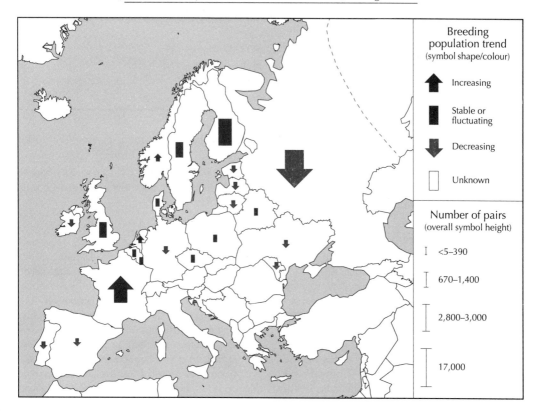

re-seeding and overgrazing. Afforestation of moorland and other open habitats can initially benefit the species through providing suitable nesting habitat while the trees are still small, but ultimately it constitutes a major habitat loss (Batten *et al*. 1990).

There is still a considerable amount of illegal persecution by gamekeepers in Europe. This happens particularly on the moors of Scotland (Bibby and Etheridge 1993) and northern England, and involves the destruction of nests as well as the killing of adult breeding birds. The species is also shot illegally in central and east Europe (L. Tomialojc *in litt*. 1993).

■ Conservation measures

The Hen Harrier would benefit from the preservation of extensive tracts of open country, particularly the favoured areas of lowland and upland heath and heather moorland, steppe, damp marsh and unimproved and marginal grasslands with low-intensity grazing. A ban on the afforestation of heather moorland and montane scrubland in countries where these habitats are under threat would also greatly assist the species.

The problem of illegal killing of Hen Harriers by gamekeepers in the United Kingdom needs to be addressed urgently by both sporting and conservation interests, and a collaborative investigation is now under way into the impact of raptor predation on populations of Red Grouse *Lagopus lagopus scoticus* in the United Kingdom.

BRIAN ETHERIDGE

163

Pallid Harrier
Circus macrourus

SPEC Category   3
Status   Endangered
Criteria   Large decline, <2,500 pairs

The Pallid Harrier is a rare and poorly known species in Europe with a rapidly contracting range and declining population. It is threatened by the wide-scale transformation of virgin steppe grasslands to agriculture. Conservation measures should combine research into the distribution and ecology of the species and its local populations with the protection of known nesting areas and the maintenance of suitable habitats.

■ Distribution and population trends

Pallid Harriers occur in the eastern part of Europe where the total population (excluding Kazakhstan west of the Ural river) is estimated at roughly 1,000–2,000 breeding pairs (Galushin in press; see table). The world population is not more than 20,000 pairs (Galushin 1993), and about a third of the breeding range lies within Europe. A small number winter in south-east Europe, North Africa and the Middle East, but most move to the Afrotropics and the Indian subcontinent (Cramp and Simmons 1980).

Almost the entire European breeding population lies within Russia (see table, map). Dispersed and fluctuating local populations occur in the lower Danube valley (Vasiliu 1968, Ciochia 1992), in central Ukraine (Strigunov 1984), along the middle and upper Don river (Vetrov 1992, Klimov and Aleksandrov 1992, Belik *et al*. 1993) and in the middle Ural river valley (Davygora 1985). The species is locally common in some parts of its Asian range, such as northern Kazakhstan (Neruchev and Makarov 1982, Solomatin 1984, Egorov 1990, Kovshar and Khrokov 1991), but it is rare now in south-west Siberia (Toropov 1983), the Altai region (Kuchin 1976, Neufeldt 1986, Berezovikov *et al*. 1992) and the Minusinsk lowlands (Kustov 1988).

The breeding range lies within the steppe, forest-steppe and semi-desert zones of Eurasia. It is contracting rapidly, and numbers are undergoing substantial declines (Davygora and Belik 1992, Belik

et al. 1993; see table, map). Some 30–50 years ago the species nested throughout the Ukraine, in the major part of southern Russia (up to the plains east of the Yenisey river) and in northern Kazakhstan (Dementiev and Gladkov 1951c). Periodically the species has invaded eastern and even western Europe, nesting, for example, in Germany and Sweden (Cramp and Simmons 1980). In 1988 (a population peak of field voles) the largest known nesting group of c.30 pairs was recorded near the middle Don river (Vetrov 1992) though none had nested there before or have since. The northernmost nesting was recorded within a forest zone near Kostroma on the upper Volga river (Kuznetsov 1994). During the last 30–40 years, however, the western limit of the breeding range has retreated greatly to the east, and remaining populations are extremely fragmented, separated sometimes by hundreds of kilometres. The species last bred in Bulgaria in 1956 (Nankinov *et al*. 1991).

The Pallid Harrier is a poorly known species, partly because of the considerable difficulties in field identification of females and immature birds, and much of the relevant literature consequently has not attempted to separate this species from Montagu's Harrier *C. pygargus*. Local fluctuations in numbers caused by yearly movements of pairs and entire breeding groups further hinders the assessment of population sizes and local distribution.

Because of the species' fairly small world population and recent declines, its global status is classified as Near Threatened (Collar *et al*. 1994).

■ Ecology

Throughout its range the Pallid Harrier prefers to nest in uncultivated grasslands. It evidently avoids very dry open sites and selects wetter areas for nesting, preferably with sparse shrubs and weeds (Osmolovskaya 1949, Davygora and Belik 1992, Belik *et al*. 1993). Exceptionally it occurs in agricultural fields (Vetrov 1992). Nests are placed in damp

| | Breeding population | | | Breeding |
	Size (pairs)	Year	Trend	range trend
Belarus	(0–0)	90	(X)	(X)
Moldova	**2–5**	88	**–1**	**0**
Romania	(0–20)	—	–1	–1
Russia	1,000–2,000	—	–1	–1
Ukraine	(10–17)	86	–2	–2
Total (approx.)	1,000–2,000			

Trends +2 Large increase   +1 Small increase   0 Stable   X Extinct
(1970–1990) –2 Large decrease   –1 Small decrease   F Fluctuating   N New breeder
Data quality **Bold**: reliable quantitative data   Normal type: incomplete quantitative data
Bracketed figures: no quantitative data   * Data quality not provided

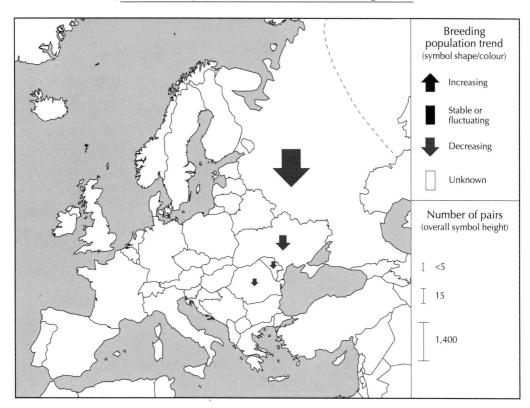

Breeding
population trend
(symbol shape/colour)

Increasing

Stable or
fluctuating

Decreasing

Unknown

Number of pairs
(overall symbol height)

<5

15

1,400

areas on the ground, and the loose groups of breeding pairs which occur can sometimes include pairs of Montagu's Harriers.

The principal prey of the Pallid Harrier is small rodents (mostly voles and mice), lizards, and small birds, especially fledglings (Osmolovskaya 1949); it is quite capable of taking larks and other passerines in flight as well as on the ground (Davygora 1985).

■ Threats

The widespread crash of the Pallid Harrier population is due to factors affecting the species throughout its range, including habitat loss and degradation through the transformation of steppe grasslands to arable agriculture, overgrazing of wet pastures, and the clearance of shrubs and tall weeds in steppeland. Pallid Harriers are more dependent on virgin steppe habitats than other harrier species and therefore suffer greatly as a result of its destruction (Belik 1991, Belik *et al.* 1993). It is also possible that the species is sensitive to pesticides and rodenticides (Davygora and Belik 1990, Belik *et al.* 1993), but specific research has not been carried out on this subject.

■ Conservation measures

The first step towards the effective conservation of the species is its incorporation into the Red Data lists of all countries within its range, and it has already been recommended as a candidate species for the second edition of the Russian Red Data book (Davygora and Belik 1990). Meanwhile, wide-ranging specific research is required to identify actual and potential nesting areas, and known nesting groups should be protected by state or local conservation law. For ground-nesting harriers the establishment of small (20–100 ha) protected areas, may be an effective conservation measure. The best example of this concerns Montagu's Harrier in the Voronezh region of south-central Russia, where 12–15 pairs have inhabited a tiny (c.20 ha) piece of totally protected steppe with some bushes amidst agricultural fields for over 30 years (Galushin *et al.* 1991). The effect of pesticides and rodenticides should be investigated on both the breeding and wintering grounds.

VLADIMIR GALUSHIN

Levant Sparrowhawk
Accipiter brevipes

SPEC Category 2
Status Rare
Criteria <10,000 pairs

The Levant Sparrowhawk, a migratory species largely confined to Europe when breeding, has a stable but small and fragmented known breeding population. The favoured habitat, which lies along river valleys, should be protected and further population studies throughout the species' range need to be initiated.

■ Distribution and population trends

Levant Sparrowhawks are restricted as breeding birds almost entirely to Europe, occupying the south-east and eastern parts of the region extending from the Balkan peninsula to the middle reaches of the Ural river and the Caspian Sea. Outside Europe the species breeds only in western Kazakhstan and Iran. The distribution is fragmented, being restricted almost entirely to river valleys. The whole population is migratory, moving to northern and eastern Africa in winter, but its precise migratory routes and winter quarters are difficult to define due partly to the problems of separating birds in the field from close relatives such as Sparrowhawk *A. nisus* and Shikra *A. badius* (Dovrat 1991).

The total European population is currently estimated to be between c.3,600 and 5,800 pairs (see table), of which probably half occur in the Don river basin in eastern Ukraine and southern Russia (Belik 1984, 1986, Belik and Vetrov 1992). There is a locally large population also in northern Greece (Bauer *et al.* 1969, Handrinos and Demetropoulos 1983), and further very small numbers of breeding birds are recorded between there and the Don river region.

The Levant Sparrowhawk remains, however, a poorly known species across the major part of its breeding range, mostly due to difficulties in field identification, and there is thus good reason to expect the discovery of further dense local populations as a result of studies conducted throughout the species' range, such as those initiated in the early 1980s by V. P. Belik and V. V. Vetrov in the Don basin. Indeed, widespread population studies are required in view of recent estimates of Levant Sparrowhawk numbers passing over Israel during migration, including 44,000 birds in the autumn of 1986 (Leshem 1990, Dovrat 1991) and over 49,000 in the spring of 1987 (Shirihai and Yekutiel 1991). These figures indicate a substantial underestimate of the breeding numbers, due presumably to the major part of the true breeding range being as yet undiscovered.

At present the size of both the known population and of the known breeding range are largely stable (Galushin 1991a), despite previous indications of a population decline in some regions (Bijleveld 1974), and possible current declines in Romania and Albania (see table, map).

■ Ecology

The Levant Sparrowhawk is highly selective in its choice of nesting habitats, rarely occurring outside areas of fragmented forest alternating with open grasslands, primarily along river valleys.

Within the most favourable habitats nesting pairs are 0.5–3.0 km away from each other (Casda 1964, Belik 1986). The species nests relatively late in the season (normally mid-May) in the taller trees (including *Populus nigra*), usually 8–15 m above ground.

The principal food comprises lizards, small fledgling birds, and large insects which include dragonflies (Odonata), grasshoppers (Orthoptera) and cicadas (Cicadidae) (Cramp and Simmons 1980, Belik 1984).

■ Threats

The agricultural and recreational development of river valleys affects the species' nesting and hunting habitats, although specific studies on the impact of these factors on the Levant Sparrowhawk have not

	Breeding population			Breeding
	Size (pairs)	Year	Trend	range trend
Albania	10–50	—	–1	(–1)
Bulgaria	(20–50)	—	(0)	(0)
Croatia	1–5 *	—	0*	0*
Greece	(1,000–1,200)	—	(0)	(0)
Hungary	5–10	—	0	0
Romania	(10–30)	—	(–2)	(–2)
Russia	1,500–3,000	—	0	0
Turkey	(10–500)	—	—	—
Ukraine	1,000–1,000	—	0	0
Total (approx.)	3,600–5,800			

Trends	+2 Large increase	+1 Small increase	0 Stable	X Extinct
(1970–1990)	–2 Large decrease	–1 Small decrease	F Fluctuating	N New breeder
Data quality	**Bold**: reliable quantitative data	Normal type: incomplete quantitative data
	Bracketed figures: no quantitative data	* Data quality not provided

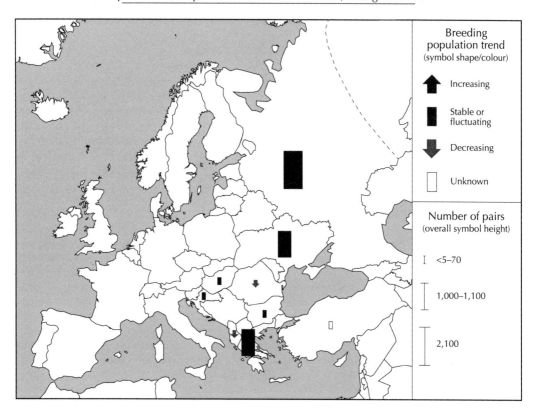

been carried out. This is, however, important, especially in view of the species' small population and its rather particular habitat requirements.

Sharp declines in lizard populations, caused for example, by extremely low winter or spring temperatures, may also diminish the number of breeding Levant Sparrowhawks (Semago 1985).

■ Conservation measures

Further population studies throughout the Levant Sparrowhawk's range are clearly of major impor-

tance, but in the meantime favoured habitats and sites should be protected. In Greece and Hungary, however, only about half of local numbers are found within Important Bird Areas, and in other countries the majority of birds live outside protected areas, so wider-scale habitat conservation measures along river valleys known to contain the species are necessary, including restrictions on the clear-felling of forests, on the cultivation of grassland and on mass tourism.

VLADIMIR GALUSHIN

Long-legged Buzzard
Buteo rufinus

SPEC Category 3
Status (Endangered)
Criteria Large decline, <2,500 pairs

Following a substantial range decline early in the twentieth century due to cultivation of steppe lands, the Long-legged Buzzard has become rare in Europe and continues to decline in numbers in Russia, largely due to habitat destruction and a decline in susliks, its main prey. Remaining steppe areas should be conserved, nesting sites should be protected and electricity pylons modified to prevent electrocution of birds.

■ Distribution and population trends

Around 20% of the Long-legged Buzzard's total range lies within Europe; the rest comprises northwest Africa, the Middle East, Kazakhstan and central Asia. In Europe it is quite rare (see table) and is concentrated in the south-east and east of the region. The main population is in Turkey (Kasparek 1992a), the northern Caucasus plains extending east of 44°E (Belik 1992b, Khokhlov 1993) and the area along the north-western border of Kazakhstan. Discontinuous populations exist in central Ukraine (Voinstvensky 1950, Strigunov 1982), the Central Chernozem Nature Reserve (in south-west Russia), former Yugoslavia, Albania, Bulgaria and Greece. In the Balkans, birds breed mostly south of the lower Danube river (Cramp and Simmons 1980). The species winters in Turkey, the Middle East, North and East Africa and northern India.

Turkey and Russia are the two European strongholds, although numbers in the former are known only very poorly (see table). The total population in European Russia is unlikely to exceed 1,500 breeding pairs (see table, map), of which about 200 pairs nest between the Volga and Ural rivers (Moseikin 1991). The Balkan population is thought to total approximately 200–300 pairs (see table), with an additional 20 pairs in the southern part of former Yugoslavia (Vasic *et al.* 1985).

The European range of the species contracted in the first half of the twentieth century due to the cultivation of steppe lands in Ukraine and southern Russia. Although geographical range has probably been relatively stable over the last 20–30 years, numbers have continued to decline slowly in southern Russia due to habitat destruction and human disturbance. East of the Volga river, however, as well as in the western part of the species' range, populations are stable or even increasing. For example, the estimated number of Long-legged Buzzards near the eastern border of Kazakhstan in the 1980s was considerably higher than in the 1950s (Lindeman 1983b), probably due to the abolition of mass raptor persecution in the former U.S.S.R. at the end of the 1960s. Vagrant Long-legged Buzzards have also been recorded more often in eastern Hungary in the 1980s than in the 1970s (Kovacs 1992) and have been found in Slovakia, Poland and Sweden. Trends in Turkey, which holds the largest European population, are unknown, as they are in Albania (see table, map).

■ Ecology

Favoured breeding habitats are open, uncultivated areas, with trees, high bushes, cliffs or hillocks for nesting. In the west of its range Long-legged Buzzard may inhabit small forests and cliffs close to open hunting sites. It builds nests readily on any kind of electricity pylons or poles running through treeless steppe, as is particularly evident along both sides of the Kazakhstan border.

Food is diverse, including lizards, snakes, small birds and large insects, but susliks *Citellus* and other small mammals are preferred. Indeed, the distribution of the Long-legged Buzzard appears to correspond with the presence of suslik and gerbil *Gerbillus* colonies (Lobachev 1961, Petrov 1964, Lindeman 1983b, Kovacs 1992).

■ Threats

The major threat to isolated Long-legged Buzzard populations is the potential destruction of unique

| | Breeding population | | | Breeding |
	Size (pairs)	Year	Trend	range trend
Albania	(0–10)	—	—	—
Bulgaria	150–250	80–90	+2	+2
Greece	40–60	—	(0)	(0)
Russia	800–1,500	—	–1	0
Turkey	(1,000–10,000)	—	—	—
Ukraine	40–50	80	0	0
Total (approx.)	2,000–12,000			

Trends +2 Large increase +1 Small increase 0 Stable X Extinct
(1970–1990) –2 Large decrease –1 Small decrease F Fluctuating N New breeder
Data quality **Bold**: reliable quantitative data Normal type: incomplete quantitative data
Bracketed figures: no quantitative data * Data quality not provided

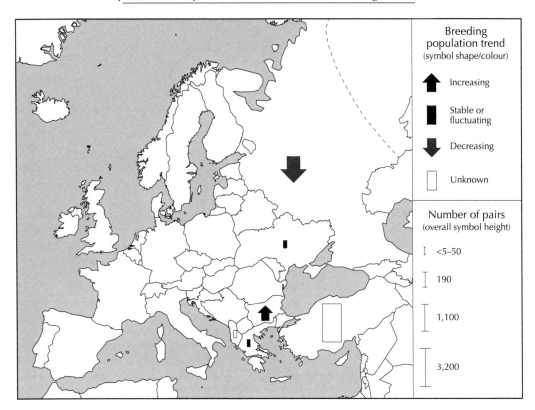

Breeding
population trend
(symbol shape/colour)

↑ Increasing

▮ Stable or
fluctuating

↓ Decreasing

▯ Unknown

Number of pairs
(overall symbol height)

I <5–50

I 190

I 1,100

I 3,200

combinations of suitable nesting and hunting habitats, either through the clearance of small forests near open grasslands or by the conversion of these grassland areas into arable agriculture. Human disturbance may also cause the birds to abandon their nesting sites, and visible nests in isolated trees are often destroyed by shepherds and other local people.

In the eastern part of the European range, the availability of suitable and safe nesting sites is insufficient. Despite an abundance of apparently adequate sites on electricity poles, many are unsafe, and relatively large numbers of birds are electrocuted. In Uzbekistan, for example, over 50% of poles are believed to be unsafe for raptors (Abdunazarov 1991).

■ Conservation measures

The most important requirement is to conserve the remaining uncultivated steppes through the establishment of reserves and support for traditional pastoral activities.

Within the western part of the range, areas with isolated nests and small populations of the Long-legged Buzzard should be designated as protected areas. For example, the Central Chernozem Reserve in the Kursk region of southern Russia supports the northernmost nest of the species in Russia (Kostin 1986).

Appropriate habitat management should ensure that suslik colonies and other prey populations are maintained in good numbers within raptor hunting areas by abandoning campaigns for the control of these rodents. Where nest-sites are limited, e.g. in the eastern part of the range, removal of isolated trees containing raptor nests should be prevented, and the installation of artificial structures suitable for nesting buzzards would be beneficial. Electric powerline poles, in contrast to complex pylons, which are not dangerous, should be equipped with protective devices to prevent electrocution of the birds (Flint et al. 1983).

Local people should be well informed of the lack of threat to livestock and of the ecological value of Long-legged Buzzards and other raptors and the need to conserve their habitat and the overall biodiversity of steppeland.

VLADIMIR GALUSHIN, ANATOLY V. DAVYGORA
AND VALERY N. MOSEIKIN

Lesser Spotted Eagle
Aquila pomarina

SPEC Category 3
Status Rare
Criteria <10,000 pairs

The known European breeding population of Lesser Spotted Eagle is small and restricted, though currently stable. It is vulnerable to habitat loss, mainly drainage of forests and meadows, and to disturbance, and consequently the forest breeding sites and adjoining open hunting areas should be maintained and protected.

■ Distribution and population trends

The western Palearctic population of Lesser Spotted Eagle (the nominate race) occurs from northern Germany east to 35°E in Russia and south to Turkey, the Caucasus and the south Caspian region. It migrates over the Bosporus (Turkey), Israel and Suez (Egypt) to winter in southern Africa. A non-migratory subspecies, *A. p. hastata* (often regarded formerly as a distinct species), inhabits northern India and adjacent countries.

The species appears to have a small and restricted European breeding population mainly concentrated in Latvia, Lithuania, Belarus, Poland and Slovakia (see table, map). Based on these figures (and assuming one fledgling per two pairs) the whole population would be c.17,000–24,000 individuals in autumn in Europe (including Turkey). The numbers of migrating birds in autumn are, however, much higher; in 1988 more than 32,000 (Shirihai and Christie 1992) crossed the Bosporus and in Israel more than 74,000 individuals were recorded at Kafr-Qassem (Tsovel

1990), the maximum figure at the latter locality being 142,000 in 1983 (Shirihai and Christie 1992). These figures therefore suggest that the breeding population size, and possibly its distribution, are underestimated. The eastern border of the nominate race's range in Russia is poorly known.

Prior to 1970 declines had occurred in the west of the range (B.-U. Meyburg *in litt.*). Overall, numbers were probably stable between 1970 and 1990 (see table, map), although there were declines recorded in Romania, Moldova, Albania and possibly Bulgaria and Greece. Gradual increases are evident in the Czech Republic and Latvia (see table, map).

■ Ecology

The Lesser Spotted Eagle is exclusively a forest-dweller in Europe. In the south it breeds largely in hilly deciduous and mixed forests, preferring forest edge and lower altitudes (below 400 m, sometimes 1,000 m), while in the northern part of central Europe it breeds in wet lowland forest on the plains. It is less dependent on wetlands than Greater Spotted Eagle *A. clanga* (B.-U. Meyburg *in litt.*).

Throughout its range the species requires neighbouring open land, which may include cultivated areas, for hunting. In central Europe birds feed mainly on small mammals, especially voles *Microtus*, but to some extent also on small to medium-sized birds, and especially on amphibians (mainly frogs *Rana temporaria*) and reptiles. In humid lowland areas amphibians can make up 42% of prey. Carrion is quite rarely taken.

The nest, constructed of large sticks, is generally placed 12–15 m above the ground in a tree. In central Europe eggs are laid at the end of April and in early May, with young fledging during late July and early August (B.-U. Meyburg *in litt.*).

■ Threats

Although not currently highly threatened, the Lesser Spotted Eagle is vulnerable to clearance of its mature forest breeding habitat and the drainage, cultivation or vegetational succession of open feeding habitats.

	Breeding population			Breeding
	Size (pairs)	Year	Trend	range trend
Albania	5–20	—	–1	(–2)
Belarus	3,000–3,500	90	0	0
Bulgaria	(60–120)	—	(–1)	(–1)
Croatia	150–250 *		0*	0*
Czech Republic	**3–6**	—	+1	+1
Estonia	150–200	—	0	0
Germany	100–100	—	**0**	**0**
Greece	50–80	—	(–1)	(–1)
Hungary	90–150	91	0	0
Latvia	800–1,500	—	+1	0
Lithuania	300–500	85–88	(0)	(0)
Moldova	**7–12**	90	**–1**	**–1**
Poland	**1,100–1,300**	—	0	0
Romania	80–200	—	–1	**0**
Russia	50–200	—	0	0
Slovakia	500–600	—	**0**	**0**
Turkey	(30–500)	—	—	—
Ukraine	**200–250**	89	**0**	**0**
Total (approx.)	6,700–9,500			

Trends   +2 Large increase   +1 Small increase   0 Stable   X Extinct
(1970–1990) –2 Large decrease   –1 Small decrease   F Fluctuating N New breeder
Data quality **Bold**: reliable quantitative data   Normal type: incomplete quantitative data
Bracketed figures: no quantitative data   * Data quality not provided

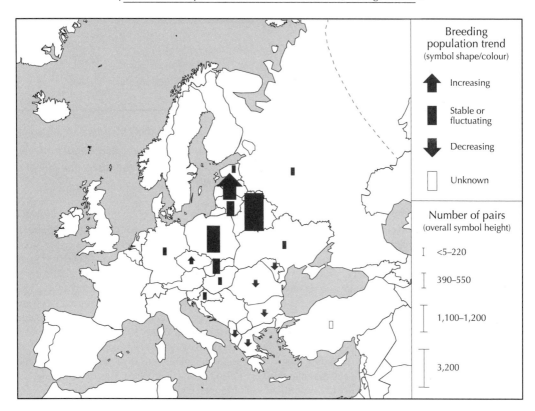

Breeding
population trend
(symbol shape/colour)

Increasing

Stable or
fluctuating

Decreasing

Unknown

Number of pairs
(overall symbol height)

<5–220

390–550

1,100–1,200

3,200

Human disturbance during the breeding period is also a problem, especially due to forestry operations. Many birds fail to breed in years when populations of fieldmice *Apodemus* are very low, or heavy losses may occur during the incubation period, the causes of which are not completely understood. Together these phenomena may result in an annual reproductive failure of 30–50% (S. Danko own data).

Large numbers of Lesser Spotted Eagles are shot while on migration through southern Europe, the Middle East and Africa, and the situation is particularly bad in Lebanon and Syria where hundreds or thousands are killed annually (B.-U. Meyburg *in litt.*).

■ Conservation measures

Most importantly, both the breeding and feeding habitats of this rare and dispersed European species should be conserved through wide-scale conservation measures. Disturbance should also be avoided during the breeding season by restricting human presence.

Measures should be taken to ensure the enforcement of this species' protected status throughout Europe, and it should be added to protected species listing elsewhere where necessary. Further research is also required to assess the true population size and distribution, including especially the eastern extension of its range in Russia, and to establish the causes of its low reproductive success.

STEFAN DANKO

Greater Spotted Eagle
Aquila clanga

SPEC Category 1
Status Endangered
Criteria Large decline, <2,500 pairs

The European range of this globally threatened species contracted during 1970–1990, and numbers continue to decline, mostly due to habitat destruction and human disturbance. Additional protected areas are required with measures designed to conserve meadows and marshes alongside blocks of undisturbed forest. Nest-sites should be guarded to prevent disturbance.

■ Distribution and population trends

The major part of the world range of the Greater Spotted Eagle extends through the southern forest zone in north European Russia and south-central Siberia as far east as the lower Amur river. However, because of its highly dispersed nature and its close similarity to the Lesser Spotted Eagle *A. pomarina* in appearance, it is difficult to make an accurate assessment of the true extent of its breeding range. About a quarter of the range lies within Europe, in a band from the Poland–Belarus border, extending eastwards between 64–65°N in the north and the edge of the forest zone in the south (which lies at the northern edge of the Black Sea in the west and at 53–56°N in the Ural region).

The species is migratory, with regular wintering areas lying around the eastern Mediterranean, including Egypt (Curry-Lindahl 1981), and in the Middle East, as well as in southern Asia. Some birds have been recorded in winter in East Africa (Cramp and Simmons 1980), and on both spring and autumn migration in southern Israel it is very rare (Shirihai and Christie 1992). It is much less frequent at migration watchpoints than is Lesser Spotted Eagle (Meyburg in prep.).

The species' total European population is very small, amounting to about 1,000 pairs. The majority are in Russia (Galushin in press; see table, map), but even here the species occurs at extremely low densities, with for example 20 pairs in 85,000 km^2 in the

St Petersburg region of north-west Russia (Malchevskiy and Pukinskiy 1983), c.30 pairs in 84,000 km^2 of the Tver region on the upper Volga (Kerdanov 1990), 10–15 pairs in 47,000 km^2 in the Moscow region (Mishchenko 1988), c.20 pairs in 160,000 km^2 in the Perm region west to the Ural mountains (Shepel 1992) and 5–7 pairs in 21,100 km^2 in the Lipetsk region in wet forests along the upper Don river and its delta (Klimov *et al.* 1990, Belik 1992b, Klimov and Aleksandrov 1992). Outside Russia, populations with 10 or more pairs occur only in Poland (Tomialojc 1990), Belarus, Romania and the Ukraine, while a few other east European countries hold smaller numbers (see table, map).

Numbers and range declined in most of Europe between 1970 and 1990, including the large Russian population (see table, map).

Due to the widespread declines which have affected Greater Spotted Eagle in Europe, and its small total world population, the species is now listed as Globally Threatened (Collar *et al.* 1994).

■ Ecology

Birds prefer to breed in wet forests bordering humid meadows, bogs, marshes and other wetlands, and human settlements are avoided. The areas occupied are generally lowland, but the species will breed at up to 1,000 m (Meyburg in prep.), being much scarcer in hill forests. Hunting takes place over wet meadows and open swamps, and the diet comprises water voles *Arvicola terrestris* and other small mammals as well as waterfowl and other middle-sized birds, frogs and snakes (Dementiev and Gladkov 1951a, Galushin 1962, Cramp and Simmons 1980).

In suitable areas, territories are 15–30 km^2 in size. The species nests 5–20 m above the ground in tall trees inside the forest, a few hundred metres from the edge. Nests are often used year after year, though many pairs use two or three nests alternately.

■ Threats

The Greater Spotted Eagle is very intolerant of permanent human presence within its breeding or

	Breeding population			Breeding
	Size (pairs)	Year	Trend	range trend
Belarus	(10–15)	90	(F)	(0)
Finland	(0–2)	92	–1	0
Latvia	1–5	—	–2	–2
Moldova	**3–5**	90	–1	–1
Poland	5–10	—	0	0
Romania	5–10	—	0	0
Russia	800–1,000	—	–1	–1
Ukraine	40–50	88	–1	–1
Total (approx.)	860–1,100			

Trends: +2 Large increase +1 Small increase 0 Stable X Extinct
(1970–1990) –2 Large decrease –1 Small decrease F Fluctuating N New breeder
Data quality: **Bold:** reliable quantitative data Normal type: incomplete quantitative data
Bracketed figures: no quantitative data * Data quality not provided

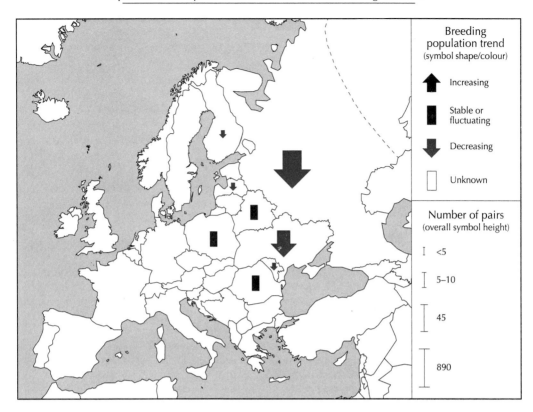

Breeding
population trend
(symbol shape/colour)

▲ Increasing

■ Stable or
fluctuating

▼ Decreasing

☐ Unknown

Number of pairs
(overall symbol height)

I <5

I 5–10

I 45

I 890

hunting habitats, and consequently birds abandon their territories once people start to live or work nearby. It is also sensitive to habitat alterations, particularly drainage of wetlands (Meyburg in prep.). Other causes of population decline are nest destruction and human disturbance during incubation and early brooding, as well as occasional shooting. Declines in the west have been linked to competition with growing numbers of Lesser Spotted Eagles, but that species is increasing only in Latvia, whereas Greater Spotted Eagle is in decline over a much larger area.

■ Conservation measures

Large protected areas may effectively conserve the species as has been shown in the Oka Nature Reserve in the Rjazan region to the south-east of Moscow, where the breeding population of 7–9 pairs has remained for 30 years (Galushin 1962, Postelnykh

1986). The protection of other important areas (for example in the Tver and Novgorod regions in Russia) should be considered in order to maintain relatively stable populations there. On a broad scale, forestry activities should be regulated to minimize disturbance, and wet meadows used as hunting areas should be maintained by traditional methods and not drained.

Known nesting sites should be guarded in May–June to prevent human disturbance. Also, the illegal shooting of birds or the removal of eggs or young from nests should be stopped and education programmes must be implemented to inform local people of the importance of conserving the species.

Surveys of Greater and Lesser Spotted Eagles, particularly in areas where their ranges coincide, are needed to clarify the trends in their populations and range sizes.

VLADIMIR GALUSHIN

Steppe Eagle
Aquila nipalensis

SPEC Category 3
Status Vulnerable
Criteria Large decline

The Steppe Eagle's European range has contracted mainly due to cultivation of virgin grassland steppes, and its population continues to decline as a result of electrocution by electricity lines, human disturbance and nest destruction. Establishment of large protected areas within the remaining natural steppelands is essential for this and other steppic species. The maintenance and protection of nesting sites and appropriate modifications of electricity lines is also required.

■ Distribution and population trends

Formerly considered as part of the Tawny/Steppe Eagle superspecies (*Aquila rapax*), the Steppe Eagle (*Aquila nipalensis*) is now considered a separate species (e.g. Sibley and Monroe 1993). The major part of the Steppe Eagle's range lies outside of Europe, extending through western and central Kazakhstan eastwards across the steppes south-east of Lake Baikal, Mongolia and central China. Within Europe some 15,000–25,000 birds breed (see table); most of these inhabit the relatively virgin steppe and semi-desert lands in Kalmykia, north-west of the Caspian Sea (Survillo 1983, Varshavski *et al.* 1983). Others mostly occur in the narrow strip of uncultivated steppes close to the Kazakhstan border, with about 250 pairs in the south-east corner of the Saratov region (Moseikin 1991), and in some years over 700 pairs nest within a 30,000 km² area in the Orenburg region south of the Ural mountains (Davygora 1992). The species also occurs in small parts of the Rostov and Stavropol regions adjacent to Kalmykia (Belik 1992b, Khokhlov 1993), and there are small populations in Ukraine and Turkey (see table, map), although the population in Ukraine may now be extinct.

The Steppe Eagle winters mostly in East Africa, the southern part of the Arabian peninsula, and in India (Curry-Lindahl 1981, Mihelsons 1982). During mild winters some eagles remain north of the Aegean Sea in Greece and Bulgaria (Nankinov 1982). Birds migrate in large numbers through Israel: up to 75,000 individuals were recorded in spring 1985 (Shirihai and Christie 1992).

The western part of the Steppe Eagle's range has contracted over the last 50–70 years. At the beginning of this century the species inhabited areas north and north-west of the Black Sea, but by the end of the 1950s it disappeared from the Crimea and south-east Ukraine (Zubarovski 1977); the last pairs recorded nesting in the Ukraine were near the Lower Dniepr river in 1982 (Sytnik 1988, Koshelev *et al.* 1991). The species is extinct in Romania (Ciochia 1992), but some individuals have been recorded in summer in Bulgaria (Nankinov 1982, Simeonov *et al.* 1990).

■ Ecology

The Steppe Eagle only inhabits uncultivated dry grassland steppes and semi-deserts, although in the eastern part of its range it sometimes lives in sand deserts. Within favourable habitats in Kalmykia, and between the Volga and Ural rivers, birds nest at high densities, with 1–4 km between pairs. However, this varies according to the density of susliks *Citellus* which are the principal prey (on average over 60% of the Steppe Eagle's diet) (Varshavski *et al.* 1983). When susliks are scarce, eagles feed on middle-sized mammals or dead saiga antelope *Saiga tatarica* and birds (Cramp and Simmons 1980, Davygora 1992).

Stick nests are constructed on the ground (preferably on gentle slopes), in low bushes or old haystacks. Less often eagles build nests in trees or on poles of electric powerlines.

■ Threats

This century, range contraction and population decline have been caused by the agricultural development of virgin steppes. At present, almost all areas suitable for arable agriculture have been ploughed. More recently the use of remaining steppe grasslands for intensive cattle- and sheep-grazing has increased, leading to disturbance of birds and destruction of their nests by people and dogs. In a study by Davygora

	Breeding population			Breeding
	Size (pairs)	Year	Trend	range trend
Russia	15,000–25,000	—	–1	–1
Turkey	(1–10)	—	—	—
Ukraine	1–5	80	–2	–2
Total (approx.)	15,000–25,000			

Trends	+2 Large increase	+1 Small increase	0 Stable	X Extinct
(1970–1990)	–2 Large decrease	–1 Small decrease	F Fluctuating	N New breeder
Data quality	**Bold**: reliable quantitative data	Normal type: incomplete quantitative data		
	Bracketed figures: no quantitative data	* Data quality not provided		

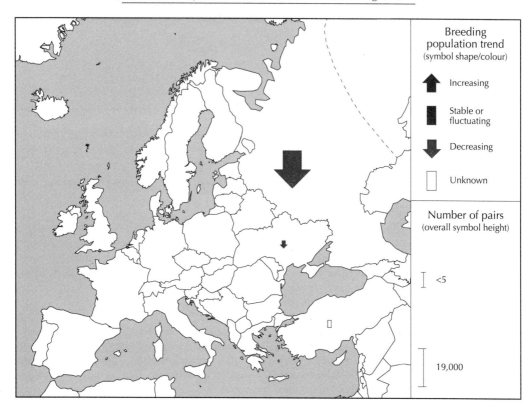

Breeding
population trend
(symbol shape/colour)

Increasing

Stable or
fluctuating

Decreasing

Unknown

Number of pairs
(overall symbol height)

<5

19,000

(1991) it was found that human disturbance of incubating birds was a major cause of egg loss, both through predation by Rooks *Corvus frugilegus* and overheating of uncovered clutches.

Another serious threat is the loss of eggs and young when old haystacks are removed or burnt; in Kalmykia, east of the Volga river, up to 18–20% of active Steppe Eagle nests have been found on the top of haystacks (Muntjanu 1977, Lindeman 1983a).

The most recent and most dangerous threat is the electrocution of large numbers of Steppe Eagles (and other raptors) by recently constructed electric powerlines which cross treeless landscapes. During surveys, 47% of Steppe Eagles recorded have been sitting on such poles (Pererva and Grazhdankin 1983), and on average 15 dead eagles (range 6–35) have been collected under every 10 km of electric powerline (Shevchenko 1976, Flint *et al*. 1983, Lopushkov 1988).

■ Conservation measures

At present there are no large nature reserves or other kinds of protected areas established within the re-

maining virgin grassland steppes of Europe, the range of the Steppe Eagle and other characteristic steppic species. This should therefore be urgently addressed. Old haystacks should be maintained, so providing attractive nest-sites. Dangerous electric powerline constructions should be either replaced with safer ones or equipped with protective devices; the latter have been designed with the help of ornithologists (Flint *et al*. 1983) and used to equip some electric powerlines in open landscapes in Kalmykia, east of the Volga river and in western Kazakhstan.

The education of herdsmen and other local people in conservation, particularly concerning ecological values and the vulnerability of the Steppe Eagle, is of great importance, especially in view of the fact that some individual Steppe Eagles enter cultivated lands and nest on stacks near agricultural fields (Davygora 1992). Also disturbance of breeding birds, especially during incubation, should be prevented.

VLADIMIR GALUSHIN

Imperial Eagle
Aquila heliaca

SPEC Category 1
Status Endangered
Criteria Large decline, <2,500 pairs

This globally threatened species is declining throughout most of its small European range. The main causes are clearance of nesting trees, disturbance whilst breeding, shortage of prey due to loss of grasslands, collisions with powerlines and shooting in the winter quarters. The management and protection of breeding sites and monitoring of the population are essential conservation measures.

■ Distribution and population trends

The Imperial Eagle (treated here as a distinct species separate from the Spanish Imperial Eagle *A. adalberti*) is sparsely distributed from central and south-east Europe into central Asia. Europe has very small breeding populations in the Carpathian mountains and Carpathian basin, the southern and eastern Balkan peninsula, and the hills and steppes of south-east Ukraine and south-west Russia. Some adults move south or south-east after breeding (Curry-Lindahl 1981), especially in severe winters, but young birds are fully migratory and winter in the Mediterranean (mainly Greece), Asia Minor and north-west Africa (Danko in press); east European young winter in Iran (Génsbøl 1991). Important migration bottlenecks include Burgas (Bulgaria), north-east Turkey and the eastern Mediterranean (Syria, Lebanon and Israel) (Shirihai and Christie 1992).

Over three-quarters of the European population is declining (see table) and the species is listed as Globally Threatened (Collar *et al.* 1994). A rapid decline began in Europe after the Second World War and is thought mostly to be continuing, although data on numbers and trends are generally poor (see table). Populations in the Ukraine and southern Russia are generally decreasing with some relatively stable local groups in favourable habitats (see table, map; Galushin 1993, V. Vetrov pers. comm. to V. Galushin). Numbers have been studied in detail only in Slovakia and Hungary where recent increases are due largely to successful conservation action (see table, map; Danko and Chavko in press, S. Danko own data).

■ Ecology

Breeding habitat in central and eastern Europe comprises hill and mountain forests (at 200–1,000 m), but also steppes, open landscapes and agricultural areas. In the Caucasus birds occur in lowland and riverine forest, semi-desert and old forest (A. V. Abuladze pers. comm. 1993).

Nesting is in high trees in deciduous forests and more rarely in mixed forest and solitary trees in flat landscapes, as is typical in Yugoslavia (Serbia) and the Former Yugoslav Republic of Macedonia; in east Ukraine and southern Russia high pines *Pinus* are greatly preferred (Vetrov 1991, Afanasiev 1993). Recently in eastern Slovakia some birds that previously bred in forest, and young pairs breeding for the first time, have also bred in solitary trees in open agricultural areas (Danko and Chavko in press). Similar movements of birds from forest to lowland have also occurred in Hungary (J. Bagyura and L. Haraszthy pers. comm.).

Imperial Eagles hunt over steppe and agricultural land, mainly on medium-sized mammals such as susliks *Citellus suslicus* and *C. citellus*, hamster *Cricetus cricetus* and hares *Lepus*, but also small rodents (*Microtus*, *Apodemus*), birds and carrion (Simeonov and Petrov 1980). In the Caucasus the main prey are hares, tortoises *Testudo*, *Agama* lizards and carrion (A. V. Abuladze pers. comm. 1993).

■ Threats

Forestry practices may be the most important threat, including deforestation, reafforestation with alien species, removal of mature trees from forest and forest edges, disturbance to breeding birds by forestry operations and increased accessibility of previously remote areas due to the construction of tracks.

	Breeding population			Breeding
	Size (pairs)	Year	Trend	range trend
Bulgaria	20–25	—	–1	–1
Croatia	1–2 *	—	0*	0*
Cyprus	2–4	—	–1	–2
Greece	**0–2**	—	–1	0
Hungary	**35–35**	91	+2	+1
Moldova	**2–3**	88	–1	–1
Romania	(30–60)	—	(–1)	0
Russia	150–300	—	–1	–1
Slovakia	**30–35**	—	0	+1
Turkey	10–50 *	—	—	—
Ukraine	40–50	—	–2	–2
Total (approx.)	320–570			

Trends	+2 Large increase	+1 Small increase	0 Stable	X Extinct
(1970–1990)	–2 Large decrease	–1 Small decrease	F Fluctuating	N New breeder
Data quality	**Bold**: reliable quantitative data	Normal type: incomplete quantitative data	
	Bracketed figures: no quantitative data	* Data quality not provided	

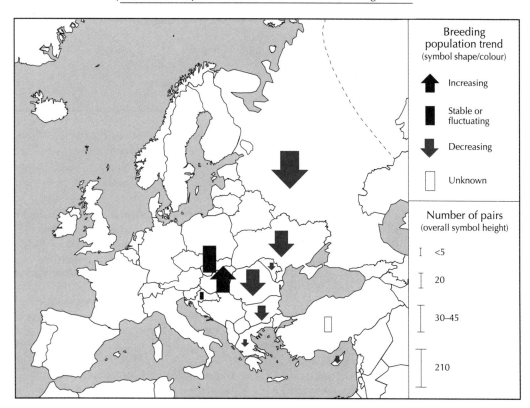

Persecution is likely to be a problem, particularly in Romania and Greece, and during migration in north-east Turkey, Lebanon and Syria (Magnin 1988, Baumgart 1991). The break-up of the U.S.S.R. has led to a relaxation of control by customs and a general lack of enforcement of the CITES regulations and thus an increase in illegal trade of birds (Flint and Sorokin 1992). The trapping and smuggling of birds out of the U.S.S.R. will probably increase in the near future.

In the last few years powerlines have been the cause of high mortality through electrocution or collision, especially in open areas (Flint *et al.* 1983).

Susliks have decreased in eastern Europe and virtually disappeared from Hungary due to overhunting and the loss and deterioration of grasslands, and this has affected the productivity of the region's Imperial Eagles.

A significant factor in winter may be secondary poisoning from, or direct ingestion of, baits intended to kill (e.g.) foxes *Vulpes vulpes* and wolves *Canis lupus*. Increases in pesticide use may affect Imperial Eagles (L. Kalabér pers. comm. 1993), though there is no direct evidence.

■ Conservation measures

Nest-guarding and habitat management for individual pairs are required, especially for nests in solitary trees. Clearance of trees at breeding sites should be prevented, as should other forestry activities outside the breeding season. In highly disturbed and clearly unsuitable areas, nesting eagles may be enticed to quieter sites through removal of nests early in their construction. Implementation of these innovative methods in eastern Slovakia has doubled breeding success (Danko in press, Danko and Chavko in press, S. Danko own data). Where necessary, old, successful nests should be secured against falling down. Artificial nests should also be erected in agricultural areas where there are increasing numbers of birds and a lack of suitable trees.

Studies of local prey availability can establish the need for protection and restoration or management of grasslands to ensure their suitability for susliks. On agricultural land, however, susliks have been replaced by hamsters, hares and Pheasant *Phasianus colchicus* as the main food source, and here pesticide use should be reduced.

Deaths caused by powerlines can be reduced by modifications to lines and posts, and educational campaigns against the shooting of eagles, mainly in southern Europe, should be organized.

STEFAN DANKO

177

Spanish Imperial Eagle
Aquila adalberti

SPEC Category 1
Status Endangered
Criteria <250 pairs

This globally threatened species has a world population of about 150 pairs, now restricted to Spain. It is threatened by illegal shooting, poisoning, trapping, nest-robbing, electrocution by powerlines and habitat degradation. Enforcement of bird protection laws, awareness campaigns, modification of electricity pylons, and habitat protection and management are essential conservation measures.

■ Distribution and population trends

The species is mainly restricted to south-west Spain where it occurs in the Guadarrama and Gredos mountains, the Tajo and Tietar river plains, central hills of Extremadura, Toledo mountains, Alcudia valley and Sierra Morena, and the Guadalquivir marshes (Doñana). In addition there have been reports of adult pairs in Salamanca, Málaga and Cádiz provinces.

In the nineteenth century the breeding range extended to southern and central Portugal, the Tingitane peninsula and Rif mountains of Morocco, and most of Spain with the exception of the Cantabrian mountains and Pyrenees (González *et al.* 1989b), but during the twentieth century its range has contracted considerably. In Morocco it has disappeared as a breeding species (Bergier 1987); one pair was recently reported (Fouarge 1992), but there is no proof of nesting. Up to 1975 there may have been 15–20 breeding pairs in Portugal (Palma 1985), but it has not bred since 1977 although individuals have been observed in recent years (Rufino 1989).

At the beginning of the twentieth century the species was relatively common in Spain, but during the last 80 years numbers declined dramatically and it is now extinct from the edges of its range: the Cordillera Penibetica, Levante and the area north of the Guadarrama mountains (González *et al.* 1989b). In the 1960s and 1970s it was close to extinction, with only 30 known pairs in the country (Garzón 1974a), but during the 1980s and 1990s there has been a slow recovery (González *et al.* 1987, González 1990), and 6–8 new breeding pairs were located in 1992, taking the total to 150 (González in press) (see table, map).

	Breeding population			Breeding
	Size (pairs)	Year	Trend	range trend
Portugal	**0–0**	—	X	X
Spain	**150–160**	93	+2	+1
Total (approx.)	150–160			

Trends +2 Large increase   +1 Small increase   0 Stable   X Extinct
(1970–1990) –2 Large decrease   –1 Small decrease   F Fluctuating   N New breeder
Data quality **Bold:** reliable quantitative data   Normal type: incomplete quantitative data
Bracketed figures: no quantitative data   * Data quality not provided

The current key breeding populations are in the Monfragüe National Park (Cáceres), Doñana National Park (Huelva) and the Royal State of Monte del Pardo (Madrid) (González 1991). Breeding density in protected areas is four times higher than at sites which have no protection (González 1991).

Although increasing, the species is considered to be Globally Threatened due to its small population size (Collar *et al.* 1994).

■ Ecology

The species inhabits forested areas in three basic landscape types: alluvial plains and dunes close to the sea in the Guadalquivir marshes, plains and hills of central Spain, and high mountain slopes of the Sistema Central (González 1991). It prefers plains but generally avoids areas subject to human disturbance, especially irrigated farmland. Rabbits *Oryctolagus cuniculus* are the main prey, and are an important factor influencing the birds' density, range and reproductive success (González 1991).

Nesting is almost always in trees, though it has twice been recorded on electricity pylons. Nest-sites used by young birds, and those newly established by adults, currently tend to be in marginal (more disturbed) habitat, either because the less disturbed areas have reached carrying capacity or because turnover rates in more disturbed habitats are higher (González *et al.* 1990, 1992).

Adults are sedentary, though the young disperse when independent, travelling distances of up to 350 km on average (Calderón *et al.* 1988, González *et al.* 1989a). During their pre-breeding period young birds tend to concentrate at a small number of localities, at which rabbits are abundant: the south-west of Madrid, the Tietar valley (Toledo), south-east of La Mancha (Ciudad Real), south-west of Bádajoz, the Guadalquivir marshes (Huelva) and La Janda plains (Cádiz) (Oria and Caballero 1992a).

■ Threats

Shooting, poisoning, trapping, electrocution by electricity pylons, breeding failure due to chemical con-

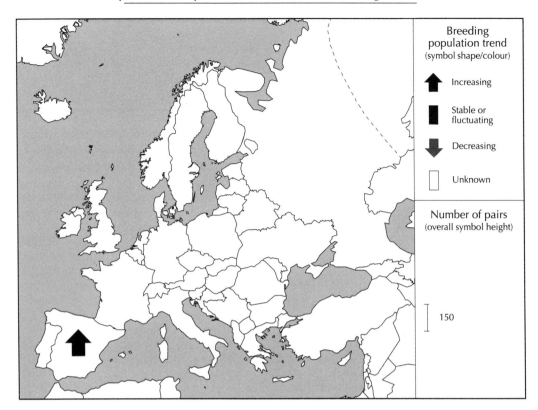

Breeding
population trend
(symbol shape/colour)

Increasing

Stable or
fluctuating

Decreasing

Unknown

Number of pairs
(overall symbol height)

150

taminants from intensive agriculture, and disturbance at the nest-site all adversely affect the species (González 1991). Electrocution is the commonest cause of non-natural death and affects mainly juveniles and immatures (10–20 cases annually: Calderón *et al.* 1988, Ferrer and Calderón 1990, Cadenas 1992, Jiménez 1992, Oria and Caballero 1992a). The decline in rabbit populations, caused by myxomatosis and viral haemorrhagic pneumonia, has also affected eagle numbers adversely (Valverde 1967, Garzón 1974a, González in press).

Changes to nesting and feeding habitat also affect the species, including tree-cutting, building of powerlines, creation of forest tracks and expansion of farmlands. MOPTMA (the Spanish government agency for hydrological and development plans), in some cases financed by the European Union, is likely to destroy or degrade much of the habitat currently available for the species outside protected areas, through the building of new roads across breeding areas and the inundation of valleys following dam construction.

■ Conservation measures

A recovery programme, developed with financial support from the EU and the Spanish Administration (Instituto para la Conservación de la Naturaleza, and the Autonomous Communities of Madrid, Andalucía, Castilla la Mancha, Castilla–León and Extremadura), is in progress in Spain and aims to increase the population to 200 breeding pairs by the beginning of the twenty-first century (González in press). Currently 35% of breeding territories are included in the network of Spanish protected areas, of which 62% are protected Important Bird Areas. The programme recommends the inclusion of all nesting territories in the Spanish network of protected areas.

The plan also recommends that new tracks and powerlines should not be constructed in forest areas where the species nests. It is suggested that electricity pylons in nesting, feeding and juvenile dispersal areas should be modified to reduce the risk of electrocution. In hunting areas it is recommended that the law is reinforced and that awareness campaigns are initiated.

Population monitoring is also necessary and should include nest surveillance, to attempt to improve survival rates of young through supplementary feeding programmes where necessary. The repopulation or reinforcement of rabbit populations in certain areas should also be considered. A captive-breeding programme was started in 1992 and it is planned to reinforce existing wild populations or to reintroduce birds to suitable habitat.

LUIS M. GONZÁLEZ

Golden Eagle
Aquila chrysaetos

SPEC Category 3
Status Rare
Criteria <10,000 pairs

This widespread but rare raptor, which mainly inhabits upland regions, is threatened by illegal killing (particularly through poisoning) and by afforestation of open hunting areas. The loss of wooded peatlands in north-east Europe threatens the continent's unique lowland population.

■ Distribution and population trends

The distribution of the Golden Eagle stretches right across the Holarctic region, with major concentrations in the eastern Palearctic and in western North America. Roughly 15–20% of the world range of the species lies within Europe.

Breeding occurs throughout upland areas in Scotland, Fennoscandia and across most of southern Europe. There is also a scattered lowland population in eastern Europe. Most birds are resident but some migrate from northern Fennoscandia to eastern Europe in winter (Cramp and Simmons 1980). The combined populations of Spain, Norway, Sweden and Turkey account for more than half the European total (see table, map). Population size is well known for most countries (Watson 1992) although the data are poor for Austria and particularly for Turkey.

Precise survey data are mostly recent and have revealed larger populations than previous 'best estimates', making interpretation of trends difficult. However, although mostly stable or increasing, recent declines have been reported in Belarus (Ivanovsky 1990) and are suspected in Greece and former Yugoslavia (Hallmann 1985, Vasic *et al.* 1985) and in Portugal, Albania, Romania and Ukraine (see table, map). In Spain the population is believed to be 30% less than 30 years ago, but is currently considered to be stable (Arroyo *et al.* 1990b). The species became extinct in the Republic of Ireland during the early part of the twentieth century (Barrington 1915).

■ Ecology

Typically the species occupies mountain landscapes where tree cover is sparse or fragmented, although in north-east Europe birds inhabit wooded peatlands at low altitudes (Zastrov 1946). Such lowland birds are exclusively tree-nesting, but elsewhere nests are predominantly on cliffs (Watson and Dennis 1992). Birds may nest at densities of 1 pair per 30 km² in parts of Scotland (Watson *et al.* 1992), but throughout continental Europe densities of lower than 1 pair per 100 km² are more usual (e.g. Haller 1982, Bergo 1984).

Across northern Europe the prey is chiefly grouse (Tetraonidae), hares *Lepus* or rabbits *Oryctolagus* (e.g. Tjernberg 1981). In the Mediterranean mountains of south-west Europe rabbits, hares and partridges *Alectoris*, as well as snakes and other reptiles (Delibes *et al.* 1975), are the main prey, with marmots *Marmota* being important in Alpine pastures (Haller 1982). In south-east Europe tortoises *Testudo* are frequently taken (Grubac 1986).

■ Threats

Historically, the greatest threats to Golden Eagles have been shooting, the poisoning and trapping of adult birds, and human interference at nests, includ-

	Breeding population			Breeding range trend
	Size (pairs)	Year	Trend	
Albania	50–120	—	–1	(–1)
Andorra	· 3–3	91	0	–1
Austria	(200–250)	—	(+1)	(+1)
Belarus	40–50	90	–1	–1
Bulgaria	130–140	70–90	+1	+1
Croatia	100–150 *	—	0*	0*
Estonia	35–35	93	0	0
Finland	220–220	92	0	0
France	255–288	91	0	0
Germany	25–30	—	+1	0
Greece	140–180	—	–1	–1
Hungary	2–2	91	N*	—
Italy	300–400	84	0	0
Latvia	7–12	—	+1	+1
Liechtenstein	1–2	—	0	0
Norway	700–1,000	90	0	0
Poland	5–10	—	0	0
Portugal	20–40	91	–1	–1
Romania	20–30	—	–1	–1
Russia	200–400	—	0	0
Slovakia	60–70	—	0	0
Slovenia	10–25	—	0	0
Spain	1,192–1,265	88	–1	–1
Sweden	600–750	87	0	0
Switzerland	200–250	90	+1	0
Turkey	(100–1,000)	—	—	—
Ukraine	6–8	88	–1	–1
United Kingdom	420–420	82–83	0	0
Total (approx.)	5,000–7,200			

Trends   +2 Large increase   +1 Small increase   0 Stable   X Extinct
(1970–1990)   –2 Large decrease   –1 Small decrease   F Fluctuating N New breeder
Data quality **Bold**: reliable quantitative data   Normal type: incomplete quantitative data
              Bracketed figures: no quantitative data   * Data quality not provided

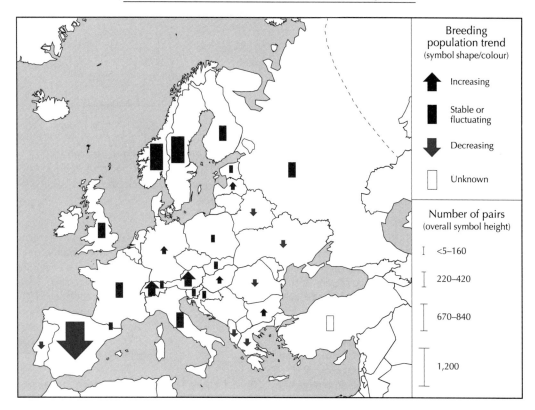

Breeding population trend
(symbol shape/colour)

▲ Increasing

■ Stable or fluctuating

▼ Decreasing

☐ Unknown

Number of pairs
(overall symbol height)

I <5–160

I 220–420

I 670–840

I 1,200

ing egg-collecting (Cramp and Simmons 1980). Some or all of these activities persist today in Scotland (RSPB and NCC 1991), Spain (Arroyo *et al.* 1990b), Italy (Fasce and Fasce 1984) and several countries in south-east Europe.

Habitat change caused by the felling of woodland and drainage of peatlands threatens already fragmented populations in north-east Europe (Ivanovsky 1990). Suppressed breeding in Scotland during the 1960s was attributed to the effects of organochlorine pesticides, although this is no longer considered a problem there (Newton and Galbraith 1991). In Scotland and Portugal reduced breeding success or loss of nesting pairs has been attributed to afforestation of the birds' previously open hunting ranges (Marquiss *et al.* 1985, Palma 1985).

■ Conservation measures

Continued vigilance against illegal killing (through the use of poisoned baits) and egg-collecting is

needed in many countries and should be coupled with educational programmes demonstrating the benefits and desirability of maintaining healthy populations of birds of prey. Site-based conservation measures are relatively ineffective for a species living at such low densities, and instead it should be ensured that general land-use policies for remote upland areas do not compromise key feeding and nesting requirements. In north-east Europe there is a special need to safeguard extensive areas of wooded peatland.

Further information on the numbers and health of the Turkish and other important but unmonitored populations is desirable.

JEFF WATSON

Booted Eagle
Hieraaetus pennatus

SPEC Category 3
Status Rare
Criteria <10,000 pairs

The Booted Eagle is a rare species in Europe and, although mostly stable, many of its small populations are declining in size and range, probably due mainly to habitat degradation and destruction. The conservation and restoration of forested areas, the enforcement of hunting laws and programmes to reduce illegal shooting, and the modification of powerlines to reduce electrocution are the major actions needed to maintain the population levels of the species.

■ Distribution and population trends

Although the Booted Eagle's world breeding range lies mainly within the Palearctic, less than half of this range falls inside Europe, where the species is considered rare, with a total of some 3,000–6,000 pairs. More than half of the European population breeds in Spain and possibly up to c.10% in each of France, Russia and Turkey, although more accurate information is needed (see table, map), and in central Europe populations are very small and fragmented. The Booted Eagle is migratory, wintering in central and southern Africa with occasional birds staying on in southern Europe and France (Cramp and Simmons 1980).

The species seems to be declining in more than half of the European countries in which it breeds, although the sizes of the populations affected and the actual decreases in numbers are in most instances very small (see table). Generally, eastern populations have been most affected, whereas in countries such as Portugal, Spain, France and Russia, with higher breeding numbers, populations appear to be stable.

However, the fact that population trends are more easily monitored in small populations could account for this result. In Spain, for example, although the overall trend is considered stable (see table), some contradictory information exists on population trends, with increases detected in some areas and decreases in others (Garzón 1977, Iribarren 1977, Muntaner 1981).

■ Ecology

Booted Eagles breed in a wide variety of habitats: mainly forested areas with clearings, including scrub and grassland, but also in open habitats with sparse trees. In mountainous areas in the south of its range, the species occurs regularly at up to 1,600 m (Garzón 1977, Veiga 1985, Carlon 1987). In the mountains of central Europe, where forests are much denser than those in the Mediterranean region, the species is almost totally absent from the hearts of extensive forests and avoids conifers. Nesting usually occurs in mature trees, although the location of these is highly variable (slopes, riverine or lowland woods, etc.). Only rarely are nests built on cliffs.

In Spain, the highest population densities are attained in the central and western parts of the evergreen Mediterranean forest zone, and in pine forests (Garzón 1973, Veiga 1985). In such areas, with optimal nesting sites and high food availability, up to 12 pairs may bred in 8 km² (Garzón 1973, Carlon 1987, Suetens 1989).

The diet of the Booted Eagle is one of the more varied amongst European raptors, and includes many small and medium-sized birds, lizards and small mammals (Cramp and Simmons 1980, Suetens 1989).

■ Threats

Habitat degradation and destruction, both in the breeding and in the wintering areas, may account for the observed declines of the Booted Eagle in Europe (Suetens 1989, Thiollay 1989). Extensive clear-felling of forests, urbanization, construction of reser-

| | Breeding population | | | Breeding |
	Size (pairs)	Year	Trend	range trend
Albania	0–5	—	–1	(–1)
Belarus	(5–15)	90	(–1)	(0)
Bulgaria	30–60	—	0	0
France	250–500	87	(0)	0
Greece	100–150	—	(–1)	(0)
Hungary	**10–10**	91	–1	–1
Moldova	**5–8**	90	–1	–1
Poland	0–5 *	—	—	—
Portugal	100–300	89	0	0
Romania	(10–80)	—	–2	–2
Russia	(200–400)	—	0	0
Slovakia	3–6	—	–1	–1
Spain	2,000–4,000	—	0	0
Turkey	(100–500)	—	—	—
Ukraine	20–24	88	–2	–1
Total (approx.)	2,800–6,100			

Trends	+2 Large increase	+1 Small increase	0 Stable	X Extinct
(1970-1990)	–2 Large decrease	–1 Small decrease	F Fluctuating	N New breeder

Data quality **Bold**: reliable quantitative data Normal type: incomplete quantitative data
Bracketed figures: no quantitative data * Data quality not provided

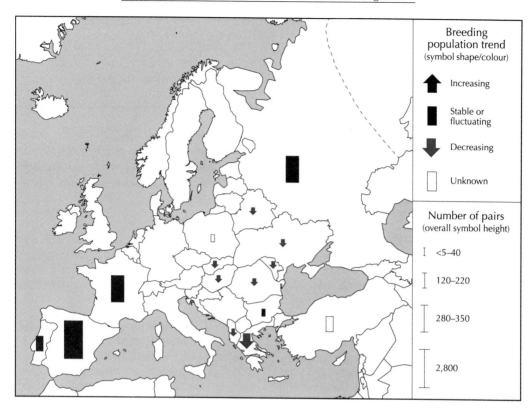

voirs, and fire are some of the major factors responsible for the destruction of forest areas. However, the partial reforestation with conifers of previously deforested areas has helped to maintain or even to increase the size of some populations locally (de Juana 1989).

Although shooting and nest-robbing may have decreased during the last 20 years, these are still, together with electrocution by powerlines, important causes of mortality in some parts of the species' range (Baldacchino 1981, Chandrinos 1981, Ferrer et al. 1986, de Juana 1989). It is also probable that organochlorine pesticides used in agriculture within the wintering areas have accumulated in Booted Eagles via their prey, and this may be having a detrimental effect on reproductive success as has been demonstrated for other bird-feeding raptors (Thiollay 1989).

■ Conservation measures

The maintenance of extensive areas with an alternation of open habitats and mature forests is essential for the conservation of the Booted Eagle, and factors responsible for forest destruction and degradation should therefore be regulated. If afforestation or deforestation is inevitable in an area, the operations should take place outside the breeding season to minimize disturbance, and the habitat change should be partial and not complete, leaving an adequate balance of open and forested areas and good numbers of mature trees. Although Booted Eagles are legally protected throughout Europe, effective enforcement of the relevant laws is required in areas where large numbers of birds concentrate and are shot during migration (Baldacchino 1981, Chandrinos 1981). There is also a need for extensive educational programmes aimed at reducing illegal persecution and nest-robbing. Modification of the design of powerlines to reduce electrocution would benefit this and several other raptor species.

Research into the species' distribution and numbers, and into habitat selection, population dynamics, local diets and the potential impact of pesticides on fertility are all needed to ensure the long-term conservation of this currently poorly known and susceptible species.

JOSÉ P. VEIGA AND JAVIER VIÑUELA

Bonelli's Eagle
Hieraaetus fasciatus

SPEC Category 3
Status Endangered
Criteria Large decline, <2,500 pairs

Numbers and range of this rare species are undergoing serious decline in Europe due to persecution, electrocution by powerlines, disturbance at nest-sites, and loss and deterioration of dry grassland and garigue habitats. Conservation measures required are nest-site protection, appropriate modification of electricity pylons, the maintenance of non-intensive pastoral farming, and the education of hunters to increase awareness of the species.

■ Distribution and population trends

Bonelli's Eagle occurs mainly outside Europe, where it is found in the Middle East, over extensive parts of southern Asia and in Africa both north and south of the Sahara (the Afrotropical race is often treated as a separate species). The resident European population is small (probably less than 1,000 pairs) and restricted to the Mediterranean region, including Portugal, Spain, southern France, Italy (Calabria, Sardinia, Sicily), Croatia, Greece (including Crete), Cyprus and Turkey. It is absent from Corsica and the Balearic Islands. Between two-thirds and three-quarters of the European population is concentrated in Spain. It should be noted that the size and trends of the Turkish population remain uncertain.

The species declined throughout most of its European range between 1970 and 1990 (see table, map). The extent of the decline in Spain, where a minimum of 15–20% of the breeding population is thought to have disappeared since 1980, is particularly significant (Arroyo *et al.* 1992). Larger (over 50%) local declines in numbers (but not range) in Spain have been recorded in Valencia, Murcia and Navarra. The species' range size has decreased and has almost disappeared in some areas in the interior of the Iberian peninsula (Real *et al.* 1991). Serious declines in number and range have also occurred in Italy

(Frugis and Schenck 1981) and Cyprus. In France, the population seems to have stabilized during the past decade after the loss of over 50% of breeding pairs (Cheylan and Siméon 1984, Cugnasse 1984).

■ Ecology

Bonelli's Eagle inhabits Mediterranean landscapes with low or little vegetation such as garigue, dry grasslands and rocky habitats. It is also often found in mosaics of open habitat with non-intensive crops, vineyards, non-irrigated orchards, small woodlands and pasture. Nesting is on rocky cliffs, with territories ranging from sea-level to 1,500 m, although rarely exceeding 1,000 m (Arroyo 1991). Juveniles and subadults can disperse over large areas and are most frequently found on low-altitude plains where prey species are abundant (Cugnasse and Cramm 1990, Real *et al.* 1991). Prey species mainly comprise rabbit *Oryctolagus cuniculus*, squirrels *Sciurus vulgaris*, partridges *Alectoris/Perdix*, Woodpigeon *Columba palumbus*, Corvidae and reptiles (Cheylan 1981, Cugnasse 1984, Arroyo 1991, Real 1991).

■ Threats

There appear to be several causes for the decline of Bonelli's Eagle. Direct persecution from shooting and trapping, and electrocution by electric powerlines seem to be the main causes of adult mortality in Spain (Real and Mañosa 1992), with electrocution also being a major threat in France (Sériot and Rocamora 1992, Cheylan in press). Juvenile birds, which tend to frequent areas more densely populated by humans, are particularly vulnerable to these threats and have a high mortality rate (c.90%) during their two first years of life in France and Spain (Real *et al.* 1992).

A decline in the availability of prey is also a significant problem (Cugnasse 1984, Real 1991), due to modern farming methods (including hedge destruction and the use of pesticides), disease epidemics (affecting rabbit populations) and over-

	Breeding population			Breeding range trend
	Size (pairs)	Year	Trend	
Albania	(0–2)	—	—	—
Croatia	5–10 *	—	0*	0*
Cyprus	10–15	—	–1	–1
France	**29–31**	92	–1	**–1**
Greece	(35–45)	—	(–1)	(0)
Italy	(15–20)	—	(–1)	(–2)
Portugal	40–60	89	(0)	–1
Spain	**675–751**	90	–1	–1
Turkey	(10–100)	—	—	—
Total (approx.)	820–1,000			

Trends   +2 Large increase   +1 Small increase   0 Stable   X Extinct
(1970-1990)   –2 Large decrease   –1 Small decrease   F Fluctuating   N New breeder
Data quality   **Bold**: reliable quantitative data   Normal type: incomplete quantitative data
Bracketed figures: no quantitative data   * Data quality not provided

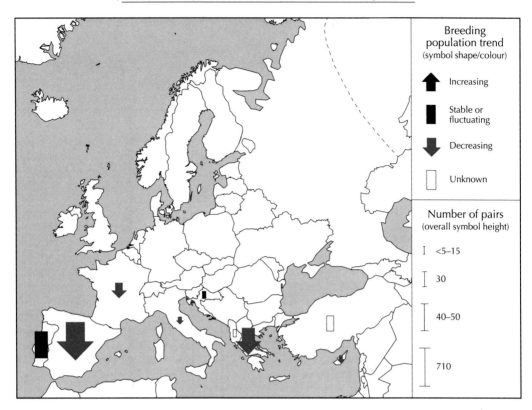

Breeding
population trend
(symbol shape/colour)

Increasing

Stable or
fluctuating

Decreasing

Unknown

Number of pairs
(overall symbol height)

<5–15

30

40–50

710

hunting. The general abandonment of traditional pastoral farming systems in many rural Mediterranean areas has led to a major reduction in the area of suitable habitat, mainly due to the natural regeneration of woodland which has followed.

Disturbance around nesting areas due to quarries, forest roads, hiking and rock-climbing is also extremely detrimental to the species.

■ Conservation measures

Both wide-scale and site-specific conservation measures are necessary to stop and reverse the decline of Bonelli's Eagle in Europe. Access restrictions and legal habitat protection are required in nesting areas to avoid disturbance and habitat destruction. In France most nests are wardened during the breeding season (FIR 1992), and in the south of France and Catalonia artificial food sources have been successfully provided for some breeding pairs (Cugnasse 1989, Iborra 1989, Real et al. 1991).

Wider-scale habitat management for the species should include: appropriate modification of the design of dangerous electricity pylons, or burial or relocation of powerlines; the use of game crops to enhance prey populations; the maintenance of extensive pastoral farming; and the preservation of hedges bordering fields. Within the EU, such measures could be promoted in appropriate areas through management agreements under the Agri-environment Regulation (EC Reg. 2078/92) of the Common Agricultural Policy. Education campaigns with the active involvement of hunting associations should also be undertaken to reduce persecution.

Research on the species' demography, including juvenile dispersal, mortality and adult recruitment, has been conducted in eastern Spain and southern France (Real and Mañosa 1992, Real et al. 1992). Such research and monitoring needs to be continued and to be extended into Portugal and eastern Mediterranean countries.

GÉRARD ROCAMORA

Osprey
Pandion haliaetus

SPEC Category 3
Status Rare
Criteria <10,000 pairs

This scarce European breeder has been declining and retracting in range for over a century, although recently some recovery has been reported. Reasons for the decline are thought to be persecution, disturbance and loss of nest-sites. Conservation measures required include protection and construction of nests, reduced water pollution, and protection from persecution on migration.

■ Distribution and population trends

About a tenth of the global range of this nearly cosmopolitan species is in Europe. The Osprey once bred over almost the whole continent, but is now mainly restricted to the north, from Scotland through Fennoscandia and from north-east Germany along the southern Baltic coasts into Siberia (Moll 1962, Glutz von Blotzheim *et al.* 1971, Génsbøl 1984). Fennoscandia and Russia are the species' strongholds (see table, map), while in southern Europe and around the Mediterranean there remain only a few isolated sites which still support the species (Cramp and Simmons 1980). European Ospreys winter mainly in tropical Africa, although some birds stay in the Mediterranean basin (Österlöf 1977).

The species disappeared from several European countries during the nineteenth and early twentieth centuries, including the United Kingdom, France, Netherlands, former Czechoslovakia, Switzerland, Austria and Italy, with populations reaching an overall low during the period of the 1930s to 1950s. Thereafter, strict protection for the Osprey was implemented in several countries and populations started to recover: after 1930 in Norway and Sweden, from the 1970s in Scotland, Finland and eastern Germany (Cramp and Simmons 1980, Klafs and Stübs 1987, Batten *et al.* 1990) and recently in the Baltic states and Russia (see table). Estimates of the species' European population range from c.3,100 pairs in the early 1970s, excluding the former U.S.S.R. (Cieslak 1980), to 5,000–5,500 pairs during the early 1980s for the whole continent (Génsbøl 1984) and more recently to 7,100–8,900 pairs (see table). In contrast, the remnant southern population occurring from the Atlantic Islands to Bulgaria was estimated at below 50 pairs during the 1970s (Cieslak 1980) and has recently declined to c.30 pairs (see table).

■ Ecology

The Osprey breeds along coasts and in forest habitats close to fresh and salt water with sufficient fish supplies. The postglacial lakelands of Scotland, Fennoscandia and northern parts of central and eastern Europe are currently the species' favoured nesting areas; although once the species bred regularly around the Mediterranean and in riparian forests of large river valleys in central and southern Europe (Cieslak 1980, Hölzinger 1987). The Osprey usually occurs in solitary pairs, although aggregations form sporadically.

Nests are generally built on the top of large trees, preferably pine, although a small proportion of birds place their nests on cliffs, on man-made constructions such as electricity pylons, and quite exceptionally on the ground. Individuals are long-lived with high site fidelity, and particular nest constructions can be used for 18 or more years.

During migration Ospreys occur occasionally in groups of dozens of birds at fresh and saline water-

| | Breeding population | | | Breeding |
	Size (pairs)	Year	Trend	range trend
Belarus	**120–180**	90	0	0
Bulgaria	3–6	—	−1	−1
Denmark	**0–2**	88	0	0
Estonia	20–25	—	+1	0
Finland	**900–1,000**	92	0	0
France	**24–26**	92	+2	+1
Germany	150–150	—	0	0
Latvia	**100–120**	—	+2	+1
Lithuania	20–30	85–88	+1	+1
Moldova	0–3	88	−1	−1
Norway	150–200	90	−1	−1
Poland	30–50	—	0	0
Portugal	**2–2**	91	−2	−2
Russia	2,500–3,500	—	0	+1
Spain	**10–16**	—	−2	−2
Canary Islands	**12–14**	87–88	0	0
Sweden	3,000–3,500	87	+1	0
Turkey	0–10 *	—	—	—
Ukraine	1–5	88	−2	−1
United Kingdom	**72–72**	91	+2	+2
Total (approx.)	7,100–8,900			

Trends +2 Large increase   +1 Small increase   0 Stable   X Extinct
(1970–1990) −2 Large decrease   −1 Small decrease   F Fluctuating   N New breeder
Data quality **Bold**: reliable quantitative data   Normal type: incomplete quantitative data
Bracketed figures: no quantitative data   * Data quality not provided

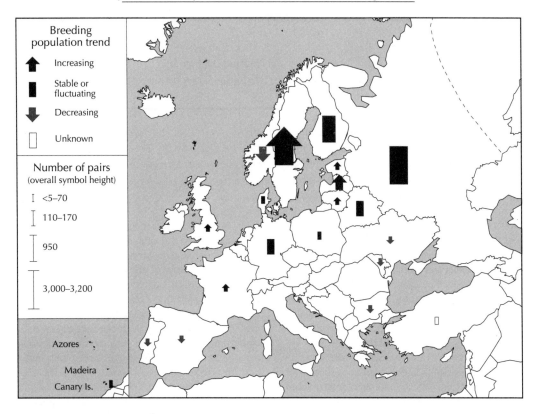

Breeding
population trend

↑ Increasing

■ Stable or
fluctuating

↓ Decreasing

☐ Unknown

Number of pairs
(overall symbol height)

<5–70

110–170

950

3,000–3,200

Azores

Madeira

Canary Is.

bodies, including fish-breeding farms and coastal waters. The species is a specialist feeder relying on medium-size fish of several species, chiefly percids and cyprinids, although during periods of unsuitable weather it may be forced to catch small mammals, waterbirds, reptiles or amphibians (Glutz von Blotzheim *et al*. 1971).

■ Threats

In the past shooting and nest destruction were the main threats to this species (Bijleveld 1974). Today, shooting still occurs, chiefly of migrant birds in Italy or at fish farms in central Europe (Chiavetta 1977), but habitat destruction (Poole 1989) and environmental pollution are the major threats. Felling old forests can cause a shortage of suitable nesting trees in otherwise suitable habitats. Contamination of birds with mercury or organochlorines (from industry and agriculture, e.g. PCBs) has reduced reproduction rates (Odsjö and Sondell 1976, Ahlgren and Eriksson 1984), and chemical pollution may cause the acidification of water-bodies and reduce fish populations (Eriksson 1986, 1987b); this may be exacerbated by the local depletion of fish stocks by intensive fisheries. In western Europe (e.g. Scotland) human disturbance at nests and egg-collecting are also threats, as

well as collisions with overhead powerlines (Hölzinger 1987, Batten *et al*. 1990).

Clearly at present the most endangered birds are those of the isolated Mediterranean populations threatened by coastal tourist developments, holiday boats and marine pollution (Terrasse and Terrasse 1977, Cieslak 1980).

■ Conservation measures

Disturbance during the breeding season may be prevented by establishing protective zones 200–300 m wide around each nest (Hemke 1983). This may be supported by nest wardening to reduce nest robberies, the rebuilding of damaged nests and the provision of artificial nests in safe locations where necessary (Poole 1989).

As the species is susceptible to toxic environmental pollutants, the levels of these may need to be lowered in some areas, as shown by the Fennoscandian Osprey population which increased after a reduction in pollutants, chiefly organochlorines and mercury (Österlöf 1977). Fish-farms visited by migrant Ospreys should use equipment to scare the birds or to prevent their access to fish stocks, instead of shooting them (Batten *et al*. 1990).

LUDWIK TOMIALOJC

Lesser Kestrel
Falco naumanni

SPEC Category   1
Status   (Vulnerable)
Criteria   Large decline

This globally threatened species has declined dramatically in its western Palearctic breeding range in recent years. The main reasons are thought to be loss of hunting areas due to agricultural intensification, the abandonment of traditional pastoral farming in Europe and in the African winter quarters, and urbanization. Loss of nest-sites through renovation of old buildings and the accumulation of toxic pesticides are very likely to have contributed.

■ Distribution and population trends

The Lesser Kestrel has a Palearctic breeding distribution southwards of 55°N, breeding from Iberia east to Mongolia and north-east China, and south to North Africa and the Levant (Hollom *et al*. 1988). In Europe, the Lesser Kestrel has a mainly Mediterranean distribution with Spain and Turkey having the largest populations, and Greece and Italy also supporting sizeable numbers (see table, map).

Most birds winter in sub-Saharan Africa, mainly from Zimbabwe south to Botswana and especially in South Africa (Cade 1982). Some overwinter in southern Europe (Negro *et al*. 1991, J. J. Negro pers. comm.) and north-west Africa (Cade 1982, Bergier 1987). Little is known about numbers wintering in West Africa (Moreau 1972, Cade 1982).

Most European populations of Lesser Kestrel have declined seriously over recent decades, including the large population of Spain where the 20,000–50,000 pairs estimated in 1980 had fallen to 4,200–5,100 by 1990 (González *et al*. 1990). Numbers may also have fallen in Greece (from 2,000

pairs in 1982 to less than 1,500 pairs in 1992: Hallmann 1985, B. Hallmann pers. comm.) and in the similarly large population in Italy (see table, map). The important Turkish population is poorly known although surveys in 1993 estimated 2,000–4,000 pairs in the central steppe (S. Parr pers. comm.). Numbers in the Ukraine and Russia are also inadequately known, although censuses and anecdotal information from the Ukraine indicate declines in these areas which must have been strongholds in the past (W. Hagemeijer pers. comm. 1993). The species is extinct or breeds only irregularly in Poland, Czech Republic, Slovakia, Hungary and Cyprus.

The species is classified as Globally Threatened by Collar *et al*. (1994) on the basis of its rapid population declines.

■ Ecology

In the western Palearctic, the Lesser Kestrel occurs in warm, open areas with short vegetation and patches of bare ground where it can easily locate prey. These include meadows, pastures, steppe habitat, non-intensively cultivated land and occasionally garigue and open woodland. In North African breeding areas and in the winter quarters birds forage in savanna, steppe, thornbush vegetation, and on open grassland or farmland (Brown 1970).

Lesser Kestrels require high prey densities, mainly large grasshoppers (Orthoptera) and beetles (Coleoptera), but sometimes also lizards (Cheylan 1991). In southern Africa it relies largely on grasshoppers and termites (Isoptera) (Siegfried and Skead 1971).

Breeding colonies used often to be of 120–250 pairs, but colonies of fewer than 10 pairs, and single pairs, may now have become more common (Biber 1990). Availability of nest-sites often limits density, even in good foraging areas (W. Hagemeijer pers. comm.). The birds nest in holes in old buildings or under roofs, in tree-holes, in earth cliffs, and sometimes in quarries or among piles of rocks (Biber 1990) or in old corvid nests in trees (in the Ukraine and Caucasus: *per* W. Hagemeijer).

	Breeding population			Breeding
	Size (pairs)	Year	Trend	range trend
Albania	100–1,000	—	–2	(–2)
Austria	**0–0**	—	X	X
Bulgaria	**60–120**	70–90	–1	–1
Croatia	5–10 *	—	0*	0*
France	**20–26**	92	–2	–2
Greece	1,000–1,500	—	(–1)	(0)
Italy	(500–1,000)	—	(–1)	(–1)
Moldova	7–12	89	–1	0
Portugal	100–200	91	–2	–2
Romania	(50–100)	—	+1	+1
Russia	(70–150)	—	–1	–1
Slovenia	**5–10**	—	–2	–2
Spain	**4,200–5,100**	90	–2	–2
Turkey	4,000–7,000	—	—	—
Ukraine	(200–300)	—	–2	–1
United Kingdom Gibraltar	10–40	—	–2	—
Total (approx.)	10,000–17,000			

Trends (1970–1990)   +2 Large increase   +1 Small increase   0 Stable   X Extinct
  –2 Large decrease   –1 Small decrease   F Fluctuating   N New breeder
Data quality   **Bold:** reliable quantitative data   Normal type: incomplete quantitative data
  Bracketed figures: no quantitative data   * Data quality not provided

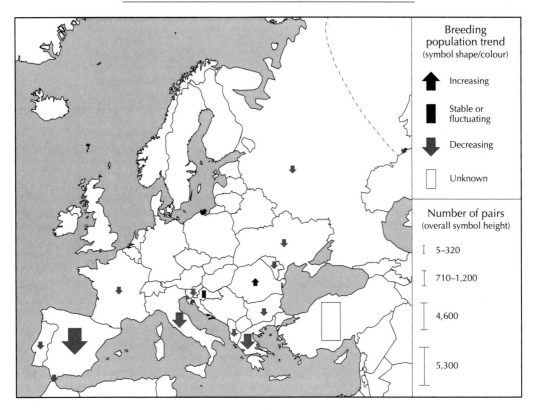

Breeding population trend
(symbol shape/colour)

⬆ Increasing

⬛ Stable or fluctuating

⬇ Decreasing

☐ Unknown

Number of pairs
(overall symbol height)

I	5–320
I	710–1,200
I	4,600
I	5,300

■ Threats

In breeding areas the main threat is believed to be the loss and reduced availability of food due to agricultural intensification, the abandonment of traditional pastoral farming, and urbanization. In Spain the loss of foraging habitat has forced the abandonment of many traditional sites (Gonzaléz et al. 1990). In the Crau (France) the number of grazing sheep has halved during the last 30 years and consequently the vegetation has grown taller and denser, which in turn has reduced grasshopper populations and rendered them less accessible.

Loss of nest-sites, primarily through destruction and restoration of buildings, has also had a serious impact in certain areas (Hallmann 1985, González et al. 1990). Eggshell thinning has been demonstrated in the Lesser Kestrel, and pesticides are known or believed to have reduced breeding success in some areas (Mendelssohn 1975a, Bijlsma et al. 1988, González et al. 1990), though it is not clear whether these are ingested in the breeding or wintering areas. Additionally, human persecution and disturbance may affect breeding birds locally (Biber 1990).

■ Conservation measures

Conservation of foraging habitat around existing colonies must receive the highest priority, and careful land-use planning should ensure the avoidance of building developments in such areas. Pesticide use should also be regulated and alternative pest-control techniques applied where possible.

Pastures should be grazed non-intensively to maintain a high diversity of vegetation and insect prey. Suitable foraging sites should be provided in cultivated farmland (including field margins with short grass and hedges). In EU countries the Agri-environment Regulation (EC Reg. 2078/92) of the Common Agricultural Policy provides the opportunity to compensate farmers for adhering to prescribed management practices which are compatible with specific environmental needs. Since Lesser Kestrels generally breed in colonies, this scheme could provide the means to manage the habitat appropriately for the species at important sites.

Restoration of houses where there are colonies should ensure that nest-sites are not destroyed, and that work is not carried out in the breeding season (April–June). New nest-sites should be provided whenever there is (or recently was) a colony, through the opening and improvement of suitable holes in walls and under roofs or by providing nest-boxes.

The scale and speed of the population decline makes further research into its causes, and the monitoring of remaining populations, urgent and essential.

JEAN-PIERRE BIBER

189

Kestrel
Falco tinnunculus

SPEC Category 3
Status Declining
Criteria Moderate decline

---

*Recent widespread declines are due mainly to agricultural intensification including crop speciali-
zation, high stocking levels, pesticides and the loss of old trees and hedgerows. Broad conservation
measures are required to regulate such agricultural practices.*

■ Distribution and population trends

Breeding occurs in all but the northernmost fringes
of Europe, with strongholds in the United Kingdom,

	Breeding population			Breeding
	Size (pairs)	Year	Trend	range trend
Albania	200–1,500	—	–1	(–1)
Andorra	30–50	91	0	–1
Austria	(7,000–7,500)	—	(0)	(0)
Belarus	700–1,000	90	F	0
Belgium	2,000–3,000	81–90	0	0
Bulgaria	500–1,000	—	0	0
Croatia	12,000–15,000 *	—	0*	0*
Cyprus	2,000–4,000	—	+1	+1
Czech Republic	9,000–13,000	—	0	**0**
Denmark	**1,800–2,500**	90	**0**	+1
Estonia	200–300	—	**–2**	0
Finland	**1,000–2,500**	92	**–2**	–1
France	**42,000–57,000**	82	(–1)	**0**
Germany	35,000–100,000	—	0	**0**
Greece	5,000–10,000	—	(0)	(0)
Hungary	3,000–4,000	—	0	0
Rep. of Ireland	(2,000–4,000)	—	(0)	(0)
Italy	(5,000–10,000)	—	(–1)	(–1)
Latvia	100–200	—	**–2**	**–2**
Liechtenstein	**15–20**	—	–1	–1
Lithuania	50–100	85–88	–1	(–1)
Luxembourg	800–1,200	—	0	0
Malta	0–0	—	X	X
Moldova	**400–600**	88	–1	**0**
Netherlands	**5,000–7,000**	79	F	**0**
Norway	2,000–4,000	90	F	**0**
Poland	1,500–2,000	—	–1	0
Portugal	1,000–10,000	89	–1	**0**
Madeira	250–500	91	**0**	**0**
Romania	3,000–5,000	—	0	**0**
Russia	50,000–90,000	—	**–2**	–1
Slovakia	4,000–5,000	—	0	0
Slovenia	1,500–2,000	—	–1	0
Spain	25,000–30,000	—	–1	–1
Canary Islands	5,000–6,000	—	0	0
Sweden	2,000–3,000	87	0	**0**
Switzerland	2,500–3,000	86–91	–1	0
Turkey	(5,000–25,000)	—	—	—
Ukraine	2,800–3,500	88	–1	–1
United Kingdom	52,000–52,000	88–91	0	**0**
Guernsey	20–40	—	0*	0*
Jersey	50–75	—	0	0
Isle of Man [1]	25–40	—	0*	0*
Gibraltar	2–3	90	N	—
Total (approx.)	290,000–490,000			

Trends   +2 Large increase   +1 Small increase   0 Stable   X Extinct
(1970–1990)   –2 Large decrease   –1 Small decrease   F Fluctuating   N New breeder
Data quality   **Bold**: reliable quantitative data   Normal type: incomplete quantitative data
    Bracketed figures: no quantitative data   * Data quality not provided
[1] Population figures are included within United Kingdom totals

France, Germany and Russia. Birds in south-west
Europe are largely resident, while those from the
north-east typically winter in southern Europe and
the Afrotropics.

Until the 1950s and 1960s numbers in Europe
appeared stable, fluctuating with winter weather and
with rodent populations. Substantial and widespread
declines then occurred (Glutz von Blotzheim *et al.*
1971, Bijleveld 1974, Cramp and Simmons 1980),
due mainly to pesticide residues in prey (Newton
1979, Shrubb 1993), though numbers around St
Petersburg (Russia) fell sharply in the 1960s despite
the scarcity of pesticides (Malchevskiy and Pukinskiy
1983). Many northern populations subsequently recovered to varying degrees (Génsbøl 1987, Shrubb
1993), but 16 countries recorded declines during
1970–1990 (see table, map), thus affecting around
45% of European numbers with known trends, including the large populations of France, Spain, Italy
and Russia, the latter having a decline of over 50%.

■ Ecology

The fairly open habitats used include forest fringes
in the north, farmland, towns, and rocky areas in the
Mediterranean, but birds avoid closed forest and
treeless habitats. Nesting is on trees, rocks, cliffs, in
treeholes and occasionally on the ground, usually
solitarily although sometimes in small colonies where
food is in good supply (e.g. Cramp and Simmons
1980, Village 1990, Shrubb 1993).

Where it is abundant in temperate Europe, the
common vole *Microtus arvalis* dominates the diet
(e.g. Cavé 1968, Shrubb 1993), but in the United
Kingdom and most of Scandinavia (where common
vole is absent) the short-tailed vole *M. agrestis* is the
most frequent prey, in addition to a wide range of
other vertebrates, including birds (Yalden and
Warburton 1979, Shrubb 1980, Korpimäki 1985,
Village 1990). In the Mediterranean region, where
voles are scarce, invertebrates (particularly
Orthoptera) predominate and lizards are also frequently taken (Thiollay 1968b,c, Lovari 1974, Rizzo
et al. 1993). Breeding densities in northern Europe
appear to be related largely to food supply, espe-

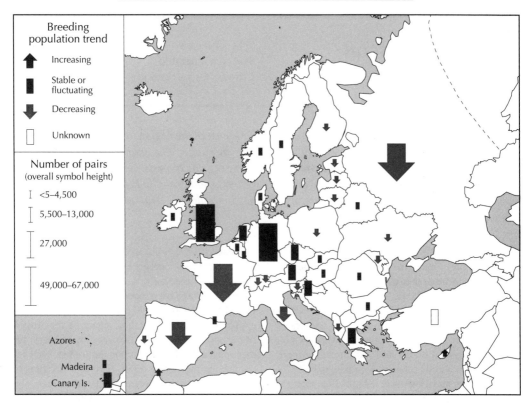

cially voles (Village 1990), though lack of nest-sites may be a limiting factor in some treeless areas (Village 1989).

■ Threats

Declines are ascribed by Shrubb (1993) mainly to persecution, pesticides, and habitat and climate change. Persecution may not currently be a major problem, but illegal hunting of raptors is common around the Mediterranean (Magnin 1991), and its effects on populations remain poorly understood. Pesticides are often implicated, either through organochlorine (e.g. DDT) or mercurial seed dressings, or through mammals poisoned with toxic baits as used in Denmark, France, Germany, Hungary and Spain (Newton 1979, Wallin *et al*. 1983, Village 1990, Shrubb 1993). These agents are no longer used, but indirect effects of modern organophosphorus pesticides on prey availability may be serious for primarily insectivorous populations (J. Garzon in Chancellor 1977, Palma 1985).

Habitat loss, chiefly through agricultural change, is probably the greatest threat. Reductions in the extent of mixed farmland, and in crop diversity, have reduced feeding opportunities. In Wales and perhaps elsewhere, high stocking rates appear to have caused declines (Shrubb 1993): heavily grazed grassland is unsuitable for voles, and vole population cycles are suppressed (Kostrzewa and Kostrzewa 1990, Ratcliffe 1990, Village 1990), affecting Kestrel breeding success (Snow 1964).

The loss of old trees (and thus nest-sites), for example through hedge removal, may be a problem, particularly in open regions (Village 1989).

■ Conservation measures

The Kestrel is highly dependent on wide-scale conservation, particularly measures which alleviate agricultural intensification. Policies are thus required which encourage mixed farming and high crop diversity, which maintain non-cultivated marginal habitats, and which decrease stocking rates and pesticide use. Within the EU countries, such measures could be promoted through extensification schemes and the development of Zonal Programmes under the Agri-environment Regulation (EC Reg. 2078/92) of the Common Agricultural Policy. The large areas of fallow land resulting from the EU Set-aside Scheme (EC Reg. 1765/92) have also been found to be advantageous through the resulting large increases in small mammal populations (R. Brown pers. comm. 1994), but the long-term future of this policy is not assured.

Kestrel populations are rather poorly monitored, and the effects of modern farming (particularly pesticides) also need further attention.

Ludwik Tomialojc and Graham Tucker

191

Red-footed Falcon
Falco vespertinus

SPEC Category 3
Status Vulnerable
Criteria Large decline

Within Europe the Red-footed Falcon breeds only in the east of the region, where almost the entire population is declining in numbers and contracting in range. The major causes of this are considered to be a decrease in the abundance of insect prey due to pesticide use, and the loss and deterioration of habitat through the conversion of wetlands and grasslands to cultivation. Conservation requires the preservation of habitats and nesting colonies and reductions in the use of pesticides.

■ Distribution and population trends

The Red-footed Falcon has a central Palearctic distribution: as a breeder it extends from east-central Europe deep into Siberia, with about half of the global range lying inside Europe, where it occurs mostly across the steppe and forest-steppe zones of the eastern part of the region (Dementiev and Gladkov 1951a, Cramp and Simmons 1980), breeding more rarely in the forest zone to approximately 63°N (Malchevskiy and Pukinskiy 1983). The approximate southern limit of the range follows the northern coasts of the Black, Azov and Caspian Seas. The species is migratory, wintering in savanna and dry grassland in Africa south of the Equator.

The main European breeding population of Red-footed Falcons is now in Hungary, southern Russia and Ukraine (see table, map). During the late nineteenth and early twentieth centuries a steady decrease in breeding numbers and some range contraction became evident across southern Fennoscandia and in central and eastern Europe, and consequently the species no longer breeds in Finland, western Belarus, Poland or Austria (Cramp and Simmons 1980, Anon. 1981, Malchevskiy and

Pukinskiy 1983, Solonen 1985, Tomialojc 1990). These decreases continue elsewhere in the breeding range and, importantly, a sharp decline and range contraction have been reported in Russia during the period from 1970 to 1990 (see table, map).

There is some uncertainty regarding the decline of the species in parts of its range. In Hungary, for example, a decline in the population has been recorded for the period 1970–1990, but a figure of 2,000–2,500 pairs given for 1949 (Glutz von Blotzheim *et al.* 1971) is practically the same as the most recent estimate (see table). In the winter quarters of southern Africa the Red-footed Falcon is considered an abundant visitor which, according to a general statement by Brown *et al.* (1982), has not shown any recent decline in numbers. The differences between breeding and wintering population trends are perhaps due to changes in the Siberian population compensating for those in Europe, although the species is reported to be scarce on its Asian breeding grounds (Dementiev and Gladkov 1951a, Gavrin *et al.* 1962).

■ Ecology

Red-footed Falcons occur in relatively warm and open habitats, for example grasslands, meadows and bogs of the European forest-steppe zone, fringed or interspersed with the copses, scattered trees and gallery forests which are used for nesting (Dementiev and Gladkov 1951a, Cramp and Simmons 1980). Further north, in the forest zone, breeding takes place in larger forest clearings, wet meadows and along forest edges.

The species is highly gregarious, tending to occur in groups throughout the year, and breeding, foraging, migration and roosting may all be communal activities (Newton 1979). Colonies can be of several hundred pairs, the birds usually nesting in old corvid nests, or occasionally in large tree-holes (Gavrin *et al.* 1962). Mixed-species colonies with corvids or

| | Breeding population | | | Breeding |
	Size (pairs)	Year	Trend	range trend
Belarus	(10–50)	90	(–2)	(–1)
Bulgaria	50–100	—	+1	+1
Croatia	5–10 *	—	0*	0*
Czech Republic	**0–5**	—	F	–2
Estonia	0–10	—	(0)	(0)
Hungary	2,200–2,200	—	–1	0
Latvia	(0–5)	—	(F)	(F)
Moldova	**120–200**	88	–1	**0**
Romania	(200–600)	—	–1	–1
Russia	15,000–40,000	—	–2	–2
Slovakia	0–30	—	F	–2
Ukraine	400–600	88	**–2**	–1
Total (approx.)	18,000–44,000			

Trends   +2 Large increase   +1 Small increase   0 Stable   X Extinct
(1970–1990)   –2 Large decrease   –1 Small decrease   F Fluctuating   N New breeder
Data quality   **Bold**: reliable quantitative data   Normal type: incomplete quantitative data
Bracketed figures: no quantitative data   * Data quality not provided

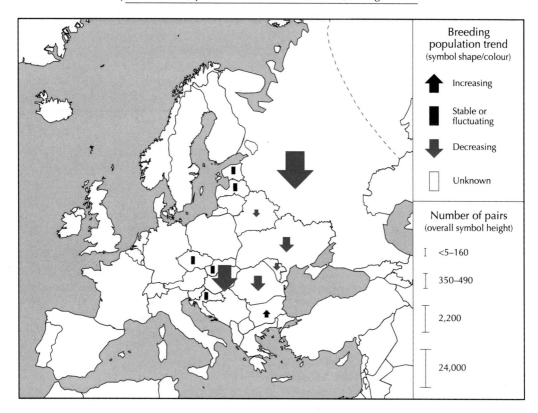

kestrels occur, and these may offer protection from nest predation (Horvath 1956, Glutz von Blotzheim *et al.* 1971).

The diet comprises large insects, such as grasshoppers, beetles, dragonflies and termites, supplemented on the breeding grounds with small vertebrates (Glutz von Blotzheim *et al.* 1971, Cramp and Simmons 1980, Hölzinger 1987). On passage and in winter, birds gather to feed in large flocks at termite and locust swarms.

■ Threats

Although there has been little research into the reasons for the decline of the Red-footed Falcon in Europe, it is suspected that an important cause is the reduction of insect prey due to the impacts of pesticides. A sharp increase in pesticide use in Africa (Newton 1979) may also have reduced prey availability for birds wintering or on passage. Habitat loss and deterioration, especially the loss of wetlands and grasslands, has reduced the availability of prey in both Europe and Africa (Hölzinger 1987).

The Red-footed Falcon is quite versatile in its choice of nesting habitat, but it is restricted by a shortage of old corvid nests. Direct human persecution sometimes occurs, for example during actions taken against corvids (Dementiev and Gladkov 1951a), and the birds' comparative tameness and habit of perching on wires while on passage makes them especially vulnerable to hunters in the Mediterranean region.

■ Conservation measures

There is a need for habitat conservation and for controls on pesticide use in the vicinity of Red-footed Falcon breeding colonies. The main breeding colonies should be protected, and studies to investigate the reasons for the species' decline should be undertaken. Similarly, work is needed to monitor the wintering populations in southern Africa and to study the feeding ecology there. Efforts should also continue to halt the killing of birds of prey in the Mediterranean region (Newton 1979, Robinson 1989).

LUDWIK TOMIALOJC

Eleonora's Falcon
Falco eleonorae

SPEC Category 2
Status Rare
Criteria <10,000 pairs

As a rare and colonial breeder on Mediterranean islands, Eleonora's Falcon is highly susceptible to egg-collecting, rat predation and disturbance (e.g. from hunting). All egg-collecting should be banned, as should hunting near colonies; efforts are needed to limit pressure from agriculture and tourism.

■ Distribution and population trends

Almost the entire breeding population (c.4,500 pairs) is concentrated on rocky islands in the Mediterranean (Walter 1979), although the breeding range extends to the Atlantic coast of Morocco and the Canary Islands. All birds winter in eastern Africa, especially Madagascar (Cramp and Simmons 1980).

Several islands in the Aegean Sea (Greece) together hold about two-thirds of European breeders, and Italy and Spain also support substantial colonies (see table, map). Exact numbers are difficult to ascertain in larger colonies (which can hold up to 300 pairs), and several Greek colonies are on remote islands not censused for many years. The numbers of pairs given in the table are thus estimates.

Numbers in Cyprus and Morocco have shown local declines since c.1960 (Walter 1979; see table, map), while some increases have been noted in Spain and on islands near Crete (Ristow *et al.* 1991). The European population seems to be stable overall (see table), but fully quantitative trend data are only available for Spain and the Canaries. With the exception of a censused population (which is increasing) in an archipelago near Crete (Ristow *et al.* 1991), the trends of other populations remain comparatively uncertain.

	Breeding population			Breeding
	Size (pairs)	Year	Trend	range trend
Croatia	100–150 *	—	0*	0*
Cyprus	100–120	—	–1	0
Greece	2,500–3,000	—	0	0
Italy	400–500	87	0	0
Spain	**599–604**	—	**+2**	**+1**
Canary Islands	**66–66**	87–88	**0**	**0**
Turkey	18–100	—	—	—
Total (approx.)	3,800–4,500			

Trends +2 Large increase +1 Small increase 0 Stable X Extinct
(1970-1990) –2 Large decrease –1 Small decrease F Fluctuating N New breeder
Data quality **Bold**: reliable quantitative data Normal type: incomplete quantitative data
Bracketed figures: no quantitative data * Data quality not provided

■ Ecology

The breeding strategy is linked to the availability of migrant birds as food for the nestlings in autumn, although food taken on the breeding grounds (from April) is otherwise mainly insects (Walter 1979, Ristow *et al.* 1983, 1986).

Breeding is colonial, on arid, rocky islands which are often small and uninhabited (Wink *et al.* 1987, Swatschek *et al.* 1993). The birds nest mainly on cliffs or steep slopes, on bare ground. Nests are often placed under small rocks or bushes, as clutches which are exposed to full sunlight have a higher failure rate (Wink *et al.* 1980, 1982).

■ Threats

Being restricted to so few breeding sites the species is extremely vulnerable. Any disturbance through tourism (e.g. building of hotels or houses near breeding cliffs) or hunting may immediately threaten the whole island population (Ristow and Wink 1985). Although many colonies are in nature reserves they are generally not monitored or guarded, and their remoteness allows hunting and nest-robbing by egg-collectors and falconers to go largely unnoticed (Ristow and Wink 1985). Local fishermen take young falcons from the nest for food, particularly in Greece and North Africa (Walter 1979, Ristow and Wink 1985).

A further threat is egg predation by rats, with losses up to 30% (Ristow and Wink 1985, Ristow *et al.* 1991). The introduction of cats and other predators could have equally detrimental consequences.

Additionally, the species is threatened during migration and in its African winter quarters by hunting, pesticides and habitat loss to deforestation and agriculture (Ristow and Wink in press).

Feeding on insects and birds, Eleonora's Falcon is high in the food chain and thus susceptible to pesticide contamination. Research to date, however, has revealed only low levels of DDE and PCBs in eggs (Clark and Peakall 1977, Ristow *et al.* 1980, Ristow and Wink in press).

■ Conservation measures

All egg-collecting, and hunting in the vicinity of colonies, should be banned and rigorously enforced.

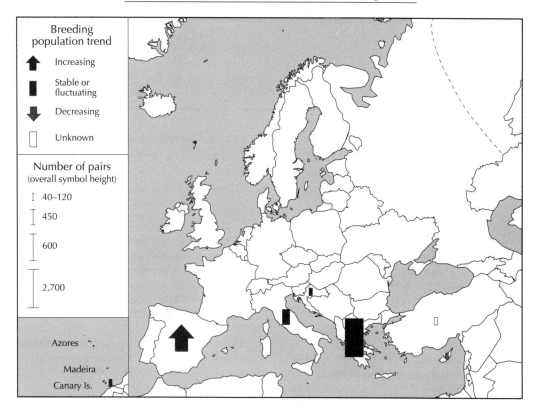

Breeding islands should be protected and not developed for tourism or agriculture. Awareness of the rarity of the species should be promoted in all countries supporting breeding (and wintering) populations in order to limit and control such detrimental activities. The control of rats by rodenticides should be considered locally, and nest-boxes could be introduced where natural sites are limited (Ristow *et al.* 1988). At some sites, wardens may be necessary to restrict access.

It is important that a thorough census be carried out on the Greek islands to ascertain the number of breeding pairs and to obtain more information on population trends.

MICHAEL WINK

Lanner
Falco biarmicus

SPEC Category 3
Status (Endangered)
Criteria Large decline, <250 pairs

The Lanner is rare and declining in Europe, where it is on the edge of its global range. Widespread persecution between the 1950s and 1970s was primarily responsible for a rapid decline in numbers. Now, habitat protection through the maintenance of inland dry grasslands in the vicinity of cliffs and a decrease in persecution through an increased public awareness of birds of prey are important conservation measures.

■ Distribution and population trends

Only a small percentage of the global population of the Lanner is known to occur in Europe where it currently breeds in the south-east and south-west of the region, including Italy (from Emilia to Calabria and Sicily), the coast of Croatia, Yugoslavia (Montenegro), Greece and southern Turkey (see map). The species is mainly sedentary.

Italy alone hosts c.50–80% of the estimated European population of 200–330 pairs (Massa *et al.* 1991; see table). Neither recent nor accurate data are available from some countries, particularly Turkey where the population could be underestimated.

The European population has apparently declined sharply during 1950–1970 (Bijleveld 1974, Chiavetta 1981). No precise figures can be given for the population trends from 1970 to 1990, but a decrease is suggested at least for Italy (see table, map) with the decline most pronounced in peripheral parts of the range.

	Breeding population			Breeding range trend
	Size (pairs)	Year	Trend	
Croatia	10–20 *	—	0*	0*
Greece	(20–40)	—	(0)	(0)
Italy	160–170	—	(–1)	(–1)
Turkey	(10–100)	—	—	—
Total (approx.)	200–330			

Trends (1970–1990) +2 Large increase +1 Small increase 0 Stable –2 Large decrease –1 Small decrease F Fluctuating X Extinct N New breeder
Data quality **Bold**: reliable quantitative data Normal type: incomplete quantitative data Bracketed figures: no quantitative data * Data quality not provided

■ Ecology

The Lanner is poorly known in Europe, with most data coming from Italy (Mebs 1959, Glutz von Blotzheim *et al.* 1971, Bonora and Chiavetta 1975, Cramp and Simmons 1980, Chiavetta 1981, Ciaccio *et al.* 1989). Birds typically frequent open dry grassland and steppe, requiring large areas of stony, bare or dry grassland for hunting, and cliffs for nesting. In the northern Apennines where the mountainous habi-tat is largely forested, the species occurs in areas comprising at least 50% agricultural fields or other open landscapes (Chiavetta 1982). Coastal areas are generally avoided, with most pairs holding inland territories 200–600 m above sea-level, and in Sicily more frequently approaching 1,000 m (Chiavetta 1981, Massa 1985).

The diet is mostly small to medium-sized birds, plus some small mammals, reptiles and large insects (Chiavetta 1982, Massa *et al.* 1991).

■ Threats

The decline in Italy during 1950–1970 was due primarily to the widespread persecution of birds of prey. Some intentional persecution at nest-sites still occurs, as well as the taking of nestlings for falconry or captivity, but the major threat is illegal shooting over the whole European range, particularly in Italy (LIPU 1991). Unintentional human disturbance from tourism and climbing during the breeding season is responsible for some breeding failures (Chiavetta 1981).

In northern Italy, because of the increase in Per-egrine numbers, competition for nest-sites is pre-sumed to occur (Chiavetta and Martelli 1991), but this is not thought to be happening in Sicily (Massa *et al.* 1991).

There is no evidence that pollution is having a serious effect on the breeding population although this has not been adequately studied.

■ Conservation measures

The European population is marginal to the Lanner's global range and may therefore be particularly sus-ceptible to ecological change and to threats. Thus the maintenance of undisturbed inland dry grasslands and cliffs is essential for conservation. Most of the key Important Bird Areas (IBAs) for Lanner are not protected but neither are they currently endangered. Breeding pairs are also scattered, and the following Italian IBAs probably include only 10–20% of the

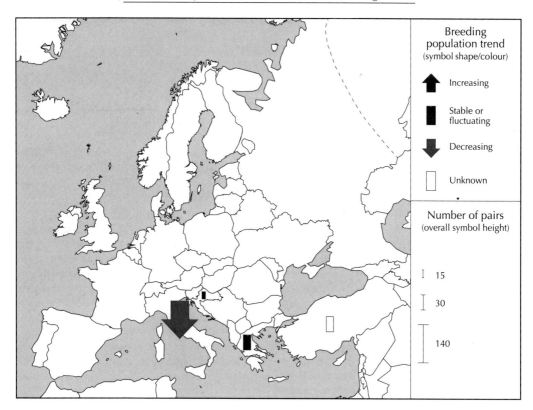

national population (Lambertini *et al.* 1991): area of Monte Sirente, Monte Velino and Montagne della Duchessa (IBA 079); Massiccio della Maiella, Montagne del Morrone and Monti Pizi (IBA 080); mountains and hills between Capracotta and Rosello (IBA 081); Le Murge di Monte Caccia (IBA 096); Valle del Ferro (IBA 102); Monte Orsomarso and Monte Verbicaro (IBA 103); area between Torrente Lipuda and Fiume Neto (IBA 104); Aspromonte (IBA 107); area between Piana degli Albanesi, Misilmeri, Ventimiglia di Sicilia e Rocca Busambra (IBA 131); Gole dell'Anapo between Palazzolo Acreide and Necropoli di Pantalica (IBA 138). Currently a more urgent requirement than habitat protection is an increase in public awareness about birds of prey, especially among hunters, farmers and shepherds.

A more detailed census of the population is needed, particularly for Turkey (Bijleveld 1974) along with the establishment of an adequate monitoring scheme.

MARCO LAMBERTINI

Saker
Falco cherrug

SPEC Category 3
Status Endangered
Criteria Large decline, <2,500 pairs

The European population has steadily declined during the twentieth century due to habitat destruction and associated decreases in prey abundance, as well as nest-robbing. Essential protective measures include the conservation of the birds' habitat and main prey, the provision of suitable nest-sites, and nest-guarding.

■ Distribution and population trends

The breeding range of the Saker extends from central Asia westwards through the steppe and forest-steppe zones of southern Russia and Ukraine. In Europe outside the former U.S.S.R., breeding occurs in Romania and Bulgaria in the Dobrogea region and adjoining areas (especially the Danube delta and some mountain areas), and on the Hungarian plains together with adjoining parts of Romania, Yugoslavia (Serbia), Croatia, Austria, Czech Republic and Slovakia; a small population is also present in Turkey (Cramp and Simmons 1980, Baumgart 1991; see table, map). Overall, Europe currently holds perhaps only 1% of the Saker's world breeding population of 35,000–45,000 pairs (Baumgart 1991).

Historical population data are sparse, partly because Sakers were frequently overlooked or misidentified. However, it is likely that Europe held some 5,000–10,000 pairs in the second half of the nineteenth century, chiefly in the steppe zone of western Kazakhstan, European Russia, Ukraine, Dobrogea and the Hungarian puszta (dry grasslands) (Baumgart *et al.* 1992).

The range clearly contracted in the late nineteenth and early twentieth centuries, the northern boundary shifting 200–300 km southwards in the Russian regions of Tula and Ryazan (Galushin 1992).

Breeding also stopped at some sites in the west, including Bohemia (Duba) in the Czech Republic, the Wienerwald in Austria (Baumgart 1991) and parts of Dobrogea and the Hungarian plains. However, widely scattered breeding pairs remain in the westernmost areas, largely in mountains and hilly country (Bagyura *et al.* 1987–1989, 1992, Baumgart 1991, Galushin 1992).

Between 1970 and 1990 this downward trend continued through most of Europe, and the present population is estimated to be 370–610 pairs. Only in Hungary has the population increased significantly (see table), although there have been recent signs of recovery in neighbouring countries (Bagyura *et al.* 1987–1989, 1992).

■ Ecology

The Saker is found mainly in open, steppe-like habitats with low vegetation. Such habitats develop in areas with low precipitation and/or chalk soils, and typically the short vegetation is maintained by sheep-grazing. Breeding may occur also in areas where forests are interspersed with steppe intrusions (Dementiev and Gladkov 1951b, Baumgart 1991). In some parts of Europe, the species is present in steppe-like areas of cultivated land.

During the breeding season the diet comprises mainly susliks (*Citellus citellus* and *C. suslicus*) (Baumgart 1991), and Sakers breed from the lowlands up to 2,000 m depending on the presence of this prey. Birds may be resident or migratory, according to the local food availability (Baumgart 1991).

The Saker usually occupies old nests of large birds (e.g. eagles, herons, corvids). In the lowlands these are normally in trees (often in riverine forest), though recently also on electricity pylons; in mountains and river canyons, nests are on cliffs.

■ Threats

Steppes and dry grasslands are being destroyed or degraded either through conversion to cultivation, afforestation, or declines in sheep-grazing leading to

	Breeding population			Breeding
	Size (pairs)	Year	Trend	range trend
Austria	5–10	—	–1	–1
Bulgaria	**20–40**	70–90	–1	–1
Croatia	10–15 *	—	0*	0*
Czech Republic	**8–12**	—	0	+1
Hungary	**80–80**	91	+2	+1
Moldova	5–7	88	–1	0
Romania	2–6	—	–1	0
Russia	80–150	—	–1	0
Slovakia	30–40	—	–2	–2
Turkey	(10–100)	—	—	—
Ukraine	(120–150)	—	–1	–1
Total (approx.)	370–610			

Trends   +2 Large increase   +1 Small increase   0 Stable   X Extinct
(1970–1990)   –2 Large decrease   –1 Small decrease   F Fluctuating   N New breeder
Data quality **Bold**: reliable quantitative data   Normal type: incomplete quantitative data
              Bracketed figures: no quantitative data   * Data quality not provided

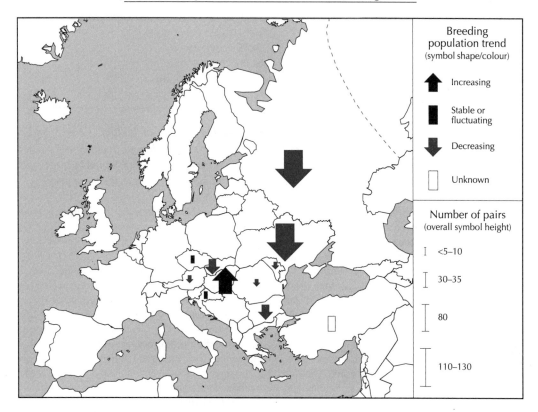

increases in vegetation cover. Such habitat transformations reduce the abundance of susliks, although increases in numbers of pigeons may compensate locally for this. In some regions the clear-felling of riverine forests may cause loss of nest-sites, and rock-climbers and tourists cause serious disturbance to some cliff-nesting birds. In consequence Sakers have mostly disappeared from lowlands, but survive in mountain areas where human impact is less intense. Thus the formerly marginal mountain breeding sites now appear to represent the species' strongholds in Europe.

As a raptor prized by falconers, Saker nestlings were frequently taken from their nests in previous decades, and sometimes still are. This happened especially between 1950 and 1980, decimating the European population, chiefly in Slovakia, Austria and Hungary (Baumgart *et al.* 1992). The trapping each year of some thousands of migrating or wintering birds in the Middle East for falconry adds to the losses, though to an unknown degree.

As a result of increasing acceptance of electricity pylons as nest-sites, electrocution of birds on pylons of certain designs in eastern Europe and Kazakhstan is a potential threat. However, pylons also provide security from disturbance and persecution, and generally contribute to the maintenance of the species' distribution in cultivated landscapes where natural nest-sites have either been lost (trees) or are lacking (cliffs) (Baumgart *et al.* 1992, Haraszthy *in litt.*)

■ Conservation measures

Throughout much of its range, the Saker is dependent on the conservation of original steppe vegetation and short grasslands. Remaining areas need to be protected from conversion to cultivation and from afforestation, and extensive livestock-grazing should be maintained to control grass and prevent vegetational succession. In addition, nest-guarding, to reduce disturbance and robbing, is necessary at susceptible sites. Provision of artificial nests, or improvement of natural ones, prevents nestlings falling from nests and provides shelter from adverse weather, thereby increasing nesting success. Based on these methods WWF projects in the Czech Republic, Slovakia and Hungary have resulted in the stabilization of these populations; indeed, in Hungary 30% of young now hatch from artificial nests (Bagyura *et al.* 1987–1989, 1992, Baumgart *et al.* 1992).

Captive breeding is frequently suggested for this species, but the reintroduction of captive-bred individuals seems inadvisable in view of the dramatic reduction in the extent of suitable habitat.

Changes in the design of electricity pylons, where necessary, would reduce the incidence of electrocution for this and many other large birds.

WOLFGANG BAUMGART

Gyrfalcon
Falco rusticolus

SPEC Category 3
Status Vulnerable
Criteria <2,500 pairs

The Gyrfalcon is a rare species in Europe where it is confined to Greenland, Iceland, Fennoscandia and northern Russia. Most of the population is thought to be stable, though declines have been recorded in Russia and northern Norway. In parts of its range the species is threatened by the illegal removal of eggs and young for falconry and by declines in numbers of grouse, the main prey.

■ Distribution and population trends

The Gyrfalcon breeds over the greater part of the circumpolar tundra regions of the world, within Europe in Greenland (from 82°N, in the interior fjord country and along the coast), Iceland, Norway (from Hardangervidda to Finnmark), Sweden (from Dalarna to Lapland), Finland (Saurola 1985) and Russia (from the Kola peninsula eastwards). Birds do not usually move outside the breeding range, although some individuals (usually juveniles) occasionally winter in the United Kingdom, France, Netherlands, Germany, southern Russia and Ukraine (Glutz von Blotzheim *et al.* 1971, Cramp and Simmons 1980).

The species is a rare breeder in Europe with only approximately 1,300 to 2,300 breeding pairs in total (see table, map). Numbers of breeding pairs vary according to the abundance of grouse and ptarmigan *Lagopus*, the main prey species (Cade 1982). The size of the Greenland population, probably the largest in Europe, is highly uncertain. Also, although the Swedish population has been estimated to be 100–200 pairs (Ahlen and Tjernberg 1992), there have been no recent surveys of the species.

Cade (1982) states that there is no indication of a long-term downward trend in numbers in recent decades in most parts of the Gyrfalcon's breeding range. Although this is supported by some of the data in the table, declines in population size and range in Russia are suggested. Local declines have also been reported from northern Norway, probably as a result of decreases in grouse numbers.

■ Ecology

Most Gyrfalcon pairs breed on cliffs, either coastal or inland, although tree-nesting has been recorded in Fennoscandia, Russia and North America (Cade 1960). Old nests of Rough-legged Buzzard *Buteo lagopus* and Raven *Corvus corvax* are often used. In Fennoscandia breeding occurs mainly in inland habitats, along river valleys and mountains, from 400 to 1,200 m above sea-level, both above and below the treeline. Ptarmigan *Lagopus mutus* and Willow Grouse *L. lagopus* constitute the main prey species as shown by Nielsen and Cade (1990) who found that in north-east Iceland grouse constituted over 80% of prey for heathland Gyrfalcons during both summer and winter months. Ducks, waders, seabirds, lemmings, voles and Arctic hares *Lepus timidus* are also utilized. Even where breeding occurs on sea cliffs close to seabird colonies, along the Norwegian coast and in Iceland, the diet is largely grouse during the summer (Nielsen and Cade 1990). The Gyrfalcon is like the Peregrine *F. peregrinus* in that certain cliffs will be used as traditional nest-sites, sometimes for centuries (Tömmeraas 1978).

■ Threats

Although the Gyrfalcon is totally protected in all the countries of Europe, a regional threat to the species is the illegal taking of eggs and young, especially in Norway, for the falconry market. In 1992 more than 35 Gyrfalcons, all collected in Fennoscandia, were confiscated by the police in Germany (Forslund 1993). Illegal shooting is an additional problem still occurring in Norway and Sweden though probably on a small scale.

Intensive hunting of grouse populations in parts of Fennoscandia may possibly affect grouse numbers and thus Gyrfalcon density (Tömmeraas 1993).

Disturbance from development near some traditional nest-sites may also cause problems locally (Tömmeraas 1993).

	Breeding population			Breeding
	Size (pairs)	Year	Trend	range trend
Denmark				
Greenland	(500–1,000)	—	(0)	(0)
Finland	**30–30**	92	0	**0**
Iceland	300–400	81–85	+1	0
Norway	300–500	90	0	0
Russia	50–200	—	–1	–1
Sweden	100–200	—	0	0
Total (approx.)	1,300–2,300			

Trends (1970–1990) +2 Large increase +1 Small increase 0 Stable –2 Large decrease –1 Small decrease F Fluctuating X Extinct N New breeder
Data quality **Bold: reliable quantitative data** Normal type: incomplete quantitative data Bracketed figures: no quantitative data * Data quality not provided

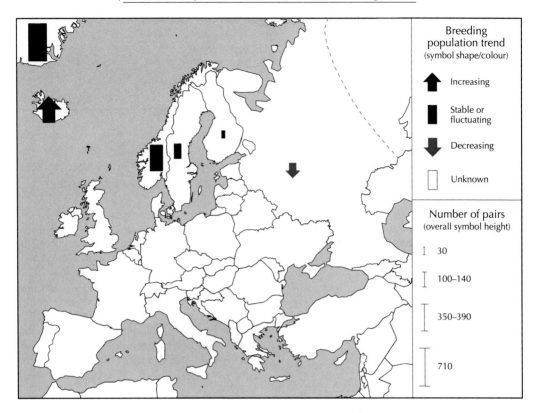

■ Conservation measures

The illegal collection of eggs and young, mainly in Iceland and Norway, for falconry purposes should be stopped by further cooperative efforts between national authorities and non-governmental nature conservation bodies. In parts of the Fennoscandian mountain range it would also be desirable to introduce more rigorous controls on snowmobile traffic, which has facilitated the illegal persecution of the species. Furthermore, the legal trade of Gyrfalcons should be more strictly controlled, for example by using DNA techniques to distinguish between wild-caught birds and those bred in captivity.

The maintenance of a healthy grouse population is important for the Gyrfalcon. Therefore, the effects of acidification through acid rain, overgrazing by reindeers *Rangifer tarandus*, and increased hunting pressure on grouse populations should be monitored and evaluated.

Roads, hydroelectric power dams and tourist establishments should not be constructed near important and traditional Gyrfalcon breeding sites.

PETER LINDBERG

201

Peregrine
Falco peregrinus

SPEC Category 3
Status Rare
Criteria <10,000 pairs

The Peregrine declined severely over much of its European range north of the Mediterranean from around 1955–1965 onwards, through widespread contamination by persistent toxic chemical residues, mainly from agriculture. It has since shown variable population recovery, mostly related to decreased exposure to these environmental pollutants as control measures have taken effect.

■ Distribution and population trends

Europe holds perhaps one fifth of the world population of this virtually cosmopolitan species, and the bulk of the nominate form, the most widespread of its 19 subspecies. Peregrines occur almost throughout Europe, though mostly at low density and highly dispersed. Northern breeding populations are strongly migratory, since their prey species mostly winter in

	Breeding population			Breeding
	Size (pairs)	Year	Trend	range trend
Albania	50–200	—	0	(0)
Andorra	3–5	91	0	–1
Austria	80–100	—	+2	+2
Belgium	0–1	81–90	0	0
Bulgaria	15–25	—	–1	–1
Croatia	150–200 *	—	0*	0*
Cyprus	4–6	—	–1	–1
Czech Republic	**0–3**	—	**0**	**0**
Denmark				
Greenland	**500–1,000**	88	0	0
Finland	**100–120**	92	+2	+1
France	**700–1,000**	85	+1	+1
Germany	**135–280**	90	+1	**(0)**
Greece	100–250	—	(0)	(0)
Rep. of Ireland	**270–270**	88–91	+2	+1
Italy	430–550	—	–1	0
Latvia	0–0	—	X	X
Malta	0–0	—	X	X
Netherlands	**0–1**	79	**0**	**0**
Norway	**150–200**	90	+2	+1
Poland	1–5 *	—	—	—
Portugal	25–50	89	–1	–1
Romania	(5–8)	—	–2	–1
Russia	400–800	—	–1	–1
Slovakia	1–10	—	–2	–2
Slovenia	**20–30**	—	+2	+2
Spain	**1,628–1,751**	85	–1	–1
Canary Islands	**9–9**	87–88	(0)	(0)
Sweden	**25–35**	90	+2	**0**
Switzerland	**120–150**	86–91	+2	+2
Turkey	(100–2,000)	—	—	—
Ukraine	(1–12)	84	–1	–1
United Kingdom	**1,200–1,200**	91	+1	+2
Isle of Man [1]	**8–12**	—	+2	0*
Gibraltar	4–5	91	**0**	0*
Total (approx.)	6,200–10,000			

Trends	+2 Large increase	+1 Small increase	0 Stable	X Extinct
(1970–1990)	–2 Large decrease	–1 Small decrease	F Fluctuating	N New breeder
Data quality	**Bold:** reliable quantitative data	Normal type: incomplete quantitative data	
	Bracketed figures: no quantitative data	* Data quality not provided	

[1] Population figures are included within United Kingdom totals

more southerly, warmer regions (Hickey 1969).

Greenland, United Kingdom, France, Spain, Italy, Russia and Turkey have the largest numbers of Peregrines, together accounting for over three-quarters of the European total (see table, map).

The Peregrine began to decline severely in numbers around 1955, in Fennoscandia and in northwest, central and eastern Europe (Hickey 1969). Numbers fell to two-fifths of pre-1950 levels in the United Kingdom, a quarter in France, a tenth in West Germany and Austria, and to still lower levels in Norway, Sweden, Finland, Switzerland, Czech Republic, Slovakia and Russia (Cade *et al*. 1988). The species was believed extinct in Belgium, Luxembourg, East Germany, Poland, Latvia, Lithuania and Estonia. This decrease bottomed by 1965 in Britain and Ireland but not until 1975 in some countries. During this period numbers also decreased slightly in Spain but apparently remained stable in much of south-west Europe, and possibly in south-east Europe, though information for the latter region is scanty (Cade *et al*. 1988).

Most of the depleted populations showed some recovery by 1991. Indeed, numbers in Britain and Ireland are now larger than ever known before, while France, Switzerland and Austria are evidently close to pre-1950 levels, and recovery is proceeding well in Germany. In some other countries recovery is much slower and, although increases outweigh decreases, overall declines were evident over the 1970–1990 period in nine countries together containing up to approximately 40% of the European total (see table).

■ Ecology

Cliffs are preferred nesting habitat, and most pairs breed on sea-cliffs and rocky offshore islands or inland crags among mountains and along river valleys. The species is absent as a breeder only from extensive areas of flat, low-lying agricultural land. It formerly nested widely in the Baltic countries where it used nests of other large birds in trees within patchy woodland. Most of the remaining population

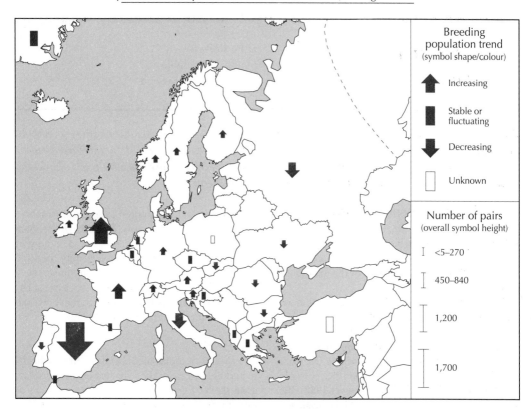

in Finland is ground-nesting, on extensive aapa mires within boreal forests. Breeding distribution and density are limited in many areas by shortage of suitable nesting cliffs. However, the Peregrine is adaptable, and the recent increase in Britain and Ireland has involved the widespread use of quarries and small cliffs, while breeding on man-made constructions and on the ground in quiet uplands is increasing (Ratcliffe 1993). Where cliffs are numerous, density is determined mainly by territorial behaviour, which is itself related to food supply (Ratcliffe 1962).

The favourite prey is the feral pigeon *Columba livia* wherever this is freely available, but Peregrines feed on an extremely wide range of other bird species, and so can winter in almost any country with good mixed bird populations.

■ Threats

The widespread post-1955 declines in Peregrine numbers were caused by food-chain contamination with persistent toxic chemical residues, mainly of agricultural organochlorine insecticides introduced between the late 1940s and mid-1950s (Ratcliffe 1993). Organo-mercury fungicides and industrial PCBs were also possible contributory factors (Newton *et al.* 1988). The restrictions and later bans on the majority of persistent organochlorines over most of Europe were followed by the general recovery in Peregrine

numbers. Lack of recovery in coastal northern Scotland may reflect contamination by marine pollutants (including PCBs) through seabird prey (Ratcliffe 1993), but the slowness of any increase in the Baltic and east European countries could result from some continuing illegal use of organochlorine pesticide hazards in European wintering areas.

As Peregrine numbers have increased, surreptitious persecution by pigeon fanciers and game preservers has been renewed, and pressure for legal controls is growing in some countries. Some nests are robbed by egg-collectors and to supply a clandestine trade for falconry.

■ Conservation measures

The most important conservation measure is to eliminate harmful food-chain pollutants, and to prevent the release into the environment of any new chemical residues with potentially damaging effects. The ban on organochlorine and other highly toxic pesticides therefore needs to be enforced.

Surveillance of nests and other direct protection measures have so far contained illegal persecution and permitted population increases, and these must therefore continue if such interference is not to get out of hand. Monitoring of breeding populations and their performance, as well as exposure to toxic pollutants, should continue.

DEREK RATCLIFFE

Black Grouse
Tetrao tetrix

SPEC Category 3
Status Vulnerable
Criteria Large decline

Population size and range are declining throughout most of Europe due mainly to habitat degradation through afforestation and agricultural intensification. Suitable habitat needs to be managed for Black Grouse, including areas of low-intensity agriculture. In some parts of lowland western and central Europe, habitat should be actively recreated.

■ Distribution and population trends

The Black Grouse is distributed across the northern Palearctic, with European birds concentrated in boreal forests and mountainous areas. Fennoscandia and Russia together hold around 90% of the total European population.

In western Europe, numbers started to fall in the latter half of the nineteenth century, and severe declines continued during 1970–1990 in western, central and eastern Europe with frequent regional extinctions. In several countries, such as Denmark (Jepsen 1989), Netherlands (Niewold 1982, Niewold and Nijland 1982) and Belgium (Ruwet 1982), the species is now practically extinct, and the heathland population of southern Sweden has already died out (Svensson *et al.* 1992).

Declines between 1970 and 1990 were most rapid

in the important Russian stronghold and also in Estonia, Latvia, Poland, Germany, Netherlands, Belgium and Slovakia. Smaller declines occurred in much of the remaining European range, including the large Finnish population. Many reductions in numbers were associated with range contractions (see table). The large Norwegian population remained stable and that in Sweden increased (Koskimies 1993b).

■ Ecology

The species occupies mosaics of different habitats, requiring open, sparsely vegetated land for display, good shelter for roosting, and sometimes shrubs or trees for feeding above the snow in winter. Habitat diversity is needed also to support the dietary requirements which vary with geography and season; edible field-layer vegetation, such as heaths *Calluna* or *Vaccinium*, is needed during winter. Logged clearings in boreal forest are occupied, but such successional stages are ephemeral, necessitating local shifts in distribution. Heathland and meadows are occupied in western and central Europe, and areas around the treeline in the central European mountains.

Black Grouse occupy a home range exceeding several square kilometres (Angelstam and Martinsson 1990, Klaus *et al.* 1990). They are gregarious, though the sexes segregate, and males form leks at traditional sites. Boreal forest populations in Fennoscandia typically show cyclic fluctuations, mainly in breeding success rather than in density, but these are not apparent further south (Angelstam *et al.* 1985, Angelstam 1988).

■ Threats

In western and (mainly lowland) central Europe, habitat fragmentation and destruction are serious threats. Local populations throughout western Europe have declined in parallel with afforestation of heathlands and their conversion to agriculture (Cramp and Simmons 1980). Thus, in the Åland archipelago in the Baltic, Haila *et al.* (1980) reported an 80% decline in numbers since the 1940s, attributed to afforestation of open, grazed heath and small agricultural

	Breeding population			Breeding range trend
	Size (pairs)	Year	Trend	
Albania	0–5		–1	(–1)
Austria	(10,000–14,000)	—	(–1)	(–1)
Belarus	15,000–25,000	90	–1	0
Belgium	**50–75**	81–90	**–2**	**–1**
Czech Republic	**1,100–2,200**	—	–1	–1
Denmark	**35–35**	89	–1	–1
Estonia	10,000–15,000	—	–2	0
Finland	**100,000–300,000**	92	–1	**0**
France	**3,000–3,000**	86	–1	**0**
Germany	1,600–1,600	85	–2	–1
Italy	10,000–15,000	82	F	(+1)
Latvia	**5,000–10,000**	—	–2	0
Liechtenstein	**120–120**	89	**0**	**0**
Lithuania	2,000–3,000	85–88	–1	–1
Netherlands	**29–40**	89–91	**–2**	**–2**
Norway	100,000–200,000	90	**0**	**0**
Poland	3,000–6,000	—	–2	–1
Romania	40–70	—	(–1)	0
Russia	100,000–1,000,000	—	–2	0
Slovakia	200–300	—	–2	–1
Slovenia	500–1,000	—	–1	–1
Sweden	200,000–400,000	87	**+1**	**0**
Switzerland	7,500–10,000	89	F	0
Ukraine	**1,000–1,300**	88	**–1**	**–1**
United Kingdom	10,000–15,000	88–91	–1	**–1**
Total (approx.)	580,000–2,000,000			

Trends	+2 Large increase	+1 Small increase	0 Stable	X Extinct
(1970–1990)	–2 Large decrease	–1 Small decrease	F Fluctuating	N New breeder

Data quality **Bold**: reliable quantitative data Normal type: incomplete quantitative data
Bracketed figures: no quantitative data * Data quality not provided

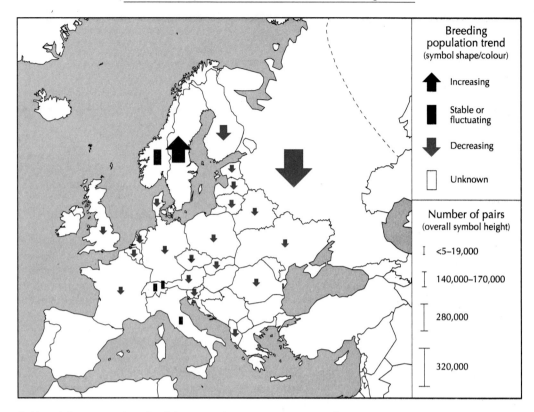

field and forest mosaics. Traditional grazing has helped maintain habitat, but recent high stocking levels of sheep have been a major contributor to destruction of birch *Betula* scrub and heather moorland which are favoured habitats in the United Kingdom (Batten *et al*. 1990). Agriculture has intensified over the last 50 years in Finland, and traditional shifting cultivation which created many suitable areas (abandoned plots with deciduous trees growing up) has been replaced by inferior conifer-dominated forest.

In central Europe eutrophication through airborne nitrogen deposition is considered a major threat to the environment (Ellenberg *et al*. 1989, Roelofs *et al*. 1989), including the Black Grouse, as it transforms heaths and peatlands into grassland unsuitable for this and other heath species.

Hunting does not seem to influence trends in boreal forest, since on average only 6% of the autumn population is shot (Bergström *et al*. 1992). However, the shooting of dominant males at leks in central Europe may perhaps alter the social structure and reduce breeding success (Batten *et al*. 1990). Black Grouse are sensitive to predation but in boreal forest have benefited locally from reductions in numbers of red foxes *Vulpes vulpes* due to the advent and spread of the disease sarcoptic mange in the 1970s (Marcström *et al*. 1988, Lindström *et al*. in press). Management of predators, including Goshawks *Accipiter gentilis*

and generalist mammals, is sometimes beneficial to Black Grouse (Angelstam 1984, Angelstam *et al*. 1984, Widén *et al*. 1987, Reynolds *et al*. 1988).

■ Conservation measures

Key localities in central Europe should be protected and managed for Black Grouse, accompanied by conservation measures in the surrounding regions aimed at maintaining mosaics of suitable habitat. These measures include low-intensity farming and reduced afforestation, as well as actively maintaining some disturbance (Niewold 1982, Niewold and Nijland 1982, Angelstam and Martinsson 1990): selective forest clearance in boreal regions, and grazing or browsing in subalpine habitats. Commercial forests should preserve areas of semi-natural habitat and maintain open clearings, open stream margins and unplanted rocky outcrops (Batten *et al*. 1990). Intensive studies of the spatial requirements of male Black Grouse in a variety of landscapes suggest that management units should involve whole, integrated landscapes rather than just specific habitats (Angelstam 1983, Willebrand 1988, Klaus *et al*. 1990).

Further research is required into the effects of isolation of patches of habitat, the minimum-area requirements of the species in different regions, and the role of dispersal. The effects of hunting also need further study (Batten *et al*. 1990).

PER ANGELSTAM

Caucasian Black Grouse
Tetrao mlokosiewiczi

SPEC Category 2
Status Insufficiently Known

The Caucasian Black Grouse has declined during the twentieth century, largely due to degradation of habitat by intensive sheep-grazing. Although current trends are unknown, it is possibly still declining. Necessary conservation measures are protection from overgrazing and disturbance through improved management in nature reserves, the creation of further protected areas, and wide-scale regulation of stocking densities.

■ Distribution and population trends

Virtually the entire world population of this resident species occurs within Europe, mainly along the Great Caucasus ridge (Russia, Georgia and Azerbaijan), but also in the Lesser Caucasus (Georgia, Armenia and Azerbaijan), and in the mountains of eastern Turkey. A tiny population of perhaps only 100 birds occurs in Iran along the border with Azerbaijan. It is estimated that roughly 70,000 birds occur in the Great Caucasus (Potapov 1984, 1987) and c.500 birds in the Lesser Caucasus (Airumian and Margarian 1974). The population in Turkey is extremely poorly known, with 'guesstimates' of 200–1,000 pairs, although results of a survey in 1993 suggest that this may be too low and that the species may be more commonly distributed within its range than previously thought (UEA Kaçkar Expedition 1993).

A decline in numbers of Caucasian Black Grouse and some local reductions in range have been apparent since the 1930s, chiefly in the lower altitudinal range of the species (Micheyev 1952, Potapov 1987). For example, in 1886–1887 the species was present on two mountains, Bermamuit (2,469 m) and Handjal (2,829 m), c.50 km beyond the edge of the species' current range, but by the 1930s it was not found there and there have been no subsequent records (Potapov 1985). The declines resulted from an increase in human activities in the mountains and an associated increase in domestic grazing animals, thus during periods of war (e.g. the Second World War and the more recent local wars) the population has tended to recover. Recovery in numbers was also noticed after the establishment of nature reserves, for example in the Teberda Reserve in the region of the Teberda river, established in 1936. The density of Caucasian Black Grouse in autumn on the north slope of the main ridge, near Mt Dombai-Ulgen (4,040 m), increased from 1.4 to 3.8 birds/km² when sheep grazing ceased (Vitovich 1977). The spring density in this reserve also increased from 0.9–1.4 birds/km² (Tkatshenko 1966) to 2.0 birds/km² (Potapov 1985). At about the same time (in the early 1980s) densities in grazed areas outside nature reserves were an order of magnitude less.

No data are available from the Caucasus for the last decade because of political unrest. Overall, however, it is believed that the population has fallen during the last 50 years, with declines possibly continuing throughout the 1970–1990 period. Population trends in Turkey are totally unknown.

■ Ecology

The species' habitat varies geographically and seasonally, but generally comprises subalpine and alpine meadows around the treeline, between 1,700 and 3,300 m (Potapov 1985, 1987). Recent work in Turkey found birds apparently confined to 1,800–3,000 m, with most seen at 2,000–2,700 m (UEA Kaçkar Expedition 1993). Within this altitudinal range birds were found to utilize slopes of reasonable grazing quality, the vast majority with *Rhododendron* and juniper *Juniperus* on them.

The species has a promiscuous mating system (Micheyev 1952, Potapov 1987) and in spring birds form leks on the steep southern slopes above the treeline. The nesting places are also mostly on southern slopes at 2,450–2,750 m on flat ledges covered with tufts of tall grass or juniper bushes, though some birds nest on northern slopes between 2,000 and 2,600 m. Newly hatched broods usually remain on flat areas at springs among alpine meadows with scattered juniper, *Rhododendron* or rose *Rosa* bushes. Caucasian Black Grouse are gregarious, staying in

| | Breeding population | | | Breeding |
	Size (pairs)	Year	Trend	range trend
Russia	P	—	—	—
Turkey	(200–1,000)	93	—	—
Total (approx.)	200–1,000			

Trends	+2 Large increase	+1 Small increase	0 Stable	X Extinct
(1970–1990)	–2 Large decrease	–1 Small decrease	F Fluctuating	N New breeder
Data quality	**Bold:** reliable quantitative data	Normal type: incomplete quantitative data		
	Bracketed figures: no quantitative data	* Not provided	P Present	

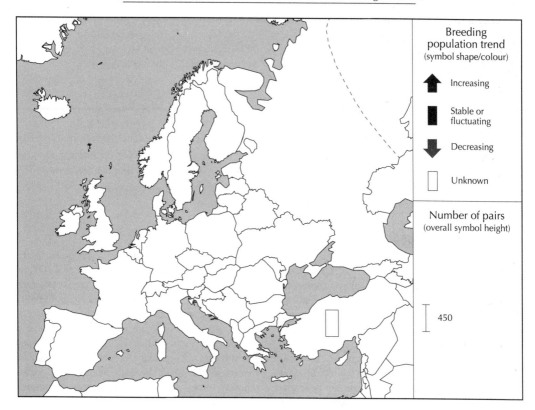

flocks in autumn and winter. In winter, birds inhabit the forest edge and clumps of dense bushes at the treeline or descend to lower altitudes.

The diet consists of buds and twigs of birch *Betula*, willow *Salix*, juniper, other trees and bushes, as well as invertebrates in early summer.

■ Threats

The main cause of the slow decline in this species is a deterioration in the suitability of the alpine meadows it occupies. This habitat is crucial for newly hatched young but is suffering from the effects of overgrazing on vegetation structure, as both lekking males and nesting females require tall grass for cover. As described above, and as recently found in Turkey (UEA Kaçkar Expedition 1993), the species does occur in grazed areas but its densities in such habitats are much lower.

Other problems associated with livestock-grazing are disturbance by sheep (of adult females both on nests and with young) and killing by herdsmen's dogs. However, Caucasian Black Grouse remain fairly numerous and seem to be able to adjust to some disturbance (Potapov 1987).

■ Conservation measures

To halt the decline of this species it is necessary to establish additional protected areas and to effect improved management on existing nature reserves, including the control of grazing levels, disturbance to breeding birds and illegal hunting. However, over 90% of the species' population lies outside these areas and it is necessary to implement wide-scale measures to reduce overgrazing and disturbance. At present these actions are difficult to achieve because of the conflicting interests of local cattle/sheep breeders and conservation authorities and, in particular, the unstable political and economic situation in the Caucasus region.

A number of key reserves have been established in the Caucasus, covering around 1,500 km² and supporting around 5,500–6,000 birds: North Caucasus (Russia: 980 km² of subalpine and alpine meadows), Teberda (Russia: 290 km² of meadows), Lagodechi (Georgia: 50 km² of meadows), Zakataly (Azerbaijan: 70 km² of meadows) and Dilijan (Armenia: 5.3 km² of meadows). While habitat protection in these areas is in general good, the main task is to control legal and illegal grazing.

Assessments of current population sizes and trends are also required, together with further information on the relationship between grazing levels and Caucasian Black Grouse population density.

ROALD L. POTAPOV

Caspian Snowcock
Tetraogallus caspius

SPEC Category 3
Status Insufficiently Known

The Caspian Snowcock has declined steadily in the Caucasian republics (Armenia, Georgia, Azerbaijan) during the twentieth century, due largely to the degradation of its habitat through grazing pressure. Current trends are, however, unknown for these regions and for the very poorly known Turkish population. The protection of areas from overgrazing, at least during the breeding season, should help to maintain and improve the population status.

■ Distribution and population trends

Perhaps about 10–15% of the global range of Caspian Snowcock lies within Europe, where the species occurs chiefly in isolated populations in Armenia, Azerbaijan and Turkey (Dementiev and Gladkov 1952, Potapov 1987). Outside Europe, the breeding range extends to the Elburz and Zagros mountains of northern and western Iran.

The Caucasus region holds almost 20 local populations, each comprising 10–35 birds. In 1964 the species was considered rare by Baziev in Transcaucasia and the population was estimated at a total of no more than 850 birds (Cramp and Simmons 1980), with most being concentrated on the Zangezur ridge (c.300 birds) and the Mrovdag ridge (nearly 200 birds) (Baziev 1978).

A decline of Caspian Snowcock in the Caucasus region was noted at the beginning of the twentieth century when the species disappeared from the Talysh mountains in Azerbaijan (Satunin 1907) and became especially noticeable in the 1960s, when it was close to local extinction on the Gegam and Aiodzor ridges in Armenia (Baziev 1978). More recent data than these are not available because of the politically unstable situation in the region.

In Turkey numbers have been roughly estimated at 200–2,000 pairs (see table), but the population of this region is very poorly known and there are no data available on population trends.

There is no information on whether or not the Iranian population is declining.

■ Ecology

The Caspian Snowcock inhabits meadows in the alpine and subalpine zones lying between 2,400 and 4,000 m, mainly on steep slopes with rocky outcrops and stony areas. South-facing slopes are preferred in summer and north-facing ones in winter, birds tending at that season to avoid areas which have a covering of snow and to gather instead on open ground with steppe-like vegetation. Nests can be placed in the open, beneath overhanging rocks, amongst stones, or in tufts of grass, usually on steep slopes (Baziev 1978).

The diet of both adults and young consists purely of plant material, especially legumes; the birds chiefly take the bulbs, flowers, fruits and seeds (Baziev 1978).

During most of the year the species is gregarious, but flocks break up and monogamous pairs are formed during the breeding season from April to June (Potapov 1987).

■ Threats

The populations of Caspian Snowcock in Armenia, Georgia and Azerbaijan are highly threatened because the high-mountain pastures on which the species feeds are being steadily degraded as a result of overgrazing by livestock (Chanmamedov 1966, Baziev 1978). The situation is particularly severe in early summer when sheep are moved up to high pastures for grazing. There is a great deal of disturbance from grazing flocks, and herdsmen's dogs also destroy the nests and some broods, as do foxes *Vulpes*, which have increased in number during the twentieth century and which may also take incubating adult females (Baziev 1978). The Turkish population remains very poorly known but may well be affected by pressures similar to those threatening Caucasian birds.

The increasing aridity and warming of the climate may also be a problem for the species (Potapov 1984).

	Breeding population			Breeding
	Size (pairs)	Year	Trend	range trend
Turkey	(200–2,000)	—	—	—
Total (approx.)	200–2,000			

Trends	+2 Large increase	+1 Small increase	0 Stable	X Extinct
(1970–1990)	−2 Large decrease	−1 Small decrease	F Fluctuating	N New breeder

Data quality **Bold**: reliable quantitative data Normal type: incomplete quantitative data
Bracketed figures: no quantitative data * Data quality not provided

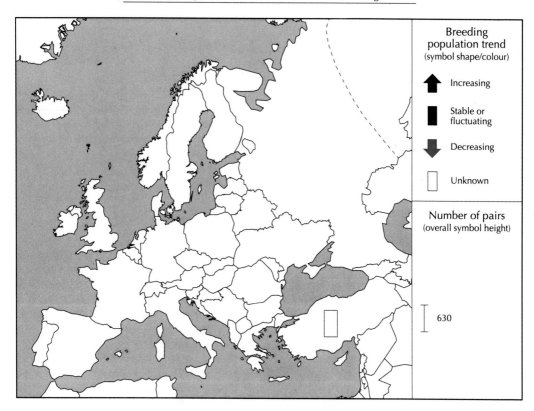

Breeding
population trend
(symbol shape/colour)

Increasing

Stable or
fluctuating

Decreasing

Unknown

Number of pairs
(overall symbol height)

630

■ Conservation measures

The Caspian Snowcock, with its dependence on the alpine and subalpine zones, requires the protection of these regions from excessive grazing pressure. Two nature reserves have been established in Armenia but these alone are not sufficient and several others are necessary, covering parts of the Karabach, Murodvag and Zanzegur ridges.

There have been one or two unsuccessful attempts at artificial rearing of young (Chanmamedov 1966), but the species is dependent ultimately on the maintenance of sufficient habitat for its survival.

Given the earlier population decline in the Caucasian republics, it is important that these and the Turkish populations are surveyed and that studies are undertaken to look at the habitat requirements and population trends.

ROALD L. POTAPOV

Chukar
Alectoris chukar

SPEC Category 3
Status Vulnerable
Criteria Large decline

The Chukar has declined over most of its range in south-east Europe, through a combination of excessive hunting, agricultural intensification, the abandonment of farming in mountain areas, and increased predation. Conservation of the species requires that hunting legislation be enforced, local management plans drawn up, and low-intensity farming maintained and, where necessary, promoted.

■ Distribution and population trends

About a tenth of the world range of the Chukar lies within Europe, where this sedentary species is restricted to the extreme south-east. The stronghold is in Cyprus, which holds about two-thirds of the European population, and most of the rest is found in Turkey, while southern Bulgaria and eastern Greece have relatively small numbers (see table, map). The species also occurs in the Caucasus mountains including those parts in Russia, but no population data are available from this region.

In all areas the populations have undergone declines since 1970. The decline in Greece had begun well before 1970, with drastic reductions in numbers or the complete disappearance of the species in southern Attica and some islands of the southern Aegean (Watson 1962, Papaevangelou 1980), but the decline seems to be relatively recent in Cyprus (Stewart and Christensen 1971).

	Breeding population			Breeding
	Size (pairs)	Year	Trend	range trend
Bulgaria	(1,000–10,000)	—	(–1)	(–1)
Cyprus	100,000–200,000	—	–1	–1
Greece	(1,000–5,000)	—	(–1)	(0)
Russia	P	—	—	—
Turkey	(50,000–200,000)	—	–1	–1
Total (approx.)	150,000–420,000			

Trends +2 Large increase +1 Small increase 0 Stable X Extinct
(1970–1990) –2 Large decrease –1 Small decrease F Fluctuating N New breeder
Data quality **Bold**: reliable quantitative data Normal type: incomplete quantitative data * Not provided
Bracketed figures: no quantitative data P Present

■ Ecology

In Europe, Chukars are primarily birds of barren arid or semi-arid hillsides with a covering of low grasses or herbs and with only occasional stunted trees and bushes (Watson 1962, Papaevangelou 1980). At lower altitudes the species inhabits rocky slopes with xerophilous bushes and shrubs, vineyards, olive-groves and agricultural land (Pantelis 1980, Papaevangelou 1980, Serez 1992). In the Turkish mountains bordering the Black Sea, Chukars even occur on forested slopes up to 2,800 m (Serez 1992).

The population density reflects the availability of water (Pantelis 1980), even though birds will move up to 10 km to drink (Watson 1962). Food taken consists of the seeds of grasses and other plants, also leaves, buds, flowers, berries, grain and occasionally insects (Watson 1962, Cramp and Simmons 1980).

Nesting takes place on the ground, usually concealed in grass or under a bush (Watson 1962, Pantelis 1980). The female birds will readily abandon the nest if they are disturbed during egg-laying, and incubating birds are at risk from predation by foxes *Vulpes vulpes*, while crows *Corvus* will take both eggs and chicks (Pantelis 1980, Papaevangelou 1980). Diurnal raptors, especially Bonelli's Eagle *Hieraaetus fasciatus*, are probably also major predators of Chukars (Watson 1962). Declines in Chukar numbers have been recorded after severe winters (Serez 1992).

■ Threats

The widespread decline of this species is due at least in part to overhunting and poaching (Watson 1962, Pantelis 1980, Papaevangelou 1980, Serez 1992). The situation in Turkey was deemed so serious that hunting was banned during the 1990–1991 season (Serez 1992). In Greece, the species has been hunted to extinction in some locations (Watson 1962), and hunting was prohibited in the 1978–1979 season to give stocks an opportunity to recover (Papaevangelou 1980). In Cyprus, hunting has been restricted and game reserves have been established (Pantelis 1980, Magnin 1987).

Agricultural intensification has also had a detrimental effect on the fortunes of the species, having caused a loss of nesting cover, the destruction of nests by machinery and poisoning through pesticides (Pantelis 1980, Papaevangelou 1980, Serez 1992). Conversely, the depletion of human populations in rural mountain areas has also led to habitat loss following the abandonment of farming,

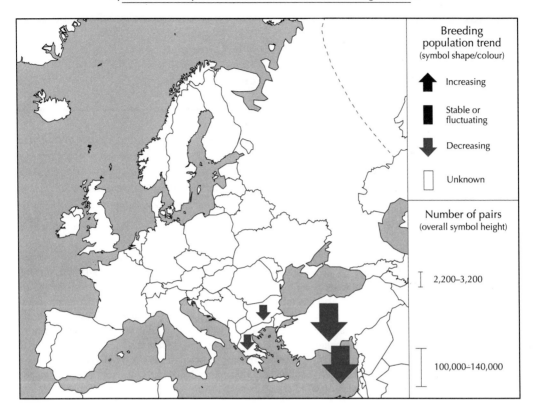

Breeding
population trend
(symbol shape/colour)

Increasing

Stable or
fluctuating

Decreasing

Unknown

Number of pairs
(overall symbol height)

2,200–3,200

100,000–140,000

and an increase in predation pressure in Greece has resulted from a sudden rise there in the numbers of foxes (Papaevangelou 1980).

■ Conservation measures

Although some steps have already been taken to control hunting (see above), there is still a need to enforce the existing legislation and to stop poaching. Further game reserves need to be established, in addition to those which already exist (Pantelis 1980, Papaevangelou 1980), and annual bag limits should be set in accord with local management plans based on autumn censuses. The participation of hunters in censuses and in habitat management should be encouraged. The restocking of low-density areas with reared partridges (Pantelis 1980, Papaevangelou

1980) should be avoided because of the risk of disease and genetic contamination.

Measures are needed to moderate the use of pesticides and the effects of other damaging aspects of modern agriculture. In Greece, financial incentives for maintaining low-intensity farming practices are available under the Agri-environment Regulation (EC Reg. 2078/92) of the EU Common Agricultural Policy, which could help to combat the abandonment of agriculture in the mountains. In addition, the EU Set-aside Scheme (EC Reg. 1765/92), which provides area payments for taking land out of production, could be used to create weedy and grassy sites suitable for Chukars to utilize as feeding and nesting areas.

N. J. AEBISCHER AND G. R. POTTS

Rock Partridge
Alectoris graeca

SPEC Category 2
Status (Vulnerable)
Criteria Large decline

The Rock Partridge, restricted to the subalpine zone of the Alps and mountainous parts of Italy and the Balkans, has declined over most of its range. Probable reasons are the abandonment of farming, the development of tourism in mountain areas, climatic change, and (in Sicily) overexploitation. In mountain regions, traditional arable and pastoral farming should be encouraged, and tourism controlled. Hunting needs careful management, with regulations enforced and the releasing of birds discouraged.

■ Distribution and population trends

This species is strictly European, its distribution being linked mainly to the Alpine range, running from France to the Balkans. Its range also extends southwards down the Apennines to Sicily, and into the Peloponnese. About half of the population occurs in the Balkans, the remainder being spread fairly evenly between the central Alps and Italy (see table, map). The species is sedentary. A natural population comprising hybrids between Rock Partridge and Red-legged Partridge *A. rufa* exists in south-east France (Bernard-Laurent 1984).

Since 1970, the population has declined in many areas, amounting to over 80% of the population (see table, map). In Switzerland, numbers have fluctuated since about 1950, although the overall trend has been downward (Lüps 1981). Since the end of the 1970s, numbers seem to have stabilized or even slightly increased locally in the south-western Alps (Schifferli *et al.* 1980, Bocca 1990, Bernard-Laurent *et al.* 1991).

	Breeding population			Breeding
	Size (pairs)	Year	Trend	range trend
Albania	1,000–5,000	—	0	(0)
Austria	1,700–1,900	—	–1	–1
Bulgaria	(5,000–10,000)	—	(–1)	(–1)
Croatia	10,000–15,000 *	—	–1*	0*
France	2,000–3,000	92	F	+1
Greece	(2,000–5,000)	—	(–1)	(0)
Italy	10,000–20,000	83	–1	0
Romania	(20–50)	—	(F)	(0)
Slovenia	(200–400)	—	(–2)	(–2)
Switzerland	(2,500–3,500)	86–91	(F)	(F)
Total (approx.)	34,000–64,000			

Trends	+2 Large increase	+1 Small increase	0 Stable	X Extinct
(1970–1990)	–2 Large decrease	–1 Small decrease	F Fluctuating	N New breeder

Data quality **Bold: reliable quantitative data** Normal type: incomplete quantitative data
Bracketed figures: no quantitative data * Data quality not provided

■ Ecology

Rock Partridges are predominantly birds of the subalpine zone, favouring sunny south-facing slopes between the treeline and the snowline (Zbinden 1984, Bernard-Laurent 1988, Bocca 1990), although in Sicily the species occurs down to sea-level (Sara 1988). It avoids dense forest, but frequents open, stunted woods, stony pastures with dwarf trees and scrub, rocky slopes and scree, interspersed with patches of short grass and low, herb-rich scrub (Bernard-Laurent 1988, de Franceschi 1988, Sara 1988). After breeding, birds may wander into the bare alpine zone, but are later forced down by snow cover. In winter they seek out steep south-exposed slopes and ridges that remain free of snow, or move to cultivated areas and farmsteads, which provide food and shelter in harsh weather (Bernard-Laurent 1988, Bocca 1990). The diet changes according to the season and the consequent shift of habitat, from a combination of plant material (young leaves, floral organs, seeds) and insects (grasshoppers, ants, Lepidoptera larvae) in the summer to mainly grass in winter (Jovetic *et al.* 1980, Didillon 1988).

Heavy snowfall in late winter can cause high mortality from starvation, and a high summer rainfall can seriously affect breeding success (Lüps 1981, Bernard-Laurent *et al.* 1991). Raptor predation seems to be one of the main causes of mortality throughout the year, although females are more vulnerable than males in the breeding season (Bernard-Laurent 1990).

■ Threats

Many causes have been advanced to explain the decline of the Rock Partridge (Lüps 1991). In the Alps and Balkans from France to Bulgaria, many suitable feeding and wintering areas provided by pastoral and arable farming (e.g. pastures, fields, hay meadows, terraces, farmsteads) have been lost as such land-uses have been abandoned and scrub or forest have taken over (Botev 1980, Jovetic *et al.* 1980, Lüps 1981, Bernard-Laurent 1988, de Franceschi 1988, Gossow *et al.* 1992). The development of the tourist industry has also led to habitat destruc-

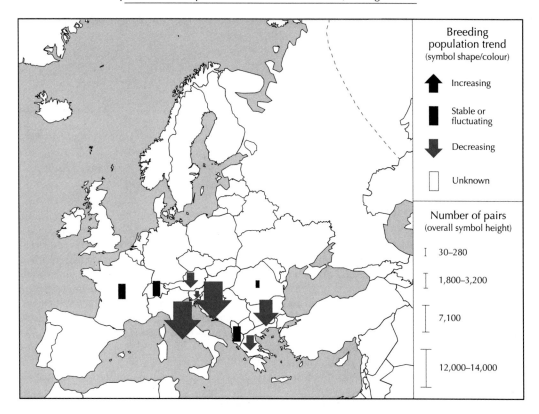

Breeding population trend
(symbol shape/colour)

↑ Increasing

■ Stable or fluctuating

↓ Decreasing

☐ Unknown

Number of pairs
(overall symbol height)

30–280

1,800–3,200

7,100

12,000–14,000

tion and, by opening up remote areas, increased disturbance during the breeding season (de Franceschi 1988, Bocca 1990).

In its alpine range, there appears to be a link between declining numbers and climatic changes such as an increase in mortality in cold wet summers and harsh winters, exacerbating the effects of habitat loss (Lüps 1981, Bocca 1990).

The Rock Partridge is now protected in many countries, and there is currently evidence of hunting having detrimental effects on populations only in Sicily (Sara 1988). Poaching occurs, but the extent and effects of this have not been quantified (Papaevangelou 1980, Brichetti 1985). Releases of reared partridges to restore numbers are always a threat to wild birds because of the risk of disease and genetic contamination (Botev 1980, Lüps 1981).

■ Conservation measures

The most important single conservation measure is to maintain and if possible to recreate the bird's favoured habitat, particularly the wintering habitats, by encouraging the traditional forms of arable and pastoral farming in mountain regions (Botev 1980,

Bernard-Laurent 1988, Bocca 1990). Within the EU, this could be achieved through management agreements developed under the Agri-environment Regulation (EC Reg. 2078/92) of the Common Agricultural Policy, or by encouraging hunters to support habitat management plans (Botev 1980) as part of a policy of drawing hunters' attention to the bird's decline (Sara 1988, Bernard-Laurent et al. 1991).

Given the Rock Partridge's comparatively low world population and its extensive decline, it is important to ensure that hunting is sustainable. In particular, existing hunting regulations must be enforced, and annual bag limits should be set according to the local bird density and reproductive success, based on autumn censuses (Sara 1988, Bocca 1990, Bernard-Laurent et al. 1991). Releases of reared Rock Partridges should be strongly discouraged.

Future habitat destruction caused by the development of the tourist industry (ski resorts, etc.) must be avoided where impacts would be serious, and the pressures of summer tourism should be reduced by controlling or discouraging access to breeding areas (Bocca 1990).

N. J. AEBISCHER AND G. R. POTTS

Red-legged Partridge
Alectoris rufa

SPEC Category 2
Status Vulnerable
Criteria Large decline

The Red-legged Partridge occurs only within the EU, and is declining in most of its range. The main threats are habitat changes on farmland brought about by both agricultural intensification and land abandonment, but overhunting and hybridization with Chukar are also problems. Traditional lowland and marginal farming should be encouraged through EU legislation.

■ Distribution and population trends

The Red-legged Partridge is found only in Europe, with about three-quarters of the total population in the Iberian peninsula. The United Kingdom (where the species was introduced in the late eighteenth century: Lever 1977) and France also hold sizeable populations, while small numbers occur in Italy and Madeira. The species is sedentary throughout its range.

Over 95% of the population is in decline, and this has probably been the case since the 1970s though it became most noticeable during the 1980s (see table, map). In contrast, the number of birds in the United Kingdom has increased since the 1980s (Marchant *et al.* 1990) but only because the decline in the wild population was masked by large-scale releasing of reared birds (Potts 1988).

	Breeding population			Breeding
	Size (pairs)	Year	Trend	range trend
Andorra	(10–20)	91	(–1)	(–1)
France	**550,000–550,000**	80	(–1)	**0**
Germany	0–0	—	X	X
Italy	(1,000–2,000)	—	(0)	(0)
Portugal	10,000–100,000	89	–1	0
Madeira	150–250	91	0	**0**
Spain	1,778,000–3,638,000	—	–1	–1
United Kingdom	90,000–250,000	88–91	0	**+1**
Isle of Man [1]	2–5	—	N	0*
Total (approx.)	2,400,000–4,500,000			

Trends (1970–1990) +2 Large increase +1 Small increase 0 Stable X Extinct
 –2 Large decrease –1 Small decrease F Fluctuating N New breeder
Data quality **Bold**: reliable quantitative data Normal type: incomplete quantitative data
 Bracketed figures: no quantitative data * Data quality not provided

■ Ecology

Essentially a bird of open ground, this species occurs in a wide range of habitats. It seems to prefer a warm, dry climate, and a combination of low vegetation for shelter and open ground for feeding. Over most of its range it is associated with arable farming, preferring low-intensity cropping with a mixture of cultivated, fallow and uncultivated ground; it also occurs on rocky mountain slopes with alternating areas of bare ground and low shrubs (Cramp and Simmons 1980). Intermediate habitats include vineyards, agricultur-

ally unimproved pastoral land and marginal hill farmland. Particularly arid or wet regions are avoided.

Breeding success depends strongly on the level of predation by corvids (on eggs) or mammals such as foxes *Vulpes vulpes* (on incubating adult birds) (Potts 1980); it depends also on chicks finding sufficient food in the form of insects (including grasshoppers, ants, bugs, beetles and aphids) and grass seeds in the cropped areas (Green 1984).

■ Threats

Habitat degradation and loss are the main reasons for the Red-legged Partridge's decline. Changes in agricultural practice have led to the disappearance of uncultivated land from much of the arable landscape, and consequently to a reduction in nesting cover and chick food. In pastoral areas pastures have been agriculturally improved (for example, re-seeded and heavily fertilized) and areas of low, herb-rich scrub converted to grassland. The disappearance of arable farming from open hill areas leads, if livestock are also removed, to the regeneration and encroachment of tall scrub and forest, and consequently to the disappearance of this partridge (Lucio and Purroy 1992).

In the Iberian peninsula, hunting pressure is also likely to have contributed to the decline through non-sustainable shooting rates encouraged by the release of reared birds. Release schemes also introduce diseases into the wild population, and hybridization with other released *Alectoris* species (especially Chukar *A. chukar*) endangers the purity of the species in Portugal (Dias 1992) and the United Kingdom (Potts 1988).

■ Conservation measures

The main requisites to halt the decline of the Red-legged Partridge are measures to stop the loss and degradation of its habitat. Thus the promotion of low-intensity agriculture in the lowlands and the maintenance of traditional farming practices in marginal hill areas are necessary. Within the EU countries, financial support for such measures could be

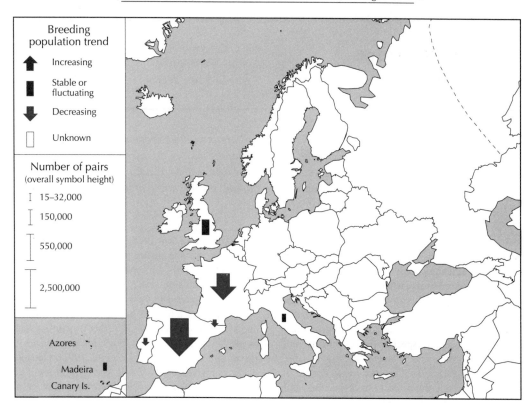

Breeding
population trend

↑ Increasing

▮ Stable or
fluctuating

↓ Decreasing

☐ Unknown

Number of pairs
(overall symbol height)

15–32,000

150,000

550,000

2,500,000

Azores

Madeira

Canary Is.

made available through the Agri-environment Regulation (EC Reg. 2078/92) of the Common Agricultural Policy. Appropriate management of set-aside land (under EC Reg. 1765/92) could also help maintain suitable habitat.

The release of any *Alectoris* species other than Red-legged Partridge was discontinued in the United Kingdom from 1993 onwards (Potts 1991), and such releases should be stopped in the rest of the EU. Sustainable hunting practices are also clearly essential and should be adopted and promoted by hunting organizations and their members.

N. J. Aebischer and G. R. Potts

Barbary Partridge
Alectoris barbara

SPEC Category 3
Status (Endangered)
Criteria Large decline, <10,000 pairs

The Barbary Partridge is restricted to only three small areas within Europe and is declining in the two most important ones, Sardinia and the Canary Islands, mainly because of excessive hunting pressure. Agricultural change has also caused habitat loss and degradation. Measures that are needed include the enforcement of hunting legislation, the creation of protected areas, and maintenance of low-intensity farming practices.

■ Distribution and population trends

Although the Barbary Partridge is restricted entirely to the west Palearctic, only a very small part of its range lies within Europe, where its small population is limited to three areas in the extreme south and west. Two of them, Sardinia and the Canary Islands, together hold over 95% of the total European numbers of this sedentary species, the remainder being found in Gibraltar and adjacent Spain (see table, map). The presence of the species in Europe is probably the result of introductions in the nineteenth century· or earlier (Lever 1987).

In Gibraltar and southern Spain, Barbary Partridge populations appear to be approximately stable (Parslow and Everett 1981). Numbers have, however, been declining at least since the 1970s in the major European populations of Sardinia and the Canary Islands (Mocci Demartis and Massoli-Novelli 1978, Martín 1987; see table, map), in parallel with trends which the species has shown outside its European range.

	Breeding population			Breeding range trend
	Size (pairs)	Year	Trend	
Italy	(3,000–10,000)	—	(–1)	(–1)
Spain	50–50	—	0	0
Canary Islands	600–1,000	—	–1	–1
United Kingdom				
Gibraltar	(50–75)	—	F	0*
Total (approx.)	3,700–11,000			

Trends   +2 Large increase   +1 Small increase   0 Stable   X Extinct
(1970–1990) –2 Large decrease   –1 Small decrease   F Fluctuating   N New breeder
Data quality   **Bold**: reliable quantitative data   Normal type: incomplete quantitative data
Bracketed figures: no quantitative data   * Data quality not provided

■ Ecology

The Barbary Partridge inhabits predominantly dry, open country with scrubby cover. It is quite adaptable, being found on steep slopes, rocky hillsides, stony terraces, unimproved agricultural land, open or degraded maquis and in woodland. The basic requirements of the species are open areas where it can feed, thorny undergrowth or rocky outcrops to afford protection from predators, and bushes, hedges or walls to provide shelter from the heat of the day (Mocci Demartis and Massoli-Novelli 1978, Finlayson and Cortes 1987, Martín 1987).

Nests are placed on the ground, usually under the concealment of a bush or in grass (Mocci Demartis and Massoli-Novelli 1978). The diet is mainly seeds of grasses and other plants, but birds also eat plant shoots and insects (Mocci Demartis 1992). Outside the breeding season, they will feed on spilt grain in stubble fields (Mocci Demartis and Massoli-Novelli 1978).

■ Threats

The decline of the Barbary Partridge in its European strongholds is primarily attributable to overhunting. In Sardinia, despite a number of regulatory measures, the pressure due to hunting (compounded by poaching) is excessive and there are too few game-wardens to enforce existing restrictions (Mocci Demartis and Massoli-Novelli 1978, Mocci Demartis 1992). In the Canary Islands, overhunting has reduced numbers to the point where the release of reared birds is increasing rapidly. This increase is potentially dangerous because of the risks of genetic contamination (de Franceschi 1988) and of introducing disease (Mocci Demartis and Massoli-Novelli 1978).

Other causes of the declines are the intensive use of pesticides, outbreaks of fire (Mocci Demartis and Massoli-Novelli 1978) and the abandonment of land which was formerly used for cultivation of cereals (A. Martín *in litt.*).

■ Conservation measures

The Barbary Partridge requires measures aimed at reducing hunting pressure. In Sardinia there is a need to enforce existing hunting legislation, to prevent poaching and to avoid the genetic contamination of wild birds by the release of reared ones. In the Canary Islands, Martín (1987) recommends a mora-

torium on hunting of one to two years to allow partridge numbers to recover. In both places, the creation of protected areas where shooting is banned would not only help the species but also safeguard its habitat (Parslow and Everett 1981).

Within the EU, governments have the opportunity to offer encouragement and financial support to low-intensity arable farming through Zonal Pro-grammes under the Agri-environment Regulation (EC Reg. 2078/92) of the EU Common Agricultural Policy. The EU Set-aside Scheme (EC Reg. 1765/92), based on area-payments for taking land out of production, could also provide winter stubbles and weedy areas suitable for the birds to feed on outside the breeding season.

N. J. AEBISCHER AND G. R. POTTS

Black Francolin
Francolinus francolinus

SPEC Category 3
Status Vulnerable
Criteria Large decline

Within Europe the Black Francolin is confined to Cyprus and Turkey. The species is especially vulnerable to hunting, which has caused declines in the population. The full protection of the species in Cyprus is required including its removal from the legal shooting list.

■ Distribution and population trends

The Black Francolin is a widespread species occurring mainly in southern Asia, from south-east Europe and the Middle East to India. Less than 5% of its global range lies within Europe (Cyprus and southern Turkey). In Cyprus the species is a fairly common resident locally and, although no precise quantitative data are available, the size of the breeding population is estimated to be between 1,000 and 2,000 pairs (see table), concentrated in the Paphos–Polis–Akamas area and on the Karpas peninsula (Boyle 1990). Data from southern Turkey are also poor but in 1987 it was estimated that there were at least 300 males along the Çukurova coast (van den Berk 1988), where the birds extend into the lower foothills of the Taurus mountains (van den Berk *in litt.* 1994). In 1991 and 1992 the population in the Göksu delta was 30–35 pairs (van den Berk *in litt.* 1994). The present Turkish population is probably less than 1,000 pairs (see table).

The distribution of the species in Cyprus has changed considerably during the nineteenth and twentieth centuries. At the beginning of the twentieth century it was quite abundant, but numbers declined thereafter through intensive hunting (Boyle 1990). Similarly it is believed that the species was well established over much of the Mediterranean zone of Turkey and has steadily declined since the second half of the nineteenth century, resulting in its current fragmented distribution (Kumerloeve 1963). Recent trends there are, however, unknown.

	Breeding population			Breeding
	Size (pairs)	Year	Trend	range trend
Cyprus	1,000–2,000	—	–1	0
Turkey	(300–1,000)	—	—	—
Total (approx.)	1,300–3,000			

Trends   +2 Large increase   +1 Small increase   0 Stable   X Extinct
(1970–1990) –2 Large decrease   –1 Small decrease   F Fluctuating   N New breeder
Data quality **Bold**: reliable quantitative data   Normal type: incomplete quantitative data
Bracketed figures: no quantitative data   * Data quality not provided

■ Ecology

The Black Francolin is found mainly in low-lying coastal areas, but also in wide, shallow valleys at altitudes of up to 400 m, up to 20 km inland on Cyprus and up to 60 km inland in southern Turkey. The species inhabits agricultural land with cereals, alfalfa, bananas, vineyards and plantations of citrus fruits and tobacco, as well as dense scrub, mainly alongside rivers with reeds. In Cyprus, the eastern population of the Karpas peninsula mainly occupies dense, high forest of juniper *Juniperus phoenicia*, but also inhabits dense scrub, especially along rivers (Flint and Stewart 1992).

Black Francolins are very shy and therefore rarely seen, but the call given by the male during the breeding season is unmistakable (Cole 1972) and helps in estimating the local population size of the species.

■ Threats

The major threat which the species faces is supposedly shooting, both in Cyprus and in Turkey (van den Berk 1988). To this the birds are highly vulnerable since they are not easily disturbed and are thus easy targets when eventually flushed at close range. A further threat in Cyprus is habitat destruction, especially in the Paphos area where citrus and tobacco plantations and other suitable vegetation cover are being destroyed, primarily in the course of developments linked to the tourist industry.

■ Conservation measures

In Turkey the Black Francolin is fully protected by law but populations in Cyprus need full protection. Indeed, the species seems to respond well to effective measures, as the Cyprus population was found to increase in numbers during 1984–1985 when it was protected from hunting by government orders, after recommendations made by the Cyprus Ornithological Society (*Cyprus Orn. Soc. (1970) Bird Reports* 1970–1990) and the Environment Association. However, despite the efforts of both local and international bodies and conservation societies, the hunting ban was subsequently lifted in 1986 after lobbying

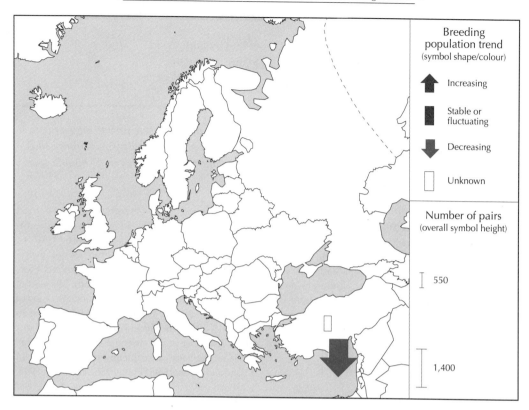

by the Hunting Association, and the species was restored to the list of birds which could be legally shot. A quota of one bird per person was allowed every Sunday and Wednesday during the shooting season. Hunting at this level has proved sufficient to cause a rapid decline in numbers, which has been especially evident from 1990 onwards. Since 1986 many attempts have been made to reverse the decision on the resumption of hunting, but these have all failed.

It is now hoped that with increased awareness of the Black Francolin's restricted European breeding range and its declining population levels, the species will be added to Appendix II of the Convention on the Conservation of European Wildlife and Natural Habitats (Bern Convention), and once again be given full protection by the government of Cyprus.

MELIS CHARALAMBIDES

Partridge
Perdix perdix

SPEC Category 3
Status Vulnerable
Criteria Large decline

The marked decline across virtually all of Europe is due mainly to agricultural intensification. Traditional ley farming should be maintained where possible, and low-intensity agriculture should be encouraged through EU legislation. Control of nest predation and provision of suitable grassy nest-sites can help greatly.

■ Distribution and population trends

Between a quarter and half the world population of the Partridge is in Europe, where it is absent only from northern Fennoscandia and northern Russia, and from parts of south-west and south-east Europe. At least a third of European birds are in Russia, and France, Poland and the United Kingdom hold a further half (Potts 1986; see table, map). Birds are

generally resident, though partially migratory (depending on snow depth) from Belarus eastwards (Dementiev and Gladkov 1952, Nikiforov 1992).

Drastic declines have occurred almost everywhere—by up to 90% in some countries (Potts 1986, Birkan and Jacob 1988; see table, map). The start of declines has depended on the local modernization of agriculture—the late 1950s in the United Kingdom and early 1970s in parts of eastern Europe (Potts 1986). The species has become extinct in Norway and is on the verge of extinction in the Republic of Ireland and Switzerland (Potts 1986, Kavenagh 1992, Schifferli 1993), and is below 20% of its pre-war level in many European countries, e.g. United Kingdom, Germany, Italy, Austria, Hungary (Potts 1986, Birkan and Jacob 1988, Dwenger 1991), though numbers have remained high in parts of northern France (Birkan and Jacob 1988) and Poland (Panek 1992). Further declines will lead to marked range contractions, as has happened in the western United Kingdom (Gibbons *et al.* 1993).

■ Ecology

The preferred habitat is open, low-intensity mixed farmland, with small fields and hedges on grassy banks which provide nesting cover (Potts 1986, Birkan and Jacob 1988). Some nesting occurs in cereals, but these are mainly important as sources of insect food and shelter for young chicks. After harvest, stubbles serve as feeding and roosting areas for coveys.

Numbers are limited by the abundance of insect prey for chicks, the amount of nesting cover and the level of predation while nesting (Potts 1980). In regions with deep or ice-covered snow, winter food availability is also limiting (Loshkarev 1976).

■ Threats

Agricultural intensification is the ultimate reason for most of the decline (Potts 1980), cropping patterns having changed from mixed farming, involving undersown grass leys and spring crops, to pure arable with a predominance of autumn crops and no

	Breeding population			Breeding
	Size (pairs)	Year	Trend	range trend
Albania	100–500	—	-2	(-2)
Andorra	(30–60)	91	(-1)	(-1)
Austria	(1,000–1,500)	—	(-1)	(-1)
Belarus	25,000–50,000	90	F	0
Belgium	9,000–18,000	81–90	-2	-2
Bulgaria	(10,000–100,000)	—	(-2)	(-2)
Croatia	15,000–20,000 *	—	-1*	0*
Czech Republic	9,000–18,000	—	-1	0
Denmark	**20,000–30,000**	87–89	-1	-1*
Estonia	4,000–10,000	—	-1	0
Finland	3,000–5,000	92	-2	-2
France	**900,000–900,000**	86	-1	0
Germany	40,000–120,000	—	-2	0
Greece	(150–300)	—	(-1)	—
Hungary	15,000–25,000	—	-1	-1
Rep. of Ireland	150–250	—	-2	-2
Italy	2,000–5,000	—	-1	(-1)
Latvia	500–3,000	—	-2	-2
Lithuania	20,000–30,000	85–88	-1	(0)
Luxembourg	80–150	—	-2	-1
Moldova	**5,500–7,000**	88	0	0
Netherlands	**20,000–25,000**	89–90	-2	-1
Norway	**0–0**	90	X	X
Poland	250,000–1,500,000	—	-2	0
Romania	40,000–60,000	—	-1	0
Russia	1,000,000–2,000,000	70–90	(-1)	(-1)
Slovakia	3,000–8,000	—	-2	-1
Slovenia	800–1,200	—	-2	-2
Spain	2,000–6,000	—	-1	-1
Sweden	5,000–15,000	87	-1	0
Switzerland	**30–50**	86–91	-2	-2
Turkey	(5,000–30,000)	—	-1	-1
Ukraine	45,000–50,000	88	-1	-1
United Kingdom	**140,000–150,000**	88–91	-2	-1
Isle of Man [1]	(30–100)	—	(0)	0*
Total (approx.)	2,600,000–5,200,000			

Trends   +2 Large increase   +1 Small increase   0 Stable   X Extinct
(1970–1990)   -2 Large decrease   -1 Small decrease   F Fluctuating   N New breeder
Data quality **Bold**: reliable quantitative data   Normal type: incomplete quantitative data
              Bracketed figures: no quantitative data   * Data quality not provided
[1] Population figures are included within United Kingdom totals

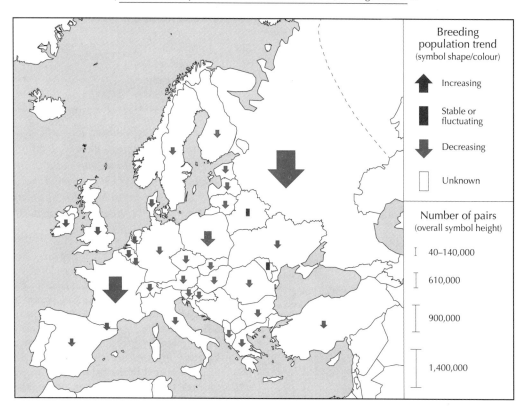

Breeding
population trend
(symbol shape/colour)

Increasing

Stable or
fluctuating

Decreasing

Unknown

Number of pairs
(overall symbol height)

40–140,000

610,000

900,000

1,400,000

overwintering stubbles. Hedges and grass banks have been removed, and herbicides have largely eliminated arable weeds that were host to insect prey (Southwood and Cross 1969, Potts 1986). Intensification has often been accompanied by increases in numbers of predatory birds and mammals; in the United Kingdom and probably elsewhere, especially in eastern Europe, the fall in keepering, which ceased to be economically viable as partridge stocks declined, exacerbated the problem (Tapper 1992).

Secondary threats are summer use of insecticides (Potts 1990), overhead irrigation of crops (Serre *et al*. 1989) and, in alpine or wetter areas, the abandonment of cereals (Lescourret and Ellison 1989). Excessive hunting may be a problem, e.g. in Italy where large-scale releases of reared birds encourage a non-sustainable shooting rate (Renzoni 1974, Potts 1985).

■ Conservation measures

Habitat restoration is the key to reversing the declines and can be achieved through the creation of grass banks, selective spraying regimes around crop edges ('conservation headlands') and predation control (Game Conservancy 1992). More generally, the species would benefit from lower intensity farming such as more overwintering stubbles, more undersowing, more spring cropping, less fertilizer and a more targeted approach to pesticide use.

EU governments can encourage appropriate habitat management through grant aid under the Agri-environment Regulation (EC Reg. 2078/92) of the Common Agricultural Policy. The EU Set-aside Scheme (EC Reg. 1765/92), based on area-payments for taking land out of production on a rotating basis, also has the potential to provide suitable habitat. Particularly valuable would be an option of mixed rotational and non-rotational set-aside land on the same farm, allowing special crops to be sown within the non-rotational area (Game Conservancy 1993).

N. J. AEBISCHER AND G. R. POTTS

221

Quail
Coturnix coturnix

SPEC Category   3
Status   Vulnerable
Criteria   Large decline

Europe's only migratory gamebird is declining over most of the region. Agricultural intensification in the breeding areas, habitat degradation in the Sahel winter quarters, and excessive exploitation around the Mediterranean seem to have affected primarily the long-distance migrants in the population, whereas irrigation in north-west Africa has benefited the formerly less common short-distance migrants wintering and breeding there. Measures are needed to promote low-intensity farming, to regulate hunting and trapping, and to prevent hybridization with released C. c. japonica.

	Breeding population			Breeding
	Size (pairs)	Year	Trend	range trend
Albania	1,000–5,000	—	–1	(–1)
Andorra	(5–10)	92	(–1)	(–1)
Austria	(300–400)	—	(–1)	(–1)
Belarus	20,000–32,000	90	F	0
Belgium	350–1,500	81–90	(–1)	(–1)
Bulgaria	(10,000–100,000)	—	(–1)	(–1)
Croatia	6,000–8,000 *		–1*	–1*
Cyprus	(100–200)	—	–1	0
Czech Republic	3,000–6,000	—	F	**0**
Denmark	**27–27**	91	F	—
Faroe Islands	(0–3)	89	F	(F)
Estonia	10–50	—	–2	–1
Finland	**0–10**	92	F	+2
France	50,000–200,000	91	F	0
Germany	(3,000–10,500)	—	(–2)	F
Greece	(300–500)	—	(–1)	(0)
Hungary	20,000–25,000	—	–1	0
Rep. of Ireland	15–70	88–91	F	+1
Italy	(5,000–10,000)	—	(–1)	(–1)
Latvia	20–100	—	F	F
Liechtenstein	**20–20**	89	F*	–2
Lithuania	(50–100)	85–88	(–1)	(–1)
Luxembourg	10–25	—	–1	–1
Malta	1–2	—	0	–1
Moldova	**4,000–6,000**	88	–1	**0**
Netherlands	**500–5,000**	79	F	F
Norway	10–100	90	F	F
Poland	5,000–10,000	—	(–2)	0
Portugal	10,000–100,000	89	–1	–1
Azores	(30,000–60,000)	—	(0)	(0)
Madeira	50–75	91	0	**0**
Romania	(30,000–50,000)	—	**–1**	–1
Russia	(100,000–1,000,000)	80–90	(–2)	(F)
Slovakia	2,000–4,500	—	–2	–1
Slovenia	1,000–2,000	—	–2	–2
Spain	320,000–435,000	—	F	F
Sweden	0–10	90	+2	0
Switzerland	300–500	86–91	–2	–1
Turkey	(50,000–350,000)	—	—	—
Ukraine	10,000–11,000	88	–2	–1
United Kingdom	**100–2,600**	88–91	F	+2
Isle of Man [1]	0–30	—	**0**	0*
Gibraltar	(1–1)	—	(N)	0*
Total (approx.)	680,000–2,400,000			

Trends   +2 Large increase   +1 Small increase   0 Stable   X Extinct
(1970–1990)   –2 Large decrease   –1 Small decrease   F Fluctuating   N New breeder
Data quality   **Bold**: reliable quantitative data   Normal type: incomplete quantitative data
      Bracketed figures: no quantitative data   * Data quality not provided
[1] Population figures are included within United Kingdom totals

■ Distribution and population trends

Roughly 10–25% of the Quail's breeding range lies within Europe, where it is widespread south of 60°N. The Iberian peninsula holds over a quarter of the European population while another half occurs in France, Russia, Hungary, Romania, Bulgaria and Turkey. Elsewhere, numbers are generally small, although this migratory species is subject to large yearly variations in abundance. Up to the 1960s, the bulk of birds wintered in the Sahel, but in recent years numbers there have decreased while there have been increases in north-west Africa (Guyomarc'h 1992).

The Quail's breeding/migratory behaviour and marked annual fluctuations make it difficult to assess population and range trends, though it seems that since 1970 up to about two-thirds of the population, mainly in central and eastern Europe, has declined by 20% or more, and half apparently by over 50% (see table, map). In the west, numbers in (e.g.) Spain and France seem variable but stable (Gallego *et al.* 1990), while a decline has been registered in Portugal (Rufino 1989; see table).

It appears that long-distance migrants, which fly directly from the Sahel into Europe, have declined in numbers. Short-distance migrants, however, have increased owing to increases in irrigated land in north-west Africa where most of them winter and remain to breed in March–April; males leave females on the nest and migrate north into Europe followed later by females and young of the year that participate in renewed breeding (Guyomarc'h and Saint-Jalme 1986, Guyomarc'h 1992, Rodriguez-Teijeiro *et al.* 1992). The extent of this migratory wave and the numbers of birds involved vary between years, though most such birds probably settle in southern Europe.

■ Ecology

This is typically a species of wide-open spaces with herbaceous vegetation just tall enough for conceal-

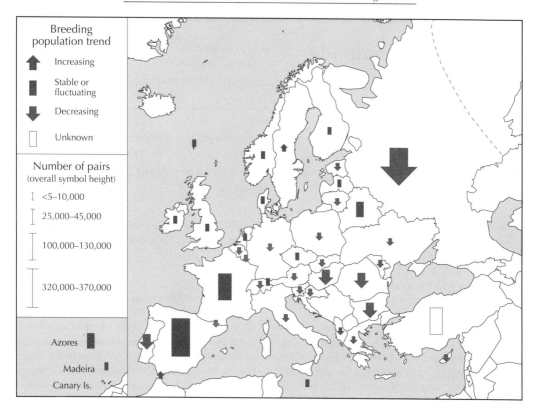

Breeding
population trend

↑ Increasing

■ Stable or
fluctuating

↓ Decreasing

☐ Unknown

Number of pairs
(overall symbol height)

I <5–10,000

I 25,000–45,000

I 100,000–130,000

I 320,000–370,000

Azores ■

Madeira ■

Canary Is.

ment. It has taken readily to agricultural land, particularly fields of clover, winter wheat and other cereals, hay, rough grass and overgrown fallow. It prefers warm, dry, sheltered areas and keeps away from trees, scrub and bare ground (Cramp and Simmons 1980, Aubrais *et al*. 1986).

Breeding success depends heavily on the availability of insect food to both adults and chicks. Birds switch to eating mainly weed seeds after breeding (Combreau and Guyomarc'h 1989, 1992, Combreau *et al*. 1990).

■ Threats

In Europe, Quails have been affected by agricultural intensification. Rough grass and uncultivated land have almost disappeared in many areas, and increased use of herbicides and insecticides has reduced the availability of weed seeds and insects (Southward and Cross 1969, Potts 1986).

Large numbers are killed every autumn upon arrival on the North African coast, particularly Egypt (Mendelssohn *et al*. 1969, Baha el Din and Salama 1991)—though Zuckerbrot *et al*. (1980) believe that the abundance of the species is related to weather and to long-term climatic fluctuations rather than to predation by man. According to Guyomarc'h (1992), declines in Europe are due to the disappearance of long-distance migrants caused by a combination of

agricultural intensification on the breeding grounds, drought in the sub-Saharan winter quarters and hunting during migration. The short-distance migrants are probably safe at present, although hunting in southern Europe may pose a threat. A much more serious danger in France is hybridization with summer releases of the non-native *japonica* race of Quail (Guyomarc'h in press).

■ Conservation measures

Wide-scale habitat conservation measures are needed on the European breeding grounds, including the maintenance and promotion of low-intensity farming methods. Within the EU, especially in Spain, financial support can be made available for such measures within Zonal Programmes developed under the Agri-environment Regulation (EC Reg. 2078/92) of the Common Agricultural Policy. Rotational set-aside schemes within the EU (under EC Reg. 1765/92) are a potential help if managed appropriately, especially by avoiding ploughing or cutting in the nesting period.

Existing hunting legislation should be enforced, and hunting reduced by making hunters and trappers aware that excessive mortality will reduce the breeding stock and ultimately jeopardize their own revenue. Releases of the race *japonica* should cease.

N. J. AEBISCHER AND G. R. POTTS

Andalusian Hemipode
Turnix sylvatica

SPEC Category   3
Status   Endangered
Criteria   Large decline, <250 pairs

The Andalusian Hemipode has almost disappeared from its former European range, largely as the result of habitat loss, and the last known stronghold in Europe is now the Doñana National Park in southern Spain. Habitat restoration is required, as is rigorous monitoring of the remnant population, and a captive-breeding scheme should be considered.

■ Distribution and population trends

The Andalusian Hemipode is widespread in Africa and Asia, but within Europe it is restricted to the south-west Mediterranean, where the subspecies *T. s. sylvatica* is an endangered taxon. It has suffered a dramatic decline throughout its former range and has almost disappeared from Europe.

This downward trend began at the end of the nineteenth century. In Sicily it declined from a healthy population in about 1880 to extinction in the 1920s, while nineteenth-century specimens are also known from Sardinia (Cramp and Simmons 1980). In Portugal it was recorded between 1890 and 1930, but the only recent observation was in 1972 and it is currently regarded as being extinct (d'Oliveira 1896, Tait 1924, Rufino 1989).

In Spain the species was common in the Andalusian coastal plains during the nineteenth century, the last known records being from Granada and Málaga in the 1910s, and from Cádiz and Sevilla in the 1960s. Now the only stronghold still known is the Doñana National Park in the Marismas del Guadalquivir (Important Bird Area 247) in Huelva province, where Andalusian Hemipodes were commonly seen and hunted during the 1960s and 1970s. However, during the 1980s a dramatic decline occurred in this area as well, and over the period from 1986 to 1992 there have been an average of only one or two records per year, including two recently shot birds (Urdiales 1993). Even considering the elusiveness of the species, the total European population, comprising birds in the Doñana National Park and the surrounding area, is estimated at just 5-10 pairs (C. Urdiales own data; see table, map).

The species is considered to be extremely sedentary in the Palearctic, though it is a partial migrant in Africa.

■ Ecology

In the past the Andalusian Hemipode was typically found in dwarf palm *Chamaerops humilis* scrub (Cramp and Simmons 1980). It also occurred in scrub and grassland and occasionally in non-intensively managed agricultural areas, including sugar-beet fields and stubble (Mountfort 1957, Bernís 1966, Noval 1975). Currently it mainly occupies two habitat types: *Halimium* scrub intermingled with small seasonal lakes surrounded by meadows, and unmanaged open woodland of cork oak *Quercus suber*, olive *Olea europaea* and mastic tree *Pistacia lentiscus* (Urdiales 1993). Both habitats are associated with sandy soils and are present in the Doñana National Park.

■ Threats

The major cause of extinction of the species over its former European range was habitat loss (Blanco and González 1992, Urdiales 1993). Scrub and grassland within former breeding areas have been lost due to the development of modern intensive agriculture, human settlement and the planting of trees, especially *Eucalyptus*.

Current threats to the minority of the remnant population that occurs outside the Doñana National Park are hunting, intensive farming practices (e.g. the recently developed Almonte–Marisma irrigation scheme) and the establishment of *Eucalyptus* plantations.

■ Conservation measures

The Andalusian Hemipode is fully protected under the laws of both Spain and Andalucía, but this is not fully effective since at least two birds have been shot in recent years (Urdiales 1993). It is therefore essential that local people's knowledge of the bird's rarity is improved.

| | Breeding population | | | Breeding |
	Size (pairs)	Year	Trend	range trend
Spain	5–10	—	-2	-2
Total (approx.)	5–10			

Trends (1970-1990): +2 Large increase +1 Small increase 0 Stable X Extinct -2 Large decrease -1 Small decrease F Fluctuating N New breeder
Data quality: **Bold**: reliable quantitative data   Normal type: incomplete quantitative data   Bracketed figures: no quantitative data   * Data quality not provided

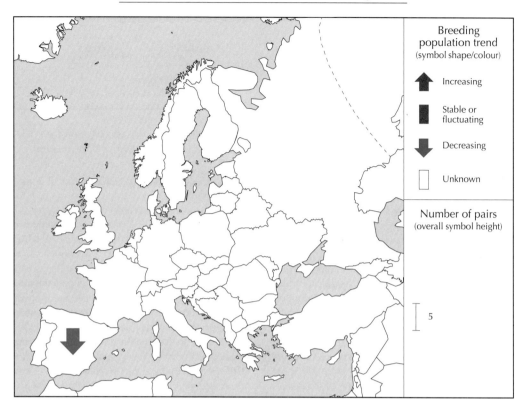

Breeding
population trend
(symbol shape/colour)

▲ Increasing

■ Stable or
fluctuating

▼ Decreasing

☐ Unknown

Number of pairs
(overall symbol height)

5

Most of the habitat within its current range is protected within the Doñana National Park and Entorno de Doñana Natural Park. Habitat restoration is needed, however, since much of the present range is either covered by plantations of *Eucalyptus* or stone pine *Pinus pinea*, or has been transformed into irrigated land and subsequently abandoned. Within the National Park the habitat restoration programme for Iberian lynx *Lynx pardina* that is currently being undertaken may benefit the Andalusian Hemipode as well since it includes the progressive removal of *Eucalyptus* groves and the clearance of pine plantations (Urdiales 1993).

Detailed monitoring of the remaining population is urgently needed and the development of a captive-breeding scheme for future reintroductions should be given consideration.

CARLOS URDIALES

Baillon's Crake
Porzana pusilla

SPEC Category 3
Status Rare
Criteria <10,000 pairs

Baillon's Crake is rare in Europe. Loss and degradation of natural marshland is the major threat to the species and efforts should be made to conserve this habitat and to manage it appropriately.

■ Distribution and population trends

Baillon's Crake is a widely distributed species in the Palearctic region but rare in Europe, with less than 10,000 breeding pairs. Two subspecies are present in Europe: the nominate race *P. p. pusilla* which occurs in Russia, mostly from the Black and Caspian Sea coasts north to 57°N (Cramp and Simmons 1980, Ilyichev and Flint 1987), and *P. p. intermedia* which is restricted to west, central and southern Europe, Belarus and Ukraine. *P. p. intermedia* generally exists in small, isolated and ephemeral breeding areas and is a scarce breeder apart from in Spain, where there are estimated to be between 3,000 and 5,000 pairs (Glutz von Blotzheim *et al.* 1973; see table, map). However, the abundance of the species in Spain is poorly known and believed to vary considerably with water-levels (J. A. Valverde pers. comm.). Landres and Urdiales (1990) report that in the Doñana marshes probably thousands of birds nest locally in years with good rains while in dry years breeding is exceptional. Also the secretive behaviour of the species has probably resulted in the underestimation of numbers in areas rarely visited by birdwatchers such as rice-fields, now extensive in Extremadura and in the west of Andalucía and lo-cally in Cataluña, Navarra and Valencia (F. Purroy pers. comm.).

The distribution and status of Baillon's Crake is uncertain as there is little quantitative information on trends, breeding range and abundance (see table), although generally the species was thought to be more numerous in the nineteenth than in the twentieth century. Earlier estimates of the population may, however, have been exaggerated because of confusion with Little Crake *P. parva* (Glutz von Blotzheim *et al.* 1973, Ilyichev and Flint 1987). It is thought that the numbers in France, Croatia and Moldova, and possibly in Romania, have declined over the period 1970–1990 (see table, map). Population trends elsewhere, although mostly uncertain, are believed to have been stable or fluctuating.

The migratory habits of Baillon's Crake are poorly known: some birds stay in western Europe, probably wintering in the Mediterranean region, while others migrate to sub-Saharan Africa (Cramp and Simmons 1980).

■ Ecology

Within Europe, Baillon's Crake occurs mainly in river deltas, marshlands and in inland wetlands in the semi-desert, steppe and forest-steppe zones. During breeding and on migration the species is restricted to vegetation at the edge of shallow water (10–50 cm), alongside lakes and estuaries, and in freshwater and brackish marshes. The species will use man-made habitats such as areas alongside fish-ponds, water channels and marshy meadows. Nesting occurs among moderately high and not too dense marshy vegetation (*Carex, Juncus, Phalaris, Scirpus, Eleocharis*) in the vicinity of open water (Glutz von Blotzheim *et al.* 1973, Cramp and Simmons 1980, Ilyichev and Flint 1987). In optimal habitats the species may occur at fairly high densities, with the nests placed only 15–50 m apart.

Birds take food mostly at the water's edge or while walking in shallow water or on floating or emergent vegetation, and the diet mainly consists of invertebrates (80–95% of the total) but also includes some plant material such as seeds; on the wintering grounds, small fish and amphibians are also taken

	Breeding population			Breeding
	Size (pairs)	Year	Trend	range trend
Albania	(0–50)	—	—	—
Bulgaria	(50–100)	—	(0)	(0)
Croatia	5–10*	—	–1*	–1*
France	10–50	90	–2	0
Germany	(25–25)	85	0	**0**
Greece	(10–50)	—	(0)	(–1)
Hungary	(30–50)	—	(0)	(0)
Moldova	30–70	88	–1	–1
Netherlands	0–20	79	F	F
Portugal	(10–100)	89	(0)	(0)
Romania	(100–1,000)	—	(–1)	(–1)
Russia	(500–2,000)	—	(0)	(+1)
Spain	3,000–5,000	—	F	F
Switzerland	(5–15)	86–91	—	0
Turkey	(0–100)	—	—	—
Ukraine	(0–1)	—	(F)	(F)
Total (approx.)	3,800–8,600			

Trends   +2 Large increase   +1 Small increase   0 Stable   X Extinct
(1970-1990) –2 Large decrease   –1 Small decrease   F Fluctuating   N New breeder
Data quality **Bold**: reliable quantitative data   Normal type: incomplete quantitative data
                   Bracketed figures: no quantitative data   * Data quality not provided

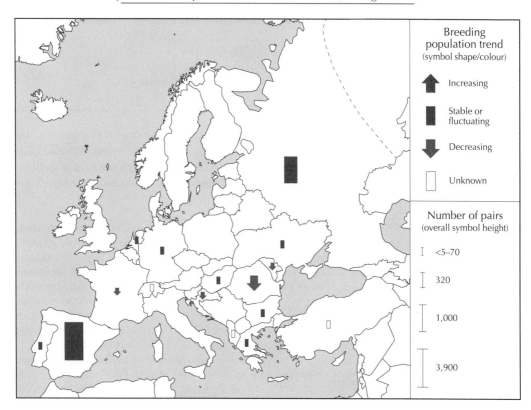

Breeding
population trend
(symbol shape/colour)

Increasing

Stable or
fluctuating

Decreasing

Unknown

Number of pairs
(overall symbol height)

<5–70

320

1,000

3,900

(Kistiakovskiy 1957, Averin and Gania 1971, Cramp and Simmons 1980).

■ Threats

The species is most threatened by the widespread loss and degradation of marshland through drainage, manifested in various ways. In particular this can involve the cutting and frequent burning of water-side vegetation at certain times of year, and large-scale reed-cutting for animal fodder is especially harmful since it is carried out during the nesting season; cutting of dry reed in autumn results in reduction of future nesting habitat, and the burning of dry reed in spring in most marshlands of eastern Europe is destroying vast areas of habitat in the deltas of the Don, Kuban, Dnieper, Dnestr and Danube rivers. Heavy grazing pressure by domestic animals is detrimental, and water-level changes (often as much as 1–3 m, caused by water discharge from river dams) may either flood nests or lead to high nest-predation when sites dry out. Changes in

climatic conditions causing cyclic droughts may also affect the species' habitat.

Mortality from collision with powerlines during night-time migration is high, and hundreds or thousands of birds may be killed in a season. The threats faced on the wintering grounds are not known.

■ Conservation measures

Although specific measures to conserve Baillon's Crake have not been identified, the general conservation of marshland through the maintenance of natural vegetation and appropriate water-levels is essential. In particular, the customary cutting and burning of vegetation near the water's edge should be regulated. Deliberate changes of water-levels in wetlands in late spring should also be avoided. The maintenance of the natural vegetation around some fish-ponds and rice-fields would also be beneficial to the species (Glutz von Blotzheim et al. 1973, Ilyichev and Flint 1987).

ALEXANDER I. KOSHELEV

Corncrake
Crex crex

SPEC Category 1
Status Vulnerable
Criteria Large decline

Though still widespread in Europe, the globally threatened Corncrake is declining steadily and often rapidly, due mainly to habitat loss and high mortality caused by the intensification and mechanization of hay and silage making. Necessary measures include the preservation of marshland, hay meadows and low-intensity farming, the promotion of appropriate hay-cutting techniques and local reductions in hunting.

■ Distribution and population trends

The breeding grounds extend right across Eurasia, north in Europe to southern Fennoscandia, and in western Russia to c.62°N. Practically all birds winter in the Afrotropics, mainly in the east (Cramp and Simmons 1980).

From the known distribution and from breeding density data for Siberia (Ilyichev and Flint 1987) less than half of the global population breeds in Europe,

	Breeding population			Breeding range trend
	Size (pairs)	Year	Trend	
Austria	400–600	—	(–1)	(–1)
Belarus	55,000–60,000	90	–1	0
Belgium	10–45	81–90	—	–1
Bulgaria	(100–1,000)	—	(–1)	(–1)
Croatia	250–300 *	—	–1*	–1*
Czech Republic	200–400	—	–1	–1
Denmark	**6–6**	91	(–1)	(–1)
Estonia	5,000–5,000	—	–1	0
Finland	**500–1,000**	92	F	**0**
France	**1,050–1,150**	92	–2	–1
Germany	(260–260)	85	–2	0
Hungary	300–500	—	–2	–2
Rep. of Ireland	**174–174**	93	–2	–2
Italy	(100–500)	—	(–1)	(–1)
Latvia	3,000–10,000	—	–2	–1
Liechtenstein	**2–4**	—	F*	0*
Lithuania	2,000–3,000	85–88	(–1)	(–1)
Luxembourg	0–10	—	–1	–1
Moldova	700–1,100	85	–1	–1
Netherlands	**50–150**	90–92	–2	–2
Norway	50–100	90	–1	**0**
Poland	6,600–7,800	—	–1	0
Romania	(3,000–6,000)	—	–1	–1
Russia	(10,000–100,000)	—	(–2)	(0)
Slovakia	600–900	—	(–1)	–1
Slovenia	(200–300)	—	(–2)	(–2)
Spain	**4–13**	90	+1	+1
Sweden	250–1,000	—	**0**	0
Switzerland	1–13	86–91	–1	–1
Turkey	(0–10)	—	—	—
Ukraine	2,000–2,500	88	–2	–2
United Kingdom	**487–487**	93	–1	–2
Isle of Man [1]	**1–1**	93	–2	0*
Total (approx.)	92,000–200,000			

Trends (1970–1990) +2 Large increase +1 Small increase 0 Stable X Extinct
−2 Large decrease −1 Small decrease F Fluctuating N New breeder
Data quality **Bold**: reliable quantitative data Normal type: incomplete quantitative data
Bracketed figures: no quantitative data * Data quality not provided
[1] Population figures are included within United Kingdom totals

with most of these in Russia, Belarus and Poland and fairly good numbers also reported from Romania and the Baltic states (see table, map). Several estimates are uncertain, however, especially for Russia.

Since the late nineteenth century, and particularly since the 1950s, numbers have declined considerably. This was first evident in Britain and Ireland, Fennoscandia and west-central Europe (Glutz von Blotzheim *et al.* 1973, Cramp and Simmons 1980), but large annual population fluctuations due to water-level and climate changes have often obscured the trend. Trends also varied considerably between different parts of western Europe (Marchant *et al.* 1990), and during the 1960s the species showed some increase in Fennoscandia as old fields were recolonized (Glutz von Blotzheim *et al.* 1973).

Between 1970 and 1990 the decline spread over the whole continent, and numbers have fallen by over 50% in 10 countries, including some of the east European strongholds (see table, map). The population of Britain, Ireland, Belgium, Netherlands and Luxembourg fell from c.8,500–10,000 calling males in 1970 to 2,000–2,700 in the early 1980s and to 1,600–2,300 in 1990 (Glutz von Blotzheim *et al.* 1973, Batten *et al.* 1990; see also Stowe *et al.* 1993).

On the basis of its widespread and rapid declines in Europe and western Siberia, the species is listed as Globally Threatened by Collar *et al.* (1994).

■ Ecology

Tall grass and herbs are a crucial requirement all year. Natural breeding habitat comprises the drier parts of extensive fens, grassy peat-bogs and other fairly open marshy lowland areas, as well as alpine meadows. Man-made habitats include wet and dry meadows, clover or rape fields, the edges of reservoirs and sometimes bushy forest clearings. On arrival in spring, when the grass is short, birds use other taller vegetation, such as marshy areas with *Carex*, *Iris* or *Glyceria*, or dry stands of grass and nettles *Urtica*. When the vegetation is sufficiently high, birds then move into grassy habitats such as

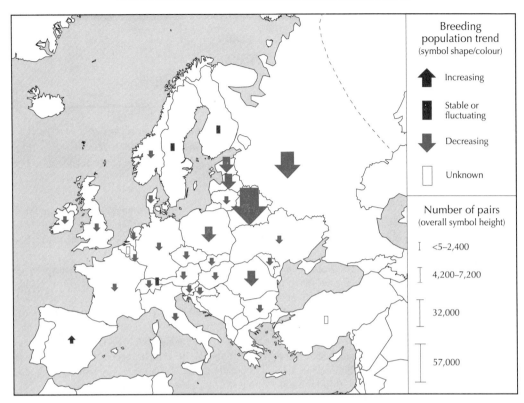

Breeding population trend
(symbol shape/colour)

Increasing

Stable or fluctuating

Decreasing

Unknown

Number of pairs
(overall symbol height)

<5–2,400

4,200–7,200

32,000

57,000

hay meadows. Nesting is on the ground, with eggs laid between mid-May and early July. The food is mainly insects, snails, earthworms and spiders (Glutz von Blotzheim *et al.* 1973, Cramp and Simmons 1980, Ilyichev and Flint 1987, Flade 1991).

▪ Threats

The main threats indicated by Glutz von Blotzheim *et al.* (1973), Hölzinger (1987), Stowe and Becker (1989), Batten *et al.* (1990), Stowe and Hudson (1991a,b) and Stowe *et al.* (1993) are: habitat loss due to drainage and agricultural intensification, especially the conversion of hay meadows into short-grass pasture or into grassland harvested for silage; use of machines for cutting hay and an associated shift to earlier and more rapidly completed harvesting, causing increased destruction of nests, adults and particularly young; hunting of eastern populations on migration and in winter; and collisions with powerlines, etc., on migration, though this is not confirmed by Stowe and Hudson (1991b).

The apparent mobility of adults suggests that protection of small areas would be inadequate to maintain populations (Batten *et al.* 1990, N. Schäffer pers. comm.).

▪ Conservation measures

Remaining marshlands of eastern Europe should be protected and managed to prevent succession to scrub, while in man-made habitats low-intensity farming should be promoted to preserve or restore mosaics of late-mowed hay meadows and stands of marsh vegetation or other tall herbs (Hölzinger 1987). A reduction in the area of grassland from which two cuts of silage are taken would also be beneficial (Green and Stowe in press). Mortality would be reduced by late harvesting of hay (preferably after mid-June) and especially by cutting from the centre of meadows outwards or from side to side (rather than from the edge inwards) and by adding bird-flushing equipment to machinery (Batten *et al.* 1990, Flade 1991, Stowe and Hudson 1991a,b). Leaving patches uncut for a day or so during harvesting may also allow birds to move elsewhere. In some cases birds may be attracted to suitable breeding areas using tape recordings (N. Schäffer pers. comm.). Within the EU countries, such habitat-management measures could be financially supported through the development of management agreements under the Agri-environment Regulation (EC Reg. 2078/92) of the Common Agricultural Policy.

Some control of predators, including cats and American mink *Mustela vison* in western Europe or foxes *Vulpes vulpes* and cats in the east, as well as a ban on hunting in eastern Europe and at migratory stopovers, may be necessary.

LUDWIK TOMIALOJC

Purple Gallinule
Porphyrio porphyrio

SPEC Category 3
Status Rare
Criteria <10,000 pairs

The Purple Gallinule occurs in small numbers in Europe. Although in Spain and Russia it is increasing in numbers and range, its populations in Turkey and Portugal are decreasing. Major threats are habitat loss and deterioration, and hunting pressure, which if removed could lead to the recovery of declining populations.

■ Distribution and population trends

This principally tropical and subtropical species occurs across a wide range, from Africa to New Zealand. Only small numbers occur in Europe, where it has a fragmented range which extends from southwest Iberia to south-east European Russia (Cramp and Simmons 1980). Spain, Italy (Sardinia) and Russia hold the largest populations (see table, map). The species is mainly resident (Cramp and Simmons 1980).

The Purple Gallinule was once widely distributed over nearly all wetlands of the Mediterranean and south Atlantic coast of the Iberian peninsula, but it experienced a rapid decline during the nineteenth century (Valverde 1960, Consellería d'Agricultura i Pesca 1988). In western Europe a large population still breeds in southern Spain where it is found in the marshes of the Guadalquivir river. This population declined strongly (Valverde 1960), before starting to increase again in the 1980s, and it was recently estimated that more than 1,000 pairs nest in the Doñana National Park of the Marismas del Guadalquivir (Important Bird Area 247) (Máñez 1991). A minimum of 62 individuals was found on the upper course of the Guadalquivir (IBA 239) at the beginning of the 1980s (Sánchez-Lafuente *et al.* 1987), increasing to 300–350 in 1990 (A. M. Sánchez-Lafuente pers. comm.). The species also breeds in lakes and reservoirs of western Andalucía (Sánchez-Lafuente *et al.* 1987, Lebrero 1991).

In Portugal the population is very small and

highly unstable. In Italy, the population is confined to the coastal wetlands of Sardinia, especially those of the Sinis peninsula and Golfo di Oristano (IBA 120) and around Cagliari (IBA 124).

In eastern Europe the largest population of at least 14,000 individuals was reported in the wetlands of the Caspian basin, in Azerbaijan (data not included in table or map) in Lake Akgyel (IBA 076), Kirov Bay (IBA 077) and water-bodies of the Shirvanskaya Steppe (IBA 078) (Grimmett and Jones 1989), though there are no recent estimates of these populations. In Russia itself only a modest population of 100–1,000 pairs is thought to occur.

In Turkey the species' status is also critically small and declining (see table), with the species being confined to the Göksu delta (IBA 052).

■ Ecology

The species lives in wetlands (including marshes, lakes and reservoirs with stable water-levels) which provide dense areas of vegetation (mainly reedmace *Typha*, rushes *Scirpus*, sedges *Carex* and reeds *Phragmites*), amongst which the birds build their nests. In the Guadalquivir marshes they feed mainly on seeds and the vegetative parts of marsh plants (Rodríguez and Hiraldo 1975). Rice-fields may constitute a seasonal source of food if situated near suitable breeding habitats (Rodríguez and Hiraldo 1975, Dementiev and Gladkov 1951c).

■ Threats

The Purple Gallinule's decline on the Iberian peninsula has been due to habitat loss and degradation through drainage, transformation into rice-fields and the natural drying of marshes, as well as to the high vulnerability of the species to hunting (Consellería d'Agricultura i Pesca 1988). These same problems, and also the use of pesticides (which may accumulate in emergent vegetation, as may heavy metals), seriously threaten the species in Sardinia today (Mocci Demartis 1972 in Cramp and Simmons 1980). In Portugal the alteration and fragmentation of habitat is also causing problems, even though the area in

	Breeding population			Breeding
	Size (pairs)	Year	Trend	range trend
Italy	(240–300)	—	(+1)	(+1)
Portugal	**5–10**	89	–1	–1
Russia	100–1,000	—	(+1)	+1
Spain	**3,000–3,500**	—	+1	+1
Turkey	100–200	90	–1	–1
Total (approx.)	3,400–5,000			

Trends +2 Large increase +1 Small increase 0 Stable X Extinct
(1970-1990) –2 Large decrease –1 Small decrease F Fluctuating N New breeder
Data quality **Bold**: reliable quantitative data Normal type: incomplete quantitative data
Bracketed figures: no quantitative data * Data quality not provided

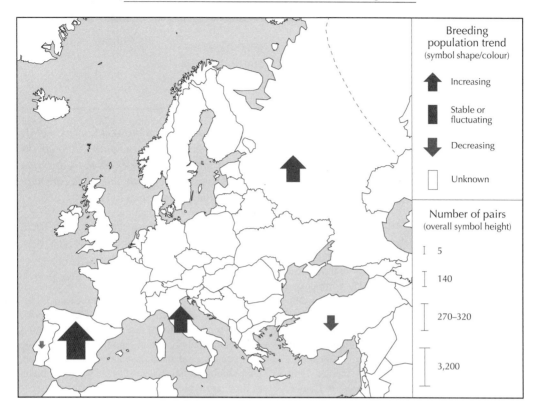

Breeding population trend
(symbol shape/colour)

- Increasing
- Stable or fluctuating
- Decreasing
- Unknown

Number of pairs
(overall symbol height)

- 5
- 140
- 270–320
- 3,200

which the species occurs is protected by law. The population in the Guadalquivir marshes is threatened principally through the disturbance of breeding birds by fishermen catching red swamp crawfish *Procambarus clarkii* (Máñez 1991), and the funnel traps used in this process sometimes also catch and kill young Purple Gallinules (Asensio 1991).

Conservation measures

As has been shown in Spain, Purple Gallinule populations may recover if hunting pressure is stopped and if the habitat is protected. By 1989 the majority of the breeding areas in Andalucía had been protected. A complementary measure which would accelerate the recovery of the species is its reintroduction to suitable wetlands, as has been carried out in Spain in the Natural Parks of Aiguamolls de l'Empordá (Cataluña) (IBA 199) and S'Albufera (IBA 280) in the Balearic Islands (Garrigós and Sargatal 1990, J. Mayol pers. comm.).

MANUEL MÁÑEZ

Crested Coot
Fulica cristata

SPEC Category   3
Status   Endangered
Criteria   <250 pairs

A small, remnant population of Crested Coot of about 50 adults occurs in south-west Europe, mainly in the marshes of the Guadalquivir river and some inland lagoons in southern Spain. Although the reasons for the species' decline during the twentieth century are not fully understood, the loss and degradation of wetland habitat are the most likely main reasons. Restoration and management of wetlands are therefore necessary to reverse the species' decline and to aid its recovery.

■ Distribution and population trends

The Crested Coot is widely distributed throughout the eastern and southern parts of Africa, but its range in the Palearctic is restricted to north-west Morocco and southern Spain (Wood 1975, Cramp and Simmons 1980). During the early part of the twentieth century it bred in Portugal (Tait 1924), and was locally common in some wetlands of southern Spain, mainly the marshes of the Guadalquivir river (Chapman and Buck 1910, Mountfort 1957) and La Janda lagoons in Cádiz (Irby 1895, Verner 1909, Yeates 1946), with a ratio of *F. cristata* to Coot *F. atra* of at least 1:10 (Valverde 1960, García *et al.* 1987).

The Iberian population has declined strongly during the twentieth century (Bernís 1972), and Crested Coot is now of only accidental occurrence in Portugal (CODA–SEO 1985). By the 1960s it had disappeared in Spain from La Janda (Alonso López 1985) and was near extinction at Doñana (Valverde 1960). This trend continued at Doñana with just 17 winter records recorded by the Biological Reserve personnel between 1977 and 1986 (García *et al.* 1987). Thereafter it showed a small recovery with 10–20 breeding pairs at Doñana in 1987 (Mañez 1991) and an estimated total of about 50 adults in 1990 (de Juana 1992) and 10–25 pairs in 1991 (see table, map).

At present the species' European breeding range is limited chiefly to some areas near the mouth of the Guadalquivir (mainly Doñana) and a few lagoons, mostly within 50 km of Doñana, although a few are over 100 km distant. This population is resident but the birds do make local movements, especially after breeding when they disperse due to the drying out of seasonal wetlands (Fernández-Palacios and Raya 1991).

■ Ecology

The three main habitats frequented by Crested Coot in Europe are: natural marshes (at Guadalquivir); marshes transformed into rice-fields and aquaculture; and small, shallow, inland lagoons, mostly steppic with mineral and alkaline waters, but sometimes lying among littoral dunes. All such wetland habitats as these are typically only semi-permanent or seasonal.

During the breeding season the species uses sheltered zones with emergent vegetation (e.g. *Scirpus*, *Phragmites*) and abundant submerged macrophytes. At other times of the year it also occurs in more open-water habitats (Wood 1975, Cramp and Simmons 1980, Fernández-Palacios and Raya 1991).

■ Threats

There are no clearly known reasons which explain the marked decline of the Crested Coot in Europe. It shares the same waters as Coot but tends to have more particular habitat requirements, especially for breeding. However, the drainage of important wetland sites, such as La Janda and parts of the marshes of the Guadalquivir, have probably had a negative impact on the species (García *et al.* 1987), together with the deterioration of remaining habitat due to changes in hydrology and water quality.

Although hunting of Crested Coot is forbidden throughout Spain, it so closely resembles the Coot (which is a game species) that it is sometimes shot (Fernández-Palacios and Raya 1991).

Strong periods of drought (e.g. 1981–1983 and 1992–1993) resulted in the drying out of suitable habitats and a marked decrease in the number of birds present (Agencia de Medio Ambiente in prep.). Clearly, with such small populations these fluctuations in climate are a threat to the continued survival of the Crested Coot in Europe.

| | Breeding population | | | Breeding |
	Size (pairs)	Year	Trend	range trend
Spain	**10–25**	91	**0**	**0**
Total (approx.)	10–25			

Trends	+2 Large increase	+1 Small increase	0 Stable	X Extinct
(1970–1990)	−2 Large decrease	−1 Small decrease	F Fluctuating	N New breeder
Data quality	**Bold**: reliable quantitative data	Normal type: incomplete quantitative data		
	Bracketed figures: no quantitative data	* Data quality not provided		

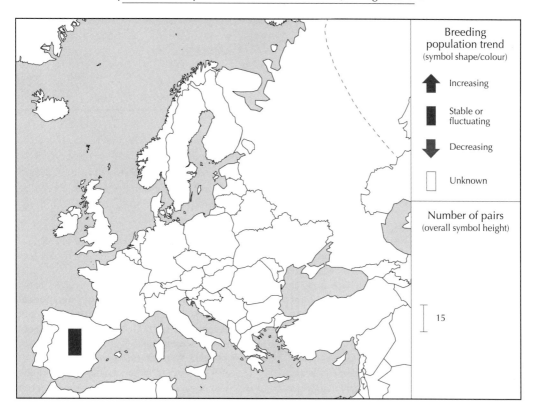

Breeding population trend
(symbol shape/colour)

Increasing

Stable or fluctuating

Decreasing

Unknown

Number of pairs
(overall symbol height)

15

Conservation measures

The entire European population occurs in Important Bird Areas (IBAs), most of which are legally protected, such as the Marismas del Guadalquivir (IBA 247), lagoons of Espera (IBA 249), Terry (IBA 250), Medina (IBA 252) and Puerto Real (IBA 253), in the provinces of Cádiz, Seville and Huelva. There is also a successful captive breeding unit, established in 1991, at Puebla del Río in the Marismas del Guadalquivir from which 22 birds were released during 1991–1992, with further birds released during 1993–1994.

However, habitat restoration and management measures are required to facilitate an increase in the population and to provide additional suitable refuges during times of drought and environmental stress.

Monitoring studies in the Andalusian region should continue and be extended to the North African population. Applied research is also essential in order to understand the natural factors involved in population regulation of the Crested Coot and to improve management measures in order to ensure the recovery and long-term survival of the species as part of the European avifauna.

JOSÉ FERNÁNDEZ-PALACIOS

Crane
Grus grus

SPEC Category 3
Status Vulnerable
Criteria Large decline

There has been a considerable decline over most of Europe during the last 300 years. Since the 1960s numbers have increased in central Europe but are probably still declining in the east where the bulk of European birds breed. Major threats include human disturbance at breeding sites, illegal shooting and drought. Conservation requires protection of, and habitat management at, breeding and wintering sites and at migratory staging posts, and improved protection from illegal hunting.

▓ Distribution and population trends

The breeding range extends from central Europe east to central Siberia. Within Europe, breeding is concentrated in the north and east, where birds are mostly migratory, although those breeding east and south of the Black Sea are perhaps resident.

The largest numbers of birds breed in Russia and Sweden, though sizeable populations also occur in Norway, Finland, Germany, Poland, the Baltic states and Belarus. A few pairs have also recently bred in France and the Czech Republic (see table, map), and irregularly in the United Kingdom (Gibbons *et al.* 1993).

There has been a marked decrease in numbers and range since the Middle Ages, with extinction in many areas during the last 100 years, for example in southern Europe, mainly due to drainage of breeding habitats (Johnsgard 1983, Alonso *et al.* 1987, Prange 1989, in press). Although central European populations have increased and spread continuously since the 1960s, declines are thought to have contin-

ued during 1970–1990 in several countries, including the large populations in Finland, Russia and Belarus (see table, map).

Cranes in Europe use two migration routes (in the west and east) and further routes pass over Russia (Libbert 1936, Alerstam and Bauer 1973, Neufeldt 1982, Prange 1986–1987, 1989, 1991, Swanberg 1986–1987, Neufeldt and Keskpaik 1987, 1989, Litvinenko and Neufeldt 1988).

Birds from parts of Fennoscandia and the Baltic states (and possibly Russia) take the west European route, wintering mainly in Spain (50,000–60,000 birds) with some in Portugal and North Africa (Alonso and Alonso 1990, Sánchez Guzmán *et al.* 1993). Central Europe is an important staging area (60,000–70,000 birds) in autumn, with the Rügen–Bock region in Germany being the most important site with up to 40,000 resting birds (Moll 1956, Prange and Mewes 1989, Prange 1991). In spring and autumn, large numbers of birds occur in France (20,000–30,000) and Spain (up to 50,000 at Laguna de Gallocanta) (Salvi 1986–1987, Prange 1989). The number of birds migrating along the west European flyway has increased since the 1960s, from about 40,000 to 70,000 (Alonso *et al.* 1987, Alonso and Alonso 1990, Prange 1991, in press).

East European populations—including parts of the Swedish and Polish, and the majority of the Finnish, Baltic and Belarus populations—migrate to Tunisia, Algeria and Libya, as well as to Turkey, Israel, Sudan and Ethiopia. The number of migrating birds on this route varies between 30,000 and 70,000, with important staging areas in Estonia (up to 30,000 birds) and in Hungary (55,000 birds at Hortobagy National Park in 1992: Fintha 1993). Although several east European populations have declined between 1970 and 1990, increasing numbers have been noted on the eastern flyway in recent years, perhaps due to western translocation of the Russian migration routes (Kovacs 1986–1987, Rinne 1986–1987, Neufeldt and Keskpaik 1989).

	Breeding population			Breeding
	Size (pairs)	Year	Trend	range trend
Belarus	1,500–2,000	90	–1	0
Czech Republic	1–5 *	—	N*	—
Denmark	**3–3**	90	(+1)	(+1)
Estonia	600–700	—	+1	0
Finland	**4,000–5,000**	92	–1	**0**
France	**1–1**	90	N	**0**
Germany	**1,300–1,600**	—	+1	**0**
Latvia	300–600	—	+2	+1
Lithuania	**200–300**	85–88	–1	–1
Norway	1,000–1,500	90	+1	**+1**
Poland	2,300–2,600	—	+1	0
Romania	0–2	—	(0)	(0)
Russia	30,000–50,000	87	–1	0
Spain	0–0	—	X	X
Sweden	10,000–15,000	87	+1	**0**
Turkey	(100–300)	—	(–1)	(–1)
Ukraine	**200–280**	88	–1	**–1**
Total (approx.)	52,000–80,000			

Trends +2 Large increase +1 Small increase 0 Stable X Extinct
(1970–1990) –2 Large decrease –1 Small decrease F Fluctuating N New breeder
Data quality **Bold**: reliable quantitative data Normal type: incomplete quantitative data
Bracketed figures: no quantitative data * Data quality not provided *

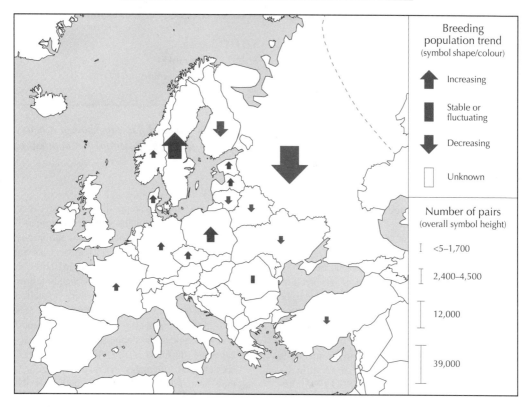

Breeding population trend (symbol shape/colour)	
▲	Increasing
▮	Stable or fluctuating
▼	Decreasing
☐	Unknown

Number of pairs (overall symbol height)

<5–1,700

2,400–4,500

12,000

39,000

■ Ecology

Breeding occurs in boreal and temperate taiga and deciduous forest zones, typically in wet habitats including bogs, swampy clearings in pine *Pinus* forest, wetlands with reeds *Phragmites* (Germany), and wet alder *Alnus* and birch *Betula* woods with standing water 20–40 cm deep. During the last 30 years the species has adapted to cultivated landscapes and will breed at small ponds in fields and meadows. Adults feed primarily on plant material but also take insects (which are particularly important for chicks) and other animal food including fish.

Foraging sites in staging and wintering areas comprise fields and meadows, including the important Spanish dehesa and Portuguese montado pastoral oak *Quercus* woodlands, where the food is mainly vegetable material (cereals, potatoes, acorns). Birds move to and from wetland roosting sites according to a fixed daily rhythm (Mewes 1980, 1989, Karlsson and Swanberg 1983, Riols 1986–1987).

■ Threats

Threats in western and central Europe include human disturbance causing lowered breeding success (Prange and Mewes 1987), and in extreme drought the nest and chicks are more accessible to predators (crows *Corvus*, wild boar *Sus scrofa*, fox *Vulpes vulpes*) due to lowered water-levels. In Europe, collisions with powerlines and shooting are common causes of mortality (Prange 1989). Shooting occurs mainly in south-east Europe and Africa, the species being well protected along the west European flyway. Birds in their first year are more affected by threats in general than are adults (Johnsgard 1983).

■ Conservation measures

Although a number of sites in Europe are protected—e.g. c.85% of staging posts and one-third of breeding areas in Germany (van der Ven 1986–1987, Prange and Mewes 1987, von Treuenfels 1989)—protection needs to be extended to further key sites, especially where the species is declining. Conservation measures at such sites should also include protection of wetlands and forests through appropriate management and water regulation.

Low-intensity agricultural practices need to be maintained in key areas such as the montados and dehesas of the Iberian peninsula and at important staging posts (e.g. Laguna de Gallocanta in Spain, Important Bird Area 192), which could be realized in the EU through Zonal Programmes under the Agri-environment Regulation (EC Reg. 2078/92) of the Common Agricultural Policy.

The species is protected in all European countries, but stricter enforcement is necessary, particularly on the key migration routes in south-east Europe.

HARTWIG PRANGE

235

Little Bustard
Tetrax tetrax

SPEC Category 2
Status Vulnerable
Criteria Large decline

Although substantial numbers still remain in Iberia, the Little Bustard has experienced a heavy population decline in most of its European range. There is, however, potential for population stability if non-intensive farming systems are restored.

■ Distribution and population trends

The Little Bustard occurs in highly fragmented populations across Europe, Morocco, Algeria and Asia (Schulz 1985). It is resident, dispersive and migratory in different regions, the degree and regularity of movements tending to become more pronounced toward the north and east of the breeding range. The total world population is estimated to be in excess of 100,000 birds, of which over 50% occur in Iberia and approximately 20% in European Russia with approximately a further 20,000 in Kazakhstan (V. Belik *in litt.* 1993). Within Spain, the species is most abundant in the provinces of Castilla–La Mancha, Madrid and Extremadura (SEO 1993). Important populations also occur in France and Sardinia (Italy).

Between the early 1950s and late 1970s, the Little Bustard declined steeply in numbers within Europe (especially in the north and east), associated with the expansion and intensification of agriculture (Belik 1992a, Moseikin 1992). Its status is still fragile, with declines noted for the 1970–1990 period in France, Spain, Italy and Ukraine, and numbers fluctuating in Russia. However, in some areas populations are showing signs of recovery, and there is potential for stability in the future, given the application of suitable conservation measures.

Although formerly classified as Globally Threatened (Collar and Andrew 1988), the global status of Little Bustard is currently listed as Near Threatened (Collar *et al.* 1994).

	Breeding population			Breeding
	Size (individuals)	Year	Trend	range trend
France	4,000–5,000	92	–2	0
Italy	2,000–2,500	88	–1	–1
Portugal	10,000–20,000	89	**0**	**0**
Russia	18,000–20,000	—	F	F
Spain	50,000–70,000	—	–1	–1
Turkey	(0–50)	—	—	—
Ukraine	8–10	78	–1	–1
Total (approx.)	84,000–120,000			

Trends +2 Large increase   +1 Small increase   0 Stable   X Extinct
(1970–1990) –2 Large decrease   –1 Small decrease   F Fluctuating   N New breeder
Data quality **Bold**: reliable quantitative data   Normal type: incomplete quantitative data
Bracketed figures: no quantitative data   * Data quality not provided

■ Ecology

Little Bustards inhabit steppe-like regions: extensive, gently undulating plains with a predominance of fairly short grass. They tolerate cold and aridity quite well, but generally avoid moist areas. Like the Great Bustard *Otis tarda*, Little Bustard tends to occur in extensive mosaics of cereal, weedy fallow and pasture (pseudo-steppe), but favours vegetation that is not too dense or higher than about 30 cm. It is less dependent on cereal crops than the Great Bustard and is most abundant in steppelands with high pasture coverage (de Juana *et al.* 1988).

Females mate with males on a displaying ground, but they nest, incubate their eggs, and raise the young alone. They often select nesting sites in fallow fields, alfalfa or cereal crop margins. During the breeding season, a vital source of food is insects which are fed to the chicks. In winter, they are attracted to crops such as alfalfa in which they can feed in flocks numbering many thousands of birds.

■ Threats

Agricultural intensification has been by far the most important cause of the overall decline of the Little Bustard and the fragmentation of its range since the end of the Second World War. Ploughing of grasslands, increased application of agro-chemicals and irrigation of dry lands has been widespread, especially in France, Italy, Russia and Ukraine (Goriup and Batten 1990, Moseikin 1992). Similar pressures are now mounting in Iberia. Moreover, the remaining steppe vegetation in eastern Europe is highly overgrazed, with all fallow and pasture land heavily utilized and disturbed by pastoralists.

Predation by Rooks *Corvus frugilegus* when females have been flushed, and trampling of nests by cattle, can both be frequent causes of egg-loss in some places (Moseikin 1992).

Shooting is a further cause of mortality, whether it occurs through deliberate poaching or opportunistically during the hunting of associated game species such as Red-legged Partridges *Alectoris rufa* and hares *Lepus europaeus*.

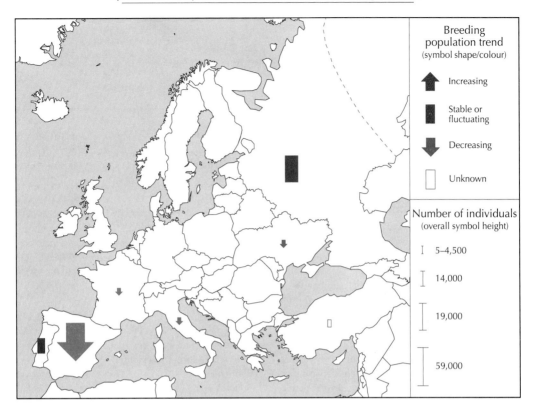

Breeding
population trend
(symbol shape/colour)

Increasing

Stable or
fluctuating

Decreasing

Unknown

Number of individuals
(overall symbol height)

5–4,500

14,000

19,000

59,000

■ Conservation measures

In most of Europe the conservation of Little Bustards is dependent on human intervention to maintain open areas of steppe or non-intensive farmland. Through management agreements, developed under the EU Agri-environment Regulation (EC Reg. 2078/92), such extensive farming practices can be supported and management plans can be prepared to benefit Little Bustards as well as other species of dry grassland regions (e.g. SEO 1992) in EU countries. However, many more such schemes are required within and beyond the EU and this will need a substantial education effort directed at policy-makers and farmers alike. Studies in Spain have emphasized the importance of maintaining and enhancing landscape diversity, which can be achieved by reducing the area of cereal crops, and increasing the area under legumes, sunflowers, vineyards and pasture (SEO 1993).

With respect to overgrazing in natural steppes, stocking densities need to be carefully regulated in areas where Little Bustards occur. Where damage to winter crops is proved to result from large feeding flocks, compensation payments should be made.

As in the case of the Great Bustard, the dispersed distribution and migratory behaviour of Little Bustards requires international cooperation for their conservation, and this could be achieved through an Agreement for dry grassland birds under the Bonn Convention (see Great Bustard).

PAUL GORIUP

Houbara Bustard
Chlamydotis undulata

SPEC Category 3
Status (Endangered)
Criteria <250 pairs

The endemic Canarian Houbara Bustard has a population of just 200–400 birds. It is threatened by the loss and degradation of habitat, and this needs to be addressed by initiating better land-use practices through management agreements with local farmers under the EU Agri-environment Regulation.

■ Distribution and population trends

The Houbara Bustard occurs from the Canary Islands (Spain), across North Africa to central Asia. The total world population is some tens of thousands of birds, which represents a considerable reduction from former numbers (Goriup 1982), and continues to decline. The distinctive subspecies *C. u. fuertaventurae* is entirely confined to the Canary Islands, chiefly Fuerteventura, with a few birds also inhabiting Lanzarote; it is resident.

Although bustards were known from Fuerteventura as early as 1402, the island was much less arid then than now, supporting woodlands and several perennial streams, so bustard habitat was probably quite limited (Collar and Goriup 1983). Available habitat increased with human colonization, and by the early 1900s von Thanner (1905) was able to purchase over 100 bustard eggs (representing at least 35 nests) in a single season. Human pressure on the land then rapidly increased, and a few decades later Bannerman (1963) considered the bird to be all but extinct. It remains possible that this was in fact never the case, though it may be that numbers fluctuate with variations in the climate, recruitment to the population being reduced during dry periods.

There are currently believed to be 200–400 birds, though a recent survey on Lanzarote suggests that this population may have increased considerably or been previously underestimated (M. Nogales pers. comm. 1994). Population trends for the 1970–1990 period are unclear since the first census was not until 1979 and subsequent counts have not presented a consistent picture. There seems to have been a gradual increase in numbers, associated with a decrease in the human rural population and with improved protection, but due to differences in survey methods this is not conclusive. Also local people have claimed that the Houbara seemed more common in the 1950s and 1960s than now (J. J. Naranjo *in litt.* 1993).

■ Ecology

In the eastern Canary Islands, Houbara Bustards inhabit arid gravelly plains and areas with low sand-dunes where shrubby vegetation (especially *Launaea arborescens* and *Lycium afrum*) can provide cover and food such as shoots and seeds, as well as beetles, grasshoppers and other insect prey (Collar and Goriup 1983). Within such habitats, abandoned rain-fed fields (gavias) with annual weeds or irrigated crops of alfalfa are often used for feeding. In 1991, the maximum extent of suitable habitat on Fuerteventura was about 34,300 ha, mainly in the north of the island, but with a significant block of 4,560 ha (13% of the total) covering the Matas Blancas (Jandía isthmus) in the south. It is not known whether or not the carrying capacity of this habitat has been reached.

On the Canary Islands, males defend individual display areas or territories which are usually c.500–1,000 m apart. Both sexes tend to be solitary in the breeding season and meet only for mating; males are probably polygynous, taking no part in rearing the young (Collins 1984a).

■ Threats

The amount of habitat available on the Canary Islands is steadily being eroded by desiccation, overgrazing, road building, tourist development and particularly by the destruction of vegetation through off-road joy-riding in jeeps; all these threats have worsened since about 1960. A few birds are poached each year by determined hunters, and any eggs found by goatherds are generally removed. A plan to construct a wind-power generating farm in the Matas Blancas with EU grant support was partly implemented during 1992, and subsequent efforts made to halt this development have been unsuccessful; resi-

	Breeding population			Breeding
	Size (pairs)	Year	Trend	range trend
Spain				
Canary Islands	**200–400**	89	—	—
Total (approx.)	200–400			

Trends   +2 Large increase   +1 Small increase   0 Stable   X Extinct
(1970–1990)   –2 Large decrease   –1 Small decrease   F Fluctuating   N New breeder
Data quality   **Bold**: reliable quantitative data   Normal type: incomplete quantitative data
   Bracketed figures: no quantitative data   * Data quality not provided

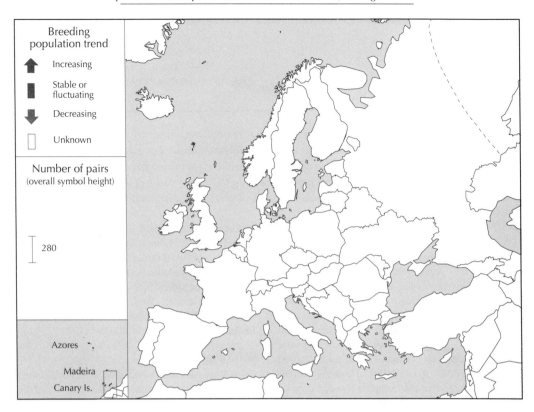

Breeding population trend

Increasing

Stable or fluctuating

Decreasing

Unknown

Number of pairs
(overall symbol height)

280

Azores

Madeira

Canary Is.

dent Houbara Bustards have been affected. The situation of the Houbara on Lanzarote is unclear.

■ Conservation measures

A recovery plan for the bird has been drafted by Domínguez and Díaz (1985) and some 2,754 ha of the Matas Blancas (8% of the total available habitat on Fuerteventura) has been designated as a Special Protection Area in accordance with the EU Wild Birds Directive.

Particular attention should be paid to the fact that in the 1988 census only five areas were found to hold ten or more bustards. Prime areas and other potential sites can be managed to encourage breeding success by developing management agreements, under the Agri-environment Regulation (EC Reg. 2078/92) of the EU Common Agricultural Policy, that aid local farmers to reduce grazing levels by erecting stock-housing units, and to restore gavias to grow fodder crops such as rape and alfalfa which are also valuable for Houbara Bustards.

The Houbara is an attractive species for birdwatchers as well as having dramatic display behaviour, and some income for local farmers could be derived by charging a modest fee for access to hides overlooking sites used for feeding and display.

PAUL GORIUP

Great Bustard
Otis tarda

SPEC Category 1
Status Declining
Criteria Moderate decline

There has been a rapid decline (including national extinctions) in much of central and eastern Europe, and a similar collapse is imminent in the Iberian stronghold. The European population can only be saved by maintaining large areas of non-intensive farming systems that preserve open habitats and substitute for former natural grasslands. In this respect, the globally threatened Great Bustard serves as a flagship for many other grassland species that are in a similar predicament.

■ Distribution and population trends

The Great Bustard occurs in highly fragmented populations across Europe, Morocco and Asia (Kollar 1988). Various populations are resident, dispersive and migratory, the degree and regularity of movements tending to become more pronounced toward the north and east of the breeding range. Allowing that the status of populations in Mongolia and China (subspecies *O. t. dybowski*) is uncertain, the total world population was estimated to be under 25,000 birds (Goriup 1987, Tucker 1991). However, current data now suggest that the European Russian population is larger than previously thought: there were 2,900 birds in the European part of the former Soviet Union in the late 1980s (Goriup 1987), but European Russia is now judged to hold 10,000–11,000 birds and the Ukraine 300–500 birds (see table, map). Thus the European total alone is now at least 26,000 birds, of which c.50% occur in Iberia, and at least a third in Russia, with the bulk of the remainder in Turkey (true population unknown) and Hungary.

Over the last 50 years, Great Bustards became extinct in western Germany, Poland, former Yugoslavia and Bulgaria, and only a few remain in Austria, Czech Republic, Slovakia and Romania. This is

part of a long-term trend, following extinction in the United Kingdom, France, Sweden, Switzerland, Italy and Greece in the 100 years before. Furthermore, most of the extant populations outside Russia have continued to decline since 1970 (see table, map).

On a world scale, the Great Bustard is classified as Globally Threatened due to current, and predicted further, declines (Collar *et al.* 1994).

■ Ecology

Great Bustards inhabit extensive, gently undulating, treeless plains with a predominance of grass (i.e. steppes). They are tolerant of the cold, but generally avoid arid or very moist areas. In the current agricultural landscape of Europe, Great Bustards require extensive mosaics of cereal, fallow and pasture (pseudo-steppe) to provide varied feeding opportunities and an abundant source of invertebrates (especially beetles, crickets and grasshoppers) which are fed to the chicks (Cramp and Simmons 1980, Martínez 1991, SEO 1992). High insecticide inputs are therefore particularly damaging. Areas with crops such as alfalfa are also favoured as these are fed upon in winter (Hidalgo and Carranza 1990).

Females mate with males on a lekking ground, and then nest, incubate the clutch of three or four eggs and raise the young alone. They often select nesting sites in cereal fields as these provide the best cover against predators (e.g. Ena *et al.* 1987, Alonso *et al.* 1990). During migration and at wintering sites, Great Bustards generally form flocks, sometimes of several hundred birds (Buzun and Golovach 1992).

■ Threats

The most important causes of the fragmentation and decline of the European population of the Great Bustard have been the widespread ploughing of grasslands and the increased applications of pesticides since the end of the Second World War; more recently, changes in cropping patterns have also been implicated (Goriup and Batten 1990, Flint and Mishchenko 1991). Currently the majority of the re-

| | Breeding population | | | Breeding |
	Size (individuals)	Year	Trend	range trend
Austria	**50–60**	93	–2	–2
Czech Republic	**7–13**	—	–2	–1
Germany	**150–150**	—	–2	–2
Hungary	**1,000–1,200**	91	–2	–2
Moldova	**2–3**	88	–1	–1
Poland	**0–0**	—	X	X
Portugal	**500–700**	89	–1	0
Romania	**10–15**	—	–2	–2
Russia	10,000–11,000	—	F	F
Slovakia	**25–40**	—	–2	–1
Spain	**13,500–14,000**	87–89	–1	–1
Turkey	145–4,000	—	—	—
Ukraine	300–500	—	–1	–1
Total (approx.)	26,000–32,000			

Trends	+2 Large increase	+1 Small increase	0 Stable	X Extinct
(1970–1990)	–2 Large decrease	–1 Small decrease	F Fluctuating	N New breeder

Data quality **Bold**: reliable quantitative data   Normal type: incomplete quantitative data
Bracketed figures: no quantitative data   * Data quality not provided

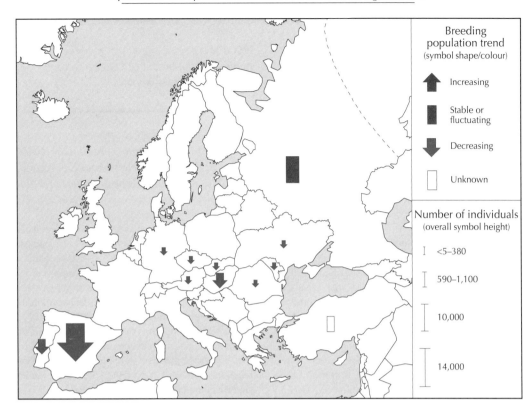

Breeding
population trend
(symbol shape/colour)

Increasing

Stable or
fluctuating

Decreasing

Unknown

Number of individuals
(overall symbol height)

<5–380

590–1,100

10,000

14,000

maining Iberian Great Bustards are threatened by agricultural intensification through EU irrigation schemes (MOPT 1992, Martín-Novella *et al*. 1993, MOPTMA 1994). In eastern and south-east Europe the remaining steppe vegetation is highly overgrazed and degraded. Turkey, for instance, has over 50 million head of low-yielding sheep, so all fallow and pasture land is heavily utilized and disturbed by pastoralists (Goriup and Parr 1985).

A further cause of Great Bustard decline is shooting, whether by direct poaching or through disturbance during hunting of other game species. In Spain, there is growing pressure to re-open trophy hunting of mature male Great Bustards, the best breeders, which could severely affect social structures.

Powerlines can cause a significant level of mortality from collisions at night or in fog, especially where such lines are at high densities, as in the vicinity of pumping stations for irrigation schemes (MOPT 1992, Martín-Novella *et al*. 1993, MOPTMA 1994).

■ Conservation measures

In most of Europe human intervention is required to maintain open areas of steppe or non-intensive farmland in order to prevent Great Bustard populations from diminishing further. Such opportunities exist in the EU through various schemes, especially through the development of Zonal Programmes under the Agri-environment Regulation (EC Reg. 2078/92) of the Common Agricultural Policy. These can provide funds to support environmentally beneficial farming through management agreements with farmers; management plans can be prepared that benefit bustards and other steppe landbirds (Goriup and Batten 1990, SEO 1992). Such schemes should be more widely used both within and beyond the EU, though this requires a substantial education effort directed at policy-makers as well as farmers.

With respect to overgrazing in natural steppes, stocking densities have to be carefully regulated in areas where Great Bustards occur.

Where appropriate, overhead powerlines should be clearly marked (e.g. with orange balls) to make them more visible to flying Great Bustards.

The dispersed distribution of Great Bustards requires international cooperation for their conservation. This could be promoted by an Agreement under the Bonn Convention for dry grassland birds (including also Little Bustard *Tetrax tetrax*), to include monitoring and research such as: regular international bustard censuses; studies of the influences of agricultural practices on dry grassland birds; the use of new telemetric techniques such as satellite- and radar-tracking to obtain data on bustard movements, population dynamics, and habitat use; and exchange of information and expertise between researchers and conservation managers of dry grassland species.

PAUL GORIUP

Avocet
Recurvirostra avosetta

SPEC Category 4, breeding; 3, winter
Status Secure, breeding; Localized, winter
Criteria Localized, winter

There have been declines in breeding populations of east and south-east Europe, but increases in North Sea countries. Through concentrating in a small number of coastal wintering sites the Avocet is highly vulnerable to their loss or degradation. Key coastal wintering sites should be suitably managed and more reserves should be established in east and south-east Europe to protect breeding habitat.

■ Distribution and population trends

Europe contains only a third to a half of the Avocet's global range, but probably over half the world population breeds in the region (Rose and Scott 1994). Breeding occurs locally in the Baltic area, along the Atlantic coast from Denmark to western France, locally in the Mediterranean and from central Europe east to the Caspian. West European birds winter on the Atlantic coast, especially of southern France, southern Iberia, Senegal and Guinea (Blomert and Engelmoer 1990); central and east European birds move mainly to the Mediterranean (Greece, Tunisia, Egypt) (Cramp and Simmons 1983, Summers *et al.* 1987).

Europe is estimated to hold 31,000–56,000 pairs, over half in the Netherlands, Denmark, Spain and Turkey (EBD 1994). Population sizes are well known except for Turkey and Russia.

The species declined in north-west Europe during the nineteenth century, becoming temporarily extinct in the United Kingdom and Sweden, before recolonizing both countries and spreading to Belgium and Norway this century (Cramp and Simmons 1983). Breeding numbers along the North Sea coast (including Sweden) increased from 1,800 pairs in 1924–1925 (van Oordt 1929) to c.10,000 pairs in 1969 (Tjallingii 1970), and 16,400–19,700 pairs in the 1980s. However, declines are reported for 1970–1990 from much of east and south-east Europe, including the large but imprecisely known population in Russia (EBD 1994).

Of greatest concern is the fact that the species is concentrated in winter, with more than 90% of European wintering numbers gathering at just 10 sites (see Important Bird Area table). The large French wintering population seems to be declining, but most of the others are increasing or fluctuating (see population table, map).

■ Ecology

Avocets inhabit estuaries, shallow bays, tidal mudflats, coastal lagoons, brackish and freshwater pools, and steppe lakes. The specialized feeding method involves sweeping the long, upcurved bill from side to side through water or loose sediment. Essential habitat requirements are water up to 15 cm deep over soft sediments (without stones or shell fragments) rich in aquatic invertebrates (Cramp and Simmons 1983). Nesting birds avoid dense vegetation, although some cover for the young is important. The Avocet is not dependent on saline habitats as long as (e.g.) grazing or flooding maintain sparse or low vegetation. Breeding tends to be in loose colonies of 10–70 pairs (Glutz von Blotzheim *et al.* 1977).

■ Threats

Loss and disturbance of breeding habitat, and the deterioration of feeding conditions at breeding and wintering sites, are the main threats, e.g. at the Evros delta in Greece (Goutner 1987).

Increased numbers in north-west Europe are presumably related to better protection, extension of breeding habitat and improvement in feeding conditions. In the United Kingdom the increase is related to habitat creation and management (Cadbury *et al.*

	Winter population			Winter
	Size (individuals)	Year	Trend	range trend
Belgium	**10–100**	89–90	+2	0
Bulgaria	**10–900**	77–91	0	0
Cyprus	1–20	—	0	0
France	**14,000–16,000**	89	–1	0
Germany	**0–811**	80–91	—	—
Greece	**1,760–6,500**	87–91	0	0
Italy	5,000–10,000	84	+2	+1
Netherlands	**0–1,000**	80–91	F	0
Portugal	**7,000–20,000**	91	F	0
Spain	**7,200–11,000**	—	F	—
Canary Islands	2–5	—	F	–1
Switzerland	**0–5**	—	F	F
Turkey	(700–700)	—	—	—
United Kingdom	**890–900**	88	+2	+2
Total (min., approx.)	37,000			

Trends	+2 Large increase	+1 Small increase	0 Stable	X Extinct
(1970–1990)	–2 Large decrease	–1 Small decrease	F Fluctuating	N New breeder

Data quality **Bold**: reliable quantitative data   Normal type: incomplete quantitative data
Bracketed figures: no quantitative data   * Data quality not provided

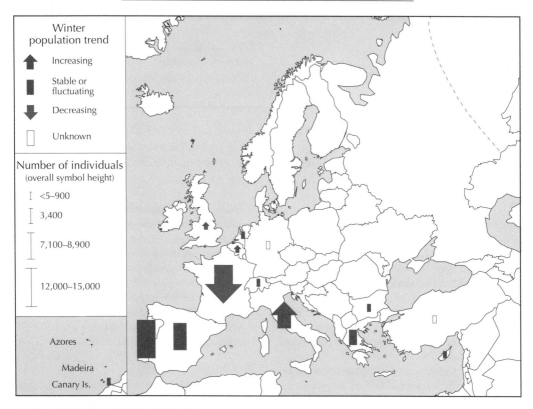

Winter population trend

↑	Increasing
■	Stable or fluctuating
↓	Decreasing
☐	Unknown

Number of individuals
(overall symbol height)

I	<5–900
I	3,400
I	7,100–8,900
I	12,000–15,000

Azores

Madeira

Canary Is.

Important Bird Areas The top ten IBAs for wintering Avocets in Europe, together holding over 90% of the total European wintering population.

France	011	Estuaire de la Seine (right bank)
	043	Estuaire de la Loire
	045	Baie et marais de Bourgneuf
	049	Marais Poitevin avec Baie de l'Aiguillon, Ponte de'Arcy, Communaux du marais Vendéen et île de Charrouin
	070	Ile d'Oléron, marais de Brouage et la Gripperie Saint-Symphorien
Greece	001	Delta Evrou (Evros Delta)
	004	Porto Lagos, Limni Vistonis (Lake Vistonis) and Coastal lagoons (Lakes of Thrace)
Italy	095	Wetlands along Golfo di Manfredonia
Portugal	010	Ria de Aveiro
	017	Tejo Estuary

1989). Much breeding habitat in the Netherlands has been created by land-claim, and in 1990 over two-thirds of Avocets in the south-west (2,700 pairs) were breeding in these temporary habitats (Meininger *et al.* 1992). Increased numbers in the Dutch Wadden Sea, holding over a quarter of the European population, are also related to extension of breeding habitat (Engelmoer and Blomert 1985), and presumably to increased food supply following eutrophication (cf.

Beukema 1992). However, such eutrophication is often temporary and present numbers will probably not be maintained.

The Avocet is more vulnerable than other waders due to its specialized requirements which cause it to concentrate outside the breeding season at a few coastal wetlands under considerable pressure from land-claim, pollution, marine farming and disturbance.

■ Conservation measures

When breeding, over 75% of Avocets in north-west and central Europe are found in Important Bird Areas, while in south-west and south-east Europe and the Ukraine this proportion is about half, and in Russia only 10%. Also, because birds are concentrated at only a few sites in winter, conservation depends largely on protection and proper management of these, as required under the EU Wild Birds Directive and promoted under the Ramsar Convention (where applicable).

Two areas need particular attention: birds breeding in the Wadden Sea (over 80% of the Dutch population) depend on correct management of saltmarshes, and in the Tejo estuary of Portugal (where over 15% of west European birds winter) there are serious threats of mercury contamination, hunting and bridge construction.

Eduard Osieck

Stone Curlew
Burhinus oedicnemus

SPEC Category 3
Status Vulnerable
Criteria Large decline

A widespread decline has occurred, particularly in western and central Europe, due to habitat loss through the abandonment of low-intensity mixed and pastoral agriculture in favour of more intensive and mainly arable farming. Low-intensity farming practices should be maintained and promoted to provide suitable habitat.

■ Distribution and population trends

The Stone Curlew's breeding range covers much of central and southern Europe, comprising a quarter to a half of its global range. The Iberian population is resident, but birds to the north and east are migratory, wintering in southern Europe, North Africa and along the southern edge of the Sahara.

Breeding strongholds lie in Russia and Spain, which together hold over 80% of European numbers. France and Portugal also support sizeable populations (see table, map).

Declines in several west European countries began as early as the second half of the nineteenth century, but were most marked after the Second World War, when the loss of lowland dry grassland and heath accelerated (Goriup 1988) and Stone Curlews disappeared from the Netherlands and western Germany (Cramp and Simmons 1983, Reichholf 1989).

During 1970–1990 numbers fell in practically all countries within the European range, including the large populations of Spain, Portugal and France. In Russia the situation is currently considered stable, but the species is poorly known there and no quantitative data on trends are available. Elsewhere in eastern Europe the species has been described as scarce and local (Dementiev and Gladkov 1951c, Gavrin *et al.* 1962) and as declining (Anon. 1981, Hölzinger 1987, Glowacinski 1992).

■ Ecology

The Stone Curlew inhabits lowland heath, semi-natural dry grassland, infertile agricultural grassland, steppe on poor soil, desert and extensive sand-dunes. It breeds on open, bare ground or areas with little vegetation (Batten *et al.* 1990), and has adapted to arable land but only where crops are short or have an open structure during the breeding season, e.g. maize, carrots, sugar beet and sunflowers (Green 1988); intensively grown cereals are normally too tall and dense in spring to be used. Communal daytime roosts in autumn and winter in Spain occupy traditional sites with some cover (e.g. shrubland, gravel pits, vineyards) and include both local birds and winter visitors (Barros in prep.).

Birds feed mainly at night on invertebrates and a few small vertebrates, preferably on sparsely vegetated grasslands but also in arable crops. In some areas, invertebrates associated with the dung of rabbits *Oryctolagus* and ungulates are important prey (Green 1988, Batten *et al.* 1990).

■ Threats

The widespread decline is attributable largely to habitat loss and degradation. A general reduction in pastoral farming on dry grassland in Europe and the continued high level of myxomatosis has reduced livestock and rabbit grazing and left much grassland unsuitable for Stone Curlews because of vegetation growth (Green and Griffiths in press). However, the major threat to dry grassland is its conversion to arable farmland and, in some areas, plantation for-

	Breeding population			Breeding range trend
	Size (pairs)	Year	Trend	
Albania	10–20	80	–1	(–1)
Austria	(4–8)	—	(–2)	(–2)
Belarus	**1–10**	90	–1	–1
Bulgaria	30–100	—	0	0
Croatia	100–200 *	—	0*	0*
Cyprus	(50–80)	—	(–1)	(–1)
Czech Republic	**1–5**	—	–2	–2
France	5,000–9,000	92	–1	(0)
Germany	1–5 *	—	–2	**0**
Greece	300–500	—	(–1)	(–1)
Hungary	200–250	—	0	0
Italy	200–500	89	–1	–1
Poland	**5–15**	—	–2	0
Portugal	1,000–10,000	89	–1	–1
Romania	(200–400)	—	(–1)	–1
Russia	(10,000–100,000)	80–90	(0)	(0)
Slovakia	(1–5)	—	–1	–1
Spain	22,000–30,000	—	–1	–1
Canary Islands	(300–500)	—	–2	–2
Turkey	(1,000–5,000)	—	—	—
Ukraine	15–30	80	–2	–1
United Kingdom	**150–160**	88	**–1**	**–1**
Total (approx.)	41,000–160,000			

Trends +2 Large increase +1 Small increase 0 Stable X Extinct
(1970–1990) –2 Large decrease –1 Small decrease F Fluctuating N New breeder
Data quality **Bold**: reliable quantitative data Normal type: incomplete quantitative data
Bracketed figures: no quantitative data * Data quality not provided

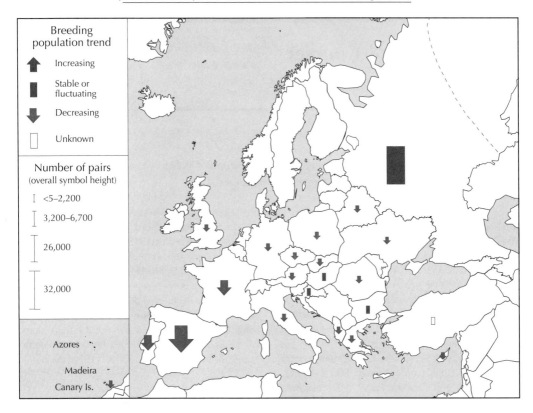

Breeding population trend

- Increasing
- Stable or fluctuating
- Decreasing
- Unknown

Number of pairs
(overall symbol height)

- <5–2,200
- 3,200–6,700
- 26,000
- 32,000

Azores

Madeira

Canary Is.

estry. An important region threatened by cultivation is the steppe lands of Spain (de Juana *et al.* 1988): three million hectares have already been destroyed through irrigation and conversion to cereals, and the government aims to extend this. Some Spanish steppes are subject to annual pesticide spraying during the Stone Curlew breeding season which kills practically all invertebrates present (Barros *et al.* 1990, Hellmich 1992a). Also, breeding success on arable land is affected by the destruction of eggs and chicks during mechanized farming operations, and traditional winter roosting sites can be subject to repeated disturbance.

Conservation measures

■ As a dispersed and migratory species the Stone Curlew requires large areas of habitat to maintain a viable population, and so depends on broad conservation measures aimed at maintaining dry grasslands and low-intensity arable farming.

Within the EU, opportunities to conserve dry grasslands and heaths exist under the Agri-environment Regulation (EC Reg. 2078/92) of the Common Agricultural Policy, which enables member states to introduce aid schemes supporting 'wildlife friendly' farming practices such as the maintenance of low-intensity grazing of existing dry grassland and the conversion of arable land back to dry grassland. Arable land taken out of production under the EU Set-aside Scheme (EC Reg. 1765/92) can also provide suitable habitat if plant cover is kept low and sparse by cultivation, mowing or grazing outside the breeding season.

At some sites, the viability of populations needs to be ensured by specific measures to protect young and eggs from egg-collectors and from damage by mechanized farming operations (Green 1988).

MELANIE HEATH

Cream-coloured Courser
Cursorius cursor

SPEC Category 3
Status Vulnerable
Criteria Large decline

The small European population of the Cream-coloured Courser is declining and mostly confined to the Canary Islands, though small numbers breed also in Turkey. Currently threatened by the destruction and degradation of habitat, it requires protection of its key sites as well as wide habitat conservation measures appropriate for semi-desert species.

■ Distribution and population trends

The Cream-coloured Courser has a fragmented distribution across North Africa (including the Canary Islands and the Cape Verde Islands) and south-west and central Asia. Presently there is little information on numbers present in Africa, and therefore it is difficult to estimate the percentage of the global population which breeds within Europe, although it is clearly marginal to the main range of the species and must be very small.

The majority of the European population occurs in the Canary Islands, on Lanzarote, Fuerteventura, Gran Canaria and Tenerife, with small numbers probably also occurring in south-east Turkey (see table, map). The maximum known population of the Canary Islands has been estimated at 250 pairs (see table), but this figure is probably lower than the actual number as no specific surveys have been carried out. Most previous observations have come from surveys of the Canarian race of Houbara Bustard *Chlamydotis undulata fuertaventurae*, which often did not cover suitable habitat for this species. Most birds occur on Fuerteventura, where the species is locally common on the plains, and it is frequently seen in Tindaya, Llanos de La Laguna and on the slopes of El Time. On Lanzarote the population is very small and is locally distributed, concentrated in the Llanos de La Mareta–Hoya de La Yegua and in Ancones–La Hondura. The species has been regularly observed on Gran Canaria (Bannerman 1963), but, although there have been some recent sightings in the south of the island (Rodríguez *et al.* 1987), these are probably of vagrants. Birds occur regularly

on Tenerife during winter and early spring, but breeding has never been proved (Martín 1987, Lorenzo and González 1993).

Bannerman (1963) reported a decline in the eastern islands of the archipelago during the first half of the twentieth century, up to 1960. In some areas of Fuerteventura declines in population size have been observed during the 1980s (K. W. Emmerson pers. comm.) and overall the population of the Canary Islands is considered to have declined considerably during the period between 1970 and 1990 (see table).

■ Ecology

The Cream-coloured Courser lives in semi-desert, sandy-rocky plains and sand-dunes, preferring areas with a sparse cover of herbaceous vegetation or low shrubs. Typically these habitats are dominated by *Frankenia* spp., *Salsola vermiculata*, *Launaea arborescens* and *Lycium intricatum*, together also with *Atriplex glauca*, *Aizoon canariense* and annual grasses. On Tenerife during the winter it occurs on sandy plains with a sparse vegetation cover of *Frankenia laevis*, *Polycarpaea nivea*, *Heliotropium ramossisimum* and *Launaea arborescens*; occasionally it has also been observed in fields of *Mesembryanthemum crystallinum* and *M. nodiflorum*.

■ Threats

In the past the eggs of Cream-coloured Courser were very heavily collected, which contributed to the rarity of the species (Bannerman 1963), but this activity has decreased substantially in recent times. Currently, the main conservation problem is the destruction and alteration of habitat, as many plains, especially those near the coast, are being destroyed through the construction of tourist resorts. Also, the building of new roads and off-road driving for recreation ('jeep safaris') are disturbing and destroying the habitats of the species.

Military exercises held in many areas of Fuerteventura lead to disturbance and habitat damage which affect Cream-coloured Coursers as well as many other species such as Houbara Bustard and

	Breeding population			Breeding
	Size (pairs)	Year	Trend	range trend
Spain				
Canary Islands	200–250	—	–2	–2
Turkey	(0–30)	—	—	—
Total (approx.)	200–280			

Trends (1970–1990): +2 Large increase, +1 Small increase, 0 Stable, X Extinct, –2 Large decrease, –1 Small decrease, F Fluctuating, N New breeder

Data quality: **Bold**: reliable quantitative data   Normal type: incomplete quantitative data   Bracketed figures: no quantitative data   * Data quality not provided

Black-bellied Sandgrouse *Pterocles orientalis* which share the same habitat.

■ Conservation measures

There is a requirement for further research, monitoring and population censuses to find out more about the population status, breeding success and habitat-use of this poorly known species. In particular, attention should be given to areas on Gran Canaria and Tenerife where the species appears regularly, but where the existence of a breeding population has never been established.

The most important areas for this species need to be protected and appropriately managed and should include sites on Lanzarote such as Jable de Famara (Important Bird Area or IBA 006), Llano de Las Honduras (IBA 007) and Llanos de la Mareta (IBA 009), as well as representative areas on Fuerteventura, including Llano de La Laguna (IBA 017), Tindaya and El Time. The majority of these areas also support other arid-habitat species of high conservation priority, such as Houbara Bustard, making their protection even more necessary. Indeed, many of the conservation measures necessary to safeguard Houbara Bustard populations would also benefit the Cream-coloured Coursers.

Many areas supporting Cream-coloured Coursers are protected at the regional level, and have been declared Natural Sites or Natural Parks, but in practice these are often poorly managed. Several sites are not adequately protected and are subject to ongoing activities that are detrimental to the birds.

JUAN ANTONIO LORENZO

Collared Pratincole
Glareola pratincola

SPEC Category 3
Status Endangered
Criteria Large decline, <10,000 pairs

Numbers have declined through most of the European range, particularly in the east. Habitat loss and degradation, the increased use of pesticides, and disturbance to colonies are the major threats. The conservation of important breeding colonies and of suitable habitat in the Sahel winter quarters is required.

■ Distribution and population trends

Collared Pratincole is patchily distributed across southern Europe, north-west Africa, Egypt and the Afrotropics, east to Kazakhstan, Iran and Pakistan. About a quarter to a half of the breeding range of the nominate (Palearctic) race lies within Europe. This race is migratory, wintering mainly on the southern edge of the Sahara, from Senegal to Ethiopia (Cramp and Simmons 1983).

Russia and Spain together hold up to 70% of the European breeding population, with Greece, Ukraine, Portugal, Romania and Turkey also supporting sizeable numbers (see table, map).

Since 1970 the species has declined in most countries within its European range, including Russia, amounting to up to c.75% of the population for which trends are known (see table, map). Only in Italy, Spain and Romania are numbers considered stable, although an apparent decline was earlier noted in Romania by Sterbetz (1974). The breeding range has also contracted in several countries (see table).

	Breeding population			Breeding
	Size (pairs)	Year	Trend	range trend
Albania	100–300	80	–1	(–1)
Bulgaria	25–50	—	–1	0
France	10–20	90	–2	0
Greece	500–1,000	—	(–1)	(–1)
Hungary	30–120	—	–2	–2
Italy	30–80	89	0	0
Portugal	250–1,000	89	–1	–1
Romania	(200–400)	—	(0)	0
Russia	(1,000–10,000)	75–90	(–1)	(0)
Spain	3,761–3,815	89	F	F
Turkey	(500–5,000)	—	—	—
Ukraine	280–420	84	–2	–2
Total (approx.)	6,700–22,000			

Trends   +2 Large increase   +1 Small increase   0 Stable   X Extinct
(1970–1990) –2 Large decrease   –1 Small decrease   F Fluctuating   N New breeder
Data quality **Bold**: reliable quantitative data   Normal type: incomplete quantitative data
Bracketed figures: no quantitative data   * Data quality not provided

■ Ecology

Breeding is colonial and occurs on steppe, semi-desert, fallow land with sparse or grazed vegetation, and late sown crops. Birds require dry, flat areas with sand or gravel soils, normally near water, with an ample supply of insects (Glutz von Blotzheim *et al.* 1977, Cramp and Simmons 1983, Calvo in press a). The northern populations occupy inland areas with halophytic vegetation, near saline rivers and salt-lakes (Glutz von Blotzheim *et al.* 1977), mainly on *Artemisia* steppe (Sterbetz 1974, Szabó 1975). Southern populations also breed among halophytic vegetation, though more typically alongside coastal or inland marshes, lagoons and rivers (Glutz von Blotzheim *et al.* 1977, Cramp and Simmons 1983, De Lope 1983, Joensen and Jerrentrup 1988, Dolz *et al.* 1990).

Birds feed within the breeding areas and also over open water, rice-fields, reedbeds and coastal Mediterranean scrub (Dolz *et al.* 1990), principally taking insects, especially beetles and grasshoppers, usually caught in flight (Cramp and Simmons 1983).

■ Threats

The loss and degradation of suitable habitat is an important reason for the decline of the species (Council of Europe 1981, Cramp and Simmons 1983). For example, the expansion and intensification of agriculture has led to drainage of wetlands, while flood-control measures and river canalization have caused the loss of riverside habitats. In such developments, areas with the peripheral halophytic vegetation that this species inhabits are among the first to be destroyed. Furthermore, in coastal Mediterranean areas the loss of habitat is accentuated by urban encroachment, particularly through tourist pressure.

The increase in the use of pesticides is believed to have contributed to the widespread decline of this and other insectivorous species (Council of Europe 1981, Cramp and Simmons 1983, Biber and Salathé 1991).   Also of concern is the poor breeding success in colonies located in areas with high levels of disturbance from agriculture and other sources (Dolz *et al.* 1990, Calvo in press a).

In large parts of the Sahel winter quarters, water-management programmes are dramatically changing the structure of the original habitat, and pesticide

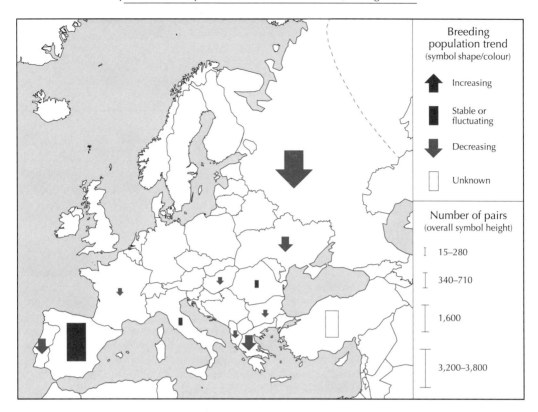

Breeding
population trend
(symbol shape/colour)

Increasing

Stable or
fluctuating

Decreasing

Unknown

Number of pairs
(overall symbol height)

15–280

340–710

1,600

3,200–3,800

use in newly planted rice-fields is decreasing their value for Palearctic migrants (Mullié *et al.* 1991).

■ Conservation measures

This migratory species requires the maintenance of suitable habitats throughout its European range and winter quarters. The protection of important colonies is clearly a priority, and where appropriate the creation of reserves may be necessary (Council of Europe 1981). Some colonies may also need measures to prevent disturbance from agricultural activity such as grazing and spraying, and in some cases a delay of just two weeks in the use of machinery may be enough to improve breeding success (Calvo in press b). Such measures could be supported in some areas of the EU by the new Agri-environment Regulation (EC Reg. 2078/92) of the Common Agricultural Policy, under which farmers would receive

financial support for adopting environmentally beneficial practices. Also, since new rice-cultivation schemes are often economically unviable, the Regulation may help to stop the conversion of land for this purpose and to promote habitat restoration where rice-farming has been abandoned on previously traditional breeding areas. Disturbance from leisure activities also needs to be minimized (Dolz *et al.* 1990).

It is necessary to obtain more information on the status of the European populations, especially in the east, and to establish their winter distribution. Further research is also needed to assess the impact of pesticides throughout the breeding and wintering range.

CARLES DOLZ

Black-winged Pratincole
Glareola nordmanni

SPEC Category 3
Status Rare
Criteria <10,000 pairs

The Black-winged Pratincole is a rare and locally declining species in Europe, threatened by the loss of steppe grassland and by the intensification of grazing on its remaining nesting grounds. An additional threat is predation by increasing numbers of corvids. Important conservation measures include the restriction of livestock-grazing at pratincole colonies, reductions in the conversion of natural steppe grassland to arable agriculture, and an assessment of the impact of predation.

■ Distribution and population trends

The Black-winged Pratincole breeds only in the Palearctic, chiefly in the steppe zone of central Eurasia. Roughly a third of its global breeding range lies within Europe, where it is mainly found in the Azov and Black Sea coastal zones of Ukraine, and in Russia along the Don and Manytsh valleys, near the Caspian lowlands. It also breeds sporadically in southern Belarus, Hungary, Romania and Armenia (Dementiev and Gladkov 1951c, Cramp and Simmons 1983; see table, map). The winter quarters lie in tropical Africa.

A conspicuous decline in breeding numbers in Romania and Ukraine started in the nineteenth century. This intensified during the 1950s (Dementiev and Gladkov 1951c, Molodan 1988), and between 1970 and 1990 the Ukrainian population almost became extinct (Molodan 1988, Chernichko *et al.* 1990, Molodan and Pozhidayeva 1991; see table, map). In contrast, in the area north of the Caucasus and in Kalmykia, numbers increased markedly during the second half of the twentieth century, reaching 5,000–7,000 pairs during the mid-1980s (Belik *et al.* in press), although by 1993 this population had stabilized or started to decline. The population to the east of the Volga river (thus lying outside Europe) appears to be fairly stable (V. N. Moseikin pers. comm.).

	Breeding population			Breeding
	Size (pairs)	Year	Trend	range trend
Belarus	**0–5**	90	N	N
Hungary	0–1	—	N*	0*
Romania	(0–10)	—	(–2)	(–1)
Russia	6,500–11,100	75–90	0	0
Ukraine	40–100	85	–2	–2
Total (approx.)	6,500–11,000			

Trends   +2 Large increase   +1 Small increase   0 Stable   X Extinct
(1970–1990) –2 Large decrease   –1 Small decrease   F Fluctuating   N New breeder
Data quality **Bold:** reliable quantitative data   Normal type: incomplete quantitative data
Bracketed figures: no quantitative data   * Data quality not provided

■ Ecology

This species usually breeds in loose colonies of two to 300 or more pairs, frequently with other waders or terns. Throughout its range it is highly dependent on saline (solonchaks) and alkaline (solonetz) steppe-like areas, situated in river valleys and along the shores of lakes or seas. It prefers drier sites than does Collared Pratincole *G. pratincola* (Kazakov *et al.* 1983, Molodan 1988), though it always deserts them if the water-bodies nearby dry up. The partial irrigation of dry steppes may help to raise Black-winged Pratincole numbers (Bulakhov 1968, Kukish 1990). For example, the creation of a network of canals in the Don and Manytsh river valleys as well as in the semi-desert Caspian lowlands is believed to have increased breeding numbers of the species (Kukish 1990, Belik *et al.* in press).

Nesting sites are selected for their low and sparse vegetation cover and birds may even breed on the bare earth of ploughed fields (Khrustov and Moseikin 1986, Molodan 1988). The diet consists of invertebrates, mostly insects (Dolgushin 1962).

■ Threats

As a colonial, ground-nesting, and highly conspicuous bird, the Black-winged Pratincole is a very vulnerable species. The main reason for its decline is the conversion of steppelands to arable agriculture. Colonies which subsequently nest in the cultivated fields are then destroyed during further agricultural operations, particularly by harrowing. The loss of steppe grassland has also led to increases in grazing pressure by livestock in areas of remaining natural steppe and, consequently, grazing can destroy up to 50% of clutches and over 30% of nestlings (Lysenko 1980, Sirenko 1980).

Breeding success has decreased recently, chiefly in the Ukrainian steppe (Molodan 1980), because of predation by increasing numbers of corvids, which thrive in the many shelter belts of trees planted during the twentieth century. Heavy rain and hail

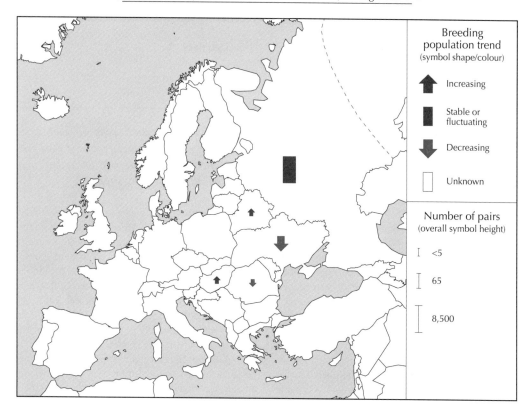

cause sporadic mass destruction of clutches (Minoranskiy 1967, Kostin 1983), and during drought years the birds regularly fail to breed (Solomatin 1973b).

■ Conservation measures

Black-winged Pratincole clearly requires full legal protection and recognition of its threatened status throughout its range. Breeding areas need to be identified and to be fully protected from conversion into arable agricultural land. Improvements in repro-ductive success may be achieved by the regulation of grazing at permanent colonies during the nesting period and by the construction of metal frames over the nests (G. Molodan pers. comm.). It is also necessary to modify agricultural operations on ploughed fields where birds have established breeding colonies (Khrustov and Moseikin 1986).

Research into the effects of predation on the pratincole by Rooks *Corvus frugilegus* is required, and it is possible that corvid numbers may need to be controlled locally.

VICTOR BELIK

Kentish Plover
Charadrius alexandrinus

SPEC Category 3
Status Declining
Criteria Moderate decline

The Kentish Plover is widespread and locally common in sandy coastal areas of south-east, southern and western Europe, but has declined markedly in most regions during recent decades. It is threatened by human disturbance, loss of habitat and locally by intense nest-predation, and consequently requires the protection and management of important breeding sites.

■ Distribution and population trends

The Kentish Plover is a widely distributed species with under a quarter of its global range in Europe where it breeds mainly in Mediterranean and Black Sea coastal areas, as well as along the western coasts as far north as south-west Sweden. It also occurs locally inland in Spain, Austria, Hungary, former Yugoslavia, Romania, Ukraine, southern Russia and Turkey. The largest breeding populations are in Spain, Ukraine, Russia and Turkey, totalling 15,000–36,000 pairs, while the total population of Fennoscandia and north-west Europe (western France northwards) is estimated at about only 1,000 pairs (see table, map).

Most European birds winter in coastal areas of the Mediterranean and along African coasts south to the Equator, with important populations in southern Spain, Sicily, Mauritania (Banc d'Arguin), north-west Morocco, Tunisia (Gulf of Gabès), Egypt (Nile Delta), southern Turkey and the Persian Gulf (Glutz von Blotzheim *et al.* 1975, Cramp and Simmons 1983, van der Have *et al.* 1988, Tinarelli 1993, Velasco and Alberto 1993). Populations of the Atlantic islands are mainly resident.

Population declines and contractions in breeding range have been reported from most regions where reliable quantitative data are available (see table, map), and the species has disappeared from many former breeding sites in north-west Europe during the last 10 years (Haftorn 1971, Glutz von Blotzheim *et al.* 1975, Sharrock 1976, Bauer and Thielcke 1982, Thibault 1983, Jönsson 1983, Christensen 1990a).

■ Ecology

In Europe the Kentish Plover breeds primarily along coasts on sand, shell banks or exposed dry mud by estuaries and saline or brackish lagoons. It also breeds on short-grazed, coastal meadows in Denmark and Sweden, on alkaline grasslands or in dried-up fish-ponds in Hungary and Austria, and on saltpans in the Mediterranean region. Birds frequently colonize new areas of coastal landfill, as, for instance, in the Wadden Sea (Rittinghaus 1961, Dybbro 1970, Cramp and Simmons 1983, Jönsson 1983, Dubois and Mahéo 1986, Spitzenberger 1988, Christensen 1990a, Szekely 1991, Hälterlein and Steinhardt 1993, Tinarelli 1993).

The nest consists of a bare or sparsely lined scrape on the ground. In suitable areas (especially if free of ground predators) it often breeds semi-colonially with locally dense populations.

Northern populations leave their breeding areas between July and September. Site-tenacity is generally strong, with adult return-rates of 75–90% in Swedish and German populations (Cramp and Simmons 1983, Jönsson 1983). However, birds (most

	Breeding population			Breeding range trend
	Size (pairs)	Year	Trend	
Albania	100–300	80	–1	(–1)
Austria	**20–25**	91	**–1**	**0**
Belgium	**55–60**	90	**–2**	**–1**
Bulgaria	50–100	—	–2	0
Croatia	100–200 *	—	0*	0*
Cyprus	20–60	—	F	0
Denmark	**18–31**	91	**–2**	**–2**
France	**1,115–1,160**	84	**0**	**0**
Germany	500–600	91	–1	0
Greece	500–1,000	—	(0)	(–1)
Hungary	100–150	—	–2	–2
Italy	(1,300–2,000)	89	(0)	(0)
Netherlands	**425–550**	89–91	**–2**	**–1**
Poland	**1–1**	—	**N**	**N***
Portugal	1,000–2,000	89	–1	–1
Azores	(100–150)	—	(–1)	(0)
Madeira	10–20	91	**0**	**0**
Romania	(400–800)	—	(–1)	–1
Russia	(1,000–10,000)	80–90	(0)	(0)
Slovenia	**40–60**	—	**0**	**0**
Spain	5,000–6,000	—	0	0
Canary Islands	**200–300**	91	**–1**	**–1**
Sweden	**8–8**	90	**–2**	**–1**
Turkey	(5,000–15,000)	—	—	—
Ukraine	4,000–5,000	85	–1	–1
United Kingdom				
Gibraltar	1–1	—	0	0*
Total (approx.)	21,000–46,000			

Trends (1970–1990) +2 Large increase +1 Small increase 0 Stable X Extinct
                     –2 Large decrease –1 Small decrease F Fluctuating N New breeder
Data quality **Bold**: reliable quantitative data Normal type: incomplete quantitative data
              Bracketed figures: no quantitative data * Data quality not provided

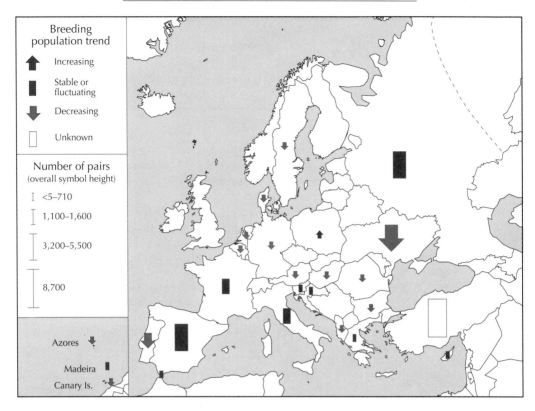

Breeding population trend

↑ Increasing

▮ Stable or fluctuating

↓ Decreasing

☐ Unknown

Number of pairs
(overall symbol height)

I <5–710

I 1,100–1,600

I 3,200–5,500

I 8,700

Azores ↓

Madeira ▮

Canary Is. ↓

often females) are also known to move long distances between two successive breeding attempts, e.g. more than 260 km from Sweden to Germany, within the same season (R. Schulz pers. comm.).

Food consists mainly of insects, crustaceans, worms and molluscs (Cramp and Simmons 1983).

▮ Threats

The main reason for the decline in north-west Europe is believed to be disturbance on the breeding grounds resulting from increased human usage of coastal areas (Dybbro 1980, Bauer and Thielcke 1982, Jönsson 1983, Meininger 1986, Schulz and Stock 1991). Many sandy beaches are exploited for tourism both in north-west and southern Europe, while other suitable breeding areas such as estuarine mudbanks are subjected to land-claim and used for industrial purposes. In Scandinavia, traditional grazing of coastal meadows has ceased in many places, resulting in the loss of suitable habitat for Kentish Plovers and other waders (Dybbro 1980, Jönsson 1983).

Intense nest-predation has been observed in several countries (Sweden, Denmark, Germany, France and Hungary: Jönsson 1989, Christensen 1990a, Schulz and Stock 1991, Szekely 1991), in some cases resulting in egg losses of up to 90% (south-west Sweden) (Christensen 1990a, Jönsson 1993). Most predation is by red fox *Vulpes vulpes*, Ameri-

can mink *Mustela vison*, Carrion Crow *Corvus corone* and gulls *Larus*.

▮ Conservation measures

To maintain the Kentish Plover as a widespread breeding bird in Europe, a large number of suitable breeding sites need to be protected from human disturbance during the breeding season. Management of traditionally grazed alkaline or saline grasslands should be improved where necessary, by grazing or cutting to keep the vegetation low, and predation should be reduced (e.g. by electric fencing around colonies), especially at vulnerable and important sites. The creation of new, predator-free breeding areas (artificial breeding islands) should be considered in relation to industrial or other exploitative activities in coastal areas (e.g. salt production).

Important stopover and wintering sites should also be protected, with restrictions on exploitation and hunting.

Monitoring of breeding and wintering populations at an international level should be initiated or enhanced in order to increase knowledge about the species' numbers and reproductive success and the threats facing it. In particular, further information is needed from certain countries in the Mediterranean and Black Sea regions.

PAUL E. JÖNSSON

Greater Sand Plover
Charadrius leschenaultii

SPEC Category 3
Status (Endangered)
Criteria <250 pairs

The numbers and population trends of Greater Sand Plover in Turkey are not well known, but it is probably a very rare breeding bird there, threatened by degradation of grassland steppe habitats and the loss of wetlands through drainage and water extraction for irrigation. Measures should be taken to conserve grassland steppes and nearby wetland habitats frequented by the species.

■ Distribution and population trends

The breeding range of the Greater Sand Plover extends from Turkey in the west, through central Asia, to Mongolia in the east, but it is very inadequately known. The subspecies *C. l. columbinus* breeds in the central plateau of Turkey and perhaps in Jordan, as well as in Afghanistan, Azerbaijan and Iran, and perhaps also locally elsewhere in the Middle East. The species is migratory, and *C. l. columbinus* probably winters mainly along the shores of the Red Sea and Gulf of Aden (Cramp and Simmons 1983); it seems likely that the birds wintering in the eastern Mediterranean (mainly Egypt) are also of this subspecies (D. Scott pers. comm.).

The occurrence of breeding in Turkey was not established until 1967, and about 100 pairs were estimated to be present in the early 1980s (Cramp and Simmons 1983). The present population probably lies between 100 and 1,000 pairs (DHKD pers. comm.), but it is likely that this rise in recorded breeding numbers is due to the better coverage of Turkey by ornithologists in recent years rather than to any real increase. The total world population of *C. l. columbinus* is unlikely to exceed 10,000 individuals (D. Scott pers. comm.), so Turkey holds an important proportion of the total population of the race.

	Breeding population			Breeding
	Size (pairs)	Year	Trend	range trend
Turkey	(100–1,000)	—	—	—
Total (approx.)	100–1,000			

Trends +2 Large increase +1 Small increase 0 Stable X Extinct
(1970-1990) -2 Large decrease -1 Small decrease F Fluctuating N New breeder
Data quality **Bold**: reliable quantitative data Normal type: incomplete quantitative data
Bracketed figures: no quantitative data * Data quality not provided

■ Ecology

During the breeding season in Europe, the Greater Sand Plover occurs mainly on the dry Anatolian plateau of central Turkey, up to at least 1,100 m. The breeding habitat comprises open sandflats, mudflats or heavily sheep-grazed steppe in the vicinity of

water, and sparsely covered with scattered low grasses and other low, salt-tolerant plants, mainly saltwort *Salsola* and wormwood *Artemisia*. During the breeding season the species feeds on insects, probably mainly beetles (Cramp and Simmons 1983).

Outside the breeding season Greater Sand Plovers are found predominantly on intertidal sand and mudflats, where they feed on marine invertebrates, especially worms and crustaceans.

■ Threats

The Turkish population of Greater Sand Plover is threatened by the destruction of breeding habitat; this is through the drainage of lakes and marshes and their conversion, together with bordering fallow steppe, to agricultural fields (e.g. Grimmett and Jones 1989). Whether widespread overgrazing of the Anatolian plateau by sheep has reduced the quality of the breeding habitat is not known.

Favoured migration staging posts, such as the Çukurova delta in southern Turkey, are under increasing pressure from hunting, tourism and industrial activities (e.g. van der Have *et al.* 1989), and are often polluted along the coasts with oil.

■ Conservation measures

The preservation of large areas of steppe habitat bordering wetlands in Turkey is needed to maintain viable breeding populations of Greater Sand Plovers. The maintenance of low-intensity sheep farming is also necessary at some sites to ensure the preferred vegetation structure for breeding.

Further drainage of Turkish wetland sites frequented by the species should be prevented. This includes Sultansazligi (Important Bird Area 030), Hotamis Sazligi (IBA 024), Eregli Sazligi (IBA 023), Karapinar Ovasi (IBA 025), Tuz Gölü (IBA 032), Kulu Gölü (IBA 027) and the whole of the Çukurova delta (IBA 050) (e.g. de Goeij *et al.* 1992, Grimmett and Jones 1989), and these sites should receive national protection.

GUIDO KEIJL

Caspian Plover
Charadrius asiaticus

SPEC Category 3
Status (Vulnerable)
Criteria Large decline

The Caspian Plover's small, marginal, poorly known and rapidly declining European breeding population is threatened mainly by loss of its desert steppe habitat through conversion to agriculture and overgrazing. Conservation measures should initially be directed towards the preservation of breeding habitat, with further studies on the species' population status and habitat requirements.

Distribution and population trends

The breeding range of the Caspian Plover lies in central Asia and marginally into Europe, extending from the Caspian Sea to the eastern side of Lake Balkhash in Kazakhstan. In the Kazakhstan, Turkestan and Uzbekistan region it is an unevenly distributed but locally common bird of clay and stone deserts. The small and scattered European population lies on the western edge of the global range in the lowlands north-west of the Caspian Sea.

Caspian Plovers are migratory, wintering in two main areas: in East Africa in the uplands of southwest Kenya and Tanzania, and further south in Botswana, Namibia and South Africa. The world population is poorly known but thought to be 10,000–100,000 birds (Rose and Scott 1994).

The species has been little studied, and there is virtually no information on the size of the European breeding population. It is known that within its European breeding range the species is rare and sporadic in occurrence (Cramp and Simmons 1983) and tends to move between breeding areas. V. Belik *in litt.* (1993) suggests that there may be 100–500 pairs in Europe, and that, although populations in the centre of the world range are stable or are decreasing only slightly, European birds on the edge of the range have declined considerably (see table).

	Breeding population			Breeding
	Size (pairs)	Year	Trend	range trend
Russia	100–500 *	—	(–2)	(–2)
Total (approx.)	100–500			

Trends (1970-1990): +2 Large increase +1 Small increase 0 Stable X Extinct –2 Large decrease –1 Small decrease F Fluctuating N New breeder
Data quality: **Bold**: reliable quantitative data   Normal type: incomplete quantitative data   Bracketed figures: no quantitative data   * Data quality not provided

Ecology

During the breeding season the birds are found in arid habitats, ranging from below sea-level in lowland desert and desert steppe up to altitudes of c.800 m and higher. Nesting birds favour habitats such as saltpans and tracts of saline soil, often subject to seasonal flooding and with sparse shrub vegetation which mostly comprises halophytic plant species (Cramp and Simmons 1983). Non-breeding birds gather in moister habitat, such as river banks or lakesides.

Caspian Plovers are predominantly insectivorous throughout the year, and the distribution of the species is thus probably related to the abundance of the insects on which it feeds.

Birds on migration and wintering are rarely seen near the coast but are mainly found inland, on open grasslands, gravel plains, semi-arid steppe and true desert (D. Scott pers. comm.), less frequently on bare cultivated and ploughed fields.

Threats

The major threat to Caspian Plovers is undoubtedly the destruction of natural steppe and grassland through overgrazing by domestic livestock and the conversion of such habitats into intensive agricultural land (D. Scott pers. comm.).

Since the European population is situated on the edge of its world range, conditions may well be suboptimal for the species within the region, making it particularly vulnerable to habitat change. It is therefore likely that a decline in the world population will be first detected in that part of the range which lies within Europe.

Conservation measures

The maintenance of large areas of suitable habitat is essential to ensure the viability of the Caspian Plover's population. The intensification of agriculture should be moderated within areas where the bird occurs as a breeder, and overgrazing should be avoided in both breeding and wintering areas. Furthermore, the establishment of desert steppe-land reserves should be considered.

Importantly, studies of the population ecology, the distribution, and the habitat and feeding requirements of the species are needed for a better understanding of its conservation needs.

GUIDO KEIJL

Spur-winged Plover
Hoplopterus spinosus

SPEC Category   3
Status   (Endangered)
Criteria   Large decline, <2,500 pairs

The population in Greece has declined rapidly, while trends in the European stronghold of Turkey are unknown. Wetland loss and alteration as well as predation by feral dogs and Yellow-legged Gulls are serious threats. Conservation measures required, particularly in Greece, include the restoration and legal delineation of protected areas.

■ Distribution and population trends

The Spur-winged Plover is resident chiefly in the Middle East and Afrotropics. Breeding occurs also in Greece, Cyprus and Turkey (see map, table), and the birds here are migratory, wintering within the species' main range to the south.

The largest European breeding population is in Turkey, especially in the coastal Marmara and Aegean regions, in the south of the country, and in central Anatolia (Kasparek 1992a). Greece also holds significant numbers, and breeding here may be long-established, although it was not proved until 1959 (Hennipman 1961). In Cyprus, a few pairs have bred irregularly at three different sites in recent years (M. Charalambides *in litt.* 1994).

Status and trends are well known for Greece and indicate a fall in numbers of over 70% between 1970 and 1993 (see table, map): 1970 (120–170 pairs: Bauer and Müller *in litt.*); 1981 (100–125 pairs: Jerrentrup 1982); 1993 (32–45 pairs: Jerrentrup 1993). The species formerly bred westwards to the delta plain of west Thessaloniki in central Macedonia (Makatsch 1962, 1969, Bauer *et al.* 1969), but during the last decade breeding has not been recorded west of the Nestos delta, the current main stronghold. Populations along the Thracian wetlands of Vistonis, Porto Lagos, Lake Mitrikou and the Evros delta have also declined seriously (H. Jerrentrup own data). No trend data are available for Turkey, although the species seems to be stable except in some areas around shallow lakes in central Anatolia where breeding varies according to water-levels (M. Kasparek *in litt.*). In contrast to the European situa-

tion are the strong increases reported in Israel and Egypt over the last 30 years (Bezzel 1985).

■ Ecology

In Europe the species does not breed at man-made wetlands such as rice-fields, dams, fish-ponds and sewage farms that are important habitats in Africa and southern Asia Minor, instead mainly utilizing natural and semi-natural habitats mostly on saline soils with halophytic vegetation and close to water. Open areas are preferred, to permit early awareness of approaching danger (Cramp and Simmons 1983). In Greece the species is found only at large coastal wetlands, in three main habitats: medium-dry saltmarsh along lagoons on more or less open ground, between the zone of *Salicornia europaea* (wet) and *Juncus acutus/J. marinus* (seasonally dry), often close to or among *Arthrocnemum radicans* shrubs; coastal sand-dunes; and sandy islands with sparse grass in the last 2–3 km of river mouths (e.g. Nestos delta) (Jerrentrup 1982, 1986, 1993). Similar areas are preferred in Turkey (Cramp and Simmons 1983, M. Kasparek *in litt.* 1994). In Cyprus breeding takes place in marshy areas, close to reedbeds in the Phasouri area, close to the shore of Lake Achna and at Lake Paralimni (M. Charalambides *in litt.* 1994).

The species feeds in the vicinity of its nesting sites, but generally in wetter areas. The chicks are fed mainly insects (various families of beetles) and other arthropods, especially spiders and myriapods (Glutz von Blotzheim *et al.* 1975).

■ Threats

The main threat throughout the European range is loss of natural and semi-natural wetlands, especially saltmarshes. This has followed drainage and land-claim (e.g. for new rice-fields), earth-works for intensifying lagoon fisheries, rubbish-dumping, and road-building (e.g. Jerrentrup 1982). During the twentieth century 73% of all wetlands in Macedonia (Greece) have been drained (Psilovikos 1992).

Intensive grazing often leads to the repeated loss of clutches from trampling. Many eggs and chicks

| | Breeding population | | | Breeding |
	Size (pairs)	Year	Trend	range trend
Cyprus	1–3	—	N	0
Greece	**32–45**	93	–2	–1
Turkey	(1,000–5,000)	—	—	—
Total (approx.)	1,000–5,000			

Trends	+2 Large increase	+1 Small increase	0 Stable	X Extinct
(1970–1990)	–2 Large decrease	–1 Small decrease	F Fluctuating	N New breeder
Data quality	**Bold**: reliable quantitative data	Normal type: incomplete quantitative data		
	Bracketed figures: no quantitative data	* Data quality not provided		

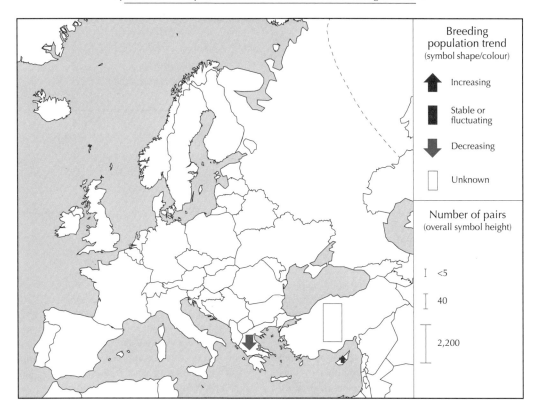

Breeding
population trend
(symbol shape/colour)

Increasing

Stable or
fluctuating

Decreasing

Unknown

Number of pairs
(overall symbol height)

<5

40

2,200

are taken by feral dogs, jackals *Canis aureus* and Yellow-legged Gulls *Larus cachinnans* (whose numbers have risen with the increasing amounts of rubbish), with up to 25% losses recorded (H. Jerrentrup own data). Tourist activities on beaches, especially off-road driving, cause further loss of nests, much disturbance and habitat degradation. The lack of any enforcement of conservation measures and the absence of legally established boundaries for most Ramsar Sites (designated under the Ramsar Convention) and Special Protection Areas (SPAs, designated under the EU Wild Birds Directive) partly explain the serious loss and deterioration of Greek wetlands (Jerrentrup 1986, Jerrentrup *et al.* 1988).

Illegal shooting is of minor significance in Greece, but may be much more serious in Turkey. The impact of increased pesticide use around the wetlands is not known.

■ Conservation measures

In Greece all breeding areas are Ramsar Sites and SPAs, and in Turkey most of the important sites are Important Bird Areas (IBAs). The major action required in Greece is immediate legal enforcement of boundaries for all Ramsar Sites and SPAs, full protection of these sites, and cessation of any further habitat loss. Integrated conservation and management authorities, with the collaboration of local and

international NGOs, should be created and equipped with the necessary authority, personnel and means to protect these areas effectively (Anon. 1986, Malakou *et al.* 1988, Tsimbos 1988). Former breeding grounds in Greece should also be restored, e.g. in the Evros and Nestos deltas (IBAs 001 and 007: Jerrentrup *et al.* 1988). In Turkey a new IBA inventory is under way and this should be followed by the development of a national wetland conservation strategy.

Lower livestock densities in marshes and on dunes would improve breeding success. A reduction in the number of rubbish dumps and their better management is also important to cut numbers of stray dogs and gulls, and additional control measures may be necessary (Walmsley 1989). Tourist activities must be controlled at coastal sites, and the wardening of key breeding areas seems to be necessary in northeast Greece and perhaps in some areas in Turkey.

In all three countries, careful monitoring is proposed in order to further research into the breeding ecology and conservation requirements. Other species, including Black-winged Stilt *Himantopus himantopus*, Avocet *Recurvirostra avosetta*, Stone Curlew *Burhinus oedicnemus*, Collared Pratincole *Glareola pratincola* and Kentish Plover *Charadrius alexandrinus*, will profit directly from the conservation measures proposed for Spur-winged Plover (Jerrentrup 1992).

Hans Jerrentrup

Sociable Plover
Chettusia gregaria

SPEC Category   1
Status   Endangered
Criteria   Large decline, <2,500 pairs

The globally threatened Sociable Plover is rare and declining in Europe due mainly to the conversion of grass steppes into arable agriculture and the consequent increase in grazing pressure on remaining grasslands. Areas of natural steppe in Europe need to be conserved, and breeding colonies must be protected from disturbance, trampling by cattle, excessive predation by Rooks, and destruction by agricultural machinery.

■ Distribution and population trends

The Sociable Plover breeds in Russia and Kazakhstan, the small numbers occurring within Europe occupying the steppes between the Volga and the Ural rivers (Khrustov and Moseikin 1986, Ilyichev and Fomin 1988, Davygora *et al.* 1989). Birds winter in desert regions from Israel and north-east Africa to north-west India (e.g. Kasparek 1992b).

In the nineteenth century, the species had a more westerly breeding distribution, extending across the steppe to the Dniepr river (Ukraine) and the Crimea (Dementiev and Gladkov 1951c, Kistiakovskiy 1957, Kozlova 1961). It was also common in the Volga region (Volga Land–Povolzhye) (Samorodov 1982) and, up to the mid-twentieth century, occurred in the Kalmykia region, west of the Volga river. In northern Kazakhstan numbers fell dramatically, by 40%, between 1930 and 1960 (Riabov 1982) after which they further halved by 1987 (Gordienko 1991).

An estimated 2,000 pairs currently breed in the Orenburg region beyond the Ural river (in Asia), the average density being one pair per 10–20 km² of steppe habitat (Davygora *et al.* 1989). Birds occur in similar densities between the Ural and Volga rivers in western Kazakhstan (Shevchenko and Debelo 1991), but, in the semi-desert areas alongside the lower Volga river in Russia, the species is now considered to be very rare, although there are no density estimates available (Chernobay 1992, V. N. Moseikin pers. comm.). Overall the species is considered to have declined over the 1970–1990 period to no more than 2,100 pairs in Europe.

Due to the rapid declines which the species has experienced in both Europe and Asia, it is listed as Globally Threatened (Collar *et al.* 1994).

■ Ecology

The Sociable Plover breeds in loose colonies of 2–30 pairs, with nests generally 20–50 m apart, often in association with other waders such as Collared Pratincole *Glareola pratincola*. The breeding habitat lies mainly in the transition zones between *Stipa* and *Artemisia* steppes with bare saline patches and near water-bodies. In steppes dominated by tall grasses the Sociable Plover settles in heavily grazed areas near villages (Cramp and Simmons 1983, Gordienko 1991). Sandy areas are avoided, but recently it has bred in ploughed fields that show similar features to natural bare-ground sites (Khrustov and Moseikin 1986, Ilyichev and Fomin 1988).

The diet consists almost entirely of insects such as grasshoppers (Orthoptera), beetles (Coleoptera) and the larvae of moths (Lepidoptera), which are taken on the ground.

■ Threats

This conspicuous ground-nesting species is vulnerable to predation and human disturbance, but is chiefly threatened by the transformation of grassland steppe habitats into arable agriculture, which has also resulted in increased grazing pressure in the remaining patches of suitable habitat. According to Gordienko (1991) about half of Sociable Plover nests which are located in heavily grazed areas perish through trampling by livestock, and many colonies established in farmland areas are destroyed during agricultural operations (Khrustov and Moseikin 1986) or are predated by Rooks *Corvus frugilegus*, which have increased considerably in these regions (Gordienko 1991).

In some areas the decline of the Sociable Plover cannot be explained, and it is possible that an increasingly dry climate during the twentieth century, both on the breeding grounds and in the winter

	Breeding population			Breeding range trend
	Size (pairs)	Year	Trend	
Russia	1,000–2,100	—	–1	–1
Total (approx.)	1,000–2,100			

Trends   +2 Large increase   +1 Small increase   0 Stable   X Extinct
(1970-1990) –2 Large decrease   –1 Small decrease   F Fluctuating   N New breeder
Data quality **Bold**: reliable quantitative data   Normal type: incomplete quantitative data
Bracketed figures: no quantitative data   * Data quality not provided

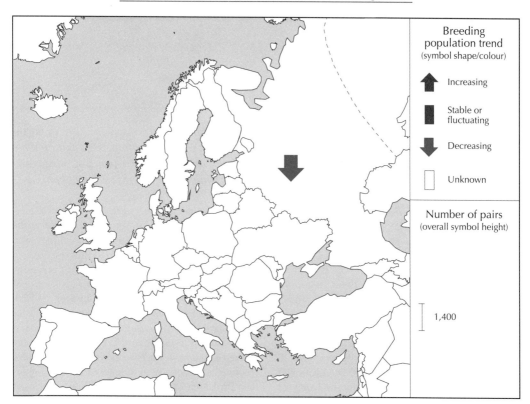

Breeding
population trend
(symbol shape/colour)

Increasing

Stable or
fluctuating

Decreasing

Unknown

Number of pairs
(overall symbol height)

1,400

quarters, may have contributed to the decline of the species (Solomatin 1973a).

■ Conservation measures

The protection of grassland steppe from conversion into arable agriculture is necessary to prevent the further decline of this species, and livestock numbers need to be regulated to manage the impact of grazing. Marginal agricultural areas are likely to come out of production in the near future and could be managed to recreate breeding habitat for Sociable Plovers.

Adequate protection of the species' breeding sites is hindered by its sporadic and irregular pattern of breeding. Each year the breeding colonies which move need to be found again, and management undertaken during the nesting period to prevent human disturbance, grazing and agricultural operations. Additionally, at regular nesting sites it may prove necessary to reduce Rook numbers.

VICTOR BELIK

Knot
Calidris canutus

SPEC Category 3, winter
Status Localized
Criteria Localized

European wintering populations from Greenland and Canada concentrate at a few sites in north-west Europe and almost all Siberian breeders stop off at the Wadden Sea in spring and autumn. Protection and management of these sites as part of an international flyway network of coastal and estuarine sites with abundant mollusc food is therefore essential to safeguard these populations.

■ Distribution and population trends

Knots are highly migratory high-Arctic breeders, with over two-thirds of the world population occurring in Europe for part of the year (Piersma and Davidson 1992). European winterers breed mostly in Canada, and about 15% in Greenland (Meltofte 1985). Almost all pass through Iceland in autumn, and through Iceland and northern Norway (Porsangerfjord and Balsfjord) in spring, wintering almost wholly on a few large estuaries in the United Kingdom and southern North Sea (Germany and Netherlands), south to western France (Dick *et al.* 1976, Davidson and Wilson 1992). Siberian breeders almost all stop off at the Wadden Sea in spring and autumn, wintering mainly in West Africa (Piersma *et al.* 1992).

A major drop in European winter numbers in the 1970s, attributed to a series of summers with severe weather in the Arctic (Boyd 1992), was followed by a slow increase through the 1980s. However, numbers in the 1990s remain about 40% lower than the early 1970s; Smit and Piersma (1989) gave a European total of 345,000 birds. The 1970s decline was greatest in France and the Republic of Ireland, distribution then being concentrated more at the Wadden Sea and British estuaries. Since the mid-1980s United Kingdom winter numbers have risen by over a quarter, apparently through further redistribution from the Netherlands and Germany, since the total European population seems to have changed little.

By 1993 almost 90% of birds wintering in Europe were in Britain. Here, the Wash alone contains over half the European winter total (in the early 1990s), with the Ribble, Humber, Thames, Alt and Dee estuaries and Morecambe Bay also supporting major populations (see Important Bird Area table). In the United Kingdom in recent years winter numbers have declined substantially in Strangford Lough (Important Bird Area 252) but the Upper Solway Flats and Marshes (IBA 133) have become more important.

Important Bird Areas The top ten IBAs for wintering Knots in Europe, together holding over 90% of the total European wintering population.

Netherlands	001	Waddenzee
	050	Oosterschelde
United Kingdom	135	Morecambe Bay
	139	Ribble and Alt Estuaries
	157	Humber Flats, Marshes and Coast
	164	The Wash
	176	Blackwater, Colne and Dengie
	206	South Thames Marshes
	210	Dee Estuary
	252	Strangford Lough and Islands

■ Ecology

Knots breed on dry tundra (Meltofte 1985) but are otherwise exclusively coastal, mostly restricted to extensive tidal flats, often predominantly of muddy sand, where they feed in large, dense flocks (Piersma and Davidson 1992). In Icelandic and Norwegian staging areas weed-covered boulder shores are also used (Davidson and Evans 1986, Alerstam *et al.* 1992). Outside the breeding season, Knots feed mainly on molluscs (Prater 1972, Goss-Custard *et al.* 1977, Alerstam *et al.* 1992). Abundant food is known to be essential for the birds to achieve successful migration and breeding (Morrison and Davidson 1990, de Goeij *et al.* in prep.).

	Winter population			Winter
	Size (individuals)	Year	Trend	range trend
Belgium	**0–200**	89–90	F	**0**
Bulgaria	0–5	77–91	0	0
Denmark	**0–10,800**	80–91	—	—
France	**17,500–17,500**	90	–2	0
Germany	**5–21,900**	80–91	—	—
Greece	40–? *	89		—
Rep. of Ireland	25,000–50,000	—	–1	—
Italy	(10)–?	84	**0**	**0**
Netherlands	**19,700–63,700**	80–91	F	**0**
Portugal	**500–1,500**	91	F	F
Spain	**300–1,679**	—	–1	—
Canary Islands	5–20	—	F	**0**
United Kingdom	**250,000–300,000**	88	F	**0**
Isle of Man[1]	**0–15**	—	F	0*
Total (min., approx.) 310,000				

Trends	+2 Large increase	+1 Small increase	0 Stable	X Extinct	
(1970-1990)	–2 Large decrease	–1 Small decrease	F Fluctuating	N New breeder	
Data quality	**Bold**: reliable quantitative data		Normal type: incomplete quantitative data		
	Bracketed figures: no quantitative data		* Data quality not provided		

[1] Population figures are included within United Kingdom totals

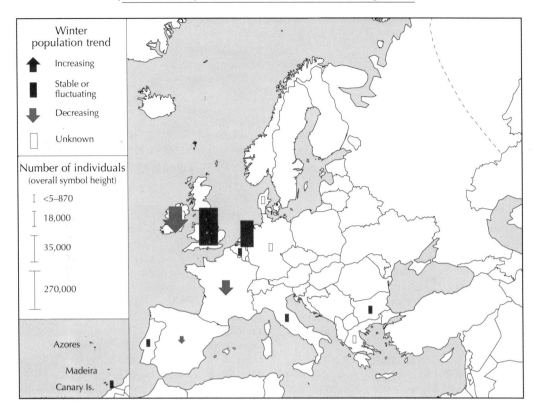

Winter population trend

- ▲ Increasing
- ■ Stable or fluctuating
- ▼ Decreasing
- ☐ Unknown

Number of individuals (overall symbol height)
- <5–870
- 18,000
- 35,000
- 270,000

Azores

Madeira

Canary Is.

■ Threats

The concentration at very few estuaries makes the Knot highly vulnerable to a range of widespread threats affecting European estuaries, notably loss and degradation of intertidal habitat through land-claim and barrage construction, and locally to rising sea-levels and erosion (Davidson *et al.* 1991). All reduce shore width and often alter sediment characteristics.

Reduction in food availability can reduce the ability of the birds to accumulate sufficient energy reserves in time to reach breeding grounds. The recent redistribution of Knots to Britain appears linked to major declines in shellfish stocks in the Wadden Sea, at least partly due to human overexploitation leading to direct reduction of food supply and indirectly to alterations in sediment character which reduce prey availability (T. Piersma pers. comm.).

Disturbance outside the breeding season from recreational activities and overflying aircraft reduces the size of areas available for foraging and increases energy use (Davidson and Rothwell 1993, Koolhaas *et al.* 1993, Kirby *et al.* 1993). Major changes in roost sites on the Dee estuary, now involving birds in feeding flights of over 20 km, have been attributed to heavy recreational pressure (Mitchell *et al.* 1988).

■ Conservation measures

An essential conservation measure is the safeguard of the network of estuaries and bays used by Knots as moulting, wintering and staging sites. Such sites need to be protected and managed to prevent further habitat losses, to minimize excessive depletion of food stocks and to avoid disturbance. The network must include sites used irregularly as emergency staging sites and cold weather refuges, and must provide sufficient alternative feeding grounds for birds forced to move by the failure of food stocks.

Almost all the European Knot population from late autumn to early spring occurs on estuaries designated or proposed (partly or wholly) as Ramsar Sites (Davidson and Piersma 1992), and many are also Special Protection Areas under the EU Wild Birds Directive. However, there is little protection for staging sites used in late spring and early autumn.

In Norway, Stabbursneset (IBA 010) and Sørkjosen (IBA 017) cover parts of the late spring staging areas, and at least nine IBAs in Iceland cover parts of the spring and autumn staging areas, notably Stokkseyri (IBA 012), Laxárvogur (IBA 021), Löngufjördur (IBA 026) and Breidafjördur (IBA 028).

Integrated management of the coastal zone, based on sustainable resource use, can contribute to network maintenance, and the development of an international flyway conservation plan for Knots would help set the agenda for future action. Conserving the dispersed breeding population requires broad ecosystem safeguard measures for Arctic tundra.

NICK DAVIDSON

Dunlin
Calidris alpina

SPEC Category 3, winter
Status Vulnerable
Criteria Large decline

Although a widespread wader, with stable breeding populations in northern temperate and Arctic latitudes, numbers wintering in Europe have declined considerably since 1970. The species is restricted to a relatively small number of estuaries outside the breeding season making it vulnerable to changes in this restricted habitat.

■ Distribution and population trends

The Dunlin is circumpolar in distribution, breeding in northern temperate and Arctic latitudes. Three races occur in Europe: *arctica*, breeding in north-east Greenland and wintering in Africa; *schinzii*, which breeds in south-east Greenland, Iceland, United Kingdom and the Baltic region, wintering primarily in southern Europe and Africa; and nominate *alpina*, which breeds across Scandinavia and Russia and winters in western Europe.

The main European breeding concentrations are in Iceland and Russia, which together hold over three-quarters of European birds (EBD 1994). Elsewhere, breeding populations in temperate latitudes have been declining (e.g. United Kingdom, Finland,

Denmark, Estonia), and in several countries (e.g. Finland, Denmark), the range is also contracting. This is especially true for the small population of *schinzii* breeding on coastal marshes around the Baltic, which have declined alarmingly in recent years (Jönsson 1988).

In winter, Dunlin are concentrated on west European coasts, notably in the Republic of Ireland, United Kingdom, France and Netherlands (see table, map). Substantial declines have been noted in France between 1970 and 1990—and in the United Kingdom, which has been closely monitored since 1970, numbers have also fallen, the population index for January 1987 being 55% of that in 1973; numbers have gradually recovered since then but are still below those of the early 1970s (Kirby *et al.* 1991).

■ Ecology

Damp or boggy habitat is required for breeding. In the north temperate zone birds often breed on saltmarshes and coastal meadows, and in the United Kingdom also on wet upland moors. Arctic breeding habitat is tussock tundra or peat-hummock tundra (Cramp and Simmons 1983). During migration the majority of adults stop off at coastal sites within Europe, while juveniles occur more often on inland muddy areas such as sewage works and river banks.

In winter, the vast majority of Dunlin concentrate at a relatively small number of large estuaries, where they prefer muddy to sandy substrates. Within Britain, for example, just nine sites hold over half the wintering population (Kirby *et al.* 1991).

■ Threats

The concentration of birds at a few key estuaries in winter makes them extremely vulnerable (Davidson *et al.* 1991). These large sites are under considerable pressures from land-claim, and in south-west England there is estimated to be little scope for Dunlin to be accommodated if there are further large-scale developments on estuaries (Clark 1989). Decreases in wintering numbers in the United Kingdom are closely correlated with the spread of *Spartina anglica*

	Winter population			Winter
	Size (individuals)	Year	Trend	range trend
Belgium	**2,000–2,500**	89–90	–2	0
Bulgaria	100–1,000	77–91	0	0
Cyprus	100–2,000	—	0	0
Czech Republic	0–10 *	—	—	—
Denmark	**0–56,500**	80–91	—	—
Faroe Islands	(0–10)	92	(F)	(0)
France	**240,000–240,000**	89	–2	0
Germany	**2,800–165,000**	80–91	—	—
Greece	**5,000–20,000**	87–91	0	0
Rep. of Ireland	100,000–150,000	—	—	—
Italy	15,500–20,000	84	0	0
Netherlands	**17,500–103,000**	80–91	F	**0**
Norway	P	—	—	—
Poland	10–50 *	—	—	—
Portugal	30,000–70,000	91	–1	**0**
Romania	500–2,000	—	+1	(+1)
Russia	(0–5,000)	—	(F)	(F)
Slovenia	0–5	—	F	0
Spain	**30,000–?**	—	F	—
Canary Islands	300–300	—	F	0
Switzerland	5–30	—	F	0
Turkey	(5,000–5,000)	—	—	—
United Kingdom	**583,000–600,000**	89	–1	**0**
Guernsey	1,000–3,000	—	—	—
Jersey	**2,000–3,000**	—	0	**0**
Isle of Man[1]	**100–250**	—	F	0*
Total (min.)	c.1,000,000			

Trends +2 Large increase +1 Small increase 0 Stable X Extinct
(1970–1990) –2 Large decrease –1 Small decrease F Fluctuating N New breeder
Data quality **Bold**: reliable quantitative data Normal type: incomplete quantitative data
Bracketed figures: no quantitative data * Data quality not provided
[1] Population figures are included within United Kingdom totals P Present

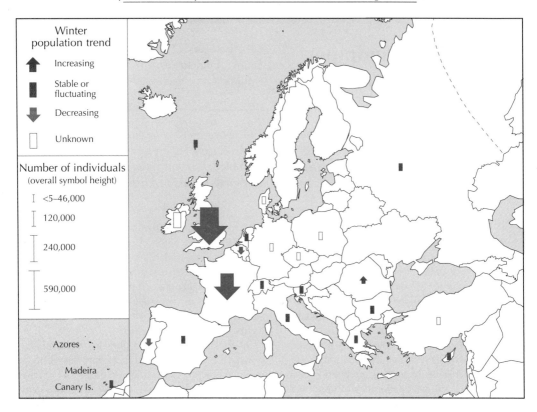

Winter
population trend

▲ Increasing

■ Stable or
fluctuating

▼ Decreasing

☐ Unknown

Number of individuals
(overall symbol height)

I <5–46,000

I 120,000

I 240,000

I 590,000

Azores

Madeira

Canary Is.

on upper mudflats and estuaries and the consequent reduction in feeding areas. Further spread of *Spartina* may have considerable impacts on Dunlin populations (Goss-Custard and Moser 1988).

Populations are also under potential threat from large-scale pollution incidents which could occur within estuaries. The nominate race is particularly vulnerable in the spring when large numbers concentrate in the northern Waddenzee prior to migration (Smit and Wolff 1981). In spring, a high proportion of the races *schinzii* and *arctica* stop off for short periods on the estuaries of the Irish Sea to fatten up (Prater 1981).

The most threatened breeding population is that of *schinzii* in Britain and around the Baltic. Here, changes in land-use, particularly the drainage of coastal marshes, intensification of farming methods and abandonment of grazing land, have caused or are likely to cause losses in breeding habitat. In Scotland, increasing afforestation of moorland has al-

ready produced a 17% decline in the Dunlin population of Caithness and Sutherland (Stroud *et al.* 1987).

■ Conservation measures

The maintenance of a network of estuarine sites for Dunlin populations outside the breeding season is essential for their survival. There is thus a need for the Waddenzee and important migration sites in the Irish Sea to be adequately protected, in addition to the wintering areas in the Republic of Ireland, United Kingdom, France and Netherlands. Many of these areas are already designated as Special Protection Areas in accordance with the EU Wild Birds Directive or as Ramsar Sites under the Ramsar Convention.

Coastal breeding sites around the Baltic are confined to wet meadows. Many of these sites are already afforded some protection, although drainage and intensification of farming practices should be avoided.

Nigel A. Clark

263

Broad-billed Sandpiper
Limicola falcinellus

SPEC Category 3
Status (Vulnerable)
Criteria Large decline

The Broad-billed Sandpiper is a poorly known and secretive breeder in inaccessible wet fens of northern Fennoscandia and eastern Europe. Although perhaps not at present seriously threatened, it is probably declining in its European stronghold of Finland. Wet fens should be preserved and its habitat requirements in both breeding and wintering grounds should be further studied in order to assess conservation requirements.

■ Distribution and population trends

The Broad-billed Sandpiper's breeding range is confined to Fennoscandia and Russia, though outside Europe the limits of the breeding range are virtually unknown (Cramp and Simmons 1983). However, on the basis of winter counts and estimates by Rose and Scott (1994) the European population is probably less than half of the global total.

Within Europe the Broad-billed Sandpiper breeds in northern Fennoscandia, including south-east Norway, northern Sweden, central and northern Finland and the Karelia and Kola peninsulas of north-west Russia. Further east the distribution is very poorly known, in part due to the secretive nature of the species and the difficulty of access to its boggy habitat. It is perhaps fairly widely distributed across northernmost Russia, but the number of known breeding localities is small. Overall, the breeding range of the Broad-billed Sandpiper is one of the least known of all European breeding birds.

European birds winter along coasts from the Arabian peninsula and East Africa to western India, and possibly in the eastern Mediterranean; the Siberian population winters east to south-east Asia, Indonesia and Australia (Cramp and Simmons 1983, Perennou and Mundkur 1991). The Azov–Black Sea region is an important staging area (P. S. Tomkovich pers. comm.).

About two-thirds of the European numbers breed in Finland, mainly in southern and central Lapland, though the distribution also extends to the alpine birch *Betula* zone in the north and to barren watershed areas dominated by open, wet peatlands in the south (Koskimies 1989). Almost a third of the population breeds in Sweden, and there are a few hundred pairs in Norway. Actual numbers in Russia may be many times higher than estimated (see table), and in fact all figures are uncertain because of the inaccessibility of wet peatlands and the species' skulking habits.

In Finland, the species probably declined between 1970 and 1990, and there may have been a range contraction associated with this. However, the species is so badly monitored—indeed no long-term trends are known in Finland (Koskimies 1989)—that recent trends are uncertain. Populations in Norway, Sweden and Russia are also poorly known although they appear to be stable (see table, map).

■ Ecology

The ecological requirements of this species are poorly understood. Dementiev and Gladkov (1951c) give its habitat in Russia as swampy hillocky marshes but state that details are unknown. In Finland the Broad-billed Sandpiper breeds in the middle of extensive, wet fens, often in loose colonies, with local densities of up to 20 pairs/km^2 (Koskimies 1989). The basic requirements seem to be small, muddy patches of water surrounded by thin peat, lightly overgrown with sedges *Carex* and dotted with half-floating tufts of cotton-grass *Eriophorum* and bog rosemary *Andromeda polifolia* (Cramp and Simmons 1983). The species breeds only in subarctic, montane and lowland zones, usually above 200 m, and probably in similar habitats throughout its range. The Broad-billed Sandpiper feeds in muddy and wet areas, with a diet consisting of invertebrates (mainly insects and small crustaceans) and seeds.

■ Threats

Potential threats to the Broad-billed Sandpiper are drainage or flooding of breeding habitats—although much habitat which is suitable for the species is probably too wet for afforestation, and may there-

| | Breeding population | | | Breeding |
	Size (pairs)	Year	Trend	range trend
Finland	(10,000–15,000)	92	(–1)	(–1)
Norway	200–1,000	90	0	**0**
Russia	(100–1,000)	70–90	(0)	(0)
Sweden	3,000–5,000	87	0	0
Total (approx.)	13,000–22,000			

Trends   +2 Large increase   +1 Small increase   0 Stable   X Extinct
(1970–1990)   –2 Large decrease   –1 Small decrease   F Fluctuating   N New breeder
Data quality   **Bold**: reliable quantitative data   Normal type: incomplete quantitative data
Bracketed figures: no quantitative data   * Data quality not provided

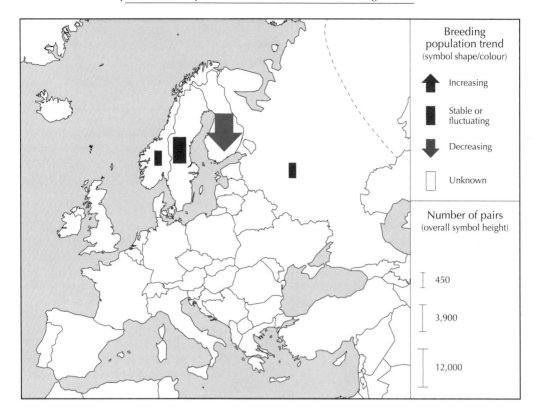

**Breeding
population trend**
(symbol shape/colour)

Increasing

Stable or
fluctuating

Decreasing

Unknown

Number of pairs
(overall symbol height)

450

3,900

12,000

fore remain safe. In Finland some of the best peatland areas have been flooded to create artificial lakes, but overall there do not seem to be any large-scale threats to the species or its breeding habitats which will have a significant impact in the near future.

No specific threats are known, either, to affect birds on migration, but drainage of wet meadows and other wetlands may destroy suitable habitats.

■ Conservation measures

Poor knowledge of the Broad-billed Sandpiper, especially on the wintering grounds, makes it difficult to plan any precise conservation measures covering the whole annual cycle. The most important conservation action within the breeding range is the preservation of wet fens. They should remain in as natural a state as possible, and as such need no management.

Census and monitoring programmes are also needed for reliable assessment of the species' distribution, population size and trends. The species' habitat requirements on the breeding grounds and in the winter quarters should also be further studied in order to assess more accurately the conservation requirements of the species.

PERTTI KOSKIMIES

Jack Snipe
Lymnocryptes minimus

SPEC Category 3, winter
Status (Vulnerable)
Criteria Large decline

This very poorly known crepuscular species is believed to have declined in its breeding areas during the twentieth century, primarily due to the loss and deterioration of habitat. Although breeding numbers may now have stabilized, some large winter populations declined between 1970 and 1990, probably through further habitat loss such as wetland drainage and associated agricultural intensification.

■ Distribution and population trends

The Jack Snipe breeds in boreal and sub-boreal zones from north-east Europe to eastern Siberia. Russia and northern Fennoscandia are the core breeding areas, with small isolated populations in southern Sweden, northern Poland, northern Belarus and the Baltic states (Okulewicz and Witkowski 1979, Nikiforov *et al.* 1989, Pedersen 1990, 1992) which are probably relics of a former more south-westerly distribution in the nineteenth century.

	Winter population			Winter
	Size (individuals)	Year	Trend	range trend
Austria	(0–2)	—	(F)	(0)
Belarus	(0–50)	90	F	F
Belgium	1–100	89–90	0	0
Czech Republic	0–2*	—	—	—
Denmark	(10,000–15,000)	—	(–1)	—
Faroe Islands	(1–50)	92	(0)	(0)
Estonia	0–10	—	0	0
Finland	0–50	92	0	0
France	(1,000–10,000)	—	—	—
Germany	(100–1,000)	—	—	—
Greece	(0–100)	—	(–2)	(–2)
Rep. of Ireland	(20,000–25,000)	—	—	—
Italy	(1,000–10,000)	—	(0)	(0)
Latvia	(0–10)	—	(F)	(F)
Netherlands	100–500	79–83	(F)	F
Poland	0–5*	—	—	—
Portugal	(10–100)	91	(0)	(0)
Romania	(0–100)	—	(0)	(0)
Russia	(0–5,000)	—	(F)	(F)
Slovakia	(5–20)	—	(0)	0
Slovenia	(5–20)	—	(F)	(0)
Spain	2,000–4,000	—	—	—
Canary Islands	(1–5)	—	(–1)	(0)
Sweden	1–50	89	0	0
Switzerland	(5–50)	—	F	—
Turkey	P	—	—	—
United Kingdom	(10,000–40,000)	84	(–1)	(0)
Guernsey	5–20	—	—	—
Jersey	1–5	—	0	0
Isle of Man[1]	(0–10)	—	(F)	0*
Total (min., approx.)	44,000			

Trends +2 Large increase +1 Small increase 0 Stable X Extinct
(1970–1990) –2 Large decrease –1 Small decrease F Fluctuating N New breeder
Data quality **Bold**: reliable quantitative data Normal type: incomplete quantitative data
Bracketed figures: no quantitative data * Data quality not provided
[1] Population figures are included within United Kingdom totals P Present

The species is migratory and up to half of the European breeding population may winter from north-west Europe to the Iberian peninsula and the Balkans (Glutz von Blotzheim *et al.* 1977, Cramp and Simmons 1983, Lack 1986, Pedersen 1991). The other half winters largely in Africa. Population sizes are very poorly known, and indeed it is suggested that numbers wintering in Germany may be substantially higher than the figures given here (see table), but no data are available to prove this. Jack Snipe may winter in countries of central and eastern Europe additional to those listed in the table.

Population trends are also difficult to assess, since little reliable information is available. However, during the nineteenth century the species' breeding population declined significantly in central and eastern Europe, resulting in a range contraction from the south-west (Tuck 1972, Cramp and Simmons 1983). Winter populations are believed to have declined simultaneously. This trend probably continued throughout the twentieth century, due to the continuing deterioration and degradation of European wetlands. Estimates of breeding numbers for the period 1970–1990, although poor, suggest that populations may have stabilized (EBD 1994). The large winter populations, however, although often known even less well, have probably declined in Denmark and the United Kingdom (see table), suggesting continued declines in at least part of the breeding population.

■ Ecology

The Jack Snipe breeds in boreal bogs, marshes and flood-plains dominated by *Carex* sedges and *Sphagnum* mosses (Okulewicz and Witkowski 1979, Cramp and Simmons 1983, Pedersen 1992, A. M. Macikunas *in litt.*, V. K. Ryabitchev *in litt.*). In southern Sweden the species inhabits semi-natural transition bogs and mires where, until the middle of the twentieth century, seasonal water-level regulations were practised in order to produce livestock fodder (Pedersen 1990).

In winter the species occurs in various brackish

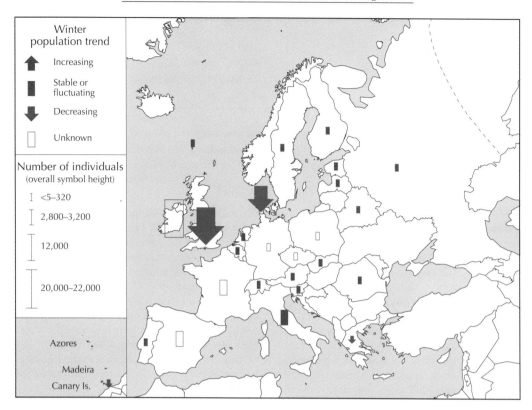

Winter population trend

- ↑ Increasing
- ▮ Stable or fluctuating
- ↓ Decreasing
- ☐ Unknown

Number of individuals
(overall symbol height)

- <5–320
- 2,800–3,200
- 12,000
- 20,000–22,000

Azores

Madeira

Canary Is.

and freshwater habitats, being most abundant in heterogeneous wetlands consisting of mosaics of moist and waterlogged mudflats with tussocks of vegetation (Sack 1961, Glutz von Blotzheim *et al.* 1977, Lack 1986, Pedersen 1989a). The species is highly crepuscular and feeds mainly on larvae and insects and sometimes seeds (Cramp and Simmons 1983). During cold spells Jack Snipe roost and feed along margins of rivers, streams and inland spring-fed meadows (Sack 1961, Lack 1986, Pedersen 1991 and in press, Velasco 1992).

■ Threats

Habitat deterioration, primarily caused by drainage for agricultural intensification, afforestation and peat extraction, is the major threat to the European breeding population (Cramp and Simmons 1983). In southern Sweden, for example, approximately 70% of the breeding sites are threatened by factors of human origin, e.g. hydrological changes, and eutrophication and habitat succession associated with drainage for water management and forestry improvements (Pedersen 1990).

The European winter population is likely to have been affected by drainage and other hydrological engineering schemes in wetlands and river systems (Glutz von Blotzheim *et al.* 1977, Cramp and Simmons 1983).

Hunting is another important factor since approximately 5% of the European population is thought to be shot during autumn migration, e.g. in France and Denmark (Pedersen 1989b).

■ Conservation measures

As a widely dispersed species when breeding and wintering, only a small part of the Jack Snipe's population occurs in Important Bird Areas (IBAs), and wide-scale habitat conservation measures are therefore required. In European breeding habitats these should include the maintenance of natural hydrological dynamics in peatbogs and boreal marshes.

In the winter quarters it is necessary to promote the conservation of large complex wetlands, unregulated streams, deltas and extensive wet grasslands, including the promotion of their sustainable use. Specific legislative measures are also necessary to limit mortality related to hunting, and a moratorium should be enforced until sustainable exploitation can be assured.

As the Jack Snipe is a highly crepuscular and readily overlooked species, this has inevitably resulted in a lack of basic, reliable, long-term population data. Further studies are therefore required to clarify its population status and distribution and the causes of its apparent decline.

MICHAEL BRINCH PEDERSEN

Great Snipe
Gallinago media

SPEC Category 2
Status (Vulnerable)
Criteria Large decline

There has been a widespread decline in the western and southern parts of the European range, principally due to loss and deterioration of flood-plain meadows and marshland. Measures should be taken to preserve the habitat of the species by ceasing the drainage of flood-plains and promoting low-intensity farming practices.

■ Distribution and population trends

The present European breeding range extends from eastern Poland to beyond the Ural mountains and from the northern Ukraine to the tundra zone near the Barents Sea. The Fennoscandian mountains hold a separate population. Outside Europe the species breeds in northern Asia east to 95°E. The species is migratory, wintering mainly in the Afrotropical region, especially the eastern part (Kozlova 1962, Cramp and Simmons 1983, Massoli-Novelli 1987).

Over three-quarters of the European population is in Russia, although Belarus and Norway also have high numbers (see table, map). A contraction in the species' range and a decline in numbers have been evident in central and eastern Europe since the second half of the nineteenth century (Glutz von Blotzheim *et al.* 1977). More rapid declines took place in the first half of the twentieth century which led to extinctions in Denmark and Germany (Cramp and Simmons 1983). During 1970–1990 the species approached the verge of extinction in western Poland, Lithuania, Latvia and Finland (Malchevskiy and Pukinskiy 1983, Strazds 1983, Tiainen 1987, Tomialojc 1990; see table, map). Importantly, in the southern part of the forest and forest-steppe zones of Russia and Ukraine, rapid declines in numbers and contractions in range continue (Anon. 1990b, Tomkovich 1992; see table, map). In northern Ukraine

the species still breeds in good numbers locally (Afanasiev *et al.* 1992), while in Belarus it is not rare though a strong decline in numbers is reported (see table). In Scandinavia, lowland breeding birds have disappeared, but there is no evidence of a decline in the montane population. In the Russian tundra zone there are no available data concerning population changes (Estafiev 1991). Only in Norway and Sweden has the population recently recovered and stabilized (Elveland and Tjernberg 1984; see table).

Due to the widespread declines of the species in Europe, its global status is listed as Near Threatened (Collar *et al.* 1994).

■ Ecology

The preferred nesting habitats are flood-plain meadows with moderately tall and uniform grasses (Nikiforov and Hybet 1981, Morozov 1990) and tussock meadows and natural fens with scattered bushes or trees in wide river valleys (Dyrcz *et al.* 1972, Malchevskiy and Pukinskiy 1983, Nikiforov *et al.* 1989, Afanasiev *et al.* 1992). In the Fennoscandian uplands (450–1,200 m) the species inhabits peatland and wet grassland with some bushes (Elveland and Tjernberg 1984, Schandy 1984) and an abundance of earthworms (Løfaldli *et al.* 1992). Similar habitats are occupied in northern Russia, where birds prefer wet grassland, peatland and tundra with scattered willow *Salix* and dwarf birch *Betula nana* shrubs (Kozlova 1962, Estafiev 1991, V. V. Morozov own data).

The Great Snipe's promiscuous mating system requires fairly large patches of boggy habitat for leks to form (Schandy 1984). Under optimal conditions, leks may be 1–5 km apart and be used for many years (Cramp and Simmons 1983). This renders the species sensitive to both natural and man-made habitat changes. Nests are either solitary or in clusters around the centre of the lek, reaching densities of 0.4–1.4 per 10 ha (Dyrcz *et al.* 1972, Afanasiev *et al.* 1992).

The diet on the breeding grounds is mostly earthworms, though Cramp and Simmons (1983) indicate

	Breeding population			Breeding range trend
	Size (pairs)	Year	Trend	
Belarus	12,000–20,000	90	–2	0
Estonia	50–100	—	–1	–1
Finland	(1–5)	92	(0)	(0)
Latvia	(5–20)	—	(0)	(F)
Lithuania	(30–50)	85–88	(–1)	(–1)
Norway	5,000–15,000	90	0	0
Poland	400–500	—	–1	–1
Russia	(150,000–250,000)	70–90	–2	(–1)
Sweden	1,000–2,000	87	0	(0)
Ukraine	400–500	—	—	–2
Total (approx.)	170,000–290,000			

Trends	+2 Large increase	+1 Small increase	0 Stable	X Extinct
(1970–1990)	–2 Large decrease	–1 Small decrease	F Fluctuating	N New breeder

Data quality **Bold**: reliable quantitative data   Normal type: incomplete quantitative data
Bracketed figures: no quantitative data   * Data quality not provided

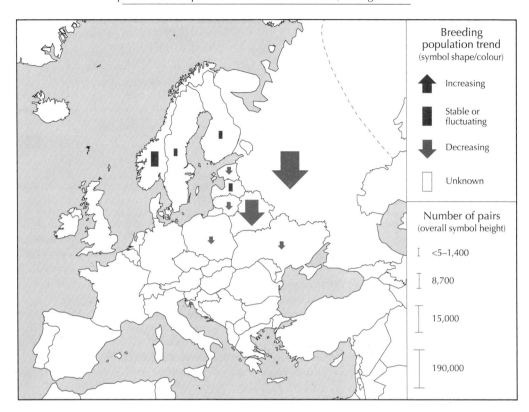

Breeding
population trend
(symbol shape/colour)

Increasing

Stable or
fluctuating

Decreasing

Unknown

Number of pairs
(overall symbol height)

<5–1,400

8,700

15,000

190,000

that molluscs and insects are also eaten. The distribution is largely determined by a trade-off between earthworm density and soil penetrability: sodden areas hold few worms, whereas dry areas are difficult to probe. Because only one adult cares for each brood, the species can breed only in very productive areas, so its distribution is limited to eutrophic habitats rich in sub-surface invertebrates (Løfaldli *et al.* 1992).

Threats

The destruction and deterioration of the Great Snipe's habitat is the major cause of its decline in central Europe and lowland Fennoscandia. In Russia and the Ukraine threats include the loss of flood-plain meadows due to the intensification of agriculture, and the submergence of river valleys in the creation of new reservoirs (Ptushenko and Inozemtsev 1968, Nikiforov and Hybet 1981, Morozov 1990). In Poland, Belarus and Russia, intensive drainage of marshland and the intensification of farming have greatly reduced the extent of suitable breeding and feeding habitat (Nikiforov and Hybet 1981, Dyrcz *et al.* 1972, Malchevskiy and Pukinskiy 1983).

Great Snipe also desert areas where land management such as grazing or mowing is abandoned and shrubs and trees are consequently allowed to invade (Elveland and Tjernberg 1984, Morozov 1990). Such

areas may be too densely vegetated for safe escape from predators (Løfaldli *et al.* 1992).

The species is still hunted in eastern Europe, and this is a greater problem in the south where it has a concentrated distribution in river valleys with suitable habitat. Large numbers are shot, and pointing dogs are used. In the tundra the species is evenly dispersed, low numbers are killed, and hunting techniques involving dogs are not used. However, the threat from shooting is probably secondary compared to that which comes from habitat destruction (Swanberg 1965, Glutz von Blotzheim *et al.* 1977).

Conservation measures

As a dispersed, promiscuous, migratory and rather specialized species the Great Snipe requires fairly large areas of suitable habitat to maintain viable local populations. It is therefore dependent on the implementation and promotion of broad conservation measures aimed at the maintenance of natural flooded river valleys, extensive peatbogs and low-intensity farming in meadows. Excessive drainage of the species' wetland habitat has to be stopped, especially in the southern part of its breeding range.

A ban on Great Snipe hunting in the south of its range and some restriction of hunting in the north are also necessary.

Vladimir V. Morozov

Woodcock
Scolopax rusticola

SPEC Category 3, winter
Status Vulnerable
Criteria Large decline

The very large French wintering population of Woodcock has declined substantially in recent years, and it seems likely that this has been matched by a decline in the east European breeding population, but there are no data to show this. The cause of the decline is not clear, but may be due to hunting. An analysis of the survival rates of Woodcock ringed throughout Europe is necessary to assess the impact of hunting.

■ Distribution and population trends

Europe holds about a third of the global breeding range of the Woodcock, with breeding occurring from Fennoscandia southwards to the Mediterranean and Canary Islands and eastwards from western Europe to Russia. Over 90% of the European breeding population occurs in Russia and Fennoscandia (EBD 1994). These populations are migratory, wintering throughout western and southern Europe, but particularly in France, Spain, the United Kingdom and Italy. The breeding populations of north-west and southern Europe are largely sedentary (Cramp and Simmons 1983).

	Winter population			Winter
	Size (individuals)	Year	Trend	range trend
Belgium	10,000–20,000	90	F	(0)
Bulgaria	(0–10)	77–91	(0)	(0)
Cyprus	(500–5,000)	—	(F)	(0)
Czech Republic	0–3 *	—	—	—
Denmark	50–50 *	—	—	—
Faroe Islands	(0–20)	92	(F)	(0)
Estonia	0–20	—	0	0
France	1,320,000–?	84	**-2**	0
Greece	(1,000–10,000)	—	(0)	(0)
Rep. of Ireland	P	—	(+1)	—
Italy	(50,000–100,000)	—	(–1)	0
Luxembourg	5–20	—	0	0
Netherlands	1,000–10,000	79–83	F	0
Poland	20–50 *	—	—	—
Portugal	(1,000–10,000)	91	(0)	(0)
Azores	(400–800)	—	(0)	(0)
Romania	(100–300)	—	(0)	(0)
Russia	(0–1,000)	—	(F)	(F)
Slovenia	(50–100)	—	(F)	(F)
Spain	646,600–680,000	—	—	—
Switzerland	(50–500)	—	(F)	(0)
Turkey	P	—	—	—
Ukraine	**1–5**	91	**+1**	**+1**
United Kingdom	(200,000–300,000)	84	(0)	(0)
Guernsey	50–200	—	—	—
Jersey	(100–100)	—	(0)	(0)
Isle of Man [1]	(100–500)	—	F	0*
Total (min.)	c.2,200,000			

Trends +2 Large increase +1 Small increase 0 Stable X Extinct
(1970–1990) –2 Large decrease –1 Small decrease F Fluctuating N New breeder
Data quality **Bold**: reliable quantitative data Normal type: incomplete quantitative data
Bracketed figures: no quantitative data * Data quality not provided
[1] Population figures are included within United Kingdom totals P Present

Small increases in numbers of breeding birds have occurred in Belgium, the Netherlands (Teixeira 1979, Cramp and Simmons 1983), Denmark (Jespersen 1946, Clausager 1972) and Ireland (Hutchinson 1989) in the last century.

The current data (see table) suggest that over 80% of the European wintering population declined in numbers between 1970 and 1990. Unfortunately no trend data are available for the large wintering population in Spain and the trend for the European population is based almost entirely on the detection of a substantial decline in the French wintering population (Yeatman-Berthelot 1991). It is likely that this decline has been matched by a decline in breeding populations in eastern Europe but there are no data to show this.

Paradoxically, breeding numbers within Europe are believed to have remained largely stable over the same 1970–1990 period (<5% of population declined) (EBD 1994), but the species is extremely difficult to census and population sizes and trends within most countries are highly uncertain. The fluctuations in Russia are, however, a cause for concern as the majority of the European breeding population is located there (EBD 1994).

■ Ecology

The preferred breeding habitat is deciduous or mixed woodland. Conifer plantations are also used up to the thicket stage (Shorten 1974, Marchant *et al*. 1990), as are large patches of bracken *Pteridium* in upland areas. An understorey and earthworm-rich soils are important (Hirons and Johnson 1987, Granval and Muys 1992) as are wide rides and small clearings (2–4 ha) in larger woods (Shorten 1974).

Habitat requirements are less specific in winter and patches of scrub often hold Woodcock during the day, as well as woodland. The species feeds in fields at night, preferring areas with permanent, frost-free pasture or long-rotation grass leys within about 1 km distance from woodland, due to the high

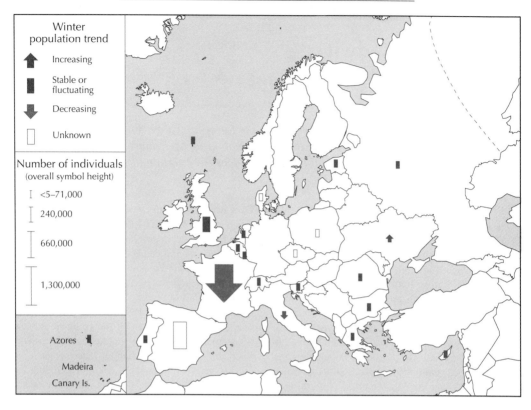

densities of invertebrate food that are available (Hirons and Bickford-Smith 1983, Granval 1988). The distribution of Woodcock in winter is determined largely by the availability of suitable nocturnal feeding areas as opposed to diurnal cover and only low densities occur in predominantly arable areas. The species is susceptible to cold winters, due to feeding sites becoming frozen (Baillie *et al.* 1986, Marchant *et al.* 1990).

■ Threats

Hunting is a cause for concern as some populations are likely to be harvested in several different areas whilst on migration, as well as on their wintering grounds. The decline in the French winter population may be linked to the high levels of Woodcock hunting there, although there is also evidence of a reduction in hunting pressure throughout Europe, with the possible exception of France, since the early 1960s (Henderson *et al.* 1993).

Increased fragmentation of large tracts of woodland in central and north-west Europe may have reduced breeding populations in some areas. For example, in the United Kingdom, where the population has declined (Gibbons *et al.* 1993), breeding habitat has been lost due to felling and fragmentation of mature woods and due to a dramatic loss of managed coppice. This was compensated to some extent by the creation of conifer plantations during the 1960s (Parslow 1967a), but the value of this habitat is now much reduced due to closure of the forest canopy.

■ Conservation measures

Information is urgently required on survival rates to determine whether hunting and/or reduced breeding success have caused population declines. A full understanding of the impact of hunting and sustainable bag limits in different countries should be sought.

The species will benefit from the planting and maintenance of large blocks of woodland. Also woodland management, such as the opening of rides and clearings and thinning to preserve the understorey, is important. Detailed research is required on the habitat requirements and the factors affecting breeding success in Fennoscandia and Russia.

ANDREW HOODLESS

Black-tailed Godwit
Limosa limosa

SPEC Category 2
Status Vulnerable
Criteria Large decline

Breeding populations are declining over most of the European range due to the loss of nesting habitat through wetland drainage and the intensification of agriculture. The conservation of lowland wet grasslands and the regulation of disturbance from certain farming activities are the main conservation measures necessary.

■ Distribution and population trends

This species' breeding range extends right across Eurasia. In Europe, two forms occur: the subspecies *L. l. islandica* breeds in Iceland, and sporadically in Ireland and Scotland, while the nominate race breeds in continental Europe from northern Italy, Hungary and Ukraine in the south, up to central Sweden, Estonia and the tributaries of the upper Volga river in the north, and from the Atlantic coast to the central European and Russian lowlands. The main wintering grounds of the north-west European populations are in West Africa south of the Sahara, although some birds winter along the Atlantic coast of north-west Europe (*islandica*) and in the Mediterranean basin. East European breeding birds winter mainly in eastern and central Africa (Beintema and Drost 1986).

Over two-thirds of the world population of the species occurs in Europe (Rose and Scott 1994).

In Europe, the largest breeding populations occur in lowland wet grasslands in the Netherlands (which holds at least a third of European numbers), northern Germany, central Poland, southern Belarus and Russia (Fediushin and Dolbik 1967, Glutz von Blotzheim *et al.* 1977, Tomialojc 1990; see table, map). Elsewhere in Europe (except for the Icelandic population) colonies are usually isolated and ephemeral, fluctuating in size depending on water-levels.

Over past centuries the Black-tailed Godwit has benefited from man-made changes to the landscape and has spread over most of central and northern Europe (Kirchner 1969, Glutz von Blotzheim *et al.* 1977). Early this century increases continued to prevail over local decreases (Cramp and Simmons 1983), but during 1970–1990 declines occurred in countries which together hold up to 85% of European breeding numbers, including important populations in the Netherlands and Russia (see table, map)—although data for Russia and Lithuania are uncertain.

■ Ecology

Historically, Black-tailed Godwits bred in extensive river valley fens, temporarily inundated margins of large lakes, damp grassy steppes, raised bogs and moorlands (Dementiev and Gladkov 1951c, Kirchner 1969, Cramp and Simmons 1983). Some of these areas still support large breeding concentrations of the species, but a significant part of the European population now breeds in secondary habitats, including lowland wet grasslands with moderately high and dense grass, coastal grazing marshes, pastures on muddy soils, damp areas around fish-ponds or sewage farms, and salt-water lagoons (Glutz von Blotzheim *et al.* 1977, Hölzinger 1987). In the Netherlands and Germany breeding also occurs sporadically in fields of sugar beet, potato and rye.

One-year-olds summer in the African winter quarters, and return to the breeding grounds for the first time at two years old, though (in the north-west European population at least) they travel by a different

| | Breeding population | | | Breeding |
	Size (pairs)	Year	Trend	range trend
Austria	**77–90**	91	F	–1
Belarus	15,000–17,000	90	0	0
Belgium	**865–910**	90	+2	0
Czech Republic	**30–60**	—	–2	–1
Denmark	**667–693**	87	+1	0
Estonia	1,000–1,000	—	–1	0
Finland	**20–20**	92	0	0
France	**85–110**	89	0	0
Germany	7,000–20,000	85	–1	0
Hungary	1,000–1,200	—	0	0
Iceland	5,000–15,000	—	(0)	+1
Rep. of Ireland	2–3	89	0	0
Italy	5–10	89	(N)	(N)
Latvia	**80–100**	—	0	+1
Lithuania	100–500	85–88	(–1)	(–1)
Netherlands	**85,000–100,000**	89–91	–1	0
Norway	100–150	90	+1	+1
Poland	6,000–8,000	—	–1	0
Romania	30–60	—	+1	+2
Russia	(10,000–100,000)	80–90	(–1)	(0)
Slovakia	25–40	—	–1	–1
Spain	0–20	—	F	F
Sweden	**275–350**	87	0	0
Ukraine	**4,500–5,000**	88	–1	–1
United Kingdom	**34–36**	88–90	0	+1
Total (approx.)	140,000–270,000			

Trends +2 Large increase +1 Small increase 0 Stable X Extinct
(1970-1990) –2 Large decrease –1 Small decrease F Fluctuating N New breeder
Data quality **Bold**: reliable quantitative data Normal type: incomplete quantitative data
Bracketed figures: no quantitative data * Data quality not provided

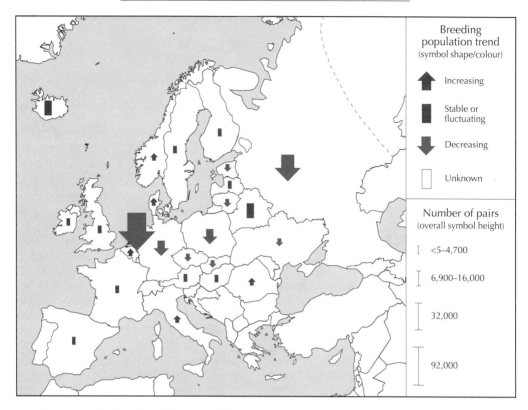

route from that taken by adults (Beintema 1986).

Black-tailed Godwits feed mainly in grasslands in spring, largely in muddy estuaries after breeding and in winter (Glutz von Blotzheim *et al.* 1977, Hale 1980, Cramp and Simmons 1983). Rice-fields are an important feeding habitat in Africa (Roux 1973) and in Portugal where 15,000 wintering birds have recently been using fields adjoining the Tagus estuary (Huggett 1992).

■ Threats

A major threat is loss of nesting habitat due to drainage of wetlands and intensification of farming practices. Detrimental activities include the conversion of wet meadows to arable land, increased drainage, increased use of fertilizers, and the artificial flooding of nesting habitats (Dementiev and Gladkov 1951c, Green *et al.* 1987). On intensively grazed pastures, the trampling of nests is a frequent cause of breeding failure (Beintema and Müskens 1987).

The species is gregarious and nests in dispersed colonies and sub-colonies as a means of defence against predators; it is therefore less likely to breed successfully in small areas of habitat which can only support isolated pairs (Batten *et al.* 1990).

The tendency for birds to congregate in large flocks at wintering, migratory stopover and roosting sites makes it vulnerable to loss of intertidal feeding habitat, human disturbances, and hunting and persecu-

tion. Drought in the West African wintering quarters may also have had a negative impact on the European population (Green *et al.* 1987).

■ Conservation measures

Breeding habitat can be improved by the raising of water-tables, low-level use of organic fertilizer, low-intensity grazing, late mowing and winter flooding (Beintema 1991a). Losses of eggs and chicks may also be prevented by leaving patches of grass unmowed alongside ditches, at the edges of meadows, and around wader colonies where feasible, although this may attract predators.

In western Europe, wide-scale changes in land-use policies are necessary, which may include payments under the Agri-environment Regulation (EC Reg. 2078/92) of the Common Agricultural Policy (Beintema 1991b) to farmers who manage grasslands for the benefit of breeding waders.

Establishment of nature reserves, including site-based measures as mentioned above, and management to prevent the succession of bushy vegetation, are recommended for the main breeding sites in eastern Europe, especially the river valleys of Biebrza in Poland and Pripjet in Belarus.

It is also necessary to ensure that migratory staging areas and wintering feeding habitats and roosts are conserved and monitored.

LUDWIK TOMIALOJC

273

Bar-tailed Godwit
Limosa lapponica

SPEC Category 3, winter
Status Localized
Criteria Localized

Bar-tailed Godwits are long-distance migrants heavily dependent on a small number of coastal wetlands on passage and in winter. The majority of the European wintering population is found at a few sites, some unprotected and seriously threatened by land-claim, pollution and disturbance.

■ Distribution and population trends

Bar-tailed Godwits breed in the high Arctic and subarctic climate zones along the edge of the Arctic Ocean from Norway to Alaska. Within Europe, 1,000–3,000 pairs breed in Norway, 5–25 in Sweden, another 200–500 are found in Finland (EBD 1994). The species also breeds in European Russia, but numbers there are highly uncertain. These European birds together with those from Asiatic Russia (from as far east as the Yamal peninsula) largely winter in west Europe (Meltofte and Lyngs 1981), with mid-winter counts indicating that this population is about 125,000 birds (Smit and Piersma 1989).

Birds breeding further east, to the western Taymyr peninsula (Rogacheva 1992), probably winter mostly in West Africa, stopping over at west European coastal wetlands (Piersma and Jukema 1990, Meltofte 1993). This African-wintering population is about 700,000 birds and is concentrated in the Banc d'Arguin in Mauritania (537,000) and the Arquipélago dos Bijagos in Guinea-Bissau (156,000).

In spring almost the whole European-wintering population congregates in the Wadden Sea (Prokosch 1988). The key wintering sites are given in the Important Bird Area table. Numbers fluctuated between 1970 and 1990 throughout much of the European wintering range, including the United Kingdom, where population indices show an increase in wintering numbers from 1971 to 1985, followed by a steady decrease to nearly the 1971 levels (Cranswick *et al.* 1992; see table, map). The French wintering population, however, has declined considerably.

Important Bird Areas The top ten IBAs for wintering Bar-tailed Godwits in Europe, together holding over 90% of the total European wintering population.

Netherlands	001	Waddenzee
	010	Groningen buitendijks
	050	Oosterschelde
Rep. of Ireland	108	Dundalk Bay
United Kingdom	124	Inner Firth of Forth and Outer Firth of Forth
	135	Morecambe Bay
	139	Ribble and Alt Estuaries
	142	Lindisfarne
	164	The Wash
	206	South Thames Marshes

■ Ecology

Outside the breeding season Bar-tailed Godwits are dependent on intertidal habitats with a preference for sheltered bays, inlets and estuaries (Cramp and Simmons 1983). Within these habitats they prefer sandy areas situated low in the intertidal zone (Ens *et al.* in press). Further inland the species occurs in small numbers (Meltofte 1993).

Breeding habitats include shrub tundra, dry hillock or moss-lichen tundra, forest tundra, although at low densities, wet river valleys and open larch woodlands near water-bodies (Rogacheva 1992). In the breeding habitat the food consists of insects, including beetles, flies, larvae of Lepidoptera, and annelid worms and occasionally seeds and berries (Cramp and Simmons 1983).

In winter, birds feed chiefly in flocks at the tide edge and in water to about 15 cm deep (Smith and Evans 1973). In western Europe food consists mainly

	Winter population			Winter
	Size (individuals)	Year	Trend	range trend
Belgium	**10–100**	89–90	F	0
Bulgaria	0–5	77–91	0	0
Denmark	**0–9,500**	80–91	—	—
France	5,000–5,000	90	–2	0
Germany	**41–14,200**	80–91	—	—
Greece	4–?*	89	—	—
Iceland	5–50	—	F	0
Rep. of Ireland	16,000–20,000	—	0	—
Italy	(11–100)	84	+1	+1
Netherlands	**6,300–33,500**	80–91	F	0
Portugal	**2,500–5,000**	91	F	0
Azores	(20–40)	—	(0)	(0)
Russia	(0–500)	—	(F)	(F)
Spain	**1,800–?**	—	F	—
Canary Islands	100–150	—	F	0
United Kingdom	**50,000–60,000**	88	F	0
Guernsey	25–50	—	—	—
Jersey	**500–500**	—	0	0
Isle of Man[1]	**2–7**	—	0	0*
Total (min., approx.)	82,000			

Trends +2 Large increase +1 Small increase 0 Stable X Extinct
(1970–1990) –2 Large decrease –1 Small decrease F Fluctuating N New breeder
Data quality **Bold**: reliable quantitative data Normal type: incomplete quantitative data
Bracketed figures: no quantitative data * Data quality not provided
[1] Population figures are included within United Kingdom totals

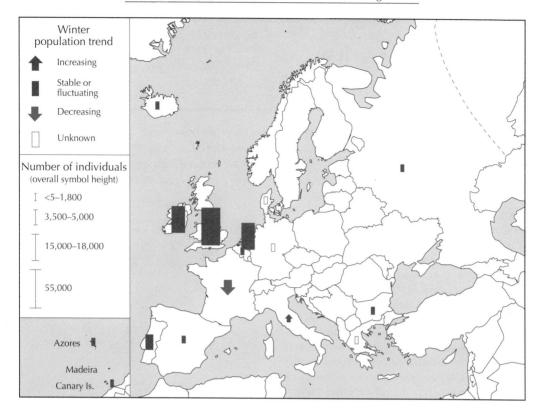

Winter
population trend

Increasing

Stable or
fluctuating

Decreasing

Unknown

Number of individuals
(overall symbol height)

<5–1,800

3,500–5,000

15,000–18,000

55,000

Azores

Madeira

Canary Is.

of large *Nereis* and *Arenicola* worms, but small worms (e.g. *Heteromastus*) and crustaceans are also taken (Boere and Smit 1981). At high tide Bar-tailed Godwits concentrate in large flocks along the edges of saltmarsh or in large, open, sandy areas close to or even in water. However, if such roost sites are unavailable, they may also roost inland, quite frequently joining flocks of Curlews *Numenius arquata*.

Bar-tailed Godwits show high site-fidelity to stopover places in succeeding years and seasons (Prokosch 1988, Piersma and Jukema 1990).

■ Threats

The species is vulnerable due its concentration at a few coastal wetlands outside the breeding season. From Africa the birds migrate in a single long-distance flight to a very small number of stop-over sites in western Europe (Piersma and Jukema 1990).

The success of the species' migration strategy depends heavily on the presence of suitable coastal wetlands where sufficient undisturbed habitat and food are available. However, many European passage and wintering sites are either poorly protected or lack any protection. Land-claim and pollution of these areas detrimentally affects the feeding conditions for the birds and reduces the number of birds which use these areas. Mitchell *et al.* (1988) also found that high-tide roosts of Bar-tailed Godwits are vulnerable to human disturbance which, if frequent,

results in a high energy expenditure which may reduce the birds' reproduction and survival rates.

■ Conservation measures

Large parts of the Wadden Sea (Netherlands, IBA 001) and key sites in the United Kingdom (see IBA table) are protected areas. However, even in these protected areas human activities such as land-claim, construction of marinas, overexploitation of shellfish stocks, oil and gas extraction, tourism, and barrage construction continue to pose a threat, leading to disturbance to foraging and roosting birds, a decrease in food-stocks and habitat deterioration. Protection measures in terms of safeguarding feeding areas, food-stocks and roosting areas should be improved in these Important Bird Areas and, in general, wise use of wetlands as agreed in the Ramsar Convention, promoted through integrated coastal zone planning. Within the EU this could be furthered by the implementation of the proposed Coastal Zone Management Strategy.

Many important passage sites in France and Portugal are unprotected as are wetlands used in winter in Guinea-Bissau, although the Banc d'Arguin in Mauritania has been designated as a National Park. Considering the relatively large importance of coastal wetlands in Guinea-Bissau strong efforts should be given to safeguard these wetlands.

Cor Smit

Slender-billed Curlew
Numenius tenuirostris

SPEC Category 1
Status Not applicable – passage migrant only

The globally threatened Slender-billed Curlew is almost certainly the rarest and most poorly known bird species in Europe, where it occurs as a passage migrant. Declines throughout the twentieth century are thought to have been caused mainly by habitat loss and hunting. The identification and protection of key sites and the implementation of effective hunting controls throughout the range of the species are essential if it is to survive.

■ Distribution and population trends

The Slender-billed Curlew is thought to breed in south-west Siberia (Ushakov 1916, 1925) from where it migrates in a west-south-west direction across eastern and southern Europe to winter in North Africa. However, because the location, and hence number, of breeding birds is unknown, and because of the erratic distribution of wintering records outside the only known regularly used wintering site of Merja Zerga on the Atlantic coast of northern Morocco, the size of the world population of the species is highly uncertain. It is, though, clear that it is very small, and Gretton (1991) suggested it to be in the order of 100–400 individuals, an estimate more recently revised to 50–270 individuals (Gretton 1994 in press a). The species is therefore classified as Globally Threatened (Collar *et al.* 1994).

Although there have been occasional recent winter records from the Arabian peninsula (which may indicate a small population wintering there), it appears that almost the entire Slender-billed Curlew population passes through Europe. Key passage countries are Russia, Ukraine, Turkey, Bulgaria, Romania, Hungary, Yugoslavia (Vojvodina), Greece and Italy (Gretton 1991; see table), while Albania (IRSNB 1992), Croatia and Spain may prove to be of similar importance (the latter two countries both have a significant number of unconfirmed records). Since the early 1980s, apart from Morocco, regular records have come only from Hungary, Greece and Italy. However, because the species is easily overlooked due to the difficulty of identification, the distribution of records is heavily influenced by the coverage given to different areas by sufficiently skilled observers, making it difficult to assess the precise importance of each country for the species.

A recent review (Gretton 1991) demonstrated that the species has undergone a dramatic decline since the nineteenth century when it was decribed as common in the Mediterranean region. Much of this decline took place during the early part of the twentieth century, but it is known that at least 16 Slender-

Confirmed records of Slender-billed Curlew in Europe

	1900–1950	1951–1970	1971–1993	Total
Albania			2	2
Austria		3	3	6
Azerbaijan			1	1
Bosnia-Herzegovina	3		1	4
Bulgaria	**4**	**6**	**9**	**19**
Russia	**11 ***	**1**	**2**	**14 ***
Croatia		2	4	6
Cyprus		2	1	3
Czech Republic	1			1
France	3	3	2	8
Germany	1	1		2
Greece	**3**	**13**	**55**	**71**
Hungary	**35**	**18**	**32**	**85**
Italy	**54**	**7**	**15**	**76**
Malta		4	1	5
Netherlands	5		2	7
Poland	1		3	4
Romania		**3**	**13**	**16**
Spain		3	3	6
Switzerland			1	1
Turkey	**2**	**14**	**13**	**29**
Ukraine	**1**	**3**	**11**	**15**
Yugoslavia	**3**	**28**	**3**	**34**
Totals	127	111	177	415

Key passage countries (10 or more records) are shown in **bold**; total number of records from these countries is 359.
* Includes the only known breeding records in 1916 and 1924 (Ushahov 1916, 1925).

billed Curlews were shot (in four European countries) between 1962 and 1987 (Gretton 1991, 1994 in press b). The population trend of the species in recent years is highly uncertain, though occasional but unconfirmed sightings of flocks give some basis for hope, such as the observation of c.150 birds in Greece in 1978 (Cramp and Simmons 1983) and 123 in Morocco in 1974–1975 (Thévenot 1989).

■ Ecology

There is only one thoroughly reliable description of the nesting habitat: extensive quaking peatbog with sedge and horsetail *Equisetum* and small scattered willows *Salix* and birches *Betula* (Ushakov 1916). In contrast to its apparently rather specialized nesting requirements, Slender-billed Curlews occur on passage in Europe in a wide range of habitats, including saltmarsh, saltpans, brackish lagoons, drained fishponds, steppe and freshwater marsh (Gretton 1991). At Merja Zerga in Morocco, the best-studied site, the birds feed mainly on sandy agricultural land and wet brackish grazing marsh close to a large coastal lagoon that is used for roosting (van den Berg 1989; Gretton 1991). Many European records have come from large wetland sites including the Danube delta, Evros delta, and Hortobágy, and it appears that a complex of undisturbed wetland habitats may be important for the species.

■ Threats

The major threats to the species have been habitat loss and hunting (Gretton 1991). The loss of wetland and steppe areas across much of Europe would have caused increasing problems for the species on passage, although it is curious that no other European migratory waterbird has suffered a decline of such magnitude. After a two-year review of the species (Gretton 1991), it was concluded that hunting was the only selective factor that could explain such a drastic decline in Slender-billed Curlew numbers. Curlews *N. arquata* were a favoured quarry species, and Slender-billed Curlews often appear to be unusually tame (hunters would be unlikely to distinguish between the two similar species). There are many records of shot Slender-billed Curlews from Hungary and Italy in the early part of the twentieth century, and even now the species continues to be shot occasionally, despite its very low numbers.

Furthermore, at such low population levels, a breakdown in social behaviour patterns is likely to exacerbate the situation, with the chances of birds pairing on the breeding grounds becoming increasingly remote.

■ Conservation measures

The effective protection and monitoring of key passage sites in Europe is a priority, including the establishment of non-hunting areas. The known key sites in Europe (with six or more records during the twentieth century) are the following: the Crimea/Azov Sea region (Ukraine, Important Bird Areas or IBAs 043, 044, 046 and 052–2), the Danube Delta (Romania, IBA 001), Lake Atanasovo (Bulgaria, IBA 010), Hortobágy (Hungary, IBA 016), Kardoskut (Hungary, IBA 025), Šoškopo in Vojvodina (Yugoslavia, IBA 035), the Evros Delta (Greece, IBA 001), Porto Lagos (Greece, IBA 004), the Axios Delta (Greece, IBA 019), the Viareggio area (Italy, IBAs 050 and 051), Golfo di Manfredonia (Italy, IBA 095), Valli di Commacchio and the Ravenna coast (Italy, IBAs 044, 046, 047 and 048). Doñana National Park in Spain may well be a key site, as there have been 34 unconfirmed records in recent winters. Increased survey efforts are needed in many areas, notably Russia, Ukraine, Turkey, Bulgaria, Albania, Croatia, Spain and Morocco, to identify further key sites—though the location of the current breeding grounds is arguably the highest priority.

Legislation providing adequate protection for the Slender-billed Curlew is needed in Russia, Ukraine, Turkey, Croatia and Yugoslavia, and the effective enforcement of existing laws is required elsewhere, notably in Italy and Greece. Furthermore, because of the potential for confusion with other large waders, all *Numenius* and godwit *Limosa* species must be strictly protected throughout the range of the Slender-billed Curlew.

The action plan for the species in Gretton (1991) is currently being updated by BirdLife International and expanded to cover all relevant countries. Some legislative measures have been taken to increase protection for the species and/or its 'look-alikes' in Italy, Morocco and Romania, but further efforts are needed. In January 1994 a workshop was held in Morocco to revise the action plan for the west Mediterranean countries (Morocco, Tunisia, Italy and the probable range states of Spain and Algeria). In 1994 the Bonn Convention Secretariat proposed a Memorandum of Understanding on the species to countries in which it is known to occur.

ADAM GRETTON

Curlew
Numenius arquata

SPEC Category 3, winter
Status Declining
Criteria Moderate decline

Although declining widely in Europe as a breeder, the large numbers in Russia, Finland and the United Kingdom appear to be stable. However, 40% of the wintering population has declined, so declines in breeding numbers may be underestimated. Loss of breeding habitat is probably the major cause, but wintering birds are affected by building developments, disturbance, pollution and hunting. Reductions in intensive farming and protection of wintering sites are a priority.

■ Distribution and population trends

The Curlew breeds throughout northern and temperate latitudes of Europe and Asia from Ireland to eastern Siberia (Dementiev and Gladkov 1951c, Cramp and Simmons 1983). Nearly half of its global breeding range is in Europe, concentrated in the north of the continent, chiefly in Finland, Sweden, United Kingdom, Republic of Ireland and northern Russia. A significant proportion winters in north-west Europe, particularly the United Kingdom, Republic of Ireland, Germany and Netherlands (see table, map).

During the late nineteenth century the Curlew started to decline in parts of central Europe (Glutz von Blotzheim *et al.* 1977, Cramp and Simmons 1983) and in the first half of this century a decrease was noted in eastern Europe in the Ukraine, Belarus and some southern and central provinces of Russia (Dementiev and Gladkov 1951c, Malchevskiy and Pukinskiy 1983). However, in north-west Europe, parts of central Europe and Fennoscandia the population simultaneously increased in size and the range expanded to the north, and to the south into Czechoslovakia and Hungary (Yeatman 1976, Glutz von Blotzheim *et al.* 1977, Cramp and Simmons 1983, Ylimaunu *et al.* 1987).

During 1970–1990 the population decline and range contraction continued in large parts of southern and central Europe as well as the southern and central regions of eastern Europe, where the Curlew now only breeds locally (EBD 1994). Furthermore, the decline has extended to populations that were previously increasing, such as those in Sweden, Norway and Estonia. However, during this period the large population in Russia increased and those in Finland and the United Kingdom remained stable, although local declines in the United Kingdom were observed (Gibbons *et al.* 1993). Thus, overall, no more than 20% of the European breeding total occurred in countries that registered population declines.

At the same time a larger fall was noted in wintering numbers, affecting some 40% of birds in Europe (see table, map). As the species is probably better monitored in winter, and as these populations are largely the same birds as those which breed in Europe (Cramp and Simmons 1983), it seems likely that some breeding declines may have been overlooked.

■ Ecology

Fens, peat-bogs, heathland, coastal marshes and wet grasslands, large river valleys and steppes are the species' preferred habitat in boreal Russia and Fennoscandia. Elsewhere, some Curlew populations have successfully colonized pastures and other agricultural grasslands to some extent in France, the

| | Winter population | | | Winter |
	Size (individuals)	Year	Trend	range trend
Austria	**170–460**	90	F	0
Belarus	(0–10)	90	F	F
Belgium	**2,000–5,000**	89–90	F	0
Bulgaria	10–200	77–91	0	0
Cyprus	1–100	—	0	0
Czech Republic	0–20 *	—	—	—
Denmark	**200–4,050**	80–91	—	—
Faroe Islands	(50–200)	92	(0)	(0)
France	**18,000–18,000**	89	–1	0
Germany	**19,700–97,200**	80–91	—	—
Greece	**1,000–2,000**	87–91	0	0
Hungary	**177–177**	91	F*	—
Iceland	50–100	—	0	0
Rep. of Ireland	(75,000–100,000)	—	(–1)	—
Italy	4,000–6,000	84–89	0	0
Netherlands	**25,300–94,400**	80–91	F	0
Poland	0–5 *	—	—	—
Portugal	2,000–3,500	91	F	0
Romania	10–50	—	(0)	(0)
Russia	(0–1,000)	—	(F)	(F)
Slovakia	(0–15)	—	—	—
Slovenia	**10–20**	—	0	0
Spain	**3,800–?**	—	0	—
Canary Islands	5–15	—	F	0
Switzerland	300–500	—	F	0
Turkey	(1,500–1,500)	—	—	—
United Kingdom	90,000–100,000	88	0	0
Guernsey	250–750	—	—	—
Isle of Man[1]	**3,500–7,000**	—	F	0*
Total (min.)	c.250,000			

Trends   +2 Large increase   +1 Small increase   0 Stable   X Extinct
(1970–1990) –2 Large decrease   –1 Small decrease   F Fluctuating   N New breeder
Data quality **Bold**: reliable quantitative data   Normal type: incomplete quantitative data
              Bracketed figures: no quantitative data   * Data quality not provided
[1] Population figures are included within United Kingdom totals

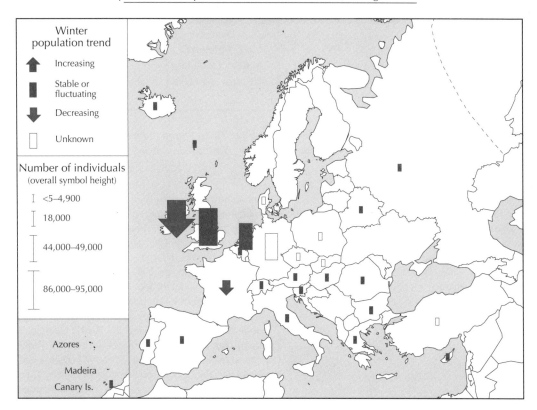

Winter population trend	
⬆	Increasing
⬛	Stable or fluctuating
⬇	Decreasing
☐	Unknown

Number of individuals
(overall symbol height)

I	<5–4,900
I	18,000
I	44,000–49,000
I	86,000–95,000

Azores

Madeira

Canary Is.

Netherlands and the United Kingdom (Parslow 1967a, Cramp and Simmons 1983, Gibbons *et al.* 1993). However, it has been shown that reproductive success is higher in semi-natural habitats than in farmland (Baines 1988, Berg 1991).

European wintering birds mostly gather at large estuaries and other extensive muddy sites.

■ Threats

In winter and during migration Curlews are sensitive to building developments on, and disturbance of, high-tide roosts, as well as local chemical pollution and hunting (Poslawski 1969, Meltofte 1986). However, it is likely that the observed decline in the European wintering population is due to the loss, degradation and fragmentation of natural and semi-natural breeding habitats caused by the widespread intensification of agricultural practices, such as drainage and the replacement of heathland, moorland and wet meadows with arable land and agriculturally improved or frequently mowed grassland. For example, in northern England densities fell from 10 to 1 pair per km[2] as marginal farmland was gradually converted to agriculturally improved grassland (Baines 1988).

These practices affect the availability of food and the breeding success of the species (Berg 1992, 1993). For example, populations breeding in mowed meadows suffer heavy mortality if the grassland is cut during the breeding season, through destruction of eggs and young (Hölzinger 1987). Predation is consistently a major cause of nest failure in agriculturally improved habitats (Baines 1989, M. Grant pers. comm.). Based on trials with artificial clutches, nest-predation may be higher in more southerly latitudes (Berg 1991), which may help to explain the recent shift of the species' breeding grounds to the north.

Increased afforestation of lower moorlands has led to habitat loss and caused population declines in the Republic of Ireland at least (Hutchinson 1989).

■ Conservation measures

In regions where the species breeds in natural and semi-natural habitats, the main conservation strategy should be to preserve extensive areas of these habitats through regulation of agricultural intensification. Drainage of wet moorlands, heath and grasslands should be prevented and afforestation of lower-altitude moorland avoided. Mowed grasslands with breeding waders should be managed so that they are cut after the incubation period.

Feeding and roosting habitats utilized by wintering and migratory birds should also be monitored and protected from land-claim, pollution and disturbance. A comprehensive assessment of the effects of hunting on Curlew populations should also be undertaken, and hunting regulations amended if necessary.

LUDWIK TOMIALOJC

Redshank
Tringa totanus

SPEC Category 2
Status Declining
Criteria Moderate decline

Much of the breeding population has declined since 1970, mainly due to habitat loss and agricultural intensification. Habitat can be secured by site-based measures together with widespread changes in land-use policies.

■ Distribution and population trends

The Redshank is distributed across the Palearctic, over half the breeding range lying within Europe. Iceland, Norway, Belarus, United Kingdom and Netherlands together hold up to three-quarters of the European breeding population; European Russia and Turkey may also have a large population but numbers are poorly known (see table, map).

Declines are known to have started in north-west

	Breeding population			Breeding
	Size (pairs)	Year	Trend	range trend
Albania	200–500	80	–1	(–1)
Austria	130–200	—	F	–1
Belarus	70,000–90,000	90	0	0
Belgium	**145–160**	90	–1	–1
Bulgaria	30–50	—	–1	–1
Croatia	40–60 *	—	0*	0*
Czech Republic	**40–60**	—	–2	–1
Denmark	**5,000–6,000**	87–89	(–1)	–1
Faroe Islands	5–10	81	(–1)	(–1)
Estonia	6,000–6,000	—	–1	0
Finland	15,000–20,000	92	+1	0
France	900–1,400	90	0	0
Germany	11,000–16,000	86	–1	0
Greece	400–800	—	(–1)	(–1)
Hungary	500–600	—	0	0
Iceland	50,000–100,000	—	(0)	0
Rep. of Ireland	(4,000–4,500)	88–91	0	+1
Italy	400–700	89	0	(–1)
Latvia	500–1,000	—	–1	+1
Lithuania	400–1,000	85–88	(–1)	(0)
Moldova	250–400	89	–1	–1
Netherlands	**24,000–36,000**	89–91	–1	0
Norway	40,000–80,000	90	0	0
Poland	**2,000–2,500**	—	–1	–1
Portugal	10–20	89	—	—
Romania	(100–400)	—	0	0
Russia	(10,000–100,000)	80–90	(–1)	(0)
Slovakia	35–70	—	(–1)	–1
Slovenia	**3–5**	—	N	N
Spain	1,200–3,500	—	–1	–1
Sweden	10,000–20,000	87	0	0
Turkey	(10,000–100,000)	—	—	—
Ukraine	6,000–7,000	88	–1	–1
United Kingdom	32,000–35,000	1980s	–1	0
Isle of Man [1]	**2–5**	—	0	0*
Total (approx.)	300,000–630,000			

Trends   +2 Large increase   +1 Small increase   0 Stable   X Extinct
(1970-1990) –2 Large decrease   –1 Small decrease   F Fluctuating   N New breeder
Data quality **Bold**: reliable quantitative data   Normal type: incomplete quantitative data
              Bracketed figures: no quantitative data   * Data quality not provided
[1] Population figures are included within United Kingdom totals

and central Europe early in the nineteenth century, following land drainage, agricultural intensification and river flood control, although Britain had marked increases between 1865 and 1940, mainly due to reduced drainage (Glutz von Blotzheim *et al.* 1977, Cramp and Simmons 1983, Stiefel and Schleufler 1984). Up to about 40% of the breeding population (for which trends are known) declined during 1970–1990, including populations in the United Kingdom, Netherlands, Germany and Russia (see table, map). Numbers in the Netherlands during 1979–1987 appear to be half of those for 1958–1962 (Osieck and Hustings 1993), and recent range decreases have occurred in several countries with small populations (see table). Large, stable populations are present only in northern regions and in Belarus.

Of the total winter population (285,000 birds for the East Atlantic Flyway: Smit and Piersma 1989), 130,000–180,000 winter in Europe, the majority occurring in the United Kingdom (over 50%), Republic of Ireland, Netherlands and Portugal (EBD 1994). The rest go mainly to Africa, especially Guinea-Bissau, Mauritania, Tunisia, Sierra Leone, Morocco and Egypt (Summers *et al.* 1987, Smit and Piersma 1989).

There are discrepancies between population trends based on breeding bird surveys and midwinter counts (Smit and Piersma 1989). Overall, European wintering populations were stable between 1970 and 1990, and, although numbers wintering in Britain fell during 1975–1988, more were recorded there in subsequent years (Batten *et al.* 1990).

■ Ecology

Breeding occurs mainly in open lowlands and valleys of temperate and steppe regions, in many different wetland habitats (water-meadows, marshes, coastal saltings, etc.) as well as drier sites near moist feeding grounds, and in steppe areas on saline lakes and at high altitudes. Highest densities (up to 100 pairs/km^2) are in coastal saltmarshes (Glutz von Blotzheim *et al.* 1977, Batten *et al.* 1990). Key requirements for breeding are a high water-table with local soil saturation, open landscapes with look-

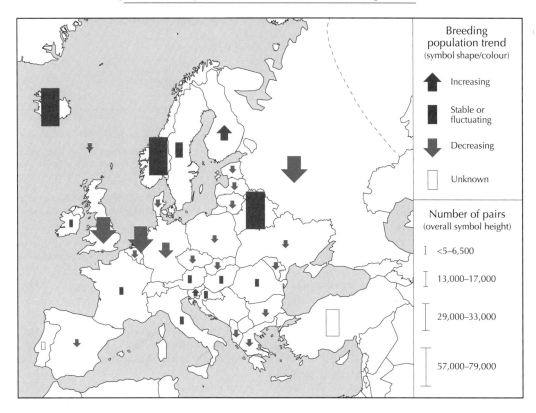

Breeding population trend
(symbol shape/colour)

⬆ Increasing

⬛ Stable or fluctuating

⬇ Decreasing

☐ Unknown

Number of pairs
(overall symbol height)

⌶ <5–6,500

⌶ 13,000–17,000

⌶ 29,000–33,000

⌶ 57,000–79,000

out posts, moderately dense tussock vegetation (preferably grass or sedge) of intermediate height, and nearby wetlands for feeding. Wintering is on coastal mudflats. Prey is mainly small crustaceans, molluscs and polychaete worms, or, for inland breeders, earthworms and cranefly larvae.

■ Threats

Loss and degradation of breeding and winter habitat are the main problems. Breeding habitat is destroyed by wetland drainage, agricultural intensification (the Redshank's tolerance to agricultural management is rather low: Beintema 1991a), flood control and afforestation (Glutz von Blotzheim et al. 1977, Cramp and Simmons 1983, Pienkowski et al. 1987). Coastal winter quarters are affected by land-claim, industrial development, dredging, pollution, human disturbance, saltworks and by Spartina encroaching on mudflats (Meininger and Mullié 1981, Smit et al. 1987, Summers et al. 1987, Batten et al. 1990).

For birds wintering in western Europe severe winters with frozen or snow-covered waters and fields can be disastrous (Davidson 1982, Marchant et al. 1990). In West Africa the clearance of mangroves for rice-growing and the construction of barrages in irrigation schemes reduce the extent of natural habitat, but may also provide suitable new habitats (Hepburn 1987, Tye and Tye 1987).

■ Conservation measures

In temperate regions, breeding habitat can be improved by raising the water-table, low-level use of organic fertilizer, low-intensity grazing, late mowing, winter flooding, and the creation of shallow pools (Davidson and Evans 1987, Batten et al. 1990, Beintema 1991b, Pienkowski 1991). However, a site-based approach is unlikely to secure enough habitat to maintain the population. Widespread changes in land-use policies are also necessary, and may include payments to farmers for the management of grassland to benefit waders (Marchant et al. 1990, Beintema 1991b). This will be costly, with payments made in Germany, for example, amounting to 1,300–2,000 DM/ha/year (Reinke 1991). However, funding for the conservation of wet grassland could be provided within the EU in appropriate areas, through the development of management agreements under the Agri-environment Regulation (EC Reg. 2078/92) of the Common Agricultural Policy.

Adequate protection of coastal sites with over 1% of total winter Redshank numbers is essential; for the East Atlantic Flyway this totals 39 sites, together holding about 90% of the population (Smit and Piersma 1989). The restoration and creation of suitable coastal habitats is also needed (Davidson and Evans 1987).

JOHANNA E. WINKELMAN

Wood Sandpiper
Tringa glareola

SPEC Category 3
Status Declining
Criteria Moderate decline

There has been a decline in some countries, especially in Finland which may hold up to half the European population. Drainage and exploitation of peatlands is the main cause, and it is therefore essential that extensive areas of the habitat are conserved.

■ Distribution and population trends

The Wood Sandpiper has a Palearctic distribution, mainly north of 55°N. Its main breeding range extends from Fennoscandia in the west through Russia to eastern Siberia. The species is a long-distance migrant, wintering in tropical and subtropical areas, with the west Palearctic population moving almost entirely to Africa, although very limited numbers probably winter in the Mediterranean and in southern Russia.

Fennoscandia and Russia west of the Urals perhaps hold a fifth to a quarter of the global population, but the size of the population in Siberia is poorly known. Very limited numbers breed in 11 other European countries, which together account for no more than 1% of the European population (see table, map).

A decline has been noted in four countries during the period 1970–1990, although the population in three of these (Denmark, Lithuania and Ukraine) totals only 150–175 pairs (see table, map). More importantly, the species has declined in Finland, which may hold up to a half the European population. European Russian and other Fennoscandian populations are now considered stable, although in

southern Sweden a drastic decline took place during the nineteenth century due to wetland drainage (SOF 1990), and by the late nineteenth and early twentieth centuries breeding had stopped almost completely in Lithuania, Poland, Germany and Ukraine, where it was once widespread (Glutz von Blotzheim *et al.* 1977, Cramp and Simmons 1983, Tomialojc 1990).

■ Ecology

In Fennoscandia and Russia the Wood Sandpiper mainly inhabits open swamps in taiga and on tundra, including bogs and marshes with stretches, or pools, of open water and damp meadows close to rivers. Typically, the vegetation of such bogs and marshes includes dwarf birch *Betula nana*, small conifers *Pinus silvestris* and/or *Picea abies*, sedge *Carex* and mosses *Sphagnum*, and in other damp areas sometimes willows *Salix* and grasses. In other parts of Europe birds occur in boggy areas such as are found along the shores of small lakes.

■ Threats

Drainage and destruction of wetlands is the major threat. In Finland vast peatland areas have already been exploited for forestry, and this has probably caused the decline in Wood Sandpiper numbers. In Sweden wetland drainage increased rapidly after 1970 (Boström 1978), and presently almost all peatlands are being considered for commercial exploitation. Vast areas are thought to be suitable for peat cutting for fuel or for afforestation, and a large proportion of wet meadows are also threatened by drainage for agriculture. In southern Sweden, Germany and Poland a decline has been noted even on unexploited wetlands, and this may be due to climate change (Glutz von Blotzheim *et al.* 1977).

The current situation regarding the status and threats to the Wood Sandpiper habitat in Russia is poorly known.

■ Conservation measures

As the Wood Sandpiper occurs in low densities it is essential that wide-scale measures are developed to conserve large areas of suitable peatland habitat,

	Breeding population			Breeding
	Size (pairs)	Year	Trend	range trend
Belarus	3,000–3,200	90	0	0
Denmark	**47–55**	87	–1	–1
Estonia	1,000–2,000	—	0	0
Finland	**200,000–300,000**	92	–1	**0**
Germany	3–5	—	0	0
Iceland	0–5	79–90	N	0
Latvia	300–500	—	0	–1
Lithuania	(50–60)	85–88	(–1)	(–1)
Norway	20,000–40,000	90	0	+1
Poland	5–10 *			—
Russia	(100,000–1,000,000)	70–90	(0)	(0)
Sweden	50,000–100,000	87	(0)	0
Ukraine	**50–60**	86	–2	–2
United Kingdom	**5–6**	88–91	**0**	–2
Total (approx.)	370,000–1,400,000			

Trends	+2 Large increase	+1 Small increase	0 Stable	X Extinct
(1970–1990)	–2 Large decrease	–1 Small decrease	F Fluctuating	N New breeder

Data quality **Bold:** reliable quantitative data   Normal type: incomplete quantitative data
Bracketed figures: no quantitative data   * Data quality not provided

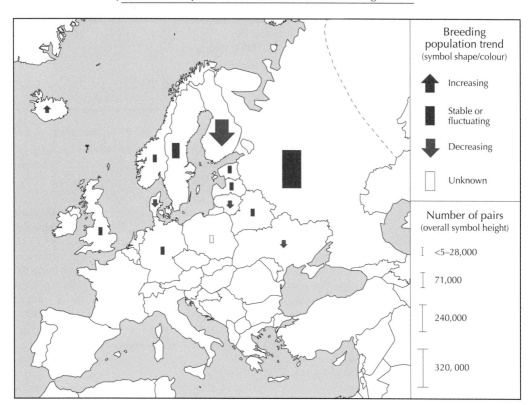

particularly in Fennoscandia and Russia and for the few remaining breeding sites in the southern parts of the breeding range. This can be achieved by prohibiting all kinds of drainage in forested areas, including small wetlands.

Further investigations are needed to identify reasons for the decline in apparently suitable habitats.

ULF KOLMODIN AND LENNART RISBERG

Little Gull
Larus minutus

SPEC Category 3
Status Declining
Criteria Moderate decline

Almost half the European population breeds in Russia, and although poorly known, is probably declining. Major threats at breeding and passage sites include drainage, flooding, recreational disturbance and pollution. Conservation measures should include control of access to breeding grounds, monitoring of pollution and management of water-levels in the breeding season.

■ Distribution and population trends

The Little Gull has three separate breeding populations: eastern Siberia, western Siberia, and from western Russia to the Baltic, with a few smaller additional colonies scattered across Europe. Russia holds roughly half the European breeders, with about another third in Finland, and colonies in Belarus, Estonia and Latvia constituting a further fifth (see table, map). Regular breeding also occurs in Norway, Sweden, Netherlands, Poland, Lithuania, Romania and Ukraine (see table, map), although breeding is often sporadic in the west and south of the main range (Cramp and Simmons 1983).

A migratory species, the Little Gull is largely coastal when not breeding. The extent of the winter quarters is not well known, but west European populations are generally found on western seaboards from the North and Irish Seas to the Mediterranean, where they join wintering eastern populations. Smaller numbers winter on the Black Sea and the southern Caspian (Cramp and Simmons 1983).

Although some population trends are uncertain and masked by fluctuations, numbers fell over the 1970–1990 period in parts of the large Russian range as well as in the better known populations of Poland, Estonia and the Ukraine (see table, map). In contrast, major increases have occurred recently in Finland,

with smaller increases in the Netherlands and parts of Russia (St Petersburg, Vologda and Moscow provinces). This may reflect a general breeding range extension to the west (Smith 1975). An increase in British observations in spring and autumn since the late 1940s (Neath and Hutchinson 1978) may indicate an increase in breeding numbers in western populations or a change in migration routes. However, overall the species showed a significant decline in just over 50% of its European population.

■ Ecology

The Little Gull breeds across many climatic zones, in Russia from steppe lakes in the south, through mixed forest and into the taiga. It breeds colonially in river valleys, lowland freshwater wetlands with lush vegetation and emergent plants, the nest being usually close to shallow water (Cramp and Simmons 1983, Batten *et al.* 1990). Wet marshes with rough grass tussocks, bog-bean *Menyanthes*, water-soldier *Stratiotes* or rushes *Juncus* are frequently used, as are small islands and sand/shingle banks, reedbeds and grazed saline marshes. Birds frequently nest close to other colonial species, e.g. Black-headed Gull *L. ridibundus*, Common Tern *Sterna hirundo* and marsh terns *Chlidonias*, though in Kazakhstan pure colonies of several hundred pairs are found (Ilyichev and Zubakin 1988). Sandy or muddy beaches with nearby fresh water are preferred at coastal wintering sites (Cramp and Simmons 1983).

A wide variety of insects forms the main food during breeding and on passage, and oligochaete worms, fish and spiders are also taken. The winter diet is less well known, but includes fish and marine invertebrates. As surface-feeders, Little Gulls will frequently accompany terns Sternidae on foraging trips (Cramp and Simmons 1983).

■ Threats

The sporadic breeding distribution of Little Gull has been linked with specific habitat requirements (Cramp and Simmons 1983), and the habit of nesting in marshy, partially flooded areas leaves them suscep-

| | Breeding population | | | Breeding |
	Size (pairs)	Year	Trend	range trend
Belarus	**1,800–2,300**	85	F	0
Estonia	1,000–2,000	—	–1	0
Finland	8,000–10,000	92	+2	+2
Latvia	**700–3,000**	—	F	–1
Lithuania	**100–200**	85–88	(0)	(0)
Netherlands	**5–40**	87–90	+1	0
Norway	0–10	90	N	N
Poland	20–60	—	–1	F
Romania	(0–5)	—	(0)	(0)
Russia	11,000–14,000	84–88	(–1)	(–1)
Sweden	75–125	87	0	0
Ukraine	100–200	80	–1	–1
Total (approx.)	23,000–32,000			

Trends +2 Large increase +1 Small increase 0 Stable X Extinct
(1970–1990) –2 Large decrease –1 Small decrease F Fluctuating N New breeder
Data quality **Bold**: reliable quantitative data Normal type: incomplete quantitative data
Bracketed figures: no quantitative data * Data quality not provided

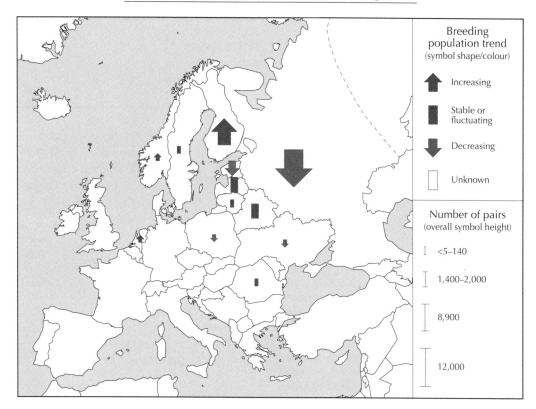

Breeding population trend
(symbol shape/colour)

↑ Increasing

▮ Stable or fluctuating

↓ Decreasing

☐ Unknown

Number of pairs
(overall symbol height)

I <5–140

I 1,400–2,000

I 8,900

I 12,000

tible to both natural and man-made flooding in the breeding season. In Sweden, the construction of dykes for agriculture has threatened some colonies (Grimmett and Jones 1989). Recreational disturbance also threatens freshwater breeding sites, for example the reconstruction of a lake for fishing has been proposed at Lake Engure in Latvia (Important Bird Area 015) (Grimmett and Jones 1989). Forestry work may also cause disturbance, as for example on the Umealven delta, Sweden (IBA 025). Water pollution (including PCBs, pesticides and heavy metals), sand extraction, intensive fishing and military training threaten the IJsselmeer, Netherlands (IBA 030), an important passage site (Grimmett and Jones 1989).

■ Conservation measures

The Little Gull is protected under the EU Wild Birds Directive and Appendix II of the Bern Convention and appropriate enforcement of this legislation is essential.

Public access restrictions and monitoring of pollution should continue at breeding, passage and wintering sites such as, in Sweden, coastal areas around Gotland (IBA 009), Lake Hornborgasjön (IBA 014), River Svartan (IBA 021), Lake

Gammelstadsviken (IBA 028) and Lake Persofjarden (IBA 028); in Latvia, Gomelis Marsh (IBA 012) and Lake Engure (IBA 015); Ujscie Wisly (mouth of the River Vistula) (Poland, IBA 023); and IJsselmeer (Netherlands, IBA 030). In particular, attention should be directed towards conservation of Little Gulls within Russia, as, although this country holds half the European breeding population, very few IBAs have been identified as holding the species.

Management of water-levels at breeding sites will be an important factor in site protection, and appropriately managed grazing will maintain vegetation at a suitable height for successful breeding. At some sites, e.g. River Svartan, Sweden (IBA 021), regular mowing and grazing is needed to control *Salix* growth. Monitoring of habitat loss and change will be necessary for the maintenance of suitable breeding areas for Little Gull throughout the breeding range and this will include changes in water-level and agricultural practices.

Recreational disturbance and industrial and domestic pollution at breeding areas should also be carefully controlled. The effects of predation, especially by newly introduced predators at breeding sites, and the impact of newly introduced flora, should also be investigated.

EMMA BRINDLEY AND ADRIAN DEL NEVO

Audouin's Gull
Larus audouinii

SPEC Category 1
Status Localized
Criteria Localized

Over 90% of the global breeding population of this Mediterranean seabird is in Europe. Although it has recently increased in numbers, the species is highly susceptible because about 90% of the European population occurs at just two Spanish colonies: the Ebro delta and the Chafarinas Islands. Rapidly increasing populations of Yellow-legged Gull threaten these colonies through competition for nest space and predation of eggs and chicks. Continued protection of colonies is therefore essential.

■ Distribution and population trends

Audouin's Gull is confined as a breeding bird to the Mediterranean, with Europe holding over 90% of the global breeding population in 1989. Over 90% of the European population is concentrated at two Spanish colonies, the Ebro delta and the Chafarinas Islands off Morocco, with other important populations in Sardinia, the Corsica–Tuscan archipelago, the Balearic Islands and the Columbretes, and a few scattered and small colonies in the eastern Mediterranean (see population table, Important Bird Area table, map). The species is partially migratory, the main winter quarters lying along the Atlantic coast of Africa, extending south to Senegal and Gambia (Hoogendoorn and Mackrill 1987, de Juana *et al.* 1987, Baillon 1989).

The species was formerly very rare (de Bournonville 1964, Makatsch 1968, King 1981), but an impressive recovery has recently taken place. The global population rose from 1,000 pairs in 1966 to 9,000–9,500 pairs in 1989 (de Juana and Varela 1993), a rate of increase of some 10% per year and not attributable to improved knowledge of the species. Important increases occurred in the protected Chafarinas colony ·which grew from c.1,000 pairs in 1976 to 2,200 pairs in 1981, and then stabilized at this level, at which point a new colony formed in the Ebro delta (Martínez and Carrera 1983). Subse-

Important Bird Areas The top ten IBAs for breeding Audouin's Gulls in Europe, together holding over 90% of the total European population.

France	153	Iles Finocchiarola et Côte de Tamarone a Barcaggio
Italy	056	Arcipelago Toscano (including Isole Capraia, Giglio, Montecristo, d'Elba and Palmaiola)
Spain	202	Delta del Ebro
	210	Islas Columbretes
	270	Islas Chafarinas
	271	Islas Vedrá y Vedranell
	274	Islas de los Freus
	277	Isla Dragonera
	285	Acantilados costeros Islas Malgrats Isla del Sech
	286	Archipiélago de Cabrera

quently, the Chafarinas colony has increased again to 3,188 pairs in 1991 and 4,440 in 1992. The number of pairs at the Ebro delta, a site which is also protected, increased from 36 in 1981 to 6,714 in 1992 (Martínez Viltata 1992), a change that can only be explained if movements from the Chafarinas are taken into account. Consequently, after taking account of other colonies in the Balearics and the Columbretes, the Spanish total alone was 12,631 pairs in 1992 (see population table).

Because it depends on continued protection of the main colonies, the species' global status is classified as Conservation Dependent (Collar *et al.* 1994).

■ Ecology

Breeding takes place in colonies on flat ground, generally on small rocky islands covered with low, scattered bushes, although the Ebro delta colony lies on the sandy tip of a thin peninsula. Away from the breeding areas birds roost on beaches, often near river mouths, and in saltpans.

Audouin's Gull is a specialized fish-eater (Wallace 1969, Witt 1977), taking clupeids and other pelagic species (Witt *et al.* 1981), mostly at night, in calm

	Breeding population			Breeding
	Size (pairs)	Year	Trend	range trend
Cyprus	10–20	—	F	0
France	**85–100**	92	F	F
Greece	(70–100)	—	(0)	(0)
Italy	500–600	86	(0)	(F)
Spain	**12,631–12,631**	92	+2	+2
Turkey	(50–50)	83	—	—
Total (approx.)	13,000–14,000			

Trends   +2 Large increase   +1 Small increase   0 Stable   X Extinct
(1970–1990)   -2 Large decrease   -1 Small decrease   F Fluctuating   N New breeder
Data quality **Bold**: reliable quantitative data   Normal type: incomplete quantitative data
              Bracketed figures: no quantitative data   * Data quality not provided

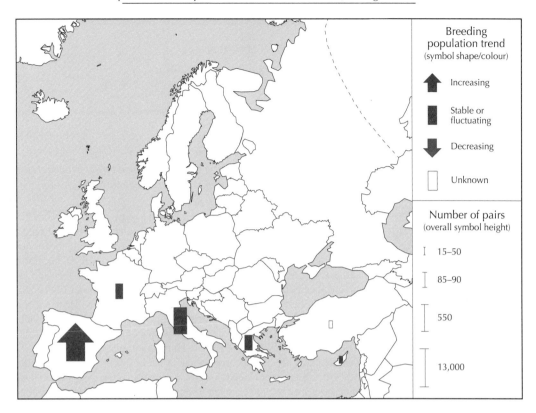

Breeding population trend
(symbol shape/colour)

▲ Increasing

■ Stable or fluctuating

▼ Decreasing

☐ Unknown

Number of pairs
(overall symbol height)

| 15–50

| 85–90

| 550

| 13,000

seas within the continental shelf. General oceano-graphic factors and related fish abundance seem to determine both the uneven breeding distribution of the species within the Mediterranean (Witt 1982), and its non-breeding areas along the north-west African coast, where winter upwellings and important fisheries occur. Birds will, however, feed on waste from fishing vessels, and indeed in Morocco the species' distribution and relative abundance throughout the year are related to commercial fishing activities (Beaubrun 1983).

■ Threats

In historic times and until recently the low population levels were considered to be due to egg-collecting (de Juana 1984, Mayol 1986), but this has virtually stopped and disturbance from fishermen, tourists and military activities is only occasional. In some colonies, including that on the Chafarinas Islands, the major threat now seems to be the rapidly increasing populations of Yellow-legged Gull *L. cachinnans*, which competes with Audouin's Gull for nesting space and predates its eggs and chicks (Bradley 1986). This is a major concern, especially since the world's population of the Audouin's Gull is concentrated in just two major colonies.

Overfishing by man could deplete the stocks of pelagic fish, at least locally (Paterson *et al.* 1992), but the species' dependence on offal from trawlers may determine breeding success in some colonies (Paterson *et al.* 1992).

■ Conservation measures

Protection of the main colonies should be maintained and expanded to cover other sites, especially in the eastern Mediterranean and on the North African coast. Additionally, protection must be given to the main stopover sites; in Spain these are Cabo de Gata (Important Bird Area 227) and Cerrillos (IBA 230) in Almería province, and in Morocco the beaches between Tamri and Agadir, the Muluya river, and the mouth of the Massa river.

More research is required to establish the effects that Yellow-legged Gulls are having on the Audouin's Gull populations and, if necessary, to establish the best means of control. The breeding distribution in the eastern Mediterranean and Algeria and the extent of the African winter quarters should also be investigated. More information is needed on the feeding ecology in both breeding and wintering areas and its relation to fisheries. Comparisons of breeding success between colonies over time should be examined.

EDUARDO DE JUANA

287

Common Gull
Larus canus

SPEC Category 2
Status Declining
Criteria Moderate decline

The majority of the world population nests in Europe, particularly Fennoscandia. Population trends of this rather poorly known species seem mixed, although numbers in the Norwegian and Danish strongholds seem to be falling. Declines may be related to competition and predation from Herring Gulls, human disturbance, pesticide use, land-claim, drainage and American mink predation.

◼ Distribution and population trends

Common Gulls breed across a broad swathe of the Palearctic and western Nearctic. Probably over half of the world total breeds in Europe, concentrated in northern Russia, Finland, Sweden and Norway, and with sizeable populations in Scotland and Denmark (Lloyd *et al*. 1991; see table, map). With some exceptions, this gull tends to nest in small dispersed groups, making censusing difficult, so numbers are not well known in much of the range. Birds move from the colder frozen areas of Fennoscandia to warmer shores in winter, south to 45°N in western Europe. Very small breeding populations have grown up in some of these wintering areas, such as southern England.

Common Gulls have apparently experienced a mix of trends in both population levels and range. There has been a general increase during the twentieth century (Cramp and Simmons 1983), but Hario (1985) recorded 70–75% declines in the Gulf of Finland in the 1970s. Between 1970 and 1990 population falls were recorded in Norway, Denmark and Estonia (Christensen 1990b, see table, map), while there was apparently an increase in the large population in Russia. Numbers in other countries holding large populations, such as Sweden, Finland and the United Kingdom remained about constant. However, overall more than 35% of the population declined.

◼ Ecology

Common Gulls often nest in small groups in areas with difficult access for mammalian ground predators (Burger and Gochfeld 1987). These habitats include shingle bars in rivers, boggy ground, small coastal islands, and the vicinity of ponds. Less usually, some birds nest on buildings (Cramp 1971, Sullivan 1985). In Scotland, some very large colonies occur on the tops of moorland hills overlooking arable land (Tasker *et al*. 1991), perhaps because these provide a relatively predator-free environment (the surrounding habitat is managed for grouse shooting) in a food-rich landscape. Two colonies in the Correen and Mortlach Hills, together holding a total of 25,000–40,000 pairs, account for about half the British population. Such large concentrations are unusual, the largest sites known elsewhere being on the coastal islands of Langenwerder (Germany) and Amager (Denmark) (Nehls 1973, Møller 1978).

In winter, Common Gulls feed in a wide range of coastal habitats and arable fields free from frost. Their main foods are invertebrates.

◼ Threats

Three reasons have been advanced for the spectacular decline in Denmark during the 1970s and early 1980s. Herring Gulls *L. argentatus* increased greatly in this period and often breed at the same sites,

	Breeding population			Breeding
	Size (pairs)	Year	Trend	range trend
Austria	**3–3**	91	**0**	**0**
Belarus	500–1,200	87	+2	+2
Belgium	15–25	81–90	+1	+1
Czech Republic	**3–7**	—	+1	+1
Denmark	**29,000–29,300**	88	–1	0
Faroe Islands	(500–1,000)	81	(0)	(0)
Estonia	10,000–15,000	—	–2	0
Finland	50,000–60,000	92	**0**	**0**
France	**23–33**	91	+2	+2
Germany	7,500–16,500	—	+1	**0**
Hungary	**4–4**	91	N*	0*
Iceland	**300–400**	—	+2	+2
Rep. of Ireland	3,000–3,000	85–87	+1	0
Latvia	**500–600**	86	F	+1
Lithuania	**100–150**	85–88	+1	+1
Moldova	0–10	88	0	–1
Netherlands	**7,000–7,000**	90	+2	**0**
Norway	100,000–200,000	90	–1	**0**
Poland	**3,500–4,300**	—	+1	+1
Russia	40,000–60,000	84–88	+1	0
Slovakia	5–10	—	N	+1
Sweden	100,000–200,000	87	**0**	**0**
Switzerland	**1–6**	86–91	**0**	**0**
United Kingdom	68,500–68,500	85–87	0	**0**
Isle of Man [1]	**1–2**	—	N	0*
Total (approx.)	420,000–670,000			

Trends +2 Large increase +1 Small increase 0 Stable X Extinct
(1970-1990) -2 Large decrease -1 Small decrease F Fluctuating N New breeder
Data quality **Bold**: reliable quantitative data Normal type: incomplete quantitative data
Bracketed figures: no quantitative data * Data quality not provided
[1] Population figures are included within United Kingdom totals

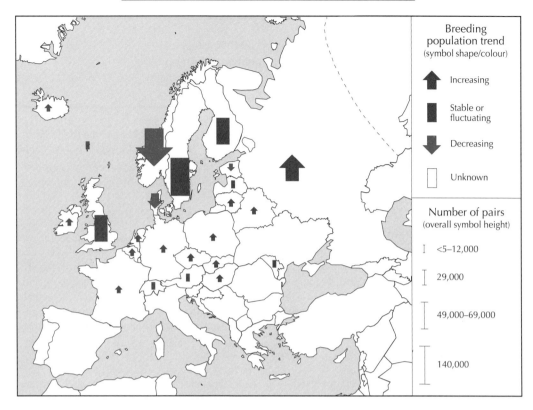

competing with Common Gulls and perhaps predating them. However, this increase in Herring Gulls has stopped without a subsequent rise in the number of Common Gulls. Human activities can have significant effects, but disturbance cannot be a major factor as most important breeding colonies (generally uninhabited isolated islands) are much better protected now than in the 1970s. However, the decline or disappearance of smaller colonies outside sanctuaries may be attributed to increased human disturbance. Agricultural pesticides may be contaminating the birds (the species feeds extensively on farmland) and reducing their reproductive success, but as yet there is no proof of this. Some colonies are known to have unsuccessful breeding for several years at a stretch (e.g. in the northern part of Jutland, Denmark) and birds have been seen sitting on empty nests (J. O. Christensen *in litt.*).

In some areas (e.g. west coast of Scotland, Norway), introduced ground predators, such as American mink *Mustela vison*, appear to have reduced the number of colonies and caused the population to move to more inaccessible sites (Craik 1990, Soikkeli 1990). Land-claim and drainage may affect other sites, both in the breeding season and in wintering areas, which would reduce both breeding and feed-

ing opportunities and lead to some reductions in breeding range (e.g. Gibbons *et al.* 1993). In northeast Scotland, forestry plantations on hills used for breeding seem likely to result in the abandonment of these sites as trees mature (Tasker *et al.* 1991), and more traditional wetland sites have also suffered from agricultural drainage or forestry plantation.

Common Gulls have not been studied in depth for (e.g.) the impact of pollutants, so some potential threats remain to be evaluated.

■ Conservation measures

Since little is known of the threats facing this species, it is difficult to identify conservation measures. Further studies are thus required, especially of the declining Norwegian and Danish populations.

Common Gulls are usually dispersed, when breeding or otherwise, so sites such as the Correen Hills in Scotland which support large colonies should be protected through measures to control further habitat change. Action to conserve the diversity of habitats in the wider countryside will help to preserve existing small colonies, and control of American mink would undoubtedly help in some areas. If the Common Gull is to be managed, monitoring schemes will be required that sample broad areas of landscape.

MARK TASKER

Ivory Gull
Pagophila eburnea

SPEC Category 3
Status (Endangered)
Criteria Large decline, <2,500 pairs

The distribution and status of this high-Arctic species are poorly known. Many breeding colonies are in highly inaccessible areas and often change location. Declines in breeding numbers are recorded from Russia but these are insufficiently understood. Outside the breeding season the species disperses, but wintering areas are also little known. A full census with subsequent monitoring of the species throughout its range are required.

■ Distribution and population trends

Ivory Gulls breed in northern and eastern Greenland, the high-Arctic zone of Canada and Russia, and in Svalbard (Blomqvist and Elander 1981, Cramp and Simmons 1983). Most birds are restricted to the pack-ice zone and are colonial in summer and dispersed in winter (Mehlum 1989, 1990, Camphuysen 1993). On current information, Europe holds about 10% of the world's breeding population of the species.

In the European parts of the Russian Arctic Ivory Gull breeds on Franz Josef Land and Severnaya Zemlya (Golovkin 1984) where the largest colony (c.700 pairs) was found in 1993 on Domashny Island (Severnaya Zemlya) and the entire archipelago was estimated to hold at least 1,000 pairs (de Korte and Volkov 1993; see table). Although Ivory Gulls are widespread breeders in Svalbard, only small colonies are known (Løvenskiold 1964, Mehlum and Fjeld 1987). Major wintering areas holding up to 35,000 individuals include the Davis Strait and Labrador Sea (Orr and Parsons 1982), Greenland Sea (Brown 1984) and the pack-ice of the Bering Sea (Trukhin and Kosygin 1987, Everett *et al.* 1989). Numbers located in wintering areas indicate that many breeding sites remain to be discovered throughout the range of the species.

It is possible that a population decline has occurred in Svalbard. At the end of the nineteenth century many colonies there were reported to have

held a hundred or more pairs, yet thorough investigations during the last 30 years have failed to locate colonies of this size (Mehlum and Fjeld 1987). The Russian population in Europe is thought to have declined during the 1970–1990 period, although the trend is uncertain (see table, map). No information is available on the population trend in Greenland.

■ Ecology

The Ivory Gull breeds exclusively in the high-Arctic zone although its breeding habitat varies considerably through its range. In Franz Josef Land and Greenland, the majority of colonies are on the ground (Salomonsen 1961, MacDonald and MacPherson 1962, Løvenskiold 1964, Tomkovich 1984, de Korte 1991), whereas in most of Svalbard and parts of Greenland colonies are located on steep cliffs on nunataks (isolated rock peaks above the snow or ice) high above the sea and often far inland (Bateson and Plowright 1959, Birkenmajer 1969, Hakala 1975, Frisch and Morgan 1979, Wright and Matthews 1980). Many colonies are small and situated on inaccessible cliffs.

Ivory Gulls are known to forage in a wide range of habitats and on a variety of food sources. Large feeding concentrations occur at the edge of sea ice and at glacier fronts, where there are high densities of surface zooplankton (Renaud and MacLaren 1982, Mehlum 1984, Ree 1986, Bradstreet 1986, Camphuysen 1991). Ivory Gulls also scavenge near human settlements and on whale or seal carcasses (Divoky 1976, Bradstreet 1977, Gjertz *et al.* 1985, Camphuysen 1991).

■ Threats

Reported declines in Ivory Gulls have been attributed to the decreasing number of polar bears *Ursus maritimus*, due to extensive hunting, as the bears' faeces and freshly killed prey are a food source for Ivory Gulls. However, recent studies have shown that the gulls' main food consists of small fish and

| | Breeding population | | | Breeding |
	Size (pairs)	Year	Trend	range trend
Denmark				
Greenland	(100–200)	83	—	(0)
Norway				
Svalbard	237–?	—	—	—
Russia	(1,000–1,500)	84–88	(–1)	(0)
Total (approx.)	1,300–1,700			

Trends   +2 Large increase   +1 Small increase   0 Stable   X Extinct
(1970–1990)   -2 Large decrease   -1 Small decrease   F Fluctuating   N New breeder
Data quality   **Bold**: reliable quantitative data   Normal type: incomplete quantitative data
  Bracketed figures: no quantitative data   * Data quality not provided

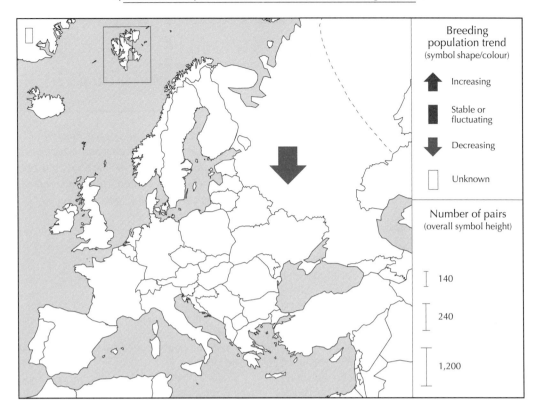

small marine invertebrates (Divoky 1976). Since the Ivory Gull competes successfully amongst gulls and skuas at feeding sites in the Arctic (Camphuysen 1991), and feeds on a wide variety of prey, it is not exceptionally vulnerable to the collapse of fish stocks or to declines in the availability of prey. However, the species' extensive use of seal and whale blubber does make it particularly vulnerable to heavy-metal contamination (*cf.* Nielsen and Dietz 1989).

The species' favoured habitats appear not to be greatly threatened, although tourism has increased in areas which were formerly highly isolated, such as eastern Svalbard, Franz Josef Land and northern and eastern Greenland, where Ivory Gulls breed on the ground, and this may cause disturbance, predation and desertion.

Overall the population declines in Svalbard and Russia are poorly documented and poorly understood.

■ Conservation measures

Fuller census studies and monitoring of breeding numbers throughout the range of the species are urgently required, as is further research to assess the main food items taken and the location of wintering areas. This will allow clarification of conservation priorities. Colonies which are among the larger (more than 50 pairs) and on flat ground (and thus more accessible) deserve special protection.

KEES CAMPHUYSEN

Gull-billed Tern
Gelochelidon nilotica

SPEC Category 3
Status (Endangered)
Criteria Large decline, <10,000 pairs

Gull-billed Terns are declining widely in Europe and are now rare, having decreased substantially since the end of the nineteenth century. The most likely reasons are loss of foraging habitats close to breeding areas, the destruction and disturbance of, and predation at, colonial nesting sites, and habitat destruction and degradation in the winter quarters. Colonies should be protected from habitat destruction and disturbance, and appropriate management of feeding areas is needed.

◼ Distribution and population trends

The cosmopolitan but very discontinuous distribution of the Gull-billed Tern ranges over Neotropical, Nearctic, Australian, Oriental, Palearctic and Afrotropical regions. The species used to be distributed more widely than at present in northern Europe but now it breeds mainly in the Mediterranean and Black Sea regions in Spain, France, Italy, Russia, Ukraine, Romania, Bulgaria, Albania, Greece and Turkey (see table, map). Single colonies remain in northern Germany (Schleswig-Holstein) and Denmark. There has been no breeding in the Netherlands since the 1950s when the site of the last colony was destroyed by the expansion of Rotterdam harbour (J. de Vlas *in litt.*).

Currently the European population is estimated to be only 7,000–16,000 pairs, with the largest numbers in Spain, Russia and Turkey. Most colonies have been decreasing since the beginning of the twentieth century, and many continued to decline between 1970 and 1990, including those in Spain, Denmark, Romania, Russia, Ukraine, Greece and Turkey (Biber 1993; see table, map). Overall approximately 95% of the European population is in countries where declines were recorded for this period, although there has been little information from the major colonies in Russia, the Ukraine and Turkey.

◼ Ecology

Gull-billed Tern colonies, often mixed with other terns and gulls, form on sand-dunes, islands, the shores of coastal and inland wetlands and pastures on polders with short grass (Goutner 1987, Biber and Salathé 1989).

The species forages over both wet and dry terrain such as beaches, dunes, freshwater or brackish wetlands, rice-fields, small dykes between ploughed fields, ditches, freshly irrigated fields, cereal and vegetable fields, orchards and even plantations (Leveque 1956, Tombal and Tombal 1986, M. Fasola and U. F. Foschi *in litt.* 1987, A. Martinez Vilalta *in litt.* 1987, M. Rendon *in litt.* 1987). The species shows considerable variation in the use of feeding sites, different habitats being used at different periods of the year, and also at different times within the breeding season.

There is also considerable geographical and seasonal variation in the diet. Birds in the Camargue take mainly crustaceans, crickets, grasshoppers, beetles and the Iberian marsh frog *Rana perezi* (Møller 1977, J.-P. Biber own data). In Denmark, voles, fish and lizards are also taken (Møller 1977) and, in the Valli di Camacchio of Italy, Bogliani *et al.* (1990) found lizards to be the main food brought to chicks. Wintering birds feed chiefly on large flying insects (Orthoptera, Coleoptera, Odonata) (Urban *et al.* 1986).

◼ Threats

A major enquiry into the Gull-billed Tern's status and distribution in Europe and Africa was conducted during the 1980s (Biber 1993), and much of the following information is drawn from this.

In the breeding areas, the main threats are the loss and degradation of foraging habitats through the intensification of agriculture, including the drainage

| | Breeding population | | | Breeding |
	Size (pairs)	Year	Trend	range trend
Albania	(0–50)	62	—	—
Bulgaria	10–30	—	0	0
Denmark	**0–2**	91	–2	–1
France	**423–423**	92	+2	0
Germany	50–60	—	**0**	**0**
Greece	50–150	—	(–1)	(–1)
Italy	**200–300**	86	0	+1
Romania	(20–40)	—	–2	–1
Russia	1,800–5,000	84–88	(–1)	(–1)
Spain	1,869–1,869	89	–1	–1
Turkey	(2,000–7,000)	—	(–1)	(0)
Ukraine	**400–800**	81	–1	–1
Total (approx.)	6,800–16,000			

Trends (1970–1990) +2 Large increase +1 Small increase 0 Stable X Extinct
  –2 Large decrease –1 Small decrease F Fluctuating N New breeder
Data quality **Bold**: reliable quantitative data Normal type: incomplete quantitative data
  Bracketed figures: no quantitative data * Data quality not provided

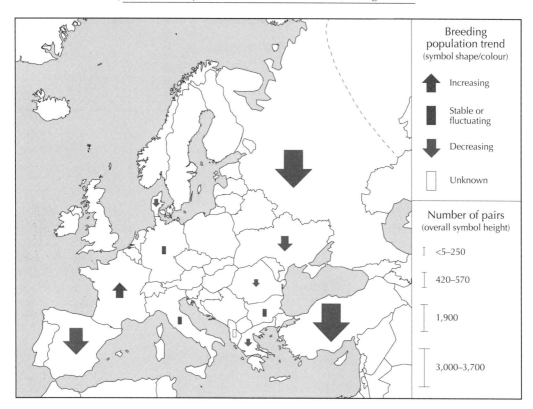

Breeding
population trend
(symbol shape/colour)

Increasing

Stable or
fluctuating

Decreasing

Unknown

Number of pairs
(overall symbol height)

<5–250

420–570

1,900

3,000–3,700

of marshes and the use of pesticides which reduce prey numbers in habitats where they are applied, such as rice-fields. Colonies have also been lost due to decreases in water-levels which allow easier access for nest predators. Predation is by foxes *Vulpes vulpes*, rats *Rattus* spp. and dogs, and eggs are taken by humans; all cause disturbance of colonies. Flooding of colonies has also caused substantial losses (up to 100%) of birds in some areas. Birds may die from accumulation of toxic chemicals. At Punta de la Banya in the Ebro delta of Spain, high mortality occurred before the 1980s and several dead birds were recorded annually through that decade (A. Martinez Vilalta *in litt.*).

Birds in the winter quarters may be subject to the toxic effects of pesticides as well as to the reduction in available food supplies which these chemicals may bring about (Biber and Salathé 1989).

■ Conservation measures

All colonies should be protected from habitat destruction and disturbance. The appropriate manage-

ment of feeding areas in the vicinity of colonies is also needed, including the protection of dunes, dry uncultivated land and marshes, and a shift to low-intensity farming practices on agricultural land should be encouraged. On farmland, overgrazing should be prevented and local controls on the use of pesticides could improve food availability and reduce the risk of poisoning. Measures may also need to be taken against predators, as for example in Spain, where electric fences are being used successfully to protect colonies (E. de Juana pers. comm.). In the Camargue, southern France, measures were taken to improve the conditions of the colony on an island, including the planting of vegetation (*Salicornia*) and the building of a ditch around the island to prevent intrusion by foxes and wild boar *Sus scrofa* (A. Johnson pers. comm.). In Italy the trapping of rats at the beginning of the breeding season has been considered (M. Fasola pers. comm.).

JEAN-PIERRE BIBER

Caspian Tern
Sterna caspia

SPEC Category 3
Status (Endangered)
Criteria Large decline, <10,000 pairs

The small and declining European population is restricted to a few groups of colonies. These colonies are often ephemeral, and susceptible to human disturbance and to destruction by wind-blown sand or flooding, and should therefore be protected from these threats. Shooting of birds on passage and on the wintering grounds should also be stopped.

■ Distribution and population trends

Less than a fifth of the Caspian Tern's breeding range is in Europe, where it occurs at a number of isolated sites. The main European breeding colonies are concentrated in the Volga delta (up to 3,000–5,000 pairs) and along the northern coast of the Black Sea (300–1,000 pairs) (Ilyichev and Zubakin 1988; see table). Important concentrations of breeding birds are also present in the northern part of the Baltic, chiefly along the Finnish, Swedish and Estonian coastlines (see table), with some movements of birds occurring between neighbouring colonies in this region (Staav 1979). The Baltic population totalled about 1,450 pairs in 1992, distributed among about 25 colonies (R. Staav pers comm.). Elsewhere only ephemeral small breeding groups or single pairs occur (Cramp 1985).

The Caspian Tern is a long-distance migrant (Mayaud 1956, Józefik 1969). Baltic and Black Sea birds winter mainly in the Niger inundation zone of interior West Africa, with a few along the West African coast and in the central Mediterranean and Nile delta. Birds from the Volga delta join wintering populations in the Persian Gulf and coasts to the east and south.

By the end of the nineteenth century the Caspian Tern was disappearing as a breeding species from Denmark, Germany and Romania (Glutz von Blotzheim and Bauer 1982). Increases have been reported from the Baltic since 1910, and during the twentieth century also from the Black and Caspian Seas, though most recent data (Cramp 1985, and see table) indicate that numbers in all three regions are below those from the 1970s (Glutz von Blotzheim and Bauer 1982, Ilyichev and Zubakin 1988, Siokhin *et al.* 1988). However, a significant problem with monitoring this species is that long-term trends in population size may be partly obscured by large local fluctuations, as (e.g.) in the Baltic.

■ Ecology

Breeding colonies usually comprise less than 100–200 pairs (Ilyichev and Zubakin 1988), although even single pairs can breed among other larids (Bergman 1980). Colonies are usually alongside coastal salt or freshwater lagoons, or on small, flat islets, within 40–50 km of clear waters rich in fish, nests being placed on sandy, rocky or short-vegetated ground (e.g. Cramp 1985).

The diet consists almost entirely of fish, usually 3–25 cm long, with a few invertebrates also being taken (Glutz von Blotzheim and Bauer 1982, Ilyichev and Zubakin 1988). Fish species eaten include Cyprinidae (such as roach *Rutilus rutilus*, dace *Leuciscus leuciscus*, ide *L. idus*, bleak *Alburnus alburnus*, rudd *Scardinius erythrophthalmus*), perch *Perca fluviatilis*, white bream *Blicca bjoerkna*, salmon and trout *Salmo*, ruffe *Gymnocephalus cernua*, pike *Esox lucius*, smelt *Osmerus eperlanus*, Clupeidae (including herring *Clupea harengus*), eel *Anguilla*, plaice *Pleuronectes* and mackerel *Scomber scombrus* (Cramp 1985).

■ Threats

Colonies are often ephemeral and are susceptible to human disturbance, flooding, wind-blown sand, fluctuations in fish stocks and predation by gulls and crows (Cramp 1985, Ilyichev and Zubakin 1988, Siokhin *et al.* 1988); some Baltic colonies have been abandoned after continued predation by American mink *Mustela vison* (R. Staav *in litt.*).

Away from colonies large numbers of birds are shot, chiefly in Romania, Italy and Malta (at fish-

	Breeding population			Breeding
	Size (pairs)	Year	Trend	range trend
Estonia	**250–250**	93	0	0
Finland	**700–750**	92	–1	–2
Russia	3,000–5,500	84–88	(–1)	(–1)
Spain	**1–1**	89	N	N
Sweden	**500–600**	87	–1	0
Turkey	(50–200)	—	(–1)	(0)
Ukraine	**250–800**	86	–1	–1
Total (approx.)	4,800–8,100			

Trends +2 Large increase +1 Small increase 0 Stable X Extinct
(1970–1990) –2 Large decrease –1 Small decrease F Fluctuating N New breeder
Data quality **Bold**: reliable quantitative data Normal type: incomplete quantitative data
Bracketed figures: no quantitative data * Data quality not provided

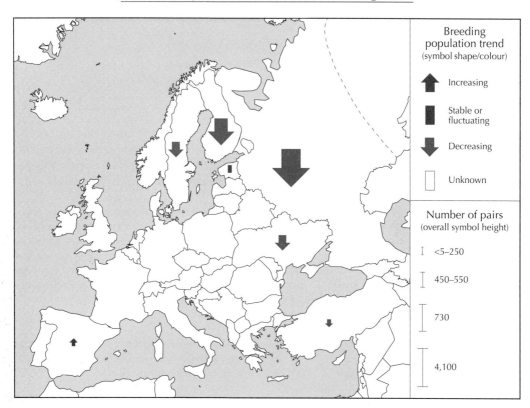

Breeding
population trend
(symbol shape/colour)

Increasing

Stable or
fluctuating

Decreasing

Unknown

Number of pairs
(overall symbol height)

<5–250

450–550

730

4,100

ponds and for sport). In winter quarters some are netted (Mayaud 1956), and in Mali many are caught on fish-hooks (Glutz von Blotzheim and Bauer 1982, R. Staav *in litt.*).

Conservation measures

All colonies should be protected from human disturbance, and where practical also from flooding and strong winds which can result in eggs being covered with sand. Measures may also be necessary to reduce predation levels locally where these are excessive.

Hunting and trapping of the species should be reduced through enforcement of existing laws, improved legislation, and public awareness and education initiatives.

LUDWIK TOMIALOJC

Sandwich Tern
Sterna sandvicensis

SPEC Category 2
Status Declining
Criteria Moderate decline

Although increasing in many countries, numbers in the Ukraine (half the European total) fell by 20–50% during 1970–1990. Main threats include land-use affecting vegetation at colonies, coastal developments, recreational disturbance, and predation. Conservation requires vegetation management, control of disturbance and predation, and continued population and productivity monitoring.

■ Distribution and population trends

The Sandwich Tern breeds mainly in north-west and south-east Europe (Batten *et al*. 1990), with other races in North and South America (Cramp 1985). European numbers and trends are generally well documented, with over three-quarters of the European population currently in the United Kingdom, Netherlands, Germany and Ukraine (see table, map); large populations also occur in France and Russia. These six countries together account for over 90% of the European total.

Outside the breeding season, western and northern populations migrate to the Atlantic seaboard of Africa (Møller 1981), while the south-eastern populations in the Black Sea move to the Mediterranean, and populations in the Caspian Sea move to the Persian Gulf (Batten *et al*. 1990).

The large populations in the United Kingdom and Netherlands, and to some extent France, increased substantially during 1970–1990, together with Estonia and Spain (see table, map). Smaller increases have also been noted in Greece and the Republic of Ireland, and it commenced breeding in

	Breeding population			Breeding
	Size (pairs)	Year	Trend	range trend
Belgium	**900–1,000**	91	N	0
Bulgaria	0–10	—	0	0
Denmark	**3,664–3,664**	90	(0)	0
Estonia	800–800	—	+2	+2
France	**6,500–6,650**	85	+1	0
Germany	21,000–21,000	85	0	0
Greece	0–50	—	(+1)	(0)
Rep. of Ireland	**1,800–1,800**	85–87	+1	0
Italy	**140–500**	86	N	N
Netherlands	**10,000–12,500**	89–91	+2	+1
Norway	0–5	90	N	N
Poland	0–300	—	F	F
Romania	500–2,000	—	F	–1
Russia	**4,000–6,000**	84–88	–1	0
Spain	**755–755**	89	+2	0
Sweden	**575–700**	89	–1	0
Ukraine	**50,000–70,000**	93	–1	–1
United Kingdom	**17,000–17,000**	85–87	+2	–1
Total (approx.)	120,000–140,000			

Trends (1970–1990) +2 Large increase +1 Small increase 0 Stable –2 Large decrease –1 Small decrease F Fluctuating X Extinct N New breeder
Data quality **Bold**: reliable quantitative data Normal type: incomplete quantitative data Bracketed figures: no quantitative data * Data quality not provided

Italy during the period. However, the Ukraine population, the largest in Europe, experienced a decline of 20–50% over the same period, following an earlier increase. Declines were also noted in Russia and Sweden, so that in total around 50% of the European population occurs in countries where declines occurred during 1970–1990.

■ Ecology

Nesting is colonial, frequently with other tern species and gulls (Batten *et al*. 1990), preferably on such sites as sand and shingle beaches (Cramp 1985), sand-dunes or rocky islets, although birds nest locally on inland freshwater lakes (as in Ireland: Cramp 1985). Bare patches of ground among vegetation are suitable as nest-sites, and tall, dense vegetation is generally avoided (A. del Nevo pers. comm.).

Small surface-shoaling marine fish are taken in plunge-dives from 5–10 m (Dunn 1972), although there is regional variation in the types of fish taken (Cramp 1985). Terns wintering in inshore West African waters may prey on fish driven to the surface by predators such as tuna (Dunn 1972). Preferred wintering areas are coastlines with mudflats, sandy beaches and rocky shores (Dunn 1972).

■ Threats

Vegetation changes seem to have led to the declines in the Ukraine (V. Serebryakov and V. Siohin pers. comm. 1994). Colonies there are frequently on islands subject for many years to grazing, but extensive pastoral agriculture has now been abandoned, causing rapid vegetation growth. In some cases designation of nature reserves has also led to inadequate grazing, as agriculture is normally forbidden.

Elsewhere, population fluctuations and movements between years are poorly understood, although birds will frequently move following disturbance to which they are highly susceptible on the breeding grounds (A. del Nevo own data).

In the Mediterranean, colonies have been threatened by development of holiday resorts and associated recreational disturbance (James 1984). The

296

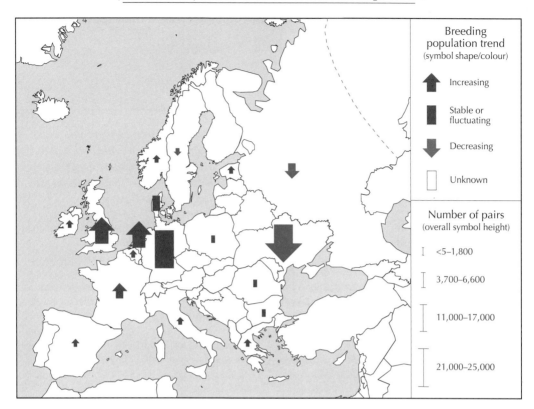

Breeding population trend (symbol shape/colour)	
↑	Increasing
▮	Stable or fluctuating
↓	Decreasing
▯	Unknown

Number of pairs (overall symbol height)	
I	<5–1,800
I	3,700–6,600
I	11,000–17,000
I	21,000–25,000

United Kingdom's populations have been affected by both human disturbance and predation by foxes *Vulpes vulpes* (Bourne and Smith 1974); indeed, persistent intrusion in the early settling period, for example by dogs, may lead to abandonment (Veen 1977). Sand-dunes and shingle beaches used as breeding sites are subject to marine and wind erosion and may quickly become unsuitable.

Birds on passage and wintering are trapped at many coastal localities in West Africa (e.g. Ntiamoa-Baidu 1991), but little is known of the effect these activities have on the breeding population.

■ Conservation measures

Vegetation at breeding sites should be managed. In the Ukraine, regular grazing outside the breeding season has been recommended (V. Serebryakov and V. Siohin pers. comm.), and plant growth should be monitored in areas where grazing has ceased.

Control of disturbance during the breeding season is vital, particularly during the early settling period when birds are most likely to desert (Lloyd *et al.* 1991). Local conservation bodies should be encouraged to produce guidelines for public visiting to colonies and for recreation in their vicinity. Important Bird Areas (IBAs) holding important colonies are, in the Ukraine, Yagorlytski and Tendra Bays (IBA 052) and Sivash Bay in the Sea of Azov (IBA

044); in the Netherlands, Griend (IBA 004) and Grevelingen (IBA 049); in Germany, Schleswig-Holsteinisches Wattenmeer (IBA 002) and Neuwerker und Sharhorner Watt (IBA 030); in the U.K., Farne Islands (IBA 143), Coquet Island (IBA 145) and the North Norfolk coast (IBA 165); and Bassin d'Arcachon et Banc d'Arguin (France, IBA 086). Disturbance levels at these and other sites should be monitored and methods sought to control this at critical times.

Predator control at breeding sites, e.g. anti-fox fencing, should be implemented where feasible. Successfully established Sandwich Tern colonies may benefit other tern species which are less aggressive in repelling predators, e.g. Roseate Terns *S. dougallii* (A. del Nevo own data).

The Sandwich Tern is protected under Annex I of the EU Wild Birds Directive and Appendix II of the Bern Convention. This protection should be enforced and extended to include marine areas as well as countries not covered by these agreements.

Continued monitoring of populations and productivity on a wide scale is also recommended for this highly mobile colonial species. A better understanding of the ecology and the threats to survival outside the breeding season is also needed to provide information for effective conservation measures.

EMMA BRINDLEY AND ADRIAN DEL NEVO

Roseate Tern
Sterna dougallii

SPEC Category 3
Status Endangered
Criteria Large decline, <2,500 pairs

The Roseate Tern suffered a dramatic population decline between 1969 and 1987 through much of its European range, particularly in the north-west. Disturbance and predation contribute to reduced breeding success. Outside the breeding season, food shortage and hunting may influence survival. To address these issues a research and conservation programme is currently aiming to understand the ecology and threats to the species and provide conservation recommendations.

■ Distribution and population trends

The Roseate Tern is a pantropical species with a small proportion (c.3%) of its global population breeding within Europe (A. del Nevo own data). The species breeds on the Portuguese Azores archipelago, where three-quarters of the European population occurs, and on islets off the east and west coasts of Britain and Ireland, and the north coast of Brittany in France (see table, map).

It is migratory, moving from breeding areas during August–September and remaining close to the Iberian and African coast to arrive in the Gulf of Guinea, its primary wintering area, during September–October. Birds remain within African coastal waters until late November or December after which their whereabouts are unknown until they return to the northern breeding colonies during April–June.

The European population of about 1,600 pairs (del Nevo *et al.* 1993) has been well documented, with the majority concentrated on the islands of Flores, Graciosa and Santa Maria in the Azores. However, the largest and most successful colony is located on the east coast of the Republic of Ireland, and there are smaller but important colonies in southern Ireland and in Brittany (see table, map). In north-west Europe two-thirds of the population experienced decline during 1970–1990, the pattern of decline varying between colonies. The Azorean population

is also believed to have declined, although the pattern of the decrease is uncertain.

■ Ecology

Roseate Terns rarely nest in isolation, gaining protection from avian and ground predators by their association with more aggressive species such as Common Tern *S. hirundo* or Sandwich Tern *S. sandvicensis*. Nest-sites tend to be concealed amongst rocks, vegetation or artificial cover, situated on isolated marine islets or islands in freshwater coastal lagoons.

Foraging is done predominantly in small, single-species groups, generally further offshore than other *Sterna* species (A. del Nevo own data). Foraging over shallow water, hydrographic features, or in association with large predatory fish (e.g. tuna and mackerel), Roseate Terns take small, shoaling prey within 1.5 m of the surface (A. del Nevo own data). In north-west Europe prey is dominated by sand-eels *Ammodytes* and a few gadoid species, but is considerably more varied in the Azores where up to twelve species of prey may be delivered to chicks (A. del Nevo own data).

■ Threats

All European colonies have been subject to variable levels of disturbance and/or predation from human activities (e.g. egg-collection) and avian and ground predators (e.g. Peregrine *Falco peregrinus*, gulls, mustelids, fox *Vulpes vulpes*) (del Nevo *et al.* 1990, Avery and del Nevo 1991, Avery *et al.* in press). Nesting Roseate Terns are particularly sensitive to human disturbance and avian or ground predators, resulting in desertion by whole colonies or shifts in subsequent seasons.

Hunting in the winter quarters has been identified as a threat to tern species and to Roseate Terns in particular. This occurs particularly between September and December in Senegal and Ghana, and involves the use of a variety of techniques such as beach snares (Dunn and Mead 1982, Anon. 1990c,

	Breeding population			Breeding
	Size (pairs)	Year	Trend	range trend
France	**81–86**	92	–2	–2
Rep. of Ireland	**454–454**	92	+1	0
Portugal				
Azores	**1,000–1,000**	92	–1	0
Madeira	5–15	91	0	0
Spain	1–2	—	N	N
Canary Islands	1–1	87	N	N
United Kingdom	**64–64**	92	–2	–1
Total (approx.)	1,600–1,600			

Trends +2 Large increase +1 Small increase 0 Stable X Extinct
(1970–1990) –2 Large decrease –1 Small decrease F Fluctuating N New breeder
Data quality **Bold:** reliable quantitative data Normal type: incomplete quantitative data
Bracketed figures: no quantitative data * Data quality not provided

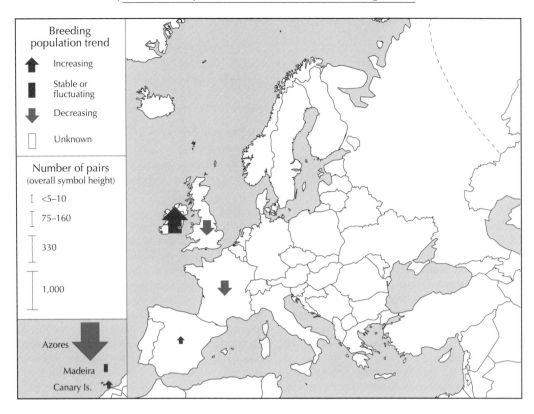

Breeding population trend

↑ Increasing

■ Stable or fluctuating

↓ Decreasing

☐ Unknown

Number of pairs
(overall symbol height)

<5–10

75–160

330

1,000

Azores

Madeira

Canary Is.

Ntiamoa-Baidu 1991, A. del Nevo own data). An average of 1.36 terns hunted per hour was recorded in Ghana during 1989 with an estimated minimum of 32 (maximum 224) Roseate Terns caught or injured during a 75-day period in September–December (A. del Nevo own data).

■ Conservation measures

Breeding Roseate Terns are fully protected under national and international law but have limited legislative protection at sea outside European territorial waters or in the coastal waters of other countries. Appropriate protective legislation and enforcement should exist for the entire range of this endangered species. Colony management has included promotion of vegetation cover, anti-predator control (e.g. rat eradication and the provision of nest-boxes and fox-proof fencing) and the reduction of human disturbance. A conservation programme is being enacted by biologists and conservationists throughout Europe and in several other countries, and a comparative quantitative assessment of reproductive ecology is being prepared from small and large colonies in the Republic of Ireland, United Kingdom, France and Azores. These studies have identified the relative threats within the European breeding range, and

in several colonies it has been possible to recommend immediate conservation action, as above.

Colony management and protection is particularly important at a number of Important Bird Areas (IBAs: see Grimmett and Jones 1989), as follows. Republic of Ireland: Rockabill (IBA 094), Lady's Island Lake (IBA 085). France: Baie de Morlaix et de Carantec (IBA 061). United Kingdom: Forth Islands (IBA 125), Coquet Island (IBA 145), Farne Islands (IBA 143), Anglesey Islands and Cemlyn Bay (IBA 213). Azores (Portugal): Coast of Flores (IBA 001) (Flores), Ilhéu de Baixo (IBA 003) and Ilhéu da Praia (IBA 004) (Graciosa), and Ilhéu da Vila do Porto and Lagoinhas (IBA 005) (Santa Maria).

Colonies which appear to have been abandoned should retain appropriate protection and management in order to permit recolonization. Breeding population and productivity monitoring should continue at selected sites.

The introduction of protective legislation and education programmes has taken place in Ghana and Senegal, the experience from this work having been extended also to other countries. It is of paramount importance for the conservation of Roseate Terns to find out where the birds wintering in the Gulf of Guinea move to after leaving there in December.

ADRIAN DEL NEVO

Little Tern
Sterna albifrons

SPEC Category 3
Status Declining
Criteria Moderate decline

The Little Tern has experienced a long-term decline throughout Europe, being a common breeder in both inland riverine sites and coastal areas during the nineteenth century. Numbers increased at the beginning of the twentieth century but declined in many countries between 1970 and 1990 probably due to disturbance and habitat loss. Breeding sites should be protected and managed appropriately.

■ Distribution and population trends

The Little Tern has a cosmopolitan distribution. In the Palearctic its breeding range extends from the Atlantic coast to central Asia, and from the Mediterranean and the Middle East north to Fennoscandia and c.57°N latitude in Russia (Cramp 1985, Ilyichev and Zubakin 1988). The largest populations occur in Russia, Turkey and Italy (see table, map). The European population winters mainly along the West African coast, as well as in East Africa, the Red Sea and the Persian Gulf.

In Europe the species has experienced a long-term decline in numbers, and some contraction of the breeding range. At one time it was a common breeder along large inland rivers as well as in coastal areas, but river canalization destroyed most inland breeding sites in western Europe during or before the nineteenth century, including those along the Rhine, Elbe, Danube and Oder rivers (Glutz von Blotzheim and Bauer 1982, Hölzinger 1987). The bird still breeds along natural sections of rivers such as the Loire and Allier in France, the Po in Italy, the Vistula in Poland, and the Dniestr, Dniepr, Don, Volga and Ural in the Ukraine and Russia (Glutz von Blotzheim and Bauer 1982, Ilyichev and Zubakin 1988).

Numbers in the north-western coastal breeding sites also declined in the late nineteenth century but subsequent protection measures resulted in recovery during the 1920s and 1930s (Parslow 1967b, Cramp 1985). By the 1950s populations had recovered throughout most of the north-west, as also in Spain and Italy (Glutz von Blotzheim and Bauer 1982). This positive trend continued between 1970 and 1990 in the United Kingdom and in Italy, amongst other countries (see table, map). However, declines were recorded for the same period in 10 countries including the large populations in Greece, Russia and Ukraine, in total amounting to up to 50% of the European population for which trends are known (see table, map).

■ Ecology

The Little Tern breeds colonially, generally in groups of 2–50 nests although exceptionally in colonies of up to 300–400 (Nadler 1976, Glutz von Blotzheim and Bauer 1982, Wesolowski *et al.* 1985). Nesting occurs only in open areas adjacent to water, preferably isolated islands or peninsulas, either on coastal sand or shingle beaches or inland on sandy islets in large rivers. Little Terns are less aggressive than larger tern species, and are particularly sensitive to disturbance, having relatively low fidelity to individual colony sites (McNicholl 1975).

On coastal beaches, sites with accumulations of mollusc shells are preferred. Dense vegetation is avoided, although birds exceptionally nest among

	Breeding population			Breeding
	Size (pairs)	Year	Trend	range trend
Albania	(500–1,000)	91	(–1)	(–1)
Belarus	**900–1,100**	85	F	**0**
Belgium	**100–110**	91	+2	**+1**
Bulgaria	60–120	—	0	0
Croatia	100–150 *	—	0*	0*
Denmark	**407–458**	88	–2	–1
Estonia	200–400	—	0	0
Finland	**50–60**	92	+2	**+1**
France	**1,091–1,183**	87	0	**0**
Germany	300–600	—	–1	0
Greece	1,000–2,000	—	(–1)	(–1)
Rep. of Ireland	**390–390**	85–87	**0**	**0**
Italy	**5,000–6,000**	86	+1	(F)
Latvia	**250–300**	—	F	F
Lithuania	100–400	85–88	(–1)	(0)
Moldova	50–70	88	0	–1
Netherlands	**275–400**	89–91	–1	**0**
Poland	1,000–1,300	—	F	0
Portugal	150–200	91	–1	–1
Romania	300–400	—	–1	0
Russia	5,000–9,000	84–88	–1	–1
Slovenia	**2–3**	—	F	F
Spain	**2,500–3,000**	—	0	0
Sweden	400–600	87	**0**	**0**
Turkey	(5,000–15,000)	—	—	—
Ukraine	**1,200–2,500**	86	–1	–1
United Kingdom	**2,400–2,400**	85–87	+1	**0**
Isle of Man ¹	**57–60**	85	+2	0*
Total (approx.)	29,000–49,000			

Trends +2 Large increase +1 Small increase 0 Stable X Extinct
(1970-1990) –2 Large decrease –1 Small decrease F Fluctuating N New breeder
Data quality **Bold**: reliable quantitative data   Normal type: incomplete quantitative data
Bracketed figures: no quantitative data   * Data quality not provided
¹ Population figures are included within United Kingdom totals

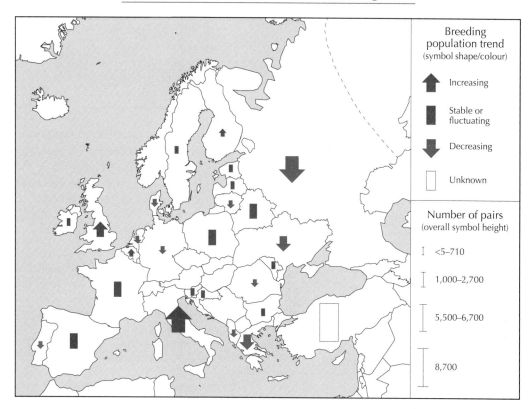

Breeding
population trend
(symbol shape/colour)

Increasing

Stable or
fluctuating

Decreasing

Unknown

Number of pairs
(overall symbol height)

<5–710

1,000–2,700

5,500–6,700

8,700

scattered low vegetation such as fields of sugar-beet or barley (Nadler 1976, Glutz von Blotzheim and Bauer 1982). In eastern Europe most colonies are located on sandy islands in rivers, although birds may sporadically breed inland on bodies of standing water such as reservoirs and fish-ponds (Ilyichev and Zubakin 1988).

The Little Tern requires clean waters rich in prey including sandeels, which constitute its main food, but also other small fish, crustaceans, pelagic molluscs and aquatic insects, the tern's diet varying both geographically and seasonally (Nadler 1976, Glutz von Blotzheim and Bauer 1982, Cramp 1985).

◼ Threats

Although difficult to prove, the decrease in numbers of this species is probably due to excessive habitat change and human disturbance. Local populations are highly unstable in both numbers and distribution (Nadler 1976, Glutz von Blotzheim and Bauer 1982, Cramp 1985) due to both natural and human factors such as flooding in rivers and from high tides, disturbance by people, boats, dogs and cattle (Knight and Hoobdan 1983), predation by gulls (many species) and rats, and habitat loss such as river canalization and development of beaches. Clearly, further canalization of natural sections of large rivers or an in-

crease in tourist pressure on coastal beaches may trigger further declines.

◼ Conservation measures

The Little Tern requires active habitat protection and site management for its conservation. Suggested measures following Knight and Hoobdan (1983), Larkins (1984), Peterson (1984) and Hölzinger (1987) include: the prevention of the canalization of natural sections of river with sandy islets; reductions in disturbance of colonies by fencing or wardening; the establishment of enclosed pens or hiding places to protect young terns from avian predators as an attempt to improve nesting success; and the establishment of appropriately managed nature reserves encompassing important colonies. In the United Kingdom, the effects of flooding of nests at high tides have been reduced at several colonies by raising nest-sites artificially or by gradually moving the nests up the beach and out of danger (Batten et al. 1990).

Active management of potential breeding sites to attract Little Terns is also possible, and in coastal regions artificial sand beaches have been created which need to be at least 6 ha in size (Larkins 1984). Elsewhere, artificial islands or anchored nesting rafts have been established on rivers (Hölzinger 1987).

LUDWIK TOMIALOJC

Whiskered Tern
Chlidonias hybridus

SPEC Category 3
Status Declining
Criteria Moderate decline

The European population of the Whiskered Tern is concentrated in eastern Europe and Spain. Although the population has fluctuated considerably, declines were noted between 1970 and 1990 in countries holding up to half of the European population, due mainly to the destruction and deterioration of the wetland habitats which the species uses. The main conservation measures proposed are the appropriate management of wetland vegetation, control of human disturbance, and enhancement of nesting opportunities on artificial water-bodies.

■ Distribution and population trends

Approximately a quarter of the global breeding range of Whiskered Tern lies within Europe, where the main breeding areas are in Romania and the forest-steppe zone of Ukraine and Russia (Mees 1979, Glutz von Blotzheim and Bauer 1982, Cramp 1985, Ilyichev and Zubakin 1988). The species also breeds in the Iberian peninsula, France and Turkey, and at a few sites which are more isolated in central Europe and Italy (see table, map). It winters mostly south of the Sahara in West Africa, but also in increasing numbers in the Mediterranean region (Glutz von Blotzheim and Bauer 1982).

Estimates of the population size vary considerably due to the highly unstable character of many breeding colonies (see table) and possibly due to variable numbers arriving to breed. For example, population estimates for Spain include more than 50,000 pairs (J. A. Valverde, after Mees 1979), 3,600 pairs (Mees 1979), more than 100,000 pairs

(A. Noval in Cramp 1985) and most recently 5,000–8,000 pairs (see table). Similarly, population estimates for Russia and Ukraine (see table) are considerably higher than previously suggested. Dementiev and Gladkov (1951c) and Ilyichev and Zubakin (1988) considered the Whiskered Tern to be a very scarce breeding species in the European part of the former Soviet Union, transitory at any particular site.

The most recent data show that declines have occurred during 1970–1990 in countries which together hold up to about half of the European breeding population (see table, map). In contrast, however, population increases have been noted between 1970 and 1990 in western Ukraine and Romania (Gorban 1991; see table), and new sites have been colonized in Lithuania, central Russia, Poland, Slovakia and Hungary (Anon. 1990a, Kapocsy 1979, Kashentseva *et al.* 1991, Dyrcz 1992). Possibly the centre of the breeding range has shifted during recent dry years towards the north and west, away from the Russian steppes, due to increasing aridity and the destruction of wetlands (Gorban 1991, V. Krivenko pers. comm.). There is thus no firm evidence for an overall population decline in central and eastern Europe, since some regional declines may have been compensated for by local increases elsewhere. Nevertheless the species is clearly at risk due to the unstable character of its breeding range.

■ Ecology

The Whiskered Tern breeds in dry climatic zones, such as the Mediterranean, and the forest-steppe, steppe and semi-desert of Eurasia (Dementiev and Gladkov 1951c, Cramp 1985). The species is gregarious and nests in small colonies on both natural and artificial water-bodies, selecting sites with fairly deep water (0.6–1.5 m) (Kapocsy 1979). Under natural conditions Whiskered Tern colonies are located on floating vegetation on standing or slow flowing,

	Breeding population			Breeding
	Size (pairs)	Year	Trend	range trend
Albania	(0–50)	91	—	—
Belarus	**0–20**	90	N	F
Bulgaria	50–500	—	0	0
Croatia	500–600 *	—	–1*	0*
France	**1,500–1,900**	92	F	0
Greece	250–400	—	(0)	(0)
Hungary	600–1,000	—	+1	0
Italy	250–450	86	–1	(–1)
Lithuania	5–10	85–88	(F)	(–1)
Poland	**30–150**	—	+1	+2
Portugal	20–100	91	–1	–1
Romania	(6,000–10,000)	—	+1	+1
Russia	10,000–13,000	84–88	–1	–1
Slovakia	0–120	—	F	F
Spain	5,000–8,000	—	–1	–1
Turkey	(1,000–5,000)	—	—	—
Ukraine	**8,000–9,000**	90	+2	+1
Total (approx.)	33,000–50,000			

Trends (1970-1990) +2 Large increase +1 Small increase 0 Stable –1 Small decrease –2 Large decrease F Fluctuating X Extinct N New breeder

Data quality **Bold**: reliable quantitative data Normal type: incomplete quantitative data Bracketed figures: no quantitative data * Data quality not provided

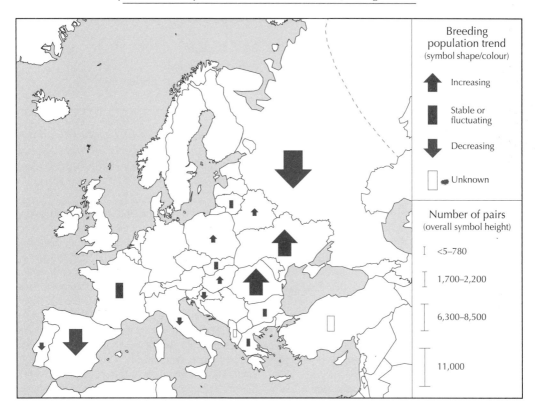

preferably clean, water of lakes, estuaries and sometimes marshes (Dementiev and Gladkov 1951c). In Hungary, up to 41% of Whiskered Tern colonies are on fish-ponds, usually those freshly filled with water and hence containing loose tussocks of *Schoenoplectus*, *Carex*, *Nymphaea* or *Stratiotes aloides* (Kapocsy 1979).

Like other *Chlidonias* terns, Whiskered Tern feeds on a variety of prey items, mostly comprising larger insects and their larvae but also including small fish and amphibians.

■ Threats

Wetland habitat loss through the drainage of marshes and the canalization of rivers is the major threat to the Whiskered Tern in Europe (Glutz von Blotzheim and Bauer 1982). Another major problem is the unsympathetic management of water-bodies, espe-

cially fish-ponds, reservoirs and some large river estuaries, involving drastic and regular reductions in the amount of emergent and floating vegetation. The increasing pressure of tourism and water-sports close to breeding colonies also causes disturbance and results in loss of nesting sites, especially in southern Europe (Kapocsy 1979, Hölzinger 1987).

■ Conservation measures

It is necessary to maintain a network of water-bodies with well developed emergent and floating vegetation to provide sufficient suitable breeding habitat for the Whiskered Tern (Kapocsy 1979). Such sites could be protected from human disturbance by the establishment of buffer zones around them (Hölzinger 1987). On intensively managed water-bodies, artificial anchored rafts may be effective in providing suitable nesting sites.

LUDWIK TOMIALOJC

Black Tern
Chlidonias niger

SPEC Category   3
Status   Declining
Criteria   Moderate decline

The decline which has occurred over most of the European range between 1970 and 1990 is due to habitat loss and deterioration through wetland drainage and natural changes in water-levels. A halt to drainage of natural marshlands, restrictions on recreational activities at breeding sites and improvement of nesting conditions on artificial water-bodies are needed.

■ Distribution and population trends

With a distribution that extends into central Asia and covers a large part of North America, roughly a quarter of the global range of Black Tern lies within Europe, where it is widespread. Breeding occurs from southern Spain and the coasts of the Mediterranean, Black and Caspian Seas, across southern northwest, central and eastern Europe, and north into southern Fennoscandia (Cramp 1985, Ilyichev and Zubakin 1988). The species winters at sea along the west coast of Africa, with concentrations occurring off Ghana.

Most of the European population occurs in the east of the continent with Russia holding around one third of the total and Estonia, Latvia, Lithuania,

Belarus, Poland, Ukraine and Romania also having high numbers of birds (see table, map).

Declines were reported during the nineteenth and early twentieth centuries, chiefly from the United Kingdom (where there has been no regular breeding since the mid-nineteenth century), Denmark, Sweden, Germany and western Poland (Glutz von Blotzheim and Bauer 1982, Cramp 1985, Dyrcz *et al.* 1991). This trend strengthened between 1970 and 1990, with rapid declines also being recorded then in Spain, France, Netherlands, Czech Republic, Slovakia, Ukraine and parts of Russia (Hölzinger 1987, Stastny *et al.* 1987, Ilyichev and Zubakin 1988; see table). Simultaneously, some local increases and range extensions have been noticed in Finland, Estonia and the St Petersburg region of Russia (Malchevskiy and Pukinskiy 1983, Solonen 1985; see table), but these in no way counterbalance the decline of the species in other parts of its breeding range (see table, map).

■ Ecology

In Europe Black Terns breed at coastal and inland lowland sites, characterized by shallow water and the presence of floating vegetation. Throughout the species' range, nesting commonly occurs on floating dead or cut vegetation which is usually protected from the wind and waves by reedbeds. Rosettes of water-soldier *Stratiotes aloides* and floating roots of water-lilies *Nymphaea* and *Nuphar* are favoured, but birds also breed occasionally on floating wood or on muddy islets (Haverschmidt 1978, Glutz von Blotzheim and Bauer 1982). In natural marshlands the species also breeds on sedge tussocks, sometimes alongside White-winged Black Terns *C. leucopterus* (Ilyichev and Zubakin 1988), or in patches of horsetail *Equisetum limosum* or sedge *Cladium mariscus*.

Colonies generally comprise a dozen or so pairs, but can total up to 200 nests in rare cases (Haverschmidt 1978). Of the three *Chlidonias* marsh terns that breed in Europe the Black Tern is the most dependent on open water, though small groups of

| | Breeding population | | | Breeding |
	Size (pairs)	Year	Trend	range trend
Albania	(100–200)	91	—	—
Belarus	**15,000–22,000**	87	**F**	**0**
Bulgaria	50–50	—	–2	–1
Croatia	100–150 *	—	–1*	0*
Czech Republic	**20–50**	—	–2	**0**
Denmark	**91–97**	91	**–2**	**–2**
Estonia	2,000–3,000	—	+1	0
Finland	**15–20**	92	**+2**	**+2**
France	**177–206**	92	**–2**	**–1**
Germany	1,500–2,000	—	–2	**0**
Greece	50–150	—	(+1)	(0)
Hungary	600–1,200	—	–1	0
Iceland	0–5	—	I	0*
Italy	120–160	86	–2	(–2)
Latvia	**2,000–3,000**	87	**F**	**F**
Lithuania	2,000–3,000	85–88	(0)	0
Moldova	300–400	88	0	–1
Netherlands	900–1,300 *	90	–2	**–2**
Poland	5,000–7,000	—	**F**	–1
Romania	(3,000–8,000)	—	0	**0**
Russia	20,000–30,000	84–88	0	0
Slovakia	40–200	—	**–2**	–1
Spain	150–200	—	–2	–2
Sweden	**175–200**	87	**0**	**0**
Turkey	(50–500)	—	—	—
Ukraine	**3,500–5,000**	88	**–2**	**–1**
Total (approx.)	57,000–88,000			

Trends	+2 Large increase	+1 Small increase	0 Stable	X Extinct
(1970-1990)	–2 Large decrease	–1 Small decrease	F Fluctuating	N New breeder
Data quality	**Bold: reliable quantitative data**	Normal type: incomplete quantitative data		
	Bracketed figures: no quantitative data	* Data quality not provided		

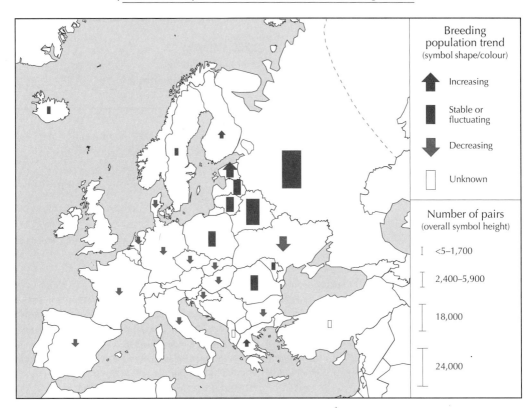

Breeding
population trend
(symbol shape/colour)

Increasing

Stable or
fluctuating

Decreasing

Unknown

Number of pairs
(overall symbol height)

<5–1,700

2,400–5,900

18,000

24,000

birds may nest on tiny pools among marshes or grasslands, and on fish-ponds (Haverschmidt 1978). On passage the species is found on extensive lakes, coastal bays, lagoons and estuaries (Glutz von Blotzheim and Bauer 1982).

Food in the breeding season mostly comprises insects and their larvae, but also includes some fish and amphibians, and in winter at sea the diet is mainly fish (Cramp 1985).

■ Threats

The main cause of the decline in Europe is habitat loss and the deterioration of nesting conditions. During the nineteenth century, river canalization and wetland drainage projects destroyed many breeding sites (Hölzinger 1987, Glutz von Blotzheim and Bauer 1982). More recently intensification of the fish-farming industry has encroached upon waterbodies so reducing the extent of the floating vegetation. Additionally, increasing water pollution may have reduced food resources (Glutz von Blotzheim and Bauer 1982).

A recent threat is increasing disturbance from recreational activities such as water-sports and tourism, which cause frequent flushing of birds from nests, increasing the risk of desertion and exposing the eggs and young to predators (Hölzinger 1987).

Natural factors such as the damage to nests by changing water-levels and the competition for nesting sites from other species (gulls, ducks or swans) may add to the threats imposed by man (Glutz von Blotzheim and Bauer 1982, Haverschmidt 1978, Hölzinger 1987).

■ Conservation measures

The European population of Black Terns continues to decline despite legislative protection of the species in most countries. Conservation requires a halt to further wetland drainage and river canalization projects that would destroy its habitat. Additionally, some areas need management to improve their suitability, for example through the provision of floating mats of cut reed for nesting, or by allowing a proportion of emergent and floating vegetation to remain on intensively managed fish-ponds. The construction of anchored rafts on ponds or canals with no emergent vegetation has been found to be effective in the Netherlands and Switzerland (Haverschmidt 1978, Hahnke and Becker 1986). Human disturbance could be reduced at established colonies.

LUDWIK TOMIALOJC

Black Guillemot
Cepphus grylle

SPEC Category 2
Status Declining
Criteria Moderate decline

Although probably stable or increasing in much of its range, Black Guillemot populations are declining in Fennoscandia. Drowning in fishing gear, shooting, and predation by introduced American mink appear to constitute particular threats, but the precise influences of these man-induced mortality factors need to be examined carefully. Improved population monitoring is required and further research into census methodology is necessary.

■ Distribution and population trends

The Black Guillemot is a northern species, distributed on both sides of the North Atlantic and in the Arctic Ocean. Approximately 200,000 pairs, around two-thirds of the world population, breed in Europe (including Greenland). In general adult Black Guillemots are mostly sedentary, although immatures may stray far from the natal area outside the breeding season, exceptionally moving more than a thousand kilometres away (Andersen-Harild 1969, Petersen 1977, 1981, Ewins 1988).

The species' European strongholds lie in Greenland and Norway, and large populations are also present in Iceland, Svalbard, United Kingdom and Russia (Nettleship and Birkhead 1985) (see table, map). Population estimates are generally poor for this species, with wide margins of error, which makes trends difficult to interpret. The Fennoscandian population, amounting to approximately a third of the total European population for which trends are known, appears to have declined between 1970 and 1990 (see table, map). Populations in the Republic of Ireland, United Kingdom and Denmark have in-

creased, while numbers in other countries appear to be stable.

■ Ecology

The Black Guillemot is more coastal in its distribution than other species of auk in Europe. It requires areas free of mammalian predators (Ewins and Tasker 1985) within which it is quite flexible in its choice of nest-site, and may use natural crevices, principally in boulder screes but also on low cliffs, as well as an array of different man-made structures.

The birds feed in shallow coastal waters during both summer and winter. The food is of benthic origin, principally butterfish *Pholis gunnellus* and other blennies (Pholidae), sand-eels (Ammodytidae) and sculpins (Cottidae) for the chicks, while the adults take a wider spectrum of food for themselves, and in particular a greater diversity of invertebrates (Bergman 1971, Bradstreet 1980, Petersen 1981, Cairns 1987a,b, Ewins 1990).

■ Threats

Human-induced mortality is higher in Black Guillemot than most other European auks, presumably because of its preference for coastal waters. Drowning in fishing nets and shooting are reported to be of particular significance in various parts of the species' range in the Scandinavian countries (Petersen 1981). The effect of fishing nets on Black Guillemots has been quantified by Petersen (1981) who found that, over a two-month summer period on Flatey Island (north-west Iceland), 1.3% of the breeders in a local population drowned in nets set for lumpsucker *Cyclopterus lumpus*. This mortality factor constituted about half of the average monthly mortality in this breeding population, for which the annual survival was 87%.

Ground predators, such as the introduced American mink *Mustela vison*, are a problem to the species in parts of Norway and Sweden (Folkestad 1982, Jönsson 1990). Although it is difficult to assess the

	Breeding population			Breeding range trend
	Size (pairs)	Year	Trend	
Denmark	**603–639**	91	+1	0
Faroe Islands	(4,000–7,000)	—	(0)	(0)
Greenland	25,000–100,000	83	—	(0)
Estonia	6–10	—	0	0
Finland	8,000–10,000	92	–1	0
Iceland	10,000–20,000	—	0	0
Rep. of Ireland	1,200–1,200	85–91	+1	0
Norway	20,000–40,000	90	–1	0
Svalbard	(5,000–50,000)	—	(0)	(0)
Russia	23,500–23,500	—	0	0
Sweden	7,000–10,000	87	–1	0
United Kingdom	19,000–19,000	85–91	+1	+1
Isle of Man [1]	**260–290**	85	+2	0*
Total (approx.)	120,000–280,000			

Trends   +2 Large increase   +1 Small increase   0 Stable   X Extinct
(1970–1990) –2 Large decrease   –1 Small decrease   F Fluctuating N New breeder
Data quality **Bold**: reliable quantitative data   Normal type: incomplete quantitative data
Bracketed figures: no quantitative data   * Data quality not provided
[1] Population figures are included within United Kingdom totals

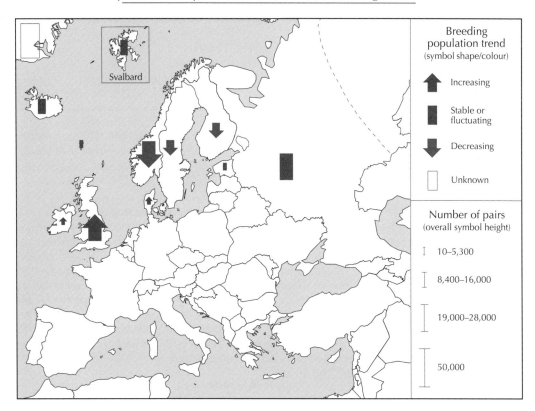

effect of mink predation on the size of Black Guille-mot populations, changes in the birds' distribution have certainly taken place (Petersen 1979). Thus, the establishment of American mink farms in the Ork-ney Islands was opposed for fear of heavy predation on the birds (Bourne 1978). Previous local extinctions of Black Guillemots in Orkney have been attributed to the arrival of rats *Rattus* (Ewins and Tasker 1985).

■ Conservation measures

Only a small proportion of the total Black Guillemot population is found within Important Bird Areas (IBAs); the Faroe Islands are the best represented in this respect, with 70% of the island's population of 4,000–7,000 breeding pairs within IBAs. Little ac-tive protection of suitable breeding sites for this species has been undertaken and this should be improved, although the needs of the species may be more appropriately addressed by wider-scale con-servation measures.

The impact of the more commonly reported mor-tality factors on Black Guillemot populations, in-cluding predation by American mink and fishing gear by-catch, need to be assessed and appropriate measures taken.

Of the core areas in Europe, monitoring is prob-ably best in the United Kingdom, although on the whole Black Guillemot populations are far from adequately censused, which is to some extent be-cause of methodological problems (Lloyd *et al.* 1991). Research into census methodology has been carried out (Cairns 1979, Petersen 1981, Ewins 1985), but this also needs to be further explored and developed.

ÆVAR PETERSEN

Puffin
Fratercula arctica

SPEC Category 2
Status Vulnerable
Criteria Large decline

The Puffin is a common North Atlantic seabird, but numbers in Norway, the Faroes, Channel Islands, France and Russia have seen a decline during the 1970–1990 period. Wise use of the sea and sustainable exploitation of fish stocks are essential for the Puffin's well-being. Additionally, ground predators must be prevented from reaching colonies.

■ Distribution and population trends

The species is restricted to colder parts of the North Atlantic and Arctic Oceans and breeds on cliffs and islands from Maine in the U.S.A. and from Britanny in France, northwards as far as there is land. The total population is estimated at 6 million pairs, of which about 95% breed in Europe. This figure includes a 'guesstimate' for Iceland which seems to have a third to a half of the global population. There are slightly fewer birds in Norway than in Iceland (Anker-Nilsson 1991) and substantial numbers in the Faroes and United Kingdom (see table, map). The Arctic and southernmost colonies are small.

During the winter, Puffins are rarely seen from land as they disperse widely over the open sea south to the Azores and Canary Islands and into the western Mediterranean.

The Puffin is one of the commonest seabirds in the region but there have been major decreases in numbers at southern colonies during the twentieth century (Harris 1984, Lloyd *et al.* 1991). Between 1970 and 1990 numbers in Iceland and the United Kingdom have remained stable or increased, but declines have been reported in the Faroes, Republic of Ireland, Norway, Channel Islands (Guernsey and Jersey), France and Russia (Barrett and Vader 1984, Lloyd *et al.* 1991; see table, map). The population in the Røst archipelago of Norway, which had approximately 600,000 breeding pairs in 1990 (Anker-Nilsson 1991), collapsed by two-thirds between 1979 and 1988 but has since been fairly stable, having only increased by 6% since then (Anker-Nilsson and Røstad 1993, T. Anker-Nilssen pers. comm.). Although the Icelandic population is thought to be stable, there is an urgent need for up-to-date information for the country.

■ Ecology

Puffins breed colonially, with nests being sited in burrows, under boulders or in cracks in cliffs. They are vulnerable to ground predators, and colonies are always on islands or inaccessible cliffs. Colonies must also be close to predictable concentrations of energy-rich fish, e.g. sand-eel *Ammodytes* spp., sprat *Sprattus sprattus*, herring *Clupea harengus* or capelin *Mallotus villosus*. Suitable breeding sites are consequently in limited supply and colonies are therefore often very large. Adults are flightless during the main moult which takes place in the late winter and early spring.

■ Threats

The main threat to the species is changes in the distribution and numbers of small fish. For example, the crash on Røst involved a long series of disastrous breeding seasons which coincided with a collapse in the stock of Norwegian spring-spawning herring, the immature stages of which are a staple food of the young birds (Harris 1984, Anker-Nilsson 1987, 1992). The reduction in this stock was mainly due to overexploitation by the fishing industry (Anker-Nilsson 1987, Vader *et al.* 1989), although a period of exceptionally cold ocean climate has severely delayed the rebuilding of the stock (Beverton 1993). Some earlier declines in Puffin numbers elsewhere, e.g. the United Kingdom, appear to have been natural (Harris 1984).

Oil pollution is also a threat to the species, par-

	Breeding population			Breeding range trend
	Size (pairs)	Year	Trend	
Denmark				
Faroe Islands	(350,000–600,000)	—	(–1)	(0)
Greenland	1,500–3,000	83	—	(0)
France	**241–255**	88	**–2**	**–2**
Iceland	2,000,000–3,000,000	—	0	0
Rep. of Ireland	18,000–18,000	85–87	–1	0
Norway	2,000,000–2,000,000	90	–2	**0**
Svalbard	(1,000–10,000)	—	(0)	(0)
Russia	20,000–20,000	—	–1	0
United Kingdom	**450,000–450,000**	85–87	**+1**	**0**
Guernsey	**200–250**	86–89	**–2**	**0**
Jersey	10–15	—	–2	–2
Isle of Man [1]	**116–116**	85	**F**	0*
Total (approx.)	4,800,000–6,100,000			

Trends   +2 Large increase   +1 Small increase   0 Stable   X Extinct
(1970–1990) –2 Large decrease   –1 Small decrease   F Fluctuating   N New breeder
Data quality   **Bold:** reliable quantitative data   Normal type: incomplete quantitative data
Bracketed figures: no quantitative data   * Data quality not provided
[1] Population figures are included within United Kingdom totals

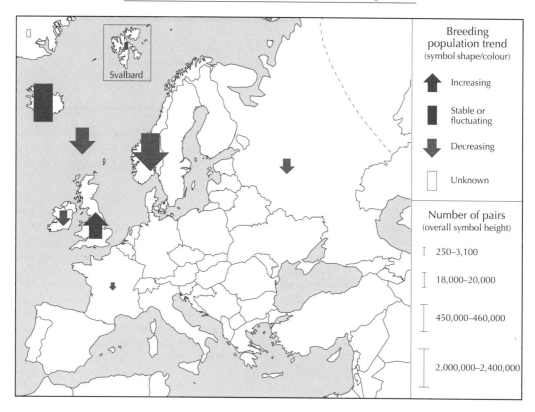

Breeding population trend
(symbol shape/colour)

Increasing

Stable or fluctuating

Decreasing

Unknown

Number of pairs
(overall symbol height)

250–3,100

18,000–20,000

450,000–460,000

2,000,000–2,400,000

ticularly when the birds are flightless. Oil from the wreck of the *Torrey Canyon* killed 85% of French Puffins in 1967, and oil from the *Amoco Cadiz* in 1978 reduced the population further (Henry and Monnat 1981). Additionally, chemicals, heavy metals and discarded netting are all potential threats (Evans 1984) but are unlikely to be the underlying cause of most major declines (Harris 1984). Adult survival in the North Sea has declined in recent years and this has coincided with a change in the number and distribution of sprat (Harris and Wanless 1991, Harris and Bailey 1992).

Non-native predators are a scourge of nesting Puffins. Rats *Rattus* have been claimed as having caused the demise of many Puffin colonies and introduced American mink *Mustela vison* are credited with killing the last few Puffins in Sweden (Harris 1984). The traditional hunting of Puffins in the Faroes and Iceland probably has little effect on population levels as it is controlled and restricted to immature birds (Petersen 1976). Soil erosion resulting from the burrowing of the birds themselves can destroy breeding habitat.

Large numbers of birds, mainly immatures, are sometimes killed by gulls (especially Herring Gull *Larus argentatus* and Great Black-backed Gull *L. marinus*) and other avian predators such as White-tailed Eagle *Haliaeetus albicilla*, Gyrfalcon *Falco rusticolus* and Peregrine *F. peregrinus*, but these losses are natural and probably do not significantly affect the populations.

■ Conservation measures

Sensible exploitation of the seas (especially of fish stocks), a reduction in the incidence of marine pollution and the prevention of ground predators from reaching colonies are the only realistic conservation measures.

Particular attention should be given to eliminating causes of high adult mortality since adult Puffins normally have high survival and low reproductive output (with only a single-egg clutch) and the loss of adults may therefore have a much greater impact on numbers than do many years of breeding failure (Vader *et al.* 1989).

MIKE HARRIS

Black-bellied Sandgrouse
Pterocles orientalis

SPEC Category 3
Status Vulnerable
Criteria Large decline

Both the population size and the range of the Black-bellied Sandgrouse are clearly declining within Europe, mainly due to changes in agricultural practices and the loss of habitat. The maintenance of traditional farming methods and the protection of lowland dry grassland are both essential for the conservation of the species.

■ Distribution and population trends

The global range of the Black-bellied Sandgrouse extends from North Africa and southern Europe through Turkey, the Middle East, Iraq, Iran and Pakistan to China (Johnsgard 1991). Within Europe it is largely sedentary and is restricted to the south and south-east (see table, map). The population sizes are generally poorly known and it is therefore difficult to estimate the proportion of the global population which occurs in Europe, although it is considered to be under a quarter of the total.

Black-bellied Sandgrouse occur in very low numbers in Portugal, Cyprus and the Canary Islands, but seem to be common in steppic habitats in Turkey, although the population trend there is unknown (Baris 1991). The largest west European population occurs in Spain, but it is believed that in the last 30 years its numbers there have halved. However, reliable data are only available for the last five years, thus making it difficult to measure precisely the rate of decline. Although it is still common in the Aragón, Castilla–La Mancha and Extremadura regions of Spain, the species is clearly declining in the north-east (Marco and García Ferré 1983) and in the south-east of the country (Pleguezuelos and Manrique 1987, Manrique and de Juana 1991).

	Breeding population			Breeding
	Size (pairs)	Year	Trend	range trend
Cyprus	(10–30)	—	(–2)	(–1)
Portugal	100–1,000	89	–1	–1
Russia	(100–1,000)	—	(0)	(0)
Spain	27,000–50,000	—	–2	–2
Canary Islands	(200–300)	—	(–1)	(–1)
Turkey	(5,000–50,000)	—	—	—
Total (approx.)	32,000–100,000			

Trends +2 Large increase +1 Small increase 0 Stable X Extinct
(1970–1990) –2 Large decrease –1 Small decrease F Fluctuating N New breeder
Data quality **Bold**: reliable quantitative data Normal type: incomplete quantitative data
Bracketed figures: no quantitative data * Data quality not provided

■ Ecology

The Black-bellied Sandgrouse is a characteristic species of dry grassland steppe. Like the Pin-tailed Sandgrouse *Pterocles alchata*, it favours open, tree-less steppes or pseudo-steppes which incorporate uncultivated areas, fallow land and arable stubbles, but it can be found at higher altitudes than that species and is more tolerant of taller vegetation (Cramp 1985). Consequently, it is found more often than the Pin-tailed Sandgrouse in natural shrub-steppes such as the Spanish páramos (de Juana *et al.* 1988). For nesting it requires bare, stony areas, such as are often found on the edges of ploughed fields, where it lays its eggs in an uncovered, bare scrape.

Black-bellied Sandgrouse are gregarious throughout the year when feeding and drinking, and form flocks which usually number no more than 30–50 birds. The diet usually consists of small seeds, though it also includes cultivated cereal seed (Christensen *et al.* 1964, Cramp 1985).

■ Threats

As with many steppeland birds, the main threat to the Black-bellied Sandgrouse is the intensification of agriculture. Ploughing of pasture and the irrigation of what was previously extensively farmed arable land has caused massive reductions in the availability of suitable habitat for the species. In the province of Almería (Spain) alone, between 1960 and 1980 the area of land under irrigation increased from 35,700 ha to 69,000 ha (Manrique and de Juana 1991), and in Extremadura 14,000 ha of prime steppeland habitat was flooded in 1989 to build La Serena dam. Now, proposed EU-funded irrigation schemes threaten to destroy more of the remaining Spanish steppelands. The increased application of agro-chemicals has also reduced the seed resources on which the species feeds, and these practices have indeed probably been responsible for the extinction of Black-bellied Sandgrouse in some areas (Canut *et al.* 1987, de Juana 1989a). Agricultural intensification also frequently involves removal of remaining marginal areas of semi-natural vegetation, further reducing food resources and nest-sites.

On the remaining grasslands, overgrazing is a frequent problem as this affects the vegetation composition and structure, reducing both food availabil-

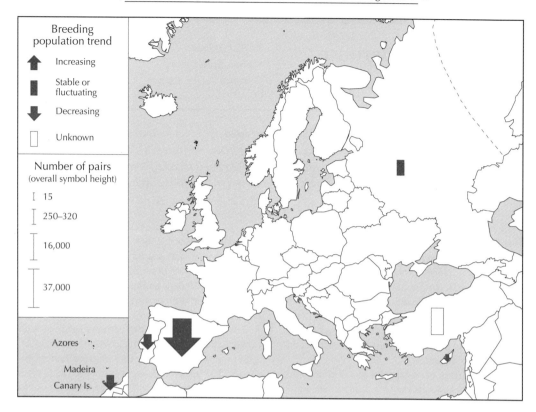

ity and cover for nesting. Conversely, the abandonment of land is also a major threat, as the open, treeless steppe habitat is quickly lost when grazing is removed completely.

Hunting, which is legal in Turkey during the breeding season, may be a problem; the species' habit of concentrating in large numbers at traditional drinking sites throughout the year means that it forms an attractive and relatively easy target.

■ Conservation measures

As with many other dry-grassland species, the conservation of the Black-bellied Sandgrouse is dependent on the maintenance of suitable habitats through the continuation of long-established, low-intensity farming systems (Batten *et al*. 1991). Within the EU, such farming systems can be maintained through Zonal Programmes developed under the Agri-environment Regulation (EC Reg. 2078/92) of the Common Agricultural Policy. These provide financial support for farmers who agree to farm according to environmentally sensitive management prescriptions. Thus, to benefit Black-bellied Sandgrouse, restrictions on grazing rates and use of herbicides and the need to maintain fallow land should be incorporated into such agreements where appropriate. Long-term, wide-scale habitat conservation can, however, be achieved only by the integration of conservation objectives into EU, national and regional agricultural policies and regulations.

Nieves de Borbón

Pin-tailed Sandgrouse
Pterocles alchata

SPEC Category 3
Status Endangered
Criteria Large decline, <10,000 pairs

The Pin-tailed Sandgrouse is a scarce species which is undergoing a widespread decline in both its population size and distribution within the European part of its range. This is due mainly to the destruction of dry grasslands which has followed the spread of intensive farming. The maintenance of low-intensity agricultural practices is required to conserve suitable habitat and to halt the decline of the species.

◼ Distribution and population trends

The breeding range of the Pin-tailed Sandgrouse extends across North Africa, southern Europe and south-west Asia. In Europe, it occurs mainly in Spain and Turkey, although small populations are present in southern France (the Crau) and in Portugal. The species is essentially sedentary, but nomadic movements can take place when environmental conditions are unfavourable.

The population of the species has declined considerably throughout its range in Europe (see table, map), particularly in Spain where its numbers have probably decreased by over half during the period between 1970 and 1990. Some regions where it was formerly much more common and widespread than at present include Catalonia (Ferrer *et al.* 1986), Navarra (Elósegui Abtasoro 1985) and eastern Andalucía (Pleguezuelos 1991). The numbers in Turkey are uncertain and trends unknown.

	Breeding population			Breeding
	Size (pairs)	Year	Trend	range trend
France	**150–170**	83	(–1)	**–1**
Portugal	10–100	89	–1	–2
Spain	5,500–11,000	—	–2	–2
Turkey	(1,000–10,000)	—	—	—
Total (approx.)	6,700–21,000			

Trends   +2 Large increase   +1 Small increase   0 Stable   X Extinct
(1970–1990)   –2 Large decrease   –1 Small decrease   F Fluctuating   N New breeder
Data quality   **Bold**: reliable quantitative data   Normal type: incomplete quantitative data
Bracketed figures: no quantitative data   * Data quality not provided

◼ Ecology

The Pin-tailed Sandgrouse is a species of steppe country, requiring dry, open grassland plains without trees or high bushes (de Juana 1989b). It favours lowland plains which comprise a mosaic of natural pastures, arable fields and uncultivated sandy or saline land (Cramp 1985). Birds hide their nests among dense grass cover in marginal, uncultivated vegetation or in extensive pastureland. In northern Spain and France, where extensive pastures are scarce, the Pin-tailed Sandgrouse is found in uncultivated

areas during the breeding season and on fallow land during autumn and winter (Cheylan *et al.* 1983, Guadalfajara and Tutor 1987). In central Spain it is known to feed on agricultural land in early summer and to move on to more natural habitats later (Casado *et al.* 1983).

The diet consists mainly of small seeds of wild flowers (Parra and Levassor 1982, Casado *et al.* 1983), but the birds will also eat green leaves and shoots. The species also visits stubble fields after harvest, and during the winter large mixed flocks of Pin-tailed Sandgrouse and Little Bustards *Tetrax tetrax* can frequently be found in large fields of alfalfa.

This species has been little studied, and only a poor knowledge exists of its ecological requirements.

◼ Threats

The Pin-tailed Sandgrouse is threatened by agricultural intensification, particularly in the form of irrigation schemes. In Turkey, there are plans to irrigate 17,000 km^2 of steppe in the south-east of the country, where the species' distribution is already limited (Baris 1991). Once such regions are irrigated, grasslands, fallow land and low-intensity crops are ploughed up and replaced with dense, fast-growing cereals that do not form suitable habitat for nesting and feeding.

Overgrazing of grassland steppes leads to reductions in both the quantities of seeds available as food and in the availability of plant cover for nesting. In contrast, the total abandonment of land may also damage the species' breeding habitat through changes in the vegetation structure.

◼ Conservation measures

As with the Black-bellied Sandgrouse *P. orientalis*, the conservation of Pin-tailed Sandgrouse is dependent on the maintenance of steppe habitats through non-intensive agricultural practices. Such farming

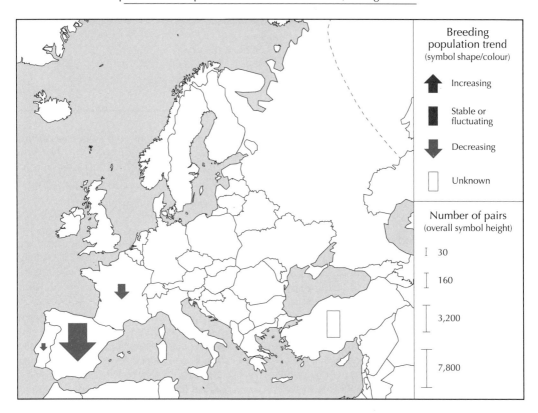

Breeding population trend
(symbol shape/colour)

Increasing

Stable or fluctuating

Decreasing

Unknown

Number of pairs
(overall symbol height)

30

160

3,200

7,800

systems can be maintained in the EU countries, where necessary, by management agreements under the Agri-environment Regulation (EC Reg. 2078/92) of the Common Agricultural Policy. Under such management agreements, restrictions on grazing rates and agro-chemical applications, and the need to maintain fallow land, would be of benefit to Pin-tailed Sandgrouse.

NIEVES DE BORBÓN

Long-toed Pigeon
Columba trocaz

SPEC Category   1
Status   Vulnerable
Criteria   <2,500 pairs

This very scarce species is endemic to the laurel forests of Madeira. Habitat loss from tree-felling has led to a decrease in numbers since the island's discovery, but the laurel forest has recently received full legal protection. Although the population of the Long-toed Pigeon is considered stable, due to conservation measures already taken, the habitat remains threatened by fires and grazing, and the pigeon is affected by illegal shooting and poisoning, and predation by black rats.

■ Distribution and population trends

Endemic to the Atlantic island of Madeira (Portugal), the distribution of the Long-toed Pigeon is directly related to the distribution of laurel forest. The area of this forest has been substantially reduced since the island's discovery in 1419, resulting in a large decline of the bird's population. Cadamosto, for example, during a visit in 1455, observed large numbers of pigeons on Madeira (Cadamosto c.1507). Jones (1988) estimated the population at 1,100–2,700 individuals, with the actual figure probably in the upper part of the range. The forest now covers only 13.5% of the island (Vieira *in litt.*), and 1993 estimates put the population at 3,500–4,900 birds (P. Oliveira *in litt.* to B. Heredia 1994, see table). However, the species is prone to considerable yearly fluctuations in population which are dependent on food availability.

Although listed as Globally Threatened by Collar and Andrew (1988), due to its small range, specialized habitat and small population, the Long-toed Pigeon has now been re-classified as Conservation Dependent (Collar *et al.* 1994), following the progress achieved by conservation measures already undertaken.

	Breeding population			Breeding
	Size (individuals)	Year	Trend	range trend
Portugal Madeira	3,500–4,950	91	**0**	**0**
Total (approx.)	3,500–4,950			

Trends   +2 Large increase   +1 Small increase   0 Stable   X Extinct
(1970-1990)   –2 Large decrease   –1 Small decrease   F Fluctuating   N New breeder
Data quality   **Bold**: reliable quantitative data   Normal type: incomplete quantitative data
            Bracketed figures: no quantitative data   * Data quality not provided

■ Ecology

The laurel forest on Madeira is the largest area of this forest-type in the world. Containing almost all of the Long-toed Pigeon's natural food resources, it is essential to the survival of the species. This dense evergreen humid forest is present mostly on the north-facing slopes of the island, though there are also isolated pockets to the south. The pigeon mainly feeds on the berries of *Laurus azorica*, which is by far the most common tree in the laurel forest, but it also eats the fruits of *Ocotea foetens*, *Persea indica*, *Appolonias barbujana*, *Myrica faya*, *Clethra arborea* and *Piconia exelsa* (Zino and Zino 1986, Jones 1988). During times of food shortage in the forest the birds move to agricultural areas where the main damage they do is to cabbage crops, but they also eat watercress and have a considerable impact on fruit trees, eating notably the young shoots of walnut trees and the flowers of plums and cherries (Bannerman and Bannerman 1966, Zino and Zino 1986, Jones 1988, Oliveira and Jones in press, Zino and Biscoito in press). In moving to agricultural land they are exposed to shooting and deliberate poisoning.

■ Threats

Laurel forest once covered most of the island of Madeira but much of it has been felled for its valuable timber, which was exported or used locally for construction. In recent times the felling has been strictly controlled, though this threat remains and must be contained. The forest is threatened by fires, which are mostly started deliberately to improve grazing for livestock, and by grazing and browsing by goats and pigs (Zino and Zino 1986, Jones 1988).

Until recently, hunting of the Long-toed Pigeon was a popular sport, with about 500 birds killed by shooting and poisoning in a single shooting season (Zino and Zino 1986). In addition, the hunting season often coincided with the height of the breeding season, thus accentuating its effect. Hunting of the species is now illegal, following its inclusion in Annex I of the EU Wild Birds Directive. However, although there is no official hunting season, it remains almost impossible to prevent illegal shooting. Farmers have always used poison as one means of limiting damage to crops by pigeons, and in the past there have been reports of over a hundred birds being

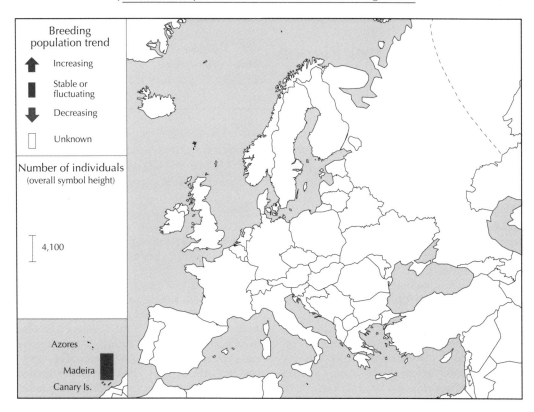

Breeding population trend

↑ Increasing

■ Stable or fluctuating

↓ Decreasing

□ Unknown

Number of individuals
(overall symbol height)

4,100

Azores

Madeira

Canary Is.

killed in one area. Now that shooting is controlled some farmers have taken to poison as their main means of defence. The Parque Natural da Madeira is doing all it can with the use of bird-scaring devices to restrict crop damage.

The black rat *Rattus rattus* is abundant within the laurel forest and takes both eggs and young of the Long-toed Pigeon (Zino 1969, Zino and Zino 1986). The Buzzard *Buteo buteo*, which is also known to take young from the nest as well as the occasional adult, has recently increased in numbers (F. J. A. Zino pers. obs.).

■ Conservation measures

The Parque Natural da Madeira (Important Bird Areas 001, 002, 003, 004 and 006) now covers almost two-thirds of the island and virtually all the laurel forest. The most important areas receive total protection as Strict Nature Reserves, or special protection as Partial Nature Reserves, and have been designated as Special Protection Areas in accordance with the EU Wild Birds Directive. It remains essential that forest fires and the felling of forest trees are prohibited and that grazing and browsing by livestock are controlled. Equally, every effort must be made to resist representations by hunters requesting special shooting permits.

The black rat population continues to be a serious problem. Although this predator will be impossible to eliminate, its numbers could be reduced by encouraging the public not to dump rubbish in the forest.

FRANCIS ZINO, MANUEL JOSÉ BISCOITO
AND PAUL ALEXANDER ZINO

Dark-tailed Laurel Pigeon
Columba bollii

SPEC Category   1
Status   Vulnerable
Criteria   <2,500 pairs

The globally threatened Dark-tailed Laurel Pigeon has a small endemic population on the Canary Islands of La Palma, La Gomera, Tenerife and El Hierro. Its range and population have decreased substantially, although probably stable at the moment. The loss and degradation of habitat, and poaching, continue to threaten the species and efforts should be made to prevent these.

■ Distribution and population trends

The Dark-tailed Laurel Pigeon is endemic to the laurel forest of the islands of La Palma, La Gomera, Tenerife and El Hierro in the Canary Island archipelago. Population figures are not well known, and are largely based on the results of a study carried out at the beginning of the 1980s which estimated the minimum population to be close to 1,200–1,300 individuals (Emmerson 1985). This included a minimum of 250–300 individuals on La Palma, concentrated principally in three areas: Finca del Canal and the Tiles and the canyons of Herradura, La Galga and Puente (San Andrés and Sauces); Barranco de Carmona (Garafia) and the Breñas mountains (Breña Alta). The population on La Gomera comprised 550–600 birds, concentrated in central parts of the island, largely within the limits of the National Park of Garajonay. At least 350–400 individuals are concentrated on Tenerife, principally in Anaga, Teno and small pockets of remaining laurel forest in the north of the island. There are also 10–15 individuals on Hierro, where the species was recently discovered breeding (Martín *et al.* 1993). Presumably the total population on the Canaries is higher than the sum of the individual estimates on each of the islands as those are likely to have been underestimated. Indeed more recent studies suggest that over 1,000 individuals occur within the National Park of Garajonay (Emmerson *et al.* 1993), raising the total population size estimate to c.1,700 individuals (see table, map).

The range has contracted substantially since the nineteenth century. Emmerson *et al.* (1986) commented that on Tenerife the Dark-tailed Laurel Pigeon

occupies just 35–40% of its original area, which gives an idea of the scale of destruction and alteration of the laurel forest on the island, and the consequent decrease in the pigeon's population (Martín *et al.* 1990).

Due to a lack of reliable and precise population figures it is very difficult to estimate the population trends of the Dark-tailed Laurel Pigeon on the Canaries between 1970 and 1990. Numbers do appear to have increased on both Tenerife and La Gomera during recent decades but this is most likely attributed to increased study effort and more extensive surveys visiting the species' preferred areas, rather than to a real change in numbers (Martín 1987).

Dark-tailed Laurel Pigeon is classified as Globally Threatened (Collar *et al.* 1994) due to declines projected to result from continued habitat destruction coupled with the effects of hunting and predation.

■ Ecology

The species principally inhabits areas of closed-canopy laurel forest preferring ravines and passes but also heath vegetation of *Myrica faya* and *Erica arborea*. On occasion it is present in open, degraded habitats including cultivated areas. The species is frugivorous, eating fruits from the laurel forest trees, but occasionally it takes invertebrates (Emmerson 1985).

The breeding season is very long, with occupied nests found in practically all months of the year. The clutch is invariably of one egg only. On Tenerife the trees most frequently used for nesting include *Erica arborea*, *E. scoparia*, *Myrica faya* and *Picconia excelsa*, and these represent 71% of nesting records (Emmerson *et al.* 1986). On the island of La Gomera 79% of known nests were in *E. arborea*, *Ilex canariensis* or *Laurus azorica* (Emmerson *et al.* 1993).

■ Threats

Habitat destruction is continuing despite legal protection for the forest (see 'Conservation Measures').

	Breeding population			Breeding
	Size (individuals)	Year	Trend	range trend
Spain Canary Islands	**1,650–1,700**	85	0	0
Total (approx.)	1,700–1,700			

Trends (1970–1990)   +2 Large increase   +1 Small increase   0 Stable   X Extinct
−2 Large decrease   −1 Small decrease   F Fluctuating   N New breeder
Data quality   **Bold**: reliable quantitative data   Normal type: incomplete quantitative data
Bracketed figures: no quantitative data   * Data quality not provided

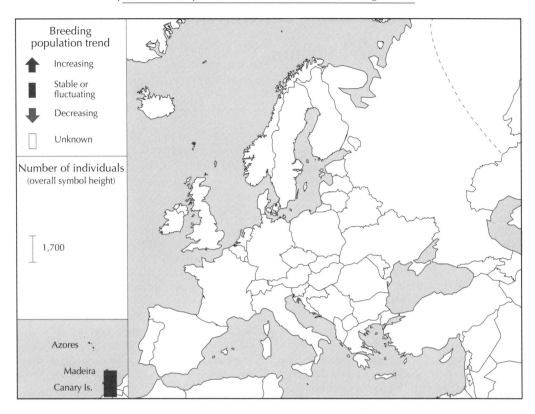

Breeding population trend

↑ Increasing

■ Stable or fluctuating

↓ Decreasing

☐ Unknown

Number of individuals
(overall symbol height)

1,700

Azores

Madeira

Canary Is.

This is principally taking place in the small pockets of remaining laurel forest in the north of Tenerife, but also on La Palma, El Hierro and, to a lesser extent, on La Gomera, both within and outside protected areas. This mainly takes the form of inappropriate forestry management and small-scale clearance for cultivation. The Dark-tailed Laurel Pigeon is much more susceptible to alterations of habitat than the White-tailed Laurel Pigeon *C. junoniae* (Emmerson 1985).

Poaching with firearms, snares and other traps, especially at drinking and feeding areas, is a frequent activity on Tenerife and La Gomera but the effects it has on populations are unknown. Rats *Rattus* and feral cats *Felis* also predate the pigeons and their eggs and young, but the extent of the problem is poorly known.

■ Conservation measures

The largest expanse of laurel forest in the Canary Islands, at Garajonay on La Gomera (Important Bird Area 051), is protected as a National Park and World Heritage Site, and is managed by the national authorities. It is likely to hold the largest population of Dark-tailed Laurel Pigeon. An adjacent area, Riscos de Hermigua y Agulo (IBA 050), is currently without protection. Other areas of forest for the pigeon on La Palma and Tenerife lie with Protected Forest Areas and Protected Landscape Areas. To date, actions by the local administration to conserve the species on the Canary Islands have comprised only production of educational materials and some wardening.

Actions are required to prevent destruction and alteration of the species' habitat. These should include better forestry management and in some cases acquisition of forested areas. Degraded areas should be restored with native species from the laurel forest in order to extend the range of the species.

Each island's population of Dark-tailed Laurel Pigeons should be censused and monitored to ascertain its current status. The effects of hunting should be studied, together with the impacts of cat and rat predation. More general studies on the species' biology, including reproduction, feeding and movements, together with effective census methodology, are required to develop management plans for the species and its habitats.

JUAN ANTONIO LORENZO

317

White-tailed Laurel Pigeon
Columba junoniae

SPEC Category 1
Status Vulnerable
Criteria <2,500 pairs

Endemic to Tenerife, La Palma and La Gomera in the Canary Islands, the White-tailed Laurel Pigeon today has a reduced population and is globally threatened, principally due to the very extensive destruction of laurel forest. Measures to protect and restore the habitat and to prevent poaching are necessary to guarantee recovery.

■ Distribution and population trends

This species is endemic to the Canary Islands where it inhabits almost exclusively the remaining laurel forest of La Palma, La Gomera and Tenerife. The population has been estimated by Emmerson (1985) as 1,200–1,480 birds (see table, map). These include 1,000–1,200 birds on La Palma, principally in the north-east of the island; 120–160 in the central part of La Gomera; and 80–120 in four distinct areas in the north-west, north, and north-east of Tenerife. However, these figures may need revision, as the current status of the species, at least on Tenerife, needs to be ascertained. During the twentieth century it was not recorded on Tenerife until the beginning of the 1970s (Collar and Stuart 1985); there is, however, an unequivocal report from 1871 by local people (Godman 1872), so the species was probably overlooked through most of the next century.

The enormous reduction in laurel forest over the last 500 years (Ceballos and Ortuño 1976) has resulted in a substantial contraction of the White-tailed Laurel Pigeon's range. Numbers are, however, believed to have been stable during 1970–1990 (see table, map), although insufficient quantitative data are available to confirm this.

The species is classified as Globally Threatened (Collar *et al.* 1994) due to further projected declines, principally through illegal hunting and continued habitat loss.

	Breeding population			Breeding
	Size (individuals)	Year	Trend	range trend
Spain Canary Islands	**1,200–1,480**	85	0	0
Total (approx.)	1,200–1,500			

Trends (1970–1990): +2 Large increase +1 Small increase 0 Stable X Extinct −2 Large decrease −1 Small decrease F Fluctuating N New breeder
Data quality: **Bold**: reliable quantitative data Normal type: incomplete quantitative data Bracketed figures: no quantitative data * Data quality not provided

■ Ecology

The White-tailed Laurel Pigeon occurs in areas with steep slopes, large escarpments and deep canyons, where it prefers mature laurel forest (Emmerson 1985, Martín 1987), but also occurs in scrubbier areas with *Myrica faya* and tree heath *Erica arborea* (generally along the lower edges of major stands of laurel forest) and in mixed pine stands (generally found along the upper edges of laurel forest).

The nest is situated on the ground, on small ledges or crevices, or beneath trunks or stones in the interior of the forest. Breeding perhaps occurs throughout the year, although there are data only from March and May–September (Bannerman 1963, Emmerson 1985, M. A. Hernández own data). There is generally just a single egg, though clutches of two occur occasionally (Pérez Padrón 1983).

The diet is fruit, buds and flower shoots of laurel forest trees, including *Ocotea foetens*, *Persea indica*, *Ilex canariensis* and *Laurus azorica*, as well as in orchards nearby to protected areas (Emmerson 1985).

■ Threats

The main threat is hunting. Although it has been prohibited since 1973 (Collar and Stuart 1985), and the number of pigeons shot illegally each year is unknown, poachers are still very active around known drinking and feeding places (Emmerson 1985) judging by the presence of hides, spent cartridges and pigeon feathers. In summer, the pigeons congregate to drink at a small number of (natural) water sources, and many birds can thus be shot with relative ease.

The destruction and degradation of laurel forest continues throughout La Palma, where the majority of the forests are privately owned. Over the past 500 years most of the forest has been destroyed through exploitation for agricultural use and ship-building. The main threats to the forest are now unregulated tree-felling and clear-cutting, the exploitation of spring-water for agriculture, and unregulated construction of vehicle tracks and roads. Although both White-tailed Laurel and Dark-tailed Laurel Pigeons *Columba bollii* are threatened by these factors, the latter species is believed to be more susceptible to habitat alteration (Emmerson 1985).

Predation by rats *Rattus* and feral cats *Felis* on eggs and chicks may be a threat in certain areas (M.

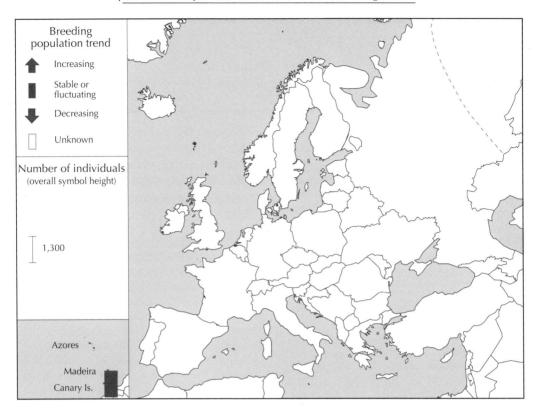

Breeding population trend

⬆ Increasing

⬛ Stable or fluctuating

⬇ Decreasing

▯ Unknown

Number of individuals
(overall symbol height)

1,300

Azores

Madeira

Canary Is.

A. Hernández own data), although there are insufficient data to assess the impact on the White-tailed Laurel Pigeon population.

■ Conservation measures

On Tenerife, the species occurs in the following protected areas, which are also Important Bird Areas (IBAs): Laderas de Tigaiga (IBA 033), Montes de Las Mercedes, Mina y Yedra, Aguirre and La Goleta y Pedro Alvarez (all IBA 035), Monte del Agua, Barranco de los Cochinos and Barranco de Cuevas Negras (all IBA 036), and Monte Verde de Santa Ursula y La Victoria (IBA 037). All of these areas are within Natural Parks and Special Protection Areas (SPAs). On La Gomera, it occurs in Riscos de Hermigua y Agulo (IBA 050) and Parque Nacional de Garajonay (IBA 051), which is a National Park, World Heritage Site and SPA (de Juana 1990). On La Palma, it occurs in El Canal y Los Tiles Biosphere Reserve (IBA 056), and at Monte Verde (IBA 052) which is partly covered by two National Parks, two Natural Parks and an SPA (de Juana 1990).

In order to prevent poaching, vigilance needs to be intensified by increasing the number of forest guards and the frequency of patrols at key sites, particularly in areas where the species drinks (Martín *et al.* 1990). Establishment of artificial drinking sites may be needed to promote dispersion of pigeons during the summer and thereby reduce their vulner-

ability to shooting (Emmerson 1985).

There is a need for coordinated management of the laurel forests which may be achieved through improved cooperation between the organizations utilizing it, i.e. local government, town councils, environmental advisors and the Institute for Conservation of the Environment (ICONA). Of all the laurel forest on Tenerife, La Palma, La Gomera and El Hierro, 40% is publicly owned. Viseconsejería de Medio Ambiente del Gobierno de Canarias manages the greater part of this forest with only National Parks being under the jurisdiction of ICONA. At least on La Palma, public organizations should try to acquire fincas (private plots of land) supporting laurel forest, with the objective of guaranteeing their conservation. It is also necessary to gradually re-forest areas of degraded laurel forest.

Prevention of hunting requires environmental education, and infractions of the law should be firmly punished.

There is a need for studies on the impact of predation by rats, cats and raptors, together with other aspects of the White-tailed Laurel Pigeon's biology such as reproduction and the consequences of displacement. Additionally, each of the island populations should be regularly monitored. Sociedad Española Ornitología–BirdLife is currently preparing a conservation plan for the species.

MIGUEL A. HERNÁNDEZ

Turtle Dove
Streptopelia turtur

SPEC Category 3
Status Declining
Criteria Moderate decline

The European population of Turtle Dove fell between 1970 and 1990, especially from the mid-1980s onwards, and particularly in western Europe. This decline is likely to be due to severe drought in the species' African wintering grounds, shooting in winter and during spring migration, and the intensification of agriculture in the breeding area. Breeding and wintering habitat should be maintained (with reductions in agricultural herbicide use), spring shooting of the species should be stopped and winter hunting regulated.

■ Distribution and population trends

The majority of the nominate race of the Turtle Dove breeds in Europe, where it is widespread. The range,

	Breeding population			Breeding range trend
	Size (pairs)	Year	Trend	
Albania	1,000–5,000	91	(–1)	(–1)
Andorra	(0–3)	83	(–1)	(0)
Austria	(8,000–10,000)	—	(0)	(0)
Belarus	60,000–80,000	90	0	0
Belgium	10,000–17,000	81–90	–1	0
Bulgaria	(20,000–50,000)	—	(–1)	(–1)
Croatia	50,000–100,000 *	—	–1*	0*
Cyprus	3,000–4,000	—	–1	0
Czech Republic	60,000–120,000	—	–1	**0**
Denmark	**2–20**	88	(+1)	(+1)
Estonia	5,000–10,000	—	+1	0
Finland	**50–100**	92	**+2**	**+1**
France	200,000–450,000	92	–2	0
Germany	45,000–150,000	—	0*	0*
Greece	10,000–30,000	—	(–1)	(0)
Hungary	100,000–200,000	—	0	0
Italy	(50,000–100,000)	—	(0)	(0)
Latvia	3,000–5,000	—	+1	+1
Liechtenstein	(1–3)	—	(0)	(0)
Lithuania	1,000–15,000	85–88	(–1)	(0)
Luxembourg	300–700	—	–1	0
Malta	2–5	—	0	0
Moldova	**2,500–4,000**	88	**–1**	**0**
Netherlands	**35,000–50,000**	79	**–1**	**0**
Poland	100,000–200,000	—	0	0
Portugal	10,000–100,000	89	–1	0
Madeira	1–5	91	**0**	**0**
Romania	(20,000–40,000)	—	–2	–1
Russia	(500,000–5,000,000)	—	(0)	(0)
Slovakia	(15,000–30,000)	—	(0)	0
Slovenia	2,000–3,000	—	0	0
Spain	790,000–1,000,000	—	–1	–1
Canary Islands	2,500–3,000	—	–1	0
Switzerland	1,000–2,500	86–91	–1	0
Turkey	(500,000–5,000,000)	—	—	—
Ukraine	20,000–22,000	86	–1	–1
United Kingdom	**75,000–75,000**	88–91	**–2**	**–1**
Guernsey [1]	10–50	—	0*	0*
Jersey [1]	40–50	—	0	0
Total (approx.)	2,700,000–13,000,000			

Trends +2 Large increase +1 Small increase 0 Stable X Extinct
(1970–1990) –2 Large decrease –1 Small decrease F Fluctuating N New breeder
Data quality **Bold: reliable quantitative data** Normal type: incomplete quantitative data
Bracketed figures: no quantitative data * Data quality not provided
[1] Population figures are included within United Kingdom totals

which covers most of Europe (except Iceland, Ireland, northern Britain and Scandinavia), extends east to Turkey and the Caspian region and encompasses the Canary Islands (Cramp 1985). Turtle Doves migrate south of the Sahara to the Sahelian and Sudanian savannas, from Senegal east to Eritrea and Ethiopia. The west European population winters in Senegal and Mali (Cramp 1985, Jarry 1992).

European breeding numbers are estimated to lie between 2,700,000 and 13,000,000 pairs, with largest numbers breeding in Spain, Russia and Turkey, which together hold over two-thirds of the total (see map, table).

Between 1970 and 1990, an increase in numbers and range was noted for the rather small Baltic population in Denmark, Estonia, Finland and Latvia. In (e.g.) Germany, Poland, Slovakia, Austria, Belarus, Hungary, Italy, Slovenia and Russia the general trend was more or less of stability (see table, map), but overall up to about 60% of the European population (for which trends are known) declined between 1970–1990, especially in the west. In the United Kingdom, France and Romania more than half of the breeding pairs were lost between 1970 and 1990 (Marchant *et al*. 1990, Yeatman-Berthelot and Jarry in press; see table). This decline started at the end of the 1970s and became more marked, particularly after 1985 (Duckworth 1992, Yeatman-Berthelot and Jarry in press).

■ Ecology

The Turtle Dove breeds at low altitudes not exceeding 500 m in the temperate zone and up to 1,000 or 1,300 m in Mediterranean areas. Its habitat includes hedges, borders of forest, groves, spinneys, coppices, young tree plantations, scrubby wasteland, woody marshes, scrub and garigue, all with agricultural areas nearby for feeding. The species feeds on a large variety of small wild seeds and cultivated grain on rather bare ground (Cramp 1985). The nest, a small platform of twigs, is generally hidden in the

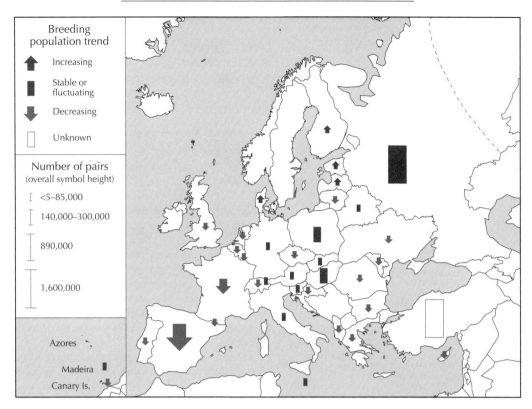

Breeding population trend	
▲	Increasing
■	Stable or fluctuating
▼	Decreasing
☐	Unknown

Number of pairs
(overall symbol height)

I	<5–85,000
I	140,000–300,000
I	890,000
I	1,600,000

Azores

Madeira

Canary Is.

lowest parts of trees. Breeding success is low, with less than half of eggs laid resulting in fledglings (Murton 1968).

In their winter quarters, Turtle Doves congregate in open savanna where both wild graminaceous seeds and cultivated rice, maize, sorghum, millet and peanuts are abundant (Morel 1987, Jarry in prep.). Birds roost communally in groups of up to several thousand, mainly in acacia woods (Morel 1987, Gore 1980, Lamarche 1980, Jarry and Baillon 1991) and close to fresh water for drinking.

■ Threats

Within Europe, the destruction of hedges is often considered to be one of the major factors limiting the species' breeding habitat (Marchant *et al*. 1990), but its decline is also likely to be caused by the use of agricultural herbicides. These chemical treatments have substantially reduced, and often eliminated, adventitious plants from farmland. These plants and their seeds provide most of the Turtle Dove's food, particularly during the spring (Yeatman-Berthelot and Jarry in press).

The main cause of the species' decline is considered to be the severe drought which has affected the African wintering range, especially in West Africa, and which has corresponded with a steep decrease of

the west European Turtle Dove population (Goodwin 1985, Skinner 1987, Marchant *et al*. 1990, Jarry 1992, Yeatman-Berthelot and Jarry in press). Also, the wintering habitat, especially the dense acacia forest, is being seriously degraded by cutting for charcoal (Jarry and Baillon 1991).

Hunting in the winter quarters, mainly in Senegal, where tens of thousands of birds are killed annually, and during spring in Morocco (more than 15,000 birds killed: El Mastour 1988) and in southwest France (over 40,000 killed: Razin and Urcun 1992, Ancer 1993, Urcun 1993) may also have contributed to, and accelerated, the decline of west European populations, especially given the species' low breeding success.

■ Conservation measures

Within Europe, measures should include the conservation and re-creation of hedges with hawthorn *Crataegus* which is a favoured tree for breeding, together with reductions in agricultural herbicides.

Special attention should be devoted to conserving acacia forests in tropical Africa which are necessary for roosting. Shooting during spring migration should be stopped in Morocco, as well as in France where it is already illegal, and hunting needs to be more tightly managed in wintering areas such as Senegal.

GUY JARRY

Barn Owl
Tyto alba

SPEC Category 3
Status Declining
Criteria Moderate decline

This widely distributed species has declined through much of north-west and central Europe, due mainly to agricultural intensification and urbanization. Traditional low-intensity farming needs to be maintained and provision made for the creation of rough-grassland field margins and for artificial nesting and roosting sites on intensively managed lands.

■ Distribution and population trends

The Barn Owl, the most widely distributed land bird in the world, breeds within all European countries except Greenland, Malta and the countries of Fennoscandia. It is most common in southern Eu-

	Breeding population			Breeding
	Size (pairs)	Year	Trend	range trend
Albania	1,000–3,000	62	(–1)	(–1)
Andorra	(0–2)	92	(–1)	(–1)
Austria	(10–20)	—	(–1)	(–1)
Belarus	(10–50)	90	(–1)	(–1)
Belgium	650–1,000	81–90	–1	–1
Bulgaria	20–50	—	(0)	(0)
Croatia	3,000–4,000 *	—	–1*	0*
Cyprus	(200–600)	—	0	0
Czech Republic	**400–700**	—	–2	–1
Denmark	20–25	90	(–2)	(–1)
France	20,000–50,000	90	(–1)	0
Germany	5,000–15,000	—	F	F
Greece	2,000–5,000	—	(0)	(0)
Hungary	1,500–2,000	—	–1	–1
Rep. of Ireland	550–800	82–85	–2	–1
Italy	(6,000–12,000)	—	(–1)	(0)
Latvia	(0–5)	—	(F)	(F)
Liechtenstein	1–3	—	–1	–1
Lithuania	10–50	85–88	(+1)	(+1)
Luxembourg	400–800	—	0	0
Malta	0–0	—	X	X
Moldova	**30–50**	89	–1	0
Netherlands	600–1,200 *	85	F	–1
Poland	1,000–4,000	—	–1	0
Portugal	1,000–10,000	89	F	0
Madeira	100–200	91	0	0
Romania	(500–1,000)	—	(–1)	0
Slovakia	400–500	—	–2	–1
Slovenia	(50–150)	—	(–2)	(–2)
Spain	50,000–90,000	—	0	0
Canary Islands	(400–500)	—	(0)	(0)
Switzerland	500–800	86–91	F	F
Turkey	(50–500)	—	—	—
Ukraine	(25–35)	90	–2	–1
United Kingdom	**4,450–4,500**	82–85	–2	–1
Guernsey [1]	10–15	—	0*	0*
Jersey [1]	**3–10**	—	F	F
Isle of Man [1]	2–7	—	0	0*
Gibraltar	(1–2)	—	—	0*
Total (approx.)	100,000–210,000			

Trends +2 Large increase   +1 Small increase   0 Stable   X Extinct
(1970-1990) –2 Large decrease   –1 Small decrease   F Fluctuating   N New breeder
Data quality **Bold**: reliable quantitative data   Normal type: incomplete quantitative data
Bracketed figures: no quantitative data   * Data quality not provided
[1] Population figures are included within United Kingdom totals

rope where winters are mild, and although extending as far north as Scotland and Denmark it is scarce in north-west and central Europe north of the 0°C mean January isotherm. It nevertheless persists in Poland, Hungary and other parts of central Europe, probably because non-intensive farming provides sufficient prey around farmyards in severe winters. First-year birds in the north occasionally disperse long distances, but European Barn Owls are basically resident.

The main strongholds are Spain, United Kingdom, France, Germany and Italy, which together hold over three-quarters of European numbers (see table, map). The Barn Owl has declined throughout much of its range since the 1950s, and during 1970–1990 the Barn Owl became extinct in Malta, and numbers fell by over 50% in seven countries and by 20–50% in a further 13 (see table). Populations are believed to be fluctuating in six countries, stable in nine and increasing in just one.

■ Ecology

The Barn Owl is predominantly a specialist feeder on small terrestrial mammals, particularly voles (Microtinae), mice (Murinae) and shrews (Soricidae), mainly restricted to open areas of rough grassland and marsh. It can also occur at relatively high density in intensively farmed or afforested regions but only where an extensive network of rough grassland feeding corridors exist, e.g. along the banks of open drainage ditches, rivers and hedges (Shawyer 1989), as well as in young forest plantations and around mature forest edge (Shaw and Dowell 1990).

Farm buildings provide the main nest- and roost-sites, although church towers are more commonly used in parts of central Europe (Pikula *et al.* 1984). Large tree cavities are frequently used in the eastern United Kingdom and Republic of Ireland, and cliff crevices are quite common sites in Scotland.

Prolonged snow cover and rainfall can restrict feeding, and this, together with cyclical changes in small mammal populations, can dramatically affect breeding success (Bunn *et al.* 1982, Shawyer 1987).

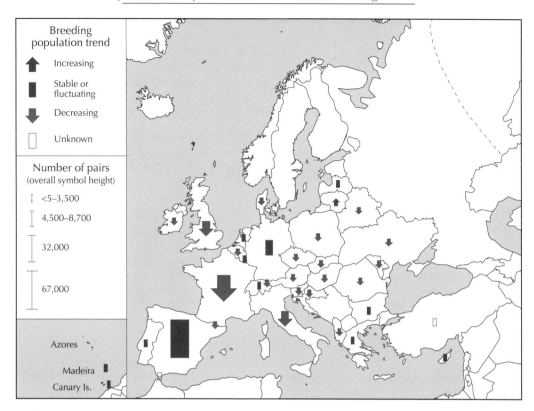

Breeding population trend

↑ Increasing

▮ Stable or fluctuating

↓ Decreasing

☐ Unknown

Number of pairs
(overall symbol height)

I <5–3,500

I 4,500–8,700

I 32,000

I 67,000

Azores

Madeira

Canary Is.

▪ Threats

The main cause of the Barn Owl's decline has been the loss and fragmentation of rough grassland foraging habitat, the result of agricultural intensification, urbanization and road development. Increased mechanization on farms, particularly in north-west Europe, resulting in the disappearance of prey-rich stackyards and straw-bedded stables, also led to a sudden loss of an important food supply on which the Barn Owl had previously depended during severe winters. The demolition of old farm buildings, their conversion to domestic accommodation, particularly in the United Kingdom and France, together with increased human usage of those which remain, is seriously reducing nesting and roosting opportunities (Shawyer 1987, van der Hut 1992).

The use of organochlorine pesticides is considered to have had some influence on numbers in the United Kingdom during the 1950s and 1960s (Newton *et al.* 1991). The possible poisoning of Barn Owls by rodenticides has also been reported in the United Kingdom (Shawyer 1985), and recent research has shown that a significant proportion of British Barn Owls contain measurable levels of different second-generation anticoagulants (Newton *et al.* 1990). Road mortality has risen dramatically in many countries as the volume and speed of traffic have increased and as Barn Owls have been attracted to hunt along road verges following the disappearance of rough grassland from farmland and the fragmentation of traditional habitats (Shawyer 1994).

▪ Conservation measures

The protection and re-establishment of rough grasslands, particularly alongside watercourses, field margins and woodland edge, is essential to provide an inter-connected network of prey-rich foraging grounds and to help reduce habitat fragmentation (Brazil and Shawyer 1989). Within the EU countries, opportunities exist for such habitat provision under the Set-aside Scheme (EC Reg. 1765/92) and the Agri-environment Regulation (EC Reg. 2078/92) of the Common Agricultural Policy. Adjacent to these habitats, suitable boxes for nesting and roosting should be placed in trees, in little-used farm buildings and in modern hay barns where nest losses are common following the removal of bales.

Further controls may be required over the use of second-generation anticoagulant rodenticides. Although the reintroduction of Barn Owls is taking place in a number of countries with mixed success, this has sometimes led to conflict with wild stock. New government regulations in the United Kingdom have been designed to make operators more aware of the potential dangers of introducing poor and incorrect genetic stock and to offer guidance (DoE 1992).

COLIN SHAWYER

Scops Owl
Otus scops

SPEC Category 2
Status (Declining)
Criteria Moderate decline

A substantial proportion of the European population is declining, due chiefly to the widespread use of agricultural pesticides. The principal conservation measures required are the reduced use of broad-spectrum and highly toxic pesticides and the preservation of old trees which provide nest-sites.

■ Distribution and population trends

Over half the global range of the Scops Owl lies within Europe, where it is widely distributed through southern Europe including Iberia, Italy, the Balkan peninsula and Turkey, as well as southern and central Russia. It also occurs in France and southern parts of central Europe. Northern birds are migratory, the southern populations of Spain and Greece are partial migrants, and the endemic subspecies *Otus scops cyprius* of Cyprus is resident (Cramp 1985).

Although the sizes of the populations are not well known, over half of Europe's breeding birds probably occur in Spain, Russia and Croatia. Other countries with particularly important numbers are Italy, Bulgaria, Greece, Cyprus and Turkey (see table, map).

	Breeding population			Breeding
	Size (pairs)	Year	Trend	range trend
Albania	2,000–5,000	62	—	—
Andorra	(0–1)	83	—	(0)
Austria	20–30	—	–2	–2
Belarus	(10–50)	90	(F)	(F)
Bulgaria	(10,000–10,000)	—	(0)	(0)
Croatia	20,000–25,000 *	—	0*	0*
Cyprus	(5,000–15,000)	—	0	0
France	1,000–10,000	76	(0)	**0**
Greece	5,000–10,000	—	(–1)	(0)
Hungary	300–400	—	+1	+1
Italy	(4,000–8,000)	—	(–1)	(–1)
Moldova	**300–500**	88	**–1**	**0**
Portugal	1,000–10,000	89	(0)	0
Romania	1,000–4,000	—	0	**0**
Russia	(5,000–50,000)	75–90	(0)	(0)
Slovakia	(20–30)	—	(0)	(0)
Slovenia	500–800	—	0	+1
Spain	30,000–34,000	—	–1	–1
Switzerland	**12–15**	88	**–2**	**–2**
Turkey	(5,000–30,000)	—	—	—
Ukraine	100–120	88	–2	–1
United Kingdom Gibraltar	(1–2)	—	(0)	0*
Total (approx.)	90,000–210,000			

Trends (1970–1990) +2 Large increase +1 Small increase 0 Stable X Extinct
  –2 Large decrease –1 Small decrease F Fluctuating N New breeder
Data quality **Bold**: reliable quantitative data Normal type: incomplete quantitative data
  Bracketed figures: no quantitative data * Data quality not provided

Up to half of the European population is decreasing, including the large populations in Spain, Greece and Italy, and the species has declined particularly rapidly in Austria, Switzerland and the Ukraine. Furthermore, a decrease in range has been noted in Spain, Italy and the Ukraine and particularly in Austria and Switzerland where the species is in danger of extinction (see table).

■ Ecology

The habitat includes all types of open woodland, riverine forest, cultivated land with trees, fruit plantations, olive-groves, and town parks and gardens; in Europe it can be found above 1,500 m (Máñez 1987, Voous 1988). Nests are typically in holes in trees or buildings, although old nests of other species (especially crows, etc., Corvidae) are sometimes used (Cramp 1985).

The food is almost entirely invertebrates, more so than in any other European owl, and consists mainly of large insects, especially crickets, etc. (Orthoptera), moths (Lepidoptera) and beetles (Coleoptera) (Koenig 1973).

■ Threats

Widespread use of agricultural pesticides is a major cause of the Scops Owl's decline (Garzón 1977): residues are accumulated from contaminated insect prey, and these may reach levels fatal to the birds when their fat reserves are depleted on migration (Burton 1973). Additionally, the widespread use of pesticides greatly reduces prey numbers (Voous 1988).

Structural changes to the habitat are also a significant threat in France and central Europe at least (Glutz von Blotzheim and Bauer 1980, Mikkola 1983), due mostly to the loss of old trees with natural nest-sites (e.g. Arlettaz 1987). On migration the species may also be affected by hunting where it is particularly intense, such as in Italy and Malta (Mikkola 1983).

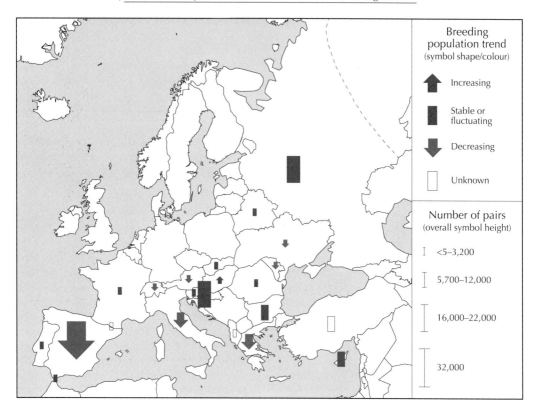

Breeding population trend
(symbol shape/colour)

▲ Increasing

■ Stable or fluctuating

▼ Decreasing

□ Unknown

Number of pairs
(overall symbol height)

<5–3,200

5,700–12,000

16,000–22,000

32,000

■ Conservation measures

Most effective would be a reduction in the use of highly toxic pesticides that are prone to accumulation in such insect predators, combined with a reduction in the use of broad-spectrum insecticides that reduce prey numbers.

The preservation of old trees would be beneficial, and the use of nest-boxes may be appropriate, as it has been demonstrated in various countries that Scops Owls readily accept these in areas with insufficient natural sites (Voous 1988).

Where there is high hunting pressure, protection of this and other legally protected species should be enforced and awareness campaigns developed to inform hunters of the need for conservation measures for this species.

MANUEL MÁÑEZ

Eagle Owl
Bubo bubo

SPEC Category 3
Status Vulnerable
Criteria Large decline

Although there have been widespread increases this owl has declined markedly in parts of southern and eastern Europe due to shooting, egg-collecting, disturbance and collision with, or electrocution by, powerlines. In areas with high human population levels, strict protection from disturbance at the nest is particularly important for this very shy species.

■ Distribution and population trends

The Eagle Owl has a very large world range, occurring across Europe and Asia in the subarctic to subtropical zones and into North Africa. Its population strongholds are thought to be in the far eastern Siberian boreal forest belt and on Sakhalin Island. It is found in much of mainland Europe, where its range extends from Portugal in the west to the Urals

	Breeding population			Breeding range trend
	Size (pairs)	Year	Trend	
Albania	50–100	62	(–1)	(–1)
Andorra	(0–2)	83	(–1)	(–1)
Austria	250–300	—	+1	+1
Belarus	250–400	90	–1	0
Belgium	20–30	81–90	N	N
Bulgaria	**100–150**		0	0
Croatia	1,000–1,500 *	—	0*	0*
Czech Republic	**600–950**	—	+2	+2
Denmark	**1–1**	89	N	—
Estonia	100–150	—	0	0
Finland	**2,000–3,000**	92	+2	+2
France	887–1,000	92	+1	+1
Germany	400–500	—	+2	+1
Greece	(200–500)	—	(–1)	(0)
Hungary	**10–10**	91	–2	–2
Italy	(100–200)	88	(–1)	(–1)
Latvia	30–50	—	0	+1
Liechtenstein	**3–3**	91	0	0
Lithuania	1–5	85–88	(–1)	(–1)
Luxembourg	1–5	—	+1	+1
Moldova	**20–30**	89	–1	0
Netherlands	**0–2**	85	N	N
Norway	1,000–3,000	90	0	**0**
Poland	130–160	—	0	0
Portugal	100–1,000	89	–1	–1
Romania	200–600	—	0	0
Russia	(2,000–20,000)	75–90	(–2)	(0)
Slovakia	300–350	—	(0)	0
Slovenia	50–100	—	0	0
Spain	520–600	—	–1	–1
Sweden	250–350	87	+1	0
Switzerland	**40–80**	89–90	+1	+1
Turkey	(500–5,000)	—	—	—
Ukraine	**150–200**	88	–2	–2
Total (approx.)	11,000–40,000			

Trends (1970–1990) +2 Large increase +1 Small increase 0 Stable X Extinct
–2 Large decrease –1 Small decrease F Fluctuating N New breeder
Data quality **Bold**: reliable quantitative data Normal type: incomplete quantitative data
Bracketed figures: no quantitative data * Data quality not provided

in the east, though it seems to be absent from all Mediterranean islands and the Canaries.

Large populations in Europe are found in Norway, Finland and Russia, which together hold between 5,000 and 26,000 pairs. In many parts of Europe the Eagle Owl has become rare or extinct as a result of direct persecution through shooting, nest robbing or disturbance. The important Russian population is reported to be in rapid decline, although numbers are poorly known (see table, map). Although the species has recently recovered in some large populations, including Norway, Finland, France and Czech Republic, and is stable or increasing elsewhere, overall nearly two-thirds of the population for which trends are known is in decline (see table). Furthermore, populations comprising up to c.60% of the total have declined rapidly.

Captive breeding and release schemes in Norway, Sweden, France, Belgium, Germany and Switzerland have supplemented or re-established some populations. For example, in the mid-1950s the entire German Eagle Owl population dropped to less than 50 pairs, but due (at least in part) to reintroduction schemes it lies now between 400 and 500 pairs (Voous 1988).

■ Ecology

The species inhabits extremely varied habitats, from boreal coniferous and mixed deciduous forests to Mediterranean scrub, wooded and grassy steppes and rocky and sandy deserts. It also occurs on steep slopes or cliff faces, usually close to open water. In the Alps it has nested at altitudes of up to 2,100 m and hunts above the treeline at up to 2,800 m (Glutz von Blotzheim and Bauer 1980).

The Eagle Owl's nest-scrapes are usually in fissures, crevices and holes, or on ledges, often protected by overhanging rocks, bushes or tree trunks. Infrequently it takes possession of the nests of other birds. Eagle Owls are strongly territorial and virtually sedentary, though some young birds disperse up to 200 km and individuals from northernmost

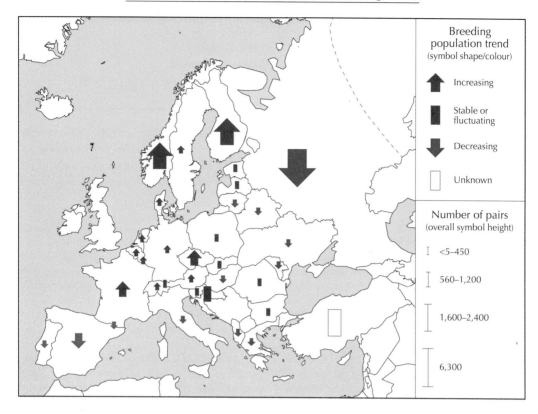

Breeding
population trend
(symbol shape/colour)

Increasing

Stable or
fluctuating

Decreasing

Unknown

Number of pairs
(overall symbol height)

<5–450

560–1,200

1,600–2,400

6,300

populations have wandered south over considerable distances in years of food scarcity. Substantial numbers of birds undertake such movements in Siberia (Dementiev and Gladkov 1951a).

Originally the main prey was probably medium-sized to large mammals, but Eagle Owls have now been forced to turn to voles and other small mammals and medium-sized birds (Voous 1988).

■ Threats

Man seems to be directly responsible for the Eagle Owl's high mortality, at least in inhabited temperate Eurasia. The species is extremely sensitive to man's presence in the vicinity of the nest and the slightest disturbance can cause desertion (Mikkola 1983). Unfortunately, cross-country skiing, mountaineering, alpinism and other popular leisure activities often take many people unknowingly close to Eagle Owl nests in otherwise remote and inaccessible areas. These sites are amongst the owl's last refuges in densely inhabited Europe.

Large numbers of owls have been killed by illegal shooting and by overhead wires, either by direct collision or by electrocution (Everett and Sharrock 1980). Ever-increasing motor traffic and railways take an additional heavy toll all year round, especially of young birds, and the level of nest-robbing by egg-collectors is relatively high.

■ Conservation measures

Since the Eagle Owl is strongly territorial and sedentary it is possible to protect it against human disturbance during the breeding season. The general public, and birdwatchers and photographers in particular, should be made more aware of the susceptibility of this species to nest disturbance. A single visit is often sufficient to cause desertion of the eggs, so the early breeding stages should not be studied or photographed. In recent years strict protection from disturbance and persecution has restored the Eagle Owl population in Sweden.

Fortunately, the species also seems capable of adapting slowly to human presence and has recently been found nesting more frequently close to villages and farms, and recently even in rubbish dumps on the outskirts of large cities (Mikkola 1983).

Eagle Owls seem to have profited from deforestation, as they now breed in small forest islands and hunt for voles and rats over the cultivated fields and grasslands which border them (Burton 1992).

HEIMO MIKKOLA

327

Snowy Owl
Nyctea scandiaca

SPEC Category 3
Status Vulnerable
Criteria <2,500 pairs

The Snowy Owl is a rare and irregular breeder on the tundra of northern Russia and in mountainous areas of Fennoscandia. It breeds only during years of peak rodent numbers, leading to often-long periods between breeding in some countries. Food scarcity within its breeding range can also lead to south-westerly eruptive movements during winter. It is essential to avoid road construction and other development in traditional breeding areas.

■ Distribution and population trends

The Snowy Owl has a circumpolar Holarctic distribution in the tundra climatic zone, with the European breeding range extending across Greenland, Iceland, southern Norway (Hardangervidda), and over the Fennoscandian mountain ridge (Sweden, Finland) to the Russian tundra. There were also breeding records on the Shetland Islands in the United Kingdom between 1967 and 1975 (Sharrock 1976, Sharrock and Rare Breeding Birds Panel 1982). The species is regularly observed on Svalbard but has never been known to breed there.

Birds regularly move across the tundra to the west and south of the normal range in response to climatic conditions and food availability. Birds winter mainly within the breeding range, but eruptive movements into central Europe occur during periods of food scarcity (Glutz von Blotzheim and Bauer 1980, Cramp 1985).

The nomadic lifestyle of the species and the dynamic nature of its breeding distribution makes the estimation of both population size and long-term trends difficult, with numbers ranging from nil to several hundred in some countries in different years (see table). In northern Finland the species was common at the beginning of the twentieth century, and in 1907 about 800 Snowy Owl eggs were collected from 100 nests. The species gradually became rarer there, probably as a result of large-scale trapping and egg-collecting (Mikkola 1983), and did not breed between 1932 and 1974. It then reappeared in Finland in 1974 when between 30 and 35 pairs bred, this probably being related to a decline in the populations of rodents on the Russian tundra which forced the birds westwards for food (Hakala *et al*. 1974).

A remarkable occurrence of breeding was recorded in 1978 in parts of northern Sweden and Norway, when about 100 nests were found and the total population size was estimated to be several hundred pairs (Persson 1978, Broo and Lindberg 1981, Wiklund and Stigh 1983, 1986). Snowy Owls have since bred in Fennoscandia in 1981, 1982, 1985 and 1987, with between 1 and 18 pairs recorded in each of these years (Solheim 1989).

In Iceland the species is rare, and Mikkola (1983) mentions a maximum breeding population of less than 10 pairs. The most recent estimate is of 0–5 pairs, with the last known breeding record being in 1973 (see also Cramp 1985). In Greenland the species is found on ice-free tundra areas but very little is known about the actual population size. The distribution of Snowy Owls on the Russian tundra is probably better known but few reports have been published in English.

■ Ecology

The Snowy Owl breeds on alpine mountain heaths and in tundra areas above the tree-line. In Fennoscandia it often selects areas with moraine or sand ridges, where the nest scrape is located on hillocks. The owls seem to have a preference for certain breeding sites but these may only be used every few decades, coinciding with years of peak rodent populations.

Egg-laying starts at the beginning of May and clutch size varies from 4 to 10 with an average of 7.7 (Watson 1957, Hagen 1960, Mikkola 1983). Incubation begins with the first egg, so the nestlings are of

| | Breeding population | | | Breeding |
	Size (pairs)	Year	Trend	range trend
Denmark				
Greenland	(0–1,000)	—	(F)	(F)
Finland	0–100	92	F	F
Iceland	0–5	79–90	—	0*
Norway	0–50	90	F	0
Russia	(?–1,000)	75–90	(F)	(F)
Sweden	1–200	87	**F**	0
Total (approx.)	?–2,400			

Trends   +2 Large increase   +1 Small increase   0 Stable   X Extinct
(1970–1990) –2 Large decrease   –1 Small decrease   F Fluctuating   N New breeder
Data quality **Bold**: reliable quantitative data   Normal type: incomplete quantitative data
Bracketed figures: no quantitative data   * Data quality not provided

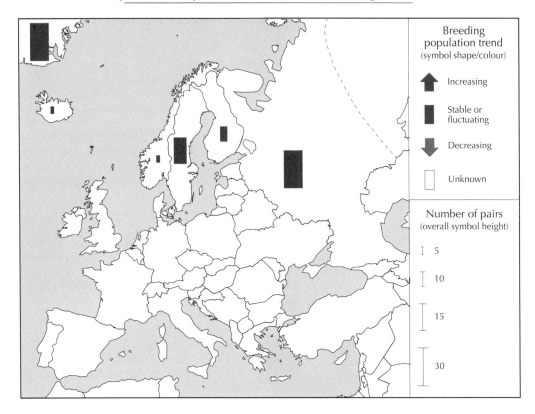

Breeding
population trend
(symbol shape/colour)

Increasing

Stable or
fluctuating

Decreasing

Unknown

Number of pairs
(overall symbol height)

5

10

15

30

markedly different sizes, with the first to hatch having the best chance of survival (Cramp 1985). The species is polygamous.

Small and medium-sized rodents form the Snowy Owl's staple food in Fennoscandia and the Norway lemming *Lemmus lemmus* is the commonest prey item in Lapland (Mikkola 1983).

■ Threats

Although currently not threatened directly, the relatively sparse and nomadic European breeding population, with its specific breeding habitat requirements, could be detrimentally affected by the impacts of human activity on the breeding grounds.

The species is relatively sensitive to disturbance by man during the egg-laying period, and increased snowmobile traffic would negatively affect reproduction, especially in Fennoscandian mountain areas.

Little is known about the long-term effects which climatic change, acidification, and overgrazing by reindeers may have on the populations of tundra rodents, the main prey.

■ Conservation measures

Although considerable time may elapse between incidences of breeding by Snowy Owls in individual regions, the major breeding areas along the Fennoscandian mountain range should be given long-term protection. It is especially important to avoid road construction, the erection of powerlines and development of tourism in the breeding areas. The regulation or prohibition of snowmobile and off-road traffic during the breeding season is also required.

Research into the effects of acidification on rodent and owl population dynamics should be carried out.

PETER LINDBERG

Little Owl
Athene noctua

SPEC Category 3
Status Declining
Criteria Moderate decline

The European population of the Little Owl has been decreasing for 30–40 years, and its range has also declined in some countries. This is likely to be due to a reduction in large insect prey populations, loss of nesting sites, and road mortality. Only measures which address conservation in the wider countryside, including the use of pesticides and the maintenance of old trees and buildings, stand a chance of reversing this decline.

■ Distribution and population trends

The Little Owl has a Palearctic distribution with between a quarter and half of its range in Europe. It is absent from Greenland, Iceland, Fennoscandia, the northern half of eastern Europe and the Macaronesian Islands (Cramp 1985). The species was introduced to the United Kingdom in the second half of the nineteenth century (Glüe and Scott 1980). The Little Owl is essentially resident, but some adults disperse over short distances in autumn and winter; most first-year birds settle within 20 km of their birthplace (Cramp 1985).

Countries supporting particularly large numbers of breeding birds are France, Spain, Italy, Romania, Ukraine, Russia and Portugal.

For the last 30–40 years, the Little Owl has been declining in most European countries (Noval 1975, Juillard 1980, Cramp 1985, Jarry 1993). Between 1970 and 1990 the decline was most marked in central and north-west Europe, but also apparent in Spain, Greece and Cyprus. Furthermore, in addition to population declines, contractions in range size have been confirmed in the Netherlands, Germany, Switzerland, Czech Republic and Moldova and are probable in several other countries (see table).

■ Ecology

In Europe, the Little Owl has a preference for lowland areas, although in Spain birds also commonly breed on the central plateau between 500 and 1,100 m (Máñez 1981, Urios *et al.* 1991). The species does not appear to have very specific habitat requirements but does avoid dense forest. It lives on the edges or in the clearings of forests, open oak woodland such as the dehesas, agricultural land, olive-groves, vegetable gardens, city parks, villages, elevated steppes and semi-deserts. Birds usually build their nests in the holes of trees, buildings or rock clefts, mounds of stones or in burrows of rabbits *Oryctolagus cuniculus*.

The species has a tendency to hunt in areas without high vegetation, either from conspicuous perches or on the ground. Large insects, especially beetles, are the major food (Cramp 1985).

■ Threats

Pesticides, which seriously reduce or eliminate populations of large insects, are a cause of the Little Owl's decline (Juillard *et al.* 1978). The direct toxic effect of chemical pollutants is also suggested as a major threat by Fuchs and Thissen (1981), although

	Breeding population			Breeding
	Size (pairs)	Year	Trend	range trend
Albania	5,000–10,000	62	0*	0*
Andorra	(0–1)	83	—	(–1)
Austria	(40–60)	—	(–2)	(–2)
Belarus	(2,000–4,000)	90	–1	(0)
Belgium	4,500–6,600	81–90	–1	–1
Bulgaria	(4,000–10,000)	—	(0)	(0)
Croatia	6,000–8,000 *	—	0*	0*
Cyprus	2,000–4,000	—	–1	0
Czech Republic	**700–1,100**	—	**–1**	**–1**
Denmark	150–150	—	–1	(–2)
France	**10,000–50,000**	90	–1	0
Germany	5,000–10,000	85	–2	–1
Greece	5,000–10,000	—	(–1)	(0)
Hungary	1,500–2,000	—	–1	–1
Italy	(10,000–50,000)	—	(0)	(0)
Latvia	10–30	—	(F)	(F)
Lithuania	(10–50)	85–88	(0)	(0)
Luxembourg	80–150	—	–1	0
Moldova	**5,000–7,000**	88	–1	–1
Netherlands	9,000–12,000 *	79	–1	–1
Poland	1,000–3,000	—	–2	0
Portugal	10,000–100,000	89	0	0
Romania	(20,000–40,000)	—	(0)	0
Russia	(10,000–100,000)	75–90	(0)	(0)
Slovakia	800–1,000	—	–1	–1
Slovenia	500–800	—	–2	–2
Spain	50,000–65,000	—	–1	–1
Switzerland	**30–40**	86–91	–2	–2
Turkey	(5,000–50,000)	—	—	—
Ukraine	11,000–12,000	88	+1	+1
United Kingdom	6,000–12,000	88–91	–1	0
Gibraltar	(3–6)	—	–1	0*
Total (approx.)	180,000–570,000			

Trends +2 Large increase +1 Small increase 0 Stable X Extinct
(1970–1990) –2 Large decrease –1 Small decrease F Fluctuating N New breeder
Data quality **Bold**: reliable quantitative data Normal type: incomplete quantitative data
Bracketed figures: no quantitative data * Data quality not provided

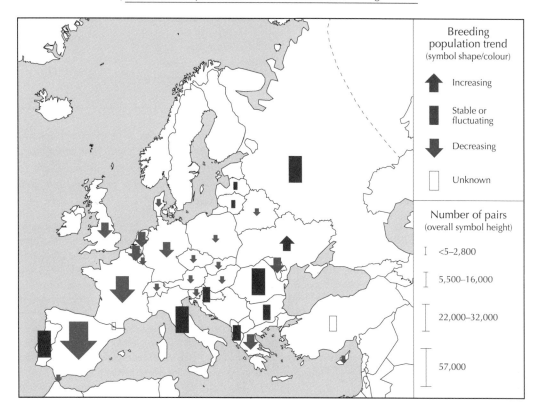

Breeding population trend (symbol shape/colour)	
↑	Increasing
▮	Stable or fluctuating
↓	Decreasing
☐	Unknown

Number of pairs (overall symbol height)	
<5–2,800	
5,500–16,000	
22,000–32,000	
57,000	

other authors do not consider that this is a factor contributing to the species' decline (Jarry 1983).

Changes in land-use practices which have brought about the elimination of old, hollow trees in orchards and hedges (Juillard 1980), together with the restoration of abandoned country houses and farm buildings, are depriving the species of nesting holes (Juillard 1984).

Road casualties are an important known cause of non-natural Little Owl mortality in Europe, as has been demonstrated in Spain (Hernández 1988), United Kingdom (Glue 1971), France (Jarry 1983), Germany and Netherlands (Exo and Hennes 1980). Hernández (1988) found that 63% of recorded road-deaths occurred on roads with roadside vegetation less than 0.5 m high, 37% with vegetation 0.5–1 m high and none on roads with vegetation of 1–3 m high. It seems that where vegetation is lacking birds perch on the road itself, and are thus more likely to be killed by vehicles.

■ Conservation measures

Only measures which address conservation in the wider countryside, across the region, stand a chance

of reversing the decline. The most effective conservation measures would be the preservation of the species' habitat, including old trees and hedges that separate fields, together with reductions in the use of pesticides. Organochlorine pesticides which eliminate the invertebrates on which the Little Owl feeds (Juillard et al. 1978) should be replaced with less aggressive products or with biological methods of pest control. Nest-boxes could also help to alleviate the scarcity of nesting sites (Juillard 1980, Voous 1988).

An advisable measure to reduce car-collision incidents is to ensure the presence of perches near roads, either by maintaining or planting trees or shrubs or, where appropriate, by establishing 2-m-high perches 10–15 m apart and 5 m from the edge of the road (Hernández 1988).

Further research is required into habitat requirements, the population size, and trends and threats.

MANUEL MÁÑEZ

Short-eared Owl
Asio flammeus

SPEC Category 3
Status (Vulnerable)
Criteria Large decline

The Short-eared Owl is a Holarctic species, with its main breeding areas in the northern United Kingdom, Fennoscandia and Russia. Although populations fluctuate according to food abundance (mainly voles), significant declines have been noted, especially in eastern Europe, probably due to habitat loss and degradation. Remaining marshlands and moorlands need to be protected and open ditches, meadows and old pastures in farmland areas maintained.

■ Distribution and population trends

The nominate form of the Short-eared Owl has a circumpolar distribution extending across the Holarctic region. In the west Palearctic the species' main breeding area is found in northern Europe, including the United Kingdom, Fennoscandia and Russia. In central and south-east Europe, breeding areas are scattered, and the species breeds only during years of high rodent density or when food is limited in its northern breeding range (Hölzinger *et al.* 1973, Bezzel 1985).

	Breeding population			Breeding
	Size (pairs)	Year	Trend	range trend
Austria	0–10	—	–1	–2
Belarus	1,500–3,000	90	–1	0
Belgium	1–6	81–90	0	0
Croatia	10–15 *	—	–1*	–1*
Czech Republic	0–5	—	F*	F*
Denmark	**3**–?	91	(0)	(0)
Estonia	100–100	—	–1	(0)
Finland	**3,000–10,000**	92	F	**F**
France	**10–100**	76	F	**–1**
Germany	100–300	—	F	0
Greece	(0–10)	—	(0)	(0)
Hungary	5–20	—	0	0
Iceland	100–200	—	0	0
Latvia	0–10	—	–2	–2
Lithuania	(20–50)	85–88	(–1)	(–1)
Moldova	10–50	85	–2	–1
Netherlands	60–140 *	79	**F**	**–1**
Norway	1,000–10,000	90	F	**0**
Poland	30–80	—	F	0
Romania	(0–20)	—	(–2)	(0)
Russia	(10,000–100,000)	75–90	(–2)	(0)
Slovakia	(15–30)	—	F*	F*
Spain	0–6	—	F	F
Sweden	2,000–7,000	87	(F)	0
Turkey	(1–50)	—	—	—
Ukraine	**150–180**	86	**–2**	**–2**
United Kingdom	1,000–3,500	88–91	(F)	**0**
Isle of Man [1]	2–5	—	0	0*
Total (approx.)	19,000–130,000			

Trends   +2 Large increase   +1 Small increase   0 Stable   X Extinct
(1970-1990) –2 Large decrease   –1 Small decrease   F Fluctuating   N New breeder
Data quality **Bold**: reliable quantitative data   Normal type: incomplete quantitative data
              Bracketed figures: no quantitative data   * Data quality not provided
[1] Population figures are included within United Kingdom totals

Russia has the largest population (see table) which breeds from the Arctic tundra to the temperate steppe and dry grassland zone in the south. In Finland and Norway the Short-eared Owl is one of the commonest owls. In Sweden the population was estimated at 5,000–10,000 pairs during good vole years in the mid-1970s (Ulfstrand and Högstedt 1976), and more recent estimates give a population of up to about 7,000 pairs (SOF 1990; see table). In Iceland the small population breeds in lowland areas.

The distribution in central and south-east Europe is more sparse (see table), and the species has disappeared from many areas as a result of drainage of marshlands. The owl is a rare breeder in small numbers in the Czech Republic, Slovakia, Hungary, Romania and Greece (see table, map).

Marked population fluctuations due to variations in food availability are typical throughout the European breeding range. In the United Kingdom, for example, the population is known to vary according to fluctuations in the numbers of small mammals, especially the short-tailed vole *Microtus agrestis* (Lockie 1955, Picozzi and Hewson 1970). Declines have, however, been noted in a significant part of the European range, particularly in central and eastern Europe, including a large decrease reported for the Russian population (see table, map).

■ Ecology

The Short-eared Owl is a ground-nester, preferring open habitats such as marshes, bogs, moorland, meadows, alpine heaths and sand-dunes. In Fennoscandia it also breeds in clear-felled forest areas which offer both open space and an abundance of voles. Owl numbers peak 3–4 years after peak vole populations, and good breeding years in Fennoscandia and Russia can be followed by eruptive movements into southern parts of Europe (Glutz von Blotzheim and Bauer 1980). In winter the owl is found in coastal lowlands, sometimes in small concentrations, and in open, cultivated areas inland (Cramp 1985).

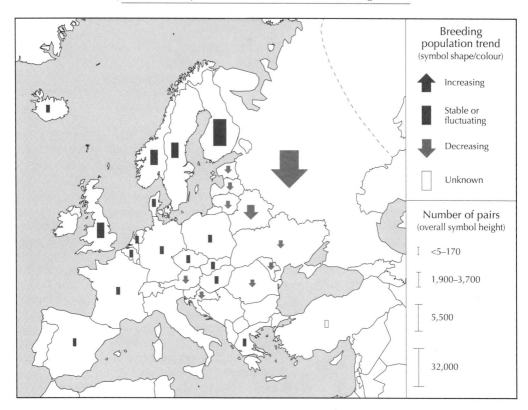

Breeding
population trend
(symbol shape/colour)

Increasing

Stable or
fluctuating

Decreasing

Unknown

Number of pairs
(overall symbol height)

<5–170

1,900–3,700

5,500

32,000

The breeding season and clutch size vary in relation to food (Korpimäki and Norrdahl 1991): there are several early breeding records from December and January during vole peaks in central Europe, and clutches vary from 2 to 14 eggs, with an average of 7.3 (Mikkola 1983). Two broods are sometimes raised and polygamy has been observed.

The owl has a nomadic lifestyle and nestlings ringed in the Netherlands and Germany have later summered in northern Norway, Sweden, Finland and in northern Russia from Arkhangelsk east to Sverdlovsk (Cramp 1985).

Threats

Drainage of wetlands and marshes in central Europe has reduced both the extent of the Short-eared Owl's breeding habitat and the numbers of voles (Voous 1960, Mikkola 1983). Also, the use of buried pipes to drain cultivated fields reduces the need for open ditches and these are important vole habitats. So, as cultivation, drainage and afforestation continue, Short-eared Owls are likely to decline further. Other possible threats such as hunting and poisoning by rodenticides are probably less important.

Although the afforestation of moorlands in the United Kingdom may have increased vole numbers and consequently the Short-eared Owl population (Sharrock 1976), the benefit is likely to be temporary. Open hunting habitat will decrease as the trees grow, and thus afforestation will probably cause the Short-eared Owl to become less common in the long term.

Conservation measures

Areas of marshland, old pastureland, meadows and moorland that support good vole habitat are important feeding areas for Short-eared Owls and for diurnal raptors and should be conserved for such species. Marshlands and moorlands thus need to be protected from destruction, drainage and afforestation, and agricultural habitats such as meadows and old pasturelands should be managed with conservation objectives in mind. Ditches with rough vegetation and other such habitats that support voles and provide nesting habitats should be maintained on farmland where possible. Within the EU countries, the Set-aside Scheme (EC Regulation 1765/92) and Zonal Programmes developed under the Agri-environment Regulation (EC Reg. 2078/92) could provide opportunities for such conservation measures.

PETER LINDBERG

Nightjar
Caprimulgus europaeus

SPEC Category 2
Status (Declining)
Criteria Moderate decline

The European population is declining in numbers and range, primarily through habitat deterioration and the application of pesticides. Maintenance of extensive areas of habitats which provide a mosaic of, and transitions between, open sparsely vegetated areas and woodland is important.

■ Distribution and population trends

Over half of the global range of the Nightjar lies in Europe, north to the boreal zone. Birds migrate to the Afrotropics in winter.

Although there are particularly large populations in Spain, Russia, Ukraine, Belarus and Greece, data from most countries are insufficiently precise for a confident comparison of numbers (see table).

	Breeding population			Breeding
	Size (pairs)	Year	Trend	range trend
Albania	2,000–4,000	81	(–1)	(–1)
Andorra	(3–5)	91	(0)	(–1)
Austria	(250–400)	—	(–1)	(–1)
Belarus	45,000–60,000	90	(0)	0
Belgium	180–250	90	–1	–1
Bulgaria	(1,000–5,000)	—	(–1)	(–1)
Croatia	3,000–4,000 *	—	–1*	–1*
Cyprus	(100–200)	—	(0)	(0)
Czech Republic	600–1,200	—	–1	**–1**
Denmark	300–300	87–89	(–1)	—
Estonia	2,000–5,000	—	–1	0
Finland	3,000–4,000	92	–1	**–1**
France	1,000–10,000	76	0	0
Germany	3,000–6,000	—	(–1)	0
Greece	(10,000–20,000)	—	(–1)	(0)
Hungary	5,000–10,000	—	0	0
Rep. of Ireland	25–25	88–91	–2	–1
Italy	(5,000–15,000)	—	(–1)	(–1)
Latvia	(3,000–5,000)	—	(–1)	(0)
Lithuania	3,000–5,000	85–88	(0)	(0)
Luxembourg	0–3	—	–1	–1
Moldova	500–700	85	–1	–1
Netherlands	450–650 *	85	**–2**	–1
Norway	100–1,000	90	–1	**0**
Poland	(1,000–5,000)	—	(0)	(0)
Portugal	1,000–10,000	89	(0)	–1
Romania	(2,000–6,000)	—	(–1)	–1
Russia	(100,000–500,000)	—	(0)	(0)
Slovakia	(900–2,000)	—	(0)	(0)
Slovenia	(500–600)	—	(0)	(0)
Spain	82,000–112,000	—	–1	–1
Sweden	2,000–5,000	87	0	0
Switzerland	50–70	86–91	–1	–1
Turkey	(1,000–10,000)	—	—	—
Ukraine	12,000–14,000	86	–2	–2
United Kingdom	**3,100–3,100**	92	**–1**	**–2**
Total (approx.)	290,000–830,000			

Trends +2 Large increase +1 Small increase 0 Stable X Extinct
(1970-1990) –2 Large decrease –1 Small decrease F Fluctuating N New breeder
Data quality **Bold**: reliable quantitative data Normal type: incomplete quantitative data
Bracketed figures: no quantitative data * Data quality not provided

The breeding population of the Nightjar is declining in numbers and range through most of Europe (see table, map). In the United Kingdom, numbers are thought to have been falling since the late nineteenth century (Marchant *et al.* 1990). Between 1950 and 1990, but especially from 1970, numbers decreased in much of north-west and northern Europe and in parts of central, southern and eastern Europe (see table, map). Previous continental declines were only at a local scale and attributable to small-scale habitat change (L. Tomialojc pers. comm.). In the United Kingdom the species is known to have decreased by about half during 1970–1981, although by 1992 it had recovered to about 75% of its 1970 level (Sharrock 1976, Gribble 1983, Morris 1993).

■ Ecology

Nightjars nest on bare or sparsely vegetated ground, often on free-draining soils (Cramp 1985), in heathland, woodland edges and clearings. Particularly in north-west Europe, Nightjars also breed in young plantations of pine *Pinus* and spruce *Picea*, as these are open and resemble early successional stages of lightly wooded heathland; open pine forests are a preferred habitat. In south-east England such plantations are used for nesting up to 10–15 years after planting (Ravenscroft 1989, Bowden and Green 1991). Open steppes are avoided save where there are bushy or forest areas, often in river valleys or on slopes (Dementiev and Gladkov 1951a). Hölzinger (1987) indicates that the species occurs mainly in areas with May–July temperatures of over 15°C and less than 260 mm of precipitation in those months.

Birds hunt for flying insects, particularly moths, in the twilight of dusk and dawn and, to a lesser extent, during the night. They roost immobile on the ground or at the nest by day (Cramp 1985, Alexander and Cresswell 1990, Bowden and Green 1991). Nesting habitats are also used for foraging, although Nightjars may range up to 6 km from the nest-site whilst feeding (Alexander and Cresswell 1990, Bowden and Green 1991) and frequently hunt over wetlands near forest. It is a territorial breeder, even in areas of high density.

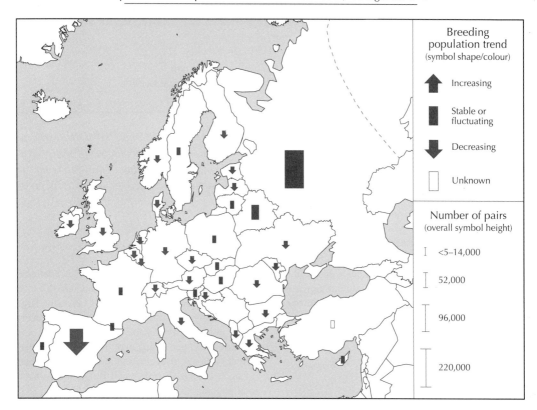

Threats

The main causes of the decline of this species are probably habitat degradation and pesticide use. The main processes involved are a reduction of the grazing of heathlands and pastoral woodlands and conversion of such habitats to arable agricultural land, vineyards, commercial forestry and built-up areas (Glutz von Blotzheim and Bauer 1980, Hölzinger 1987). Increasing recreational use of heathlands and death on roads may also be contributory factors (Hölzinger 1987). Loss of diversity of foraging areas, for example by drainage of wetlands, and loss of small woods and open areas within woodland would be expected to affect populations. Afforestation provides suitable habitat, sometimes on a large scale, but only for 15–20% of the forestry cycle (Ravenscroft 1989, Bowden and Green 1991). Nightjar populations in planted forests with an uneven age structure are thus likely to be very unstable.

Hölzinger (1987) stressed the coincidence in timing between increased pesticide use and the start of the species' strong decline in central Europe. Cockchafers *Melolontha melolontha* formerly emerged in large numbers in early spring, and the loss of this food source appears to have affected Nightjars and other birds feeding on large insects.

Nitrogenous pollutants in rain may lead to eutrophication of dry-land breeding areas, triggering quicker vegetational succession and denser forests than previously. This factor may adversely affect several open-country species (L. Tomialojc pers. comm.). Climate change might affect the geographical range of the species in future, but there is insufficient knowledge of the effects of temperature and rainfall to predict the degree and location of such effects.

Conservation measures

The maintenance of extensive areas of habitats which provide a mosaic of, and transitions between, open, sparsely vegetated areas and woodland is important for the conservation of this species. Thus, in north-west Europe management of heathland to produce the optimal mixture of open ground and woodland is needed (Burgess *et al.* 1990). Management of commercial forests should aim to retain a mixture of young and mature stands and open habitats and wetlands within afforested areas. In Spain the continuation of extensive traditional farming in the dehesas (open oak woodland) is of importance. A reduction in pesticide use and in general environmental pollution is also necessary.

RHYS GREEN

Kingfisher
Alcedo atthis

SPEC Category   3
Status   Declining
Criteria   Moderate decline

The north European range has expanded this century, but populations have recently fallen in several countries. Numbers are severely depleted by harsh winters, but the overall decline is attributable to industrial and agricultural pollution and to canalization of rivers. The curbing of pollution and the promotion of sensitive habitat management are required particularly in countries with large or declining populations.

■ Distribution and population trends

The Kingfisher has a vast breeding range, from the western Palearctic to Japan, Sri Lanka, Indochina, Sulawesi and the Solomon Islands. About a quarter to a third of the world population lives in Europe, where Kingfishers range almost everywhere south of 60°N except for Scotland, southern Norway, parts of east European Russia and Turkey.

Reliable breeding population data are available for Jersey, Netherlands, Denmark, Finland, Moldova and Czech Republic (see table). Russia has the largest population and, although its exact size is uncertain, it probably amounts to 20–50% of the total (see table, map). Other strongholds include the United Kingdom, Spain, Italy, Poland and Romania, while Portugal, France, Germany and Bulgaria also have good populations.

In winter the eastern half of the European range is vacated, and migrants move into western and southern Europe (southern Sweden and west of a line from Rostock to the Danube delta), with the Republic of Ireland, United Kingdom, France, Spain and Italy holding the largest populations. Some Kingfishers winter on east Mediterranean and North African seashores.

The range has expanded in northern Europe during the twentieth century, with increases in Denmark, Sweden, Finland and Estonia. However, numbers decreased during 1970–1990 in a number of countries with important populations, including the United Kingdom, Spain, Germany, Italy and Bulgaria (see table, map). In total, population size declines have been noted in 12 countries, constituting up to about 40% of the European population in which trends are known.

■ Ecology

Breeding Kingfishers generally occupy lowlands (usually below 650 m) where they require stretches of running fresh water which is unpolluted, shallow, translucent, partly shaded and not turbulent, with reedy or woody cover at the edges providing plenty of low perches (Cramp 1985). However, in the Caucasus they breed on mountain lakes at up to 2,000 m (Dementiev and Gladkov 1951). The species inhabits streams with a flow of at least 1 million gallons per day, also occasionally ditches, canals and the

	Breeding population			Breeding range trend
	Size (pairs)	Year	Trend	
Albania	100–500	81	(–1)	(–1)
Andorra	(0–2)	83	(0)	(–1)
Austria	280–320	—	–1	–1
Belarus	1,700–2,000	90	0	**0**
Belgium	200–350	81–90	0	–1
Bulgaria	(1,000–10,000)	—	(–1)	(–1)
Croatia	1,500–2,000 *	—	0*	0*
Czech Republic	**300–700**	—	F*	**0**
Denmark	**100–200**	87–89	(0)	(0)
Estonia	200–400	—	–1	0
Finland	**0–20**	92	F	F
France	1,000–10,000	76	F	F
Germany	1,000–10,000	—	–1	**0**
Greece	(100–1,000)	—	(–1)	(0)
Hungary	800–1,000	—	0	0
Rep. of Ireland	900–1,600	88–91	(0)	0
Italy	(4,000–8,000)	—	(–1)	(–1)
Latvia	300–400	—	F	0
Lithuania	200–500	85–88	(0)	(0)
Luxembourg	50–80	—	0	0
Moldova	**500–700**	88	–1	**–1**
Netherlands	**125–250**	79	F	**F**
Norway	0–10	90	F	0
Poland	4,000–8,000	—	F	0
Portugal	1,000–10,000	89	(0)	0
Romania	2,000–4,000	—	+1	+1
Russia	(10,000–100,000)	—	(0)	(0)
Slovakia	(700–1,300)	—	(–1)	–1
Slovenia	400–600	—	–2	–2
Spain	7,800–9,500	—	–1	–1
Sweden	10–100	87	F	0
Switzerland	150–200	77–78	F	F
Turkey	(100–1,000)	—	—	—
Ukraine	1,500–1,800	85	0	0
United Kingdom	3,600–6,000	88–91	–1	**0**
Jersey	**0–2**	—	F	F
Total (approx.)	46,000–190,000			

Trends   +2 Large increase   +1 Small increase   0 Stable   X Extinct
(1970–1990)   –2 Large decrease   –1 Small decrease   F Fluctuating   N New breeder
Data quality   **Bold**: reliable quantitative data   Normal type: incomplete quantitative data
Bracketed figures: no quantitative data   * Data quality not provided

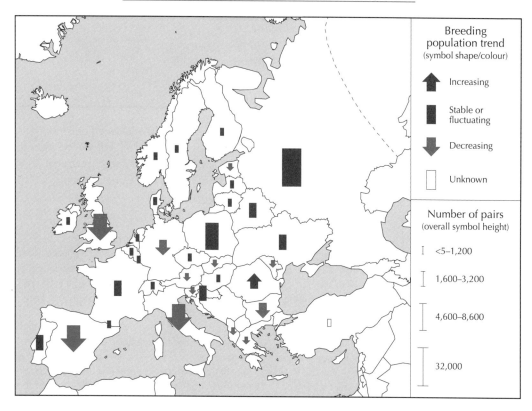

borders of lakes, with abundant minnows *Phoxinus phoxinus*, bullheads *Cottus gobio*, roach *Rutilus rutilus* and other fish 3–7 cm long (Cramp 1985).

Kingfishers are strongly territorial and summer territories must include a low, perpendicular bank of stone-free sandy or clay soil for nest-burrow excavation. In winter Kingfishers require ice-free water for fishing, and many move to estuaries, harbours and seashores. They are very vulnerable to icy conditions and die in large numbers in severe winters (Cramp 1985).

■ Threats

The effects of hard winters can outweigh all other threats to Kingfishers' survival. In the severe winters of 1961–1962 and 1962–1963 the species was almost totally extirpated in parts of Europe including Britain (Dobinson and Richards 1964, Lack 1986). Numbers in Wales fell to about 15% and in England to 5% of previous levels (Smith 1969). Although breeding productivity is high (Morgan and Glue 1977), recovery took up to nine years.

The species' response to weather may mask other influences on the population, but a long-term decline has been noted in many countries and it is generally attributed to chemical and biological pollution of rivers. The two principal sources of freshwater pollution are industrial waste disposal and agricultural chemical runoff. In England and Wales, a significant correlation between low Kingfisher density and high levels of pollution has been demonstrated (Meadows 1972).

Increasing the efficiency of drainage systems by the canalization of streams and the clearance of emergent vegetation is also highly detrimental to Kingfishers (Hölzinger 1987), most likely through loss of nesting habitat, although loss of feeding habitat and feeding efficiency, and declines in fish numbers, may also contribute.

■ Conservation measures

The Kingfisher is an excellent and easily monitored indicator of the health of river ecosystems.

The species seems set to decline further from current levels unless the degradation of rivers and streams can be stopped. Effective conservation must therefore be mediated through industry, agriculture and water authorities.

HILARY FRY

Bee-eater
Merops apiaster

SPEC Category 3
Status Declining
Criteria Moderate decline

The Bee-eater is declining in several of its strongholds in south-west and south-east Europe. Although the causes of these declines are uncertain, thousands of birds fall every year to Mediterranean hunters, and mortality in several countries, including Malta and Cyprus, could be reduced by legislation and its effective enforcement. The population status may also be improved by increasing the availability of nesting sites through appropriate local management.

■ Distribution and population trends

About half of the Bee-eater's breeding range is in Europe, and half in North Africa and western Asia. The species winters entirely in sub-Saharan Africa apart from small numbers which move to India. Birds return to Europe in mid-April and depart in late August, allowing time for only a single brood. Breeding occurs from Belarus and nearly 58°N in Russia, south to the warm coastal lowlands of France, Iberia, the larger Mediterranean islands, Italy and the Balkan peninsula, throughout the interior of Turkey and east to the Caspian Sea.

Reliable counts have been made in a few countries with relatively small populations such as Poland and Moldova but, unfortunately, estimates of population sizes in stronghold countries other than Ukraine are incomplete (see table). On the basis of minimal population estimates, about a quarter of the European population occurs in Spain and an eighth in each of Portugal, Romania, Turkey and Ukraine (see table, map). Using maximum estimates, Portugal and Turkey each hold about a quarter of the population, Bulgaria and Russia nearly an eighth each, and Spain and Romania an eighth together (see table).

Although the range and abundance of the Bee-eater fluctuated between 1970 and 1990, the species is considered to have declined in Portugal, Bulgaria, Greece and the Czech Republic (see table, map) amounting to over half of the population for which trends were estimated. In contrast, however, increases were noted in some countries, including Spain, Ukraine and France (see table, map). The trend in the important Turkish population is unknown. In Cyprus, 30–100 pairs nested in the 1970s, but breeding ceased in the early 1980s as a result of shooting—though up to 15 nests were found in 1991–1992 when spring shooting stopped for two years (M. A. Charalambides *in litt.* 1993).

■ Ecology

Being dependent on large insect prey, the Bee-eater is a species of warm climates, and its northern breeding limit coincides closely with the 21°C July isotherm. The birds need elevated perches such as trees or telegraph wires from which to pursue flying insects, and are commonest in sunny, warm areas with low-intensity agriculture: valleys and lowlands with pasture, grassland, open fields or steppe, with olives, cork oaks, vines, clover and wheat, as well as some open water. Such habitats support the favoured prey of airborne bees (*Bombus*, *Apis*), ants, dragonflies and small beetles (Fry 1984).

Within suitable habitats the species requires well-drained soils for nest-burrows, usually in steep banks of stone-free loam, compacted sand or soft sandstone. Breeding is generally in colonies, where num-

	Breeding population			Breeding range trend
	Size (pairs)	Year	Trend	
Albania	1,000–2,000	81	—	—
Austria	30–60	—	F	F
Belarus	(0–20)	90	(N)	(F)
Bulgaria	(5,000–50,000)	—	(–1)	(–1)
Croatia	1,000–1,500 *	—	0*	0*
Cyprus	15–30	91–92	0	0
Czech Republic	**3–10**	—	–1	–1
France	3,500–5,000	90	+1	+1
Germany	1–10	—	F	0
Greece	(2,000–3,000)	—	(–1)	(–1)
Hungary	1,000–3,000	—	0	0
Italy	2,000–4,000	—	(0)	(+1)
Moldova	**2,000–3,000**	88	**0**	**0**
Poland	**50–80**	—	+1	+2
Portugal	10,000–100,000	89	–1	0
Romania	10,000–20,000	—	0	**0**
Russia	(5,000–50,000)	—	(0)	F
Slovakia	700–1,000	—	+1	+1
Slovenia	**10–20**	—	F	F
Spain	23,000–30,000	—	+1	+1
Switzerland	**0–2**	91	N	N
Turkey	(10,000–100,000)	—	—	—
Ukraine	**10,000–12,000**	85	+1	0
Total (approx.)	86,000–380,000			

Trends	+2 Large increase	+1 Small increase	0 Stable	X Extinct
(1970–1990)	–2 Large decrease	–1 Small decrease	F Fluctuating	N New breeder

Data quality **Bold:** reliable quantitative data   Normal type: incomplete quantitative data   Bracketed figures: no quantitative data   * Data quality not provided

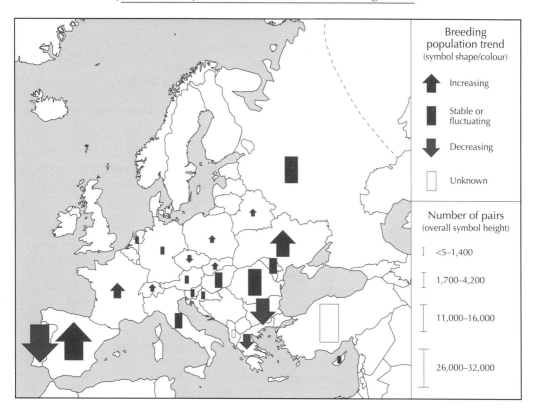

Breeding
population trend
(symbol shape/colour)

↑ Increasing

■ Stable or
fluctuating

↓ Decreasing

☐ Unknown

Number of pairs
(overall symbol height)

I <5–1,400

I 1,700–4,200

I 11,000–16,000

I 26,000–32,000

bers of nests are typically in single figures, but colonies comprising hundreds of 'pairs' occur (up to about a quarter of nests are attended by three or more adults) (Fry 1984).

■ Threats

The Bee-eater appears not to be unduly threatened on the African wintering grounds. However, it is or has been regarded as a pest by beekeepers in Algeria and South Africa, and thousands are killed every year in Egypt (Fry 1984). In the past, autumn migrants have also been treated as apiary pests in Moldova (Yakubanis and Litvak 1962), Hungary (Szederkenyi *et al.* 1956), Russia (Kraft and Korelov 1938) and Azerbaijan (Atakishiev 1971) and killed accordingly, but present attitudes there are unknown. In Malta 2,500 migrating Bee-eaters are shot annually (Woldhek 1979), and in Cyprus 4,000–6,000 are

shot every year, mainly in autumn (M. A. Charalambides *in litt.* 1993).

Loss of nest-sites is perhaps a threat, as may be the depletion of food supplies through increased use of pesticides, although no data are available on these questions.

■ Conservation measures

It is doubtful whether food availability for Bee-eater populations can be increased by way of habitat management, and some evidence suggests that they are in any case limited not by food but by nest-site availability. If so, reproductive potential would be enhanced by providing small sand cliffs free of vegetation, erosion and interference. Annual mortality could be reduced by legislation and its effective enforcement, particularly in Malta, Cyprus and other countries with high levels of hunting.

HILARY FRY

Roller
Coracias garrulus

SPEC Category 2
Status (Declining)
Criteria Moderate decline

There has been a dramatic decline in population size and range in many European countries between 1970 and 1990. The most important factor is considered to have been the loss of habitat through agricultural intensification, and possibly climatic change and persecution (mainly on migration). It is most important to conserve the Roller's habitat throughout the breeding and wintering range, mainly through the maintenance of low-intensity farming practices.

■ Distribution and population trends

The Roller is restricted to the Palearctic, breeding from north-west Africa and the Iberian peninsula eastwards through the Mediterranean to the western Himalayas. Over half of the world breeding range lies within Europe, where the strongholds are in Spain, Russia, Ukraine, Romania, Bulgaria and Turkey, which together hold about 90% of the European breeding population (see table, map). The species winters in the Afrotropical region, mainly in eastern and south-east Africa (Cramp 1985, Glutz von Blotzheim and Bauer 1990).

At the end of the nineteenth century, the Roller began to decline in several countries in western and northern Europe, leading to its disappearance from Sweden and Germany (Glutz von Blotzheim and

Bauer 1980, Robel 1991). In the former East Germany there were still 150–200 pairs in 1961, but by 1991 this population was extinct (Robel 1991). Between 1970 and 1990 numbers declined in practically all countries, including Spain, Ukraine and Bulgaria (see table, map), with several recording rapid declines, in most cases supported by quantitative data (see table). In the well-studied population of Styria (Austria), overall numbers dropped dramatically by more than 90% between 1967 and 1985 (Samwald and Samwald 1989). Although the large population in Russia is thought to be stable, no quantitative data on trends are available and its status is thus uncertain. Trends in the large Turkish population are unknown.

■ Ecology

The Roller is predominantly a lowland species, favouring open, sunny habitats (steppes, meadows) with scattered, mature trees (e.g. oaks *Quercus*) and clearings and heaths (Cramp 1985). It breeds in sandy banks, in walls, and in nest-holes of Black Woodpecker *Dryocopus martius* or Green Woodpecker *Picus viridis*, but also in suitable nest-boxes (Cramp 1985). It inhabits avenues, tree-lined river banks and orchards in parts of its range, but avoids intensive cultivation.

Birds hunt from open perches on trees, posts and overhead wires, overlooking bare or sparsely vegetated ground or short vegetation which provides little cover for prey. It takes mainly insects, particularly medium-sized to large beetles (Coleoptera) and crickets (Orthoptera).

■ Threats

The main cause of the recent widespread decline is considered to be the loss of suitable habitat (Bracko 1986, Samwald 1989). In Styria the loss of traditional meadows and pastures in favour of maize fields is thought to be the most important factor causing the decrease of breeding numbers in the last 30 years. Indeed, in one district within Styria, maize

	Breeding population			Breeding
	Size (pairs)	Year	Trend	range trend
Albania	20–100	81	(–1)	(–1)
Austria	**8–8**	91	**–2**	**–2**
Belarus	900–1,600	90	–2	(0)
Bulgaria	(1,000–5,000)	—	(–1)	(–1)
Croatia	50–100 *	—	–1*	–1*
Cyprus	300–800	—	0	0
Czech Republic	**0–3**	—	**–2**	**–2**
Estonia	150–200	—	–2	–1
France	**450–540**	90	**0**	**0**
Greece	(50–200)	—	(–1)	(–1)
Hungary	300–600	—	–2	–2
Italy	(300–500)	—	(–1)	(–1)
Latvia	10–100	—	–2	–2
Lithuania	150–200	85–88	(–1)	(–1)
Moldova	**500–800**	88	**+1**	**0**
Poland	200–300	—	–2	–1
Portugal	100–1,000	91	–1	–1
Romania	(2,000–4,000)	—	0	**0**
Russia	(10,000–100,000)	—	(0)	(0)
Slovakia	25–40	—	–2	–2
Slovenia	**5–10**	—	**–2**	**–2**
Spain	4,000–10,000	—	–1	–1
Turkey	(5,000–50,000)	—	—	—
Ukraine	**3,000–3,500**	83	**–2**	**–1**
Total (approx.)	29,000–180,000			

Trends (1970–1990): +2 Large increase +1 Small increase 0 Stable X Extinct
−2 Large decrease −1 Small decrease F Fluctuating N New breeder
Data quality: **Bold**: reliable quantitative data Normal type: incomplete quantitative data
Bracketed figures: no quantitative data * Data quality not provided

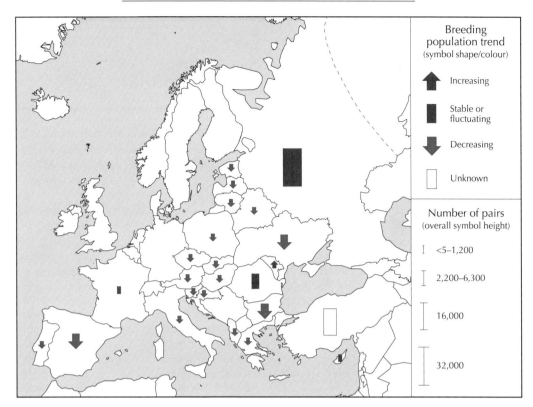

Breeding
population trend
(symbol shape/colour)

Increasing

Stable or
fluctuating

Decreasing

Unknown

Number of pairs
(overall symbol height)

<5–1,200

2,200–6,300

16,000

32,000

acreage increased by about 64% between 1966 and 1986, and during the same period the initial Roller population of 86 pairs decreased by about 60% (Samwald and Samwald 1989). Intensification of agriculture is also a major threat in southern Europe. As an example, vast irrigation projects are threatening the small population in the Crau (southern France), involving the transformation of the original steppe into maize fields, market gardens and orchards.

The use of pesticides in modern agriculture is reducing abundance of large insect prey and may therefore be an important factor in the Roller's decline. In Styria the relationship between food supply and breeding success is currently being studied.

In Sweden, on the edge of the Roller's former breeding range, it was supposed that climatic changes affecting food supply were responsible for the species' extinction (Durango 1946), but in central parts of the breeding range (Styria) there is no correlation between climatic changes and the Roller's poor fortunes (Samwald and Samwald 1989).

The Roller is also threatened by sustained persecution in Italy, Oman and elsewhere (Fry *et al.* 1992).

■ Conservation measures

The reversal of the Roller's widespread European decline can only be achieved through wide-scale

changes in agricultural practices, involving the promotion of non-intensive farming and the transformation of intensively used farmland back into pastures and meadows with scattered trees. Within the European Union, such practices could be implemented through management agreements under the Agri-environment Regulation (EC Reg. 2078/92) of the Common Agricultural Policy. In southern Austria, a project for the conservation of low-intensity grazed meadows was established in the breeding areas of the Roller in order to stop its decline (Ehrlich and Samwald 1990), and it is planned to extend this; since the beginning of this project the Roller population has been maintained at eight pairs (up to 1993).

As a migratory species the Roller also requires conservation in its winter quarters where a major threat is thought to be the very heavy or excessive agricultural utilization of savannah regions, particularly overgrazing which destroys or degrades the vegetation cover of trees and bushes. It is also necessary to stop the persecution of migrants in southern Europe and south-west Asia.

Locally, other measures, such as the provision of artificial nest-boxes, may help to support the species, but only in areas with already healthy populations.

OTTO SAMWALD

Wryneck
Jynx torquilla

SPEC Category 3
Status Declining
Criteria Moderate decline

Almost half the Wryneck population was in decline during 1970–1990. The main cause seems to be loss and degradation of grassland near forest nesting habitat due to agricultural intensification and increases in pesticide use which affect ant populations, the preferred food. Maintenance of low-intensity farming and reduction in pesticide use are therefore necessary conservation measures.

■ Distribution and population trends

Wrynecks are distributed right across the Palearctic, occurring over the Mediterranean, steppe and forest zones of Eurasia. In Europe the breeding range extends from Iberia, Italy, northern Greece and the Caucasus in the south to well beyond the Arctic Circle in Fennoscandia, though only reaching 65°N in north-east European Russia. European birds win-

	Breeding population			Breeding
	Size (pairs)	Year	Trend	range trend
Albania	(0–200)	62	(–1)	(–1)
Andorra	(0–1)	83	(0)	(–1)
Austria	(2,000–3,000)	—	(–1)	(–1)
Belarus	80,000–130,000	90	0	0
Belgium	5–9	81–90	–1	–1
Bulgaria	(5,000–10,000)	—	(0)	(0)
Croatia	8,000–10,000 *		0*	0*
Czech Republic	2,500–5,000	—	–1	0
Denmark	**150–300**	88	(+1)	(+1)
Estonia	10,000–20,000	—	0	0
Finland	30,000–50,000	92	–2	0
France	(5,000–10,000)	90	–1	–1
Germany	10,000–40,000	—	–1	0
Greece	(100–200)	—	(0)	(0)
Hungary	20,000–25,000	—	0	0
Italy	(20,000–40,000)	—	(–1)	(0)
Latvia	2,000–5,000	—	–1	–1
Liechtenstein	10–15	—	–1	–1
Lithuania	7,000–10,000	85–88	(0)	(0)
Luxembourg	80–100	—	–1	–1
Moldova	**3,500–4,500**	89	–1	0
Netherlands	**100–200**	79	–1	–1
Norway	2,000–10,000	90	–1	+1
Poland	(4,500–13,000)	—	(0)	(0)
Portugal	100–1,000	89	(0)	(0)
Romania	(4,000–10,000)	—	–2	–1
Russia	(50,000–500,000)	—	(0)	(0)
Slovakia	(2,500–4,000)	—	(–1)	0
Slovenia	2,000–3,000	—	–1	–1
Spain	46,000–53,000	—	–1	–1
Sweden	10,000–20,000	87	–1	0
Switzerland	2,000–3,000	86–91	–1	–1
Turkey	(100–1,000)	—	—	—
Ukraine	20,000–22,000	88	–1	–1
United Kingdom	**0–10**	88–90	–2	–2
Total (approx.)	350,000–1,000,000			

Trends (1970–1990): +2 Large increase +1 Small increase 0 Stable –1 Small decrease –2 Large decrease F Fluctuating X Extinct N New breeder
Data quality **Bold**: reliable quantitative data Normal type: incomplete quantitative data Bracketed figures: no quantitative data * Data quality not provided

ter in Africa, principally between the Sahara and the Equator.

During the nineteenth century the species was fairly numerous in preferred habitats through most of its range, but there has been a widespread and long-term decline. By about 1830 some fall in numbers was noticed in England followed by a dramatic decline leading to an almost-complete disappearance by the 1960s (Monk 1963, Peal 1968). During the twentieth century, serious declines were reported from north-west and central Europe, including northern France, Belgium, Luxembourg, Denmark, northern and western Germany, Switzerland and Austria (Peitzmeier 1951, Glutz von Blotzheim and Bauer 1980, Hölzinger 1987). Simultaneously, but chiefly from the 1940s to the 1960s, numbers and range increased in the north, including Scotland, parts of Fennoscandia and the St Petersburg province of Russia (Glutz von Blotzheim and Bauer 1980, Malchevskiy and Pukinskiy 1983, Cramp 1985), probably due to climatic amelioration.

Data for 1970–1990 (see table, map) suggest a continuation and spread of the decline to nearly all of western, southern and central Europe and Fennoscandia. Declines have been reported in countries which together hold up to nearly half the population, including the large populations of Germany, Spain, Italy and Ukraine, with severe declines having been reported in the large Finnish population and also in Romania and the United Kingdom (see table, map). Numbers in Russia are probably stable but this is uncertain, and trends in Turkey are unknown.

■ Ecology

The Wryneck is widespread over most of lowland Europe, and also occurs in low numbers in mountainous areas (Glutz von Blotzheim and Bauer 1980). Breeding occurs in a variety of forest-types, from dry pine *Pinus* stands to riparian forest. Dense forest blocks are avoided, the birds tending to settle along south-facing forest edges, or in clear-felled or burned patches. Where summers are relatively cold or humid, localities with dry sandy soil are preferred (Peal

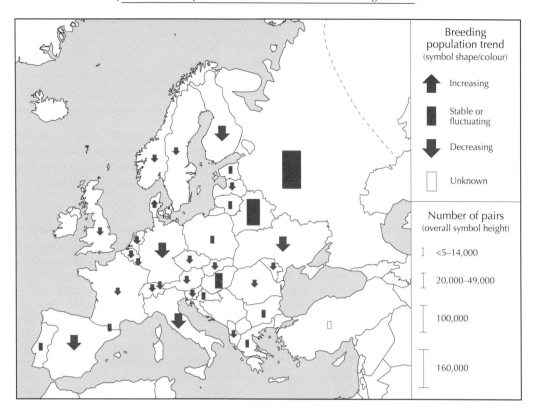

Breeding
population trend
(symbol shape/colour)

Increasing

Stable or
fluctuating

Decreasing

Unknown

Number of pairs
(overall symbol height)

<5–14,000

20,000–49,000

100,000

160,000

1968, Batten *et al.* 1990). The species easily adapts to traditional (low-intensity) managed habitats and breeds in partly deforested valleys, orchards, parks and the edges of human settlements (Dementiev and Gladkov 1951a, Menzel 1962, Glutz von Blotzheim and Bauer 1980). Wrynecks nest in natural or old woodpecker tree-holes, including holes taken over from smaller birds (Glutz von Blotzheim and Bauer 1980), and, more sporadically, holes in the ground or in walls of timber buildings (Dementiev and Gladkov 1951a, Glutz von Blotzheim and Bauer 1980).

Wrynecks are specialized insectivores, primarily taking the larvae and pupae of ants in grasslands (Glutz von Blotzheim and Bauer 1980, Cramp 1985). During bad weather, or in northern localities, other insects, spiders and even tadpoles and berries may be brought to nestlings (Pokrovskaya 1963). The specialized diet makes the species sensitive to climatic influences which affect insect availability. The clutch size is large (usually 7–11 eggs) but high losses occur during the post-fledging period. Nestlings differ much in size, as an adaptation to the unpredictable food supply (Malchevskiy and Pukinskiy 1983).

■ Threats

The main cause of the decline is the reduced abundance of ants in grasslands due to agricultural intensification which has in many areas transformed semi-natural grasslands and fallow lands into intensively managed fields. Excessive use of pesticides also causes reductions in ant numbers (Hölzinger 1987, Batten *et al.* 1990). Regional cooling of the spring and summer climate may also influence food resources (Peitzmeier 1951, Glutz von Blotzheim and Bauer 1980).

Other reasons suggested for Wryneck declines are the shortage of nest-sites, loss of nesting and feeding habitat, and increased mortality during migration or in winter (Hölzinger 1987).

■ Conservation measures

Reversal of the downward population trend in Europe seems to depend on the maintenance of adequate insect numbers, especially ants, and the conservation of sufficient suitable nesting sites. Thus it is necessary to: reduce the use of pesticides in agricultural areas and orchards; maintain low-intensity managed meadows, pastures and orchards, and prevent their conversion into intensively managed open fields or commercial forestry plantations; and to preserve suitable nesting sites in woods and along forest edges. Where nest-sites are limiting, the use of nest-boxes may be beneficial and has been successful in north-east Europe (Menzel 1962, Malchevskiy and Pukinskiy 1983, Hölzinger 1987, Batten *et al.* 1990).

LUDWIK TOMIALOJC

Grey-headed Woodpecker
Picus canus

SPEC Category 3
Status Declining
Criteria Moderate decline

The Grey-headed Woodpecker has declined significantly in parts of east and central Europe where it is threatened by modern forestry practices resulting in the destruction of old natural woodland and the subsequent establishment of even-aged and often coniferous stands. Conservation measures should include the preservation of natural woodland and changes in forestry practices including the extension of rotation periods and avoidance of large-scale clear felling.

■ Distribution and population trends

Grey-headed Woodpeckers are distributed throughout a band embracing the Eurasian continent, from the Atlantic coast in western France to the Pacific coast in eastern Russia. The range extends to central Fennoscandia but the species is absent from southern Europe. Although accurate population figures for large parts of Asia are not presently available, it is estimated that Europe includes roughly a quarter of the global breeding range.

The species is resident, with the main European population concentrated in central and eastern Europe,

particularly Russia and Romania where about half the European population occurs, although Germany and Belarus also hold significant numbers (see table, map).

Up to about 50% of the European population of the species was in decline during 1970–1990, including the important populations in Germany and Romania (see table, map). However, the knowledge of numerical trends throughout the European range is poor, partly due to the difficulty of surveys and the scattered distribution.

A widespread change in the extent of the range is not apparent (see table), but decreases have been observed at regional and local levels (Erhard and Wink 1987).

■ Ecology

To provide the differing habitat requirements for nesting and feeding, the Grey-headed Woodpecker is dependent on woodland with a high level of structural diversity which must include many borders between areas of different height and age (Südbeck 1993). These mosaics are typically found in natural successional stages of unmanaged climax forest. Old stands of trees are required for both nesting and roosting; these can be in deciduous forest, especially where beech *Fagus sylvatica* (in central Europe) and aspen *Populus tremula* (in Fennoscandia) provide nest-sites (Glutz von Blotzheim and Bauer 1980; Hågvar *et al.* 1990), or in orchards, parks and riverine forest fringes. Areas with short vegetation such as glades, meadows, forest edges and recently afforested areas are also needed since the species is a ground feeder, taking mainly ants, especially *Lasius* and *Formica*.

Mountain regions are preferred, possibly because of the high structural diversity of natural forest stands in such areas (Scherzinger 1982). In winter the species exhibits a stronger dependence on rough-barked trees with numerous broken branches.

	Breeding population			Breeding range trend
	Size (pairs)	Year	Trend	
Albania	10–50	81	(–1)	(–1)
Austria	(2,000–4,000)	—	(0)	(0)
Belarus	10,500–17,000	90	0	0
Belgium	8–10	81–90	0	0
Bulgaria	(500–1,000)	—	(0)	(0)
Croatia	1,500–2,000 *		0*	0*
Czech Republic	3,000–6,000	—	0	**0**
Estonia	1,000–2,000	—	+1	0
Finland	1,500–2,000	92	0	**0**
France	1,000–10,000	76	(0)	0
Germany	11,000–30,000	—	–1	**0**
Greece	(50–200)	—	(0)	(0)
Hungary	600–600	—	0	0
Italy	(500–1,000)	82	(0)	(0)
Latvia	800–1,500	—	+1	+1
Liechtenstein	**1–1**	91	(0)	(0)
Lithuania	50–200	85–88	(–1)	(0)
Luxembourg	50–80	—	+1	0
Moldova	**200–400**	89	**–1**	**–1**
Norway	1,000–2,500	90	0	**0**
Poland	1,000–2,000	—	+1	0
Romania	20,000–60,000	—	–1	**0**
Russia	(10,000–100,000)	—	(0)	(0)
Slovakia	(1,500–2,000)	—	(0)	(0)
Slovenia	1,000–2,000	—	0	0
Sweden	(200–400)	87	0	0
Switzerland	400–600	86–91	–1	–1
Turkey	(100–1,000)	—	—	—
Ukraine	2,000–2,100	89	–1	–1
Total (approx.)	71,000–250,000			

Trends (1970–1990) +2 Large increase +1 Small increase 0 Stable X Extinct
  –2 Large decrease –1 Small decrease F Fluctuating N New breeder
Data quality **Bold**: reliable quantitative data Normal type: incomplete quantitative data
  Bracketed figures: no quantitative data * Data quality not provided

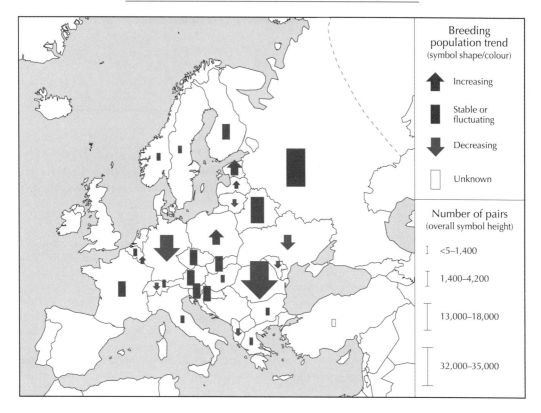

Breeding population trend
(symbol shape/colour)

- Increasing
- Stable or fluctuating
- Decreasing
- Unknown

Number of pairs
(overall symbol height)

- <5–1,400
- 1,400–4,200
- 13,000–18,000
- 32,000–35,000

■ Threats

The main factors attributed as being responsible for the Grey-headed Woodpecker's decline are the clearance of old deciduous woodland (e.g. Laske *et al.* 1991, GOMn 1989) and the large-scale conversion of these woodlands to coniferous plantations, resulting in habitat loss and isolation (Angelstam 1990).

High levels of nutrient input (e.g. from agriculture) are believed to reduce habitat suitability for ants and may consequently be reducing food supplies for the Grey-headed Woodpecker (Schmid 1993).

Recent changes in forestry practice are detrimentally affecting the species with the shortening of the rotation period resulting in the loss of potential nesting trees and therefore a marked reduction in the time-span during which the Grey-headed Woodpecker can use a given tract of forest. Additionally, forestry practices throughout Europe favour even-aged and monospecific forests with inadequate levels of internal structural diversity for the species (Scherzinger 1982).

Local declines in Grey-headed Woodpecker populations may also be caused by losses of orchards through the expansion of villages (Ullrich 1987) and decreases in the extent and quality of riverine forests through clearance and replanting of commercial monocultures, flood-prevention schemes, canalization and damming (Spitznagel 1990).

■ Conservation measures

The establishment of protected areas is insufficient to fully conserve the Grey-headed Woodpecker. A reduction in the intensity of forestry management is also required throughout Europe in order to maintain and build a network of old deciduous woodland with a sufficiently high degree of structural and species diversity (mosaic-cycle concept, Scherzinger 1991). Thus clear cutting of older woodland should generally be avoided, or, where this is not possible, should be carried out over small areas in order to maintain mosaics of habitat suitable for the species. Rotation periods in modern forestry should be extended and the replacement of deciduous forests with conifer stands should be halted and reversed.

Outside forests, a reduction in nutrient input and the maintenance of adjacent, nutrient-poor grassland areas are required to improve feeding opportunities for the species, and the extension of edge habitats could increase the area of existing habitat.

A monitoring scheme should be established to assess accurately the population trends of the Grey-headed Woodpecker in Europe. Further research on the influence of modern forestry and agricultural land-use on the distribution and frequency of the species should be carried out.

PETER SÜDBECK

Green Woodpecker
Picus viridis

SPEC Category   2
Status   Declining
Criteria   Moderate decline

Almost half the European population of Green Woodpecker was in decline during 1970–1990. The major causes are a reduction in nest-sites through the loss of old deciduous trees and a reduction in food availability through the loss of heaths, orchards and semi-natural non-fertilized grasslands. The maintenance and restoration of diverse landscapes containing both nest-sites and foraging areas is the major conservation measure necessary.

■ Distribution and population trends

Over three-quarters of the global range of the Green Woodpecker lies in Europe, where it is widely distributed but absent from some northern and eastern parts, Ireland, Greenland, and the Macaronesian Islands (Blume 1980). The species is resident.

Although quantitative data on population sizes and trends are scarce, over half of the European

	Breeding population			Breeding
	Size (pairs)	Year	Trend	range trend
Albania	1,000–2,000	81	(–1)	(–1)
Andorra	(20–35)	91	(–1)	(–1)
Austria	(5,000–10,000)	—	(0)	(0)
Belarus	9,000–13,000	90	0	0
Belgium	2,800–4,800	81–90	–1	0
Bulgaria	(5,000–50,000)	—	(0)	(0)
Croatia	15,000–20,000 *	—	0*	0*
Czech Republic	9,000–18,000	—	–1	**0**
Denmark	**300–500**	87–89	(–1)	(+1)
Estonia	500–1,000	—	–1	–1
France	100,000–1,000,000	76	(0)	**0**
Germany	30,000–100,000	—	–1	**0**
Greece	(5,000–10,000)	—	(0)	(0)
Hungary	10,000–15,000	—	–1	0
Italy	5,000–10,000	—	0	0
Latvia	50–100	—	–2	–2
Liechtenstein	**20–25**	—	–1	–1
Lithuania	500–1,000	85–88	(–1)	(–1)
Luxembourg	250–400	—	0	0
Moldova	**10–25**	89	+1	**0**
Netherlands	**3,000–4,500**	79	–1	–1
Norway	2,000–10,000	90	–1	**0**
Poland	3,500–7,000	—	0	0
Portugal	10,000–100,000	89	(0)	0
Romania	10,000–40,000	—	0	**0**
Russia	(10,000–100,000)	—	(0)	(0)
Slovakia	(1,200–2,000)	—	(0)	0
Slovenia	1,500–2,500	—	0	0
Spain	65,500–95,600	—	–1	–1
Sweden	25,000–50,000	87	–1	0
Switzerland	2,000–3,000	86–91	–1	–1
Turkey	(1,000–10,000)	—	—	—
Ukraine	**1,700–1,900**	89	–1	–1
United Kingdom	15,000–15,000	88–91	0	**0**
Total (approx.)	350,000–1,700,000			

Trends   +2 Large increase   +1 Small increase   0 Stable   X Extinct
(1970–1990)   –2 Large decrease   –1 Small decrease   F Fluctuating   N New breeder
Data quality   **Bold**: reliable quantitative data   Normal type: incomplete quantitative data
                Bracketed figures: no quantitative data   * Data quality not provided

population is thought to occur in France, Spain and Germany, while Portugal, United Kingdom, Sweden, Russia, Croatia, Romania and Bulgaria also hold substantial numbers (see table, map).

Between 1970 and 1990 up to nearly half the European population declined, this trend being particularly important in the large populations of Spain and Germany.

Decreases in central Europe started in some regions in the 1950s and became stronger at the beginning of the 1960s (e.g. Paszkowski 1977, Blume 1984). In other countries (e.g. Switzerland) decreases were noted only from the 1980s onwards (e.g. Winkler 1987, Zbinden 1989), while in others such as (probably) France, the species has remained stable (see table, map).

■ Ecology

An essential habitat requirement is the combination of old deciduous trees (for nesting) with nearby feeding grounds which have an abundance of ants (*Lasius, Formica*), the main food. Such habitat is usually in semi-open landscapes, with small woodlands, hedgerows, scattered old trees, forest edges and flood-plain forests; foraging areas include grassland, heaths, plantations, orchards and village lawns. Favoured nest-trees include oak *Quercus*, beech *Fagus*, willow *Salix* and fruit trees in western and central Europe and aspens *Populus* in the north (Petersen 1945, Mildenberger 1984, Knorre 1986, Hagvar *et al.* 1990).

■ Threats

The Green Woodpecker's habitat is threatened throughout Europe, and the species is suffering from the clearance of semi-open landscapes, and the loss of small woodlands, orchards, old hedgerows and solitary trees. Nest-sites have disappeared through intensive forestry, which has resulted in harvesting of old deciduous stands, the clear-felling of flood-plain forests, large-scale afforestation with conifers

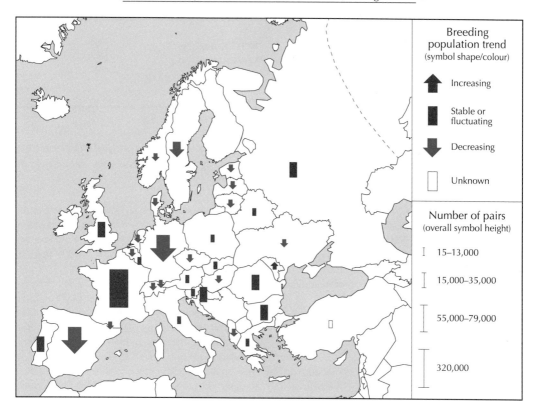

Breeding
population trend
(symbol shape/colour)

Increasing

Stable or
fluctuating

Decreasing

Unknown

Number of pairs
(overall symbol height)

15–13,000

15,000–35,000

55,000–79,000

320,000

(e.g. in Fennoscandia: Stenberg 1989) and the cultivation of non-native tree species (e.g. *Eucalyptus* in Spain and Portugal: Tellería and Galarza 1990).

The quality of feeding habitat is threatened by high nutrient input to agricultural land (especially meadows and heaths) which decreases the abundance of ants (SOVON 1987, Havelka and Ruge 1993). Additionally, the enlargement of fields has reduced the area taken up by hedgerows, field edges, etc. In northern Germany, for example, the Green Woodpecker was formerly a typical breeding bird of rural villages, foraging on surrounding meadows, pastures, orchards and gardens (Brinkmann 1933), but due to declines in the numbers of ants it is now relatively more abundant in sufficiently open and diverse deciduous forests (Keßler 1986).

The threats from long-term habitat change can be accentuated by short-term changes such as unfavourable winter weather, in particular by heavy and long-lasting snow cover, which restricts foraging. Even under normal conditions it may take over ten years for populations to recover from high winter mortality, but in suboptimal habitat long-term population decline is likely to be accelerated, possibly to critical levels (Blume 1984 and pers. comm., Sharrock 1976, Zang and Heckenroth 1986).

■ Conservation measures

Wide-scale habitat conservation needs to be undertaken to maintain the essential close juxtaposition of habitat elements required for nesting and feeding within structurally diverse landscapes. This should include the conservation of old trees for nesting in woodlands, orchards and villages and the maintenance and restoration of feeding grounds such as small meadows, pastures, orchards and heaths.

PETER SÜDBECK

Three-toed Woodpecker
Picoides tridactylus

SPEC Category 3
Status Declining
Criteria Moderate decline

Some populations of Three-toed Woodpecker are declining, mainly because of the intensive exploitation of forests which renders them largely unsuitable as habitat; old or dead trees in mature coniferous or mixed forest are required for feeding and nesting. In the long term the species may be seriously threatened by the loss of forest through acid rain.

■ Distribution and population trends

There are two distinct subspecies of Three-toed Woodpecker in Europe, both resident: the nominate form is a widespread breeder in the boreal forests of northern Europe, while *alpinus* is restricted to the mountains of Europe. Other forms occur in northern Asia and the Nearctic.

P. t. alpinus is restricted to several isolated breeding areas in the mountain forests of the Alps, Shumava (Czech Republic), the Carpathians and some mountain areas in Croatia, Bulgaria and Greece. Some breeding areas such as Schwarzwald (south-west Germany), the Sudety mountains (Poland/Czech Republic) and western Serbia (Yugoslavia) were deserted in earlier decades (Glutz von Blotzheim and Bauer 1980, Stastny *et al.* 1987). However, with the exception of the population in the Ukrainian Car-

pathians the subspecies is now considered to be stable, although this conclusion is highly dependent on estimates of numbers and trends for Romania (see table). In total, there are c.12,000–19,000 pairs of *alpinus* in Europe.

During 1970–1990 the Swedish and Finnish populations in boreal forests, totalling 20,000–35,000 pairs of the nominate subspecies, declined by more than 20% (see table, map) and declines have also been noted in the west Lithuanian–Belarus–Polish population (Wesolowski and Tomialojc 1986). In total up to about 40% of the European population of the species occurs in countries that recorded declines over the 1970–1990 period.

■ Ecology

Three-toed Woodpeckers occur in the interior of old and dark mixed or coniferous forests. The nominate form occupies conifer-dominated boreal forests (taiga) with spruce *Picea*, pine *Pinus* and alder *Alnus*, and prefers damp areas such as peat bogs or sites near lakes or rivers (Dementiev and Gladkov 1951). The mountain race breeds in spruce and fir *Abies* forests (sometimes mixed with broad-leaved trees) at 650–1,900 m in central Europe (Glutz von Blotzheim and Bauer 1980), and particularly on steep, spruce-dominated slopes (Hess 1983). For food (largely bark-living beetles, moths, etc.) and nesting, both races require abundant old wood resulting from fire, forestry, etc. (Glutz von Blotzheim and Bauer 1980, Cramp 1985). Nest-holes are generally in dead spruce or pine trees over 25 cm in diameter, c.5 m above ground; younger trees stands are thus usually unsuitable. A Norwegian study (Hogstad 1971) suggests that winter territory size is inversely related to the density of dead trees.

■ Threats

Three-toed Woodpecker may benefit from limited disturbance to its habitat; Dementiev and Gladkov (1951) suggested it was less numerous in untouched parts of the Siberian taiga than in burnt areas or those partly exploited by man. However, intensively ex-

	Breeding population			Breeding range trend
	Size (pairs)	Year	Trend	
Albania	(10–50)	81	—	—
Austria	(2,000–3,000)	—	(0)	(0)
Belarus	9,000–14,000	90	0	0
Bulgaria	(50–100)	—	(0)	(0)
Croatia	500–1,000 *	—	0*	0*
Czech Republic	300–500 *	—	—	—
Estonia	200–500	—	0	0
Finland	15,000–20,000	92	–1	**0**
France	10–100	76	0	0
Germany	450–700	—	(0)	**0**
Greece	(50–100)	—	(0)	(0)
Italy	(50–100)	82	(0)	(0)
Latvia	1,000–2,000	—	F	+1
Liechtenstein	**25–25**	—	·0	0
Lithuania	(30–50)	85–88	(–1)	(0)
Norway	5,000–10,000	90	0	**0**
Poland	200–500	—	–1	**0**
Romania	(2,000–6,000)	—	(0)	(0)
Russia	(10,000–100,000)	—	(0)	(0)
Slovakia	(800–1,200)	—	(0)	0
Slovenia	(100–200)	—	(0)	(0)
Sweden	5,000–15,000	87	–1	0
Switzerland	1,000–1,500	86–91	0	0
Ukraine	**300–400**	88	–1	–1
Total (approx.)	53,000–180,000			

Trends (1970-1990) +2 Large increase +1 Small increase 0 Stable X Extinct
–2 Large decrease –1 Small decrease F Fluctuating N New breeder
Data quality **Bold**: reliable quantitative data Normal type: incomplete quantitative data
Bracketed figures: no quantitative data * Data quality not provided

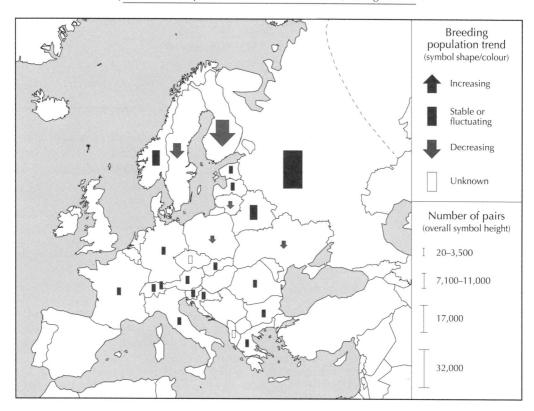

ploited forest is undoubtedly unsuitable due to the scarcity of nest trees or dead wood (Glutz von Blotzheim and Bauer 1980, Cramp 1985).

In the long term the widespread death of spruce and fir stands from acid rain in central Europe, though temporarily benefiting the bird through an increase in dead wood, may be a serious threat.

■ Conservation measures

Favoured habitats, such as patches of old spruce- or fir-dominated forest with abundant dead wood in mountains or in damp lowlands, should be protected from intensive management. These protected forest blocks should cover at least 50 ha, an area large enough for a single pair.

Within intensively managed mature forests some dying or dead trees should be left. Where there is insufficient dead wood, cutting single mature spruces to a height of c.10 m and leaving them to decay may provide suitable nest-sites.

LUDWIK TOMIALOJC

Dupont's Lark
Chersophilus duponti

SPEC Category 3
Status Vulnerable
Criteria Large decline

Approximately half of the global population of this Mediterranean species is concentrated in Spain. Although population trends are poorly known, regional declines have been noted due to the increase of dry cultivation, widespread irrigation and afforestation. The maintenance of non-intensive farming, including sheep-grazing, is required.

■ Distribution and population trends

The geographical distribution of Dupont's Lark, although fragmented, is markedly Mediterranean. The most important populations are in Spain, as well as in Morocco and Algeria, where they breed principally on plateaus dominated by *Stipa* grass and *Artemisia* scrub, but the breeding range also extends to Tunisia, Libya and Egypt (Cramp 1988). The total population size is unknown, since, although there are good estimates of the numbers present in Spain, populations in North Africa have not been quantified. Nevertheless, extrapolations based on censuses conducted on the Hauts Plateaux in Morocco (Suárez *et al.* 1989) suggest that approximately half of the population breeds in Europe. The species is sedentary, although birds may make seasonal movements in the most extreme climatic zones (Suárez and Garza 1989).

The entire European population is concentrated in Spain (Garza and Suárez 1990; see table, map), although historical records exist from Portugal (Irby 1875, in Cramp 1988). Trends are poorly known, but some regional declines were observed between 1970 and 1990. In the Ebro valley the species probably declined due to increased cultivation of natural shrub-steppe areas (see 'Threats', below), while in other places, such as the shrub-steppes of Sistema Ibérico, increases are likely to have occurred following the abandonment of cultivation in the 1960s (Gutiérrez *et al.* 1993).

| | Breeding population | | | Breeding |
	Size (pairs)	Year	Trend	range trend
Spain	13,000–15,000	—	–1	–1
Total (approx.)	13,000–15,000			

Trends   +2 Large increase   +1 Small increase   0 Stable   'X Extinct
(1970-1990)   –2 Large decrease   –1 Small decrease   F Fluctuating   N New breeder
Data quality   **Bold: reliable quantitative data**   Normal type: incomplete quantitative data
Bracketed figures: no quantitative data   * Data quality not provided

■ Ecology

The Dupont's Lark breeds from sea-level to 1,600 m, although the largest known populations in Spain (accounting for approximately 70% of the total) are found between 800 m and 1,200 m (Suárez *et al.* 1982). During the breeding season birds occupy flat or gently undulating areas, sparsely covered with shrubs. Studies show that the floristic composition of this shrub-steppe is unimportant (Suárez *et al.* 1982, Garza and Suárez 1990), but its optimal structure is 20–50 cm high with a ground cover of approximately 30% (Tellería *et al.* 1988, Garza and Suárez 1990).

During winter Dupont's Larks tend to remain in the breeding habitats (Suárez and Garza 1989, Manrique *et al.* 1990), but in dry, cultivated regions some birds have been observed in fallow land and crops (e.g. Cramp 1988).

The species feeds principally on insects (beetles and Lepidoptera larvae) and seeds (Cramp 1988). The chicks are fed only on invertebrates, predominantly Lepidoptera larvae, grasshoppers (Acrididae) and spiders (Herranz *et al.* 1993).

■ Threats

The population of Dupont's Lark in the Ebro valley (Important Bird Areas 177, 178, 179, 181 and 186) is threatened by widescale irrigation projects and the expansion of dry cultivation, which are leading to the destruction of the natural shrub-steppe habitat, while in the shrub-steppes of the Sistema Ibérico (IBAs 053, 054, 056, 070, 071, 073, 075, 193 and 194) afforestation plans, financed with help from the EU (EC Regulation 2080), may constitute a significant threat.

Reductions in sheep-grazing are also a threat, since the consequent growth of shrub vegetation cover may lead to the loss of habitat suitable for Dupont's Larks. Additionally, the absence of control measures over potential predators such as feral dogs can occasionally have negative effects on populations (Suárez *et al.* 1993).

Since a small minority of birds appear to winter in areas of cereal cultivation in dry areas (see above), the complete abandonment of this type of farming

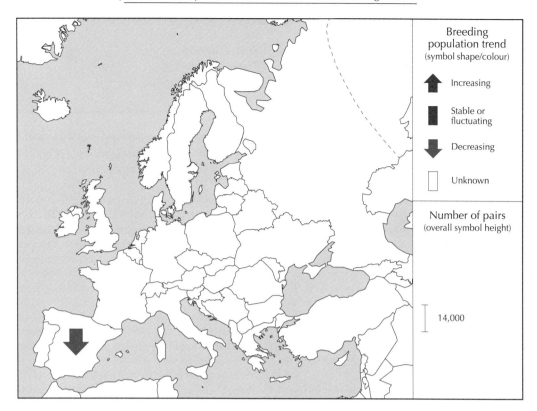

Breeding population trend
(symbol shape/colour)

Increasing

Stable or fluctuating

Decreasing

Unknown

Number of pairs
(overall symbol height)

14,000

through reforms in the context of the EU Common Agricultural Policy may have some negative effect on the species.

■ Conservation measures

The conservation requirements for Dupont's Lark are similar to those for Tawny Pipit *Anthus campestris*, and consequently it is necessary to maintain non-intensive farming, including extensive sheep-grazing, in almost all areas where Dupont's Lark occurs. The species could also benefit from an increase in the area of land which is left fallow or under stubble. Such measures could be promoted through their incorporation into Zonal Programmes developed under the Agri-environment Regulation (EC Reg. 2078/92) of the EU Common Agricultural Policy.

FRANCISCO SUÁREZ AND JUAN J. OÑATE

Calandra Lark
Melanocorypha calandra

SPEC Category   3
Status   (Declining)
Criteria   Moderate decline

The Calandra Lark has decreased in most European countries where it occurs, probably due to the loss of suitable habitat through the intensification of agriculture. Low-intensity farming practices should be maintained in dry cereal crop areas to provide suitable habitat for this species.

■ Distribution and population trends

Calandra Larks are distributed around the Mediterranean and Black Seas, northern parts of the Middle East, North Africa and in the steppes of central Asia (Cramp 1988). They are mainly resident in Europe, but migratory and partially migratory populations in central Asia move southwards in winter. Less than half of the breeding range lies within Europe, but there is probably a slight increase in numbers in Europe in winter.

Most of the European population breeds in Russia and Spain, and sizeable numbers also occur in Turkey (see table, map).

The species is decreasing across most of its European range, with the exception of populations in some countries of eastern Europe. Russian breeding numbers appear to be stable, although quantitative data are not available (see table, map).

	Breeding population			Breeding
	Size (pairs)	Year	Trend	range trend
Albania	(300–800)	81	(–1)	(–1)
Bulgaria	(1,000–5,000)	—	(0)	(0)
Croatia	100–150 *	—	0*	0*
Cyprus	200–600	—	–1	0
France	200–400	90	–2	0
Greece	2,000–5,000	—	(–1)	(–1)
Italy	(5,000–15,000)	86	(–1)	(–1)
Moldova	**3,500–5,000**	90	**–1**	**–1**
Portugal	10,000–100,000	89	–1	–1
Romania	(20,000–40,000)	—	(0)	0
Russia	(1,000,000–10,000,000)	—	(0)	(0)
Slovenia	(0–0)	—	(X)	(X)
Spain	1,030,000–3,400,000	—	–1	–1
Turkey	(100,000–1,000,000)	—	—	—
Ukraine	(400–1,500)	84	(–2)	(–2)
Total (approx.)	2,200,000–15,000,000			

Trends   +2 Large increase   +1 Small increase   0 Stable   X Extinct
(1970–1990) –2 Large decrease   –1 Small decrease   F Fluctuating N New breeder
Data quality **Bold**: reliable quantitative data   Normal type: incomplete quantitative data
Bracketed figures: no quantitative data   * Data quality not provided

■ Ecology

The Calandra Lark occurs on lowland plains and upland plateaus, avoiding rocky, saline and infertile soils and semi-desert areas. Its most typical habitats are grassland and farmland, ranging from virgin steppe to cultivated crops. In fact the density of this species is highest in extensively farmed cereal crops (Tellería *et al.* 1988). It generally avoids shelterbelts, long-term set-aside areas or forest edges, although in the north-eastern part of its European range it sometimes occurs among shrubs, bushes or even well scattered low trees (Cramp 1988). In the west and south the species is found almost exclusively in cultivated areas (Wadley 1951, Bannerman 1953, de Juana *et al.* 1988), but it cannot live in intensively farmed areas such as irrigated cereal, sugar-beet, sunflower or maize crops. In Spain it is scarce or absent in highland steppe areas, such as the páramos and the Ebro valley, and in coastal areas (de Juana *et al.* 1988, Suárez *et al.* 1991).

Wintering areas in Spain are fallow and stubble fields (Tellería *et al.* 1988). The selection of winter habitat in croplands appears to be more closely related to food accessibility and risk of predation rather than to the abundance of food (Díaz 1991). Birds will use the bill to dig for pupae, and the diet is largely insects in summer but seeds and grass shoots in winter (Cramp 1988).

■ Threats

The decline of this species in Europe is related mainly to agricultural intensification, including the irrigation of steppe habitats in Spain and the intensification of traditional cereal crops (Yeatman 1976). Other factors which may also have contributed to the decline include hunting (for example in France: Yeatman 1976), regeneration of scrub vegetation in old fields due to reductions in extensive livestock rearing, and the afforestation of abandoned croplands (de Juana *et al.* 1988).

■ Conservation measures

Only a small proportion of the European Calandra Lark population is within protected areas, and this, combined with the dispersed and nomadic character of the species, means that broad habitat conservation measures are required. These should include the maintenance of traditional land-use practices such as low-intensity cereal cultivation and low-intensity

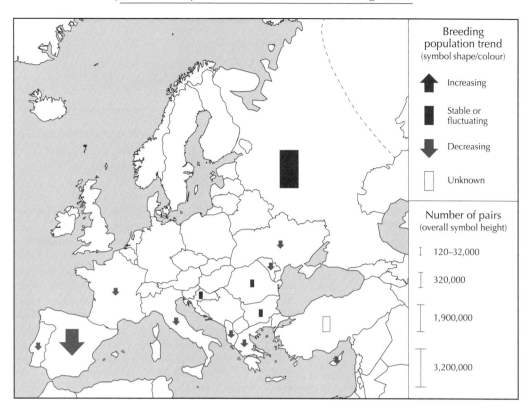

Breeding population trend
(symbol shape/colour)

Increasing

Stable or fluctuating

Decreasing

Unknown

Number of pairs
(overall symbol height)

120–32,000

320,000

1,900,000

3,200,000

livestock rearing. The development of Zonal Programmes under the Agri-environment Regulation (EC Reg. 2078/92) of the EU Common Agricultural Policy provide opportunities to make such extensive farming of cereal crops profitable.

A broader and deeper knowledge of the biological processes affecting the distribution and abundance of the Calandra Lark is needed. This is especially important to ensure that management practices for this bird do not conflict with the maintenance of habitat features that are important for other threatened species (Tellería *et al*. in press).

MARIO DÍAZ ESTEBAN

Black Lark
Melanocorypha yeltoniensis

SPEC Category 3
Status (Vulnerable)
Criteria Large decline

The considerable decline has been due principally to the cultivation of virgin steppe grasslands. The Black Lark remains under threat, mainly through the degradation of remaining dry grasslands due to overgrazing and trampling by cattle and sheep. These areas should be protected and controls on grazing levels need to be established.

■ Distribution and population trends

The major part of the Black Lark's breeding range extends across the semi-deserts of northern Kazakhstan up to the Altai foothills. Within Europe the species extends as a breeder east of the Volga river along the border between Russia and Kazakhstan, an area which constitutes not more than 10% of its total world range. Over the last 30–40 years the western limit of the breeding range has retreated 100–200 km to the east and is now close to the border with Kazakhstan. There have also been smaller yearly fluctuations. The species is a partial migrant, wintering either within the breeding range or undertaking short-range movements to the south and west. Large numbers of birds sometimes wander outside the regularly occupied areas, and vagrants have been recorded far to the west and north of the principal breeding and wintering grounds in both summer and winter (Dementiev and Gladkov 1954b, Cramp 1988).

Despite the yearly population fluctuations which occur as a result of the species' nomadic nature, breeding numbers declined overall in Europe between 1970 and 1990 to less than 10,000 pairs (see table, map). Nevertheless, some populations in favourable habitats may have remained stable; these include parts of the proposed Orenburg Nature Reserve and the south-eastern corner of the Saratov region, which supports 2,000–4,000 breeding pairs in c.20,000 km² of grass steppe.

| | Breeding population | | | Breeding |
	Size (pairs)	Year	Trend	range trend
Russia	(6,000–10,000)	—	(–1)	(–1)
Total (approx.)	6,000–10,000			

Trends   +2 Large increase   +1 Small increase   0 Stable   X Extinct
(1970–1990)   –2 Large decrease   –1 Small decrease   F Fluctuating   N New breeder
Data quality   **Bold**: reliable quantitative data   Normal type: incomplete quantitative data
Bracketed figures: no quantitative data   * Data quality not provided

■ Ecology

The most typical habitat of the Black Lark is dry grassland dominated by *Artemisia* plant associations within the southern steppe sub-zone (lying between the typical steppe zone and the semi-desert zone in south Russia) and semi-desert zone. It avoids dense high grasses, preferring to nest in mosaics of short grass with low *Artemisia* shrubs and solonchaks (areas of largely unvegetated saline soils), ideally with water nearby. The moderate grazing of virgin steppe has therefore been rather favourable to the Black Lark (Dinesman 1960), but birds are unable to breed in cultivated fields.

Nests are placed on the ground, either in the open or close to tussocks, in shallow depressions which can be natural or excavated and are lined with dry grass and other materials (Moiseev 1980). Both during the breeding season and in winter males considerably outnumber females (Dementiev and Gladkov 1954b, Moiseev 1980).

The diet consists of small insects and seeds, and in winter birds may need to break snow cover to reach food (Krivitski 1962). Severe winters which produce a thick snow cover can result in high rates of mortality.

■ Threats

During the first half of the twentieth century, and particularly in the 1950s and 1960s, the ploughing of dry steppe grasslands destroyed favourable Black Lark habitat, resulting in a breeding range contraction and population decline. Today most virgin steppe lands suitable for arable agriculture have already been cultivated and those remaining are used for pasture. They are now threatened by the degradation of grassland through overgrazing and trampling, due to the intensification of cattle and sheep farming.

■ Conservation measures

Dry grassland areas need to be protected both through nature reserves and with the aid of broader land-use policies. Recently the Orenburg Nature Reserve in the southern steppe of the Orenburg region was proposed, and it is hoped that this designation will be officially recognized in 1994; this area already supports nesting Black Larks on dispersed fragments of

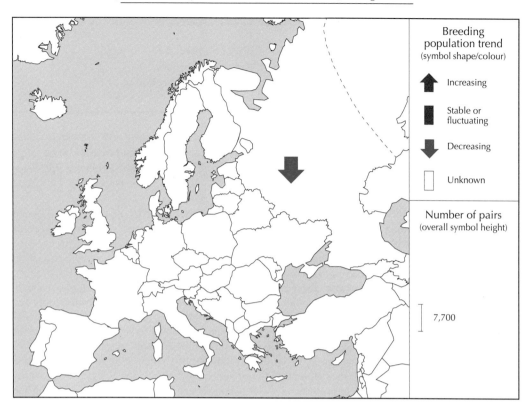

Breeding population trend
(symbol shape/colour)

▲ Increasing

■ Stable or fluctuating

▼ Decreasing

□ Unknown

Number of pairs
(overall symbol height)

7,700

suitable habitat (Geide 1989). Dry grasslands in the south-eastern part of the Saratov region along the border with Kazakhstan are also an important area for Black Lark and should be protected. The destruc-tion of remaining grassland habitat by cultivation or overgrazing has been prevented in some areas in eastern Europe, but these areas will take some years to regenerate.

VLADIMIR GALUSHIN, ANATOLY V. DAVYGORA AND
VALERY N. MOSEIKIN

Short-toed Lark
Calandrella brachydactyla

SPEC Category   3
Status   Vulnerable
Criteria   Large decline

The majority of the European Short-toed Lark population is decreasing due to the loss and degradation of its habitat through the expansion and intensification of agriculture. Its conservation should include the encouragement of low-intensity farming practices and extensive livestock-rearing, aimed at maintaining dry grasslands.

■ Distribution and population trends

The distribution of the Short-toed Lark lies around the Mediterranean and Black Seas and extends eastwards to the steppes of central Asia. The species is chiefly migratory, birds from Europe wintering mainly in the Sahel and Red Sea coastal zones of Africa, with the exception of a sedentary or partially migratory population in Greece (Cramp 1988; see table).

The greater part of the total European population breeds in the Iberian peninsula, though sizeable numbers also occur in Russia. The species appears to be decreasing over much of its range, and this includes the large population of Spain together with those in France, Hungary, Ukraine, Albania and Malta (see table, map). It has disappeared from central France during the twentieth century (Cramp 1988). Numbers are, however, considered to be stable in Portugal and even to be showing a slight increase in Russia, and between 1970 and 1990 the species has been discovered to breed in Switzerland and Slovakia, although in both these cases the numbers

involved are very small. In other countries of central and eastern Europe, the species is either very scarce or absent.

■ Ecology

The habitat occupied by Short-toed Larks is mainly dry, open plains and uplands, terraces, slopes and undulating foothills. The diet consists largely of seeds and insects (these latter in summer and for nestlings) which the birds take from the ground or from low plants (Cramp 1988). In some areas birds can also occupy low, bushy garigue incorporating patches of bare soil (Cramp 1988). In Spain the species occurs at high densities in steppe habitats, from sand-dunes to upland shrub-steppes (de Juana *et al.* 1988). It may also occupy low-intensity farmed croplands where it selects ploughed fields in which to nest (Tellería *et al.* 1988). However, it cannot adapt to breeding within intensively cultivated areas, and therefore the high-level usage of agro-chemicals and the cultivation of pastures and marginal land may make areas unsuitable for the species.

Although Lesser Short-toed Lark *Calandrella rufescens* has a similar geographical distribution to that of Short-toed Lark, the latter occurs at lower densities than Lesser Short-toed Lark in saline areas and may even be completely absent from them. In late autumn in the Camargue (southern France), Short-toed Lark also inhabits stubbles and fallows (Cramp 1988).

■ Threats

The decline of this species in the Iberian peninsula is thought to be related to the fragmentation and loss of traditional croplands and dry grasslands which has followed the expansion and intensification of agriculture. In particular this has involved the substitution of traditional low-intensity farming by the cultivation of dense, irrigated crops, the regeneration of tall grassland and scrub in traditional pastures due to reduction or cessation of extensive livestock-grazing, and the afforestation of abandoned croplands. All of these factors have reduced the extent of

	Breeding population			Breeding
	Size (pairs)	Year	Trend	range trend
Albania	(1,000–3,000)	81	(–1)	(–1)
Bulgaria	(5,000–10,000)	—	(0)	(0)
Croatia	1,000–1,500 *	—	0*	0*
Cyprus	300–800	—	0	0
France	1,000–10,000	76	–1	–1
Greece	(20,000–40,000)	—	(0)	(0)
Hungary	**10–15**	90	–1	–1
Italy	(15,000–30,000)	—	(0)	(0)
Malta	2,000–3,000	—	–1	–1
Portugal	100,000–1,000,000	89	(0)	0
Romania	(5,000–10,000)	—	(0)	(0)
Russia	(100,000–1,000,000)	—	(+1)	(0)
Slovakia	1–10 *	—	N*	N*
Spain	2,200,000–2,600,000	—	–1	–1
Switzerland	**0–1**	89–90	N	N
Turkey	(10,000–100,000)	—	—	—
Ukraine	(7,000–11,000)	84	(–1)	(–1)
Total (approx.)	2,500,000–4,800,000			

Trends	+2 Large increase	+1 Small increase	0 Stable	X Extinct
(1970–1990)	–2 Large decrease	–1 Small decrease	F Fluctuating	N New breeder

Data quality   **Bold:** reliable quantitative data   Normal type: incomplete quantitative data
Bracketed figures: no quantitative data   * Data quality not provided

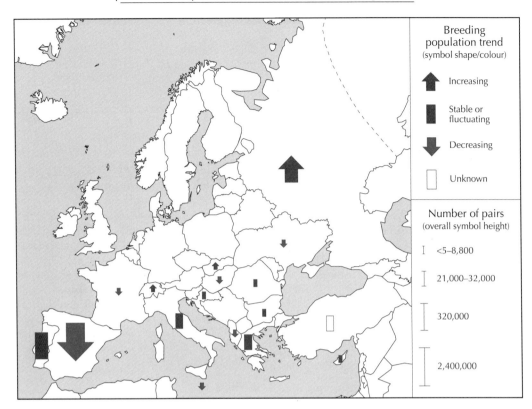

suitable habitat for the species (de Juana *et al*. 1988), and these general conclusions are likely to be more widely applicable also to populations in the rest of the species' range across Europe. The construction of residential complexes in coastal areas of south-east Spain may also be a threat to the Iberian populations (de Juana *et al*. 1988).

■ Conservation measures

A very small part of the European Short-toed Lark breeding population occurs within Important Bird Areas (IBAs), and much of the population in Russia and the Iberian peninsula is not covered by any conservation measures. As a dispersed and migratory species, the Short-toed Lark requires large areas of suitable habitat to maintain its population levels, and must therefore rely on broad conservation meas-

ures aimed at the maintenance and expansion of dry grasslands and low-intensity croplands. Within the EU, such conservation measures could be promoted through the development of Zonal Programmes under the Agri-environment Regulation (EC Reg. 2078/92) of the Common Agricultural Policy. Appropriate management of short-term set-aside land (under EC Regulation 1765/92) may also help where this reintroduces the practice of holding some land temporarily fallow within intensive cereal farmland. The application of these ideas in the non-EU countries of central and eastern Europe would be also valuable.

Further research on the biological processes underlying the patterns of the species' distribution and abundance are required, in order that suitable management practices to conserve the species can be prescribed (Tellería *et al*. in press).

MARIO DÍAZ ESTEBAN

Lesser Short-toed Lark
Calandrella rufescens

SPEC Category 3
Status Vulnerable
Criteria Large decline

The Lesser Short-toed Lark is declining over substantial parts of its range in Europe, primarily due to the loss and deterioration of steppe habitats through afforestation, urban developments and the intensification of agriculture. Protection of steppe habitats is therefore an essential conservation measure, together with the maintenance of appropriate low-intensity farming practices.

■ Distribution and population trends

The Lesser Short-toed Lark breeds and winters from the Canary Islands eastwards across North Africa, Spain, southern Russia, Turkey, the Middle East and Iran (Cramp 1988) in a band lying between 25 and 50°N. Less than half of its world range is within Europe, where it breeds in four main areas: the Canary Islands, the Iberian peninsula, the Ukraine and southern Russia, and Turkey. The species is mainly resident with the exception of birds breeding in Russia and the Ukraine which are migratory and probably winter in Iraq and Iran.

Spain and Russia hold the largest breeding populations, accounting for approximately 90% of the European total (see table, map). The species is, however, also numerous in the Canary Islands, Ukraine and Turkey. The small Portuguese population is highly localized (Rufino 1989).

Numbers of Lesser Short-toed Larks breeding on the Canary Islands, the Iberian peninsula and probably in the Ukraine declined between 1970 and 1990 (see table, map). The Russian population was probably stable, although no quantitative data on trends are available.

	Breeding population			Breeding
	Size (pairs)	Year	Trend	range trend
Portugal	10–100	90	—	—
Russia	(100,000–1,000,000)	—	(0)	(0)
Spain	230,000–260,000	—	–1	–1
Canary Islands	17,000–19,000	—	–1	–1
Turkey	(10,000–100,000)	—	—	—
Ukraine	(10,000–17,000)	84	(–1)	(0)
Total (approx.)	370,000–1,400,000			

Trends +2 Large increase +1 Small increase 0 Stable X Extinct
(1970–1990) –2 Large decrease –1 Small decrease F Fluctuating N New breeder
Data quality **Bold**: reliable quantitative data Normal type: incomplete quantitative data
Bracketed figures: no quantitative data * Data quality not provided

■ Ecology

The Lesser Short-toed Lark occupies flat or slightly undulating steppe areas which incorporate a large proportion of bare ground. It is mainly a lowland species (breeding from sea-level to 600 m) but may occupy steeply sloping hillsides and the Trans-

caucasian race *pseudobaltica* ascends to alpine meadows at 3,000 m. Unlike several other larks, the Lesser Short-toed Lark avoids crops and high scrub vegetation during the breeding season.

On the Iberian peninsula the species occurs in the continental arid steppes of the Ebro valley and southeast coast, in habitats which include scattered and dispersed patches of cereal crops, fallow land and areas subject to extensive grazing. It is absent from the colder, more continental inland steppes of central Spain (Tellería *et al*. 1988).

■ Threats

Land-use changes which have come about through irrigation, afforestation and locally through urban development schemes in steppe areas are serious local threats in the Iberian peninsula (Suárez *et al*. 1993) which may be affecting large areas (Yanes in press). The ploughing-up of steppe, favoured by some aspects of the EU Common Agricultural Policy, is also a short-term threat in Iberia. The abandonment of cultivation in the semi-arid steppes may, however, favour the species in some areas, by allowing some initial regeneration of scrub and so increasing the extent of suitable habitat.

Along the Iberian coastline the species is threatened by urban development and by the commercial extraction of sand (Manrique and de Juana 1991); sand from the south-east of the peninsula is used for plastic greenhouse farming. The abandonment of traditional grazing is also a threat in Iberia, especially in the Ebro valley, since this allows scrub to develop to a height beyond the optimum level for the species.

The high rate of nest destruction (up to 80%) by foxes, dogs, reptiles and other predators also forms a threat to the species locally.

■ Conservation measures

An objective of primary importance for the conservation of this species is to increase the area of semi-arid steppe habitat which is either under protection or, within the EU, which is covered by management

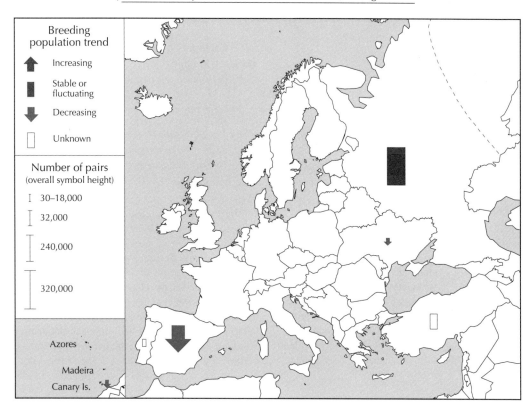

Breeding population trend

↑ Increasing

■ Stable or fluctuating

↓ Decreasing

□ Unknown

Number of pairs
(overall symbol height)

30–18,000

32,000

240,000

320,000

Azores

Madeira

Canary Is.

agreements under the Agri-environment Regulation (EC Reg. 2078/92) of the Common Agricultural Policy.

On the Canary Islands and coastal parts of the Iberian peninsula, actions causing the destruction of semi-arid steppe habitats, such as urban development, sand extraction and intensive cropping should be restricted. Similarly, the afforestation of steppe areas of high conservation interest should be avoided. Consequently, grants should not be available for forestry schemes in such areas.

The maintenance of traditional grazing practices is also required to avoid excessive shrub regeneration and the consequent degradation of habitat quality for Lesser Short-toed Larks as well as for other steppe species. Such practices could be supported in the EU through the development of Zonal Programmes under the Agri-environment Regulation, as above.

The effects of nest predators on Lesser Short-toed Larks should be monitored in protected and non-protected areas.

JUAN MANRIQUE AND MIGUEL YANES

Crested Lark
Galerida cristata

SPEC Category 3
Status (Declining)
Criteria Moderate decline

Although an abundant species, the Crested Lark declined in population size and range in most of western and central Europe between 1970 and 1990. This decrease may be attributed mainly to agricultural intensification and a decrease in extensive livestock rearing. Low-intensity farming should be maintained and promoted to provide suitable habitat.

■ Distribution and population trends

The Crested Lark is widely distributed across the continental west Palearctic south of the boreal zone. It also breeds around the Sahara desert and in large oases in Africa, along the coast of the Arabian peninsula, and in the steppes of central Asia and the Indian subcontinent (Cramp 1988). Population size data are not available outside Europe but it seems that Europe includes less than half of the total breeding range. The species appears to be mainly resident except in northern Russia, where it is a summer visitor.

The European breeding strongholds are in Turkey and Spain, which together hold more than two-thirds of the Crested Lark's European population (see table). Italy, Russia, Romania and Bulgaria also support sizeable numbers.

The Crested Lark has expanded its European range over recent centuries into various man-modified areas which simulate its original desert habitat (Cramp 1988). Although the range and population size have fluctuated during the twentieth century, a marked decline has occurred over the last few decades, especially in central Europe (Cramp 1988). The species has become extinct as a breeding bird in Norway (the last breeding record was in 1972: Cramp 1988) and has shown a reduction in both breeding population size and range in most European countries during 1970–1990, including the significant populations in Spain and Italy. The trend of the large Turkish population is unknown (see table, map).

■ Ecology

The Crested Lark's basic habitat is open, dry, flat or gently sloping lowland areas with very low or sparse vegetation that covers no more than 50% of the ground (Cramp 1988). The species inhabits man-modified areas that resemble semi-desert habitats, including low-intensity cereal crops. Urban and industrial wastelands, railway yards, gravel pits and refuse dumps are also occupied. Dense cereals are avoided, but nesting will occur in traditionally cultivated fields with short and well-spaced crops, in pastures with sparse grass, in asparagus fields and in vineyards (Abs 1963). In Spain birds occupy traditional low-intensity croplands and open grasslands as well as other rural areas and sand-dunes. Crested Larks are replaced by Thekla Lark *G. theklae* in natural, open habitats such as steppes and dehesas (de Juana *et al.* 1988, Tellería *et al.* 1988, Tellería *et al.* in press.); hybridization with this species has been suggested to occur (Abs 1963, Niethammer 1955).

	Breeding population			Breeding range trend
	Size (pairs)	Year	Trend	
Albania	10,000–20,000	81	(–1)	(–1)
Austria	(150–200)	—	(–1)	(–1)
Belarus	3,500–4,000	90	F	0
Belgium	100–100	—	–1	–1
Bulgaria	(100,000–1,000,000)	—	(0)	(0)
Croatia	20,000–25,000 *	—	0*	0*
Cyprus	30,000–60,000	—	0	0
Czech Republic	1,100–2,200	—	–2	–1
Denmark	**300–500**	87–89	–1	–1
Estonia	(50–100)	—	(0)	(0)
France	(1,000–10,000)	76	(–1)	0
Germany	6,000–13,500	—	–2	0
Greece	40,000–70,000	—	(–1)	(–1)
Hungary	50,000–60,000	—	+1	0
Italy	(200,000–400,000)	—	(–1)	(–1)
Latvia	10–50	—	(–1)	F
Lithuania	10–20	85–88	(–1)	(–1)
Moldova	**18,000–25,000**	90	**0**	+1
Netherlands	**400–450**	85	–2	–2
Norway	**0–0**	—	X	X
Poland	4,000–8,000	—	–2	0
Portugal	10,000–100,000	89	(0)	(0)
Romania	(100,000–300,000)	—	0	0
Russia	(100,000–1,000,000)	—	(0)	(0)
Slovakia	(1,000–2,000)	—	(–1)	(–1)
Slovenia	800–1,000	—	–1	–1
Spain	400,000–1,000,000	—	–1	–1
Sweden	**3–3**	89	–2	–2
Switzerland	**0–0**	86–91	X	X
Turkey	(1,000,000–10,000,000)	—	—	—
Ukraine	15,000–18,000	88	–1	–1
Total (approx.)	2,100,000–14,000,000			

Trends +2 Large increase +1 Small increase 0 Stable X Extinct
(1970–1990) –2 Large decrease –1 Small decrease F Fluctuating N New breeder
Data quality **Bold**: reliable quantitative data Normal type: incomplete quantitative data
Bracketed figures: no quantitative data * Data quality not provided

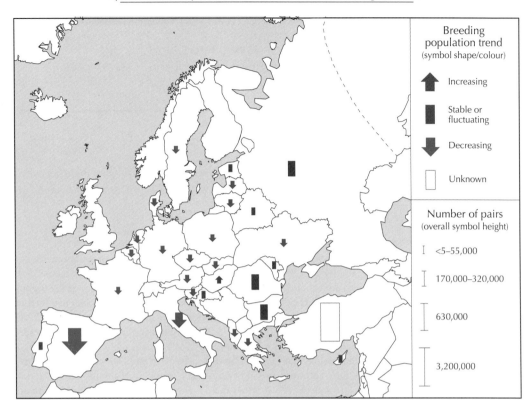

Breeding population trend (symbol shape/colour)
Increasing
Stable or fluctuating
Decreasing
Unknown

Number of pairs (overall symbol height)

<5–55,000

170,000–320,000

630,000

3,200,000

■ Threats

The decline of Crested Lark in the western and central parts of its European range can be attributed to agricultural intensification. The irrigation and substitution of traditional low-intensity farmland by dense and fast-growing crops, the destruction of vineyards, the regeneration of scrub vegetation in old fields due to reductions in extensive livestock rearing, and the afforestation of abandoned croplands have all reduced the extent of suitable habitat for the species. The decrease in numbers observed in Somme (north-east France) at the beginning of the 1960s was attributed to mechanical agriculture and use of pesticides (Triplet 1981), whereas in Belgium the decrease from mid-century onwards was apparently linked to reduced populations of insects formerly associated with horses and their dung (Lippens and Wille 1972).

■ Conservation measures

Only a tiny proportion of the Crested Lark population occurs in Important Bird Areas, and the species therefore clearly requires broad conservation measures, including the maintenance of traditional low-intensity farming practices. Mosaics of non-irrigated cereal crops, including short-term set-aside lands (under EC Regulation 1765/92), arable lands and wide margins between crops without any chemical treatments, should be maintained. The development of Zonal Programmes under the Agri-environment Regulation (EC Reg. 2078/92) of the EU Common Agricultural Policy provides a good opportunity to achieve this.

As with some other agricultural species, a broader and deeper understanding of the biological processes affecting the distribution and abundance of this species is required to ensure that prescribed conservation practices do not conflict with the habitat requirements of other Species of European Conservation Concern (Tellería et al. in press).

MARIO DÍAZ ESTEBAN

Thekla Lark
Galerida theklae

SPEC Category 3
Status   Vulnerable
Criteria   Large decline

Although it is still an abundant bird in the Iberian peninsula, both the population and the range of the Thekla Lark have decreased over the period from 1970 to 1990. The species is currently threatened by loss of habitat resulting from afforestation and from the intensification of agriculture. The maintenance of fallow land, which may be achieved through the EU Set-aside Scheme, would be of benefit.

■ Distribution and population trends

The Thekla Lark occurs in south-west Europe, North Africa (mainly the north-west) and in north-east Africa. Europe probably comprises just under half of its total global range, but no estimates of the African populations are available. The European range encompasses south-east France, the Balearic Islands, and a large part of the Iberian peninsula, where the species is abundant in the mountains along the Mediterranean coast, especially in the south-east. Throughout the distributional range birds appear to be sedentary or to move only short distances outside the breeding season, for example it seems that there may be some altitudinal migration in Spain (Cramp 1988).

Although precise data are not available, it is believed that Spain harbours more than 90% of the total European population and smaller numbers occur in France (Yeatman-Berthelot 1991) and Portugal (Rufino 1989; see table, map). Population trends and distribution changes in recent years are poorly known, but it has been suggested that a decrease has occurred in the Spanish population (see table).

| | Breeding population | | | Breeding |
	Size (pairs)	Year	Trend	range trend
France	(10–100)	76	0	**0**
Portugal	10,000–100,000	89	(0)	0
Spain	1,400,000–1,600,000	—	–1	–1
Total (approx.)	1,400,000–1,700,000			

Trends   +2 Large increase   +1 Small increase   0 Stable   X Extinct
(1970–1990)   –2 Large decrease   –1 Small decrease   F Fluctuating   N New breeder
Data quality   **Bold**: reliable quantitative data   Normal type: incomplete quantitative data
                     Bracketed figures: no quantitative data   * Data quality not provided

■ Ecology

The optimum habitat for Thekla Larks is open scrub of low to medium height in arid or semi-arid terrain. In agricultural habitats, it exclusively occupies remnants of fallow land; in the cultivated and inhabited areas, which it largely avoids, it is replaced by Crested Lark *G. cristata* (Tellería *et al.* 1988, Diaz *et al.* in press). Throughout most of its range Thekla Lark occurs on stony soils where there is a considerable proportion of bare ground (de Juana 1980), but it is also found on sandy soils with pasture and stable dune formations near the coast (Manrique 1992). It occupies flat to very steep areas, from sea-level to 2,000 m.

The diet consists mainly of insects and seeds. These are often taken by searching under stones rather than, as in Crested Lark, by digging (Cramp 1988).

■ Threats

Given that Thekla Larks avoid forest formations, the species will be detrimentally affected in the medium term by the abandonment of agriculture over large parts of the south and south-east of the Iberian peninsula which were formerly under non-intensive cultivation and grazing, and the subsequent afforestation of these areas under EU and national policies.

Agricultural intensification (especially the loss of fallow land) and associated irrigation projects in the steppe habitats of Spain will also continue to have a negative impact on established populations. Overgrazing is causing declines in populations in some parts of south-west Iberia.

■ Conservation measures

The conservation status of the Thekla Lark in Europe may be favoured by implementation of the Set-aside Scheme (EC Reg. 1765/92) and the development of Zonal Programmes under the Agri-environment Regulation (EC Reg. 2078/92) of the EU Common Agricultural Policy, with the objective of maintaining non-intensive farming systems, especially medium-term fallow land. The abandonment of cropland, mainly in steppe areas, and the recovery of steppe vegetation with large shrubs will also be appropriate. The maintenance of medium-height scrub through low grazing pressure may also be beneficial and

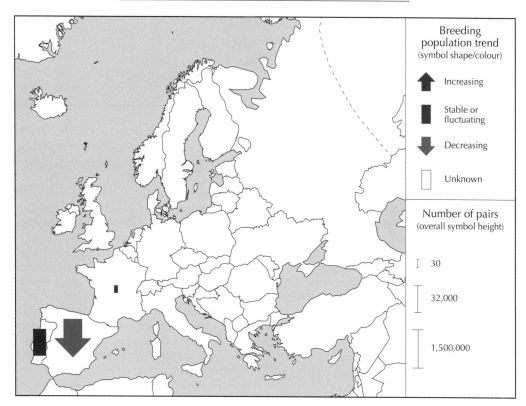

guarantee the species' viability and stability, especially in areas where populations are fragmented and numbers are low. Additionally, in order to maintain suitable habitat and to reduce its fragmentation, afforestation and irrigation developments should be restricted.

JUAN MANRIQUE AND MIGUEL YANES

Woodlark
Lullula arborea

SPEC Category 2
Status Vulnerable
Criteria Large decline

A widespread decline in population size and range is in progress, major causes being the loss and deterioration of dry grassland and heath. This dispersed and migratory species requires extensive networks of habitat throughout Europe to maintain its population, primarily through the continuation of low-intensity pastoral farming.

■ Distribution and population trends

Over three-quarters of the Woodlark's global range lies within Europe, where it breeds from southern Fennoscandia south to the Mediterranean, and from western and central Europe east to the Urals. It is partly migratory, wintering in the western and southern parts of its breeding range as well as North Africa and the Middle East.

	Breeding population			Breeding
	Size (pairs)	Year	Trend	range trend
Albania	2,000–5,000	81	—	—
Andorra	6–12	92	–1	0
Austria	(170–210)	—	(–2)	(–2)
Belarus	12,000–17,000	90	–1	0
Belgium	450–550	81–90	–1	–1
Bulgaria	(10,000–100,000)	—	(0)	(0)
Croatia	10,000–12,000 *	—	0*	0*
Cyprus	600–1,200	—	0	0
Czech Republic	600–1,100	—	–1	–1
Denmark	**200–400**	87	–1	–1
Estonia	2,000–2,000	—	–2	0
Finland	**800–1,000**	92	–2	–2
France	10,000–100,000	76	(–1)	0
Germany	25,000–35,000	—	–1	**0**
Greece	(4,000–10,000)	—	(0)	(0)
Hungary	2,000–2,000	—	–1	0
Italy	(20,000–40,000)	—	(0)	(0)
Latvia	(1,000–6,000)	—	(–1)	(0)
Lithuania	5,000–10,000	85–88	0	0
Luxembourg	40–60	—	–2	–1
Moldova	**1,500–3,000**	90	**0**	**0**
Netherlands	**2,700–3,500**	80	**+1**	**0**
Norway	50–200	90	0	–1
Poland	15,000–30,000	—	0	0
Portugal	100,000–1,000,000	89	(0)	0
Romania	(30,000–50,000)	—	0	0
Russia	(10,000–100,000)	—	(0)	(F)
Slovakia	(1,000–1,500)	—	(0)	(0)
Slovenia	800–1,000	—	–1	–1
Spain	560,000–1,300,000	—	–1	–1
Sweden	1,000–3,000	87	0	0
Switzerland	**250–300**	77–79	–1	–1
Turkey	(10,000–100,000)	—	—	—
Ukraine	4,500–5,200	86	–1	–1
United Kingdom	**550–550**	92	–2	–2
Total (approx.)	840,000–2,900,000			

Trends +2 Large increase +1 Small increase 0 Stable X Extinct
(1970-1990) –2 Large decrease –1 Small decrease F Fluctuating N New breeder
Data quality **Bold**: reliable quantitative data Normal type: incomplete quantitative data
Bracketed figures: no quantitative data * Data quality not provided

Countries with particularly large breeding populations are Spain and Portugal, which together hold over three-quarters of the total European numbers (see table, map). Large populations are also present in France, Germany, Italy, Russia, Romania and Bulgaria. Turkey may well hold a large population but numbers are poorly known there.

Populations have fluctuated widely during the twentieth century in north-west and central Europe (Glutz von Blotzheim and Bauer 1985, Bowden and Hoblyn 1990), with several countries experiencing long-term decline. Indeed during 1970–1990 up to three-quarters of the total breeding population declined (see table, map).

For that part of the European population for which trends are known, up to two-thirds are also experiencing reductions in range size, with contractions of particular concern recorded in Spain (which may well hold over half the world population) and France. Additionally in the United Kingdom and Finland the northern limit of the range has receded (Koskimies 1989, Batten *et al.* 1990), and breeding has ceased in the Republic of Ireland (Sharrock 1976).

■ Ecology

The Woodlark's habitat varies but is usually grazed and on poor soil. The basic requirements are bare ground intermingled with short grass for feeding, with areas of longer vegetation for nesting and roosting, and trees or bushes for song-posts (Glutz von Blotzheim and Bauer 1985, Sitters 1986, Bowden 1990).

In the south of the range, areas occupied stretch from river valleys to mountains at 2,000 m, in a wide variety of habitats encompassing open oak *Quercus* woodland, sclerophyllous vegetation, open upland pastures, vineyards and olive-groves (Koffan 1960, Glutz von Blotzheim and Bauer 1985).

In northern latitudes Woodlarks are found mainly on lowland heath and clear-felled and re-stocked conifer plantations on sandy soil. In eastern Europe other habitats include open pine *Pinus* forest, mixed

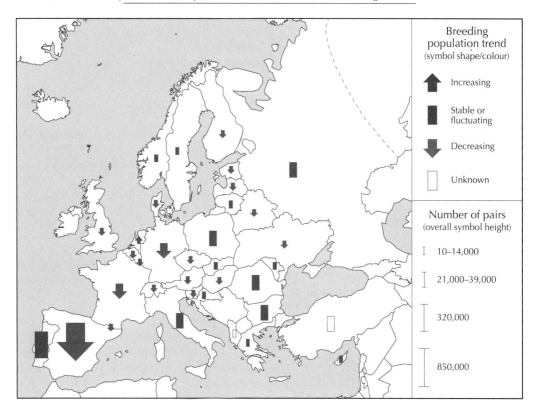

Breeding
population trend
(symbol shape/colour)

Increasing

Stable or
fluctuating

Decreasing

Unknown

Number of pairs
(overall symbol height)

10–14,000

21,000–39,000

320,000

850,000

or broadleaf forest clearings and open oak woodland extending to the edges of dunes (Koffan 1960, Pätzold 1971, Cramp 1988).

■ Threats

The main causes of the recent decline are habitat loss and deterioration. In southern and central Europe threats include loss of dry grassland to intensive arable agriculture, invasion of fallow land and abandoned pasture by tall grass and scrub, replacement of traditional vineyards and orchards by intensive farmland, and reduction of pastoral activity in woodland (Glutz von Blotzheim and Bauer 1985). Afforestation is also a potential threat.

In northern Europe large areas of lowland heath have been built on or converted to intensive agriculture. Afforestation has also reduced the extent of many heathlands although it does provide a temporarily suitable habitat immediately after planting, and again after the area is felled and replanted (Mackowicz 1970, Bowden 1990). Furthermore, tall grasses and scrub have increased on many remaining heathlands due to reduced grazing. Severe winters in north-west Europe may also have caused local extinctions where numbers have already been reduced by habitat loss or deterioration (Sharrock 1976, Koskimies 1989, Batten et al. 1990).

■ Conservation measures

The maintenance of extensive areas of suitable habitat throughout Europe is essential for the conservation of this dispersed species. To achieve this the promotion and continuation of low-intensity pastoral farming is necessary.

In north-west Europe, favoured habitats such as dunes and heath should continue to be protected (Bijlsma et al. 1985) from afforestation, urbanization and mass tourism (Ledant and Jacob 1980). In England it is proposed that young plantations can be managed to keep them suitable for Woodlarks for longer (Bowden and Hoblyn 1990), a measure which could be applied to populations elsewhere.

MELANIE HEATH

365

Skylark
Alauda arvensis

SPEC Category 3
Status Vulnerable
Criteria Large decline

Agricultural intensification has caused widespread decline, particularly in western Europe. Wide-scale measures are needed to encourage mixed farming, the maintenance of stubbles over winter and low agro-chemical use. In the EU, appropriately managed set-aside land may be beneficial.

■ Distribution and population trends

The Skylark has a huge distribution across upper and lower middle latitudes, from Ireland to the Pacific. It is widespread and abundant in Europe, occurring in all regions except Iceland and Greenland and the tundra of Fennoscandia and Russia. Strongholds include the United Kingdom, Spain, Denmark, Germany, Poland, Russia and Bulgaria (see table, map).

In the past the species benefited from the clearance of forests, and until recently from the increase in arable farmland. However, there was a widespread decline during 1970–1990, particularly in western Europe, with falls of over 50% in the United Kingdom, Netherlands and Germany (see table, map).

■ Ecology

Skylarks are characteristic ground-nesting birds of open temperate and boreal habitats. Although highest densities are often found in saltmarshes, coastal grazing marshes and sand-dunes, most birds now occur on farmland even though density is often low (e.g. O'Connor and Shrubb 1986, Karlsson and Kjellén 1988, Schläpfer 1988, Tellería *et al.* 1988). Within agricultural habitats, cereals, root crops and young leys are preferred (O'Connor and Shrubb 1986, Williamson 1967). Highest densities in Switzerland were found to occur where high crop diversity provides a mosaic of habitats suitable for nesting throughout the breeding season (Schläpfer 1988, Jenny 1990a,b,c). Individual pairs make up to three or exceptionally four nesting attempts in one year; the first pairs having eggs in early April and the last broods being fed in late July (Cramp 1988).

In the breeding season, invertebrates, particularly adult beetles (Carabidae, Elateridae, Chrysomelidae and Curculionidae) predominate in the diet (Green 1978), while young chicks are fed Lepidoptera and Hymenoptera larvae and spiders (Poulsen 1993). Outside the breeding season Skylarks are mostly herbivorous, taking a great variety of leaves, seeds and cereal grain (Green 1978, 1980).

■ Threats

Agricultural intensification is probably the major cause of declines. Firstly, widespread reductions in crop diversity have reduced opportunities for nesting in optimal habitat structures and thus the likelihood of successfully raising multiple broods (O'Connor and Shrubb 1986, Schläpfer 1988). Secondly, sowing of cereals in spring has been replaced

	Breeding population			Breeding
	Size (pairs)	Year	Trend	range trend
Albania	500–1,000	81	—	—
Andorra	50–150	91	0	0
Austria	(40,000–50,000)	—	(–1)	(–1)
Belarus	1,200,000–1,700,000	90	0	0
Belgium	100,000–140,000	81–90	–1	0
Bulgaria	(1,000,000–10,000,000)	—	(0)	(0)
Croatia	200,000–250,000 *	—	0*	0*
Czech Republic	800,000–1,600,000	—	–1	**0**
Denmark	**13,000,000–13,000,000**	83	(–1)	(0)
Faroe Islands	5–10	81	(–1)	(–1)
Estonia	100,000–200,000	—	–1	0
Finland	**300,000–400,000**	92	**–1**	**0**
France	(300,000–1,300,000)	90	–1	**0**
Germany	4,900,000–4,900,000	85	–2	–1
Greece	2,000–5,000	—	(0)	(0)
Hungary	150,000–300,000	—	–1	0
Rep. of Ireland	490,000–490,000	88–91	(–1)	(0)
Italy	(500,000–1,000,000)	—	(–1)	(0)
Latvia	**1,100,000–1,800,000**	—	**0**	**0**
Liechtenstein	**35–35**	89	**–2**	**–2**
Lithuania	150,000–200,000	85–88	0	0
Luxembourg	10,000–15,000	—	–1	0
Moldova	**50,000–70,000**	89	**0**	**0**
Netherlands	**150,000–175,000**	79	**–2**	**0**
Norway	100,000–500,000	90	–1	**0**
Poland	5,000,000–9,000,000	—	(0)	(0)
Portugal	100,000–1,000,000	89	–1	–1
Romania	(600,000–1,000,000)	—	0	0
Russia	1,000,000–10,000,000	—	0	0
Slovakia	(200,000–400,000)	—	(0)	0
Slovenia	8,000–12,000	—	–2	–2
Spain	2,000,000–6,000,000	—	–1	–1
Sweden	700,000–1,000,000	87	**–1**	**0**
Switzerland	40,000–50,000	86–91	–1	0
Turkey	(50,000–500,000)	—	—	—
Ukraine	900,000–1,000,000	88	+1	+1
United Kingdom	**2,100,000–2,100,000**	88–91	–2	**0**
Guernsey [1]	25–100	—	0*	0*
Jersey [1]	(100–200)	—	0	(0)
Isle of Man [1]	(100–200)	—	(–1)	0*
Total (approx.)	37,000,000–160,000,000			

Trends (1970–1990) +2 Large increase +1 Small increase 0 Stable –2 Large decrease –1 Small decrease F Fluctuating X Extinct N New breeder
Data quality **Bold**: reliable quantitative data Normal type: incomplete quantitative data Bracketed figures: no quantitative data * Data quality not provided
[1] Population figures are included within United Kingdom totals

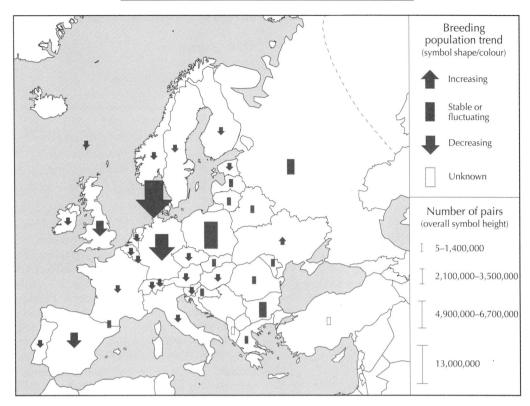

Breeding
population trend
(symbol shape/colour)

Increasing

Stable or
fluctuating

Decreasing

Unknown

Number of pairs
(overall symbol height)

5–1,400,000

2,100,000–3,500,000

4,900,000–6,700,000

13,000,000

in many regions by autumn sowing; this has meant the loss of grain and weed seeds on winter stubbles, and of the spring-sown grain itself (Green 1978). Furthermore, intensive winter cereal tend to be unsuitable breeding habitat (Wilson and Browne 1993, Poulsen 1993), probably being too tall and dense for nesting (Schläpfer 1988) or having much reduced invertebrate food resources compared with other habitats (Jenny 1990a, Poulsen 1993, Tucker 1993).

Thirdly, intensive grassland habitats are frequently unsuitable, due to high fertilizer applications leading to vegetation that is too tall and dense for nesting, as well as high nest failure rates through high stocking rates or frequent mowing (Busche 1989).

Lastly, the current high levels of insecticide and herbicide use on farmland have undoubtedly reduced weed seed and invertebrate food resources (Potts 1986) and may have contributed to the Skylark's decline. Skylark densities have been found to be higher on organic compared to conventional farmland in Denmark (Braae *et al.* 1988) and in the United Kingdom, where nesting success was also higher (Wilson 1993, Wilson and Brown 1993), but in both cases factors other than pesticide inputs may also be involved.

■ Conservation measures

Clearly, the Skylark is mostly dependent on wide-scale conservation measures, including the mainte-

nance of crop diversity and the practice of leaving stubble fields over winter, as well as a reduction in the use of fertilizers, herbicides and pesticides. Such measures could be supported in the EU countries through management agreements under the Agri-environment Regulation (EC Reg. 2078/92) of the Common Agricultural Policy, or through short-term set-aside of land (EC Reg. 1765/92). Set-aside land in the United Kingdom has indeed been found to hold high densities of Skylarks (Poulsen 1993, Wilson and Browne 1993), but successful nesting depends on farmers not cutting or cultivating this land between late April and the end of June. However, initial management rules in the United Kingdom (MAFF 1992) resulted in cutting and ploughing at the peak of the Skylark's breeding season in 1993, and many nests were undoubtedly destroyed (Mead and Wilson 1993). These rules have changed, and farmers are now permitted to delay cutting and cultivation until July and to employ selective herbicides to control pernicious weeds at an earlier date.

Until proven otherwise, pesticides should be regarded as a likely cause of the Skylark's decline. Tighter controls of broad-spectrum herbicide and insecticide use should therefore be implemented, combined with the promotion of integrated systems of pest control that reduce the need for pesticides.

GRAHAM TUCKER

Sand Martin
Riparia riparia

SPEC Category   3
Status   Declining
Criteria   Moderate decline

The Sand Martin relies naturally for nesting on newly eroded banks of rivers, streams, lake edges or sea-cliffs. In areas with a high human population these are often greatly modified and most birds use man-made sites, particularly quarries, for nesting. During the 1970–1990 period severe declines were recorded in western Europe, almost certainly associated with drought on the wintering grounds.

■ Distribution and population trends

Sand Martins breed throughout the temperate, boreal and subarctic regions of both the Palearctic and Nearctic. The distribution is patchy in some areas as the species is not normally found in heavily forested

	Breeding population			Breeding
	Size (pairs)	Year	Trend	range trend
Albania	2,000–5,000	81	(F)	0*
Austria	(9,000–15,000)	—	(–1)	(–1)
Belarus	(200,000–250,000)	90	(0)	0
Belgium	3,750–5,200	81–90	–1	–1
Bulgaria	(10,000–100,000)	—	(0)	(0)
Croatia	25,000–30,000 *	—	0*	0*
Czech Republic	18,000–36,000	—	0	0
Denmark	20,000–40,000	87–89	–1	0
Estonia	20,000–50,000	—	+1	0
Finland	80,000–120,000	92	–1	0
France	10,000–100,000	76	F	0
Germany	50,000–130,000	—	–1	0
Greece	10,000–20,000	—	(–1)	(0)
Hungary	60,000–80,000	—	0	0
Rep. of Ireland	16,000–24,000	—	(+1)	(0)
Italy	8,000–9,000	88	–1	–1
Latvia	30,000–100,000	—	0	0
Lithuania	**15,000–20,000**	85–88	(0)	0
Luxembourg	100–140	—	–1	–1
Moldova	6,500–7,000	85	–1	–1
Netherlands	**9,000–12,000**	87	**–2**	**–2**
Norway	100,000–250,000	90	0	**0**
Poland	150,000–300,000	—	0	0
Portugal	10,000–100,000	89	F	+1
Romania	(30,000–50,000)	—	0	0
Russia	(1,000,000–10,000,000)—		(0)	(0)
Slovakia	(15,000–30,000)	—	(+1)	0
Slovenia	150–250	—	F	F
Spain	540,000–750,000	—	–1	–1
Sweden	100,000–250,000	87	0	**0**
Switzerland	**3,000–5,000**	80	**F**	**F**
Turkey	(10,000–100,000)	—	—	—
Ukraine	140,000–150,000	88	–1	–1
United Kingdom	85,000–270,000	88–91	(–2)	**–1**
Guernsey [1]	25–50	—	0*	0*
Jersey [1]	40–50	—	+1	+1
Isle of Man [1]	**125–175**	90	+2	0*
Total (approx.)	2,800,000–14,000,000			

Trends   +2 Large increase   +1 Small increase   0 Stable   X Extinct
(1970–1990)   –2 Large decrease   –1 Small decrease   F Fluctuating   N New breeder
Data quality   **Bold**: reliable quantitative data   Normal type: incomplete quantitative data
Bracketed figures: no quantitative data   * Data quality not provided
[1] Population figures are included within United Kingdom totals

areas nor where the underlying geology prevents the formation of sandy, vertical banks for nesting. Europe comprises only a small part of the total breeding range and probably contains less than 20% of the global population. Largest European populations occur in Russia and Spain, although substantial numbers are present also in the United Kingdom, Norway, Sweden, Poland, Belarus and Ukraine (see table, map). Sand Martins are not easy to count accurately, but, with the exception of Spain, they seem possibly to be less common in the southern third of the continent, probably because of the drier climate.

Palearctic populations winter mainly in the Sahel zone of Africa (from Senegal eastwards) and in East Africa south to Mozambique. Breeding populations in the east extend much further south in winter than do western populations.

In western Europe, particularly in Britain and Ireland, Sand Martins suffered a severe setback over the winter of 1968/9. This was due to drought conditions on the wintering grounds in the Sahel region (Cowley 1979, Mead 1979), and the population fell by more than 75%. The population in the United Kingdom continued at a low level and received another setback in the 1983/4 winter so that in 1984 it was estimated that numbers amounted to only 10% of the peak level in the mid-1960s (Jones 1987); the number of occupied 10-km squares dropped by 25% between 1970 and 1990 (Gibbons *et al.* 1993). Persson (1987) recorded the lowest populations in his study area in south-west Sweden in 1985 and postulated that populations crashed every dozen years or so. Overall numbers declined in much of north-west Europe during the 1970–1990 period as well as in some south European countries, including the important population in Spain (see table, map). East European populations may not have been as severely affected by conditions in Africa since the areas where they winter have not been so drought-stricken, although numbers fell between 1970–1990 in the

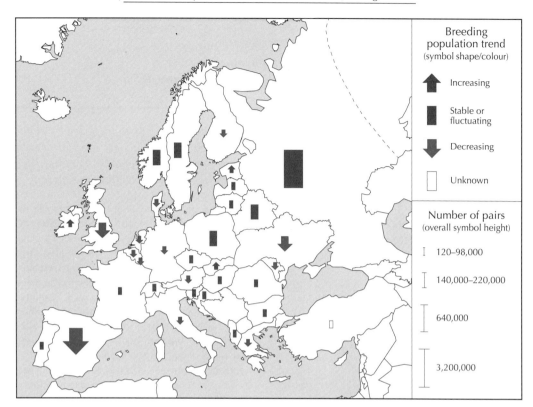

Legend:

Breeding population trend (symbol shape/colour)

- Increasing
- Stable or fluctuating
- Decreasing
- Unknown

Number of pairs (overall symbol height)

- 120–98,000
- 140,000–220,000
- 640,000
- 3,200,000

Ukraine (see table, map). The large Russian population is poorly known but believed to be stable (see table).

■ Ecology

Sand Martins feed in the lower air space on flying and drifting invertebrates. The ecology of the ground underlying their feeding areas is not important provided that suitable food items either arise from it or drift over it from elsewhere. Many agricultural crops provide excellent sites but urban areas and forest are generally not good. Locally, the summer distribution is restricted by the availability of suitable nesting sites lying within 10–15 km of suitable feeding areas. Sand Martins nest colonially, and single colonies often contain more than 100 pairs and provide breeding sites for over 1% of the birds within 50 km. Natural sites for nesting are restricted to newly eroded banks of rivers, streams, lake edges or sea-cliffs, but over a considerable part of their range within Europe the birds are mostly dependent on man's incidental provision of suitable sites in quarries, as natural sites are almost all destroyed by river and stream management.

Drought in the winter quarters probably drasti-cally reduces the available feeding area for the species in the later part of the winter and the early spring (Mead 1979).

■ Threats

Work within quarries may be very detrimental to breeding but workmen are often affectionately disposed to the birds and take measures to protect them. Modern farming techniques, through the use of pesticides, may restrict food supply over farmland, and thus impact on the species. Further declines may occur if drought conditions return to the wintering area.

■ Conservation measures

Since local distribution depends crucially on the presence of nesting sites, the provision of deliberately constructed sites, even importing ballast, can make a real difference (du Feu 1993). The acquisition of spent quarries by conservation bodies in order to protect nesting sites is also appropriate. Indeed, the species is afforded legal protection within the United Kingdom from disturbance during the working of quarries. Management of flood alteration schemes to provide nest-sites is also important.

CHRIS MEAD

Swallow
Hirundo rustica

SPEC Category 3
Status Declining
Criteria Moderate decline

Populations have declined in many parts of Europe, probably due partly to the loss of suitable habitat through the intensification of agriculture, although climatic variations, especially in the wintering areas, may also be significant. Low-intensity farming practices should be maintained and promoted, to provide pastures and other foraging areas and suitable farm buildings for nesting.

■ Distribution and population trends

The Swallow breeds across most of Eurasia, North Africa and North America. Perhaps c.15% of the world range lies within Europe, where almost the whole of the region is occupied excepting mainly the tundra zone north of c.67°N. Although some population sizes are poorly known, particularly large populations probably occur in Russia, Germany, Poland and Bulgaria, and also United Kingdom, France, Spain, Portugal, Italy, Czech Republic, Croatia, Ukraine and Belarus (see map, table). European birds winter mainly in Africa, though a very few winter in southern and western Europe, and regularly in southern Spain and Portugal.

Fluctuations in population size are not unusual but there has been a widespread decline during 1970–1990 in many areas, including Fennoscandia, most of north-west and central Europe, the Baltic states, Romania, Ukraine, Spain, Italy and Croatia (see table, map; also Cramp 1988, Marchant *et al.* 1990). The population appears stable in Russia but no quantitative data on trends are available. Range has remained largely stable with small contractions in some countries including Spain, Austria, Romania and Ukraine (see table).

■ Ecology

Breeding occurs in a variety of habitats but not generally in arid, heavily built-up or wooded areas. The preferred habitats for feeding are pastures, meadows and areas of water where flying insects are most abundant; grazing animals are desirable as they disturb insects, making them available to Swallows in flight. For nest-sites, the species is almost entirely dependent on human artefacts, usually open buildings and particularly those housing livestock (Møller 1985). A source of mud is also necessary for nest building.

■ Threats

Changes in farming practices, such as the abandonment of traditional beef and milk production in Denmark (Møller 1983, 1985) and loss of suitable feeding areas on farms in Westphalia, Germany (Loske and Lederer 1987), have been implicated in the population decline. Intensive livestock rearing,

	Breeding population			Breeding range trend
	Size (pairs)	Year	Trend	
Albania	20,000–50,000	91	(–1)	(–1)
Andorra	20–30	92	–1	–1
Austria	(250,000–300,000)	—	(–1)	(–1)
Belarus	800,000–830,000	90	0	0
Belgium	70,000–130,000	81–90	–1	0
Bulgaria	(500,000–5,000,000)	—	(0)	(0)
Croatia	500,000–600,000 *	—	–1*	0*
Cyprus	200,000–600,000	—	0	0
Czech Republic	400,000–800,000	—	–1	**0**
Denmark	200,000–300,000	87–89	–1	(0)
Faroe Islands	0–1	—	F	F
Estonia	100,000–200,000	—	–1	**0**
Finland	**150,000–200,000**	92	**–1**	**0**
France	1,000,000–?	76	–1	**0**
Germany	1,000,000–2,000,000	—	–2	**0**
Greece	20,000–50,000	—	(–1)	(0)
Hungary	150,000–200,000	—	0	0
Iceland	0–5	—	I	0*
Rep. of Ireland	210,000–210,000	88–91	(–1)	(0)
Italy	(500,000–1,000,000)	—	(–1)	(0)
Latvia	117,000–475,000	—	0	0
Liechtenstein	50–80	—	–1	–1
Lithuania	**20,000–40,000**	85–88	(–1)	0
Luxembourg	10,000–15,000	—	–1	0
Moldova	**25,000–35,000**	88	**–1**	**–1**
Netherlands	100,000–500,000	79	–2	**0**
Norway	100,000–400,000	90	–1	**0**
Poland	1,500,000–2,900,000	—	0	0
Portugal	1,000,000–1,000,000	89	(0)	0
Romania	(200,000–500,000)	—	–1	**–1**
Russia	(1,000,000–10,000,000)	—	(0)	(0)
Slovakia	(200,000–400,000)	—	–1	0
Slovenia	200,000–300,000	—	0	0
Spain	783,000–812,000	—	–1	–1
Sweden	200,000–400,000	87	–1	**0**
Switzerland	100,000–150,000	86–91	–1	0
Turkey	(100,000–1,000,000)	—	—	—
Ukraine	800,000–850,000	88	–1	–1
United Kingdom	610,000–610,000	88–91	–1	**0**
Guernsey [1]	40–100	—	0*	0*
Jersey [1]	1,000–1,500	—	0	0
Isle of Man [1]	500–1,000	—	(0)	0*
Gibraltar	0–0	—	X	X
Total (approx.)	13,000,000–33,000,000			

Trends +2 Large increase +1 Small increase 0 Stable X Extinct
(1970–1990) –2 Large decrease –1 Small decrease F Fluctuating N New breeder
Data quality **Bold:** reliable quantitative data Normal type: incomplete quantitative data
Bracketed figures: no quantitative data * Data quality not provided
[1] Population figures are included within United Kingdom totals

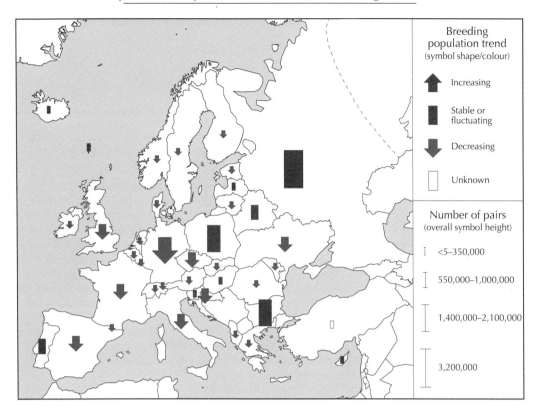

Breeding population trend
(symbol shape/colour)

- Increasing
- Stable or fluctuating
- Decreasing
- Unknown

Number of pairs
(overall symbol height)

I	<5–350,000
I	550,000–1,000,000
I	1,400,000–2,100,000
I	3,200,000

land drainage, improved hygiene in agriculture and the use of herbicides and insecticides all reduce the supply of insect food, and suitable nest-sites are often scarcer on large, modern farms.

The Swallow is also susceptible to changes in climate. Bad weather reduces insect numbers, so affecting breeding success and (especially during migration) increasing mortality. Conditions in the wintering areas have an important effect on breeding success in Europe: Møller (1989) found that low rainfall in the wintering area was associated with high winter mortality and with small clutch sizes the following season in Denmark.

■ **Conservation measures**

This species requires the maintenance of large areas of suitable habitat throughout Europe, which can be achieved by the continuation and promotion of traditional, low-intensity farming. Particular needs include extensive livestock rearing, especially of cattle, a reduction in pesticide use, and the preservation of wetland areas and water-bodies. Long-term monitoring of population sizes and further research into the effects of climatic variation are also required.

ANGELA TURNER

Tawny Pipit
Anthus campestris

SPEC Category 3
Status Vulnerable
Criteria Large decline

Numbers have declined over most of the European range during 1970–1990. The main threat is loss of habitat due to agricultural intensification and the abandonment of extensive sheep-grazing.

■ Distribution and population trends

The Tawny Pipit's breeding range extends from southern Sweden and Estonia south through western Europe to Iberia and north-west Africa, east through central and southern Europe to central Asia. Almost half its range is in Europe.

Over half the European breeding population is concentrated in Spain, although France, Italy, Greece, Hungary, Romania, Russia and Turkey (although poorly known), also have large numbers (see table, map). Ranges and populations in (e.g.) Sweden, Germany and the Netherlands have declined since the nineteenth century (Cramp 1988), and numbers in more than three-quarters of the occupied Euro-

pean countries (for which trends are known) fell between 1970 and 1990 (see table, map). Information on the large Russian, Italian and Greek populations is poor, however, and trends in Turkey are unknown. Decreases seem to be most pronounced in central Europe with particularly large declines noted for example in Germany (Bauer and Thielcke 1982) and the Netherlands (Teixeira 1979). The range of the species also appears to have undergone a noticeable reduction.

West Palearctic populations are mostly migratory, wintering mainly south of the Sahara in the Sahel, but also in the Aegean region and Turkey.

■ Ecology

The Tawny Pipit's preferred habitat is generally open, with a sparse and broken herb cover, bare sandy patches and elevated perches for singing. In southern Europe this is often sheep-grazed land, with occasional low shrubs, and also dry grasslands with thickets of thyme *Thymus* (de Juana 1980). In Spain, the habitat is similar to that of Dupont's Lark *Chersophilus duponti* and Black-eared Wheatear *Oenanthe hispanica* in that it includes flat or slightly undulating areas, a high proportion of bare soil and patches of pasture and/or shrubs. Occasionally nesting occurs in cleared forest habitats such as open juniper *Juniperus* woods. In Iberia it is not present in the most arid steppes of the south-east or the Ebro valley, but occurs principally in the inland mountains and plateaus (páramos) (Tellería *et al.* 1988). Further north and east in Europe the Tawny Pipit also breeds in arable fields on poor, sandy soils, coastal sand-dunes, heaths, steppes and semi-arid desert (Cramp 1988).

The diet is mainly invertebrates.

■ Threats

The exact causes of the decline in Europe are not clear, but in Iberia and most of the rest of Europe decreases are considered to be due primarily to habitat loss through conversion to forestry, agricultural intensification or abandonment of farmland. These land-use changes result in the loss of suitable grassland, either through conversion to intensive

	Breeding population			Breeding
	Size (pairs)	Year	Trend	range trend
Albania	(2,000–5,000)	81	—	—
Austria	(10–20)	—	(–2)	(–2)
Belarus	3,000–8,000	90	F	0
Bulgaria	(350–1,000)	—	(0)	(0)
Croatia	3,000–6,000 *	—	0*	0*
Czech Republic	**40–80**	—	–2	–2
Denmark	**29–31**	89	(–1)	(–1)
Estonia	50–50	—	–1	0
Finland	(0–3)	92	–2	–2
France	(10,000–30,000)	89	0	**0**
Germany	460–650	—	–2	**0**
Greece	(10,000–20,000)	—	(0)	(0)
Hungary	10,000–20,000	—	0	0
Italy	(15,000–40,000)	—	(–1)	(–1)
Latvia	200–500	—	(0)	(0)
Lithuania	(100–300)	85–88	(0)	(0)
Luxembourg	0–1	—	–1	–1
Moldova	**4,000–5,500**	88	**0**	**0**
Netherlands	**60–80**	79	–2	–2
Poland	5,000–10,000	—	0	0
Portugal	1,000–10,000	89	–1	–1
Romania	(15,000–30,000)	—	0	(0)
Russia	(10,000–100,000)	—	(0)	(0)
Slovakia	70–150	—	–1	–1
Slovenia	50–100	—	F	F
Spain	400,000–640,000	—	–1	–1
Sweden	150–300	87	**–1**	**0**
Switzerland	**1–2**	86–91	F	F
Turkey	(50,000–500,000)	—	—	—
Ukraine	1,500–2,000	88	–1	–1
Total (approx.)	540,000–1,400,000			

Trends   +2 Large increase   +1 Small increase   0 Stable   X Extinct
(1970–1990) –2 Large decrease   –1 Small decrease   F Fluctuating   N New breeder
Data quality **Bold**: reliable quantitative data   Normal type: incomplete quantitative data
Bracketed figures: no quantitative data   * Data quality not provided

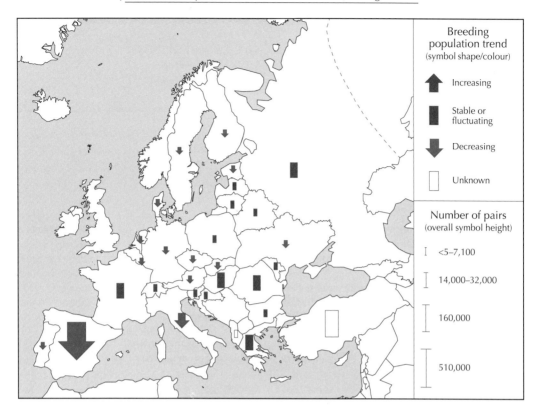

**Breeding
population trend**
(symbol shape/colour)

▲ Increasing

■ Stable or
fluctuating

▼ Decreasing

▯ Unknown

Number of pairs
(overall symbol height)

I <5–7,100

I 14,000–32,000

I 160,000

I 510,000

arable crops or plantations or through the growth of vegetation with the reduction or abandonment of grazing. It is expected that such habitat loss will continue through support from EU development funds, and will therefore continue to have a considerable impact on Tawny Pipit and other dry grassland bird populations.

There may also be factors operating other than habitat loss, however (e.g. climate change and the use of pesticides and fertilizers that, directly or indirectly, affect insect populations: Glutz von Blotzheim and Bauer 1985, Hölzinger 1987), as declines have occurred in some areas which have not suffered marked habitat changes (Tomialojc 1990,

Dyrcz *et al.* 1991). Research would be necessary to establish this.

■ Conservation measures

Action should centre on the maintenance of low-intensity grazing practices in order to restrict the development of dense vegetation cover. Within the EU, such measures could be supported by management agreements under the Agri-environment Regulation (EC Reg. 2078/92) of the Common Agricultural Policy. Additionally, the abandonment of marginal crops in flat areas could favour the species, providing that such sites are converted to sheep grazing and not to forestry plantation.

FRANCISCO SUÁREZ

Radde's Accentor
Prunella ocularis

SPEC Category 3
Status (Vulnerable)
Criteria <2,500 pairs

A rare and poorly known species, Radde's Accentor is restricted in Europe to isolated localities in the arid mountains of Armenia and Turkey. Its low abundance is likely to stem from its specialized ecology and the degradation of its habitat by overgrazing. To maintain the species, conservation of its breeding habitat, chiefly subalpine xerophytic thorny scrub, is necessary.

■ Distribution and population trends

Radde's Accentor is mainly a resident species with a range that extends through areas characterized by a continental climate from central and eastern Turkey across the Armenian and Iranian highlands (Loskot 1988). Northern birds (from Armenia, eastern Turkey and north-west Iran) winter in the southern parts of the species' range.

Within Turkey the species is found in the high mountains in the east and south-east, including: Nemrut Dag, Samdi Dag, Cilo Dag (Beaman 1986, Martins 1989) and Kavusshap Dag (R. F. Porter pers. comm.); also on Bü Agri Dagi (Mt Ararat), but only on the basis of an old record (Sushkin 1914). It is also patchily distributed in the Toros Daglari (Taurus mountain chain), including Ala Daglari (Gaston 1968, Beaman 1986, Martins 1989), and in the mountains of the eastern Black Sea region (Beaman 1986, Martins 1989, Kasparek 1992a), and it occurs on Erciyas Dagi (Mt Argeus), an isolated volcano in central Anatolia (Kasparek 1992a). On current knowledge it is thought that Turkey may hold 500–5,000 pairs, but the species is probably more widely distributed in the country than the records so far suggest (Beaman 1986), and extrapolation from transect counts in the south-east suggest that true populations could be considerably higher (R. F. Porter pers. comm.). Extrapolations from local estimates on Aragats Mountain suggest there may be some 100 pairs nesting in Armenia.

There is no information available on population trends, although it is strongly believed that the increasing intensity of pastoral farming is degrading the species' breeding habitats, probably with detrimental effects on the population levels.

■ Ecology

Radde's Accentor breeds only on high mountain massifs, between 2,000 and 3,000 m above sea-level, and local breeding groups can therefore often be dozens or hundreds of kilometres apart. Summer post-breeding nomadic movements are characteristic of the species (Loskot 1988), and some adults and juveniles move then into the alpine zones, e.g. to 3,250 m on Aragats Mountain (Loskot 1988), to 3,125 m on the Gegamskiy ridge in Armenia (Lyayster and Sosnin 1942) and to 3,300 m in the Elburz mountains of northern Iran (Norton 1958). Movements to the lower mountains occur in winter, usually below 1,000 m.

The species breeds exclusively in the narrow subalpine zone of xerophytic vegetation, comprising scattered, mostly thorny low bushes with dense crowns, such as juniper *Juniperus hemisphaerica* and barberry *Berberis iberica*, usually in stream valleys and on slopes. The nests are found exclusively in juniper or barberry bushes, 16–40 cm above the ground (Gaston 1968, Loskot 1988). Additional habitat requirements include scattered grass (amounting to less than 30% coverage), patches of bare ground, a nearby water source, and rocks or large boulders to provide shade during the heat of the day. Sites with a dense covering of bushes, high grass and herbaceous vegetation are avoided, even by non-breeding birds.

The species specializes in collecting small seeds and invertebrates (mainly insects) on the ground in low grassy vegetation, along streams and among snow, rocks and scrub (Cramp 1988, Loskot 1988). Birds also collect prey (mainly caterpillars) on twigs of *Juniperus* and *Astragalus*, and flying insects are sometimes taken. Seeds of Labiatae (*Ziziphora*, *Ajuga*) and Rosaceae (*Potentilla*) predominated in the stomachs of adult birds taken in July; among invertebrate food, Hymenoptera (especially small ants) and Coleoptera are particularly favoured (Loskot 1988).

Although little is known about the species' breeding biology is appears to have a rather low reproduc-

	Breeding population			Breeding
	Size (pairs)	Year	Trend	range trend
Turkey	(500–5,000)	—	—	—
Total (approx.)	500–5,000			

Trends +2 Large increase +1 Small increase 0 Stable X Extinct
(1970–1990) –2 Large decrease –1 Small decrease F Fluctuating N New breeder
Data quality **Bold**: reliable quantitative data Normal type: incomplete quantitative data
Bracketed figures: no quantitative data * Data quality not provided

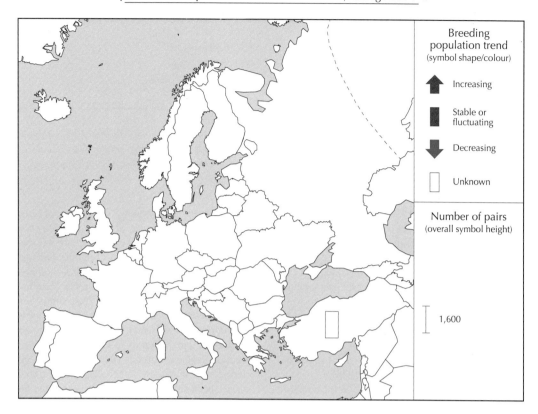

Breeding
population trend
(symbol shape/colour)

Increasing

Stable or
fluctuating

Decreasing

Unknown

Number of pairs
(overall symbol height)

1,600

tive potential as Loskot (1988) found only 3–4 eggs in each of six first- and second-brood clutches.

■ Threats

The main factor controlling the vegetation in the subalpine zone is grazing (Gaston 1968). Moderate levels are believed not to reduce the breeding success of Radde's Accentor and may create suitable conditions for foraging. The main threat to the species is habitat degradation, through intensive pastoral farming, and the associated increases in burning and cutting of bushes, which serve as the only secure nesting places for the bird. Intensive cattle-grazing

also increases the risk of nest predation by weasels *Mustela nivalis* and corvids, chiefly Magpies *Pica pica* (Loskot 1988).

■ Conservation measures

Ways need to be found to ensure the conservation of patches of suitable breeding habitat (in particular, scattered clumps of *Juniperus* or *Berberis* bushes) in low-intensity, traditionally managed summer montane pastures.

Further censuses and monitoring of the species' populations are required, as is research into potential threats.

VLADIMIR LOSKOT

Black-throated Accentor
Prunella atrogularis

SPEC Category 3
Status (Vulnerable)
Criteria <2,500 pairs

The Black-throated Accentor, a rare and extremely poorly known bird, is confined in Europe to spruce forests in the northern Ural mountains and the eastern coast of the White Sea. Numbers probably total a few thousand birds. Trends are unknown but the forest habitat of the species has potential for exploitation and needs to be monitored.

■ Distribution and population trends

The Black-throated Accentor comprises two subspecies; the nominate form concentrated in the northern part of the Ural mountains with an isolated population on the eastern coast of the White Sea; and the subspecies *P. a. huttoni* in central Asia with a range encompassing the Altai mountains, the south-west part of Sayan (Russia), Saur (Kazakhstan and China), Dzhungarskiy Alatau and Ketmen' (Kazakhstan), Tian-Shan (Kyrgyzstan) and the northern part of Alai mountain system (Kyrgyzstan and Tajikistan) (Portenko and Viettinghoff-Scheel 1976).

Within Europe the species breeds in the coniferous montane forests of the northern regions of the Urals from 59°40´N almost to 68°N (Danilov 1960, Danilov *et al.* 1984). Its breeding range extends as far west as Ust-Patoka in the lower course of the Stshugor river (Dmokhovsky 1933) and as far east as the Labytnangi region (Danilov *et al.* 1984). Small isolated colonies have been found near the Arctic Circle on the eastern coast of the Mezen' Bay on the White Sea, which are also the northernmost sites with spruce *Picea* (Spangenberg and Leonovich 1958).

The western subspecies winters mostly in southeast central Asia between the Tedzhen valley (southeast Turkmenistan) in the west and the Ili valley (south-east Kazakhstan) in the east (Meklenburtsev 1954, Gavrilov 1972), as well as in Iran (Hüe and Etchécopar 1970) and Afghanistan (Paludan 1959). During migration birds have been recorded in areas between the eastern coast of the Caspian Sea (Isakov and Vorobiev 1940) and Barnaul (south-west Siberia) (Velizhanin 1928).

The knowledge of the population size of the Ural subspecies is extremely poor. The majority of birds breed in the highest parts of the Urals, between Telposiz and Narodnaya peaks. On the western slopes of the subpolar Urals, in the upper catchment area of the river Bolshaya Synya, densities of 0.1–3.0 birds per 10 ha have been recorded in summer (Estafiev 1977, 1981). Early in September this form is a common migrant in the eastern parts of the northern Urals (Portenko 1937), and indeed in late October 1882 a loose flock of up to 150 birds was encountered near Orenburg (Zarudny 1888). However, given current densities and the limited distribution of the Ural subspecies, its total population size must be low, and probably of the order of a few thousand individuals (see table, map).

■ Ecology

The Black-throated Accentor breeds mainly in mountain spruce forests, often also containing birch *Betula*, fir *Abies*, pine *Pinus* or larch *Larix*, with a ground cover of either moss or grass. It is more numerous at the upper treeline, chiefly in the sparsely forested and dwarf-tree zones, with boulders or isolated rocks (Portenko 1937, Estafiev 1977, 1981). Birds forage mostly in neighbouring wet meadows intermixed with willow *Salix* bushes, in scattered forest beside streams and marshy sites, as well as in subalpine stands of larch and birch. The diet mainly consists of insects, though birds will also take other arthropods (Cramp 1988).

In the subpolar Urals birds arrive on the breeding grounds in early June. Full clutches have been found in late June, and the last individuals have departed for the winter quarters by mid-September (Estafiev 1982). Studies have shown that the breeding success of the Asian subspecies averages 56% (*n*=140) (Kovshar' 1979).

■ Threats

In general the forest habitat of Black-throated Accentor (forest–tundra zone and forest islands in tundra zone) is little exploited and the species is not currently threatened.

	Breeding population			Breeding
	Size (pairs)	Year	Trend	range trend
Russia	(1,000–2,000)	—	—	—
Total (approx.)	1,000–2,000			

Trends   +2 Large increase   +1 Small increase   0 Stable   X Extinct
(1970-1990)   –2 Large decrease   –1 Small decrease   F Fluctuating   N New breeder
Data quality **Bold**: reliable quantitative data   Normal type: incomplete quantitative data
              Bracketed figures: no quantitative data   * Data quality not provided

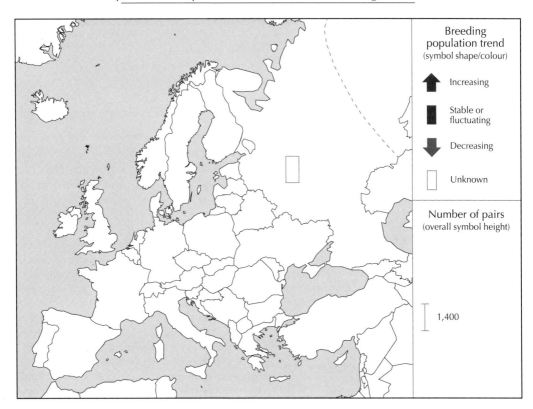

Breeding population trend
(symbol shape/colour)

▲ Increasing

■ Stable or fluctuating

▼ Decreasing

□ Unknown

Number of pairs
(overall symbol height)

1,400

■ Conservation measures

All northern forests are protected by Russian nature conservation laws. Indeed one new large reserve, the Pechoro-Ilich Biosphere Reserve (7,000 km²), lies in the southern part of the Black-throated Accentor's range in the Urals. Also the National Park of the Komi Republic (12,000 km²) is being established on the western slopes of the Urals, to the north of Pechoro-Ilich. The establishment of this park and maintenance of its habitat on the western slopes of the northern and subpolar Urals would be of considerable benefit to the conservation of the rare western subspecies.

Clearly, further studies of the Black-throated Accentor's breeding and wintering ecology are necessary in order to clarify the species' population status, to assess threats and to identify further necessary conservation measures. There is potential for exploitation of the Ural habitat to occur in future, and any such activities should be monitored.

VLADIMIR LOSKOT

Redstart
Phoenicurus phoenicurus

SPEC Category 2
Status Vulnerable
Criteria Large decline

Although widespread, the Redstart has declined markedly since the late 1960s, especially in European mid-latitudes. It is likely that this has been caused by the decline of mature forests, and a general loss of trees in secondary habitats, combined with drought in the winter quarters. The preservation of mature trees in forests and secondary habitats, and conservation measures in the wintering areas, are therefore necessary.

■ Distribution and population trends

The Redstart has a Palearctic distribution, its breeding range extending from the Atlantic and Mediterranean coasts to central Siberia, and from southern Europe north to the shores of the Arctic (Dementiev and Gladkov 1954b, Cramp 1988). The species is widespread, being absent only from oceanic islands and treeless habitats such as tundra and steppe, but is usually fairly scarce and distributed unevenly. It is migratory, wintering in the African Sahel zone and south-west Arabia.

More than half of the global breeding range is in Europe, with strongholds in the United Kingdom, France, Germany, Fennoscandia, Romania and Russia (see table, map). In previous centuries the species benefited from forest fragmentation, overgrazing and the creation of parkland in Europe. Consequently during the first half of the twentieth century the Redstart was fairly numerous and showed local increases with the exception of the United Kingdom, where declines had already been noted by the 1940s (Cramp 1988, Glutz von Blotzheim and Bauer 1988).

A sharp decline in population was evident in 1968–1969, and was especially severe in the middle European latitudes including France, Germany, Switzerland, Poland and Denmark (Berndt and Winkel 1979, Berthold *et al.* 1986, Dyrcz *et al.* 1991). During the 1970–1990 period less severe and non-synchronous local declines occurred over almost all countries from Fennoscandia to the Mediterranean, affecting in total up to approximately 80% of the European population. Increases have recently been reported only from the United Kingdom, the Provence region of France (Glutz von Blotzheim and Bauer 1988), Finland and Croatia (see table, map).

■ Ecology

Prior to man's widespread impact on European forests, the Redstart occurred in fairly open deciduous and coniferous forests and woods, preferably with natural and burnt clearings (Dementiev and Gladkov 1954b). The species now breeds also in secondary habitats including areas with scattered mature trees such as parkland, orchards, woody pastures, and gardens in human settlements.

The Redstart is versatile in its choice of nest-sites, which include tree-holes, and cavities in rock and in

	Breeding population			Breeding range trend
	Size (pairs)	Year	Trend	
Albania	(500–1,000)	81	—	—
Andorra	(3–6)	92	(0)	–1
Austria	(5,000–8,000)	—	(–1)	(–1)
Belarus	50,000–60,000	90	0	0
Belgium	6,300–7,400	81–90	–1	0
Bulgaria	(500–5,000)	—	(0)	(0)
Croatia	5,000–7,000 *	—	+1*	—
Czech Republic	30,000–60,000	—	–1	**0**
Denmark	14,000–160,000	—	–1	(–1)
Estonia	10,000–20,000	—	–1	0
Finland	**300,000–400,000**	92	**+1**	0
France	100,000–1,000,000	76	(–1)	**0**
Germany	100,000–1,000,000	—	–2	**0**
Greece	(2,000–5,000)	—	(–1)	(0)
Hungary	8,000–12,000	—	–1	–1
Rep. of Ireland	1–4	88–91	(0)	(0)
Italy	(30,000–50,000)	—	(–1)	(–1)
Latvia	60,000–100,000	—	0	0
Liechtenstein	10–30	—	–1	–1
Lithuania	1,000–15,000	85–88	(–1)	(0)
Luxembourg	7,500–10,000	—	0	0
Moldova	**35,000–50,000**	88	**0**	**0**
Netherlands	33,000–45,000	79	**–1**	**0**
Norway	50,000–500,000	90	–1	**0**
Poland	40,000–100,000	—	–2	0
Portugal	100–1,000	89	(0)	(0)
Romania	200,000–300,000	—	–1	–1
Russia	(100,000–1,000,000)	—	(–1)	(0)
Slovakia	(9,000–15,000)	—	–1	–1
Slovenia	3,000–5,000	—	–2	–2
Spain	75,000–94,000	—	–1	–1
Sweden	100,000–300,000	87	–1	**0**
Switzerland	10,000–15,000	86–91	–2	–1
Turkey	(10,000–100,000)	—	—	—
Ukraine	(9,000–10,000)	86	–1	–1
United Kingdom	90,000–330,000	88–91	+2	**–1**
Total (approx.)	1,500,000–5,800,000			

Trends (1970–1990) +2 Large increase +1 Small increase 0 Stable F Fluctuating X Extinct N New breeder
-2 Large decrease –1 Small decrease

Data quality **Bold**: reliable quantitative data Normal type: incomplete quantitative data
Bracketed figures: no quantitative data * Data quality not provided

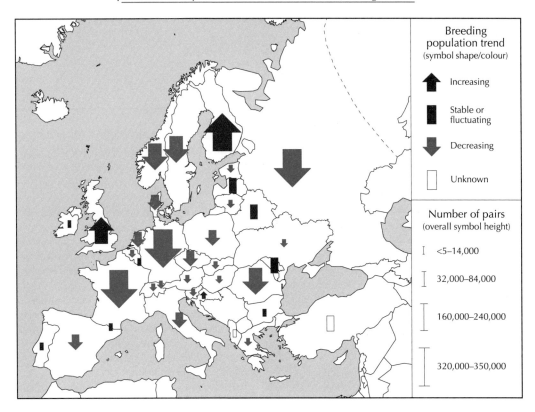

Breeding population trend (symbol shape/colour)

- Increasing
- Stable or fluctuating
- Decreasing
- Unknown

Number of pairs (overall symbol height)

- <5–14,000
- 32,000–84,000
- 160,000–240,000
- 320,000–350,000

buildings amongst trees. In boreal forests with few available tree-holes it nests in ground-holes or among tree roots (Siivonen 1935, Dementiev and Gladkov 1954b). The species has high breeding success (70–78%), at least in man-made habitats and northern forests (Järvinen 1978, Menzel 1984, Glutz von Blotzheim and Bauer 1988).

The diet varies according to the time of year and the habitat, but comprises fairly big insects (Coleoptera, Lepidoptera, Hymenoptera), spiders, other invertebrates and some fruits (Cramp 1988).

■ Threats

The slow, long-term decline of the Redstart seems to be the result of habitat loss in Europe, through the disappearance of old forests and of mature trees from secondary habitats.

The sharp decline in Redstart numbers in Europe after 1968–1969, coinciding with a severe drought in the Sahel zone (Berndt and Winkel 1979, Bruderer and Hirschi 1984), strongly suggests that decreases are at least partly due to habitat deterioration in the winter quarters. In addition, dead birds have been collected in connection with high-dose application of dieldrin and erolosulfan in tsetse fly control operations in Nigeria (Koeman et al. 1978), suggesting a possible but unproven link with pesticide use in the wintering areas.

■ Conservation measures

Measures should include the conservation of mature, fairly open deciduous and mixed forests, the conservation of mature trees in secondary habitats, and a reduction in the use of insecticides in the winter quarters. Additionally, the density of the species may be increased locally in suitable habitat by the provision of nest-boxes (Dementiev and Gladkov 1954b, Enemar 1980, Menzel 1984).

LUDWIK TOMIALOJC

Güldenstädt's Redstart *Phoenicurus erythrogaster* – see p. 389

Fuerteventura Chat
Saxicola dacotiae

SPEC Category 2
Status Vulnerable
Criteria <2,500 pairs

This very rare species comprises only 650–850 breeding pairs and is endemic to the island of Fuerteventura in the Canary Islands. Although it is vulnerable because of its small population size and its restriction to a single island, there are no currently known threats to the species. The main conservation measures suggested include the study of its biology and regular monitoring.

■ Distribution and population trends

The Fuerteventura Chat is an endemic passerine restricted to the island of Fuerteventura in the Canarian archipelago. Alegranza and Montaña Clara, two small islands to the north of Lanzarote, may have supported the species at the beginning of the twentieth century, but subsequent searches have failed to locate it; these birds were claimed to belong to a separate race, *S. d. murielae* (Bannerman 1913), but there is now doubt about the validity of this form (Collar and Stuart 1985).

Population size was estimated by Collar and Stuart (1985) as 50–150 pairs, while Collins (1984b) estimated 100–200 pairs. In both these cases the values were based on observations of the species in areas where the species was then known to occur. Subsequently, a formally designed sample survey carried out in 1985 provided a revised population estimate of 650–850 pairs (Bibby and Hill 1987), and recent observations from Canarian ornithologists indicate that the current figure may be even higher.

Insufficient data are available to provide a reliable assessment of population trends between 1970 and 1990, although there is no evidence of any major population change. The apparent increase indicated by a comparison of the estimates made during the 1980s is almost certainly a result of the different methodologies involved and does not reflect a real increase in numbers.

	Breeding population			Breeding
	Size (pairs)	Year	Trend	range trend
Spain				
Canary Islands	**750–850**	87	0	0
Total (approx.)	750–850			

Trends	+2 Large increase	+1 Small increase	0 Stable	X Extinct
(1970–1990)	–2 Large decrease	–1 Small decrease	F Fluctuating	N New breeder
Data quality	**Bold**: reliable quantitative data	Normal type: incomplete quantitative data	
	Bracketed figures: no quantitative data	* Data quality not provided	

■ Ecology

The species is widely distributed, although discontinuously, throughout the island, from mountain areas to the coast. It mainly occupies rocky or stony hillsides with very scarce vegetation cover, typically of aulaga *Launaea arborescens*, saltwort *Salsola vermiculata* and box-thorn *Lycium intricatum*, with succulent spurge *Euphorbia obtusifolia* and ragwort *Senecio kleinia*. It is also found on the edge of malpaís (lava flow) with vegetation, barrancos (watercourses) with or without water, and cultivated areas and gardens. Areas known to hold the species but at predicted low density include both the coastal plains, especially in the north and east, and the main central plains as well as the sand-covered isthmus linking the Jandía peninsula.

It feeds mainly on the ground (Bibby and Hill 1987), often among annual and herbaceous vegetation.

■ Threats

As population trends are not known, it is difficult to evaluate the real effect of potential threats on the species. The rapid development of tourist resorts does not seem, at least to date, to have had any detrimental effect. Similarly, the impact of predation by introduced mammals such as cats, rats *Rattus*, ground-squirrels and hedgehogs *Atelerix alginus* is also unknown. The long-term and continuing desertification of Fuerteventura, which 500 years ago was lush and well-wooded in places (Collar and Stuart 1985), together with water extraction and grazing by domestic and feral goats, are the most likely factors to damage the future prospects of the Fuerteventura Chat (Bibby and Hill 1987).

■ Conservation measures

The Fuerteventura Chat remains one of the scarcest species breeding in the western Palearctic and is one of the few single-island endemics to occur in the region (Bibby and Hill 1987). Its global status is classified as Near Threatened by Collar *et al.* (1994). The main conservation measures required are further studies of the species' biology, which is practically unknown, and monitoring of its numbers. In order to limit desertification of Fuerteventura the large-scale elimination of grazing animals (principally goats)

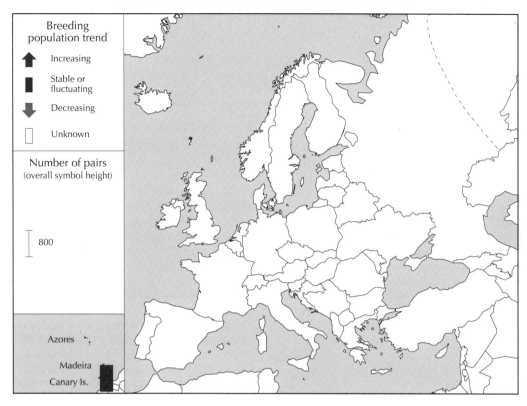

Breeding population trend

- ↑ Increasing
- ■ Stable or fluctuating
- ↓ Decreasing
- ☐ Unknown

Number of pairs
(overall symbol height)

800

Azores

Madeira

Canary Is.

would probably be required, but this would be extremely difficult. The widespread distribution of Fuerteventura Chats over most of the island makes it difficult to formulate an adequate conservation strategy. Key sites should, however, be protected. Only three of the areas important for the species are currently recognized under the new law of natural areas in the Canary Islands (La Nueva Lay de Espacios Naturales de Canarias) which has not yet been approved by Parliament. These are Parque Natural de Jandía (Important Bird Area 021), Parque Rural de Betancuria (IBA 016) and Paisaje Protegido de Malpaís Grande (IBA 019).

Morro Tabaiba and Morro Rincones are of great importance for the species but are not afforded any protection, and efforts are being made to include them under the new law. Many other areas with high densities of the species (especially rocky slopes of the interior of the mountains) are also unprotected. Ajuí–Betancuria (IBA 016) is a hunting refuge, established each year and does not necessarily have permanent status.

GUILLERMO DELGADO CASTRO

Stonechat
Saxicola torquata

SPEC Category 3
Status (Declining)
Criteria Moderate decline

The Stonechat is declining in much of north-west Europe and in parts of central Europe due to habitat loss through the intensification of agriculture. Low-intensity farming practices should be maintained and promoted to provide suitable habitat for the species.

■ Distribution and trends

The many races of Stonechat breed right across Eurasia and through a large part of Africa. Europe contains under a quarter of the global range of the species, which is distributed there from north-west Europe across southern Europe to the Caucasus, and throughout southern parts of central and eastern Europe, as well as in northern Russia (Dementiev and Gladkov 1954b, Cramp 1988, Glutz von Blotzheim and Bauer 1988). In Europe, populations

	Breeding population			Breeding
	Size (pairs)	Year	Trend	range trend
Albania	1,500–3,000	91	—	—
Andorra	20–40	91	0	0
Austria	(3,000–5,000)	—	(0)	(0)
Belgium	**1,150–1,400**	81–90	–1	–1
Bulgaria	(10,000–100,000)	—	(0)	(0)
Croatia	10,000–20,000 *	—	0*	0*
Czech Republic	2,500–5,000	—	0	**0**
Denmark	**1–1**	91	**F**	0
Finland	0–3	92	**N**	N
France	(100,000–1,000,000)	76	(–1)	**0**
Germany	800–3,700	—	–2	**0**
Greece	50,000–100,000	—	(0)	(0)
Hungary	70,000–80,000	—	+1	0
Rep. of Ireland	7,000–18,000	88–91	(–1)	(0)
Italy	(200,000–300,000)	—	(+1)	(0)
Liechtenstein	**25–25**	89	**+2**	**+2**
Luxembourg	120–180	—	–1	–1
Moldova	**4,500–6,000**	88	**0**	**0**
Netherlands	**1,800–2,300**	82	**–2**	–1
Norway	0–100	90	**N***	N
Poland	3,000–6,000	—	+1	+1
Portugal	10,000–100,000	89	(0)	0
Romania	(50,000–100,000)	—	(0)	0
Russia	(10,000–100,000)	—	(0)	(0)
Slovakia	(22,000–45,000)	—	+1	+1
Slovenia	8,000–12,000	—	+1	+1
Spain	300,000–700,000	—	–1	–1
Switzerland	**200–250**	77–79	**F**	**0**
Turkey	(10,000–100,000)	—	—	—
Ukraine	2,000–3,500	86	0	0
United Kingdom	9,000–23,000	88–91	(–2)	**0**
Guernsey	15–30	—	0*	0*
Jersey	5–10	—	–2	–2
Isle of Man [1]	90–180	—	**F**	0*
Total (approx.)	890,000–2,800,000			

Trends +2 Large increase   +1 Small increase   0 Stable   X Extinct
(1970–1990) –2 Large decrease   –1 Small decrease   F Fluctuating   N New breeder
Data quality **Bold**: reliable quantitative data   Normal type: incomplete quantitative data
Bracketed figures: no quantitative data   * Data quality not provided
[1] Population figures are included within United Kingdom totals

in the south and west are resident, while the others are partially or wholly migratory, moving in winter to the Mediterranean basin. The most northerly European birds (belonging to the west Siberian and central Eurasian race *maura*) apparently winter in South-East Asia (Dhondt 1983, Cramp 1988).

Data collated for this review suggest that up to nearly two-thirds of the European Stonechat population has declined during 1970–1990 (see table, map). The decline was noticed in the United Kingdom and western parts of Germany in the 1940s (Magee 1965, Hölzinger 1987) and spread over most of north-west Europe during the 1960s and 1970s, although several local or temporary increases were reported during this time (Glutz von Blotzheim and Bauer 1988). The decline is now evident over most of western Europe, and is affecting the important populations in France and Spain (Hölzinger 1987, Cramp 1988; see table, map).

Numbers in (for example) Poland, Hungary and Italy have risen, however, and the species' range has increased in Poland during the last 20–30 years (Glutz von Blotzheim and Bauer 1988, Tomialojc 1990, Dyrcz *et al.* 1991; see table). In the Czech Republic and Slovakia the species' population declined in the 1970s but has since stabilized and started to recover in the latter (Stastny *et al.* 1987; see table).

It should be noted that monitoring of the population size of the Stonechat only began fairly recently in most countries, so estimates of its abundance and trends may be subject to some inaccuracies.

■ Ecology

Across its range the Stonechat breeds in diverse, yet structurally similar, habitats, nesting mainly at ground level, and rarely at up to 1.2 m, in dense bushes (Frankenvoort and Hubatsch 1966). Its optimal habitat requirements comprise open areas of fallow or wasteland, on sunny southern slopes, with scattered bushes, trees or artificial structures (e.g. poles or wires) which can be used as song-posts or for perching. In temperate latitudes of Europe the original nesting habitat was probably moorland or early suc-

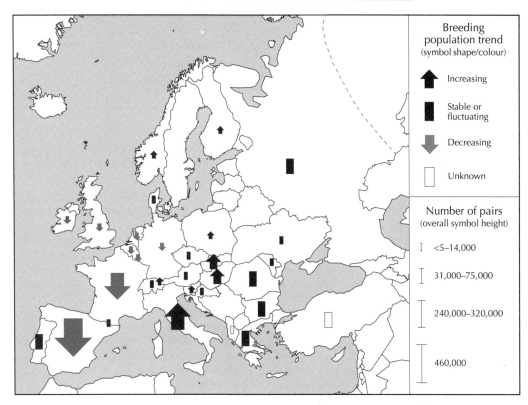

Breeding
population trend
(symbol shape/colour)

Increasing

Stable or
fluctuating

Decreasing

Unknown

Number of pairs
(overall symbol height)

<5–14,000

31,000–75,000

240,000–320,000

460,000

cessional stages after large-scale forest fires (Mildenberger 1950). Moorland, although reduced in area, still provides some suitable habitat together with heathland, Mediterranean garigue or maquis, and secondary vegetation associated with quarries and embankments alongside roads, railway lines, canals, vineyards and other warm slopes. Dry areas with poor soils are most frequently occupied.

■ Threats

The most important threat to the Stonechat is the intensification of traditionally managed habitat through changes in farming practices (Magee 1965, Hölzinger 1987). The creation of large open fields, the destruction of hedges and bushes, the transformation of pastures to arable fields, the afforestation of fallow land and moorland, and the destruction of structurally diverse vegetation by uncontrolled fire and human disturbance have all reduced the availability of habitat suitable for the species (Magee 1965, Glutz von Blotzheim and Bauer 1988).

Climate may also be responsible for large fluctuations and decreases in population size (Glutz von Blotzheim and Bauer 1988), as short-term decreases

have been observed after severe winters. Consequently, a recent series of warm summers in central Europe may have led to an extension of the species' northern breeding limit (Glutz von Blotzheim and Bauer 1988, Tomialojc 1990, Dyrcz et al. 1991).

■ Conservation measures

The conservation of the Stonechat in Europe is dependent primarily on wide-scale conservation measures aimed at the preservation of its habitat through the promotion of non-intensive farming practices (Magee 1965, Hölzinger 1987, Glutz von Blotzheim and Bauer 1988). Suggested measures include the preservation of scattered trees, bushes and hedges in fields, avoidance of afforestation of moorland and fallow areas, and maintenance of strips of infrequently mown grass (cut every 3–4 years) among intensively managed grasslands. In some countries the illegal but customary practice of burning grass on the slopes of dams and embankments should be prevented. However, traditional fire management in heathland and maquis areas is beneficial to the species but can be recommended only if legal and properly controlled.

LUDWIK TOMIALOJC

Cyprus Pied Wheatear
Oenanthe cypriaca

SPEC Category 2
Status Rare
Criteria <10,000 pairs

The endemic Cyprus Pied Wheatear numbers 3,000–7,000 pairs which are widely distributed on the island. While the species is not immediately threatened, it undoubtedly suffers from illegal trapping by Cypriot bird-limers and mist-netters, and from shooting. Closer monitoring to evaluate this threat and the enforcement of legislation to reduce it are necessary.

■ Distribution and population trends

The Cyprus Pied Wheatear is considered by some (e.g. Cramp 1988) to be a race of Pied Wheatear *O. pleschanka*, but others (notably Sluys and van den Berg 1982) have strongly advocated treatment of it as a distinct species. By contrast with *O. pleschanka*, which is widely distributed from eastern Europe across to central Asia, the Cyprus Pied Wheatear is entirely confined to Cyprus where the population, estimated at 3,000–7,000 pairs, was apparently stable between 1970 and 1990 (see table).

The species migrates between October and November, apparently on a broad front, to overwinter in southern Sudan and Ethiopia (Vaurie 1959, Urban and Brown 1971). In addition to migratory movements, altitudinal movements have been recorded within Cyprus (Flint and Stewart 1992). Direct observations (Bannerman and Bannerman 1971), supported by bird-lime capture data (see Threats, below), show that males precede females on spring migration. There is some evidence of natal site-fidelity by first-time breeders (Flint and Stewart 1992).

	Breeding population			Breeding
	Size (pairs)	Year	Trend	range trend
Cyprus	3,000–7,000	—	0	0
Total (approx.)	3,000–7,000			

Trends   +2 Large increase   +1 Small increase   0 Stable   X Extinct
(1970-1990)   –2 Large decrease   –1 Small decrease   F Fluctuating   N New breeder
Data quality   **Bold**: reliable quantitative data   Normal type: incomplete quantitative data
Bracketed figures: no quantitative data   * Data quality not provided

■ Ecology

The Cyprus Pied Wheatear is widespread on the island, chiefly in the hills and mountains up to c.1,800 m (Bannerman and Bannerman 1971). It is especially numerous on rough, rocky, open ground with scattered trees and bushes, but also occurs in montane pine forest. Although it is least common on the central plain (Stewart and Christensen 1971), its habitat embraces open lowland terrain, including cultivated land, woodland and plantations, built-up areas and suburban gardens. Trees are a significant habitat requirement, their tops being used as song-posts in the breeding season, though other high vantage points will suffice, such as buildings, boulders or overhead wires (Flint and Stewart 1992). The mainstay of the diet is surface invertebrates, supplemented seasonally by berries, and there is one breeding-season record of a bird carrying a lizard (Cramp 1988).

Breeding generally starts during the latter half of April on the plains, in early May at c.600 m in the hills, and in mid-May at 1,500–1,800 m in the Troodos forest (Ashton-Johnson 1961). Nesting birds occur in dense neighbourhood groups, especially in the hills and mountains, such that four or five singing males are often heard from one point (Christensen 1974). Accordingly, territories are relatively small, and the case of a male singing c.70 m from its nest was presumed to be typical. The nest, usually in a hole (in a wide variety of natural and man-made sites), is attended by both sexes of the monogamous pair (Ashton-Johnson 1961). Although usually single-brooded, there is one record of a double brood and a wider incidence of second broods may have been overlooked. There are records of individual families (adults and offspring) staying together for two months or more after fledging (Flint and Stewart 1992).

■ Threats

There are no major threats to the habitat of the Cyprus Pied Wheatear. Indeed, the species has shown itself adaptable to man-made alterations of habitat, especially in its readiness to exploit settled areas. The only known threat on Cyprus arises from the activities of bird-catchers using lime-sticks and mist-nets, and from shooting at migration times. In March and April 1968 at Paralimni, the main bird-liming region located in the south-east of the island, Horner and Hubbard (1982) registered the capture by bird-liming of 371 Cyprus Pied Wheatears. Of 351 sexed, 57% were males; these arrived between 10 March and 25 April, while the passage period for females started later (18 March–13 April). For both sexes, spring passage was heavy for a period of c.20 days.

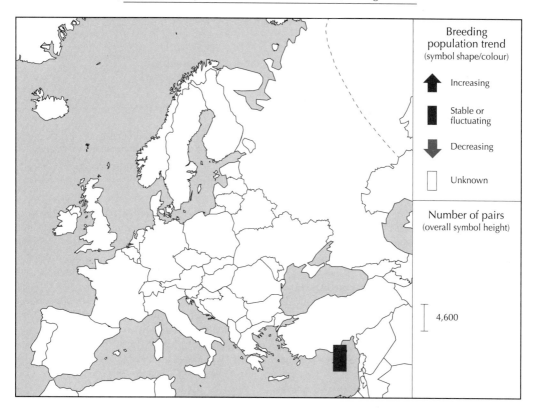

Breeding
population trend
(symbol shape/colour)

Increasing

Stable or
fluctuating

Decreasing

Unknown

Number of pairs
(overall symbol height)

4,600

The mortality inflicted on Cyprus Pied Wheatears by hunters using mist-nets and guns has not been examined. Since the introduction of legislation, the use of mist-nets has declined somewhat, but the same cannot be said for bird-liming which, although also illegal, is still very common in the parts of Cyprus where the practice is traditional (Magnin 1987, Sigg 1991).

■ Conservation measures

The conservation measures which are urgently required of Cyprus will benefit all migrants (and wintering birds) including Cyprus Pied Wheatears. Pressure needs to be kept up on the Cypriot authorities to implement and enforce existing laws against trapping. The Cyprus Pied Wheatear is fully protected by Law no. 24 of 1988 which implements the Bern Convention, of which Cyprus is a Contracting Party and under which the species is protected (Appendix II of the Convention).

Controls are needed on the use of lime-sticks, on the import, sale, and use of mist-nets, and on the trafficking and sale of birds as food in restaurants. In addition, there is a need for wider and more systematic monitoring of bird-trapping activities by independent observers (Magnin 1987, Sigg 1991).

EUAN DUNN

Black-eared Wheatear
Oenanthe hispanica

SPEC Category 2
Status Vulnerable
Criteria Large decline

Numbers have declined during 1970 to 1990 in several west European countries, including Spain, which has the largest population. The species has probably been adversely affected by changes in its winter habitat due to drought in the Sahel, but intensification of agriculture and changes in forestry practices have undoubtedly reduced suitable breeding habitat.

■ Distribution and population trends

The Black-eared Wheatear has a Mediterranean distribution in Europe, its breeding range extending east to south-west Asia and south to north-west Africa. On the basis of the range, over half the world population occurs in Europe. There are two clearly differentiated subspecies: *O. h. hispanica* in the west, and *O. h. melanoleuca* in the east.

The largest national population is in Spain, which holds over three-quarters of the European breeding population; Turkey, Croatia, Greece and Portugal also have large numbers (see table, map). Numbers of *O. h. hispanica* have fallen in the large populations of Portugal and Spain, also in Italy (Yeatman 1976, Mestre *et al.* 1987; see table, map). This subspecies has also undergone a reduction in range size. *O. h. melanoleuca* however, appears to be stable in both numbers and range, although in most countries information is poor and Turkey's population trends are unknown.

All birds winter on the southern edge of the Sahara, in a belt stretching right across Africa from Senegal to Ethiopia.

	Breeding population			Breeding
	Size (pairs)	Year	Trend	range trend
Albania	5,000–10,000	91	—	—
Bulgaria	(1,000–10,000)	—	(0)	(0)
Croatia	40,000–60,000 *	—	0*	0*
France	100–500	90	0	0
Greece	30,000–60,000	—	(0)	(0)
Italy	(1,000–2,000)	—	(–1)	(–1)
Portugal	10,000–100,000	89	–1	–1
Romania	(30–100)	—	+1	**+2**
Russia	P	—	—	—
Spain	513,000–620,000	—	–1	–1
Turkey	(50,000–500,000)	—	—	—
Total (approx.)	650,000–1,400,000			

Trends +2 Large increase +1 Small increase 0 Stable X Extinct
(1970-1990) -2 Large decrease -1 Small decrease F Fluctuating N New breeder
Data quality **Bold**: reliable quantitative data   Normal type: incomplete quantitative data
Bracketed figures: no quantitative data   * Not provided   P Present

■ Ecology

The species breeds and winters from sea-level to 2,400 m in open habitats with scattered shrubs (Panow 1974, Suárez 1988). Occasionally it also breeds in open forests of juniper *Juniperus thurifera* or holm oak *Quercus ilex*, and in open farmland including extensively managed olive-groves and vineyards. The most important habitat requirements are low vegetation cover, incorporating a large proportion of bare ground with shrubs (*Thymus, Lavandula, Salvia,* etc.) used for nesting and perching (Loskot 1983, Suárez 1980, 1988).

The diet consists of various invertebrates, principally Hymenoptera, Coleoptera and Lepidoptera larvae (Loskot 1983, Suárez 1987).

■ Threats

The decline of the European population has been attributed to drought-induced habitat changes in the Sahel winter quarters (Mestre *et al.* 1987). However, in Iberia there are two other imminent threats. Firstly, the intensification of agriculture, principally through new irrigation schemes, and the redistribution and amalgamation of farmland ownership. Secondly, the abandonment of extensive pastoralism and forestry, both of which result in an increase in vegetation cover and thus a reduction of suitable habitat. Nest predation by foxes *Vulpes* and feral dogs may also be a problem locally (Suárez and Manrique 1992).

■ Conservation measures

Recent increases in the number of sheep-grazing within Iberia have to some extent been favourable. However, in the near future, ageing rural populations and falling farm incomes may lead to further loss of extensive pastoral farmland through land abandonment or agricultural intensification. Areas subject to extensive sheep-grazing therefore need to be conserved through support for traditional pastoral farming methods.

FRANCISCO SUÁREZ

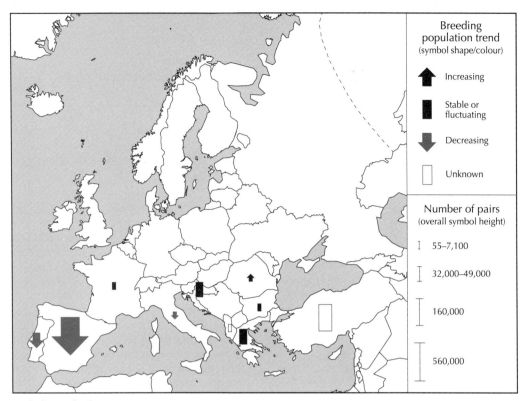

Legend (upper map)

Breeding population trend
(symbol shape/colour)

- Increasing
- Stable or fluctuating
- Decreasing
- Unknown

Number of pairs
(overall symbol height)

- 55–7,100
- 32,000–49,000
- 160,000
- 560,000

- **Black-eared Wheatear**

- **Black Wheatear** (next page)

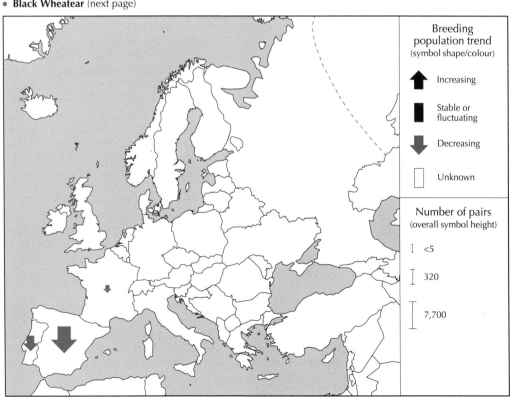

Legend (lower map)

Breeding population trend
(symbol shape/colour)

- Increasing
- Stable or fluctuating
- Decreasing
- Unknown

Number of pairs
(overall symbol height)

- <5
- 320
- 7,700

Black Wheatear
Oenanthe leucura

SPEC Category 3
Status Endangered
Criteria Large decline, <10,000 pairs

Rare in Europe, the Black Wheatear has suffered a widespread decline in range and numbers, perhaps through poor reproductive success of birds breeding in natural cavities, loss of suitable habitats, and severe winters. Necessary conservation measures are the protection of favoured habitats from afforestation and the preservation of abandoned buildings and caves.

■ Distribution and population trends

The Black Wheatear is restricted to southern Europe and north-west Africa. A quarter to half of the global breeding range lies within southern Europe, although it is scarce in this region. The majority of birds reside in Portugal and Spain, but a small population also occurs in the eastern French Pyrenees (see table). The species is mainly sedentary throughout its breeding range, although some individuals disperse after breeding, and partial altitudinal migration occurs in some mountainous regions (Cramp 1988).

The Black Wheatear declined throughout its European range between 1970 and 1990 (see table; map on previous page). In France this seems to be part of a long-term trend; Prodon (1985) stated that in the eighteenth and nineteenth centuries the species was more frequent in southern France, and in the 1950s approximately 100 breeding pairs were recorded in the region (Yeatman 1976). A decline in numbers and in the extent of the breeding range is also suggested in Spain and Portugal (see table), although there is little quantitative information available to support this. The Black Wheatear was mentioned by many authors as occurring in Gibraltar during the eighteenth and nineteenth centuries, but it had become extinct there by the 1950s (Cortés *et al.* 1980).

	Breeding population			Breeding
	Size (pairs)	Year	Trend	range trend
France	**2–5**	90	–2	–2
Portugal	100–1,000	89	–1	–1
Spain	4,000–15,000	—	–1	–1
Total (approx.)	4,100–16,000			

Trends +2 Large increase +1 Small increase 0 Stable X Extinct
(1970-1990) –2 Large decrease –1 Small decrease F Fluctuating N New breeder
Data quality **Bold**: reliable quantitative data Normal type: incomplete quantitative data
Bracketed figures: no quantitative data * Data quality not provided

■ Ecology

The habitat frequented by the Black Wheatear varies throughout its range and includes boulder-strewn sea cliffs, mountainous regions and arid stony plateaus. The basic requirements are rock walls, denuded soil or low or sparse scrub, and scattered rocks (de Juana 1980, Cramp 1988). In Spain the species reaches relatively high densities on high arid plateaus in areas of deep canyons and ravines with eroded slopes and an abundance of caves. In one such area, Hoya de Guadix (37°11´N 3°43´W), the highest density for the species of 3.8 breeding pairs per linear km of gully has been recorded (Soler *et al.* 1983).

Nesting occurs in canyons and gullies and around ruined buildings, locally in abandoned caves excavated historically by man for housing. Large numbers of stones are placed (mainly by males) inside or in front of the nest holes, an activity which may allow adjustment of reproductive activities to the quality of partners (Moreno *et al.* in press). Birds occasionally roost at the breeding site throughout the year.

■ Threats

Nest predation by snakes, rats *Rattus* spp. and foxes *Vulpes vulpes* is a common cause of reproductive failure in the Black Wheatear. Nests placed in ruined buildings and abandoned man-made caves are safer, and so breeding success there is higher than in natural cavities. Thus, the disappearance of derelict buildings and of abandoned caves in southern Spain could be a significant reason for the decline, at least locally. Cavities positioned above ground-level may be the safest from predators, although no nests higher than 3.7 m have ever been recorded, probably because of the birds' need to carry stones up to the nest (Lindén *et al.* in prep.).

Afforestation has reduced the suitability of preferred areas such as canyons and gullies, and severe winters, such as in 1985, may also cause extinctions locally (Cramp 1988).

■ Conservation measures

The preservation of abandoned buildings and man-made caves is essential for the conservation of the Black Wheatear, as these are invariably preferred over natural formations. In addition, favoured habitats such as arid stony plateaus, canyons and gullies should be protected from afforestation.

MANUEL SOLER

Güldenstädt's Redstart
Phoenicurus erythrogaster

SPEC Category 3
Status Insufficiently Known

The nominate Caucasian race of Güldenstädt's Redstart is rare and little known, forming an isolated population restricted to south-east Europe. It occupies a narrow range of habitats, in which it has low numbers and low reproductive rates. Winter habitats have also deteriorated recently. Its future depends on the maintenance of berry-bearing sea buckthorn bushes in the Caucasus mountains, the main source of winter food.

■ Distribution and population trends

There are two subspecies of Güldenstädt's Redstart. The Asian race, *P. e. grandis*, is widely distributed across the highlands of southern Siberia and central Asia, where mountainous areas surround the deserts of Mongolia and western China (Neufeldt and von Vietinghoff-Scheel 1984). The nominate subspecies is restricted to the Caucasus.

Birds in the Caucasus breed exclusively in the zone just below the snow-line between 2,800 and 3,700 m, and after the breeding season both adults and juveniles roam nomadically across the upper zones of alpine vegetation between 3,500 and 3,800 m. In winter, birds concentrate at clumps of berry-bearing bushes alongside rivers, usually at middle altitudes, though some have been recorded in the foothills (300 m) up to 60 km from the known breeding sites (Lorenz 1887).

Güldenstädt's Redstart occurs at low densities as a breeder. For example in narrow gorges 1–5 km long only one, two, or occasionally three pairs were found (Beme 1926, Baziev and Chunikhin 1963, Molamusov 1967, Lipkovich 1985, Nasrullaev 1990, Timofeev 1990, V. Loskot own data). Thus, based on the size of the breeding area and the density, total numbers of the nominate Caucasus subspecies may be roughly estimated at only 2,500–3,000 birds. The main part of this population is on the northern slopes of the central Caucasus, between Elbrus and Kazbek, following the distribution of maximum ice cover. The largest wintering aggregations, comprising up to 113 individuals in 30 ha, have been recorded within this area (Gizel'don river valley in the Terek basin), which contains bushes of sea buckthorn *Hippophae rhamnoides* (Drozdov and Zlotin 1962). Population trends are unknown.

■ Ecology

Nesting takes place in the upper ice-covered parts of gorges, at the base of rock walls, in rock crevices and on screes composed of large stones, often adjacent to areas of moraine sediment (Baziev and Chunikhin 1963, Lipkovich 1985). Patches of vegetation, typical of the snow-line belt, or alpine meadows with cold-tolerant grasses and sedges, are also required nearby. Pairs generally breed over 1 km apart.

It seems that Güldenstädt's Redstarts in the Caucasus may be characterized by a rather low reproductive rate: clutches found so far have contained not more than 4 eggs, and on average only 3.2 nestlings (n=12) have been found (Baziev and Chunikhin 1963, Lipkovich 1985, V. Loskot own data).

During summer, the diet is exclusively arthropods, mostly insects and spiders. In winter, however, birds rely primarily, and perhaps usually solely, on eating the berries and seeds of *Hippophae rhamnoides* (Beme 1926, Dementiev and Gladkov 1954b); midges can be an important food at times, birds having been seen taking large numbers near water in January–February (Drozdov and Zlotin 1962).

■ Threats

The main threat to Güldenstädt's Redstart in the Caucasus is the recent reduction in the distribution of *Hippophae rhamnoides* bushes due largely to pressure from building development (Amirkhanov *et al.* 1988). Additionally, local people collect large amounts of berries for food, often removing whole twigs rather than just the berries and so damaging the bushes.

■ Conservation measures

As in the case of another restricted-range species of the Caucasus, the Great Rosefinch *Carpodacus rubicilla*, the conservation of the species' wintering grounds and maintenance of sufficient *Hippophae rhamnoides* bushes and berries for food is essential. This is especially urgent in the upper region of the Terek river basin, where the major part of the Caucasus population of Güldenstädt's Redstart winters.

VLADIMIR LOSKOT

Rock Thrush
Monticola saxatilis

SPEC Category 3
Status (Declining)
Criteria Moderate decline

The Rock Thrush has suffered a long-term decline since the nineteenth century, especially in the northern part of its range. The causes of this decline are not certain, although the loss of habitat and climatic changes are likely reasons. Conservation of suitable montane areas is necessary to maintain populations, together with further research into the species' habitat requirements and into the reasons for the decline in numbers.

■ Distribution and population trends

The Rock Thrush is a Palearctic migrant, breeding in temperate and warm latitudes from Iberia across Eurasia to Mongolia, north to Ukraine and Lake Baikal and south to North Africa and Iran. European populations winter in Africa south of the Sahara.

Within Europe, breeding takes place in countries surrounding the Mediterranean and Black Seas, from eastern Portugal to the Ukraine, Turkey and the Caucasus. Greece and Turkey hold about half of the total numbers which breed in Europe, although Spain, Italy, Croatia, Albania and Bulgaria also have important populations (see table, map). Only relict populations now breed in central and eastern Europe. The size of the populations in many countries is poorly known, including the important ones in Italy, Bulgaria and Turkey.

The species has experienced a long-term decline in central Europe, and disappeared, for example, from Germany and Belgium as early as the end of the nineteenth century (Lippens and Willé 1972, Makatsch 1981). This decline has continued and spread throughout Europe, and the species is currently at risk of extinction in several countries in central and eastern Europe including Poland, Austria, Slovakia, Hungary and Ukraine (Tomialojc 1976, Cramp 1988). Numbers and range seem to be stable in south-east Europe, but there is no information on trends from several countries with significant populations such as Albania and Turkey.

■ Ecology

The Rock Thrush generally breeds on rocky mountain slopes and stony hills at altitudes of up to 3,800 m, always near patches of herbs or small shrubs which are used as foraging sites (Dementiev and Gladkov 1954b, Harrison 1982, Cramp 1988). Steep and sunny slopes are preferred, but birds can also be found at lower altitudes, especially in eastern Europe, where they inhabit steppe grasslands with stony outcrops (Dementiev and Gladkov 1954b). The wintering habitat in Africa consists of stony savanna and steppe areas.

Rock Thrushes feed mainly on insects such as beetles, grasshoppers and caterpillars, the usual foraging technique being to watch for prey from a perch before sallying to the ground to take it (Schmidt and Farkas 1974). Birds usually nest in crevices in crags, rock walls and ruins, or under boulders on steep ground.

■ Threats

The decline within the northern part of the Rock Thrush's European breeding range may be due to a change towards a cooler climate (Yeatman 1976), although this is questionable since other species are expanding northwards (Cramp 1988). Another possible major threat is the loss of suitable habitat for breeding and wintering. Extensive afforestation and developments linked to the tourist industry in moun-

	Breeding population			Breeding range trend
	Size (pairs)	Year	Trend	
Albania	2,000–5,000	81	—	—
Andorra	(50–80)	92	(–1)	(–1)
Austria	(30–60)	—	(–1)	(–1)
Bulgaria	(1,000–5,000)	—	(0)	(0)
Croatia	3,000–5,000 *	—	+1*	+1*
France	(500–1,000)	90	–1	**0**
Greece	10,000–20,000	—	(0)	(0)
Hungary	20–50	—	–2	–2
Italy	(5,000–10,000)	—	(–1)	(–1)
Moldova	**400–600**	89	**–1**	**–1**
Poland	0–10 *	—	—	—
Portugal	100–1,000	89	–1	–1
Romania	100–400	—	0	0
Russia	P	—	—	—
Slovakia	30–60	—	–2	**–2**
Slovenia	(200–500)	—	(0)	(0)
Spain	3,500–4,800	—	–1	–1
Switzerland	500–700	86–91	0	0
Turkey	(5,000–50,000)	—	—	—
Ukraine	20–50	86	–2	–1
Total (approx.)	31,000–100,000			

Trends (1970–1990): +2 Large increase +1 Small increase 0 Stable X Extinct –2 Large decrease –1 Small decrease F Fluctuating N New breeder
Data quality: **Bold:** reliable quantitative data Normal type: incomplete quantitative data Bracketed figures: no quantitative data * Not provided P Present

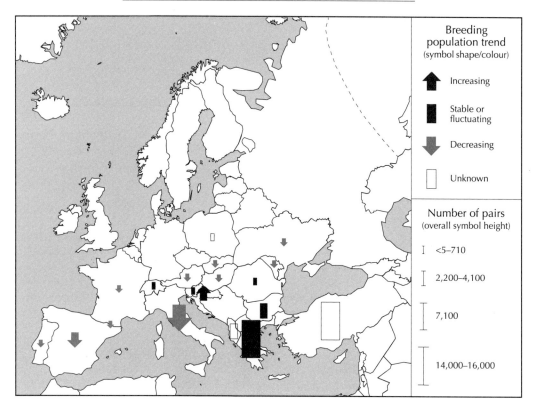

Breeding
population trend
(symbol shape/colour)

Increasing

Stable or
fluctuating

Decreasing

Unknown

Number of pairs
(overall symbol height)

<5–710

2,200–4,100

7,100

14,000–16,000

tain areas of southern Europe are resulting in the destruction of habitat (Yeatman 1976), and so may have adverse effects on the species, although there is a lack of specific information on this.

Overgrazing may also reduce the extent and quality of suitable feeding habitat locally. Conversely, the abandonment of traditional livestock rearing and other agricultural practices in mountain areas may also be a problem because of the expansion of unsuitable shrublands or forests which follows from this—a problem which has occurred notably in Spain and possibly elsewhere.

Conservation measures

The maintenance of adequate populations of the Rock Thrush through its present European range requires the conservation of extensive montane areas with a low cover of vegetation. In such areas there needs to be suitable management of land-uses such as forestry, grazing and cultivation, including the strict regulation of tourist-related developments, especially in the Mediterranean region where this species has its European strongholds.

The causes of the decline of the Rock Thrush remain largely unexplained, and further research is therefore necessary to establish the precise habitat requirements of the species and to investigate the causes and effects of habitat deterioration and destruction.

ALEJANDRO SÁNCHEZ

Blue Rock Thrush
Monticola solitarius

SPEC Category 3
Status (Vulnerable)
Criteria Large decline

Although quantitative data are lacking, the larger European populations of the Blue Rock Thrush probably declined during the 1970–1990 period. The major threat is habitat destruction due to coastal development for tourism and the construction of reservoirs. Habitat conservation measures are needed, in part through coastal-zone planning, and further research into the reasons for the species' decline is required.

■ Distribution and population trends

The Blue Rock Thrush's range extends across the southern Palearctic and Oriental regions. Approximately a quarter of the global breeding range lies within Europe, mainly in the south, with the Iberian peninsula holding a third of the European breeding population and countries bordering the Aegean Sea holding a further third. Birds also occur more sparsely in the southernmost parts of north-west and central Europe. Movements comprise long-distance and partial migration and altitudinal dispersion. European populations winter in Mediterranean countries and south to 5°N in Africa and the Middle East; some (mainly males) remain in or near the breeding areas all year, moving to lower altitudes in winter (Glutz von Blotzheim and Bauer 1988).

Portugal, Spain, Italy, Greece and Turkey support the largest numbers, but population size estimates are highly uncertain in several countries, although figures for some of the smaller populations tend to be more accurate (see map, table).

	Breeding population			Breeding
	Size (pairs)	Year	Trend	range trend
Albania	(1,000–2,000)	81	—	—
Andorra	3–5	92	N	0
Bulgaria	(50–150)	—	(+1)	(0)
Croatia	3,000–5,000 *	—	0*	0*
Cyprus	100–300	—	0	0
France	100–1,000	90	(0)	**0**
Greece	5,000–20,000	—	(0)	(0)
Italy	(10,000–20,000)	—	(–1)	(0)
Malta	200–500	—	–1	–1
Portugal	1,000–10,000	89	(0)	0
Russia	P	—	—	—
Slovenia	(10–30)	—	(0)	(0)
Spain	12,500–16,800	—	–1	–1
Switzerland	**20–25**	86–91	**0**	**0**
Turkey	(5,000–50,000)	—	—	—
United Kingdom Gibraltar	20–35	—	0	0*
Total (approx.)	38,000–130,000			

Trends (1970–1990) +2 Large increase +1 Small increase 0 Stable X Extinct
-2 Large decrease -1 Small decrease F Fluctuating N New breeder
Data quality **Bold: reliable quantitative data** Normal type: incomplete quantitative data
Bracketed figures: no quantitative data * Not provided P Present

No overall long-term population trend can be reliably demonstrated since there are no comparative censuses. However, over 1970–1990 the species probably declined in parts of France (Glutz von Blotzheim and Bauer 1988), Spain (F. Purroy pers. comm.), Italy and Malta (see table, map).

■ Ecology

The species inhabits rocky montane and coastal areas, always with some vertical structures (such as rock faces, quarries or buildings) and rich in crags, holes and crevices for nesting. Diverse vegetation may cover between 20% and 80% of the area. The proximity of water is a regular feature but it does not normally form a substantial component of the habitat. Foraging areas (bare ground and drought-resistant grasses) typically border the rocky areas or are intermixed with them. In winter birds are often found near olive-groves.

Three main habitat types are used in Spain: sea cliffs or other rocky coastlines, mountain valleys with deep gorges and canyons, and buildings such as castles, churches and ruins, even in the centres of towns (Hellmich 1992b). In Switzerland, the species mostly inhabits quarries (Cramp 1988, Glutz von Blotzheim and Bauer 1988).

■ Threats

Along the Spanish Mediterranean coast and in the Balearic Islands areas of rocky and scrubby habitat are being destroyed due to tourist and industrial developments. In the interior of Spain the recent construction of reservoirs along riverine systems has flooded many hectares of canyons and gorges frequented by the species (F. Purroy pers. comm.). However, in parts of Portugal (the Algarve) and Spain (e.g. the Mediterranean coast and Mallorca), the species nests in buildings, including those under construction, thereby possibly compensating for the loss of coastal habitats (Cary 1973, J. Hellmich pers. comm.).

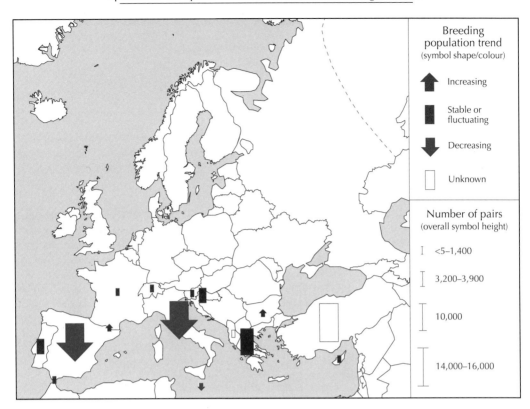

Breeding population trend
(symbol shape/colour)

↑ Increasing

■ Stable or fluctuating

↓ Decreasing

□ Unknown

Number of pairs
(overall symbol height)

I <5–1,400

I 3,200–3,900

I 10,000

I 14,000–16,000

In Malta nests are still robbed of their eggs for commercial use and the catching of birds is likely to be a significant threat (Sultana and Gauci 1982), although elsewhere it is probably unimportant (J. Hellmich pers. comm.). The local shift of birds in Malta towards inaccessible coastal areas is believed to be due to human disturbance (Sultana and Gauci 1982).

■ Conservation measures

Actions to conserve this species should include the protection of habitat in coastal regions and along inland river systems. Census and monitoring work to obtain basic information on numbers is greatly needed, especially in Portugal, Italy, Greece and Turkey. It is also imperative to conduct further research into the reasons for the species' decline, especially where no obvious causes are apparent, such as in parts of Spain and Gibraltar.

JOACHIM HELLMICH

Aquatic Warbler
Acrocephalus paludicola

SPEC Category 1
Status Endangered
Criteria Large decline, <10,000 pairs

The disappearance of this globally threatened species from western Europe and its dramatic decline in central Europe is due mainly to habitat loss through agricultural intensification. Measures are needed to preserve the remaining suitable habitat, especially fen mires, and to support non-intensive farming practices such as hand-scything and grazing in these areas.

■ Distribution and population trends

The Aquatic Warbler has a small breeding range, almost restricted to the west Palearctic at 50–60°N, though the eastern and southern limits are poorly known. At least three-quarters of the global breeding range is in Europe, with strongholds in Poland,and possibly Russia, which together may support over 90% of the world population (see table, map).

Estimates of breeding populations are complicated by the mating system, which combines polygyny and promiscuity, so it is difficult to convert counts of singing males into numbers of breeding females (Dyrcz and Zdunek 1993, Cramp 1992). The species may also occasionally be overlooked or underestimated due to its habit of singing mostly at dusk and infrequently at dawn.

Aquatic Warblers are migratory, probably wintering in West Africa (Curry-Lindahl 1981, By 1990). They occur regularly on autumn passage at coastal sites in the Netherlands, Belgium, France, United Kingdom and Portugal (By 1990).

The disjunct breeding range in Europe is the remains of a distribution which was once more continuous. Since about 1930 the species has become extinct in the former Yugoslavia, Bulgaria, Romania, Italy, Slovakia, Austria, France and the Netherlands, and is now almost extinct in Germany (Schulze-Hagen 1991). Furthermore, between 1970 and 1990 the remaining central European populations (including Poland) seem mostly to have declined,

though in Hungary numbers increased (see table, map). The Russian population is thought to be stable but its present status and size are uncertain, and there is also very little information for Belarus (where it may be extinct) and Ukraine.

The current population in Europe is possibly as few as 3,740 singing males, and the species is much the rarest and most threatened migratory passerine in the west Palearctic. It is classified as Globally Threatened (Collar *et al.* 1994) due to its small world population and further projected declines.

■ Ecology

The generally preferred breeding habitat is fen mire in river valleys, typically comprising open moorland with scattered sedge *Carex* (Wawrzyniak and Sohns 1977, Sellin 1989, Dyrcz 1993). Birds are also locally numerous in partially drained hay meadows dominated by the grasses *Molinia caerulea* or *Calamagrostis neglecta* (Dyrcz *et al.* 1984). In the Chelm district of south-east Poland the breeding marshes are calcareous, dominated by *Cladium mariscus*. In the Odra estuary and some coastal sites birds breed in the sedge-like, salt-tolerant plant community dominated by *Puccinellia* and *Spergularia* (Dyrcz and Czeraszkiewicz in press).

Throughout its range the Aquatic Warbler requires habitat rich in large insects and spiders (Schulze-Hagen *et al.* 1989) and is unusual amongst passerines in that the male never feeds the incubating female or young, so access to abundant food by the female is essential (Dyrcz 1993).

■ Threats

The highly specific requirements of the Aquatic Warbler mean that the frequent loss of habitat, mainly due to land drainage associated with agricultural and industrial development and the abandonment of traditional farming practices, is a serious threat (Dyrcz and Czeraszkiewicz in press). Areas affected include the Biebrza and Chelm marshes in Poland where the cessation of traditional hand-scything is resulting in the succession of marshland to scrub (Dyrcz and

	Breeding population			Breeding
	Size (pairs)	Year	Trend	range trend
Belarus	(0–0)	90	(X)	(X)
Germany	30–100	—	–2	–1
Hungary	**150–200**	90	+2	0
Latvia	(10–50)	—	(0)	(0)
Lithuania	(50–200)	85–88	(–1)	(–1)
Poland	2,500–7,500	—	–1	–1
Russia	(1,000–10,000)	70–90	(0)	(0)
Ukraine	1–10	90	F	F
Total (approx.)	3,700–18,000			

Trends +2 Large increase   +1 Small increase   0 Stable   X Extinct
(1970–1990) –2 Large decrease   –1 Small decrease   F Fluctuating   N New breeder
Data quality **Bold**: reliable quantitative data   Normal type: incomplete quantitative data
Bracketed figures: no quantitative data   * Data quality not provided

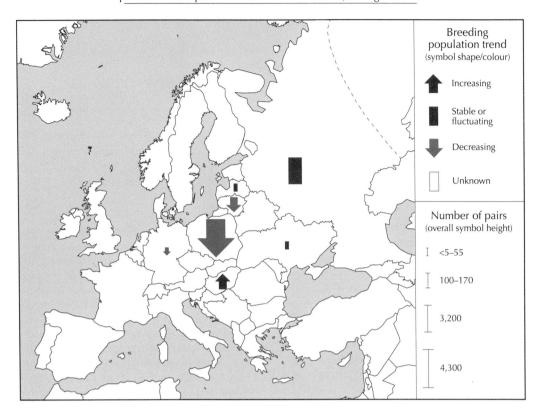

Breeding
population trend
(symbol shape/colour)

Increasing

Stable or
fluctuating

Decreasing

Unknown

Number of pairs
(overall symbol height)

<5–55

100–170

3,200

4,300

Czeraszkiewicz in press). Similarly in the Odra estuary the abandonment of extensive livestock-grazing is resulting in the expansion of dense reedbeds, which are unsuitable for the species.

The increasing use of insecticides close to breeding areas may reduce the high insect richness which is essential for successful breeding (Dyrcz 1993). Additionally, pollution from chemical factories has resulted in the loss of breeding grounds in the meadows near Jasienica in the Odra estuary (Dyrcz and Czeraszkiewicz in press).

■ Conservation measures

It is essential that full protection is given to important breeding grounds which remain unprotected,

such as the Odra estuary and (in Asiatic Russia) the Ob valley. It is also essential to stop vegetational succession by cutting and burning small areas and allowing low-intensity mowing and grazing outside the breeding season. Buffer zones should be established around protected areas where non-intensive farming and the more restricted use of insecticides are promoted.

The monitoring of singing males at selected, important breeding sites is necessary in order to learn more about population trends (Dyrcz and Czeraszkiewicz in press).

ANDRZEJ DYRCZ

Olivaceous Warbler
Hippolais pallida

SPEC Category 3
Status (Vulnerable)
Criteria Large decline

Within Europe, the Olivaceous Warbler has a mainly Mediterranean distribution, with Greece and Turkey supporting the largest populations. Numbers fluctuate considerably from year to year, but the Greek and Romanian populations appears to have declined between 1970 and 1990. This is probably due to habitat loss, particularly through the intensification of agriculture.

■ Distribution and population trends

The global distribution of the Olivaceous Warbler includes the southern Iberian peninsula, the Balkans, Turkey, northern parts of the Middle East, North Africa, parts of the Sahara and west-central Africa, and south-west and west-central Asia. Europe contains roughly a third of the world range, the major part of the European population being found in the south-east, with Greece and Turkey holding the largest numbers (see table, map). The species is migratory and winters in bushy steppe areas right across Africa, mainly south of the Sahara and north of the Equator.

Long-term population trends are poorly known, as numbers fluctuate widely and few quantitative data are available. It is believed, however, that numbers in Greece and Romania declined between 1970 and 1990, in total amounting to at least three-quarters of the population for which trends are known (see table, map). The smaller populations in Hungary, Croatia and Bulgaria increased. In Hungary this seems to have been a long-term increase, for Voous (1960) described the species' dispersal northwards into river valleys from as early as 1935. Populations appear to be stable in other European countries, but trends are unknown in Turkey.

	Breeding population			Breeding
	Size (pairs)	Year	Trend	range trend
Albania	10,000–20,000	81	(F)	(–1)
Bulgaria	(1,000–10,000)	—	(+1)	(+1)
Croatia	6,000–9,000 *	—	+1*	+1*
Cyprus	4,000–10,000	—	0	0
Greece	100,000–150,000	—	(–1)	(0)
Hungary	200–250	—	+2	+2
Portugal	100–1,000	89	(0)	0*
Romania	(2,000–5,000)	—	(–1)	(0)
Russia	P	—	—	—
Spain	500–1,300	—	(0)	(0)
Turkey	(500,000–5,000,000)	—	—	—
Total (approx.)	620,000–5,200,000			

Trends	+2 Large increase	+1 Small increase	0 Stable	X Extinct
(1970-1990)	–2 Large decrease	–1 Small decrease	F Fluctuating	N New breeder
Data quality	**Bold**: reliable quantitative data	Normal type: incomplete quantitative data	
	Bracketed figures: no quantitative data	* Not provided	P Present

■ Ecology

The Olivaceous Warbler's habitat chiefly comprises hedges, tall brambles, and brushwood consisting of willow *Salix* and tamarisk *Tamarix* (Jonsson 1982) as well as forest edges, orchards, olive-groves, poplar *Populus* plantations, gardens and parks with deciduous trees and rich undergrowth. It even occurs within villages and towns provided that some suitably dense vegetation is present for nesting. It generally avoids closed woods, preferring an alternating open and closed vegetation structure and dry biotopes of maquis or sclerophyllous scrub. Breeding occurs from sea-level up to 1,000–1,500 m, but the preference is for moist environments at lower altitudes, such as riparian woods and scrub, and edges of woodland on valley slopes (B. Hallmann own data). These habitats are rich in insects, on which the species feeds. In Greece, high breeding densities are found in river valleys, around lakes and on moist plains in the north. The smaller coastal valleys of the Aegean islands also attract considerable numbers of Olivaceous Warblers, provided that lush vegetation is present.

■ Threats

The suggested decline of the Olivaceous Warbler in Greece is likely to be due to the widespread destruction of its habitat. The clearance and burning of bushes, groves and hedges, and the drainage of land for agricultural expansion has been intensified in recent years (Baldock and Long 1987). The use of pesticides in these habitats may also adversely affect the species; aerial spraying of insecticide over scrubland against gypsy moth *Lymantria* (to anticipate the potential problem of diminishing fodder for goat-grazing), and over olive-groves, is increasing and may detrimentally affect many passerines.

Factors operating in the species' winter quarters, including drought and the use of pesticides, may also be responsible for the yearly population fluctuation in Greece.

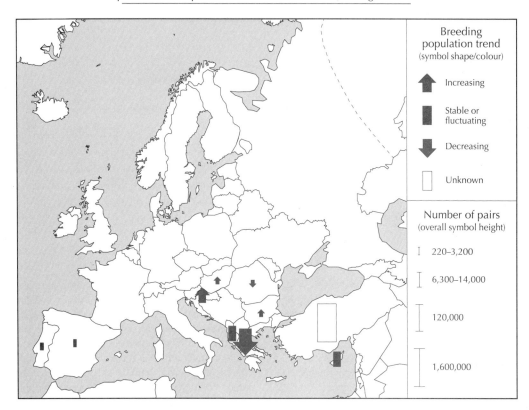

■ Conservation measures

The maintenance of traditional low-intensity farm-land with hedges, scrub and small wooded groves is needed to conserve this species. The retention of a high groundwater-table along river valleys and around lakes, and the conservation of moist scrub habitats in the plains is also essential. Such measures would also favour a rich diversity of other flora and fauna within these habitats and in traditional Mediterranean farmland.

Given the poor state of knowledge on the Olivaceous Warbler's population status, a programme of census and monitoring studies should be undertaken for this and for other similarly little-studied species of the region.

BEN HALLMANN

Olive-tree Warbler
Hippolais olivetorum

SPEC Category 2
Status (Rare)
Criteria <10,000 pairs

The current population status of this rare near-endemic to south-east Europe is poorly known, but there is some suggestion of an increase in range and numbers in Bulgaria. Although there are no apparent threats to its main habitats of open woodland and olive-groves and other cultivated trees, these are likely to be subject to forestry practices and agricultural intensification, with potentially detrimental impacts. Studies of such potential threats are therefore urgently needed; in the meantime, pesticide use should be avoided and persistent toxic compounds and aerial spraying banned.

■ Distribution and population trends

The Olive-tree Warbler occurs almost exclusively in south-east Europe with its range just creeping into Syria. There is no recent information on the numbers in Syria but they are unlikely to be more than 5% of the population and probably very much less. The species winters in East and south-east Africa.

On the basis of minimum population figures, well over half of the European total numbers occurs in Greece, with smaller populations in Croatia, Albania, Bulgaria and Turkey (see table, map). Some previous literature references to breeding in Iran and Israel were probably erroneous (e.g. Simms 1985). The available data must be treated with extreme caution for there have been no attempts to survey populations in any part of the breeding range. Some random counts in western Turkey in the 1960s and 1970s (R. F. Porter own data) suggest that the population there is likely to lie within the upper part of the population estimate which is given here. Notwithstanding this, the little information available suggests that between 1970 and 1990 numbers were stable in Greece and Croatia, but increased slightly (as did range) in Bulgaria (see table, map). There is no information available about trends over a longer time scale.

■ Ecology

The Olive-tree Warbler is a poorly known species. It occurs as a breeder in a wide range of open woodland habitats, notably oaks, pines, olives and fruit plantations (especially almond), and also in vineyards and scrub (Voous 1960, Kumerloeve 1961, Simms 1985). It is essentially a bird of the warm east Mediterranean coastlands and Greek islands, where it can be found in both the coastal plains, flat lands and hillsides. In Greece a study of bird communities in two olive plantations showed a density of 3.5 pairs per 10 ha in an old dense plantation (with 140–160 trees per ha) whereas none were found in a more sparse plantation (40–90 trees per ha). The inference from this study was that the dominant bird species of denser olive plantations are those which are typical of natural woodland and that such plantations may act as a substitute (Wietfeld 1981). Observations in western Turkey (R. F. Porter own data) suggest that relatively high densities may be found in damp woodlands (17 out of 35 singing males were in such habitat).

The diet has not been studied but is known to include insects and fig *Ficus* in autumn (Cramp 1992).

In the East African winter quarters Olive-tree Warblers occur largely in *Acacia* savanna and dry bush country (Cramp 1992).

■ Threats

The main habitat of dense or open woodland that the species' occupies in Europe and in winter in Africa is probably not currently threatened, except perhaps by local building developments in Europe, e.g. for tourism, and by fires. However, the ecology of the species is poorly known and changes in habitat structure, especially thinning or clearance of woodland and agricultural intensification in olive-groves and fruit plantations, may well have detrimental

	Breeding population			Breeding
	Size (pairs)	Year	Trend	range trend
Albania	(1,000–3,000)	81	—	—
Bulgaria	(100–1,000)	—	(+1)	(+1)
Croatia	500–1,000 *	—	0*	0*
Greece	(5,000–10,000)	—	(0)	(0)
Turkey	(1,000–10,000)	—	—	—
Total (approx.)	7,600–25,000			

Trends	+2 Large increase	+1 Small increase	0 Stable	X Extinct
(1970–1990)	–2 Large decrease	–1 Small decrease	F Fluctuating	N New breeder
Data quality	**Bold**: reliable quantitative data	Normal type: incomplete quantitative data		
	Bracketed figures: no quantitative data	* Data quality not provided		

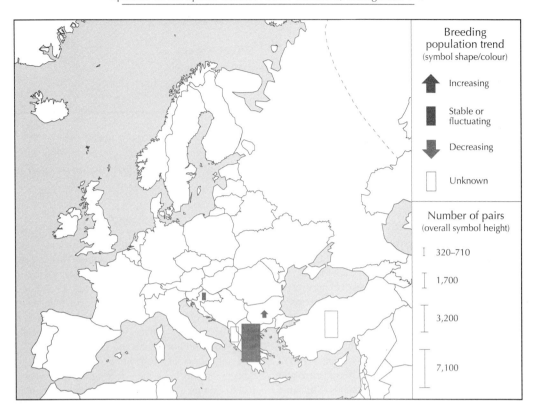

Breeding
population trend
(symbol shape/colour)

Increasing

Stable or
fluctuating

Decreasing

Unknown

Number of pairs
(overall symbol height)

320–710

1,700

3,200

7,100

effects. In particular, agricultural pesticide use, for example against olive flies *Dacus oleae*, may decrease insect prey numbers considerably. Also the aerial spraying of pesticides against forest pests such as the caterpillars of the gypsy moth *Lymantria dispar* is becoming more commonplace in Greece (B. Hallman pers. comm. 1994).

It is conceivable that bird trapping on the Greek islands may be having some impact on Olive-tree Warbler populations.

■ Conservation measures

As one of the least-studied European birds, any current assessment of its threats and conservation requirements must be treated with caution. However, it is possible to see that, with the production of fruits and olives being an important component of south-east Europe's agriculture (Greece, for example, having 706,800 ha under olives, and in Turkey 10% of the cultivated land being devoted to the production of tree crops, chiefly olives, fruit and

vines: Blake *et al*. 1987), the maintenance of a major component of the Olive-tree Warbler's habitat will be through normal economic (and cultural) factors. These are likely to continue to be favourable, although it is essential that funding to assist olive production (through, for example the EU 'oils and fat' regimes) should favour old traditional plantations and management. The intensification of forestry and agricultural practices may well be detrimental and should therefore be urgently studied. In the meantime, the use of broad-spectrum pesticides should be avoided wherever possible through the encouragement of integrated pest control measures. Toxic products of high persistence in the environment, and the use of aerial spraying, should also be banned for the benefit of this and many other species affected by these practices. A survey of the Olive-tree Warbler's population status is also clearly needed as well as further studies of the species' ecological requirements, especially its relationship with the various forms of olive plantations.

RICHARD PORTER

Dartford Warbler
Sylvia undata

SPEC Category 2
Status Vulnerable
Criteria Large decline

The major part of the global population of Dartford Warbler occurs in Spain where the species is suffering from a slow and progressive decline of suitable habitat. It is necessary to develop wide-scale conservation measures for the bird's habitat throughout its range and to further investigate its population size and habitat requirements in Iberia.

■ Distribution and population trends

The Dartford Warbler is restricted to the western part of the Mediterranean region, and almost the entire population breeds within Europe, except for that part which breeds in a narrow belt across north-west Africa from Morocco to Tunisia. The species is mainly resident, although the young disperse over quite large distances (Bibby 1979). Populations breeding in montane regions migrate altitudinally during the winter to warm lowland areas (Sánchez 1989), and some French populations leave the northern part of their range for more southern latitudes (Muntaner *et al.* 1983), some European birds then reaching north-west Africa (Tellería 1981, Cramp 1992).

Spain harbours probably more than three-quarters of the world population of Dartford Warblers, although the exact numbers are unknown. Large populations also occur in the south of France and in Italy and Portugal.

Available data suggest that, at least in some parts of Spain, this species has suffered a slow but progressive decline since the early 1970s (Muntaner *et al.* 1983). Throughout the rest of its range, populations appear to be stable or fluctuating (see table, map). In the United Kingdom there has been quite a large contraction of the breeding range during the twentieth century (Simms 1985), although between 1970 and 1990 the range increased and the population fluctuated in size.

	Breeding population			Breeding
	Size (pairs)	Year	Trend	range trend
Andorra	(10–20)	92	(0)	0
France	100,000–1,000,000	76	(F)	0
Italy	(10,000–30,000)	—	(0)	(0)
Portugal	10,000–100,000	89	(0)	0
Spain	1,700,000–3,000,000	—	–1	–1
United Kingdom	**1,100–1,100**	92	F	+2
Jersey [1]	**10–20**	92	–2	–2
Total (approx.)	1,800,000–4,100,000			

Trends   +2 Large increase   +1 Small increase   0 Stable   X Extinct
(1970–1990)   –2 Large decrease   –1 Small decrease   F Fluctuating   N New breeder
Data quality   **Bold**: reliable quantitative data   Normal type: incomplete quantitative data
Bracketed figures: no quantitative data   * Data quality not provided
[1] Population figures are included within United Kingdom totals

■ Ecology

The preferred habitat of Dartford Warblers in southern Europe is Mediterranean maquis. This is composed of a variety of dense sclerophyllous and thorny bushes of low to moderate height (up to 150 cm), including *Cistus*, *Halimium* and *Genista*. In the north of its range typical habitats are lowland heath (up to 60–150 cm tall) dominated by gorse *Ulex* and heaths *Erica* and *Calluna* (Bibby and Tubbs 1975).

Large areas of heath always contain a higher density of territories than do fragmented, isolated pieces (Simms 1985). The species shows some preference for maritime regions and islands but in the south of its range it extends to uplands, reaching 900 m in the Pyrenees (Afree 1975, Muntaner *et al.* 1983), 1,700 m in the Sistema Central mountains of the Iberian peninsula (Tellería and Potti 1984, Sánchez 1991) and up to 1,950 m in the Sierra Nevada (Pleguezuelos 1992). Outside the breeding season and mainly in winter, Dartford Warblers can also be found in open agricultural plains with some scrub.

■ Threats

The main threats to the species are the destruction, fragmentation and degradation of its habitat throughout its range, as a result of agricultural intensification, forestry and urban development (Bibby and Tubbs 1975, Batten *et al.* 1990, Santos and Alvarez 1990). There have consequently been heavy losses in some of the most valuable habitats in Spain including the Mediterranean maquis (de Juana *et al.* 1988).

The frequent fires that occur during the summer months in vast areas of scrub in Spain (548,427 ha between 1989 and 1992: ICONA 1993) are highly detrimental to this species. Also, plant disease has affected some areas of scrub inhabited in the United Kingdom (Simms 1985) and in the south of Spain (20,010 ha affected in south-west Spain during 1990–1991: ICONA 1991).

Given that the species is resident for the most

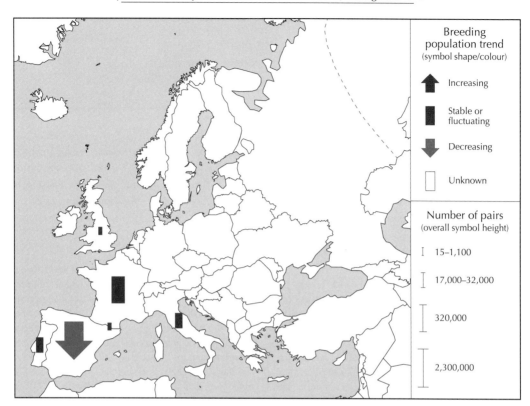

Breeding
population trend
(symbol shape/colour)

Increasing

Stable or
fluctuating

Decreasing

Unknown

Number of pairs
(overall symbol height)

15–1,100

17,000–32,000

320,000

2,300,000

part, harsh winters cause declines in the population which frequently reduce numbers to critical levels (Simms 1985).

■ Conservation measures

It is necessary to promote studies to further investigate the habitat requirements of this warbler in the south of its range. Mediterranean maquis, and lowland heaths which support key populations, should be conserved. The protection of such areas may be improved by their designation as Special Protection Areas in accordance with the EU Wild Birds Directive. Measures under the EU Agri-environment Regulation (EC Reg. 2078/92) could also be used to reduce the destruction or fragmentation of large shrubland areas through overgrazing or other detrimental agricultural activities. Fire prevention and the control of reforestation, invasive trees and plant diseases are also necessary for the conservation of these habitats.

FRANCISCO J. CANTOS

Cyprus Warbler *Sylvia melanothorax* – see p. 437

Orphean Warbler
Sylvia hortensis

SPEC Category   3
Status   Vulnerable
Criteria   Large decline

The Orphean Warbler is a patchily distributed species that is declining in its European stronghold in Spain, as well as in Italy. The loss and deterioration of habitat through agricultural intensification is thought to be the main reason for the decline of the species, although this is not certain. Further studies of the species' habitat requirements are necessary, but the maintenance of traditional, low-intensity management of olives, fruits and cork oaks, the main habitats of the species, are prudent conservation measures.

■ Distribution and population trends

The Orphean Warbler has a patchy breeding range that extends across southern Europe, north-west Africa, Asia Minor, Transcaucasia and south-central Asia. Probably about half of the species' world range lies within Europe, although the exact distribution is poorly known. The species is migratory, with European birds moving to Africa, just south of the Sahara, in winter. The wintering range of the western race *hortensis* lies in a band from Senegal across to western Sudan, and the race breeding in south-east Europe, *crassirostris*, winters in eastern Sudan and Ethiopia (Cramp 1992).

The most important European stronghold is on the Iberian peninsula where Spain has more than 80% of the total European population (see table, map). Coastal parts of Croatia, Greece (including the islands) and Turkey locally harbour good numbers of birds (see table, map), but little is known about either the distribution or population sizes in these countries (see table).

Population trends also are poorly known, but declines have been suggested for the 1970–1990 period in the important Spanish population and in Italy, where numbers have fallen rapidly (see table, map).

	Breeding population			Breeding range trend
	Size (pairs)	Year	Trend	
Albania	(1,000–2,000)	81	—	—
Bulgaria	(100–1,000)	—	(+1)	(+1)
Croatia	10,000–15,000 *	—	0*	0*
France	(500–1,000)	90	F	0
Greece	(3,000–10,000)	—	(0)	(0)
Italy	(1,000–2,000)	—	(–2)	(–1)
Portugal	100–1,000	89	(0)	(0)
Spain	170,000–440,000	—	–1	–1
Switzerland	**10–15**	86–91	**0**	**0**
Turkey	(5,000–50,000)	—	—	—
Total (approx.)	190,000–520,000			

Trends	+2 Large increase	+1 Small increase	0 Stable	X Extinct
(1970–1990)	–2 Large decrease	–1 Small decrease	F Fluctuating	N New breeder

Data quality   **Bold**: reliable quantitative data   Normal type: incomplete quantitative data
Bracketed figures: no quantitative data   * Data quality not provided

■ Ecology

Orphean Warblers occur in a range of open woodland habitats, usually dominated by oaks *Quercus*, especially cork oak *Q. suber*. They are also present in groves of olives and fruit trees, with open areas of richly structured and often grazed maquis vegetation, mostly on warm south- and west-facing slopes, as well as in park-like habitats such as non-intensive farmland with hedges and trees. In south-east Europe, such habitats are often shared with the Olive-tree Warbler *Hippolais olivetorum*. Orphean Warblers breed mainly in lower middle altitudes but they also occupy mountain foothills as well as coastal zones.

Like Barred Warbler *S. nisoria* and Whitethroat *S. communis*, the territorial and courtship behaviour of Orphean Warbler often includes flying over low maquis and open spaces between clumps of trees where it climbs up to sing.

Food taken chiefly comprises invertebrates, but also berries, gathered at all levels from low scrub to high oaks (Cramp 1992).

■ Threats

The loss and deterioration of woodlands through agricultural intensification, including those under fruit or olive production, is probably the main potential threat to the species. Also, diminishing grazing levels in maquis and within groves of trees decreases the open character and structure of the habitats which the species requires. Small fires may temporarily destroy habitat but may be beneficial in the long term by opening up woods and brushwood areas.

■ Conservation measures

The Orphean Warbler's habitat requirements need to be further studied in order to ascertain more fully the reasons for its declines and for the apparent gaps in its distribution, as well as to identify the conservation measures which need to be undertaken. Meanwhile, low-intensity land-use practices and the

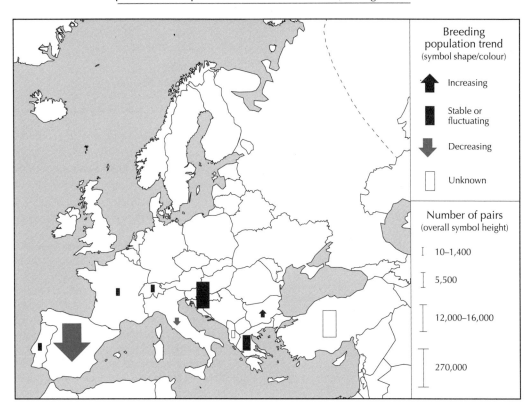

traditional management of olives, fruit trees and orchards should be maintained, as these are likely to be important components of the species' habitat. One mechanism for achieving this objective, within the EU, is the Agri-environment Regulation (EC Reg. 2078/92) of the Common Agricultural Policy, which includes proposals for the support of traditional olive-farming systems.

BEN HALLMANN

Spotted Flycatcher
Muscicapa striata

SPEC Category 3
Status Declining
Criteria Moderate decline

This widespread and common species has declined in over a quarter of its population. Reasons are uncertain but may include a spell of cooler and wetter summers in Europe, and habitat degradation and possibly droughts in Africa. Further research is needed, but a reduction in pesticide use and the protection of favoured habitats are prudent conservation measures.

■ Distribution and population trends

Breeding occurs through most of Europe, with the exception of the northern tundra and central and southern Turkey. The Spotted Flycatcher is a trans-Saharan migrant, the majority wintering south of the Equator.

The European strongholds are in Sweden, Finland, Russia and Belarus (see table, map), which together hold about 70% of the population.

Breeding numbers fluctuate markedly, as reported from the United Kingdom, Finland and Russia (Dementiev and Gladkov 1954b, Peklo 1987), so it is difficult to judge population trends, but data suggest that during 1970–1990 between a quarter and a half of the European population experienced some decline, including the sizeable populations in the United Kingdom, Finland (Koskimies 1993a), Germany and Spain (see table, map). In the United Kingdom, despite marked short-term fluctuations, substantial declines have occurred, at least in farmland and woodland, and by 1988 numbers were down to nearly a quarter of the level in the 1960s (Marchant et al. 1990). Comparison between atlas data for 1968–1972 and 1988–1991 showed a range decline of 2% in Britain and 18% in Ireland (Gibbons et al. 1993). A clear (but not strong) decline has taken place in Finland over the last 50 years (Koskimies 1993a).

In contrast, long-term data in Sweden and the Netherlands indicate stable but fluctuating populations (Hustings 1988, SOVON 1988), and although an overall decline was observed in Germany this was not the case in Rheinland (Mildenberger 1984) or Bavaria (Wüst 1986). A decline was also previously reported in Denmark (DOFF 1989), but during 1970–1990 the population there was stable overall (see table). A 19-year study in a protected primeval forest in Poland also recorded a stable population (Tomialojc and Wesolowski in prep.).

■ Ecology

This widespread species is dependent on exposed perches and adequate space to make aerial sallies for flying insects. It thus normally avoids both open areas and dense forests. Typically it occurs in habitats with well-spaced mature trees, such as fairly open forest, parkland, wooded farmland, orchards

| | Breeding population | | | Breeding |
	Size (pairs)	Year	Trend	range trend
Albania	(2,000–5,000)	81	—	—
Andorra	(20–60)	92	(0)	0
Austria	(25,000–40,000)	—	(0)	(0)
Belarus	1,350,000–1,450,000	90	0	0
Belgium	10,000–14,000	81–90	0	0
Bulgaria	(1,000–10,000)	—	(0)	(0)
Croatia	20,000–25,000 *	—	+1*	0*
Cyprus	(10–30)	—	(0)	(0)
Czech Republic	30,000–60,000	—	–1	**0**
Denmark	7,000–92,000	87–89	0*	—
Estonia	100,000–200,000	—	(0)	0
Finland	**2,000,000–3,000,000**	92	**–1**	**0**
France	100,000–1,000,000	76	(0)	0
Germany	200,000–600,000	—	–1	**0**
Greece	10,000–30,000	—	(0)	(0)
Hungary	80,000–120,000	—	0	0
Rep. of Ireland	30,000–30,000	88–91	(–1)	(0)
Italy	(50,000–200,000)	—	(0)	(0)
Latvia	200,000–400,000	—	0	0
Liechtenstein	150–250	—	0	0
Lithuania	10,000–20,000	85–88	(–1)	(0)
Luxembourg	800–1,000	—	0	0
Malta	3–5	—	0	0
Moldova	**17,000–25,000**	88	**0**	**0**
Netherlands	**50,000–100,000**	79	**–1**	**0**
Norway	100,000–500,000	90	0	**0**
Poland	(150,000–300,000)	—	0	0
Portugal	100–1,000	89	(0)	(0)
Romania	(50,000–100,000)	—	0	**0**
Russia	(1,000,000–10,000,000)	—	(0)	(0)
Slovakia	(65,000–150,000)	—	(0)	**0**
Slovenia	15,000–20,000	—	0	0
Spain	640,000–690,000	—	–1	–1
Sweden	500,000–1,200,000	87	**0**	**0**
Switzerland	30,000–60,000	86–91	0	0
Turkey	(5,000–50,000)	—	—	—
Ukraine	95,000–105,000	88	–1	–1
United Kingdom	130,000–130,000	88–91	–2	**0**
Guernsey [1]	20–50	—	0*	0*
Jersey [1]	40–50	—	0	0
Isle of Man [1]	25–50	—	0	0*
Total (approx.)	7,100,000–21,000,000			

Trends (1970–1990): +2 Large increase +1 Small increase 0 Stable –1 Small decrease –2 Large decrease F Fluctuating X Extinct N New breeder

Data quality: **Bold**: reliable quantitative data Normal type: incomplete quantitative data Bracketed figures: no quantitative data * Data quality not provided

[1] Population figures are included within United Kingdom totals

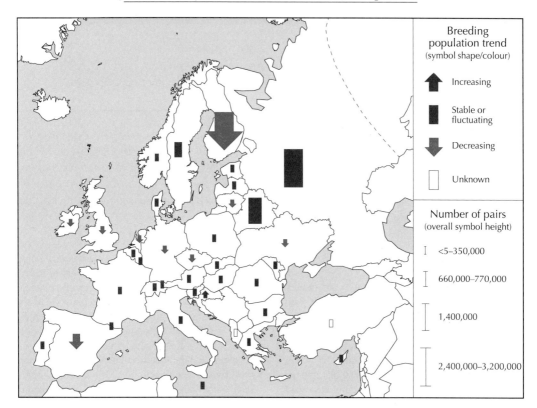

Breeding
population trend
(symbol shape/colour)

Increasing

Stable or
fluctuating

Decreasing

Unknown

Number of pairs
(overall symbol height)

<5–350,000

660,000–770,000

1,400,000

2,400,000–3,200,000

and gardens at up to 2,000 m (Dementiev and Gladkov 1954b, Peklo 1987, Cramp and Perrins 1993). Deciduous woodlands are mostly preferred, but in northern Europe it occurs in spruce *Picea* or pine *Pinus*. In denser habitats it prefers woodland edges, clearings and glades or occurs alongside streams or open water where there is sufficient space and prey for hunting (Cramp and Perrins 1993).

Nests are located mainly in holes and crevices in trees, man-made constructions and rocks (Malchevskiy and Pukinskiy 1983, Golovan 1985), and are fairly open and vulnerable to predation, especially from corvids, rodents and woodpeckers (Glutz von Blotzheim and Bauer 1993).

The food is chiefly Diptera and Hymenoptera (Cramp and Perrins 1993), and in bad weather items may be taken directly from vegetation, or from the ground, while in autumn berries may be eaten (Dementiev and Gladkov 1954b, Davies 1977, Malchevskiy and Pukinskiy 1983). Sensitivity to weather is such, however, that broods often starve to death after a week of cool, wet conditions (Crick in Gibbons *et al.* 1993), and breeding success is significantly higher in warm summers.

■ Threats

There are no clearly demonstrated threats, and the observed declines may be due to weather influenc-

ing breeding success or winter survival (Marjakangas 1982, Marchant *et al.* 1990). The early periods of recent summers have been relatively cool and wet, at least in the United Kingdom, and there is also some correlation between large declines in British Spotted Flycatcher populations and failures of the Sahel rains in 1983 and 1984 (Marchant *et al.* 1990). However, there was only a small decline in the species in 1969, when the Sahel rains failed and caused a crash in Whitethroats *Sylvia communis* and Sand Martins *Riparia riparia* (Winstanley *et al.* 1974, Cowley 1979). Furthermore, the lack of a widespread European decline in the species suggests that local factors may be involved.

There is some evidence that the United Kingdom decline is more evident in the south and may be due to habitat degradation or, more plausibly, to the widespread use of insecticides (Marchant *et al.* 1990). The loss of trees in farmland is widespread and may also be a factor leading to local declines.

■ Conservation measures

As the reasons for the decline are uncertain, the main requirement is for further research. The species would meanwhile benefit from the protection of its favoured mature woodland habitats, a reduced use of broad-spectrum insecticides, and the maintenance of mature trees in farmland, parkland and gardens.

LUDWIK TOMIALOJC

405

Semi-collared Flycatcher
Ficedula semitorquata

SPEC Category 2
Status (Endangered)
Criteria Large decline, <10,000 pairs

The Semi-collared Flycatcher breeds in low numbers in the Balkans, Turkey and the Caucasus. Its population status is very poorly known, but numbers are considered to be declining in Greece. Main habitats, chiefly comprising old beech and riparian woodlands, are restricted to small parts of the region and are highly threatened by forestry, changes in land-use and their vulnerability to hydrological changes. The protection of the species therefore depends primarily on the conservation of this habitat. Nest-box provision is of local benefit.

■ Distribution and population trends

The Semi-collared Flycatcher breeds in the Balkans, Turkey, an area adjoining the northern and eastern part of the Black Sea, the Caucasus and north-west Iran, roughly 70% of the world range lying within Europe. The species has a localized distribution within its overall range, since its habitat of old, moist forest is naturally restricted in extent. The winter quarters lie south of the Sahara, but the fact that the population is small and restricted, combined with identification difficulties and the previous treatment of the species as a race of *Ficedula albicollis*, has resulted in there being only an incomplete knowledge of the migration routes and exact wintering areas (Cramp and Perrins 1993). During spring migration, the species is common in Egypt but scarce in adjacent zones of North Africa.

The species is very poorly known, and population sizes are uncertain throughout its breeding range. In Greece, it occurs in the north, and overall numbers are declining locally in the central mainland and in the Peloponnese. In Bulgaria, it breeds mainly in the mountains in the central and western parts of the country and along the Black Sea coast; populations are thought to be stable. The species' population status in Russia and trends in Turkey are unknown.

	Breeding population			Breeding
	Size (pairs)	Year	Trend	range trend
Bulgaria	(500–5,000)	—	(0)	(0)
Greece	(1,000–5,000)	—	(–1)	(0)
Russia	P	—	—	—
Turkey	(1,000–10,000)	—	—	—
Total (approx.)	2,500–20,000			

Trends (1970-1990) +2 Large increase +1 Small increase 0 Stable X Extinct -2 Large decrease -1 Small decrease F Fluctuating N New breeder

Data quality **Bold**: reliable quantitative data   Normal type: incomplete quantitative data   Bracketed figures: no quantitative data   * Not provided   P Present

■ Ecology

In Greece, the preferred habitat of Semi-collared Flycatcher is mostly old, riparian woods of plane *Platanus orientalis* and alder *Alnus glutinosa* along streams and rivers, mostly in hilly country at lower altitudes. Other old, deciduous woods without much undergrowth, including parks and orchards (Hollom *et al.* 1988), are also used. As human habitation in Greece is traditionally situated close to springs or running water, together with large, shady plane trees, it is not unusual for birds to occur within villages and towns. Even a few large trees near a spring within a village may support breeders. Such environments are also plentiful in food.

In Bulgaria, the species prefers two main habitats: old beech *Fagus sylvatica* forests from sea-level to 1,500 m, and, along the Black Sea coast, old riparian woods (longozes) dominated by ash *Fraxinus oxyphylla* and oak *Quercus pedunculiflora*. Breeding also occurs in mixed forests of beech and spruce *Picea abies* and in coniferous forests of pine *Pinus nigra* and spruce (Donchev 1961, 1970, 1974, Paspaleva-Antonova 1964, P. Iankov pers. comm.). The species takes insects, hunting for them mainly from the crowns of large trees.

Semi-collared Flycatchers nest chiefly in tree-holes, especially in plane trees, a species which sheds branches easily, and also in alder. Nest-boxes are freely used in Bulgaria (Donchev 1961, Paspaleva-Antonova 1964), the optimum height being 2.5–4.5 m (P. Iankov pers. comm.). Breeding has also been successful in a wooden pylon in the central Balkans (Georgiev and Alexandrov 1988). Bulgarian breeders arrive in mid-April (Paspaleva-Antonova 1964), build nests in early May (Georgiev and Alexandrov 1988) and incubate to mid-June (Donchev 1961), though early young hatch by mid-May (Paspaleva-Antonova 1964).

■ Threats

Although the large plane trees and gallery woodland along streams, and certainly those in and near villages, have been traditionally respected and pro-

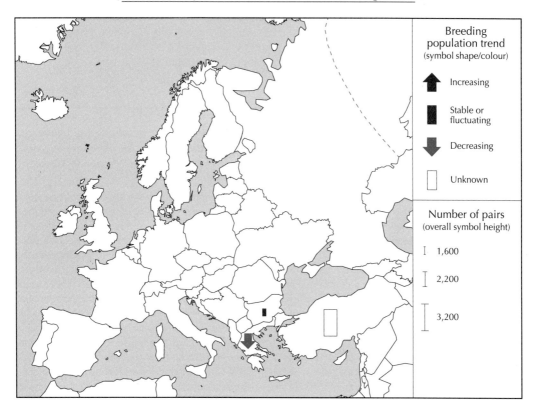

Breeding
population trend
(symbol shape/colour)

Increasing

Stable or
fluctuating

Decreasing

Unknown

Number of pairs
(overall symbol height)

1,600

2,200

3,200

tected, these old forests are currently threatened by exploitation for the production of timber. This has become more prevalent recently in several regions in Greece including Thessalia and Thrace (B. Hallmann own data). This habitat is also threatened by changing agricultural practices and by related hydrological alteration, and by the construction of large reservoirs. Mature forests supporting Semi-collared Flycatchers are also being destroyed by forestry and forest-fires. There may be other damaging factors operating outside the breeding areas since the desertion of some sites traditionally used for nesting cannot be explained.

■ Conservation measures

In order to conserve the Semi-collared Flycatcher's habitat, important areas of riparian woodland (par-

ticularly with large, old trees) need to be protected. Many of these woodlands are presently drying out as groundwater is extracted for agriculture, and such activities should be carefully managed in valleys and plains where these woods survive. Old *Platanus* woodlands should also be protected from exploitation for firewood. In Bulgaria, populations of Semi-collared Flycatcher increase locally after the provision of nest-boxes (P. Iankov *in litt.* 1994).

Further research into the species' distribution, population status and ecology is clearly required.

BEN HALLMANN

Corsican Nuthatch
Sitta whiteheadi

SPEC Category 2
Status Vulnerable
Criteria <2,500 pairs

The Corsican Nuthatch has an extremely limited range and a very small population size. Endemic to the island of Corsica, it depends mainly on Corsican pine forests and its conservation relies on the appropriate management of this habitat.

■ Distribution and population trends

The Corsican Nuthatch is endemic to the island of Corsica (France). It belongs to an 'old' group of three closely related Mediterranean nuthatches ('Mesogean Nuthatches') which includes the relict Algerian Nuthatch *S. ledanti* and the Krüper's Nuthatch *S. krueperi*. Restricted to the coniferous mountain forests of Corsica, this bird has an extremely limited range. In the late 1950s, Löhrl (1960, 1961) gave a first, approximate population-size estimate of 3,000 breeding pairs, based on a forest area of 437.5 km². In the early 1980s, Brichetti and Di Capi (1985) estimated a population of 2,000 pairs based on an area of suitable forest habitat of 240 km². Löhrl's estimate of forest area was probably much more all-embracing than that of Brichetti and Di Capi since the area of suitable forest habitat certainly was not halved between the late 1950s and the early 1980s.

Although in some areas populations are known to have decreased during recent decades due to forest exploitation or burning, there is no evidence for a significant global reduction in suitable habitat area, or of an overall population or range decline.

The species' global status is classified as Near Threatened because of its small world population size and range (Collar *et al.* 1994).

	Breeding population			Breeding
	Size (pairs)	Year	Trend	range trend
France	2,000–3,000	90	0	**0**
Total (approx.)	2,000–3,000			

Trends   +2 Large increase   +1 Small increase   0 Stable   X Extinct
(1970–1990) –2 Large decrease   –1 Small decrease   F Fluctuating   N New breeder
Data quality **Bold**: reliable quantitative data   Normal type: incomplete quantitative data
             Bracketed figures: no quantitative data   * Data quality not provided

■ Ecology

The optimal habitat of the species is highly specialized and fragmented, consisting of old stands of Corsican pine *Pinus nigra laricio*, located between 1,000 and 1,500 m, with abundant dead and rotting trunks for nest-sites. Suboptimal habitats include forests where Corsican pine is associated with cluster pine *P. pinaster*, balsam fir *Abies alba* or beech *Fagus sylvatica* and younger stands or exploited forest of Corsican pine. Average densities in these habitats are much lower than those in optimal habitat (0.24 compared to 1.13 pairs/10 ha: Brichetti and Di Capi 1985). Another suboptimal habitat in which Corsican Nuthatch occurs is cluster pine forests above 800 m: in the south of Corsica, point counts gave much lower contact frequencies (29%) in such forests than in Corsican pine forests (62%) (Rocamora in prep.). Beck (in press) also found the species in cluster pine forests, and with much lower densities than in Corsican pine forests. He also found higher average densities in Corsican pine forest than those given by Brichetti and Di Capi (1985). This suggests that the current population size estimate of 2,000 pairs, which does not take into account cluster pine forests, should be considered a minimum (see table, map).

Nesting takes place in dead or rotten, mature trees of Corsican pine, and the nest itself is often built in feeding excavations or uncompleted nest-holes of Great Spotted Woodpecker *Dendrocopos major*, a species which may prey on the nestlings of Corsican Nuthatch.

The Corsican Nuthatch is sedentary except for altitudinal movements in winter, and it may then be found in forests of holm oak *Quercus ilex* or sweet chestnut *Castanea sativa* (Thibault 1983). Adults can remain territorial during winter and high densities have been found then in cluster pine forest (Matthysen and Adriensen 1989).

Food during the winter is probably mainly pine seeds, and in the breeding season insects.

■ Threats

Factors limiting the local distribution and population size of the Corsican Nuthatch are avalanches, which reduce the area of woodland and break off many dead trees; forest burning, which can destroy extensive areas of suitable feeding habitat; and the felling of older, dead or rotten trees in commercially managed forests (Brichetti and Di Capi 1987). Although less than a third of the area of Corsican pine is

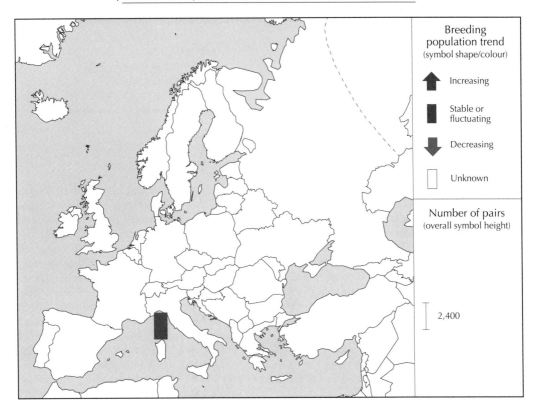

Breeding
population trend
(symbol shape/colour)

▲ Increasing

■ Stable or
fluctuating

▼ Decreasing

☐ Unknown

Number of pairs
(overall symbol height)

2,400

intensively managed at present, and forest fires are uncommon at high altitudes, these two factors are considered to be the major threats. Furthermore, the very limited range and population size of the species makes it highly vulnerable to these and to less predictable threats such as disease or climatic change. Indeed, global warming in future decades could reduce the area of Corsican pine on the island and thus be a major threat to the nuthatch's survival.

■ Conservation measures

Due to its highly specialized habitat, conservation of the Corsican Nuthatch is dependent on the suitable management of Corsican pine forests. Proposed management measures mainly consist of leaving dead or rotten trees which do not present any risk of spreading disease to the remaining trees and which are essential for nest-sites (Brichetti and Di Capi 1987,

Beck in press). Excessive fragmentation of optimal habitats should also be avoided by planning forest rotational systems in a way that allows felling of contiguous plots (Beck in press).

The prevention of forest fires is important, particularly in cluster pine forests which are more sensitive to fires than Corsican pine. These conservation measures should be applied as a priority in the 'Forêts Domaniales' area (Rocamora in prep., including Important Bird Area 147), where more than half of the nuthatch population is concentrated, and extended to all public forests managed by the Office National des Forêts within the boundaries of the 'Parc Naturel Régional de la Corse'. Such a management agreement between the relevant partners would be enough to guarantee the future of the species and to declare the area as a Special Protection Area in accordance with the EU Wild Birds Directive.

GÉRARD ROCAMORA

Red-backed Shrike
Lanius collurio

SPEC Category 3
Status (Declining)
Criteria Moderate decline

There is a widespread and continuing decline in range and numbers in Europe, probably due mainly to loss and deterioration of habitat, and (in north-west Europe) climatic changes. Measures should be taken to conserve the habitat by maintaining low-intensity farming.

■ Distribution and population trends

Between a quarter and half of the global breeding range is in Europe, extending across the continent from southern Fennoscandia south to the north Mediterranean region. A large proportion of the European total breeds in eastern Europe, with particularly large numbers in Poland, Russia, Ukraine, Croatia, Romania and Bulgaria (see table, map). Spain, and Germany also have sizeable populations. The species is migratory, wintering mainly in Africa.

A widespread fall in numbers was noted in up to about 50% of the European population during 1970–1990 (see table, map). This decline was evident in parts of all the European regions, though key populations in Russia, Romania and Bulgaria are currently considered stable. The decline has been most severe in north-west Europe where the species has been decreasing for over a century (Ash 1970). Sweden lost over 50% of its population during 1970–1990 (see table), where the species decreased considerably during the 1980s, especially in western and northern parts, owing to a low reproductive rate (Olsson in press). In the United Kingdom it is now probably extinct as a regular breeder. Only in Norway has a general upward trend in numbers occurred, though local increases have been noted in France, Belgium, Netherlands and Germany. In parts of Belgium and France numbers increased in the mid-1980s, in France, at least, without obvious changes to the habitat (Van Nieuwenhuyse and Vandekerkhove 1989, N. Lefranc pers. comm.). In the Netherlands (at Bargerveen peat-more reserve: Van Berkel 1991) and Germany (at a former waste deposit in Berlin: Ratzke and Schreck 1992) habitat improvements induced a significant rise in numbers.

	Breeding population			Breeding
	Size (pairs)	Year	Trend	range trend
Albania	10,000–30,000	81	—	—
Andorra	(50–70)	92	(0)	0
Austria	(10,000–15,000)	—	(–1)	(0)
Belarus	50,000–70,000	90	0	0
Belgium	550–900	81–90	0	–1
Bulgaria	(100,000–1,000,000)	—	(0)	(0)
Croatia	200,000–300,000 *	—	–1*	0*
Czech Republic	25,000–50,000	—	–1	**0**
Denmark	1,500–3,000	86	–1	(–1)
Estonia	20,000–20,000	—	–1	0
Finland	**50,000–80,000**	92	**–1**	**0**
France	70,000–?	76	–1	**0**
Germany	130,000–220,000	—	**–1**	**0**
Greece	20,000–50,000	—	(–1)	(–1)
Hungary	60,000–90,000	—	0	0
Italy	(30,000–60,000)	—	(–1)	(–1)
Latvia	20,000–40,000	—	(0)	0
Liechtenstein	40–60	—	–1	0
Lithuania	5,000–10,000	85–88	(–1)	(–1)
Luxembourg	4,000–5,000	—	–1	–1
Moldova	**60,000–80,000**	88	**0**	**0**
Netherlands	**150–220**	—	**–1**	**–2**
Norway	5,000–10,000	90	**0**	**+1**
Poland	80,000–300,000	—	–1	**0**
Portugal	100–1,000	89	–1	–1
Romania	(600,000–1,000,000)	—	0	**0**
Russia	(100,000–1,000,000)	—	(0)	(0)
Slovakia	(65,000–130,000)	—	–1	**0**
Slovenia	20,000–30,000	—	F	F
Spain	240,000–500,000	—	–1	–1
Sweden	20,000–100,000	87	**–2**	0
Switzerland	8,000–12,000	86–91	0	0
Turkey	(50,000–500,000)	—	—	—
Ukraine	200,000–210,000	86	–1	–1
United Kingdom	**0–1**	88–91	**–2**	**–2**
Total (approx.)	2,300,000–5,900,000			

Trends	+2 Large increase	+1 Small increase	0 Stable	X Extinct
(1970–1990)	–2 Large decrease	–1 Small decrease	F Fluctuating	N New breeder

Data quality **Bold**: reliable quantitative data Normal type: incomplete quantitative data
Bracketed figures: no quantitative data * Data quality not provided

■ Ecology

Preferred habitats in eastern Europe are open, meadow landscapes, typically with scattered bushes, hedgerows, roadside verges and forest edges. Birds are also present at lower densities in young pine–birch forest plantations and peat-bogs with bushes (Malchevskiy and Pukinskiy 1983). In western and central Europe the species occurs in open areas including heath, non-intensive cultivation, fallow land, pasture, scrub, young plantations, and waste ground and orchards with scattered bushes (Lefranc 1979, Jakober and Stauber 1987a). Additional suitable habitats in southern Europe are vineyards, sclerophyllous vegetation on hills and lower mountains, and sparsely wooded pasture.

Breeding territories are about 1.5 ha (1.0–3.5 ha), much smaller than for Great Grey Shrike *L. excubitor* (N. Lefranc pers. comm.). Climatic features have a strong influence on distribution.

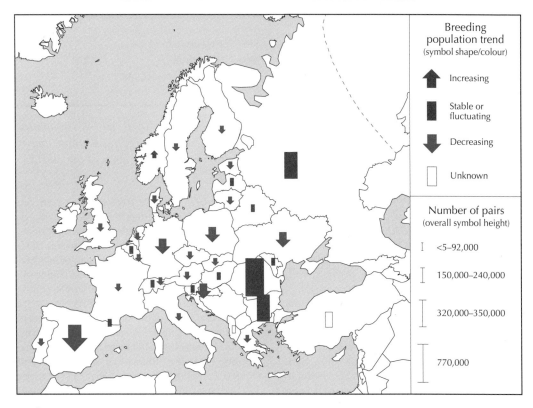

Breeding
population trend
(symbol shape/colour)

Increasing

Stable or
fluctuating

Decreasing

Unknown

Number of pairs
(overall symbol height)

<5–92,000

150,000–240,000

320,000–350,000

770,000

■ Threats

The destruction and deterioration of habitat are thought to be the major causes of the Red-backed Shrike's decline in Europe (Jakober and Stauber 1981, 1987b). Increases in the area of cultivated land, the intensification of farming (including the increased use of pesticides), and afforestation may all have resulted in the reduction of suitable habitat (Jakober and Stauber 1987b, Kowalski 1992). In intensively farmed areas with few bushes, adults have problems feeding young because of energy expended in foraging at long distances from the nest (Diehl 1971, Lügger 1992). Ellenberg (1986) and Maréchal (1993) suggest that the triggering factor for population decline is heavy application of inorganic nitrogen fertilizer causing vegetation to grow early, dense and high.

Although habitat destruction is undoubtedly affecting Red-backed Shrikes in some areas, they are disappearing from parts of north-west Europe where apparently suitable habitat remains and Ellenberg (1986) states that some areas of available habitat are not used. Climate may be a factor accounting for the decline and the contraction of range in the west (Durango 1950, Peakall 1962, Lefranc 1973), for wetter, cooler summers may have reduced the activity and perhaps abundance of insect food (Bibby 1973, Lefranc 1973). Some doubt remains, however,

about the importance of changes in abundance of certain food items, as the birds appear to utilize a wide range of prey (Ash 1970, Jakober and Stauber 1987a, Cramp and Perrins 1993, Lefranc 1993, Wagner 1993).

■ Conservation measures

The Red-backed Shrike requires wide-scale habitat conservation through the promotion of low-intensity farming. This may be implemented in the EU countries through management agreements under the Agri-environment Regulation (EC Reg. 2078/92) of the Common Agricultural Policy. D. Van Nieuwenhuyse et al. (in prep.) state that management or creation of suitable habitats can be achieved by providing open grasslands with a mixture of tall and low vegetation (through mixing the timing and location of mowing and grazing) with thorny shrubs; prey accessibility can be improved by providing artificial perches. Other suggested measures include the conservation of hedges and bushes bordering fields, the planting of bushes in intensively managed orchards and vineyards, and the maintenance of fallow areas (Hölzinger 1987, Kowalski 1992). Reductions in the use of broad-spectrum insecticides may also be appropriate. In western Germany, Jakober and Stauber (1987c) suggest linking fragments of suitable habitat by a series of protected areas.

MELANIE HEATH

Lesser Grey Shrike
Lanius minor

SPEC Category 2
Status (Declining)
Criteria Moderate decline

Range and population have contracted considerably over the last 200 years, and this continues, probably due mainly to a long series of wet summers in western and central Europe, and to reductions in numbers of large insects. Decreases in pesticide use, restoration of low-intensity farming and research on the impact of corvids are required.

■ Distribution and population trends

The Lesser Grey Shrike has only a small part of its range extending outside Europe to central Asia (Dementiev and Gladkov 1954, Panow 1983), with the main European populations in the steppe zones of south-central Europe up to 55°N (see table, map). The main winter quarters are in southern Africa.

Following forest clearance and fragmentation before 1600, chiefly in central Europe and Russia, the range expanded northwards and birds still occur only in man-made habitats at these latitudes (Malchevskiy and Pukinskiy 1983, Viksne 1983). However, after reaching its maximum northern extent by the eighteenth century, the range contracted between c.1850 and c.1945 in western, north-central and northern parts (Glutz von Blotzheim and Bauer 1993), and numbers fell dramatically (Lefranc 1978, Bauer and Thielcke 1982, Viksne 1983, Glutz von Blotzheim

and Bauer 1993). Despite some regional recoveries during 1920–1960, a further sharp decline was evident over 1970–1990, affecting up to a third of the European population (Niehuis 1990, Tomialojc 1992) (see table, map). Breeding was last recorded in Switzerland in 1972 and in Germany in 1978 (Glutz von Blotzheim and Bauer 1993, Lefranc in press). It is also now extinct in the Czech Republic.

The species is now very rare and almost extinct in parts of western Europe, Poland, Slovakia, Belarus, western Ukraine, the Baltic states and its forest zone breeding grounds in Russia (e.g. near Ryazan and Oriel) (Panow 1983, Glutz von Blotzheim and Bauer 1993). Knowledge of the status is generally poor and data sometimes conflict, partly due to sharp, periodic, climate-induced fluctuations, affecting particularly the large populations of Russia, Romania and Turkey. Thus, D. Munteanu suggests high numbers for Romania and no decline (see table), while a dramatic decline with only isolated populations surviving is suggested by others (G. G. Buzzard in Cramp and Perrins 1993, P. Weber pers. comm.).

■ Ecology

The Lesser Grey Shrike is well adapted to the continental climate, characterized by hot summers with little rain (Lefranc in press). It occurs in open lowlands and hills (Cramp and Perrins 1993, N. Lefranc pers. comm.) in steppe, forest-steppe and Mediterranean zones. Suitable habitat is provided by orchards, groves, parks, woodland edges and overgrown ditches, even if close to human settlement or cultivation. Birds are patchily distributed, even within optimal breeding habitat, nesting in clusters or widely scattered pairs, and always in trees (Panow 1983).

Lesser Grey Shrikes are specialized insectivores: beetles may comprise up to 97% of prey items, and grasshoppers can also be very important. Prey is taken from the ground and air; the species requires few perches and often hovers. Unlike other shrikes, food hoarding is rare, making the species vulnerable to prolonged cold or wet spells (Panow 1983) when they may even cannibalize their own young (Lefranc 1980, Panow 1983, Cramp and Perrins 1993).

	Breeding population			Breeding
	Size (pairs)	Year	Trend	range trend
Albania	(2,000–5,000)	81	—	—
Austria	5–10	—	–2	–1
Belarus	(50–200)	90	(–1)	(–2)
Bulgaria	(1,000–10,000)	—	(0)	(0)
Croatia	3,000–4,000 *	—	0*	0*
Czech Republic	0–0	—	X	X
France	25–40	90	**–2**	–2
Germany	0–0	—	X	X
Greece	2,000–3,000	—	(–1)	(–1)
Hungary	5,000–8,000	—	–1	0
Italy	(1,000–2,000)	—	(–1)	(–1)
Latvia	(0–5)	—	(0)	(0)
Lithuania	(10–20)	85–88	(–1)	(0)
Moldova	**10,000–15,000**	88	**–1**	**–1**
Poland	10–50	—	–2	–2
Romania	(30,000–70,000)	—	(0)	0
Russia	(10,000–100,000)	—	(0)	(0)
Slovakia	220–330	—	–2	–2
Slovenia	20–30	—	–2	–2
Spain	45–90 *	—	–1	–1
Switzerland	**0–0**	—	X	X
Turkey	(10,000–100,000)	—	—	—
Ukraine	3,000–3,500	86	–1	–1
Total (approx.)	77,000–320,000			

Trends +2 Large increase +1 Small increase 0 Stable X Extinct
(1970–1990) –2 Large decrease –1 Small decrease F Fluctuating N New breeder
Data quality **Bold**: reliable quantitative data Normal type: incomplete quantitative data
Bracketed figures: no quantitative data * Data quality not provided

412

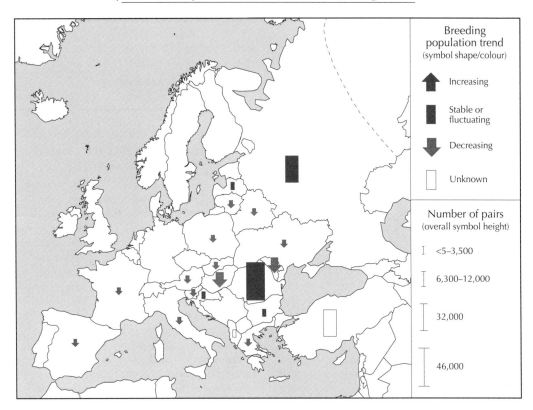

Breeding
population trend
(symbol shape/colour)

Increasing

Stable or
fluctuating

Decreasing

Unknown

Number of pairs
(overall symbol height)

<5–3,500

6,300–12,000

32,000

46,000

■ Threats

The intensification of agriculture and the predominance of monocultures, replacing mosaics of crops interspersed with groups of trees, may have contributed to the decline in western and central Europe (Hölzinger 1987, Niehuis 1990). However, such changes have occurred far less extensively in the east of the species' range, yet it has also declined there (Tomialojc 1992).

Climatic fluctuations (temperature and rainfall) are thought to be one of the main causes of the decline in western and central Europe as breeding success is depressed by wet summers (Lefranc 1978, 1980, Bauer and Thielcke 1982, Glutz von Blotzheim and Bauer 1993). Declines in eastern Europe are, however, taking place while the climate is becoming drier rather than wetter.

A more recent threat is the decline in availability of large insects due to pollution and insecticide use, a factor known to influence other bird species with a similar diet (Hölzinger 1987). The almost complete disappearance of cockchafers *Melolontha melolontha* from European agricultural habitats exemplifies this, and increased pesticide use along the migratory routes and in parts of the winter quarters (Namibia, Botswana) may also have adverse effects (Glutz von Blotzheim and Bauer 1993).

Lesser Grey Shrikes suffer high losses due to nest predation by natural predators, including corvids, and disturbance by humans (Cramp and Perrins 1993). In many central European countries, shrikes were historically persecuted as predators of songbirds and this attitude is locally present even today (Hölzinger 1987). In Slavonic areas including Hungary the bird's prominent perching left it vulnerable to small boys with catapults, and such killing continues although it is currently much less common.

■ Conservation measures

A decrease in the use of agricultural pesticides would probably be the most effective conservation measure. Additionally, in western and central Europe (eastern Poland or Slovakia are marginal exceptions), beneficial effects would be had from the restoration of mosaics of orchards, arable fields and grassland managed at low intensity, as well as a reduction in recreation pressure on remaining suitable habitats. Within the EU, where the species is now rare, such measures would be promoted through appropriate development of Zonal Programmes under the Agri-environment Regulation (EC Reg. 2078/92) of the Common Agricultural Policy.

Studies of the possible influence of corvids on nesting success and post-fledging survival are required, as is improved censusing and monitoring of core populations in eastern and south-east Europe.

LUDWIK TOMIALOJC

Great Grey Shrike
Lanius excubitor

SPEC Category 3
Status Declining
Criteria Moderate decline

The widespread decline over most of the European range during 1970–1990 was due to habitat loss through agricultural intensification, including increased use of pesticides. Measures should therefore be taken to maintain low-intensity farming practices and reduce agro-chemical use.

■ Distribution and population trends

The Great Grey Shrike has a Holarctic distribution, with probably less than a quarter of its breeding range in Europe, where three races breed: most belong to the Euro-Siberian race *excubitor*, while birds in Iberia and southern France belong to *meridionalis* and those in the Canary Islands are *koenigi*. The European breeding range extends from the Mediterranean and Black Sea coasts north to the White Sea beyond the Arctic Circle, and from Portugal, France and Netherlands eastwards into Siberia. Population strongholds are in Russia, Fennoscandia, Portugal and Spain (see table, map), with highest local densities reported in the eastern part of central Europe (Dyrcz *et al.* 1991). Most populations are either partially migratory or short-distance migrants, except in the south where birds are sedentary.

	Breeding population			Breeding
	Size (pairs)	Year	Trend	range trend
Andorra	(0–1)	83	(F)	0
Austria	**12–15** ·	90	–2	–2
Belarus	600–1,200	90	0	0
Belgium	130–160	81–90	–1	–1
Czech Republic	1,000–2,000	—	–1	**0**
Denmark	**10–11**	90	+1	0
Estonia	200–400	—	0	0
Finland	5,000–10,000	92	–1	**–1**
France	1,000–10,000	76	–1	–1
Germany	3,000–4,500	—	–2	**0**
Latvia	100–150	—	–1	0
Lithuania	(25–50)	85–88	(–1)	(0)
Luxembourg	· 50–100	—	–1	–1
Netherlands	**15–40**	79	–1	–1
Norway	5,000–10,000	90	0	+1
Poland	2,000–6,000	—	F	(0)
Portugal	10,000–100,000	89	(0)	0
Romania	(1,000–3,000)	—	–2	–1
Russia	(100,000–1,000,000)	—	(0)	(0)
Slovakia	500–1,000	—	–1	0
Spain	200,000–250,000	—	–1	0
Canary Islands	1,000–1,500	—	–1	0
Sweden	· 1,000–10,000	87	(0)	0
Switzerland	**0–0**	86	X	X
Ukraine	**900–1,200**	88	–1	–1
Total (approx.)	330,000–1,400,000			

Trends	+2 Large increase	+1 Small increase	0 Stable	X Extinct
(1970–1990)	–2 Large decrease	–1 Small decrease	F Fluctuating	N New breeder
Data quality	**Bold:** reliable quantitative data	Normal type: incomplete quantitative data		
	Bracketed figures: no quantitative data	* Data quality not provided		

As a species of fairly open habitats the Great Grey Shrike formerly benefited from forest clearance. Thus in the mid-nineteenth century it was a very rare breeder in eastern Poland but is now widespread and fairly abundant (Tomialojc 1990). However, the first signs of population decline were reported early in the twentieth century from France, Germany and Switzerland (Glutz von Blotzheim 1964, Yeatman 1976), and led to disappearance from Switzerland and about a tenfold drop in numbers in the neighbouring Baden-Württemberg region of Germany (Hölzinger 1987).

Between 1970 and 1990 this downward trend was apparent over much of Europe, particularly in north-west Europe, the south-western part of central Europe and Spain, strongest declines being noted in Germany, Austria and Romania (see table, map). Numbers in Russia probably remained stable, although the population is very poorly known (see table); at least around Moscow, the species has recently entered a steep decline with some local extinctions (Butiev *et al.* 1990).

■ Ecology

The Great Grey Shrike is dispersed in semi-open habitats, comprising mosaics of scattered trees, bushes and short grassland. In northern and north-east Europe the species mainly inhabits edges of forests and peat-bogs, partly deforested river valleys, and (sporadically) parks and orchards (Dementiev and Gladkov 1954b). In central Europe it occurs in meadows and fields with scattered trees, orchards, parkland and heathland (Hölzinger 1987). The nominate race differs from other shrike species by generally nesting high in trees rather than in bushes (Panow 1983). The treatment of *meridionalis* as a full species may be justified as it differs in a number of ways in its ecology and habitat, preferring semi-open scrub and nesting in bushes or small trees (Isenmann and Bouchet 1993).

The main food is insects (most notably beetles), but small vertebrates (mainly voles, especially *Microtus arvalis* and *M. agrestis*) are also taken (although not by *meridionalis*: Glutz von Blotzheim 1964), especially when climatic conditions are harsh,

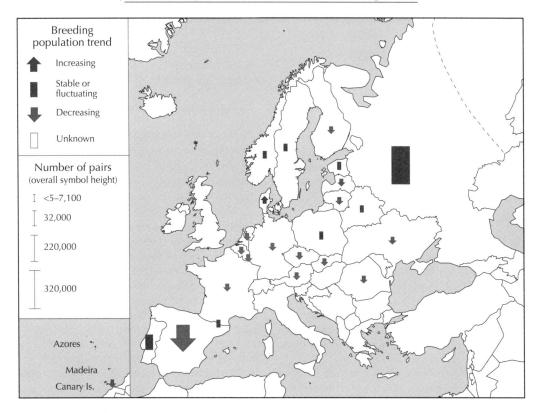

Breeding
population trend

↑ Increasing

■ Stable or
fluctuating

↓ Decreasing

☐ Unknown

Number of pairs
(overall symbol height)

I <5–7,100

I 32,000

I 220,000

I 320,000

Azores

Madeira

Canary Is.

such as during snowy winters or wet summers when they may form a significant part of the diet (Hölzinger 1987). Small passerine birds are taken mainly as fledglings and during snowy periods.

The species is difficult to conserve as pairs have territories of 25–100 ha in the breeding season, and whilst single in winter they occupy large areas.

■ Threats

Agricultural intensification has degraded or destroyed much suitable Great Grey Shrike habitat and fragmented populations. The removal of hedges, trees and orchards has led to fewer nest-sites and perches and reduced food availability. The increased use of pesticides and herbicides also reduces the amount of insect food and may reduce numbers of passerines which are an important food source during adverse conditions. The cessation of agricultural activity can also have detrimental effects, e.g. removal of sheep-grazing may lead to invasion of scrub leaving the habitat unsuitable for Great Grey Shrikes.

The destruction of peatbogs with scattered pines is thought to explain the recent declines in the vicinity of Moscow.

It is possible that adverse factors such as bad spring weather, hard winters and low vole numbers contribute to the extinction of isolated populations in sub-optimal habitats, and such populations can also suffer from development schemes such as road-building and industry (N. Lefranc pers. comm.). Disturbance by humans, cars and dogs attracts the attention of nest-robbing corvids and thus increases predation (Hölzinger 1987, Kowalski 1992).

■ Conservation measures

The Great Grey Shrike requires broad habitat conservation measures which include: the maintenance of low-intensity farming practices; reductions in the use of agro-chemicals in agriculture; preservation of patches of moorland, heathland, fallowlands with juniper *Juniperus* and peat-bogs with dwarf trees for nesting; prevention of excessive afforestation of fallowlands or low-quality pastures; restoration of orchards composed of standard rather than dwarf trees, and of rows of trees in agricultural areas; and reductions in human disturbance at nests by limiting access by visitors to certain areas only (Hölzinger 1987, Kowalski 1992).

In the European Union, the Agri-environment Regulation (EC Reg. 2078/92) provides an opportunity to support farmers who implement some of these measures. In eastern Europe, land-tenure agreements could be used to protect some preferred habitats when converted from state to private ownership.

Ludwik Tomialojc

Woodchat Shrike
Lanius senator

SPEC Category 2
Status Vulnerable
Criteria Large decline

Declines have occurred virtually throughout Europe. Loss and degradation of habitat through agricultural intensification, afforestation, large fires and the abandonment of charcoal-making are the main threats. Traditional management of Mediterranean scrub and pastoral woodlands, reduced use of insecticides and herbicides, and prevention of hunting are among the necessary conservation measures.

■ Distribution and population trends

The Woodchat Shrike is restricted almost entirely to the west Palearctic, mainly within the Mediterranean region. Roughly three-quarters of its range is in Europe, where it is well represented in Spain, Portugal, southern France, Italy, Croatia, Greece and Turkey (see table, map). Its range also extends north in western Europe within the 19°C July isotherm (Cramp and Perrins 1993). The species mainly winters south of the Sahara, but north of the Equator.

The species has declined by over 20% in up to c.90% of its European population. The decline has been dramatic in the north and west of the European breeding range in the last decades, especially in Belgium, south-west Germany (Ullrich 1971), Switzerland, Poland, Czech Republic, Slovakia and Italy (Po valley) (see table, map). It has disappeared from

the Netherlands (last bred 1984), Austria (1963) (Cramp and Perrins 1993) and Belgium (1982, though a few pairs may be overlooked). Numbers also decreased during 1970–1990 in the strongholds of France and Spain (see table, map), with severe declines in southern France (Lefranc 1980), and in the northern third of Spain (Ceballos and Purroy 1981) and Cataluña (Muntaner *et al.* 1983).

■ Ecology

In the Mediterranean region, suitable areas contain scattered trees or shrubs interspersed with large clearings of short or sparse herbaceous vegetation. Such habitats include undeveloped Mediterranean scrubland with some extensive livestock-grazing, and woodlands such as dehesas in Spain and montados in Portugal that are dominated by holm oak *Quercus ilex* and cork oak *Q. suber* on grazed grassland (Bernís 1971, Herrera 1980, Lefranc 1980, Rabaça 1983). The species also occupies irrigated and other cultivated areas with olives, almonds and fruit trees (Lefranc 1980, Ceballos and Purroy 1981, Muñoz-Cobo 1987, 1992). Birds seem to avoid homogenous pine plantations. Outside the Mediterranean, Woodchats are typical of traditional enclosed orchards which are grazed low by stock, and here it usually nests in fruit trees or poplars whereas around the Mediterranean it uses both trees and bushes.

Perches are required for the hunting of arthropods, and dry projecting branches seem to be preferred (Ullrich 1971, Herrera 1980, Lefranc 1980, Magdaleno and Muñoz-Cobo 1993).

Winter habitat is savanna with scattered *Acacia*, and birds may frequent patches of cultivation with suitable perches (Moreau 1972, Lefranc 1980).

■ Threats

The species' decline has been attributed to loss and degradation of breeding habitat (mainly in the Mediterranean region) and of wintering habitat in the Sahel. In the Mediterranean, its habitat is being made unsuitable through afforestation with conifers and

	Breeding population			Breeding range trend
	Size (pairs)	Year	Trend	
Albania	(2,000–5,000)	81	—	—
Andorra	(0–1)	83	(F)	0
Belgium	0–0	—	X	X
Bulgaria	(300–3,000)	—	(+1)	(+1)
Croatia	20,000–30,000 *	—	0*	0*
Cyprus	(2–5)	—	N	0
Czech Republic	**0–3**	—	-2	-2
France	10,000–100,000	76	(-1)	-1
Germany	1–150	—	-2	**0**
Greece	5,000–20,000	—	(-1)	(-1)
Italy	(5,000–10,000)	—	(-1)	(-1)
Luxembourg	**1–3**	—	-1	-1
Malta	2–3	—	0	0
Netherlands	0–0	—	X	X
Poland	10–50	—	-2	-2
Portugal	10,000–100,000	89	(0)	0
Romania	(10–20)	—	(+1)	+1
Slovakia	1–25	—	-2	-2
Spain	390,000–860,000	—	-1	-1
Switzerland	**30–50**	86–91	-2	-2
Turkey	(5,000–50,000)	—	—	—
Ukraine	1–10	84	-2	-2
United Kingdom Gibraltar	**0–1**	—	F	0*
Total (approx.)	450,000–1,200,000			

Trends +2 Large increase +1 Small increase 0 Stable X Extinct
(1970–1990) -2 Large decrease -1 Small decrease F Fluctuating N New breeder
Data quality **Bold:** reliable quantitative data Normal type: incomplete quantitative data
Bracketed figures: no quantitative data * Data quality not provided

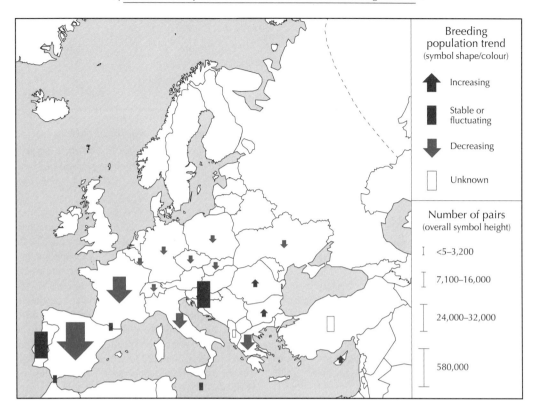

Breeding population trend (symbol shape/colour)

Increasing

Stable or fluctuating

Decreasing

Unknown

Number of pairs (overall symbol height)

<5–3,200

7,100–16,000

24,000–32,000

580,000

increases in the density and cover of scrub following the abandonment of traditional charcoal-making. Large fires are not a problem in the dehesas, but in areas of holm oak and riparian vegetation they render the habitat unsuitable (Prodon *et al*. 1984). Riparian vegetation is also being lost or degraded through river canalization. The replacement of traditional methods of cultivation, e.g. of olives and oranges, by intensive techniques with associated widespread use of herbicides and insecticides has led to the elimination of bordering shrubs and herbaceous cover and to low insect numbers (Lefranc 1980, Gil-Delgado 1981, Muñoz-Cobo 1990).

Heavy rain in the breeding season may have short-term consequences by delaying egg-laying and decreasing reproductive success (Ullrich 1971, Lefranc 1980, Magdaleno and Muñoz-Cobo 1993). It may also decrease insect activity, thereby affecting hunting and thus breeding success.

The species is hunted around ponds in summer and on migration in Italy (Lefranc 1980), southern and eastern Spain (Muntaner *et al*. 1983, Muñoz-Cobo 1984) and North Africa, which may be affecting the population, as with other shrikes (Lefranc 1980). Prolonged drought in the Sahel, and changes in agricultural practices in the winter quarters, may contribute to population declines in the long term (Lefranc 1980).

■ Conservation measures

Most important is the maintenance of traditional methods of livestock-rearing and fruit-growing in the Mediterranean. Clearance of tall scrubland is beneficial and should be carried out in the traditional way, by extensive livestock-grazing. In the dehesas and similar pastoral woodlands it is necessary to prune oak groves carefully (leaving protruding branches), to maintain minimal shrub cover, and to reduce pesticide application to the trees. In olive-groves, use of herbicides and insecticides should be controlled, soil-rotation practices should be used and unploughed field margins with boundaries of trees, shrubs and herbaceous vegetation maintained (Muñoz-Cobo 1987). Monoculture crops should be diversified wherever possible and woodland maintained at roadsides in rural areas, as well as in irrigated cereal cultivation. Such beneficial habitat management practices could be supported in the EU by their inclusion within Zonal Programmes developed under the Agri-environment Regulation (EC Reg. 2078/92) of the Common Agricultural Policy.

Hunting bans should be enforced in Europe and protection from hunting is required also in North Africa, where there are currently no controls. Research into the impact of potential threats on the wintering grounds is needed.

JOAQUIN MUÑOZ-COBO

Masked Shrike
Lanius nubicus

SPEC Category 2
Status (Vulnerable)
Criteria Large decline

In Europe the Masked Shrike has a breeding distribution restricted to the south-east, where its population is small and seemingly declining. The loss and degradation of suitable habitat is the most likely cause of the decline. The maintenance of traditional farmland with large hedges and old trees is required for the conservation of this species.

■ Distribution and population trends

The Masked Shrike's world breeding range comprises parts of the Former Yugoslav Republic of Macedonia, Greece, Bulgaria, Turkey, Cyprus, the Levant region and parts of Iraq and western Iran. At least half of this range lies within Europe, where the minimum population estimate is approximately 7,500 pairs, these being concentrated mainly in Turkey and Cyprus (see table, map). All populations are migratory, wintering just south of the Sahara in a narrow belt from Sudan and Ethiopia across to eastern Mali (Cramp and Perrins 1993).

There are few data on population sizes or trends, especially for the main European population in Turkey. In Greece and Cyprus numbers are declining, while an increase is reported from Bulgaria (see table, map).

	Breeding population			Breeding
	Size (pairs)	Year	Trend	range trend
Bulgaria	(50–100)	—	(+1)	(+1)
Cyprus	2,000–4,000	—	–1	0
Greece	(600–2,000)	—	(–1)	(–1)
Turkey	(5,000–50,000)	—	—	—
Total (approx.)	7,700–56,000			

Trends   +2 Large increase   +1 Small increase   0 Stable   X Extinct
(1970–1990) –2 Large decrease   –1 Small decrease   F Fluctuating   N New breeder
Data quality **Bold**: reliable quantitative data   Normal type: incomplete quantitative data
              Bracketed figures: no quantitative data   * Data quality not provided

■ Ecology

The Masked Shrike, like most *Lanius* species, inhabits open, lowland areas with hedges, solitary trees and groves, and edges of woodland, preferably mixed or deciduous. However, the species is the most woodland-bound of the European shrike species, often living and hunting in and under trees rather than in hedges or brushwood, and this is true in the winter quarters as well as on the breeding grounds. A rich vegetation structure is an important habitat requirement, and the species therefore occurs frequently around the edges of orchards, olive-groves and poplar plantations. Where the undergrowth is sparse, Masked Shrikes will also settle inside these plantations, such as in the older poplar stands of the Nestos delta (Jerrentrup 1986). The species has, indeed, shown local expansions into plantations and orchards.

Nests are sited mainly in the lower branches of large trees, but may also be placed in the crowns of smaller trees. Masked Shrikes prey on large insects (mainly grasshoppers and beetles), lizards and small passerine birds, hunting under trees and on the ground; insects are sometimes pursued in flight (Cramp and Perrins 1993).

■ Threats

The disappearance of groves and individual large trees from traditional farmland is probably the major cause of the Masked Shrike's decline. Furthermore, the general degradation of these rich habitats due to burning, clearance, drainage and the use of pesticides has an overall detrimental effect on a large group of bird species, of which the Masked Shrike is among the most sensitive. Decreased levels of grazing allow denser undergrowth to form in open woodland, which reduces feeding opportunities for this species.

Throughout much of Turkey and some parts of the Middle East and Africa, shooting during autumn migration at the end of August is a threat to all shrike species. Masked Shrike is also shot on its breeding grounds in Syria, and in Greece shooting is a major problem since these birds are thought by local people to be harmful.

■ Conservation measures

Traditional farmland, managed at low intensity, particularly where it occurs in diverse landscapes, should be maintained, and where old trees and small groves are present these should be preserved. Within the EU, this may be achieved through the development of management agreements under the Agri-environment Regulation (EC Reg. 2078/92) of the Common Agricultural Policy.

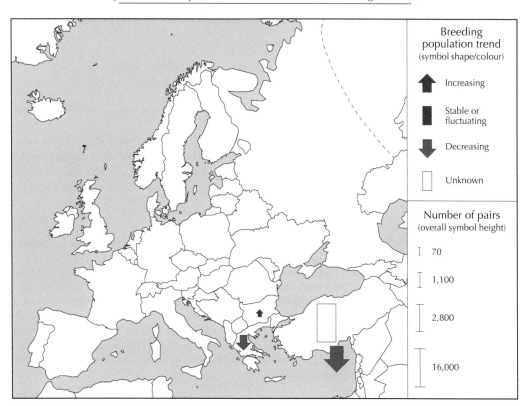

Breeding
population trend
(symbol shape/colour)

Increasing

Stable or
fluctuating

Decreasing

Unknown

Number of pairs
(overall symbol height)

70

1,100

2,800

16,000

All shrikes require legal protection from shooting, and the existing hunting laws which give the species such protection should be rigorously enforced.

Population assessments should be conducted throughout the Masked Shrike's breeding range and its precise conservation status needs to be ascertained.

BEN HALLMANN

Siberian Jay *Perisoreus infaustus* – see p. 436

Chough
Pyrrhocorax pyrrhocorax

SPEC Category 3
Status Vulnerable
Criteria Large decline

Numbers are decreasing in about 90% of the population and the distribution is contracting in many areas. Choughs are strongly associated with traditional pastoral farming, but, as some populations are now barely viable, other factors such as persecution, predation and bad weather combine to influence survival even where land-use appears suitable. Action is required to influence farming policy supported by direct conservation action.

■ Distribution and population trends

The Chough occurs in the Palearctic and north-east Ethiopia. Within Europe it breeds in the Republic of Ireland, western United Kingdom, north-west France (Brittany) and southern Europe from Iberia and the Canary Islands (La Palma only) eastwards through Sardinia (not Corsica), Italy, Sicily, Greece, Turkey and the Caucasus. The African distribution comprises two populations, one in the Moroccan High Atlas mountains and one in the mountains of Bale Province, Ethiopia.

Over three-quarters of the European population is concentrated in Turkey, Spain, Greece (Crete holds the largest Mediterranean island population, B. Massa pers. comm.) and France (see table, map). However, most populations are small, isolated and declining, though many areas remain unsurveyed, especially in Turkey where trends are unknown. Choughs were lost from Austria in the early 1950s and are now gone from most of Switzerland. Marked declines have been also reported in Portugal by Farinha (1991), where the entire population is confined to just five breeding areas. In total about 90% of the population

for which trends are estimated occurs in countries where declines were recorded.

The continuing contractions in range and the Chough's sedentary nature have led to the existence now of many small, isolated populations, some of doubtful viability, for instance in southern Portugal (Farinha 1991), Brittany (P. Le'Flock pers. comm.), the Swiss Alps (E. Thaler-Kottek pers. comm.) and in Sardinia (B. Massa pers. comm.).

■ Ecology

Choughs nest in caves, rock crevices and recesses and in artefacts which mimic these conditions. They feed principally on soil-living, surface-active and dung-associated invertebrates in extensive natural and semi-natural pastures grazed by domestic livestock (e.g. Roberts 1982, Warnes and Stroud 1989). In Europe, a combination of these features is mostly confined to remote mountain or coastal areas. Optimum feeding conditions occur in a range of arid to temperate vegetation types where there are abundant prey, with bare ground and short or open vegetation. Many studies have reported strong seasonal shifts in diet, both in invertebrates and to include cereals, seeds and fruit (Garcia Dory 1983, McCracken *et al.* 1992, Blanco *et al.* in press).

Choughs are not migratory, although in winter some of the mountain populations, such as those in the Pyrenees and the Cantabrian Mountains, move to the foothills, often forming flocks of several hundred birds.

■ Threats

The overwhelming factor associated with the recent decline of this species is the loss of traditional livestock farming—through abandonment, or conversion to forestry, tourist-related developments, or intensive or specialist farming. In north-west Europe and in mountain areas the cessation of seasonally high grazing pressure results in denser vegetation which in turn makes soil-invertebrate prey unavail-

| | Breeding population | | | Breeding |
	Size (pairs)	Year	Trend	range trend
Albania	(0–50)	81	—	—
Andorra	(200–300)	91	(0)	(0)
France	(800–2,000)	90	(–1)	**0**
Greece	1,000–5,000	—	(–1)	(0)
Rep. of Ireland	**810–810**	92	**+1**	**0**
Italy	(500–1,000)	—	(–2)	(–1)
Portugal	**100–150**	90	**–2**	**–2**
Spain	7,000–9,800	—	–1	–1
Canary Islands	300–400	—	–1	0
Switzerland	**40–60**	86–91	**0**	**0**
Turkey	(5,000–50,000)	—	—	—
United Kingdom	**340–340**	86–91	**0**	**0**
Isle of Man [1]	**49–60**	82	**0**	**0***
Total (approx.)	16,000–70,000			

Trends	+2 Large increase	+1 Small increase	0 Stable	X Extinct
(1970–1990)	–2 Large decrease	–1 Small decrease	F Fluctuating	N New breeder

Data quality **Bold**: reliable quantitative data Normal type: incomplete quantitative data
Bracketed figures: no quantitative data * Data quality not provided
[1] Population figures are included within United Kingdom totals

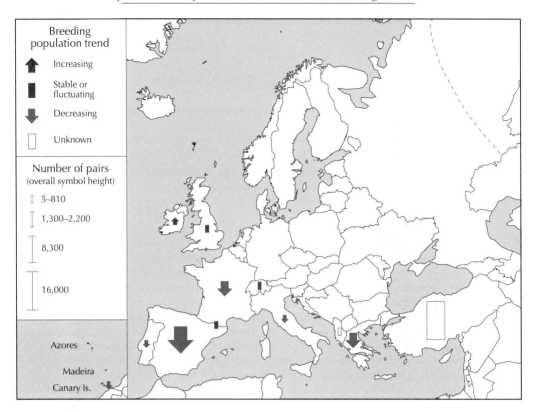

The legend of the map reads:

Breeding population trend
- Increasing
- Stable or fluctuating
- Decreasing
- Unknown

Number of pairs (overall symbol height)
- 5–810
- 1,300–2,200
- 8,300
- 16,000

Azores

Madeira

Canary Is.

able to Choughs. The continuing collapse of transhumance livestock systems is of crucial importance in southern Europe particularly in Spain and Greece. In coastal and mountain areas tourist developments generate excessive disturbance (e.g. Spain, Portugal) and compete for key Chough habitat such as sand-dunes, sand grassland and machair (Scotland, Ireland), mato and maquis vegetation (southern Europe) and cliffs and caves (Portugal, Pyrenees).

■ Conservation measures

The conservation of surviving areas of traditional extensive pastoral farmland is essential. The restricted distribution of Choughs in most European countries means that special measures to support pastoral farming on natural and semi-natural vegetation in long-established breeding areas can be clearly targeted through agricultural policy. For example, management agreements with farmers could be developed in EU countries under the Agri-environment Regulation (EC Reg. 2078/92) of the Common Agricultural Policy, with the objective of maintaining areas of extensive pastureland for domestic livestock (Bignal and Curtis 1989). Even in Iberia and Greece, where Choughs are more widely distributed and where nearly three-quarters of the European population occurs, the basic requirement is to prevent detrimental land-use change in key areas. To complement this, it has proved possible in the United Kingdom to provide artificial nest-sites in areas that do not have nest-sites but which are otherwise suitable (Bignal and Bignal 1987).

ERIC BIGNAL

Blue Chaffinch
Fringilla teydea

SPEC Category 1
Status Vulnerable
Criteria <2,500 pairs

This endemic species of the Canary Islands is restricted to woods of Canarian pine on Tenerife and Gran Canaria. Though common on Tenerife, it has declined on Gran Canaria almost to the level of extinction, principally because of habitat destruction. The species requires continued protection and maintenance of its habitat on Tenerife and the implementation of a conservation programme on Gran Canaria.

■ Distribution and population trends

The Blue Chaffinch is endemic to the Canary Islands where it is restricted to Tenerife (nominate *teydea*) and Gran Canaria (subspecies *polatzeki*) with a total population estimated to be around 1,000–1,500 pairs (see table, map). On Tenerife, where the majority of the species' global population occurs, it is common in the appropriate habitat, though the number of birds is very poorly known. It has been recorded throughout much of the extensive Canarian pine *Pinus canariensis* woodland in the north, north-east and southern parts of the island. The most recent population estimate of the race on Gran Canaria is just 180–260 individuals (Moreno 1991), confined to only two distinct and isolated patches of Canarian pine woodland in the north-west and south-west of the island.

It appears that by dispersing and/or being patchily distributed or concentrated in its pine forest habitat, this species has given varying impressions of its abundance to different observers over the last hundred years on Gran Canaria and Tenerife, ranging from rare to common (Collar and Stuart 1985). On Tenerife substantial replanting was carried out in the 1940s and this was followed by an increase in the Blue Chaffinch population (Hüe and Etchécopar 1958). In the 1980s birds were fairly common in all areas, including both natural and mature reforested pine woods (Martín 1987). On Gran Canaria the species was reported to be very rare and decreasing in the first half of the twentieth century and it appears still to be declining (Martín 1979, Nogales 1985).

	Breeding population			Breeding range trend
	Size (pairs)	Year	Trend	
Spain Canary Islands	1,000–1,500	—	0	0
Total (approx.)	1,000–1,500			

Trends (1970-1990) +2 Large increase +1 Small increase 0 Stable X Extinct −2 Large decrease −1 Small decrease F Fluctuating N New breeder
Data quality **Bold**: reliable quantitative data Normal type: incomplete quantitative data Bracketed figures: no quantitative data * Data quality not provided

■ Ecology

The Blue Chaffinch inhabits Canarian pine woods almost exclusively, at altitudes which range from 700 to 2,000 m, and include both natural and old replanted forest (Martín 1979, 1987). The birds remain at high altitude even when there is snow cover and only occasionally leave the limits of the forest to feed in adjacent areas during periods of severe cold weather. The distribution of birds within the forest can be patchy and may depend on the type of undergrowth and the presence of mature pine trees. The species seems to prefer areas with an undergrowth of the shrub escobón *Chamaecytisus proliferus*, since this sustains caterpillars that are frequently fed to the young (Martín 1979). Blue Chaffinches occur less often in pine woods that are in association with faya *Myrica faya* and tree-heath *Erica arborea* (Martín 1987).

The diet is mainly seeds (principally of Canarian pine) and invertebrates. Birds spend much time foraging on the ground as well as in trees, and extract pine seeds from open cones. Breeding occurs from April to July, and adults feed the young mainly on adult and larval insects as well as on pine seeds (Martín *et al.* 1990, Blanco and González 1992).

■ Threats

The two major causes of the species' decline in the past were hunting and habitat destruction (Martín 1979). At the beginning of the twentieth century, shooting by collectors was considered to be widespread and very intensive; one collector alone killed 76 birds on Gran Canaria and 122 on Tenerife over a short period of time (von Thanner 1910). Pine woods have suffered considerably from destruction and from the removal of undergrowth (Lack and Southern 1949, Volsøe 1951, Martín 1979, Martín *et al.* 1990).

The Blue Chaffinch is not currently threatened on Tenerife (Blanco and González 1992), even though it is still kept as a cage-bird. However, the population

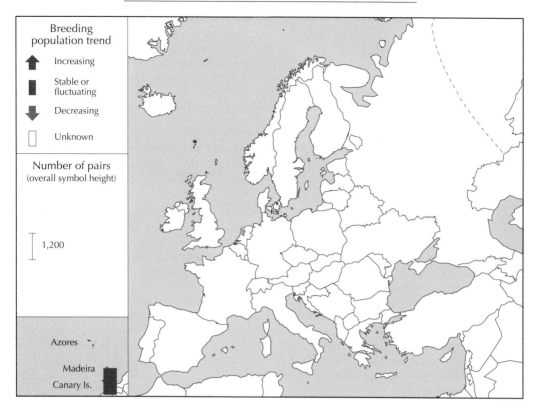

Breeding population trend

↑ Increasing

■ Stable or fluctuating

↓ Decreasing

☐ Unknown

Number of pairs
(overall symbol height)

1,200

Azores

Madeira

Canary Is.

on Gran Canaria, with its small insular range, is endangered and is included in the Canary Islands' Red Data list (Martín *et al.* 1990). Problems include habitat fragmentation, scarcity of suitable habitat, and the effects of forest fires. The piping of water from forested slopes—which in the early 1960s was judged to be reducing the number of places where the birds could drink in high summer—has now resulted in all streams running dry on Gran Canaria, although there are still several viable drinking places that Blue Chaffinches use. Predation of adults, eggs and young appears to be an additional risk (Rodríguez and Moreno 1993).

■ Conservation measures

The Blue Chaffinch and its habitat are currently protected by national and regional laws, and recently this species was added to Annex I of the EU Wild Birds Directive. The reafforestation of several tens of thousands of hectares with Canarian pine on Tenerife in the mid-1950s is considered to be the reason why good numbers are still present on this island (Collar and Stuart 1985).

However, the endemic subspecies *polatzeki* on Gran Canaria requires specific and wide-scale conservation measures to guarantee its survival, including the preservation and reconstruction of large areas of suitable habitat, particularly through reafforestation with Canarian pine (Martín *et al.* 1990). The creation of corridors between isolated patches of pine wood is also needed. Since 1991, the Canarian Government has operated a conservation programme for this race which includes proposals for further studies of its ecology (especially its breeding success and habitat requirements), species and habitat protection, habitat management (including reafforestation in poor areas and the installation of pipes to create permanent artificial water supplies), control of introduced predators, captive breeding, translocation of individuals and public education.

The continued protection of the species and the maintenance of suitable habitat are required on Tenerife, whilst on Gran Canaria the implementation of the conservation programme is essential to maintain the species' current global status, which is listed as Conservation Dependent (Collar *et al.* 1994).

FELIPE RODRÍGUEZ

Scottish Crossbill
Loxia scotica

SPEC Category 1
Status Insufficiently Known

Population size and trends are extremely poorly known, though the original habitat of native Scottish pinewoods has undoubtedly declined dramatically over the last few hundred years. Regeneration through statutory protection and a reduction of red deer numbers would reduce further habitat loss, while appropriate management of pine plantations would increase the amount of suitable habitat.

■ Distribution and population trends

The Scottish Crossbill has only recently been given specific status, having been previously considered conspecific with Common Crossbill *L. curvirostra* (ó 1976, Voous 1978). It is confined to Scotland, with core areas to the north-west of the Great Glen and in Strathspey and Deeside (Nethersole-Thompson 1975, Knox 1986).

Population guesses for the twentieth century indicate that numbers are small. During the 1930s to 1950s hundreds of pairs were reported nesting in upper Strathspey alone, while in the 1970s the entire population was put at 320 pairs, though perhaps as many as 1,500 adults (Nethersole-Thompson 1975). Batten *et al.* (1990) gave 300–1,000 pairs (for 1988) in their table of population estimates, though in the text they state that up to 1,250 pairs may in fact be present. The species appears subject to strong fluctuations in population size and/or to distributional shifts, both presumably due to changes in food availability, but there are no complete surveys in different years to demonstrate which type of change is actually happening. Between 1933 and 1942 the numbers nesting in Strathspey appeared to fluctuate by a factor of 40 in synchrony with the pine-cone crop (Nethersole-Thompson 1975), but at this time it was not appreciated that Common Crossbill was raising the overall Highland crossbill population in invasion years.

Due to the dramatic loss of suitable habitat it seems certain that the population and range have decreased during the past few hundred years, although in the recent past there has probably been some increase since the time of maximum forest clearance (Knox 1987). However, given the nomadic nature of crossbills, the large local variation in numbers in relation to food supply, and the difficulties of identification (Knox 1990a) and therefore of censusing, it is difficult to assess population size with any accuracy and recent trends cannot be estimated. Consequently, its European Threat Status is classed as Insufficiently Known and Collar *et al.* (1994) describe its global status as Data Deficient.

■ Ecology

The primary habitat is native forests of Scots pine *Pinus sylvestris*, where birds feed on pine-cone seeds (Lack 1944). Other tree species used occasionally for foraging include Norway and Sitka spruce *Picea abies* and *P. sitchensis*, Douglas fir *Pseudotsuga menziesii* and larch *Larix decidua*. Pine and larch plantations only become really attractive as habitat when more than c.80 years old (Knox 1987). If cone crops fail, birds may exploit, for example, birch *Betula pubescens*, rowan *Sorbus aucuparia* and weeds (Nethersole-Thompson 1975).

Nesting is solitary or in groups of 2–6 pairs, usually in Scots pine. Nests are placed 50–400 m apart, at a maximum density of one per 1.8 ha (Nethersole-Thompson 1975).

The population appears to maintain its integrity despite large, repeated invasions of Common Crossbills and subsequent sympatric breeding, so hybridization cannot have happened to any significant extent in the past—nor is there any recent evidence of this, although it does remain a possibility (Knox 1976, 1990b).

■ Threats

Native pinewoods have declined from an estimated 1.5 million ha a few hundred years ago (McVean and Ratcliffe 1962) to 12,000 ha now (Bain 1987). The remaining forest is no longer being destroyed at the same rate, and most has some statutory protection, though not all receives adequate management, and there has been underplanting with exotic conifers.

| | Breeding population | | | Breeding |
	Size (pairs)	Year	Trend	range trend
United Kingdom	(300–1,250)	88	—	0
Total (approx.)	300–1,300			

Trends   +2 Large increase   +1 Small increase   0 Stable   X Extinct
(1970–1990)   –2 Large decrease   –1 Small decrease   F Fluctuating   N New breeder
Data quality   **Bold**: reliable quantitative data   Normal type: incomplete quantitative data
Bracketed figures: no quantitative data   * Data quality not provided

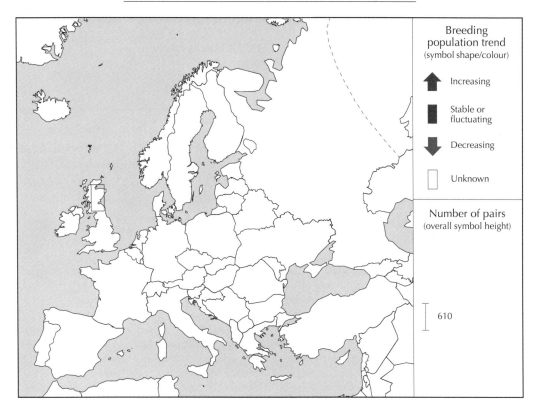

Breeding
population trend
(symbol shape/colour)

Increasing

Stable or
fluctuating

Decreasing

Unknown

Number of pairs
(overall symbol height)

610

Many very old plantations and stands of pine and larch around large houses are being felled, and where replanted are unlikely to be allowed to grow so old again (Knox 1987). Numbers of red deer *Cervus elaphus* are still too high in most forests, and they prevent regeneration of trees (Ratcliffe 1990).

After the First World War the Forestry Commission increased the area of pine woodland in Scotland, but this is now being replaced with faster-growing spruce, so the area of pines is again diminishing. Common Crossbill has a bill adapted for spruce cones and, following invasions from the continent, may therefore settle and breed in the area more frequently, thus increasing the chances of hybridization.

■ Conservation measures

Further research is needed to assess the population status of the species. In the meantime, however, steps should be taken to protect and to manage correctly the remaining native pine forest and other areas of old timber, so limiting further loss of habitat due to felling or underplanting. Red deer numbers should also be drastically reduced and the remaining deer excluded with fences placed so as to permit the spread of native pinewoods beyond current boundaries as well as encouraging regeneration within the present woodland area.

In an attempt to increase the amount of forest suitable for Scottish Crossbills, landowners should be encouraged to consider the Forestry Commission's Woodland Grant Scheme which makes provision for the creation of pinewood (Forestry Commission 1989). However, as the understanding of the Scottish Crossbill's habitat requirements are poor, further work is also required to ensure that appropriate woodland management is instigated.

RON SUMMERS

Trumpeter Finch
Bucanetes githagineus

SPEC Category 3
Status Rare
Criteria <10,000 pairs

Although stable in the Canary Islands and slightly increasing in the Iberian peninsula, the Trumpeter Finch remains susceptible in Europe due to the small size of its mostly isolated population. However, its sedentary nature and localized occurrence in areas with poor soils make possible its conservation through the protection of key sites. The species could be further protected in continental Spain if the capture of finches was prohibited and trapping laws were more effectively enforced.

■ Distribution and population trends

Europe harbours 10–15% of the global range of Trumpeter Finch, where it is almost entirely restricted to the Canary Islands (see table, map). The largest numbers there are on the islands of Lanzarote and Fuerteventura, but birds are also present on Alegranza, La Graciosa, Tenerife, Isla de Lobos, Gran Canaria and La Gomera. Breeding occurs in south-east Spain (Almería and Murcia provinces) and Turkey, and there is some evidence of nesting in Greece. The migration patterns of the species are not precisely known, but the Iberian population seems to undertake short-range winter movements from the interior towards the coastal zones (Manrique and Miralles 1988).

Populations in the Canaries are considered to be stable (see table, map) although quantitative historical data are lacking (Osborne 1986, Martín 1987). The population of the Iberian peninsula, however, increased in size and range between 1970 and 1990 (Castanedo *et al.* 1987, 1989, Manrique and Miralles 1988, Sánchez *et al.* 1991). The expansion has occurred from the main nucleus in the arid zones of Almería, eastwards along the coastal mountain chains to the Manga del Mar Menor in Murcia. There has also been a north-west spread towards Granada (Guadix depression), but this expansion of range did not persist (M. Soler pers. comm.). Very recently, the main population in Almería has decreased, though this may be a short-term fluctuation associated with rainfall (J. Manrique and M. Yanes own data), as

probably occurs in north-west Africa (Heim de Balsac and Mayaud 1962).

The species' population size in Turkey is uncertain and population trends are unknown.

■ Ecology

The Trumpeter Finch has an extremely localized distribution in Europe. During the breeding season the species uses habitats that are characterized by the absence of tree cover, with sparse scrub (below 100 cm high and covering 15–50% of the land) (Cuyás 1971, Manrique and Miralles 1988), including poorly vegetated, erosion-prone, uncultivated areas (García 1972). In the Canary Islands, the species also nests on sandy plains with halophytic and xerophytic scrub (de Juana 1990). Nests are sited among rocks, under vegetation clumps and in holes in earth banks and stone walls, including houses. The birds require water, and thus often concentrate around the few existing springs.

Diet is not well known but adults eat many crucifer seeds during the breeding season, including *Moricandia foetida* and *Euzomodendron bourgaeanum* (J. Manrique own data).

During the winter on the Iberian peninsula, the species forms flocks that frequent flat, sandy coastal zones with sparse, very low vegetation cover; they can then also occur in and around ramblas (dry watercourses), small villages and industrial areas.

■ Threats

Although the Trumpeter Finch is a rare bird in the European context, it is presently neither declining nor seriously threatened. It is, however, susceptible in Europe due to the small size and probable isolation of the population.

Over large parts of the south-east of the Iberian peninsula the species is trapped with nets at water sources. The legal capture of other finch species is permitted in this way by some Spanish Regional Governments during the autumn (Garrido and Alba

	Breeding population			Breeding
	Size (pairs)	Year	Trend	range trend
Spain	100–300	—	+1	+1
Canary Islands	4,000–5,000	—	0	0
Turkey	(0–50)	—	—	—
Total (approx.)	4,100–5,400			

Trends   +2 Large increase   +1 Small increase   0 Stable   X Extinct
(1970–1990)   –2 Large decrease   –1 Small decrease   F Fluctuating   N New breeder
Data quality   **Bold**: reliable quantitative data   Normal type: incomplete quantitative data
Bracketed figures: no quantitative data   * Data quality not provided

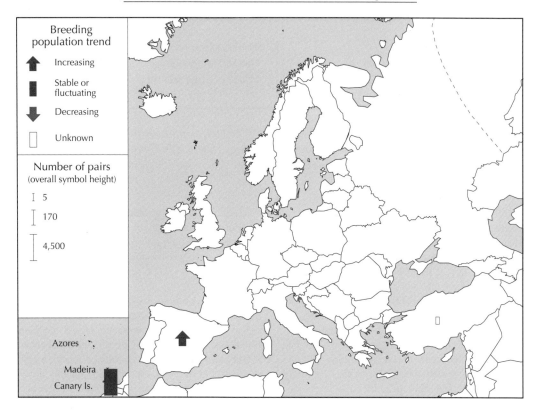

Breeding
population trend

▲ Increasing

▆ Stable or
fluctuating

▼ Decreasing

☐ Unknown

Number of pairs
(overall symbol height)

5

170

4,500

Azores

Madeira

Canary Is.

1985, Castanedo *et al.* 1989), and Trumpeter Finches may be illegally taken in the process. Development of the tourist industry and the uncontrolled use of four-wheel-drive vehicles may also threaten the habitat of the species on some islands in the short term (e.g. Jable Itsmo de la Jandía, Fuerteventura: de Juana 1990).

■ Conservation measures

A large part of the island population is found in Special Protection Areas which have been designated under the EU Wild Birds Directive, especially on the island of Fuerteventura. On the Canaries the species occurs in many Important Bird Areas (IBAs) including, on Fuerteventura, Jandía (IBAs 012, 021), Lajares (IBA 013), Betancuria (IBA 016), Pozo Negro (IBA 022), Isla de Lobos (IBA 023) and Dunas de Corralejo (IBA 024); on Lanzarote, Islotes del Norte de Lanzarote (IBA 001), Riscos de Famara

(IBA 002) and Salinas de Janubio (IBA 003); and on La Gomera, Acantilados de Alajeró. On the Iberian mainland, Cabo de Gata–Níjar (IBA 226), Sierra Alhamilla (IBA 228) and Desierto de Tabernas (IBA 229) support the species but, overall, less than half of the population is located in areas receiving some form of legal protection. The continued protection of Cabo de Gata–Níjar Natural Park, together with the enlargement of the Tabernas Desert and Sierra de Alhamilla Natural Areas in Almería, would permit the protection of the areas with the peninsula's greatest density of Trumpeter Finches and the most suitable habitats.

The prohibition of the capture of finches, complemented by improved enforcement measures against trappers, particularly in the provinces of Almería, Murcia and Granada, would also be beneficial to Trumpeter Finch populations.

JUAN MANRIQUE AND MIGUEL YANES

Great Rosefinch *Carpodacus rubicilla* – see p. 438

Rock Bunting
Emberiza cia

SPEC Category 3
Status Vulnerable
Criteria Large decline

The Rock Bunting is not uncommon throughout most of its range in Mediterranean and central Europe. Although the population is stable in most countries, numbers in Spain and Italy, the species' European strongholds, declined between 1970 and 1990. Local habitat destruction appears to be the only threat at present.

■ Distribution and population trends

The Rock Bunting's range extends from the northern Mediterranean, central Europe and north-west Africa, eastwards across Turkey and central Asia into China. The largest European populations occur in the Iberian peninsula, Italy, Greece (except for the southern Aegean islands) and Turkey (see table, map). As with some other *Emberiza* species, the Rock Bunting has quite a localized distribution, and overall populations seem rather small when compared with the extent of the apparently suitable habitat which is available. The species is partially migratory with some European breeding birds wintering at lower altitudes (below 600 m) near breeding sites.

Numbers appear to be stable in most European countries, although the important Spanish population declined between 1970 and 1990, and populations are also believed to have decreased in Italy and

Ukraine. There is little information available concerning trends in Turkey. It may be that the species' range is expanding towards the north in central Europe (Hungary) (see table).

■ Ecology

The Rock Bunting occurs in a variety of relatively dry habitats, from rocky slopes and bare ravines with sparse shrub vegetation to rather closed old pine forest with little undergrowth (Cramp and Perrins 1994b). However, it most typically prefers the edges of forest and rocky zones. It breeds mainly above 1,000 m, but in ravines, on islands in the Aegean and in the pine forests of Thrace it is also present at lower altitudes, e.g. down to 100 m above sea-level at Dedia in Thrace.

The diet consists of seeds, mainly of grasses (Gramineae), and other plant material, and in the breeding season also invertebrates (Cramp and Perrins 1994b).

In winter, Rock Buntings occurs in mixed flocks with other *Emberiza* species in all kinds of open country at lower altitudes. Wintering birds feed on the ground close to hedges, bushes, copses and wayside trees (Cramp and Perrins 1994b).

■ Threats

No threats to the species have been definitely identified, and overall the reasons for the declines in Spain and Italy are very poorly understood. Habitat loss following the expansion of skiing resorts and other developments may be of local significance, while reduced grazing levels may also lead to vegetation growth and decrease the suitability of habitat. Similarly, forest exploitation destroys habitat and open areas under the canopy are replaced by low shrubs and thicker undergrowth. It may well be that birds are favoured by forest fires and related soil erosion that create an open forest structure and by forestry practices which produce a similar result.

	Breeding population			Breeding
	Size (pairs)	Year	Trend	range trend
Albania	(5,000–10,000)	81	—	—
Andorra	(200–500)	92	(0)	0
Austria	100–150	—	0	0
Bulgaria	(1,000–10,000)	—	(0)	(0)
Croatia	1,000–2,000 *	—	0*	0*
France	1,000–10,000	76	(0)	(0)
Germany	280–1,200	—	0	**0**
Greece	(10,000–20,000)	—	(0)	(0)
Hungary	100–120	—	+1	+1
Italy	(30,000–60,000)	—	(–1)	(0)
Portugal	100,000–1,000,000	89	(0)	0
Romania	200–1,000	—	(0)	(0)
Slovakia	150–250	—	0	**0**
Slovenia	1,000–2,000	—	0	0
Spain	820,000–2,000,000	—	–1	–1
Switzerland	1,000–2,500	86–91	0	0
Turkey	(100,000–1,000,000)	—	—	—
Ukraine	(1–10)	78	(–1)	(–1)
United Kingdom Gibraltar	1–3	—	F	0*
Total (approx.)	1,100,000–4,100,000			

Trends +2 Large increase +1 Small increase 0 Stable X Extinct
(1970–1990) –2 Large decrease –1 Small decrease F Fluctuating N New breeder
Data quality **Bold:** reliable quantitative data Normal type: incomplete quantitative data
Bracketed figures: no quantitative data * Data quality not provided

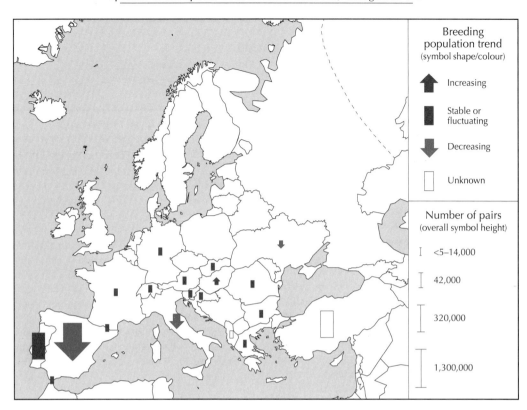

Breeding population trend (symbol shape/colour)

- Increasing
- Stable or fluctuating
- Decreasing
- Unknown

Number of pairs (overall symbol height)

- <5–14,000
- 42,000
- 320,000
- 1,300,000

■ Conservation measures

The conservation status of the Rock Bunting's habitat is generally good and subject to little change, and on the basis of current knowledge, there are no clear conservation measures that can be described. The occurrence of the species at low densities in apparently suitable habitat needs to be better understood as do the declines reported in Spain and Italy. The populations in several countries, including Turkey, Greece, Italy and Spain, should be better monitored.

BEN HALLMANN

Cinereous Bunting
Emberiza cineracea

SPEC Category 2
Status (Vulnerable)
Criteria <2,500 pairs

The Cinereous Bunting is one of Europe's rarest and least known breeding species. Although there are no reliable population estimates, recent records do not indicate any significant decline in numbers or retraction of range. However, further development of tourism in the west of its range and large-scale changes in land use in the east are potentially important threats.

■ Distribution and population trends

Virtually the entire global population of Cinereous Bunting occurs within the western Palearctic, with most birds (c.500–5,000 pairs) of both subspecies (*E. c. cineracea* and *E. c. semenowi*) breeding in Turkey. The nominate western race breeds from Mytilene (Greece) in the Aegean Sea eastwards and southwards to Develi and Kilis in Turkey. The eastern race *E. c. semenowi* is reported to breed from the Gaziantep area in south-east Turkey eastwards to the Turkish borders with Iran and Iraq. Outside Turkey, only two other small populations still exist, neither exceeding c.100 pairs. The first, of the race *E. c. cineracea*, is on the Greek island of Mytilene and is part of the ancient stronghold of this subspecies along the Turkish west coast. The second, involving the subspecies *E. c. semenowi*, is isolated in the Zagros mountains of western Iran. The species is migratory, apparently wintering in southern Sudan, Eritrea and Yemen.

Reliable estimates on both past and current population sizes are lacking. However, analysis of all known records of this species revealed no obvious decline in numbers nor any retraction of the breeding range (de Knijff 1991). Also, records from the major migration route through Israel suggest that numbers have remained unchanged over the past few decades.

The species' global status is classified as Near Threatened because of its small world population size (Collar *et al.* 1994).

	Breeding population			Breeding
	Size (pairs)	Year	Trend	range trend
Greece	(50–100)	—	(0)	(0)
Turkey	(500–5,000)	—	—	—
Total (approx.)	550–5,100			

Trends (1970–1990) +2 Large increase +1 Small increase 0 Stable X Extinct
  −2 Large decrease −1 Small decrease F Fluctuating N New breeder
Data quality **Bold**: reliable quantitative data Normal type: incomplete quantitative data
  Bracketed figures: no quantitative data * Data quality not provided

■ Ecology

Although initially described as a breeding bird of grassy slopes intermixed with shrubs and rocky outcrops at relatively high altitudes (Paludan 1938, Kumerloeve 1961), Cinereous Buntings of both races are known to breed at lower altitudes on slopes with lusher vegetation grazed by sheep and goats. Recently, the species was also found breeding in sheltered valleys which were partly cultivated with orchards and small fields around Gaziantep in Turkey, a habitat shared with Cretzschmar's Bunting *Emberiza caesia* and Black-headed Bunting *E. melanocephala*. Males have also quite frequently been heard calling from the ruins of Pergamum in western Turkey during the breeding season.

The Cinereous Bunting's breeding ecology is virtually unknown, although Chappuis *et al.* (1973) made some observations on *E. c. semenowi* in eastern Turkey, where birds were found breeding in May at a density of 12 pairs in 30 ha.

The diet is little known but seems to be principally seeds and small invertebrates (Cramp and Perrins 1994b).

■ Threats

The Cinereous Bunting is a very poorly studied species, and its status and the effects of habitat destruction on its population are unknown. Even in well-watched places such as Mytilene and western Turkey, where its habitat is being rapidly destroyed due to development for tourism, there are no recent data on the effects of this on population sizes. In the central and eastern parts of Turkey there is currently no obvious habitat loss since breeding occurs mainly on slopes which are too steep for agricultural development, but increasing use of the land for grazing by sheep and goats could adversely affect the area.

The long dry spells which have occurred in the wintering stronghold might have affected the population, but the sparse data available do not indicate any reduction in numbers.

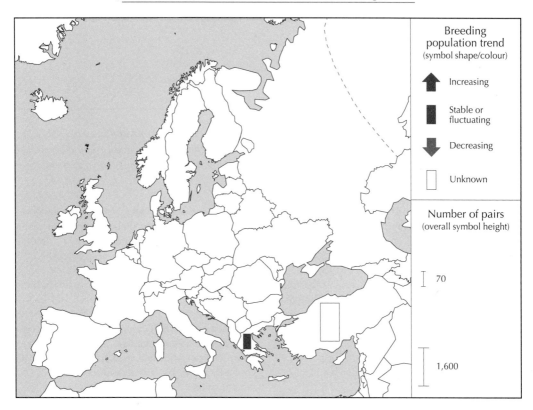

Breeding
population trend
(symbol shape/colour)

▲ Increasing

■ Stable or
fluctuating

▼ Decreasing

□ Unknown

Number of pairs
(overall symbol height)

70

1,600

■ Conservation measures

Much more information about the Cinereous Bunting's current distribution and population size is urgently required in order to develop effective conservation measures. Such data would permit the identification of Important Bird Areas for the protection of the species. Further information on the breeding ecology is also required, and the actual location of the wintering grounds needs to be more firmly established. It is likely that the speed and nature of the development of Turkey's interior will eventually determine the Cinereous Bunting's destiny.

PETER DE KNIJFF

Ortolan Bunting
Emberiza hortulana

SPEC Category 2
Status (Vulnerable)
Criteria Large decline

A massive decline is occurring in many countries, and only southern Europe and Fennoscandia still hold large populations. The main reasons for the decline are changes in agriculture and landscape structure. Conservation measures must address the main habitat requirements such as the maintenance of trees, small fields and rich crop diversities.

■ Distribution and population trends

The breeding range extends from the northern Mediterranean to the Arctic Circle and from the western seaboard of Europe to central Asia. The species has a localized distribution with many isolated populations. It is a trans-Saharan migrant, wintering in the highlands of Guinea, Ivory Coast, Nigeria and Ethiopia.

The Turkish population is poorly known but seems to comprise over half the European total (see table). Spain, Sweden, Finland, Poland, Russia and Bulgaria also hold substantial numbers.

	Breeding population			Breeding
	Size (pairs)	Year	Trend	range trend
Albania	(1,000–3,000)	81	—	—
Andorra	(3–5)	92	(0)	(0)
Austria	10–20	—	–2	–2
Belarus	1,000–3,000	90	F	F
Belgium	**0–3**	91	**–2**	**–2**
Bulgaria	(10,000–100,000)	—	(0)	(0)
Croatia	1,500–2,500 *	—	0*	0*
Czech Republic	**200–300**	—	**–1**	**–1**
Denmark	**0–1**	—	—	—
Estonia	5,000–10,000	—	0	0
Finland	**150,000–200,000**	92	**0**	**0**
France	10,000–23,000	90	–2	–1
Germany	2,000–3,500	—	–1	**0**
Greece	20,000–30,000	—	(–1)	(0)
Hungary	10–30	—	–1	–1
Italy	(4,000–8,000)	—	(–1)	(–1)
Latvia	(500–2,000)	—	(0)	(+1)
Lithuania	(100–500)	85–88	(–1)	(–1)
Moldova	**6,000–8,000**	88	**–1**	**–1**
Netherlands	**25–35**	85	**–2**	**–2**
Norway	100–500	90	–1	**–1**
Poland	60,000–120,000	—	0	0
Portugal	1,000–10,000	89	–1	–1
Romania	(10,000–30,000)	—	(–1)	(–1)
Russia	(10,000–100,000)	—	(0)	(0)
Slovakia	(1–5)	—	–1	**–1**
Slovenia	(300–500)	—	(–1)	(–1)
Spain	200,000–225,000	—	–2	–1
Sweden	25,000–100,000	87	(0)	+1
Switzerland	**200–250**	77–79	**–1**	**–1**
Turkey	(1,000,000–10,000,000)—	—	—	—
Ukraine	800–2,500	88	–1	–1
Total (approx.)	1,500,000–11,000,000			

Trends +2 Large increase +1 Small increase 0 Stable X Extinct
(1970-1990) –2 Large decrease –1 Small decrease F Fluctuating N New breeder
Data quality **Bold: reliable quantitative data** Normal type: incomplete quantitative data
Bracketed figures: no quantitative data * Data quality not provided

Until a few centuries ago the Ortolan Bunting was a typical bird of tree-lined country roads in central Europe (Steiner and Hüni-Luft 1971, Meier-Peithmann 1992), but many of these populations are now decreasing or extinct (von Bülow 1990, Kutzenberger 1991, Meier-Peithmann 1992). In the Czech Republic and Slovakia, Hudec and Stastny (1992) show that in the early nineteenth century the species was extremely rare, but between 1860 and 1880 became a frequent bird in farmland with sparse trees. The population increased up to 1960 within the Czech Republic, but a decline there since 1970 has left only a few sites still occupied.

Since 1970 population trends have differed regionally: while massive declines and local extinctions have occurred in western and central Europe, most notably in Spain, numbers in the north and north-east, especially Finland but also north-west Russia, have remained stable (see table, map). Trends in the huge Turkish population are unknown.

■ Ecology

The species utilizes various habitats over its European range. In most parts it inhabits open farmland where sparse trees and a high diversity of cereal and root crops are important (Conrads 1968, Lang *et al.* 1990); indeed, most nests are found in cereal fields. In southern Europe breeding is mainly in rocky meadows with shrubs and olive orchards (Lovaty 1991, Kumerloeve 1962), and in the south-east it occupies higher altitudes, between 700 and 3,000 m (Kumerloeve 1962, 1989).

In Sweden, rocky grassland sites with isolated oak *Quercus* and pine *Pinus* trees are the main habitats (Stolt 1974). In Finland, the population is most dense in non-intensive arable land with scattered trees, poles or other song-posts; in the north, it breeds in clearings of drier forests and rarely in natural habitats such as grassy meadows and around lakes, and on the driest open peatlands (Koskimies 1989). Individuals often return to the same breeding places each year (P. Keusch pers. comm. 1992).

Single trees are an important component of Ortolan

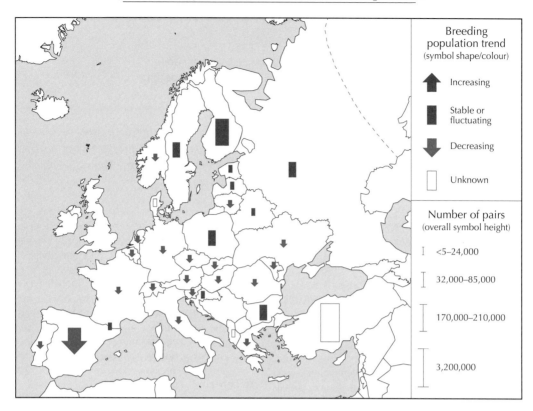

Breeding
population trend
(symbol shape/colour)

Increasing

Stable or
fluctuating

Decreasing

Unknown

Number of pairs
(overall symbol height)

<5–24,000

32,000–85,000

170,000–210,000

3,200,000

Bunting territories as song-posts (only in southern France are rocks also utilized) (Lovaty 1991) and as a source of insects (Conrads 1968).

◼ Threats

Agricultural changes are mainly responsible for the dramatic declines in central European farmland areas. Amalgamation of fields and the consequent loss of hedges (especially isolated trees), together with reductions in crop diversity, are the main factors (Lang *et al.* 1990, Kutzenberger 1991, Meier-Peithmann 1992). In addition, the expansion of settlements and increases in human disturbance during the breeding season may threaten populations locally.

In Austria, road development is an additional significant threat, and almost 90 breeding sites near or along tree-lined roads were destroyed between 1960 and 1990 (Steiner and Hüni-Luft 1971, Kutzenberger 1991). The Mediterranean population in France has declined because of the intensification of sheep-grazing (Lovaty 1991), and about 50,000 migrant Ortolan Buntings are trapped each year in south-west France (O. Claessons pers. comm.).

The importance of threats such as agricultural changes in the wintering quarters is poorly known.

◼ Conservation measures

The Ortolan Bunting's breeding habitat requires urgent conservation measures, especially in arable farming landscapes (Portugal, Spain, Italy, Poland and Fennoscandia). The most important requirements are to maintain or develop non-intensive farming systems which have small fields, high crop diversity, tree-lined tracks or field borders, and low levels of pesticide use. The presence of trees near junctions of field borders is of high importance, because here different crops may meet and optimum breeding places are often found. The maintenance or development of non-intensive farming in pastoral or semi-natural landscapes (especially in Spain, southern France, Greece and Turkey) is also required. Such measures could be supported within the EU by Zonal Programmes developed under the Agri-environment Regulation (EC Reg. 2078/92) of the Common Agricultural Policy. However, similar schemes which give financial support for environmentally beneficial management practices need to be developed in other parts of the species' range.

Given that the species is listed in Annex I of the EU Wild Birds Directive and that it is declining in much of its range, there is a need to stop the trapping of the species in south-west France. Further research into the species' ecology in its winter quarters is required, as this may be important in explaining current population trends.

HARALD KUTZENBERGER

Black-headed Bunting
Emberiza melanocephala

SPEC Category 2
Status (Vulnerable)
Criteria Large decline

Although the Black-headed Bunting's world distribution is quite restricted it is a very common bird in the south-east of Europe. Numbers and trends are known only poorly, but the large population in Greece is declining, probably as a result of the intensification of agriculture. The maintenance of low-intensity farming practices is therefore necessary for this species.

■ Distribution and population trends

The range of the Black-headed Bunting is concentrated in Europe; it extends from southern Italy eastwards, including most of the Balkans and Turkey, to the Caspian region, eastern Ukraine and western and southern Iran. The species is fully migratory, with the whole population wintering in western and central India (Cramp and Perrins 1994b).

Black-headed Buntings are numerous in Europe, with Turkey holding most birds and large populations occurring also in Albania, Greece, Bulgaria and probably Croatia (see table, map). Population trends are poorly known, and in Turkey there is no trend estimate available (see table, map). However, in Greece, which has the second largest population, the species is believed to be declining. Numbers in other countries are probably mostly stable, while some expansion of both population size and range has been reported in Bulgaria and Romania (see table).

■ Ecology

The habitat of the species is open areas with scattered bushes, trees and hedges, mainly on arable land, but places occupied also include pastures, vineyards, orchards and open scrubland. It breeds at high densities from sea-level to 1,200 m (but also breeds on plains above this altitude), preferring low-intensity managed farmland with weeds and thistles, which provide an ample supply of seeds and insects. The birds feed generally in open fields, pastures, wastelands and roadsides, and nests are placed in vegetation close to the ground, usually in a dense bush.

Black-headed Buntings spend a relatively short time on the breeding grounds and probably have time to raise no more than a single brood: the spring arrival of adults takes place in late April or early May, and the birds leave between late July and mid-September, most having departed for India by mid-August (Cramp and Perrins 1994b).

■ Threats

Low-intensity farming provides some benefit to Black-headed Buntings but they are believed to be adversely affected by more intense agricultural practices such as the burning and clearing of hedges and coppices, the use of pesticides, and the amalgamation of small fields into larger units. In Greece, such agricultural intensification continues and is probably responsible for the decline of the species there.

Illegal catching, caging and liming have been reported from several islands in the Aegean.

■ Conservation measures

The maintenance of low-intensity arable land and lightly grazed pastures with widespread coppices and hedges would be beneficial for the species. Such farming practices and habitats could be maintained in Greece, where the species is perhaps most threatened, through Zonal Programmes developed under the Agri-environment Regulation (EC Reg. 2078/92) of the EU Common Agricultural Policy.

Given the poor state of knowledge on the Black-headed Bunting, population sizes and trends should be carefully monitored throughout the whole of its range in Europe, and the impacts of intensive agriculture in general and pesticide use in particular should be investigated.

The hunting of the species in Greece should be halted through strict enforcement of the existing bird protection laws.

BEN HALLMANN

| | Breeding population | | | Breeding |
	Size (pairs)	Year	Trend	range trend
Albania	10,000–30,000	81	—	—
Bulgaria	(5,000–50,000)	—	(+1)	(+1)
Croatia	15,000–20,000 *	—	0*	0*
Cyprus	1,000–3,000	—	0	0
Greece	100,000–200,000	—	(−1)	(0)
Italy	(2,000–4,000)	—	(0)	(0)
Romania	(10–30)	—	(+1)	+1
Russia	(1,000–10,000)	—	(0)	(0)
Turkey	(1,000,000–10,000,000)	—	—	—
Ukraine	(1–20)	78	(−1)	(−1)
Total (approx.)	1,100,000–10,000,000			

Trends   +2 Large increase   +1 Small increase   0 Stable   X Extinct
(1970-1990)   −2 Large decrease   −1 Small decrease   F Fluctuating   N New breeder
Data quality **Bold**: reliable quantitative data   Normal type: incomplete quantitative data
              Bracketed figures: no quantitative data   * Data quality not provided

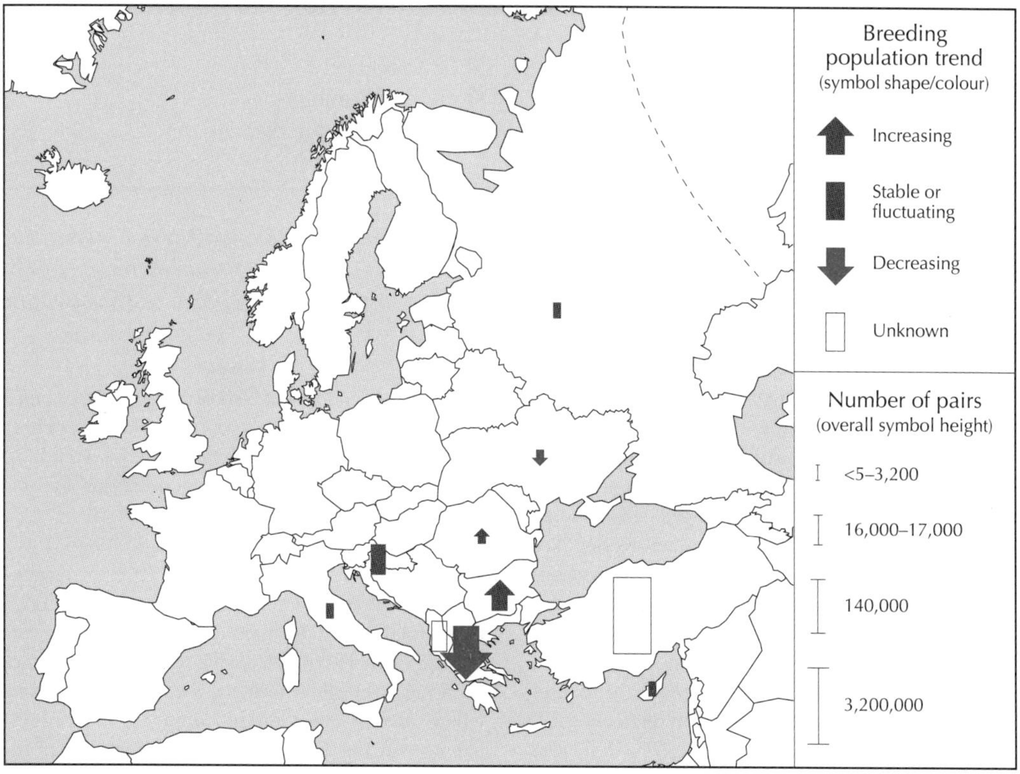
Breeding population trend
(symbol shape/colour)
Increasing
Stable or fluctuating
Decreasing
Unknown
Number of pairs
(overall symbol height)
<5–3,200
16,000–17,000
140,000
3,200,000

• **Black-headed Bunting**

• **Siberian Jay** (next page)

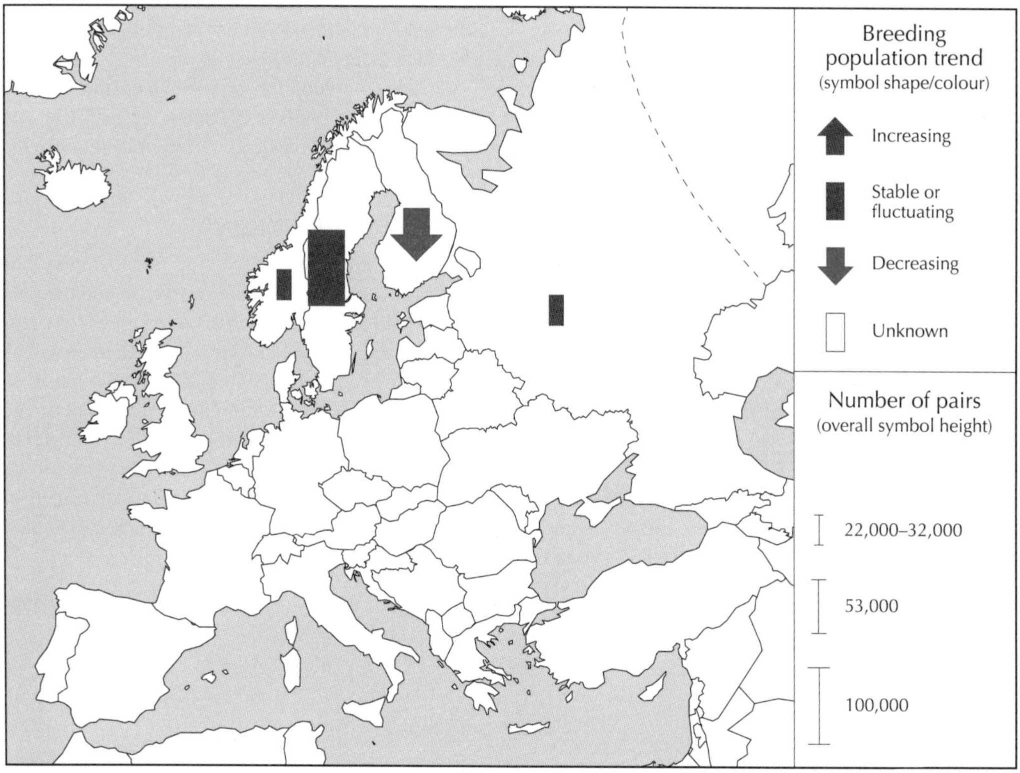
Breeding population trend
(symbol shape/colour)
Increasing
Stable or fluctuating
Decreasing
Unknown
Number of pairs
(overall symbol height)
22,000–32,000
53,000
100,000

Siberian Jay
Perisoreus infaustus

SPEC Category 3
Status (Declining)
Criteria Moderate decline

There has been a considerable reduction in numbers and range of the Siberian Jay in Finland, due mainly to the destruction and fragmentation of extensive areas of mature boreal coniferous forest. Large areas with climax stages of this habitat need to be maintained for the effective conservation of the species.

■ Distribution and population trends

The Siberian Jay occurs throughout the north Palearctic where it is restricted to northern boreal coniferous forest (taiga). Although overall knowledge of the species is poor, the European distribution includes Norway, Sweden, Finland and Russia (see table; map on previous page) and comprises perhaps a quarter of the world range. The species is resident but young birds have occurred outside the breeding range as vagrants during the autumn.

Declines have been confined primarily to Finland, where quantitative data reliably indicate a fall in the population (Järvinen *et al.* 1977, Helle and Järvinen 1986), with numbers having declined by two-thirds between the 1940s and the 1970s (Väisänen *et al.* 1986). This decline continued between 1970 and 1990 (see table). Little information on population trends is available from Russia, while in Norway and Sweden the species remains stable, and in the south of Sweden may even be expanding its range slightly.

	Breeding population			Breeding range trend
	Size (pairs)	Year	Trend	
Finland	**40,000–70,000**	92	–1	**–1**
Norway	10,000–50,000	90	0	**0**
Russia	(10,000–100,000)	—	(0)	(0)
Sweden	(50,000–200,000)	87	0	0
Total (approx.)	110,000–420,000			

Trends +2 Large increase +1 Small increase 0 Stable X Extinct
(1970–1990) –2 Large decrease –1 Small decrease F Fluctuating N New breeder
Data quality **Bold**: reliable quantitative data Normal type: incomplete quantitative data
Bracketed figures: no quantitative data * Data quality not provided

■ Ecology

Siberian Jays require extensive areas of mature coniferous forest, consisting primarily of Scots pine *Pinus sylvestris* (Haila *et al.* 1987) and Norway spruce *Picea abies*, but also of larch *Larix decidua* and downy birch *Betula pubescens*, and rich in lichens. The favoured habitat is dense stands of natural forest with only local modification by man (Cramp and Perrins 1994a).

■ Threats

The loss of habitat and its deterioration through fragmentation are the main causes of decline (Helle and Järvinen 1986). Extensive areas of forest have been clear-felled in northern Sweden and Finland, which results—in addition simply to loss of the habitat—in the fragmentation of remaining prime forest and increased accessibility to nest predators, e.g. Ravens *Corvus corax* (Blomgren 1964, Lindgren 1975). Furthermore, the younger successional stages of coniferous forest after felling are unsuitable for Siberian Jays, and also attract additional nest predators, such as Jay *Garrulus glandarius*.

Clearly, the adoption of such intensive forestry practices in other parts of Europe is a possibility, and this would then constitute a major threat to the species.

■ Conservation measures

Because of the requirement for large, continuous areas of mature boreal coniferous forest and the long recovery time needed for clear-felled areas to regenerate to a stage of sufficient maturity, there is a need for the long-term planning of forest exploitation so that refugia of mature forest can be maintained. The creation of new edges within mature forest, such as through the construction of power lines, should be minimized. An evaluation is needed of the effects of forest fragmentation on the species, and this should include studies of predation.

JAN EKMAN

Cyprus Warbler
Sylvia melanothorax

SPEC Category   2
Status   Rare
Criteria   <10,000 pairs

There have recently been small increases in population size and range due mainly to the creation of suitable habitat following the clearance and opening-up of forests, but this Cyprus endemic remains globally rare. Major threats are the destruction of low, dense Cistus scrub for tourist development and for conversion to plantations, and killing by liming, netting and shooting.

■ Distribution and population trends

Although globally rare, and restricted as a breeder entirely to Cyprus, the Cyprus Warbler has a population of more than 4,000 pairs and is a common and widespread species on the island. It occurs mainly in the Troodos and Kyrenia mountains (up to c.1,400 m), the Karpas and Akamas peninsulas, and coastal lowlands with suitable vegetation cover. It is absent from areas where the average annual rainfall is less than c.340 mm and therefore does not occur on the central Mesaoria plain, except for the eastern and western coastal areas of Famagusta and Morphou; the distributional limits closely follow the 340–350 mm isohyets in the central plain, where in certain areas the breeding range overlaps with that of Spectacled Warbler *S. conspicillata* (Flint and Stewart 1992).

The population has recently increased with the creation of suitable habitat by the clearance and opening-up of forests, and birds have spread into new areas of mainly cultivated land, citrus plantations, and areas near inland water such as small artificial lakes and dams.

Some birds leave the island in winter, with such records coming mainly from low acacia scrub and bush habitats in Israel, Egypt and the Red Sea hills of northern Sudan (Nikolaus 1987, Cramp 1992).

	Breeding population			Breeding
	Size (pairs)	Year	Trend	range trend
Cyprus	4,000–8,000	–	+1	+1
Total (approx.)	4,000–8,000			

Trends   +2 Large increase   +1 Small increase   0 Stable   X Extinct
(1970–1990) –2 Large decrease   –1 Small decrease   F Fluctuating   N New breeder
Data quality **Bold:** reliable quantitative data   Normal type: incomplete quantitative data
Bracketed figures: no quantitative data   * Data quality not provided

■ Ecology

The breeding habitat is primarily low dense scrub, but birds occur also in a wide variety of habitats with some low scrub, including open areas within pine forests, forest edges, areas of golden oak *Quercus alnifolia*, and citrus and other orchards. Scrub composed of *Cistus villosus*, *C. creticus* and *C. parviflorus* is especially favoured, mainly in the Troodos foothills, and breeding densities appear to increase with the proportion of ground covered by *Cistus* scrub (Bacon and Bacon 1982). Nests are generally low in bushes, usually *Cistus*, *Genista sphacelata* or *Calycotome villosa* (Flint and Stewart 1992).

During the breeding season the main food is caterpillars and other insects, and in autumn and winter fruits of *Myrtus communis*, *Pistacia lentiscus*, *Pistacia terebinthus* and *Ficus carica*.

■ Threats

Millions of small birds, including Cyprus Warblers, are still killed each year on Cyprus by liming, netting and shooting (Magnin 1987, Flint and Stewart 1992), especially near forest edges, orchards and other plantations.

The clearance of suitable habitat, especially *Cistus* scrub, for the development of tourism and the establishment of orchards, vineyards, etc., will adversely affect the species if it continues at the present rate. The over-use of agricultural pesticides may also prove to be a major threat if not controlled in the near future.

■ Conservation measures

The Cyprus Warbler is fully protected by Cyprus Law no. 24 of 1988 which implements the Convention on the Conservation of European Wildlife and Natural Habitats (Bern Convention), under which the species is protected (Appendix II of the Convention). Hunters generally ignore the identity of birds they kill, however (Flint and Stewart 1992). Any use of lime-sticks and mist-nets is also now prohibited, but this is not properly enforced. The development of tourism should be strictly regulated, especially in ecologically sensitive areas, and environmental impact studies should precede any major tourist or industrial project.

MELIS CHARALAMBIDES

437

Great Rosefinch
Carpodacus rubicilla

SPEC Category 3
Status (Endangered)
Criteria Large decline, <2,500 pairs

This poorly known, rare species is restricted in Europe to the high Caucasus mountains, where it is believed to have declined. This may have been caused by the over-exploitation by humans of its main winter food plant, as well as by increased predation by Alpine Choughs and by trapping for the cagebird trade. The conservation of berry-producing bushes is required, together with research into the population status and ecology of the species and a moratorium on bird trapping.

■ Distribution and population trends

The Great Rosefinch occurs in two separate areas of central Asia, one extending east from the Tien Shan and Hindu Kush mountain ranges to eastern Tibet, and the second in the high parts of the Altai, Sayan, Tannu Ola and Khangay ranges (Dementiev and Gladkov 1954a). In addition, about 10–20% of its global range lies within Europe, in the Caucasus (traversing southern Russia and Georgia), where about 500–1,500 pairs of the nominate form *C. r. rubicilla* breed (Loskot 1991).

The species breeds only in the highest parts of the main Caucasus range, mainly on the northern slopes of the central Caucasus, between the El'brus and Kazbek mountains, in Kabardino-Balkarskaya, northern Ossetia and Dagestan.

The species is believed to have declined in numbers in Europe, but this is based only on old data indicating a decrease in the size of winter flocks. Maximum winter flock sizes of 150–200 individuals were recorded in the late nineteenth century (Lorenz 1887, Beme 1925) compared to maximum flock sizes of only 40–60 birds in 1960 (Drozdov and Zlotin 1962, Molamusov 1967).

■ Ecology

Great Rosefinches nest at 3,000–3,500 m, within a narrow belt of patchy vegetation on cliffs and screes just below the zone of snow and glaciers. They feed in the alpine and subalpine belts, at about 2,500–2,700 m in summer and 1,900–2,000 m in winter, in exceptionally severe winters occurring lower down in the foothills, up to 60 km from breeding sites.

The species mainly inhabits sunny alpine meadows, where birds will perch on ledges of rocks and crags. Roosting and nesting occur in crevices and niches of cracked rocks, situated at the foot of glaciers (Loskot 1991). During the daytime birds aggregate in flocks to feed, in various nival grasslands and alpine meadows, as well as in small clusters of birch *Betula* on large scree slopes or steep rock faces, or on isolated ledges overgrown with creeping *Rhododen-*

dron. During the winter the birds often concentrate in the thickets of berry-producing shrubs, such as sea buckthorn *Hippophae rhamnoides*, barberry *Berberis iberica* and roses *Rosa* spp., which constitute the basic winter food.

■ Threats

The most important factor to have affected the species is a reduction of *Hippophae rhamnoides* bushes, which over recent decades have suffered considerably due to overexploitation, resulting in a loss of bushes and in a reduction in available berries due to picking by local people. Large amounts of berries have been collected in recent years for medical purposes.

Nests situated in crevices with broad entrances are highly vulnerable to Alpine Choughs *Pyrrhocorax graculus* which take the eggs and chicks. Numbers of Alpine Choughs in the region have increased recently due to the abundance of food near several tourist and alpinist camps, and they may thus constitute a further threat to the species.

An increasing number of Great Rosefinches are being trapped in winter and kept as cagebirds.

■ Conservation measures

The conservation of the winter habitats that are rich in *Hippophae rhamnoides* bushes is a critical requirement, especially in the river valleys bordering the Kabardino-Balkarian and North Ossetian highland reserves, where the majority of European Great Rosefinches winter. Measures should therefore be introduced to ensure sustainable exploitation of *Hippophae* berries.

An accurate census of the species and the monitoring of its population trends should also be undertaken, together with an investigation into the effects of trapping and into the impact made by predation from Alpine Choughs. Until then a complete ban on catching and keeping birds should be implemented.

VLADIMIR LOSKOT

438

SPECIES OF EUROPEAN CONSERVATION CONCERN, CATEGORY 4

Species with a Favourable Conservation Status but concentrated in Europe
(more than half their global population or range in Europe)

Summaries by Euan Dunn

Mediterranean Shearwater *Puffinus yelkouan* occupies a breeding range confined to the Mediterranean where it nests on islets, using crevices or excavated burrows. It is likely that over 75% of its breeding population is in Europe. It disperses throughout the Mediterranean and partially into the western Atlantic outside the breeding season. Breeding status is poorly known, especially in the eastern Mediterranean, but highest numbers are found in Italy and possibly Turkey (where, however, population estimates vary thirty-fold). Between 1970 and 1990 numbers were apparently stable in Italy, but for much of the range there is little information and no trends are known for Turkey. In fact for a very large proportion of the population in the eastern Mediter-

	Breeding population			Breeding range trend
	Size (pairs)	Year	Trend	
Populations >5% of European total				
Greece	(1,000–2,000)	—	(0)	(0)
Italy	(11,000–18,000)	—	(0)	(0)
Spain	3,300–5,000	—	–1	–1
Turkey	(1,000–30,000)	—	—	—
Additional populations in decline				
Malta	500–1,000	—	–1	0
Total of above	16,800–56,000			
European total	18,000–57,000			

ranean, breeding sites remain unknown. The only reasonably certain declines were recorded in Malta and Spain, collectively representing at most c.20% of the known breeding population.

Shag *Phalacrocorax aristotelis* breeds widely in Europe along rocky sea-coasts with access to sheltered inshore feeding grounds. Over 75% of the species' range is in Europe. In the Mediterranean and Black Seas it is mainly resident, but is dispersive elsewhere. The United Kingdom accounts for almost half the total European population, while Iceland, Republic of Ireland, United Kingdom, France and Norway together support all but c.10% of the European population. Census data are good for these strongholds. Between 1970 and 1990, the majority of the population increased, though nearly a quarter declined, including the important Norwegian breeding population.

	Breeding population			Breeding range trend
	Size (pairs)	Year	Trend	
Populations >5% of European total				
France	5,000–5,500	88	+2	+1
Iceland	8,000–9,000	75	+1	0
Rep. of Ireland	8,300–8,300	85–87	+1	0
Norway	15,000–15,000	90	–1	0
United Kingdom	39,000–39,000	85–87	+1	0
Additional populations in decline				
Albania	20–? *	—	—	–1*
Bulgaria	10–50	—	–1	0
Denmark				
Faroe Islands	(1,000–2,000)	—	(–1)	(0)
Greece	(200–400)	—	(–1)	(0)
Russia	1,000–1,500	84–88	–1	0
Spain	1,660–2,700	—	–1	–1
Ukraine	250–400	78	–2	–2
United Kingdom				
Gibraltar	3–5	91	–1	—
Total of above	79,000–84,000			
European total	85,000–93,000			

Whooper Swan *Cygnus cygnus* breeds in Iceland, Fennoscandia and north-east Europe, mainly in swampy lakes and river deltas. With the exception of Iceland, where the species is a partial migrant, populations are wholly migratory, wintering in north-west Europe or else in the region extending from south-east Europe to the Caspian and Aral Seas. Typical wintering habitat comprises coastal and inland wetlands and floodland providing suitable grazing of aquatic plants and grass, but foraging also occurs in stubbles, winter cereals and other arable crops. About 80% of the European wintering population is accounted for by the Republic of Ireland, United Kingdom, Denmark and Russia. Between 1970 and 1990, the Russian population apparently

	Winter population			Winter
	Size (individuals)	Year	Trend	range trend
Populations >5% of European total				
Denmark	6,700–6,700 *	—	—	—
Rep. of Ireland	**10,000–11,000**	—	+1	—
Russia	(10,000–70,000)	—	(F)	(0)
United Kingdom	**7,500–7,500**	88	**0**	**0**
Total of above	34,000			
European total	40,000			

fluctuated. In the same period, numbers were stable in the United Kingdom and increased in the Republic of Ireland, while no trends were established for Denmark. No negative trends emerged anywhere in Europe, where the majority of the wintering population appeared to be stable or increasing during 1970–1990.

Pink-footed Goose *Anser brachyrhynchus* breeds only in Europe, occurring in Greenland, Iceland and Svalbard, mainly on tundra. All populations migrate to north-west Europe in winter, with the United Kingdom supporting exclusively birds from Greenland and Iceland. The vast majority of the breeding population occurs in Svalbard and Iceland and, with improved conditions for feeding and survival on the wintering grounds, populations have increased steadily in recent years, markedly so in Iceland.

	Breeding population			Breeding
	Size (pairs)	Year	Trend	range trend
Populations >5% of European total				
Denmark				
Greenland	2,500–5,000	—	+1	+1
Iceland	15,000–25,000	60–87	+2	+2
Norway				
Svalbard	**30,000–30,000**	—	+1	+1
Total of above	48,000–60,000			
European total	48,000–60,000			

Pochard *Aythya ferina* breeds in north-west, central and eastern Europe, Fennoscandia, parts of southern Europe and marginally in Iceland, mainly in freshwater pools, lakes and slow-moving streams with fringing cover. Especially in winter it also uses brackish or salt water. It is migratory or partially so, moving mainly to southern parts of the range, some even to the Middle East and northern Afrotropics. About a third of the European population is known to breed in Russia and c.80% is accounted for by Poland, Russia, Czech Republic, Hungary, Romania and Ukraine. The population in these countries was mostly stable between 1970 and 1990, though numbers have declined in the Czech Republic and Romania and increased substantially in Ukraine. Away from these core areas, there have been small but widespread increases in both numbers and range, notably in north-west and eastern Europe. Norway and Italy are recent additions to the breeding range.

	Breeding population			Breeding
	Size (pairs)	Year	Trend	range trend
Populations >5% of European total				
Czech Republic	10,000–20,000	—	–1	**0**
Germany	23,000–23,000	—	+1	**+1**
Hungary	20,000–30,000	—	0	**0**
Poland	40,000–70,000	—	0	**0**
Romania	20,000–40,000	—	–1	**–1**
Russia	90,000–100,000	—	0	**0**
Ukraine	25,000–28,000	88	+2	**0**
Additional populations in decline				
Finland	**12,000–15,000**	92	–1	**0**
France	2,650–3,000	90	–1	**+1**
Rep. of Ireland	(20–20)	88–91	–1	**0**
Moldova	**800–1,200**	89	+1	**–1**
Sweden	1,000–1,500	87	–1	**0**
Total of above	240,000–330,000			
European total	270,000–370,000			

These advances continue an overall trend of considerable range expansion, especially in northern and western Europe, over the last 150 years.

Honey Buzzard *Pernis apivorus* occurs widely through mainland Europe which accounts for over 75% of the species' breeding range. It favours secluded forests interspersed with clearings and open ground, and winters in tropical Africa. About two-thirds of the European population is in Russia, with significant numbers also in Germany, France and Sweden. Over much of the range, including Russia, numbers were stable during 1970–1990, although c.10% of the population is declining. Numbers have increased in France and apparently decreased in Germany. Among other countries undergoing decline, Finland holds a significant population.

	Breeding population			Breeding
	Size (pairs)	Year	Trend	range trend
Populations >5% of European total				
France	**8,000–12,000**	82	(+1)	+1
Germany	(6,000–9,000)	—	–1	**0**
Russia	70,000–100,000	—	0	0
Sweden	5,000–10,000	87	**0**	**0**
Additional populations in decline				
Andorra	(0–1)	91	(0)	(–1)
Bulgaria	50–100	—	–1	0
Finland	**4,000–5,000**	92	–1	**0**
Moldova	**30–50**	89	**–1**	**0**
Ukraine	320–350	88	–1	–1
Total of above	93,000–140,000			
European total	110,000–160,000			

Red Kite *Milvus milvus* has almost its entire world breeding population in Europe, with just a few tens of pairs in Morocco. Its habitat comprises lowland areas or mountain valleys with extensive open areas for hunting, close to woodland with mature trees for nesting. Populations from north and central Europe are migratory, wintering predominantly in the Mediterranean basin. The small British population is sedentary. Over 90% of the European population breeds in Germany, France and Spain, with around two-thirds in Germany alone. During 1970–1990, the French population increased, the German population was apparently stable, while the Spanish population and range decreased. This is part of a strong decline since the nineteenth century, which is continuing in south-west and eastern Europe. During 1970–1990, about 20% of the European population was in decline. There are, however, signs of a recovery in central and north-west Europe, with countries such as Denmark, Belgium, Czech Republic and Austria being recolonized during 1970–1990.

	Breeding population			Breeding
	Size (pairs)	Year	Trend	range trend
Populations >5% of European total				
France	**2,300–2,900**	82	+1	**0**
Germany	12,000–25,000	—	0	**0**
Spain	3,000–7,000	—	–1	–1
Additional populations in decline				
Belarus	(0–10)	90	(–2)	(–2)
Italy	(70–100)	—	(–1)	(–1)
Latvia	0–5	—	–1	(–1)
Lithuania	1–2	85–88	(–1)	(–1)
Moldova	**1–1**	90	0	–1
Portugal	100–300	89	–1	–1
Romania	(10–20)	—	–1	**–1**
Russia	0–50	—	–1	–1
Slovakia	10–20	—	–1	–1
Ukraine	**5–8**	88	**–2**	**–1**
Total of above	17,000–35,000			
European total	19,000–37,000			

Montagu's Harrier *Circus pygargus* has a scattered distribution in north-west, central and southern Europe, being more widespread in the east. Its habitat embraces lowland heath, rough grassland, dunes, cereal fields and young conifer plantations. It is migratory, wintering widely in the savanna of Africa. About 75% of the European population lies in Russia, with c.10% in France, and smaller but significant numbers in Spain. During 1970–1990 numbers increased in Russia and fluctuated in France. Elsewhere there are no clear overall trends, consistent with the opportunistic settlement pattern of this species, especially in fringe areas. Overall, c.8% of the European population was in decline during 1970–1990, about half (Spain, Germany, Netherlands) declining rapidly. Trends are unknown in Turkey which has an estimated maximum 1,000 pairs.

	Breeding population			Breeding
	Size (pairs)	Year	Trend	range trend
Populations >5% of European total				
France	2,500–5,000	90	F	+1
Russia	20,000–30,000	—	+1	+1
Additional populations in decline				
Denmark	**50–54**	87	**0**	**–1**
Germany	300–500	86	**–2**	**0**
Greece	5–10	—	(0)	(–1)
Latvia	50–150	—	(–1)	(–1)
Lithuania	10–100	85–88	(–1)	(–1)
Moldova	**3–6**	88	**–1**	**0**
Netherlands	**6–12**	89–91	**–2**	**–2**
Portugal	400–900	89	–1	–1
Romania	0–0	—	X	X
Spain	1,000–1,300	—	**–2**	–2
Ukraine	200–240	89	–1	–1
United Kingdom	**6–12**	90–91	**–1**	**–1**
Total of above	25,000–38,000			
European total	26,000–42,000			

Caucasian Snowcock *Tetraogallus caucasicus* is endemic to the Caucasus, where its distribution is restricted to the alpine and subalpine zones of the High Caucasus and neighbouring ranges. It inhabits mountain slopes with an abundance of rocks, alpine meadows, clumps of bushes and patches of melting snow. The species remains mostly between 2,300 and 4,000 m, but does undergo seasonal altitudinal migration, wintering at lower altitudes. The total population size was estimated to be 164,000 individuals in spring and 278,000 in autumn. These totals are considerably lower than an earlier estimate of 410,000. There is no indication of a population decline, but the species' status is very poorly known.

Spotted Crake *Porzana porzana* is thinly scattered throughout most of Europe, but more widespread in the east, inhabiting lowland swamps and fens, overgrown edges of lakes and rivers, and upland bogs. It is mainly migratory, wintering in southern Europe and eastern Africa south of the Sahara. The status is poorly known, but about two-thirds of the European population is found in Russia and Belarus, with significant numbers also in France, Romania and Ukraine. Probably reflecting a longer-term trend, about a quarter of the European population apparently declined during 1970–1990, some of it rapidly, including a marked, well-authenticated decrease in the Ukraine. Declines were also recorded in France, Romania and various other countries with smaller populations. Elsewhere, the species seems to be stable or fluctuating, the only definitely known increase having occurred in Finland where the maximum population is put at 2,000 pairs.

	Breeding population			Breeding
	Size (pairs)	Year	Trend	range trend
Populations >5% of European total				
Belarus	24,000–28,000	90	0	0
France	1,000–10,000	76	–1	0
Romania	(5,000–20,000)	—	(–1)	–1
Russia	(10,000–100,000)	—	(0)	(0)
Ukraine	(4,200–4,800)	88	–2	–2
Additional populations in decline				
Austria	(0–20)	—	–2	–1
Czech Republic	20–40	—	–1	**–1**
Denmark	**123–123**	89	–1	(0)
Italy	(50–200)	—	(–1)	(–1)
Latvia	(200–1,000)	—	(–1)	(–1)
Lithuania	600–1,000	85–88	–1	(–1)
Moldova	250–350	88	–1	–1
Poland	2,500–3,500	—	–1	0
Sweden	100–300	87	–1	**0**
United Kingdom	10–21	88–90	0	–1
Total of above	48,000–170,000			
European total	52,000–180,000			

Little Crake *Porzana parva* occurs principally in eastern Europe and only sporadically elsewhere in mainland Europe, typically in freshwater wetlands with tall emergent vegetation. Over 75% of the world range is in Europe. The wintering grounds are not well known but the species migrates mainly to Africa, variously to Senegal, north-east and East Africa south to the Equator. Populations and trends are not well understood, but Russia, Ukraine, Belarus, Austria and Romania together account for the vast majority of the population, with Russia by far the biggest stronghold. Apparently over a quarter of the European population declined during 1970–1990, markedly so in the Ukraine, also to some extent in Romania. Several other countries with smaller populations also suffered declines, some of them rapid. Against this there was an increase in Russia. During the same period, apart from new breeding in Finland, no other country registered an increase.

	Breeding population			Breeding
	Size (pairs)	Year	Trend	range trend
Populations >5% of European total				
Austria	4,000–6,000	—	0	0
Belarus	(2,000–3,000)	90	(F)	(0)
Romania	(3,000–6,000)	—	(–1)	–1
Russia	(10,000–100,000)	—	(+1)	(+1)
Ukraine	(3,500–4,000)	88	–2	–2
Additional populations in decline				
Croatia	100–150 *	—	–1*	–1*
Czech Republic	4–8	—	–1	1
Estonia	10–20	—	(–2)	(0)
France	10–100	76	–2	0
Greece	(10–50)	—	(0)	(–1)
Italy	(20–50)	—	(–1)	(–1)
Latvia	50–100	—	–1	F
Moldova	150–250	88	–1	–1
Slovakia	(70–150)	—	(–1)	(0)
Slovenia	(1–5)	—	(–2)	(–2)
Sweden	1–10	—	–1	0*
Total of above	23,000–120,000			
European total	25,000–120,000			

Golden Plover *Pluvialis apricaria* breeds in Iceland and northern Europe, mainly on upland moors, heaths and peatlands. Over 75% of the species' wintering range is in Europe. The species is migratory or, at lower latitudes, partially so, wintering mainly in southern (especially south-west) Europe. Nearly half the European breeding population is found in Iceland, with Norway accounting for a further quarter. These two countries, along with Finland, Sweden, Russia and the United Kingdom, hold all but 1% of the European population. During 1970–1990, most of the core population was stable but c.15% showed declines, notably in Finland and the United Kingdom. Some of the small southern populations also declined, continuing a long-term downward trend in the southern part of the range.

	Breeding population			Breeding
	Size (pairs)	Year	Trend	range trend
Populations >5% of European total				
Finland	**50,000–80,000**	92	–1	**0**
Iceland	200,000–300,000	—	(0)	0
Norway	100,000–200,000	90	0	**0**
Russia	(10,000–100,000)	80–90	(0)	(+1)
Sweden	50,000–75,000	87	0	0
United Kingdom	23,000–23,000	88–91	–1	**0**
Additional populations in decline				
Denmark	**5–5**	87	–1	–1
Faroe Islands	300–1,000	81	(–1)	(0)
Germany	**20–30**	—	–1	**0**
Rep. of Ireland	(350–350)	88–91	(–1)	0
Lithuania	**60–70**	85–88	(0)	–1
Total of above	430,000–780,000			
European total	440,000–790,000			

Range apparently expanded in Russia, but the only actual population increase was recorded in Latvia.

Purple Sandpiper *Calidris maritima* breeds in Russia, Fennoscandia and Greenland, with Europe accounting for over 75% of the world range. It breeds on coastal and upland tundra, and is a migrant or partial migrant, wintering on coasts which are mostly, however, within the breeding latitudes. Iceland and Norway together make up about three-quarters of the European population, with Greenland, Svalbard, Sweden and Russia accounting for almost all the remainder. There is no evidence that the main populations were other than stable during 1970–1990, although information is generally poor. The only exception was the small Faroese population which appeared to undergo a rapid decline during this period.

	Breeding population			Breeding
	Size (pairs)	Year	Trend	range trend
Populations >5% of European total				
Denmark				
Greenland	(2,000–10,000)	—	(0)	(0)
Iceland	10,000–30,000	—	(0)	0
Norway	10,000–20,000	90	0	**0**
Svalbard	(1,000–10,000)	—	(0)	(0)
Russia	(1,000–10,000)	80–90	(0)	(0)
Additional populations in decline				
Denmark				
Faroe Islands	(0–20)	81	(–2)	(–1)
Total of above	24,000–80,000			
European total	25,000–83,000			

Ruff *Philomachus pugnax* breeds in Europe mainly in Fennoscandia and the eastern countries, and sparsely in the north-west. Habitat varies from lowland tundra in the north to wet grasslands and coastal marshes further south. It is migratory, wintering extensively in sub-Saharan Africa, and to a small extent also in southern and western Europe. Russia accounts for the vast majority (over 90%) of the European breeding population. The remainder is widely distributed, with significant numbers in Norway, Sweden and Finland. Though there is little hard evidence, the core population in Russia is probably stable. During 1970–1990, however, numbers dwindled and their range contracted rapidly in several other countries, notably Finland. Though the proportion of the European population in decline did not

	Breeding population			Breeding
	Size (pairs)	Year	Trend	range trend
Populations >5% of European total				
Russia	(1,000,000–10,000,000)	80–90	(0)	(0)
Additional populations in decline				
Denmark	**540–540**	80	–1	–1
Finland	**30,000–50,000**	92	–2	–2
Germany	600–760	3	–1	**0**
Latvia	(50–200)	—	–2	–2
Netherlands	**400–800**	89–91	–2	–2
Poland	150–300	—	–2	–2
Ukraine	1–5	86	–2	–2
Total of above	1,000,000–10,000,000			
European total	1,100,000–10,000,000			

exceed a few percent, it represents a continuation of the marked range contraction seen over the last 200 years, especially in the south. The only increase occurred in Norway.

Whimbrel *Numenius phaeopus* breeds in Europe chiefly in Iceland, Fennoscandia and the eastern countries, nesting on lowland and upland tundra, moors and peat-bogs. It winters mainly along Afrotropical coasts. Nearly two-thirds of the European population occurs in Iceland, with a further quarter in Finland, and significant numbers also in Russia. During 1970–1990, numbers in Iceland and Russia apparently remained stable (though a modest range increase apparently occurred in Russia), but increased in Finland. Small increases in population are also indicated in the United Kingdom and Estonia, and during the same period the species started breeding in Greenland. The only known declines occurred in the Faroes and Belarus, but these populations together represent only c.1% of the European total.

	Breeding population			Breeding
	Size (pairs)	Year	Trend	range trend
Populations >5% of European total				
Finland	**50,000–80,000**	92	+1	**0**
Iceland	100,000–200,000	—	(0)	0
Russia	(10,000–30,000)	80–90	(0)	(+1)
Additional populations in decline				
Belarus	20–50	90	–1	0
Denmark				
Faroe Islands	(2,000–3,000)	81	(–1)	(0)
Total of above	160,000–310,000			
European total	180,000–340,000			

Great Skua *Stercorarius skua* breeds only in Europe, being confined to Iceland, Faroes, northern Scotland and Fennoscandia. It nests on coastal moorland, grassland and tundra. It is a pelagic migrant south of the breeding grounds, wintering mainly in the Atlantic south of Britain and Ireland as far as the tropics, but also in the western Mediterranean. Status is generally well known. All but a few percent of the total population is found in the United Kingdom (which holds nearly 60% of the total) and Iceland (nearly 40%). During 1970–1990, numbers and range increased in the United Kingdom. In Iceland, numbers remained stable, but there was a range increase. During the same period, numbers fluctuated on the Faroes, increased on Svalbard, and the species colonized Norway and Russia, reflecting a general expansion in the north of the range.

	Breeding population			Breeding
	Size (pairs)	Year	Trend	range trend
Populations >5% of European total				
Iceland	**5,400–5,400**	84–85	0	+1
United Kingdom	**7,900–7,900**	85–87	+1	+1
Total of above	13,000–13,000			
European total	14,000–14,000			

Mediterranean Gull *Larus melanocephalus* breeds only in Europe, mainly in the east and southeast, but also increasingly further to the west and north. It breeds coastally or inland in the hinterland of steppe lakes, marshes and deltas. It is migratory, wintering chiefly in the Mediterranean, but also in the Black Sea, the Atlantic and North Sea coasts of Europe, and the Baltic. Over 90% of the breeding population is found in the Ukraine where it showed a rapid increase in numbers and range between 1970 and 1990. The population in Greece apparently remained stable but contracted somewhat in range, while the small Romanian population decreased rapidly in numbers and range. However, these are the exceptions to a general north-west expansion which saw widespread increases in numbers (rapidly so in the United Kingdom, France and Netherlands), and colonization of several new countries, most notably Russia where the maximum population is c.13,300 pairs. This overall range expansion continues the pattern which first became conspicuous in the 1960s. No trend data are available for Turkey, which holds the biggest population in south-east Europe after the Ukraine and Greece.

	Breeding population			Breeding
	Size (pairs)	Year	Trend	range trend
Populations >5% of European total				
Ukraine	**180,000–336,000**	83	+2	+2
Additional populations in decline				
Greece	2,000–5,000	—	0*	(–1)
Romania	(0–5)	—	(–2)	(–2)
Total of above	180,000–340,000			
European total	180,000–360,000			

Lesser Black-backed Gull *Larus fuscus* breeds mainly in Iceland, north-west Europe, Fennoscandia and eastern Europe. It is mostly marine, frequenting coastal waters and breeding in low vegetation such as heathland on islands, dunes, and other coastal fringes, but some birds nest on inland moorland. Some are resident, but most migrate, mainly to the Mediterranean and especially to Afrotropical coasts, also to large African inland lakes. About 40% of the European population is found in the United Kingdom. Other major concentrations occur in Iceland, Netherlands and France (each c.10%), followed in importance by Sweden and Norway. Between 1970 and 1990, the key populations (representing c.75% of the European total) in the United Kingdom, Iceland, France and Netherlands all increased, rapidly so in the last three cases. A significant feature of this pattern, with the probable exception of Germany, is the overall upward trend in countries bordering the southern North Sea. The increase in Iceland was accompanied by a marked range expansion. In the

	Breeding population			Breeding
	Size (pairs)	Year	Trend	range trend
Populations >5% of European total				
France	**23,563–23,563**	88	+2	0
Iceland	25,000–35,000	—	+2	+2
Netherlands	**24,000–24,000**	90	+2	0
Norway	10,000–20,000	90	–1	0
Sweden	15,000–20,000	87	–1	0
United Kingdom	86,000–86,000	85–87	+1	0
Additional populations in decline				
Denmark				
Faroe Islands	(5,000–9,000)	81	(–1)	(0)
Estonia	250–300	—	–1	0
Finland	**6,000–7,000**	92	–2	0
Russia	700–2,300	84–88	–1	0
Total of above	200,000–230,000			
European total	200,000–240,000			

same period, numbers declined in the Faroes, Norway, Sweden, Russia and Estonia, and rapidly so in Finland. Collectively, these countries represent up to about a quarter of the population in decline. Elsewhere, there were notable rapid increases in Denmark and Spain, and new breeding records for Greenland, Poland and Portugal.

Great Black-backed Gull *Larus marinus* breeds mainly in Greenland, Iceland, Fennoscandia and north-west Europe, with Europe representing over 75% of the species' range. It frequents sea coasts and offshore waters, nesting on small islands, stacks and cliffs. Populations breeding north of the Arctic Circle migrate (south and west) after the breeding season, while southern populations are dispersive. The biggest proportion of the European population occurs in Norway (30%), followed by the United Kingdom, Iceland, Sweden, Russia and Greenland, these six countries accounting for more than 80% of the European total. During 1970–1990, populations in the United Kingdom, Norway and Sweden were stable. The Russian population increased, while that in Iceland (representing up to a fifth of the European total) decreased. Apart from Greenland where trends

	Breeding population			Breeding
	Size (pairs)	Year	Trend	range trend
Populations >5% of European total				
Denmark				
Greenland	(1,000–20,000)	83	—	(0)
Iceland	15,000–30,000	—	–1	0
Norway	30,000–50,000	90	0	0
Russia	8,200–10,000	84–88	+1	0
Sweden	10,000–15,000	87	0	0
United Kingdom	**20,000–20,000**	85–87	0	0
Total of above	84,000–150,000			
European total	97,000–160,000			

are unknown, information is generally good. In countries other than those holding core populations, the prevailing trend was of increase: rapid in France, Denmark and Estonia, slower in Finland, Republic of Ireland and Slovenia. During the same period, the species colonized Germany.

Razorbill *Alca torda* occurs in Fennoscandia, north-west Europe and Iceland, these regions together accounting for over 75% of the world population. It lives on rocky sea coasts, breeding on cliff ledges and under boulders. Northern populations migrate outside the breeding season, while southern ones are both migratory as far as the Mediterranean (mainly immatures) and dispersive (adults). Iceland holds over two-thirds of the European total, followed in importance by the United Kingdom and Norway, these three countries together supporting over 90%

	Breeding population			Breeding
	Size (pairs)	Year	Trend	range trend
Populations >5% of European total				
Iceland	300,000–400,000	—	+1	0
Norway	20,000–40,000	90	–1	0
United Kingdom	80,000–80,000	85–87	+1	0
Additional populations in decline				
France	**39–43**	88	–2	0
Rep. of Ireland	**11,000–11,000**	85–87	–1	0
United Kingdom				
Jersey [1]	1–5	—	–1	–1
Total of above	410,000–530,000			
European total	430,000–560,000			

445

of the European population. Trends in the core populations indicate that numbers increased in Iceland and the United Kingdom between 1970 and 1990, but declined in Norway. Decreases were also noted in the Republic of Ireland and France. Overall, c.5–10% of the European population declined during the period. Elsewhere, significant increases were recorded in Sweden and Finland, reflecting general recovery in the Baltic after declines earlier in the twentieth century, attributed to egg-collecting, disturbance and cold weather. Trends in Greenland are poorly known.

Stock Dove

Stock Dove *Columba oenas* occurs throughout Europe (which accounts for over 75% of the range), mainly in woodland-edge habitat, parks and farmland with mature trees or other habitats offering suitable nest-hole sites. Migratory status varies from wholly migratory in northern Europe to resident or dispersive in the south. The United Kingdom supports between a third and a half of the European population, while c.80–90% is made up by this country along with Spain, Netherlands, Germany, Russia, Belarus and Romania. Between 1970 and 1990 there was a marked increase in numbers in the United Kingdom and Netherlands, with more modest increases in the Republic of Ireland, Belgium and Denmark. These increases reflect a pattern of recovery in western Europe from setbacks in the 1950s and 1960s. During 1970–1990, the German population fluctuated, while declines were recorded in Spain and Belarus. Eighteen other countries with smaller populations, notably in northern, central and south-east Europe, also showed modest declines. In total, about a fifth of the European population declined during 1970–1990.

	Breeding population			Breeding
	Size (pairs)	Year	Trend	range trend
Populations >5% of European total				
Belarus	25,000–32,000	90	–1	0
Germany	50,000–80,000	—	F	0
Netherlands	**30,000–40,000**	79	**+2**	**+1**
Romania	(20,000–40,000)	—	(0)	0
Russia	(10,000–100,000)	—	(0)	(0)
Spain	36,000–54,400	—	–1	–1
United Kingdom	240,000–240,000	88–91	+2	0
Additional populations in decline				
Albania	(500–1,000)	62	(–1)	(–1)
Austria	(1,000–1,200)	—	(–1)	(–1)
Bulgaria	(200–400)	—	(–1)	(–1)
Croatia	1,000–1,500 *	—	–1*	–1*
Czech Republic	3,000–6,000	—	–1	0
Finland	6,000–7,000	92	–1	–1
France	1,000–10,000	76	–1	0
Greece	(1,000–1,500)	—	(0)	(–1)
Italy	(100–300)	—	(–2)	(–1)
Latvia	150–200	—	–1	0
Lithuania	(100–200)	85–88	(–1)	(0)
Moldova	**120–180**	88	**–1**	**–1**
Norway	1,000–10,000	90	–1	0
Slovakia	3,500–5,500	—	–1	–1
Slovenia	(200–300)	—	(–2)	(–2)
Switzerland	500–1,000	86–91	–1	–1
Turkey	(1,000–10,000)	—	(–1)	—
Ukraine	**850–1,000**	88	**–1**	**–1**
Total of above	430,000–640,000			
European total	460,000–700,000			

Woodpigeon

Woodpigeon *Columba palumbus* occurs throughout Europe (which constitutes over 75% of the world range), flourishing in a mosaic of woodland and open ground, notably farmland, parks and suburban gardens. Migratory status varies from mainly migratory in the north of the range to mainly resident in the south. Highest numbers occur in north-west and eastern Europe, and Fennoscandia. The United Kingdom, France and Germany together account for about half the European total, while c.80–90% is comprised by these countries plus Republic of Ireland, Norway, Sweden, Netherlands, Poland and Russia. Between 1970 and 1990, populations in these strongholds were mostly stable, though increasing numbers were recorded in the Netherlands, Norway and Germany. The increase in Norway suggests consolidation of the expansion into Fennoscandia witnessed in the twentieth century, although

	Breeding population			Breeding
	Size (pairs)	Year	Trend	range trend
Populations >5% of European total				
France	1,000,000–?	90	(0)	**0**
Germany	1,000,000–4,000,000	—	+1	**0**
Rep. of Ireland	(660,000–800,000)	88–91	(0)	0
Netherlands	**500,000–800,000**	79	**+1**	**0**
Norway	100,000–1,000,000	90	+1	**+1**
Poland	300,000–1,000,000	—	0	**0**
Russia	(100,000–1,000,000)	—	(0)	(0)
Sweden	500,000–1,000,000	87	**0**	**0**
United Kingdom	2,200,000–2,700,000	88–91	(0)	**0**
Additional populations in decline				
Austria	(25,000–30,000)	—	(–1)	(0)
Bulgaria	(2,500–25,000)	—	(–1)	(–1)
Total of above	6,400,000–12,000,000			
European total	7,700,000–14,000,000			

the Finnish population is stable. Over Europe as a whole, the prevailing pattern is one of stable or slightly improving population status, with negligible declines during 1970–1990.

Tawny Owl *Strix aluco* breeds widely in Europe. It is sedentary and inhabits deciduous and coniferous woodland and orchards, and other wooded cultivated and urban areas. Half to three-quarters of the European population is found in Spain, United Kingdom, France, Germany, Poland, Russia and Croatia. The population appears to have been stable over a wide area during 1970–1990, although c.8% of the population has shown a small decline.

	Breeding population			Breeding
	Size (pairs)	Year	Trend	range trend
Populations >5% of European total				
Croatia	20,000–25,000 *	—	0*	0*
France	50,000–150,000	90	0	**0**
Germany	50,000–150,000	—	0	**0**
Poland	65,000–75,000	—	0	0
Russia	(10,000–100,000)	75–90	(0)	(0)
Spain	45,000–61,000	—	0	0
United Kingdom	20,000–20,000	88–91	–1	**0**
Additional populations in decline				
Albania	2,000–4,000	62	(–1)	(–1)
Andorra	**15–20**	92	**0**	–1
Estonia	1,000–1,200	—	–1	0
Finland	**1,500–2,500**	92	–1	**0**
Italy	(5,000–10,000)	—	–1	(–1)
Moldova	**650–800**	89	**–1**	**–1**
Total of above	270,000–600,000			
European total	360,000–800,000			

Plain Swift *Apus unicolor* breeds only in Europe, being confined to Madeira and the Canary Islands where it frequents mountainous areas, breeding in caves and rock crevices. Most are migratory, presumably to Africa though the precise wintering grounds are not known. During 1970–1990, the Madeiran population of 1,000–2,000 pairs was stable. There were no population estimates for the Canary Islands during this period.

	Breeding population			Breeding
	Size (pairs)	Year	Trend	range trend
Populations >5% of European total				
Portugal				
Madeira	1,000–2,000	91	0	0
Spain				
Canary Islands	P	—	—	—
Total of above	1,000–2,000			
European total	1,000–2,000			

Syrian Woodpecker *Dendrocopos syriacus* occurs in eastern and south-east Europe, largely replacing Great Spotted Woodpecker *D. major* in open lowland country such as wooded farmland, vineyards, orchards, parkland, and open deciduous woodland. Though a sedentary species, it has shown a strong capacity for range expansion. Highest numbers are found in Romania, Bulgaria and Turkey, representing perhaps c.80% of the European population. With the exception of Romania, where a well-documented increase in numbers occurred between 1970 and 1990, status in these strongholds is little known, notably in Turkey. During the same period, the range continued to expand into central and eastern Europe, a trend which began around the end of the nineteenth century. Thus during 1970–1990 numbers increased rapidly in the Ukraine and Poland, less rapidly in Slovakia, Czech Republic, Austria,

	Breeding population			Breeding
	Size (pairs)	Year	Trend	range trend
Populations >5% of European total				
Bulgaria	(10,000–100,000)	—	(0)	(0)
Romania	(80,000–150,000)	—	+1	+1
Turkey	(10,000–100,000)	—	—	—
Additional populations in decline				
Albania	1,000–3,000	81	(–1)	(–1)
Greece	(5,000–10,000)	—	(–1)	(0)
Moldova	**5,000–7,000**	90	**+1**	**–1**
Total of above	110,000–370,000			
European total	120,000–390,000			

and apparently Croatia, and breeding began in Belarus. The increase in Moldova was accompanied by some range contraction. Population declines probably occurred in Albania and Greece, and overall c.5% of the European population declined during the period.

447

Middle Spotted Woodpecker *Dendrocopos*

medius is widespread in eastern and south-east Europe, and more scattered further west, its European range accounting for more than 75% of the world population. The species is largely sedentary, but is to some extent nomadic outside the breeding season. Around 75% of the European population is found collectively in Germany, Poland, Hungary, Belarus, Russia, Croatia, Romania and Turkey. Knowledge of population status is generally poor throughout the range, with data lacking for some key countries. Numbers in the strongholds appear to be mostly stable, with the exception of Croatia where there may be a small decline. However, in other areas, notably to the north and west of the main distribution, many smaller populations showed declines between 1970 and 1990, and breeding ceased in one (Sweden). This continues the pattern of widespread, peripheral range contraction suffered by the species in the twentieth century. Overall, about a quarter of the European population declined between 1970 and 1990.

	Breeding population			Breeding
	Size (pairs)	Year	Trend	range trend
Populations >5% of European total				
Belarus	5,500–9,000	90	0	0
Croatia	8,000–10,000 *	—	–1*	0*
Germany	9,000–19,000	—	0	**0**
Hungary	5,000–7,000	—	0	0
Poland	8,000–15,000	—	0	(0)
Romania	(3,000–10,000)	—	(0)	0
Russia	(1,000–10,000)	—	(0)	(0)
Turkey	(1,000–10,000)	—	—	—
Additional populations in decline				
Albania	2,000–5,000	81	(–1)	(–1)
Austria	(600–1,000)	—	(–1)	(–1)
France	100–1,000	76	(–1)	0
Italy	(300–500)	—	(–1)	(0)
Lithuania	50–200	85–88	(–1)	(0)
Moldova	**450–600**	90	**–1**	**–1**
Spain	650–680	—	–1	–1
Sweden	**0–0**	90	**X**	**X**
Ukraine	1,000–1,200	89	–1	–1
Total of above	46,000–100,000			
European total	53,000–120,000			

White-winged Lark *Melanocorypha leucoptera*

breeds in the steppe belt which extends through Kazakhstan to eastern Europe, with up to 100,000 pairs thought to breed in Russia. It is a short-distance migrant, birds in the west of the range spreading through the northern hinterland of the Black Sea as far as Romania, with wintering habitat extending to the forest–steppe zone. More than 50% of the wintering range is in Europe, but the relative status in different countries is not known.

Berthelot's Pipit *Anthus berthelotii*

breeds only in Europe, being confined to, and essentially sedentary in, the Canary Islands and Madeira. It breeds at most altitudes, especially on rocky, scrubby ground. Available evidence suggests that populations on both island groups were stable during 1970–1990.

	Breeding population			Breeding
	Size (pairs)	Year	Trend	range trend
Populations >5% of European total				
Portugal				
Madeira	1,000–1,500	91	**0**	**0**
Spain				
Canary Islands	15,000–20,000	—	0	0
Total of above	16,000–22,000			
European total	16,000–22,000			

Meadow Pipit *Anthus pratensis* is widespread in northern Europe, favouring open, thinly vegetated ground such as moors, pastures and dunes. Europe accounts for more than 75% of its world range. It is resident or a partial migrant in the west of its range and wholly migratory (travelling as far as the Middle East) in the north and east. About 90% of the European population is held by Iceland, Republic of Ireland, United Kingdom, Fennoscandia and Russia. Between 1970 and 1990, numbers were mostly stable in these strongholds, though they fluctuated in Iceland and increased in Finland. This balance of trends prevailed elsewhere over much of the range. However, a rapid increase in numbers recorded in the Czech Republic and Austria is part of a continuing expansion there. The relatively few regions experiencing modest declines in 1970–1990 are all coastal, namely the Netherlands, Belgium, Denmark, Estonia and Lithuania.

	Breeding population			Breeding
	Size (pairs)	Year	Trend	range trend
Populations >5% of European total				
Finland	**1,000,000–1,500,000**	92	**+1**	**0**
Iceland	500,000–1,000,000	—	F	0
Rep. of Ireland	(750,000–750,000)	88–91	(0)	(0)
Norway	1,000,000–5,000,000	90	0	**0**
Russia	(1,000,000–10,000,000)	—	(0)	(0)
Sweden	500,000–1,000,000	87	**0**	**0**
United Kingdom	(2,000,000–2,000,000)	88–91	(0)	**0**
Additional populations in decline				
Belgium	28,000–42,000	81–90	–1	0
Denmark	3,000–40,000	87–89	–1	(0)
Estonia	50,000–100,000	—	–1	0
Lithuania	10,000–15,000	85–88	(–1)	(0)
Netherlands	**70,000–100,000**	79	**–1**	**0**
Total of above	6,900,000–22,000,000			
European total	7,500,000–23,000,000			

Dunnock *Prunella modularis* breeds widely throughout Europe (except regions directly bordering the Mediterranean) which constitutes over 75% of its world range. The habitat ranges from gardens and parks with good shrub cover to wooded tundra, montane scrub and forests including conifer plantations. Western and southern populations are resident or at most dispersive, while those in the north and east migrate, principally to the Mediterranean. About two-thirds of the European population is accounted for by the Republic of Ireland, United Kingdom, Sweden, Germany and Russia. Between 1970 and 1990, population trends for Germany were unknown, but other key populations were stable (Republic of Ireland, Sweden, Russia) or declined (United Kingdom). Declines were also recorded in Austria and Denmark. Estimates of the proportion of the European population in decline vary markedly (11–28%) due to wide-ranging population estimates for some

	Breeding population			Breeding
	Size (pairs)	Year	Trend	range trend
Populations >5% of European total				
Germany	1,000,000–4,000,000	—	—	**0**
Rep. of Ireland	(680,000–680,000)	88–91	(0)	(0)
Russia	(1,000,000–10,000,000)	—	(0)	(0)
Sweden	1,000,000–2,500,000	87	**0**	**0**
United Kingdom	2,100,000–2,100,000	88–91	**–1**	**0**
Additional populations in decline				
Austria	(70,000–100,000)	—	(–1)	(+1)
Denmark	20,000–200,000	87–89	–1	(+1)
Total of above	5,900,000–20,000,000			
European total	8,700,000–27,000,000			

key countries. Elsewhere in the range, numbers were mostly stable, but populations increased rapidly in Finland and Hungary, and more slowly in the Netherlands, Estonia and Czech Republic. Some of these increases (e.g. Finland, Czech Republic) reflect longer-term upward trends.

Key to tables (see p. 34)

Trends	+2 Large increase	+1 Small increase	0 Stable	X Extinct
	–2 Large decrease	–1 Small decrease	F Fluctuating	N New breeder

Data quality   **Bold**: reliable quantitative data   Normal type: incomplete quantitative data
Bracketed figures: no quantitative data   * Data quality not provided
[1] Population figures included within United Kingdom totals   P Present

Robin *Erithacus rubecula* is widespread in Europe which represents more than 75% of its world range. Its habitat varies from deciduous and coniferous forest to the more broken cover of gardens, parks and hedgerows. Movements of different populations intergrade from wholly migratory in the far north to largely sedentary in the extreme south. The strongholds of the species are Sweden, United Kingdom, France, Germany, Russia and Romania, these countries together accounting for c.65–80% of the European population. For 1970–1990, Russian estimates of numbers are crude (varying tenfold) and trends are uncertain. Overall during this period, however, populations in the core of the distribution, as elsewhere in the species' European range, were predominantly stable, or less often fluctuating (notably

	Breeding population			Breeding
	Size (pairs)	Year	Trend	range trend
Populations >5% of European total				
France	3,000,000–6,000,000	90	F	0
Germany	1,500,000–7,800,000	—	0	0
Romania	5,000,000–1,000,000	—	0	0
Russia	(10,000,000–100,000,000)	—	(0)	(0)
Sweden	3,000,000–6,000,000	87	0	0
United Kingdom	4,500,000–4,500,000	88–91	0	0
Additional populations in decline				
Albania	10,000–30,000	81	—	(–1)
Total of above	27,000,000–130,000,000			
European total	40,000,000–150,000,000			

France), with negligible declines. There was evidence of increasing numbers in Norway, Spain and Portugal, and a spread of breeding to Gibraltar.

Thrush Nightingale *Luscinia luscinia* occurs mainly in central and eastern Europe, and southern Fennoscandia. Its habitat is dense, damp thickets, often riverine or swampy, with good ground cover. It winters in East Africa, mostly south of the Equator. Russia, Ukraine, Belarus, Latvia, Poland, Romania and Denmark together hold about c.80% of European numbers. Between 1970 and 1990, this core population was largely stable but increases were recorded in Denmark and Poland. At the same time, numbers increased rapidly in Norway and Finland, more slowly in Estonia, and some range expansion occurred in Sweden. Collectively, these increases are evidence of a longer-term spread to the west and north. Small declines affected Lithuania and Hun-

	Breeding population			Breeding
	Size (pairs)	Year	Trend	range trend
Populations >5% of European total				
Belarus	160,000–175,000	90	0	0
Denmark	11,000–120,000	87–89	+1	(+1)
Latvia	50,000–150,000	—	0	0
Poland	45,000–65,000	—	+1	+1
Romania	(75,000–200,000)	—	(0)	0
Russia	(100,000–1,000,000)	—	(0)	(0)
Ukraine	250,000–300,000	86	0	0
Additional populations in decline				
Hungary	50–100	—	–1	0
Lithuania	10,000–15,000	85–88	(–1)	(0)
Total of above	700,000–2,000,000			
European total	820,000–2,200,000			

gary, but these were insignificant in terms of the total European population.

Nightingale *Luscinia megarhynchos* is widespread in southern and western Europe, complementing the more northerly and easterly distribution of Thrush Nightingale *L. luscinia*. Habitat varies from moist thickets with rank herbage to drier areas such as bushy dunes and maquis. It winters in the Afrotropics. About 80% of the European population is held by France, Spain, Italy, Croatia and Bulgaria. Of these, numbers were stable during 1970–1990 in France, Spain and Bulgaria, and probably increased in Italy and Croatia. There was also some increase in numbers and range in the Czech Republic and Austria. Contractions in numbers and/or range were recorded in parts of the north-west of the range (notably United Kingdom and Netherlands) and the south-east (notably Greece and Albania), affecting c.5% of the European population.

	Breeding population			Breeding
	Size (pairs)	Year	Trend	range trend
Populations >5% of European total				
Bulgaria	(100,000–500,000)	—	(0)	(0)
Croatia	200,000–400,000 *	—	+1*	—
France	1,000,000–?	76	(0)	0
Italy	(500,000–1,000,000)	—	(+1)	(0)
Spain	450,000–1,700,000	—	0	0
Turkey	(50,000–500,000)	—	—	—
Additional populations in decline				
Albania	20,000–50,000	81	(–1)	(–1)
Andorra	20–50	91	0	–1
Belgium	2,400–3,200	81–90	–1	–1
Greece	100,000–150,000	—	(–1)	(–1)
Luxembourg	250–300	—	–1	–1
Netherlands	**7,500–10,000**	79	+1	**–1**
Ukraine	(100–150)	86	–1	–1
United Kingdom	**5,000–6,000**	88–91	**–1**	**–1**
Total of above	2,400,000–4,300,000			
European total	2,700,000–5,000,000			

Whinchat *Saxicola rubetra* breeds in Fennoscandia and north-west, central, eastern and parts of south-east Europe, in heath, scrub and grassland. More than 75% of its breeding range lies within Europe. Whinchats are trans-Saharan migrants, wintering mainly in tropical Africa. Between 1970 and 1990 the largest European populations, in eastern Europe and Fennoscandia, which together account for nearly 90% of the total numbers, have remained mostly stable, though the species has declined throughout much of the remainder of Europe. Overall, c.20% of the population was in decline during the period, notably in north-west and central Europe.

	Breeding population			Breeding
	Size (pairs)	Year	Trend	range trend
Populations >5% of European total				
Belarus	550,000–650,000	90	0	0
Finland	**300,000–400,000**	92	–1	**0**
Latvia	300,000–500,000	—	0	0
Norway	100,000–500,000	90	0	**0**
Poland	150,000–300,000	—	0	0
Romania	(200,000–300,000)	—	(0)	0
Russia	(100,000–1,000,000)	—	(0)	(0)
Sweden	200,000–500,000	87	**0**	0
Additional populations in decline				
Austria	(5,000–8,000)	—	(–1)	(–1)
Belgium	**350–500**	81–90	**–2**	**–1**
Denmark	1,000–21,000	87–89	(–1)	(–1)
France	10,000–100,000	76	–1	**0**
Germany	10,000–70,000	—	–2	**0**
Italy	(10,000–15,000)	86	(–1)	(0)
Liechtenstein	**50–60**	90	–1	–1
Lithuania	2,000–5,000	85–88	(–1)	(0)
Luxembourg	120–150	—	–1	–1
Netherlands	**700–1,100**	83	**–2**	**–2**
Slovakia	(10,000–20,000)	—	–1	0
Spain	15,000–20,000	—	–1	–1
Switzerland	5,000–7,000	86–91	–2	–1
United Kingdom	(14,000–28,000)	88–91	(–1)	**0**
Total of above	2,000,000–4,400,000			
European total	2,100,000–4,700,000			

Ring Ouzel *Turdus torquatus* has a scattered distribution, mainly in the United Kingdom, Fenno-scandia and central, southern and eastern Europe. Europe accounts for over 75% of the world breeding range. In northern Europe it inhabits steep rocky slopes, gullies and moorland, elsewhere often alpine, coniferous forest. Most birds migrate to winter in the Mediterranean basin, though some southern populations may be resident. Austria and Romania together hold almost half the European population, while these two countries along with Norway, Germany, Switzerland, Italy and Ukraine account for c.80%. Although information is often sparse, these key populations appear to have been stable during 1970–1990, or, in the case of Italy, probably increased. In the same period most populations elsewhere were also stable, although declines were recorded in Spain, Andorra and the Republic of

	Breeding population			Breeding
	Size (pairs)	Year	Trend	range trend
Populations >5% of European total				
Austria	(50,000–80,000)	—	(0)	(0)
Germany	9,000–25,000	—	(0)	**0**
Italy	(10,000–20,000)	83	(+1)	(0)
Norway	10,000–100,000	90	0	**0**
Romania	60,000–100,000	—	0	**0**
Switzerland	(15,000–25,000)	86–91	—	(0)
Ukraine	16,000–19,000	86	0	0
Additional populations in decline				
Andorra	(50–70)	92	(–1)	(–1)
Rep. of Ireland	(150–350)	88–91	(–1)	(–1)
Spain	6,000–7,000	—	–1	–1
United Kingdom	(5,500–11,000)	88–91	(0)	**–1**
Total of above	180,000–390,000			
European total	200,000–450,000			

Ireland, while range contracted in the United Kingdom. Together, these reductions affected only c.2–3% of total European numbers.

Blackbird *Turdus merula* occurs widely throughout Europe in a broad range of habitats including all types of woodland, scrub, parks, gardens and thinly vegetated uplands. Northern populations are migratory (moving south and west), those further south are mainly resident. The breeding strongholds are widely distributed, over two-thirds of the total population occurring in the United Kingdom, Germany, Czech Republic, Croatia, Bulgaria, Spain and Italy. With the exception of the United Kingdom, which registered a decline in numbers during 1970–1990, status in these core populations was generally healthy, with numbers apparently either stable (Germany, Czech Republic) or increasing (Croatia, Bulgaria, Spain, Italy). Increases also occurred in a few other countries with significant populations (Estonia, Netherlands, Hungary, Switzerland, Ukraine) and there was a rapid increase in Slovenia. Apart from the United Kingdom, only the small Albanian popula-

	Breeding population			Breeding
	Size (pairs)	Year	Trend	range trend
Populations >5% of European total				
Bulgaria	(1,000,000–10,000,000)—		(+1)	(+1)
Croatia	2,000,000–2,500,000 *—		+1*	0*
Czech Republic	2,000,000–4,000,000 —		0	0
Germany	7,000,000–20,000,000 —		0	0
Italy	(2,000,000–5,000,000) —		(+1)	(+1)
Spain	2,300,000–5,900,000 —		+1	+1
United Kingdom	4,700,000–4,700,000	88–91	–1	0
Additional populations in decline				
Albania	10,000–40,000	81	(–1)	(–1)
Total of above	21,000,000–52,000,000			
European total	31,000,000–70,000,000			

tion declined in the same period. Nevertheless, these reductions together represent c.7–15% of the European population in decline, reflecting the United Kingdom's status as a major breeding area. Elsewhere in Europe, numbers and distribution during 1970–1990 were predominantly stable.

Fieldfare *Turdus pilaris* breeds in northern, central and eastern Europe, typically in deciduous or mixed woodland. It is a migrant, vacating its northern breeding grounds to winter widely through Europe south to the Mediterranean, typically in such open country as provides foraging in rough pastures, arable fields, and bushes and trees bearing berries and other fruit. Over 75% of the world wintering range lies within Europe, but knowledge of wintering status in the various countries of its range is generally either poor or unavailable, and therefore no data table is given here. However, the evidence that exists suggests that the United Kingdom supports the largest population, with significant numbers elsewhere in western, central and south-east Europe. During 1970–1990, wintering populations fluctuated over a wide area and no clear regional trends emerged.

Song Thrush *Turdus philomelos* breeds widely throughout Europe, except for regions directly bordering the Mediterranean. In western Europe it inhabits woodland, parks and gardens, in northern and eastern Europe preferring moist, mossy, coniferous or mixed forest with ample undergrowth. It is mostly resident but northern populations are partially or entirely migratory, some moving as far as North Africa and the Middle East in winter. Over 75% of the world population breeds and winters within Europe. Germany and Sweden together support a quarter to a third of the European breeding population, while these two countries along with the United Kingdom, France, Finland and Belarus account for over a half. During 1970–1990 numbers in the core populations were stable except for France (fluctuating) and United Kingdom (rapid decline, representing c.5–10% of the European population). Slower declines were recorded in the Republic of Ireland,

	Breeding population			Breeding
	Size (pairs)	Year	Trend	range trend
Populations >5% of European total				
Belarus	700,000–800,000	90	0	0
Finland	**1,000,000–2,000,000**	92	**0**	**0**
France	(400,000–2,000,000)	90	(F)	0
Germany	1,700,000–5,000,000	—	0	0
Sweden	1,500,000–3,000,000	87	**0**	**0**
United Kingdom	1,100,000–1,100,000	88–91	–2	0
Additional populations in decline				
Andorra	(10–20)	92	(–1)	0
Belgium	150,000–250,000	81–90	0	–1
Rep. of Ireland	(320,000–320,000)	88–91	(–1)	(0)
Netherlands	**100,000–125,000**	79	**–1**	**0**
Total of above	7,000,000–15,000,000			
European total	11,000,000–24,000,000			

Netherlands and Andorra. Overall, c.10% of the European population declined during the period. Elsewhere in Europe, the evidence points to widespread stability between 1970 and 1990.

Redwing *Turdus iliacus* breeds mainly in Fenno-scandia, the Baltic states and western Russia, typically in birch or mixed woodland, and often where scrub predominates. It migrates after the breeding season to winter chiefly in north-west and south-west Europe and in the Mediterranean region. On the wintering grounds it favours rough pastures, arable fields, hedges and open woodland, as well as olive-groves and vineyards, these together providing a mixed diet of terrestrial invertebrates, berries and fruit (frugivory dominates in the south). Europe accounts for more than 50% of the wintering range. Data are not available for a number of countries and therefore no table is presented here. However, although exact proportions cannot be estimated, the information that does exist suggests that over 90% of the European wintering population is accounted for by Spain, Portugal, United Kingdom, Republic of Ireland, Italy and the Czech Republic. Foremost among these are Spain and the United Kingdom which together hold about three-quarters of the wintering population, while Spain alone supports possibly half. During 1970–1990, populations fluctuated across much of the wintering range, and allowing for the paucity of data from a number of key countries, no significant regional trends were recorded.

Mistle Thrush *Turdus viscivorus* is widespread in Europe, inhabiting woodland (often conifers), parkland and gardens with tall trees. Over 75% of the world breeding and wintering range lies within Europe. Movements vary from migratory in the north and east of the range to resident or dispersive in the west and south. Germany, Spain, United Kingdom, Belarus and Croatia together support over half of the European breeding population. For 1970–1990, numbers probably increased in Germany, but populations in other key countries were stable or fluctuated. During the same period, the majority of the population elsewhere in Europe was likewise stable, indicating that the expansion seen earlier in the twentieth century in north-west Europe has largely ceased. Increases were recorded in the Republic of Ireland

	Breeding population			Breeding
	Size (pairs)	Year	Trend	range trend
Populations >5% of European total				
Belarus	120,000–160,000	90	F	0
Croatia	100,000–150,000 *	—	0*	0*
Germany	250,000–1,000,000	—	+1	**0**
Spain	330,000–790,000	—	0	0
United Kingdom	250,000–250,000	88–91	0	**0**
Additional populations in decline				
Estonia	2,000–5,000	—	–1	0
Italy	(50,000–100,000)	—	(–1)	(–1)
Netherlands	**25,000–35,000**	79	–1	**–1**
Ukraine	5,000–6,000	88	–1	0
Total of above	1,100,000–2,500,000			
European total	1,800,000–4,100,000			

and Denmark, and a rapid increase in Hungary, while modest declines occurred in the Netherlands, Italy, Ukraine and Estonia.

Grasshopper Warbler *Locustella naevia* is widely distributed in middle, temperate latitudes of Europe, being absent from most of Fennoscandia and southern Europe. It favours rough grassland, scrub, fringes of marshes and other wet areas with good ground cover. All European populations migrate to sub-Saharan Africa, but the precise wintering grounds are poorly known. Census data are generally poor for the key countries of France, Germany, Russia and Latvia, which together support c.75% or more of the European population. A relatively small proportion (c.5%) of the European total declined between 1970 and 1990, though the reductions were rapid in the United Kingdom and Romania. Meanwhile, populations and range expanded in Estonia, Denmark, Fennoscandia, and markedly in Hungary. The Czech Republic also showed clear

	Breeding population			Breeding
	Size (pairs)	Year	Trend	range trend
Populations >5% of European total				
France	(10,000–100,000)	76	(F)	(F)
Germany	100,000–200,000	—	0	**0**
Latvia	(30,000–80,000)	—	(0)	0
Russia	(100,000–1,000,000)	—	(0)	(0)
Additional populations in decline				
Austria	(1,500–1,700)	—	(–1)	(0)
Belgium	880–1,580	81–90	–1	–1
Lithuania	5,000–8,000	85–88	(–1)	(0)
Moldova	1,600–2,000	86	–1	–1
Romania	(1,000–5,000)	—	(–2)	(–2)
United Kingdom	(11,000–11,000)	88–91	–2	**–1**
Total of above	260,000–1,400,000			
European total	320,000–1,500,000			

range expansion. These changes are consistent with the pattern of spread in central and northern Europe, which mostly began around the 1950s.

453

River Warbler *Locustella fluviatilis* occurs in central and eastern Europe, these regions accounting for over 75% of its world breeding range. It requires dense, moist ground-cover including wooded swamps, often alder carr or willow scrub, typically along rivers, streams, ponds and ditches. It migrates to the eastern Afrotropics, but the limits of its wintering grounds are obscure. At least a half (possibly much more) of the European population is found jointly in Russia and Belarus. Latvia, Poland and Hungary together support most of the remainder. Between 1970 and 1990, this core population was apparently stable. Modest declines were recorded in Lithuania and Moldova, but elsewhere there were several gains: numbers and range increased in Estonia, Germany, Austria and Bulgaria, with more rapid

	Breeding population			Breeding
	Size (pairs)	Year	Trend	range trend
Populations >5% of European total				
Belarus	100,000–140,000	90	0	0
Hungary	50,000–100,000	—	0	0
Latvia	50,000–100,000	—	0	0
Poland	50,000–100,000	—	0	0
Russia	(100,000–1,000,000)	—	(0)	(0)
Additional populations in decline				
Lithuania	8,000–10,000	85–88	(–1)	(0)
Moldova	1,700–2,300	86	–1	–1
Romania	(200–1,000)	—	(0)	(–1)
Total of above	360,000–1,500,000			
European total	400,000–1,500,000			

expansion by the small pockets of distribution in Sweden and Finland. This continues the pattern of European spread, mainly west and north-west, since the 1950s.

Savi's Warbler *Locustella luscinioides* occurs mainly in eastern and south-east Europe, but is also widely scattered further to the west and north. Its typical habitat is extensive wet reedbeds fringing marshes, floodlands, lakes and rivers. It winters in sub-Saharan Africa north of the forest zone, but the precise limits are not known. Hungary and Romania account for at least half the European population, with the inclusion of Russia and Poland making up c.80%. Between 1970 and 1990, numbers increased in Poland and were stable in Russia, Hungary and Romania. Although declines were recorded in several other countries during the same period, most conspicuously in the Netherlands, these did not significantly affect overall numbers in Europe. In the United Kingdom's small population, range expanded but numbers decreased. The establishment of this satellite population coincided with range expansion in the western and northern parts of the distribution, especially from the 1960s. During 1970–1990, this spread appears to have stabilized in France, but

	Breeding population			Breeding
	Size (pairs)	Year	Trend	range trend
Populations >5% of European total				
Hungary	30,000–60,000	—	0	0
Poland	8,000–20,000	—	+1	0
Romania	70,000–130,000	—	(0)	0
Russia	(10,000–100,000)	—	(0)	(0)
Additional populations in decline				
Belgium	18–28	81–90	–1	–1
Croatia	2,000–2,500 *	—	–1*	0*
Greece	(500–1,000)	—	(0)	(–1)
Italy	(1,000–2,000)	—	(–1)	(–1)
Moldova	3,500–5,000	86	–1	0
Netherlands	**1,000–1,600**	79	**–2**	–1
Portugal	100–1,000	89	–1	–1
United Kingdom	**10–20**	88–91	**–2**	+2
Total of above	130,000–320,000			
European total	140,000–370,000			

continued in Denmark, Germany, Poland, Finland (being a new breeding species in this period), Latvia and Estonia. Range expansion also occurred in Austria, Czech Republic and Ukraine.

Sedge Warbler *Acrocephalus schoenobaenus* is widespread in Europe except for the south where it is thinly distributed. Its habitat includes drier reedbed margins, often with emergent scrub, overgrown ditches, and cover away from water such as hedgerows, nettlebeds and farm crops. It winters widely in Africa south of the Sahara. Russia supports an estimated 35–75% of the total European population (although estimates vary tenfold), while the inclusion with Russia of the United Kingdom, Finland, Hungary and Romania accounts for 80% or more. During 1970–1990, numbers were apparently stable in Russia, Hungary and Romania, though the breeding range may have contracted somewhat in Romania. Numbers increased in Finland (extending a long-term pattern of spread) and declined in the United Kingdom. Populations also declined in various other countries, most widely in north-west Europe. Of these, the most rapid declines occurred in Belgium, Germany and the Netherlands, and altogether a possible maximum 12% of the European total was in decline during this period. In numerical

	Breeding population			Breeding
	Size (pairs)	Year	Trend	range trend
Populations >5% of European total				
Finland	**300,000–500,000**	92	**+1**	**0**
Hungary	150,000–200,000	—	0	0
Romania	500,000–1,000,000	—	(0)	–1
Russia	(1,000,000–10,000,000)	70–90	(0)	(0)
United Kingdom	270,000–270,000	88–91	–1	**0**
Additional populations in decline				
Belgium	500–600	81–90	–2	–2
Croatia	15,000–20,000 *	—	–1*	0*
Denmark	442–11,000	87–89	(–1)	(–1)
France	10,000–100,000	76	–1	–1
Germany	12,000–20,000	—	–2	**0**
Greece	(500–1,000)	—	(–1)	(–1)
Italy	(30–100)	—	(–1)	(–1)
Luxembourg	0–5		–1·	–1
Moldova	5,000–7,000	86	–1	–1
Netherlands	**12,000–18,000**	79	**–2**	**–1**
Total of above	2,300,000–12,000,000			
European total	2,800,000–13,000,000			

terms, this was matched by gains recorded in Norway, Austria and Ukraine. In most of Europe, however, the majority of the population was stable.

Marsh Warbler *Acrocephalus palustris* occurs mainly in central, eastern and south-east Europe, but also increasingly in southern Fennoscandia. Its typical habitat is rank herbaceous vegetation by ditches or marshes and sometimes also standing cereals. It winters in East and south-east Africa. Europe accounts for more than 75% of the breeding range. About half the European population occurs in Germany, Russia and Romania, while these along with Poland, Latvia, Czech Republic and Belarus account for c.75%. The majority of this core population during 1970–1990 was stable, with numbers fluctuating in Germany and declining in the Czech Republic. The United Kingdom and Moldova also suffered losses but collectively these declines do not seriously affect overall numbers in Europe. Elsewhere in the range, the most significant pattern during

	Breeding population			Breeding
	Size (pairs)	Year	Trend	range trend
Populations >5% of European total				
Belarus	80,000–130,000	90	0	0
Czech Republic	80,000–160,000	—	–1	**0**
Germany	150,000–500,000	—	F	**0**
Latvia	70,000–120,000	—	0	**0**
Poland	50,000–200,000	—	0	0
Romania	400,000–600,000	—	0	–1
Russia	(100,000–1,000,000)	70–90	(0)	(0)
Additional populations in decline				
Moldova	4,500–6,000	86	–1	–1
United Kingdom	**12–12**	88–89	**–1**	**–1**
Total of above	930,000–2,700,000			
European total	1,300,000–3,400,000			

1970–1990 was a continuing northward expansion, rapid in Sweden, Finland and Estonia, slower in Denmark and Norway. Increases also occurred in France, Liechtenstein and Ukraine.

Reed Warbler *Acrocephalus scirpaceus* occurs widely in Europe, but is more scattered in the Mediterranean region and absent in the far north. It is largely confined to reedbeds and winters widely in the Afrotropics. Romania supports over half the European population, mainly in the extensive Danube delta reedbeds, while Romania and Sweden together account for about two-thirds. Between 1970 and 1990, numbers were stable in Romania and increased in Sweden. During the same period, c.5% of the European population declined, apparently most widely in the south and east of the range although evidence of trends was generally poor. Elsewhere, the most striking trend, evident from earlier in the twentieth century, was of increasing numbers in north-west and northern Europe, being rapid in the United Kingdom and Netherlands, and slower in the Republic of Ireland, Denmark, Nor-

| | Breeding population | | | Breeding |
	Size (pairs)	Year	Trend	range trend
Populations >5% of European total				
Romania	1,500,000–2,500,000	—	0	0
Sweden	250,000–500,000	87	+1	0
Additional populations in decline				
Albania	2,000–5,000	81	—	(–1)
Belgium	5,500–8,800	81–90	–1	–1
Croatia	8,000–12,000 *	—	–1*	0*
Germany	100,000–200,000	—	–1	**0**
Greece	10,000–20,000	—	(0)	(–1)
Italy	(30,000–60,000)	—	(–1)	(0)
Luxembourg	120–150	—	–1	–1
Moldova	5,000–7,000	86	–1	–1
Ukraine	(3,000–5,000)	88	(–1)	(–1)
Total of above	1,900,000–3,300,000			
European total	2,400,000–4,400,000			

way, Finland (also rapid range expansion), Lithuania, Latvia and Estonia. Switzerland also registered an increase.

Icterine Warbler *Hippolais icterina* is widespread in Europe except for the far west and south. It inhabits open and edge woodland with rich undergrowth, also orchards, parks and gardens. The wintering grounds are in sub-Saharan Africa, mainly south of the Equator. Over 75% of the breeding range is in Europe, especially in Russia which holds an estimated 50–75% of the European population. Belarus also supports significant numbers which increased during 1970–1990, as did the population in neighbouring Ukraine. With Russian population estimates varying tenfold, trends there in 1970–1990 are hard to detect but numbers apparently remained stable. In the north of the range there were some notable increases (Denmark, Sweden, Finland), but declines in Estonia, also in France, Belgium and Germany. However, with the exception of Germany,

| | Breeding population | | | Breeding |
	Size (pairs)	Year	Trend	range trend
Populations >5% of European total				
Belarus	570,000–600,000	90	+1	0
Russia	(1,000,000–10,000,000)	—	(0)	(0)
Additional populations in decline				
Belgium	9,500–14,000	81–90	–1	–1
Estonia	20,000–50,000	—	–1	0
France	1,000–10,000	90	–1	**0**
Germany	100,000–250,000	—	–1	**0**
Liechtenstein	**10–10**	89	–1	0
Slovenia	(1–5)	—	(–2)	(–2)
Switzerland	150–200	86–91	–1	–1
Total of above	1,700,000–11,000,000			
European total	2,100,000–12,000,000			

most of the populations in decline were relatively minor and do not seriously affect the overall European picture.

Melodious Warbler *Hippolais polyglotta* is confined to the south-west, central and north-west of mainland Europe. It inhabits woodland and shrub thickets, often near water and winters in tropical West Africa north of the Equator. Europe represents over 75% of the breeding range, with around half the European total in Spain and well over 90% accounted for by the combined populations of Spain, Portugal and Italy. The quality of trend data is generally low, but there are no indications that this core population is other than stable. Elsewhere in Europe, the range expansion to the north and north-east, which started in the 1930s, continued during

| | Breeding population | | | Breeding |
	Size (pairs)	Year	Trend	range trend
Populations >5% of European total				
France	100,000–1,000,000	90	+2	**+1**
Italy	(50,000–150,000)	—	(0)	(0)
Portugal	100,000–1,000,000	89	(0)	0
Spain	700,000–1,500,000	—	(0)	(0)
Total of above	950,000–3,700,000			
European total	950,000–3,700,000			

1970–1990. During the latter period, the species spread markedly in France and Switzerland, started breeding in Belgium and Germany, and thereafter expanded its range rapidly in Germany. No declines were recorded anywhere.

Marmora's Warbler *Sylvia sarda* breeds only in Europe where it is confined mainly to the Balearic Islands (Spain), Corsica (France) and Sardinia (Italy). Its habitat is dry heath and scrub (maquis and garigue), up to c.1,000 m on Corsica. The Balearics population (*balearica*) is mostly sedentary, the rest (nominate *sarda*) being partial migrants to North Africa. Highest numbers are found in Spain, followed by France and Italy. Between 1970 and 1990 the Span-

	Breeding population			Breeding
	Size (pairs)	Year	Trend	range trend
Populations >5% of European total				
France	(10,000–20,000)	90	(0)	**0**
Italy	(5,000–10,000)	—	(0)	(0)
Spain	14,000–25,000	—	+1	+1
Total of above	29,000–55,000			
European total	29,000–55,000			

ish population increased, while the others apparently remained stable.

Subalpine Warbler *Sylvia cantillans* occurs across southern Europe from Portugal to western Turkey, mainly on dry slopes covered with dense scrub, also in open woodland (especially oak *Quercus*) with scattered bushes. It winters on the southern edge of the Sahara. Over 75% of the breeding range is in Europe and of this the vast majority (c.80%) is found in Spain, with significant numbers also in Greece. On the available evidence, numbers in these strongholds were stable during 1970–1990. Elsewhere in Europe during this period, trends are

	Breeding population			Breeding
	Size (pairs)	Year	Trend	range trend
Populations >5% of European total				
Greece	100,000–300,000	—	(0)	(0)
Spain	1,100,000–2,300,000	—	0	0
Total of above	1,200,000–2,600,000			
European total	1,300,000–3,000,000			

poorly known (e.g. no information for Albania and Turkey), but, other than indications of some increase in Bulgaria, numbers were apparently stable.

Sardinian Warbler *Sylvia melanocephala* occurs throughout southern Europe from the Canary Islands through the Mediterranean to Turkey. It is a typical inhabitant of low scrub (maquis), but also occurs in areas with taller undergrowth and trees. In different parts of the range, some are partial migrants (mainly to North Africa), others sedentary. Around a third of the European population occurs in Spain, and the addition to this of Portugal, France, Italy and Greece accounts for all but a few percent of the European total. Between 1970 and 1990 there was evidence of an increase and spread in Spain. During the same period the rest of the core population was apparently stable except for France where numbers

	Breeding population			Breeding
	Size (pairs)	Year	Trend	range trend
Populations >5% of European total				
France	200,000–1,000,000	90	F	**0**
Greece	500,000–1,000,000	—	(0)	(0)
Italy	(300,000–600,000)	—	(0)	(+1)
Portugal	100,000–1,000,000	89	(0)	0
Spain	990,000–1,900,000	—	+1	+1
Total of above	2,100,000–5,500,000			
European total	2,200,000–5,800,000			

fluctuated. Elsewhere in Europe, there are some gaps in knowledge of status (Croatia, Albania, Turkey), but numbers and range generally remained stable or expanded (Malta, Slovenia, Bulgaria).

Rüppell's Warbler *Sylvia rueppelli* breeds only in Europe where it is confined to southern Greece and Turkey, occupying dry scrub on rocky hillsides and also open oak *Quercus* forest with dense undergrowth. It winters in Chad and Sudan. No trends are known for Turkey, which supports the highest numbers, while the population in Greece seems to have been stable during 1970–1990.

	Breeding population			Breeding
	Size (pairs)	Year	Trend	range trend
Populations >5% of European total				
Greece	(3,000–10,000)	—	(0)	(0)
Turkey	(5,000–50,000)	—	—	—
Total of above	8,000–60,000			
European total	8,000–60,000			

Barred Warbler *Sylvia nisoria* occurs mainly in central, eastern and south-east Europe, typically in a stratified habitat of herb layer and bushes (often thorny), interspersed with taller trees. It winters in eastern Africa south of the Sahara. Wide-ranging estimates suggest that Russia supports about half the European population, while the addition of Poland, Hungary, Moldova and Romania accounts for four-fifths or more. The little available evidence indicates that between 1970 and 1990 numbers were stable in Poland, Russia and Romania, while (on better evidence) they increased in Hungary and decreased somewhat in Moldova. With mild reductions reported also in Denmark, Germany, Czech Republic and Ukraine, a possible 3–14% of the European population declined during this period. Against this, numbers increased markedly in Finland, less rapidly in Estonia, Italy and Slovenia, and the species spread anew to Norway. Across the breeding range, there-

	Breeding population			Breeding
	Size (pairs)	Year	Trend	range trend
Populations >5% of European total				
Hungary	20,000–40,000	—	+1	0
Moldova	22,000–30,000	86	–1	–1
Poland	20,000–30,000	—	(0)	(0)
Romania	(20,000–500,000)	—	(0)	**0**
Russia	(100,000–1,000,000)	—	(0)	(0)
Additional populations in decline				
Czech Republic	1,500–3,000	—	–1	**0**
Denmark	**9–10**	89	**–1**	**–1**
Germany	5,000–10,000	—	–1	**0**
Ukraine	2,700–3,300	88	–1	–1
Total of above	190,000–1,600,000			
European total	230,000–1,700,000			

fore, status fluctuated during 1970–1990, the most consistent regional feature being the gains made in Fennoscandia and north-east Europe. The expansion in Finland continues the pattern of spread there since the species first established itself in the 1920s.

Whitethroat *Sylvia communis* occurs widely in Europe, typically in open cover exposed to the sun, and consisting variously of tall herbage, bushes, thickets, field margins and woodland edge. It winters widely in Africa, especially in the Sahel and in other semi-arid regions further south and east. Poland, Russia, Belarus, Ukraine, Romania, Spain, United Kingdom and Denmark together support about three-quarters of European numbers. Between 1970 and 1990, numbers were apparently stable in the strongholds of Russia, Belarus and Poland, also in Romania, increased in the Ukraine and declined in Spain and Denmark. Elsewhere in Europe, rapid declines were recorded in Germany, Switzerland and Slovenia, with slower declines in several other countries, notably (in terms of population size) France, Belgium, Netherlands, Czech Republic and Greece. In sum, about a fifth of the European population was in decline during this period. This began with a sudden, steep decline, especially noticeable in western and central Europe, from the mid- to late 1960s through the 1970s. Other noteworthy trends during 1970–1990 were the modest increases in Sweden and Estonia, the Swedish gains reflecting continuing recovery from the crash there of 1969.

	Breeding population			Breeding
	Size (pairs)	Year	Trend	range trend
Populations >5% of European total				
Belarus	400,000–450,000	90	0	0
Denmark	140,000–1,600,000	87–89	(–1)	(0)
Poland	1,000,000–2,000,000	—	0	0
Romania	(500,000–1,000,000)	—	0	**0**
Russia	(1,000,000–10,000,000)	—	(0)	(0)
Spain	450,000–600,000	—	–1	–1
Ukraine	350,000–370,000	88	+1	0
United Kingdom	670,000–670,000	88–91	0	**0**
Additional populations in decline				
Albania	5,000–20,000	81	(–1)	(–1)
Andorra	(5–10)	92	(–1)	0
Austria	(5,000–10,000)	—	(–1)	(0)
Belgium	75,000–90,000	81–90	–1	–1
Czech Republic	90,000–180,000	—	–1	**0**
France	100,000–1,000,000	76	–1	(0)
Germany	200,000–500,000	—	**–2**	**0**
Greece	100,000–200,000	—	(–1)	(0)
Rep. of Ireland	(20,000–40,000)	—	(–1)	(0)
Liechtenstein	**3–3**	89	–2	0
Netherlands	**80,000–95,000**	79	**–1**	**0**
Slovenia	2,000–3,000	—	–2	–2
Switzerland	800–1,000	86–91	–2	–2
United Kingdom Jersey	5–10	—	–2	–2
Total of above	5,200,000–19,000,000			
European total	6,400,000–22,000,000			

Garden Warbler *Sylvia borin* occurs widely throughout Europe except the extreme south. It favours deciduous woodland with a dense shrub or scrub layer, found mainly in clearings or at the woodland edge. It winters extensively in Africa south of the Sahara. More than 75% of the species' breeding range is in Europe, with about half the European population concentrated in France, Germany, Sweden and Finland. Numbers in Russia may exceed the population of any of these individually, but, with Russian population estimates varying tenfold, its relative status is hard to assess. Apart from Sweden, where numbers have increased, populations in all these strongholds are thought to have been stable between 1970 and 1990, likewise in Latvia (which supports a significant population). Populations were also mostly stable elsewhere in Europe during the same period. Exceptions were the increases re-

	Breeding population			Breeding
	Size (pairs)	Year	Trend	range trend
Populations >5% of European total				
Finland	**1,000,000–2,000,000**	92	**0**	**0**
France	2,000,000–3,300,000	90	(0)	(0)
Germany	1,000,000–2,000,000	—	0	**0**
Latvia	500,000–700,000	—	0	0
Russia	(500,000–5,000,000)	—	(0)	(0)
Sweden	1,000,000–3,000,000	87	**+1**	0
Additional populations in decline				
Hungary	10,000–30,000	—	–1	0
Liechtenstein	30–100	—	–1	–1
Moldova	5,500–7,000	86	–1	–1
Total of above	6,000,000–16,000,000			
European total	8,500,000–21,000,000			

corded in the United Kingdom, Belgium, Estonia and Czech Republic, and declines in Liechtenstein, Hungary and Moldova. However, these losses were insignificant in terms of the overall European population.

Blackcap *Sylvia atricapilla* occurs throughout Europe, mainly in mature deciduous woodland with a moderate shrub understorey, also in plantations, parks, gardens and other suburban habitats offering suitable cover. Populations vary from sedentary to migratory, with widely dispersed wintering grounds in the Mediterranean and Africa, both north and south of the Sahara. Over 75% of the breeding range is in Europe, with about two-thirds of the European population held collectively by Spain, France, Germany, Italy, Russia, Belarus, Romania and Bulgaria. Between 1970 and 1990, this core population was apparently mostly stable, but increased in Germany and Spain. Elsewhere in Europe, numbers in the majority of countries were stable or increasing, with the few cases of decline relatively unimportant in terms of the overall European population. A marked increase was recorded in the United Kingdom, with smaller increases in the Republic of Ireland, Belgium, Netherlands, Denmark, Sweden, Estonia,

	Breeding population			Breeding
	Size (pairs)	Year	Trend	range trend
Populations >5% of European total				
Belarus	900,000–950,000	90	0	0
Bulgaria	(500,000–5,000,000)	—	(0)	(0)
France	1,000,000–?	76	(0)	0
Germany	2,500,000–5,000,000	—	+1	**0**
Italy	(2,000,000–5,000,000)	—	(0)	(0)
Romania	1,000,000–2,000,000	—	**0**	**0**
Russia	(1,000,000–10,000,000)	—	(0)	(0)
Spain	850,000–1,500,000	—	+1	+1
Additional populations in decline				
Albania	20,000–50,000	81	—	(–1)
Croatia	800,000–1,000,000 *	—	+1*	–1*
Moldova	60,000–80,000	86	–1	–1
Total of above	11,000,000–31,000,000			
European total	16,000,000–41,000,000			

Czech Republic and Ukraine. These changes represent a trend of widespread gains in western and northern Europe, with some central and eastern populations also showing signs of increase.

Key to tables (see p. 34)

Trends	+2 Large increase	+1 Small increase	0 Stable	X Extinct
	–2 Large decrease	–1 Small decrease	F Fluctuating	N New breeder

Data quality **Bold**: reliable quantitative data   Normal type: incomplete quantitative data
Bracketed figures: no quantitative data   * Data quality not provided
[1] Population figures included within United Kingdom totals   P Present

Bonelli's Warbler *Phylloscopus bonelli* occurs mainly in southern Europe, in open woodland, commonly of oak *Quercus* but also mixed forest including conifers, up to c.2,000 m. It winters on the southern edge of the Sahara. More than 75% of the species' breeding range is in Europe, chiefly in Spain which accounts for some 70–80% of European numbers. France also holds a significant population. Between 1970 and 1990, numbers in these strongholds, as in most other parts of Europe, were apparently stable. The only decline, albeit small and unsubstantiated, was recorded in Germany's relatively minor population, while Bulgaria experienced

	Breeding population			Breeding
	Size (pairs)	Year	Trend	range trend
Populations >5% of European total				
France	100,000–1,000,000	76	(0)	0
Spain	1,100,000–2,700,000	—	0	0
Additional populations in decline				
Germany	1,500–5,000	—	–1	0
Total of above	1,200,000–3,700,000			
European total	1,300,000–4,000,000			

a small increase in numbers and range. The species also gained a breeding foothold in the Netherlands, in keeping with the northerly spread which began in the mid-twentieth century but which now appears to have all but halted.

Wood Warbler *Phylloscopus sibilatrix* is widely distributed through Europe except for Iberia and much of the Mediterranean region. It inhabits deciduous, mixed and coniferous forest (in eastern Europe), typically with a closed canopy and of mixed ages to produce stratified foliage. It winters in sub-Saharan Africa from Sierra Leone east to Uganda. Over 75% of the breeding range is in Europe, chiefly in Russia, with Belarus and Latvia also holding significant numbers. Their combined populations, representing c.80% of the European total, were apparently stable between 1970 and 1990, but this assessment relies heavily on Russian population estimates which vary tenfold. Elsewhere in Europe, the majority of populations were likewise stable during this period, with a few on the increase but only one

	Breeding population			Breeding
	Size (pairs)	Year	Trend	range trend
Populations >5% of European total				
Belarus	2,400,000–2,600,000	90	0	0
Latvia	**1,000,000–1,300,000**	—	0	**0**
Russia	10,000,000–100,000,000	—	(0)	(0)
Additional populations in decline				
Moldova	35,000–50,000	86	–1	–1
Total of above	13,000,000–100,000,000			
European total	15,000,000–110,000,000			

(Moldova) showing some decline. Increase was rapid in Finland, slower in Belgium, Sweden, Norway and Ukraine. Modest range expansion accompanied the population increases in Finland and Norway. The main regional trend is stability with a continuation of the spread in Fennoscandia seen in recent decades.

Goldcrest *Regulus regulus* breeds widely in Europe except in the south where it is more scattered. Its optimum habitat is tall, dense stands of conifers, especially spruce *Picea*, but it also uses mixed woods. Mainland European populations winter both within the breeding range and also south of it as far as the Mediterranean, while birds breeding on the Azores are mostly sedentary. Russian population estimates, despite varying tenfold, show that Russia supports much the biggest proportion, perhaps half or more, of the European breeding numbers. The other European strongholds are Sweden and Germany. There is good evidence that the Swedish population was stable between 1970 and 1990, as was probably the case in Germany and perhaps also in Russia. The majority of the population elsewhere in Europe was also stable, or at most fluctuating, with only a minor-

	Breeding population			Breeding
	Size (pairs)	Year	Trend	range trend
Populations >5% of European total				
Germany	1,000,000–2,000,000	—	0	0
Russia	(10,000,000–100,000,000)	—	(0)	(0)
Sweden	1,000,000–3,000,000	87	**0**	**0**
Additional populations in decline				
Liechtenstein	500–1,000	—	(–1)	0
Ukraine	3,500–4,000	88	0	–1
United Kingdom				
Jersey	10–100	—	–2	–2
Total of above	12,000,000–110,000,000			
European total	17,000,000–120,000,000			

ity showing increases in numbers and/or in breeding range (Republic of Ireland, Denmark, Czech Republic, Hungary), or declines (Liechtenstein, Ukraine, Jersey).

Tenerife Goldcrest *Regulus teneriffae* is endemic to the Canary Islands, occurring on Tenerife, La Gomera, La Palma and El Hierro, but absent from Gran Canaria, Lanzarote and Fuerteventura. It is sedentary, apart from possible local altitudinal movements. Its main habitat is pinewoods with or without a dense understorey of tree-heath (especially *Erica arborea*), but it also occurs in pure tree-heath and laurel forest.

	Breeding population			Breeding
	Size (pairs)	Year	Trend	range trend
Populations >5% of European total				
Spain				
Canary Islands	**23,000–24,000**	—	**0**	**0**
European total	23,000–24,000			

Firecrest *Regulus ignicapillus* breeds mainly in central and eastern Europe, with a more fragmented distribution to the west and south. Compared with Goldcrest *R. regulus*, it is less dependent on tall conifers, occurring in a variety of woodland types and making extensive use of understorey. Northern and eastern populations are mainly migratory, wintering in western Europe and the Mediterranean region, while southern populations are mainly resident. Europe accounts for over 75% of the range, with Spain supporting about a third of the European breeding population and Germany about a quarter. Spain and Germany, along with Switzerland, Austria, Italy and Romania, together support c.80% of the total. Although the data reflect the difficulty of censusing this species, it appears that between 1970 and 1990 this core population was stable or, in the case of Austria, increased. During the same period, the small populations in Liechtenstein and the Ukraine declined, but the majority of the population in other

	Breeding population			Breeding
	Size (pairs)	Year	Trend	range trend
Populations >5% of European total				
Austria	(150,000–250,000)	—	(+1)	(+1)
Germany	700,000–1,500,000	—	0	0
Italy	(100,000–300,000)	—	(0)	(0)
Romania	(150,000–250,000)	—	(0)	**0**
Spain	910,000–2,000,000	—	0	0
Switzerland	350,000–400,000	86–91	0	0
Additional populations in decline				
Liechtenstein	400–600	—	–1	0
Ukraine	(50–150)	88	(–1)	–1
Total of above	2,400,000–4,700,000			
European total	2,700,000–5,500,000			

parts of Europe was stable. Small increases in numbers and range occurred in Portugal, France, Netherlands and Denmark, while the United Kingdom's small, fluctuating population appeared to undergo a moderate range expansion. Taken together, these changes are consistent with the known spread of the species north and west. During 1970–1990, Hungary was a new addition to the breeding distribution.

Collared Flycatcher *Ficedula albicollis* breeds only in Europe, mainly in the east, with a scattered distribution in the south-east, central and Baltic regions. Its typical habitat is mature, open, deciduous woodland and parkland, also to some extent orchards and shady gardens. It winters mainly south of the Equator in east-central Africa. About a third of the European population is found in Romania, with over 80% comprised by Russia, Moldova, Czech Republic, Slovakia, Hungary, Romania and Ukraine. Between 1970 and 1990, this core population was stable or, in the case of Moldova, increased. Numbers in Poland also increased during the same period. Elsewhere in Europe, numbers were stable in some countries and declined in others, rapidly in Germany, more slowly in Austria, Croatia and the small Swiss population. Collectively, however, these de-

	Breeding population			Breeding
	Size (pairs)	Year	Trend	range trend
Populations >5% of European total				
Czech Republic	25,000–50,000	—	0	**0**
Hungary	70,000–80,000	—	0	0
Moldova	**20,000–30,000**	88	**+1**	**+1**
Romania	100,000–300,000	—	0	**0**
Russia	(5,000–50,000)	—	(0)	(0)
Slovakia	(70,000–150,000)	—	0	**0**
Ukraine	20,000–25,000	90	0	0
Additional populations in decline				
Austria	(2,000–3,000)	—	(–1)	(0)
Croatia	10,000–20,000 *	—	–1*	0*
Germany	3,400–16,000	—	–2	**0**
Switzerland	**15–25**	86–91	–1	–1
Total of above	330,000–720,000			
European total	340,000–760,000			

clines amounted to only c.5% of the European population.

Pied Flycatcher *Ficedula hypoleuca* breeds throughout central and eastern Europe and Fenno-scandia, more patchily further west and south-west. It favours mature deciduous and mixed woodland, also parks and gardens. It winters in West Africa. Over 75% of the breeding range is in Europe, with Sweden, Finland and Russia together accounting for about two-thirds of the European population. This proportion increases to c.80% with the addition of Norway, Latvia and Belarus. There is good evidence that numbers increased during 1970–1990 in Sweden and Finland, while remaining stable in the other strongholds. Elsewhere in Europe, there were increases and range expansions in Belgium, Netherlands, Luxembourg, Lithuania, Estonia, Austria and Czech Republic (where there was also a marked range expansion). These trends indicate increases along a broad front in the north and north-west of the range, and also to some extent in central Europe. At

	Breeding population			Breeding
	Size (pairs)	Year	Trend	range trend
Populations >5% of European total				
Belarus	750,000–800,000	90	0	0
Finland	**1,000,000–1,500,000**	92	**+1**	**0**
Latvia	300,000–400,000	—	0	0
Norway	200,000–1,000,000	90	0	**0**
Russia	1,000,000–10,000,000	—	(0)	(0)
Sweden	1,000,000–2,000,000	87	**+1**	**0**
Additional populations in decline				
Denmark	2,000–32,000	87–89	(–1)	(–1)
Liechtenstein	3–10	—	–2	–1
Moldova	**400–700**	88	**–1**	**–1**
Romania	(100–5,000)	—	–1	–1
Spain	130,000–350,000	—	–1	–1
Total of above	4,400,000–16,000,000			
European total	4,900,000–17,000,000			

the same time, declines affected Spain, Denmark, Moldova and Romania, and the small Liechtenstein population, but collectively amounting to no more than c.3% of the European population in decline.

Sombre Tit *Parus lugubris* has a relatively confined distribution in Europe, chiefly in the southeast. It is resident in dry, open woodland and scrub, mainly in mountain areas. Over 75% of the species' range is in Europe, with Bulgaria supporting 75% of the European population, and all but a few percent accounted for by Greece, Bulgaria and Turkey. No trends are known for Turkey (or Albania), but the little available information suggests that numbers in Bulgaria and Greece, as elsewhere in Europe, were

	Breeding population			Breeding
	Size (pairs)	Year	Trend	range trend
Populations >5% of European total				
Bulgaria	(100,000–500,000)	—	(0)	(0)
Greece	10,000–30,000	—	(0)	(0)
Turkey	(10,000–100,000)	—	—	—
Total of above	120,000–630,000			
European total	130,000–640,000			

stable between 1970 and 1990. No declines were reported.

Crested Tit *Parus cristatus* is found only in Europe, widely distributed except in the extreme north and south-east. The United Kingdom supports a separate race in the Scottish Highlands. The species is highly sedentary over most of its range, rarely straying outside its typical habitat of mature pinewood in the north, and mixed woods further south. Highest numbers are in Russia (estimates vary tenfold but represent perhaps a quarter or more of the European population). Together, Spain, Portugal, Germany, Russia, Latvia and Belarus account for at least 75% of the European total. This core population appeared stable during 1970–1990, with the exception of Spain which registered an increase in numbers and range. Elsewhere in Europe, the only declines recorded were in Sweden and the Czech Republic, together representing about 5% of the European population in decline. The minor expansion seen in other parts of the western range earlier in the twentieth century (including the United Kingdom) appears to have

	Breeding population			Breeding
	Size (pairs)	Year	Trend	range trend
Populations >5% of European total				
Belarus	640,000–660,000	90	0	0
Germany	200,000–500,000	—	0	**0**
Latvia	300,000–370,000	—	0	0
Portugal	100,000–1,000,000	89	(0)	0
Russia	(1,000,000–10,000,000)	—	(0)	(0)
Spain	860,000–1,500,000	—	**+1**	**+1**
Additional populations in decline				
Czech Republic	80,000–160,000	—	–1	**0**
Sweden	150,000–500,000	87	**–1**	0
Total of above	3,300,000–15,000,000			
European total	3,900,000–16,000,000			

halted, with the majority of countries recording stable populations during 1970–1990. However, there was a marked increase in the small Hungarian population and smaller increases in Italy and Denmark, with the Finnish population fluctuating. The Danish data are consistent with a continuing pattern of northward spread in this region which included also expansion in Finland up to the 1950s.

Blue Tit *Parus caeruleus* occurs throughout Europe in (mostly lowland) woodland of all types, but especially open deciduous or mixed woods, parks and gardens with trees. Most populations are resident, but those in central and northern Europe make irregular eruptive movements in autumn and winter. Over 75% of the species' range is in Europe, with highest numbers in the United Kingdom and Germany. Together these may support up to a quarter of the European population and two-thirds to three-quarters including Spain, Portugal, Republic of Ireland, Denmark, Czech Republic and Slovakia. Between 1970 and 1990, numbers increased in the United Kingdom and were apparently stable (or, in the case of Denmark, fluctuating) in most of the other strongholds. The exception was the Czech Republic where numbers declined and, apart from the small Liechtenstein population, no other declines were reported during the period. Rather, most of the

	Breeding population			Breeding
	Size (pairs)	Year	Trend	range trend
Populations >5% of European total				
Czech Republic	800,000–1,600,000	—	–1	**0**
Denmark	290,000–2,900,000	87–89	(F)	(+1)
Germany	2,000,000–4,000,000	—	0	**0**
Rep. of Ireland	(900,000–900,000)	88–91	(0)	(0)
Portugal	1,000,000–1,000,000	89	(0)	0
Slovakia	(700,000–1,500,000)	—	(0)	0
Spain	930,000–3,600,000	—	0	0
United Kingdom	3,500,000–3,500,000	88–91	+1	**0**
Additional populations in decline				
Liechtenstein	100–200	—	–1	0
Total of above	10,000,000–19,000,000			
European total	14,000,000–28,000,000			

rest of Europe mirrored the stability of the core population during 1970–1990. The main regional trend to emerge was of population increase and range expansion in the north-east fringes, markedly so in Finland, slower in Estonia. Numbers also rose in the Netherlands and the Ukraine.

Krüper's Nuthatch *Sitta krueperi* occurs only in Europe and is confined to the south-east where it inhabits mature conifer forest (notably pines *Pinus*) from sea-level up to the tree-line. It is chiefly sedentary but shows some altitudinal movement in winter. Apart from a few hundred pairs in Greece, the vast majority of the population is found in Turkey. The little available evidence suggests that numbers in Greece were stable in 1970–1990, but the status of

	Breeding population			Breeding
	Size (pairs)	Year	Trend	range trend
Populations >5% of European total				
Turkey	(10,000–100,000)	—	—	—
European total	10,000–100,000			

the Turkish population is not known. There are no census data for Russia and Georgia.

Rock Nuthatch *Sitta neumayer* has a restricted distribution in Europe (which accounts for over 75% of its world range), being confined to dry, rocky, or thinly scrub-covered slopes up to 2,000 m in the south-east. The Turkish population, though by far the biggest, is poorly censused and no trends are known. The smaller but significant population in Greece was apparently stable from 1970 to 1990. Little is known about the comparatively small populations in Albania and Croatia, though the latter is thought to have been stable during the period. The

	Breeding population			Breeding
	Size (pairs)	Year	Trend	range trend
Populations >5% of European total				
Greece	10,000–30,000	—	(0)	(0)
Turkey	(50,000–500,000)	—	—	—
Total of above	60,000–530,000			
European total	65,000–540,000			

only country showing any increase in numbers and range was Bulgaria, a continuation of the spread which began there before 1970. There are no data for Armenia, Azerbaijan and Georgia.

Short-toed Treecreeper *Certhia brachydactyla* occurs throughout much of Europe but is mostly absent in the north, north-west, east and parts of the south-east. It inhabits mature, mainly deciduous and mixed woodland, parks and avenues, making more use of conifers in Mediterranean countries. It is sedentary throughout its range, of which Europe accounts for more than 75%. Highest numbers are found in Spain, followed by France, Germany, Portugal and Italy, these together accounting for c.80% of the European total. This core population was apparently stable between 1970 and 1990, although range may have contracted in Italy. Elsewhere in Europe during the same period, the vast majority of the population was likewise stable. Declines in numbers and/or range only affected Liechtenstein, Austria, Ukraine and Jersey, and negligibly so in terms of overall European numbers. The only known increase was in Denmark.

	Breeding population			Breeding
	Size (pairs)	Year	Trend	range trend
Populations >5% of European total				
France	500,000–2,000,000	90	(0)	0
Germany	300,000–1200,000	—	0	0
Italy	(100,000–500,000)	—	(0)	(–1)
Portugal	100,000–1,000,000	89	(0)	0
Spain	1,000,000–3,300,000	—	0	0
Additional populations in decline				
Austria	(10,000–15,000)	—	(0)	(–1)
Liechtenstein	20–50	—	–1	0
Ukraine	**200–300**	88	**–1**	**–1**
United Kingdom Jersey	200–500	—	–1	–1
Total of above	2,000,000–8,000,000			
European total	2,400,000–8,700,000			

Jackdaw *Corvus monedula* occurs widely throughout Europe except the far north. Its habitat, strongly dictated by its hole-nesting requirements, varies from mature woodland, parks and avenues, to cliffs and tall city buildings, with access to open ground for feeding. Populations in northern and western Europe are mostly resident, those further east more migratory but wintering almost entirely within the breeding range. By far the biggest breeding populations occur in Russia, Bulgaria and Turkey. Estimates vary widely, but these three together account for perhaps 50–80% of the European total. Other strongholds are the United Kingdom, Spain and Belarus. During 1970–1990 there were no trend data for Turkey, but numbers increased rapidly in the United Kingdom, more slowly in Spain (also with some range expansion) and Belarus, and were apparently stable in Russia and Bulgaria. Apart from this core population, rapid increases were also recorded in the Ukraine and Slovenia, and slower ones in the Republic of Ireland, Denmark, Italy and Croatia. Overall, therefore, c.8–30% of the European population was increasing between 1970 and 1990. Declines affected less than 2% of the European population, principally in France, Germany, Finland and the Czech Republic (rapid decline). Broad regional trends are difficult to discern, but some of the most important increases are in western Europe and most of the declines in central Europe.

	Breeding population			Breeding
	Size (pairs)	Year	Trend	range trend
Populations >5% of European total				
Belarus	350,000–400,000	90	+1	0
Bulgaria	(1,000,000–5,000,000)	—	(0)	(0)
Russia	(1,000,000–10,000,000)	—	(0)	(0)
Spain	423,600–533,000	—	+1	+1
Turkey	(1,000,000–10,000,000)	—	—	—
United Kingdom	430,000–430,000	88–91	+2	0
Additional populations in decline				
Austria	(2,500–4,000)	—	(–1)	(–1)
Czech Republic	10,000–20,000	—	–2	–1
Finland	40,000–60,000	92	–1	0
Germany	55,000–150,000	—	–1	–1
Liechtenstein	**11–14**	89	**–1**	**0**
Portugal	1,000–10,000	89	–1	–1
Slovakia	(3,000–5,000)	—	(0)	–1
Switzerland	**950–1,000**	89	**–1**	**–1**
Total of above	4,300,000–27,000,000			
European total	5,500,000–29,000,000			

Key to tables (see p. 34)					Data quality	**Bold:** reliable quantitative data Normal type: incomplete quantitative data
Trends	+2 Large increase	+1 Small increase	0 Stable	X Extinct		Bracketed figures: no quantitative data * Data quality not provided
	–2 Large decrease	–1 Small decrease	F Fluctuating	N New breeder	¹ Population figures included within United Kingdom totals	P Present

464

Spotless Starling *Sturnus unicolor* has a limited European distribution, confined to the south-west of the continent and to Corsica, Sardinia, Sicily. It requires old trees or buildings for nest-holes, situated in woodland or dwellings with access variously to short grass and herbage, cultivated areas or degraded coastal scrub. It is resident or a partial short-distance migrant, subject to nomadic dispersal. Spain accounts for c.70–80% of the European population, Spain and Portugal together supporting over 90%. Next in importance is Italy (i.e. Sardinia and Sicily), followed by France (southern mainland and Corsica), then Gibraltar. Between 1970 and 1990, num-

	Breeding population			Breeding
	Size (pairs)	Year	Trend	range trend
Populations >5% of European total				
Portugal	100,000–1,000,000	89	(0)	0
Spain	2,000,000–2,250,000	—	+1	+1
Total of above	2,100,000–3,300,000			
European total	2,200,000–3,400,000			

bers and range increased in Spain and range increased in France. During the same period, numbers in Italy and Gibraltar were apparently stable. The expansion in Spain has been to the north and east, probably from the 1950s, resulting in southern France being colonized by at least 1985.

Chaffinch *Fringilla coelebs* is widespread in Europe, occupying deciduous, mixed and coniferous woods up to the treeline, also parks and gardens. It is mainly sedentary in the west and south, more migratory further north and east, but wintering chiefly within the breeding range. Breeding strongholds are the United Kingdom, Sweden, Finland, Russia, Belarus, Germany and Czech Republic, which together account for half to two-thirds of the European total. During 1970–1990, numbers in this core population, as in most other parts of the range, appeared stable. Only Finland, holding up to c.8% of the European total population, suffered a small decline. Modest

	Breeding population			Breeding
	Size (pairs)	Year	Trend	range trend
Populations >5% of European total				
Belarus	**5,400,000–5,600,000**	90	0	0
Czech Republic	4,000,000–8,000,000	—	0	**0**
Finland	**6,000,000–9,000,000**	92	–1	**0**
Germany	7,000,000–14,000,000	—	0	**0**
Russia	(10,000,000–100,000,000)	—	(0)	0
Sweden	7,500,000–15,000,000	87	**0**	0
United Kingdom	5,800,000–5,800,000	88–91	**0**	**0**
Total of above	46,000,000–160,000,000			
European total	78,000,000–230,000,000			

increases in numbers and range were recorded in Spain, Denmark, Croatia and Ukraine.

Serin *Serinus serinus* occurs widely in mainland Europe except for much of the east and most of Fennoscandia. It inhabits parks, gardens and open country with scattered clumps of trees, preferring conifers in dry, sunny situations. Birds in the centre and south of the range are mainly sedentary, those further north more migratory, wintering south to North Africa and the Middle East. Over 75% of the breeding range lies in Europe, chiefly Spain (nearly half the European population). Spain, Germany, Portugal, Ukraine, Czech Republic and France together support c.90% of the European total. During 1970–1990, numbers and range increased rapidly in the Ukraine, more slowly in Spain. However, numbers apparently fell in Germany, representing declining status in up to a quarter of the European population. Otherwise, population and/or range declines affected only small marginal populations in the north of the range. By contrast, several other countries outside the core population registered expansion of numbers and range during 1970–1990, or recruited the species to breed. These changes are a continuation of slow expansion, mainly northward, since the early

	Breeding population			Breeding
	Size (pairs)	Year	Trend	range trend
Populations >5% of European total				
Czech Republic	450,000–900,000	—	0	**0**
France	100,000–1,000,000	76	(0)	0
Germany	2,000,000–4,000,000	—	–1	**0**
Portugal	1,000,000–1,000,000	89	(0)	0
Spain	4,100,000–6,600,000	—	+1	+1
Ukraine	600,000–650,000	86	**+2**	**+2**
Additional populations in decline				
Belgium	650–1,200	81–90	–1	–1
Estonia	50–100	—	**–1**	–1
Finland	(0–3)	92	0	–2
Sweden	**5–15**	87	**–1**	0
Total of above	8,300,000–14,000,000			
European total	8,900,000–16,000,000			

nineteenth century. In summary, during 1970–1990, range contracted in Fennoscandia (reversing earlier small gains), but continued expanding on many other fronts: in the Baltic (Latvia, Lithuania), north-west (United Kingdom, Netherlands), south-west (Andorra, Spain, Italy, also Canary Islands), central (Liechtenstein, Hungary), south-east (Moldova, Croatia, Cyprus) and eastern Europe (Belarus, Ukraine).

Canary *Serinus canaria* is confined to the Canary Islands, Madeira and the Azores, occupying fruit plantations, other cultivated areas with trees and shrubs and open scrubby areas. It is resident, showing only local movements. Highest numbers, representing about two-thirds of the world population, are found on the Canary Islands, followed in order of importance by the Azores and Madeira. Numbers everywhere appeared to be stable during 1970–1990.

	Breeding population			Breeding
	Size (pairs)	Year	Trend	range trend
Populations >5% of European total				
Portugal				
Azores	(30,000–60,000)	—	(0)	(0)
Spain				
Canary Islands	80,000–90,000	—	0	0
Total of above	110,000–150,000			
European total	110,000–160,000			

Citril Finch *Serinus citrinella* is confined to Europe, having a fragmented distribution in central and south-west regions. It inhabits montane areas, favouring light coniferous woodland interspersed with alpine meadows and other open ground; on Corsica and Sardinia it is found on scrubby, rocky slopes. Some southern populations are sedentary, elsewhere movements are mainly short-distance or altitudinal. Spain supports c.80% of the world population, with Switzerland the only other significant stronghold. During 1970–1990, numbers and range increased in Spain. In terms of the overall European population,

	Breeding population			Breeding
	Size (pairs)	Year	Trend	range trend
Populations >5% of European total				
Spain	225,000–230,000	—	+1	**+1**
Switzerland	(5,000–30,000)	86–91	—	(0)
Additional populations in decline				
Austria	(5,000–7,000)	—	(−1)	(0)
Liechtenstein	200–300	—	−1	(0)
Total of above	240,000–270,000			
European total	240,000–290,000			

none of the changes elsewhere was significant, although the data are often too poor to be certain of trends.

Greenfinch *Carduelis chloris* occurs widely in Europe, favouring open areas with tall trees, including woodland edge, farmland with hedgerows, parks and suburban gardens. Most populations are partial migrants (as far as North Africa), except for some in the south which appear to be resident or dispersive. The bulk of the population is well distributed in Europe which accounts for more than 75% of the world range. About 75% of the European breeding population accrues to Spain, Portugal, United Kingdom, France, Germany, Denmark, Czech Republic and Ukraine. During 1970–1990, numbers were stable in Portugal, United Kingdom, France and Germany, increased in Spain, Ukraine and probably Denmark, but declined in the Czech Republic. Other declines during this period were recorded in Belgium and Andorra. Elsewhere, outside the core population, numbers in most countries were stable, but there were some notable gains. The long-term popu-

	Breeding population			Breeding
	Size (pairs)	Year	Trend	range trend
Populations >5% of European total				
Czech Republic	500,000–1,000,000	—	−1	**0**
Denmark	200,000–2,000,000	87–89	(+1)	(+1)
France	1,000,000–1,000,000	76	(0)	**0**
Germany	2,000,000–4,000,000	—	0	**0**
Portugal	1,000,000–1,000,000	89	(0)	0
Spain	1,060,000–3,600,000	—	+1	+1
Ukraine	800,000–950,000	86	+1	+1
United Kingdom	560,000–560,000	88–91	0	**0**
Additional populations in decline				
Andorra	(20–50)	91	(−1)	0
Belgium	40,000–80,000	81–90	−1	0
Total of above	7,200,000–14,000,000			
European total	9,800,000–21,000,000			

lation increase and range expansion continued in Fennoscandia, with Estonia also showing a rise in numbers. Other notable increases occurred in the Netherlands, Switzerland and Cyprus, while the Canary Islands were colonized during the period.

Siskin *Carduelis spinus* occurs mainly in central and eastern Europe and Fennoscandia, occupying lowland and montane coniferous (especially spruce *Picea*) or mixed forest. Northern populations are mostly migratory (moving as far as North Africa and the Middle East) while some southern ones may be resident. More than 75% of the species' world range is in Europe, with the United Kingdom, Norway, Sweden, Finland and Russia together accounting for c.80% of European numbers. Northern populations are known to undergo marked fluctuations and this is evident in the data for the core population in 1970–1990: numbers fluctuated throughout Fennoscandia, accompanied by some range expansion in the case of Finland. Range also expanded markedly in the United Kingdom, along with a modest increase in numbers. Meanwhile the huge Russian population was apparently stable, but the census estimates allow a wide latitude for status changes.

	Breeding population			Breeding
	Size (pairs)	Year	Trend	range trend
Populations >5% of European total				
Finland	500,000–1,500,000	92	F	**0**
Norway	100,000–1,000,000	90	F	**+1**
Russia	(1,000,000–10,000,000)	—	(0)	(0)
Sweden	400,000–1,000,000	87	F	0
United Kingdom	(310,000–310,000)	88–91	(+1)	**+2**
Total of above	2,300,000–14,000,000			
European total	2,700,000–15,000,000			

Elsewhere in Europe, as in the strongholds, no steady declines were recorded during 1970–1990 and most populations were either stable or fluctuating. Most fluctuations were on the southern fringes where the breeding range is especially prone to expansion and contraction. Population increases in the Republic of Ireland, Netherlands, Luxembourg and Denmark, and the colonization of the Faroes, endorse the upward trend in much of north-west Europe during 1970–1990.

Linnet *Carduelis cannabina* occupies most of Europe except the far north. It favours open scrub and heath with a dry sunny aspect, also cultivated areas with bushes, young plantations and woodland edge. It is a partial migrant, most birds wintering in the breeding range or slightly south of it, especially in the Mediterranean. The breeding strongholds are Spain, United Kingdom, France, Denmark, Germany, Ukraine and Turkey, together accounting for c.80% of the European population. Between 1970 and 1990, numbers and range increased in Spain, Ukraine and probably Denmark, these being the only gains in Europe during the period. At the same time, a similar proportion (c.20%) of the European population was in decline, markedly so in the United Kingdom, Netherlands and Finland, more slowly in Estonia, Norway, Sweden, Belgium, Germany, Switzerland, Czech Republic, Slovakia and Malta. Overall, these show a general contraction of range in Fennoscandia and declining numbers in north-west and central Europe. Other populations outside the strongholds, including much of eastern and south-

	Breeding population			Breeding
	Size (pairs)	Year	Trend	range trend
Populations >5% of European total				
Denmark	160,000–1,800,000	87–89	(+1)	(+1)
France	1,000,000–?	76	(0)	**0**
Germany	450,000–900,000	—	–1	**0**
Spain	1,700,000–3,300,000	—	+1	+1
Turkey	(1,000,000–10,000,000)	—	—	—
Ukraine	900,000–1,000,000	86	+1	+1
United Kingdom	540,000–540,000	88–91	–2	**0**
Additional populations in decline				
Belgium	60,000–130,000	81–90	–1	0
Czech Republic	60,000–120,000	—	–1	**0**
Estonia	20,000–50,000	—	–1	0
Finland	15,000–20,000	92	–2	**–2**
Malta	20–30	—	–1	–1
Netherlands	**60,000–130,000**	79	–2	**0**
Norway	10,000–15,000	90	–1	**0**
Slovakia	(40,000–60,000)	—	(–1)	0
Sweden	100,000–250,000	87	**–1**	0
Switzerland	30,000–60,000	86–91	–1	0
Total of above	6,100,000–18,000,000			
European total	7,100,000–21,000,000			

east Europe, were essentially stable during 1970–1990.

Parrot Crossbill *Loxia pytyopsittacus* is confined to Europe, occurring in mature pine forest in the north-east and Fennoscandia. It is resident and dispersive, also making eruptive movements mainly south-west as far as north-west Europe, which can lead to small numbers breeding sporadically in new areas (e.g. Belgium during 1970–1990). Population estimates are generally broad, partly because numbers fluctuate locally from year to year, and partly from the difficulty of distinguishing this species from the more widespread Crossbill *L. curvirostra*. The vast majority of European Parrot Crossbills breed in Norway, Sweden, Finland and Russia. Dur-

	Breeding population			Breeding
	Size (pairs)	Year	Trend	range trend
Populations >5% of European total				
Finland	10,000–100,000	92	F	F
Norway	10,000–100,000	90	F	**0**
Russia	(10,000–100,000)	—	(0)	(0)
Sweden	10,000–50,000	87	**0**	0
Total of above	40,000–350,000			
European total	42,000–360,000			

ing 1970–1990, numbers fluctuated in Norway and Finland and were stable in Sweden and perhaps also in Russia. No declines were reported anywhere in Europe during the period.

Yellowhammer *Emberiza citrinella* occurs widely in Europe except in the south-west and south-east. Its typical habitat is open country, especially cultivated areas with hedges, plantations, scrub, rough grassland and parkland. It is sedentary to migratory (in the far north of the range), but mostly a partial migrant, wintering largely within the breeding range. Highest numbers are found in the United Kingdom, Denmark, Poland, Czech Republic and Russia, these together supporting c.75% of the European population. Between 1970 and 1990, this core population, like most of the population elsewhere in Europe, was apparently stable. However, parts of the range, notably in central and north-west Europe, have suffered declining numbers and some range contraction during the twentieth century. Between 1970 and 1990 this trend was evident in, e.g., Republic of Ireland, Belgium, Netherlands (rapid decline), Germany and Austria, also in Italy and Latvia. In terms of overall European numbers, these declines are relatively small, representing c.5% of the total population in decline.

	Breeding population			Breeding
	Size (pairs)	Year	Trend	range trend
Populations >5% of European total				
Czech Republic	2,000,000–4,000,000	—	0	**0**
Denmark	260,000–2,600,000	87–89	(0)	(0)
Poland	2,500,000–5,000,000	—	0	0
Russia	(10,000,000–100,000,000)	—	(0)	(0)
United Kingdom	1,200,000–1,200,000	88–91	0	**0**
Additional populations in decline				
Austria	(200,000–250,000)	—	(–1)	(0)
Belgium	21,000–38,000	81–90	–1	0
Germany	1,000,000–3,500,000	—	–1	**0**
Rep. of Ireland	(180,000–180,000)	88–91	(–1)	(0)
Italy	(20,000–50,000)	—	(–1)	(0)
Latvia	80,000–160,000	—	–1	0
Liechtenstein	**30–30**	89	–1	–1
Netherlands	**22,000–28,000**	79	**–2**	**–1**
United Kingdom Isle of Man [1]	100–200	—	–2	0*
Total of above	17,000,000–117,000,000			
European total	23,000,000–125,000,000			

Cirl Bunting *Emberiza cirlus* is distributed through north-west, south-west and south-east Europe. It is mainly sedentary breeding principally in heath, scrub and agricultural habitats. Spain, France, Italy and Turkey together hold the vast majority of the population. Though generally not well studied (e.g. no trend data available for Turkey), this core population appears to have been stable (France, Italy) or to have increased (Spain) during 1970–1990. Numbers have also increased, and range expanded, in Croatia and Romania, and breeding has spread to Austria and Hungary, but there has been a substantial decrease in the small population in the United Kingdom. This is consistent with long-term range contraction in north-

	Breeding population			Breeding
	Size (pairs)	Year	Trend	range trend
Populations >5% of European total				
France	100,000–1,000,000	76	(0)	(0)
Italy	(300,000–600,000)	—	(0)	(0)
Spain	500,000–800,000	—	+1	+1
Turkey	(100,000–1,000,000)	—	—	—
Additional populations in decline				
United Kingdom	**230–230**	89–91	**–2**	**–2**
Jersey	8–8	92	–2	–2
Total of above	1,000,000–3,400,000			
European total	1,100,000–3,900,000			

west Europe, including extinction in Belgium, while range appears to have spread north in parts of central and south-east Europe.

Cretzschmar's Bunting *Emberiza caesia* has a restricted European distribution in the south-east where it inhabits barren, rocky hillsides or open scrub, often near gardens. It winters in north-east Africa south to Sudan and perhaps also in western Arabia. Over 75% of the world breeding range is in Europe, mainly in Turkey, with Greece and Cyprus also holding significant numbers. Information for Turkey is sparse, with no trends known for 1970–1990 (nor for the small population in Albania). During the

	Breeding population			Breeding
	Size (pairs)	Year	Trend	range trend
Populations >5% of European total				
Cyprus	3,000–5,000	—	0	0
Greece	5,000–15,000	—	(0)	(0)
Turkey	(10,000–100,000)	—	—	—
Total of above	18,000–120,000			
European total	18,000–120,000			

same period, numbers in Greece and Cyprus were apparently stable.

Corn Bunting *Miliaria calandra* is widespread in Europe except Fennoscandia and the north-east. Its habitat is open country, often cultivated areas supplied with song-posts such as fences and bushes. It is resident to partially migratory, wintering chiefly within the breeding range. Highest numbers are found in Spain and Turkey which together support two-thirds or more of the European population. These, along with other strongholds in Portugal, France, Italy, Greece and Bulgaria, support c.90% of the total. No trends are known for the major Turkish population between 1970 and 1990, but during this period numbers rose in Spain. Populations in Portugal, France and Bulgaria were stable, but those in Italy and Greece declined. Elsewhere in Europe, there have been widespread population declines and range contraction in the twentieth century, most conspicuously since the 1960s. The regions most affected are central and north-west Europe. In central Europe between 1970 and 1990, marked reductions in numbers and range were recorded in Germany, Switzerland, Austria and Czech Republic, with lesser declines in Poland, Slovakia and Hungary. In north-west Europe, the most dramatic declines were in the Republic of Ireland, United Kingdom and Netherlands, with Belgium and Denmark also affected. Range also contracted in northern breeding areas (Sweden, Latvia, Lithuania) and in the south-east and east (Moldova, Ukraine), although numbers may have increased in Croatia. In sum, the reductions represent about a quarter of the European population in decline during 1970–1990

	Breeding population			Breeding
	Size (pairs)	Year	Trend	range trend
Populations >5% of European total				
Bulgaria	(100,000–1,000,000)	—	(0)	(0)
France	100,000–1,000,000	76	(0)	0
Greece	300,000–500,000	—	(–1)	(0)
Italy	(200,000–600,000)	—	(–1)	(–1)
Portugal	100,000–1,000,000	89	(0)	0
Spain	1,440,000–4,300,000	—	+1	+1
Turkey	(1,000,000–10,000,000)	—	—	—
Additional populations in decline				
Austria	(250–400)	—	(–2)	(–1)
Belgium	3,000–5,500	81–90	–1	–1
Czech Republic	700–1,400	—	–2	–1
Denmark	11,000–120,000	87–89	(–1)	(–1)
Germany	10,000–40,000	—	–2	–1
Hungary	8,000–12,000	—	–1	0
Rep. of Ireland	(30–30)	88–91	–2	–2
Latvia	(5–20)	—	(–1)	(–1)
Liechtenstein	**10–10**	90	–1	–2
Lithuania	50–100	85–88	(–2)	(–1)
Luxembourg	50–250	—	0	–1
Malta	400–600	—	–1	–1
Moldova	**1,500–3,000**	88	**–1**	**–1**
Netherlands	**100–200**	89	**–2**	**–2**
Poland	150,000–200,000	—	(–1)	(0)
Slovakia	(3,000–14,000)	—	–1	**–1**
Spain				
Canary Islands	P*	—	(–1)	(–1)
Sweden	**5–10**	—	**–1**	–1
Switzerland	200–250	86–91	–2	–2
Ukraine	4,000–7,000	86	–1	–1
United Kingdom	16,000–23,000	93	–2	**–1**
Total of above	3,500,000–19,000,000			
European total	3,600,000–19,000,000			

(c.2% declining rapidly), with the rest mostly stable and only the substantial Spanish population reliably showing expansion.

SPEC category

1   Species of global conservation concern, i.e. classified as Globally Threatened, Conservation Dependent or Data Deficient (Collar *et al.* 1994).

2   Concentrated in Europe and with an Unfavourable Conservation Status.

3   Not concentrated in Europe but with an Unfavourable Conservation Status.

4   Concentrated in Europe and with a Favourable Conservation Status.

For SPEC categories given as, for example, '4/2', the first number is the SPEC category relating to the breeding population, while the second number relates to the winter population.

[w] Category relates to winter populations.

European Threat Status

E	Endangered	L	Localized
V	Vulnerable	Ins	Insufficiently Known
R	Rare	S	Secure
D	Declining	( )	Status provisional

Population decline, size and localization criteria upon which species qualify as having an Unfavourable Conservation Status are indicated in **bold** type.

Population declines

These are based on summed population totals of countries that recorded population declines (see Box 5 on p. 30). Winter population declines are only given for selected well monitored species (Anatidae, Haemato-podidae, Charadriidae and Scolopacidae). ? indicates that the entire European population occurs in countries where trends are unknown.

Minimum breeding population

Rounded to two significant figures, and only given if less than 1 million pairs.

[ind] Population figures refer to individuals.

Localized

In such species, more than 90% of the population occurs at ten sites or fewer.
B Localized when breeding.
W Localized in winter.

Notes:

[1] Decline criterion not met because a higher proportion of the population is increasing.

[2] Small population size criterion not met because the European population is marginal to a large non-European population.

[3] Population total and conservation assessment includes data for the Caucasus region of Russia, Georgia, Armenia and Azerbaijan taken from the species' account.

[4] Occurs in the region only on passage.

Population sizes and trends do not include Armenia, Azerbaijan, Georgia, Bosnia and Herzegovina, Yugoslavia and Former Yugoslav Republic of Macedonia unless otherwise indicated.

	SPEC category	European Threat Status	% of breeding population				% of winter pop. size declined by:		Minimum breeding population (pairs)	Local-ized
			size declined by:		range declined by:					
			>20%	>50%	>20%	>50%	>20%	>50%		
Red-throated Diver *Gavia stellata*	3	V	**88**	0	0	0			61,000	
Black-throated Diver *Gavia arctica*	3	V	**96**	0	0	0			120,000	
Great Northern Diver *Gavia immer*		(S)	0	0	0	0			500 [2]	
White-billed Diver *Gavia adamsii*		(S)	0	0	0	0			50 [2]	
Little Grebe *Tachybaptus ruficollis*		S	21	2	10	2	15	4	67,000	
Great Crested Grebe *Podiceps cristatus*		S	3	0	1	0	2	0	340,000	
Red-necked Grebe *Podiceps grisegena*		S	29	0	30	0	0	0	28,000	
Slavonian Grebe *Podiceps auritus*		(S)	30	7	2	0	0	0	15,000	
Black-necked Grebe *Podiceps nigricollis*		S	9	0	5	0	1	0	39,000	
Fulmar *Fulmarus glacialis*		S	0	0	0	0				
Fea's Petrel *Pterodroma feae*	1	E	0	0	0	0			**150**	
Zino's Petrel *Pterodroma madeira*	1	E	0	0	0	0			**20**	
Bulwer's Petrel *Bulweria bulwerii*	3	V	**33**	**22**	22	0			**7,500**	
Cory's Shearwater *Calonectris diomedea*	2	(V)	**78**	**32**	21	0			140,000	
Great Shearwater *Puffinus gravis*									0 [4]	
Sooty Shearwater *Puffinus griseus*									0 [4]	
Manx Shearwater *Puffinus puffinus*	2	(L)	0	0	0	0			270,000	B
Yelkouan Shearwater *Puffinus yelkouan*	4	S	21	0	18	0			18,000	
Little Shearwater *Puffinus assimilis*	3	V	**36**	**15**	15	**15**			**2,700**	
White-faced Storm-petrel *Pelagodroma marina*	3	L	0	0	0	0			16,000	B

Appendix 1: Conservation Status of All European Species

	SPEC category	European Threat Status	% of breeding population				% of winter pop. size declined by:		Minimum breeding population (pairs)	Local-ized
			size declined by:		range declined by:					
			>20%	>50%	>20%	>50%	>20%	>50%		
Storm Petrel *Hydrobates pelagicus*	2	(L)	3	0	1	0			280,000	B
Leach's Storm-petrel *Oceanodroma leucorhoa*	3	(L)	0	0	0	0			91,000	B
Madeiran Storm-petrel *Oceanodroma castro*	3	V	41	0	0	0			**3,300**	
Gannet *Sula bassana*	2	L	0	0	0	0			230,000	B
Cormorant *Phalacrocorax carbo*		S	1	1	4	1	0	0	140,000	
Shag *Phalacrocorax aristotelis*	4	S	24	0	3	0			85,000	
Pygmy Cormorant *Phalacrocorax pygmeus*	2	V	65	5	5	5	0	0	**6,400**	
White Pelican *Pelecanus onocrotalus*	3	R	10	0	0	0			**3,400**	
Dalmatian Pelican *Pelecanus crispus*	1	V	19	6	6	6			**960**	
Bittern *Botaurus stellaris*	3	(V)	79	3	4	1			19,000	
Little Bittern *Ixobrychus minutus*	3	(V)	92	7	23	6			37,000	
Night Heron *Nycticorax nycticorax*	3	D	41	0	11	0			51,000	
Squacco Heron *Ardeola ralloides*	3	V	66	5	8	2			12,000	
Cattle Egret *Bubulcus ibis*		S	0	0	0	0			67,000	
Little Egret *Egretta garzetta*		S	31	5	10	0			31,000	
Great White Egret *Egretta alba*		S	5	0	2	0			12,000	
Grey Heron *Ardea cinerea*		S	4	1	1	0			130,000	
Purple Heron *Ardea purpurea*	3	V	99	4	9	4			49,000	
Black Stork *Ciconia nigra*	3	R	9	0	5	0			**6,500**	
White Stork *Ciconia ciconia*	2	V	52	38	24	0			120,000	
Glossy Ibis *Plegadis falcinellus*	3	D	58	17	42	0			14,000	
Spoonbill *Platalea leucorodia*	2	E	77	34	14	0			**5,200**	
Greater Flamingo *Phoenicopterus ruber*	3	L	0	0	0	0			28,000	B
Mute Swan *Cygnus olor*		S	0	0	1	0	0	0	49,000	
Bewick's Swan *Cygnus columbianus*	3 [w]	L [w]	0	0	0	0	17	0	3,000 [2]	W
Whooper Swan *Cygnus cygnus*	4 [w]	S	0	0	0	0	0	0	6,300 [2]	
Bean Goose *Anser fabilis*		S	0	0	1	0	0	0	83,000	
Pink-footed Goose *Anser brachyrhynchus*	4	S	0	0	0	0	0	0	48,000	
White-fronted Goose *Anser albifrons*		S	0	0	0	0	0	0	50,000	
Lesser White-fronted Goose *Anser erythropus*	1	V	3	0	2	0	2	2	**1,000**	
Greylag Goose *Anser anser*		S	2	0	0	0	1	0	56,000	
Barnacle Goose *Branta leucopsis*	4/2	L [w]	0	0	0	0	0	0	9,800 [2]	W
Brent Goose *Branta bernicla*	3	V	0	0	0	0	0	0	**1,100**	W
Red-breasted Goose *Branta ruficollis*	1	L [w]					0	0	**0**	W
Ruddy Shelduck *Tadorna ferruginea*	3	V	73	0	2	0	79	0	6,100 [2]	
Shelduck *Tadorna tadorna*		S	4	0	4	0	0	0	38,000	
Wigeon *Anas penelope*		S	0	0	0	0	13	3	260,000	
Gadwall *Anas strepera*	3	V	79	1	2	1	5	1	75,000	
Teal *Anas crecca*		S	0	0	0	0	23	9		
Mallard *Anas platyrhynchos*		S	9	0	7	0	1	1		
Pintail *Anas acuta*	3	V	99	0	0	0	53	28	170,000	
Garganey *Anas querquedula*	3	V	96	0	5	0			640,000	
Shoveler *Anas clypeata*		S	0	0	3	2	8	0	96,000	
Marbled Teal *Marmaronetta angustirostris*	1	E	100	100	100	100	100	100	**200**	
Red-crested Pochard *Netta rufina*	3	D	57	0	1	0	3	3	14,000	
Pochard *Aythya ferina*	4	S	22	0	11	0	32	0	270,000	
Ferruginous Duck *Aythya nyroca*	1	V	82	2	81	0	92	79	11,000	
Tufted Duck *Aythya fuligula*		S	0	0	0	0	14	0	620,000	
Scaup *Aythya marila*	3 [w]	L [w]	2	2	2	0	5	0	47,000	W
Eider *Somateria mollissima*		S	9	0	0	0	0	0	740,000	
King Eider *Somateria spectabilis*		S	0	0	0	0			44,000	
Steller's Eider *Polysticta stelleri*	1	L [w]	?	?	?	?	0	0	1 [2]	W
Harlequin Duck *Histrionicus histrionicus*	3	V	0	0	0	0			**2,200**	
Long-tailed Duck *Clangula hyemalis*		S	0	0	0	0			370,000	
Common Scoter *Melanitta nigra*		S	1	0	0	0	0	0	100,000	
Velvet Scoter *Melanitta fusca*	3 [w]	L [w]	12	0	0	0	0	0	69,000	W
Barrow's Goldeneye *Bucephala islandica*	3	E	0	0	0	0			**200**	
Goldeneye *Bucephala clangula*		S	1	0	14	0	0	0	240,000	
Smew *Mergus albellus*	3	V	0	0	87	0	24	24 [1]	8,100 [2]	
Red-breasted Merganser *Mergus serrator*		S	2	0	0	0	3	0	58,000	
Goosander *Mergus merganser*		S	4	0	0	0	0	0	52,000	

	SPEC category	European Threat Status	% of breeding population				% of winter pop. size declined by:		Minimum breeding population (pairs)	Local-ized
			size declined by:		range declined by:					
			>20%	>50%	>20%	>50%	>20%	>50%		
White-headed Duck *Oxyura leucocephala*	1	E	0	0	0	0	3	3	210	
Honey Buzzard *Pernis apivorus*	4	S	10	0	0	0			110,000	
Black-winged Kite *Elanus caeruleus*	3	V	0	0	0	0			1,100	
Black Kite *Milvus migrans*	3	V	73	1	70	1			75,000	
Red Kite *Milvus milvus*	4	S	20	0	20	0			19,000	
White-tailed Eagle *Haliaeetus albicilla*	3	R	2	1	2	0			3,300	
Lammergeier *Gypaetus barbatus*	3	E	6	0	0	0			200	
Egyptian Vulture *Neophron percnopterus*	3	E	98	2	99	2			2,800	
Griffon Vulture *Gyps fulvus*	3	R	18	2	13	2			9,300	
Cinereous Vulture *Aegypius monachus*	3	V	7	1	1	1			1,000	
Short-toed Eagle *Circaetus gallicus*	3	R	8	0	7	0			5,900	
Marsh Harrier *Circus aeruginosus*		S	3	0	3	0			48,000	
Hen Harrier *Circus cyaneus*	3	V	70	1	70	0			22,000	
Pallid Harrier *Circus macrourus*	3	E	100	1	100	1			1,000	
Montagu's Harrier *Circus pygargus*	4	S	8	5	7	4			26,000	
Goshawk *Accipiter gentilis*		S	11	1	3	0			130,000	
Sparrowhawk *Accipiter nisus*		S	4	0	2	0			270,000	
Levant Sparrowhawk *Accipiter brevipes*	2	R	1	1	1	1			3,600	
Buzzard *Buteo buteo*		S	3	0	1	0			740,000	
Long-legged Buzzard *Buteo rufinus*	3	(E)	81	0	81	0			2,000	
Rough-legged Buzzard *Buteo lagopus*		S	0	0	0	0			91,000	
Lesser Spotted Eagle *Aquila pomarina*	3	R	5	0	3	0			6,700	
Greater Spotted Eagle *Aquila clanga*	1	E	98	1	98	1			860	
Steppe Eagle *Aquila nipalensis*	3	V	100	0	100	0			15,000	
Imperial Eagle *Aquila heliaca*	1	E	86	13	74	14			320	
Spanish Imperial Eagle *Aquila adalberti*	1	E	0	0	0	0			150	
Golden Eagle *Aquila chrysaetos*	3	R	30	0	30	0			5,000	
Booted Eagle *Hieraaetus pennatus*	3	R	6	2	2	1			2,800	
Bonelli's Eagle *Hieraaetus fasciatus*	3	E	94	0	95	2			820	
Osprey *Pandion haliaetus*	3	R	3	0	3	0			7,100	
Lesser Kestrel *Falco naumanni*	1	(V)	99	73	83	70			10,000	
Kestrel *Falco tinnunculus*	3	D	47	20	30	0			290,000	
Red-footed Falcon *Falco vespertinus*	3	V	100	93	94	91			18,000	
Merlin *Falco columbarius*		S	9	0	1	0			34,000	
Hobby *Falco subbuteo*		S	10	2	4	0			58,000	
Eleonora's Falcon *Falco eleonorae*	2	R	3	0	0	0			3,800	
Lanner *Falco biarmicus*	3	(E)	84	0	84	0			200	
Saker *Falco cherrug*	3	E	80	8	47	8			370	
Gyrfalcon *Falco rusticolus*	3	V	9	0	9	0			1,300	
Peregrine *Falco peregrinus*	3	R	41[1]	0	34[1]	0			6,200	
Barbary Falcon *Falco pelegrinoides*		S	0	0	0	0			6[2]	
Hazel Grouse *Bonasa bonasia*		S	18	1	1	0				
Red/Willow Grouse *Lagopus lagopus*		S	30	0	5	0				
Ptarmigan *Lagopus mutus*		S	2	0	0	0			480,000	
Black Grouse *Tetrao tetrix*	3	V	69	51	5	0			580,000	
Caucasian Black Grouse *Tetrao mlokosiewiczi*	2	Ins	?	?	?	?			71,000[3]	
Capercaillie *Tetrao urogallus*		(S)	13	1	12	0			580,000	
Caucasian Snowcock *Tetraogallus caucasicus*	4	S	0	0	0	0			164,000[ind,3]	
Caspian Snowcock *Tetraogallus caspius*	3	Ins	?	?	?	?			200	
Chukar *Alectoris chukar*	3	V	100	0	99	0			150,000	
Rock Partridge *Alectoris graeca*	2	(V)	84	1	20	1			34,000	
Red-legged Partridge *Alectoris rufa*	2	V	96	0	80	0				
Barbary Partridge *Alectoris barbara*	3	(E)	99	0	99	0			3,700	
See-see *Ammoperdix griseogularis*		(S)	?	?	?	?			100[2]	
Black Francolin *Francolinus francolinus*	3	V	100	0	0	0			1,300[2]	
Partridge *Perdix perdix*	3	V	99	37	49	2				
Quail *Coturnix coturnix*	3	V	64	50	14	0			680,000	
Pheasant *Phasianus colchicus*		S	21	4	2	0				
Andalusian Hemipode *Turnix sylvatica*	3	E	100	100	100	100			5	
Water Rail *Rallus aquaticus*		(S)	32	0	20	0			110,000	
Spotted Crake *Porzana porzana*	4	S	27	8	20	8			52,000	

	SPEC category	European Threat Status	% of breeding population				% of winter pop. size declined by:		Minimum breeding population (pairs)	Local-ized
			size declined by:		range declined by:					
			>20%	>50%	>20%	>50%	>20%	>50%		
Little Crake *Porzana parva*	4	(S)	28	14 [1]	28	14 [1]			25,000	
Baillon's Crake *Porzana pusilla*	3	R	13	1	13	0			**3,800**	
Corncrake *Crex crex*	1	V	99	56	16	3			92,000	
Moorhen *Gallinula chloropus*		S	10	0	3	0			790,000	
Purple Gallinule *Porphyrio porphyrio*	3	R	4	0	4	0			**3,400**	
Coot *Fulica atra*		S	19	2	20	0				
Crested Coot *Fulica cristata*	3	E	0	0	0	0			**10**	
Crane *Grus grus*	3	V	72	0	1	0			52,000	
Demoiselle Crane *Anthropoides virgo*		S	0	0	0	0			15,000	
Little Bustard *Tetrax tetrax*	2	V	67	5	62	0			84,000 [ind]	
Houbara Bustard *Chlamydotis undulata*	3	(E)	?	?	?	?			**200**	
Great Bustard *Otis tarda*	1	D	61	5	59	5			26,000 [ind]	
Oystercatcher *Haematopus ostralegus*		S	12	0	9	0	0	0	200,000	
Black-winged Stilt *Himantopus himantopus*		S	22	0	8	0			21,000	
Avocet *Recurvirostra avosetta*	4/3 [w]	L [w]	31	25 [1]	6	0	39 [1]	0	31,000	**W**
Stone Curlew *Burhinus oedicnemus*	3	V	74	1	61	1			41,000	
Cream-coloured Courser *Cursorius cursor*	3	V	100	100	100	100			200 [2]	
Collared Pratincole *Glareola pratincola*	3	E	75	5	19	5			**6,700**	
Black-winged Pratincole *Glareola nordmanni*	3	R	1	1	1	1			**6,500**	
Little Ringed Plover *Charadrius dubius*		(S)	7	0	1	0			110,000	
Ringed Plover *Charadrius hiaticula*		S	13	0	9	0	0	0	95,000	
Kentish Plover *Charadrius alexandrinus*	3	D	43	4	42	1			21,000	
Greater Sand Plover *Charadrius leschenaultii*	3	(E)	0	0	0	0			**100**	
Caspian Plover *Charadrius asiaticus*	3	(V)	100	100	100	100			100 [2]	
Dotterel *Charadrius morinellus*		(S)	0	0	0	0			25,000	
Golden Plover *Pluvialis apricaria*	4	S	17	0	0	0			440,000	
Grey Plover *Pluvialis squatarola*		(S)	0	0	0	0	0	0	10,000	
Spur-winged Plover *Hoplopterus spinosus*	3	(E)	97	0	0	0			**1,000**	
Red-wattled Plover *Hoplopterus indicus*		S	0	0	0	0			10 [2]	
Sociable Plover *Chettusia gregaria*	1	E	100	0	100	0			**1,000**	
White-tailed Plover *Chettusia leucura*		(S)	?	?	?	?			<10 [2]	
Lapwing *Vanellus vanellus*		(S)	26	5	5	0				
Knot *Calidris canutus*	3 [w]	L [w]					16	6	10,000	**W**
Sanderling *Calidris alba*		S	0	0	0	0	0	0	17,000	
Little Stint *Calidris minuta*		(S)	0	0	0	0			100,000	
Temminck's Stint *Calidris temminckii*		(S)	0	0	1	0				
Curlew Sandpiper *Calidris ferruginea*									0 [4]	
Purple Sandpiper *Calidris maritima*	4	(S)	0	0	0	0	8	0	25,000	
Dunlin *Calidris alpina*	3 [w]	V [w]	3	0	0	0	92	26	390,000	
Broad-billed Sandpiper *Limicola falcinellus*	3	(V)	75	0	75	0			13,000	
Ruff *Philomachus pugnax*	4	(S)	3	3	3	3				
Jack Snipe *Lymnocryptes minimus*	3 [w]	(V) [w]	0	0	0	0	95	0	22,000	
Snipe *Gallinago gallinago*		(S)	13	4	1	0	14	0		
Great Snipe *Gallinago media*	2	(V)	96	96	89	0			170,000	
Pintail Snipe *Gallinago sterna*		S	0	0	0	0			1,000 [2]	
Woodcock *Scolopax rusticola*	3 [w]	V [w]	3	1	1	0	86	83		
Black-tailed Godwit *Limosa limosa*	2	V	86	0	4	0	6	0	140,000	
Bar-tailed Godwit *Limosa lapponica*	3 [w]	L [w]	0	0	0	0	6	6	2200 [2]	**W**
Whimbrel *Numenius phaeopus*	4	(S)	1	0	0	0			180,000	
Slender-billed Curlew *Numenius tenuirostris*	1								0 [4]	
Curlew *Numenius arquata*	3 [w]	D [w]	21	0	1	0	41	0	120,000	
Spotted Redshank *Tringa erythropus*		S	0	0	0	0	0	0	24,000	
Redshank *Tringa totanus*	2	D	40	0	14	0	3	0	300,000	
Marsh Sandpiper *Tringa stagnatilis*		(S)	0	0	0	0			10,000	
Greenshank *Tringa nebularia*		S	0	0	0	0	11	0	61,000	
Green Sandpiper *Tringa ochropus*		(S)	0	0	0	0			230,000	
Wood Sandpiper *Tringa glareola*	3	D	53	0	0	0			370,000	
Terek Sandpiper *Xenus cinereus*		(S)	0	0	0	0			10,000	
Common Sandpiper *Actitis hypoleucos*		S	1	0	0	0	12	0	500,000	
Turnstone *Arenaria interpres*		S	1	0	0	0	0	0	27,000	
Red-necked Phalarope *Phalaropus lobatus*		(S)	19	0	19	0			160,000	

Birds in Europe: Their Conservation Status

	SPEC category	European Threat Status	% of breeding population — size declined by: >20%	>50%	range declined by: >20%	>50%	% of winter pop. size declined by: >20%	>50%	Minimum breeding population (pairs)	Local-ized
Grey Phalarope *Phalaropus fulicarius*		(S)	6	0	6	0			640 [2]	
Pomarine Skua *Stercorarius pomarinus*		(S)	0	0	0	0			1,000 [2]	
Arctic Skua *Stercorarius parasiticus*		(S)	22	0	0	0			26,000	
Long-tailed Skua *Stercorarius longicaudus*		(S)	0	0	0	0			13,000	
Great Skua *Stercorarius skua*	4	S	0	0	0	0			14,000	
Great Black-headed Gull *Larus ichthyaetus*		S	0	0	0	0			24,000	
Mediterranean Gull *Larus melanocephalus*	4	S	0	0	1	0			180,000	
Little Gull *Larus minutus*	3	D	**53**	0	**54**	0			23,000	
Sabine's Gull *Larus sabini*		S	0	0	0	0			100 [2]	
Black-headed Gull *Larus ridibundus*		S	24	10	9	0				
Slender-billed Gull *Larus genei*		(S)	0	0	0	0			41,000	
Audouin's Gull *Larus audouinii*	1	L	0	0	0	0			13,000	**B**
Common Gull *Larus canus*	2	D	37	2	0	0			420,000	
Lesser Black-backed Gull *Larus fuscus*	4	S	24	3	0	0			200,000	
Herring Gull *Larus argentatus*		S	23	3	0	0			900,000	
Yellow-legged Gull *Larus cachinnans*		(S)	0	0	0	0			>10,000	
Armenian Gull *Larus armenicus*		(S)	?	?	?	?			2,000 [2]	
Iceland Gull *Larus glaucoides*		(S)	?	?	?	?			10,000	
Glaucous Gull *Larus hyperboreus*		S	0	0	0	0			27,000	
Great Black-backed Gull *Larus marinus*	4	S	21	0	0	0			97,000	
Ross's Gull *Rhodostethia rosea*		S	0	0	0	0			0 [2]	
Kittiwake *Rissa tridactyla*		S	32	0	0	0				
Ivory Gull *Pagophila eburnea*	3	(E)	**100**	0	0	0			**1,300**	
Gull-billed Tern *Gelochelidon nilotica*	3	(E)	**95**	0	**61**	0			**6,800**	
Caspian Tern *Sterna caspia*	3	(E)	**97**	0	**87**	**15**			**4,800**	
Sandwich Tern *Sterna sandvicensis*	2	D	**53**	0	**61**	0			120,000	
Roseate Tern *Sterna dougallii*	3	E	**71**	9	9	5			**1,600**	
Common Tern *Sterna hirundo*		S	21	0	10	0			200,000	
Arctic Tern *Sterna paradisaea*		S	22	0	0	0			430,000	
Little Tern *Sterna albifrons*	3	D	**50**	2	**45**	0			29,000	
Whiskered Tern *Chlidonias hybridus*	3	D	**49**	0	**48**	0			33,000	
Black Tern *Chlidonias niger*	3	D	13	**12**	18	2			57,000	
White-winged Black Tern *Chlidonias leucopterus*		S	6	6	7	6			19,000	
Guillemot *Uria aalge*		S	17	10	4	0				
Brünnich's Guillemot *Uria lomvia*		S	18	18 [1]	0	0				
Razorbill *Alca torda*	4	S	9	0	0	0			430,000	
Black Guillemot *Cepphus grylle*	2	D	**36**	0	0	0			120,000	
Little Auk *Alle alle*		(S)	0	0	0	0				
Puffin *Fratercula arctica*	2	V	**49**	**41**	0	0				
Black-bellied Sandgrouse *Pterocles orientalis*	3	V	**100**	**99**	**100**	**99**			32,000	
Pin-tailed Sandgrouse *Pterocles alchata*	3	E	**100**	**98**	**100**	**98**			**6,700**	
Rock Dove *Columba livia*		S	1	0	0	0				
Stock Dove *Columba oenas*	4	S	20	0	11	0			460,000	
Woodpigeon *Columba palumbus*	4	S	0	0	0	0				
Long-toed Pigeon *Columba trocaz*	1	V	0	0	0	0			**3,500** [ind]	
Dark-tailed Laurel Pigeon *Columba bollii*	1	V	0	0	0	0			**1,700** [ind]	
White-tailed Laurel Pigeon *Columba junoniae*	1	V	0	0	0	0			**1,200** [ind]	
Collared Dove *Streptopelia decaocto*		(S)	25	0	0	0				
Turtle Dove *Streptopelia turtur*	3	D	**60**	13	**42**	0				
Rufous Turtle Dove *Streptopelia orientalis*		(S)	0	0	0	0			5,000 [2]	
Laughing Dove *Streptopelia senegalensis*		(S)	0	0	0	0			5,000 [2]	
Great Spotted Cuckoo *Clamator glandarius*		S	3	0	3	0			56,000	
Cuckoo *Cuculus canorus*		S	14	0	1	0				
Oriental Cuckoo *Cuculus saturatus*		(S)	0	0	0	0			1,000 [2]	
Barn Owl *Tyto alba*	3	D	**40**	6	10	0			100,000	
Striated Scops Owl *Otus brucei*		(S)	?	?	?	?			5 [2]	
Scops Owl *Otus scops*	2	(D)	**47**	0	**41**	0			90,000	
Eagle Owl *Bubo bubo*	3	V	**65**	**57**	9	1			11,000	
Brown Fish Owl *Ketupa zeylonensis*		(S)	?	?	?	?			1 [2]	
Snowy Owl *Nyctea scandiaca*	3	V	0	0	0	0			**<2,500**	

Appendix 1: Conservation Status of All European Species

	SPEC category	European Threat Status	% of breeding population size declined by: >20%	>50%	range declined by: >20%	>50%	% of winter pop. size declined by: >20%	>50%	Minimum breeding population (pairs)	Local-ized
Hawk Owl *Surnia ulula*		(S)	0	0	0	0			14,000	
Pygmy Owl *Glaucidium passerinum*		(S)	0	0	0	0			33,000	
Little Owl *Athene noctua*	3	D	57	4	43	0			180,000	
Tawny Owl *Strix aluco*	4	S	8	0	2	0			360,000	
Ural Owl *Strix uralensis*		(S)	0	0	0	0			110,000	
Great Grey Owl *Strix nebulosa*		S	0	0	0	0			1,700 [2]	
Long-eared Owl *Asio otus*		S	2	0	1	0			200,000	
Short-eared Owl *Asio flammeus*	3	(V)	77	74	1	1			19,000	
Tengmalm's Owl *Aegolius funereus*		(S)	2	0	1	0			37,000	
Nightjar *Caprimulgus europaeus*	2	(D)	46	4	40	5			290,000	
Red-necked Nightjar *Caprimulgus ruficollis*		S	0	0	0	0			100,000	
Plain Swift *Apus unicolor*	4	S	0	0	0	0			> 10,000	
Swift *Apus apus*		S	11	0	2	0				
Pallid Swift *Apus pallidus*		(S)	22	0	3	0			17,000	
Alpine Swift *Apus melba*		(S)	13	0	13	0			46,000	
White-rumped Swift *Apus caffer*		S	0	0	0	0			30 [2]	
Little Swift *Apus affinis*		(S)	?	?	?	?			500 [2]	
White-breasted Kingfisher *Halcyon smyrnensis*		(S)	?	?	?	?			100 [2]	
Kingfisher *Alcedo atthis*	3	D	43	1	33	1			46,000	
Pied Kingfisher *Ceryle rudis*		(S)	?	?	?	?			200 [2]	
Blue-cheeked Bee-eater *Merops superciliosus*		(S)	0	0	0	0			200 [2]	
Bee-eater *Merops apiaster*	3	D	54	0	19	0			86,000	
Roller *Coracias garrulus*	2	(D)	44	20	40	1			29,000	
Hoopoe *Upupa epops*		S	13	0	8	0			670,000	
Wryneck *Jynx torquilla*	3	D	47	10	24	0			350,000	
Grey-headed Woodpecker *Picus canus*	3	D	47	0	4	0			71,000	
Green Woodpecker *Picus viridis*	2	D	44	0	21	0			350,000	
Black Woodpecker *Dryocopus martius*		S	7	0	1	0			270,000	
Great Spotted Woodpecker *Dendrocopos major*		S	1	0	0	0				
Syrian Woodpecker *Dendrocopos syriacus*	4	(S)	5	0	5	0			120,000	
Middle Spotted Woodpecker *Dendrocopos medius*	4	S	25	0	9	0			53,000	
White-backed Woodpecker *Dendrocopos leucotos*		S	7	3	7	0			34,000	
Lesser Spotted Woodpecker *Dendrocopos minor*		S	19	4	5	1			170,000	
Three-toed Woodpecker *Picoides tridactylus*	3	D	39	0	1	0			53,000	
Desert Lark *Ammomanes deserti*		(S)	?	?	?	?			15 [2]	
Dupont's Lark *Chersophilus duponti*	3	V	100	0	100	0			13,000	
Calandra Lark *Melanocorypha calandra*	3	(D)	51	0	51	0				
Bimaculated Lark *Melanocorypha bimaculata*		(S)	?	?	?	?			5,000 [2]	
White-winged Lark *Melanocorypha leucoptera*	4 [w]	(S)	0	0	0	0			10,000	
Black Lark *Melanocorypha yeltoniensis*	3	(V)	100	0	100	0			6,000 [2]	
Short-toed Lark *Calandrella brachydactyla*	3	V	90	0	90	0				
Lesser Short-toed Lark *Calandrella rufescens*	3	V	72	0	69	0			370,000	
Crested Lark *Galerida cristata*	3	(D)	61	1	60	0				
Thekla Lark *Galerida theklae*	3	V	99	0	99	0				
Woodlark *Lullula arborea*	2	V	75	0	68	0			840,000	
Skylark *Alauda arvensis*	3	V	69	19	19	0				
Shore Lark *Eremophila alpestris*		(S)	2	0	2	0			110,000	
Sand Martin *Riparia riparia*	3	D	35	3	29	0				
Crag Martin *Ptyonoprogne rupestris*		S	0	0	0	0			130,000	
Swallow *Hirundo rustica*	3	D	58	8	16	0				
Red-rumped Swallow *Hirundo daurica*		S	0	0	0	0			45,000	
House Martin *Delichon urbica*		S	16	1	1	0				
Tawny Pipit *Anthus campestris*	3	V	86	0	85	0			540,000	
Berthelot's Pipit *Anthus berthelotii*	4	S	0	0	0	0			16,000	
Olive-backed Pipit *Anthus hodgsoni*		(S)	0	0	0	0			3,100 [2]	
Tree Pipit *Anthus trivialis*		S	8	0	2	0				

Birds in Europe: Their Conservation Status

	SPEC category	European Threat Status	% of breeding population size declined by:		range declined by:		% of winter pop. size declined by:		Minimum breeding population (pairs)	Local-ized
			>20%	>50%	>20%	>50%	>20%	>50%		
Pechora Pipit *Anthus gustavi*		(S)	0	0	0	0			1,000 [2]	
Meadow Pipit *Anthus pratensis*	4	S	2	0	0	0				
Red-throated Pipit *Anthus cervinus*		(S)	0	0	12	0			17,000	
Rock Pipit *Anthus petrosus*		S	0	0	0	0				
Water Pipit *Anthus spinoletta*		S	2	0	0	0			380,000	
Yellow Wagtail *Motacilla flava*		S	0	0	0	0				
Citrine Wagtail *Motacilla citreola*		(S)	0	0	0	0			100,000	
Grey Wagtail *Motacilla cinerea*		(S)	8	0	0	0			490,000	
Pied Wagtail *Motacilla alba*		S	1	0	0	0				
Yellow-vented Bulbul										
Pycnonotus xanthopygos		(S)	?	?	?	?			5,000 [2]	
Waxwing *Bombycilla garrulus*		(S)	0	0	1	0			130,000	
Dipper *Cinclus cinclus*		(S)	21	0	17	0			110,000	
Wren *Troglodytes troglodytes*		S	0	0	0	0				
Dunnock *Prunella modularis*	4	S	28	0	0	0				
Siberian Accentor *Prunella montanella*		(S)	0	0	0	0			100 [2]	
Radde's Accentor *Prunella ocularis*	3	(V)	?	?	?	?			**500**	
Black-throated Accentor *Prunella atrogularis*	3	(V)	?	?	?	?			**1,000**	
Alpine Accentor *Prunella collaris*		S	0	0	0	0			47,000	
Rufous Bush Robin *Cercotrichas galactotes*		S	7	0	0	0			19,000	
Robin *Erithacus rubecula*	4	S	0	0	0	0				
Thrush Nightingale *Luscinia luscinia*	4	S	1	0	0	0			820,000	
Nightingale *Luscinia megarhynchos*	4	(S)	5	0	5	0				
Siberian Rubythroat *Luscinia calliope*		(S)	0	0	0	0			10 [2]	
Bluethroat *Luscinia svecica*		S	1	0	1	0			530,000	
Red-flanked Bluetail *Tarsiger cyanurus*		(S)	1	1	1	1			100 [2]	
White-throated Robin *Irania gutturalis*		(S)	?	?	?	?			5,000 [2]	
Black Redstart *Phoenicurus ochruros*		S	0	0	0	0				
Redstart *Phoenicurus phoenicurus*	2	V	**83**	**20**	**31**	0				
Güldenstädt's Redstart										
Phoenicurus erythrogaster	3	Ins	?	?	?	?			**2,500** [ind,3]	
Whinchat *Saxicola rubetra*	4	S	18	2	1	0				
Fuerteventura Chat *Saxicola dacotiae*	2	V	0	0	0	0			**750**	
Stonechat *Saxicola torquata*	3	(D)	**64**	1	**35**	0			890,000	
Isabelline Wheatear *Oenanthe isabellina*		(S)	0	0	0	0			200,000	
Wheatear *Oenanthe oenanthe*		S	18	0	11	0				
Pied Wheatear *Oenanthe pleschanka*		(S)	2	0	0	0			110,000	
Cyprus Pied Wheatear *Oenanthe cypriaca*	2	R	0	0	0	0			**3,000**	
Black-eared Wheatear *Oenanthe hispanica*	2	V	**88**	0	**88**	0			650,000	
Desert Wheatear *Oenanthe deserti*		(S)	?	?	?	?			? [2]	
Finsch's Wheatear *Oenanthe finschii*		(S)	?	?	?	?			1,000 [2]	
Red-tailed Wheatear										
Oenanthe xanthoprymna		(S)	?	?	?	?			100 [2]	
Black Wheatear *Oenanthe leucura*	3	E	**100**	0	**100**	0			**4,100**	
Rock Thrush *Monticola saxatilis*	3	(D)	**39**	0	**37**	0			31,000	
Blue Rock Thrush *Monticola solitarius*	3	(V)	**71**	0	**40**	0			38,000	
White's Thrush *Zoothera dauma*		(S)	0	0	0	0			100 [2]	
Ring Ouzel *Turdus torquatus*	4	S	3	0	6	0			200,000	
Blackbird *Turdus merula*	4	S	15	0	0	0				
Black-throated Thrush *Turdus ruficollis*		(S)	0	0	0	0			1,000 [2]	
Fieldfare *Turdus pilaris*	4 [w]	S	1	0	0	0				
Song Thrush *Turdus philomelos*	4	S	13	10	1	0				
Redwing *Turdus iliacus*	4 [w]	S	0	0	0	0				
Mistle Thrush *Turdus viscivorus*	4	S	5	0	4	0				
Cetti's Warbler *Cettia cetti*		S	6	0	6	0			410,000	
Fan-tailed Warbler *Cisticola juncidis*		(S)	0	0	0	0				
Graceful Warbler *Prinia gracilis*		(S)	?	?	?	?			500 [2]	
Lanceolated Warbler *Locustella lanceolata*		(S)	0	0	0	0			10,000	
Grasshopper Warbler *Locustella naevia*	4	S	6	4	4	0			320,000	
River Warbler *Locustella fluviatilis*	4	S	2	0	0	0			400,000	
Savi's Warbler *Locustella luscinioides*	4	(S)	5	1	0	0			140,000	

Appendix 1: Conservation Status of All European Species

	SPEC category	European Threat Status	% of breeding population size declined by: >20%	>50%	range declined by: >20%	>50%	% of winter pop. size declined by: >20%	>50%	Minimum breeding population (pairs)	Localized
Moustached Warbler *Acrocephalus melanopogon*		(S)	1	0	15	0			78,000	
Aquatic Warbler *Acrocephalus paludicola*	1	E	**69**	1	**69**	0			**3,700**	
Sedge Warbler *Acrocephalus schoenobaenus*	4	(S)	12	1	19	0				
Paddyfield Warbler *Acrocephalus agricola*		S	0	0	0	0			110,000	
Blyth's Reed Warbler *Acrocephalus dumetorum*		(S)	0	0	0	0			110,000	
Marsh Warbler *Acrocephalus palustris*	4	S	6	0	31	0				
Reed Warbler *Acrocephalus scirpaceus*	4	S	7	0	0	0				
Great Reed Warbler *Acrocephalus arundinaceus*		(S)	6	0	37[1]	0				
Olivaceous Warbler *Hippolais pallida*	3	(V)	**82**	0	10	0			620,000	
Booted Warbler *Hippolais caligata*		(S)	0	0	0	0			10,000	
Upcher's Warbler *Hippolais languida*		(S)	0	0	0	0			1,000[2]	
Olive-tree Warbler *Hippolais olivetorum*	2	(R)	0	0	0	0			**7,600**	
Icterine Warbler *Hippolais icterina*	4	S	6	0	0	0				
Melodious Warbler *Hippolais polyglotta*	4	(S)	0	0	0	0			950,000	
Marmora's Warbler *Sylvia sarda*	4	(S)	0	0	0	0			29,000	
Dartford Warbler *Sylvia undata*	2	V	**93**	0	**93**	0				
Spectacled Warbler *Sylvia conspicillata*		(S)	0	0	0	0			200,000	
Subalpine Warbler *Sylvia cantillans*	4	S	0	0	0	0				
Ménétries's Warbler *Sylvia mystacea*		(S)	0	0	0	0			1,100[2]	
Sardinian Warbler *Sylvia melanocephala*	4	S	0	0	0	0				
Cyprus Warbler *Sylvia melanothorax*	2	R	0	0	0	0			**4,000**	
Rüppell's Warbler *Sylvia rueppelli*	4	(S)	0	0	0	0			8,000[2]	
Desert Warbler *Sylvia nana*		(S)	0	0	0	0			1,000[2]	
Orphean Warbler *Sylvia hortensis*	3	V	**94**	1	**94**	0			190,000	
Barred Warbler *Sylvia nisoria*	4	(S)	14	0	11	0			230,000	
Lesser Whitethroat *Sylvia curruca*		S	25	0	1	0				
Whitethroat *Sylvia communis*	4	S	20	3	8	0				
Garden Warbler *Sylvia borin*	4	S	0	0	0	0				
Blackcap *Sylvia atricapilla*	4	S	0	0	5	0				
Green Warbler *Phylloscopus nitidus*		(S)	?	?	?	?			1,000[2]	
Greenish Warbler *Phylloscopus trochiloides*		(S)	0	0	0	0			120,000	
Arctic Warbler *Phylloscopus borealis*		(S)	0	0	0	0				
Yellow-browed Warbler *Phylloscopus inornatus*		S	0	0	0	0			<10,000[2]	
Bonelli's Warbler *Phylloscopus bonelli*	4	S	0	0	0	0				
Wood Warbler *Phylloscopus sibilatrix*	4	(S)	0	0	0	0				
Mountain Chiffchaff *Phylloscopus sindianus*		(S)	?	?	?	?			1,000[2]	
Chiffchaff *Phylloscopus collybita*		(S)	0	0	0	0				
Willow Warbler *Phylloscopus trochilus*		S	0	0	0	0				
Goldcrest *Regulus regulus*	4	(S)	0	0	0	0				
Tenerife Goldcrest *Regulus teneriffae*	4	S	0	0	0	0			23,000	
Firecrest *Regulus ignicapillus*	4	S	0	0	0	0				
Spotted Flycatcher *Muscicapa striata*	3	D	45	2	10	0				
Red-breasted Flycatcher *Ficedula parva*		(S)	1	0	0	0				
Semi-collared Flycatcher *Ficedula semitorquata*	2	(E)	**67**	0	0	0			**2,500**	
Collared Flycatcher *Ficedula albicollis*	4	S	5	2	0	0			340,000	
Pied Flycatcher *Ficedula hypoleuca*	4	S	3	0	3	0				
Bearded Tit *Panurus biarmicus*		(S)	2	1	2	1			250,000	
Long-tailed Tit *Aegithalos caudatus*		S	1	0	1	0				
Marsh Tit *Parus palustris*		S	10	0	2	0				
Sombre Tit *Parus lugubris*	4	(S)	0	0	0	0			130,000	
Willow Tit *Parus montanus*		(S)	2	0	0	0				
Siberian Tit *Parus cinctus*		(S)	0	0	0	0			240,000	
Crested Tit *Parus cristatus*	4	S	6	0	0	0				
Coal Tit *Parus ater*		S	4	0	0	0				
Blue Tit *Parus caeruleus*	4	S	6	0	0	0				
Azure Tit *Parus cyanus*		(S)	0	0	0	0			10,000	

Birds in Europe: Their Conservation Status

	SPEC category	European Threat Status	% of breeding population size declined by: >20%	>50%	range declined by: >20%	>50%	% of winter pop. size declined by: >20%	>50%	Minimum breeding population (pairs)	Local-ized
Great Tit *Parus major*		S	0	0	0	0				
Krüper's Nuthatch *Sitta krueperi*	4	(S)	0	0	0	0			10,000	
Corsican Nuthatch *Sitta whiteheadi*	2	V	0	0	0	0			**2,000**	
Nuthatch *Sitta europaea*		S	1	0	1	0				
Eastern Rock Nuthatch *Sitta tephronota*		(S)	?	?	?	?			500 [2]	
Rock Nuthatch *Sitta neumayer*	4	(S)	0	0	0	0			65,000	
Wallcreeper *Tichodroma muraria*		(S)	0	0	0	0			13,000	
Treecreeper *Certhia familiaris*		S	15	0	2	0				
Short-toed Treecreeper *Certhia brachydactyla*	4	S	0	0	6	0				
Penduline Tit *Remiz pendulinus*		(S)	0	0	0	0			140,000	
Golden Oriole *Oriolus oriolus*		S	17	0	6	0				
Red-backed Shrike *Lanius collurio*	3	(D)	**53**	2	23	0				
Lesser Grey Shrike *Lanius minor*	2	(D)	**33**	0	25	0			77,000	
Great Grey Shrike *Lanius excubitor*	3	D	**64**	1	2	0			330,000	
Woodchat Shrike *Lanius senator*	2	V	**93**	0	**93**	0			450,000	
Masked Shrike *Lanius nubicus*	2	(V)	**98**	0	33	0			7,700 [2]	
Jay *Garrulus glandarius*		(S)	0	0	0	0				
Siberian Jay *Perisoreus infaustus*	3	(D)	**36**	0	**36**	0			110,000	
Azure-winged Magpie *Cyanopica cyana*		S	0	0	0	0			250,000	
Magpie *Pica pica*		S	0	0	0	0				
Nutcracker *Nucifraga caryocatactes*		(S)	2	0	0	0			150,000	
Alpine Chough *Pyrrhocorax graculus*		(S)	10	0	0	0			58,000	
Chough *Pyrrhocorax pyrrhocorax*	3	V	**92**	6	**68**	1			16,000	
Jackdaw *Corvus monedula*	4	(S)	2	0	2	0				
Rook *Corvus frugilegus*		S	1	0	0	0				
Carrion Crow *Corvus corone*		S	0	0	0	0				
Raven *Corvus corax*		(S)	3	0	1	0			280,000	
Starling *Sturnus vulgaris*		S	27	3	0	0				
Spotless Starling *Sturnus unicolor*	4	S	0	0	0	0				
Rose-coloured Starling *Sturnus roseus*		(S)	1	1	1	1			15,000	
House Sparrow *Passer domesticus*		S	24	0	0	0				
Spanish Sparrow *Passer hispaniolensis*		(S)	0	0	0	0				
Dead Sea Sparrow *Passer moabiticus*		(S)	0	0	0	0			510 [2]	
Tree Sparrow *Passer montanus*		S	16	2	0	0				
Pale Rock Sparrow *Carpospiza brachydactyla*		(S)	0	0	0	0			100 [2]	
Yellow-throated Sparrow *Petronia xanthocollis*		(S)	?	?	?	?			50 [2]	
Rock Sparrow *Petronia petronia*		S	3	1	2	1			860,000	
Snowfinch *Montifringilla nivalis*		(S)	0	0	0	0			23,000	
Chaffinch *Fringilla coelebs*	4	S	8	0	0	0				
Blue Chaffinch *Fringilla teydea*	1	V	0	0	0	0			**1,000**	
Brambling *Fringilla montifringilla*		S	0	0	0	0				
Red-fronted Serin *Serinus pusillus*		(S)	?	?	?	?			10,000	
Serin *Serinus serinus*	4	S	26	0	0	0				
Canary *Serinus canaria*	4	S	0	0	0	0			110,000	
Citril Finch *Serinus citrinella*	4	S	3	0	0	0			240,000	
Greenfinch *Carduelis chloris*	4	S	6	0	0	0				
Goldfinch *Carduelis carduelis*		(S)	13	0	9	0				
Siskin *Carduelis spinus*	4	S	0	0	0	0				
Linnet *Carduelis cannabina*	4	S	23	10	0	0				
Twite *Carduelis flavirostris*		S	0	0	0	0			170,000	
Redpoll *Carduelis flammea*		(S)	2	0	0	0				
Arctic Redpoll *Carduelis hornemanni*		(S)	0	0	0	0			110,000	
Two-barred Crossbill *Loxia leucoptera*		(S)	0	0	0	0			11,000	
Crossbill *Loxia curvirostra*		S	0	0	0	0			840,000	
Scottish Crossbill *Loxia scotica*	1	Ins	?	?	0	0			**300**	
Parrot Crossbill *Loxia pytyopsittacus*	4	S	0	0	0	0			42,000	
Crimson-winged Finch *Rhodopechys sanguinea*		(S)	?	?	?	?			10,000	
Desert Finch *Rhodospiza obsoleta*		(S)	?	?	?	?			1,000 [2]	

	SPEC category	European Threat Status	% of breeding population				% of winter pop. size declined by:		Minimum breeding population (pairs)	Local-ized
			size declined by:		range declined by:					
			>20%	>50%	>20%	>50%	>20%	>50%		
Mongolian Trumpeter Finch										
Bucanetes mongolicus		(S)	?	?	?	?			10[2]	
Trumpeter Finch *Bucanetes githagineus*	3	R	0	0	0	0			**4,100**	
Scarlet Rosefinch *Carpodacus erythrinus*		(S)	0	0	0	0				
Great Rosefinch *Carpodacus rubicilla*	3	(E)	**100**	**0**	0	0			**500**[3]	
Pine Grosbeak *Pinicola enucleator*		S	0	0	0	0			44,000	
Bullfinch *Pyrrhula pyrrhula*		S	8	6	0	0				
Hawfinch *Coccothraustes coccothraustes*		S	3	0	0	0			920,000	
Lapland Bunting *Calcarius lapponicus*		(S)	0	0	0	0				
Snow Bunting *Plectrophenax nivalis*		(S)	15	0	0	0			690,000	
Yellowhammer *Emberiza citrinella*	4	(S)	7	0	0	0				
Cirl Bunting *Emberiza cirlus*	4	(S)	0	0	0	0				
Rock Bunting *Emberiza cia*	3	V	**88**	0	**85**	0				
Cinereous Bunting *Emberiza cineracea*	2	(V)	0	0	0	0			**550**	
Ortolan Bunting *Emberiza hortulana*	2	(V)	**49**	**41**	**45**	0				
Grey-necked Bunting *Emberiza buchanani*		(S)	?	?	?	?			1,000[2]	
Cretzschmar's Bunting *Emberiza caesia*	4	(S)	0	0	0	0			18,000	
Rustic Bunting *Emberiza rustica*		(S)	5	0	0	0				
Little Bunting *Emberiza pusilla*		(S)	0	0	0	0			110,000	
Yellow-breasted Bunting *Emberiza aureola*		(S)	1	0	1	1			10,000	
Reed Bunting *Emberiza schoeniclus*		S	29	9	5	0				
Red-headed Bunting *Emberiza bruniceps*		S	0	0	0	0			1,000[2]	
Black-headed Bunting										
Emberiza melanocephala	2	(V)	**81**	0	0	0				
Corn Bunting *Miliaria calandra*	4	(S)	28	2	10	0				

The following lists include all SPECs known to breed regularly in the geopolitical units covered by this review.
SPEC Categories, given for each species, are as follows:

1 Species of global conservation concern, i.e. classified as Globally Threatened, Conservation Dependent or Data Deficient (Collar *et al.* 1994).

2 Concentrated in Europe and with an Unfavourable Conservation Status.

3 Not concentrated in Europe but with an Unfavourable Conservation Status.

4 Concentrated in Europe and with a Favourable Conservation Status.

For SPEC categories given as, for example, '4/2', the first number is the SPEC category relating to the breeding population, while the second number relates to the winter population.

[w] Category relates to winter populations.

Species in **bold** occur in only one geopolitical unit in Europe.

ALBANIA

4 *Puffinus yelkouan*	3 *Tetrao tetrix*	3 *Melanocorypha calandra*	4 *Sylvia communis*
4 *Phalacrocorax aristotelis*	2 *Alectoris graeca*	3 *Calandrella*	4 *Sylvia borin*
2 *Phalacrocorax pygmeus*	3 *Perdix perdix*	*brachydactyla*	4 *Sylvia atricapilla*
1 *Pelecanus crispus*	3 *Coturnix coturnix*	3 *Galerida cristata*	4 *Phylloscopus bonelli*
3 *Botaurus stellaris*	4 *Porzana porzana*	2 *Lullula arborea*	4 *Phylloscopus sibilatrix*
3 *Ixobrychus minutus*	3 *Porzana pusilla*	3 *Alauda arvensis*	4 *Regulus regulus*
3 *Nycticorax nycticorax*	4/3 *Recurvirostra avosetta*	3 *Riparia riparia*	4 *Regulus ignicapillus*
3 *Ardeola ralloides*	3 *Burhinus oedicnemus*	3 *Hirundo rustica*	3 *Muscicapa striata*
3 *Ardea purpurea*	3 *Glareola pratincola*	3 *Anthus campestris*	4 *Ficedula albicollis*
3 *Ciconia nigra*	3 *Charadrius alexandrinus*	4 *Prunella modularis*	4 *Ficedula hypoleuca*
3 *Ciconia ciconia*	3[w] *Scolopax rusticola*	4 *Erithacus rubecula*	4 *Parus lugubris*
3 *Plegadis falcinellus*	2 *Tringa totanus*	4 *Luscinia megarhynchos*	4 *Parus cristatus*
2 *Platalea leucorodia*	4 *Larus melanocephalus*	2 *Phoenicurus phoenicurus*	4 *Parus caeruleus*
3 *Tadorna ferruginea*	3 *Gelochelidon nilotica*	4 *Saxicola rubetra*	4 *Sitta neumayer*
3 *Anas strepera*	3 *Sterna albifrons*	3 *Saxicola torquata*	4 *Certhia brachydactyla*
3 *Anas querquedula*	3 *Chlidonias hybridus*	2 *Oenanthe hispanica*	3 *Lanius collurio*
3 *Netta rufina*	3 *Chlidonias niger*	3 *Monticola saxatilis*	2 *Lanius minor*
4 *Aythya ferina*	4 *Columba oenas*	3 *Monticola solitarius*	2 *Lanius senator*
1 *Aythya nyroca*	4 *Columba palumbus*	4 *Turdus torquatus*	3 *Pyrrhocorax pyrrhocorax*
4 *Pernis apivorus*	3 *Streptopelia turtur*	4 *Turdus merula*	4 *Corvus monedula*
3 *Milvus migrans*	3 *Tyto alba*	4[w] *Turdus pilaris*	4 *Fringilla coelebs*
3 *Haliaeetus albicilla*	2 *Otus scops*	4 *Turdus philomelos*	4 *Serinus serinus*
3 *Gypaetus barbatus*	3 *Bubo bubo*	4 *Turdus viscivorus*	4 *Carduelis chloris*
3 *Neophron percnopterus*	3 *Athene noctua*	4 *Locustella luscinioides*	4 *Carduelis spinus*
3 *Gyps fulvus*	4 *Strix aluco*	4 *Acrocephalus*	4 *Carduelis cannabina*
3 *Circaetus gallicus*	2 *Caprimulgus europaeus*	*schoenobaenus*	4 *Emberiza citrinella*
2 *Accipiter brevipes*	3 *Alcedo atthis*	4 *Acrocephalus palustris*	4 *Emberiza cirlus*
3 *Buteo rufinus*	3 *Merops apiaster*	4 *Acrocephalus scirpaceus*	3 *Emberiza cia*
3 *Aquila pomarina*	2 *Coracias garrulus*	3 *Hippolais pallida*	2 *Emberiza hortulana*
3 *Aquila chrysaetos*	3 *Jynx torquilla*	2 *Hippolais olivetorum*	4 *Emberiza caesia*
3 *Hieraaetus pennatus*	3 *Picus canus*	4 *Hippolais icterina*	2 *Emberiza melanocephala*
3 *Hieraaetus fasciatus*	2 *Picus viridis*	4 *Sylvia cantillans*	4 *Miliaria calandra*
1 *Falco naumanni*	4 *Dendrocopos syriacus*	4 *Sylvia melanocephala*	
3 *Falco tinnunculus*	4 *Dendrocopos medius*	3 *Sylvia hortensis*	
3 *Falco peregrinus*	3 *Picoides tridactylus*	4 *Sylvia nisoria*	

ANDORRA

4 *Pernis apivorus*	3 *Coturnix coturnix*	3 *Athene noctua*	3 *Alauda arvensis*
3 *Circaetus gallicus*	4 *Columba oenas*	4 *Strix aluco*	3 *Hirundo rustica*
3 *Aquila chrysaetos*	4 *Columba palumbus*	2 *Caprimulgus europaeus*	4 *Prunella modularis*
3 *Falco tinnunculus*	3 *Streptopelia turtur*	3 *Alcedo atthis*	4 *Erithacus rubecula*
3 *Falco peregrinus*	3 *Tyto alba*	3 *Jynx torquilla*	4 *Luscinia megarhynchos*
2 *Alectoris rufa*	2 *Otus scops*	2 *Picus viridis*	2 *Phoenicurus phoenicurus*
3 *Perdix perdix*	3 *Bubo bubo*	2 *Lullula arborea*	4 *Saxicola rubetra*

3 *Saxicola torquata*
3 *Monticola saxatilis*
3 *Monticola solitarius*
4 *Turdus torquatus*
4 *Turdus merula*
4 *Turdus philomelos*
4 *Turdus viscivorus*
4 *Hippolais polyglotta*
2 *Sylvia undata*
4 *Sylvia cantillans*

4 *Sylvia melanocephala*
4 *Sylvia communis*
4 *Sylvia borin*
4 *Sylvia atricapilla*
4 *Phylloscopus bonelli*
4 *Regulus regulus*
4 *Regulus ignicapillus*
3 *Muscicapa striata*
4 *Ficedula hypoleuca*
4 *Parus cristatus*

4 *Parus caeruleus*
4 *Certhia brachydactyla*
3 *Lanius collurio*
3 *Lanius excubitor*
2 *Lanius senator*
3 *Pyrrhocorax pyrrhocorax*
3 *Corvus monedula*
4 *Fringilla coelebs*
4 *Serinus serinus*
4 *Serinus citrinella*

4 *Carduelis chloris*
4 *Carduelis spinus*
4 *Carduelis cannabina*
4 *Emberiza citrinella*
4 *Emberiza cirlus*
3 *Emberiza cia*
2 *Emberiza hortulana*
4 *Miliaria calandra*

AUSTRIA

3 *Botaurus stellaris*
3 *Ixobrychus minutus*
3 *Nycticorax nycticorax*
3 *Ardea purpurea*
3 *Ciconia nigra*
2 *Ciconia ciconia*
2 *Platalea leucorodia*
3 *Anas strepera*
3 *Anas acuta*
3 *Anas querquedula*
3 *Netta rufina*
4 *Aythya ferina*
1 *Aythya nyroca*
4 *Pernis apivorus*
3 *Milvus migrans*
4 *Milvus milvus*
3 *Gyps fulvus*
4 *Circus pygargus*
3 *Aquila chrysaetos*
3 *Falco tinnunculus*
3 *Falco cherrug*
3 *Falco peregrinus*
3 *Tetrao tetrix*
2 *Alectoris graeca*
3 *Perdix perdix*
3 *Coturnix coturnix*
4 *Porzana porzana*
4 *Porzana parva*
1 *Crex crex*

1 *Otis tarda*
4/3 *Recurvirostra avosetta*
3 *Burhinus oedicnemus*
3 *Charadrius alexandrinus*
3* *Scolopax rusticola*
2 *Limosa limosa*
3* *Numenius arquata*
2 *Tringa totanus*
4 *Larus melanocephalus*
2 *Larus canus*
4 *Columba oenas*
4 *Columba palumbus*
3 *Streptopelia turtur*
3 *Tyto alba*
2 *Otus scops*
3 *Bubo bubo*
3 *Athene noctua*
4 *Strix aluco*
3 *Asio flammeus*
2 *Caprimulgus europaeus*
3 *Alcedo atthis*
3 *Merops apiaster*
2 *Coracias garrulus*
3 *Jynx torquilla*
3 *Picus canus*
2 *Picus viridis*
4 *Dendrocopos syriacus*
4 *Dendrocopos medius*
3 *Picoides tridactylus*

3 *Galerida cristata*
2 *Lullula arborea*
3 *Alauda arvensis*
3 *Riparia riparia*
3 *Hirundo rustica*
3 *Anthus campestris*
4 *Anthus pratensis*
4 *Prunella modularis*
4 *Erithacus rubecula*
4 *Luscinia megarhynchos*
2 *Phoenicurus phoenicurus*
4 *Saxicola rubetra*
3 *Saxicola torquata*
3 *Monticola saxatilis*
4 *Turdus torquatus*
4 *Turdus merula*
4* *Turdus pilaris*
4 *Turdus philomelos*
4* *Turdus iliacus*
4 *Turdus viscivorus*
4 *Locustella naevia*
4 *Locustella fluviatilis*
4 *Locustella luscinioides*
4 *Acrocephalus
    schoenobaenus*
4 *Acrocephalus palustris*
4 *Acrocephalus scirpaceus*
4 *Hippolais icterina*
4 *Sylvia nisoria*

4 *Sylvia communis*
4 *Sylvia borin*
4 *Sylvia atricapilla*
4 *Phylloscopus bonelli*
4 *Phylloscopus sibilatrix*
4 *Regulus regulus*
4 *Regulus ignicapillus*
3 *Muscicapa striata*
4 *Ficedula albicollis*
4 *Ficedula hypoleuca*
4 *Parus cristatus*
4 *Parus caeruleus*
4 *Certhia brachydactyla*
3 *Lanius collurio*
2 *Lanius minor*
3 *Lanius excubitor*
4 *Corvus monedula*
4 *Fringilla coelebs*
4 *Serinus serinus*
4 *Serinus citrinella*
4 *Carduelis chloris*
4 *Carduelis spinus*
4 *Carduelis cannabina*
4 *Emberiza citrinella*
4 *Emberiza cirlus*
3 *Emberiza cia*
2 *Emberiza hortulana*
4 *Miliaria calandra*

AZORES

3 *Bulweria bulwerii*
2 *Calonectris diomedea*
2 *Puffinus puffinus*
3 *Puffinus assimilis*
3 *Oceanodroma castro*

3 *Coturnix coturnix*
3 *Charadrius alexandrinus*
3* *Scolopax rusticola*
3 *Sterna dougallii*
4 *Columba palumbus*

4 *Erithacus rubecula*
4 *Turdus merula*
4 *Sylvia atricapilla*
4 *Regulus regulus*
4 *Fringilla coelebs*

4 *Serinus canarinus*
4 *Carduelis chloris*

BELARUS

3 *Gavia arctica*
3 *Botaurus stellaris*
3 *Ixobrychus minutus*
3 *Nycticorax nycticorax*
3 *Ciconia nigra*
2 *Ciconia ciconia*
3 *Anas strepera*
3 *Anas acuta*
3 *Anas querquedula*
4 *Aythya ferina*
1 *Aythya nyroca*

3 *Mergus albellus*
4 *Pernis apivorus*
3 *Milvus migrans*
4 *Milvus milvus*
3 *Haliaeetus albicilla*
3 *Circaetus gallicus*
3 *Circus cyaneus*
4 *Circus pygargus*
3 *Aquila pomarina*
1 *Aquila clanga*
3 *Aquila chrysaetos*

3 *Hieraaetus pennatus*
3 *Pandion haliaetus*
3 *Falco tinnunculus*
3 *Falco vespertinus*
3 *Tetrao tetrix*
3 *Perdix perdix*
3 *Coturnix coturnix*
4 *Porzana porzana*
4 *Porzana parva*
1 *Crex crex*
3 *Grus grus*

3 *Burhinus oedicnemus*
3 *Glareola nordmanni*
4 *Pluvialis apricaria*
3* *Calidris alpina*
4 *Philomachus pugnax*
3* *Lymnocryptes minimus*
2 *Gallinago media*
3* *Scolopax rusticola*
2 *Limosa limosa*
4 *Numenius phaeopus*
3* *Numenius arquata*

2 *Tringa totanus*
3 *Tringa glareola*
4 *Larus melanocephalus*
3 *Larus minutus*
2 *Larus canus*
3 *Sterna albifrons*
3 *Chlidonias hybridus*
3 *Chlidonias niger*
4 *Columba oenas*
4 *Columba palumbus*
3 *Streptopelia turtur*
3 *Tyto alba*
2 *Otus scops*
2 *Bubo bubo*
3 *Athene noctua*
4 *Strix aluco*
3 *Asio flammeus*
2 *Caprimulgus europaeus*
3 *Alcedo atthis*
3 *Merops apiaster*

2 *Coracias garrulus*
3 *Jynx torquilla*
3 *Picus canus*
2 *Picus viridis*
4 *Dendrocopos syriacus*
4 *Dendrocopos medius*
3 *Picoides tridactylus*
3 *Galerida cristata*
2 *Lullula arborea*
3 *Alauda arvensis*
3 *Riparia riparia*
3 *Hirundo rustica*
3 *Anthus campestris*
4 *Anthus pratensis*
4 *Prunella modularis*
4 *Erithacus rubecula*
4 *Luscinia luscinia*
2 *Phoenicurus phoenicurus*
4 *Saxicola rubetra*
4 *Turdus merula*

4ᵂ *Turdus pilaris*
4 *Turdus philomelos*
4ᵂ *Turdus iliacus*
4 *Turdus viscivorus*
4 *Locustella naevia*
4 *Locustella fluviatilis*
4 *Locustella luscinioides*
4 *Acrocephalus schoenobaenus*
4 *Acrocephalus palustris*
4 *Acrocephalus scirpaceus*
4 *Hippolais icterina*
4 *Sylvia nisoria*
4 *Sylvia communis*
4 *Sylvia borin*
4 *Sylvia atricapilla*
4 *Phylloscopus sibilatrix*
4 *Regulus regulus*
4 *Regulus ignicapillus*
3 *Muscicapa striata*

4 *Ficedula albicollis*
4 *Ficedula hypoleuca*
4 *Parus cristatus*
4 *Parus caeruleus*
3 *Lanius collurio*
2 *Lanius minor*
3 *Lanius excubitor*
4 *Corvus monedula*
4 *Fringilla coelebs*
4 *Serinus serinus*
4 *Carduelis chloris*
4 *Carduelis spinus*
4 *Carduelis cannabina*
4 *Loxia pytyopsittacus*
4 *Emberiza citrinella*
2 *Emberiza hortulana*
4 *Miliaria calandra*

BELGIUM

3 *Botaurus stellaris*
3 *Ixobrychus minutus*
3 *Nycticorax nycticorax*
3 *Ciconia nigra*
2 *Ciconia ciconia*
4ᵂ *Cygnus cygnus*
3 *Anas strepera*
3 *Anas querquedula*
4 *Aythya ferina*
4 *Pernis apivorus*
3 *Milvus migrans*
4 *Milvus milvus*
3 *Circus cyaneus*
3 *Falco tinnunculus*
3 *Falco peregrinus*
3 *Tetrao tetrix*
3 *Perdix perdix*
3 *Coturnix coturnix*
4 *Porzana porzana*
1 *Crex crex*
4/3 *Recurvirostra avosetta*
3 *Charadrius alexandrinus*
3ᵂ *Calidris alpina*
3ᵂ *Scolopax rusticola*

2 *Limosa limosa*
3ᵂ *Numenius arquata*
2 *Tringa totanus*
4 *Larus melanocephalus*
2 *Larus canus*
4 *Larus fuscus*
2 *Sterna sandvicensis*
3 *Sterna albifrons*
4 *Columba oenas*
4 *Columba palumbus*
3 *Streptopelia turtur*
3 *Tyto alba*
3 *Bubo bubo*
4 *Athene noctua*
4 *Strix aluco*
3 *Asio flammeus*
2 *Caprimulgus europaeus*
3 *Alcedo atthis*
3 *Jynx torquilla*
3 *Picus canus*
2 *Picus viridis*
4 *Dendrocopos medius*
3 *Galerida cristata*
2 *Lullula arborea*

3 *Alauda arvensis*
3 *Riparia riparia*
3 *Hirundo rustica*
4 *Anthus pratensis*
4 *Prunella modularis*
4 *Erithacus rubecula*
4 *Luscinia megarhynchos*
2 *Phoenicurus phoenicurus*
4 *Saxicola rubetra*
3 *Saxicola torquata*
4 *Turdus torquatus*
4 *Turdus merula*
4ᵂ *Turdus pilaris*
4 *Turdus philomelos*
4 *Turdus viscivorus*
4 *Locustella naevia*
4 *Locustella luscinioides*
4 *Acrocephalus schoenobaenus*
4 *Acrocephalus palustris*
4 *Acrocephalus scirpaceus*
4 *Hippolais icterina*
4 *Hippolais polyglotta*
4 *Sylvia communis*

4 *Sylvia borin*
4 *Sylvia atricapilla*
4 *Phylloscopus bonelli*
4 *Phylloscopus sibilatrix*
4 *Regulus regulus*
4 *Regulus ignicapillus*
3 *Muscicapa striata*
4 *Ficedula hypoleuca*
4 *Parus cristatus*
4 *Parus caeruleus*
4 *Certhia brachydactyla*
3 *Lanius collurio*
3 *Lanius excubitor*
4 *Corvus monedula*
4 *Fringilla coelebs*
4 *Serinus serinus*
4 *Carduelis chloris*
4 *Carduelis spinus*
4 *Carduelis cannabina*
4 *Loxia pytyopsittacus*
4 *Emberiza citrinella*
2 *Emberiza hortulana*
4 *Miliaria calandra*

BULGARIA

4 *Phalacrocorax aristotelis*
2 *Phalacrocorax pygmeus*
1 *Pelecanus crispus*
3 *Botaurus stellaris*
3 *Ixobrychus minutus*
3 *Nycticorax nycticorax*
3 *Ardeola ralloides*
3 *Ardea purpurea*
3 *Ciconia nigra*
2 *Ciconia ciconia*
3 *Plegadis falcinellus*
2 *Platalea leucorodia*
3 *Tadorna ferruginea*
3 *Anas strepera*
3 *Anas acuta*

3 *Anas querquedula*
3 *Netta rufina*
4 *Aythya ferina*
1 *Aythya nyroca*
4 *Pernis apivorus*
3 *Milvus migrans*
3 *Haliaeetus albicilla*
3 *Neophron percnopterus*
3 *Gyps fulvus*
3 *Circaetus gallicus*
4 *Circus pygargus*
2 *Accipiter brevipes*
3 *Buteo rufinus*
3 *Aquila pomarina*
1 *Aquila heliaca*

3 *Aquila chrysaetos*
3 *Hieraaetus pennatus*
3 *Pandion haliaetus*
1 *Falco naumanni*
3 *Falco tinnunculus*
3 *Falco vespertinus*
3 *Falco cherrug*
3 *Falco peregrinus*
3 *Alectoris chukar*
2 *Alectoris graeca*
3 *Perdix perdix*
3 *Coturnix coturnix*
4 *Porzana porzana*
4 *Porzana parva*
3 *Porzana pusilla*

1 *Crex crex*
4/3 *Recurvirostra avosetta*
3 *Burhinus oedicnemus*
3 *Glareola pratincola*
3 *Charadrius alexandrinus*
3ᵂ *Scolopax rusticola*
2 *Tringa totanus*
4 *Larus melanocephalus*
2 *Gelochelidon nilotica*
2 *Sterna sandvicensis*
3 *Sterna albifrons*
3 *Chlidonias hybridus*
3 *Chlidonias niger*
4 *Columba oenas*
·4 *Columba palumbus*

3 Streptopelia turtur
3 Tyto alba
2 Otus scops
3 Bubo bubo
3 Athene noctua
4 Strix aluco
2 Caprimulgus europaeus
3 Alcedo atthis
3 Merops apiaster
2 Coracias garrulus
3 Jynx torquilla
3 Picus canus
2 Picus viridis
4 Dendrocopos syriacus
4 Dendrocopos medius
3 Picoides tridactylus
3 Melanocorypha calandra
3 Calandrella
   brachydactyla
3 Galerida cristata
2 Lullula arborea

3 Alauda arvensis
3 Riparia riparia
3 Hirundo rustica
3 Anthus campestris
4 Prunella modularis
4 Erithacus rubecula
4 Luscinia megarhynchos
2 Phoenicurus phoenicurus
4 Saxicola rubetra
3 Saxicola torquata
2 Oenanthe hispanica
3 Monticola saxatilis
3 Monticola solitarius
4 Turdus torquatus
4 Turdus merula
4 Turdus philomelos
4 Turdus viscivorus
4 Locustella fluviatilis
4 Locustella luscinioides
4 Acrocephalus
   schoenobaenus

4 Acrocephalus palustris
4 Acrocephalus scirpaceus
3 Hippolais pallida
2 Hippolais olivetorum
4 Hippolais icterina
4 Sylvia cantillans
4 Sylvia melanocephala
3 Sylvia hortensis
4 Sylvia nisoria
4 Sylvia communis
4 Sylvia borin
4 Sylvia atricapilla
4 Phylloscopus bonelli
4 Phylloscopus sibilatrix
4 Regulus regulus
4 Regulus ignicapillus
3 Muscicapa striata
2 Ficedula semitorquata
4 Parus lugubris
4 Parus cristatus
4 Parus caeruleus

4 Sitta neumayer
4 Certhia brachydactyla
3 Lanius collurio
2 Lanius minor
2 Lanius senator
2 Lanius nubicus
4 Corvus monedula
4 Fringilla coelebs
4 Serinus serinus
4 Carduelis chloris
4 Carduelis spinus
4 Carduelis cannabina
4 Emberiza citrinella
4 Emberiza cirlus
3 Emberiza cia
2 Emberiza hortulana
2 Emberiza melanocephala
4 Miliaria calandra

CANARY ISLANDS

3 Bulweria bulwerii
2 Calonectris diomedea
2 Puffinus puffinus
3 Puffinus assimilis
3 Pelagodroma marina
2 Hydrobates pelagicus
3 Oceanodroma castro
3 Neophron percnopterus
3 Pandion haliaetus
3 Falco tinnunculus
2 Falco eleonorae

3 Falco pelegrinoides
3 Alectoris barbara
3 Chlamydotis undulata
3 Burhinus oedicnemus
3 Cursorius cursor
3 Charadrius alexandrinus
3 Sterna dougallii
3 Pterocles orientalis
1 Columba bollii
1 Columba junoniae
3 Streptopelia turtur

3 Tyto alba
4 Apus unicolor
3 Calandrella rufescens
4 Anthus berthelotii
4 Erithacus rubecula
2 Saxicola dacotiae
4 Turdus merula
4 Sylvia melanocephala
4 Sylvia atricapilla
4 Regulus regulus
4 Regulus teneriffae

4 Parus caeruleus
3 Lanius excubitor
3 Pyrrhocorax pyrrhocorax
4 Fringilla coelebs
1 Fringilla teydea
4 Serinus serinus
4 Serinus canaria
4 Carduelis chloris
4 Carduelis cannabina
3 Bucanetes githagineus
4 Miliaria calandra

CROATIA

2 Calonectris diomedea
4 Puffinus yelkouan
4 Phalacrocorax aristotelis
3 Botaurus stellaris
3 Ixobrychus minutus
3 Nycticorax nycticorax
3 Ardeola ralloides
3 Ardea purpurea
3 Ciconia nigra
2 Ciconia ciconia
2 Platalea leucorodia
3 Anas strepera
3 Anas querquedula
3 Netta rufina
4 Aythya ferina
1 Aythya nyroca
4 Pernis apivorus
3 Milvus migrans
4 Milvus milvus
3 Haliaeetus albicilla
3 Gyps fulvus
3 Circaetus gallicus
4 Circus pygargus
2 Accipiter brevipes
3 Aquila pomarina
1 Aquila heliaca
3 Aquila chrysaetos

3 Hieraaetus fasciatus
1 Falco naumanni
3 Falco tinnunculus
3 Falco vespertinus
2 Falco eleonorae
3 Falco biarmicus
3 Falco cherrug
3 Falco peregrinus
2 Alectoris graeca
3 Perdix perdix
3 Coturnix coturnix
4 Porzana parva
3 Porzana pusilla
1 Crex crex
3 Burhinus oedicnemus
3 Charadrius alexandrinus
3ʷ Scolopax rusticola
2 Tringa totanus
3 Sterna albifrons
3 Chlidonias hybridus
3 Chlidonias niger
4 Columba oenas
4 Columba palumbus
3 Streptopelia turtur
3 Tyto alba
2 Otus scops
3 Bubo bubo

3 Athene noctua
4 Strix aluco
3 Asio flammeus
2 Caprimulgus europaeus
3 Alcedo atthis
3 Merops apiaster
2 Coracias garrulus
3 Jynx torquilla
3 Picus canus
2 Picus viridis
4 Dendrocopos syriacus
4 Dendrocopos medius
3 Picoides tridactylus
3 Melanocorypha calandra
3 Calandrella
   brachydactyla
3 Galerida cristata
2 Lullula arborea
3 Alauda arvensis
3 Riparia riparia
3 Hirundo rustica
3 Anthus campestris
4 Prunella modularis
4 Erithacus rubecula
4 Luscinia megarhynchos
2 Phoenicurus phoenicurus
4 Saxicola rubetra

3 Saxicola torquata
2 Oenanthe hispanica
3 Monticola saxatilis
3 Monticola solitarius
4 Turdus torquatus
4 Turdus merula
4 Turdus philomelos
4 Turdus viscivorus
4 Locustella naevia
4 Locustella fluviatilis
4 Locustella luscinioides
4 Acrocephalus
   schoenobaenus
4 Acrocephalus palustris
4 Acrocephalus scirpaceus
3 Hippolais pallida
2 Hippolais olivetorum
4 Hippolais icterina
4 Hippolais polyglotta
4 Sylvia cantillans
4 Sylvia melanocephala
3 Sylvia hortensis
4 Sylvia nisoria
4 Sylvia communis
4 Sylvia borin
4 Sylvia atricapilla
4 Phylloscopus sibilatrix

4 Regulus regulus
4 Regulus ignicapillus
3 Muscicapa striata
4 Ficedula albicollis
4 Parus lugubris
4 Parus cristatus
4 Parus caeruleus
4 Sitta neumayer
4 Certhia brachydactyla
3 Lanius collurio
2 Lanius minor
2 Lanius senator
4 Corvus monedula
4 Fringilla coelebs
4 Serinus serinus
4 Carduelis chloris
4 Carduelis spinus
4 Carduelis cannabina
4 Emberiza citrinella
4 Emberiza cirlus
3 Emberiza cia
2 Emberiza hortulana
2 Emberiza melanocephala
4 Miliaria calandra

CYPRUS

4 Phalacrocorax aristotelis
3 Gyps fulvus
1 Aquila heliaca
3 Hieraaetus fasciatus
3 Falco tinnunculus
2 Falco eleonorae
3 Falco peregrinus
3 Alectoris chukar
3 Francolinus francolinus
3 Coturnix coturnix
3 Burhinus oedicnemus
3 Charadrius alexandrinus
3 Hoplopterus spinosus
1 Larus audouinii
3 Pterocles orientalis
4 Columba palumbus
3 Streptopelia turtur
3 Tyto alba
2 Otus scops
3 Athene noctua
2 Caprimulgus europaeus
3 Merops apiaster
2 Coracias garrulus
3 Melanocorypha calandra
3 Calandrella brachydactyla
3 Galerida cristata
2 Lullula arborea
3 Hirundo rustica
4 Luscinia megarhynchos
2 **Oenanthe cypriaca**
3 Monticola solitarius
4 Acrocephalus scirpaceus
3 Hippolais pallida
2 **Sylvia melanothorax**
3 Muscicapa striata
4 Certhia brachydactyla
2 Lanius senator
2 Lanius nubicus
4 Corvus monedula
4 Fringilla coelebs
4 Serinus serinus
4 Carduelis chloris
4 Carduelis cannabina
4 Emberiza caesia
2 Emberiza melanocephala
4 Miliaria calandra

CZECH REPUBLIC

3 Botaurus stellaris
3 Ixobrychus minutus
3 Nycticorax nycticorax
3 Ardea purpurea
2 Ciconia nigra
2 Ciconia ciconia
2 Platalea leucorodia
3 Anas strepera
3 Anas acuta
3 Anas querquedula
3 Netta rufina
4 Aythya ferina
1 Aythya nyroca
4 Pernis apivorus
3 Milvus migrans
4 Milvus milvus
3 Haliaeetus albicilla
3 Circus cyaneus
4 Circus pygargus
3 Aquila pomarina
3 Falco tinnunculus
3 Falco vespertinus
3 Falco cherrug
3 Falco peregrinus
3 Tetrao tetrix
3 Perdix perdix
3 Coturnix coturnix
4 Porzana porzana
4 Porzana parva
1 Crex crex
3 Grus grus
1 Otis tarda
4/3 Recurvirostra avosetta
3 Burhinus oedicnemus
3ᵂ Scolopax rusticola
2 Limosa limosa
3ᵂ Numenius arquata
2 Tringa totanus
4 Larus melanocephalus
2 Larus canus
3 Chlidonias niger
4 Columba oenas
4 Columba palumbus
3 Streptopelia turtur
3 Tyto alba
3 Bubo bubo
3 Athene noctua
4 Strix aluco
4 Asio flammeus
2 Caprimulgus europaeus
3 Alcedo atthis
3 Merops apiaster
2 Coracias garrulus
3 Jynx torquilla
3 Picus canus
2 Picus viridis
4 Dendrocopos syriacus
4 Dendrocopos medius
3 Picoides tridactylus
3 Galerida cristata
2 Lullula arborea
3 Alauda arvensis
3 Riparia riparia
3 Hirundo rustica
3 Anthus campestris
4 Anthus pratensis
4 Prunella modularis
4 Erithacus rubecula
4 Luscinia luscinia
4 Luscinia megarhynchos
2 Phoenicurus phoenicurus
4 Saxicola rubetra
3 Saxicola torquata
4 Turdus torquatus
4 Turdus merula
4ᵂ Turdus pilaris
4 Turdus philomelos
4ᵂ Turdus iliacus
4 Turdus viscivorus
4 Locustella naevia
4 Locustella fluviatilis
4 Locustella luscinioides
4 Acrocephalus schoenobaenus
4 Acrocephalus palustris
4 Acrocephalus scirpaceus
4 Hippolais icterina
4 Sylvia nisoria
4 Sylvia communis
4 Sylvia borin
4 Sylvia atricapilla
4 Phylloscopus sibilatrix
4 Regulus regulus
4 Regulus ignicapillus
3 Muscicapa striata
4 Ficedula albicollis
4 Ficedula hypoleuca
4 Parus cristatus
4 Parus caeruleus
4 Certhia brachydactyla
3 Lanius collurio
3 Lanius excubitor
2 Lanius senator
4 Corvus monedula
4 Fringilla coelebs
4 Serinus serinus
4 Carduelis chloris
4 Carduelis spinus
4 Carduelis cannabina
4 Emberiza citrinella
2 Emberiza hortulana
4 Miliaria calandra

DENMARK

3 Botaurus stellaris
3 Ixobrychus minutus
3 Ciconia nigra
2 Ciconia ciconia
4/2 Branta leucopsis
3 Anas strepera
3 Anas acuta
3 Anas querquedula
3 Netta rufina
4 Aythya ferina
4 Pernis apivorus
4 Milvus milvus
3 Circus cyaneus
3 Circus pygargus
3 Pandion haliaetus
3 Falco tinnunculus
3 Tetrao tetrix
3 Perdix perdix
3 Coturnix coturnix
4 Porzana porzana
1 Crex crex
3 Grus grus
4/3 Recurvirostra avosetta
3 Charadrius alexandrinus
4 Pluvialis apricaria
3ᵂ Calidris alpina
4 Philomachus pugnax
3ᵂ Scolopax rusticola
2 Limosa limosa
3ᵂ Numenius arquata
2 Tringa totanus
4 Tringa glareola
4 Larus melanocephalus
2 Larus canus
4 Larus fuscus
4 Larus marinus

3 Gelochelidon nilotica
2 Sterna sandvicensis
3 Sterna albifrons
3 Chlidonias niger
4 Alca torda
2 Cepphus grylle
4 Columba oenas
4 Columba palumbus
3 Streptopelia turtur
3 Tyto alba
3 Bubo bubo
3 Athene noctua
4 Strix aluco
3 Asio flammeus
2 Caprimulgus europaeus
3 Alcedo atthis
3 Jynx torquilla

2 Picus viridis
3 Galerida cristata
2 Lullula arborea
3 Alauda arvensis
3 Riparia riparia
3 Hirundo rustica
3 Anthus campestris
4 Anthus pratensis
4 Prunella modularis
4 Erithacus rubecula
4 Luscinia luscinia
2 Phoenicurus phoenicurus
4 Saxicola rubetra
3 Saxicola torquata
4 Turdus torquatus
4 Turdus merula
4^w Turdus pilaris

4 Turdus philomelos
4^w Turdus iliacus
4 Turdus viscivorus
4 Locustella naevia
4 Locustella luscinioides
4 Acrocephalus schoenobaenus
4 Acrocephalus palustris
4 Acrocephalus scirpaceus
4 Hippolais icterina
4 Sylvia nisoria
4 Sylvia communis
4 Sylvia borin
4 Sylvia atricapilla
4 Phylloscopus sibilatrix
4 Regulus regulus
4 Regulus ignicapillus

3 Muscicapa striata
4 Ficedula hypoleuca
4 Parus cristatus
4 Parus caeruleus
4 Certhia brachydactyla
3 Lanius collurio
3 Lanius excubitor
4 Corvus monedula
4 Fringilla coelebs
4 Carduelis chloris
4 Carduelis spinus
4 Carduelis cannabina
4 Loxia pytyopsittacus
4 Emberiza citrinella
2 Emberiza hortulana
4 Miliaria calandra

ESTONIA

3 Gavia arctica
3 Botaurus stellaris
3 Ciconia nigra
2 Ciconia ciconia
4^w Cygnus cygnus
4/2 Branta leucopsis
3 Anas strepera
3 Anas acuta
3 Anas querquedula
4 Aythya ferina
3^w Aythya marila
3^w Melanitta fusca
4 Pernis apivorus
3 Milvus migrans
3 Haliaeetus albicilla
3 Circaetus gallicus
3 Circus cyaneus
3 Circus pygargus
3 Aquila pomarina
3 Aquila chrysaetos
3 Pandion haliaetus
3 Falco tinnunculus
3 Falco vespertinus
3 Tetrao tetrix
3 Perdix perdix
3 Coturnix coturnix
4 Porzana porzana
4 Porzana parva

1 Crex crex
3 Grus grus
4/3 Recurvirostra avosetta
4 Pluvialis apricaria
3^w Calidris alpina
4 Philomachus pugnax
3^w Lymnocryptes minimus
2 Gallinago media
3^w Scolopax rusticola
2 Limosa limosa
4 Numenius phaeopus
3^w Numenius arquata
2 Tringa totanus
3 Tringa glareola
3 Larus minutus
2 Larus canus
4 Larus fuscus
4 Larus marinus
3 Sterna caspia
2 Sterna sandvicensis
3 Sterna albifrons
3 Chlidonias niger
4 Alca torda
2 Cepphus grylle
4 Columba oenas
4 Columba palumbus
3 Streptopelia turtur
3 Bubo bubo

4 Strix aluco
3 Asio flammeus
2 Caprimulgus europaeus
3 Alcedo atthis
2 Coracias garrulus
3 Jynx torquilla
3 Picus canus
2 Picus viridis
3 Picoides tridactylus
3 Galerida cristata
2 Lullula arborea
3 Alauda arvensis
3 Riparia riparia
3 Hirundo rustica
3 Anthus campestris
4 Anthus pratensis
4 Prunella modularis
4 Erithacus rubecula
4 Luscinia luscinia
2 Phoenicurus phoenicurus
4 Saxicola rubetra
4 Turdus merula
4^w Turdus pilaris
4 Turdus philomelos
4^w Turdus iliacus
4 Turdus viscivorus
4 Locustella naevia
4 Locustella fluviatilis

4 Locustella luscinioides
4 Acrocephalus schoenobaenus
4 Acrocephalus palustris
4 Acrocephalus scirpaceus
4 Hippolais icterina
4 Sylvia nisoria
4 Sylvia communis
4 Sylvia borin
4 Sylvia atricapilla
4 Phylloscopus sibilatrix
4 Regulus regulus
3 Muscicapa striata
4 Ficedula hypoleuca
4 Parus cristatus
4 Parus caeruleus
3 Lanius collurio
3 Lanius excubitor
4 Corvus monedula
4 Fringilla coelebs
4 Serinus serinus
4 Carduelis chloris
4 Carduelis spinus
4 Carduelis cannabina
4 Loxia pytyopsittacus
4 Emberiza citrinella
2 Emberiza hortulana

FAROE ISLANDS

3 Gavia stellata
2 Puffinus puffinus
2 Hydrobates pelagicus
3 Oceanodroma leucorhoa
2 Sula bassana
4 Phalacrocorax aristotelis
4/2 Branta leucopsis
3 Anas acuta
3 Coturnix coturnix

4 Pluvialis apricaria
4 Calidris maritima
3^w Calidris alpina
4 Numenius phaeopus
3^w Numenius arquata
2 Tringa totanus
4 Stercorarius skua
2 Larus canus
4 Larus fuscus

4 Larus marinus
4 Alca torda
2 Cepphus grylle
2 Fratercula arctica
4 Columba palumbus
3 Alauda arvensis
3 Hirundo rustica
4 Anthus pratensis
4 Erithacus rubecula

4 Turdus torquatus
4 Turdus merula
4^w Turdus iliacus
4 Sylvia borin
4 Sylvia atricapilla
4 Regulus regulus
4 Fringilla coelebs
4 Carduelis spinus

FINLAND

3 Gavia stellata
3 Gavia arctica
3 Botaurus stellaris
4ʷ Cygnus cygnus
1 Anser erythropus
4/2 Branta leucopsis
3 Anas strepera
3 Anas acuta
3 Anas querquedula
4 Aythya ferina
3ʷ Aythya marila
3ʷ Melanitta fusca
3 Mergus albellus
4 Pernis apivorus
3 Milvus migrans
3 Haliaeetus albicilla
3 Circus cyaneus
3 Circus pygargus
1 Aquila clanga
3 Aquila chrysaetos
3 Pandion haliaetus
3 Falco tinnunculus
3 Falco rusticolus
3 Falco peregrinus
3 Tetrao tetrix
3 Perdix perdix
3 Coturnix coturnix
4 Porzana porzana
4 Porzana parva

1 Crex crex
3 Grus grus
4 Pluvialis apricaria
4 Calidris maritima
3ʷ Calidris alpina
3 Limicola falcinellus
4 Philomachus pugnax
3ʷ Lymnocryptes minimus
2 Gallinago media
3ʷ Scolopax rusticola
3 Limosa limosa
3ʷ Limosa lapponica
4 Numenius phaeopus
3ʷ Numenius arquata
2 Tringa totanus
3 Tringa glareola
3 Larus minutus
2 Larus canus
4 Larus fuscus
3 Larus marinus
3 Sterna caspia
3 Sterna albifrons
3 Chlidonias niger
4 Alca torda
2 Cepphus grylle
4 Columba oenas
4 Columba palumbus
3 Streptopelia turtur
3 Bubo bubo

3 Nyctea scandiaca
3 Strix nebulosa
3 Strix aluco
3 Asio flammeus
2 Caprimulgus europaeus
3 Alcedo atthis
3 Jynx torquilla
3 Picus canus
3 Picoides tridactylus
2 Lullula arborea
3 Alauda arvensis
3 Riparia riparia
3 Hirundo rustica
3 Anthus campestris
4 Anthus pratensis
4 Prunella modularis
4 Erithacus rubecula
4 Luscinia luscinia
2 Phoenicurus phoenicurus
4 Saxicola rubetra
3 Saxicola torquata
4 Turdus torquatus
4 Turdus merula
4ʷ Turdus pilaris
4 Turdus philomelos
4ʷ Turdus iliacus
4 Turdus viscivorus
4 Locustella naevia
4 Locustella fluviatilis

4 Locustella luscinioides
4 Acrocephalus schoenobaenus
4 Acrocephalus palustris
4 Acrocephalus scirpaceus
4 Hippolais icterina
4 Sylvia nisoria
4 Sylvia communis
4 Sylvia borin
4 Sylvia atricapilla
4 Phylloscopus sibilatrix
4 Regulus regulus
3 Muscicapa striata
4 Ficedula hypoleuca
4 Parus cristatus
4 Parus caeruleus
3 Lanius collurio
3 Lanius excubitor
3 Perisoreus infaustus
4 Corvus monedula
4 Fringilla coelebs
4 Serinus serinus
4 Carduelis chloris
4 Carduelis spinus
4 Carduelis cannabina
4 Loxia pytyopsittacus
4 Emberiza citrinella
2 Emberiza hortulana

FRANCE

2 Calonectris diomedea
2 Puffinus puffinus
4 Puffinus yelkouan
2 Hydrobates pelagicus
2 Sula bassana
4 Phalacrocorax aristotelis
3 Botaurus stellaris
3 Ixobrychus minutus
3 Nycticorax nycticorax
3 Ardeola ralloides
3 Ardea purpurea
3 Ciconia nigra
2 Ciconia ciconia
3 Plegadis falcinellus
2 Platalea leucorodia
3 Phoenicopterus ruber
3 Anas strepera
3 Anas acuta
3 Anas querquedula
3 Netta rufina
4 Aythya ferina
4 Pernis apivorus
3 Elanus caeruleus
3 Milvus migrans
4 Milvus milvus
3 Gypaetus barbatus
3 Neophron percnopterus
3 Gyps fulvus
3 Circaetus gallicus
3 Circus cyaneus
4 Circus pygargus
3 Aquila chrysaetos

3 Hieraaetus pennatus
3 Hieraaetus fasciatus
3 Pandion haliaetus
1 Falco naumanni
4 Falco tinnunculus
3 Falco peregrinus
3 Tetrao tetrix
2 Alectoris graeca
2 Alectoris rufa
3 Perdix perdix
3 Coturnix coturnix
4 Porzana porzana
4 Porzana parva
3 Porzana pusilla
1 Crex crex
3 Grus grus
2 Tetrax tetrax
4/3 Recurvirostra avosetta
3 Burhinus oedicnemus
3 Glareola pratincola
3 Charadrius alexandrinus
4 Philomachus pugnax
3ʷ Scolopax rusticola
2 Limosa limosa
3ʷ Numenius arquata
2 Tringa totanus
4 Larus melanocephalus
1 Larus audouinii
2 Larus canus
4 Larus fuscus
4 Larus marinus
3 Gelochelidon nilotica

2 Sterna sandvicensis
3 Sterna dougallii
3 Sterna albifrons
3 Chlidonias hybridus
3 Chlidonias niger
4 Alca torda
2 Fratercula arctica
3 Pterocles alchata
4 Columba oenas
4 Columba palumbus
3 Streptopelia turtur
3 Tyto alba
3 Otus scops
3 Bubo bubo
3 Athene noctua
4 Strix aluco
3 Asio flammeus
2 Caprimulgus europaeus
3 Alcedo atthis
3 Merops apiaster
3 Coracias garrulus
3 Jynx torquilla
3 Picus canus
2 Picus viridis
4 Dendrocopos medius
3 Picoides tridactylus
3 Melanocorypha calandra
3 Calandrella brachydactyla
3 Galerida cristata
3 Galerida theklae
2 Lullula arborea

3 Alauda arvensis
3 Riparia riparia
3 Hirundo rustica
4 Anthus campestris
4 Anthus pratensis
4 Prunella modularis
4 Erithacus rubecula
4 Luscinia megarhynchos
2 Phoenicurus phoenicurus
4 Saxicola rubetra
3 Saxicola torquata
2 Oenanthe hispanica
3 Oenanthe leucura
3 Monticola saxatilis
3 Monticola solitarius
4 Turdus torquatus
4 Turdus merula
4ʷ Turdus pilaris
4 Turdus philomelos
4 Turdus viscivorus
4 Locustella naevia
4 Locustella luscinioides
4 Acrocephalus schoenobaenus
4 Acrocephalus palustris
4 Acrocephalus scirpaceus
4 Hippolais icterina
4 Hippolais polyglotta
4 Sylvia sarda
2 Sylvia undata
4 Sylvia cantillans
4 Sylvia melanocephala

3 *Sylvia hortensis*
4 *Sylvia communis*
4 *Sylvia borin*
4 *Sylvia atricapilla*
4 *Phylloscopus bonelli*
4 *Phylloscopus sibilatrix*
4 *Regulus regulus*
4 *Regulus ignicapillus*
3 *Muscicapa striata*

4 *Ficedula albicollis*
4 *Ficedula hypoleuca*
4 *Parus cristatus*
4 *Parus caeruleus*
2 **Sitta whiteheadi**
4 *Certhia brachydactyla*
3 *Lanius collurio*
2 *Lanius minor*
3 *Lanius excubitor*

2 *Lanius senator*
3 *Pyrrhocorax pyrrhocorax*
4 *Corvus monedula*
4 *Sturnus unicolor*
4 *Fringilla coelebs*
4 *Serinus serinus*
4 *Serinus citrinella*
4 *Carduelis chloris*
4 *Carduelis spinus*

4 *Carduelis cannabina*
4 *Emberiza citrinella*
4 *Emberiza cirlus*
3 *Emberiza cia*
2 *Emberiza hortulana*
4 *Miliaria calandra*

GERMANY

2 *Sula basana*
3 *Botaurus stellaris*
3 *Ixobrychus minutus*
3 *Nycticorax nycticorax*
3 *Ardea purpurea*
3 *Ciconia nigra*
2 *Ciconia ciconia*
3 *Anas strepera*
3 *Anas acuta*
3 *Anas querquedula*
3 *Netta rufina*
4 *Aythya ferina*
1 *Aythya nyroca*
3ʷ *Aythya marila*
4 *Pernis apivorus*
3 *Milvus migrans*
4 *Milvus milvus*
3 *Haliaeetus albicilla*
3 *Circus cyaneus*
4 *Circus pygargus*
3 *Aquila pomarina*
3 *Aquila chrysaetos*
3 *Pandion haliaetus*
3 *Falco tinnunculus*
3 *Falco peregrinus*
3 *Tetrao tetrix*
2 *Alectoris rufa*
3 *Perdix perdix*
3 *Coturnix coturnix*
4 *Porzana porzana*
4 *Porzana parva*
3 *Porzana pusilla*
1 *Crex crex*

3 *Grus grus*
1 *Otis tarda*
4/3 *Recurvirostra avosetta*
3 *Burhinus oedicnemus*
3 *Charadrius alexandrinus*
4 *Pluvialis apricaria*
3ʷ *Calidris alpina*
4 *Philomachus pugnax*
3ʷ *Scolopax rusticola*
2 *Limosa limosa*
3ʷ *Numenius arquata*
2 *Tringa totanus*
3 *Tringa glareola*
4 *Larus melanocephalus*
2 *Larus canus*
4 *Larus fuscus*
4 *Larus marinus*
3 *Gelochelidon nilotica*
2 *Sterna sandvicensis*
3 *Sterna albifrons*
3 *Chlidonias niger*
4 *Alca torda*
4 *Columba oenas*
4 *Columba palumbus*
3 *Streptopelia turtur*
3 *Tyto alba*
4 *Bubo bubo*
3 *Athene noctua*
4 *Strix aluco*
3 *Asio flammeus*
2 *Caprimulgus europaeus*
3 *Alcedo atthis*
3 *Merops apiaster*

3 *Jynx torquilla*
3 *Picus canus*
3 *Picus viridis*
2 *Dendrocopos medius*
3 *Picoides tridactylus*
3 *Galerida cristata*
2 *Lullula arborea*
3 *Alauda arvensis*
3 *Riparia riparia*
3 *Hirundo rustica*
3 *Anthus campestris*
4 *Anthus pratensis*
4 *Prunella modularis*
4 *Erithacus rubecula*
4 *Luscinia luscinia*
4 *Luscinia megarhynchos*
2 *Phoenicurus phoenicurus*
4 *Saxicola rubetra*
4 *Saxicola torquata*
4 *Turdus torquatus*
4 *Turdus merula*
4ʷ *Turdus pilaris*
4 *Turdus philomelos*
4ʷ *Turdus iliacus*
4 *Turdus viscivorus*
4 *Locustella naevia*
4 *Locustella fluviatilis*
4 *Locustella luscinioides*
1 *Acrocephalus paludicola*
4 *Acrocephalus schoenobaenus*
4 *Acrocephalus palustris*
4 *Acrocephalus scirpaceus*

4 *Hippolais icterina*
4 *Hippolais polyglotta*
4 *Sylvia nisoria*
4 *Sylvia communis*
4 *Sylvia borin*
4 *Sylvia atricapilla*
4 *Phylloscopus bonelli*
4 *Phylloscopus sibilatrix*
4 *Regulus regulus*
4 *Regulus ignicapillus*
3 *Muscicapa striata*
4 *Ficedula albicollis*
4 *Ficedula hypoleuca*
4 *Parus cristatus*
4 *Parus caeruleus*
4 *Certhia brachydactyla*
3 *Lanius collurio*
3 *Lanius excubitor*
2 *Lanius senator*
4 *Corvus monedula*
4 *Fringilla coelebs*
4 *Serinus serinus*
4 *Serinus citrinella*
4 *Carduelis chloris*
4 *Carduelis spinus*
4 *Carduelis cannabina*
4 *Emberiza citrinella*
4 *Emberiza cirlus*
3 *Emberiza cia*
2 *Emberiza hortulana*
4 *Miliaria calandra*

GIBRALTAR

4 *Phalacrocorax aristotelis*
1 *Falco naumanni*
3 *Falco tinnunculus*
3 *Falco peregrinus*
3 *Alectoris barbara*
3 *Coturnix coturnix*

3 *Charadrius alexandrinus*
3 *Tyto alba*
2 *Otus scops*
3 *Athene noctua*
4 *Erithacus rubecula*
4 *Luscinia megarhynchos*

3 *Monticola solitarius*
4 *Turdus merula*
4 *Sylvia melanocephala*
4 *Sylvia atricapilla*
4 *Parus caeruleus*
2 *Lanius senator*

4 *Sturnus unicolor*
4 *Fringilla coelebs*
4 *Serinus serinus*
4 *Carduelis chloris*
3 *Emberiza cia*

GREECE

2 *Calonectris diomedea*
4 *Puffinus yelkouan*
2 *Hydrobates pelagicus*
4 *Phalacrocorax aristotelis*
2 *Phalacrocorax pygmeus*
3 *Pelecanus onocrotalus*

1 *Pelecanus crispus*
3 *Ixobrychus minutus*
3 *Nycticorax nycticorax*
3 *Ardeola ralloides*
3 *Ardea purpurea*
3 *Ciconia nigra*

2 *Ciconia ciconia*
3 *Plegadis falcinellus*
2 *Platalea leucorodia*
3 *Tadorna ferruginea*
3 *Anas strepera*
3 *Anas querquedula*

3 *Netta rufina*
4 *Aythya ferina*
1 *Aythya nyroca*
4 *Pernis apivorus*
3 *Milvus migrans*
3 *Haliaeetus albicilla*

3 Gypaetus barbatus	1 Larus audouinii	3 Hirundo rustica	4 Phylloscopus sibilatrix
3 Neophron percnopterus	3 Gelochelidon nilotica	3 Anthus campestris	4 Regulus regulus
3 Gyps fulvus	2 Sterna sandvicensis	4 Prunella modularis	4 Regulus ignicapillus
3 Aegypius monachus	3 Sterna albifrons	4 Erithacus rubecula	3 Muscicapa striata
3 Circaetus gallicus	3 Chlidonias hybridus	4 Luscinia megarhynchos	2 Ficedula semitorquata
3 Circus pygargus	3 Chlidonias niger	2 Phoenicurus phoenicurus	4 Parus lugubris
2 Accipiter brevipes	4 Columba oenas	4 Saxicola rubetra	4 Parus cristatus
3 Buteo rufinus	4 Columba palumbus	3 Saxicola torquata	4 Parus caeruleus
3 Aquila pomarina	3 Streptopelia turtur	2 Oenanthe hispanica	4 Sitta krueperi
1 Aquila heliaca	3 Tyto alba	3 Monticola saxatilis	4 Sitta neumayer
3 Aquila chrysaetos	2 Otus scops	3 Monticola solitarius	4 Certhia brachydactyla
3 Hieraaetus pennatus	3 Bubo bubo	4 Turdus torquatus	3 Lanius collurio
3 Hieraaetus fasciatus	3 Athene noctua	4 Turdus merula	2 Lanius minor
1 Falco naumanni	4 Strix aluco	4ᵂ Turdus pilaris	2 Lanius senator
3 Falco tinnunculus	3 Asio flammeus	4 Turdus philomelos	2 Lanius nubicus
2 Falco eleonorae	2 Caprimulgus europaeus	4 Turdus viscivorus	3 Pyrrhocorax pyrrhocorax
3 Falco biarmicus	3 Alcedo atthis	4 Locustella luscinioides	4 Corvus monedula
3 Falco peregrinus	3 Merops apiaster	4 Acrocephalus	4 Fringilla coelebs
3 Alectoris chukar	2 Coracias garrulus	schoenobaenus	4 Serinus serinus
2 Alectoris graeca	3 Jynx torquilla	4 Acrocephalus palustris	4 Carduelis chloris
3 Perdix perdix	3 Picus canus	4 Acrocephalus scirpaceus	4 Carduelis cannabina
3 Coturnix coturnix	3 Picus viridis	3 Hippolais pallida	4 Emberiza citrinella
4 Porzana parva	4 Dendrocopos syriacus	2 Hippolais olivetorum	4 Emberiza cirlus
3 Porzana pusilla	4 Dendrocopos medius	4 Sylvia cantillans	3 Emberiza cia
4/3 Recurvirostra avosetta	3 Picoides tridactylus	4 Sylvia melanocephala	2 Emberiza cineracea
3 Burhinus oedicnemus	3 Melanocorypha calandra	4 Sylvia rueppelli	2 Emberiza hortulana
3 Glareola pratincola	3 Calandrella	3 Sylvia hortensis	4 Emberiza caesia
3 Charadrius alexandrinus	brachydactyla	4 Sylvia nisoria	2 Emberiza melanocephala
3 Hoplopterus spinosus	3 Galerida cristata	4 Sylvia communis	4 Miliaria calandra
3ᵂ Scolopax rusticola	3 Lullula arborea	4 Sylvia borin	
2 Tringa totanus	3 Alauda arvensis	4 Sylvia atricapilla	
4 Larus melanocephalus	3 Riparia riparia	4 Phylloscopus bonelli	

GREENLAND

3 Gavia stellata	3 Haliaeetus albicilla	3ᵂ Calidris alpina	2 Cepphus grylle
3ᵂ Cygnus columbianus	3 Falco rusticolus	4 Numenius phaeopus	2 Fratercula arctica
4 Anser brachyrhynchus	3 Falco peregrinus	4 Larus fuscus	3 Nyctea scandiaca
4/2 Branta leucopsis	4 Pluvialis apricaria	4 Larus marinus	4 Anthus pratensis
3 Branta bernicla	3ᵂ Calidris canutus	3 Pagophila eburnea	4ᵂ Turdus pilaris
3 Histrionicus histrionicus	4 Calidris maritima	4 Alca torda	4ᵂ Turdus iliacus

GUERNSEY

2 Puffinus puffinus	4 Columba oenas	4 Erithacus rubecula	4 Sylvia borin
2 Hydrobates pelagicus	4 Columba palumbus	3 Saxicola torquata	4 Sylvia atricapilla
2 Sula bassana	3 Streptopelia turtur	4 Turdus merula	4 Regulus regulus
4 Phalacrocorax aristotelis	3 Tyto alba	4 Turdus philomelos	3 Muscicapa striata
3 Falco tinnunculus	3 Alauda arvensis	4 Turdus viscivorus	4 Parus caeruleus
4 Larus fuscus	3 Riparia riparia	4 Acrocephalus	4 Certhia brachydactyla
4 Larus marinus	3 Hirundo rustica	schoenobaenus	4 Fringilla coelebs
4 Alca torda	4 Anthus pratensis	4 Acrocephalus scirpaceus	4 Carduelis chloris
2 Fratercula arctica	4 Prunella modularis	4 Sylvia communis	4 Carduelis cannabina

HUNGARY

2 Phalacrocorax pygmeus	3 Plegadis falcinellus	4 Pernis apivorus	1 Aquila heliaca
3 Botaurus stellaris	2 Platalea leucorodia	3 Milvus migrans	3 Aquila chrysaetos
3 Ixobrychus minutus	3 Anas strepera	4 Milvus milvus	3 Hieraaetus pennatus
3 Nycticorax nycticorax	3 Anas acuta	3 Haliaeetus albicilla	3 Falco tinnunculus
3 Ardeola ralloides	3 Anas querquedula	3 Circaetus gallicus	3 Falco vespertinus
3 Ardea purpurea	3 Netta rufina	4 Circus pygargus	3 Falco cherrug
3 Ciconia nigra	4 Aythya ferina	2 Accipiter brevipes	3 Perdix perdix
2 Ciconia ciconia	1 Aythya nyroca	3 Aquila pomarina	3 Coturnix coturnix

4 *Porzana porzana*
4 *Porzana parva*
3 *Porzana pusilla*
1 *Crex crex*
1 *Otis tarda*
4/3 *Recurvirostra avosetta*
3 *Burhinus oedicnemus*
3 *Glareola pratincola*
3 *Glareola nordmanni*
3 *Charadrius alexandrinus*
4 *Philomachus pugnax*
3ᵂ *Scolopax rusticola*
2 *Limosa limosa*
3ᵂ *Numenius arquata*
2 *Tringa totanus*
4 *Larus melanocephalus*
2 *Larus canus*
3 *Chlidonias hybridus*
3 *Chlidonias niger*
4 *Columba oenas*
4 *Columba palumbus*
3 *Streptopelia turtur*
3 *Tyto alba*
2 *Otus scops*

3 *Bubo bubo*
3 *Athene noctua*
4 *Strix aluco*
3 *Asio flammeus*
2 *Caprimulgus europaeus*
4 *Alcedo atthis*
3 *Merops apiaster*
2 *Coracias garrulus*
3 *Jynx torquilla*
3 *Picus canus*
2 *Picus viridis*
4 *Dendrocopos syriacus*
4 *Dendrocopos medius*
3 *Calandrella brachydactyla*
3 *Galerida cristata*
2 *Lullula arborea*
3 *Alauda arvensis*
3 *Riparia riparia*
3 *Hirundo rustica*
3 *Anthus campestris*
4 *Prunella modularis*
4 *Erithacus rubecula*
4 *Luscinia luscinia*

4 *Luscinia megarhynchos*
2 *Phoenicurus phoenicurus*
4 *Saxicola rubetra*
3 *Saxicola torquata*
3 *Monticola saxatilis*
4 *Turdus merula*
4ᵂ *Turdus pilaris*
4 *Turdus philomelos*
4 *Turdus viscivorus*
4 *Locustella naevia*
4 *Locustella fluviatilis*
4 *Locustella luscinioides*
1 *Acrocephalus paludicola*
4 *Acrocephalus schoenobaenus*
4 *Acrocephalus palustris*
4 *Acrocephalus scirpaceus*
3 *Hippolais pallida*
4 *Hippolais icterina*
4 *Sylvia nisoria*
4 *Sylvia communis*
4 *Sylvia borin*
4 *Sylvia atricapilla*
4 *Phylloscopus sibilatrix*

4 *Regulus regulus*
4 *Regulus ignicapillus*
3 *Muscicapa striata*
4 *Ficedula albicollis*
4 *Ficedula hypoleuca*
4 *Parus cristatus*
4 *Parus caeruleus*
4 *Certhia brachydactyla*
3 *Lanius collurio*
2 *Lanius minor*
4 *Corvus monedula*
4 *Fringilla coelebs*
4 *Serinus serinus*
4 *Carduelis chloris*
4 *Carduelis spinus*
4 *Carduelis cannabina*
4 *Emberiza citrinella*
4 *Emberiza cirlus*
3 *Emberiza cia*
2 *Emberiza hortulana*
4 *Miliaria calandra*

ICELAND

3 *Gavia stellata*
2 *Puffinus puffinus*
2 *Hydrobates pelagicus*
3 *Oceanodroma leucorhoa*
2 *Sula bassana*
4 *Phalacrocorax aristotelis*
4ᵂ *Cygnus cygnus*
4 *Anser brachyrhynchus*
4/2 *Branta leucopsis*
3 *Anas strepera*
3 *Anas acuta*

4 *Aythya ferina*
3ᵂ *Aythya marila*
3 *Histrionicus histrionicus*
3 **Bucephala islandica**
3 *Haliaeetus albicilla*
3 *Falco rusticolus*
4 *Pluvialis apricaria*
4 *Calidris maritima*
3ᵂ *Calidris alpina*
2 *Limosa limosa*
4 *Numenius phaeopus*

3ᵂ *Numenius arquata*
2 *Tringa totanus*
3 *Tringa glareola*
4 *Stercorarius skua*
2 *Larus canus*
4 *Larus fuscus*
4 *Larus marinus*
3 *Chlidonias niger*
4 *Alca torda*
2 *Cepphus grylle*
2 *Fratercula arctica*

4 *Columba palumbus*
3 *Nyctea scandiaca*
3 *Asio flammeus*
3 *Hirundo rustica*
4 *Anthus pratensis*
4 *Turdus merula*
4ᵂ *Turdus pilaris*
4ᵂ *Turdus iliacus*
4 *Fringilla coelebs*

ISLE OF MAN

2 *Puffinus puffinus*
2 *Hydrobates pelagicus*
4 *Phalacrocorax aristotelis*
3 *Circus cyaneus*
3 *Falco tinnunculus*
3 *Falco peregrinus*
2 *Alectoris rufa*
3 *Perdix perdix*
3 *Coturnix coturnix*
1 *Crex crex*
3ᵂ *Scolopax rusticola*
3ᵂ *Numenius arquata*
2 *Tringa totanus*
2 *Larus canus*

4 *Larus fuscus*
4 *Larus marinus*
3 *Sterna albifrons*
4 *Alca torda*
2 *Cepphus grylle*
2 *Fratercula arctica*
4 *Columba oenas*
4 *Columba palumbus*
3 *Tyto alba*
3 *Asio flammeus*
3 *Alauda arvensis*
3 *Riparia riparia*
3 *Hirundo rustica*
4 *Anthus pratensis*

4 *Prunella modularis*
4 *Erithacus rubecula*
4 *Saxicola rubetra*
3 *Saxicola torquata*
4 *Turdus merula*
4ᵂ *Turdus pilaris*
4 *Turdus philomelos*
4 *Turdus viscivorus*
4 *Locustella naevia*
4 *Acrocephalus schoenobaenus*
4 *Sylvia communis*
4 *Sylvia borin*
4 *Sylvia atricapilla*

4 *Phylloscopus sibilatrix*
4 *Regulus regulus*
3 *Muscicapa striata*
4 *Parus caeruleus*
3 *Pyrrhocorax pyrrhocorax*
4 *Corvus monedula*
4 *Fringilla coelebs*
4 *Carduelis chloris*
4 *Carduelis spinus*
4 *Carduelis cannabina*
4 *Emberiza citrinella*

ITALY

2 *Calonectris diomedea*
4 *Puffinus yelkouan*
2 *Hydrobates pelagicus*
4 *Phalacrocorax aristotelis*
3 *Botaurus stellaris*

3 *Ixobrychus minutus*
3 *Nycticorax nycticorax*
3 *Ardeola ralloides*
3 *Ardea purpurea*
2 *Ciconia ciconia*
3 *Plegadis falcinellus*

2 *Platalea leucorodia*
3 *Anas strepera*
3 *Anas querquedula*
3 *Netta rufina*
4 *Aythya ferina*
1 *Aythya nyroca*

4 *Pernis apivorus*
3 *Milvus migrans*
4 *Milvus milvus*
3 *Neophron percnopterus*
3 *Gyps fulvus*
3 *Circaetus gallicus*

4 Circus pygargus
3 Aquila chrysaetos
3 Hieraaetus fasciatus
1 Falco naumanni
3 Falco tinnunculus
2 Falco eleonorae
3 Falco biarmicus
3 Falco peregrinus
3 Tetrao tetrix
2 Alectoris graeca
2 Alectoris rufa
3 Alectoris barbara
3 Perdix perdix
3 Coturnix coturnix
4 Porzana porzana
4 Porzana parva
1 Crex crex
3 Porphyrio porphyrio
2 Tetrax tetrax
4/3 Recurvirostra avosetta
3 Burhinus oedicnemus
3 Glareola pratincola
3 Charadrius alexandrinus
3[w] Scolopax rusticola
2 Limosa limosa
2 Tringa totanus
4 Larus melanocephalus
1 Larus audouinii
3 Gelochelidon nilotica

2 Sterna sandvicensis
3 Sterna albifrons
3 Chlidonias hybridus
3 Chlidonias niger
4 Columba oenas
4 Columba palumbus
4 Streptopelia turtur
3 Tyto alba
2 Otus scops
3 Bubo bubo
3 Athene noctua
4 Strix aluco
2 Caprimulgus europaeus
3 Alcedo atthis
3 Merops apiaster
2 Coracias garrulus
3 Jynx torquilla
3 Picus canus
2 Picus viridis
4 Dendrocopos medius
3 Picoides tridactylus
3 Melanocorypha calandra
3 Calandrella brachydactyla
3 Galerida cristata
2 Lullula arborea
3 Alauda arvensis
3 Riparia riparia
3 Hirundo rustica

3 Anthus campestris
4 Prunella modularis
4 Erithacus rubecula
4 Luscinia megarhynchos
2 Phoenicurus phoenicurus
4 Saxicola rubetra
3 Saxicola torquata
2 Oenanthe hispanica
3 Monticola saxatilis
3 Monticola solitarius
4 Turdus torquatus
4 Turdus merula
4[w] Turdus pilaris
4 Turdus philomelos
4 Turdus viscivorus
4 Locustella luscinioides
4 Acrocephalus schoenobaenus
4 Acrocephalus palustris
4 Acrocephalus scirpaceus
4 Hippolais polyglotta
4 Sylvia sarda
2 Sylvia undata
4 Sylvia cantillans
4 Sylvia melanocephala
3 Sylvia hortensis
4 Sylvia nisoria
4 Sylvia communis
4 Sylvia borin

4 Sylvia atricapilla
4 Phylloscopus bonelli
4 Phylloscopus sibilatrix
4 Regulus regulus
4 Regulus ignicapillus
3 Muscicapa striata
4 Ficedula albicollis
4 Parus cristatus
4 Parus caeruleus
4 Certhia brachydactyla
3 Lanius collurio
2 Lanius minor
2 Lanius senator
3 Pyrrhocorax pyrrhocorax
4 Corvus monedula
4 Sturnus unicolor
4 Fringilla coelebs
4 Serinus serinus
4 Serinus citrinella
4 Carduelis chloris
4 Carduelis spinus
4 Carduelis cannabina
4 Emberiza citrinella
4 Emberiza cirlus
3 Emberiza cia
2 Emberiza hortulana
2 Emberiza melanocephala
4 Miliaria calandra

JERSEY

4 Phalacrocorax aristotelis
3 Falco tinnunculus
4 Larus fuscus
4 Larus marinus
4 Alca torda
2 Fratercula arctica
4 Columba oenas
4 Columba palumbus
3 Streptopelia turtur
3 Tyto alba

3 Alcedo atthis
3 Alauda arvensis
3 Riparia riparia
3 Hirundo rustica
4 Anthus pratensis
4 Prunella modularis
4 Erithacus rubecula
3 Saxicola torquata
4 Turdus merula
4 Turdus philomelos

4 Turdus viscivorus
4 Acrocephalus schoenobaenus
4 Acrocephalus scirpaceus
2 Sylvia undata
4 Sylvia communis
4 Sylvia borin
4 Sylvia atricapilla
4 Regulus regulus
3 Muscicapa striata

4 Parus caeruleus
4 Certhia brachydactyla
4 Fringilla coelebs
4 Serinus serinus
4 Carduelis chloris
4 Carduelis cannabina
4 Emberiza citrinella
4 Emberiza cirlus
2 Emberiza melanocephala
4 Miliaria calandra

LATVIA

3 Gavia arctica
3 Botaurus stellaris
3 Ixobrychus minutus
3 Ciconia nigra
2 Ciconia ciconia
4[w] Cygnus cygnus
3 Anas strepera
3 Anas acuta
3 Anas querquedula
4 Aythya ferina
4 Pernis apivorus
3 Milvus migrans
4 Milvus milvus
3 Haliaeetus albicilla
3 Circaetus gallicus
3 Circus cyaneus
4 Circus pygargus
3 Aquila pomarina
1 Aquila clanga
3 Aquila chrysaetos

3 Pandion haliaetus
3 Falco tinnunculus
3 Falco vespertinus
3 Tetrao tetrix
3 Perdix perdix
3 Coturnix coturnix
3 Porzana porzana
4 Porzana parva
1 Crex crex
3 Grus grus
4 Pluvialis apricaria
3[w] Calidris alpina
4 Philomachus pugnax
2 Gallinago media
3[w] Scolopax rusticola
2 Limosa limosa
4 Numenius phaeopus
3[w] Numenius arquata
2 Tringa totanus
3 Tringa glareola

3 Larus minutus
2 Larus canus
3 Sterna albifrons
3 Chlidonias niger
4 Columba oenas
4 Columba palumbus
3 Streptopelia turtur
3 Tyto alba
3 Bubo bubo
3 Athene noctua
4 Strix aluco
3 Asio flammeus
2 Caprimulgus europaeus
3 Alcedo atthis
3 Coracias garrulus
3 Jynx torquilla
3 Picus canus
2 Picus viridis
4 Dendrocopos medius
3 Picoides tridactylus

3 Galerida cristata
2 Lullula arborea
3 Alauda arvensis
3 Riparia riparia
3 Hirundo rustica
3 Anthus campestris
4 Anthus pratensis
4 Prunella modularis
4 Erithacus rubecula
3 Luscinia luscinia
2 Phoenicurus phoenicurus
4 Saxicola rubetra
4 Turdus merula
4[w] Turdus pilaris
4 Turdus philomelos
4[w] Turdus iliacus
4 Turdus viscivorus
4 Locustella naevia
4 Locustella fluviatilis
4 Locustella luscinioides

1 *Acrocephalus paludicola*
4 *Acrocephalus schoenobaenus*
4 *Acrocephalus palustris*
4 *Acrocephalus scirpaceus*
4 *Hippolais icterina*
4 *Sylvia nisoria*
4 *Sylvia communis*

4 *Sylvia borin*
4 *Sylvia atricapilla*
4 *Phylloscopus sibilatrix*
4 *Regulus regulus*
4 *Regulus ignicapillus*
3 *Muscicapa striata*
4 *Ficedula hypoleuca*
4 *Parus cristatus*

4 *Parus caeruleus*
3 *Lanius collurio*
2 *Lanius minor*
3 *Lanius excubitor*
4 *Corvus monedula*
4 *Fringilla coelebs*
4 *Serinus serinus*
4 *Carduelis chloris*

4 *Carduelis spinus*
4 *Carduelis cannabina*
4 *Loxia pytyopsittacus*
4 *Emberiza citrinella*
2 *Emberiza hortulana*
4 *Miliaria calandra*

LIECHTENSTEIN

4 *Pernis apivorus*
3 *Milvus migrans*
3 *Aquila chrysaetos*
3 *Falco tinnunculus*
3 *Tetrao tetrix*
3 *Coturnix coturnix*
1 *Crex crex*
3ᵂ *Scolopax rusticola*
3ᵂ *Numenius arquata*
4 *Columba oenas*
4 *Columba palumbus*
3 *Streptopelia turtur*
3 *Tyto alba*
3 *Bubo bubo*
4 *Strix aluco*

3 *Jynx torquilla*
3 *Picus canus*
2 *Picus viridis*
3 *Picoides tridactylus*
3 *Alauda arvensis*
3 *Hirundo rustica*
4 *Prunella modularis*
4 *Erithacus rubecula*
4 *Luscinia megarhynchos*
2 *Phoenicurus phoenicurus*
4 *Saxicola rubetra*
3 *Saxicola torquata*
4 *Turdus torquatus*
4 *Turdus merula*
4ᵂ *Turdus pilaris*

4 *Turdus philomelos*
4 *Turdus viscivorus*
4 *Locustella naevia*
4 *Acrocephalus palustris*
4 *Acrocephalus scirpaceus*
4 *Hippolais icterina*
4 *Sylvia communis*
4 *Sylvia borin*
4 *Sylvia atricapilla*
4 *Phylloscopus bonelli*
4 *Regulus regulus*
4 *Regulus ignicapillus*
3 *Muscicapa striata*
4 *Ficedula hypoleuca*
4 *Parus cristatus*

4 *Parus caeruleus*
4 *Certhia brachydactyla*
3 *Lanius collurio*
4 *Corvus monedula*
4 *Fringilla coelebs*
4 *Serinus serinus*
4 *Serinus citrinella*
4 *Carduelis chloris*
4 *Carduelis spinus*
4 *Carduelis cannabina*
4 *Emberiza citrinella*
4 *Miliaria calandra*

LITHUANIA

3 *Gavia arctica*
3 *Botaurus stellaris*
3 *Ixobrychus minutus*
3 *Ciconia nigra*
2 *Ciconia ciconia*
4ᵂ *Cygnus cygnus*
3 *Anas strepera*
3 *Anas acuta*
3 *Anas querquedula*
4 *Aythya ferina*
1 *Aythya nyroca*
4 *Pernis apivorus*
3 *Milvus migrans*
4 *Milvus milvus*
3 *Haliaeetus albicilla*
3 *Circaetus gallicus*
3 *Circus cyaneus*
4 *Circus pygargus*
3 *Aquila pomarina*
3 *Pandion haliaetus*
3 *Falco tinnunculus*
3 *Tetrao tetrix*
3 *Perdix perdix*
3 *Coturnix coturnix*
4 *Porzana porzana*
4 *Porzana parva*
1 *Crex crex*

3 *Grus grus*
4 *Pluvialis apricaria*
3ᵂ *Calidris alpina*
4 *Philomachus pugnax*
2 *Gallinago media*
3ᵂ *Scolopax rusticola*
2 *Limosa limosa*
3ᵂ *Numenius arquata*
2 *Tringa totanus*
3 *Tringa glareola*
3 *Larus minutus*
2 *Larus canus*
3 *Sterna albifrons*
3 *Chlidonias hybridus*
3 *Chlidonias niger*
4 *Columba oenas*
4 *Columba palumbus*
3 *Streptopelia turtur*
3 *Tyto alba*
3 *Bubo bubo*
3 *Athene noctua*
4 *Strix aluco*
3 *Asio flammeus*
2 *Caprimulgus europaeus*
3 *Alcedo atthis*
2 *Coracias garrulus*
3 *Jynx torquilla*

3 *Picus canus*
2 *Picus viridis*
4 *Dendrocopos medius*
3 *Picoides tridactylus*
3 *Galerida cristata*
2 *Lullula arborea*
3 *Alauda arvensis*
3 *Riparia riparia*
3 *Hirundo rustica*
3 *Anthus campestris*
4 *Anthus pratensis*
4 *Prunella modularis*
4 *Erithacus rubecula*
4 *Luscinia luscinia*
2 *Phoenicurus phoenicurus*
4 *Saxicola rubetra*
4 *Turdus merula*
4ᵂ *Turdus pilaris*
4 *Turdus philomelos*
4ᵂ *Turdus iliacus*
4 *Turdus viscivorus*
4 *Locustella naevia*
4 *Locustella fluviatilis*
4 *Locustella luscinioides*
1 *Acrocephalus paludicola*
4 *Acrocephalus schoenobaenus*

4 *Acrocephalus palustris*
4 *Acrocephalus scirpaceus*
4 *Hippolais icterina*
4 *Sylvia nisoria*
4 *Sylvia communis*
4 *Sylvia borin*
4 *Sylvia atricapilla*
4 *Phylloscopus sibilatrix*
4 *Regulus regulus*
3 *Muscicapa striata*
4 *Ficedula hypoleuca*
4 *Parus cristatus*
4 *Parus caeruleus*
3 *Lanius collurio*
2 *Lanius minor*
3 *Lanius excubitor*
4 *Corvus monedula*
4 *Fringilla coelebs*
4 *Serinus serinus*
4 *Carduelis chloris*
4 *Carduelis spinus*
4 *Carduelis cannabina*
4 *Emberiza citrinella*
2 *Emberiza hortulana*
4 *Miliaria calandra*

LUXEMBOURG

3 *Ixobrychus minutus*
3 *Ciconia nigra*
3 *Anas querquedula*
4 *Pernis apivorus*
3 *Milvus migrans*

4 *Milvus milvus*
3 *Circus cyaneus*
4 *Circus pygargus*
3 *Falco tinnunculus*
3 *Perdix perdix*

3 *Coturnix coturnix*
1 *Crex crex*
3ᵂ *Scolopax rusticola*
4 *Columba oenas*
4 *Columba palumbus*

3 *Streptopelia turtur*
3 *Tyto alba*
3 *Bubo bubo*
3 *Athene noctua*
4 *Strix aluco*

Birds in Europe: Their Conservation Status

2 *Caprimulgus europaeus*
3 *Alcedo atthis*
3 *Jynx torquilla*
3 *Picus canus*
2 *Picus viridis*
4 *Dendrocopos medius*
4 *Lullula arborea*
3 *Alauda arvensis*
3 *Riparia riparia*
3 *Hirundo rustica*
3 *Anthus campestris*
4 *Anthus pratensis*
4 *Prunella modularis*

4 *Erithacus rubecula*
4 *Luscinia megarhynchos*
2 *Phoenicurus phoenicurus*
4 *Saxicola rubetra*
3 *Saxicola torquata*
4 *Turdus merula*
4ᵂ *Turdus pilaris*
4 *Turdus philomelos*
4 *Turdus viscivorus*
4 *Locustella naevia*
4 *Acrocephalus schoenobaenus*
4 *Acrocephalus palustris*

4 *Acrocephalus scirpaceus*
4 *Sylvia communis*
4 *Sylvia atricapilla*
4 *Phylloscopus sibilatrix*
4 *Regulus regulus*
4 *Regulus ignicapillus*
3 *Muscicapa striata*
4 *Ficedula hypoleuca*
4 *Parus cristatus*
4 *Parus caeruleus*
4 *Certhia brachydactyla*
3 *Lanius collurio*
3 *Lanius excubitor*

2 *Lanius senator*
4 *Corvus monedula*
4 *Fringilla coelebs*
4 *Serinus serinus*
4 *Carduelis chloris*
4 *Carduelis spinus*
4 *Carduelis cannabina*
4 *Emberiza citrinella*
4 *Miliaria calandra*

MADEIRA

1 **Pterodroma feae**
1 **Pterodroma madeira**
3 *Bulweria bulwerii*
2 *Calonectris diomedea*
2 *Puffinus puffinus*
3 *Puffinus assimilis*
3 *Pelagodroma marina*

3 *Oceanodroma castro*
3 *Falco tinnunculus*
2 *Alectoris rufa*
3 *Coturnix coturnix*
3 *Charadrius alexandrinus*
3ᵂ *Scolopax rusticola*
3 *Sterna euclata*

3 *Sterna dougallii*
1 **Columba trocaz**
3 *Streptopelia turtur*
3 *Tyto alba*
4 *Apus unicolor*
4 *Anthus berthelotii*
4 *Erithacus rubecula*

4 *Turdus merula*
4 *Sylvia atricapilla*
4 *Regulus ignicapillus*
4 *Fringilla coelebs*
4 *Serinus canaria*
4 *Carduelis chloris*
4 *Carduelis cannabina*

MALTA

2 *Calonectris diomedea*
4 *Puffinus yelkouan*
2 *Hydrobates pelagicus*
3 *Coturnix coturnix*

3 *Streptopelia turtur*
3 *Calandrella brachydactyla*
3 *Monticola solitarius*

4 *Sylvia melanocephala*
3 *Muscicapa striata*
2 *Lanius senator*
4 *Fringilla coelebs*

4 *Serinus serinus*
4 *Carduelis chloris*
4 *Carduelis cannabina*
4 *Miliaria calandra*

MOLDOVA

2 *Phalacrocorax pygmeus*
3 *Botaurus stellaris*
3 *Ixobrychus minutus*
3 *Nycticorax nycticorax*
3 *Ardeola ralloides*
3 *Ardea purpurea*
3 *Ciconia nigra*
2 *Ciconia ciconia*
3 *Plegadis falcinellus*
3 *Platalea leucorodia*
3 *Tadorna ferruginea*
3 *Anas strepera*
3 *Anas querquedula*
3 *Netta rufina*
4 *Aythya ferina*
1 *Aythya nyroca*
4 *Pernis apivorus*
4 *Milvus migrans*
4 *Milvus milvus*
3 *Neophron percnopterus*
3 *Circaetus gallicus*
3 *Circus cyaneus*
3 *Circus macrourus*
4 *Circus pygargus*
3 *Aquila pomarina*
1 *Aquila clanga*
1 *Aquila heliaca*

3 *Hieraaetus pennatus*
3 *Pandion haliaetus*
1 *Falco naumanni*
3 *Falco tinnunculus*
3 *Falco vespertinus*
3 *Falco cherrug*
3 *Perdix perdix*
3 *Coturnix coturnix*
4 *Porzana porzana*
4 *Porzana parva*
3 *Porzana pusilla*
1 *Crex crex*
1 *Otis tarda*
4/3 *Recurvirostra avosetta*
2 *Tringa totanus*
2 *Larus canus*
3 *Sterna albifrons*
3 *Chlidonias niger*
4 *Columba oenas*
4 *Columba palumbus*
3 *Streptopelia turtur*
3 *Tyto alba*
2 *Otus scops*
3 *Bubo bubo*
3 *Athene noctua*
4 *Strix aluco*
3 *Asio flammeus*

2 *Caprimulgus europaeus*
3 *Alcedo atthis*
3 *Merops apiaster*
2 *Coracias garrulus*
3 *Jynx torquilla*
3 *Picus canus*
2 *Picus viridis*
4 *Dendrocopos syriacus*
4 *Dendrocopos medius*
4 *Melanocorypha calandra*
3 *Galerida cristata*
2 *Lullula arborea*
3 *Alauda arvensis*
3 *Riparia riparia*
3 *Hirundo rustica*
3 *Anthus campestris*
4 *Anthus pratensis*
4 *Erithacus rubecula*
4 *Luscinia luscinia*
2 *Phoenicurus phoenicurus*
4 *Saxicola rubetra*
3 *Saxicola torquata*
3 *Monticola saxatilis*
4 *Turdus merula*
4 *Turdus philomelos*
4 *Locustella naevia*
4 *Locustella fluviatilis*

4 *Locustella luscinioides*
4 *Acrocephalus schoenobaenus*
4 *Acrocephalus palustris*
4 *Acrocephalus scirpaceus*
4 *Hippolais icterina*
4 *Sylvia nisoria*
4 *Sylvia communis*
4 *Sylvia borin*
4 *Sylvia atricapilla*
4 *Phylloscopus sibilatrix*
3 *Muscicapa striata*
4 *Ficedula albicollis*
4 *Ficedula hypoleuca*
4 *Parus caeruleus*
3 *Lanius collurio*
2 *Lanius minor*
4 *Corvus monedula*
4 *Fringilla coelebs*
4 *Serinus serinus*
4 *Carduelis chloris*
4 *Carduelis cannabina*
4 *Emberiza citrinella*
2 *Emberiza hortulana*
4 *Miliaria calandra*

NETHERLANDS

3 Botaurus stellaris	4/3 Recurvirostra avosetta	3 Jynx torquilla	4 Sylvia communis
3 Ixobrychus minutus	3 Charadrius alexandrinus	2 Picus viridis	4 Sylvia borin
3 Nycticorax nycticorax	3ᵂ Calidris alpina	3 Galerida cristata	4 Sylvia atricapilla
3 Ardea purpurea	4 Philomachus pugnax	2 Lullula arborea	4 Phylloscopus bonelli
2 Ciconia ciconia	3ᵂ Scolopax rusticola	3 Alauda arvensis	4 Phylloscopus sibilatrix
2 Platalea leucorodia	2 Limosa limosa	3 Riparia riparia	4 Regulus regulus
3 Anas strepera	3ᵂ Numenius arquata	3 Hirundo rustica	4 Regulus ignicapillus
3 Anas acuta	2 Tringa totanus	3 Anthus campestris	3 Muscicapa striata
3 Anas querquedula	4 Larus melanocephalus	4 Anthus pratensis	4 Ficedula hypoleuca
3 Netta rufina	3 Larus minutus	4 Prunella modularis	4 Parus cristatus
4 Aythya ferina	2 Larus canus	4 Erithacus rubecula	4 Parus caeruleus
1 Aythya nyroca	4 Larus fuscus	4 Luscinia megarhynchos	4 Certhia brachydactyla
4 Pernis apivorus	2 Sterna sandvicensis	2 Phoenicurus phoenicurus	3 Lanius collurio
3 Milvus migrans	3 Sterna albifrons	4 Saxicola rubetra	3 Lanius excubitor
4 Milvus milvus	3 Chlidonias niger	3 Saxicola torquata	4 Corvus monedula
3 Circus cyaneus	4 Columba oenas	4 Turdus merula	4 Fringilla coelebs
4 Circus pygargus	4 Columba palumbus	4ᵂ Turdus pilaris	4 Serinus serinus
3 Falco tinnunculus	3 Streptopelia turtur	4 Turdus philomelos	4 Carduelis chloris
3 Falco peregrinus	3 Tyto alba	4 Turdus viscivorus	4 Carduelis spinus
3 Tetrao tetrix	3 Bubo bubo	4 Locustella naevia	4 Carduelis cannabina
3 Perdix perdix	3 Athene noctua	4 Locustella luscinioides	4 Emberiza citrinella
3 Coturnix coturnix	4 Strix aluco	4 Acrocephalus	2 Emberiza hortulana
4 Porzana porzana	3 Asio flammeus	schoenobaenus	4 Miliaria calandra
4 Porzana parva	2 Caprimulgus europaeus	4 Acrocephalus palustris	
3 Porzana pusilla	3 Alcedo atthis	4 Acrocephalus scirpaceus	
1 Crex crex	3 Merops apiaster	4 Hippolais icterina	

NORWAY

3 Gavia stellata	3 Grus grus	3 Nyctea scandiaca	4 Acrocephalus
3 Gavia arctica	4/3 Recurvirostra avosetta	4 Strix aluco	schoenobaenus
2 Hydrobates pelagicus	4 Pluvialis apricaria	3 Asio flammeus	4 Acrocephalus palustris
3 Oceanodroma leucorhoa	4 Calidris maritima	2 Caprimulgus europaeus	4 Acrocephalus scirpaceus
2 Sula bassana	3ᵂ Calidris alpina	3 Alcedo atthis	4 Hippolais icterina
4 Phalacrocorax aristotelis	3 Limicola falcinellus	3 Jynx torquilla	4 Sylvia nisoria
4ᵂ Cygnus cygnus	4 Philomachus pugnax	3 Picus canus	4 Sylvia communis
1 Anser erythropus	3ᵂ Lymnocryptes minimus	2 Picus viridis	4 Sylvia borin
4/2 Branta leucopsis	2 Gallinago media	3 Picoides tridactylus	4 Sylvia atricapilla
3 Anas strepera	3ᵂ Scolopax rusticola	2 Lullula arborea	4 Phylloscopus sibilatrix
3 Anas acuta	2 Limosa limosa	3 Alauda arvensis	4 Regulus regulus
3 Anas querquedula	3ᵂ Limosa lapponica	3 Riparia riparia	3 Muscicapa striata
4 Aythya ferina	4 Numenius phaeopus	3 Hirundo rustica	4 Ficedula hypoleuca
3ᵂ Aythya marila	3ᵂ Numenius arquata	4 Anthus pratensis	4 Parus cristatus
3ᵂ Melanitta fusca	2 Tringa totanus	4 Prunella modularis	4 Parus caeruleus
3 Mergus albellus	3 Tringa glareola	4 Erithacus rubecula	3 Lanius collurio
4 Pernis apivorus	4 Stercorarius skua	4 Luscinia luscinia	3 Lanius excubitor
3 Haliaeetus albicilla	3 Larus minutus	2 Phoenicurus phoenicurus	3 Perisoreus infaustus
3 Circus cyaneus	2 Larus canus	4 Saxicola rubetra	4 Corvus monedula
3 Aquila chrysaetos	4 Larus fuscus	3 Saxicola torquata	4 Fringilla coelebs
3 Pandion haliaetus	4 Larus marinus	4 Turdus torquatus	4 Carduelis chloris
3 Falco tinnunculus	2 Sterna sandvicensis	4 Turdus merula	4 Carduelis spinus
3 Falco rusticolus	4 Alca torda	4ᵂ Turdus pilaris	4 Carduelis cannabina
3 Falco peregrinus	2 Cepphus grylle	4 Turdus philomelos	4 Loxia pytyopsittacus
3 Tetrao tetrix	2 Fratercula arctica	4ᵂ Turdus iliacus	4 Emberiza citrinella
3 Coturnix coturnix	4 Columba oenas	4 Turdus viscivorus	2 Emberiza hortulana
4 Porzana porzana	4 Columba palumbus	4 Locustella naevia	
1 Crex crex	3 Bubo bubo		

POLAND

3 Botaurus stellaris	3 Ardea purpurea	4ᵂ Cygnus cygnus	3 Anas querquedula
3 Ixobrychus minutus	3 Ciconia nigra	3 Anas strepera	3 Netta rufina
3 Nycticorax nycticorax	2 Ciconia ciconia	3 Anas acuta	4 Aythya ferina

Birds in Europe: Their Conservation Status

1 *Aythya nyroca*
4 *Pernis apivorus*
3 *Milvus migrans*
4 *Milvus milvus*
3 *Haliaeetus albicilla*
3 *Circaetus gallicus*
3 *Circus cyaneus*
4 *Circus pygargus*
3 *Aquila pomarina*
1 *Aquila clanga*
3 *Aquila chrysaetos*
3 *Hieraaetus pennatus*
3 *Pandion haliaetus*
3 *Falco tinnunculus*
3 *Falco peregrinus*
3 *Tetrao tetrix*
3 *Perdix perdix*
3 *Coturnix coturnix*
4 *Porzana porzana*
4 *Porzana parva*
1 *Crex crex*
3 *Grus grus*
3 *Burhinus oedicnemus*
3 *Charadrius alexandrinus*
3[w] *Calidris alpina*
4 *Philomachus pugnax*
3[w] *Lymnocryptes minimus*
2 *Gallinago media*
3[w] *Scolopax rusticola*
2 *Limosa limosa*

3[w] *Numenius arquata*
2 *Tringa totanus*
3 *Tringa glareola*
4 *Larus melanocephalus*
3 *Larus minutus*
2 *Larus canus*
4 *Larus fuscus*
2 *Sterna sandvicensis*
3 *Sterna albifrons*
3 *Chlidonias hybridus*
3 *Chlidonias niger*
4 *Columba oenas*
4 *Columba palumbus*
3 *Streptopelia turtur*
3 *Tyto alba*
3 *Bubo bubo*
3 *Athene noctua*
4 *Strix aluco*
3 *Asio flammeus*
2 *Caprimulgus europaeus*
3 *Alcedo atthis*
3 *Merops apiaster*
2 *Coracias garrulus*
3 *Jynx torquilla*
3 *Picus canus*
2 *Picus viridis*
4 *Dendrocopos syriacus*
4 *Dendrocopos medius*
3 *Picoides tridactylus*
3 *Galerida cristata*

2 *Lullula arborea*
3 *Alauda arvensis*
3 *Riparia riparia*
3 *Hirundo rustica*
3 *Anthus campestris*
4 *Anthus pratensis*
4 *Prunella modularis*
4 *Erithacus rubecula*
4 *Luscinia luscinia*
4 *Luscinia megarhynchos*
2 *Phoenicurus phoenicurus*
4 *Saxicola rubetra*
3 *Saxicola torquata*
3 *Monticola saxatilis*
4 *Turdus torquatus*
4 *Turdus merula*
4[w] *Turdus pilaris*
4 *Turdus philomelos*
4[w] *Turdus iliacus*
4 *Turdus viscivorus*
4 *Locustella naevia*
4 *Locustella fluviatilis*
4 *Locustella luscinioides*
1 *Acrocephalus paludicola*
4 *Acrocephalus schoenobaenus*
4 *Acrocephalus palustris*
4 *Acrocephalus scirpaceus*
4 *Hippolais icterina*
4 *Sylvia nisoria*

4 *Sylvia communis*
4 *Sylvia borin*
4 *Sylvia atricapilla*
4 *Phylloscopus bonelli*
4 *Phylloscopus sibilatrix*
4 *Regulus regulus*
4 *Regulus ignicapillus*
3 *Muscicapa striata*
4 *Ficedula albicollis*
4 *Ficedula hypoleuca*
4 *Parus cristatus*
4 *Parus caeruleus*
4 *Certhia brachydactyla*
3 *Lanius collurio*
2 *Lanius minor*
3 *Lanius excubitor*
2 *Lanius senator*
4 *Corvus monedula*
4 *Fringilla coelebs*
4 *Serinus serinus*
4 *Carduelis chloris*
4 *Carduelis spinus*
4 *Carduelis cannabina*
4 *Loxia pytyopsittacus*
4 *Emberiza citrinella*
2 *Emberiza hortulana*
4 *Miliaria calandra*

PORTUGAL

2 *Calonectris diomedea*
3 *Oceanodroma castro*
4 *Phalacrocorax aristotelis*
3 *Botaurus stellaris*
3 *Ixobrychus minutus*
3 *Nycticorax nycticorax*
3 *Ardeola ralloides*
3 *Ardea purpurea*
3 *Ciconia nigra*
2 *Ciconia ciconia*
2 *Platalea leucorodia*
3 *Anas strepera*
3 *Anas querquedula*
3 *Netta rufina*
4 *Aythya ferina*
4 *Pernis apivorus*
3 *Elanus caeruleus*
3 *Milvus migrans*
4 *Milvus milvus*
3 *Neophron percnopterus*
3 *Gyps fulvus*
3 *Circaetus gallicus*
3 *Circus cyaneus*
4 *Circus pygargus*
3 *Aquila chrysaetos*
3 *Hieraaetus pennatus*
3 *Hieraaetus fasciatus*
3 *Pandion haliaetus*
1 *Falco naumanni*
3 *Falco tinnunculus*

3 *Falco peregrinus*
2 *Alectoris rufa*
3 *Coturnix coturnix*
3 *Porzana pusilla*
3 *Porphyrio porphyrio*
2 *Tetrax tetrax*
1 *Otis tarda*
4/3 *Recurvirostra avosetta*
3 *Burhinus oedicnemus*
3 *Glareola pratincola*
3 *Charadrius alexandrinus*
2 *Tringa totanus*
4 *Larus fuscus*
3 *Sterna albifrons*
3 *Chlidonias hybridus*
3 *Pterocles orientalis*
3 *Pterocles alchata*
4 *Columba oenas*
4 *Columba palumbus*
3 *Streptopelia turtur*
3 *Tyto alba*
2 *Otus scops*
3 *Bubo bubo*
3 *Athene noctua*
4 *Strix aluco*
2 *Caprimulgus europaeus*
3 *Alcedo atthis*
3 *Merops apiaster*
2 *Coracias garrulus*
3 *Jynx torquilla*

2 *Picus viridis*
3 *Melanocorypha calandra*
3 *Calandrella brachydactyla*
3 *Calandrella rufescens*
3 *Galerida cristata*
3 *Galerida theklae*
2 *Lullula arborea*
3 *Alauda arvensis*
3 *Riparia riparia*
3 *Hirundo rustica*
3 *Anthus campestris*
4 *Prunella modularis*
4 *Erithacus rubecula*
4 *Luscinia megarhynchos*
2 *Phoenicurus phoenicurus*
4 *Saxicola rubetra*
3 *Saxicola torquata*
2 *Oenanthe hispanica*
3 *Oenanthe leucura*
3 *Monticola saxatilis*
3 *Monticola solitarius*
4 *Turdus merula*
4 *Turdus philomelos*
4 *Turdus viscivorus*
4 *Locustella luscinioides*
4 *Acrocephalus scirpaceus*
3 *Hippolais pallida*
4 *Hippolais polyglotta*
2 *Sylvia undata*

4 *Sylvia cantillans*
4 *Sylvia melanocephala*
3 *Sylvia hortensis*
4 *Sylvia communis*
4 *Sylvia borin*
4 *Sylvia atricapilla*
4 *Phylloscopus bonelli*
4 *Regulus ignicapillus*
3 *Muscicapa striata*
4 *Ficedula hypoleuca*
4 *Parus cristatus*
4 *Parus caeruleus*
4 *Certhia brachydactyla*
3 *Lanius collurio*
3 *Lanius excubitor*
2 *Lanius senator*
3 *Pyrrhocorax pyrrhocorax*
4 *Corvus monedula*
4 *Sturnus unicolor*
4 *Fringilla coelebs*
4 *Serinus serinus*
4 *Carduelis chloris*
4 *Carduelis cannabina*
4 *Emberiza citrinella*
4 *Emberiza cirlus*
3 *Emberiza cia*
2 *Emberiza hortulana*
4 *Miliaria calandra*

REPUBLIC OF IRELAND

3 Gavia stellata
2 Puffinus puffinus
2 Hydrobates pelagicus
3 Oceanodroma leucorhoa
2 Sula bassana
4 Phalacrocorax aristotelis
3 Anas strepera
3 Anas querquedula
4 Aythya ferina
3 Circus cyaneus
3 Falco tinnunculus
3 Falco peregrinus
3 Perdix perdix
3 Coturnix coturnix
1 Crex crex
4 Pluvialis apricaria
3ʷ Calidris alpina

3ʷ Scolopax rusticola
2 Limosa limosa
3ʷ Numenius arquata
2 Tringa totanus
2 Larus canus
4 Larus fuscus
4 Larus marinus
2 Sterna sandvicensis
3 Sterna dougallii
3 Sterna albifrons
4 Alca torda
2 Cepphus grylle
2 Fratercula arctica
4 Columba oenas
4 Columba palumbus
3 Tyto alba
2 Caprimulgus europaeus

3 Alcedo atthis
3 Alauda arvensis
3 Riparia riparia
3 Hirundo rustica
4 Anthus pratensis
4 Prunella modularis
4 Erithacus rubecula
2 Phoenicurus phoenicurus
4 Saxicola rubetra
4 Saxicola torquata
4 Turdus torquatus
4 Turdus merula
4 Turdus philomelos
4 Turdus viscivorus
4 Locustella naevia
4 Acrocephalus
     schoenobaenus

4 Acrocephalus scirpaceus
4 Sylvia communis
4 Sylvia borin
4 Sylvia atricapilla
4 Phylloscopus sibilatrix
4 Regulus regulus
3 Muscicapa striata
4 Ficedula hypoleuca
4 Parus caeruleus
3 Pyrrhocorax pyrrhocorax
4 Corvus monedula
4 Fringilla coelebs
4 Carduelis chloris
4 Carduelis spinus
4 Carduelis cannabina
4 Emberiza citrinella
4 Miliaria calandra

ROMANIA

2 Phalacrocorax pygmeus
3 Pelecanus onocrotalus
1 Pelecanus crispus
3 Botaurus stellaris
3 Ixobrychus minutus
3 Nycticorax nycticorax
3 Ardeola ralloides
3 Ardea purpurea
3 Ciconia nigra
2 Ciconia ciconia
3 Plegadis falcinellus
2 Platalea leucorodia
3 Tadorna ferruginea
3 Anas strepera
3 Anas acuta
3 Anas querquedula
3 Netta rufina
4 Aythya ferina
1 Aythya nyroca
4 Pernis apivorus
3 Milvus migrans
3 Milvus milvus
3 Haliaeetus albicilla
3 Neophron percnopterus
3 Circaetus gallicus
3 Circus macrourus
2 Accipiter brevipes
3 Aquila pomarina
1 Aquila clanga
1 Aquila heliaca
3 Aquila chrysaetos
3 Hieraaetus pennatus
1 Falco naumanni
3 Falco tinnunculus
3 Falco vespertinus
3 Falco cherrug
3 Falco peregrinus

3 Tetrao tetrix
2 Alectoris graeca
3 Perdix perdix
3 Coturnix coturnix
4 Porzana porzana
4 Porzana parva
3 Porzana pusilla
1 Crex crex
3 Grus grus
1 Otis tarda
4/3 Recurvirostra avosetta
3 Burhinus oedicnemus
3 Glareola pratincola
3 Glareola nordmanni
3 Charadrius alexandrinus
3ʷ Scolopax rusticola
2 Limosa limosa
3ʷ Numenius arquata
2 Tringa totanus
4 Larus melanocephalus
3 Larus minutus
3 Gelochelidon nilotica
2 Sterna sandvicensis
3 Sterna albifrons
3 Chlidonias hybridus
3 Chlidonias niger
4 Columba oenas
4 Columba palumbus
3 Streptopelia turtur
3 Tyto alba
2 Otus scops
3 Bubo bubo
3 Athene noctua
4 Strix aluco
3 Asio flammeus
2 Caprimulgus europaeus
3 Alcedo atthis

3 Merops apiaster
2 Coracias garrulus
3 Jynx torquilla
3 Picus canus
2 Picus viridis
4 Dendrocopos syriacus
4 Dendrocopos medius
3 Picoides tridactylus
3 Melanocorypha calandra
3 Calandrella
     brachydactyla
3 Galerida cristata
2 Lullula arborea
3 Alauda arvensis
3 Riparia riparia
3 Hirundo rustica
3 Anthus campestris
4 Anthus pratensis
4 Prunella modularis
4 Erithacus rubecula
4 Luscinia luscinia
4 Luscinia megarhynchos
2 Phoenicurus phoenicurus
4 Saxicola rubetra
3 Saxicola torquata
2 Oenanthe hispanica
3 Monticola saxatilis
4 Turdus torquatus
4 Turdus merula
4ʷ Turdus pilaris
4 Turdus philomelos
4 Turdus viscivorus
4 Locustella naevia
4 Locustella fluviatilis
4 Locustella luscinioides
4 Acrocephalus
     schoenobaenus

4 Acrocephalus palustris
4 Acrocephalus scirpaceus
3 Hippolais pallida
4 Hippolais icterina
4 Sylvia nisoria
4 Sylvia communis
4 Sylvia borin
4 Sylvia atricapilla
4 Phylloscopus sibilatrix
4 Regulus regulus
4 Regulus ignicapillus
3 Muscicapa striata
4 Ficedula albicollis
4 Ficedula hypoleuca
4 Parus lugubris
4 Parus cristatus
4 Parus caeruleus
4 Certhia brachydactyla
3 Lanius collurio
2 Lanius minor
3 Lanius excubitor
2 Lanius senator
4 Corvus monedula
4 Fringilla coelebs
4 Serinus serinus
4 Carduelis chloris
4 Carduelis spinus
4 Carduelis cannabina
4 Emberiza citrinella
4 Emberiza cirlus
3 Emberiza cia
2 Emberiza hortulana
2 Emberiza melanocephala
4 Miliaria calandra

RUSSIA

3 Gavia stellata
3 Gavia arctica
4 Phalacrocorax aristotelis

2 Phalacrocorax pygmeus
3 Pelecanus onocrotalus
1 Pelecanus crispus

3 Botaurus stellaris
3 Ixobrychus minutus
3 Nycticorax nycticorax

3 Ardeola ralloides
3 Ardea purpurea
3 Ciconia nigra

Birds in Europe: Their Conservation Status

2 Ciconia ciconia
3 Plegadis falcinellus
2 Platalea leucorodia
3ᵂ Cygnus columbianus
4ᵂ Cygnus cygnus
1 Anser erythropus
4/2 Branta leucopsis
3 Branta bernicla
3 Tadorna ferruginea
3 Anas strepera
3 Anas acuta
3 Anas querquedula
3 Netta rufina
4 Aythya ferina
1 Aythya nyroca
3ᵂ Aythya marila
1 Polysticta stelleri
3ᵂ Melanitta fusca
3 Mergus albellus
1 Oxyura leucocephala
4 Pernis apivorus
3 Milvus migrans
4 Milvus milvus
3 Haliaeetus albicilla
3 Gypaetus barbatus
3 Neophron percnopterus
3 Gyps fulvus
3 Aegypius monachus
3 Circaetus gallicus
3 Circus cyaneus
3 Circus macrourus
4 Circus pygargus
2 Accipiter brevipes
3 Buteo rufinus
3 Aquila pomarina
1 Aquila clanga
1 Aquila heliaca
3 Aquila chrysaetos
3 Hieraaetus pennatus
3 Pandion haliaetus
1 Falco naumanni
3 Falco tinnunculus
3 Falco vespertinus
3 Falco cherrug
3 Falco rusticolus
3 Falco peregrinus
3 Tetrao tetrix

2 Tetrao mlokosiewiczi
4 Tetraogallus caucasicus
3 Tetraogallus caspius
3 Alectoris chukar
3 Perdix perdix
4 Coturnix coturnix
4 Porzana porzana
4 Porzana parva
3 Porzana pusilla
1 Crex crex
3 Porphyrio porphyrio
3 Grus grus
2 Tetrax tetrax
1 Otis tarda
4/3 Recurvirostra avosetta
3 Burhinus oedicnemus
3 Glareola pratincola
3 Glareola nordmanni
3 Charadrius alexandrinus
3 Charadrius asiaticus
4 Pluvialis apricaria
1 Chettusia gregaria
4 Calidris maritima
3ᵂ Calidris alpina
3 Limicola falcinellus
4 Philomachus pugnax
3ᵂ Lymnocryptes minimus
2 Gallinago media
3ᵂ Scolopax rusticola
2 Limosa limosa
3ᵂ Limosa lapponica
4 Numenius phaeopus
3ᵂ Numenius arquata
2 Tringa totanus
3 Tringa glareola
4 Larus melanocephalus
3 Larus minutus
2 Larus canus
4 Larus fuscus
4 Larus marinus
3 Pagophila eburnea
3 Gelochelidon nilotica
3 Sterna caspia
2 Sterna sandvicensis
3 Sterna albifrons
3 Chlidonias hybridus
3 Chlidonias niger

4 Alca torda
2 Cepphus grylle
2 Fratercula arctica
3 Pterocles orientalis
4 Columba oenas
4 Columba palumbus
3 Streptopelia turtur
2 Otus scops
3 Bubo bubo
3 Nyctea scandiaca
3 Athene noctua
4 Strix aluco
3 Asio flammeus
2 Caprimulgus europaeus
3 Alcedo atthis
3 Merops apiaster
2 Coracias garrulus
3 Jynx torquilla
3 Picus canus
2 Picus viridis
4 Dendrocopos medius
3 Picoides tridactylus
3 Melanocorypha calandra
**4ᵂ Melanocorypha
   leucoptera**
**3 Melanocorypha
   yeltoniensis**
3 Calandrella
   brachydactyla
4 Calandrella rufescens
4 Galerida cristata
2 Lullula arborea
3 Alauda arvensis
3 Riparia riparia
3 Hirundo rustica
3 Anthus campestris
4 Anthus pratensis
4 Prunella modularis
3 Prunella atrogularis
4 Erithacus rubecula
4 Luscinia luscinia
4 Luscinia megarhynchos
2 Phoenicurus phoenicurus
**3 Phoenicurus
   erythrogaster**
4 Saxicola rubetra
3 Saxicola torquata

3 Oenanthe hispanica
3 Monticola saxatilis
3 Monticola solitarius
4 Turdus torquatus
4 Turdus merula
4ᵂ Turdus pilaris
3 Turdus philomelos
4ᵂ Turdus iliacus
4 Turdus viscivorus
4 Locustella naevia
4 Locustella fluviatilis
4 Locustella luscinioides
1 Acrocephalus paludicola
4 Acrocephalus
   schoenobaenus
4 Acrocephalus palustris
4 Acrocephalus scirpaceus
3 Hippolais pallida
4 Hippolais icterina
4 Sylvia nisoria
4 Sylvia communis
4 Sylvia borin
4 Sylvia atricapilla
4 Phylloscopus sibilatrix
4 Regulus regulus
3 Muscicapa striata
2 Ficedula semitorquata
4 Ficedula albicollis
4 Ficedula hypoleuca
4 Parus cristatus
4 Parus caeruleus
3 Lanius collurio
2 Lanius minor
3 Lanius excubitor
3 Perisoreus infaustus
4 Corvus monedula
4 Fringilla coelebs
4 Serinus serinus
4 Carduelis chloris
4 Carduelis spinus
4 Carduelis cannabina
4 Loxia pytyopsittacus
3 Carpodacus rubicilla
4 Emberiza citrinella
2 Emberiza hortulana
2 Emberiza melanocephala
4 Miliaria calandra

SLOVAKIA

2 Phalacrocorax pygmeus
3 Botaurus stellaris
3 Ixobrychus minutus
3 Nycticorax nycticorax
3 Ardeola ralloides
3 Ardea purpurea
3 Ciconia nigra
2 Ciconia ciconia
2 Platalea leucorodia
3 Anas strepera
3 Anas acuta
3 Anas querquedula
3 Netta rufina
4 Aythya ferina
1 Aythya nyroca
4 Pernis apivorus

3 Milvus migrans
4 Milvus milvus
3 Circaetus gallicus
4 Circus pygargus
3 Aquila pomarina
1 Aquila heliaca
3 Aquila chrysaetos
3 Hieraaetus pennatus
3 Falco tinnunculus
3 Falco vespertinus
3 Falco cherrug
3 Falco peregrinus
3 Tetrao tetrix
3 Perdix perdix
3 Coturnix coturnix
4 Porzana porzana

4 Porzana parva
1 Crex crex
1 Otis tarda
4/3 Recurvirostra avosetta
3 Burhinus oedicnemus
3ᵂ Scolopax rusticola
2 Limosa limosa
3ᵂ Numenius arquata
2 Tringa totanus
2 Larus canus
3 Chlidonias hybridus
3 Chlidonias niger
4 Columba oenas
4 Columba palumbus
3 Streptopelia turtur
3 Tyto alba

2 Otus scops
3 Bubo bubo
3 Athene noctua
4 Strix aluco
3 Asio flammeus
2 Caprimulgus europaeus
3 Alcedo atthis
3 Merops apiaster
2 Coracias garrulus
3 Jynx torquilla
3 Picus canus
2 Picus viridis
4 Dendrocopos syriacus
4 Dendrocopos medius
3 Picoides tridactylus

3 Calandrella
   brachydactyla
3 Galerida cristata
2 Lullula arborea
3 Alauda arvensis
3 Riparia riparia
3 Hirundo rustica
3 Anthus campestris
4 Anthus pratensis
4 Prunella modularis
4 Erithacus rubecula
4 Luscinia luscinia
4 Luscinia megarhynchos
2 Phoenicurus phoenicurus
4 Saxicola rubetra

3 Saxicola torquata
3 Monticola saxatilis
4 Turdus torquatus
4 Turdus merula
4ʷ Turdus pilaris
4 Turdus philomelos
4ʷ Turdus iliacus
4 Turdus viscivorus
4 Locustella naevia
4 Locustella fluviatilis
4 Locustella luscinioides
4 Acrocephalus
   schoenobaenus
4 Acrocephalus palustris
4 Acrocephalus scirpaceus

4 Hippolais icterina
4 Sylvia nisoria
4 Sylvia communis
4 Sylvia borin
4 Sylvia atricapilla
4 Phylloscopus sibilatrix
4 Regulus regulus
4 Regulus ignicapillus
3 Muscicapa striata
4 Ficedula albicollis
4 Ficedula hypoleuca
4 Parus cristatus
4 Parus caeruleus
4 Certhia brachydactyla
3 Lanius collurio

2 Lanius minor
3 Lanius excubitor
2 Lanius senator
4 Corvus monedula
4 Fringilla coelebs
4 Serinus serinus
4 Carduelis chloris
4 Carduelis spinus
4 Carduelis cannabina
4 Emberiza citrinella
3 Emberiza cia
2 Emberiza hortulana
4 Miliaria calandra

SLOVENIA

3 Botaurus stellaris
3 Ixobrychus minutus
3 Nycticorax nycticorax
3 Ciconia nigra
2 Ciconia ciconia
3 Anas querquedula
4 Aythya ferina
1 Aythya nyroca
4 Pernis apivorus
3 Milvus migrans
3 Haliaeetus albicilla
3 Circaetus gallicus
3 Aquila chrysaetos
1 Falco naumanni
3 Falco tinnunculus
3 Falco peregrinus
3 Tetrao tetrix
2 Alectoris graeca
3 Perdix perdix
3 Coturnix coturnix
4 Porzana porzana
4 Porzana parva
1 Crex crex
3 Charadrius alexandrinus
3ʷ Scolopax rusticola
3ʷ Numenius arquata
2 Tringa totanus

4 Larus cachinnans
3 Sterna albifrons
4 Columba oenas
4 Columba palumbus
3 Streptopelia turtur
3 Tyto alba
2 Otus scops
3 Bubo bubo
3 Athene noctua
4 Strix aluco
2 Caprimulgus europaeus
3 Alcedo atthis
3 Merops apiaster
2 Coracias garrulus
3 Jynx torquilla
3 Picus canus
2 Picus viridis
4 Dendrocopos syriacus
4 Dendrocopos medius
3 Picoides tridactylus
3 Galerida cristata
2 Lullula arborea
3 Alauda arvensis
3 Riparia riparia
3 Hirundo rustica
3 Anthus campestris
4 Prunella modularis

4 Erithacus rubecula
4 Luscinia megarhynchos
2 Phoenicurus phoenicurus
3 Saxicola rubetra
3 Saxicola torquata
3 Monticola saxatilis
3 Monticola solitarius
4 Turdus torquatus
4 Turdus merula
4ʷ Turdus pilaris
4 Turdus philomelos
4 Turdus viscivorus
4 Locustella naevia
4 Locustella fluviatilis
4 Locustella luscinioides
4 Acrocephalus
   schoenobaenus
4 Acrocephalus palustris
4 Acrocephalus scirpaceus
4 Hippolais icterina
4 Hippolais polyglotta
4 Sylvia cantillans
4 Sylvia melanocephala
4 Sylvia nisoria
4 Sylvia communis
4 Sylvia borin
4 Sylvia atricapilla

4 Phylloscopus bonelli
4 Phylloscopus sibilatrix
4 Regulus regulus
4 Regulus ignicapillus
3 Muscicapa striata
4 Ficedula albicollis
4 Parus lugubris
4 Parus cristatus
4 Parus caeruleus
4 Certhia brachydactyla
3 Lanius collurio
2 Lanius minor
4 Corvus monedula
4 Fringilla coelebs
4 Serinus serinus
4 Serinus citrinella
4 Carduelis chloris
4 Carduelis spinus
4 Carduelis cannabina
4 Emberiza citrinella
4 Emberiza cirlus
3 Emberiza cia
2 Emberiza hortulāna
4 Miliaria calandra

SPAIN

2 Calonectris diomedea
4 Puffinus yelkouan
2 Hydrobates pelagicus
4 Phalacrocorax aristotelis
3 Botaurus stellaris
3 Ixobrychus minutus
3 Nycticorax nycticorax
3 Ardeola ralloides
3 Ardea purpurea
3 Ciconia nigra
2 Ciconia ciconia
3 Plegadis falcinellus
2 Platalea leucorodia
3 Phoenicopterus ruber
3 Anas strepera
3 Anas acuta
3 Anas querquedula

1 Marmaronetta
   angustirostris
3 Netta rufina
4 Aythya ferina
1 Aythya nyroca
1 Oxyura leucocephala
4 Pernis apivorus
3 Elanus caeruleus
3 Milvus migrans
4 Milvus milvus
3 Gypaetus barbatus
3 Neophron percnopterus
3 Gyps fulvus
3 Aegypius monachus
3 Circaetus gallicus
3 Circus cyaneus
4 Circus pygargus

1 **Aquila adalberti**
3 Aquila chrysaetos
3 Hieraaetus pennatus
3 Hieraaetus fasciatus
3 Pandion haliaetus
1 Falco naumanni
3 Falco tinnunculus
2 Falco eleonorae
3 Falco peregrinus
2 Alectoris rufa
3 Alectoris barbara
3 Perdix perdix
3 Coturnix coturnix
3 **Turnix sylvatica**
4 Porzana porzana
4 Porzana parva
3 Porzana pusilla

1 Crex crex
3 Porphyrio porphyrio
3 **Fulica cristata**
2 Tetrax tetrax
1 Otis tarda
4/3 Recurvirostra avosetta
3 Burhinus oedicnemus
3 Glareola pratincola
3 Charadrius alexandrinus
3ʷ Scolopax rusticola
2 Limosa limosa
3ʷ Numenius arquata
2 Tringa totanus
4 Larus melanocephalus
1 Larus audouinii
4 Larus fuscus
3 Gelochelidon nilotica

Birds in Europe: Their Conservation Status

3 *Sterna caspia*
2 *Sterna sandvicensis*
3 *Sterna dougallii*
3 *Sterna albifrons*
3 *Chlidonias hybridus*
3 *Chlidonias niger*
3 *Pterocles orientalis*
3 *Pterocles alchata*
4 *Columba oenas*
4 *Columba palumbus*
3 *Streptopelia turtur*
3 *Tyto alba*
2 *Otus scops*
3 *Bubo bubo*
3 *Athene noctua*
4 *Strix aluco*
3 *Asio flammeus*
2 *Caprimulgus europaeus*
3 *Alcedo atthis*
3 *Merops apiaster*
3 *Coracias garrulus*
3 *Jynx torquilla*
2 *Picus viridis*
4 *Dendrocopos medius*

3 **Chersophilus duponti**
3 *Melanocorypha calandra*
3 *Calandrella brachydactyla*
3 *Calandrella rufescens*
3 *Galerida cristata*
3 *Galerida theklae*
2 *Lullula arborea*
3 *Alauda arvensis*
3 *Riparia riparia*
3 *Hirundo rustica*
3 *Anthus campestris*
3 *Prunella modularis*
4 *Erithacus rubecula*
4 *Luscinia megarhynchos*
2 *Phoenicurus phoenicurus*
4 *Saxicola rubetra*
3 *Saxicola torquata*
2 *Oenanthe hispanica*
3 *Oenanthe leucura*
3 *Monticola saxatilis*
3 *Monticola solitarius*
4 *Turdus torquatus*
4 *Turdus merula*

4 *Turdus philomelos*
4 *Turdus viscivorus*
4 *Locustella naevia*
4 *Locustella luscinioides*
4 *Acrocephalus schoenobaenus*
4 *Acrocephalus palustris*
4 *Acrocephalus scirpaceus*
3 *Hippolais pallida*
4 *Hippolais polyglotta*
4 *Sylvia sarda*
2 *Sylvia undata*
4 *Sylvia cantillans*
4 *Sylvia melanocephala*
3 *Sylvia hortensis*
4 *Sylvia communis*
4 *Sylvia borin*
4 *Sylvia atricapilla*
4 *Phylloscopus bonelli*
4 *Phylloscopus sibilatrix*
4 *Regulus regulus*
4 *Regulus ignicapillus*
3 *Muscicapa striata*
4 *Ficedula hypoleuca*

4 *Parus cristatus*
4 *Parus caeruleus*
4 *Certhia brachydactyla*
3 *Lanius collurio*
2 *Lanius minor*
3 *Lanius excubitor*
2 *Lanius senator*
3 *Pyrrhocorax pyrrhocorax*
4 *Corvus monedula*
4 *Sturnus unicolor*
4 *Fringilla coelebs*
4 *Serinus serinus*
4 *Serinus citrinella*
4 *Carduelis chloris*
4 *Carduelis spinus*
4 *Carduelis cannabina*
3 *Bucanetes githagineus*
4 *Emberiza citrinella*
4 *Emberiza cirlus*
3 *Emberiza cia*
2 *Emberiza hortulana*
4 *Miliaria calandra*

SVALBARD

3 *Gavia stellata*
4 *Anser brachyrhynchus*
4/2 *Branta leucopsis*
3 *Branta bernicla*

4 *Pluvialis apricaria*
3ᵂ *Calidris canutus*
4 *Calidris maritima*
3ᵂ *Calidris alpina*

4 *Stercorarius skua*
3 *Pagophila eburnea*
4 *Alca torda*
2 *Cepphus grylle*

2 *Fratercula arctica*

SWEDEN

3 *Gavia stellata*
3 *Gavia arctica*
3 *Botaurus stellaris*
4ᵂ *Cygnus cygnus*
1 *Anser erythropus*
4/2 *Branta leucopsis*
3 *Anas strepera*
3 *Anas acuta*
3 *Anas querquedula*
4 *Aythya ferina*
3ᵂ *Aythya marila*
3ᵂ *Melanitta fusca*
3 *Mergus albellus*
4 *Pernis apivorus*
3 *Milvus migrans*
4 *Milvus milvus*
3 *Haliaeetus albicilla*
3 *Circus cyaneus*
4 *Circus pygargus*
3 *Aquila chrysaetos*
3 *Pandion haliaetus*
3 *Falco tinnunculus*
3 *Falco rusticolus*
3 *Falco peregrinus*
3 *Tetrao tetrix*
3 *Perdix perdix*
3 *Coturnix coturnix*
4 *Porzana porzana*
4 *Porzana parva*
1 *Crex crex*

3 *Grus grus*
4/3 *Recurvirostra avosetta*
3 *Charadrius alexandrinus*
4 *Pluvialis apricaria*
4 *Calidris maritima*
3ᵂ *Calidris alpina*
3 *Limicola falcinellus*
4 *Philomachus pugnax*
3ᵂ *Lymnocryptes minimus*
2 *Gallinago media*
3ᵂ *Scolopax rusticola*
2 *Limosa limosa*
3ᵂ *Limosa lapponica*
4 *Numenius phaeopus*
3ᵂ *Numenius arquata*
2 *Tringa totanus*
3 *Tringa glareola*
3 *Larus minutus*
2 *Larus canus*
4 *Larus fuscus*
4 *Larus marinus*
3 *Sterna caspia*
2 *Sterna sandvicensis*
3 *Sterna albifrons*
3 *Chlidonias niger*
4 *Alca torda*
2 *Cepphus grylle*
4 *Columba oenas*
4 *Columba palumbus*
3 *Bubo bubo*

3 *Nyctea scandiaca*
4 *Strix aluco*
3 *Asio flammeus*
2 *Caprimulgus europaeus*
3 *Alcedo atthis*
3 *Jynx torquilla*
3 *Picus canus*
2 *Picus viridis*
3 *Picoides tridactylus*
3 *Galerida cristata*
2 *Lullula arborea*
3 *Alauda arvensis*
3 *Riparia riparia*
3 *Hirundo rustica*
3 *Anthus campestris*
4 *Anthus pratensis*
4 *Prunella modularis*
4 *Erithacus rubecula*
4 *Luscinia luscinia*
2 *Phoenicurus phoenicurus*
4 *Saxicola rubetra*
4 *Turdus torquatus*
4 *Turdus merula*
4ᵂ *Turdus pilaris*
4 *Turdus philomelos*
4ᵂ *Turdus iliacus*
4 *Turdus viscivorus*
4 *Locustella naevia*
4 *Locustella fluviatilis*

4 *Acrocephalus schoenobaenus*
4 *Acrocephalus palustris*
4 *Acrocephalus scirpaceus*
4 *Hippolais icterina*
4 *Sylvia nisoria*
4 *Sylvia communis*
4 *Sylvia borin*
4 *Sylvia atricapilla*
4 *Phylloscopus sibilatrix*
4 *Regulus regulus*
3 *Muscicapa striata*
4 *Ficedula albicollis*
4 *Ficedula hypoleuca*
4 *Parus cristatus*
4 *Parus caeruleus*
3 *Lanius collurio*
3 *Lanius excubitor*
3 *Perisoreus infaustus*
4 *Corvus monedula*
4 *Fringilla coelebs*
4 *Serinus serinus*
4 *Carduelis chloris*
4 *Carduelis spinus*
4 *Carduelis cannabina*
4 *Loxia pytyopsittacus*
4 *Emberiza citrinella*
2 *Emberiza hortulana*
4 *Miliaria calandra*

SWITZERLAND

3 Ixobrychus minutus
3 Ardea purpurea
2 Ciconia ciconia
3 Anas strepera
3 Anas acuta
3 Anas querquedula
3 Netta rufina
4 Aythya ferina
1 Aythya nyroca
4 Pernis apivorus
3 Milvus migrans
4 Milvus milvus
4 Circus pygargus
3 Aquila chrysaetos
3 Falco tinnunculus
3 Falco peregrinus
3 Tetrao tetrix
2 Alectoris graeca
3 Perdix perdix
3 Coturnix coturnix
4 Porzana porzana
4 Porzana parva
3 Porzana pusilla
1 Crex crex
3ᵂ Scolopax rusticola
3ᵂ Numenius arquata

4 Larus melanocephalus
2 Larus canus
4 Columba oenas
4 Columba palumbus
3 Streptopelia turtur
3 Tyto alba
2 Otus scops
3 Bubo bubo
3 Athene noctua
4 Strix aluco
2 Caprimulgus europaeus
3 Alcedo atthis
3 Merops apiaster
3 Jynx torquilla
3 Picus canus
2 Picus viridis
4 Dendrocopos medius
3 Picoides tridactylus
3 Calandrella brachydactyla
2 Lullula arborea
3 Alauda arvensis
3 Riparia riparia
3 Hirundo rustica
3 Anthus campestris
4 Anthus pratensis

4 Prunella modularis
4 Erithacus rubecula
4 Luscinia megarhynchos
2 Phoenicurus phoenicurus
4 Saxicola rubetra
3 Saxicola torquata
3 Monticola saxatilis
3 Monticola solitarius
4 Turdus torquatus
4 Turdus merula
4ᵂ Turdus pilaris
4 Turdus philomelos
4 Turdus viscivorus
4 Locustella naevia
4 Locustella luscinioides
4 Acrocephalus schoenobaenus
4 Acrocephalus palustris
4 Acrocephalus scirpaceus
4 Hippolais icterina
4 Hippolais polyglotta
3 Sylvia hortensis
4 Sylvia nisoria
4 Sylvia communis
4 Sylvia borin
4 Sylvia atricapilla

4 Phylloscopus bonelli
4 Phylloscopus sibilatrix
4 Regulus regulus
4 Regulus ignicapillus
3 Muscicapa striata
4 Ficedula albicollis
4 Ficedula hypoleuca
4 Parus cristatus
4 Parus caeruleus
4 Certhia brachydactyla
3 Lanius collurio
2 Lanius senator
3 Pyrrhocorax pyrrhocorax
4 Corvus monedula
4 Fringilla coelebs
4 Serinus serinus
4 Serinus citrinella
4 Carduelis chloris
4 Carduelis spinus
4 Carduelis cannabina
4 Emberiza citrinella
4 Emberiza cirlus
3 Emberiza cia
2 Emberiza hortulana
4 Miliaria calandra

TURKEY

4 Puffinus yelkouan
2 Phalacrocorax pygmeus
3 Pelecanus onocrotalus
1 Pelecanus crispus
1 Botaurus stellaris
3 Ixobrychus minutus
3 Nycticorax nycticorax
3 Ardeola ralloides
3 Ardea purpurea
3 Ciconia nigra
2 Ciconia ciconia
3 Plegadis falcinellus
3 Platalea leucorodia
3 Phoenicopterus ruber
3 Tadorna ferruginea
3 Anas strepera
3 Anas acuta
3 Anas querquedula
1 Marmaronetta angustirostris
3 Netta rufina
4 Aythya ferina
1 Aythya nyroca
3ᵂ Melanitta fusca
1 Oxyura leucocephala
4 Pernis apivorus
3 Milvus migrans
3 Haliaeetus albicilla
3 Gypaetus barbatus
3 Neophron percnopterus
3 Gyps fulvus
3 Aegypius monachus
3 Circaetus gallicus
4 Circus pygargus
2 Accipiter brevipes

3 Buteo rufinus
3 Aquila pomarina
1 Aquila heliaca
3 Aquila chrysaetos
3 Hieraaetus pennatus
3 Hieraaetus fasciatus
3 Pandion haliaetus
1 Falco naumanni
3 Falco tinnunculus
2 Falco eleonorae
3 Falco biarmicus
3 Falco cherrug
3 Falco peregrinus
2 Tetrao mlokosiewiczi
3 Tetraogallus caspius
3 Alectoris chukar
3 Francolinus francolinus
3 Perdix perdix
3 Coturnix coturnix
4 Porzana porzana
4 Porzana parva
3 Porzana pusilla
1 Crex crex
3 Porphyrio porphyrio
3 Grus grus
2 Tetrax tetrax
1 Otis tarda
4/3 Recurvirostra avosetta
3 Burhinus oedicnemus
3 Cursorius cursor
3 Glareola pratincola
3 Charadrius alexandrinus
3 Hoplopterus spinosus
2 Tringa totanus
4 Larus melanocephalus

1 Larus audouinii
3 Gelochelidon nilotica
3 Sterna caspia
3 Sterna albifrons
3 Chlidonias hybridus
3 Chlidonias niger
3 Pterocles orientalis
3 Pterocles alchata
4 Columba oenas
4 Columba palumbus
3 Streptopelia turtur
3 Tyto alba
2 Otus scops
3 Bubo bubo
3 Athene noctua
4 Strix aluco
3 Asio flammeus
2 Caprimulgus europaeus
3 Alcedo atthis
3 Merops apiaster
2 Coracias garrulus
3 Jynx torquilla
3 Picus canus
2 Picus viridis
4 Dendrocopos syriacus
4 Dendrocopos medius
3 Melanocorypha calandra
3 Calandrella brachydactyla
3 Calandrella rufescens
3 Galerida cristata
2 Lullula arborea
3 Alauda arvensis
3 Riparia riparia
3 Hirundo rustica

3 Anthus campestris
4 Prunella modularis
3 Prunella ocularis
4 Erithacus rubecula
4 Luscinia megarhynchos
2 Phoenicurus phoenicurus
4 Saxicola rubetra
3 Saxicola torquata
2 Oenanthe hispanica
3 Monticola saxatilis
3 Monticola solitarius
4 Turdus torquatus
4 Turdus merula
4 Turdus philomelos
4 Turdus viscivorus
4 Locustella luscinioides
4 Acrocephalus schoenobaenus
4 Acrocephalus palustris
4 Acrocephalus scirpaceus
3 Hippolais pallida
2 Hippolais olivetorum
4 Hippolais icterina
4 Sylvia cantillans
4 Sylvia melanocephala
4 Sylvia rueppelli
3 Sylvia hortensis
4 Sylvia nisoria
4 Sylvia communis
4 Sylvia borin
4 Sylvia atricapilla
4 Phylloscopus bonelli
4 Phylloscopus sibilatrix
4 Regulus regulus
4 Regulus ignicapillus

3 *Muscicapa striata*
2 *Ficedula semitorquata*
4 *Parus lugubris*
4 *Parus caeruleus*
4 *Sitta krueperi*
4 *Sitta neumayer*
4 *Certhia brachydactyla*

3 *Lanius collurio*
2 *Lanius minor*
2 *Lanius senator*
2 *Lanius nubicus*
3 *Pyrrhocorax pyrrhocorax*
4 *Corvus monedula*
4 *Fringilla coelebs*

4 *Serinus serinus*
4 *Carduelis chloris*
4 *Carduelis spinus*
4 *Carduelis cannabina*
3 *Bucanetes githagineus*
4 *Emberiza citrinella*
4 *Emberiza cirlus*

3 *Emberiza cia*
2 *Emberiza cineracea*
2 *Emberiza hortulana*
4 *Emberiza caesia*
2 *Emberiza melanocephala*
4 *Miliaria calandra*

UKRAINE

4 *Phalacrocorax aristotelis*
2 *Phalacrocorax pygmeus*
1 *Pelecanus crispus*
3 *Botaurus stellaris*
3 *Ixobrychus minutus*
3 *Nycticorax nycticorax*
3 *Ardeola ralloides*
3 *Ardea purpurea*
3 *Ciconia nigra*
2 *Ciconia ciconia*
3 *Plegadis falcinellus*
2 *Platalea leucorodia*
3 *Tadorna ferruginea*
3 *Anas strepera*
3 *Anas acuta*
3 *Anas querquedula*
3 *Netta rufina*
4 *Aythya ferina*
1 *Aythya nyroca*
3ʷ *Aythya marila*
4 *Pernis apivorus*
3 *Milvus migrans*
4 *Milvus milvus*
3 *Haliaeetus albicilla*
3 *Neophron percnopterus*
3 *Gyps fulvus*
3 *Aegypius monachus*
3 *Circaetus gallicus*
3 *Circus cyaneus*
3 *Circus macrourus*
4 *Circus pygargus*
2 *Accipiter brevipes*
3 *Buteo rufinus*
3 *Aquila pomarina*
1 *Aquila clanga*
1 *Aquila heliaca*
3 *Aquila chrysaetos*
3 *Hieraaetus pennatus*
3 *Pandion haliaetus*

1 *Falco naumanni*
3 *Falco tinnunculus*
3 *Falco vespertinus*
3 *Falco cherrug*
3 *Falco peregrinus*
3 *Tetrao tetrix*
3 *Perdix perdix*
3 *Coturnix coturnix*
4 *Porzana porzana*
4 *Porzana parva*
3 *Porzana pusilla*
1 *Crex crex*
3 *Grus grus*
2 *Tetrax tetrax*
1 *Otis tarda*
4/3 *Recurvirostra avosetta*
3 *Burhinus oedicnemus*
3 *Glareola pratincola*
3 *Glareola nordmanni*
3 *Charadrius alexandrinus*
4 *Philomachus pugnax*
2 *Gallinago media*
3ʷ *Scolopax rusticola*
2 *Limosa limosa*
3ʷ *Numenius arquata*
2 *Tringa totanus*
3 *Tringa glareola*
4 *Larus melanocephalus*
3 *Larus minutus*
3 *Gelochelidon nilotica*
3 *Sterna caspia*
2 *Sterna sandvicensis*
3 *Sterna albifrons*
3 *Chlidonias hybridus*
3 *Chlidonias niger*
4 *Columba oenas*
4 *Columba palumbus*
3 *Streptopelia turtur*
3 *Tyto alba*

2 *Otus scops*
3 *Bubo bubo*
3 *Athene noctua*
4 *Strix aluco*
3 *Asio flammeus*
2 *Caprimulgus europaeus*
3 *Alcedo atthis*
3 *Merops apiaster*
2 *Coracias garrulus*
3 *Jynx torquilla*
3 *Picus canus*
2 *Picus viridis*
4 *Dendrocopos syriacus*
4 *Dendrocopos medius*
3 *Picoides tridactylus*
3 *Melanocorypha calandra*
3 *Calandrella
    brachydactyla*
3 *Calandrella rufescens*
3 *Galerida cristata*
2 *Lullula arborea*
3 *Alauda arvensis*
3 *Riparia riparia*
3 *Hirundo rustica*
3 *Anthus campestris*
4 *Anthus pratensis*
4 *Prunella modularis*
4 *Erithacus rubecula*
4 *Luscinia luscinia*
4 *Luscinia megarhynchos*
2 *Phoenicurus phoenicurus*
4 *Saxicola rubetra*
3 *Saxicola torquata*
2 *Monticola saxatilis*
4 *Turdus torquatus*
4 *Turdus merula*
4ʷ *Turdus pilaris*
4 *Turdus philomelos*
4ʷ *Turdus iliacus*

4 *Turdus viscivorus*
4 *Locustella naevia*
4 *Locustella fluviatilis*
4 *Locustella luscinioides*
1 *Acrocephalus paludicola*
4 *Acrocephalus
    schoenobaenus*
4 *Acrocephalus palustris*
4 *Acrocephalus scirpaceus*
4 *Hippolais icterina*
4 *Sylvia nisoria*
4 *Sylvia communis*
4 *Sylvia borin*
4 *Sylvia atricapilla*
4 *Phylloscopus sibilatrix*
4 *Regulus regulus*
4 *Regulus ignicapillus*
3 *Muscicapa striata*
4 *Ficedula albicollis*
4 *Ficedula hypoleuca*
4 *Parus cristatus*
4 *Parus caeruleus*
4 *Certhia brachydactyla*
3 *Lanius collurio*
2 *Lanius minor*
3 *Lanius excubitor*
2 *Lanius senator*
4 *Corvus monedula*
4 *Fringilla coelebs*
4 *Serinus serinus*
4 *Carduelis chloris*
4 *Carduelis spinus*
4 *Carduelis cannabina*
4 *Emberiza citrinella*
3 *Emberiza cia*
2 *Emberiza hortulana*
2 *Emberiza melanocephala*
4 *Miliaria calandra*

UNITED KINGDOM

3 *Gavia stellata*
3 *Gavia arctica*
2 *Puffinus puffinus*
2 *Hydrobates pelagicus*
3 *Oceanodroma leucorhoa*
2 *Sula bassana*
4 *Phalacrocorax aristotelis*
3 *Botaurus stellaris*
4ʷ *Cygnus cygnus*
3 *Anas strepera*
3 *Anas acuta*
3 *Anas querquedula*
3 *Netta rufina*

4 *Aythya ferina*
3ʷ *Aythya marila*
4 *Pernis apivorus*
4 *Milvus milvus*
3 *Haliaeetus albicilla*
3 *Circus cyaneus*
4 *Circus pygargus*
3 *Aquila chrysaetos*
3 *Pandion haliaetus*
3 *Falco tinnunculus*
3 *Falco peregrinus*
3 *Tetrao tetrix*
2 *Alectoris rufa*

3 *Perdix perdix*
3 *Coturnix coturnix*
4 *Porzana porzana*
1 *Crex crex*
4/3 *Recurvirostra avosetta*
3 *Burhinus oedicnemus*
3 *Pluvialis apricaria*
4 *Calidris maritima*
3ʷ *Calidris alpina*
4 *Philomachus pugnax*
3ʷ *Scolopax rusticola*
2 *Limosa limosa*
4 *Numenius phaeopus*

3ʷ *Numenius arquata*
2 *Tringa totanus*
3 *Tringa glareola*
4 *Stercorarius skua*
4 *Larus melanocephalus*
2 *Larus canus*
4 *Larus fuscus*
4 *Larus marinus*
2 *Sterna sandvicensis*
3 *Sterna dougallii*
3 *Sterna albifrons*
4 *Alca torda*
2 *Cepphus grylle*

2 *Fratercula arctica*
4 *Columba oenas*
4 *Columba palumbus*
3 *Streptopelia turtur*
3 *Tyto alba*
3 *Athene noctua*
4 *Strix aluco*
3 *Asio flammeus*
2 *Caprimulgus europaeus*
3 *Alcedo atthis*
3 *Jynx torquilla*
2 *Picus viridis*
2 *Lullula arborea*
3 *Alauda arvensis*
3 *Riparia riparia*

3 *Hirundo rustica*
4 *Anthus pratensis*
4 *Prunella modularis*
4 *Erithacus rubecula*
4 *Luscinia megarhynchos*
2 *Phoenicurus phoenicurus*
4 *Saxicola rubetra*
3 *Saxicola torquata*
4 *Turdus torquatus*
4 *Turdus merula*
4ʷ *Turdus pilaris*
4 *Turdus philomelos*
4ʷ *Turdus iliacus*
4 *Turdus viscivorus*
4 *Locustella naevia*

4 *Locustella luscinioides*
4 *Acrocephalus schoenobaenus*
4 *Acrocephalus palustris*
4 *Acrocephalus scirpaceus*
2 *Sylvia undata*
4 *Sylvia communis*
4 *Sylvia borin*
4 *Sylvia atricapilla*
4 *Phylloscopus sibilatrix*
4 *Regulus regulus*
4 *Regulus ignicapillus*
3 *Muscicapa striata*
4 *Ficedula hypoleuca*
4 *Parus cristatus*

4 *Parus caeruleus*
3 *Lanius collurio*
3 *Pyrrhocorax pyrrhocorax*
4 *Corvus monedula*
4 *Fringilla coelebs*
4 *Serinus serinus*
4 *Carduelis chloris*
4 *Carduelis spinus*
4 *Carduelis cannabina*
1 **Loxia scotica**
4 *Emberiza citrinella*
4 *Emberiza cirlus*
4 *Miliaria calandra*

Species with particularly poorly monitored breeding populations in Europe

For definitions of SPEC category and European Threat Status, see Appendix 1 (p. 470). Species of global conservation concern (SPEC category 1) are shown in **bold**.

[1] Minimum percentage of the breeding population estimate that is based on non-quantitative data (i.e. verification code 1) or has no data quality code provided.

[2] Minimum percentage of the breeding population that has population size trend estimates based on non-quan-

titative data (i.e. verification code 1), or has no trend quality code provided, or no trend estimates.

No data were collected for the Caucasus region of Armenia, Azerbaijan, Georgia and Russia, or for Bosnia and Herzegovina, Yugoslavia and Former Yugoslav Republic of Macedonia; populations in these regions are thus not taken into account here.

	SPEC category	European Threat Status	% with poor population size data [1]	% with poor population trend data [2]
Great Northern Diver *Gavia immer*	—	(S)	40	100
White-billed Diver *Gavia adamsii*	—	(S)	100	100
Slavonian Grebe *Podiceps auritus*	—	(S)	0	65
Cory's Shearwater *Calonectris diomedea*	2	(V)	4	72
Manx Shearwater *Puffinus puffinus*	2	(L)	9	89
Storm Petrel *Hydrobates pelagicus*	2	(L)	61	80
Leach's Storm-petrel *Oceanodroma leucorhoa*	3	(L)	11	100
Bittern *Botaurus stellaris*	3	(V)	56	63
Little Bittern *Ixobrychus minutus*	3	(V)	57	63
Long-legged Buzzard *Buteo rufinus*	3	(E)	49	51
Lesser Kestrel *Falco naumanni*	**1**	**(V)**	**8**	**53**
Lanner *Falco biarmicus*	3	(E)	20	100
Caucasian Black Grouse *Tetrao mlokosiewiczi*	2	Ins	100	100
Capercaillie *Tetrao urogallus*	—	(S)	1	70
Caspian Snowcock *Tetraogallus caspius*	3	Ins	100	100
Rock Partridge *Alectoris graeca*	2	(V)	53	53
Barbary Partridge *Alectoris barbara*	3	(E)	82	81
See-see *Ammoperdix griseogularis*	—	(S)	100	100
Water Rail *Rallus aquaticus*	—	(S)	40	52
Little Crake *Porzana parva*	4	(S)	78	65
Houbara Bustard *Chlamydotis undulata*	3	(E)	0	100
Little Ringed Plover *Charadrius dubius*	—	(S)	53	58
Greater Sand Plover *Charadrius leschenaultii*	3	(E)	100	100
Caspian Plover *Charadrius asiaticus*	3	(V)	100	100
Dotterel *Charadrius morinellus*	—	(S)	51	51
Grey Plover *Pluvialis squatarola*	—	(S)	100	100
Spur-winged Plover *Hoplopterus spinosus*	3	(E)	97	100
White-tailed Plover *Chettusia leucura*	—	(S)	100	100
Lapwing *Vanellus vanellus*	—	(S)	51	50
Little Stint *Calidris minuta*	—	(S)	100	100
Temminck's Stint *Calidris temminckii*	—	(S)	99	99
Purple Sandpiper *Calidris maritima*	4	(S)	20	60
Broad-billed Sandpiper *Limicola falcinellus*	3	(V)	74	74
Ruff *Philomachus pugnax*	4	(S)	91	91
Jack Snipe *Lymnocryptes minimus*	3 [w]	(V)[w]	50	50
Snipe *Gallinago gallinago*	—	(S)	57	69
Great Snipe *Gallinago media*	2	(V)	87	0
Whimbrel *Numenius phaeopus*	4	(S)	7	64
Marsh Sandpiper *Tringa stagnatilis*	—	(S)	100	100
Green Sandpiper *Tringa ochropus*	—	(S)	43	51
Terek Sandpiper *Xenus cinereus*	—	(S)	99	99
Red-necked Phalarope *Phalaropus lobatus*	—	(S)	66	72
Grey Phalarope *Phalaropus fulicarius*	—	(S)	94	94
Pomarine Skua *Stercorarius pomarinus*	—	(S)	100	100
Arctic Skua *Stercorarius parasiticus*	—	(S)	43	64
Long-tailed Skua *Stercorarius longicaudus*	—	(S)	92	80
Slender-billed Gull *Larus genei*	—	(S)	0	71
Armenian Gull *Larus armenicus*	—	(S)	100	100
Iceland Gull *Larus glaucoides*	—	(S)	0	100

	SPEC category	European Threat Status	% with poor population size data [1]	% with poor population trend data [2]
Ivory Gull *Pagophila eburnea*	3	(E)	82	100
Gull-billed Tern *Gelochelidon nilotica*	3	(E)	30	56
Caspian Tern *Sterna caspia*	3	(E)	1	64
Little Auk *Alle alle*	—	(S)	0	97
Collared Dove *Streptopelia decaocto*	—	(S)	58	43
Rufous Turtle Dove *Streptopelia orientalis*	—	(S)	100	0
Laughing Dove *Streptopelia senegalensis*	—	(S)	100	0
Oriental Cuckoo *Cuculus saturatus*	—	(S)	100	100
Striated Scops Owl *Otus brucei*	—	(S)	100	100
Scops Owl *Otus scops*	2	(D)	54	59
Hawk Owl *Surnia ulula*	—	(S)	74	78
Pygmy Owl *Glaucidium passerinum*	—	(S)	40	76
Ural Owl *Strix uralensis*	—	(S)	92	93
Short-eared Owl *Asio flammeus*	3	(V)	53	68
Tengmalm's Owl *Aegolius funereus*	—	(S)	35	62
Nightjar *Caprimulgus europaeus*	2	(D)	44	62
Pallid Swift *Apus pallidus*	—	(S)	59	50
Alpine Swift *Apus melba*	—	(S)	59	74
Little Swift *Apus affinis*	—	(S)	100	100
White-breasted Kingfisher *Halcyon smyrnensis*	—	(S)	100	100
Pied Kingfisher *Ceryle rudis*	—	(S)	100	100
Blue-cheeked Bee-eater *Merops superciliosus*	—	(S)	100	100
Roller *Coracias garrulus*	2	(D)	65	58
Syrian Woodpecker *Dendrocopos syriacus*	4	(S)	89	25
Desert Lark *Ammomanes deserti*	—	(S)	100	100
Calandra Lark *Melanocorypha calandra*	3	(D)	52	52
Bimaculated Lark *Melanocorypha bimaculata*	—	(S)	100	100
White-winged Lark *Melanocorypha leucoptera*	4 ᵂ	(S)	100	100
Black Lark *Melanocorypha yeltoniensis*	3	(V)	100	100
Crested Lark *Galerida cristata*	3	(D)	72	70
Shore Lark *Eremophila alpestris*	—	(S)	98	98
Olive-backed Pipit *Anthus hodgsoni*	—	(S)	100	100
Pechora Pipit *Anthus gustavi*	—	(S)	100	100
Red-throated Pipit *Anthus cervinus*	—	(S)	58	58
Citrine Wagtail *Motacilla citreola*	—	(S)	100	100
Grey Wagtail *Motacilla cinerea*	—	(S)	59	28
Yellow-vented Bulbul *Pycnonotus xanthopygos*	—	(S)	100	100
Waxwing *Bombycilla garrulus*	—	(S)	83	83
Dipper *Cinclus cinclus*	—	(S)	56	23
Siberian Accentor *Prunella montanella*	—	(S)	100	100
Radde's Accentor *Prunella ocularis*	3	(V)	100	100
Black-throated Accentor *Prunella atrogularis*	3	(V)	100	100
Nightingale *Luscinia megarhynchos*	4	(S)	34	59
Siberian Rubythroat *Luscinia calliope*	—	(S)	100	100
Red-flanked Bluetail *Tarsiger cyanurus*	—	(S)	99	99
White-throated Robin *Irania gutturalis*	—	(S)	100	100
Güldenstädt's Redstart *Phoenicurus erythrogaster*	3	Ins	100	100
Stonechat *Saxicola torquata*	3	(D)	47	53
Isabelline Wheatear *Oenanthe isabellina*	—	(S)	100	100
Pied Wheatear *Oenanthe pleschanka*	—	(S)	97	95
Finsch's Wheatear *Oenanthe finschii*	—	(S)	100	100
Red-tailed Wheatear *Oenanthe xanthoprymna*	—	(S)	100	100
Rock Thrush *Monticola saxatilis*	3	(D)	47	84
Blue Rock Thrush *Monticola solitarius*	3	(V)	50	66
White's Thrush *Zoothera dauma*	—	(S)	100	100
Black-throated Thrush *Turdus ruficollis*	—	(S)	100	100
Fan-tailed Warbler *Cisticola juncidis*	—	(S)	3	98
Graceful Warbler *Prinia gracilis*	—	(S)	100	100
Lanceolated Warbler *Locustella lanceolata*	—	(S)	100	100
Savi's Warbler *Locustella luscinioides*	4	(S)	14	64
Moustached Warbler *Acrocephalus melanopogon*	—	(S)	73	88
Sedge Warbler *Acrocephalus schoenobaenus*	4	(S)	40	63
Blyth's Reed Warbler *Acrocephalus dumetorum*	—	(S)	94	90
Great Reed Warbler *Acrocephalus arundinaceus*	—	(S)	47	51
Olivaceous Warbler *Hippolais pallida*	3	(V)	82	99
Booted Warbler *Hippolais caligata*	—	(S)	100	100

	SPEC category	European Threat Status	% with poor population size data [1]	% with poor population trend data [2]
Upcher's Warbler *Hippolais languida*	—	(S)	100	100
Olive-tree Warbler *Hippolais olivetorum*	2	(R)	100	100
Melodious Warbler *Hippolais polyglotta*	4	(S)	4	73
Marmora's Warbler *Sylvia sarda*	4	(S)	52	52
Spectacled Warbler *Sylvia conspicillata*	—	(S)	5	75
Ménétries's Warbler *Sylvia mystacea*	—	(S)	100	100
Rüppell's Warbler *Sylvia rueppelli*	4	(S)	100	100
Desert Warbler *Sylvia nana*	—	(S)	100	100
Barred Warbler *Sylvia nisoria*	4	(S)	57	65
Green Warbler *Phylloscopus nitidus*	—	(S)	100	100
Greenish Warbler *Phylloscopus trochiloides*	—	(S)	83	83
Arctic Warbler *Phylloscopus borealis*	—	(S)	100	100
Wood Warbler *Phylloscopus sibilatrix*	4	(S)	0	67
Mountain Chiffchaff *Phylloscopus sindianus*	—	(S)	100	100
Chiffchaff *Phylloscopus collybita*	—	(S)	61	62
Goldcrest *Regulus regulus*	4	(S)	64	66
Red-breasted Flycatcher *Ficedula parva*	—	(S)	82	78
Semi-collared Flycatcher *Ficedula semitorquata*	2	(E)	100	100
Bearded Tit *Panurus biarmicus*	—	(S)	23	89
Sombre Tit *Parus lugubris*	4	(S)	92	100
Willow Tit *Parus montanus*	—	(S)	1	79
Siberian Tit *Parus cinctus*	—	(S)	53	53
Azure Tit *Parus cyanus*	—	(S)	96	100
Krüper's Nuthatch *Sitta krueperi*	4	(S)	100	100
Eastern Rock Nuthatch *Sitta tephronota*	—	(S)	100	100
Rock Nuthatch *Sitta neumayer*	4	(S)	84	100
Wallcreeper *Tichodroma muraria*	—	(S)	92	28
Penduline Tit *Remiz pendulinus*	—	(S)	82	69
Red-backed Shrike *Lanius collurio*	3	(D)	51	24
Lesser Grey Shrike *Lanius minor*	2	(D)	74	76
Masked Shrike *Lanius nubicus*	2	(V)	74	74
Jay *Garrulus glandarius*	—	(S)	50	51
Siberian Jay *Perisoreus infaustus*	3	(D)	55	9
Nutcracker *Nucifraga caryocatactes*	—	(S)	39	52
Alpine Chough *Pyrrhocorax graculus*	—	(S)	45	73
Jackdaw *Corvus monedula*	4	(S)	58	69
Raven *Corvus corax*	—	(S)	65	46
Rose-coloured Starling *Sturnus roseus*	—	(S)	99	99
Spanish Sparrow *Passer hispaniolensis*	—	(S)	92	86
Dead Sea Sparrow *Passer moabiticus*	—	(S)	98	0
Pale Rock Sparrow *Carpospiza brachydactyla*	—	(S)	100	0
Yellow-throated Sparrow *Petronia xanthocollis*	—	(S)	100	100
Snowfinch *Montifringilla nivalis*	—	(S)	90	69
Red-fronted Serin *Serinus pusillus*	—	(S)	100	100
Goldfinch *Carduelis carduelis*	—	(S)	37	63
Redpoll *Carduelis flammea*	—	(S)	92	92
Arctic Redpoll *Carduelis hornemanni*	—	(S)	96	100
Two-barred Crossbill *Loxia leucoptera*	—	(S)	91	91
Scottish Crossbill *Loxia scotica*	**1**	**Ins**	**100**	**100**
Crimson-winged Finch *Rhodopechys sanguinea*	—	(S)	100	100
Desert Finch *Rhodospiza obsoleta*	—	(S)	100	100
Scarlet Rosefinch *Carpodacus erythrinus*	—	(S)	69	71
Great Rosefinch *Carpodacus rubicilla*	3	(E)	100	100
Lapland Bunting *Calcarius lapponicus*	—	(S)	72	83
Snow Bunting *Plectrophenax nivalis*	—	(S)	1	78
Yellowhammer *Emberiza citrinella*	4	(S)	50	58
Cirl Bunting *Emberiza cirlus*	4	(S)	41	56
Cinereous Bunting *Emberiza cineracea*	2	(V)	100	100
Ortolan Bunting *Emberiza hortulana*	2	(V)	68	71
Grey-necked Bunting *Emberiza buchanani*	—	(S)	100	100
Cretzschmar's Bunting *Emberiza caesia*	4	(S)	56	83
Rustic Bunting *Emberiza rustica*	—	(S)	95	95
Little Bunting *Emberiza pusilla*	—	(S)	95	95
Yellow-breasted Bunting *Emberiza aureola*	—	(S)	99	99
Black-headed Bunting *Emberiza melanocephala*	2	(V)	90	100
Corn Bunting *Miliaria calandra*	4	(S)	39	58

The following listing gives the annexes/appendices of the Wild Birds Directive and the Bern and Bonn Conventions appropriate to Species of European Conservation Concern. For definitions of SPEC categories and European Threat Status, see Appendix 1 (p. 470).

EU Wild Birds Directive

The list below incorporates amendments to the Annexes of the Council Directive (79/409/EEC) of 6 March 1991 (91/244/EEC), 8 June 1994 (94/24/EC) and 29 August 1994 (94/C241/08) taking account of the expected accession of Austria, Finland, Norway and Sweden on 1 January 1995.

Annex I

The Directive requires that species listed in Annex I 'shall be the subject of special conservation measures concerning their habitat in order to ensure their survival and reproduction in their area of distribution' and that 'Member States shall classify in particular the most suitable territories in number and size as special protection areas for the conservation of these species, taking into account their protection requirements in the geographical sea and land area where this Directive applies'.

In addition, 'Member States shall take similar measures for regularly occurring migratory species not listed in Annex I, bearing in mind their need for protection in the geographical sea and land area where this Directive applies, as regards their breeding, moulting and wintering areas and staging posts along their migration routes'.

Annex II

'The species referred to in Annex II/1 may be hunted in the geographical sea and land area where the Directive applies'. 'Species referred to in Annex II/2 may be hunted only in Member States in respect of which they are indicated' (see p. 510).

Annex III

For species listed in Annex III/1 Member States shall not prohibit 'the sale, transport for sale, keeping for sale and the offering for sale of live or dead birds and of any readily recognizable parts or derivatives of such birds', provided that the birds have been legally killed or captured or otherwise legally acquired. Member States may for the species listed in Annex III/2, allow within their territory the activities referred to above, making provision for certain restrictions, provided the birds have been legally killed or captured or otherwise legally acquired. The activities referred to above are prohibited for all other species of naturally occurring wild birds in the European territory of EU Member States.

Bern Convention

The list below incorporates additions made by the Standing Committee in December 1987.

Parties undertake to take appropriate and necessary measures for the conservation of the habitats of wild flora and fauna, especially those on Appendices I (plants) and II, and to give special attention to the protection of areas of importance for the migratory species on Appendices II and III, and to prohibit the deliberate damage or destruction of sites for species listed in Appendix II.

Parties undertake to regulate any exploitation of the wild fauna specified in Appendix III and prohibit blameworthy means of capture and killing.

Bonn Convention

The list below incorporates amendments by the Conference of the Parties in 1985, 1988, 1991 and 1994.

Appendix I: 'Species in danger of extinction throughout all or major parts of their range'

Parties to the Convention undertake to provide immediate protection to species included in Appendix I, and Range States should conserve and, where feasible and appropriate, restore those habitats of the species which are of importance in removing it from danger of extinction.

Appendix II: 'Species which would benefit from international cooperation in their conservation and management'

Parties to the Convention shall 'conclude Agreements covering the conservation and management of migratory species included in Appendix II'. Each Agreement should, where appropriate, provide for the 'maintenance of a network of suitable habitats appropriately disposed in relation to migratory routes'.

	SPEC category	European Threat Status	Wild Birds Directive	Bern Convention	Bonn Convention
Red-throated Diver *Gavia stellata*	3	V	I	II	II
Black-throated Diver *Gavia arctica*	3	V	I	II	II
Fea's Petrel *Pterodroma feae*	1	E	I	II	
Zino's Petrel *Pterodroma madeira*	1	E	I	II	
Bulwer's Petrel *Bulweria bulwerii*	3	V	I	II	
Cory's Shearwater *Calonectris diomedea*	2	(V)	I	II	
Manx Shearwater *Puffinus puffinus*	2	(L)		II	
Yelkouan Shearwater *Puffinus yelkouan*	4	S	I [1]	II	
Little Shearwater *Puffinus assimilis*	3	V	I	II [2]	
White-faced Storm-petrel *Pelagodroma marina*	3	L	I	II	

Birds in Europe: Their Conservation Status

	SPEC category	European Threat Status	Wild Birds Directive	Bern Convention	Bonn Convention
Storm Petrel *Hydrobates pelagicus*	2	(L)	I	II	
Leach's Storm-petrel *Oceanodroma leucorhoa*	3	(L)	I	II	
Madeiran Storm-petrel *Oceanodroma castro*	3	V	I	II	
Gannet *Sula bassana*	2	L		III	
Shag *Phalacrocorax aristotelis*	4	S	I [3]	III	
Pygmy Cormorant *Phalacrocorax pygmeus*	2	V	I	II	II
White Pelican *Pelecanus onocrotalus*	3	R	I	II	I & II
Dalmatian Pelican *Pelecanus crispus*	1	V	I	II	I & II
Bittern *Botaurus stellaris*	3	(V)	I	II	II
Little Bittern *Ixobrychus minutus*	3	(V)	I	II	II
Night Heron *Nycticorax nycticorax*	3	D	I	II	
Squacco Heron *Ardeola ralloides*	3	V	I	II	
Purple Heron *Ardea purpurea*	3	V	I	II	II
Black Stork *Ciconia nigra*	3	R	I	II	II
White Stork *Ciconia ciconia*	2	V	I	II	II
Glossy Ibis *Plegadis falcinellus*	3	D	I	II	II
Spoonbill *Platalea leucorodia*	2	E	I	II	II
Greater Flamingo *Phoenicopterus ruber*	3	L	I	II	II
Bewick's Swan *Cygnus columbianus*	3 [w]	L [w]	I	II	II
Whooper Swan *Cygnus cygnus*	4 [w]	S	I	II	II
Pink-footed Goose *Anser brachyrhynchus*	4	S	II/2	III	II
Lesser White-fronted Goose *Anser erythropus*	1	V	I	II	II
Barnacle Goose *Branta leucopsis*	4/2	L [w]	I	II	II
Brent Goose *Branta bernicla*	3	V	II/2	III	II
Red-breasted Goose *Branta ruficollis*	1	L [w]	I	II	II
Ruddy Shelduck *Tadorna ferruginea*	3	V	I	II	II
Gadwall *Anas strepera*	3	V	II/1	III	II
Pintail *Anas acuta*	3	V	II/1 & III/2	III	II
Garganey *Anas querquedula*	3	V	II/1	III	II
Marbled Teal *Marmaronetta angustirostris*	1	E	I	II	II
Red-crested Pochard *Netta rufina*	3	D	II/2	III	II
Pochard *Aythya ferina*	4	S	II/1 & III/2	III	II
Ferruginous Duck *Aythya nyroca*	1	V	I	III	II
Scaup *Aythya marila*	3 [w]	L [w]	II/2 & III/2	III	II
Steller's Eider *Polysticta stelleri*	1	L [w]		II	II
Harlequin Duck *Histrionicus histrionicus*	3	V		II	II
Velvet Scoter *Melanitta fusca*	3 [w]	L [w]	II/2	III	II
Barrow's Goldeneye *Bucephala islandica*	3	E		II	II
Smew *Mergus albellus*	3	V	I [10]	II	II
White-headed Duck *Oxyura leucocephala*	1	E	I	II	I & II
Honey Buzzard *Pernis apivorus*	4	S	I	II	II
Black-winged Kite *Elanus caeruleus*	3	V	I	II	II
Black Kite *Milvus migrans*	3	V	I	II	II
Red Kite *Milvus milvus*	4	S	I	II	II
White-tailed Eagle *Haliaeetus albicilla*	3	R	I	II	I
Lammergeier *Gypaetus barbatus*	3	E	I	II	II
Egyptian Vulture *Neophron percnopterus*	3	E	I	II	II
Griffon Vulture *Gyps fulvus*	3	R	I	II	II
Cinereous Vulture *Aegypius monachus*	3	V	I	II	II
Short-toed Eagle *Circaetus gallicus*	3	R	I	II	II
Hen Harrier *Circus cyaneus*	3	V	I	II	II
Pallid Harrier *Circus macrourus*	3	E	I	II	II
Montagu's Harrier *Circus pygargus*	4	S	I	II	II
Levant Sparrowhawk *Accipiter brevipes*	2	R	I	II	II
Long-legged Buzzard *Buteo rufinus*	3	(E)	I	II	II
Lesser Spotted Eagle *Aquila pomarina*	3	R	I	II	II
Greater Spotted Eagle *Aquila clanga*	1	E	I	II	II
Steppe Eagle *Aquila nipalensis*	3	V		II	II
Imperial Eagle *Aquila heliaca*	1	E	I	II	II
Spanish Imperial Eagle *Aquila adalberti*	1	E	I	II	II
Golden Eagle *Aquila chrysaetos*	3	R	I	II	II
Booted Eagle *Hieraaetus pennatus*	3	R	I	II	II
Bonelli's Eagle *Hieraaetus fasciatus*	3	E	I	II	II
Osprey *Pandion haliaetus*	3	R	I	II	II
Lesser Kestrel *Falco naumanni*	1	(V)	I	II	II

Appendix 4: Wild Birds Directive, Bern Convention and Bonn Convention

	SPEC category	European Threat Status	Wild Birds Directive	Bern Convention	Bonn Convention
Kestrel *Falco tinnunculus*	3	D		II	II
Red-footed Falcon *Falco vespertinus*	3	V		II	II
Eleonora's Falcon *Falco eleonorae*	2	R	I	II	II
Lanner *Falco biarmicus*	3	(E)	I	II	II
Saker *Falco cherrug*	3	E		II	II
Gyrfalcon *Falco rusticolus*	3	V	I [10]	II	II
Peregrine *Falco peregrinus*	3	R	I	II	II
Black Grouse *Tetrao tetrix*	3	V	I [4] & II/2 & III/2 [5]	III	
Caucasian Black Grouse *Tetrao mlokosiewiczi*	2	Ins		III	
Caucasian Snowcock *Tetraogallus caucasicus*	4	S			
Caspian Snowcock *Tetraogallus caspius*	3	Ins		III	
Chukar *Alectoris chukar*	3	V	II/2	III	
Rock Partridge *Alectoris graeca*	2	V	I [6] & II/1	III	
Red-legged Partridge *Alectoris rufa*	2	(V)	II/1 & III/1	III	
Barbary Partridge *Alectoris barbara*	3	(E)	I & II/2 & III/1	III	
Black Francolin *Francolinus francolinus*	3	V		III	
Partridge *Perdix perdix*	3	V	I [7] & II/1 & III/1	III	
Quail *Coturnix coturnix*	3	V	II/2	III	II
Andalusian Hemipode *Turnix sylvatica*	3	E	I	II	
Spotted Crake *Porzana porzana*	4	S	I	II	II
Little Crake *Porzana parva*	4	(S)	I	II	II
Baillon's Crake *Porzana pusilla*	3	R	I	II	II
Corncrake *Crex crex*	1	V	I	II	
Purple Gallinule *Porphyrio porphyrio*	3	R	I	II	
Crested Coot *Fulica cristata*	3	E	I	II	
Crane *Grus grus*	3	V	I	II	II
Little Bustard *Tetrax tetrax*	2	V	I	II	
Houbara Bustard *Chlamydotis undulata*	3	(E)	I	II	I
Great Bustard *Otis tarda*	1	D	I	II	I & II
Avocet *Recurvirostra avosetta*	4/3 [w]	L [w]	I	II	II
Stone Curlew *Burhinus oedicnemus*	3	V	I	II	II
Cream-coloured Courser *Cursorius cursor*	3	V	I	II	
Collared Pratincole *Glareola pratincola*	3	E	I	II	II
Black-winged Pratincole *Glareola nordmanni*	3	R		II	II
Kentish Plover *Charadrius alexandrinus*	3	D		II	II
Greater Sand Plover *Charadrius leschenaultii*	3	(E)		II	II
Caspian Plover *Charadrius asiaticus*	3	(V)		III	II
Golden Plover *Pluvialis apricaria*	4	S	I & II/2 & III/2	III	II
Spur-winged Plover *Hoplopterus spinosus*	3	(E)	I	II	II
Sociable Plover *Chettusia gregaria*	1	E		III	II
Knot *Calidris canutus*	3 [w]	L [w]	II/2	III	II
Purple Sandpiper *Calidris maritima*	4	S		II	II
Dunlin *Calidris alpina*	3 [w]	V [w]		II	II
Broad-billed Sandpiper *Limicola falcinellus*	3	(V)		II	II
Ruff *Philomachus pugnax*	4	(S)	I & II/2	III	II
Jack Snipe *Lymnocryptes minimus*	3 [w]	(V) [w]	II/1 & III/2	III	II
Great Snipe *Gallinago media*	2	(V)	I	II	II
Woodcock *Scolopax rusticola*	3 [w]	V [w]	II/1 & III/2	III	II
Black-tailed Godwit *Limosa limosa*	2	V	II/2	III	II
Bar-tailed Godwit *Limosa lapponica*	3 [w]	L [w]	I [10] & II/2	III	II
Whimbrel *Numenius phaeopus*	4	(S)	II/2	III	II
Slender-billed Curlew *Numenius tenuirostris*	1	S	I	II	I & II
Curlew *Numenius arquata*	3 [w]	D [w]	II/2	III	II
Redshank *Tringa totanus*	2	D	II/2	III	II
Wood Sandpiper *Tringa glareola*	3	D	I	II	II
Great Skua *Stercorarius skua*	4	S		III	
Mediterranean Gull *Larus melanocephalus*	4	S	I	II	II
Little Gull *Larus minutus*	3	D		II	
Audouin's Gull *Larus audouinii*	1	L	I	II	I & II
Common Gull *Larus canus*	2	D	II/2	III	
Lesser Black-backed Gull *Larus fuscus*	4	S	II/2		
Great Black-backed Gull *Larus marinus*	4	S	II/2		
Ivory Gull *Pagophila eburnea*	3	(E)		II	
Gull-billed Tern *Gelochelidon nilotica*	3	(E)	I	II	
Caspian Tern *Sterna caspia*	3	(E)	I	II	II

	SPEC category	European Threat Status	Wild Birds Directive	Bern Convention	Bonn Convention
Sandwich Tern *Sterna sandvicensis*	2	D	I	II	II
Roseate Tern *Sterna dougallii*	3	E	I	II	II
Little Tern *Sterna albifrons*	3	D	I	II	II
Whiskered Tern *Chlidonias hybridus*	3	D	I	II	
Black Tern *Chlidonias niger*	3	D	I	II	II
Razorbill *Alca torda*	4	S		III	
Black Guillemot *Cepphus grylle*	2	D		III	
Puffin *Fratercula arctica*	2	V		III	
Black-bellied Sandgrouse *Pterocles orientalis*	3	V	I	II	
Pin-tailed Sandgrouse *Pterocles alchata*	3	E	I	II	
Stock Dove *Columba oenas*	4	S	II/2	III	
Woodpigeon *Columba palumbus*	4	S	I [8] & II/1 & III/1		
Long-toed Pigeon *Columba trocaz*	1	V	I	III	
Dark-tailed Laurel Pigeon *Columba bollii*	1	V	I	II	
White-tailed Laurel Pigeon *Columba junoniae*	1	V	I	II	
Turtle Dove *Streptopelia turtur*	3	D	II/2	III	
Barn Owl *Tyto alba*	3	D		II	
Scops Owl *Otus scops*	2	(D)		II	
Eagle Owl *Bubo bubo*	3	V	I	II	
Snowy Owl *Nyctea scandiaca*	3	V	I	II	
Little Owl *Athene noctua*	3	D		II	
Tawny Owl *Strix aluco*	4	S		II	
Short-eared Owl *Asio flammeus*	3	(V)	I	II	
Nightjar *Caprimulgus europaeus*	2	(D)	I	II	
Plain Swift *Apus unicolor*	4	S		II	
Kingfisher *Alcedo atthis*	3	D	I	II	
Bee-eater *Merops apiaster*	3	D		II	II
Roller *Coracias garrulus*	2	(D)	I	II	II
Wryneck *Jynx torquilla*	3	D		II	
Grey-headed Woodpecker *Picus canus*	3	D	I	II	
Green Woodpecker *Picus viridis*	2	D		II	
Syrian Woodpecker *Dendrocopos syriacus*	4	(S)	I	II	
Middle Spotted Woodpecker *Dendrocopos medius*	4	S	I	II	
Three-toed Woodpecker *Picoides tridactylus*	3	D	I	II	
Dupont's Lark *Chersophilus duponti*	3	V	I	II	
Calandra Lark *Melanocorypha calandra*	3	(D)	I	II	
White-winged Lark *Melanocorypha leucoptera*	4 [w]	(S)		II	
Black Lark *Melanocorypha yeltoniensis*	3	(V)		II	
Short-toed Lark *Calandrella brachydactyla*	3	V	I	II	
Lesser Short-toed Lark *Calandrella rufescens*	3	V		II	
Crested Lark *Galerida cristata*	3	(D)		III	
Thekla Lark *Galerida theklae*	3	V	I	II	
Woodlark *Lullula arborea*	2	V	I	III	
Skylark *Alauda arvensis*	3	V	II/2	III	
Sand Martin *Riparia riparia*	3	D		II	
Swallow *Hirundo rustica*	3	D		II	
Tawny Pipit *Anthus campestris*	3	V	I	II	
Berthelot's Pipit *Anthus berthelotii*	4	S		II	
Meadow Pipit *Anthus pratensis*	4	S		II	
Dunnock *Prunella modularis*	4	S		II	
Radde's Accentor *Prunella ocularis*	3	(V)		II	
Black-throated Accentor *Prunella atrogularis*	3	(V)		II	
Robin *Erithacus rubecula*	4	S		II	II
Thrush Nightingale *Luscinia luscinia*	4	S		II	II
Nightingale *Luscinia megarhynchos*	4	(S)		II	II
Redstart *Phoenicurus phoenicurus*	2	V		II	II
Güldenstädt's Redstart *Phoenicurus erythrogaster*	3	Ins		II	
Whinchat *Saxicola rubetra*	4	S		II	II
Fuerteventura Chat *Saxicola dacotiae*	2	V	I	II	II
Stonechat *Saxicola torquata*	3	(D)		II	II
Cyprus Pied Wheatear *Oenanthe cypriaca*	2	R		II	II
Black-eared Wheatear *Oenanthe hispanica*	2	V		II	II
Black Wheatear *Oenanthe leucura*	3	V	I	II	II
Rock Thrush *Monticola saxatilis*	3	(D)		II	II
Blue Rock Thrush *Monticola solitarius*	3	(V)		II	II

Appendix 4: Wild Birds Directive, Bern Convention and Bonn Convention

	SPEC category	European Threat Status	Wild Birds Directive	Bern Convention	Bonn Convention
Ring Ouzel *Turdus torquatus*	4	S		II	II
Blackbird *Turdus merula*	4	S	II/2	III	II
Fieldfare *Turdus pilaris*	4 [w]	S	II/2	III	II
Song Thrush *Turdus philomelos*	4	S	II/2	III	II
Redwing *Turdus iliacus*	4 [w]	S	II/2	III	II
Mistle Thrush *Turdus viscivorus*	4	S	II/2	III	II
Grasshopper Warbler *Locustella naevia*	4	S		II	II
River Warbler *Locustella fluviatilis*	4	S		II	II
Savi's Warbler *Locustella luscinioides*	4	(S)		II	II
Aquatic Warbler *Acrocephalus paludicola*	1	E	I	II	II
Sedge Warbler *Acrocephalus schoenobaenus*	4	(S)		II	II
Marsh Warbler *Acrocephalus palustris*	4	S		II	II
Reed Warbler *Acrocephalus scirpaceus*	4	S		II	II
Olivaceous Warbler *Hippolais pallida*	3	(V)		II	II
Olive-tree Warbler *Hippolais olivetorum*	2	(R)	I	II	II
Icterine Warbler *Hippolais icterina*	4	S		II	II
Melodious Warbler *Hippolais polyglotta*	4	(S)		II	II
Marmora's Warbler *Sylvia sarda*	4	(S)	I	II	II
Dartford Warbler *Sylvia undata*	2	V	I	II	II
Subalpine Warbler *Sylvia cantillans*	4	S		II	II
Sardinian Warbler *Sylvia melanocephala*	4	S		II	II
Cyprus Warbler *Sylvia melanothorax*	2	R		II	II
Rüppell's Warbler *Sylvia rueppelli*	4	(S)	I	II	II
Orphean Warbler *Sylvia hortensis*	3	V		II	II
Barred Warbler *Sylvia nisoria*	4	(S)	I	II	II
Whitethroat *Sylvia communis*	4	S		II	II
Garden Warbler *Sylvia borin*	4	S		II	II
Blackcap *Sylvia atricapilla*	4	S		II	II
Bonelli's Warbler *Phylloscopus bonelli*	4	S		II	II
Wood Warbler *Phylloscopus sibilatrix*	4	(S)		II	II
Goldcrest *Regulus regulus*	4	(S)		II	II
Tenerife Goldcrest *Regulus teneriffae*	4	S		II	II
Firecrest *Regulus ignicapillus*	4	S		II	II
Spotted Flycatcher *Muscicapa striata*	3	D		II	II
Semi-collared Flycatcher *Ficedula semitorquata*	2	(E)	I	II	II
Collared Flycatcher *Ficedula albicollis*	4	S	I	II	II
Pied Flycatcher *Ficedula hypoleuca*	4	S		II	II
Sombre Tit *Parus lugubris*	4	(S)		II	
Crested Tit *Parus cristatus*	4	S		II	
Blue Tit *Parus caeruleus*	4	S		II	
Krüper's Nuthatch *Sitta krueperi*	4	(S)	I	II	
Corsican Nuthatch *Sitta whiteheadi*	2	V	I	II	
Rock Nuthatch *Sitta neumayer*	4	(S)		II	
Short-toed Treecreeper *Certhia brachydactyla*	4	S		II	
Red-backed Shrike *Lanius collurio*	3	(D)	I	II	
Lesser Grey Shrike *Lanius minor*	2	(D)	I	II	
Great Grey Shrike *Lanius excubitor*	3	D		II	
Woodchat Shrike *Lanius senator*	2	V		II	
Masked Shrike *Lanius nubicus*	2	(V)		II	
Siberian Jay *Perisoreus infaustus*	3	(D)		II	
Chough *Pyrrhocorax pyrrhocorax*	3	V	I	II	
Jackdaw *Corvus monedula*	4	(S)	II/2		
Spotless Starling *Sturnus unicolor*	4	S		II	
Chaffinch *Fringilla coelebs*	4	S	I [9]	III	
Blue Chaffinch *Fringilla teydea*	1	V	I	II	
Serin *Serinus serinus*	4	S		II	
Canary *Serinus canaria*	4	S		III	
Citril Finch *Serinus citrinella*	4	S		II	
Greenfinch *Carduelis chloris*	4	S		II	
Siskin *Carduelis spinus*	4	S		II	
Linnet *Carduelis cannabina*	4	S		II	
Scottish Crossbill *Loxia scotica*	1	Ins	I	II	
Parrot Crossbill *Loxia pytyopsittacus*	4	S		II	
Trumpeter Finch *Bucanetes githagineus*	3	R	I	III	
Great Rosefinch *Carpodacus rubicilla*	3	(E)			

	SPEC category	European Threat Status	Wild Birds Directive	Bern Convention	Bonn Convention
Yellowhammer *Emberiza citrinella*	4	(S)		II	
Cirl Bunting *Emberiza cirlus*	4	(S)		II	
Rock Bunting *Emberiza cia*	3	V		II	
Cinereous Bunting *Emberiza cineracea*	2	(V)	I	II	
Ortolan Bunting *Emberiza hortulana*	2	(V)	I	III	
Cretzschmar's Bunting *Emberiza caesia*	4	(S)	I	II	
Black-headed Bunting *Emberiza melanocephala*	2	(V)		II	
Corn Bunting *Miliaria calandra*	4	(S)		III	

[1] *P. y. mauritanicus* only
[2] *P. a. baroli* only
[3] *P. a. desmarestii* only
[4] *T. t. tetrix* only
[5] *T. t. britannicus* only
[6] *A. g. saxatilis* and *A. g. whitaken* only
[7] *P. p. italica* and *P. p. hispaniensis* only
[8] *C. p. azorica* only
[9] *F. c. ombriosa* only
[10] Inclusion dependent on the accession of Austria, Finland, Norway and Sweden on 1 January 1995, and does not come into effect until then.

Hunting of SPECs listed in Annex II/2 of the EU Wild Birds Directive according to Member State

- Member States which under Article 7(3) may authorize hunting of the species listed.
- M Males only may be hunted, as above.

	Belgium	Denmark	Germany	Greece	Spain	France	Ireland	Italy	Luxembourg	Netherlands	Portugal	U.K.	Austria	Sweden	Finland	Norway
Pink-footed Goose *Anser brachyrhynchus*	•	•				•					•					•
Brent Goose *Branta bernicla*		•	•													
Red-crested Pochard *Netta rufina*				•	•											
Scaup *Aythya marila*	•	•	•	•		•	•			•			•			
Velvet Scoter *Melanitta fusca*		•	•			•	•					•		•	•	•
Black Grouse *Tetrao tetrix*	•		M			M	•					•		•	•	•
Chukar *Alectoris chukar*			•													
Barbary Partridge *Alectoris barbara*				•				•								
Quail *Coturnix coturnix*				•	•			•			•		•			
Golden Plover *Pluvialis apricaria*	•	•		•		•	•		•	•		•				•
Knot *Calidris canutus*		•						•								•
Ruff *Philomachus pugnax*						•		•								•
Black-tailed Godwit *Limosa limosa*	•							•								
Bar-tailed Godwit *Limosa lapponica*	•							•				•				
Whimbrel *Numenius phaeopus*	•							•				•				•
Curlew *Numenius arquata*	•					•	•					•				
Redshank *Tringa totanus*	•					•	•									
Common Gull *Larus canus*	•	•											•	•		•
Lesser Black-backed Gull *Larus fuscus*	•	•														
Great Black-backed Gull *Larus marinus*	•	•												•	•	•
Stock Dove *Columba oenas*				•	•	•					•					•
Turtle Dove *Streptopelia turtur*				•	•	•		•			•		•			
Skylark *Alauda arvensis*					•	•		•								
Blackbird *Turdus merula*					•	•		•			•		•			
Fieldfare *Turdus pilaris*				•	•	•		•			•		•	•	•	•
Song Thrush *Turdus philomelos*				•	•	•		•			•					
Redwing *Turdus iliacus*				•	•	•		•			•					•
Mistle Thrush *Turdus viscivorus*				•	•	•					•					
Jackdaw *Corvus monedula*					•	•			•				•		•	

PHASE 1 QUESTIONNAIRE – INSTRUCTIONS

Where data are available (for example from the European Atlas Questionnaire) then these have been entered onto the database and the enclosed questionnaire has been partially filled in with these data.

PART 1 – DATA

Part 1 of the questionnaire consists of tables for all species, other than vagrants (i.e. species outside their normal migratory range), occurring in Europe or occurring in your country if more detailed information is available. Section A covers breeding populations and section B covers mid-winter populations.

These tables have been filled in where data are available. Where data are unavailable the missing values are indicated by a full stop. PLEASE ENSURE THAT AN ANSWER IS GIVEN TO ALL MISSING VALUES. If a value is incorrect, cross it out and place the correct value immediately below. To make your entries clear please do not use a black pen.

Please fill in the table according to the criteria below or where data have been entered please check that these are correct.

Migrant Status (MGS)

Indicate the migratory status of the breeding population of your country as follows:

R Resident   P Partly migratory (i.e. part of
M Migratory   the population is migratory)

Here migratory populations are defined as those that undergo movements at predictable times and in predictable directions between breeding and one or more wintering areas.

Habitats

Using the two-figure CORINE codes given [not included here] list each of the habitats used by at least 10% of the population, when either feeding or nesting. Separate each habitat-type with a comma.

Habitat verification (HBV)

Indicate whether or not you consider that the species' habitat use is adequately described by the available CORINE codes by entering **Y** or **N** respectively.

Population size (POPMIN & POPMAX)

Give as accurate an estimate as possible of the current size of the breeding and mid-winter populations of each species.

For breeding populations express estimates as breeding PAIRS (or breeding females if more appropriate, but indicate this in Part 2 – NOTES [not included here]). For mid-winter populations give estimates of the number of INDIVIDUALS. Indicate the range of each estimate using the minimum (POPMIN) and maximum (POPMAX) population size columns. If an exact count is available, then enter this in both POPMIN and POPMAX population size columns. Past counts may be used if you consider that their estimates remain reasonably valid, otherwise you should reassess the situation using currently available data. Details of out-of-date counts may, however, be given in Part 2 (NOTES).

Even if quantitative data are unavailable please still answer this question because even very rough estimates are valuable for monitoring and conservation purposes. We suggest that you calculate approximate minimum and maximum totals using likely densities and the total area of the country. As you will see, the accuracy of this estimate will be summarized in the next question.

For wintering seabirds, include all birds within your country's official coastal waters.

Year of estimate (YRC)

Where population size estimates are based on counts or surveys, etc., please give year of count or survey.

Population size verification (PSV)

Indicate the reliability and accuracy of the information supplied on population size according to the following three categories:

1 Species poorly known, with no quantitative data available.
2 Species generally well known, but only poor or incomplete quantitative data available.
3 Reliable quantitative data available (e.g. atlas, survey or monitoring data) for whole period and region.

Population size trend (PST)

Please indicate what is thought to have been the <u>overall</u> trend in population size over the period 1970–1990 according to the following guidelines:

+2   Large increase of at least 50%
+1   Small increase of at least 20% but less than 50%
 0   Stable with no overall change of more than 20%
−1   Small decrease of at least 20% but less than than 50%
−2   Large decrease of at least 50%

F   Fluctuating, with changes of at least 20%, but no clear trend
N   New breeder within period
X   Gone extinct within period

Population trend verification (PTV)

Indicate the reliability and accuracy of the information supplied on population size trends using the same three verification codes given under population size verification.

Range size trend (RST)

Indicate what is thought to have been the <u>overall</u> trend in range size (i.e. the area over which the species regularly occurs) over the period 1970–1990 using the same categories as for population size trend.

Range trend verification (RTV)

Indicate the reliability and accuracy of the information supplied on range trend using the same three verification codes as given above.

Proportion in Important Bird Area sites (IBA)

Indicate to the nearest 10% the percentage of the population within your country/region that occurs within designated Important Bird Areas (cf. Grimmett, R. F. A. and Jones, T. A. (1989) *Important Bird Areas in Europe*. Cambridge, U.K.: International Council for Bird Preservation).

Where available a database printout of the IBA populations of those species mentioned in the text of the IBA book is enclosed (Appendix 2).

If some birds within Important Bird Areas are also dependent on some habitats outside these areas, for example for feeding, please give details of the numbers and habitats involved in Part 2 (NOTES).

References (REFS)

Please indicate the references used to complete the questions on Population size, Population size trend and Range size trend. To do this enter the code that relates to the full reference given in Part 3 (REFERENCES) of the questionnaire and follow each reference with an indication of those questions to which it relates using the following codes:

PS   Population Size   RT   Range Trend
PT   Population Trend

If a reference relates to more than one question, separate the two-letter codes with '/'; if more than one reference is given, separate each reference code with a comma (e.g. '12PS,15PT/RT,23PT,24RT').

Extra species

If you consider that there are additional species for which data should be included please add them at the bottom of the questionnaire using the full scientific name. Please ensure that you answer all questions.

[Forms for Part 2 (notes) and Part 3 (references) are not shown here.]

CONSERVATION OF DISPERSED SPECIES IN EUROPE PHASE 1 QUESTIONNAIRE

PART 1 SECTION ... − .... POPULATIONS

COUNTRY: ....

Species	MGS	Habitats	HBV	POPMIN	POPMAX	YRC	PSV	PST	PTV	RST	RTV	IBA	Refs
Example	P	34, 82	Y	10,000	12,500	90	3	+1	1	0	2	10	17PS,3RT

GLOSSARY

Agri-environment Regulation   EU Council Regulation 2078/92 on 'agricultural production methods compatible with the requirements of the protection of the environment and the maintenance of the countryside'. This regulation updates and broadens the previous EU schemes for supporting environmentally sensitive farming (e.g. ESAs, see below) and extensification. The regulation includes an aid scheme to promote environmental measures including reduction of pollution from agriculture, extensification of crop, sheep and cattle farming (including conversion of arable land into extensive grassland), long-term set-aside, and, through management agreements, the maintenance of farming practices beneficial to the environment. These measures are implemented at national or regional levels through the development of Zonal Programmes.

Bern Convention   Convention on the Conservation of European Wildlife and Natural Habitats. See p. 21 and Appendix 4 (p. 505).

Bonn Convention   Convention on the Conservation of Migratory Species of Wild Animals. See p. 21 and Appendix 4 (p. 505).

Conservation Dependent   A species which does not qualify as Globally Threatened but is the focus of a continuing conservation programme, the cessation of which would result in the species qualifying as Globally Threatened (Collar *et al.* 1994).

Data Deficient   A species for which there is inadequate information to make a direct, or indirect, assessment of its risk of global extinction (Collar *et al.* 1994).

Dehesa   Spanish name for wooded pastoral habitats in Iberia dominated by oaks *Quercus*. Growth of scrub ('maquis') is controlled and pasture maintained by extensive rotational cultivation and/or grazing. In Portugal this habitat is called 'montado'.

Environmentally Sensitive Area (ESA)   Area within which farmers received European Community support (under Council Reg. 797/85, as amended by Reg. 2328/91) for management agreements that maintained environmentally beneficial farming practices. This scheme is now superseded by the Agri-environment regulation (see above).

European Union (EU)   Member states: Belgium, Denmark, France, Germany, Greece, Ireland, Italy, Luxembourg, Netherlands, Portugal, Spain, United Kingdom. On 1 January 1995 Austria, Norway, Finland and Sweden will accede to the Union.

EU Wild Birds Directive   Directive and Resolution of the Council of the European Community on the Conservation of Wild Birds. See p. 22 and Appendix 4 (p. 505).

Global conservation concern   Applied to species whose global status is classified as Globally Threatened, Conservation Dependent or Data Deficient according to the new IUCN criteria used by Collar *et al.* (1994). These species are Species of European Conservation Concern (SPEC) category 1.

Globally Threatened   A species at risk of global extinction and classed as Critical, Endangered or Vulnerable under the new IUCN criteria used by Collar *et al.* (1994).

IBA   Important Bird Area, as listed in *Important Bird Areas in Europe* (Grimmett and Jones 1989).

Maquis   Dense, mostly evergreen shrub community 1–3 m high, characteristic of the Mediterranean region.

Montado   See 'dehesa'.

Near Threatened   Unofficial category used by Collar *et al.* (1994) to identify species thought to be close to meeting the new IUCN criteria thresholds for Globally Threatened status.

Ramsar Convention   Convention on Wetlands of International Importance Especially as Waterfowl Habitat.

Ramsar Site   Site designated for the Ramsar List of Wetlands of International Importance. The importance of a wetland for waterfowl is a prime criterion for designation, though wetlands may also be designated on the basis of their representativeness or uniqueness, or their importance for plants and animals other than waterfowl (Ramsar Convention Bureau 1990).

Set-aside   Land taken out of production through supply-control measures within EC Reg. 1765/92, 'a support system for producers of certain arable crops'. A long-term (20-year) set-aside scheme is available for the promotion of environmental benefits through the Agri-environment regulation (see above).

SPEC   Species of European Conservation Concern, as defined in this review (see p. 27).

Special Protection Area (SPA)   Site classified by Member States of the EU for the conservation of wild birds as required under Article 4 of the EU Wild Birds Directive.

Unfavourable Conservation Status   Applied to species with European Threat Status classed as Endangered, Vulnerable, Rare, Declining, Localized or Insufficiently Known (see p. 28 for criteria).

DATA REFERENCES: SOURCE CODES

The following lists contain literature source codes for data given in the individual species' population tables (Species of European Conservation Concern, categories 1–3, pp. 55–438; due to shortage of space and time it has not been possible to list sources for category 4 species). For each species, and for each country under that species, numbers are given which cross-refer to the country-by-country list of data references (p. 524). The country-by-country section lists sources separately for breeding and winter, so it is necessary to note whether the species being considered contains breeding or winter data (all data are for breeding except where 'winter' is indicated in the lists below). Additional general references (unnumbered) are sometimes given in the country-by-country list for countries (e.g. Russia) where most population data are not referenced individually or where one source is used for most or all species (e.g. United Kingdom). Where no source is specified the data are personal assessments by the national coordinator and contributors (see p. 25 for a description of the process of data collection).

Gavia stellata
Denmark	
Faroe Islands	1
Finland	5
Iceland	4
Latvia	19
Norway	
Svalbard	1
Sweden	7
United Kingdom	29

Gavia arctica
Belarus	2,9
Finland	4
Latvia	10,11,19
Lithuania	2,4
Sweden	7
United Kingdom	29

Pterodroma feae
Portugal	
Madeira	3,9,12,17

Pterodroma madeira
Portugal	
Madeira	3,9,12,17

Bulweria bulwerii
Portugal	
Azores	2,3,5
Madeira	3,11,12
Spain	
Canary Islands	11

Calonectris diomedea
Albania	9
France	21
Greece	15
Italy	18
Portugal	8,12
Azores	1,3,5
Madeira	3,10,12,15
Spain	28,75,77,79,112
Canary Islands	11

Puffinus puffinus
Denmark	
Faroe Islands	6
France	35,42,49
United Kingdom	12,25,29
Isle of Man	4,5,8

Puffinus assimilis
Portugal	
Azores	2,3,5
Madeira	3,5,12
Spain	
Canary Islands	11

Pelagodroma marina
Portugal	
Madeira	3,8,12
Spain	
Canary Islands	11

Hydrobates pelagicus
Denmark	
Faroe Islands	5,7
France	35
Italy	2,4,16,17
Spain	14,75,77,88,112,132
Canary Islands	11
United Kingdom	29
Isle of Man	4,8

Oceanodroma leucorhoa
Denmark	
Faroe Islands	2
United Kingdom	12,29

Oceanodroma castro
Portugal	12
Azores	2,3,5
Madeira	3,8,12
Spain	
Canary Islands	11

Sula bassana
Denmark	
Faroe Islands	2,9
France	40
Germany	16
Iceland	8,24
United Kingdom	14

Phalacrocorax pygmeus
Albania	1,3,4,5,9
Bulgaria	1,13
Greece	2,12
Hungary	4
Italy	11
Romania	5
Slovakia	1
Turkey	13,20

Pelecanus onocrotalus
Albania	1,3,4,5,9
Greece	3
Romania	3,5
Russia	3
Turkey	2,9

Pelecanus crispus
Albania	1,2,3,4,5,9
Bulgaria	2,8,13
Greece	3,4
Romania	3,5
Russia	3
Turkey	2,13,14
Ukraine	6

Botaurus stellaris
Albania	5,9
Belarus	14
Belgium	1,3,15
Bulgaria	1,13
Czech Republic	9
Denmark	25,26
France	12,48,49
Germany	2,6,8
Latvia	10
Lithuania	2,4
Netherlands	5,12,14
Poland	19,26,37,45,54
Portugal	9
Spain	79,87,130
Sweden	7
Turkey	19
United Kingdom	28

Ixobrychus minutus
Albania	1,3,4,5,9
Belarus	14
Belgium	3,15
Bulgaria	13
Czech Republic	9
Denmark	26
France	12
Germany	2,20
Greece	14
Latvia	8,10,11
Lithuania	2,4
Netherlands	1,5
Poland	26,29,37,45,54
Portugal	11
Spain	20,33,79,94
Switzerland	2
Turkey	18

Nycticorax nycticorax
Albania	1,3,4,5,9,11
Belarus	3
Belgium	1,3,15
Bulgaria	13
Croatia	1
Czech Republic	9
France	36
Germany	2
Greece	5
Italy	12
Netherlands	5,12,14
Poland	22,45,54
Portugal	5
Romania	5,31,33,34
Spain	35,38

Turkey 18
Ukraine 17

Ardeola ralloides
Albania 1,3,4,5,9,11
Bulgaria 13
Croatia 1
France 36,45,49
Greece 5
Italy 12
Romania 5,31
Spain 35,38
Ukraine 33

Ardea purpurea
Albania 3,4,5,9,11
Bulgaria 1,13,20
Croatia 1
Czech Republic 9
France 19,27,28
Germany 2
Greece 5
Italy 12
Netherlands 5,7,12,13,14
Poland 22,45
Spain 87
Switzerland 15,18
Ukraine 17,18,33

Ciconia nigra
Albania 5,9
Austria 9
Belarus 15
Belgium 3,11,13,15
Bulgaria 13,15
Czech Republic 9
Denmark 25
France 28
Germany 4,6,22
Latvia 14,18
Lithuania 2,4
Poland 4,45,60
Romania 23
Slovakia 15
Spain 18,40
Ukraine 9,14,50

Ciconia ciconia
Albania 5,9,13
Austria 12
Belarus 16
Belgium 1,3,15
Bulgaria 11,13
Czech Republic 8,9
Denmark 12,25
France 20,41
Germany 1,7,14
Hungary 1
Italy 29
Latvia 5,10
Lithuania 2,4
Netherlands 5,12,13,14

Poland 7,30,45,46
Portugal 4
Romania 10,12,13,17,21,37
Slovakia 16,17
Slovenia 3
Spain 52,81
Switzerland 3
Turkey 10,16
Ukraine 13

Plegadis falcinellus
Albania 5,9,11,13
Bulgaria 1,13,20
France 40
Greece 5
Romania 5
Spain 70
Ukraine 34,36

Platalea leucorodia
Albania 1,3,4,11
Austria 7
Bulgaria 1,13,20
Czech Republic 5
Denmark 25
France 40
Greece 5
Italy 8
Latvia 20
Netherlands 3,5,9,12,13,14
Romania 5,31,34
Spain 87
Ukraine 48

Phoenicopterus ruber
France 30
Spain 5,17,39,73,87
Turkey 12,14

Cygnus columbianus
(WINTER)
Belgium 2,4
Bulgaria 1,2
Denmark 1
Estonia 2
France 1,5
Germany 1,4
Latvia 1
Lithuania 2
Netherlands 6
Romania 2,4
Slovakia 1
Spain 8,13
Ukraine 2
United Kingdom 1,5
Isle of Man 1

Anser erythropus
Sweden 2

Branta leucopsis
(WINTER)
Belgium 2,4
Denmark 4
France 5
Germany 5
Netherlands 3,4,6
Romania 1,7
Spain 6,11
United Kingdom 1,4,5
Isle of Man 1

Branta bernicla
Denmark
Greenland 4
Norway
Svalbard 2

Branta ruficollis
(WINTER)
Bulgaria 1,2,3
Germany 2
Greece 2,3
Netherlands 6
Romania 3,4,6
Ukraine 2

Tadorna ferruginea
Albania 8
Bulgaria 7,13
Turkey 8,11
Ukraine 24,29

Anas strepera
Albania 3,5,8
Belarus 14
Belgium 1,3,15
Bulgaria 7,13
Czech Republic 2
Denmark 13,21
France 31,49,50
Germany 2,6,20
Iceland 4,6,7
Italy 6
Latvia 10,15,19
Lithuania 2,4
Netherlands 12,13,14
Poland 21,22,33,40,45,53,54
Spain 28,48,79,94,111
Sweden 7
Switzerland 15,18
Ukraine 2,29
United Kingdom 6

Anas acuta
Belarus 14
Bulgaria 7,13
Czech Republic 9
Denmark 7,12
Faroe Islands 1

France 37
Germany 6,20
Iceland 4,6,7,21
Latvia 10,19
Lithuania 2,4
Netherlands 5
Poland 19,21,23,45,54,58,59
Romania 40
Spain 111,133
Sweden 7
Ukraine 23,29
United Kingdom 28

Anas querquedula
Albania 8
Belgium 1,3,15
Bulgaria 7,13
Czech Republic 2
Denmark 12,13,21
France 1,49,50
Germany 20
Italy 6
Latvia 19,22
Lithuania 2,4
Netherlands 5,12,13,14
Poland 3,21,26,29,33,40,
45,54,59
Spain 31,111,133
Sweden 6
Switzerland 15,18
Ukraine 4,23,29
United Kingdom 15,20,
27,28

Marmaronetta angustirostris
Spain 111,133
Turkey 6,17,19

Netta rufina
Albania 4
Bulgaria 7,13
Croatia 2
Czech Republic 4,9
Denmark 12,21
France 12,37,49,50
Germany 2,6,20
Italy 6
Latvia 19
Netherlands 3,5,12,13,14
Poland 11,23,45,54
Portugal 6
Romania 31
Spain 28,37,79,89,109,
111,129,133
Switzerland 7
Ukraine 29
United Kingdom 1,25

Aythya nyroca
Albania 1,4,5,8,9,11
Belarus 14

Bulgaria	7,13
Czech Republic	9
Italy	6,15,25
Latvia	19
Lithuania	2,4
Netherlands	12,13,14
Poland	45,53,54
Spain	111
Switzerland	9
Ukraine	3,29

Aythya marila
(WINTER)

Austria	1
Belgium	2,4
Bulgaria	1,2
Denmark	2,3
Estonia	1
France	4
Germany	3,4
Greece	3
Iceland	1,2,3,4
Italy	1
Lithuania	1,3
Netherlands	1
Norway	2
Portugal	1,2,3,4,5,6
Romania	4,5
Slovenia	1
Spain	6,7,12
Switzerland	2,3,5,6,7
Ukraine	2
United Kingdom	1,5
Isle of Man	1

Polysticta stelleri
(WINTER)

Denmark	10
Lithuania	3
Norway	1
Russia	1,2
Sweden	1

Histrionicus histrionicus

Iceland	4,9,10

Melanitta fusca
(WINTER)

Austria	1
Belgium	2,4
Bulgaria	1,2
Denmark	2
Estonia	1
France	4,5
Germany	3
Italy	1
Latvia	2
Lithuania	3
Netherlands	2,6
Norway	2
Romania	1,7

Slovenia	1
Spain	6,7,12
Switzerland	1,2,3,5,6,7
Ukraine	2
United Kingdom	3
Isle of Man	1

Bucephala islandica

Iceland	5,9,23

Mergus albellus

Belarus	5,10
Sweden	6

Oxyura leucocephala

Spain	6,9,112,128
Turkey	5,15

Elanus caeruleus

France	40
Portugal	11
Spain	80

Milvus migrans

Albania	3,4,12
Austria	2,4
Belarus	14
Belgium	1,3,15
Bulgaria	1,10,13
Czech Republic	7,9
France	23,24,25
Germany	10,20
Latvia	10,11,19
Liechtenstein	5
Lithuania	2,4
Luxembourg	1
Netherlands	13
Poland	1,4,45,54
Romania	8,36
Slovakia	7
Slovenia	4
Spain	80
Sweden	6
Switzerland	5,17
Turkey	3
Ukraine	49,53

Haliaeetus albicilla

Albania	4,11,12
Austria	2
Belarus	7
Bulgaria	1,13
Croatia	2
Czech Republic	7,9,10
Denmark	17,26
Finland	8
Germany	10,11
Greece	12
Denmark	
Greenland	5

Iceland	12,13
Latvia	3,10,19
Lithuania	2,4
Poland	23,45
Romania	36
Sweden	3
Ukraine	51,53
United Kingdom	28

Gypaetus barbatus

Albania	12
France	22,24,25
Spain	63,64,69,80
Turkey	3

Neophron percnopterus

Albania	1,3,4,12
Bulgaria	1,5
France	22,40,49
Italy	9
Romania	36
Spain	100
Canary Islands	4,10,12
Ukraine	53

Gyps fulvus

Albania	3,4,11
Bulgaria	4
France	22,24,40,48
Italy	27
Portugal	3
Spain	12,32,116
Turkey	3
Ukraine	53

Aegypius monachus

Albania	9
Greece	10
Spain	53,57,68,127
Turkey	3
Ukraine	1,53

Circaetus gallicus

Albania	3,4,9,11,12
Belarus	6
Bulgaria	5
France	23,24,49
Italy	24
Latvia	9,10
Lithuania	2,4
Poland	17,19,35,45
Romania	4,36
Slovakia	7
Spain	80
Ukraine	16,51,53

Circus cyaneus

Belarus	14
Belgium	3,15

Czech Republic	7,9
Denmark	17
Finland	6
France	23,49
Germany	2,18
Rep. of Ireland	3
Latvia	8,10,19
Lithuania	2,4
Netherlands	2,5,12,14
Poland	23,45,54
Spain	80
Sweden	6
Ukraine	53
United Kingdom	3,15
Isle of Man	4,6

Circus macrourus

Belarus	9
Ukraine	16,53

Accipiter brevipes

Albania	9,12
Bulgaria	5,13
Turkey	3
Ukraine	47

Buteo rufinus

Albania	3,4,12
Bulgaria	12,13
Turkey	3
Ukraine	53

Aquila pomarina

Albania	12
Belarus	14
Bulgaria	13,20
Czech Republic	7,9
Germany	20
Greece	9
Latvia	3,4,6,10
Lithuania	1,2,4
Poland	8,45,47,60
Romania	36
Slovakia	3,7
Turkey	3
Ukraine	11,16,53

Aquila clanga

Belarus	9
Latvia	10,12,19
Poland	35,45,53,54
Romania	8
Ukraine	53

Aquila nipalensis
No specific sources provided

Aquila heliaca
Albania	9,12
Bulgaria	13,16
Greece	9
Romania	8,36
Slovakia	7
Ukraine	46

Aquila adalberti
Spain	56,57,58,59

Aquila chrysaetos
Albania	3,4,9,11,12
Austria	2
Belarus	9
Bulgaria	13,14
Finland	9
France	23,24,49
Germany	2,3
Italy	10
Latvia	2,3,10,19
Liechtenstein	5
Poland	23,35,45,54
Romania	8,36
Slovakia	7
Spain	11,13
Sweden	9
Switzerland	6
Turkey	3
Ukraine	16,53
United Kingdom	4

Hieraaetus pennatus
Albania	9,12
Belarus	9
Bulgaria	1,13
France	7,24,49
Greece	9
Poland	23,35,45,54
Romania	8,36
Slovakia	7
Spain	80
Turkey	3
Ukraine	5,16,53

Hieraaetus fasciatus
Albania	4,9,12
France	22,24
Greece	9
Spain	10,80
Turkey	3

Pandion haliaetus
Belarus	18
Bulgaria	1,13
Denmark	17
Finland	7
France	22,24
Germany	8
Latvia	3,7,11
Lithuania	2,4

Poland	23,45,54
Spain	80
Canary Islands	4,5,9
Sweden	7
Ukraine	11,53
United Kingdom	28

Falco naumanni
Albania	9,12
Bulgaria	6,13
France	1,22,24
Italy	7
Portugal	1
Romania	7
Russia	2
Spain	54
Ukraine	10
United Kingdom	
Gibraltar	1,2

Falco tinnunculus
Albania	3,9,12
Austria	2
Belarus	9
Belgium	1,3,15
Bulgaria	13
Czech Republic	7
Denmark	17
Finland	6
France	23,24,49
Germany	10
Rep. of Ireland	3
Latvia	6,10,11
Liechtenstein	2,5
Lithuania	2,4
Portugal	
Madeira	1
Netherlands	12,13,14
Poland	5,45
Portugal	11
Romania	25,36
Slovakia	7
Spain	78,80
Canary Islands	4
Sweden	7
Switzerland	16
Ukraine	7,53
United Kingdom	15,19
Gibraltar	1,2,3
Isle of Man	4

Falco vespertinus
Belarus	9
Bulgaria	5,13
Czech Republic	7,9
Latvia	10,15,19
Slovakia	7
Ukraine	53

Falco eleonorae
Italy	28
Spain	80
Canary Islands	4

Falco biarmicus
Albania	1,9,10,12
Italy	19

Falco cherrug
Albania	12
Austria	2
Bulgaria	5,9
Czech Republic	7,9
Romania	36
Slovakia	7
Ukraine	32,53

Falco rusticolus
Iceland	1,14
Sweden	11

Falco peregrinus
Albania	4,9,12
Austria	2
Belarus	9
Belgium	3,10,15
Bulgaria	13,17
Czech Republic	7,9
Denmark	17
Greenland	2
Finland	10
France	22,24
Germany	10,13
Latvia	10,19
Netherlands	12,13,14
Poland	23,45,54
Romania	8,36,38
Slovakia	7
Spain	62,80
Canary Islands	4
Sweden	5
Switzerland	17
Turkey	3
Ukraine	53
United Kingdom	3,15,24
Gibraltar	1,2,3
Isle of Man	4

Tetrao tetrix
Albania	5
Austria	13
Belarus	8
Belgium	1,3,15
Czech Republic	3,9
Denmark	10,11,16
France	3
Germany	2,18,20
Italy	5,14
Latvia	1,19
Liechtenstein	1

Lithuania	2,4
Netherlands	5,12,13,14
Poland	31,41,45,54
Slovakia	12
Sweden	6
Switzerland	10
Ukraine	19,20,28,52
United Kingdom	1,11,13

Alectoris chukar
Bulgaria	13,20

Alectoris graeca
Albania	5,9
Austria	3
Bulgaria	13,20
France	2,3,16,34,49
Germany	3
Italy	22
Romania	20,32,41

Alectoris rufa
France	1,48,49
Portugal	11
Madeira	1
Spain	83
United Kingdom	13,15,25
Isle of Man	4

Alectoris barbara
Spain	98
Canary Islands	10,13
United Kingdom	
Gibraltar	1,2

Perdix perdix
Albania	5,9
Belarus	14
Belgium	1,3,15
Bulgaria	13,20
Denmark	9,27
France	1,13,48,49
Germany	20
Italy	7,20
Latvia	10,19
Lithuania	2,4
Netherlands	4,12,13,14
Poland	42,43,45
Romania	22
Spain	79,82
Sweden	6
Switzerland	8
Ukraine	19,43
United Kingdom	13,15,23, 25
Isle of Man	4

Coturnix coturnix
Albania	1,4,5,9,11
Andorra	1

Belarus 14
Belgium 1,3,15
Bulgaria 13
Denmark 12,26,27
  Faroe Islands 4
France 1,49
Germany 20
Latvia 10,19
Liechtenstein 3
Lithuania 2,4
Netherlands 12,13,14
Poland 36,45
Portugal 11
  Madeira 1
Spain 42
Sweden 7
Ukraine 19,44
United Kingdom 15,25
  Gibraltar 3
  Isle of Man 4

Turnix sylvatica
Spain 70,131

Porzana pusilla
Albania 5,9
Bulgaria 13
France 1,8,13,49
Germany 15,20
Netherlands 12,13,14
Portugal 11
Spain 37,49,79,133

Crex crex
Belarus 14
Belgium 1,3,14,15
Bulgaria 3,13
Denmark 12,21
France 6,13,31
Germany 20
Rep. of Ireland 2
Italy 31
Latvia 10,19
Liechtenstein 3
Lithuania 2,4
Netherlands 5,12,14
Poland 5,12,13,45
Spain 23,24
Sweden 6
Switzerland 15,18
Ukraine 19,39
United Kingdom 8,10,15,16,29
  Isle of Man 4,10

Porphyrio porphyrio
Portugal 10
Spain 16,70,79
Turkey 17

Fulica cristata
Spain 36,70,79,113

Grus grus
Belarus 4
Czech Republic 6
Denmark 12,26
Finland 3
France 40
Germany 2,8
Latvia 10
Lithuania 2,4
Poland 4,6,28,45
Spain 2
Sweden 7
Ukraine 19

Tetrax tetrax
France 17
Italy 23,26
Russia 2
Spain 25
Ukraine 19

Chlamydotis undulata
Spain
  Canary Islands 7,12,13

Otis tarda
Austria 6
Bulgaria 13
Czech Republic 7,9
Germany 8,17
Poland 45,54
Romania 27
Russia 2
Slovakia 8,10,11
Spain 67
Turkey 4
Ukraine 19

Recurvirostra avosetta
(WINTER)
Belgium 3,4
Bulgaria 2
France 5
Germany 4
Greece 3
Italy 2,4
Netherlands 5
Portugal 1,2,3,4,5,6
Spain 2,14
United Kingdom 1,5

Burhinus oedicnemus
Albania 5,8,9
Austria 8
Belarus 9
Bulgaria 13
Czech Republic 9

France 1,39
Greece 6,14
Italy 30
Poland 15,23,45
Portugal 11
Romania 11
Spain 25,50,79
  Canary Islands 10,13
Ukraine 19
United Kingdom 7,15,28

Cursorius cursor
Spain
  Canary Islands 10,12,13,14

Glareola pratincola
Albania 3,8,9
Bulgaria 13
France 4,12,14
Greece 6,13,14
Hungary 3
Italy 30
Romania 30
Spain 79,89,90,94,133
Turkey 1
Ukraine 19,35

Glareola nordmanni
Belarus 3
Ukraine 19,35

Charadrius alexandrinus
Albania 3,4,5,9
Bulgaria 13
Denmark 5,7,8,12,26
France 18,49
Germany 12
Italy 30
Netherlands 5,12,14
Poland 2,45
Romania 30,31
Spain 1,8,94,102,118
  Canary Islands 8,10,12
Sweden 4
Turkey 1
Ukraine 19,35

Charadrius asiaticus
Russia 1

Hoplopterus spinosus
Greece 6,8,11

Chettusia gregaria
Russia 1

Calidris canutus
(WINTER)
Belgium 4
Bulgaria 2
Denmark 5,6,11
France 2,3,5
Germany 4
Greece 4
Italy 3
Netherlands 5,6
Portugal 1,2,3,4,5,6
Spain 2,14
United Kingdom 1,5
  Isle of Man 1

Calidris alpina
(WINTER)
Belgium 3,4
Bulgaria 2
Denmark 5,6,11
France 2,3,5
Germany 4
Greece 3
Italy 3,4
Netherlands 5,6
Portugal 1,2,3,4,5,6
Romania 4
Spain 2,14
United Kingdom 2
  Isle of Man 1

Limicola falcinellus
Sweden 7

Lymnocryptes minimus (WINTER)
Belgium 4
Denmark 5,7,8,9
France 5
Greece 1
Latvia 3
Netherlands 6
Spain 1,10
United Kingdom 3
  Isle of Man 1

Gallinago media
Belarus 14
Latvia 10,19
Lithuania 2,4
Poland 9,15,16,19,21,23,32,45,54
Sweden 6
Ukraine 21,40

Scolopax rusticola
(WINTER)
Belgium 1,4
Bulgaria 2
Denmark 5

France 5
Netherlands 6
Spain 3,4,5,9
Ukraine 1
United Kingdom 3
  Isle of Man 1

Limosa limosa
Austria 5
Belarus 14
Belgium 3,5,15
Czech Republic 9
Denmark 4,12,14
France 18,43
Germany 19,22
Italy 30
Latvia 10,19
Lithuania 2,4
Netherlands 5,12,14
Poland 9,21,45,54,58,59
Spain 1,110
Sweden 7
Ukraine 19,26,40
United Kingdom 15,28
Iceland 4

Limosa lapponica
(WINTER)
Belgium 3,4
Bulgaria 2
Denmark 5,6,11
France 3,5
Germany 4
Greece 4
Iceland 5
Italy 3
Netherlands 5,6
Portugal 1,2,3,4,5,6
  Azores 1
Spain 2,14
United Kingdom 1,5
  Isle of Man 1

Numenius arquata
(WINTER)
Austria 2
Belgium 3,4
Bulgaria 2
Denmark 5,6,11
France 2,3,5
Germany 4
Greece 3
Iceland 1,5
Italy 3,4
Netherlands 5,6
Portugal 1,2,3,4,5,6
Romania 4
Slovakia 2
Spain 2,14
United Kingdom 3,5
  Isle of Man 1

Tringa totanus
Albania 3,4,6,8,9
Austria 5
Belarus 14
Belgium 3,5,15
Bulgaria 13
Denmark 27
  Faroe Islands 1
France 18
Germany 19,22
Iceland 20
Italy 30
Latvia 10
Lithuania 2,4
Netherlands 5,10
Poland 9,21,34,45,54,59
Portugal 13
Slovenia 5
Spain 20,33,72,94,102
Sweden 6
Ukraine 19,38
United Kingdom 15,22
  Isle of Man 4

Tringa glareola
Belarus 14
Denmark 3,12
Germany 2,19
Iceland 2,3,19
Latvia 2,10,19
Lithuania 2,4
Poland 27,45
Sweden 7
Ukraine 19,27
United Kingdom 28

Larus minutus
Belarus 9,11
Denmark 12,20,21
Latvia 10,19,21
Lithuania 2,4
Netherlands 12,13,14
Poland 23,25,45,54
Sweden 7
Ukraine 19

Larus audouinii
France 21,26
Italy 13
Spain 21,22,71

Larus canus
Austria 4
Belarus 12
Belgium 1,2,3,9,15
Czech Republic 1
Denmark 7,20
  Faroe Islands 1
France 21,48,49
Germany 9
Iceland 18
Latvia 10,21

Lithuania 2,4
Netherlands 3,12,14
Poland 10,11,26,45,54,57
Slovakia 6
Sweden 7
Switzerland 15,18
United Kingdom 12,25
  Isle of Man 3,4,8

Pagophila eburnea
Denmark
  Greenland 1,3,6

Gelochelidon nilotica
Albania 5,9
Bulgaria 7,13
Denmark 12,13,20,21,26
France 1,40
Germany 2,9
Greece 1,14
Italy 13
Romania 11
Spain 79,90
Ukraine 19,35

Sterna caspia
Finland 1
Spain 79,88
Sweden 8
Ukraine 19,35

Sterna sandvicensis
Albania 5
Belgium 1,3,15
Bulgaria 7,13
Denmark 7,13,19,26
France 21,35,49
Germany 2,9,20
Greece 1,7
Italy 13
Netherlands 5,11,12,14
Poland 23,45,54
Romania 5,11
Spain 22,88,89
Sweden 10
Ukraine 19,35
United Kingdom 14

Sterna dougallii
France 35,46
Rep. of Ireland 4
Portugal
  Azores 4
  Madeira 2,4
Spain 88,89
  Canary Islands 11
United Kingdom 14,28,32

Sterna albifrons
Albania 3,4,5,9
Belarus 9,12
Belgium 1,3,15
Bulgaria 7,13
Denmark 7,12,19,26
Finland 2
France 21,35
Germany 2,9
Greece 1,14
Italy 13
Latvia 10,17,19,21
Lithuania 2,4
Netherlands 5,12,14
Poland 16,23,45,54,57,58
Portugal 2,12
Romania 11
Spain 7,79
Sweden 7
Turkey 7
Ukraine 19,35
United Kingdom 14
  Isle of Man 2,4,8

Chlidonias hybridus
Albania 3,5
Belarus 13,17
Bulgaria 7,13
France 10,25
Italy 13
Lithuania 2,4
Poland 35,45,53
Spain 16,79,94,133
Ukraine 19,22,45

Chlidonias niger
Albania 3,5
Belarus 12
Bulgaria 13
Czech Republic 9
Denmark 12,15
France 1,10,44
Germany 5
Iceland 15,19
Italy 13
Latvia 10,21
Lithuania 2,4
Netherlands 5,12,14
Poland 14,16,21,33,40,45,54
Spain 16,72,89
Sweden 7
Ukraine 12,19

Cepphus grylle
Denmark 1,2,25
  Faroe Islands 2
  Greenland 1
Iceland 15,16,17
Norway
  Svalbard 1
Sweden 6
United Kingdom 5,13
  Isle of Man 4,8,9

Fratercula arctica
Denmark
  Faroe Islands 2,3,8
  Greenland 1
France 21,35
Iceland 22
Norway 1
  Svalbard 1
United Kingdom 14
  Isle of Man 4,8

Pterocles orientalis
Portugal 11
Spain 25,79

Pterocles alchata
France 40,48
Portugal 11
Spain 25,79

Columba trocaz
Portugal
  Madeira 6,7,13,14

Columba bollii
Spain
  Canary Islands 6

Columba junoniae
Spain
  Canary Islands 6

Streptopelia turtur
Albania 3,5,9
Andorra 2
Belarus 14
Belgium 1,3,15
Bulgaria 13
Denmark 12,26
France 49
Germany 20
Latvia 10,19
Lithuania 2,4
Netherlands 12,13,14
Poland 4,45
Portugal 11
  Madeira 16
Romania 16
Spain 108
  Canary Islands 1,3,10,13
Ukraine 19
United Kingdom 12,15

Tyto alba
Albania 5,9
Andorra 1
Belarus 9
Belgium 3,4,15
Bulgaria 13,19
Denmark 12,26
France 1,10,38,48,49
Germany 20
Hungary 2
Latvia 10,19
Lithuania 2,4
Netherlands 3,5,12,14
Poland 36,45,48,54
Portugal 11
  Madeira 1
Spain 20
  Canary Islands 4
Switzerland 17
Ukraine 42
United Kingdom 15,21,26
  Gibraltar 1
  Isle of Man 4

Otus scops
Albania 3,5,9
Andorra 2
Belarus 1,9
Bulgaria 13
France 10
Portugal 11
Romania 6
Switzerland 1
Ukraine 42
United Kingdom
  Gibraltar 1,3

Bubo bubo
Albania 1,5
Andorra 2
Belarus 9
Belgium 3,6,7,8,15
Bulgaria 13,18
Czech Republic 9
Denmark 22
Finland 6
France 10,49
Germany 20
Italy 5
Latvia 10,19
Lithuania 2,4
Netherlands 3
Poland 23,45,48,54,60
Portugal 11
Romania 17
Spain 79,86
Sweden 7
Switzerland 11
Ukraine 42

Nyctea scandiaca
Iceland 11,19
Sweden 1,7,11

Athene noctua
Albania 3,5,9
Andorra 2
Belarus 14
Belgium 1,3,15
Bulgaria 13
Denmark 12,27
France 10,48,49
Germany 22
Latvia 10,11
Lithuania 2,4
Netherlands 5,12,14
Poland 36,45,48
Portugal 11
Spain 93
Switzerland 17
Ukraine 42
United Kingdom 15,25
  Gibraltar 1

Asio flammeus
Belarus 14
Belgium 1,3,15
Denmark 12,21,26
France 1,48
Germany 2,20
Latvia 10,19
Lithuania 2,4
Netherlands 5,12,14
Poland 9,23,45,48,54
Spain 94,110
Sweden 7
Ukraine 42
United Kingdom 15,25
  Isle of Man 4

Caprimulgus europaeus
Albania 3,5,9
Belarus 14
Belgium 1,3,15,17
Bulgaria 13
Denmark 12,27
France 10,47,49
Germany 20
Latvia 19
Lithuania 2,4
Netherlands 5,12,14
Poland 45
Portugal 11
Spain 4
Sweden 6
Switzerland 20
Ukraine 37,42
United Kingdom 9,25

Alcedo atthis
Albania 4,5,9
Andorra 2
Belarus 9
Belgium 1,3,15
Bulgaria 13
Denmark 12,27
France 15,48,49
Germany 20
Latvia 10,16
Lithuania 2,4
Netherlands 5,12,14
Poland 45,49
Portugal 11
Romania 39
Spain 20,33,117
Sweden 7
Switzerland 4
Ukraine 42
United Kingdom 15,25

Merops apiaster
Albania 3,4,5,9
Belarus 9,14
Bulgaria 13
Czech Republic 9
Denmark 12,21
France 15,49
Germany 20
Italy 3
Netherlands 5,12,14
Poland 18,38,45,50,55,56
Portugal 11
Romania 1
Slovakia 14
Slovenia 2
Spain 121,122
Sweden 7
Switzerland 12
Ukraine 42,49

Coracias garrulus
Albania 5,9
Austria 11
Belarus 14
Bulgaria 13
France 1,40
Germany 8
Latvia 10,11,19
Lithuania 2,4
Poland 23,25,45,51,54
Portugal 11
Romania 14,16
Slovenia 1
Spain 122
Ukraine 15,37,42

Jynx torquilla
Albania 5
Andorra 2
Belarus 14
Belgium 1,3,15
Bulgaria 13
Denmark 3,12
France 1,10,49
Germany 20
Latvia 10
Lithuania 2,4
Netherlands 5,12,14
Poland 45
Portugal 11
Romania 14,16
Spain 27,30
Sweden 6

Ukraine 42
United Kingdom 25,28

_____

Picus canus
Albania 3,5,9,11
Belarus 14
Belgium 3,15
Bulgaria 13
France 10,48,49
Germany 20
Italy 5
Latvia 13
Lithuania 2,4
Poland 45,52
Romania 2,16
Sweden 6
Ukraine 42

_____

Picus viridis
Albania 3,5,9
Belarus 9,14
Belgium 1,3,15
Bulgaria 13
Denmark 27
France 10,48,49
Germany 20
Latvia 10,13
Liechtenstein 2,3
Lithuania 2,4
Netherlands 5,12,14
Poland 45,61
Portugal 11
Romania 2,16
Spain 19,45,61,105,107,
123,124,125,135
Sweden 6
Ukraine 42
United Kingdom 12,15,25

_____

Picoides tridactylus
Albania 4,5
Belarus 9
Bulgaria 13
France 10
Germany 3
Italy 5
Latvia 11,13
Liechtenstein 2,3
Lithuania 2,4
Poland 23,24,44,45
Romania 15,28,29
Sweden 6
Ukraine 41

_____

Chersophilus duponti
Spain 47,85,120

_____

Melanocorypha calandra
Albania 4,5,9
Bulgaria 13

France 1,11,15,48
Italy 1
Portugal 11
Spain 65,76,104,119,125
Ukraine 37

_____

Calandrella brachydactyla
Albania 5,9
Bulgaria 13
France 1,11,15,49
Hungary 3
Portugal 11
Slovakia 2
Spain 65,95,103,104
125,126
Switzerland 15,18
Ukraine 37

_____

Calandrella rufescens
Portugal 11
Spain 65,119,126
Canary Islands 1,10,12,13
Ukraine 37

_____

Galerida cristata
Albania 4,5,9
Belarus 14
Belgium 1,3,15
Bulgaria 13
Denmark 27
France 11
Germany 20
Latvia 10,19
Lithuania 3,4
Netherlands 6,12,14
Poland 45
Portugal 11
Spain 51,76,95,96,104,125
Sweden 10
Ukraine 37,42

_____

Galerida theklae
France 1,11,48
Portugal 11
Spain 43,65,66,103,119,
125,126

_____

Lullula arborea
Albania 5,9
Andorra 1
Austria 1
Belarus 14
Belgium 1,3,15
Bulgaria 13
Denmark 23
France 1,11
Germany 20
Latvia 10
Lithuania 3,4

Netherlands 5,12,14
Poland 45
Portugal 11
Romania 14,16
Spain 4,26,45,46,55,66,95,
96,101,103,115,125
Sweden 6
Switzerland 2
Ukraine 42
United Kingdom 15,25,28

_____

Alauda arvensis
Albania 5,9
Belarus 14
Belgium 3,15
Bulgaria 13
Denmark 6
Faroe Islands 1
France 11,48
Germany 20
Latvia 10
Lithuania 3,4
Netherlands 5,12,14
Poland 45
Portugal 11
Spain 19,46,76,95,103,
104,114,125,134
Sweden 7
Ukraine 37,42
United Kingdom 12,15
Isle of Man 4

_____

Riparia riparia
Albania 1,3,5,9,11
Belarus 14
Belgium 1,3,12,15
Bulgaria 13
Denmark 27
France 11
Germany 2,20
Rep. of Ireland 3
Italy 21
Latvia 10,16
Lithuania 3,4
Netherlands 5,8,12,14
Poland 14,45
Portugal 11
Romania 1
Spain 27
Sweden 6
Switzerland 19
Ukraine 37,42
United Kingdom 15,25
Isle of Man 4

_____

Hirundo rustica
Albania 3,5,9
Andorra 1
Belarus 14
Belgium 1,3,15,16
Bulgaria 13
Denmark 27
Faroe Islands 1

France 11
Germany 20
Iceland 19
Latvia 10
Lithuania 3,4
Netherlands 5,12,14
Poland 45
Portugal 11
Spain 15
Sweden 6
Ukraine 37,42
United Kingdom 12,15
Gibraltar 1
Isle of Man 4

_____

Anthus campestris
Albania 1,3,5,9
Austria 8
Belarus 14
Bulgaria 13
Czech Republic 9
Denmark 12,21
France 11,49
Germany 2,20
Latvia 10
Lithuania 3,4
Netherlands 5,12,14
Poland 45,49
Portugal 11
Spain 55,101,103,114,115,
125,126,134
Sweden 7
Switzerland 15,18
Ukraine 37,42

_____

Phoenicurus phoenicurus
Albania 5,7,9
Andorra 1
Belarus 14
Belgium 3,15
Bulgaria 13
Denmark 24,27
France 11
Germany 20
Latvia 10
Lithuania 3,4
Netherlands 5,12,14
Poland 45
Portugal 11
Romania 2,9,16
Spain 4,55,66,103,115
Sweden 6
Ukraine 42
United Kingdom 12,15
Isle of Man 4

_____

Phoenicurus erythrogaster
No specific sources provided

Saxicola dacotiae
Spain
  Canary Islands   2

Saxicola torquata
Albania   3,5,9
Belgium   1,3,15
Bulgaria   13
Denmark   12,21,26
France   11,49
Germany   20
Liechtenstein   4
Netherlands   5,12,14
Poland   22,45,55
Portugal   11
Spain   19,41,55,61,91,103,
     114,123,125,126
Switzerland   2
Ukraine   8,42
United Kingdom   15,25
  Isle of Man   4

Oenanthe hispanica
Albania   3,5,9,11
Bulgaria   13
France   11
Portugal   11
Spain   46,55,65,92,95,101,
     103,115,119,125,126

Oenanthe leucura
France   11,40,49
Portugal   11
Spain   20,27

Monticola saxatilis
Albania   5,9,11
Andorra   1
Bulgaria   13
France   11,49
Poland   23,45
Portugal   11
Spain   91,103,134
Ukraine   31,42

Monticola solitarius
Albania   5,7,9
Andorra   1
Bulgaria   13
France   11,48,49
Portugal   11
Spain   103
United Kingdom
  Gibraltar   1

Acrocephalus
  paludicola
Belarus   9
Germany   8
Hungary   3

Latvia   10,19
Lithuania   3,4
Poland   19,20,45,60
Ukraine   42

Hippolais pallida
Albania   4,5,9,11
Bulgaria   13
Portugal   11
Spain   29

Hippolais olivetorum
Albania   4,5,7,9,11
Bulgaria   13

Sylvia undata
Andorra   1
France   47,48
Portugal   11
Spain   4,19,26,45,46,55,61,
     74,103,107,114,115,124
United Kingdom   15,28,31

Sylvia hortensis
Albania   5,7,9,11
Bulgaria   13
France   47,49
Portugal   11
Spain   45,46,66,95,96,101,
     103,107,115

Muscicapa striata
Albania   5,7,9
Andorra   1
Belarus   14
Belgium   1,3,15
Bulgaria   13
Denmark   27
France   47
Germany   20
Latvia   10
Lithuania   3,4
Netherlands   5,12,13,14
Poland   45
Portugal   11
Romania   2,9,16
Spain   29,41,46,51,61,66,
     99,103,106,123,136
Sweden   6
Ukraine   30,37,42
United Kingdom   12,15
  Isle of Man   4

Ficedula semitorquata
Bulgaria   13

Sitta whiteheadi
France   5,48,49

Lanius collurio
Albania   5,7,9,11
Andorra   1
Belarus   14
Belgium   1,3,15
Bulgaria   13
Denmark   3,12
France   33,47,49
Germany   20
Latvia   10
Lithuania   3,4
Netherlands   5,12,14
Poland   39,45
Portugal   11
Romania   14,16
Slovakia   9
Spain   41,91,123
Sweden   6
Ukraine   37,42
United Kingdom   25,27,28

Lanius minor
Albania   5,7,9
Belarus   9
Bulgaria   13
France   32,40,47,48,49
Germany   20
Latvia   10
Lithuania   3,4
Poland   23,45
Slovakia   5
Spain   79,94
Switzerland   14
Ukraine   37,42

Lanius excubitor
Andorra   2
Austria   10
Belarus   9
Belgium   1,3,15
Denmark   12,21,26
France   1,47,48,49
Germany   2,20
Latvia   10,19
Lithuania   3,4
Netherlands   5,12,14
Poland   39,45
Portugal   11
Romania   18,24,26
Spain   45,103,119,124,
     125,126,137
  Canary Islands   13
Sweden   6
Switzerland   14
Ukraine   42

Lanius senator
Albania   5,7,9
Andorra   2
Bulgaria   13
Czech Republic   9
France   47,49
Germany   21

Poland   23,45
Portugal   11
Romania   40
Slovakia   13
Spain   29,45,46,51,61,66,95,
     96,101,103,115,119,125
Ukraine   42
United Kingdom
  Gibraltar   1

Lanius nubicus
Bulgaria   13

Perisoreus infaustus
Sweden   6

Pyrrhocorax
  pyrrhocorax
Andorra   1
France   1,40,47,48
Greece   16
Rep. of Ireland   1
Portugal   7
Spain   34,44,109
Switzerland   13
United Kingdom   2,17,25
  Isle of Man   1,4,7

Fringilla teydea
Spain
  Canary Islands   10

Loxia scotica
United Kingdom   18,30

Bucanetes githagineus
Spain   79,84
  Canary Islands   10,13

Carpodacus rubicilla
No specific sources provided

Emberiza cia
Albania   5,7,9,10
Andorra   1
Austria   14
Bulgaria   13
France   47,48
Germany   20
Portugal   11
Romania   19,35
Slovakia   4
Spain   3,4,19,45,55,60,97,
     101,103,105,115,134
Ukraine   25,42

Data References: Source Codes

Emberiza cineracea
No specific sources provided

Emberiza hortulana

Albania	3,5,7,9
Andorra	1
Belarus	14

Belgium	1,3,15
Bulgaria	13
Czech Republic	9
Denmark	18
France	1,9,29,47
Germany	8
Latvia	10,19
Lithuania	3,4

Netherlands	5,12,14
Poland	39,45
Portugal	11
Spain	45,55,101,103, 115,134
Sweden	6
Switzerland	2
Ukraine	42

Emberiza melanocephala

Albania	5,7,9
Bulgaria	13

DATA REFERENCES: COUNTRY-BY-COUNTRY LIST

This list comprises details of literature sources used in compiling the population tables for individual species. The code numbers given with the majority of references, and the system of cross-referencing, are explained on p. 514. For details of references cited in the text, see p. 551.

ALBANIA

Breeding
1. CATSADORAKIS, G. (1987) [*The National Park of Prespa.*] Elliniki Etairia. (In Greek.)
2. CRIVELLI, A. J. (1994) The importance of the former U.S.S.R. for the conservation of pelican populations nesting in the Palearctic. In A. J. Crivelli, V. G. Krivenko and V. G. Vinogradov, eds. *Pelicans in the former U.S.S.R.* Slimbridge, U.K.: International Waterfowl and Wetlands Research Bureau (Spec. Publ. 27).
3. CROCKFORD, N. J. AND SUTHERLAND, W. J. (1991) Some Albanian Important Bird Areas (unpublished).
4. GRIMMETT, R. F. A. AND JONES, T. A. (1989) *Important bird areas in Europe.* Cambridge, U.K.: International Council for Bird Preservation (Techn. Publ. 9).
5. LAMANI, F. AND PUZANOV, V. (1962) [Inventory of the Birds of Albania.] *Bul. U. Sh. Tirane, Ser. Shk. Nat.* 16: 100–117. (In Albanian.)
6. MAKATSCH, W. (1950) [*The birdlife of Macedonia.*] Leipzig: Akademische Verlagsgesellschaft Geest and Portkig, K-G. (In German.)
7. MATVEJEV, S. D. AND VASIC, V. F. (1973) [*Catalogue of the fauna of Yugoslavia. IV/3, Aves Ljubliana.*] (In Serbo-Croat.)
8. NOWAK, E. (1980) [Waterbirds and wetlands of Albania: status, changes, use and protection.] *Beitr. Vogelkunde* 26: 65–103. (In German.)
9. NOWAK, E. (1989) Provisional species list of the birds of Albania (manuscript).
10. REISER, O. AND VON FÜHRER, L. (1896) [*Materials for Ornis Balcanica IV.*] Vienna: Montenegro. (In German.)
11. SHEPHERD, M. (1975) *Let's look at Montenegro.* Ornitholidays guide no. 5.
12. ZEKO, I. (1963) [Inventory of the birds of Albania.] *Bul. U. Sh. Tirane, Ser. Shk. Nat.* 17: 96–99. (In Albanian.)
13. ZEKO, I. AND LAMANI, F. (1966) [Ornithological data from the reserve of Kunës.] *Bul. U. Sh. Tirane, Ser. Shk. Nat.* 20: 3–14. (In Albanian.)

ANDORRA

Breeding
1. ADN (in prep.) Atlas of breeding birds in Andorra 1992–1996. Associació per a la Defensa de la Natura.
2. MUNTANER, J., FERRER, X. AND MARTÍNEZ-VILLALTA, A. (1983) [*Atlas of the breeding birds of Cataluña and Andorra.*] Barcelona: Ketres. (In Catalan.)

AUSTRIA

Breeding
1. BERG, H.-M., ZELZ, S. AND ZUNA-KRATKY, T. (1992) [Two important occurrences of Woodlark *Lullula arborea* in Lower Austria.] *Vogelkundliche Nachrichten aus Ostösterreich* 3–4: 1–6. (In German.)
2. GAMAUF, A. (1991) [*Birds of prey in Austria: populations, threats, laws.*] Vienna: Umweltbundesamt (Monogr. 29). (In German.)
3. HAFNER, F. (1990) [*Alectoris graeca*: an almost unknown bird.] *Natur und Land.* 76: 15–18. (In German.)
4. KILZER, R. AND BLUM, V. (1991) [*Atlas of breeding birds of Vorarlberg.*] Bregenz: Vorarlberger Landschaftspflegefonds/Österreichische Gesellschaft für Vogelkunde Landesstelle Vorarlberg. (In German.)
5. KOHLER, B. AND RAUER, J. (1992) [Results of 1991 census of *Vanellus vanellus, Limosa limosa* and *Tringa totanus* in Seewinkel.] *Vogelkundliche Nachrichten aus Ostösterreich* 1: 11–17. (In German.)
6. KOLLAR, H. P. (1989) [Population trend of *Otis tarda* in Marchfeld, Lower Austria.] *Egretta* 32: 73–75. (In German.)
7. MÜLLER, C. Y. (1984) [Population trends and migration of *Platalea leucorodia* in Austria and Hungary.] *Egretta* 27: 45–67. (In German.)
8. PROKOP, P. (1989) [Bird populations of the military training area Grossmittel.] Pp.93–111 in K. Farasin, G. Schramayr, A. Kaltenbach, F. Tiedmann, P. Prokop, F. M. Grünweis and M. Hauser, eds. [*Study on biotopes of the military training area Grossmittel.*] Vienna: Umweltbundesamt (Monogr. 10). (In German.)
9. SACKL, P. (1985) [The Black Stork *Ciconia nigra* in Austria: expansion, population dynamics and distribution.] *Vogelwelt* 106: 121–141. (In German.)
10. SACKL, P. AND LAUERMANN, H. (1990) [Distribution and population trend of *Lanius excubitor* in Waldviertel.] *Vogelkundliche Nachrichten aus Ostösterreich* 4: 1–5. (In German.)
11. SAMWALD, O. AND SAMWALD, F. (1989) [Population numbers, phenology, breeding biology and decline of the Roller *Coracias garrulus* in Styria, Austria.] *Egretta* 32: 37–57. (In German.)
12. SCHIFTER, H. (1989) [Status of *Ciconia ciconia* in Austria 1988.] *Vogelschutz in Österreich* 4: 38–39. (In German.)
13. SCHMALZER, A. (1990) [*Black Grouse in Mühlviertel.*] Linz, Austria: Amt der oö. Landesregierung. (In German.)
14. WÖHL, E. (1989) [The Rock Bunting *Emberiza cia* L. as a breeding bird in Styria, Austria.] *Egretta* 32: 12–16. (In German.)

Wintering
1. AUBRECHT, G. AND BÖCK, F. (1985) [*Austrian waters as wintering areas for waterfowl, 3.*] Vienna: Bundesministeriums für Gesundheit und Umweltschutz (Grüne Reihe). (In German.)
2. KILZER, R. AND BLUM, V. (1991) [*Atlas of breeding birds of Vorarlberg.*] Bregenz: Vorarlberger Land-

schaftspflegefonds/Österreichische Gesellschaft für Vogelkunde Landesstelle Vorarlberg. (In German.)

BELARUS

Breeding

1. BIRYUKOV, V. P. (1990a) [Breeding of Scops Owl in northern Byelorussia.] *Protected Animals of Byelorussia* 1: 24. (In Russian.)

2. BIRYUKOV, V. P. (1990b) [The breeding of Black-throated Diver in Byelorussia.] *Protected Animals of Byelorussia* 1: 25–28. (In Russian.)

3. DOLBIK, M. S. (1985) [Revision of the composition and distribution of Byelorussian avifauna.] *Arch. Byel. Acad. Sci. Ser. Biol. Sci.* 34: 85–89. (In Russian.)

4. DOROFEEV, A. M. (1982) [Common Crane in Byelorussia.] Pp.68–74 in I. N. Neufeldt, ed. [*Cranes of the U.S.S.R., I.*] Leningrad: Nauka. (In Russian.)

5. GRICHIK, V. V. (1990) [Breeding Smew in Byelorussia.] *Protected Animals of Byelorussia* 1: 30. (In Russian.)

6. IVANOVKSY, V. V. (1990a) [Status of Short-toed Eagle in Byelorussia.] *Protected Animals of Byelorussia* 1: 42–48. (In Russian.)

7. IVANOVSKY, V. V. (1990b) [Status of White-tailed Eagle in Byelorussia.] *Protected Animals of Byelorussia* 2: 25–28. (In Russian.)

8. IVANYUTENKO, A. N. AND BYCHKOV, V. P. (1989) [Distribution of Black Grouse in Byelorussia.] Pp.244 in L. M. Sushchenia, ed. *Abstrs. VI Zool. Conf. Byel. SSR.* Minsk: Nauka. (In Russian.)

9. KOZLOV, V. A., SUSHCHENIA, L. M. AND PARFENOV, V. I. (1981) [*Red Data Book of Byelorussia SSR: rare and endangered plants and animals.*] Minsk: Byel. Encyclopedia Press. (In Russian.)

10. KOZULIN, A. V. (1990) [Isolated colony of Smew in Pripiat Polessie region.] *Protected Animals of Byelorussia* 2: 28–29. (In Russian.)

11. NAUMCHIK, A. V. (1982) [*Protected plants and animals of Byelorussia.*] Minsk: Byel. NIINTI. (In Russian.)

12. NAUMCHIK, A. V. (1989) [Distribution of Larids in different habitats in Byelorussia.] Pp.150–151 in M. Zalakevicius, ed. *Abstrs. XII East. Baltic Orn. Conf.* Vilnius: Mintis Publ. (In Russian.)

13. NIKIFOROV, M. E. AND KOZULIN, A. V. (1990) [New breeding bird species in Byelorussia.] *Protected Animals of Byelorussia* 1: 4–7. (In Russian.)

14. NIKIFOROV, M. E., YAMINSKY, B. V. AND SHKLIAROV, L. P. (1989) [*Birds of Byelorussia: handbook to nests and eggs.*] Minsk: Vysheishaya Shkola Publ. (In Russian.)

15. SAMUSENKO, I. E. (1987) [Distribution and numbers of Black Stork in Byelorussia.] Pp.143–144 in T. V. Koshkina, ed. *Impact of human transformation of landscapes of populations of terrestrial vertebrates: All-Union Symposium.* Moscow: Nauka (abstracts). (In Russian.)

16. SAMUSENKO, I. E. AND LEVANOVICH, A. M. (1990) [Some aspects of distribution and population dynamics of White Stork in Byelorussia.] Pp.129–146 in B. P. Savitsky and E. G. Samusenko, eds. [*Storks: distribution, ecology and conservation.*] Minsk: Nauka i Tekhnika Publ. (In Russian.)

17. SHOKALO, S. I. (1990) [Whiskered Tern: breeding species in Byelorussia.] *Protected Animals of Byelorussia* 2: 36–37. (In Russian.)

18. TISHECHKIN, A. K. AND IVANOVSKY, V. V. (1993) [Status and breeding performance of the Osprey *Pandion haliaetus* in northern Byelorussia.] *Ornis Fenn.* 69: 149–154.

BELGIUM

Breeding

1. ANSELIN, A. AND DEVOS, K. (1992) Population estimates of breeding birds in Flanders 1989–1991. Flemmish contribution to BirdLife International's Dispersed Species Project. V. Z. W. Vlavcio in cooperation with Koninklijk Belgisch Institut voor Natuurwetenschappen–Institut Royal des Sciences Naturelles de Belgique, Brussels (unpublished).

2. CLOTUCHE, E., DEEVINGT, W. AND FOUARGE, J. P. (1989) [New breeding of the Common Gull *Larus canus* in the Meuse valley.] *Aves* 26: 212–213. (In French.)

3. DEVILLERS, P., ROGGEMAN, W., TRICOT, J., DEL MARMOL, P., KERWIJN, C., JACOB, J.-P. AND ANSELIN, A., EDS. (1988) [*Atlas of the breeding birds of Belgium.*] Brussels: Institut Royal des Sciences Naturelles de Belgique. (In French.)

4. DEVOS, K., MEIRE, P., MAES, P., BENOY, L., GABRIESEL, J., DE SCHEEMAEKER, F., DE SMET, W. AND VAN IMPE, J. (1991) [Breeding populations of waders in Belgium, 1989–1990.] *Oriolus* 57: 43–56. (In Dutch.)

5. DE DOE, J. (1991) [Better years for the Barn Owl, 1988–1989.] *Wielewaal* 57: 141–147. (In Dutch.)

6. DOUCET, J. (1989) [The reappearance of nesting Eagle Owls *Bubo bubo* in Wallonie—its reintroduction in Western Europe.] *Aves* 26: 137–158. (In French.)

7. GÉE, L. H. (1989) [The Eagle Owl *Bubo bubo*: status in Wallonie in 1988 and 1989.] *Aves* 26: 214–219. (In French.)

8. GÉE, L. H. AND WEISS, J. (1987) [Present status of the Eagle Owl *Bubo bubo* in Belgium and adjoining regions.] *Aves* 24: 49–63. (In French.)

9. JACOB, J. P. AND LOLY, P. (1986) [The Common Gull *Larus canus* breeding in the region of Liège—status of the breeding population in Wallonie in 1986.] *Aves* 23: 188–189. (In French.)

10. LAMBERT, M. AND CLOTUCHE, E. (1987) [Renewed breeding of the Peregrine *Falco peregrinus* in Belgium.] *Aves* 24: 169–176. (In French.)

11. OVERAL, B. (1989) [A waited event in Belgium: the proof of the breeding of the Black Stork *Ciconia nigra*.] *Aves* 26: 122–125. (In French.)

12. PIERRE, P. (1985) [Recent evolution of status of Sand Martin *Riparia riparia* in Belgian Lorraine.] *Aves* 22: 107–114. (In French.)

13. PIERRE, P. (1989) [Actual status of Black Stork *Ciconia nigra* in Wallonie.] *Aves* 25: 183–189. (In French.)

14. RYELANDT, P. (1990) [Status of Corncrake *Crex crex* in Fagne and Ramenne.] *Aves* 27: 245–261. (In French.)

15. VLAVICO, V. Z. W. (1989) [*Birds in Flanders: presence and distribution.*] Bornem: IMP. (In Dutch.)

16. WALRAVENS, M. AND LANGHENDRIES, R. (1985) [Nesting of the House Martin in the south and east of the Brussels region.] *Aves* 22: 3–34. (In French.)

17. DE WAVRIN, H. (1990) [Nightjar *Caprimulgus europaeus*

in Wallonie and Brussels.] *Aves* 27: 137–158. (In French.)

Wintering

1. VAN DEN BOSSCHE, W. (1991) [A study on the presence of the Woodcock in Flanders.] Report for Flemish Minister of Environment, Nature Conservation and Land-use, Koninklijk Belgisch Institut voor Natuurwetenschappen, Brussels. (In Dutch.)
2. IWRB (INTERNATIONAL WATERFOWL AND WETLANDS RESEARCH BUREAU) (1980–1990) Waterfowl counts from database in Hasselt, Belgium and database Centrale Ornithologique Aves, Liège, Belgium.
3. DE PUTTER, G., DE SCHUYTER, T., WILLEMYNS, F. AND DE SCHEEMAEKER, F. (1989) [Some total counts of waders along the Flemish North Sea coast, September 1988–February 1989.] *Mergus* 3: 64–88. (In Dutch.)
4. VLAVICO, V. Z. W. (1989) [*Birds in Flanders: presence and distribution.*] Bornem: IMP. (In Dutch.)

BULGARIA

Breeding

1. BOEV, N., ED. (1985) [*Red Data Book of the people's republic of Bulgaria. 2: animals.*] Sofia: BAS Publishing House. (In Bulgarian.)
2. CRIVELLI, A. J. (1994) The importance of the former U.S.S.R. for the conservation of pelican populations nesting in the Palearctic. In A. J. Crivelli, V. G. Krivenko and V. G. Vinogradov, eds. *Pelicans in the former U.S.S.R.* Slimbridge, U.K.: International Waterfowl and Wetlands Research Bureau (Spec. Publ. 27).
3. IANKOV, P. (in press) [Distribution and numbers of the Corncrake *Crex crex* L. in Bulgaria.] *Ecologia.* (In Bulgarian.)
4. IANKOV, P. AND PROFIROV, L. (1991) [Current status of the Griffon Vulture *Gyps fulvus* population in Bulgaria.] *Ecologia* 24: 44–52. (In Bulgarian.)
5. IANKOV, P., MICHEV, T., PROFIROV, L. AND IVANOV, B. (1990) National Bank for Ornithological Information at the Bulgarian Society for the Protection of Birds (unpublished data).
6. IANKOV, P., PETROV, T., MICHEV, T. AND PROFIROV, L. (1993) Distribution and numbers of the Lesser Kestrel *Falco naumanni* Fleisher in Bulgaria. Pp.1–8 in R. D. Chancellor, ed. *Proceedings of the IV World Conference on Birds of Prey and Owls, Berlin 10–17 May 1992.* London: B.-U. Meyburg and the World Working Group on Birds of Prey and Owls.
7. NANKINOV, D., SIMEONOV, S., MICHEV, T. AND IVANOV, B. (in press) [*The fauna of Bulgaria. 2: Aves.*] Sofia: BAS Publishing House. (In Bulgarian.)
8. MICHEV, T. (1981) [The Dalmatian Pelican *Pelecanus crispus* Bruch., its numbers and population dynamics in the Srebarna Nature Reserve in Southern Dobrudja.] Pp.516–527 in S. Nedialkov, ed. *Regional Symposium on Project 8 MAB, 1985.* Sofia: BAS Publishing House (MAB Report). (In Bulgarian.)
9. MICHEV, T. AND PETROV, T. (1985) [Distribution and numbers of the Saker *Falco cherrug* Grey, 1834 in Bulgaria.] Pp.314–324 in S. Nedialkov, ed. *International Symposium on MAB Project 8, 1985, Blagoevgrad, Bulgaria.* Sofia: BAS Publishing House (MAB Report). (In Bulgarian.)
10. MICHEV, T. AND PETROV, T. (1987) [A contribution to the distribution of the Black Kite *Milvus migrans migrans* (Voddaert 1783) in Bulgaria.] Pp.164–177 in S. Nedialkov, ed. *International Symposium of the Role of Wetlands in preserving genetic material, Srebarna, Bulgaria.* Sofia: BAS Publishing House. (In Bulgarian.)
11. MICHEV, T. AND STOJANOVA, L. (1986) [Nesting distribution and numbers of the White Stork *Ciconia nigra* L. 1758 in Bulgaria.] *Ecologia* 18: 17–26. (In Bulgarian.)
12. MICHEV, T., VATEV, I., SIMEONOV, P. AND PROFIROV, L. (1984) [Distribution and nesting of the Long-legged Buzzard *Buteo rufinus* (Cretzchmar, 1827) in Bulgaria.] *Ecologia* 13: 74–82. (In Bulgarian.)
13. MICHEV, T., IANKOV, P. AND PROFIROV, L. (1990) The atlas of breeding birds in Bulgaria. Distribution maps with questionnaire to European Ornithological Atlas Committee (manuscript).
14. MICHEV, T., PETROV, T., PROFIROV, L., IANKOV, P. AND GAVRAILOV, S. (1989) [Distribution and nature protection status of the Golden Eagle *Aquila chrysaetos chrysaetos* L. 1758 in Bulgaria.] *Bull. Mus. South Bulgaria* 15: 79–87. (In Bulgarian.)
15. PETROV, T., IANKOV, P., MICHEV, T. AND PROFIROV, L. (1991) [Distribution and numbers of the Black Stork *Ciconia nigra* L. in Bulgaria.] *Bull. Mus. South Bulgaria* 17: 25–32. (In Bulgarian.)
16. PETROV, T., IANKOV, P., DARAKCHIEV, A., NIKOLOV, K., MICHEV, T., PORFIROV, L. AND MILCHEV, B. (1993a) State of the Imperial Eagle (*Aquila heliaca savigny*) in Bulgaria in the period between 1890 and 1993 (unpublished report).
17. PETROV, T., IANKOV, P., KOLTCHAKOV, R., MICHEV, T., PROFIROV, L. AND NYAGOLOV, K. (1993b) [Numbers, distribution and preservation of the Peregrine *Falco peregrinus* in Bulgaria.] Pp.1–8 in R. D. Chancellor, ed. *Proceedings of the IV World Conference on Birds of prey and Owls, Berlin 10–17 May 1992.* London: B.-U. Meyburg and the World Working Group on Birds of Prey and Owls.
18. SIMEONOV, S. AND MICHEV, T. (1985) [On the present distribution and abundance of the Eagle Owl *Bubo bubo* L. in Bulgaria.] *Ecologia* 15: 60–65. (In Bulgarian.)
19. SIMEONOV, S., MICHEV, T. AND SIMEONOV, P. (1981) [Materials on the nesting distribution and the diet of the Barn Owl *Tyto alba scopoli* in Bulgaria.] *Ecologia* 8: 49–54. (In Bulgarian.)
20. SIMEONOV, S., MICHEV, T. AND NANKINOV, D. (1990) [*The fauna of Bulgaria. 1: Aves, 20.*] Sofia: BAS Publishing House. (In Bulgarian.)

Wintering

1. NANKINOV, D., SIMEONOV, S., MICHEV, T. AND IVANOV, B. (in press) [*The fauna of Bulgaria. 2: Aves.*] Sofia: BAS Publishing House. (In Bulgarian.)
2. MICHEV, T., IVANOV, B., PROFIROV, L., NANKINOV, D. AND POMACOV, V. (1977–1991) Mid-winter counts of birds in Bulgaria. Institute of Ecology (manuscript).
3. MICHEV, T., POMAKOV, V., NANKINOV, D., IVANOV, B. AND PROFIROV, L. (1991) A short note on wild geese in Bulgaria during the period 1977–1989. *Ardea* 79: 167–168.

CROATIA

Breeding

1. MIKUSKA, T. (1993) *in litt.* to BirdLife International.
2. SCHNEIDER-JACOBY, M. AND VASIC, V. F. (1989) The Red-breasted Pochard *Netta rufina*, breeding and wintering in Yugoslavia. *Wildfowl* 40: 39–44.

CZECH REPUBLIC

Breeding

1. CHYTIL, J. AND MACHÁCEK, P. (1991) [Regular nesting of Common Gull *Larus canus* in South Moravia.] *Sylvia* 28: 129–131. (In Czech.)
2. FIALA, V. (1982) [Status of waterfowl in Czech Republic.] *Acta Sci. Nat. Brno.* 16: 1–49. (In German.)
3. HANUS, V., BOUCHNER, M. AND FISER, Z. (1979) [Present status of Black Grouse in the Czech Republic.] *Myslivost* 4: 78–79. (In Czech.)
4. HORA, J. (1982) [Population of Red-crested Pochard *Netta rufina* (Pallas, 1773) in the Trebon region in 1974–1979.] Pp.21–38 in J. Zeman, ed. *Proceedings on contributions to ornithological research in South Bohemia.* Ceske Budejovice: Jihoceské Muzeum. (In Czech.)
5. KLOUBEC, B. (1988) [The first breeding of Spoonbill *Platalea leucorodia* L. in Bohemia.] Pp.133–139 in J. Sitko and P. Trpak, eds. *Proc. Conf. Waterbirds 1987.* Prevov: SZN Praha. (In Czech.)
6. KURKA, P. (1991) [The first documented breeding of Crane *Grus grus* in Czechoslovakia.] *Sylvia* 28: 89–94. (In Czech.)
7. MRLÍK, V. AND DANKO, S. (1990) [Numbers of nesting pairs of birds of prey in Czechoslovakia in 1988.] *Sylvia* 27: 71–78. (In Czech with English summary.)
8. REJMAN, B. (1990) [1989—Year of the stork in the Czech Republic.] *Panurus (Pardubice)* 3: 107–112. (In Czech.)
9. STASTNY, K., RANDÍK, A. AND HUDEC, K. (1987) [*Atlas of the breeding distribution of birds in Czechoslovakia 1973–1977.*] Prague: Academia. (In Czech.)
10. TRPÁK, P. (1987) [Project *Haliaeetus*—a successful reintroduction of an extinct species.] *Památky a príroda* 12: 545–554. (In Czech.)

DENMARK

Breeding

1. ASBIRK, S. (1978) [Breeding numbers and habitat selection of Danish Black Guillemots *Cepphus grylle*.] *Dansk Ornit. Foren. Tidsskr.* 72: 161–178. (In Danish.)
2. ASBIRK, S. (1988) [The breeding population of the Black Guillemot *Cepphus grylle* in Denmark 1978–1987.] *Dansk Ornit. Foren. Tidsskr.* 82: 131–133. (In Danish.)
3. ASBIRK, S. AND BRAAE, L. (1988) [Status and trends of birds.] Pp.64–70 in S. Asbirk, ed. [*The nature in Denmark.*] Copenhagen: Miljøministeriet Skov-og Naturstyrelsen. (In Danish.)
4. ASBIRK, S., BRØGGER-JENSEN, S. AND FALK, K. (1989) [Status of the breeding populations of some scarce bird species in Denmark.] *Dansk Ornit. Foren. Tidsskr.* 83: 103–104. (In Danish.)

5. BILEDGAARD, K. (1992) pers. comm.
6. BRAAE, L. AND KAYSER, B. (1985) [How many birds are breeding in Denmark?] *Fugle* 5: 30–31. (In Danish.)
7. CHRISTENSEN, J. O., ED. (1988) [*Status of breeding gulls and terns in Denmark 1988.*] Copenhagen: Dansk Ornitologisk Forening. (In Danish.)
8. CHRISTENSEN, J. O., ED. (1990) [*Status of breeding populations of gulls and terns and others in Denmark 1988.*] Copenhagen: Dansk Ornitologisk Forening. (In Danish.)
9. CLAUSAGER, I. (1974) [Marking of gamebirds 1950–1973.] *Dansk Vildtforskning* 117: 41–47. (In Danish.)
10. DEGN, H. J. (1973) [Distribution of Black Grouse *Tetrao tetrix* in Denmark 1973.] *Danske Vildtundersøgelser* 22. (In Danish.)
11. DEGN, H. J. (1978) [Trends for population of Black Grouse *Tetrao tetrix* in Denmark until 1978.] *Danske Vildtundersøgelser* 31. (In Danish.)
12. DYBBRO, T. (1976) [*Distribution of Danish breeding birds.*] Copenhagen: Dansk Ornitologisk Forening. (In Danish.)
13. DYBBRO, T. (1985) [*Status of Danish bird locations.*] Copenhagen: Dansk Ornitologisk Forening. (In Danish.)
14. DYBBRO, T. AND JØRGENSEN, O. H. (1971) [The distribution of Black-tailed Godwit *Limosa limosa*, Dunlin *Calidris alpina*, Ruff *Philomachus pugnax* and Avocet *Recurvirostra avosetta* in Denmark 1970.] *Dansk Ornit. Foren. Tidsskr.* 65: 116–128. (In Danish.)
15. FLENSTED, K. (1992) pers. comm.
16. JEPSEN, P. U. (1989) [*Status of Black Grouse* Tetrao tetrix *in Denmark 1989.*] Rønde: Miljøministeriets Vildtforvaltning. (In Danish.)
17. JØRGENSEN, H. E. (1989) [*Raptors of Denmark.*] Copenhagen: Frederikshus. (In Danish.)
18. LAURSEN, K. (1989) Estimates of sea duck winter populations of the western Palearctic. *Dan. Rev. Game Biol.* 13: 6.
19. MARDAL, W. (1974) [Report on terns.] *Feltornitologen* 16: 4–7. (In Danish.)
20. MØLLER, A. P. (1978) [Distribution, population size and changes in gulls *Larinae* breeding in Denmark, with a review of the situation in other parts of Europe.] *Dansk Ornit. Foren. Tidsskr.* 72: 15–39. (In Danish.)
21. MUNK, M., CHRISTENSEN, R., SKOV, H. AND SMIDT, J. (1991) [The Danish Bird Report 1989.] *Dansk Ornit. Foren. Tidsskr.* 85: 109–144. (In Danish.)
22. OLSEN, R. M. (1991) [Rare birds in Denmark and Greenland in 1989.] *Dansk Ornit. Foren. Tidsskr.* 85: 20–34. (In Danish.)
23. ØSTERGAARD, E. (1988) [*Birds at night in Ringkøbing Amt 1986–1987.*] Lokalafdeling and Ringkøbing: Dansk Ornitologisk Forening. (In Danish.)
24. PETERSEN, B. S. AND BØRGGER-JENSEN, S. (1992) [The populations of Common Danish Woodland birds 1976–1990.] *Dansk Ornit. Foren. Tidsskr.* 86: 137–154. (In Danish.)
25. SKOV, H., MUNK, M., CHRISTENSEN, R., LINDBALLE, P. AND SMIDT, J. (1992) [The Danish Bird Report 1990.] *Dansk Ornit. Foren. Tidsskr.* 86: 209–242. (In Danish.)
26. SØRENSEN, U. G. (in prep.) [Rare breeding birds in Denmark.] (In Danish.)
27. SØRENSEN, U. G. AND CHRISTENSEN, R. (1991) Data

collected for the European Ornithological Atlas Committee (unpublished).

Wintering

1. BEEKMAN, J. H., DIRKSEN, S. P. AND SLAGBOOM, T. H. (1985) Population size and breeding success of Bewick's Swans wintering in Europe in 1983–1984. *Wildfowl* 36: 5–12.
2. JENSEN, F. P., ED. (in prep.) [*Birds in the coastal waters of Denmark.*] Copenhagen: Skov-og Naturstyrelsen, Miljøministeriet.
3. LAURSEN, K. (1989) Estimates of sea duck winter populations of the western Palearctic. *Dan. Rev. Game Biol.* 13: 6.
4. MADSEN, J. (1987) Status and trends of goose populations in the western Palearctic in the 1980s. *Ardea* 79: 113–122.
5. MELTOFTE, H. (1981) [*Wader counts in Denmark 1974–1978.*] Copenhagen: Fregningsstyrelsen, Miljøministeriet.
6. MELTOFTE, H., BLEW, J., KRIKKE, J., RÖSNER, H.-U. AND SMIT, C. (in prep.) Numbers and distribution of waterbirds in the Wadden Sea. *Wader Study Group Bull.* (Suppl.).
7. PEDERSEN, M. B. (1989a) [Wintering strategy of the Jack Snipe in Denmark.] *Dansk Ornit. Foren. Tidsskr.* 83: 69–73.
8. PEDERSEN, M. B. (1989b) [Changes in the occurrence of the roosting and moulting Snipes and Jack Snipes on inland habitats in Denmark.] *Dansk Ornit. Foren. Tidsskr.* 83: 75–82.
9. PEDERSEN, M. B. (1991) Winter population estimates of Jack Snipe and Common Snipe in Denmark. *Dansk Ornit. Foren. Tidsskr.* 85: 173–174.
10. PIHL, S. (1993) pers. comm. to M. Munk.
11. SMIT, C. J. AND PIERSMA, T. (1989) Numbers, midwinter distribution, and migration of wader populations using the East Atlantic flyway. Pp.24–63 in H. Boyd and J.-Y. Pirot, eds. *Flyways and reserve networks for waterbirds.* Slimbridge: International Waterfowl and Wetlands Research Bureau (Spec. Publ. 9).

Faroe Islands
Breeding

1. BLOCH, D. AND SØRENSEN, S. (1984) [*Checklist of Faroese birds.*] Tórshavn: Føroya Skúlabókagrunnur.
2. GRIMMETT, R. F. A. AND JONES, T. A. (1989) *Important bird areas in Europe.* Cambridge, U.K.: International Council for Bird Preservation (Techn. Publ. 9).
3. HARRIS, M. P. (1984) *The Puffin.* Calton, U.K.: T. and A. D. Poyser.
4. JENSEN, J. K. AND KAMPP, K. (1990) [Breeding records of the Quail in the Faroes.] *Dansk Ornit. Foren. Tidsskr.* 84: 71–76. (In Danish with English summary.)
5. MARTIN, A. R. (1989) *in litt* to S. Sørenson.
6. OLSEN, B. (1992) pers. comm. to S. Sørenson.
7. OLSEN, B. AND JENSEN, J.-K. (1992) pers. comm. to S. Sørenson.
8. OLSEN, B. AND MORTENSEN, E. (1992) pers. comm. to S. Sørenson.
9. OLSEN, B. AND PERMIN, M. (1974) [The population of Gannet on Mykines Hólmur 1972.] *Dansk Ornit. Foren. Tidsskr.* 68: 39–42. (In Danish with English summary.)

Greenland
Breeding

1. EVANS, P. G. H. (1984) The seabirds of Greenland: their status and conservation. Pp.49–84 in J. P. Croxall, P. G. H. Evans and R. W. Schreiber, eds. *Status and conservation of the world's seabirds.* Cambridge, U.K.: International Council for Bird Preservation (Techn. Publ. 2).
2. FALK, K. AND MØLLER, S. (1988) Status of the Peregrine Falcon in South Greenland: Population density and reproduction. Pp.37–43 in T. J. Cade, J. H. Enderson, C. G. Thelander and C. M. White, eds. *Peregrine Falcon populations: their management and recovery.* Sacramento: The Peregrine Fund Inc.
3. HJORT, C., HÅKANSSON, E. AND STEMMERIK, L. (1983) Bird observations around the Nordøst vandet polynya, North-east Greenland 1980. *Dansk Ornit. Foren. Tidsskr.* 77: 107–114.
4. HJORT, C., HÅKANSSON, E. AND MØLGAARD, P. (1987) Brent Geese *Branta bernicla*, Snow Geese *Anser caerulescens* and Barnacle Geese *Branta leucopsis* on Kilen, Kronprins Christian Land, North-east Greenland, 1985. *Dansk Ornit. Foren. Tidsskr.* 81: 121–128.
5. KAMPP, K. AND WILLE, F. (1990) [The White-tailed Eagle population in Greenland.] *Dansk Ornit. Foren. Tidsskr.* 84: 37–44. (In Danish.)
6. WRIGHT, N. J. R. AND MATTHEWS, D. W. (1980) New nesting colonies of the Ivory Gull *Pagophila eburnea* in southern East Greenland. *Dansk Ornit. Foren. Tidsskr.* 74: 59–64.

ESTONIA
General

VEROMANN, H. AND LEIBAK, E., EDS. (in press) *Birds of Estonia: numbers, distribution and phenology.*

Wintering

1. KURESOO, A. (1985) [Wintering of waterfowl in Estonia.] *Communications of the Baltic Commission for the study of Bird Migration* 17: 63–79. (In Russian.)
2. KURESOO, A. (1991) Present status of Mute Swan *Cygnus olor*, Whooper swan *C. cygnus* and Bewick's Swan *C. bewickii* wintering in the Eastern Baltic Region. *Wildfowl* 1: 214–217.

FINLAND
Breeding

1. HARIO, M., KASTEPOLD, T., KILPI, M., STAAV, R. AND STJERNBERG, T. (1987) [Status of the Caspian Tern *Sterna caspia* in the Baltic.] *Ornis Fenn.* 64: 154–157.
2. HONGELL, H. (1989) [Ecology of the Little Tern *Sterna albifrons*.] *Ornis Botnica* 10: 138–168. (In Finnish with English summary.)
3. KARLIN, A. (1985) [Crane research in Finland.] *Lintumies* 20: 111–118. (In Finnish with English summary.)
4. PAKARINEN, R. (1989) [A survey of the Black-throated Diver population in 1985–86 in Finland.] *Lintumies* 24: 2–11. (In Finnish with English summary.)
5. PAKARINEN, R. AND JÄRVINEN, O. (1984) [The Red-throated Diver *Gavia stellata* in Finland: a ecological population analysis of its status and population trends.]

Lintumies 19: 46–54. (In Finnish with English summary.)

6. SAUROLA, P. (1985) [Finnish birds of prey: status and population changes.] *Ornis Fenn.* 62: 64–72. (In Finnish.)

7. SAUROLA, P. (1990) [The Osprey—symbol of bird protection and monitoring.] *Lintumies* 25: 80–86. (In Finnish with English summary.)

8. STJERNBERG, T., KOIVUSAARI, J. AND NUUJA, I. (1990) [Population trends and nesting success of the White-tailed Eagle in Finland in 1970–89.] *Lintumies* 25: 65–75. (In Finnish with English summary.)

9. VIROLAINEN, E. AND RASSI, P. (1990) [Population trends of Finnish Golden Eagles in 1970–89.] *Lintumies* 25: 59–64. (In Finnish with English summary.)

10. WIKMAN, M. (1990) [The Peregrine Falcon in Finland 1980–89.] *Lintumies* 25: 54–58. (In Finnish with English summary.)

FRANCE

Breeding

1. DE BEAUFORT, F., ED. (1983) [*Red book of the endangered species of France. 1: vertebrates.*] Paris: Secretariat Faune Flore. Muséum Hist. Nat. Paris.

2. BERNARD-LAURENT, A., LEONARD, P. AND LEONARD, Y. (1992) [*Ecological study of the Rock Partridge.*] Paris: ONC/CNERA Annual Report 1991. (In French.)

3. BERTELSEN, J. AND SIMONSEN, N. H. (1986) *Documentation on bird hunting and the conservation status of the species involved: situation in 1986.* Copenhagen: Game and Wildlife Administration.

4. BLONDEL, J. AND ISENMANN, P. (1981) [*Guide to birds of the Camargue.*] Paris: Delachaux et Niestlé. (In French.)

5. BRICHETTI, P. AND DI CAPI (1987) Distribution, population and breeding ecology of the Corsican Nuthatch *Sitta whiteheadi. Riv. Ital. Orn. Milano* 55: 3–26.

6. BROYER, J. (1987) [Distribution of Corncrakes *Crex crex* in France.] *Alauda* 55: 10–19. (In French.)

7. CARLON, J. (1987) [Numbers, distribution and density of the Booted Eagle in the Atlantic Pyrenees.] *Alauda* 55: 89–92. (In French.)

8. CHAPPUIS, M. (1991) pers. comm.

9. CLAESSENS, O. (1992) [The status of the Ortolan Bunting (*Emberiza hortulana*) in France and Europe.] *Alauda* 60: 65–76. (In French.)

10. CRAMP, S., ED. (1985) *The birds of the western Palearctic*, 4. Oxford: Oxford University Press.

11. CRAMP, S., ED. (1988) *The birds of the western Palearctic*, 5. Oxford: Oxford University Press.

12. CRAMP, S. AND SIMMONS, K. E. L., EDS. (1977) *The birds of the western Palearctic*, 1. Oxford: Oxford University Press.

13. CRAMP, S. AND SIMMONS, K. E. L., EDS. (1980) *The birds of the western Palearctic*, 2. Oxford: Oxford University Press.

14. CRAMP, S. AND SIMMONS, K. E. L., EDS. (1983) *The birds of the western Palearctic*, 3. Oxford: Oxford University Press.

15. CRUON, R. AND NICOLAU-GUILLAUMET, P. (1985) [French Ornithology Notes.] *Alauda* 13: 33–63. (In French.)

16. CRUVEILLE, M. H. (1987) [Mountain galliformes status in France.] *Colloque Galliformes de Montagne. ONC*: 11–20. (In French.)

17. DALLARD, R. (1989) [*Breeding birds of the Vendres lagoon.*] Montepellier: Assoc. des Basses plaines de l'Aude/GRIVE. (In French.)

18. DUBOIS, P. AND MAHÉO, R. (1986) [*Nesting waders of France.*] Rochefort: Ministère de l'Environnement/Ligue pour la Protection des Oiseaux/BIROE. (In French.)

19. DUHAUTOIS, L. (1984) [Inventory of Purple Heron populations in France: evaluation of the breeding numbers of Bittern and Little Bittern: breeding season 1983.] SNPN, Directorate for the Protection of Nature, State Secretariat for the Environment and the Quality of Life (unpublished). (In French.)

20. DUQUET, M. (1990) [*Status of the White Stork* (Ciconia ciconia) *and the Black Stork* (Ciconia nigra) *in France.*] Rochefort: Ministère de l'Environnement/Ligue pour la Protection des Oiseaux. (In French.)

21. EVANS, P. (1987) *in litt.*

22. FIR (1991) [Endangered Raptors Survey, 19.] (In French.)

23. FIR/UNAO (1984) [*Status of diurnal and non-rupicolous nesting raptors in France 1979–1982.*] Paris: Ministère de l'Environnement Enquete/FIR/UNAO. (In French.)

24. GÉNSBØL, B. (1987) *Collins guide to the birds of prey of Britain and Europe, North Africa and the Middle East.* London: Collins.

25. GRIMMETT, R. F. A. AND JONES, T. A. (1989) *Important bird areas in Europe.* Cambridge, U.K.: International Council for Bird Preservation (Techn. Publ. 9).

26. GUYOT, I., LAUNAY, G. AND VIDAL, P. (1985) [Breeding seabirds of the French Midi and Corsica: change and importance of numbers.] *Annuales du Crop* 2. (In French.)

27. HAFNER, H., JOHNSON, A. AND WALMSLEY, J. G. (1989) [*Tour du Valat Ornithological Annual Report.*] Arles: Tour du Valat. (In French.)

28. JACOB, J.-P., LAFONTAINE, R. M., CHIWY, B., DEVILLERS, P., DE VISSCHER, M.-N. AND LEDANT, P.-P. (1985) [Information sheets on the species listed in Annex I of Directive 79/409/CEE.] Institute Royal des Sciences Naturelles Belgique (unpublished). (In French.)

29. JARRY, G. (in prep.) Data for the forthcoming Atlas of nesting birds of France. Paris: CRBPO (unpublished).

30. JOHNSON, A. (1993) *in litt.* to BirdLife International.

31. LANG, B. AND BROYER, J. (1992) [National survey of the Corncrake. Ligue pour la Protection des Oiseaux/ONC 1991–1992: first results.] *Bull. mens. ONC* 168: 2. (In French.)

32. LEFRANC, N. (1978) [The Lesser Grey Shrike *Lanius minor* in France.] *Alauda* 46: 193–208. (In French.)

33. LEFRANC, N. (1979) [Contribution to the ecology of the Red-backed Shrike (*Lanius collurio L.* in the middle Vosges.] *Oiseau et R.F.O.* 449: 245–298. (In French.)

34. MAGNANY, Y., CRUVEILLE, L., CHEYLAN, L. AND COLLARD, P. (1990) [Between Levan and the Mediterranean—Black Grouse, Rock Partridge, Hare and Marmot, status and changes in their numbers.] *Bull. mens. ONC* 150: 7–15. (In French.)

35. MAOUT, J. (1990) [Status of seabird populations of

Brittany.] *Penn ar Bed* 136: 1–9, 41–42. (In French.)

36. MARION, L. (1991) [*National inventory of the heronries of France.*] MNHN/Université de Rennes/SNPN/ Ministère de l'Environnement. (In French.)

37. MNHN/ONC (1989) [*Distribution and timing of the pre-breeding migration and breeding of hunted water-birds in France.*] Paris: Secrétariat d'Etat a l'Environnement (Rep. 88). (In French.)

38. MULLER, Y. (1987) [Status of the Barn Owl (*Tyto alba*) in church belfries: changes in numbers over a 10-year study.] *Ciconia* 11: 11–12. (In French.)

39. PIERSMA, T. (1986) Breeding waders in Europe. A review of population size estimates and a bibliography of information sources. *Bull. Wader Study Group* 48 (Suppl.): 1–116.

40. ROCAMORA, G. AND THAURONT, M. (1991) [*French inventory of important bird areas, 23.*] Paris: Ministère de l'Environnement/DPN/Ligue pour la Protection des Oiseaux/CIPO. (In French.)

41. SCHIERER, A. (1992) [Population of the White Stork in Alsace.] Pp.53–58 in J.-L. Mériaux, A. Schierer, C. Tombal and J.-C. Tombal, eds. [*The storks of Europe.*] Metz: Institut Européen d'Ecologie/AMBE. (In French.)

42. SIORAT, F. (1992) [*Changes in the numbers of the Gannet, Puffin and Manx Shearwater in l'Artchipel des Sept-Isles (Bretagne).*] Rochefort: Convention Sretrie-Ministère de l'Environment/Ligue pour la Protection des Oiseaux. (In French.)

43. TROLLIET, B. AND IBANEZ, F. (1990) [Numbers of Black-tailed Godwits, *Limosa limosa*, nesting in the Vendée.] *Oiseau et R.F.O.* 60: 207–211. (In French.)

44. TROTIGNON, J. (1992) [Status and protection of breeding 'guifettes' in France.] Report by Ministère de l'Environnment-DPN/Ligue pour la Protection des Oiseaux.

45. WALLACE, J., HAFNER, H. AND DUNCAN, P. (1987) [Tree-dwelling herons in the Camargue.] *Oiseau et R.F.O.* 57: 39–43. (In French.)

46. WYNDE, R., ED. (1993) *Roseate Tern News 7*. Sandy, U.K.: Royal Society for the Protection of Birds.

47. YEATMAN, L. (1976) [*Atlas of breeding birds of France.*] Paris: Société Ornithologique de France. (In French.)

48. YEATMAN-BERTHELOT, D. (1991) [*Atlas of wintering birds in France.*] Paris: Société Ornithologique de France. (In French.)

49. YEATMAN-BERTHELOT, D. AND JARRY, G. (in press) [*New atlas of breeding birds of France (1985–1989).*] Paris: Société Ornithologique de France. (In French.)

50. YÉSOU, P. (1983) [Anatidae and wetlands of France.] *Bull. Sci. Techn. ONC.* (In French.)

Wintering

1. BEEKMAN, J. H., DICKSEN, S. P. AND SLAGBOOM, T. H. (1985) Population size and breeding success of Bewick's Swans wintering in Europe in 1983–1984. *Wildfowl* 36: 5–12.

2. JACOB, J.-P., LAFONTAINE, R. M., CHIWY, B., DEVILLERS, P., DE VISSCHER, M.-N. AND LEDANT, P.-P. (1985) [Information sheets on the species listed in Annex I of Directive 79/409/CEE.] Institute Royal des Sciences Naturelles Belgique (unpublished). (In French.)

3. MAHÉO, R. (1993) pers. comm.

4. ROCAMORA, G. AND MAILLET, N. (1991) [Mid-winter counts for ducks and coots in France—1990.] DPN/UNAO/Ligue pour la Protection des Oiseaux. (In French.)

5. YEATMAN-BERTHELOT, D. (1991) [*Atlas of wintering birds in France.*] Paris: Société Ornithologique de France. (In French.)

GERMANY

General

Most population figures are based on preliminary data for the atlas of breeding birds (Rheinwald 1993, see below). This work was published too late to permit incorporation of its final data for most species where there were discrepancies, although figures for some species (indicated by the use of code 20 in the list of source codes) were updated if the new figures varied considerably from those originally used.

Breeding

1. ANON. (1988) Bonn Convention on the Conservation of Migratory Species of Wild Animals. An agreement under Article IV and V for *Ciconia ciconia*.

2. BAUER, S. AND THIELCKE, G. (1982) [Threatened breeding birds in West Germany and Berlin: population trends, threats and conservation measures.] *Vogelwarte* 31: 183–191. (In German.)

3. BEZZEL, E., LECHNER, F. AND RANFTL, H. (1980) [*Working atlas of breeding birds of Bavaria.*] Greven: Kilda Verlag. (In German.)

4. BOETTCHER-STREIM, W. (1992) Changes in the European population of the Black Stork. *Orn. Beob.* 89: 235–244.

5. CRAMP, S., ED. (1985) *The birds of the western Palearctic*, 4. Oxford: Oxford University Press.

6. CRAMP, S. AND SIMMONS, K. E. L., EDS. (1977) *The birds of the western Palearctic*, 1. Oxford: Oxford University Press.

7. DORNBUSCH, M. (1989) Population trends and protection of the White Stork, *Ciconia ciconia*, in the German Democratic Republic. Pp.61–64 in G. Rheinwald, J. Ogden and H. Schulz, eds. [*White Stork: status and conservation. Proceedings of the 1st International Stork Conservation Symposium, Walsrode, 14–19 October 1985.*] Braunschweig: Dachverband Deutscher Avifaunisten (Schriftenreihe 10). (In German.)

8. DORNBUSCH, M. (1991) verbally to G. Rheinwald.

9. EVANS, P. (1987) *in litt.* to G. Rheinwald.

10. GÉNSBØL, B. (1987) *Collins guide to the birds of prey of Britain and Europe, North Africa and the Middle East.* London: Collins.

11. GRIMMETT, R. F. A. AND JONES, T. A. (1989) *Important bird areas in Europe.* Cambridge, U.K.: International Council for Bird Preservation (Techn. Publ. 9).

12. HÄLTERLEIN, B. AND STEINHARDT, B. (1993) [Breeding bird populations on the German North Sea coast in 1991: 5th Report of the Seabird Protection Working Group.] *Seevögel* 14: 1–5. (In German.)

13. HARASZTHY, L. (1989) pers. comm.

14. HECKENROTH, H. (1989) Situation of the White Stork in the Federal Republic of Germany. Pp.60 in G. Rheinwald, J. Ogden and H. Schulz, eds. [*White Stork: status and conservation. Proceedings of the first International Stork Conservation Symposium, Walsrode,*

14–19 October 1985.] Braunschweig: Dachverband Deutscher Avifaunisten (Schriftenreihe 10). (In German.)

15. HILDESHEIM, P. B. (1990) verbally to G. Rheinwald.
16. HÜPPOP, O. (1991) *in litt.* to G. Rheinwald.
17. LITZBORSKI, H. (1993) [Conservation project 'Great Bustard' in Brandenburg, Germany.] *Ber. Vogelschutz* 31: 61–66. (In German with English summary.)
18. MÜLLER, F. (1990) verbally to G. Rheinwald.
19. PIERSMA, T. (1986) Breeding waders in Europe. A review of population size estimates and a bibliography of information sources. *Bull. Wader Study Group* 48 (Suppl.): 1–116.
20. RHEINWALD, G. (1993) [Atlas of the distribution and frequency of the breeding birds of Germany—maps of 1985.] Berlin: Dachverband Deutscher Aviafaunisten (No. 12). (In German.)
21. ULLRICH, B. (1991) verbally to G. Rheinwald.
22. WITT, K. (1991) *in litt.* to G. Rheinwald.

Wintering

1. BEEKMAN, J. H., DIRKSEN, S. P. AND SLAGBOOM, T. H. (1985) Population size and breeding success of Bewick's Swans wintering in Europe in 1983–84. *Wildfowl* 36: 5–12.
2. GALL, T. (1991) *in litt.* to G. Rheinwald.
3. LAURSEN, K. (1989) Estimates of sea duck winter populations of the western Palearctic. *Dan. Rev. Game Biol.* 13: 6.
4. MELTOFTE, H., BLEW, J., KRIKKE, J., RÖSNER, H.-U. AND SMIT, C. (in prep.) Numbers and distribution of waterbirds in the Wadden Sea. *Wader Study Group Bull.* (Suppl.).
5. ROSE, P. M. AND TAYLOR, V. (1993) *Western Palearctic and south-west Asia waterfowl census 1993*. Slimbridge, U.K.: International Waterfowl and Wetlands Research Bureau.

GREECE

Breeding

1. ANON. (1985) [Ramsar Wetlands Zonation project: Evros Delta.] Athens: Ministry of Environment, Regional Planning and Public Works (unpublished report). (In Greek.)
2. CATSADORAKIS, G., GERAKIS, A. P. AND PAPAYANNIS, T. (1988) Prespa National Park, Florina, Greece: data for zoning protected areas according to Directive 79/409/EC. Athens: The Friends of Prespa (unpublished report).
3. CRIVELLI, A. J. (1987) The ecology and behaviour of the Dalmatian pelican, *Pelecanus crispus* Bruch: a world endangered species. Unpublished report by Station Biologique de la Tour du Valat for Commission of the European Community.
4. CRIVELLI, A. J. (1994) pers. comm. to BirdLife International.
5. CRIVELLI, A. J., JERRENTRUP, H. AND HALLMANN, B. (1986) Preliminary results of a complete census of breeding colonial wading birds in Greece, spring 1985–1986. *Bull. Hell. Orn. Soc.* 4: 31–33.
6. GOUTNER, V. (1983) The distribution of waders *Charadrii* in the Evros Delta (Greece) during the breeding season. *Sci. Annals, Fac. Sciences, Univ. Thessa-*

loniki 23: 37–78.

7. GOUTNER, V. (1988) The Lesser Crested Tern in the Evros delta (Greece): a case of pairing with the Sandwich Tern? *Kartlerung Mediterr. Brutvogel* 1: 7–12.
8. GRIMMETT, R. F. A. AND JONES, T. A. (1989) *Important bird areas in Europe*. Cambridge, U.K.: International Council for Bird Preservation (Techn. Publ. 9).
9. HALLMANN, B. (1985) Status and conservation problems of birds of prey in Greece. Pp.55–59 in I. Newton and R. D. Chancellor, eds. *Conservation studies on raptors*. Cambridge, U.K.: International Council for Bird Preservation (Techn. Publ. 5).
10. HALLMANN, B. (1993) pers. comm. To BirdLife International.
11. JERRENTRUP, H. (1993) *in litt.* to BirdLife International.
12. JERRENTRUP, H., GAETHLICH, M., HOLM JOENSEN, A., NOHR, H. AND BRØGGER-JENSEN, S. (1988) *Urgent action plan to safeguard three endangered bird species in Greece and the European Community: Pygmy Cormorant* (Phalacrocorax pygmaeus)*; Great White Egret* (Egretta alba)*; White-tailed Eagle* (Haliaeetus albicilla). Arhus: Naturhistorisk Museum.
13. JOENSEN, A. H. AND JERRENTRUP, H. (1988) The Agios Mamas Lagoon, Halkidiki, Greece, an area of international importance for breeding waders. *Natura Jutlandica* 22: 185–188.
14. PERGANTIS, P. (1986) [Zoning and delineation of areas to be protected in Amvrakikos (Greece) according to the Directive 79/409/EC.] Pp.1–73 in T. Papayannis, ed. [*Amvrakikos Gulf: development of resources and environmental protection, phase B.*] Athens: Ministry of Environment, Reg. Planning and Public Works. (In Greek.)
15. RISTOW, D. AND WINK, M. (1989) Cory's Shearwater—a clever energy conserver among our birds. *Nature Bull. Hell. Soc. Prot. Nature* 46/47: 31–34.
16. SCHMID, W. AND REICHENECKER, H. (1988) [The breeding birds of the Vikos/Voidomatis valley and Mt Astraka/Gamila in the Pindus mountains, Province Ioannina, Central Greece.] *Kartierung Mediterr. Brutvogel* 1: 17–24. (In German.)

Wintering

1. CRAMP, S. AND SIMMONS, K. E. L., EDS. (1983) *The birds of the western Palearctic*, 3. Oxford: Oxford University Press.
2. HANDRINOS, G. I. (1990) The status of geese in Greece. *Ardea* 79: 175–178.
3. HELLENIC ORNITHOLOGICAL SOCIETY (HOS) (1987) Midwinter waterfowl Census, Greece 1987 (unpublished).
4. HELLENIC ORNITHOLOGICAL SOCIETY (HOS) (1989) Midwinter Waterfowl Census 1989 (unpublished).

HUNGARY

Breeding

1. JAKAB, B. (in press) [Evaluation of the 1989 White Stork *Ciconia ciconia* census.] *Madártani Tájékoztató*. (In Hungarian.)
2. KALOTÁS, Z. (1987) [Results of the 1985 population survey of the Barn Owl *Tyto alba*.] *Madártani Tájékoztató* 1: 7–9. (In Hungarian.)

3. KONYHÁS, S. AND KOVÁCS, G. (1990) [Breeding census results in 1990 in the Hortobágy.] *Madártani Tájékoztató* 3: 9–13. (In Hungarian.)

4. KOVÁCS, G. (in press) [Breeding of the Pygmy Cormorant *Phalacrocorax pygmeus* in a heronry.] *Madártani Tájékoztató*. (In Hungarian.)

ICELAND

Breeding

1. CADE, T. J. (1982) *The falcons of the world.* London: Collins.

2. GALBRAITH, C. A. AND THOMPSON, P. S. (1981) [The Wood Sandpiper *Tringa glareola* breeding in Iceland.] *Náttúrufraedingurinn* 51: 164–168. (In Icelandic with English summary.)

3. GARDARSSON, A. (1969) [Suspected breeding of the Wood Sandpiper *Tringa glareola* in Iceland.] *Náttúrufraedingurinn* 39: 10–16. (In Icelandic with English summary.)

4. GARDARSSON, A. (1975) [The birds of Icelandic wetlands.] *Rit Landverndar* 4: 100–134. (In Icelandic with English summary.)

5. GARDARSSON, A. (1978) [Distribution and numbers of the Barrow's Goldeneye *Bucephala islandica* in Iceland.] *Náttúrufraedingurinn* 48: 162–191. (In Icelandic with English summary.)

6. GARDARSSON, A. (1979) [Duck populations of the Myvatn-Laxa in 1977–78.] *Fjolrit Natturuverndarrads* 5: 127–136. (In Icelandic with English summary.)

7. GARDARSSON, A. (1984) [Duck populations of Myvatn and Laxa 1979–1982.] *Fjolrit Natturuverndarrads* 14: 145–153. (In Icelandic with English summary.)

8. GARDARSSON, A. (1989) [A survey of Gannet *Sula bassana* colonies in Iceland.] *Bliki* 7: 1–22. (In Icelandic with English summary.)

9. GARDARSSON, A. AND EINARSSON, A. (in press) *Responses of breeding duck populations to changes in food supply. Aquatic birds in the trophic web of lakes.* New Brunswick, Canada: Sackville.

10. GUDMUNDSSON, F. (1971) [The Harlequin Duck (*Histrionicus histrionicus*) in Iceland.] *Náttúrufraedingurinn* 41: 1–28, 64–98. (In Icelandic with English summary.)

11. GUDMUNDSSON, F. (1984) [The haunts of the Snowy Owl.] *Bliki* 3: 50–53. (In Icelandic.)

12. ICELANDIC SOCIETY FOR THE PROTECTION OF BIRDS (1974–1991) [Annual census of the White-tailed Eagle population in Iceland] (unpublished confidential reports).

13. MAGNUSSON, K. G. (1989) [The breeding of White-tailed Eagles in 1987.] *Bliki* 7: 63–64. (In Icelandic.)

14. NIELSEN, O. K. (1986) Population ecology of the Gyr Falcon in Iceland with comparative notes on the Merlin and the Raven. New York: Cornell University (Ph.D. thesis).

15. PETERSEN, Æ. (1979) [The breeding birds of Flatey and some adjoining islets, in Breidafjordur, north-west Iceland.] *Náttúrufraedingurinn* 49: 229–256. (In Icelandic with English summary.)

16. PETERSEN, Æ. (1981) Breeding biology and feeding ecology of Black Guillemots. Oxford: Oxford University (Ph.D. thesis).

17. PETERSEN, Æ. (1989) [The natural history of the Breidafjördur Islands.] *Arbok Ferdafelags Islands* 1989: 17–52. (In Icelandic.)

18. PETERSEN, Æ. AND THORSTENSEN, S. (1990) [Birdlife at Akureyri airport and surrounding wetland areas, north Iceland, 1987.] *Bliki* 9: 7–20. (In Icelandic.)

19. PETURSSON, G. AND OLAFSSON, E. (1984) [Rare birds in Iceland in 1982.] *Bliki* 3: 15–44. (In Icelandic with English summary.)

20. PIERSMA, T. (1986) Breeding waders in Europe. A review of population size estimates and a bibliography of information sources. *Bull. Wader Study Group* 48 (Suppl.): 1–116.

21. SKARPHÉDINSSON, K. H. AND GUDMUNDSSON, G. A. (1989) [The birdlife of Skogar and vicinity, north Iceland.] *Bliki* 9: 49–66. (In Icelandic with English summary.)

22. SKARPHÉDINSSON, K. H., THORISSON, S. AND LEIFSSON, P. (1989) [The birds of Seley, east Iceland.] *Bliki* 7: 49–58. (In Icelandic with English summary.)

23. THORSTENSEN, S. (1983) [Breeding localities of Barrow's Goldeneye *Bucephala islandica* west of Fljotsheidi, north Iceland.] *Bliki* 2: 44–47. (In Icelandic with English summary.)

24. WANLESS, S. (1987) *A survey of the numbers and breeding distribution of the North Atlantic Gannet* Sula bassana *and an assessment of the changes which have occurred since Operation Seafarer 1969/1970.* Peterborough, U.K.: Nature Conservancy Council (Publ. 4).

Wintering

1. ANON. (1973) [The Icelandic Christmas bird count: results for 1972, south-west Iceland.] Icelandic Natural History Museum (unpublished report). (In Icelandic.)

2. GARDARSSON, A. (1975) [The birds of Icelandic wetlands.] *Rit Landverndar* 4: 100–134. (In Icelandic with English summary.)

3. PETERSEN, Æ. AND HJARTARSON, G. (1989) [The Icelandic Christmas bird counts: some general points, and results for 1987.] *Fjolrit Natturufraedistofnunar* 11: 42. (In Icelandic with English summary.)

4. PETERSEN, Æ. AND HJARTARSON, G. (1991) [The Icelandic Christmas bird count: results for 1988.] *Fjolrit Natturufraedistofnunar* 18: 38. (In Icelandic with English summary.)

5. PETURSSON, G. AND OLAFSSON, E. (1984) [Rare birds in Iceland in 1982.] *Bliki* 3: 15–44. (In Icelandic with English summary.)

ITALY

Breeding

1. BACCETTI, N. AND MESCHINI, E. (1986) [The Atlas Project of the breeding birds of Tuscany: past and present distributions of some species.] *Riv. Ital. Orn.* 56: 67–78. (In Italian.)

2. BACCETTI, N., FARRONATO, I., RANDI, E., SPINA, F. AND TORRE, A. (1988) [Contribution to the knowledge of the status of the Storm Petrel *Hydrobates pelagicus* in Italy.] *Riv. Ital. Orn.* 58: 197–198. (In Italian.)

3. BORDIGNON, L. (1984) [Northern limit of the distribution of the Bee-eater *Merops apiaster* in Italy: results of an inquiry.] *Riv. Ital. Orn.* 54: 215–220. (In Italian.)

4. BRICHETTI, P. (1979) [Geographical distribution of

breeding birds in Italy, Corsica and Malta. 1: introduction, Podicipedidae, Procellaridae and Hydrobatidae.] *Natura Bresciana* 16: 82–158. (In Italian.)

5. BRICHETTI, P., ED. (1982–1988) [Atlas of the breeding birds of the Italian Alpine zone.] *Riv. Ital. Orn.* 52(1–2): 3–50; 53(3–4): 101–144; 56(1–2): 3–39; 58(1–2): 3–39. (In Italian.)

6. BRICHETTI, P., CANOVA, L. AND SAINO, N. (1984) [Status and distribution of breeding Anatidae in Italy and Corsica.] *Avocetta* 8: 19–42. (In Italian.)

7. BRICHETTI, P., DE FRANCESCHI, P. AND BACCETTI, N., EDS. (1992) [*Fauna of Italy, XXIX. Aves, 1: Gaviidae–Phasianidae.*] Bologna: Edizioni Calderini.

8. CANOVA, L. AND FASOLA, M. (1989) [First nesting of Spoonbill *Platalea leucorodia* in Italy.] *Riv. Ital. Orn.* 59: 265–267. (In Italian.)

9. CORTONE, P. AND LIBERATORI, F. (1989) [Updated status of the Egyptian Vulture *Neophron percnopterus* in the Italian peninsula.] *Riv. Ital. Orn.* 59: 49–59. (In Italian.)

10. FASCE, P. AND FASCE, L. (1984) [*The Golden Eagle* Aquila chrysaetos *in Italy: ecology and conservation.*] Parma, Italy: Lega Italiana Protezione Uccelli (Scientific Series). (In Italian.)

11. FASOLA, M. AND BARBIERI, F. (1981) [First breeding record of the Pygmy Cormorant *Phalacrocorax pygmeus* in Italy.] *Avocetta* 5: 155–156. (In Italian.)

12. FASOLA, M., BARBIERI, F., PRIGIONI, C. AND BOGLIANI, G. (1981) [First census of heronries in Italy, 1981.] *Avocetta* 5: 107–132. (In Italian.)

13. FASOLA, M., ED. (1986) [Distribution and population of Laridae and Sternidae breeding in Italy.] *Ric. Biol. Selv.* 11 (Suppl): 1–179. (In Italian.)

14. DE FRANCESCHI, P. (1988) [Status of galliform populations in Italy: recent and current research—problems of management and perspectives for the future.] *Ric. Biol. Selv. (Suppl.)* 14: 129–168. (In Italian.)

15. GUSTIN, M. (1988) [Breeding of Ferruginous Duck *Aythya nyroca* in Oristano province (west Sardinia).] *Riv. Ital. Orn.* 58: 191. (In Italian.)

16. MASSA, B. AND CATALISANO, A. (1986) An observation on the Mediterranean Storm Petrel *Hydrobates pelagicus* at Marettimo isle. *Avocetta* 10: 125–127.

17. MASSA, B. AND CATALISANO, A. (1992) [Status and conservation of the Storm Petrel *Hydrobates pelagicus* in Sicily.] Pp.135–142 in E. Torre, ed. [*Study of the population and conservation of the marine avifauna of the Mediterranean.*] Regione Sardegna: Alghero. (In Italian.)

18. MASSA, B., LO VALVO, M. AND LA MANTIA, T. (1982) [Census of the Cory's Shearwater *Calonectris diomedea* of Linosa islet with the capture–recapture method.] Pp.236–240 in M. Pandolfi and S. Frugis, eds. *Atti I Sem. Ital. Cens. Faun.* Urbino, Italy: Urbino University. (In Italian.)

19. MASSA, B., LO VALVO, F., SIRACUSA, M. AND CIACCIO, A. (1991) [The Lanner (*Falco biarmicus feldeggii* Schiegel) in Italy: status, biology and taxonomy.] *Naturalista Sicil.* 15: 27–63. (In Italian.)

20. MATTEUCCI, C. AND TOSO, S. (1984) [Distribution and status of Italian populations of Partridge *Perdix perdix*.] Pp.29–34 in F. Dessì Fulgheri and T. Mingozzi, eds. *Atti Seminario 'Biology of Galliformes'*. Cosenza: Calabria University. (In Italian.)

21. MONGINI, E., MARCHETTI, C. AND BALDACCINI, N. E. (1988) [An investigation of the distribution, number and characteristics of Sand Martin *Riparia riparia* colonies in Italy.] *Avocetta* 12: 83–94. (In Italian.)

22. PETRETTI, F. (1985) [The Rock Patridge *Alectoris graeca* in the Appennines.] World Wildlife Fund–Italy. (In Italian.)

23. PETRETTI, F. (1988) An inventory of steppe habitats in southern Italy. Pp.125–143 in P. D. Goriup, ed. *Ecology and conservation of grassland birds*. Cambridge, U.K.: International Council for Bird Preservation (Techn. Publ. 7).

24. PETRETTI, F. AND PETRETTI, A. (1980) [Status and conservation of the Short-toed Eagle *Circaetus gallicus* in Italy.] *Rapaces Mediterranean: Atti Con. Evisa.* (In Italian.)

25. SAINO, N. AND BIDDAU, L. (1989) [Confirmed breeding of the Ferruginous Duck *Aythya nyroca* in Emilia Romagna (north-east Romagna).] *Riv. Ital. Orn.* 59: 292–293. (In Italian.)

26. SCHENK, H. AND ARESU, M. (1985) On the distribution, numbers and conservation of the Little Bustard in Sardinia (Italy), 1971–1982. *Bustard Studies* 2: 161–164.

27. SCHENK, H., ARESU, M. AND SERRA, G. (1987) [Ecology and conservation of Griffon Vulture *Gyps fulvus* in north-western Sardinia, 1971–1984.] *Ric. Biol. Selv.* 12 (Suppl): 217–233. (In Italian.)

28. SPINA, F., SCHENK, H. AND MASSA, B. (1981) Conservation and status of Eleonora's Falcon *Falco eleonorae* in Italy. Pp.143–156 in *Proceedings Thessaloniki Conference on Birds of Prey* V.

29. TALLONE, G. AND CAMANNI, S. (1993) [The White Stork *Ciconia ciconia* L.: a case of recent recolonization in Italy.] *Ric. Biol. Selv.* 21 (Suppl): 239–248. (In Italian.)

30. TINARELLI, R. AND BACCETTI, N. (1989) Breeding waders in Italy. *Wader Study Group Bull.* 56: 7–15.

31. TOUT, P. (1992) *in litt.* to R. E. Green.

Wintering

1. BRICHETTI, P., DE FRANCESCHI, P. AND BACCETTI, N., EDS. (1992) [*Fauna of Italy, XXIX. Aves, 1: Gaviidae–Phasianidae.*] Bologna: Edizioni Calderini.

2. GUSTIN, M. (in press) [Wintering of the Shelduck *Tadorna tadorna* and Avocet *Recurvirostra avosetta* in the Margherita of Savoia saltpans (Apulia).] *Riv. Ital. Orn.*

3. SMIT, C. J. (1984) Waders along the Mediterranean: a summary of present knowledge. First Conference on birds wintering in the Mediterranean region. *Ric. Biol. Selv.* 10 (Suppl.): 297–318.

4. TINARELLI, R. (1989) [Wintering of waders in the Adriatic coastal wetlands from the Adige Delta to the saline of Cervia.] *Avocetta* 13: 41–46. (In Italian.)

LATVIA

Breeding

1. ANON. (1989) [Game statistics in the Latvian SSR.] Pp.225 in J. Vanags, ed. *Medibu gads*. Riga, Latvia: Avots Publishers. (In Latvian.)

2. BERGMANIS, U. AND AVOTINS, A. (1990) [Avifauna of the Teici Reserve and its surroundings.] *Putni daba* 3: 71–87. (In Latvian.)

3. BERGMANIS, U., KREILIS, M., KEMLERS, A., LIPSBERGS, J. AND PETRINS, A. (1990a) [First results of raptor monitoring in Latvia.] *Putni daba* 3: 148–153. (In Latvian.)

4. BERGMANIS, U., PETRINS, A. AND STRAZDS, M. (1990b) Lesser Spotted Eagle in Latvia: numbers, distribution and ecology. *Baltic Birds* 5: 35–38.

5. JANAUS, M. AND STIPNIECE, A. (1989) [50-year (1934–1984) population trends of the White Stork in Latvia.] Pp.145–152 in G. Rheinwald, J. Ogdem and H. Schulz, eds. [*White Stork: status and conservation. Proceedings of the first International Stork Symposium, Walsrode, 14–18 October 1985.*] Braunschweig: Dachverband Deutscher Avifaunisten (Schriftenreihe 10). (In German.)

6. KEMLERS, E. AND KEMLERS, A. (1987) [Birds of prey Falconiformes in the vicinity of Kuldiga.] *Retie augi un dzivnieki* 8: 31–46. (In Latvian.)

7. KREILIS, M. (1990) [The Osprey in Latvia: numbers, distribution and breeding biology.] Conference on Baltic Birds 6 (unpublished). (In Latvian.)

8. LIPSBERGS, J., KACALOVA, O., OZOLS, G., RUCE, I. AND SULCS, A. (1990) [*Scientific/popular Red Data Book of Latvia: Animals.*] Riga, Latvia: Zinatne Publishing House. (In Latvian.)

9. PETRINS, A. AND BERGMANIS, U. (1986) [The Short-toed Eagle *Circaetus gallicus* Gm. in Latvia.] Pp.57–72 in T. A. Zorenko, ed. [*Protection, ecology and ethology of animals.*] Riga, Latvia: Latvian State University. (In Latvian.)

10. PRIEDNIEKS, J., STRAZDS, M., PETRINS, A. AND STRAZDS, A. (1989) [*Latvian breeding bird atlas 1980–1984.*] Riga, Latvia: Zinatne Publishing House. (In Latvian.)

11. PRIEDNIEKS, J., STRAZDS, M. AND KLAVINS, A. (1990) Results of repeated Latvian breeding bird atlas programme. Pp.157–161 in K. Stastny and V. Bejcek, eds. *Bird census and atlas studies. Proc. XIth Int. Conf. on Bird Census and Atlas Work.* Prague: Institute of Applied Ecology and Ecotechnology, Agricultural University.

12. STRAZDS, M. (1989) [News review.] *Putni daba* 2: 174–182. (In Latvian.)

13. STRAZDS, M. (1990) [Occurrence of woodpeckers in Latvia.] Unpublished. (In Latvian.)

14. STRAZDS, M. (in prep.) The status of the Black Stork in Latvia: research history and development of populations. In K. Brouwer, C. King and M. Strazds, eds. *The Black Stork in the changing world.* Proceedings of the First International Black Stork Conservation and Ecology Symposium, Riga, Latvia.

15. STRAZDS, M. AND CELMINS, A. (1987) [Avifaunal novelties.] *Putni daba* 1: 94–96. (In Latvian.)

16. STRAZDS, M. AND STRAZDS, A. (1990) [Changes in the avifauna of the Gauja river (1938–1988).] *Putni daba* 3: 38–70. (In Latvian.)

17. STRAZDS, M. AND STRAZDS, A. (1991) [Breeding bird fauna of the western Latvian coast.] Annual conference of Latvian Ornithological Society, Riga, Latvia (unpublished report). (In Latvian.)

18. STRAZDS, M., LIPSBERGS, J. AND PETRINS, A. (1990) Black Stork in Latvia: numbers, distribution and ecology. *Baltic Birds* 5: 174–179.

19. VIKSNE, J., ED. (1983) [*Birds of Latvia: territorial distribution and numbers.*] Riga, Latvia: Zinatne Publishing House. (In Latvian.)

20. VIKSNE, J. AND JANAUS, M. (1982) [First breeding attempt of the White Spoonbill *Platalea leucorodia* L. in Latvia.] *Retie augi un dzivnieki* 3: 45–46. (In Latvian.)

21. VIKSNE, J. AND JANAUS, M. (1989) [Colonies of gulls, terns and the Grey Heron in Latvia in 1986.] *Putni daba* 2: 55–71. (In Latvian.)

22. VIKSNE, J. AND MEDNIS, A. (1978) [*The future of Latvian waterfowl.*] Riga, Latvia: Zinatne Publishing House. (In Latvian.)

Wintering

1. STIPNIECE, A. (1990) [Results of the mid-winter waterfowl census in Latvia (1987–1989).] *Putni daba* 3: 27–37. (In Latvian.)

2. STIPNIECE, A. (1991) [The waterfowl mid-winter counts in Latvia (1990–1991).] Unpublished. (In Latvian.)

3. VARERINS, G. (1991) [Latvian wintering bird atlas. Preliminary results of years 1982/1983–1989/1990.] Annual conference of Latvian Ornithological Society, Riga, Latvia (unpublished report). (In Latvian.)

LIECHTENSTEIN

Breeding

1. GOVERNMENT OF LIECHTENSTEIN (1990) [*Game counts 1989.*] Vaduz: Regierung de Fürstentums Liechtenstein. (In German.)

2. WILLI, G. (1984) [*A study of the natural history of the principality of Liechtenstein: the breeding birds of the Alpine Region, 4.*] Vaduz: Regierung des Fürstentums Liechtenstein. (In German.)

3. WILLI, G. (1990) [The birds of the Ruggeles Riet.] *BZG Berichte* 18: 177–212. (In German.)

4. WILLI, G. (1993) [The avifauna of the Rhine.] *BZG Berichte* 20: 65–109. (In German.)

5. WILLI, G. AND BROGGI, M. F. (1983) [The birds of the principality of Liechtenstein compared with neighbouring regions: I, Gaviiformes–Falconiformes.] *BZG Berichte* 12: 61–117. (In German.)

LITHUANIA

Breeding

1. DANKO, S. (1993) *in litt.* to BirdLife International.

2. LOGMINAS, V., ED. (1990) [*The birds of Lithuania. 1: non-passeriformes.*] Vilnius: Mokslas Publ. (In Lithuanian.)

3. LOGMINAS, V., ED. (1991) [*The birds of Lithuania. 2: passeriformes.*] Vilnius: Mokslas Publ. (In Lithuanian.)

4. MIERAUSKAS, P. (1993) Data from Lithuanian Atlas of breeding birds (unpublished). (In Lithuanian.)

Wintering

1. LOGMINAS, V., ED. (1990) [*The birds of Lithuania. 1: non-passeriformes.*] Vilnius: Mokslas Publ. (In Lithuanian.)

2. RAUDONIKIS, L., KURLAVICIUS, P. AND MIERAUSKAS, P. (1993) Unpublished data.

3. SVAZAS, S., RAUDONIKIS, L., VAITKUS, G. AND PAREIGIS, V. (1989) [*Wintering waterfowl in Lithuania in 1989.*] Vilnius: Institute of Ecology. (In Lithuanian.)

LUXEMBOURG

General

MELCHIOR, E., MENTGEN, E., PELTZER, R., SCHMITT, J. AND WEISS, J. (1987) [*Atlas of breeding birds in Luxembourg.*] Luxembourg: Letzebuerger Natur a vulleschutzliga. (In German, French and English.)

Breeding

1. PELTZER, R. (1983) [Breeding distribution of the Black Kite *Milvus migrans* in Luxembourg.] *Regulus* 14: 224–228. (In German.)

MALTA

General

MALTA ORNITHOLOGICAL SOCIETY (1966–1992) Daily logs of bird observations. Unpublished data.

SULTANA, J. (1989) Birds. Pp.138–142 in P. J. Schembri and J. Sultana, eds. *Red Data Book for the Maltese Islands.* Malta: Environment Division, Ministry of Education.

SULTANA, J. AND GAUCI, C. (1982) *A new guide to the birds of Malta.* Valetta: Maltese Ornithological Society.

NETHERLANDS

Breeding

1. BEKHUIS, J. (1990) [How long will Little Bitterns breed in the Netherlands?] *Limosa* 63: 47–50. (In Dutch.)
2. BEKHUIS, J. AND ZIJLSTRA, M. (1991) [Increase of the Dutch breeding population of the Hen Harrier *Circus cyaneus.*] *Limosa* 64: 143–153. (In Dutch.)
3. BEKHUIS, J., BIJLSMA, R. G., VAN DIJK, A. J. AND HUSTINGS, F. (1985–1992) *in litt.* Data from the archives of Samenwerkende Organisaties Vogelonderzoek Nederland (SOVON) transmitted for SOVON by J. Bekhuis and F. Hustings (unpublished).
4. BIJLSMA, R. G. (1990) Population trends in Black Grouse, Grey Partridge, Pheasant and Quail in the Netherlands. Pp.16–43 in J. T. Lumey and Y. R. Hoogeveen, eds. [*The future of wild Galliformes in the Netherlands.*] Amersfoort: Organisatie-commissie Nederlandse Wilde Hoenders. (In Dutch.)
5. HUSTINGS, F. (1992) [Number and status of some Dutch breeding birds in 1960–1991, documentation of a revised Red List.] Arnhem: Samenwerkende Organisaties Vogelonderzoek Nederland (unpublished). (In Dutch.)
6. HUSTINGS, F., BEKHUIS, J., BIJLSMA, R. G. AND POST, F. (1992) [Decrease in the Crested lark population in the Netherlands.] *Vogeljaar* 40: 145–156. (In Dutch.)
7. VAN DER KOOIJ, H. (1990) [The 1989 breeding season of the Dutch Purple Heron.] *Vogeljaar* 38: 158–161. (In Dutch.)
8. LEYS, H. N. (1988) [Breeding bird survey of Sand Martin in 1987 in the Netherlands.] *Vogeljaar* 36: 97–111. (In Dutch.)
9. OSIECK, E. R. AND DE VRIES, C. N. (1987) [Increase of Spoonbill.] *Limosa* 60: 155. (In Dutch.)
10. OSIECK, E. R. AND HUSTINGS, F. (1994) [*Red data and important birds in the Netherlands.*] Zeist: Vogelbescherming Nederland (Techn. Rep.'12). (In Dutch.)
11. ROOTH, J. (1989) [Numbers of Sandwich Tern *Sterna sandvicensis* breeding in the Netherlands in 1961–1988.] *Limosa* 62: 121–124. (In Dutch.)
12. SOVON (1987) [*Atlas of the birds of the Netherlands.*] Arnhem: Samenwerkende Organisaties Vogelonderzoek Nederland. (In Dutch.)
13. SOVON (1988) [New estimates of breeding bird numbers in the Netherlands.] *Limosa* 61: 155–162. (In Dutch.)
14. TEIXEIRA, R. M., ED. (1979) [*Atlas of Dutch breeding birds.*] Deventer: Vereniging tot Behoud Natuurmonumenten in Nederland/Stichting Ornithologisch Veldonderzoek Nederland. (In Dutch.)

Wintering

1. BUESINK, H. (1991) [*Evaluation of waterfowl counts in the Netherlands.*] Arnhem: Rijksinstituut voor Natuurbeheer (RIN-report 91/31). (In Dutch.)
2. VAN DIJK, J., CAMPHUYSEN, C. J. AND PLATTEEUW, M. (1993) *in litt.*
3. EBBINGE, B. S., VAN DEN BERGH, L. M. J., ROOTH, J. AND TIMMERMAN, A. (1987) [Distribution and numbers of wild geese in the Netherlands.] *Levende Nat.* 88: 162–178. (In Dutch.)
4. GEESE WORKING GROUP (1983–1991) [Geese counts.] *Limosa* 56–64. (In Dutch with English summary.)
5. MELTOFTE, H., BLEW, J., KRIKKE, J., RÖSNER, H.-U. AND SMIT, C. (in prep.) Numbers and distribution of waterbirds in the Wadden Sea. *Wader Study Group Bull.* (Suppl.).
6. SOVON (1987) [*Atlas of the birds of the Netherlands.*] Arnhem: Samenwerkende Organisaties Vogelonderzoek Nederland. (In Dutch.)

NORWAY

General

All population sizes and trends are taken from:

GJERSHAUG, J. O., THINGSTAD, P. G., ELDØY, S. AND BYRKJELAND, S., EDS. (1994) *Norwegian bird atlas.* Kloebu: Norsk Ornitologisk Forening. (In Norwegian.)

Breeding

1. ANKER-NILSSEN, T. (1992) [Food supply as a determinant of reproduction and population development in Norwegian Puffins *Fratercula artica.*] Trondheim: Trondheim University (Ph.D. thesis). (In Norwegian.)

Wintering

1. FRANTZEN, B. (1993) *in litt.* to BirdLife International.
2. LAURSEN, K. (1989) Estimates of sea duck winter populations of the western Palearctic. *Dan. Rev. Game Biol.* 13: 6.

Svalbard

Breeding

1. NORWEGIAN POLAR RESEARCH INSTITUTE (unpublished database).
2. PIROT, J.-Y., LAURSEN, K., MADSEN, J. AND MONVAL, J.-Y. (1989) Population estimates of swans, geese, ducks and Eurasian Coot (*Fulica atra*) in the western Palearctic and Sahelian Africa. Pp.14–63 in H. Boyd and J.-Y. Pirot, eds. *Flyways and reserve networks for water*

birds. Slimbridge, U.K.: International Waterfowl and Wetlands Research Bureau (Spec. Publ. 9).

POLAND

Breeding
1. ADAMSKI, A. (1992) *in litt.*
2. BASZANOWSKI, P. (1992) *in litt.*
3. BEDNORZ, J. (1989) [The Notec valley as a zoogeographical corridor for waterbirds.] *Beitr. Vogelkunde* 35: 75–79. (In German.)
4. BEDNORZ, J. (1992) *in litt.*
5. BETLEJA, J. (1992) *in litt.*
6. BOBROWICZ, G. (1992) *in litt.*
7. BOGUCKI, Z. (1992) *in litt.*
8. BREWKA, B., KELLER, M., MIROWSKI, M., RODZIEWICZ, M. AND WÓJCIK, J. (1991) [Polish Working Group on Lesser and Greater Spotted Eagles: report no. 1.]*Notatki Orn.* 32: 167–171. (In Polish.)
9. BUCZEK, T. (1992) *in litt.*
10. BUKACINSKA, M. (1992) *in litt.*
11. BUKACINSKI, D. (1992) *in litt.*
12. CEMPULIK, P. (1991) [Population trends, status and conservation of the Corncrake in Poland.] *Vogelwelt* 112: 40–45. (In German.)
13. CEMPULIK, P. (1992) *in litt.*
14. CHMIELEWSKI, S. (1992) *in litt.*
15. CHMIELEWSKI, S., DOMBROWSKI, A., SMOLENSKI, T. AND ZAWADZKI, J. (1987) Breeding waders in lower Bug valley. *Wader Study Group Bull.* 51: 27.
16. CHYLARECKI, P., WINIECKI, A. AND WYPYCHOWSKI, K. (in press) [Birds breeding in the middle Warta valley (Uniejów–Splawie and Santok.] *Prace Zakl. Biol. i Ekol. Ptaków UAM.* (In Polish.)
17. CIESLAK, M. (1992) *in litt.*
18. DOMASZEWICZ, A. (1992) *in litt.*
19. DYRCZ, A. (1992) *in litt.*
20. DYRCZ, A. AND CZERASZKIEWICZ, R. (1992) Report concerning numbers, distribution, conservation and threats of the Aquatic Warbler *Acrocephalus paludicola* in Poland. Gdansk: Ogólnopolskie Towarzystwo Ochrony Ptaków (unpublished).
21. DYRCZ, A., OKULEWICZ, J., WITKOWSKI, J., JESIONOWSKI, J., NAWROCKI, P. AND WINIECKI, A. (1984) Birds of the fens in Biebrza Marshquiles: a faunistic approach. *Acta Orn.* 20: 1–108.
22. DYRCZ, A., GRABINSKI, W., STAWARCZYK, T. AND WITKOWSKI, J. (1991) [*Birds of Silesia: monograph of the fauna.*] Wroclaw: Wroclaw University. (In Polish.)
23. GLOWACINSKI, Z., ED. (1992a) [*Polish Red Data Book of animals.*] Warszaw: Panstowowe Wydawnictwo Rolniczei i Lesne. (In Polish.)
24. GLOWACINSKI, Z. (1992b) *in litt.*
25. GÓRSKI, A. (1992) *in litt.*
26. GÓRSKI, W., ED. (1991) [*Breeding sites of wetland birds and their protection in the centre of the Pomeranian region.*] Slupsk: Wyzsza Szkola Pedagoglczna. (In Polish.)
27. GROMADZKI, M. (1986) Some problems of wetland protection in northern Poland. *Vår Fågelv.* 11 (Suppl): 57–60.
28. GROMADZKI, M., SZYMKIEWICZ, M. AND SZOSTAKOWSKA, A. (in press) The status of the Common Crane *Grus*

grus in northern Poland. Proc. Palearctic Crane Workshop, Tallin. *Aquila.*
29. HORDOWSKI, J. (1991) [*Distribution and number of breeding birds in the Przemysl province.*] Bolestraszyce: Zakl. Fizjogr. i Arbor. Bolestraszyce. (In Polish.)
30. JAKUBIEC, Z., ED. (1985) [Population of White Stork *Ciconia ciconia* L. in Poland.] *Studia Naturae (Ser. A)* 28: 5–263. (In Polish.)
31. JAMROZY, G. (1991) [The occurrence of the Capercaillie *Tetrao urogallus* L., the Black Grouse *Tetrao tetrix* L. and the Hazel Grouse *Bonasia bonasia* L. in the Polish Carpathians.] *Prz. Zool.* 35: 361–369. (In Polish.)
32. JANISZEWSKI, T., KUCZYNSKI, L., WYPYCHOWSKI, K., CHYLARECKI, P. AND WINIECKI, A. (in press) [Preliminary results of avifaunal studies of the area of Jeziorsko reservoir (central Poland).] *Prace Zakl. Biol. i Ekol. Ptaków UAM.* (In Polish.)
33. JERMACZEK, A., CZWALGA, T., KRZYSKOW, T. AND STANKO, R. (1990) [The birds of the Kostrzynski Retention Reservoir during the breeding seasons 1987–1989.]*Lubuski Prz. przyrodn.* 1: 3–37. (In Polish.)
34. KICHALAK, P. (1992) *in litt.*
35. KOMISJA FAUNISTYCZNA SEKCJI ORNITOLOGICZNEJ PTZOOL. (1977) [Rare birds recorded in Poland in 1985.] *Notatki Orn.* 29: 53–65. (In Polish.)
36. KOPIJ, G. (1992) *in litt.*
37. KUPCZYK, M. (1992) *in litt.*
38. KUREK, H. (1992) *in litt.*
39. KUZNIAK, S. (1992) *in litt.*
40. MAJEWSKI, P. (1983) Evaluation of the role of the Slonsk Reserve, Poland for waterfowl. *Acta Orn.* 19: 227–235.
41. MARKOWSKI, J. (1992) *in litt.*
42. OLECH, B. (1988) Changes in numbers of partridges in Poland in 1964–1984. Pp.111–122 in *Proc. Third Common Partridge Intern. Symp. Kikol, Warsaw, Poland 1985.* Warsaw: Polish Hunting Association.
43. OLECH, B. (1992) *in litt.*
44. PIOTROWSKA, M. (1992) *in litt.*
45. POLISH ORNITHOLOGICAL ATLAS DATABASE (1986–1992) Ornithological Station, Gdansk, Poland (unpublished).
46. PROFUS, P., JAKUBIEC, Z. AND MIELCZAREK, P. (1989) [The situation of the White Stork in Poland: status in 1984.] Pp.81–97 in G. Rheinwald, J. Ogden and H. Schutz, eds. *Proceedings I International Stork Conservation Symposium.* Bonn: Dachverband Deutscher Avifaunisten (Schriftenreihe 10). (In German.)
47. RODZIEWICZ, M. (1992) *in litt.*
48. RUPRECHT, A. L. AND SZWAGRZAK, A. (1988) [Atlas of Polish owls, Strigiformes.] *Studia Naturae (Ser. A)* 32: 7–153. (In Polish.)
49. SIKORA, A. (1992) *in litt.*
50. SIKORA, A. (in press) [Nesting of Bee-eater in northern Poland.] *Notatki Orn.* (In Polish.)
51. SOSNOWSKI, J. (1992) *in litt.*
52. STAJSZCZYK, M. (1992) *in litt.*
53. STAWARCZYK, T. (1992) *in litt.*
54. TOMIALOJC, L. (1990) [*The birds of Poland: their distribution and abundance.*] Warsaw: Panstwowe Wydawnictwo Naukowe. (In Polish.)
55. WALASZ, K. AND MIELCZAREK, P., EDS. (1992) [*The atlas of breeding birds in Malopolska 1985–1991.*] Wroclaw: Biologica Silesiae. (In Polish.)
56. WAWERSKI, J. (1992) *in litt.*

57. WESOLOWSKI, T., GLAZEWSKA, E., NAWROCKA, B., NAWROCKI, P. AND OKONSKA, K. (1984) [Distribution and numbers of waders, gulls and terns nesting in the middle course of the Vistula.] *Acta Orn.* 20: 159–185. (In Polish.)

58. WINIECKI, A. (1992) *in litt.*

59. WINIECKI, A., CIERZNIAK, T., PTASZYK, J. AND ZIMOWSKI, M. (1992) [Birds breeding in the Warta valley (Splawie–Santok, west Poland).] *Prace Zakl. Biol. i Ekol. Ptaków UAM* 1: 57–82. (In Polish.)

60. WÓJCIAK, J. (1992) *in litt.*

61. WOJCIECHOWSKI, Z. (1992) *in litt.*

PORTUGAL

Breeding

1. ARAÚJO, A. (1990) [Data on the evolution of the breeding population of Lesser Kestrel *Falco naumanni* in Portugal, with special reference to the period 1975–1990.] Pp.71–81 in J. L. González and M. Merino, eds. [*The Lesser Kestrel* Falco naumanni *in Iberia: situation, problems and biological aspects.*] Madrid: Instituto Nacional para la Conservación de la Naturaleza (Serie Técnica). (In Spanish.)

2. ARAÚJO, A. AND PINA, J. P. (1984) [The population of *Sterna albifrons* in the Algarve coast.] *Boletim da LPN* 18: 37–47. (In Portuguese.)

3. ARAÚJO, A., NEVES, R. AND RUFINO, R. (in press) [The breeding population of Griffon Vulture *Gyps fulvus* in Portugal: situation in 1989, trends and threats.] [First national conference on Raptors, Porto 1992.] (In Portuguese.)

4. CANDEIAS, D. AND ARAÚJO, A. (1989) The White Stork in Portugal. Pp.19–27 in G. Rheinwald, J. Ogden and H. Schulz, eds. [*White Stork: status and conservation. Proceedings of the 1st International Stork Conservation Symposium, Walsrode, 14–19 October 1985.*] Braunschweig: Dachverband Deutscher Avifaunisten (Schriftenreihe 10). (In German.)

5. CANDEIAS, D., RUFINO, R. AND ARAÚJO, A. (1987) [Breeding herons in Portugal.] Anexe 6.6 in H. Hafner, P. J. Dugan and V. Boy, eds. Herons and wetlands in the Mediterranean: development of indices for quality assessment and management of Mediterranean ecosystems. Commission European Communities/Station Biologique de la Tour du Valat (unpublished). (In French.)

6. CATRY, P. (1991) pers. comm.

7. FARINHA, J. C. AND TEIXEIRA, A. M. (1989) The Chough in Portugal: status and distribution. Pp.25–28 in *Chough and land-use in Europe. Proceedings of an international workshop on the conservation of the Chough* Pyrrhocorax pyrrhocorax *in the European Community.* Scottish Chough Study Group.

8. GRANADEIRO, J. P. (1989) [Contribution to the knowledge of Cory's Shearwater *Calonectris diomedea borealis* (Cory 1981) breeding biology on Berlenga Island.] Lisbon: Faculty of Sciencies of Lisbon (Degree thesis). (In Portuguese.)

9. NEVES, R., ED. (1990) [Ornithological news.] *Airo* 2 (Suppl.): 4. (In Portuguese.)

10. RAMOS, J. A. (1989) [Ecology and conservation of Purple Gallinule *Porphyrio porphyrio* with special reference to Ludo, 'Ría Formosa' Natural Park.] Algarve: Algarve University (Degree thesis). (In Portuguese.)

11. RUFINO, R., ED. (1989) [*Atlas of breeding birds of continental Portugal.*] Lisbon: CEMPRA/SNPRCN. (In Portuguese.)

12. TEIXEIRA, A. M. (1984) [Seabirds of the Portuguese coastline.] *Boletim da LPN* 18: 105–115. (In Portuguese.)

13. TEIXEIRA, A. M. (1986) Wintering mortality of seabirds on the Portuguese coast. Pp.409–419 in MEDMARAVIS and X. Monbailliu, eds. *Mediterranean marine avifauna: population studies and conservation.* Paris: Springer-Verlag (NATO ASI Series G Ecological Sciences, 12).

Wintering

1. CEMPA (1980) [*Winter waterfowl and wader counts: January 1980.*] Lisbon: CEMPA/SEA. (In Portuguese.)

2. CEMPA (1981) [*Winter waterfowl and wader counts: January 1981.*] Lisbon: CEMPA/SEA. (In Portuguese.)

3. CEMPA (1982) [*Winter waterfowl and wader counts: January 1982.*] Lisbon: CEMPA/SEA. (In Portuguese.)

4. RUFINO, R. (1988) [*Winter waterfowl and wader counts: January 1988.*] Lisbon: CEMPA/SNPRCN. (In Portuguese.)

5. RUFINO, R. (1989) [*Winter waterfowl and wader counts: January 1989.*] Lisbon: CEMPRA/SNPRCN. (In Portuguese.)

6. RUFINO, R. AND NEVES, R. (1986) [*Winter waterfowl and wader counts: January 1986.*] Lisbon: CEMPA/SNPRCN. (In Portuguese.)

Azores

Breeding

1. BANNERMAN, D. A. AND BANNERMAN, W. M. (1966) *Birds of the Atlantic islands, 3: a history of the birds of the Azores.* Edinburgh, U.K.: Oliver and Boyd.

2. GRIMMETT, R. F. A. AND JONES, T. A. (1989) *Important bird areas in Europe.* Cambridge, U.K.: International Council for Bird Preservation (Techn. Publ. 9).

3. MONTEIRO, L. (1993) *in litt.* to BirdLife International.

4. DEL NEVO, A. J., DUNN, E. K., MEDEIROS, F. M., LE GRAND, G., AKERS, P. AND MONTEIRO, L. R. (1990) Status, distribution and conservation of Garajau Rosado *Sterna dougallii* and Garajau Comum *Sterna hirundo* in the Azores. Sandy, U.K.: Royal Society for the Protection of Birds (preliminary report).

5. SNPRCN (1990) [*Portuguese Red Data Book. 1: mammals, birds, reptiles and amphibians.*] Lisbon: Serviço Nacional de Parques Reservas e Conservação de Natureza.

Wintering

1. LE GRAND, G. (1983) Checklist of the birds of the Azores. *Arquipélago* 4: 49–58.

Madeira

Breeding

1. BANNERMAN, D. A. AND BANNERMAN, W. M. (1965) *Birds of the Atlantic Islands, 2: a history of the birds of Madeira, the Desertas and the Porto Santo Islands.* Edinburgh and London: Oliver and Boyd.

2. BOURNE, W. R. P. (1991) Roseate Terns and other

seabirds at Madeira. *Sea Swallow* 39: 49–53.

3. GRIMMETT, R. F. A. AND JONES, T. A. (1989) *Important bird areas in Europe*. Cambridge, U.K.: International Council for Bird Preservation (Techn. Publ. 9).

4. DEN HARTOG, J. C., NORREVANG, A. AND ZINO, P. A. (1984) Bird observations in the Selvagens Islands (21–23 October 1978 and 27 May-7 June 1981). *Bol. Mus. Mun. Funchal* 36: 111–141.

5. JENSEN, A. (1981) Ornithological winter observations on Selvagem Grande. *Bocagiana* 62: 1–7.

6. JONES, M. (1988) *A survey of the distribution, density and habitat preferences of the Long-toed Pigeon* Columba trocaz *in Madeira*. Cambridge, U.K.: International Council for Bird Preservation (Study Rep. 32).

7. JONES, M. (1990) A survey of the distribution, density and habitat preferences of the Long-toed Pigeon. *Bol. Mus. Mun. Funchal* 42: 71–86.

8. JOUANIN, C. AND ROUX, F. (1965) [Contribution to the study of the biology of *Pelagodroma marina hypoleuca* (Webb, Berthelot and Mougin-Tandon).] *Bol. Mus. Mun. Funchal* 19: 16–42. (In French.)

9. JOUANIN, C., ROUX, F. AND ZINO, P. A. (1969) [Visit to the breeding grounds of *Pterodroma mollis* 'deserta'.] *Oiseau* 39: 161–175. (In French.)

10. MOUGIN, J.-L. AND ROUX, F. (1988) [The stability of the population of Cory's Shearwater *Calonectris diomedea borealis* on the island of Selvagem Grande (30°09′N, 15°52′W) from 1983 to 1986.] *Bocagiana* 16: 1–6. (In French.)

11. ZINO, F. (in prep.) *Biology, ecology and behaviour of Bulwer's Petrel* Bulweria bulwerii *in the archipelago of Madeira*.

12. ZINO, F. AND BISCOITO, M. (1994) Breeding seabirds in the Madeira archipelago. Pp.172–185 in D. N. Nettleship, J. Burger and M. Gochfeld, eds. *Seabirds on islands: threats, case studies, and action plans*. Cambridge, U.K.: BirdLife International (BirdLife Conservation Series no. 1).

13. ZINO, F. AND ZINO, P. A. (1986) An account of the habitat, feeding habitats, density, breeding and need of protection of the Long-toed Wood Pigeon, *Columba trocaz*. *Bocagiana* 97: 1–16.

14. ZINO, P. A. (1969) [Observations on *Columba trocaz*.] *Oiseau et R.F.O.* 39: 3–4. (In French.)

15. ZINO, P. A. (1985) A short history of the Shearwater hunt on Great Salvage and recent developments on this island. *Bocagiana* 84: 14.

16. ZINO, P. A. (1991) Breeding of the Turtle Dove *Streptopelia turtur* in Madeira. *Bocagiana* 146: 1–4.

17. ZINO, P. A. AND ZINO, F. (1986) Contribution to the study of the petrels of the genus *Pterodroma* in the archipelago of Madeira. *Bol. Mus. Mun. Funchal* 38: 141–165.

REPUBLIC OF IRELAND

General

Population sizes are based on data, which have been modified for the Republic of Ireland by D. W. Gibbons, from Gates *et al.* (1993) except for species where specific references are given.

GATES, S., GIBBONS, D. W. AND MARCHANT, J. H. (1993) Population estimates for breeding birds in Britain and Ireland. Pp.462–475 in D. W. Gibbons, J. B. Reid and R. A. Chapman, eds. *The new atlas of breeding birds in Britain and Ireland: 1988–1991*. London: T. and A. D. Poyser.

Population size and range trends are largely based on information from the following sources:

GIBBONS, D. W., REID, J. B. AND CHAPMAN, R. A., EDS. (1993) *The new atlas of breeding birds in Britain and Ireland: 1988–1991*. London: T. and A. D. Poyser.

GRIMMETT, R. F. A. AND JONES, T. A. (1989) *Important bird areas in Europe*. Cambridge, U.K.: International Council for Bird Preservation (Techn. Publ. 9).

HUTCHINSON, C. D. (1989) *Birds in Ireland*. Calton, U.K.: T. and A. D. Poyser.

LLOYD, C. S., TASKER, M. L. AND PARTRIDGE, K. E. (1991) *The status of seabirds in Britain and Ireland*. London: T. and A. D. Poyser.

SHARROCK, J. T. R., ED. (1976) *The atlas of breeding birds in Britain and Ireland*. Calton, U.K.: T. and A. D. Poyser.

SHEPPARD, R. (in prep.) *Ireland's wetland wealth*. Dublin.

WHILDE, A. (in prep.) The Irish Red Data Book.

Breeding

1. IRISH WILDBIRD CONSERVANCY (1992) Unpublished data.
2. IRISH WILDBIRD CONSERVANCY (1993) pers. comm. to G. Williams. Subsequently Sheppard, R. and Green, R. E. (in press) Status of the Corncrake in Ireland in 1993. *Irish Birds*.
3. MEARNE, O. J. (1993) *in litt.*
4. WYNDE, R., ED. (1993) *Roseate Tern News 7*. Sandy, U.K.: Royal Society for the Protection of Birds.

ROMANIA

Breeding

1. ANTAL, V. AND SZOMBATH, Z. (1971) [Census of *Riparia riparia* L. and *Merops apiaster* L. colonies along the Mures between Tirgu Mures and Pecica-Arad county.] Pp.301–308 in Muzeul de Stiintele Naturii Bacau, ed. *Studii si Comunicari*. Bacau: Muzeul de Stiintele Naturii Bacau. (In Romanian.)
2. BÉRES, I. (1983) [Bird community of an isolated forest at Maramures.] *Analele Banatului, St. Nat.* 1: 117–122. (In Romanian.)
3. CRIVELLI, A. J. (1994) The importance of the former U.S.S.R. for the conservation of pelican populations nesting in the Palearctic. In A. J. Crivelli, V. G. Krivenko and V. G. Vinogradov, eds. *Pelicans in the former U.S.S.R.* Slimbridge, U.K.: International Waterfowl and Wetlands Research Bureau (Spec. Publ. 27).
4. GOMBOS, A. (1982) [Contribution to the knowledge of Short-toed Eagle *Circaetus g. gallicus* Gmel. distribution in Romania.] *Marisia* 12: 187–199. (In Romanian.)
5. INSTITUTUL DE CERCETARI SI PROIECTARI DELTA DUNARII TULCEA (1993) [The populations of colonial bird species.] (Unpublished). (In Romanian.)
6. KALABÉR, L. (1975) [Range of Scops Owl *Otus scops* L. in Romania.] *Nymphaea* 3: 141–171. (In Romanian.)
7. KALABÉR, L. (1977) [Status of Lesser Kestrel *Falco naumanni* in Romania.] *Gerfaut* 67: 437–446. (In Romanian.)

8. KALABÉR, L. (1984) Status of diurnal birds of prey in Romania and the problem of their protection. *Bull. World Working Group on Birds of Prey* 2: 37–43.

9. KELEMEN, A. AND SZOMBATH, Z. (1975) [Phenological study of the Muscicapidae family, 1: genera *Sylvia*, *Muscicapa* and *Phoenicurus*.] *Nymphaea* 3: 245–257. (In Romanian.)

10. KISS, A. (1979) [The status of the White Stork population *Ciconia ciconia* L. in Timis county, in summer 1976.] *Tibiscus. Stiinte Naturale. Muzeul Banatului Timisoara*: 217–273. (In Romanian.)

11. KISS, J. B. (1977) [New ornithological observation on Sacalin Island.] *Zoologie* 5: 459–465. (In Romanian.)

12. KISS, J. B. AND MARINOV, M. (1990) [White Stork *Ciconia ciconia* breeding status in the Danube delta in the period 1980–1989.] *Bull. inf. SOR* 2: 4–5. (In Romanian.)

13. KLEMM, W. (1983) [Status of the White Stork *Ciconia ciconia* in Romania.] *Ökol. Vögel* 5: 283–293. (In Romanian.)

14. KORODI GÁL, J. (1957) [Ornithological studies in some broad-leaved woods in Transylvania.] *Studii si Cercetari de Biologie Cluj* 8: 319–329. (In Romanian.)

15. KORODI GÁL, J. (1958) [Data concerning the knowledge of bird populations in different types of forests in the Bihor Mountains.] *Studia Universitatum. Babes Bolyai* 3: 169–181. (In Romanian.)

16. KORODI GÁL, J. (1964) [Research on bird ecology in some oak and mixed plain forests in Transylvania.] *Vertebrata Hungarica* 6: 41–71.

17. KOVÁTS, L. (1968) [Data on White Stork *Ciconia ciconia* L. distribution in south-east Transylvania.] *Comunicari de Zoologie*: 61–70. (In Romanian.)

18. KOVÁTS, L. (1970a) [Contribution to the knowledge of Grey Shrike *Lanius excubitor* L. distribution in Transylvania.] *Caiet cu Comunicari. Muzeul Tarii Crisurilor, Sectia de Stiinte Naturale* 8: 113–124. (In Romanian.)

19. KOVÁTS, L. (1970b) [*Emberiza cia cia* L., the Rock Bunting in Bihor county.] *Revista Muzeelor* 7: 49–54. (In Romanian.)

20. LINTIA, D. (1955) [*Birds of Romania, 3*.] Bucuresti: Ed. Academiei RPR. (In Romanian.)

21. LUTSCH, H. (1990) [Breeding status of the White Stork in Brasov county, 1990.] *Bull. inf. SOR* 4: 12–13. (In Romanian.)

22. MANOLACHE, L. (1970) [Distribution of Partridge *Perdix perdix* L. in Romania and its range in forest areas.] *Comunicari de Zoologie*: 210–218. (In Romanian.)

23. MANOLACHE, L. AND RÖSLER, R. (1963) [Contribution to the knowledge of Black Stork *Ciconia nigra* L. distribution in R.P.R.] *Natura Ser. Biologie* 4: 84–85. (In Romanian.)

24. MATIES, M. (1968) [Biometrical, morphological and systematic research concerning the *Lanius excubitor* L. population in the Socialist Republic of Romania.] *Studii si Comunicai Istorie-Stiintele Naturii, Muzeul Pitesti*: 213–226. (In Romanian.)

25. MATIES, M. (1974) [Contribution to the knowledge of the present status of diurnal birds of prey, Falconiformes, in Arges county during the 1967–1973 period.] *Nymphaea* 2: 129–136. (In Romanian.)

26. MATIES, M. AND CIOCHIA, V. (1980) [First data on breeding of Grey Shrike *Lanius excubitor* L. in Oltenia and Muntenia.] *Studii si Comunicari, Muzeul Pitesti* 5: 191–196. (In Romanian.)

27. MUNTEANU, D. (1979) [Great Bustard: past, present, future.] *Ocrotirea naturii si a mediului inconjurator* 23: 155–162. (In Romanian.)

28. MUNTEANU, D. (1982) [Avifauna of Vladeasa Mountain.] *Nymphaea* 10: 269–281. (In Romanian.)

29. MUNTEANU, D. (1986) [Research on bird populations in the Retezat Mountains, 1.] *Studii si Cercetari de Biol., Ser. Biol. Anim.* 38: 87–90. (In Romanian.)

30. PAPADOPOL, A. (1968) [The Charadriiformes of Romania. 2: single ecology of breeding species.] *Trav. Mus. Hist. Nat. Grigore Antipa* 9: 511–527. (In Romanian.)

31. PAPADOPOL, A. (1971) [Ornithological research in the salt lakes region of the north-east part of the Romanian Plain, 1.] *Trav. Mus. Hist. Nat. Grigore Antipa* 11: 363–392. (In Romanian.)

32. PASPALEVA, M. (1977) [Red-rumped Swallow *Hirundo daurica*, Subalpine Warbler *Sylvia cantilans*, Rock Partridge *Alectoris graeca* and Blyth's Reed Warbler *Acrocephalus dumetorum dumetorum* in Romania.] *Alauda* 45: 238. (In French.)

33. POLIS, R. (1973) [Ardeidae colonies in north-west Romania.] *Nymphaea* 1: 41–69. (In Romanian.)

34. POLIS, R. (1976) [Observations on the avifauna of Cefa-Bihor county.] *Nymphaea* 4: 195–225. (In Romanian.)

35. POPESCU, M. (1969) [Cirl Bunting *Emberiza cirlus* L. in Oltenia.] *Revista Muzeelor* 6: 75–76. (In Romanian.)

36. PUSCARIU, V. AND FILIPASCU, A. (1975) The situation of birds of prey in Romania, 1970–1974. Pp.149–152 in R. D. Chancellor, ed. *World Conference on Birds of Prey, 1975, Vienna*. Cambridge, U.K.: Intenational Council for Bird Preservation.

37. ROMANIAN ORNITHOLOGICAL SOCIETY (1991) [White Stork *Ciconia ciconia* in Mures county, 1990.] *Bull. inf. SOR* 1: 8–9. (In Romanian.)

38. SZOMBATH, Z. (1990) [*Falco peregrinus*.] *Bull. inf. SOR* 2: 6. (In Romanian.)

39. SZOMBATH, Z. AND GOMBOS, A. (1975) [Observation on Kingfisher *Alcedo atthis* L. along the Mures Valley.] *Nymphaea* 3: 179–190. (In Romanian.)

40. TALPEANU, M. AND PASPALEVA, M. (1981) [Qualitative changes recorded in Romanian avifauna during the last three decades.] *Trav. Mus. Hist. Nat. Grigore Antipa* 23: 243–257. (In Romanian.)

41. VASILIU, G. D. (1968) [Check-list of Romanian birds.] *Alauda* (Suppl): 1–120. (In French.)

Wintering

1. LINTIA, D. (1954) [*Birds of Romania, 2*.] Bucuresti: Ed. Academiei RPR. (In Romanian.)

2. MUNTEANU, D. AND MARINOV, M. (in prep.) The Mute Swan *Cygnus olor* and the Whooper Swan *Cygnus cygnus* wintering in Romania (unpublished).

3. MUNTEANU, D., WEBER, P., SZABÓ, J., GOGU-BOGDAN, M. AND MARINOV, M. (1991) A note on the present status of geese in Romania. *Ardea* 79: 165–166.

4. ROMANIAN ORNITHOLOGICAL SOCIETY (1990/1991) Mid-winter counts of waterfowl and geese for the International Waterfowl and Wetlands Research Bureau (unpublished).

5. RÜGER, A., PRENTICE, C. AND OWEN, M. (1986) *Results*

of the IWRB International Waterfowl Census 1967–1983. Slimbridge, U.K.: International Waterfowl and Wetlands Research Bureau (Spec. Publ. 6).

6. SUTHERLAND, W. J. AND CROCKFORD, N. J. (1993) Factors affecting the feeding distribution of Red-breasted Geese Branta ruficollis wintering in Romania. Biol. Conserv. 63: 61–65.

7. VASILIU, G. D. (1968) [Check-list of Romanian birds.] Alauda (Suppl): 1–120. (In French.)

RUSSIA

General

ESTAFIEV, A. A. (1991) [Fauna and ecology of waders of the Boshezemelskaja tundra and the Yugorsky peninsula.] Leningrad: Nauka. (In Russian.)

FLINT, V. E. AND GOLOVKIN, A. N., EDS. (1990) [Birds of the U.S.S.R.: Alcidae.] Moscow: Nauka. (In Russian.)

ILYICHEV, V. D. AND FLINT, V. E., EDS. (1982) [Birds of the U.S.S.R.: Gaviiformes, Podicipediformes, Procellariiformes.] Moscow: Nauka. (In Russian.)

ILYICHEV, V. D. AND ZUBAKIN, V. A., EDS. (1988) [Birds of the U.S.S.R.: Laridae.] Moscow: Nauka. (In Russian.)

KRIVENKO, V. G. (1991) [Waterfowl and its preservation.] Moscow: Agropromizdat. (In Russian.)

MALCHEVSKIY, A. S. AND PUKINSKIY, Y. B. (1983) [Birds of the Leningrad region and adjacent territories, 1.] Leningrad: Leningrad University. (In Russian.)

POTAPOV, R. L. AND FLINT, V. E., EDS. (1987) [Birds of the U.S.S.R.: Galliformes, Gruiformes.] Leningrad: Nauka. (In Russian.)

Breeding

1. BELIK, V. P. (1994) in litt.
2. BELIK, V. P. AND GALUSHIN, V. (1993) in litt.
3. CRIVELLI, A. J. (1994) The importance of the former U.S.S.R. for the conservation of pelican populations nesting in the Palearctic. In A. J. Crivelli, V. G. Krivenko and V. G. Vinogradov, eds. Pelicans in the former U.S.S.R. Slimbridge, U.K.: International Waterfowl and Wetlands Research Bureau (Spec. Publ. 27).

Wintering

1. FRANTZEN, B. (1993) in litt. to BirdLife International.
2. KOZYAKIM, A. (1994) pers. comm. to V. Krivenko and V. Vinogradov.

SLOVAKIA

Breeding

1. DANKO, S. (in prep.) [Occurrence and breeding of Pygmy Cormorant Phalacrocorax pygmaeus in Czechoslovakia] (In Slovak.)

2. DANKO, S. (in press) [Short-toed Lark Calandrella brachydactyla: a new species for the avifauna of Czechoslovakia.] Sylvia. (In Slovak.)

3. DANKO, S. (1990) [The present knowledge from the research of Lesser Spotted Eagle Aquila pomarina in Czechoslovakia.] Buteo 5: 37–48. (In Slovak with English summary.)

4. KRISTIN, A. (1991a) [On the present status and ecology of Rock Bunting Emberiza cia in Czechoslovakia.] Sylvia 28: 115–120. (In Slovak with English summary.)

5. KRIŠTÍN, A. (1991b) [Breeding status and breeding ecology of Lesser Grey Shrike Lanius minor in central Slovakia, CSFR.] Orn. Mitt. 43: 131–133. [In German.]

6. MATOUSEK, B., MATOUSEK, F. AND KUBÁN, V. (1984) [The first nesting of the Common Gull Larus canus in Czechoslovakia.] Acta. Rer. Natur. Mus. Nat. Slov. Bratislava 30: 199–203. (In Slovak with German summary.)

7. MRLÍK, V. AND DANKO, S. (1990) [Numbers of birds of prey nesting pairs in Czechoslovakia, in 1988.] Sylvia 27: 71–78. (In Czech with English summary.)

8. POLIAK, M. (1989) [New knowledge on biology and captive breeding of Great Bustard.] Pp.238–249 in J. Lukásek, I. Otáhal and P. Trpák, eds. [Proceedings Conference on Safeguarding, keeping and rearing, Novy Jicín, 1987.] Novy Jicín: State Institute for Nature Conservancy in Prague/Regional Natural History Museum. (In Slovak with German summary.)

9. RANDÍK, A. (1968) [Distribution of Red-backed Shrike Lanius collurio in Slovakia.] Cs. ochr. prírody Bratislava 7: 201-217. [In Slovak with English summary.]

10. RANDÍK, A. (1970) [Status of Great Bustard Otis tarda in Czechoslovakia.] Ochrana fauny Bratislava 4: 190-191. (In Slovak with German summary.)

11. RANDÍK, A. (1978) [Distribution, protection and management of Great Bustard Otis tarda in Czechoslovakia and Europe.] Cs. ochrana prírody, Bratislava 18: 17–38. (In Slovak with English summary.)

12. SABADOS, K. (1982) [Possibilities of improving game management and intensifying the protection of the Capercaillie and the Black Grouse in Slovakia.] Folia venatoria Bratislava 12: 307–314. (In Slovak.)

13. SALAJ, J. (1990) [Distribution and nesting of Lanius senator L. in the basins of south Slovakia in 1983–1987.] Biologia, Bratislava 45: 127–131. (In Slovak with English summary.)

14. SALAJ, J. (1991) [Distribution and nesting of Merops apiaster in the territory of Rimavská, Lucenská and Ipel'ská Basins in the years 1961–1989.] Biologia, Bratislava 46: 157–167. (In Slovak with English summary.)

15. ŠTOLLMANN, A. (1975) [Black Stork Ciconia nigra in Slovakia in 1971.] Acta Rer. Natur. Mus. Nat. Slov. Bratislava 21: 231–235. (In Slovak with German summary.)

16. ŠTOLLMANN, A. (1979) [Distribution, population, dynamics and conservation of White Stork in Slovakia.] Pannonicum 1: 31–34. [In Slovak.]

17. ŠTOLLMAN, A. (1987) [Chronology of White Stork Ciconia ciconia L. in Slovakia.] Ochrana prírody Bratislava 8: 9–42. (In Slovak with English summary.)

Wintering

1. PACENOVSKY, S. (1985) [Further occurrence of the Bewick's Swan Cygnus bewickii in eastern Slovakia.] Milvus 2: 112–113. (In Slovak with German summary.)

2. STOLLMAN, A. (1968) [The wintering of the Curlew Numenius arquata in the vicinity of Komárno.] Vertebrat. zprávy, Notulae vertebratologicae 2: 61–62. (In Slovak with German summary.)

SLOVENIA

Breeding

1. BRACKO, F. (1986) [Rapid population decline of Roller *Coracias garrulus* in Slovenia.]*Acrocephalus* 7: 49–52. (In Slovenian with English summary.)
2. GREGORI, J. (1990) [Bee-eater *Merops apiaster* in Slovenia.] *Acrocephalus* 43–44: 3. (In Slovenian.)
3. JEZ, M. (1987) [White Stork *Ciconia ciconia* in Slovenia in 1979.] *Varstvo narave* 13: 79. (In Slovenian.)
4. KOZINC, B. (1990) [Nesting of Black Kite *Milvus migrans* near Lesce.] *Acrocephalus* 48: 57. (In Slovenian.)
5. SERE, D. (1985) [Redshank *Tringa totanus* breeds in Slovenia.] *Acrocephalus* 25: 35. (In Slovenian.)

Wintering

1. BIBIC, A. (1988) [Birds at reservoirs in north-eastern Slovenia.] *Acrocephalus* 26: 35–36. (In Slovenian.)

SPAIN

Breeding

1. ALBERTO, I. J. AND VELASCO, V. (1988) [Waders wintering in Spain.] Pp.71–78 in J. L. Tellería, ed. [*Wintering birds of the Iberian peninsula.*] Madrid: Sociedad Española de Ornitología (Monogr. 1). (In Spanish.)
2. ALONSO, J. A. AND ALONSO, J. C., EDS. (1990) [*Distribution and demography of the Common Crane in Spain.*] Madrid: Instituto Nacional para la Conservación de la Naturaleza/CSIC (In Spanish.)
3. ALVAREZ, A. (1983) [Comparison of the methods of strip survey, IKA and IPA applied to a mountain coniferous forest in León.] Pp.107–112 in F. J. Purroy, ed. [*Proc. VII Int. Con. Bird Census Work.*] León: León University. (In Spanish.)
4. ALVAREZ, A. (1989) [Avifauna of understorey vegetation in the Cordillera Cantábrica.] Léon: León University (Ph.D. thesis). (In Spanish.)
5. AMA (AGENCIA DE MEDIO AMBIENTE) (1990) [Record breeding of Flamingos in Fuente Piedra.] *Quercus* 56: 38. (In Spanish.)
6. AMA (AGENCIA DE MEDIO AMBIENTE) (1992) *in litt.* to A. J. Green.
7. AMAT, J. A. (1981) [The duck community of Doñana National Park (Marismas del Guadalquivir, south-west Spain).] *Doñana Acta Vert.* 8: 125–158. (In Spanish.)
8. AMAT, J. A. (1993) Status of the Kentish Plover in Spain. *Wader Study Group Kentish Plover Project Newsletter* 2: 2–4.
9. AMIGOS DE LA MALVASÍA (1989) [Increase of the Spanish population of White-headed Duck.] *Quercus* 37: 6. (In Spanish.)
10. ARROYO, B. (1991) [Results of the national census of Bonelli's Eagle.] *Quercus* 70: 17. (In Spanish.)
11. ARROYO, B. AND GARZA, V. (1988) [The Golden Eagle *Aquila chrysaetos.*] *Quercus* 28: 14–19. (In Spanish.)
12. ARROYO, B., FERREIRO, E. AND GARZA, V. (1990a) [*Second national survey of the Griffon Vulture* Gyps fulvus*: population, distribution, range and conservation.*] Madrid: Instituto Nacional para la Conservación de la Naturaleza. (In Spanish.)
13. ARROYO, B., FERREIRO, E. AND GARZA, V. (1990b) [*The*

Golden Eagle Aquila chrysaetos *in Spain: census, range, breeding and conservation.*] Madrid: Instituto Nacional para la Conservación de la Naturaleza. (In Spanish.)
14. BARCENA, F., TEIXEIRA, A. M. AND BERMEJO, A. (1984) Breeding seabird populations in the atlantic sector of the Iberian peninsula. Pp.335–345 in J. P. Croxall, P. G. H. Evans and R. W. Schreiber, eds. *Status and conservation of the world's seabirds.* Cambridge, U.K.: International Council for Bird Preservation (Techn. Publ. 2).
15. BERNÍS, F. (1988) [Urban avifauna in the Iberian plateaus.] Pp.27–171 in F. Bernís, ed. [*Birds of urban and agricultural areas in the Iberian plateaus.*] Madrid: Sociedad Española de Ornitología (Monogr. 2). (In Spanish.)
16. BLANCO, J. A. AND GONZÁLEZ, J. L., EDS. (1992) [*Red data book of Spanish vertebrates.*] Madrid: Instituto Nacional para la Conservación de la Naturaleza. (In Spanish.)
17. BLASCO, M., LUCENA, J. AND RODRÍGUEZ, J. (1979) [*The Flamingos* Phoenicopterus ruber *of Fuente de Piedra.*] Madrid: Instituto Nacional para la Conservación de la Naturaleza (Naturalia Hispánica 23). (In Spanish.)
18. BOETTCHER-STREIM, W. (1992) Changes in the European population of the Black Stork. *Orn. Beob.* 89: 235–244.
19. BONGIORNO, S. F. (1982) Land use and summer bird populations in north-western Galicia, Spain. *Ibis* 124: 1–20.
20. CARNERO, J. J. AND PERIS, S. (1988) [Atlas of breeding birds of the Salamanca Province.] Salamanca: Exma Diputación de Salamanca. (In Spanish.)
21. CARRERA, E. (1987) [*Gulls.*] Barcelona: Ed. Cyan. (In Catalan.)
22. CARRERA, E. (1988) [Wintering of gulls and terns in the Iberian peninsula.] Pp.79–96 in J. L. Tellería, ed. [*Wintering birds of the Iberian peninsula.*] Madrid: Sociedad Española de Ornitología (Monogr. 1). (In Spanish.)
23. CHACÓN, G. (1993) [The Corncrake in the Iberian peninsula and Balearics.] *Quercus* 83: 26–29. (In Spanish.)
24. CHACÓN, G., FERNÁNDEZ, J. AND MARTÍNEZ, F. (1985) [The discovery of a breeding population of Corncrake *Crex crex* in Spain.] *Alytes* 3: 180–182. (In Spanish.)
25. CONSEJERIA DE AGRICULTURA (1987) [*First International congress of steppic birds.*] León: Junta de Castilla y León. (In Spanish.)
26. COSTA, L. (1984) [The bird community of a pine forest in Doñana National Park (south-west Spain).] *Doñana Acta Vert.* 2: 151–183. (In Spanish.)
27. CRAMP, S., ED. (1988) *The birds of the western Palearctic,* 5. Oxford: Oxford University Press.
28. CRAMP, S. AND SIMMONS, K. E. L., EDS. (1977) *The birds of the western Palearctic,* 1. Oxford: Oxford University Press.
29. CUADRADO, M. (1986) [The breeding and wintering bird communities of a wild olive (*Olea europaea* var. *sylvestris*) woodland in southern Spain.] *Doñana Acta Vert.* 13: 71–85. (In Spanish.)
30. DELGADO, J. A. AND BARBA, E. (1987) [Breeding birds in orange groves.]*Mediterranea* 9: 29–40. (In Spanish.)
31. DOLZ, J. AND GÓMEZ, J. A. (1990) [Census of wintering wildfowl in Spain: January 1988.] *Garcilla* 77: 6–28. (In Spanish.)

541

32. DONÁZAR, J. A. AND FERNANDEZ, C. (1990) Population trends of the Griffon Vulture (*Gyps fulvus*) in northern Spain between 1969 and 1989 in relation to conservation measures. *Biol. Conserv.* 53: 83–91.

33. ELÓSEGUI, J. (1985) [*Atlas of breeding birds of Navarra.*] Pamplona: Caja de Ahorros de Navarra. (In Spanish.)

34. FARINHA, J. C. (1991) [*Urgent measures for the conservation of the Chough* Pyrrhocorax pyrrhocorax *in Portugal.*] Lisbon: Serviço Nacional de Parques, Reservas e Conservação da Natureza (Studies in Biology and Nature Conservation 2). (In Portuguese.)

35. See 38.

36. FERNÁNDEZ, J. M. (1993) *in litt.* to BirdLife International.

37. FERNÁNDEZ, M., PASCUAL, J. A. AND DA CRUZ, H. (1990) [*Spanish wetlands of international importance.*] Madrid: Miraguano/Federación de Amigos de la Tierra. (In Spanish.)

38. FERNÁNDEZ-ALCAZAR, G. AND FERNÁNDEZ-CRUZ, M. (1991) [Status of heron colonies in Spain.] *Quercus* 60: 8–16. (In Spanish.)

39. FERNÁNDEZ CRUZ, M. AND MARTÍN-NOVELLA, C. (1988) [Revision and updating of the wintering of Greater Flamingos (*Phoenicopterus ruber roseus*) in the Iberian peninsula.] Pp.23–53 in J. L. Tellería, ed. [*Wintering birds of the Iberian peninsula.*] Madrid: Sociedad Española de Ornitología (Monogr. 2). (In Spanish.)

40. FERRERO, J. J., ROMÁN, J. A., PIZARRO, V. M. AND RODRIGUEZ, A. (1991) [Studies about the Black Stork in Extremadura: population census (1988).] *Alytes* 5: 9–18. (In Spanish.)

41. GALARZA, A. (1987) [Seasonal description of passerine communities in a coastal farmland of the Basque Country.] *Munibe (Cien. Nat.)* 39: 3–8. (In Spanish.)

42. GALLEGO, S., RODRIQUEZ-TEIJEIRO, J. D. AND PUIG-CERVER, M. (1990) [The Quail.] *Trofeo* 241: 40–43. (In Spanish.)

43. GARCÍA, L. AND PURROY, F. J. (1973) [Evaluation of bird communities by the parcel method: results obtained in the Mediterranean scrub of Punta del Sabinar (Almería).] *Bol. Est. Cent. Ecol.* 2: 41–49. (In Spanish.)

44. GARCIA DORY, M. A. (1983) [Data on the ecology of the genus *Pyrrhocorax* (*P. pyrrhocorax* and *P. graculus*) in the mountains of Covadonga National Park, Asturias.] *Alytes* 1: 411–448. (In Spanish.)

45. GARNICA, R. (1983) [Bird community study in holm oaks in the Duero Basin in León Province.] Léon: León University (Ph.D. thesis). (In Spanish.)

46. GARNICA, R. AND PURROY, F. J. (1990) [Breeding bird communities in the Spanish oak forests.] *Testudo. Revista científica de ANSE* 1: 81–89. (In Spanish.)

47. GARZA, V. AND SUÁREZ, F. (1990) [Distribution, population and habitat selection of Dupont's Lark *Chersophilus duponti* on the Iberian peninsula.] *Ardeola* 37: 3–12. (In Spanish.)

48. GEDEB (1986) [*Descriptive study of the flora and vertebrate fauna in the Ebro Dam.*] Burgos: Eisa. (In Spanish.)

49. GÉROUDET, P. (1978) [*Large shorebirds, gamebirds and rails of Europe.*] Paris: Delachaux et Niestlé. (In French.)

50. GÉROUDET, P. (1982) [*Waders, sandgrouse and pigeons of Europe.*] Paris: Delachaux et Niestlé. (In French.)

51. GIL-DELGADO, J. A. (1979) [Bird communities of orange groves, Sagunto (Valencia).] Valencia: Valencia University (Ph.D. thesis). (In Spanish.)

52. GÓMEZ MANZANEQUE, A. (in press) [Present status of the White Stork in Spain.] Actes du colloque internationel des Cicognes Blanches d'Europe. Metz, France. (In French.)

53. GONZÁLEZ, J. L. (1994) pers. comm. to BirdLife International.

54. GONZÁLEZ, J. L. AND MANUEL, M. (1990) [*The Lesser Kestrel* Falco naumanni *in the Iberian peninsula.*] Madrid: Instituto Nacional para la Conservación de la Naturaleza. (In Spanish.)

55. GONZÁLEZ, J. M. (1975) [Vertebrate descriptions in the area of Mora de Rubiellos (Teruel).] *Bol. Est. Cent. Ecol.* 4: 63–81. (In Spanish.)

56. GONZÁLEZ, L. M. (1989) [Biology, ecology and conservation of Spanish Imperial Eagle.] *Quercus* 43: 4–15. (In Spanish.)

57. GONZÁLEZ, L. M. (1990) [Survey of the breeding populations of Spanish Imperial Eagle and Black Vulture in Spain.] *Quercus* 58: 16–22. (In Spanish.)

58. GONZÁLEZ, L. M., ED. (in press) [*Recovery plan for the Spanish Imperial Eagle* Aquila adalberti.] Madrid: Instituto Nacional para la Conservación de la Naturaleza. (In Spanish.)

59. GONZÁLEZ, L. M., GONZÁLEZ, J. L., GARZÓN, J. AND HEREDIA, B. (1978) [Census and distribution of the Spanish Imperial Eagle *Aquila adalberti* in Spain during 1981–1986.] *Bol. Estación Central de Ecología* 16: 99–109. (In Spanish.)

60. GUITIÁN, J. (1984) [Ecology of a passerine community in a mountain forest of western Cordillera Cantábrica.] Santiago, Galicia: Santiago de Compostela University (Ph.D. thesis). (In Spanish.)

61. HARO, M. AND VARGAS, J. M. (1982) [Breeding birds in the *Abies pinsapo* forests (Málaga, Spain).] *Mon. Trab. de Zoología* 3–4: 105–119. (In Spanish.)

62. HEREDIA, B., HIRALDO, F., GONZÁLEZ, L. M. AND GONZÁLEZ, J. L. (1988) Status, ecology and conservation of the Peregrine Falcon in Spain. Pp.219–226 in T. J. Cade, J. H. Enderson, C. G. Thelander and C. M. White, eds. *Peregrine falcon populations: their management and recovery.* Boise, U.S.A.: The Peregrine Fund.

63. HEREDIA, R. (1989) [Census of the Pyrenean population of Lammergeier.] *Quercus* 40: 14–15. (In Spanish.)

64. HEREDIA, R. (1991) [The results of Lammergeier reproduction in 1990.] *Quercus* 62: 17. (In Spanish.)

65. HERNÁNDEZ, F. AND PELA O ZUECO, E. (1987) [Steppic bird communities in the plains of the mid Ebro valley.] Pp.379–393 in Consejeria de Agricultura, ed. [*First International Congress on steppic birds.*] León: Junta de Castilla y León. (In Spanish.)

66. HERRERA, C. M. (1980) [Seasonal evolution of the passerine communities in two holm oak forests in western Andalucía.] *Ardeola* 25: 143–180. (In Spanish.)

67. HIDALGO DE TRUCIO, S. J. AND CARRANZA, J. (1990) [*The ecology and behaviour of Great Bustard* Otis tarda.] Salamanca: Extremadura-Caja Salamanca University. (In Spanish.)

68. HIRALDO, F. (1974) [Breeding colonies and census of Black Vultures *Aegypius monachus* in Spain.] *Naturalia Hispanica* 2: 3–31. (In Spanish.)

69. HIRALDO, F., DELIBES, M. AND CALDERÓN, J. (1979) [*The Lammergeier* Gypaetus barbatus: *systematics, taxonomy, biology, distribution and protection.*] Madrid: Instituto Nacional para la Conservación de la Naturaleza (Monogr. 22). (In Spanish.)

70. HUERTA, A. AND RODRÍGUEZ, J. L. (1988) [*SOS for the Spanish fauna: a hundred species endangered with extinction.*] Madrid: Ed. Fondo Natural. (In Spanish.)

71. ICONA (INSTITUTO NACIONAL PARA LA CONSERVACIÓN DE LA NATURALEZA) (1993) Coordinated Action Plan for the conservation of Audoin's Gull (unpublished report).

72. JACOB, J. P. AND CLOTUCHE, E. (1989) [Spreading and regression of bird species in Europe.] *Aves* 26. (In French.)

73. JOHNSON, A. (1993) *in litt.* to BirdLife International.

74. JORDANO, P. (1985) [The annual cycle of frugivorous passerines in southern Spanish Mediterranean shrubland: the wintering season and yearly variations.] *Ardeola* 32: 69–94. (In Spanish.)

75. DE JUANA, E. (1984) The status and conservation of seabirds in the Spanish Mediterranean. Pp.347–361 in J. P. Croxall, P. G. H. Evans and R. W. Schreiber, eds. *Status and conservation of the world's seabirds.* Cambridge, U.K.: International Council for Bird Preservation (Techn. Publ. 2).

76. DE JUANA, E. (1988) [La Serena, a steppic area of Extremadura of singular importance.] *La Garcilla* 71–72: 26–27. (In Spanish.)

77. DE JUANA, E., ED. (1990) [*Important bird areas in Spain.*] Madrid: Sociedad Española de Ornitología (Monogr. 3). (In Spanish.)

78. DE JUANA, E., VARELA, J. AND WITT, H.-H. (1984) The conservation of seabirds at the Chafarinas islands. Pp.363–370 in J. P. Croxall, P. G. H. Evans and R. W. Schreiber, eds. *Status and conservation of the world's seabirds.* Cambridge, U.K.: International Council for Bird Preservation (Techn. Publ. 2).

79. DE JUANA, E., DE JUANA, F. AND CALVO, S. (1988) [Wintering of birds of prey in the Iberian peninsula.] Pp.97–122 in J. L. Tellería, ed. *Wintering birds of the Iberian peninsula.* Madrid: Sociedad Española de Ornitología (Monogr. 1). (In Spanish.)

80. DE JUANA, F. (1989) [Diurnal birds of prey in Spain.] *Ecología* 3: 237–292. (In Spanish.)

81. LÁZARO, E., CHOZAS, P. AND FERNÁNDEZ-CRUZ, M. (1986) [Breeding population of the White Stork Ciconia ciconia in Spain: 1984 National Census.] *Ardeola* 33: 131–169. (In Spanish.)

82. LLAMAS, O. (1988) [The Grey Partridge.] *Trofeo* 220: 12–17. (In Spanish.)

83. LUCIO, A. (1989) [Bioecology of the Red-legged Partridge in the León Province.] Léon: León University (Ph.D. thesis). (In Spanish.)

84. MANRIQUE, J. AND MIRALLES, J. M. (1988) [The Trumpeter Finch *Bucanetes githagineus*.] *Quercus* 32: 34–36. (In Spanish.)

85. MANRIQUE, J., SUÁREZ, F. AND GARZA, V. (1990) [The Dupont's Lark in Spain.] *Quercus* 57: 6–11. (In Spanish.)

86. MAÑEZ, M. (1987) [Owls.] Pp.103–107 in Federación de Amigos de la Tierra, ed. [*Annual ornithology, 87: raptors.*] Madrid: Ed. Miraguano. (In Spanish.)

87. MARTÍ, R., MARTÍN-NOVELLA, C. AND FERNÁNDEZ-CRUZ, M. (1988) [Endangered waterfowl.] *Quercus* 34: 37–41. (In Spanish.)

88. MARTÍNEZ, A. (1988) [The importance of the Ebro Delta.] *La Garcilla* 73: 29. (In Spanish.)

89. MARTÍNEZ, A. (1989) [The importance of the Ebro delta.] *La Garcilla* 74: 19–24. (In Spanish.)

90. MARTÍNEZ-VILALTA, A. (1991) [First national census of breeding Black-winged Stilt, Avocet, Pratincole and Gull-billed Tern, 1989.] *Ecología* 5: 321–327. (In Spanish.)

91. MARTINO, J. (1986) [*Structural analysis of breeding and wintering bird communities in Sajambre valley (León).*] León: Excma. Diputación Provincial de León. (In Spanish.)

92. MESTRE, P., PERIS, S., SANTOS, T., SUÁREZ, F. AND SOLER, B. (1987) The decline of the Black-eared Wheatear *Oenanthe hispanica* on the Iberian peninsula. *Bird Study* 34: 239–243.

93. MIKKOLA, H. (1983) *Owls of Europe.* Calton, U.K.: T. and A. D. Poyser.

94. MUNTANER, J., FERRER, X. AND MARTÍNEZ-VILLALTA, A. (1983) [*Atlas of the breeding birds of Cataluña and Andorra.*] Barcelona: Ketres. (In Catalan.)

95. MUÑOZ-COBO, J. (1987) [Bird communities of Jaen olive groves.] Madrid: Universidad Complutense de Madrid (Ph.D. thesis). (In Spanish.)

96. MUÑOZ-COBO, J. (1990) [Dynamics of breeding birds in the old olive trees of Jaen.] *Revista Científica de ANSE* 1: 99–117. (In Spanish.)

97. OBESO, J. R. (1985) [Passerine communities and frugivorism in medium altitudes of the Sierra de Cazorla.] Oviedo, Asturias: Oviedo University (Ph.D. thesis). (In Spanish.)

98. PARSLOW, J. L. F. AND EVERETT, M. J. (1981) [*Birds in need of special protection in Europe.*] Strasbourg: Council of Europe (Nature and Environment Series 24). (In French.)

99. PEDROCCHI-RENAULT, C. (1973) [Studies in the coniferous forests of the Central Pyrenees. A: Pine forest with *Ilex* in San Juan de la Peña. 2: Use of grid methods in the study of density of breeding birds.] *Pirineos* 109: 73–77. (In Spanish.)

100. PEREA, J. L., MORALES, M. AND VELASCO, J. (1990) [*The Egyptian Vulture in Spain.*] Madrid: Instituto Nacional para la Conservación de la Naturaleza. (In Spanish.)

101. PERIS, S., SUAREZ, F. AND TELLERÍA, J. L. (1975) [Ornithological study of Maranchón juniper woodland (*Juniperus thurifera* L.): description of the vegetation and application of the parcel method.] *Ardeola* 22: 3–27. (In Spanish.)

102. PIERSMA, T. (1986) Breeding waders in Europe. A review of population size estimates and a bibliography of information sources. *Bull. Wader Study Group* 48 (Suppl.): 1–116.

103. POTTI, J. (1985) [Bird communities of Macizo de Ayllón (Sistema central).] Madrid: Universidad Complutense de Madrid (Ph.D. thesis). (In Spanish.)

104. POTTI, J. AND GARRIDO, G. (1986) [Seasonal dynamics of an agricultural bird community in Central Spain.] *Alytes* 4: 29–48. (In Spanish.)

105. PURROY, F. J. (1974) [Contribution to the ornithologi-

cal knowledge of the Pyrenean pine forests.] *Ardeola* 20: 245–261. (In Spanish.)

106. PURROY, F. J. (1975) [Annual evolution of the avifauna of a mixed wood of coniferous and deciduous trees in Navarra.] *Ardeola* 21: 669–697. (In Spanish.)

107. PURROY, F. J. (1977) [Breeding avifauna in beechwoods, *Quercus pubescens* forests and holm oak forests of the Pyrenees.] *Bol. Est. Cent. Ecol.* 6: 93–103. (In Spanish.)

108. PURROY, F. J. (1988) [The decrease of the Turtle Dove.] *Trofeo* 219: 10–14. (In Spanish.)

109. PURROY, F. J. (in prep.) Spanish ornithological atlas.

110. Saez-Royuela, R. (1990) [*INCAFO's guide to the birds of the Iberian peninsula.*] Madrid: INCAFO. (In Spanish.)

111. SAEZ-ROYUELA, R. AND SANTOS, T., EDS. (1985) [*Study of migrating biology of the Order Anseriformes in Spain.*] Madrid: Instituto Nacional para la Conservación de la Naturaleza (Monogr. 38). (In Spanish.)

112. SALVADOR, J. (1991) [The atlas of the seabirds of the Balearic Islands.] (In Spanish.)

113. SANCHEZ, E. (1992) [First reintroduction of 22 *Fulica cristata* in Spain.] *Quercus* 77: 11. (In Spanish.)

114. SANTOS, T. AND SUAREZ, F. (1983) The bird communities of the heathlands of Palencia. The effects of coniferous plantations. Pp.172–179 in F. J. Purroy, ed. *Proc. VII Int. Con. Bird Census Work.* León: León University.

115. SANTOS, T., SUAREZ, F. AND TELLERÍA, J. L. (1983) The bird communities of Iberian juniper woodlands (*Juniperus thurifera* L.). Pp.79–88 in F. J. Purroy, ed. *Proc. VII Int. Con. Bird Census Work.* León: León University.

116. SEO (SOCIEDAD ESPAÑOLA DE ORNITOLOGÍA) (1981) [The first survey of the breeding colonies of the Griffon Vulture *Gyps fulvus* in the Iberian peninsula.] *Ardeola* 26–27: 165–312. (In Spanish.)

117. SHARROCK, J. T. R., ED. (1976) *The atlas of breeding birds in Britain and Ireland.* Calton, U.K.: T. and A. D. Poyser.

118. DE SOUZA, J. A. AND DOMÍNGUEZ, J. (1989) [Effectiveness and distribution of the Kentish Plover (*Charadrius alexandrinus*) in Galicia.] *Ecología* 3: 305–311. (In Spanish.)

119. SUÁREZ, F. (1980) [Introduction to the study of the bird community in two peninsular steppic areas, the Iberic steppe and the steppe of the central depression of the Ebro Valley.] *Bol. Est. Cent. Ecol.* 9: 53–62. (In Spanish.)

120. SUÁREZ, F. AND GARZA, V. (1989) [Wintering of Dupont's Lark, *Chersophilus duponti*, in the Iberian peninsula.] *Ardeola* 36: 107–110. (In Spanish.)

121. TELLERÍA, J. L. (1979) [The postnuptial migration of the Bee-eater *Merops apiaster* in the Gibraltar Strait in 1977.] *Alauda* 47: 139–150. (In French.)

122. TELLERÍA, J. L. (1981) [*Bird migration on the Gibraltar Strait, 2.*] Madrid: Universidad Complutense de Madrid. (In Spanish.)

123. TELLERÍA, J. L. AND GALARZA, A. (1990) [Avifauna and landscape in northern Spain: effects of exotic tree reforestations.] *Ardeola* 37: 229–245. (In Spanish.)

124. TELLERÍA, J. L. AND GARZA, V. (1983) Methodological features of a study of a Mediterranean forest bird

community. Pp.89–92 in F. J. Purroy, ed. *Proc. VII Int. Con. Bird Census Work.* León: León University.

125. TELLERÍA, J. L., SANTOS, T., ALVAREZ, G. AND SÁEZ-ROYUELA, G. (1988a) [Avifauna of the cereal cultivations in the interior of Spain.] Pp.173–317 in F. Bernís, ed. [*Birds of urban and agricultural areas.*] Madrid: Sociedad Española de Ornitología (Monogr. 2). (In Spanish.)

126. TELLERÍA, J. L., SUÁREZ, F. AND SANTOS, T. (1988b) Bird communities of the Iberian shrubsteppes: seasonality and structure along a climatic gradient. *Holarctic Ecol.* 11: 171–177.

127. TEWES, E. (1991) [The Black Vulture in Mallorca.] *Quercus* 66: 15–17. (In Spanish.)

128. TORRES-ESQUIVIAS, J. A., ARENA, R. AND AYALA, J. M. (1986) [The historical evolution of White-headed Duck in Spain.] *Oxyura* 3: 5–17. (In Spanish.)

129. TROYA, A. AND BERNUÉS, M., EDS. (1990) [*Spanish wetlands included in the Ramsar Treaty.*] Madrid: Instituto Nacional para la Conservación de la Naturaleza. (In Spanish.)

130. URDIALES, C. (1991) pers. comm.

131. URDIALES, C. (1992) *in litt.* to BirdLife International.

132. URIOS, V., ESCOBAR, J. V., PARDO, R. AND GÓMEZ, J. A. (1991) [*Atlas of breeding birds in Valencia.*] Valencia: Generalitat Valenciana, Consellería d'Agricultura i Pesca. (In Spanish.)

133. VALVERDE, J. A. (1960) [Vertebrates of the Guadalquivir marshes.] *Arch. Inst. Aclim. Almería* 9: 1–168. (In Spanish.)

134. ZAMORA, R. (1987) [Temporal dynamics and habitat selection of passerines in the high mountain of Sierra Nevada.] Granada: Granada University (Ph.D. thesis). (In Spanish.)

135. ZAMORA, R. AND CAMACHO, I. (1984a) [Seasonal changes in a bird community in a stand of holm oaks in Sierra Nevada, Spain.] *Doñana Acta Vert.* 2: 129–150. (In Spanish.)

136. ZAMORA, R. AND CAMACHO, I. (1984b) [Seasonal changes in a bird community in a holm oak stand in Sierra Nevada (Spain).] *Doñana Acta Vert.* 2: 25–43. (In Spanish.)

137. ZÚÑIGA, J. M., SOLER, M. AND CAMACHO, I. (1982) [*Status of the terrestrial avifauna of Hoya de Guadix: ecological aspects.*] Granada: Granada University (New series: Monogr. of Zoology Dept.). (In Spanish.)

Wintering

1. AGUILAR, A. L. (1980) [Annual variation of bird populations in the Middle Extremadurian Guadiana.] Madrid: Universidad Complutense de Madrid (Ph.D. thesis). (In Spanish.)

2. ALBERTO, I. J. AND VELASCO, V. (1988) [Waders wintering in Spain.] Pp.71–78 in J. L. Tellería, ed. [*Wintering birds of the Iberian peninsula.*] Madrid: Sociedad Española de Ornitología (Monogr. 1). (In Spanish.)

3. ALVAREZ, A. (1989) [Avifauna of understorey vegetation in the Cordillera Cantábrica.] Léon: León University (Ph.D. thesis). (In Spanish.)

4. ARROYO, B. AND TELLERÍA, J. L. (1984) [Wintering of birds in the Gibraltar area.] *Ardeola* 30: 23–31. (In Spanish.)

5. COSTA, L. AND PURROY, F. J. (1992) [Breeding and wintering bird communities in birch forests of the Cantabrian Mountains.] *Munibe (Cien. Nat.)* 41: 101–105. (In Spanish.)

6. DOLZ, J. C. AND GANS, J. G. (1991) [Census of wintering wildfowl in Spain: January 1989.] Madrid: Sociedad Española de Ornitología (unpublished). (In Spanish.)

7. DOLZ, J. C. AND GÓMEZ, J. A. (1988) [Ducks and Coots wintering in Spain.] Pp.23–54, in J. L. Tellería, ed. [*Wintering birds of the Iberian peninsula.*] Madrid: Sociedad Española de Ornitología (Monogr. 1). (In Spanish.)

8. DOLZ, J. C. AND GÓMEZ, J. A. (1990) [Census of wintering wildfowl in Spain: January 1988.] *La Garcilla* 77: 6–28. (In Spanish.)

9. GARNICA, R. AND BÉCARES, J. (1985) Preliminary data on the winter population of Woodcock (*Scolopax rusticola*) in León province, Spain. *IWRB Woodcock and Snipe Res. Group, Newsletter* 11: 40–46.

10. DE JUANA, E. (1980) [*Ornithological atlas of La Rioja.*] Logroño: Instituto de Estudios Riojanos. (In Spanish.)

11. SAEZ-ROYUELA, R. (1990) [*INCAFO's guide to the birds of the Iberian peninsula.*] Madrid: INCAFO. (In Spanish.)

12. SAEZ-ROYUELA, R. AND SANTOS, T., EDS. (1985) [*A study of the migration biology of the Order Anseriformes in Spain.*] Madrid: Instituto Nacional para la Conservación de la Naturaleza (Monogr. 38). (In Spanish.)

13. SEO (SOCIEDAD ESPAÑOLA DE ORNITOLOGÍA) (1987) [*Counts of wintering wildfowl: 1985–1987.*] Madrid: Instituto Nacional para la Conservación de la Naturaleza (Sér. Técnica). (In Spanish.)

14. VELASCO, T. AND ALBERTO, L. J. (in press) Number, main localities and distribution maps of waders wintering in Spain. *Wader Study Group Bull.*

Canary Islands
Breeding

1. ANON. (1980) [Basic atlas of the Canary Islands.] (In Spanish.)

2. BIBBY, C. J. AND HILL, D. A. (1987) Status of the Fuerteventura Stonechat *Saxicola docotiae. Ibis* 129: 491–498.

3. CARRASCAL, L. M. (1987) [Relationship between birds and vegetation structure in the pine plantations of Tenerife, Canary Islands.] *Ardeola* 37: 193–224.

4. DELGADO, G., TRUJILLO, N., CARRILLO, J., SANTANA, F., QUILIS, V., NOGALES, M., TRUJILLO, O., EMMERSON, K. AND HERNANDEZ, E. (1988) [Census of the birds of prey in the Canaries archipelago.] Tenerife: Museo de Ciencias Naturales de Santa Cruz de Tenerife (unpublished report). (In Spanish.)

5. DIAZ, G., TRUJILLO, O. AND HERNANDEZ, E. (1986) [Status of the Osprey *Pandion haliaetus* in the Canary Islands.] *Bol. Est. Cent. Ecol.* 29: 67–72. (In Spanish.)

6. EMMERSON, K. W. (1985) [Study of the biology and ecology of Bolle's Laurel Pigeon *Columba bollii* and Laurel Pigeon *Columba junoniae* with a view towards their conservation, 2.] Madrid: Instituto Nacional para la Conservación de la Naturaleza (unpublished report). (In Spanish.)

7. EMMERSON, K. W. (1990) [Census of the Canarian Houbara population *Chlamydotis undulata fuerteventura* on Fuerteventura.] Tragsatec—Ornistudio SL (unpublished). (In Spanish.)

8. EMMERSON, K. W., LORENZO, J. A., BARONE, R., TRUJILLO, O. AND DELGADO, G. (1991) [Census of the breeding waterbirds in the Canary Islands.] Tragsatec—Ornistudio SL (unpublished). (In Spanish.)

9. HERNANDEZ, E., MARTÍN, A., DIAZ, G. AND TRUJILLO, O. (1987) [The Osprey *Pandion haliaetus* in the Canary Islands: status and biology.] *Vieraea* 17: 203–207. (In Spanish.)

10. MARTÍN, A. (1987) [*Atlas of the breeding birds of the island of Tenerife.*] Santa Cruz de Tenerife: Instituto de Estudios Canarios (Monogr. 32). (In Spanish.)

11. MARTÍN, A., NOGALES, M., QUILIS, V., DELGADO, G., HERNANDEZ, E., TRUJILLO, O. AND SANTANA, F. (1987) [Status and distribution of the seabirds breeding in the Canary Islands with view of their conservation.] La Laguna: Depto. Biologia Animal Univ. (unpublished). (In Spanish.)

12. MARTÍN, A., HERNANDEZ, E., NOGALES, M., QUILIS, V., TRUJILLO, O. AND DELGADO, G. (1989) [*Red data book of terrestrial vertebrates in the Canary Islands.*] Tenerife: Caja Insular de Ahorros de Canarias. (In Spanish.)

13. OSBORNE, P. E. (1986) *Survey of the birds of Fuerteventura, Canary Islands, with special reference to the status of the Canarian Houbara Bustard Chlamydotis undulata.* Cambridge, U.K.: International Council for Bird Preservation (Study Rep. 10).

14. RODRÍGUEZ, F., DÍAZ, G., ALMEIDA, R. S. AND NOGALES, I. (1987) [Ornithological news: Cream-coloured Coursor (*Cursorius cursor*)]. *Ardeola* 34: 284. (In Spanish.)

SWEDEN
Breeding

1. BROO, B. AND LINDBERG, P. (1981) [*The development of the Ritsem area: effects on the fauna, especially birds of prey.*] Stockholm: Swedish Environmental Protection Board (SNV-PM 1435). (In Swedish.)

2. VAN ESSEN, L. (1986) [The Lesser White-fronted Goose *Anser erythropus* Project.] *Fauna och Flora* 81: 175–176. (In Swedish.)

3. GERDEHAG, P. AND HELANDER, B. (1988) [*The White-tailed Eagle* Haliaeetus albicilla.] Skövde, Sweden: Bonnier. (In Swedish.)

4. JÖNSSON, P. E. (1991) [The Kentish Plover *Charadrius alexandrinus* in Scania, South Sweden, 1990: a report from a conservation project.] *Anser* 30: 41–50. (In Swedish.)

5. LINDBERG, P. (1986) [The Peregrine Falcon *Falco peregrinus* Project.] *Fauna och Flora* 81: 171–172. (In Swedish.)

6. RISBERG, L. (1991) *in litt.* to T. Larssen.

7. SOF (1990) [*Swedish birds.*] Second revised edition. Stockholm: Sveriges Ornitologiska Förening. (In Swedish.)

8. STAAV, R. (1988) [The Caspian Tern *Sterna caspia* Project in 1986 and 1987.] *Vår Fågelv.* 47: 97–100. (In Swedish.)

9. TJERNBERG, M. (1990) [The Golden Eagle *Aquila chrysaetos* in Sweden: distribution, population and

545

threats.] *Vår Fågelv.* 49: 337–348. (In Swedish.)

10. TYRBERG, T. (1990) [Records of rare and uncommon birds in Sweden 1989.] *Vår Fågelv.* 49: 389–428. (In Swedish.)

11. WIKLUND, C. G. AND STIGH, J. (1983) Nest defence and evolution of reversed sexual size dimorphism in Snowy Owls *Nyctea scandiaca*. *Ornis Scand.* 14: 58–62.

Wintering

1. SOF (1990) [*Swedish birds.*] Second edition. Stockholm: Sveriges Ornitologiska Förening. (In Swedish.)

SWITZERLAND
Breeding

1. ARLETTAZ, R. (1990) [Relict breeding population of *Otus scops* in central Valais, Swiss Alps.] *Nos Oiseaux* 40: 321–343. (In French.)

2. BIBER, O. (1984) [Distribution and numbers of eleven endangered breeding species in Switzerland.] *Orn. Beob.* 81: 1–28. (In German with English summary.)

3. BOETTCHER, W. (1991) [Report of the Swiss Society for the White Stork for 1990.] *Jahresbulletin.* (In German.)

4. GLUTZ VON BLOTZHEIM, U. N. AND BAUER, K. M., EDS. (1980) [*Handbook of the birds of central Europe, 9.*] Wiesbaden: Akademische Verlagsgesellschaft. (In German.)

5. GLUTZ VON BLOTZHEIM, U. N., BAUER, K. AND BEZZEL, E., EDS. (1971) [*Handbook of the birds of central Europe, 4.*] Frankfurt: Akademische Verlagsgesellschaft. (In German.)

6. HALLER, H. (1988) [Long-term trends in the Swiss breeding population of the Golden Eagle *Aquila chrysaetos* in Switzerland.] *Orn. Beob.* 85: 225–244. (In German with English summary.)

7. HAURI, R. (1989) [On the occurrence of *Netta rufina* in Switzerland 1974–1988 especially on Lake Thoune, with notes on its breeding biology.] *Orn. Beob.* 86: 69–87. (In German with English summary.)

8. JENNY, M. (1992) [The Grey Partridge, symbol of a traditional Landscape.] In N. Zbinden, T. Imhof and H. Pfister, eds. *Ornithological guidelines for landscape planning.* Sempach: Swiss Institute of Ornithology. (In German.)

9. LEUZINGER, H. (1992) [First breeding record of *Aythya nyroca* in Switzerland.] *Orn. Beob.* 89: 60–63. (In German.)

10. MARTI, C. (1987) [Status and conservation of Tetraonides in Switzerland.] Pp.331–337 in *Actes Coll. Galliformes de montagne.* St-Just-La-Penue. (In French.)

11. MOSIMANN, P. (in prep).

12. SCHELBERT, E. (1992) [First breeding record of *Merops apiaster* in Switzerland.] *Orn. Beob.* 89: 63–65. (In German.)

13. SCHIFFERLI, A., GÉROUDET, P., WINKLER, R., JACQUAT, B., PRAZ, J.-C. AND SCHIFFERLI, L. (1980) *Distribution atlas of breeding birds of Switzerland.* Sempach: Station Ornitologique Suisse de Sempach (database).

14. SCHMID, H. (1987) [Ornithological records in Switzerland for 1985 and 1986.] *Orn. Beob.* 84: 227–233. (In German.)

15. SCHMID, H. (1989) [Important ornithological events in Switzerland in 1987 and 1988.] *Orn. Beob.* 86: 163–170. (In German with English summary.)

16. SCHMID, H. (1990a) [The status of the Kestrel *Falco tinnunculus* in Switzerland.] *Orn. Beob.* 87: 327–349. (In German with English summary.)

17. SCHMID, H. (1990b) [*Diurnal and nocturnal birds of prey.*] Sempach: Swiss Institue of Ornithology. (In German, French and Italian.)

18. SCHMID, H. (1991) [Important ornithological events in Switzerland 1989 and 1990.] *Orn. Beob.* 88: 101–109. (In German with English summary.)

19. SIEBER, O. (1982) [Population size and distribution of the Sand Martin *Riparia riparia* 1980 in Switzerland.] *Orn. Beob.* 79: 25–38. (In German with English summary.)

20. SIERRO, A. (1991) [Ecology of *Camprimulgus europaeus* in Valais, Swiss Alps: biotopes, distribution and protection.] *Nos Oiseaux* 41: 209–235. (In French.)

Wintering

1. AUBRECHT, G., LEUZINGER, H., SCHIFFERLI, L. AND SCHUSTER, S. (1990) [Influx of Velvet Scoters *Melanitta fusca* on to waters at the northern edge of the Alps in 1985/86 and 1988/90.] *Orn. Beob.* 87: 89–97. (In German with English summary.)

2. MARTI, C. AND SCHIFFERLI, L. (1987) [Inventory of the wetlands of international importance for waterfowl in Switzerland: first revision 1986.] *Orn. Beob.* 84: 11–47. (In German with English summary.)

3. SCHIFFERLI, L. (1990) *Waterfowl.* Sempach: Swiss Institute of Ornithology (Special Issue).

4. SCHIFFERLI, L. (1992a) [Wintering distribution and numbers of Divers (*Gavia arctica, G. stellata, G. immer*) in Switzerland and adjacent waters, 1969/70–1978/79.] *Orn. Beob.* 77: 231–240. (In German with English summary.)

5. SCHIFFERLI, L. (1992b) [Wintering waterfowl in Switzerland, mid-January 1988–1991.] *Orn. Beob.* 89: 81–91. (In German with English summary.)

6. SUTER, W. (1991) [Wintering waterfowl on Swiss lakes: predicting bird and species numbers from lake qualities.] *Orn. Beob.* 88: 111–140. (In German with English summary.)

7. SUTER, W. AND SCHIFFERLI, L. (1988) [Waterfowl wintering in Switzerland and on adjacent waters: numbers and trends 1967–1987 in a European context.] *Orn. Beob.* 85: 261–298. (In German with English summary.)

TURKEY
Breeding

1. CRAMP, S. AND SIMMONS, K. E. L., EDS. (1983) *The birds of the western Palearctic,* 3. Oxford: Oxford University Press.

2. CRIVELLI, A. J. (1994) The importance of the former U.S.S.R. for the conservation of pelican populations nesting in the Palearctic. In A. J. Crivelli, V. G. Krivenko and V. G. Vinogradov, eds. *Pelicans in the former U.S.S.R.* Slimbridge, U.K.: International Waterfowl and Wetlands Research Bureau (Spec. Publ. 27).

3. GÉNSBØL, B. (1987) *Collins guide to the birds of prey of Britain and Europe, North Africa and the Middle*

East. London: Collins.

4. GORIUP, P. D. AND PARR, D. (1981) *Report on a survey of bustards in Turkey, 1981*. Cambridge, U.K.: International Council for Bird Preservation (Study Rep. 1).

5. GREEN, A. (1993) *in litt.* to BirdLife International.

6. GRIMMETT, R. F. A. AND JONES, T. A. (1989) *Important bird areas in Europe*. Cambridge, U.K.: International Council for Bird Preservation (Techn. Publ. 9).

7. JAMES, P. C. (1984) The status and conservation of seabirds in the Mediterranean Sea. Pp.371–375 in J. P. Croxall, P. G. H. Evans and R. W. Schreiber, eds. *Status and conservation of the world's seabirds*. Cambridge, U.K.: International Council for Bird Preservation (Techn. Publ. 2).

8. KASPAREK, M. (1985) [*The Sultan marshes: natural history of a bird paradise in Anatolia*.] Heidelberg: Kasparek. (In German.)

9. KASPAREK, M. (1993) pers. comm. to BirdLife International.

10. KASPAREK, M. AND KILIÇ, A. (1989) Breeding distribution and population trends of the White Stork *Ciconia ciconia* in Turkey. Pp.297–307 in G. Rheinwald, J. Ogden and H. Schulz, eds. *Proceedings of the First International Stork Symposium*. Bonn: Dachverbendes Deutscher Avifauner (Schriftenreihe 10).

11. KASPAREK, M. AND VAN DER VEN, J. (1983) *Birds of Turkey. 1: Ercek Gölü*. Heidelburg: Kasparek.

12. KILIÇ, A. (1988) The Eregli marshes: a new nesting site for the Greater Flamingo *Phoenicopterus ruber* in Turkey. *Zool. Middle East* 2: 39–45.

13. KILIÇ, A. AND KASPAREK, M. (1990) The Eregli marshes (unpublished report).

14. KIRWAN, G. (1993) pers. comm. to BirdLife International.

15. KIRWAN, G. (in press) Breeding status and distribution of the White-headed Duck *Oxyura leucocephalus* in Turkey. *Sandgrouse*.

16. KUMERLOEVE, H. (1976) Basis of the White Stork breeding population *Ciconia ciconia* L. (1758) in Turkey (1974). *Bonn. Zool. Beitr.* 27: 172–217.

17. MAGNIN, G. (1990) pers. comm.

18. MAGNIN, G. AND DOGAL HAYATI KORUMA DERNEGI (1993) pers. comm.

19. SCHEPERS, F. J., STEWART, J. J. AND MEININGER P. L. (1989) *Breeding birds of the Gösku delta*. Istanbul: Dogal Hayati Koruma Dernegi (DHKD) (preliminary report).

20. VAN DER VEN, J. A. (1988) Draft lists of the distribution of birds of particular conservation concern in Europe.

UKRAINE

Breeding

1. ABULADZE, A. V. (1993) *in litt.* to BirdLife International.

2. ARDAMATSKAYA, T. B. (1965) [Ecology and seasonal distribution of *Anas strepera* in the north-western shores of the Black Sea.] Pp.14–16 in [*Collection of Ornithological News*.] Alma-ata. (In Russian.)

3. ARDAMATSKAYA, T. B. (1984) [*Dynamics and numbers of breeding waterbirds on Tenorov and Yagurlitsk islands in the Black Sea: status of resources available for waterbirds*.] Moscow: Nauka. (In Russian.)

4. ARDAMATSKAYA, T. B. AND SABINERSKY, B. V. (1968)

[*Resources of water birds in the U.S.S.R. and their reproduction*.] Moscow: Moscow Union of Nature Researchers. (In Russian.)

5. AVERIN, V. G. (1991) [The ornithology of the Kharkov region.] *Bull. Biol. Kharkov Univ.* 46: 243–293. (In Russian.)

6. CRIVELLI, A. J. (1994) The importance of the former U.S.S.R. for the conservation of pelican populations nesting in the Palearctic. In A. J. Crivelli, V. G. Krivenko and V. G. Vinogradov, eds. *Pelicans in the former U.S.S.R*. Slimbridge, U.K.: International Waterfowl and Wetlands Research Bureau (Spec. Publ. 27).

7. GAVRILENKO, N. J. (1929) [*Birds of Poltava region*.] Poltava Hunting Union Publishing House. (In Ukrainian.)

8. GAVRILENKO, N. J. (1965) [Distribution of *Saxicola torquata* in the Ukraine.] *Ornithology* 7: 463. (In Russian.)

9. GOLOVAC, O. F., GRISCENKO, V. N. AND SEREBRIAKOV, V. V. (1990) [Actual numbers, distribution and migration of Black Stork in the Ukraine.] Pp.191–203 in E. G. Samusienko, ed. [*Storks: distribution, ecology and conservation*.] Minsk: Nauka i Tekhnika. (In Russian.)

10. GORBAN, I. (1993) pers. comm. to V. Belik.

11. GORBAN, J. M. (1985) *Current data on status of eagles in west Ukraine*. World Working Group on Birds of Prey and the International Council for Bird Preservation.

12. GORBAN, J. M. (1989) [Population dynamics of *Chlidonias niger* and factors affecting it in western Ukraine.] *Slupsk* 1992: 101–103. (In Polish.)

13. GORBAN, J. M. (1990a) [White Stork in western Ukraine: numbers, ecology and protection.] Pp.80–84 in E. G. Samusienko, ed. [*Storks: distribution, ecology and conservation*.] Minsk: Nauka i Tekhnika. (In Russian.)

14. GORBAN, J. M. (1990b) [Numbers of Black Stork in western Ukraine.] Pp.204–205 in E. G. Samusienko, ed. [*Storks: distribution, ecology and conservation*.] Minsk: Nauka i Tekhnika. (In Russian.)

15. GORBAN, J. M. (1992) [Recent numbers and distribution of *Coracias garrulus*.] Pp.33–34 in [*Birds of the Rivo region*.] (In Ukrainian.)

16. GRABAR, O. O. (1941) [Birds of prey of Puykarpatya territory.] *Zorya, Usgorod*: 114–148. (In Ukrainian.)

17. GULAY, V. J. (1975) [Structure of populations and number of water and swamp birds of the Upper Southern Bug.] *Zool. News* 6: 69–71. (In Russian.)

18. GULAY, V. J. (1981) [Breeding of *Ardea purpurea* in the Upper Southern Bug.] Pp.65–66 in [*Distribution and breeding of shore birds in U.S.S.R.*.] Moscow: Nauka. (In Russian.)

19. KISTYAKIROSKY, O. B. (1957) [*Fauna of the Ukraine: birds, 4: Galliformes, Columbiformes, Gruiformes, Charadriiformes*.] Kiev: Academy of Science of Ukraine. (In Ukrainian.)

20. KISTYAKIROSKY, O. B. (1952) [Valuable birds of Ukrainian Polissya.] Pp.11–34 in [*Works of the Institute of Zoology of the Academy of Science of Ukraine*.] Kiev: Academy of Science of Ukraine. (In Ukrainian.)

21. KLESTON, N. L. (1993) pers. comm. to I. Gorban.

22. KLESTOV, N. L. (1977) [Concerning some changes in the avifauna of the Kiev and Cherkasy regions after the building of Kaniv reservoirs.] Pp.147–148 in M. A.

Voinstvensky, ed. [*VII All Union Ornithological Conference, Kiev.*] Kiev: Naukova Dumka. (In Russian.)

23. KLESTOV, N. L. (1983) [*Avifauna of the middle Dniepr and its changes according to the gidro building.*] Kiev; Academy of Science of Ukraine. (In Russian.)

24. KOREZUKOV, A. J., KOSHELEV, A. J. AND CHERNICHENKO, J. J. (1991) [*Rare birds of the Black Sea coastal area.*] Kiev and Odessa: Lybid. (In Russian.)

25. KOSTIN, Y. V. (1983) [*Birds of Crimea.*] Moscow: Nauka. (In Russian.)

26. LESNICKY, V. V. (1982) [Current situation and dynamics of swamp avifauna of Ukrainian Polissya.] Kiev: Institute of Zoology of the Academy of Science of Ukraine (thesis). (In Russian.)

27. LESNICKY, V. V. (1980) [Breeding of *Tringa nebularia* Gunn. in the Ukraine.] Pp.155–156 in [*Materials of the second meeting on Charadrii, Moscow.*] Moscow: Nauka. (In Russian.)

28. LUGOVOY, A. E. (1986) [*Protection and breeding of* Lyrurus tetrix *in Ukrainian Carpathians.*] Lviv: Lviv Forest Institute. (In Russian.)

29. LYSENKO, V. J. (1992) [*Fauna of the Ukraine: birds, 5: Anseriformes.*] Kiev: Naukova Dumka. (In Russian.)

30. PEKLO, A. M. (1987) [*Fauna of the U.S.S.R.: Flycatchers.*] Kiev: Naukova Dumka. (In Russian.)

31. PORTENKO, L. A. (1928) [Birds of the Podillya region.] *Bull. M.O.D.N.* 37: 92–204. (In Russian.)

32. PROKOPENKO, C. AND PEKLO, A. (1989) *in litt.* to W. Baumgart.

33. SEREBRAKOV, V. V. AND GRISHCHENKO, V. N. (1989) [*Number of colonial species of* Ardea *in the Ukraine in 1986.*] Ufa: Bashkiz. (In Russian.)

34. SHCKEGOLEV, J. V. (1977) [Dynamics of the *Plegadis falcinellus* population and other Ciconiiformes in the Dniester delta.] Pp.346 in M. A. Voinstvensky, ed. [*VII All Union Ornithological Conference, Kiev.*] Kiev: Naukova Dumka. (In Russian.)

35. SIOHIN, V. D., CHERNICHENKO, J. J., ARDAMATSKAYA, J. B. ET AL. (1988) [*Colonial swamp birds of the south of Ukraine.*] Kiev: Naukova Dumka. (In Russian.)

36. SMOGORZSHEVSKY, L. A. (1953) [*The biology and distribution of* Plegadis falcinellus *L. in the Ukraine.*] Kiev: Kiev University. (In Russian.)

37. SOMOV, N. N. (1897) [*Avifauna of Kharkov region.*] Kharkov: Collection of Nature Investigator's Society. (In Russian.)

38. SREBRODOLSKA, N. J. (1961a) [*Biology of Charadrii in West Ukrainian Polissya.*] Lviv: Lviv University (Rep. 2). (In Ukrainian.)

39. SREBRODOLSKA, N. J. (1961b) [*Biology of* Rallus *in West Ukrainian Polissya.*] Lviv: Lviv University. (In Ukrainian.)

40. SREBRODOLSKA, N. J. (1981) [Shortening of Charadrii's areals in the western Polissya.] In [*VIII All Union Ornithological Conference.*] Kishineu. (In Russian.)

41. STRAUTMAN, F. J. (1954) [*Birds of the Soviet Carpathians.*] Kiev: Academy of Science of Ukraine. (In Russian.)

42. STRAUTMAN, F. J. (1963) [*Birds of western Ukraine, 1–2.*] Lvov: Lvov University. (In Ukrainian.)

43. TALPOSH, V. S. (1965) [Birds of Zakarpatya region.] Pp.92–100 in [*Animals of Ukraine.*] Kiev. (In Ukrainian.)

44. TALPOSH, V. S. (1969) [Changes in avifauna of Zakarpatija region in the twentieth century.] In [*Ornithology in the U.S.S.R.*] Ashkhabad, 'ILYM'. (In Russian.)

45. TALPOSH, V. S. (1977) [Breeding of *Chlidonias hybrida* Pal. in western Ukraine.] *Zool. Bull.* 4: 83–86. (In Russian.)

46. VETROV, V. V. (1993) pers. comm. to V. Galushin.

47. VETROV, V. V. AND BELIK, V. (1994) pers. comm. to V. Galushin.

48. VOISTVENSKY, M. A. (1953) [*Birds of the Danube delta.*] Kiev: Kiev University (Rep. 3). (In Russian.)

49. ZARYDNY, N. A. (1911) [Some notes about ornithology in the Kharkov region.] *Ornit. Bull.* 3/4: 272–277. (In Russian.)

50. ZHEZHERIN, V. J. (1961) [Distribution of *Ciconia nigra* in the Volyn region.] *Works Zool. Mus. Ukraine* 30: 82–84. (In Ukrainian.)

51. ZHEZHERIN, V. J. (1968a) [Birds of prey in the Ukraine: their work in the hunting industry.] In [*Collection of works of the First Conference on the Development of Hunting Economy.*] Kiev. (In Russian.)

52. ZHEZHERIN, V. J. (1968b) [*Tetrao urogallus, Lyrurus tetrix, Tetrastes bonasia* in the Ukraine.] In [*Collection of works of the First Conference on the Development of the Hunting Economy.*] Kiev. (In Russian.)

53. ZUBAROVSKY, V. M. (1977) [*Fauna of the Ukraine, 5: birds of prey.*] Kiev: Naukova Dumka. (In Ukrainian.)

Wintering

1. KISTYAKIROSKY, O. B. (1957) [*Fauna of the Ukraine: birds, 4: Galliformes, Columbiformes, Gruiformes, Charadriiformes.*] Kiev: Academy of Science of Ukraine. (In Ukrainian.)

2. LYSENKO, V. J. (1992) [*Fauna of the Ukraine: birds, 5: Anseriformes.*] Kiev: Naukova Dumka. (In Russian.)

UNITED KINGDOM

General

Range trends are based on data taken from Gibbons *et al.* (1993). Population sizes are based on data, modified for the U.K. by D. W. Gibbons, from Gates *et al.* (1993), except for Roseate Tern and Corncrake.

GATES, S., GIBBONS, D. W. AND MARCHANT, J. H. (1993) Population estimates for breeding birds in Britain and Ireland. Pp.462–475 in D. W. Gibbons, J. B. Reid and R. A. Chapman, eds. *The new atlas of breeding birds in Britain and Ireland: 1988–1991.* London: T. and A. D. Poyser.

GIBBONS, D. W., REID, J. B. AND CHAPMAN, R. A., EDS. (1993) *The new atlas of breeding birds in Britain and Ireland: 1988–1991.* London: T. and A. D. Poyser.

Breeding

1. BRITISH TRUST FOR ORNITHOLOGY (1992) Population estimates (unpublished).

2. BULLOCK, I. D., DREWETT, D. R. AND MICKLEBURGH, S. P. (1983) The Chough in Britain and Ireland. *Brit. Birds* 76: 377–401.

3. CADBURY, C. J., ELLIOTT, G. AND HARBARD, P. (1988) Birds of prey conservation in the U.K. *RSPB Conserv. Rev.* 2: 9–16.

4. DENNIS, R. H., ELLIS, P. M., BROAD, R. A. AND LANGSLOW, D. R. (1984) The status of the Golden Eagle in Britain. *Brit. Birds* 77: 592–607.

5. EWINS, P. J. AND TASKER, M. L. (1985) The breeding distribution of Black Guillemots *Cepphus grylle* in Orkney and Shetland, 1982–1984. *Bird Study* 32: 186–193.

6. FOX, A. D. (1988) Breeding status of the Gadwall in Britain and Ireland. *Brit. Birds* 81: 51–66.

7. GREEN, R. E. (1988) Stone-curlew conservation. *RSPB Conserv. Rev.* 2: 30–33.

8. GREEN, R. E. (in prep) The decline of the Corncrake *Crex crex* continues.

9. GRIBBLE, F. C. (1983) Nightjars in Britain and Ireland in 1981. *Bird Study* 30: 165–176.

10. HUDSON, A. V., STOWE, T. J. AND ASPINALL, S. J. (1990) Status and distribution of Corncrakes in Britain in 1988. *Brit. Birds* 83: 173–187.

11. HUDSON, P. (1989) Black Grouse in Britain. *Game Conserv. Rev.* 20: 119–124.

12. HUDSON, R. AND MARCHANT, J. H. (1984) Population estimates for British breeding birds. *BTO Research Report* 13: 1–94.

13. LACK, P. (1986) *The atlas of wintering birds in Britain and Ireland*. Calton, U.K.: T. and A. D. Poyser.

14. LLOYD, C. S., TASKER, M. L. AND PARTRIDGE, K. E. (1991) *The status of seabirds in Britain and Ireland*. London: T. and A. D. Poyser.

15. MARCHANT, J. H., HUDSON, R., CARTER, S. P. AND WHITTINGTON, P. (1990) *Population trends in British breeding birds*. Tring, U.K.: British Trust for Ornithology.

16. MAYES, E. AND STOWE, T. (1989) The status and distribution of the Corncrake in Ireland, 1988. *Irish Birds* 4: 1–12.

17. MONAGHAN, P., BIGNAL, E., BIGNAL, S., EASTERBEE, N. AND MCKAY, C. R. (1989) The distribution and status of the Chough in Scotland in 1986. *Scott. Birds* 15: 114–118.

18. NETHERSOLE-THOMPSON, D. (1975) *Pine Crossbills: a Scottish contribution*. Berkhamsted, U.K.: T. and A. D. Poyser.

19. NEWTON, I. (1984) Raptors in Britain—a review of the last 150 years. *BTO News* 131: 6–7.

20. OWEN, M., ATKINSON-WILLES, G. L. AND SALMON, D. G. (1986) *Wildfowl in Great Britain*. Second edition. Cambridge, U.K.: Cambridge University Press.

21. PERCIVAL, S. (1991) Population trends in British Barn Owls: a review of some possible causes. *Brit. Wildlife* 2: 131–140.

22. PIERSMA, T. (1986) Breeding waders in Europe. A review of population size estimates and a bibliography of information sources. *Bull. Wader Study Group* 48 (Suppl.): 1–116.

23. POTTS, G. R. (1986) *The Partridge: pesticides, predation and conservation*. London: Collins.

24. RATCLIFFE, D. (1980) *The Peregrine Falcon*. Calton, U.K.: T. and A. D. Poyser.

25. SHARROCK, J. T. R., ED. (1976) *The atlas of breeding birds in Britain and Ireland*. Calton, U.K.: T. and A. D. Poyser.

26. SHAWYER, C. R. (1987) *The Barn Owl in the British Isles: its past, present and future*. London: Hawk Trust.

27. SPENCER, R. AND RARE BREEDING BIRDS PANEL (1989) Rare breeding birds in the United Kingdom in 1987.

Brit. Birds 82: 477–504.

28. SPENCER, R. AND RARE BREEDING BIRDS PANEL (1990) Rare breeding birds in the United Kingdom in 1988. *Brit. Birds* 83: 353–390.

29. STROUD, D. A., MUDGE, G. P. AND PIENKOWSKI, M. W. (1990) *Protecting internationally important bird sites: a review of the EEC Special Protection Area network in Great Britain*. Peterborough, U.K.: Nature Conservancy Council.

30. THOM, V. M. (1986) *Birds in Scotland*. Calton, U.K.: T. and A. D. Poyser.

31. WESTERHOFF, D. V. (1989) Results of the 1988 survey of Dartford Warbler *Sylvia undata* in the New Forest. *Hampshire Bird Report*: 77–78.

32. WYNDE, R., ED. (1993) *Roseate Tern News 7*. Sandy, U.K.: Royal Society for the Protection of Birds.

Wintering

1. BATTEN, L. A., BIBBY, C. J., CLEMENT, P., ELLIOTT, G. D. AND PORTER, R. F., EDS. (1990) *Red data birds in Britain: action for rare, threatened and important species*. London: T. and A. D. Poyser.

2. KIRBY, J. J., FERNS, J. R., WATERS, R. J. AND PRYS-JONES, R. P. (1991) *Wader and wildfowl counts 1990–91*. Slimbridge, U.K.: Wildfowl and Wetlands Trust.

3. LACK, P. (1986) *The atlas of wintering birds in Britain and Ireland*. Calton, U.K.: T. and A. D. Poyser.

4. SALMON, D. G., PRYS-JONES, R. P. AND KIRBY, J. S. (1988) *Wildfowl and Wader Counts 1987–1988: the results of the National Wildfowl Counts and Birds of Estuaries Enquiry*. Slimbridge, U.K.: Wildfowl and Wetlands Trust.

5. SALMON, D. G., PRYS-JONES, R. P. AND KIRBY, J. S. (1989) *Wildfowl and Waders Counts 1988–1989: the results of the National Wildfowl Counts and Birds of Estuaries Enquiry in the United Kingdom*. Slimbridge, U.K.: Wildfowl and Wetlands Trust.

Isle of Man

Breeding

1. BULLOCK, I. D., DREWETT, D. R. AND MICKLEBURGH, S. P. (1983) The Chough on the Isle of Man. *Peregrine* 5: 229–237.

2. CULLEN, J. P. (1980) A review of the status of terns in the Isle of Man. *Peregrine* 5: 68–73.

3. CULLEN, J. P. (1984) Nesting of the Common Gull in a Manx gravel pit. *Peregrine* 5: 284.

4. CULLEN, J. P. AND JENNINGS, P. P. (1986) *Birds of the Isle of Man*. Douglas, Isle of Man: Bridgeen.

5. JENNINGS, P. P. (1983) The recent status of the Manx Shearwater on the Calf of Man. *Peregrine* 5: 225.

6. MCINTYRE, J. AND CULLEN, J. P. (1978) Nesting of the Hen Harrier in the Isle of Man. *Peregrine* 4: 283–284.

7. MOORE, A. S. (1985) The Chough in the Isle of Man. *Peregrine* 6: 43–45.

8. MOORE, A. S. (1987) The numbers and distribution of seabirds breeding on the Isle of Man during 1985–1986. *Peregrine* 6: 64–80.

9. MOORE, A. S. (1989) Black Guillemots in the Isle of Man in 1987. *Peregrine* 6: 71–73.

10. THORPE, J. P. (1989) Breeding of the Corncrake in the Isle of Man. *Peregrine* 6: 76–77.

Wintering

1. CULLEN, J. P. AND JENNINGS, P. P. (1986) *Birds of the Isle of Man.* Douglas, Isle of Man: Bridgeen.

Gibraltar

Breeding

1. CORTES, J. E., FINLAYSON, J. C., GARCIA, E. F. J. AND MOSQUERA, M. A. J. (1980) *The birds of Gibraltar.* Gibraltar: Gibraltar Books.
2. FINLAYSON, J. C. AND CORTES, J. E. (1987) The birds of the Strait of Gibraltar. *Alectoris 6.* (Special edition.)
3. STRAIT OF GIBRALTAR BIRD OBSERVATORY (1987–) Gib. Ornith. Monthly 1987–1988, Quarterly 1989–present (unpublished reports).

Guernsey

General

LLOYD, C. S., TASKER, M. L. AND PARTRIDGE, K. E. (1991) *The status of seabirds in Britain and Ireland.* London: T. and A. D. Poyser.

Jersey

General

DOBSON, R. (1952) *The birds of the Channel Islands.* London: Staples Press.

LE SUEUR, F. (1976) *A natural history of Jersey.* London: Phillimore.

LONG, R. (1981) Review of birds in the Channel Islands, 1951–1980. *Brit. Birds* 74: 327–344.

MILTON, N. (1992) The status and distribution of Red Data Birds in the Channel Islands. Unpublished report to the Royal Society of Protection of Birds.

YOUNG, H. G., ALLAN, J. M., BUXTON, I. AND PAINTIN, A. (1991) A systematic list of the birds recorded in Jersey in 1991. Pp.3–32 in *Jersey Bird Report 1991.* Jersey: Societé Jersiaise.

TEXT REFERENCES

ABDUNAZAROV, B. B. (1991) [Methods of prevention of bird loss on electric powerlines.] Pp.5–6 in V. M. Galushin, ed. [*Abstracts 10th U.S.S.R. Ornithological Conference, part 2.*] Vitebsk, Minsk: Nauka i Tekhnika. (In Russian.)

ABS, M. (1963) [Comparative studies of Crested (*Galerida cristata* L.) and Thekla Larks (*Galerida theklae* A. E. Brehm).] *Bonn. Zool. Beitr.* 14: 1–128. (In German.)

ABULADZE, A. V. (1993) Seasonal migration of the Black Stork in east Pontica. Abstracts of 1st International Black Stork Conservation and Ecology Symposium.

ADAMYAN, M. S. (1989) [Breeding of *Anas angustirostris* in the Armenian SSR.] *Biol. J. Armenia* 8: 778–780. (In Russian.)

AFANASIEV, V. T. (1993) [Nesting of the Imperial Eagle in the Sumsk region, northern Ukraine.] *Berkut* 2: 11. (In Russian.)

AFANASIEV, V. T., GAVRIS, G. G. AND KLESTOV, N. L. (1992) [*Avifauna of Desna River flood-plain and its preservation.*] Kiev. (In Russian.)

AFREE, G. (1975) [Census and geographical distribution of warblers of the genus *Sylvia* in the Midi region, France.] *Alauda* 43: 229–262. (In French.)

AHLEN, I. AND TJERNBERG, M. (1992) [*Species accounts: endangered and rare vertebrates in Sweden 1992. Database of endangered species.*] Uppsala: Sveriges Lantbruksuniversitet. (In Swedish.)

AHLGREN, C.-G. AND ERIKSSON, M. O. G. (1984) [The exposure to mercury and organochlorines on Osprey, *Pandion haliaetus*, in south-west Sweden.] *Vår Fågelv.* 43: 299–305. (In Swedish.)

AIRUMIAN, K. A. AND MARGARIAN, N. A. (1974) [Resources of the game birds in Armenia.] Theses of 6 All-Union Ornithological Conference, Moscow. (In Russian.)

ALERSTAM, T. AND BAUER, C. A. (1973) [A radar study of the spring migration of the crane (*Grus grus*) over the southern Baltic area.] *Vogelwarte* 27: 1–16. (In German.)

ALERSTAM, T., GUDMUNDSSON, G. A. AND JOHANNESSON, K. (1992) Resources for long distance migration: intertidal exploitation of *Littorina* and *Mytilus* by Knots *Calidris canutus* in Iceland. *Oikos* 65: 179–189.

ALEXANDER, I. AND CRESSWELL, B. (1990) Foraging by nightjars *Caprimulgus europaeus* away from their nesting areas. *Ibis* 132: 568–574.

ALONSO, J. A. AND ALONSO, J. C., EDS. (1990) [*Distribution and demography of the Common Crane in Spain.*] Madrid: Instituto Nacional para la Conservación de la Naturaleza, CSIC. (In Spanish.)

ALONSO, J. A., ALONSO, J. C., MARTÍNEZ-VICENTE, I. S. AND BAUTISTA, L. M. (1987) Simulation of a Common Crane population model. Pp.277–283 in *Proc. 1987 International Crane Workshop Qiqihar, China*. Baraboo, W.I.: International Crane Foundation.

ALONSO, J. C., ALONSO, J. A. AND NAVERO, M. A. (1990) [The Great Bustard population in Villafáfila and Raso de Villapando.] Pp.25–52 in J. C. Alonso and J. A. Alonso, eds. [*Demographic parameters, habitat selection and distribution of the Great Bustard in three regions of Spain.*] Mulridó: Instituto Nacional para la Conservación de la Naturaleza. (In Spanish.)

ALONSO LÓPEZ, J. A. (1985) [The birds of southern Cadiz: Gibraltar area and Comarca de la Janda.] Madrid: Universidad Complutense de Madrid. (Ph.D. thesis). (In Spanish.)

AMA (in prep.) [Recovery plan of the Crested Coot *Fulica cristata* in Andalucía.] Agencia de Medio Ambiente, Junta de Andalucía. (In Spanish.)

AMAT, J. A. (1982) The nesting biology of ducks in the Marismas of the Guadalquivir, south-western Spain. *Wildfowl* 33: 94–104.

AMAT, J. A. AND RAYA, C. (1989) [Birds on the red list: White-headed Duck.] *Garcilla* 75: 8–11. (In Spanish.)

AMAT, J. A. AND SORIGUER, R. C. (1984) Kleptoparasitism of Coots by Gadwall. *Ornis Scand.* 15: 188–194.

AMBE (1992) [The distribution of the Black Stork in France.] Pp.243–244 in J.-L. Mériaux, A. Schierer, C. Tombal and J.-C. Tombal, eds. [*The storks of Europe.*] Metz: Institut Européen d'Ecologie/AMBE. (In French.)

AMIRKHANOV, A. M., KUCHIEV, I. T., VEINBERG, P. I. AND KOMAROV, Y. E. (1988) [*North-Ossetian Reservation.*] Moscow: Agropromizdat. (In Russian.)

AMORES, F. AND FRANCO, A. (1981) [Feeding and ecology of the Short-toed Eagle in southern Spain.] *Alauda* 49: 59–64. (In Spanish.)

ANCER (1993) [Remarks and opinions of hunters on shooting the Turtle Dove during May in the Médoc.] Association Nationale pour une Chasse Ecologiquement Responsable (unpublished report). (In French.)

ANDERSEN-HARILD, P. (1969) [Some results of ringing Black Guillemot (*Cepphus grylle*) in Denmark.] *Dansk Ornit. Foren. Tidsskr.* 63: 105–110. (In Danish with English summary.)

ANDERSSON, A., LINDBERG, P., NILSSON, S. G. AND PETTERSSON, A. (1980) [Breeding success of the Black-throated Diver *Gavia arctica* in Sweden lakes.] *Vår Fågelv.* 39: 96–110. (In Swedish with English summary.)

ANGELSTAM, P. (1983) Population dynamics of tetraonids, especially the Black Grouse *Tetrao tetrix* L., in boreal forests. Uppsala: Uppsala University (Ph.D. thesis).

ANGELSTAM, P. (1988) Population dynamics in Tetraonids: the role of extrinsic factors. International Ornithological Congress.

ANGELSTAM, P. (1990) Factors determining the composition and persistence of local woodpecker assemblages in taiga forest in Sweden: a case for landscape ecological studies. Pp.147–164 in A. Carlson and G. Aulén, eds. *Conservation and management of woodpecker populations*. Uppsala: Swedish University of Agricultural Sciences, Dept. of Wildlife Ecology (Rep. 17).

ANGELSTAM, P. AND MARTINSSON, B. (1990) [The importance of appropriate spatial and temporal scales in population studies: conserving lessons based on the population dynamics of Black Grouse in boreal forest in Sweden.] Pp.82–96 in J. T. Lumeij and Y. R. Hoogeveen, eds. [*The occurrence of wild gamebirds in the Netherlands.*] Amersfoort: Organisatiecommississie Nederlandse Wilde Hoendrs. (In Swedish.)

ANGELSTAM, P. AND MIKUSINSKI, G. (1994) Woodpecker assemblages in natural and managed boreal and hemi-boreal forest—a review. *Ann. Zool. Fennici* 31: 157–172.

ANGELSTAM, P., LINDSTRÖM, E. AND WIDÉN, P. (1984) Role of predation in short-term population fluctuations of some birds and mammals in Fennoscandia. *Oecologia (Berlin)* 62: 199–208.

ANGELSTAM, P., LINDSTRÖM, E. AND WIDÉN, P. (1985) Synchronous short-term population fluctuations of some birds and mammals in Fennoscandia: occurrence and distribution. *Holarctic Ecology* 8: 285–298.

ANKER-NILSSEN, T. (1987) The breeding performance of Puffins *Fratercula arctica* on Røst, northern Norway in 1979–1985. *Fauna Norv. Ser. C, Cinclus* 10: 21–38.

ANKER-NILSSEN, T. (1991) [Census of Puffins in the area at risk from oil pollution from the central Norwegian continental shelf.] Pp.13–18 in J. A. Børresen and K. A. Moe, eds. [*AKUP Annual Report 1990.*] Oslo: Ministry of Oil and Energy. (In Norwegian.)

ANKER-NILSSEN, T. (1992) Food supply as a determinant of reproduction and population development in Norwegian Puffins *Fratercula arctica*. Trondheim: Trondheim University (Ph.D. thesis).

ANKER-NILSSEN, T. AND RØSTAD, O. W. (1993) Census and monitoring of Puffins *Fratercula arctica* on Røst, north Norway, 1979–1988. *Ornis Scand.* 24: 1–9.

ANON. (1981) [*Red Data Book of Belarussian SSR: rare and vulnerable species of animals and plants.*] Minsk: Belorusskaya Sovetskaya Entsiklopedia. (In Belarussian.)

ANON. (1986) Delineation studies of Ramsar sites in Greece: Evros delta, Mitrikou Lake, Vistonis Lake, Nestos delta. Athens: Ministry of Environment.

ANON. (1990a) [*Fauna of Lithuania: birds.*] Vilnius: Mokslas. (In Lithuanian.)

ANON. (1990b) [Distribution of rare breeding birds in regions of the central non-chernozem zone of the European part of the RSFSR (Suppl.).] Pp.178–182 in V. T. Butjev, ed. [*Rare bird species of the central European Russia.*] Moscow: U.S.S.R. Ornithological Society, Moscow Division. (In Russian.)

ANON. (1990c) [*The capture of terns by children in Senegal: preliminary report for the Secretary of State of the Environment, WWF France.*] Rochefort, France: Ligue Française pour la Protection des Oiseaux. (In French.)

ANON. (1992a) The stock of colonial bird species in the Danube delta. Tulcea: Institutul de Cercetari se Proiectari Delta Dunarii (unpublished).

ANON. (1992b) *The environment in Europe and North-America: annotated statistics 1992.* New York: United Nations (United Nations Statistical Commission and Economic Commission for Europe Conference of European Statisticians Statistical Standards and Studies no. 42)

ANSTEY, S. (1989)*The status and conservation of the White-headed Duck* Oxyura leucocephala. Slimbridge, U.K.: International Wildfowl Research Bureau (Spec. Publ. 10).

ARDAMATSKAYA, T. B. AND SABINEVSKY, B. V. (1990) The distribution and status of waterfowl in the northern Black Sea region in winter. Pp.39–42 in G. V. T. Matthews, ed. *Managing waterfowl populations.* Slimbridge, U.K.: International Waterfowl and Wetlands Research Bureau (Spec. Publ. 12).

ARLETTAZ, R. (1987) [Status of the relict population of *Otus scops* in central Valais.] *Stat. Orn. Suisse*: 1–32. (In French.)

ARROYO, B. (1991) [Results of the national census of Bonelli's Eagle.] *Quercus* 70: 17. (In Spanish.)

ARROYO, B., FERREIRO, E. AND GARZA, V. (1990a) [*Second national survey of the Griffon Vulture* Gyps fulvus: *population, distribution, range and conservation.*] Madrid: Instituto Nacional para la Conservación de la Naturaleza. (In Spanish.)

ARROYO, B., FERREIRO, E. AND GARZA, V. (1990b) [*The Golden Eagle* Aquila chrysaetos *in Spain: census, range, breeding and conservation.*] Madrid: Instituto Nacional para la Conservación de la Naturaleza. (In Spanish.)

ARROYO, B., FERREIRO, E. AND GARZA, V. (1992) [Birds of the red list: Bonelli's Eagle.] *Garcilla* 83: 8–9. (In Spanish.)

ASENSIO, J. M. (1991) Impact of the capture of 'cangrejo rojo' on other animal populations in Brazo del Este. Pp.107–115 in Andalus, ed. [*Workshop on wetlands in Andalucia.*] Málaga: Asoc. Andalus/Fund. Bios./Finca el Retiro.

ASH, J. S. (1970) Observations on a decreasing population of Red-backed Shrikes.*Brit. Birds* 63: 185–205, 225–239.

ASHTON-JOHNSON, J. F. R. (1961) Notes on the breeding birds of Cyprus. *Ool. Rec.* 35: 33–39.

ATAKISHIEV, T. A. (1971) On the biological characteristics of bee pests in Azerbaijan. *Uchenye zap. Kazanskogo Veterinarnago Inst.* 109: 266–269. (In Russian.)

ATKINSON-WILLES, G. L. (1976) The numerical distribution of ducks, swans and coots as a guide in assessing the importance of wetlands in midwinter. Pp.199–255 in M. Smart, ed. *Proc. Int. Conf. on the Conservation of Wetlands and Waterfowl, Heiligenhafen.* Slimbridge, U.K.: International Waterfowl and Wetlands Research Bureau.

AUBRAIS, O., HEMON, Y. A. AND GUYOMARC'H, J.-C. (1986) [Habitat use in the Quail (*Coturnix coturnix coturnix*) at the onset of the breeding period.] *Gibier Faune Sauvage* 3: 317–342. (In French.)

AUKES, P., VAN DEN BERK, V. M., CRONAU, J. P., VAN DORP, D., ÖZESMI, U. AND VAN WINDEN, A. C. J. (1988) The Çukurova deltas: geomorphology, hydrology, climate, biotopes and human impact. Pp.13–32 in T. M. van der Have, V. M. van der Berk, J. P. Cronau and M. J. Langeveld, eds. *South Turkey Project: a survey of waders and waterfowl in the Çukurova deltas, spring 1987.* Zeist, Netherlands: Working Group International Wader and Waterfowl Research (WIWO Rep. 22).

AULÉN, G. (1988) *Ecology and distribution history of the White-backed Woodpecker* Dendrocopus leucotos *in Sweden.* Uppsala, Sweden: Swedish University of Agricultural Sciences (Rep. 14).

AVERIN, Y. V. AND GANIA, I. M. (1971) [*Birds of Moldavia*, 2.] Kishiniev: Shtiintsa. (In Russian.)

AVERY, M. I. AND DEL NEVO, A. J. (1991) Action for Roseate Terns. *RSPB Cons. Rev.* 5: 54–59.

AVERY, M. I., COULTHARD, N. D., DEL NEVO, A. J., LEROUX, A., MEDEIROS, F. M., MERNE, O., MORALEE, A., NTIAMOA-BAIDU, Y., O'BRIAIN, M. AND WALLACE, E. (in prep.) *A recovery plan for Roseate Terns in the east Atlantic: an international programme.*

AVERY, M., GIBBONS, D. W., PORTER, R., TEW, T., TUCKER, G. M. AND WILLIAMS, G. (in press) Revising the U.K. Red Data List: the biological basis of U.K. conservation priorities. *Ibis* 137 (Suppl. 1).

BACON, P. AND BACON, E. (1982) Some notes on Cyprus Warbler territories. *COS (1970) Rep.* 13: 48–51.

BAGYURA, J., HARASZTHY, L., KALLAY, G. AND MOLNAR, L. (1987–1989) [The Hungarian Ornithological Society's activities with respect to the protection of the Saker Falcon.] Report for the WWF Project no. 3649).

BAHA EL DIN, S. M. AND SALAMA, W. (1991) *The catching of birds in North Sinai, autumn 1990*. Cambridge, U.K.: International Council for Bird Preservation (Study Rep. 45).

BAILLIE, S. R., CLARK, N. A. AND OGILVIE, M. A. (1986) *Cold weather movements of waterfowl and waders: an analysis of ringing recoveries*. Peterborough, U.K.: Nature Conservancy Council (CSD Report no. 650).

BAILLON, F. (1989) [New wintering record of Audouin's Gull *Larus audouinii* Payr. in Senogambia.] *Oiseau et R.F.O.* 59: 296–304. (In French.)

BAIN, C. (1987) *Native pinewoods in Scotland: a review 1957–1987*. Edinburgh: Royal Society for the Protection of Birds.

BAINES, D. (1988) The effects of improvement of upland grassland on the distribution and density of breeding wading birds (Charadriiformes) in northern England. *Biol. Conserv.* 45: 221–236.

BAINES, D. (1989) The effects of improvement of upland, marginal grasslands on the breeding success of Lapwings *Vanellus vanellus* and other waders. *Ibis* 131: 497–506.

BALDACCHINO, A. E. (1981) [Status of raptors in Malta.] Pp.17–18 in G. Cheylan and G. C. Thibault, eds. [*Mediterranean raptors I*]. Aix-en-Provence, France: Parc Naturel Régional de la Corse/Centre de Recherche Ornithologique de Provence. (In French.)

BALDOCK, D. (1990) *Agriculture and habitat loss in Europe*. Gland, Switzerland: WWF International.

BALDOCK, D. AND LONG, T. (1987) The Mediterranean environment under pressure: the influence of the CAP on Spain and Portugal and the IMP in France, Greece and Italy. Institute for European Environmental Policy (Report to World Wildlife Fund).

BANCROFT, G. T. (1989) Status and conservation of wading birds in the Everglades. *Amer. Birds* 43: 1258–1265.

BANNERMAN, D. A. (1913) Description of *Saxicola dacotiae murielae* and *Acantis harterti* subspecies from the Canary Islands. *Bull. Brit. Orn. Club* 33: 37–39.

BANNERMAN, D. A. (1953) *The birds of the British Isles*, 2. Edinburgh: Oliver and Boyd.

BANNERMAN, D. A. (1963) *Birds of the Atlantic Islands*, 1. Edinburgh: Oliver and Boyd.

BANNERMAN, D. A. AND BANNERMAN, W. M. (1965) *Birds of the Atlantic Islands*, 2: *a history of the birds of Madeira, the Desertas and the Porto Santo Islands*. Edinburgh: Oliver and Boyd.

BANNERMAN, D. A. AND BANNERMAN, W. M. (1966) *Birds of the Atlantic islands*, 3: *a history of the birds of the Azores*. Edinburgh, U.K.: Oliver and Boyd.

BANNERMAN, D. A. AND BANNERMAN, W. M. (1968) *Birds of the Atlantic Islands*, 4: *history of the birds of the Cape Verde Islands*. Edinburgh: Oliver and Boyd.

BANNERMAN, D. A. AND BANNERMAN, W. M. (1971) *Handbook of the birds of Cyprus*. Edinburgh and London: Oliver and Boyd.

BARBRAUD, C. AND BARBRAUD, J. C. (in press) [Short-toed Eagle *Circaetus gallicus*.] In D. Berthelot and G. Jarry, eds. [*New atlas of breeding birds in France 1985–1989*.]

Paris: Société Ornithologique de France. (In French.)

BARIS, Y. S. (1991) Conservation problems of steppic avifauna in Turkey. Pp.93–96 in P. D. Goriup, L. A. Batten and J. A. Norton, eds. *The conservation of lowland dry grassland birds in Europe*. Peterborough, U.K.: Joint Nature Conservation Committee.

BARRETT, R. T. (1979) Small oil spill kills 10–20,000 seabirds in north Norway. *Mar. Pollut. Bull.* 10: 253–255.

BARRETT, R. T. AND VADER, W. (1984) The status and conservation of seabirds in Norway. Pp.323–333 in J. P. Croxall, ed. *Status and conservation of the world's seabirds*. Cambridge, U.K.: International Council for Bird Preservation (Techn. Publ. 2).

BARRINGTON, R. M. (1915) The last Irish Golden Eagle. *Irish Naturalist* 24: 63.

BARROS, C. (in prep.) [Contribution to the study of the biology and ecology of the Stone Curlew *Burhinus oedicnemus* in La Serena, Badajoz.] Madrid: Facultad de Biologia, Universidad Complutense de Madrid (Ph.D. thesis). (In Spanish.)

BARROS, C., BORBÓN, M. N. AND GARZA, V. (1990) [Impact of pesticide use on the birds of La Serena (Badajoz), spring-summer 1990.] Madrid: Sociedad Española de Ornitología/Agencia de Medio Ambiente, Extremadura (unpublished). (In Spanish.)

BATESON, P. P. G. AND PLOWRIGHT, R. C. (1959) The breeding biology of the Ivory Gull in Spitsbergen. *Brit. Birds* 52: 105–114.

BATTEN, L. A., BIBBY, C. J., CLEMENT, P., ELLIOTT, G. D. AND PORTER, R. F., EDS. (1990) *Red data birds in Britain: action for rare, threatened and important species*. London: T. and A. D. Poyser.

BATTEN, L. A., GORIUP, P. D., GRIMMETT, R., HOUSDEN, S., MARTÍN-NOVELLA, C., POTTS, D., TEMPLE LANG, J. AND TUCKER, G. M. (1991) Recommendations of the seminar. Pp.5–8 in P. D. Goriup, L. A. Batten and J. A. Norton, eds. *The conservation of lowland dry grassland birds in Europe*. Peterborough, U.K.: Joint Nature Conservation Committee.

BAUER, K. M. AND GLUTZ VON BLOTZHEIM, U. N., EDS. (1968) [*Handbook of the birds of central Europe, 2.*] Frankfurt au Main: Akademische Verlagsgesellschaft. (In German.)

BAUER, K. M. AND GLUTZ VON BLOTZHEIM, U. N. (1987) [*Handbook of the birds of central Europe, 1.*] Second edition. Wiesbaden: Aula-Verlag. (In German.)

BAUER, S. AND THIELCKE, G. (1982) [Threatened breeding birds in West Germany and Berlin: population trends, threats and conservation measures.] *Vogelwarte* 31: 183–191. (In German.)

BAUER, W., HELVERSEN, O. V., HODGE, M. AND MARTENS, J. (1969) *Catalogue of the fauna of Greece, 2: birds.* Thessaloniki.

BAUMGART, W. (1991a) [*The Saker Falcon.*] Third edition. Wittenberg Lutherstadt: Ziemsen Verlag. (In German.)

BAUMGART, W. (1991b) Raptor problems in Syria. *Bull. World Working Group on Birds of Prey* 14 (Newsl.): 15–16.

BAUMGART, W., GAMAUF, A., BAGYURA, J., HARASZTHY, L., CHAVKO, J. AND PEKLO, A. (1992) Biology and status of the Saker Falcon *Falco cherrug* in eastern Europe. In B.-U. Meyburg, ed. *Abstracts IV World Conference on Birds of Prey, Berlin*. Berlin: B.-U. Meyburg World

Working Group on Birds of Prey and Owls.

BAZIEV, D. H. (1978) [*The snowcocks of the Caucasus.*] St Petersburg: Nauka. (In Russian.)

BAZIEV, Z. K. AND CHUNIKHIN, S. P. (1963) [On the ecology of the Güldenstädt's Redstart in Kabardino-Balkariya.] *Ornitologiya* 6: 235–237. (In Russian.)

BEAMAN, M. (1986) Turkey: Bird Report 1976–81. *Sandgrouse* 8: 1–41.

BEAMAN, M. AND PORTER, R. F. (1985) Status of birds of prey in Turkey. *Bull. World Working Group on Birds of Prey* 3: 52–56.

BEAUBRUN, P.-C. (1983) [Audouin's Gull *Larus audouinii* Payr. on the Moroccan coasts.] *Oiseau et R.F.O.* 53: 209–226. (In French.)

BECK, N. (in press) [*Conservation of the Corsican Nuthatch and forest management.*] Parc Naturel Régional et des Réserves Naturelles de la Corse. (In French.)

BEEKMAN, J. H., VAN EERDEN, M. R. AND DIRKSEN, S. (1991) Bewick's Swans *Cygnus columbianus bewickii* utilising the changing resource of *Potomogeton pectinatus* during the autumn in the Netherlands. Pp.238–248 in J. Sears and P. J. Bacon, eds. *Third IWRB International Swan Symposium, Oxford 1989*. Wildfowl (Suppl. 1).

BEINTEMA, A. J. (1986) Where in Africa do subadult Black-tailed Godwits spend the summer? *Wader Study Group Bull.* 47: 10.

BEINTEMA, A, J. (1988) Conservation of grassland bird communities in the Netherlands. Pp.105–111 in P. D. Goriup, ed. *Ecology and conservation of grassland birds.* Cambridge, U.K.: International Council for Bird Preservation (Techn. Publ. 7).

BEINTEMA, A. J. (1991a) Status and conservation of meadow birds in the Netherlands. *Wader Study Group Bull.* 61 (Suppl.): 12–13.

BEINTEMA, A. J. (1991b) What makes a meadow bird a meadow bird? *Wader Study Group Bull.* 61 (Suppl.): 3–5.

BEINTEMA, A. J. AND DROST, N. (1986) Migration of the Black-tailed Godwit. *Gerfaut* 77: 37–62.

BEINTEMA, A. J. AND MÜSKENS, G. J. D. M. (1987) Nesting success of birds breeding in Dutch agricultural grasslands. *J. Appl. Ecol.* 24: 743–758.

BELIK, V. P. (1984) [The Levant Sparrowhawk.] Pp.54–56 in Priroda. (In Russian.)

BELIK, V. P. (1986) [The Levant Sparrowhawk along the Don river.] Pp.128–143 in V. D. Ilyichev, ed. [*Recent problems in ornithology*]. Moscow: Nauka. (In Russian.)

BELIK, V. P. (1991) [Steppe ploughing and birds of the lower Don river plains: problems of adaptations.] Pp.109–111 in A. N. Khokhlov, ed. [*Recent data on bird species, distribution and ecology in the northern Caucasus.*] Stavropol: Stavropol Pedagogical Insitute. (In Russian.)

BELIK, V. P. (1992a) Distribution, numbers and some features of the ecology of the Little Bustard in the south-east of the European part of the U.S.S.R. *Bustard Studies* 5: 73–77.

BELIK, V. P. (1992b) [Distribution and numbers of rare birds in the Rostov region: materials to the Red Data Book of the North Caucasus.] Pp.21–68 in A. N. Khokhlov and V. I. Malandzia, eds. [*Caucasus Ornithological News*, 4.] Stavropol: Menzbir Ornithological Society, North-Caucasus Division. (In Russian.)

BELIK, V. P. AND VETROV, V. V. (1992) The Levant Sparrowhawk *Accipiter brevipes* within the former U.S.S.R. Pp.5 in B.-U. Meyburg, ed. *Abstracts IV World Conference on Birds of Prey, Berlin*. Berlin: B.-U. Meyburg World Working Group on Birds of Prey and Owls.

BELIK, V. P., KAZAKOV, B. A. AND PETROV, V. S. (1993) [Status of Pallid Harriers in the southern part of European Russia.] *Caucasus Orn. News* 5: 3–13. (In Russian.)

BELIK, V. P., KHOKHLOV, A. N., KUKISH, A. I., TILBA, P. A. AND KOMAROV, J. E. (in press) [Rare birds of the northern Caucasus in need of particular conservation.] (In Russian.)

BEME, L. B. (1925) [Materials on the biology of Caucasian birds.] Pp.1–26 in Anon., ed. *On the biology of North Caucasian animals.* Vladikavkaz: Tipografiya Ingushetii 'Svet'. (In Russian.)

BEME, L. B. (1926) [New data on the nesting of *Phoenicurus erythrogastra erythrogastra* Güld. in Central Caucasus.] *Nachrichten des Gorsky Pädagogischen Institut, Vladikavkaz* 3: 250–258. (In Russian.)

BENGTSON, S.-A. (1971) Habitat selection of duck broods in the Lake Myvatn area, north-east Iceland. *Ornis Scand.* 2: 17–26.

BENGTSON, S.-A. (1972) Breeding ecology of the Harlequin Duck *Histrionicus histrionicus* (L.) in Iceland. *Ornis Scand.* 3: 1–19.

BENGTSON, S.-A. AND ULFSTRAND, S. (1971) Food resources and breeding frequency of the Harlequin Duck *Histrionicus histrionicus* in Iceland. *Oikos* 22: 235–239.

BEREZOVIKOV, N. N., LUKHTANOV, A. G. AND STARIKOV, S. V. (1992) [Birds of the Buchtarma valley (southern Altai).] Pp.160–178 in E. N. Kurochkin, ed. [*Modern Ornithology 1991.*] Moscow: Nauka. (In Russian.)

VAN DEN BERG, A. B. (1989) Habitat of Slender-billed Curlews in Morocco. *Brit. Birds* 83: 1–7.

BERG, A. (1991) Ecology of Curlews *Numenius arquata* and Lapwings *Vanellus* on farmland. Uppsala: Swedish University of Agricultural Sciences (Dissertation 20).

BERG, A. (1992) Factors affecting nest-site choice and reproductive success of Curlews *Numenius arquata* on farmland. *Ibis* 134: 44–51.

BERG, A. (1993) Food resources and foraging success of Curlews *Numenius arquata* in different farmland habitats. *Ornis Fenn.* 70: 22–31.

BERGIER, P. (1985) The breeding of the Egyptian Vulture *Neophron percnopterus* in Provence (SE France) from 1979 to 1983. *Bull. World Working Group on Birds of Prey* 2: 77–78.

BERGIER, P. (1987) [*The diurnal raptors of Morocco, status, distribution and ecology.*] Aix-en-Provence: CEEP (Annales 3). (In French.)

BERGIER, P. AND CHEYLAN, G. (1989) [Status, breeding success and feeding habits of the Egyptian Vulture *Neophron percnopterus* in Mediterranean France.] *Alauda* 48: 75–97. (In French.)

BERGMAN, G. (1971) [A marginal population of the Black Guillemot *Cepphus grylle*: food, breeding success, diurnal rhythm, and habits.] *Commentationes Biologicae* 42: 1–26. (In German with English summary.)

BERGMAN, G. (1977) Birds of prey: the situation in Finland. Pp.96–103 in R. D. Chancellor, ed. *Proceedings of the I World Conference on Birds of Prey, Vienna, 1975*. Cambridge, U.K.: International Council for Bird Preservation.

BERGMAN, G. (1980) Single-breeding versus colonial breeding in the Caspian Tern, the Common Tern and the Arctic Tern. *Ornis Fenn.* 57: 141–152.

BERGO, G. (1984) Population size, spacing and age structure of Golden Eagle *Aquila chrysaetos* (L.) in Hordaland, west Norway. *Fauna Norv. Ser. C, Cinclus* 7: 106–108.

BERGSTRÖM, R., HULDT, H. AND NILSSON, U. (1992) *Swedish game—biology and management.* Swedish Hunters' Association. Uppsala: Almkvist and Wiksell.

VAN DEN BERK, V. (1988) The Black Francolin in Turkey. *Sandgrouse* 10: 51–57.

VAN DEN BERK, V., VAN DEN BERK, N., BILJSMA, R. G. AND DE RODER, F. E. (1985) *The importance of some wetlands in Turkey as transient wintering areas for waterbirds.* Zeist, Netherlands: Stichting WIWO (Publ. 6).

BERNARD-LAURENT, A. (1984) [Natural hybridization between Rock Partridge (*Alectoris graeca saxatilis*) and Red-legged Partridge (*Alectoris rufa rufa*) in the Alpes-Maritimes.] *Gibier Faune Sauvage* 2: 79–96. (In French.)

BERNARD-LAURENT, A. (1988) [Autumn and winter movements of the hybrid partridge (*Alectoris graeca saxatilis* x *Alectoris rufa rufa*) in the southern French Alps and its habitat requirements.] *Gibier Faune Sauvage* 5: 171–186. (In French.)

BERNARD-LAURENT, A. (1990) Mortality factors and survival rates of hybrid partridges in the French Alps. Pp.108–116 in S. Myrberget, ed. *Trans. 19th IUGB Congress.* Trondheim: Norwegian Institute for Nature Research.

BERNARD-LAURENT, A., LÉONARD, P. AND REITZ, F. (1991) [Rock Partridge (*Alectoris graeca saxatilis*) hunting mortality: factors of variation and management prospects for hunted populations.] *Gibier Faune Sauvage* 9: 1–25. (In French.)

BERNDT, R. AND WINKEL, W. (1979) [On population dynamics in the Blue Tit (*Parus caeruleus*), Nuthatch (*Sitta europaea*), Redstart (*Phoenicurus phoenicurus*) and Wryneck (*Jynx torquilla*) in central European study areas from 1927 to 1978.] *Vogelwelt* 100: 55–69. (In German.)

BERNES, C. (1993) *The Nordic environment—present state, trends and threats.* Nordic Council of Ministers (Nord 1993: 12).

BERNÍS, F. (1966) [The Black Vulture *Aegypius monachus* in Iberia.] *Ardeola* 12: 19–44. (In Spanish.)

BERNÍS, F. (1966) [*Iberian migratory birds*, 1.] Madrid: Sociedad Española de Ornitología. (In Spanish.)

BERNÍS, F. (1971) [*Iberian migrating birds*, 7/8.] Madrid: Sociedad Española de Ornitología. (In Spanish.)

BERNÍS, F. (1972) [Short notes on geography, migration and demography of some censused waterbirds.] *Ardeola* 17–18: 207–230. (In Spanish.)

BERNÍS, F. (1983) Migration of the Common Griffon Vulture in the western Palearctic. Pp.185–196 in S. R. Wilbur and J. A. Jackson, eds. *Vulture biology and management.* Berkeley: California University.

BERTELSEN, J. AND SIMONSEN, N. H. (1986) *Documentation on bird hunting and the conservation status of the species involved: situation in 1986.* Copenhagen: Game and Wildlife Administration.

BERTHOLD, P., FLIEGE, G., QUERNER, U. AND WINKLER, H. (1986) [The development of songbird populations in central Europe: analysis of trapping data.] *J. Orn.* 127:

397–437. (In German.)

BEUKEMA, J. J. (1992) Long-term and recent changes in the benthic macrofauna living on tidal flats in the western part of the Wadden Sea. *Neth. J. Sea Res. Publ. Ser.* 20: 135–141.

BEVERTON, R. J. H. (1993) The Rio convention and rational harvesting of natural fish resources: the Barents Sea experience in context. Pp.44–63 in O. T. Sandlund and P. J. Schei, eds. *Proceedings of the Norway/UNEP Expert Conference on Biodiversity, 24–28 May 1993.* Trondheim: Directorate for Nature Management/Norwegian Institute for Nature Research (NINA).

BEZZEL, E. (1985) [*Compendium of the birds of Middle Europe.*] Wiesbaden: Aula-Verlag. (In German.)

BIANKI, V. (1992) Seaducks of the White Sea. *IWRB Seaduck Bull.* 2: 23–29.

BIBBY, C. J. (1973) The Red-backed Shrike: a vanishing British species. *Bird Study* 20: 103–110.

BIBBY, C. J. (1979) Breeding biology of the Dartford Warbler *Sylvia undata* in England. *Ibis* 121: 41–52.

BIBBY, C. J. AND ETHERIDGE, B. (1993) Status of the Hen Harrier *Circus cyaneus* in Scotland in 1988–89. *Bird Study* 40: 1–11.

BIBBY, C. J. AND HILL, D. A. (1987) Status of the Fuerteventura Stonechat *Saxicola dacotiae. Ibis* 129: 491–498.

BIBBY, C. AND DEL NEVO, A. (1992) The first record of Fea's Petrel *Pterodroma feae* from the Azores. *Bull. Brit. Orn. Club* 111: 183–186.

BIBBY, C. J. AND TUBBS, C. R. (1975) Status, habitats and conservation of the Dartford Warbler in England. *Brit. Birds* 67: 177–195.

BIBER, J.-P. (1990) *Action plan for the conservation of western Lesser Kestrel Falco naumanni populations.* Cambridge, U.K.: International Council for Bird Preservation (Study Rep. 41).

BIBER, J. P. (1993) Status and distribution of the Gull-billed Tern *Gelochelidon nilotica* (Gmelin, 1789) in the western Palearctic. Preliminary results of an inquiry. Pp.87–95 in J. S. Aguilar, X. Monbailliu and A. M. Paterson, eds. *Status and conservation of seabirds: ecogeography and Mediterranean Action Plan. Proceedings II Mediterranean Seabird Symposium, Mallorca, 1989.* Madrid: Sociedad Española de Ornitología/BirdLife/MEDMARAVIS.

BIBER, J. P. AND SALATHÉ, S. (1991) Threats to migratory birds. Pp.17–35 in T. Salathé, ed. *Conserving migratory birds.* Cambridge, U.K.: International Council for Bird Preservation (Techn. Publ. 12).

BIBER, J. P. AND SALATHÉ, T. (1989) [Analysis of bird migration in the European Community.] International Council for Bird Preservation Report to the Commission of the European Communities, Directorate-General for the Environment, Nuclear Safety and Civil Protection (contract no. B6610–62–88). Unpublished. (In French.)

BIGNAL, E. AND BIGNAL, S. (1987) *The provision of nesting sites for Choughs.* Peterborough, U.K.: Nature Conservancy Council (Chief Scientist Directorate Rep. 765).

BIGNAL, E. AND CURTIS, D. J., EDS. (1989) *Choughs and land-use in Europe. Proceedings of an international workshop on the conservation of the Chough Pyrrhocorax pyrrhocorax in the EC, 11–14 November 1988.* Tarbento, U.K.: Scottish Chough Study Group.

BIJLEVELD, M. (1974) *Birds of prey in Europe*. London: Macmillan.

BIJLSMA, R. G., LENSINK, T. AND POST, F. (1985) [The Woodlark *Lullula arborea* as a breeding bird in the Netherlands in 1970–84.] *Limosa* 58: 89–96. (In Dutch.)

BIJLSMA, S., HAGEMEIJER, E. J. M., VERKLEY, G. J. M. AND ZOLLINGER, R. (1988) [*Ecological aspects of the Lesser Kestrel* Falco naumanni *in Extremadura (Spain).*] Nijmegen: Vakgroep Experimentele Zoölogie, Katholieke University (Report Werkgroep Dieroecologie 285). (In Dutch.)

BIRKAN, M. AND JACOB, M. (1988) [*The Grey Partridge.*] Paris: Hatier. (In French.)

BIRKENMAJER, K. (1969) [Observations of Ivory Gulls *Pagophila eburnea* (Phipps) in south-west Spitsbergenu.] *Polska akad. nauk, Acta orn.* 11: 461–476. (In Polish.)

BLACK, J. M. AND MADSEN, J. (1993) Red-breasted Goose: conservation and research needs. *IWRB Goose Research Group Bull.* 4: 8–15.

BLACK, J. M., DEERENBERG, C. AND OWEN, M. (1991) Foraging behaviour and site selection of Barnacle Geese *Branta leucopsis* in a traditional and newly colonised spring staging habitat. *Ardea* 79: 349–358.

BLAKE, G., DEWDNEY, J. AND MITCHELL, J. (1987) *The Cambridge atlas of the Middle East and North Africa*. Cambridge, U.K.: Cambridge University Press.

BLANCO, G., FARGALLO, J. A. AND CUEVAS, A. (in press) Consumption rates of olives by Choughs *Pyrrhocorax pyrrhocorax* in central Spain: variations and importance. *Bird Study*.

BLANCO, J. A. AND GONZÁLEZ, J. L., EDS. (1992) [*Red data book of Spanish vertebrates.*] Madrid: Instituto Nacional para la Conservación de la Naturaleza. (In Spanish.)

BLOMERT, A.-M. AND ENGELMOER M. (1990) The Banc d'Arguin, Mauritania, as a meeting point for Avocets during spring migration. *Ardea* 78: 185–192.

BLOMGREN, A. (1964) [*The Siberian Jay.*] Stockholm: Wahlströms. (In Swedish.)

BLOMQVIST, S. AND ELANDER, M. (1981) Sabine's Gull (*Xema sabini*), Ross's Gull (*Rhodostethia rosea*) and Ivory Gull (*Pagophila eburnea*) in the Arctic: a review. *Arctic* 34: 122–132.

BLUME, D. (1984) [Population decline of Green Woodpecker (*Picus viridis*): a signal of alarm?.] *Orn. Mitt.* 36: 3–7. (In German.)

BOCCA, M. (1990) [*The Rock Partridge* Alectoris graeca *and the Ptarmigan* Lagopus mutus *in the Aosta Valley: distribution, ecology, reproduction and management.*] Aosta: Assessorato Regionale all'Agricoltura, Foreste e Ambiente Naturale. (In Italian.)

BOERE, G. C. AND SMIT, C. J. (1981) Bar-tailed Godwit (*Limosa lapponica* L.). Pp.170–179 in C. J. Smit and W. J. Wolff, eds. *Birds of the Wadden Sea*. Rotterdam: Balkema.

BOETTCHER-STREIM, W. (1992) [Changes in the European populations of the Black Stork *Ciconia nigra*.] *Orn. Beob.* 89: 235–244. (In German.)

BOGLIANI, G., FASOLA, M., CANOVA, L. AND SAINO, N. (1990) Food and foraging rhythm of a specialised Gull-billed Tern population *Gelochelidon nilotica*. *Ethology, Ecology and Evolution* 2: 175–181.

BONNET, J., TERRASSE, M., BAGNOLINI, C. AND PINNA, J. L. (1990) [Reintroduction and spread of Griffon Vulture (*Gyps fulvus*) in the Grands Causses de Massif Central.] *Oiseau et R.F.O.* 60: 181–206. (In French.)

BONORA, M. AND CHIAVETTA, M. (1975) [Contribution to the study of Lanner *Falco biarmicus feldeggii* in Italy.] *Nos Oiseaux* 33: 153–168. (In French.)

BORODIN, A. M. (1984) [*Red data book of the U.S.S.R.: rare and endangered species of animals and plants*, 1: *animals.*] Second edition. Moscow: Promyshlennost. (In Russian.)

BOSTRÖM, U. (1978) [The effects of wetland drainage on the bird fauna.] *Proceedings of the First Nordic Congress of Ornithology*, 1977. *Anser* 3 (Suppl): 52–56. (In Danish with English summary.)

BOTEV, N. (1980) Preservation and breeding of the Rock Partridge (*Alectoris graeca* Meis) in People's Republic of Bulgaria. Pp.11–17 in C. L. Coles, M. Reydellet, G. van Tuyll, L. van Maltzahn and J. Bugalho, eds. *Partridges of the Alectoris genus*. Paris: International Council for Game and Wildlife Conservation.

BOURNE, W. R. P. (1955) The birds of the Cape Verde Islands. *Ibis* 97: 508–556.

BOURNE, W. R. P. (1957) The breeding birds of Bermuda. *Ibis* 99: 94–105.

BOURNE, W. R. P. (1965) The missing Petrels. *Bull. Brit. Orn. Club* 85: 97–105.

BOURNE, W. R. P. (1978) Mink and wildlife. *BTO News* 91: 1–2.

BOURNE, W. R. P. AND SMITH, A. J. M. (1974) Threats to Scottish Sandwich Terns. *Biol. Conserv.* 6: 222–224.

DE BOURNONVILLE, D. (1964) [Observations of an important Audouin's Gull: *Larus audouinii* Payraudeau—colony off the coast of Corsica.] *Gerfaut* 54: 439–453. (In French.)

BOWDEN, C. G. R. (1990) Selection of foraging habitats by Woodlarks (*Lullula arborea*) nesting in pine plantations. *J. Appl. Ecol.* 27: 410–419.

BOWDEN, C. G. R. AND GREEN, R. E. (1991) The ecology of nightjars on pine plantations in Thetford Forest. Sandy, U.K.: Royal Society for the Protection of Birds (unpublished report).

BOWDEN, C. G. R. AND HOBLYN, R. (1990) The increasing importance of restocked conifer plantations for Woodlarks in Britain: implications and consequences. *RSPB Conserv. Rev.* 4: 26–31.

BOYD, H. (1992) Arctic summer conditions and British Knot numbers: an exploratory analysis. *Wader Study Group Bull.* 64 (Suppl.): 144–152.

BOYLE, P. (1990) On the distribution and status of the Black Francolin *Francolinus francolinus* in Cyprus. *Zool. Middle East* 4: 17–21.

BRAAE, L., NOHR, H. AND PETERSEN, B. S. (1988) [*The bird fauna of conventional and organic farmland.*] Copenhagen: Miljøministeriet, Miljøstyrelsen (Miljøprojekt 12). (In Dutch.)

BRACKO, F. (1986) [Rapid population decrease of Roller *Coracias garrulus* in Slovenia.] *Acrocephalus* 7: 49–52. (In Slovenian with English summary.)

BRADLEY, P. (1986) The breeding biology of Audouin's Gull on the Chafarinas Islands. Pp.221–230 in MEDMARAVIS and X. Monbailliu, eds. *Mediterranean marine avifauna*. Berlin and Heidelberg: Springer-Verlag (NATO ASI Ser. G. 12).

BRADSTREET, M. S. W. (1977) Feeding ecology of seabirds

along fast-ice edges in Wellington Channel and Resolute Passage, N.W.T. Report by LGL Ltd for the Polar Gas Project (unpublished).

BRADSTREET, M. S. W. (1980) Thick-billed Murres and Black Guillemots in the Barrow Strait area, N.W.T., during spring: distribution and habitat use. *Can. J. Zool.* 58: 2120–2140.

BRADSTREET, M. S. W. (1986) Importance of ice edges to high-Arctic seabirds. Pp.991–1000 in H. Ouellet, ed. *Proc. Int. Orn. Congr. 19.* Ottawa.

BRAGIN, A. B. (1981) [On the breeding of the Goldeneye in nest-boxes.] *Ornithologiya* 16: 22–32. (In Russian.)

BRAZIL, M. AND SHAWYER, C. R. (1989) *The Barn Owl.* London: The Hawk Trust.

BRICHETTI, P. (1985) [Current distribution of Galliformes in Italy.] Pp.15–27 in F. Dessi Fulgheri and T. Mingozzi, eds. *Atti sem. Biologia Galliformi.* Arcavata: Calabria University. (In Italian.)

BRICHETTI, P. AND DI CAPI, C. (1985) Distribution, population and breeding ecology of the Corsican Nuthatch, *Sitta whiteheadi* Sharpe. *Riv. Ital. Orn.* 55: 3–26.

BRICHETTI, P. AND DI CAPI, C. (1987) Conservation of the Corsican Nuthatch *Sitta whiteheadi* Sharpe and proposals for habitat management. *Conservation* 39: 13–21.

BRINKMAN, R., KÖHLER, B., HEUNS, J.-U. AND RÖSLER, S. (1990) [*Menderes Delta*]. Hannover, Germany: Institut für Landschaftspflege und Naturschutz. (In German.)

BRINKMANN, M. (1933) [*The avifauna of north-west Germany.*] Hildesheim. (In German.)

BROO, B. AND LINDBERG, P. (1981) [*The development of the Ritsem area: effects on the fauna, especially birds of prey.*] Stockholm: Swedish Environmental Protection Board (SNV-PM 1435). (In Swedish.)

BROOKE, M. (1990) *The Manx Shearwater.* London: T. and A. D. Poyser.

BROWN, L. (1970) *African birds of prey.* Boston: Houghton Mifflin Company.

BROWN, L. H. AND AMADON, D. (1968) *Eagles, hawks and falcons of the world.* Hamlyn House, Feltham, U.K.: Country Life Books.

BROWN, L. H., URBAN, E. K. AND NEWMAN, K. (1982) *The birds of Africa,* 1. London and New York: Academic Press.

BROWN, M. J., LINTON, E. AND REES, E. C. (1992) Causes of mortality among wild swans in Britain. *Wildfowl* 36: 5–12.

BROWN, R. G. B. (1984) Seabirds in the Greenland, Barents and Norwegian Seas, February-April 1982. *Polar Res.* 2: 1–18.

BRUDERER, B. AND HIRSCHI, W. (1984) [Long-term population development of Redstart *Phoenicurus phoenicurus* and Pied Flycatcher *Ficedula hypoleuca* (based on Swiss ringing data and nest-box records).] *Orn. Beob.* 81: 285–302. (In German.)

BUCKLE, A. AND ZINO, F. J. A. (1989) Saving Europe's rarest bird. *Roundel* 5: 112–116.

BUCKLEY, P. A. AND BUCKLEY, F. G. (1984) Seabirds of the north and middle Atlantic coasts of the United States: their status and conservation. Pp.101–133 in J. P. Croxall, P. G. H. Evans and R. W. Schreiber, eds. *Status and conservation of the world's seabirds.* Cambridge, U.K.: International Council for Bird Preservation (Techn. Publ. 2).

BULAKHOV, V. L. (1968) [Shaping the avifauna of the Dneprodzerzhinskiy reservoir.] *Ornitologiya* 9: 178–187. (In Russian.)

VON BÜLOW, B. (1990) [Distribution and habitats of the Ortolan Bunting *Emberiza hortulana* L. 1758 on the edge of the Hohe Mark near Haltern/Westfalen.] *Charadrius* 26: 151–189. (In German.)

BUNDY, G. (1976) Breeding biology of the Red-throated Diver. *Bird Study* 23: 249–256.

BUNN, D. S., WARBURTON, A. B. AND WILSON, R. D. S. (1982) *The Barn Owl.* Calton, U.K.: T. and A. D. Poyser.

BURGER, J. AND GOCHFELD, M. (1987) Nest-site selection by mew gulls (*Larus canus*): a comparison of marsh and dry-land colonies. *Wilson Bull.* 99: 673–687.

BURGESS, N., EVANS, C. AND SORENSON, J. (1990) Heathland management for Nightjars. *RSPB Conserv. Rev.* 4: 32–35.

BURTON, J. A. (1973) *Owls of the world.* London: Eurobook.

BURTON, J. A., ED. (1992) *Owls of the world.* London: Peter Lowe, Eurobook Ltd.

BUSCHE, G. (1989) [Population crash of the Skylark *Alauda arvensis* in the Schleswig-Holstein lowlands.] *Vogelwelt* 110: 51–59. (In German.)

BUTIEV, V. T., ZUBAKIN, V. A., ILIYASHENKO, V. Y., LEBEDEVA, E. A. AND MISTSHENKO, A. L., EDS. (1990) [*Rare birds of the centre of non-chernozem region.*] Moscow: CNIL GLAVOKHOTY RSFR. (In Russian.)

BUZUN, V. A. AND GOLOVACH, O. F. (1992) The Great Bustard in Crimea: preliminary information about its distribution and numbers, the structure of the population and behaviour. *Bustard Studies* 5: 33–51.

BY, R. A. (1990) Migration of Aquatic Warbler in western Europe. *Dutch Birding* 12: 165–181.

CADAMOSTO, L. (c.1507) [*Description of Cadamosto's visit to Madeira in 1455.*] Lisbon: Academia Portuguesa da História. (Manuscript, published 1948.) (In Portugese.)

CADBURY, C. J., HILL, D., PARTRIDGE, J. AND SORENSEN, J. (1989) The history of the Avocet population and its management in England since recolonisation. *RSPB Conserv. Rev.* 3: 9–13.

CADBURY, J. (1992) This illegal killing must stop: a review of bird of prey persecution and poison abuse. *RSPB Conserv. Rev.* 6: 28–35.

CADE, T. J. (1960) Ecology of the Peregrine and Gyr Falcon populations in Alaska. *Univ. Calif. Publ. Zool.* 63: 151–290.

CADE, T. J. (1982) *The falcons of the world.* London: Collins.

CADE, T. J., ENDERSON, J., THELANDER, C. AND WHITE, C., EDS. (1988) *Peregrine Falcon populations: their management and recovery.* Boise, Idaho: Peregrine Fund Inc.

CADENAS, R. (1992) [Spanish Imperial Eagle breeding population in Doñana National Park.] Huelva: Instituto Nacional para la Conservación de la Naturaleza (unpublished report). (In Spanish.)

CAIRNS, D. (1979) Censusing hole-nesting auks by visual counts. *Bird Banding* 50: 358–395.

CAIRNS, D. (1987a) Diet and foraging ecology of Black Guillemots in north-eastern Hudson Bay. *Can. J. Zool.* 65: 1257–1263.

CAIRNS, D. (1987b) The ecology and energetics of chick provisioning by Black Guillemots. *Condor* 89: 627–635.

CALDERÓN, J., CASTROVIEJO, J., GARCÍA, L. AND FERRER, M. (1988) [The Imperial Eagle *Aquila adalberti*: juvenile dispersion, age structure and mortality.] *Doñana Acta Vert.* 15: 79–98. (In Spanish.)

CALVO, B. (in press a) Preferred feeding habitats of Collared Pratincoles *Glareola pratincola* in a breeding area. *Colonial Waterbirds.*

CALVO, B. (in press b) Effects of agricultural land-use on the breeding of Collared Pratincole *Glareola pratincola* in south-west Spain. *Biol. Conserv.*

CAMPBELL, L. H. (1984) The impact of changes in sewage treatment on seaducks wintering in the Firth of Forth, Scotland. *Biol. Conserv.* 28: 173–180.

CAMPBELL, L. H. AND TALBOT, T. R. (1987) Breeding status of Black-throated Divers in Scotland. *Brit. Birds* 80: 1–8.

CAMPHUYSEN, C. J. (1991) [Distribution, diet and feeding behaviour of the Ivory Gull *Pagophila eburnea* around west Spitsbergen.] *Sula* 5: 125–137. (In Dutch.)

CAMPHUYSEN, C. J. (1993) Summer distribution of seabirds and marine mammals in the Greenland Sea, 1985–90. *Sula* 7 (Spec. Issue): 45–64.

CANUT, J., GARCÍA-FERRÉ, D. AND MARCO, J. (1987) [Wintering areas and population trends in steppic species.] Pp.395–419 in [*I International Congress on Steppic Birds.*] León: Junta de Castilla y León. (In Spanish.)

CARBAJO MOLINERO, F. AND FERRERO CANTISÁN, J. J. (1985) Ecology and status of the Black-shouldered Kite in Extremadura, western Spain. Pp.137–141 in I. Newton and R. D. Chancellor, eds. *Conservation studies on raptors*. Cambridge, U.K.: International Council for Bird Preservation (Techn. Publ. 5).

CARLON, J. (1987) [Numbers, distribution and density of the Booted Eagle in the Atlantic Pyrenees.] *Alauda* 55: 89–92. (In French.)

CARY, P. (1973) *A guide to birds of southern Portugal.* Lisbon.

CASADO, M. A., LEVASSOR, C. AND PARRA, C. (1983) [Summer diet of the Pin-tailed Sandgrouse *Pterocles alchata* (L.) in central Spain.] *Alauda* 51: 203–209. (In Spanish.)

CASDA, A. (1964) [Breeding of the Levant Sparrowhawk in Debrecen-Nagyerdö.] *Aquila* 69–70: 248–251. (In Hungarian.)

CASTANEDO, J. L., GARCÍA, P. AND HERNÁNDEZ, A. J. (1987) [Ornithological news.] *Ardeola* 34: 292. (In Spanish.)

CASTANEDO, J. L., FERNÁNDEZ MARTÍN, M. P., GUARDIOLA, A. AND HERNÁNDEZ NAVARRO-ANSE, A. J. (1989) [Ornithological news.] *Ardeola* 36: 263. (In Spanish.)

CASTROVIEJO, J. (1993) *Memoria—Map of the Doñana National Park*. Andalucía: Consejo Superior de Investigaciones Científicas/Agencia de Medio Ambiente de la Junta de Andalucía.

CAVÉ, A. J. (1968) The breeding of the Kestrel, *Falco tinnunculus* L., in the reclaimed area Oostelijk Flecoland. *Netherlands J. Zool.* 18: 313–407.

CAVÉ, A. J. (1981) Purple Heron survival and drought conditions in the wintering area in tropical West Africa. In J. W. Woolfenden, ed. *Progress Report 1980*. Arhem, Netherlands: Inst. Ecol. Res.

CAVÉ, A. J. (1983) Purple Heron survival and drought in tropical West Africa. *Ardea* 71: 217–224.

CEBALLOS, L. AND ORTUÑO, F. (1976) [*Study of the vegetation and forest flora of the western Canary Islands.*] Santa Cruz de Tenerife: Excmo. Cabildo Insular. (In Spanish.)

CEBALLOS, O. AND DONÁZAR, J. A. (1988) [Activity, home range, habitat use and parental care by a pair of Egyptian Vultures (*Neophron percnopterus*) during the post-fledg-ing period.] *Ecología* 2: 275–291. (In Spanish.)

CEBALLOS, O. AND DONÁZAR, J. A. (1989) Factors influencing the breeding density and nest-site selection of the Egyptian Vulture (*Neophron percnopterus*). *J. Orn.* 130: 353–359.

CEBALLOS, O. AND DONÁZAR, J. A. (1990) Roost-tree characteristics, food habits and seasonal abundance of roosting Egyptian Vultures in northern Spain. *J. Raptor Res.* 24: 19–25.

CEBALLOS, P. AND PURROY, F. J. (1981) [*Birds of our countryside and woodlands.*] Madrid: Instituto Nacional para la Conservación de la Naturaleza. (In Spanish.)

CEC (1994) *Special Protection Areas*. Brussels: Commission of the European Communities.

CHANCELLOR, R. D., ED. (1977) *World conference on birds of prey, Vienna 1975*. Cambridge, U.K.: International Council for Bird Preservation.

CHANDRINOS, G. (1981) [Status of large breeding Falconiformes in Greece.] Pp.11–13 in G. Cheylan and G. C. Thibault, eds. [*Mediterranean raptors I*]. Aix-en-Provence, France: Parc Naturel Régional de la Corse/Centre de Recherche Ornithologique de Provence. (In French.)

CHANMAMEDOV, A. I. (1966) [On the biology of Caspian Snowcock *Tetraogallus caspicus*.] *Izv. A.N. Az. SSR Ser. Biol.* 3: 50–54. (In Russian.)

CHAPDELAINE, G., LAPORTE, P. AND NETTLESHIP, D. N. (1987) Population, productivity, and DDT contamination trends of Northern Gannets (*Sula bassanus*) at Bonaventure Island, Quebec, 1967–1984. *Can. J. Zool.* 65: 2922–2926.

CHAPMAN, A. AND BUCK, W. J. (1910) *Unexplored Spain.* London.

CHAPPUIS, C., HEIM DE BALSAC, H. AND VIELLIARD, J. (1973) [Distribution, reproduction, vocalizations and affinities of Cinereous Bunting *Emberiza cineracea*.] *Bonn. Zool. Beitr.* 24: 302–316. (In German.)

CHARMAN, K. (1979) The seasonal pattern of food utilization by *Branta bernicla* on the coast of south-east England. Pp.64–76 in M. Smart, ed. *Proceedings of First Techn. Meeting Western Palearctic Migr. Bird Management*. Slimbridge, U.K.: International Waterfowl and Wetlands Research Bureau.

CHERNICHKO, I. I., GRINCHENKO, A. B., ZHMUD, M. E. AND MOLODAN, G. N. (1990) [The numbers of colonial waders in the southern Ukraine during 1984–1985.] *Ornitologiya* 24: 165–166. (In Russian.)

CHERNOBAY, V. F. (1986) [Fishponds of the steppe zone as ornithological reserves.] Pp.319–320 in [*Studies of U.S.S.R. birds, their conservation and rational use, 2.*] Leningrad: Nauka. (In Russian.)

CHERNOBAY, V. F. (1992) [Rare and vanishing vertebrates.] Pp.90–106 in Anon. ed. [*Red Data Book: Rare and protected plants and animals of the Volgograd region.*] Kniga. (In Russian.)

CHEYLAN, G. (1981) [Role of trophic resource abundance in determining the reproductive success of Bonelli's Eagle, *Hieraaetus fasciatus*, in Provence.] Pp.95–99 in G. Cheylan and G. C. Thibault, eds. [*Mediterranean raptors I*]. Aix-en-Provence, France: Parc Naturel Régional de la Corse/Centre de Recherche Ornithologique dc Provence. (In French.)

CHEYLAN, G. (1991) [The Lesser Kestrel (*Falco naumanni*)

in France: current status and decrease.] *Faune de Provence (CEEP)* 12: 45–49. (In French.)

CHEYLAN, G. (in press) [Bonelli's Eagle.] In D. Yeatman-Berthelot and G. Jarry, eds. [*New atlas of breeding birds of France 1984–1989.*] Paris: Société Ornithologique Française. (In French.)

CHEYLAN, G. AND D. SIMÉON (1984) [Reproduction of Bonelli's Eagle in Provence.] *Bull. Cemt, Rech. Orn. Provence* 6: 36–37. (In French.)

CHEYLAN, G., BENCE, P., BOUTIN, J., DHERMAIN, F., OLIOSO, G. AND VIDAL, P. (1983) [Environment use by the birds of the Crau.] *Biol. Ecol. Medit.* 10: 83–106. (In French.)

CHIAVETTA, M. (1977) Diurnal birds of prey ringed in Europe and in northern Africa shot in Italy from 1969 to 1973. Considerations on the effect of shooting and status of the Italian breeding population. Pp.272–274 in R. D. Chancellor, ed. *Proceedings of the I World Conference on Birds of Prey, Vienna 1975.* Cambridge, U.K.: International Council for Bird Preservation.

CHIAVETTA, M. (1981) [*Raptors of Italy and Europe.*] Milano: Rizzoli. (In Italian.)

CHIAVETTA, M. (1982) [Eleven years of observation on Peregrine *Falco peregrinus* and Lanner *F. biarmicus* in a northern Appennine area: considerations on the population dynamics.] *Proc. I Conv. Ital. Orn., 1981 Aulla.* (In Italian.)

CHIAVETTA, M. AND MARTELLI, D. (1991) [Dynamics of a Lanner *Falco biarmicus* population in the northern Appennines in the last twenty years.] Bologna: INFS. (In Italian.)

CHRISTENSEN, G. C., BOHL, W. H. AND BUMP, G. (1964) A study and review of the common Indian sandgrouse and the Imperial sandgrouse. *U.S. Fish Wildl. Serv. Spec. Sci. Rep.* 84: 1–7.

CHRISTENSEN, J. O., ED. (1990a) [*Status of breeding populations of gulls and terns and others in Denmark 1988.*] Copenhagen: Dansk Ornitologisk Forening. (In Danish.)

CHRISTENSEN, J. O. (1990b) [Presentation of 'Mage-og Ternegruppen'.] *Dansk Ornit. Foren. Tidsskr.* 84: 94–96. (In Danish.)

CHRISTENSEN, S. J. (1974) Notes on the plumage of the female Cyprus Pied Wheatear. *Ornis Scand.* 5: 47–52.

CIACCIO, A., DIMARCA, A., LO VALVO, M. AND SIRACUSA, M. (1989) [Preliminary data on the biology of Lanner in Sicily.] *Ric. Biol. Selv.* 12 (Suppl.): 45–55. (In Italian.)

CIESLAK, M. (1980) [European populations of Osprey *Pandion haliaetus* (L., 1758): the present state and threats.] *Przeglad Zoologiczny* 24: 123–135. (In Polish.)

CIOCHIA, V. (1992) *Pasarile clocitoare din Romania.* Bucuresti: Editura Stiintifica.

CLARK, A. L. AND PEAKALL, D. B. (1977) Organochlorine residues in Eleonora's Falcon, its eggs and its prey. *Ibis* 119: 353–358.

CLARK, N. A. (1989) *Wader migration and distribution in southwest estuaries.* Tring, U.K.: British Trust for Ornithology (Res. Rep. 40).

CLAUSAGER, I. (1972) [*The breeding population of the Woodcock (*Scolopax rusticola*) in Denmark.*] Danske Vildtundersogelser (No. 19). (In Danish.)

CLAUSEN, P. (1991) Light-bellied Brent Goose *Branta bernicla hrota*: phenology, distribution, habitat choice and feeding ecology in Denmark in the 1980s. Zoology Department, Aarhus University (M.Sc. thesis).

CODA–SEO (1985) [*The status of birds in the Iberian peninsula.*] Madrid: Baleares y Macaronesia. (In Spanish.)

COLE, L. R. (1972) On the call of the Black Partridge. *COS (1970) Rep.* 2: 104.

COLLAR, N. J. AND ANDREW, A. (1988) *Birds to watch: the ICBP world check-list of threatened birds.* Cambridge, U.K.: International Council for Bird Preservation (Techn. Publ. 8).

COLLAR, N. J. AND GORIUP, P. D. (1983) Report of the ICBP Fuerteventura Houbara Expedition, 1979. *Bustard Studies* 1: 1–92.

COLLAR, N. J. AND STUART, S. N. (1985) *Threatened birds of Africa and related islands: the ICBP/IUCN Red Data book.* Cambridge, U.K.: International Council for Bird Preservation and International Union for Conservation of Nature.

COLLAR, N. J., CROSBY, M. J. AND STATTERSFIELD, A. J. (1994) *Birds to watch 2: the world list of threatened birds.* Cambridge, U.K.: BirdLife International (BirdLife Conservation Series no. 4).

COLLINS, D. R. (1984a) A study of the Canarian Houbara (*Chlamydotis undulata fuertaventurae*), with special reference to its behaviour and ecology. London: London University (M.Phil. thesis).

COLLINS, D. R. (1984b) Studies of west Palearctic birds, 187. Canary Islands Stonechat. *Brit. Birds* 77: 467–474.

COMBREAU, O. AND GUYOMARC'H, J.-C. (1989) [Seasonal variation in food selection in captive Quail (*Coturnix coturnix coturnix*).] *Cathiers d'Éthologie appliquée* 9: 321–338. (In French.)

COMBREAU, O. AND GUYOMARC'H, J.-C. (1992) Energy intake, breeding success and growth in captive Quail (*Coturnix coturnix coturnix*) in relation to diet. *Gibier Faune Sauvage* 9: 677–692.

COMBREAU, O., FOUILLET, P. AND GUYOMARC'H, J.-C. (1990) [Contribution to the study of the diet and food selection by young Quail (*Coturnix coturnix coturnix*) in the Mon-Saint-Michel Bay.] *Gibier Faune Sauvage* 7: 159–174. (In French.)

COMMITTEE OF EXPERTS FOR LAKE MYVATN RESEARCH (1991) *Effects of the operations of Kísildjan Inc. on the Lake Myvatn biota.* Reykjavik: Ministry of the Environment (mimeographed report).

CONRADS, K. (1968) [On the ecology of the Ortolan Bunting on the edge of the Westfälischen Bucht.] *Vogelwelt* 2 (Suppl.): 7–21. (In German.)

CONSELLERÍA D'AGRICULTURA I PESCA (1988) [Reintroduction project of the Crested Coot in the l'Albufera National park.] Valencia: Generalitat Valenciana. (In Spanish.)

CORTÉS, J. E., FINLAYSON, J. C., MOSQUERA, M. A. AND GARCÍA, E. F. J. (1980) *The birds of Gibraltar.* Gibraltar: Gibraltar Bookshop.

COUNCIL OF EUROPE (1981) [*Birds in need of special protection in Europe.*] Strasbourg: Council of Europe (Collection Sauvegarde de la Nature. 24). (In French.)

COWLEY, E. (1979) Sand Martin population trends in Britain, 1965–1978. *Bird Study* 26: 113–116.

CRAIK, J. C. A. (1990) The price of mink. *Scottish Bird News* 18: 4–5.

CRAMP, S. (1971) Gulls nesting on buildings in Britain and Ireland. *Brit. Birds* 64: 476–487.

CRAMP, S., ED. (1985) *The birds of the western Palearctic*, 4. Oxford: Oxford University Press.

CRAMP, S., ED. (1988) *The birds of the western Palearctic*, 5. Oxford: Oxford University Press.

CRAMP, S., ED. (1992) *The birds of the western Paleartic*, 6. Oxford: Oxford University Press.

CRAMP, S. AND PERRINS, C. M., EDS. (1993) *The birds of the western Palearctic*, 7. Oxford: Oxford University Press.

CRAMP, S. AND PERRINS, C. M., EDS. (1994a) *The birds of the western Palearctic*, 8. Oxford: Oxford University Press.

CRAMP, S. AND PERRINS, C. M., EDS. (1994b) *The birds of the western Palearctic*, 9. Oxford: Oxford University Press.

CRAMP, S. AND SIMMONS, K. E. L., EDS. (1977) *The birds of the western Palearctic*, 1. Oxford: Oxford University Press.

CRAMP, S. AND SIMMONS, K. E. L., EDS. (1980) *The birds of the western Palearctic*, 2. Oxford: Oxford University Press.

CRAMP, S. AND SIMMONS, K. E. L., EDS. (1983) *The birds of the western Palearctic*, 3. Oxford: Oxford University Press.

CRANSWICK, P. A., KIRBY, J. S. AND WATERS, R. J. (1992) *Wildfowl and wader counts 1991–92*. Slimbridge and Thetford: Wildfowl and Wetlands Trust and British Trust for Ornithology.

CRIVELLI, A. J. (1987) The ecology and behaviour of the Dalmatian Pelican *Pelecanus crispus* Bruch, a world endangered species. Commission of the European Communities, DG XII (unpublished report).

CRIVELLI, A. J. (1994) The importance of the former U.S.S.R. for the conservation of pelican populations nesting in the Palearctic. In A. J. Crivelli, V. G. Krivenko and V. G. Vinogradov, eds. *Pelicans in the former U.S.S.R.* Slimbridge, U.K.: International Waterfowl and Wetlands Research Bureau (Spec. Publ. 27).

CRIVELLI, A. J. AND SCHREIBER, R. W. (1984) Status of the Pelecanidae. *Biol. Conserv.* 30: 147–156.

CRIVELLI, A. J., JERRENTRUP, H. AND HALLMANN, B. (1988a) Preliminary results of a complete census of breeding colonial wading birds in Greece, spring 1985–1986. *Bull. Hell. Orn. Soc.* 4: 31–33.

CRIVELLI, A. J., JERRENTRUP, H. AND MITCHEV, T. (1988b) Electric power-lines: a cause of mortality in *Pelecanus crispus* Bruch, a world endangered bird species in Porto-Lago, Greece. *Colonial Waterbirds* 11: 301–305.

CRIVELLI, A. J., FOCARDI, S., FOSSI, C., LEONZIO, C., MASSI, A. AND RENZONI, A. (1989) Trace elements and chlorinated hydrocarbons in eggs of *Pelecanus crispus* a world endangered bird species nesting at Lake Mikri Prespa, north-western Greece. *Environ. Pollut.* 61: 235–247.

CRIVELLI, A. J., CATSADORAKIS, G., JERRENTRUP, H., HATZILACOS, D. AND MITCHEV, T. (1991a) Conservation and management of pelicans nesting in the Palearctic. Pp.137–152 in T. Salathé, ed. *Conservation of migratory birds*. Cambridge, U.K.: International Council for Bird Preservation (Tech. Publ. 12).

CRIVELLI, A. J., LESHEM, Y., MITCHEV, T. AND JERRENTRUP, H. (1991b) Where do Palearctic Great White Pelican (*Pelecanus onocrotalus*) presently overwinter? *Rev. Ecol. (Terre Vie)* 46: 145–171.

CRIVELLI, A. J., MITCHEV, T. AND G. CATSADORAKIS (1991c) Preliminary results on the wintering of Dalmatian Pelican, *Pelecanus crispus*, in Turkey. *Zool. Middle East* 5: 11–20.

CROXALL, J. P., EVANS, P. G. H. AND SCHREIBER, R. W., EDS. (1984) *Status and conservation of the world's seabirds*. Cambridge, U.K.: International Council for Bird Preservation (Techn. Publ. 2).

CUGNASSE, J. M. (1984) [Bonelli's Eagle, *Hieraaetus fasciatus*, in Languedoc-Roussillon.] *Nos Oiseaux* 37: 223–232. (In French.)

CUGNASSE, J. M. (1989) [Protection strategy for Bonelli's Eagles (*Hieraaetus fasciatus*) in Languedoc-Roussillon, France.] *Laufever Seminarbeitr.* 1: 65–66. (In German.)

CUGNASSE, J. M. AND CRAMM, P. (1990) [Wandering Bonelli's Eagle *Hieraaetus fasciatus* in France.] *Alauda* 58: 59–66. (In French.)

CURRY-LINDAHL, K. (1981) *Bird migration in Africa*, 1. London: Academic Press.

CUYÁS, J. (1971) [Some notes on birds observed during three visits to the Canary Islands (1964 and 1967).] *Ardeola* (Spec. vol.): 103–153. (In Spanish.)

DALLINGA, J. H. AND SCHOENMAKERS, S. (1989) [Population changes of the White Stork *Ciconia ciconia* since the 1850s in relation to food resources.] Pp.231–262 in G. Rheinwald, J. Ogden and H. Schulz, eds. [*White stork: status and conservation. Proceedings of the first international stork conservation symposium, Walsrode 14–19 October 1985.*] Braunschweig: Dachverband Deutscher Avifaunisten (Schriftenreihe 10). (In German.)

DANILOV, N. N. (1960) [The avifauna of the Middle Urals and the Transuralia and the history of its formation.] *Trudy Probl. and Temat. Sovetstshaniy Zool. Inst., Leningrad* 9: 73–80. (In Russian.)

DANILOV, N. N., RYZHANOVSKIY, V. N. AND RYABITSEV, V. K. (1984) [*Birds of Yamal.*] Moscow: Nauka. (In Russian.)

DANKO, S. (in press) [Results to date of the ringing of the Imperial Eagle (*Aquila heliaca*) in the north-western part of its breeding area.] Birds of Prey Bulletin 5. (In German.)

DANKO, S. AND CHAVKO, J. (in press) Breeding of the Imperial Eagle in Slovakia. Birds of Prey Bulletin 5.

DAVIDSON, N. C. (1982) Changes in the body condition of Redshanks during mild winters: an inability to regulate reserves? *Ring. Migr.* 4: 51–62.

DAVIDSON, N. C. AND EVANS, P. R., EDS. (1986) *The ecology of migrant Knots in North Norway during May 1985*. Durham: Department of Zoology, Durham University (Report SRG 86/1).

DAVIDSON, N. C. AND EVANS, P. R. (1987) Habitat restoration and creation: its role and potential in the conservation of waders. *Wader Study Group Bull.* 49 (Suppl.): 139–145.

DAVIDSON, N. C. AND EVANS, P. R. (1988) Pre-breeding accumulation of fat and muscle protein by arctic-breeding shorebirds Pp.342–352 in *Acta XIX Congr. Int. Orn.*

DAVIDSON, N. C. AND PIERSMA, T. (1992) The migration of Knots: conservation needs and implications. *Wader Study Group Bull.* 64 (Suppl.): 198–209.

DAVIDSON, N. C. AND ROTHWELL, P. I. (1993) Disturbance to waterfowl on estuaries. *Wader Study Group Bull.* 68 (Special Issue): 97–106.

DAVIDSON, N. C. AND WILSON, J. R. (1992) The migration

system of European-wintering Knots *Calidris canutus islandica*. *Wader Study Group Bull.* 64 (Suppl.): 39–51.

DAVIDSON, N. C., D'A LAFOLEY, D., DOODY, J. P., WAY, L. S., GORDON, J., KEY, R., DRAKE, C. M., PIENKOWSKI, M. W., MITCHEL, R. AND DUFF, K. L. (1991) *Nature conservation and estuaries in Great Britain*. Peterborough, U.K.: Nature Conservancy Council.

DAVIES, N. B. (1977) Prey selection and search strategy of the Spotted Flycatcher. *Anim. Behav.* 25: 1016–1033.

DAVYGORA, A. V. (1985) [Hunting behaviour of harriers.] *Ornitologiya* 20: 182–183. (In Russian.)

DAVYGORA, A. V. (1991) [Analysis of a disturbance factor and its influence upon the Steppe Eagle south of the Ural mountains.] Pp.65–67 in [*Materials of the 10th U.S.S.R. Ornithological Conference, 1.*] Minsk. (In Russian.)

DAVYGORA, A. V. (1992) [The Steppe Eagle.] Pp.41–47 in [*Priroda Nature, 3.*] (In Russian.)

DAVYGORA, A. V. AND BELIK, V. P. (1990) [The Pallid Harrier as a candidate for the Red Data Books of the U.S.S.R. and Russian Federation.] Pp.50–52 in V. I. Il'yashenko, ed. [*Results of studies on rare animals.* Moscow: TSNIL Glavokhota RSFSR. (In Russian.)

DAVYGORA, A. V. AND BELIK, V. P. (1992) The Pallid Harrier *Circus macrourus* as an endangered species in the western Paleartic. Pp.17 in B.-U. Meyburg, ed. *Abstracts IV World Conference on Birds of Prey, Berlin*. Berlin: B.-U. Meyburg World Working Group on Birds of Prey and Owls.

DAVYGORA, A. V., GAVLIUK, E. V. AND KORNEV, S. V. (1989) [Sociable Plover in the steppe of the Cis-Urals.] Pp.88–90 in V. I. Il'yashenko and L. N. Mazin, eds. [*Rare and protected animals.*] Moscow: TSNIL Glavokhota RSFSR. (In Russian.)

DE KNIJFF, P. (1991) Little-known west Palearctic birds: Cinereous Bunting. *Birding World* 4: 384–391.

DELIBES, M., CALDERÓN, J. AND HIRALDO, F. (1975) [Prey selection and food habits of the Golden Eagle (*Aquila chrysaetos*) in Spain.] *Ardeola* 21: 285–303. (In Spanish.)

DE LOPE, F. (1983) [The birds of Vegas Bajas del Guadiana.] *Doñana Acta Vert.* 10: 91–121. (In Spanish.)

DEMENTIEV, G. P. AND GLADKOV, N. A., EDS. (1951a) [*Birds of the Soviet Union, 1.*] Moscow: Sovetskaya Nauka. (In Russian.)

DEMENTIEV, G. P. AND GLADKOV, N. A., EDS. (1951b) [*Birds of the Soviet Union, 2.*] Moscow: Sovetskaya Nauka. (In Russian.)

DEMENTIEV, G. P. AND GLADKOV, N. A., EDS. (1951c) [*Birds of the Soviet Union, 3.*] Moscow: Sovetskaya Nauka. (In Russian.)

DEMENTIEV, G. P. AND GLADKOV, N. A., EDS. (1952) [*Birds of the Soviet Union, 4.*] Moscow: Sovetskaya Nauka. (In Russian.)

DEMENTIEV, G. P. AND GLADKOV, N. A., EDS. (1954a) [*Birds of the Soviet Union, 5.*] Moscow: Sovetskaya Nauka. (In Russian.)

DEMENTIEV, G. P. AND GLADKOV, N. A., EDS. (1954b) [*Birds of the Soviet Union, 6.*] Moscow: Sovetskaya Nauka. (In Russian.)

DHKD (Dogal Hayati Koruma Dernegi) (1992) *Towards integrated management in the Göksu delta, a protected special area in Turkey*. Istanbul, Turkey: Dogal Hayati Koruma Dernegi.

DHONDT, A. A. (1983) Variation in the number of overwintering Stonechats possibly caused by natural selection. *Ring. Migr.* 4: 155–158.

DIAS, D. (1992) Rock (*Alectoris graeca*) and Chukar (*A. chukar*) Partridge introductions in Portugal and their possible hybridisation with Red-legged Partridges (*A. rufa*): a research project. *Gibier Faune Sauvage* 9: 781–784.

DÍAZ, M. (1991) [Granivorous animal communities in areas of cereal crops in the Iberian peninsula.] Madrid: Universidad Complutense de Madrid (Ph.D. thesis). (In Spanish.)

DÍAZ, M., NAVESO, M. A. AND REBALLO, E. (in press) [Impact of agricultural intensification on the steppe bird communities in the northern plateau of Palencia-Valladolid.] *Aegypius*. (In Spanish.)

DICK, W. J. A., PIENKOWSKI, M. W., WALTNER, M. AND MINTON, C. D. T. (1976) Distribution and geographical origins of Knot *Calidris canutus* wintering in Europe and Africa. *Ardea* 64: 22–47.

DIDILLON, M. C. (1988) [Diet of a hybrid partridge (*Alectoris graeca saxatilis* × *Alectoris rufa rufa*) in the Alpes-Maritimes.] *Gibier Faune Sauvage* 5: 149–170. (In French.)

DIEHL, B. (1971) [Energy requirements of nestling and fledgling Red-backed Shrike.] *Eko polska* 19: 235–248. (In Polish.)

DINESMAN, L. G. (1960) [*Changes in the environment of lowland area north-west of the Caspian Sea.*] Moscow. (In Russian.)

DIRKSEN, S. AND BEEKMAN, J. H. (1991) Population size, breeding success and distribution of Bewick's Swan *Cygnus columbianus bewickii* wintering in Europe 1986–87. Pp.120–124 in J. Sears and P. J. Bacon, eds. *Third IWRB International Swan Symposium, Oxford 1989*. Wildfowl (Suppl. 1).

DIVOKY, G. J. (1976) The pelagic feeding habits of Ivory and Ross's Gull. *Condor* 78: 85–90.

DMOKHOVSKY, A. V. (1933) [Birds of the middle and lower Pechora region.] *Bull. Soc. Nat., Moskou. Ser. Biol.* 42: 214–242. (In Russian.)

DOBINSON, H. M. AND RICHARDS, A. J. (1964) The effects of the severe winter of 1962/63 on the birds of Britain. *Brit. Birds* 57: 373–434.

DoE (Department of the Environment) (1992) *Code of practice for the release of captive bred Barn Owls in Britain*. London: Department of the Environment.

DOFF (1989) [*Breeding Bird Report 1988.*] Copenhagen: Dansk Ornitologisk Forenings Fugleregistrerringsgruppe. (In Danish.)

DOLGUSHIN, I. A. (1960) [*The birds of Kazakhstan, 1.*] Alma-Ata: Akademii Nauk Kazakhskoy SSR. (In Russian.)

DOLGUSHIN, I. A. (1962) [Waders.] Pp.40–245 in I. A. Dolgushin, ed. [*The birds of Kazakhstan, 2.*] Alma-Ata: Akademii Nauk Kazakhskoy SSR. (In Russian.)

DOLZ, J. C., DIES, I. AND BELLIURE, J. (1990) [Colonies of Collared Pratincole (*Glareola pratincola* Linn 1766) in the Valencian community.] *Medi Natural* 1–2: 69–80. (In Spanish.)

DOLZ GARCÍA, J. C., GIMÉNEZ RIPOLL, M. AND HUERTAS PEDRERO, J. (1991) Status of some threatened Anatidae species in the Comunidad Valenciana, east Spain. *IWRB Threatened Waterfowl Res. Group Newsl.* 1: 7–8.

DOMÍNGUEZ, F. AND DÍAZ, G. (1985) [*Plan for the recu-*

peration of the Canarian Houbara.] Santa Cruz de Tenerife: Servício Provincial del Instituto Nacional para la Conservación de la Naturaleza. (In Spanish.)

DONÁZAR, J. A. AND CEBALLOS, O. (1988) [Food habits and breeding success of the Egyptian Vulture *Neophron percnopterus* in Navarra.] *Ardeola* 35: 3–14. (In Spanish.)

DONÁZAR, J. A. AND FERNANDEZ, C. (1990) Population trends of the Griffon Vulture (*Gyps fulvus*) in northern Spain between 1969 and 1989 in relation to conservation measures. *Biol. Conserv.* 53: 83–91.

DONÁZAR, J. A., CEBALLOS, O. AND FERNANDEZ, C. (1985) Factors influencing the distribution and abundance of seven cliff-nesting raptors: a multivariate study. Pp.545–549 in B.-U. Meyburg and R. D. Chancellor, eds. *Raptors in the modern World: proceedings of the III World conference on birds of prey and owls. Eilat, Israel 22–27 March 1987.* Berlin and London: World Working Group on Birds of Prey and Owls.

DONCHEV, S. (1961) [The birds of Vitosha Mountain.] *Bull. Inst. Zool. and Museum* 10: 59–137. (In Bulgarian with German summary.)

DONCHEV, S. (1970) [The birds of Western Balkan Range.] *Bull. Inst. Zool. and Museum* 31: 45–92. (In Bulgarian with German summary.)

DONCHEV, S. (1974) [The birds of Central and Eastern Balkan Range.] *Bull. Inst. Zool. and Museum* 41: 33–63. (In Bulgarian with German summary.)

DORNBUSCH, M. (1992) [Ethology and diet of the Black Stork.] Pp.217–220 in J.-L. Mériaux, A. Schierer, C. Tombal and J.-C. Tombal, eds. [*The storks of Europe.*] Metz: Institute Europeen d'Ecologie/AMBE. (In German.)

DOVRAT, E. (1991) The Kefar Kassem raptor migration survey, autumns 1977–1987: a brief summary. Pp.13–30 in D. Yekutiel, ed. *Raptors in Israel: passage and wintering populations.* Eilat: International Birdwatching Center, Eilat.

DROZDOV, N. N. AND ZLOTIN, R. I. (1962) [On the geography of the winter population of birds in the subalpine belt of the Central Caucasus.] *Ornitologiya* 5: 193–207. (In Russian.)

DUBOIS, P. AND MAHÉO, R. (1986) [*Nesting waders of France.*] Rochefort: Ministère de l'Environnement/LPO/BIROE. (In French.)

DUCKWORTH, W. (1992) Decline of the Turtle Dove in the Saltford area. *Bristol Orn.* 21: 64–66.

DU FEU, C. (1993) *Nestboxes.* Thetford: British Trust for Ornithology.

DUHAUTOIS, L. (1984a) [Inventory of heron populations, 1983 season: Population estimates of the Great Bittern and the Little Bittern.] S.N.P.N., Direction de la protection de la nature, Secrétariat Etat à l'Environnement et à la Qualité de la Vie. (In French.)

DUHAUTOIS, L. (1984b) [*Marsh herons of France: status in 1983.*] Paris: Société Nationale Protection Nature. (In French.)

DUNN, E. K. (1972) Effect of age on the fishing ability of Sandwich Terns *Sterna sandvicensis. Ibis* 114: 360–366.

DUNN, E. K. AND MEAD, C. J. (1982) Relationship between sardine fisheries and recovery rates of ringed terns in West Africa. *Seabird* 6: 98–104.

DURANGO, S. (1946) [The Roller (*Coracias g. garrulus* L.) in Sweden.] *Vår Fågelv.* 5: 145–190. (In Swedish with English summary.)

DURANGO, S. (1950) The influence of climate on the distribution and breeding success of the Red-backed Shrike. *Fauna och Flora* 46: 49–78.

DURINCK, J., SKOV, H. AND ANDELL, P. (1992) Action preparatory to the establishment of a protected areas network in the German Bight and the Baltic Sea. Copenhagen: Ornis Consult (unpublished report).

DURINCK, J., SKOV, H., JENSEN, F. P. AND PIHL, J. (1994) *Important marine areas for wintering seabirds in the Baltic Sea.* Copenhagen: Ornis Consult.

DWENGER, R. (1991) [*The Grey Partridge.*] Wittenberg Lutherstadt: Ziemsen Verlag. (In German.)

DYBBRO, T. (1970) The Kentish Plover *Charadrius alexandrinus* as a breeding bird in Denmark. *Dansk Ornit. Foren. Tidsskr.* 64: 205–222. (In Danish with English summary.)

DYBBRO, T. (1980) [*Threatened Danish birds.*] Copenhagen: Dansk Ornitologisk Forening. (In Danish.)

DYRCZ, A. (1992) [*Chlidonias hybridus.*] Pp.188–189 in Z. Glowacinski, ed. [*Polish Red Data Book of Animals.*] Warszawa: PWRIL. (In Polish.)

DYRCZ, A. (1993) Nesting biology of the Aquatic Warbler *Acrocephalus paludicola* on the Biebrza marshes (NE Poland). *Vogelwelt* 114: 2–15.

DYRCZ, A. AND CZERASZKIEWICZ, R. (in press) Report concerning number, distribution, conservation and threats of the Aquatic Warbler *Acrocephalus paludicola* in Poland. *Notatki Orn.*

DYRCZ, A. AND ZDUNEK, W. (1993) Breeding ecology of the Aquatic Warbler *Acrocephalus paludicola* on the Biebrza marshes, NE Poland. *Ibis* 135: 181–189.

DYRCZ, A., OKULEWICZ, J., TOMIALOJC, L. AND WITKOWSKI, J. (1972) [Breeding avifauna of the Biebrza Marshes and adjacent territories.] *Acta Orn.* 13: 343–422. (In Polish.)

DYRCZ, A., OKULEWICZ, J., WITKOWSKI, J., JESIONOWSKI, J., NAWROCKI, P. AND WINIECKI, A. (1984) Birds of fens in Biebrza Marshes. Faunistic approach. *Acta Orn.* 20: 1–108.

DYRCZ, A., GRABINSKI, W., STAWARCZYK, T. AND WITKOWSKI, J. (1991) [*Birds of Silesia: a faunistic monograph.*] Wroclaw: Wroclaw University. (In Polish.)

EBBINGE, B. (1982) The status of *Branta leucopsis* in 1980–81. *Aquila* 89: 151–161.

EBBINGE, B. (1991) The impact of hunting on mortality rates and spatial distribution of geese wintering in the western Palearctic. *Ardea* 79: 197–210.

EBD (European Bird Database) (1994) BirdLife International/European Bird Census Council European Bird Database. Cambridge, U.K.

VAN EERDEN, M. R. AND ZIJLSTRA, M. (1986) [Nature of the IJsselmeer area: prognosis for some nature of the IJsselmeer area following construction of Markerwaard.] Lelystad, Netherlands: Rijkdienst voor de IJsselmeerpolders (unpublished report). (In Dutch.)

EGDELL, J. M. (1993) *Impact of agricultural policy on Spain and its steppe regions.* Sandy, U.K.: Royal Society for the Protection of Birds.

EGOROV, V. A. (1990) [Data on birds of prey in Kalbin upland (eastern Kazakhstan).] Pp.53–62 in L. V. Viktorov, ed. [*Fauna and ecology of animals.*] Tver: Tver State University. (In Russian.)

EHRLICH, H. AND SAMWALD, O. (1990) [A native resource for the Roller (*Coracias garrulus*) in Styria, Austria.]

Vogelschutz in Österreich 5: 31–33. (In German.)

EINARSSON, A. (1988) Distribution and movements of Barrow's Goldeneye *Bucephala islandica* young in relation to food. *Ibis* 130: 153–163.

EINARSSON, A. (1990) Settlement into breeding habitats by Barrow's Goldeneyes *Bucephala islandica*: evidence for temporary oversaturation of preferred habitat. *Ornis Scand.* 21: 7–16.

EINARSSON, A. (1991) [*Salmon in the upper part of the River Laxá. Probable effects of salmon planting on the biota.*] Reykjavik: Nature Conservation Council (mimeographed report 22). (In Icelandic.)

ELLENBERG, H. (1986) [Why does the Red-backed Shrike decline in central Europe? Considerations on the effects of pesticides and landscape changes in wintering and breeding areas.] *Corax* 12: 34–46. (In German.)

ELLENBERG, H., RÜGER, A. AND VAUK, G. (1989) [*Eutrophication: the most serious threat in nature conservation.*] Norddeutsche Naturschutzakademie (Berichte 2). (In German.)

EL MASTOUR, A. (1988) [The Turtle Dove (*Streptopelia turtur*): biology, ecology and hunting legislation in Morocco.] *Bull. mens. ONC* 127: 43–45. (In French.)

ELÓSEGUI, I. (1989) [*Griffon Vulture and Egyptian Vulture: bibliographic synthesis and research.*] Acta Biologica Montana. Pau: Pau University (Série Documents de Travail 3). (In French.)

ELÓSEGUI, J. (1985) [*Atlas of breeding birds of Navarra.*] Pamplona: Caja de Ahorros de Navarra. (In Spanish.)

ELVELAND, J. AND TJERNBERG, M. (1984) [The vegetation on some display grounds of the Great Snipe *Gallinago media* in Sweden.] *Memoranda Soc. Fauna Flora fenn.* 60: 125–140. (In Finnish.)

EMMERSON, K. W. (1985) [The study of the biology and ecology of the Bolle's Pigeon *Columba bollii* and the White-tailed Laurel Pigeon *Columba junoniae* with views on their conservation, 2.] Santa Cruz de Tenerife: Ornistudio S.L. (unpublished). (In Spanish.)

EMMERSON, K. W., MARTÍN, A., DELGADO, G. AND QUILIS, V. (1986) Distribution and some aspects of the breeding biology of Bolle's Pigeon (*Columba bollii*) on Tenerife. *Vogelwelt* 107: 52–65.

EMMERSON, K. W., BARONE, R. B., LORENZO, J. A. AND NARANJO, J. J. (1993) [The census and analysis of the ornithological community of the National Park of Garajonay.] Santa Cruz de Tenerife: Ornistudio S.L. (unpublished). (In Spanish.)

ENA, V., MARTÍNEZ, A. AND THOMAS, D. H. (1987) Breeding success of the Great Bustard *Otis tarda* in Zamora Province, Spain, in 1984. *Ibis* 129: 364–370.

ENEMAR, A. (1980) [A trial with special nestboxes to get the Redstart to breed at higher than normal density in subalpine birch forest in southern Lapland.] *Vår Fågelv.* 39: 231–236. (In Swedish.)

ENGELMOER, M. AND BLOMERT, A.-M. (1985) [*Breeding biology of the Avocet along the Frisian Wadden Sea coast, 1983 season.*] Lelystad, Netherlands: Rijksdienst voor de IJsselmeerpolders. (RIJP Rep., 1985–39abw). (In Dutch.)

ENS, B. J., WINTERMANS, G. J. M. AND SMIT, C. J. (1993) [Distribution of wintering waders in the Dutch Wadden Sea.] *Limosa* 66: 137–144. (In Dutch.)

EPFT (1989) *Wetlands of Turkey.* Ankara, Turkey: Environmental Problems Foundation of Turkey.

ERHARD, R. AND WINK, M. (1987) [Fluctuations of breeding populations in the Bonn area: analysis of grid mapping in 1975 and 1985.] *J. Orn.* 128: 477–484. (In German.)

ERIKSSON, M. O. G. (1985) Prey detectability for fish-eating birds in relation to fish density and water transparency. *Ornis Scand.* 16: 1–7.

ERIKSSON, M. O. G. (1986) Fish delivery, production of young, and nest density of Osprey (*Pandion haliaetus*) in south-west Sweden. *Can. J. Zool.* 64: 1961–1965.

ERIKSSON, M. O. G. (1987a) [The production of young in Black-throated Diver *Gavia arctica* in south-west Sweden.] *Vår Fågelv.* 46: 172–186. (In Swedish with English summary.)

ERIKSSON, M. O. G. (1987b) Some effects of freshwater acidification on birds in Sweden. Pp.183–190 in A. W. Diamond and F. L. Filion, eds. *The value of birds.* Cambridge, U.K.: International Council for Bird Preservation (Techn. Publ. 6).

ERIKSSON, M. O. G. (1994) Susceptibility of freshwater acidification by two species of loon: Red-throated Loon *Gavia stellata* and Arctic Loon *Gavia arctica* in south-west Sweden. *Hydrobiologia* 279/280: 439–444.

ERIKSSON, M. O. G. AND SUNDBERG, P. (1991) The choice of fishing lakes by the Red-throated Diver *Gavia stellata* and Black-throated Diver *G. arctica* during the breeding season in south-west Sweden. *Bird Study* 38: 135–144.

ERIKSSON, M. O. G., ARVIDSSON, B. L. AND JOHANSSON, I. (1988) [Habitat characteristics of Red-throated Diver, *Gavia stellata*, breeding lakes in south-west Sweden.] *Vår Fågelv.* 47: 122–132. (In Swedish with English summary.)

ERIKSSON, M. O. G., BLOMQUIST, D., HAKE, M. AND JOHANSSON, O. (1990) Parental feeding in the Red-throated Diver *Gavia stellata. Ibis* 132: 1–13.

ERIKSSON, M. O. G., JOHANSSON, I. AND AHLGREN, C.-G. (1992) Levels of mercury in eggs of Red-throated Diver *Gavia stellata* and Black-throated Diver *Gavia arctica* in south-west Sweden. *Ornis Svecica* 2: 29–36.

VON ESSEN, L. (1991) A note on the Lesser White-fronted Goose *Anser erythropus* in Sweden and the results of a re-introduction scheme. *Ardea* 79: 305–306.

VON ESSEN, L. (1993) [Project description and results until November 1992.] Swedish Hunters Association (unpublished). (In Swedish.)

ESTAFIEEV, A. A. (1991) [*Fauna and ecology of waders of Bolshezemelskaya tundra and Yugorski peninsula.*] Leningrad: Nauka. (In Russian.)

ESTAFJEV, A. A. (1977) [Birds of the western slope of the Cis-Polar Urals.] *Trudy Komi Filiala Akad. Nauk SSR, Syktyvkar* 34: 44–101. (In Russian.)

ESTAFJEV, A. A. (1981) [Present state, distribution and protection of birds in the taiga zone of the Pechora river basin.] *Acad. Sci USRR, Syktyvkar* (Scientific Reports) 68: 1–54. (In Russian.)

ESTAFJEV, A. A. (1982) [Time of arrival, breeding and departure of birds nesting in the tiaga zone of the Pechora river basin.] Pp.25–34 in M. I. Braude, ed. [*Fauna of Ural mountains and adjacent territories*]. Sverd Urals University. (In Russian.)

EVANS, M. I. (1994) *Important Bird Areas in the East.* Cambridge, U.K.: BirdLife International

Conservation Series no. 2).

EVANS, P. G. H. (1984) Status and conservation of seabirds in north-west Europe (excluding Norway and the U.S.S.R.). Pp.293–321 in J. P. Croxall, P. G. H. Evans and R. W. Schreiber, eds. *Status and conservation of the world's seabirds*. Cambridge, U.K.: International Council for Bird Preservation (Techn. Publ. 2).

EVERETT, M. AND SHARROCK, J. T. R. (1980) The European atlas: owls. *Brit. Birds* 73: 239–256.

EVERETT, W. T., WARD, M. L. AND BOGLIANI, J. J. (1989) Birds observed in the Central Bering Sea pack-ice in February and March 1983. *Gerfaut* 79: 159–166.

EWINS, P. (1985) Colony attendance and censusing of Black Guillemots *Cepphus grylle* in Shetland. *Bird Study* 32: 176–185.

EWINS, P. (1988) An analysis of ringing recoveries of Black Guillemots *Cepphus grylle* in Britain and Ireland. *Ring. Migr.* 9: 95–102.

EWINS, P. (1990) The diet of Black Guillemots *Cepphus grylle* in Shetland. *Holarctic Ecol.* 13: 90–97.

EWINS, P. J. AND TASKER, M. L. (1985) Breeding distribution of Black Guillemot *Cepphus grylle* in Orkney and Shetland, 1982–1984. *Bird Study* 32: 186–193.

EXO, K.-M. AND HENNES, R. (1980) [A contribution to the population of the Little Owl *Athene noctua*: an analysis of ringing recoveries from Germany and the Netherlands.] *Die Vogelwarte* 30: 162–179. (In German.)

FABER, F. (1822) [*Introduction to the ornithology of Iceland, or history of the birds of Iceland.*] Copenhagen. (In German.)

FARINHA, J. C. (1991) [*Urgent measures for the conservation of the Chough* Pyrrhocorax pyrrhocorax *in Portugal.*] Lisbon: Servicio Nacional de Parques, Reservas e Conservaçao da Natureza (Estudos de Biología e Conservaçao da Natureza 2). (In Portuguese.)

FASCE, P. AND FASCE, L. (1984) [*The Golden Eagle in Italy.*] Parma: Lega Italiana Protezione Uccelli. (In Italian.)

FASCE, P., FASCE, L. AND TORRE, J. (1989) Census and observations on the biology of the Bearded Vulture *Gypaetus barbatus* on Corsica. Pp.336–341 in B.-U. Meyburg and R. Chancellor, eds. *Raptors in the modern World: proceedings of the III World conference on birds of prey and owls. Eilat, Israel 22–27 March 1987*. Berlin and London: World Working Group on Birds of Prey and Owls.

FASOLA, M. (1986) Resource use of foraging herons in agricultural and non-agricultural habitats in Italy. *Colonial Waterbirds* 9: 139–148.

FASOLA, M., BARBIERI, F., PRIGIONI, C. AND BOGLIANI, G. (1981) [Herons in Italy, 1981.] *Avocetta* 5: 107–131. (In Italian.)

FEDIUSHIN, A. V. AND DOLBIK, M. S. (1967) [*Birds of Belarus.*] Minsk: Nauka i Tekhnika. (In Russian.)

[...]EZ, C. (1991) [*Census of cliff-nesting raptors in Golden Eagle, Bonelli's Eagle, Egyptian Vul-[...]ine Falcon.*] Pamplona: Servicio de Medio [...] de Navarra. (In Spanish.)

[...]ND FERNÁNDEZ-CRUZ, M. (1991) [...]Spain.] *Quercus* 60: 8–16.

[...]AYA, C. (1991) [Biology of [...]cristata*) in Cádiz and other [...]quivir.] Pp.97–117 in Agencia

de Medio Ambiente, ed. [*Plan for the use and management of nature reserves in Cádiz lagoons.*] Sevilla: Agencia de Medio Ambiente, Junta de Andalucía. (In Spanish.)

FERRER, M. AND CALDERÓN, J. (1990) The Spanish Imperial Eagle *Aquila adalberti* Brehm 1861 in Doñana National Park (South West Spain): a study of population dynamics. *Biol. Conserv.* 51: 151–161.

FERRER, M., DE LA RIVA, M. AND CASTROVIEJO, J. (1986) [Birds die on electric poles of Doñana.] *Trophy* 191.

FERRER, M., DE LA RIVA, M. AND CASTROVIEJO, J. (1991) Electrocution of raptors on power-lines in south-western Spain. *J. Field Orn.* 62: 181–190.

FERRER, M., GUYONNE, J. AND CHACÓN, M. L. (1993) [Avian mortality in electric power-lines: present situation in Spain.] *Quercus* 94: 20–29. (In Spanish.)

FERRER, M., MARTÍNEZ-VILALTA, A. AND MUNTANER, J. (1986) [*Natural history of Catalonia: Birds.*] Barcelona: Enciclopèdia Catalana. (In Catalan.)

FERRERO, J. J. AND ROMAN, J. A. (1987) [Studies of the Black Stork in Extremadura. II: nest sites and nesting habitat.] *Alytes* 5: 19–46. (In Spanish.)

FÉSÜS, I., MÁRKUS, F., SZABÓ, G., TÖLGYESI, I., VARGA, Z. AND VERMES, L. (1990–1991) *Interaction between agriculture and the environment in Hungary*. Cambridge, U.K.: International Union for Conservation of Nature and Natural Resources (Env. Res. Ser. 5).

FIEDLER, G. AND WISSNER, A. (1980) [Overhead cables as a lethal threat for White Storks *Ciconia ciconia*.] *Ökol. Vögel* 2: 59–109. (In German.)

FINLAYSON, J. C. AND CORTES, J. E. (1987) The birds of the Strait of Gibraltar. *Alectoris* 6: 1–74.

FINLAYSON, M., ED. (1992a) *Wetland conservation and management in the lower Volga, Russia*. Slimbridge, U.K.: International Waterfowl and Wetlands Research Bureau. (Spec. Publ. 18).

FINLAYSON, M. (1992b) *A strategy and action plan to conserve the wetlands of the Lower Volga*. Slimbridge, U.K.: International Waterfowl and Wetlands Research Bureau.

FINLAYSON, C. M., HOLLIS, G. E. AND DAVIS, T. J., EDS. (1992) *Managing Mediterranean wetlands and their birds: proceedings of an International Waterfowl and Wetlands Research Bureau international symposium, Grado, Italy, February 1991*. Slimbridge, U.K.: International Waterfowl and Wetlands Research Bureau (Spec. Publ. 20).

FINTHA, J. (1993) Resting cranes in Hungary. Int. Crane Conference 21–24 January, Orellana La Vieja, Spain.

FIR (1992) [Supervision of threatened raptor's eyries.]*Bull. du Fonds d'Intervention pour les Rapaces* 21: 10–17. (In French.)

FIR/UNAO (1984) [*Estimation of numbers of nesting diurnal and non-rock-dwelling raptors in France: survey 1979–1982.*] Paris: Ministère de l'Environnement. (In French.)

FISCHER, W. (1984) [*The Sea Eagle,Haliaeetus.*] Wittenberg Lutherstadt: Ziemsen Verlag. (In German.)

FIUCZYNSKI, D. AND WENDLAND, P. (1968) [Population dynamics of Black Kite (*Milvus migrans*) in Berlin: observations from 1952–1967.] *J. Orn.* 109: 462–471. (In German.)

FLADE, M. (1991) [The habitat of Corncrakes in the breeding season in three European valleys (Aller, Save,

Biebrza).] *Vogelwelt* 112: 16–40. (In German.)

FLINT, P. R. AND STEWART, P. F. (1992) *The birds of Cyprus*. Second edition. Tring, U.K.: British Ornithologists' Union (Check-list 6).

FLINT, V. AND MISHCHENKO, A. L. (1991) The Great Bustard in the U.S.S.R.: status and conservation. Pp.89–92 in P. D. Goriup, L. A. Batten and J. A. Norton, eds. *The conservation of lowland dry grassland birds in Europe*. Peterborough, U.K.: Joint Nature Conservation Committee.

FLINT, V. AND SOROKIN, A. G. (1992) The legal situation of birds of prey in the former U.S.S.R. *Bull. World Working Group on Birds of Prey* 16/17: 7–8.

FLINT, V. E., GRAZHDANKIN, A. V., KOSTIN, A. B., PERERVA, V. I. AND DOBROV, S. G. (1983) [Prevention of loss of raptors on electric power-lines.] Pp.21–25 in V. E. Flint, ed. [*Conservation of raptors*.] Moscow: Nauka. (In Russian.)

FOLKESTAD, A. O. (1982) The effect of Mink predation on some seabird species. *Viltrapport* 21: 42–49.

FORESTRY COMMISSION (1989) *Native pinewoods grants and guidelines*. Edinburgh: Forestry Commission.

FORSLUND, M. (1993) [Bird Crime Guard.] *Vår Fågelv.* 2: 17–19. (In Swedish.)

FOUARGE, J. P. (1992) [Record of two Imperial Eagles *Aquila heliaca adalberti* in the region of Chechaouen.] *Porphyrio* 4: 25–28. (In French.)

FOX, A. D. (1988) Breeding status of the Gadwall in Britain and Ireland. *Brit. Birds* 81: 51–66.

FOX, A. D. AND SALMON, D. G. (1989) The winter status and distribution of the Gadwall in Britain and Ireland. *Bird Study* 36: 37–44.

DE FRANCESCHI, P. (1988) [Status of Galliformes population in Italy. Recent and current research. Problems of management and perspectives for the future.] *Ric. Biol. Selv. (Suppl.)* 14: 129–168. (In Italian.)

FRANKENVOORT, W. AND HUBATSCH, H. (1966) [*Our Stonechat*.] Wittenberg Lutherstadt: Ziemsen Verlag. (In German.)

FRANTZEN, B. (1985) [Occurrences of Steller's Eider *Polysticta stelleri* in Finmark in the period 1970 to 1984.] *Vår Fuglefauna* 8: 15–18. (In Norwegian.)

FRANTZEN, B. AND HENRIKSEN, G. (1992) [Steller's Eider in Finnmark 1985–1992.] *Fauna* 45: 100–107. (In Norwegian.)

FRISCH, T. AND MORGAN, W. C. (1979) Ivory Gull colonies in south-eastern Ellesmere Island, Arctic Canada. *Can. Field-Nat.* 93: 173–174.

FRUGIS, S. AND SCHENCK, H. (1981) Red list of Italian birds. *Avocetta* 5: 133–141.

FRY, C. H. (1984) *The bee-eaters*. Calton, U.K.: T. and A. D. Poyser.

FRY, C. H., FRY, K. AND HARRIS, H. (1992) *Kingfishers, bee-eaters and rollers: a handbook*. London: Christopher Helm.

FULLER, R. J., HILL, D. AND TUCKER, G. M. (1991) Feeding the birds down on the farm: perspectives from Britain. *Ambio* 20: 232–237.

FURNESS, R. W. (1987) Seabirds as monitors of the marine environment. Pp.217–230 in A. W. Diamond and F. L. Filion, eds. *The value of birds*. Cambridge, U.K.: International Council for Bird Preservation (Techn. Publ. 6).

FURNESS, R. W., GREENWOOD, J. J. D. AND JARVIS, P. J.

(1993) Can birds be used to monitor the environment? Pp.1–41 in R. W. Furness and J. D. D. Greenwood, eds. *Birds as monitors of environmental change*. London: Chapman and Hall.

GALLEGO, S., RODRIGUEZ-TEIJEIRO, J. D. AND PUIGCERVER, M. (1990) [The Quail.] *Trofeo* 241: 40–43. (In Spanish.)

GALUSHIN, V. M. (1962) [The Greater Spotted Eagle in the Oka river valley and its predatory pressure upon populations of some birds.] Pp.115–151 in S. P. Naumov, ed. [*Collection of papers*.] Moscow: Moscow Pedagogical Institute (No. 186).

GALUSHIN, V. M. (1982) [Adaptations of birds of prey to recent human influences.] *Zool. Zh.* 61: 1088–1096. (In Russian.)

GALUSHIN, V. M. (1991a) Status and protection of birds of prey in the U.S.S.R. Pp.35–38 in M. Stubbe, ed. *The population biology of raptors and owls*, 2. Halle, Germany: Martin-Luther University.

GALUSHIN, V. M. (1991b) The status and protection of birds of prey in the European part of the U.S.S.R. *Bull. World Working Group on Birds of Prey* 14 (Newsl.): 9–10.

GALUSHIN, V. M. (1992) The Saker Falcon *Falco cherrug* in European Russia and Ukraine. In B.-U. Meyburg, ed. *Abstracts IV World Conference on Birds of Prey, Berlin*. Berlin: B.-U. Meyburg World Working Group on Birds of Prey and Owls.

GALUSHIN, V. (1993) Status and distribution of the Pallid Harrier. Pp.4 in *Abstracts Ecology and Conservation of Pallid Harriers, Raptor Research Foundation First European Meeting, Canterbury*. Canterbury: Kent University.

GALUSHIN, V. M. (in press) Long-term changes in birds of prey populations within European Russia and neighbouring countries. In W. Hagemeijer and T. Verstrael, eds. *Bird Numbers 1992: distribution, monitoring and ecological aspects*. Proceedings 12th International Conference of IBCC and EOAC. Voorburg: SOVON–CBS.

GALUSHIN, V. M., TURCHIN, V. G., ZLYDNEVA, O. V. AND SUPONEVA, E. I. (1991) [The Montagu's Harrier in the Kamennaya steppe (Voronezh region).] Pp.136–138 in V. M. Galushin, ed. [*Abstracts 10th U.S.S.R. Ornithological Conference, part 2*.] Vitebsk, Minsk: Nauka i Tekhnika. (In Russian.)

GAME CONSERVANCY (1992) *Wild partridge management*. Fordingbridge, U.K.: Game Conservancy Ltd.

GAME CONSERVANCY (1993) *Game, set-aside and match*. Fordingbridge, U.K.: Game Conservancy Trust (Factsheet 3).

GARCÍA, L. (1972) [Verification of the first breeding of Trumpeter Finch *Rodopechys githaginea* in south-west Europe.] *Ardeola* 16: 215–222. (In Spanish.)

GARCÍA, L., CALDERÓN, J. AND CASTROVIEJO, J. (1987) [Wintering and occasional records of some bird species in the Doñana National Park, 1985–1986.] Patronato del Parque Nacional de Doñana. (In Spanish.)

GARCIA DORY, M. A. (1983) [Data on the ecology of the genus *Pyrrhocorax* (*P. pyrrhocorax* and *P. graculus*) in the mountains of Covadonga National Park, Asturi... *Alytes* 1: 411–448. (In Spanish.)

GARDARSSON, A. (1975) [The birds of Icelandic wetl... *Rit Landverndar* 4: 100–134. (In Icelandic with... summary.)

GARDARSSON, A. (1978) [Distribution and num...

Barrow's Goldeneye *Bucephala islandica* in Iceland.] *Náttúrufraedingurinn* 48: 162–191. (In Icelandic with English summary.)

GARDARSSON, A. (1979) Waterfowl populations of Lake Myvatn and recent changes in numbers and food habits. *Oikos* 32: 250–270.

GARDARSSON, A. AND EINARSSON, A. (in press) Responses of breeding duck populations to changes in food supply. *Hydrobiologia.*

GARRIDO, M. AND ALBA, E. (1985) [Ornithological news.] *Ardeola* 32: 424. (In Spanish.)

GARRIGÓS, B. AND SARGATAL, J. (1990) [Crested Coot Project, July 1989–1990.] DEPANA. (In Spanish.)

GARZA, V. AND SUÁREZ, F. (1990) [Distribution, population and habitat selection of Dupont's Lark *Chersophilus duponti* on the Iberian peninsula.] *Ardeola* 37: 3–12. (In Spanish.)

GARZÓN, J. (1973) [Contribution to the status, diet and conservation of Falconiformes in central Spain.] *Ardeola* 19: 279–330.

GARZÓN, J. (1974a) [Census of Imperial Eagle.] *Adena* 2: 11–19. (In Spanish.)

GARZÓN, J. (1974b) [A contribution to the study of status, feeding and protection of Falconiformes in central Spain.] *Ardeola* 19: 279–330. (In Spanish.)

GARZÓN, J. (1977) Birds of prey in Spain, the present situation. Pp.159–170 in R. D. Chancellor, ed. *Proceedings of the World Conference on Birds of Prey, Vienna 1975.* Cambridge, U.K.: International Council for Bird Preservation.

GASTON, A. (1968) The birds of the Ala Dagh Mountains, southern Turkey. *Ibis* 110: 17–26.

GAVRILOV, E. I. (1972) [Black-throated Accentor *Prunella atrogularis* Brandt.] Pp.349–357 in M. N. Korelov and A. F. Kovshar, eds. [*The birds of Kazakhstan*, 4]. Alma-Ata: Akademii Nauk Kazakhskoy SSR. (In Russian.)

GAVRIN, V. F., DOLGUSHIN, N. A. AND KORELOV, M. N. (1962) [*The birds of Kazakhstan*, 2.] Alma-Ata: Akademii Nauk Kazakhskoy SSR. (In Russian.)

GEIDE, G. M. (1989) [Birds and mammals of the proposed Orenburg steppe reserve.] Pp.17–18 in [*Materials of the 1st regional conference of Orenburg naturalists.*] Orenburg. (In Russian.)

GÉNSBØL, B. (1987) *Birds of prey in Britain and Europe.* London: Collins.

GÉNSBØL, B. (1988) [*Guide to diurnal raptors (Europe, North Africa and the Middle East).*] Paris: Delachaux et Niestlé. (In French.)

GÉNSBØL, B. (1991) [*Birds of Prey.*] München: BLV Verlagsgesellschaft. (In German.)

GÉNSBØL, B. (1984) *Birds of prey of Britain and Europe, North Africa and the Middle East.* London: Collins.

~RGE, M. (1992) *The land use, ecology and conserva-* *Broadland.* Chichester: Packard.

AND ALEXANDROV, D. (1988) [A contribu- ~una of Vasiliovska Mountain.] *Orn. Inf.* 'In Bulgarian.)

~nal and nocturnal raptors in Niestlé (1965–1984). (In

ND CHAPMAN, R. A. (1993) birds in Britain and Ireland .: T. and A. D. Poyser.

GILBERT, G. ET AL. (in prep.) Vocal individuality as a census tool.

GIL-DELGADO, J. (1981) Breeding bird community in orange groves. Pp.100–106 in F. J. Purroy, ed. *Proceedings VII International Conference Bird Census Work.* León: León University.

GJERTZ, I., MEHLUM, F. AND GABRIELSEN, G. W. (1985) Food samples analysis of seabirds collected during 'Lance'-cruise in ice-filled waters in eastern Svalbard 1984. *Norsk Polarinst. Rapp.* 23.

GLOWACINSKI, Z., ED. (1992) [*Polish Red Data Book of animals.*] Warszaw: Panstowowe Wydawnictwo Rolniczei i Lesne. (In Polish.)

GLUE, D. (1971) Ringing recovery circumstances of some small birds of prey. *Bird Study* 18: 137–146.

GLUE, D. AND SCOTT, D. (1980) Breeding biology of the Little Owl. *Brit. Birds* 73: 167–180.

GLUTZ VON BLOTZHEIM, U. N., ED. (1964) [*The breeding birds of Switzerland.*] Aarau: Schweizerische Vogelwarte Sempach. (In German.)

GLUTZ VON BLOTZHEIM, U. N. AND BAUER, K. M., EDS. (1980) [*Handbook of the birds of central Europe*, 9.] Wiesbaden: Akademische Verlagsgesellschaft. (In German.)

GLUTZ VON BLOTZHEIM, U. N. AND BAUER, K. M., EDS. (1982) [*Handbook of the birds of central Europe*, 8.] Wiesbaden: Akademische Verlagsgesellschaft. (In German.)

GLUTZ VON BLOTZHEIM, U. N. AND BAUER, K. M., EDS. (1985) [*Handbook of the birds of central Europe*, 10.] Wiesbaden: Aula-Verlag. (In German.)

GLUTZ VON BLOTZHEIM, U. N. AND BAUER, K. M., EDS. (1988) [*Handbook of the birds of central Europe*, 11.] Wiesbaden: Aula-Verlag. (In German.)

GLUTZ VON BLOTZHEIM, U. N. AND BAUER, K. M., EDS. (1993) [*Handbook of the birds of central Europe*, 13.] Wiesbaden: Aula-Verlag. (In German.)

GLUTZ VON BLOTZHEIM, U. N., BAUER, K. M. AND BEZZEL, E., EDS. (1971) [*Handbook of the birds of central Europe*, 4.] Frankfurt: Akademische Verlagsgesellschaft. (In German.)

GLUTZ VON BLOTZHEIM, U. N., BAUER, K. M. AND BEZZEL, E., EDS. (1973) [*Handbook of the birds of central Europe*, 5.] Frankfurt: Akademische Verlagsgesellschaft. (In German.)

GLUTZ VON BLOTZHEIM, U. N., BAUER, K. M. AND BEZZEL, E., EDS. (1975) [*Handbook of European birds*, 6.] Wiesbaden: Akademische Verlagsgesellschaft. (In German.)

GLUTZ VON BLOTZHEIM, U. N., BAUER, K. M. AND BEZZEL, E., EDS. (1977) [*Handbook of the birds of central Europe*, 7.] Wiesbaden: Akademische Verlagsgesellschaft. (In German.)

GODMAN, F. (1872) Notes on the resident and migratory birds of Madeira and the Canaries. *Ibis* 3: 209–224.

DE GOEIJ, P. J., VAN DER HAVE, T. M., KEIJL, G. O., VAN ROOMEN, M. W. J. AND RUITERS, P. S. (1992) The network of wetlands for waterbird migration in the eastern Mediterranean. Pp.70–72 in C. M. Finlayson, G. E. Hollis and T. J. Davis, eds. *Managing Mediterranean wetlands and their birds: proceedings of an International Waterfowl and Wetlands Research Bureau international symposium, Grado, Italy, February 1991.* Slimbridge, U.K.:

International Waterfowl and Wetlands Research Bureau (Spec. Publ. 20).

GOLOVAN, V. I. (1985) [The data on the biology of the Spotted Flycatcher in the north-west of U.S.S.R.] Pp.10–22 in I. V. Prokofyeva, ed. [*Ecology and breeding*.] Leningrad. (In Russian.)

GOLOVATSH, O. F., GRISHTSHENKO, V. AND SEREBRIAKOV, V. V. (1990) [Actual number, distribution and migration of the Black Stork in Ukraine.] Pp.191–203 in B. P. Savickij and E. G. Samusienko, eds. [*Storks: distribution, ecology, conservation*.] Minsk: Nauka i Tekhnika. (In Russian.)

GOLOVKIN, A. N. (1984) Seabirds nesting in the U.S.S.R.: the status and protection of populations. Pp.473–486 in J. P. Croxall, P. G. H. Evans and R. W. Schreiber, eds. *Status and conservation of the world's seabirds*. Cambridge, U.K.: International Council for Bird Preservation (Techn. Publ. 2).

GOMERSALL, C. H. (1986) Breeding performance of the Red-throated Diver *Gavia stellata* in Shetland. *Holarctic Ecol*. 9: 277–284.

GOMN (1989) [Atlas of the breeding birds of Normandy.] *Cormoran* 7. (In French.)

GONZÁLEZ, J. L. AND MERINO, M. (1988) [Census of the breeding population of the Black Stork in Spain.] *Quercus* 30: 12–17. (In Spanish.)

GONZÁLEZ, J. L., GARZÓN, P. AND MERINO, M. (1990) [Census of the Lesser Kestrel population of Spain.] *Quercus* 49: 6–12. (In Spanish.)

GONZÁLEZ, L. M. (1990) [Survey of the breeding populations of Spanish Imperial Eagle and Black Vulture in Spain.] *Quercus* 58: 16–22. (In Spanish.)

GONZÁLEZ, L. M. (1991) [*Natural history of the Spanish Imperial Eagle* Aquila adalberti *Brehm, 1861*.] Madrid: Instituto Nacional para la Conservación de la Naturaleza, Ministerio de Agricultura (Colección Técnica). (In Spanish.)

GONZÁLEZ, L. M., ED. (in press) [*Recovery plan for the Spanish Imperial Eagle (Aquila adalberti)*.] Madrid: Instituto Nacional para la Conservación de la Naturaleza. (In Spanish.)

GONZÁLEZ, L. M., GONZÁLEZ, J. L., GARZÓN, J. AND HEREDIA, B. (1986) [Evolution of the Black Vulture population in the Iberian peninsula during the period 1974–1984.] In *IV Cong. Int. Aves de Presa del Mediterraneo. Evora, September 1986, Portugal*. (In Spanish.)

GONZÁLEZ, L. M., GONZÁLEZ, J. L., GARZÓN, J. AND HEREDIA, B. (1987) [Census and geographic distribution of Spanish Imperial Eagle *Aquila adalberti* in Spain during 1981–1986.] *Bol. Est. Cent. Ecol*. 31: 99–110. (In Spanish.)

GONZÁLEZ, L. M., HEREDIA, B., GONZÁLEZ, J. L. AND ALONSO, J. C. (1989a) Juvenile dispersal of the Spanish Imperial Eagle (*Aquila adalberti*). *J. Field Orn*. 60: 369–379.

GONZÁLEZ, L. M., HIRALDO, F., DELIBES, M. AND CALDERÓN, J. (1989b) Reduction in the range of the Spanish Imperial Eagle (*Aquila adalberti*) since AD 1850. *J. Biogeogr*. 16: 305–315.

GONZÁLEZ, L. M., BUSTAMANTE, J. AND HIRALDO, F. (1990) Factors influencing the present distribution of the Spanish Imperial Eagle *Aquila adalberti*. *Biol. Conserv*. 51: 311–320.

GONZÁLEZ, L. M., BUSTAMANTE, J. AND HIRALDO, F. (1992) Nesting habitat selection by the Spanish Imperial Eagles *Aquila adalberti*. *Biol. Conserv*. 59: 45–50.

GOODMAN, S. M. AND MEININGER, P. L. (1989) *The birds of Egypt*. Oxford: Oxford University Press.

GOODWIN, D. (1985) Turtle Dove decline. *Brit. Birds* 78: 598.

GORBAN, I. M. (1991) [Fluctuations in the Whiskered Tern breeding range.] Pp.160 in V. M. Galushin, ed. [*Abstracts 10th U.S.S.R. Ornithological Conference, part 2*.] Vitebsk, Minsk: Nauka i Tekhnika. (In Russian.)

GORDIENKO, N. S. (1991) [Biology and numbers of Sociable Plover in Kustanay steppe.] *Ornitologiya* 25: 54–61. (In Russian.)

GORE, M. E. J. (1980) Millions of Turtle-Doves. *Malimbus* 2: 78.

GORIUP, P. D. (1982) Houbara Bustard research and conservation in Pakistan. Pp.267–272 in P. D. Goriup and H. Vardhan, eds. *Bustards in Decline*. Jaipur: TWSI.

GORIUP, P. D. (1987) Some notes on the status and management of bustards with special reference to the European species. Pp.7–26 in S. Farago, ed. *Proceedings of the symposium on the Great Bustard* (Otis tarda): *nure cnservancy and beeding of the potected secies*. Budapest: Conseil International de la Chasse et de la Conservation du Gibier.

GORIUP, P. D., ED. (1988) *Ecology and conservation of grassland birds*. Cambridge, U.K.: International Council for Bird Preservation (Techn. Publ. 7).

GORIUP, P. D. AND BATTEN, L. (1990) The conservation of steppic birds: a European perspective. *Oryx* 24: 215–223.

GORIUP, P. D. AND PARR, D. F. (1985) Results of the ICBP survey of Turkey, 1981. *Bustard Studies* 2: 77–98.

GORIUP, P. D. AND SCHULZ, H. (1991) Conservation management of the White Stork: an international need and opportunity. Pp.97–127 in T. Salathé, ed. *Conserving migratory birds*. Cambridge, U.K.: International Council for Bird Preservation (Techn. Publ. 12).

GORIUP, P. D., BATTEN, L. A. AND NORTON, J. A., EDS. (1991) *The conservation of lowland dry grassland birds in Europe*. Peterborough, U.K.: Joint Nature Conservation Committee.

GOSS-CUSTARD, J. D. AND MOSER, M. E. (1988) Rates of change in the numbers of Dunlin *Calidris alpina*, wintering in British estuaries in relation to *Spartina anglica*. *J. Appl. Ecol*. 25: 95–109.

GOSS-CUSTARD, J. D., JONES, R. E. AND NEWBERY, P. E. (1977) The ecology of the Wash. I: the distribution and diet of wading birds (Charadrii). *J. Appl. Ecol*. 14: 681–700.

GOSSOW, H., HAFNER, F., PSEINER-PETRJANOS, S., VONKILCH, G. AND WATZINGER, G. (1992) The status of Grey Partridge (*Perdix perdix*) and Rock Partridge (*Alectoris graeca*) populations in relation to human land use in Austria: a review. *Gibier Faune Sauvage* 9: 515–521.

GÖTMARK, F., NEERGAARD, R. AND ÅHLUND, M. (1989) Nesting ecology and management of the Arctic Loon in Sweden. *J. Wildl. Manage*. 53: 1025–1031.

GÖTMARK, F., NEERGAARD, R. AND ÅHLUND, M. (1990) Predation of artificial and real Arctic Loon nests in Sweden. *J. Wildl. Manage*. 54: 429–432.

GOUTNER, V. (1987a) Breeding population and distribution changes of Avocets and Red-winged Pratincoles in the

Evros delta, Greece, 1980–1987. *Wader Study Group Bull.* 51: 26.

GOUTNER, V. (1987b) Vegetation preferences by colonies of Mediterranean Gulls (*Larus melanocephalus*) and Gull-billed Terns (*Gelochelidon nilotica*) in the Evros delta. *Seevögel* 8: 29–31.

GRANVAL, P. (1988) [Influence of the availability and accessibility of earthworms on the choice of habitats used by Woodcock (*Scolopax rusticola* L.).] Pp.60–66 in P. Havet and G. Hirons, eds. *Proc. 3rd European Woodcock and Snipe Workshop*. Slimbridge, U.K.: International Waterfowl and Wetlands Research Bureau. (In French.)

GRANVAL, P. AND MUYS, B. (1992) Management of forest soils and earthworms to improve Woodcock (*Scolpax* sp.) habitats: a literature survey. *Gibier Faune Sauvage* 9: 243–255.

GRASTVEIT, J. (1975) [Cleaning of oil damaged birds.] *Lappmeisen* 1: 22–25. (In Norwegian.)

GREEN, A. J. (1993) *The status and conservation of the Marbled Teal* Marmaronetta angustirostris. Slimbridge, U.K.: International Waterfowl and Wetlands Research Bureau (Spec. Publ. 23).

GREEN, A. J. AND ANSTEY, S. (1992) The status of the White-headed Duck *Oxyura leucocephala. Bird Conserv. Internatn.* 2: 185–201.

GREEN, A. J., HILTON, G. M., HUGHES, B., FOX, A. D. AND YARAR, M. (1993) *The ecology and behaviour of the White-headed Duck* Oxyura leucocephala *at Burdur Gölü, Turkey, February–March 1993*. Slimbridge, U.K.: Widlfowl and Wetlands Trust.

GREEN, I. A. AND MOORHOUSE, C. N. (1989) White-headed Duck in Turkey. A study of their breeding status and distribution (unpublished report).

GREEN, R. (1978) Factors affecting the diet of farmland Skylarks *Alauda arvensis. J. Anim. Ecol.* 47: 913–928.

GREEN, R. E. (1980) Food selection by Skylarks and grazing damage to sugar beet seedlings. *J. Appl. Ecol.* 17: 613–630.

GREEN, R. E. (1984) The feeding ecology and survival of partridge chicks (*Alectoris rufa* and *Perdix perdix*) on arable farmland in East Anglia. *J. Appl. Ecol.* 21: 817–830.

GREEN, R. E. (1988) Stone Curlew conservation. *RSPB Conserv. Rev.* 2: 30–33.

GREEN, R. (1992) The ornithological importance of the Danube delta and Lakes Razim Sinue. Pp.61–70 in IUCN, ed. *Conservation status of the Danube delta*. Norwich, U.K.: Page Brothers (IUCN Environmental Status Rep. 4).

GREEN, R. E. AND GRIFFITHS, G. H. (1994) Use of preferred nesting habitat of Stone Curlews *Burhinus oedicnemus* in relation to vegetation structure. *J. Zool., Lond.* 233: 457–471.

GREEN, R. E. AND HIRONS, G. J. M. (1991) The relevance of population studies to the conservation of threatened birds. Pp.594–633 in C. M. Perrins, J.-D. Lebreton and G. J. M. Hirons, eds. *Bird population studies: relevance to conservation and management*. Oxford, U.K.: Oxford University Press.

GREEN, R. E., CADBURY, C. J. AND WILLIAMS, J. (1987) [Floods threaten Black-tailed Godwits breeding in the Ouse Washes.] *RSPB Conserv. Rev.* 1: 14–16.

GRETTON, A. (1991) *The ecology and conservation of the Slender-billed Curlew* (Numenius tenuirostris). Cam-

bridge, U.K.: International Council for Bird Preservation (Monogr. 6).

GRETTON, A. (in press a) An estimate of the current population of the Slender-billed Curlew. In *Plan to save* Numenius tenuirostris. Brussels: European Commission.

GRETTON, A. (in press b) Slender-billed Curlew database: an update. In *Plan to save* Numenius tenuirostris. Brussels: European Commission.

GRIBBLE, F. C. (1983) Nightjars in Britain and Ireland in 1981. *Bird Study* 30: 165–176.

GRIMMETT, R. F. A. AND JONES, T. A. (1989) *Important bird areas in Europe*. Cambridge, U.K.: International Council for Bird Preservation (Techn. Publ. 9).

GRUBAC, B. R. (1986) The Golden Eagle (*Aquila chrysaetos chrysaetos*) in south-eastern Yugoslavia. *Larus* 38/39: 95–135.

GRUBAC, B. (1991) Present status of vultures in Macedonia. Pp.139–147 in Instituto Nacional para la Conservación de la Naturaleza, ed. *I International Cogress on scavanging birds*. Madrid: Instituto Nacional para la Conservación de la Naturaleza.

GRUBAC, R. B. (1991) Status and biology of the Bearded Vulture *Gypaetus barbatus aureus* in Macedonia. *Birds of Prey Bull.* 4: 101–117.

GUADALFAJARA, R. AND TUTOR, E. (1987) [Study of the habitat requirements of Sandgrouse in the steppes of the Ebro depression, Spain.] Pp.241–254 in Consejeria de Agricultura, ed. [*First International Congress on Steppic birds*.] León: Junta de Castilla y León. (In Spanish.)

GUDMUNDSSON, F. (1971) [The Harlequin Duck (*Histrionicus histrionicus*) in Iceland.] *Náttúrufraedingurinn* 41: 1–28, 64–98. (In Icelandic with English summary.)

GUDMUNDSSON, F. (1979) The past status and exploitation of the Myvatn waterfowl populations. *Oikos* 32: 232–249.

GURNEY, J. H. (1913) *The Gannet, a bird with a history*. London: H. F. and G. Witherby.

GÜRPINAR, T. AND WILKINSON, W. H. N. (1970) Wildfowl status in Turkey. Pp.174–176 in Y. A. Isakov, ed. *Proceedings of the International Regional Meeting on Conservation of Wildfowl Resources, Leningrad, U.S.S.R., 25–30 September 1968*.

GUTIÉRREZ, A., JIMÉNEZ, B., MALO, J. E., LEVASSOR, C., PECO, B. AND SUÁREZ, F. (1993) [The changes in the countryside: lessons for the future.] *Quercus* 88: 14–17. (In Spanish.)

GUYOMARC'H, J.-C. (1992) [Structure, functioning and microevolution in Quail (*Coturnix c. coturnix*) populations of the western Palearctic.] *Gibier Faune Sauvage* 9: 387–401. (In French.)

GUYOMARC'H, J.-C. (in press) [The Quail (*Coturnix coturnix coturnix*).] In M. Berthelot and G. Jarry, eds. [*Atlas of breeding birds 1985–1989.*] Paris: Société Ornithologique de France. (In French.)

GUYOMARC'H, J.-C. AND SAINT-JALME, M. (1986) [Reproduction in the Quail (*Coturnix coturnix*). II: growth and sexual maturation in chicks.] *Gibier Faune Sauvage* 3: 281–295. (In French.)

GUYOT, A. (1990) [First confirmed breeding of Black-winged Kite *Elanus caeruleus* in France.] *Nos Oiseaux* 40: 465–477. (In French.)

HAFNER, H. (1977) [Contribution to the ecology of four species of heron (*Egretta g. garzetta, Ardeola r. ralloides, A. i. ibis, Nycticorax nycticorax*).] Toulouse: Paul Sabatier

University (thesis). (In French.)

HAFNER, H. (1980) [Ecological studies of four nesting herons *Egretta garzetta, Ardeola ralloides, Ardea purpurea* and *Nycticorax nycticorax* in the Camargue.] *Bonn. Zool. Beitr.* 31: 249-287. (In French.)

HAFNER, H. AND FASOLA, M. (1992a) Workshop on colonial waterbirds in the Mediterranean: a summary. *Colonial Waterbirds* 15: 159–160.

HAFNER, H. AND FASOLA, M. (1992b) The relationship between feeding habitat and colonial-nesting Ardeidae. Pp.194–201 in C. M. Finlayson, G. E. Hollis and T. J. Davis, eds. *Managing Mediterranean wetlands and their birds: proceedings of an International Waterfowl and Wetlands Research Bureau international symposium, Grado, Italy, February 1991.* Slimbridge, U.K.: International Waterfowl and Wetlands Research Bureau (Spec. Publ. 20).

HAFNER, H. AND WALLACE, J. P. (1988) Population changes in Camargue Ardeids. The effect of climatic conditions in the wintering areas. *Bull. Col. Waterbird Soc.* 12: 29.

HAFNER, H., BOY, V. AND GORY, G. (1982) Feeding methods, flock size and feeding success in the Little Egret *Egretta garzetta* and the Squacco Heron *Ardeola ralloides* in Camargue, southern France. *Ardea* 70: 45–54.

HAFTORN, S. (1971) [*Birds of Norway.*] Oslo: Universitetsforlaget. (In Norwegian.)

HAGA, A. (1980) [Management of the Red-throated Diver and Crane in south-eastern Norway.] *Fauna Norv. Ser. C, Cinclus* 33: 129–136. (In Norwegian with English summary.)

HAGEN, Y. (1960) [Snowy Owl on the Hardangervidda in the summer of 1959.] *Medd. Stall.-Viltunders* 2: 1–25. (In Swedish.)

HÅGVAR, S., HÅGVAR, G. AND MØNNESS, E. (1990) Nest site selection in Norwegian woodpeckers. *Holarctic Ecol.* 13: 156–165.

HAHNKE, H. AND BECKER, T. (1986) [Artificial nest-sites for the Black Tern: an effective contribution to species preservation.] *Falke* 33: 116–122. (In German.)

HAILA, Y., JÄRVINEN, O. AND VÄISÄNEN, R. A. (1980) Effects of changing forest structure on long-term trends in bird populations in south-west Finland. *Ornis Scand.* 11: 12–22.

HAILA, Y., JÄRVINEN, O. AND RAIVIO, S. (1987) Quantitative versus qualitative distribution patterns of birds in the western Palearctic taiga. *Ann. Zool. Fenn.* 24: 179–194.

HAKALA, A. V. K. (1975) An Ivory Gull colony at Lardyfjellet, Spitsbergen. *Sterna* 14: 91–94.

HAKALA, A., KAIKUSALO, A. AND RIKKONEN, M. (1974) [The return of the Snowy Owl.] *Suomen Luonto* 33: 278–280. (In Swedish.)

HÅKANSON, L. (1980) The quantitative impact of pH, bioproduction and Hg-contamination on the Hg-content of fish (pike). *Environ. Pollut. Serv. Bull.* 1: 285–304.

HALE, W. G. (1980) *Waders.* London: Collins.

HALLER, H. (1982) [Dispersion and population dynamics of Golden Eagles *Aquila chrysaetos* in the Central Alps.] *Der Ornithologische Beobachter* 79: 163–211. (In German.)

HALLMANN, B. (1985) Status and conservation problems of birds of prey in Greece. Pp.55–59 in I. Newton and R. D. Chancellor, eds. *Conservation studies on raptors.* Cambridge, U.K.: International Council for Bird Preservation

(Techn. Publ. 5).

HALLMANN, B. (1993) Black Vulture conservation in Greece (unpublished report).

HÄLTERLEIN, B. AND STEINHARDT, B. (1993) [Breeding bird populations on the German North Sea coast in 1991: 5th Report of the Seabird Protection Working Group.] *Seevögel* 14: 1–5. (In German.)

HAMPICKE, U. (1978) Agriculture and conservation—ecological and social aspects. *Agriculture and the Environment* 4: 25–42.

HANCOCK, J. AND ELLIOT, H. (1978) *The herons of the world.* London: Harper and Row.

HANCOCK, J. AND KUSHLAN, J. (1984) *The herons handbook.* London: Croom Helm.

HANCOCK, J. A., KUSHLAN, J. A. AND KAHL, M. P. (1992) *Storks, ibises and spoonbills of the world.* London: Academic Press.

HANDRINOS, G. I. (1985a) Migrant raptors shot in Greece. *Bull. World Working Group on Birds of Prey* 2: 153–156.

HANDRINOS, G. I. (1985b) The status of vultures in Greece. Pp.103–115 in I. Newton and R. D. Chancellor, eds. *Conservation studies on raptors.* Cambridge, U.K.: International Council for Bird Preservation (Techn. Publ. 5).

HANDRINOS, G. I. (1991) The status of geese in Greece. *Ardea* 79: 175–178.

HANDRINOS, G. AND DEMETROPOULOS, A. (1983) *Birds of prey of Greece.* Athens: P. Efstathiadis and Sons S.A.

HARDY, A. R., STANLEY, P. I. AND GREIG-SMITH, P. W. (1987) Birds as indicators of the intensity of use of agricultural pesticides in the U.K. Pp.119–132 in A. W. Diamond and F. L. Filion, eds. *The value of birds.* Cambridge, U.K.: International Council for Bird Preservation (Techn. Publ. 6).

HARIO M. (1985) [Factors affecting the breeding success of gulls in the Gulf of Finland.] *Soumen Riista* 32: 23–31. (In Finnish.)

HARRIS, M. P. (1984) *The Puffin.* Calton, U.K.: T. and A. D. Poyser.

HARRIS, M. P. AND BAILEY, R. S. (1992) Mortality rates of Puffin *Fratercula arctica* and Guillemot *Uria aalge* and fish abundance in the North Sea. *Biol. Conserv.* 60: 39–46.

HARRIS, M. P. AND WANLESS, S. (1991) Population studies and conservation of Puffins *Fratercula arctica.* Pp.230–248 in C. M. Perrins, J.-D. Lebreton and G. J. M. Hirons, eds. *Bird population studies.* Oxford: Oxford University Press.

HARRISON, C. (1982) *An atlas of the birds of the western Palearctic.* London: Collins.

HARRISON, P. (1983) *Seabirds: an identification guide.* Beckenham, U.K.: Croom Helm.

HARVEY, P. (1983) *Breeding seabird populations, Isles of Scilly.* Taunton, U.K.: Nature Conservancy Council.

HAURI, R. (1973) [On the occurrence of Red-crested Pochard *Netta rufina* in the Aare land south of Bern.] *Orn. Beob.* 70: 57–66. (In German.)

VAN DER HAVE, T. M., VAN DEN BERK, V., CRONAU, J. AND LANGEVELD, M., EDS. (1988) *South Turkey project: a survey of waders and waterfowl on the Cukurova deltas, spring 1987.* Zeist, Netherlands: Foundation Working Group International Wader and Waterfowl Research.

VAN DER HAVE, T. M., VAN DEN BERK, V. M., CRONAU, J. P. AND LANGEVELD, M. J. (1989) Importance of the Çukurova deltas, southern Turkey, for migrating waders and other waterbirds in spring. *Sandgrouse* 11: 76–88.

HAVELKA, P. AND RÜGE, K. (1993) [Population trends of woodpeckers (Picidae) in the Federal Republic of Germany.] *Veröff. Natursch. Landschaftspfl. Bad.-Wurtt.* 67: 33–38. (In German.)

HAVERSCHMIDT, F. (1978) [*The Black Tern* Chlidonias niger.] Wittenberg Lutherstadt: Ziemsen Verlag. (In German.)

HEIM DE BALSAC, H. AND MAYAUD, N. (1962) [*The birds of north-west Africa*.] Paris: Paul Leclevalier. (In French.)

HELANDER, B. (1977) [The White-tailed Eagle in Sweden.] Pp.319–329 in R. D. Chancellor, ed. *World conference on birds of prey, Vienna 1975*. Cambridge, U.K.: International Council for Bird Preservation. (In Swedish.)

HELANDER, B. (1983) *Reproduction of the White-tailed Sea Eagle* Haliaeetus albicilla *(L.) in Sweden, in relation to food and residue levels of organochlorine and mercury compounds in the eggs*. Stockholm: University of Stockholm/Swedish Society for the Conservation of Nature.

HELANDER, B. AND GÄRDEHAG, P. (1989) [*The Sea Eagle*.] Stockholm. (In Swedish.)

DEN HELD, J. J. (1981) Population changes in the Purple Heron in relation to drought in the wintering area. *Ardea* 69: 185–191.

HELLE, P. AND JÄRVINEN, O. (1986) Population trends of north Finnish landbirds in relation to their habitat selection and changes in forest structure. *Oikos* 46: 107–115.

HELLMICH, J. (1992a) [Impact of pesticide use: a case study on Great Bustard.] *Ardeola* 39: 7–22. (In Spanish.)

HELLMICH, J. (1992b) [Habitat and territory of the Blue Rock Thrush (*Monticola s. solitarius* in a sierra of Extremadura.] XI Jornadas Ornitológicas Españolas, Mérida, Spain, January 1992 (poster). (In Spanish.)

HEMKE, E. (1983) [On the nesting of the Osprey in the German Democratic Republic.] *Lounais-Hameen Luonto* 69: 32–35. (In Finnish.)

HENDERSON, I. G., PEACH, W. J. AND BAILLIE, S. R. (1993) *The hunting of Snipe and Woodcock in Europe: a ringing recovery analysis*. Thetford: British Trust for Ornithology (Research Rep. 115).

HENNIPMAN, E. (1961) [Results of the Dutch biological expedition to Turkey in 1959.] *Levende Nat.* 64: 3–27. (In Dutch.)

HENRY, J. AND MONNAT, J. Y. (1981) [*Marine birds of the French Atlantic*.] Brest: Societé pour l'Etude et la Protection de la Nature en Bretagne. (In French.)

HEPBURN, I. R. (1984) *Migratory bird hunting in European Community countries*. Brussels: Federation of Hunting Associations of the EEC.

HEPBURN, I. R. (1987) Conservation of wader habitats in coastal West Africa. *Wader Study Group Bull.* 49 (Suppl.): 125–127.

HEREDIA, B. (1991a) [Coordinated action plan.] Pp.117–124 in R. Heredia and B. Heredia, eds. [*The Bearded Vulture* (Gypaetus barbatus) *in the Pyrenees: ecological characteristics and biological conservation*.] Madrid: Instituto Nacional para la Conservación de la Naturaleza. (In Spanish.)

HEREDIA, R. (1991b) [Distribution and population status.] Pp.27–37 in R. Heredia and B. Heredia, eds. [*The Bearded Vulture* (Gypaetus barbatus) *in the Pyrenees: ecological characteristics and biological conservation*.] Madrid: Instituto Nacional para la Conservación de la Naturaleza.

(In Spanish.)

HEREDIA, R. (1991c) [Juvenille dispersal.] Pp.67–76 in R. Heredia and B. Heredia, eds. [*The Bearded Vulture* (Gypaetus barbatus) *in the Pyrenees: ecological characteristics and biological conservation*.] Madrid: Instituto 2Nacional para la Conservación de la Naturaleza.

HEREDIA, R. (1991d) [Feeding.] Pp.79–88 in R. Heredia and B. Herdia, eds. [*The Bearded Vulture* (Gypaetus barbatus) *in the Pyrenees: ecological characteristics and biological conservation*.] Madrid: Instituto Nacional para la Conservación de la Naturaleza. (In Spanish.)

HEREDIA, R. (1991e) [Supplementary feeding.] Pp.101–108 in R. Heredia and B. Heredia, eds. [*The Bearded Vulture* (Gypaetus barbatus) *in the Pyrenees: ecological characteristics and biological conservation*.] Madrid: Instituto Nacional para la Conservación de la Naturaleza. (In Spanish.)

HEREDIA, R. AND DONÁZAR, J. A. (1990) High frequency of polyandrous trios in an endangered population of lammergeiers *Gypaetus barbatus* in northern Spain. *Biol. Conserv.* 53: 163–171.

HERNÁNDEZ, M. (1988) Road mortality of the Little Owl (*Athene noctua*) in Spain. *J. Raptor Res.* 22: 81–84.

HERRANZ, J., YANES, M. AND SUÁREZ, F. (1993) [First records on the diet of Dupont's Lark, *Chersophilus duponti*, nestlings in the Iberian peninsula.] *Ardeola* 40: 77–79. (In Spanish.)

HERRERA, C. (1980) [Composition and structure of two passerine Mediterranean communities.] *Doñana Acta Vertebrata* 7: 1–340. (In Spanish.)

HESS, R. (1983) [Distribution, density and habitat of *Picoides tridactylus alpinus* in Kanton Schwyz.] *Orn. Beob.* 80: 153–182. (In German.)

HICKEY, J. J. (1969) *Peregrine Falcon populations: their biology and decline*. Madison and London: Wisconsin Press University.

HIDALGO DE TRUCIO, S. J. AND CARRANZA, J. (1990) [*The ecology and behaviour of Great Bustard* Otis tarda.] Salamanca: Extremadura-Caja Salamanca University. (In Spanish.)

HILL, D. (1988) Population dynamics of the Avocet (*Recurvirostra avosetta*) breeding in Britain. *J. Anim. Ecol.* 57: 669–683.

HIRALDO, F. (1974) [Breeding colonies and census of Black Vultures *Aegypius monachus* in Spain.] *Naturalia Hispanica* 2: 3–31. (In Spanish.)

HIRALDO, F. (1976) The diet of Black Vulture *Aegypius monachus* in the Iberian peninsula. *Doñana Acta Vert.* 3: 19–31.

HIRALDO, F. (1983) Breeding biology of the Cinereous Vulture. Pp.197–216 in S. R. Wilbur and J. A. Jackson, eds. *Vulture biology and management*. Berkeley: California Press University.

HIRALDO, F., DELIBES, M. AND CALDERÓN, J. (1979) [*The Lammergeier* Gypaetus barbatus*: systematics, taxonomy, biology, distribution and protection*.] Madrid: Instituto Nacional para la Conservación de la Naturaleza (Monogr. 22). (In Spanish.)

HIRONS, G. AND BICKFORD-SMITH, P. (1983) The diet and behaviour of Eurasian Woodcock wintering in Cornwall. Pp.11–17 in H. Kalchreuter, ed. *Proc. 2nd European Woodcock and Snipe Workshop*. Slimbridge, U.K.: International Waterfowl and Wetlands Research Bureau.

HIRONS, G. AND JOHNSON, T. H. (1987) A quantitative analysis of habitat preferences of Woodcock, *Scolopax rusticola*, in the breeding season. *Ibis* 129: 371–381.

HJORT, C., HÅKANSSON, E. AND MØLGAARD, P. (1987) Brent Geese *Branta bernicla*, Snow Geese *Anser caerulescens* and Barnacle Geese *Branta leucopsis* on Kilen, Kronprins Christian Land, north-east Greenland, 1985. *Dansk Ornit. Foren. Tidsskr.* 81: 121–128.

HOGSTAD, O. (1971) Stratification in winter feeding of *Dendrocopos major* and *Picoides tridactylus*. *Ornis Scand.* 2: 143–146.

HOLLIS, E. G. (1992) The causes of wetland loss and degradation in the Mediterranean. Pp.83–90 in C. M. Finlayson, G. E. Hollis and T. J. Davis, eds. *Managing Mediterranean wetlands and their birds: proceedings of an International Waterfowl and Wetlands Research Bureau international symposium, Grado, Italy, February 1991.* Slimbridge, U.K.: International Waterfowl and Wetlands Research Bureau (Spec. Publ. 20).

HOLLIS, G. E., ADAMS, W. M. AND AMINU-KANO, M. (1993) *The Hadejia-Nguru Wetlands: environment, economy and sustainable development of a Sahelian floodplain wetland.* Gland, Switzerland: International Union for Conservation of Nature and Natural Resources.

HOLLOM, P. A. D., PORTER, R. F., CHRISTENSEN, S. AND WILLIS, I. (1988) *Birds of the Middle East and North Africa.* Calton, U.K.: T. and A. D. Poyser.

HÖLZINGER, J., ED. (1987) [*Birds of Baden-Württemberg*, 1: *threats and conservation.*] Karlsruhe: E. Ulmer Verlag. (In German.)

HÖLZINGER, J., MICKLEY, M. AND SCHILHANSL, K. (1973) [Studies on the reproductive biology and diet of Short-eared Owls (*Asio flammeus*) at a breeding site in south Germany with comments on the species' occurrence in central Europe.] *Anz Orn. Ges. Bayern* 12: 176–197. (In German.)

HOOGENDOORN, W. AND MACKRILL, E. J. (1987) Audouin's Gull in south-western Palearctic. *Dutch Birding* 9: 99–107.

HORNER, K. O. AND HUBBARD, J. P. (1982) An analysis of birds limed in spring at Paralimni, Cyprus. *Cyprus Orn. Soc.* (1982) Rep. 76: 54–104.

HORVÁTH, L. (1956) The life of the Red-footed Falcon in the Ohat forest. *Acta Congr. Int. Orn. Basel* 11: 583–587.

HOS (1992) *Greek threatened areas project.* Athens: Hellenic Ornithological Society (unpublished annual report).

HUDEC, K. AND STASTNY, K. (1992) [The Ortolan Bunting in Czechoslovakia.] In [*Symposium on the Ortolan Bunting, Vienna 4–6 July 1992.*] Vienna: Universität für Bodenkultur. (In German.)

HUDSON, A. V. AND FURNESS, R. W. (1989) The behaviour of seabirds foraging at fishing boats around Shetland. *Ibis* 131: 225–237.

HUDSON, R. (1976) Ruddy Ducks in Britain. *Brit. Birds* 69: 132–143.

HUDSON, R., TUCKER, G. M. AND FULLER, R. J. (1994) Lapwing *Vanellus vanellus* populations in relation to agricultural changes: a review. Pp.1–33 in G. M. Tucker, S. M. Davies and R. J. Fuller eds. *The ecology and conservation of Lapwings.* Peterborough, U.K.: Joint Nature Conservation Committee (U.K. Nature Conservation, no. 9).

HÜE, F. AND ETCHÉCOPAR, R. D. (1958) [A month of ornithological research on the Canary Islands.] *Terre et Vie* 105: 186–219. (In French.)

HÜE, F. AND ETCHÉCOPAR, R. D. (1970) [*Birds of Proche and Moyen Orient.*] Paris: Boubée and Cie. (In French.)

HUGGETT, D. (1992) The implications of the proposed second road bridge across the Tagus estuary, Portugal. Sandy, U.K.: Royal Society for the Protection of Birds (unpublished report).

HUGHES, B. (1991) The status of the North American Ruddy Duck *Oxyura jamaicensis* in Great Britain. Pp.162–163 in D. Stroud and D. Glue, eds. *Britain's birds in 1989–1990: the conservation and monitoring review.* Thetford, U.K.: British Trust for Ornithology and Nature Conservancy Council.

HUGHES, R. H. AND HUGHES, J. S. (1992) *A directory of African wetlands.* Cambridge, U.K.: World Conservation Union/United Nations Environment Programme/World Conservation Monitoring Centre.

HUSTINGS, F. (1988) *European monitoring studies of breeding birds.* Beek, Netherlands: Samenwerkende Organisaties Vogelonderzoek Nederland.

VAN DER HUT, R. M. G., DE JONG, J. AND OSIECK, E. R. (1992a) [*Biology and conservation of the Spoonbill* Platalea leucorodia *in the Netherlands: towards a conservation plan.*] Zeist, Netherlands: Vogelbescherming (Techn. Rapport 6). (In Dutch.)

VAN DER HUT, R. M. G., DE JONG, J. AND OSIECK, E. R. (1992b) [*Biology and conservation of the Barn Owl* Tyto alba*: towards a conservation plan.*] Zeist: Vogelbescherming Nederland (Techn. Rapport 7). (In Dutch.)

HUTCHINSON, C. D. (1989) *Birds in Ireland.* Calton, U.K.: T. and A. D. Poyser.

IANKOV, P., HRISTOV, H. AND AVRAMOV, S. (1992) Changes in status of the Black Vulture in Bulgaria during 1980–90. In B.-U. Meyburg, ed. *Abstracts IV World Conference on Birds of Prey, Berlin.* Berlin: B.-U. Meyburg World Working Group on Birds of Prey and Owls.

IBORRA, O. (1989) [First balance of artificial feeding of three Bonelli's Eagle pairs *Hieraaetus fasciatus* in Provence.] *Faune de Provence (CEEP)* 10: 31–38. (In French.)

ICBP (1992) *Putting biodiversity on the map: priority areas for global conservation.* Cambridge, U.K.: International Council for Bird Preservation.

ICONA (1991) [*Forest oak decline in Spain (1990–1991).*] Madrid: Informe Interno del Instituto Nacional para la Conservación de la Naturaleza (MAPA). (In Spanish.)

ICONA (1993a) [*Forest fires in Spain during 1992.*] Madrid: Informe Interno del Instituto Nacional para la Conservación de la Naturaleza (MAPA). (In Spanish.)

ICONA (1993b) The spread of the Ruddy Duck in Spain and its impact on the White-headed Duck. *IWRB TWRG Newsl.* 3: 3–4.

ILYICHEV, V. D. AND FLINT, V. E., EDS. (1987) [*Birds of U.S.S.R.: Galliformes and Gruiformes.*] St Petersburg: Nauka. (In Russian.)

ILYICHEV, V. D. AND FOMIN, V. E. (1988) [*Avifauna and environmental changes.*] Moscow: Nauka. (In Russian.)

ILYICHEV, V. D. AND ZUBAKIN, V. A., EDS. (1988) [*Birds of U.S.S.R.: gulls and terns.*] Moscow: Nauka. (In Russian.)

IMBODEN, C. (1994) Birds as indicators of unsustainability. Pp.61–68 in G. Bennett, ed. *Conserving Europe's natural heritage: towards a European ecological network.* London: Graham and Trotman.

IRBY, L. H. (1895) *Ornithology of the Straits of Gibraltar.* Second edition. London: R. H. Porter.

IRIBARREN, J. J. (1977) The present status of birds of prey in Navarra (Spain). Pp.381–387 in R. D. Chancellor, ed. *Proceedings of the World Conference on Birds of Prey, Vienna 1975.* Cambridge, U.K.: International Council for Bird Preservation.

IRSNB (1992) [*Preparation of a plan to save* Numenius tenuirostris *sub-plan.* 7: Albania (project 7.4).] Unpublished. (In French.)

ISAKOV, Y. A. (1970) Wintering of waterfowl in the U.S.S.R. Pp.239–254 in Y. A. Isakov, ed. *Proceedings of the International Regional Meeting on Conservation of Wildfowl Resources, Leningrad, U.S.S.R., 25–30 September 1968.*

ISAKOV, Y. A. AND VOROBIEV. K. A. (1940) [Review of the wintering and migrating birds in southern Caspian Sea.] *Transact. Hassan-Kuli Orn. State Reserve, Moskva* 1: 5–159. (In Russian.)

ISENMANN, P. AND BOUCHET, M. A. (1993) [The Mediterranean Grey Shrike *Lanius excubitor meridionales* distribution in France and its taxonomic status.] *Alauda* 61: 223–227. (In French.)

IUCN (1990) *Environmental status reports 1988/1989.* 1: *Czechoslovakia, Hungary, Poland.* Cambridge, U.K.: International Union for Conservation of Nature and Natural Resources.

IUCN (1991) *Environmental status reports 1990.* 2: *Albania, Bulgaria, Romania, Yugoslavia.* Cambridge, U.K.: International Union for Conservation of Nature and Natural Resources.

IUCN (1992) *Conservation status of the Danube delta.* Cambridge, U.K.: International Union for Conservation of Nature and Natural Resources.

IUCN COMMISSION ON NATIONAL PARKS AND PROTECTED AREAS (1994) *Parks for life: action for protected areas in Europe.* Gland, Switzerland and Cambridge, U.K.: International Union for Conservation of Nature and Natural Resources.

IUCN/UNEP/WWF (1991) *Caring for the Earth. A strategy for sustainable living.* Gland, Switzerland: International Union for Conservation of Nature and Natural Resources/United Nations Environment Program/World Wide Fund for Nature.

IVANOVSKY, V. V. (1990) [The Golden Eagle: dweller of Lithuania.] *Musu Gamta* 5: 12–13, 31. (In Lithuanian.)

IVANOVSKY, V. V. AND SAMUSENKO, I. E. (1990) [Attraction of the Black Stork by means of artificial nests.] Pp.212–215 in B. P. Savitzky and E. G. Samusenko, eds. [*Storks: distribution, ecology, conservation.*] (In Russian.)

JAKOBER, H. AND STAUBER, W. (1981) [Habitat requirements of the Red-backed Shrike: a contribution to the protection of an endangered species.] *Ökol. Vögel* 3: 223–247. (In German.)

JAKOBER, H. AND STAUBER, W. (1987a) [Habitat requirements of the Red-backed Shrike and conservation measures.] *Beih. Veröff. Naturschutz Landschaftspflege* 48: 25–53. (In German.)

JAKOBER, H. AND STAUBER, W. (1987b) [On the population dynamics of the Red-backed Shrike.] *Beih. Veröff. Naturschutz Landschaftspflege* 48: 71–78. (In German.)

JAKOBER, H. AND STAUBER, W. (1987c) [Dispersion processes in a population of Red-backed Shrike.] *Beih. Veröff.*

Naturschutz Landschaftspflege 48: 119–130. (In German.)

JAMES, P. C. (1984) The status and conservation of seabirds in the Mediterranean Sea. Pp.371–375 in J. P. Croxall, P. G. H. Evans and R. W. Schreiber, eds. *Status and conservation of the world's seabirds.* Cambridge, U.K.: International Council for Bird Preservation (Techn. Publ. 2).

JARRY, G. (1983) [Fluctuations of breeding areas and population densities of western European birds under the direct or indirect influence of man.] *C. R. Soc. Biogéogr.* 59: 87–104. (In French.)

JARRY, G. (1992) [Biology of the Turtle Dove in its wintering grounds in Senegal.] Paris: Centre de Recherches sur la Biologie des Populations d'Oiseaux (unpublished report). (In French.)

JARRY, G. (in prep.) [Distribution and ecology of Turtle Dove populations wintering in the western Senegal.] Paris: Centre de Recherches sur la Biologie des Populations d'Oiseaux. (In French.)

JARRY, G. AND BAILLON, F. (1991) [Wintering Turtle Doves (*Streptopelia turtur*) in Senegal: study of a population in the Nianing region.] CRBPO/ORSTOM (unpublished report). (In French.)

JÄRVINEN, A. (1978) [Population dynamics of the Redstart in a subarctic area.] *Ornis Fenn.* 55: 69–76. (In Finnish.)

JÄRVINEN, O., KUUSELA, K. AND VÄISÄNEN, R. A. (1977) Effects of modern forestry on the numbers of breeding birds in Finland in 1945–1975. *Silva Fennica* 11: 284–294. (In Finnish with English summary.)

JENKIN, P. M. (1957) The filter-feeding and food of flamingos (*Phoenicopteri*). *Phil. Trans. R. Soc. Lond. B* 240: 410–493.

JENKINS, D. (1984) *Agriculture and the environment. Proceedings of ITE Symposium No. 13.* Cambridge, U.K.: Natural Environment Research Council.

JENNY, M. (1990a) [Diet of the Skylark *Alauda arvensis* in an area of intensive agriculture in central Switzerland.] *Orn. Beob.* 87: 31–53. (In German.)

JENNY, M. (1990b) [Population dynamics of the Skylark *Alauda arvensis* in an area of intensive agriculture in central Switzerland.] *Orn. Beob.* 87: 153–163. (In German.)

JENNY, M. (1990c) [Territoriality and reproductive biology of the Skylark *Alauda arvensis* in an area of intensive agriculture in central Switzerland.] *J. Orn.* 131: 241–265. (In German.)

JENSEN, A. (1981) Ornithological winter observations on Selvagem Grande. *Bocagiana* 62: 1–7.

JEPSEN, P. U. (1989) [*The status of the Black Grouse in Denmark.*] Miljøministeriets vildtforvaltning, Vildtreservatskontoret. (In Danish.)

JERRENTRUP, H. (1982) [Ecological surveys of internationally important wetlands in north-east Greece.] Heidelberg: Heidelberg University (Dipl. thesis). (In German.)

JERRENTRUP, H. (1986) [The Nestos delta ecosystem: natural zones and related animal communities, nature conservation and human activities.] *Biologia Gallo-hellenica* 12: 315–334. (In German.)

JERRENTRUP, H. (1992) The fauna of Lake Vistonis and the Porto Lagos Area. Pp.363–373 in P. A. Gerakis, ed. *Conservation and management of Greek wetlands.* Gland, Switzerland: International Union for Conservation of Nature and Natural Resources.

JERRENTRUP, H. (1993) [On the status of the Spur-winged

Plover (*Hoplopterus spinosus*) in the Nestos delta in 1993.] Hrysoupolis: European Natural Heritage Fond (unpublished report). (In German.)

JERRENTRUP, H., GAETHLICH, M., HOLM JOENSEN, A., NOHR, H. AND BROGGER-JENSEN, S. (1988) *Urgent action plan to safeguard three endangered bird species in Greece and the European Community:* Pygmy Cormorant (Phalacrocorax pygmaeus)*; Great white egret* (Egretta alba)*; White tailed eagle* (Haliaeetus albicilla). Arhus: Naturhistorisk Museum.

JESPERSEN, P. (1946) *The breeding birds of Denmark.* Copenhagen.

JIMÉNEZ, J. (1990) [*Survey of Spanish Imperial Eagle and Black Vulture populations in Ciudad Real.*] Ciudad Real: Consejeria de Agricultura. (In Spanish.)

JIMÉNEZ, J. (1992) [*Census of Spanish Imperial Eagle and Black Vulture populations in Ciudad Real.*] Ciudad Real: Consejeria de Agricultura. (In Spanish.)

JOENSEN, A. H. (1972) Studies on oil pollution and seabirds in Denmark 1968–1971. *Dan. Rev. Game Biol.* 6: 1–32.

JOENSEN, A. H. AND HANSEN, E. B. (1977) Oil pollution and seabirds in Denmark 1971–1976. *Dan. Rev. Game Biol.* 10: 1–31.

JOENSEN, A. J. AND JERRENTRUP, H. (1988) The Agios mamas lagoon, Haldikiki, Greece, an area of international importance for breeding waders. *Nat. Jutlandica* 22: 185–188.

JOHNSGARD, P. A. (1983) *Cranes of the world.* Bloomington: Indiana University Press.

JOHNSGARD, P. A. (1991) *Bustards, hemipodes, and sandgrouse: birds of dry places.* Oxford: Oxford University Press.

JOHNSON, A. R. (1982) Construction of a breeding island for flamingos in the Camargue. Pp.204–208 in *Managing wetlands and their birds.* International Waterfowl and Wetlands Research Bureau: Slimbridge, U.K.

JOHNSON, A. R. (1983) [Behavioural ecology of Greater Flamingo (*Phoenicopterus ruber rosens* Pallas) in the Camargue and western Palearctic.] Toulouse: Paul Sabatier University (unpublished thesis). (In French.)

JOHNSON, A. R. (1989a) [Movements of Greater Flamingos *Phoenicopterus ruber roseus* in the western Palearctic.] *Terre et Vie, Rev. Ecol.* 44: 75–94. (In French.)

JOHNSON, A. R. (1989b) Population studies and conservation of Greater Flamingos in the Camargue. Pp.49–63 in A. L. Spaans, ed. [*Wetlands and waterbirds.*] Wageningen: Pucdoc. (In French.)

JOHNSON, A. R. (1991) Conservation of breeding flamingos in the Camargue (southern France). *Species* 17: 33–34.

JOHNSON, A. R. (1992) The western Mediterranean population of flamingos: is it at risk? Pp.215–219 in C. M. Finlayson, G. E. Hollis and T. J. Davis, eds. *Managing Mediterranean wetlands and their birds: proceedings of an International Waterfowl and Wetlands Research Bureau international symposium, Grado, Italy, February 1991.* Slimbridge, U.K.: International Waterfowl and Wetlands Research Bureau (Spec. Publ. 20).

JONES, G. (1987) Selection against large size in the Sand Martin *Riparia riparia* during a dramatic population crash. *Ibis* 129: 274–280.

JONES, M. (1988) *A survey of the distribution, density and habitat references of the Long-toed Pigeon* Columba trocaz *in Madeira.* Cambridge, U.K.: International Council for Bird Preservation (Study Rep. 32).

JONES, T. A. AND HUGHES, J. M. R. (in press) Wetlands inventories and wetland loss studies: an European perspective. Proceedings of the 35th Meeting of the International Waterfowl and Wetlands Research Bureau Executive Board.

JÖNSSON, G. (1987) [*History of the Laxá Hydropower Station.*] Akureyri: Landsvirkjun. (In Icelandic.)

JÖNSSON, L. (1982) *Birds of the Mediterranean and Alps.* London: Croom Helm.

JÖNSSON, P. E. (1983) [The Kentish Plover *Charadrius alexandrinus* in Sweden: status and breeding ecology.] *Anser* 22: 209–230. (In Swedish with English summary.)

JÖNSSON, P. E. (1988) [Ecology of the southern Dunlin.] Lund: Lund University (Ph.D. thesis). (In Swedish.)

JÖNSSON, P. E. (1989) [The Kentish Plover *Charadrius alexandrinus* in Skåne, south Sweden, 1989: a report from a conservation project.] *Anser* 28: 251–258. (In Swedish with English summary.)

JÖNSSON, P. E. (1990) [Mink: a serious threat for Black Guillemots on Hallands Väderö.] *Anser* 29: 278–281. (In Swedish with English summary.)

JÖNSSON, P. E. (1993) [The Kentish Plover Project: report for 1992.] *Anser* 32: 29–34. (In Swedish with English summary.)

JÖRGENSEN, H. E., MADESEN, J. AND CLAUSEN, P. (1994) [Staging and wintering Geese in Denmark.] Denmark: National Environment Research Institute (unpublished report).

JOUANIN, C. AND ROUX, F. (1965) [Contribution to the study of the biology of *Pelagodroma marina hypoleuca* (Webb, Berthelot and Mouquin-Tandon).] *Bul. Mus. Mun. Funchal* 19: 16–42. (In French.)

JOUANIN, C., ROUX, F. AND ZINO, P. A. (1969) [Visit to the breeding grounds of *Pterodroma mollis 'deserta'.*] *Oiseau et R.F.O.* 39: 161–175. (In French.)

JOUANIN, C., MOUGIN, J.-L., ROUX, F. AND ZINO, A. (1979) [Bulwer's Petrel *Bulweria bulwerii* in the archipelago of Madeira and on the Selvagem Islands.] *Oiseau et R.F.O.* 49: 165–184.

JOVETIC, R., TRPKOV, B. AND RIZOVSKI, R. (1980) [Some biological characteristics of the partridge (*Alectoris graeca graeca* Meisner) and possibilities for rearing in Yugoslavia.] Pp.141–147 in C. L. Coles, M. Reydellet, G. van Tuyll, L. van Maltzahn and J. Bugalho, eds. *Partridges of the Alectoris genus.* Paris: International Council for Game and Wildlife Conservation. (In French.)

JÓZEFIK, M. (1969) Caspian Tern in Poland—the biology of migration period. *Acta Orn.* 11: 381–443.

DE JUANA, E. (1980) [*Ornithological atlas of La Rioja.*] Logroño: Instituto de Estudios Riojanos. (In Spanish.)

DE JUANA, E. (1984) The status and conservation of seabirds in the Spanish Mediterranean. Pp.347–361 in J. P. Croxall, P. G. H. Evans and R. W. Schreiber, eds. *Status and conservation of the world's seabirds.* Cambridge, U.K.: International Council for Bird Preservation (Techn. Publ. 2).

DE JUANA, E. (1989a) [Dry grassland birds in Spain.] Pp.197–221 in [*Seminar on arid zones in Spain.*] Madrid: Real Academia de Ciencias Exactas, Físicas y Naturales. (In Spanish.)

DE JUANA, E. (1989b) [The birds of the Spanish steppes.] Pp.199–221 in [*Seminar on the arid lands of Spain.*] Madrid: Real Academia de Ciencias Exactas, Físicas y

Naturales. (In Spanish.)

DE JUANA, E. (1989c) [Diurnal birds of prey in Spain.] *Ecología* 3: 237–292. (In Spanish.)

DE JUANA, E., ED. (1990) [*Important bird areas in Spain.*] Madrid: Sociedad Española de Ornitología (Monogr. 3). (In Spanish.)

DE JUANA, E. (1992) [Birds of Spain.] *Garcilla* 84: 40. (In Spanish.)

DE JUANA, E. AND DE JUANA, F. (1984) [Livestock and the distribution and abundance of the Griffon Vulture and Black Vulture in Spain.] Pp.32–45 in Centre Recerca Protecció Rapinyaires, ed. [*Mediterranean raptors II.*] Barcelona: CRPR. (In Spanish.)

DE JUANA, E. AND VARELA, J. M. (1993) [The world breeding population of the Audouin's Gull *Larus audouinii.*] Pp.71–85 in J. S. Aguilar, X. Monbailliu and A. M. Paterson, eds. *Status and conservation of seabirds: ecogeography and Mediterranean Action Plan. Proceedings II Mediterranean Seabird Symposium, Mallorca, 1989.* Madrid: Sociedad Española de Ornitología/ BirdLife/MEDMARAVIS.

DE JUANA, E., BRADLEY, P. M., VARELA, J. AND WITT, H.-H. (1987) [Migratory requirements of Audouin's Gull *Larus audouinii.*] *Ardeola* 34: 15–24. (In Spanish.)

DE JUANA, E., MARTÍN-NOVELLA, C., NAVESO, M. A., PAIN, D. AND SEARS J. (1993) Farming and birds in Spain: threats and opportunities for conservation. *RSPB Conserv. Rev.* 7: 67–73.

DE JUANA, E., SANTOS, T., SUÁREZ, F. AND TELLERÍA, J. L. (1988) Status and conservation of steppe birds and their habitats in Spain. Pp.113–123 in P. D. Goriup, ed. *Ecology and conservation of grassland birds.* Cambridge, U.K.: International Council for Bird Preservation (Techn. Publ. 7).

JUILLARD, M. (1980) [Distribution, biotops and breeding sites of the Little Owl, *Athene noctus*, in Switzerland.] *Nos Oiseaux* 35: 309–337. (In French.)

JUILLARD, M. (1984) [*The Little Owl.*] Pragins, Switzerland: Société Romande pour l'Etude et la Protection des Oiseaux. (In French.)

JUILLARD, M., PRAZ, J.-C., ETOURNAD, A. AND BEAUD, P. (1978) [Data on the contamination of raptors and their eggs of Switzerland romande by organochlored biocides, as PCB and heavy metals.] *Nos Oiseaux* 34: 189–206. (In French.)

KAPOCSY, G. (1979) [*White-winged and Whiskered Terns.*] Wittenberg Lutherstadt: Ziemsen Verlag. (In German.)

KARLSSON, A. AND SWANBERG, P. O. (1983) [Hornborgasjöns Cranes.] In *Hornborgadokument Nr. 5, Ref. Naturvardsenheten, Mariestad.* (In Swedish.)

KARLSSON, S. AND KJELLÉN, N. (1988) [Skylark *Alauda arvensis* L.] *Vår Fågelv.* 12 (Suppl.): 245–254. (In Swedish.)

KASHENTSEVA, T. A., KOTYUKOV, Y. V. AND IVANCHEV, V. P. (1991) [Whiskered Tern *Chlidonias hybridus*, a new breeding species of the south-east of Mestchera depression, Ryazan region.] *Ornitologiya* 25: 161. (In Russian.)

KASPAREK, M. (1985) [*The Sultan Marshes: natural history of a bird paradise in Anatolia*]. Heidelberg, Germany: Max Kasparek Verlag. (In German.)

KASPAREK, M. (1992a) [*Birds of Turkey.*] Heidelberg: Verlag. (In German.)

KASPAREK, M. (1992b) Status of the Sociable Plover

Chettusia gregaria and White-tailed Plover *C. leucura* in Turkey and the Middle East. *Sandgrouse* 14: 2–15.

KAVENAGH, B. (1992) Irish Grey Partridge (*Perdix perdix*) population survey 1991, with special reference to population and habitat use in cutaway bogland. *Gibier Faune Sauvage* 9: 503–514.

KAZAKOV, B. A., PEKLO, A. M., TILBA, P. A. AND BELIK, V. P. (1983) [Waders of the northern Caucasus.] *Soobsh. 4. Vestnik Zoologii* 2: 47–54. (In Russian.)

KELLER, M. AND PROFUS, P. (1992) [Present situation, reproduction and food of the Black Stork in Poland.] Pp.227–236 in J.-L. Mériaux, A. Schierer, C. Tombal and J.-C. Tombal, eds. [*The storks of Europe.*] Metz: Institut Européen d'Ecologie/AMBE. (In Polish.)

KERDANOV, D. A. (1990) [A number of birds of prey in the Kalinin region.] Pp.120–124 in V. T. Butjev, ed. [*Rare bird species in the central European Russia.*] Moscow: U.S.S.R. Ornithological Society, Moscow Division.

KERTELL, K. (1991) Disappearance of the Steller's Eider from the Yukon-Kuskowim delta, Alaska. *Arctic* 44: 177–184.

KEÂLER, A. (1986) [Actual population size of the Green Woodpecker (*Picus viridis*) with additional remarks on the distribution in the Oldenburg area.] *Jahresber. Orn. Arbeitsgem. Oldenb.* 10: 23–27. (In German.)

KHOKHLOV, A. N. (1993) [Animals in Stavropol region.] Stavropol: Menzbir Ornithological Society, North-Caucasus Division. (In Russian.)

KHRUSTOV, A. AND MOSEIKIN, V. (1986) [Conservation of rare birds in the Saratov region.] *Okhota Okh. Khoz.* 9: 22–25. (In Russian.)

KILIÇ, A. AND KASPAREK, M. (1990) *The Eregli marshes.* Unpublished report to International Council for Bird Preservation and the World Wide Fund for Nature.

KING, W. B. (1981) *Endangered birds of the world. The ICBP Red Data Book.* Washington, D.C.: International Union for the Conservation of Nature and Natural Resources.

KIRBY, J. S., FERNS, P. R., WATERS, R. J. AND PRYS-JONES, R. P. (1991) *Wader and wildfowl counts 1990–1991.* Slimbridge, U.K.: Wildfowl and Wetlands Trust.

KIRBY, J. S., CLEE, C. AND SEAGER, V. (1993a) Impact and extent of recreational disturbance to wader roosts on the Dee estuary: some preliminary results. *Wader Study Group Bull.* 68 (Special Issue): 53–58.

KIRBY, J., EVANS, R. AND FOX, A. D. (1993b) A review of the status and distribution of wintering seaducks in Britain and Ireland. *Aquatic Conserv.* 3: 105–137.

KIRCHNER, K. (1969) [*The Black-tailed Godwit Limosa limosa.*] Wittenberg Lutherstadt: Ziemsen Verlag. (In German.)

KIRWAN, G. (in press) The breeding status and distribution of the White-headed Duck on the central plateau, Turkey. *Sandgrouse.*

KISTIAKOVSKIY, A. B. (1957) [*Fauna of the Ukraine.* 4: birds.] Kiev: AN USSR. (In Ukrainian.)

KLAFS, G. AND STÜBS, J., EDS. (1987) [*The avifauna of Mecklemburg.*] Jena: G. Fischer Verlag. (In German.)

KLAUS, S., BERGMANN, H.-H., MARTI, C., MÜLLER, F., WIESNER, J. AND VITOVI'C, O. A. (1990) [*The Black Grouse Tetrao tetrix and T. mlokosiewiczi.*] Wittenberg Lutherstadt: Ziemsen Verlag. (In German.)

KLIMOV, S. M. AND ALEKSANDROV, V. N. (1992) [*Rare*

animals of the Lipetsk region.] Lipetsk: Lipetsk State Pedagogical Institute. (In Russian.)

KLIMOV, S. M., SARYCHEV, V. S. AND NEDOSEKIN, V. Y. (1990) [Recent status of rare birds in the Lipetsk region. Pp.45–47 in V. T. Butjev, ed. [Rare animals in the Lipetsk region.] Moscow: U.S.S.R. Ornithological Society, Moscow Division. (In Russian.)

KNIGHT, R. C. AND HOOBDAN, P. C. (1983) A guide to Little Tern conservation. Sandy, U.K.: Royal Society for the Protection of Birds.

KNORRE, D. V., GRÜN, G., GÜNTHER, R. AND SCHMIDT, K. (1986) [The avifauna of Thüringen.] Wiesbaden: Aula-Verlag. (In German.)

KNOX, A. G. (1976) The taxonomic status of the Scottish Crossbill Loxia sp. Bull. Brit. Orn. Club 96: 15–19.

KNOX, A. G. (1986) Common Crossbill Loxia curvirostra, Scottish Crossbill L. scotica. Pp.400–403 in P. Lack, ed. The atlas of wintering birds in Britain and Ireland. Calton, U.K.: T. and A. D. Poyser.

KNOX, A. G. (1987) Crossbills: their general biology and some conservation problems. Pp.64–74 in E. Cameron, ed. Glen Tamar: its human and natural history. Proceedings of symposium at Glen Tamar House, November 1983. Peterborough, U.K.: Nature Conservancy Council.

KNOX, A. G. (1990a) Identification of Crossbill and Scottish Crossbill. Brit. Birds 83: 89–94.

KNOX, A. G. (1990b) The sympatric breeding of Common and Scottish Crossbills Loxia curvirostra and L. scotica and the evolution of crossbills. Ibis 132: 454–466.

KOEMAN, J. H., DE BOEAR, W. M. J., FEITH, A. F., DE IONGH, H. H., SLIETHOFF, P. C., NA'ISA, B. K. AND SPIELBERGER, U. (1978) Three years observation on side-effects of helicopter applications of insecticide to exterminate Glossina species in Nigeria. Environ. Pollut. 15: 31–59.

KOENIG, L. (1973) [The behaviour of Otus scops (Linné 1758).] Z. Tierpsychol. Beih 13: 1–24. (In German.)

KOFFAN, K. (1960) Observations on the nesting of the Woodlark (Lullula arborea). Acta Zool. Acad. Sci. Hung. 6: 371–412.

VAN DER KOIJ, H. (1992) [The 1991 breeding season of the Purple Heron.] Vogeljaar 40: 119–121. (In Dutch.)

KOLLAR, H. P. (1988) [Protection of species and habitats taking Great Bustard as an example.] Verein für Ökologie und Umweltforschung 11. (In German.)

KONDRATIEV, A. Y. (1991) The distribution and status of Bewick's Swans Cygnus bewickii, Tundra Swans C. columbianus and Whooper Swans C. cygnus in the extreme north-east of the U.S.S.R. Pp.56–61 in J. Sears and P. J. Bacon, eds. Third IWRB International Swan Symposium, Oxford 1989. Wildfowl (Suppl. 1).

KOOLHAAS, A., DEKINGA, A. AND PIERSMA, T. (1993) Disturbance of foraging Knots by aircraft in the Dutch Wadden Sea in August-October 1992. Wader Study Group Bull. 68 (Special Issue): 20–22.

KORPIMÄKI, E. (1985) Diet of the Kestrel Falco tinnunculus during the breeding season. Ornis Fenn. 62: 130–137.

KORPIMÄKI, E. AND NORRDAHL, K. (1991) Numerical and functional responses of kestrels, short-eared owls and long-eared owls to vole densities. Ecology 72: 814–826.

DE KORTE, J. (1991) Frans Josef Land, August 1991. Circump. J. 6: 70–76.

DE KORTE, J. AND VOLKOV, A. (1993) Large colony of Ivory Gulls Pagophila eburnea at Domastiny Island, Severnaya Zemlya. Sula 7: 107–110.

KOSHELEV, A. I., KORZJUKOV, A. I., LOBKOV, V. A. AND PERESADJKO, L. B. (1991) [Survey of populations of rare bird species in the Odessa region.] Pp.9–36 in [Rare birds north of the Black Sea.] Odessa, Kiev: Lybid. (In Russian.)

KOSKIMIES, P. (1989) Distribution and numbers of Finnish breeding birds: appendix to Suomen lintuatlas. Helsinki: SLY:n Lintutieto Oy.

KOSKIMIES, P. (1993a) [Population sizes and recent trends of breeding and wintering birds in Finland.] Linnut 28: 6–15. (In Finnish.)

KOSKIMIES, P. (1993b) Population sizes and recent trends of breeding birds in the nordic countries. Helsinki: National Board of Waters and the Environment.

KOSTIN, A. B. (1986) [Nesting of the Long-legged Buzzard in the Central-Chernozem Reserve.] Pp.229–231 in V. D. Ilyichev, ed. [Actual problems in ornithology.] Moscow: Nauka. (In Russian.)

KOSTIN, Y. V. (1983) [Birds of the Crimea.] Moscow: Nauka. (In Russian.)

KOSTRZEWA, R. AND KOSTRZEWA, A. (1990) The relationship of spring and summer weather with the density and breeding performance of the Buzzard Buteo buteo, Goshawk Accipiter gentilis and Kestrel Falco tinnunculus. Ibis 132: 550–559.

KOVACS, G. (1986–1987) Staging and summering of cranes (Grus grus) in the Hortobagy in 1975–1985. Aquila 93/94: 153–169.

KOVACS, G. (1992) Occurrence of the Long-legged Buzzard (Buteo rufinus) in Hortobagy between 1976 and 1991. Aquila 99: 41–48.

KOVSHAR', A. F. (1979) [Song birds of the subalpine zone of Tian-Shan.] Alma-Ata: Akademii Nauk Kazakhskoy SSR. (In Russian.)

KOVSHAR, A. F. AND KHROKOV, V. V. (1991) [The birds of principal landscapes in the Pavlodar Zairtyshje.] Pp.89–91 in L. G. Vartapetov, ed. [Abstracts Ornithological Problems in Siberia.] Barnaul: Altai University. (In Russian.)

KOWALSKI, H. (1992) [Population numbers of Shrike species in Germany: causes of decline, status, conservation strategies.] J. Orn. 133: 321–322. (In German.)

KOZLOVA, E. V. (1961) [Fauna of the U.S.S.R.: Birds 2, part 1.2. Charadriiformes: Suborder waders.] Moscow/Leningrad: AN USSR. (In Russian.)

KOZLOVA, E. V. (1962) [Fauna of the U.S.S.R.: Charadriiformes—Limicolae.] Moscow/Leningrad: Akademii Nauk. (In Russian.)

KRAFT, J. A. AND KORELOV, M. N. (1938) [Concerning chemical methods and Merops apiaster L. in apiaries in Uzbekistan.] Bull. Univ. Asie Centr. 22: 165–168. (In Russian.)

KRAPIVNYJ, A. P. (1957) [Ecology of the Black Stork.] Biul. Inst. Biol. 2: 242–249. (In Russian.)

KRIVENKO, V. G. (1984) [Recent abundance of the waterfowl in the central region of the U.S.S.R..] Pp.8–11 in V. G. Krivenko, ed. [Proceedings of the All-Union seminar on present status of waterfowl resources.] Moscow: TSNIL Glavokhota RSFSR. (In Russian.)

KRIVENKO, V. G. (1990) Effect of climate on the dynamics of waterfowl numbers and their ranges. Pp.182–186 in G. V. T. Matthews, ed. Managing waterfowl populations. Slimbridge, U.K.: International Waterfowl and Wetlands

Research Bureau (Spec. Publ. 12).

KRIVENKO, V. G. (1991a) [Climatic variability and water-fowl populations.] Moscow. (In Russian.)

KRIVENKO, V. G. (1991b) [Waterfowl and its preservation.] Moscow: Agropromizdat. (In Russian.)

KRIVENKO, V. G., KRIVONOSOV, G. A., RUSANOV, G. M., MOSHONKIN, N. N., NIKEROV, Y. N., RAVKIN, E. S. AND AKSENOV, A. P. (1991) [The state of environment of the Volga delta, Volga/Akhtubin valley and western steppe-like territories.] Pp.67–84 in [Terrestrial vertebrates]. Moscow: MBIV. (In Russian.)

KRIVENKO, V. G., CRIVELLI, A. J. AND VINOGRADOV, V. G. (1994) Historical changes and present status of Pelecanus crispus and Pelecanus onocrotalus numbers and distribution in the former U.S.S.R.: a synthesis with recommendations for their conservation. In A. J. Crivelli, V. G. Krivenko and V. G. Vinogradov, eds. Pelicans in the former U.S.S.R. Slimbridge, U.K.: International Waterfowl and Wetlands Research Bureau (Spec. Publ. 27).

KRIVITSKI, I. A. (1962) [Wintering birds in the Kurgaldzhin Reserve.] Ornitologia 4: 208–216. (In Russian.)

KROL, W. (1983) The status of eagles in Poland. Bull. World Working Group on Birds of Prey 1: 61–67.

KUCHEL, C. R. (1977) Some aspects of the behaviour and ecology of Harlequin Ducks breeding in Glacier National Park. Montana: Montana University (M.Sc. thesis).

KUCHIN, A. P. (1976) [The birds of the Altai.] Barnaul: Altai Publishing House. (In Russian.)

KUKISH, A. I. (1990) [Influence of irrigation on colonial birds of Saprin lakes.] Pp.12–21 in A. I. Kukish, ed. [Fauna and ecology of animals under the impact of irrigation.] Elista. (In Russian.)

KUMERLOEVE, H. (1961) [Identification of the avifauna of Asia Minor.] Bonn. Zool. Beitr. 12: 1–318. (In German.)

KUMERLOEVE, H. (1962) [On the breeding distribution of the two Ortolan Bunting species Emberiza hortulana L. and Emberiza caesia Cretschmar in Asia Minor.] Bonn. Zool. Beitr. 13: 327–332. (In German.)

KUMERLOEVE, H. (1963) [Breeding distribution of the Black Francolin Francolinus francolinus in the Middle East.] Vogelwelt 84: 129–137.

KUMERLOEVE, H. (1989) [Ortolan Bunting Emberiza hortulana breeding at high altitudes in Anatolia (Turkey).] Oiseau et R.F.O. 59. (In French.)

KURZYNSKI, J. AND ZAJAC, T. (1993) [Nest protection zones for rare birds: an attempt to standardize methods.] Chronmy Przyr. Ojcz. 49: 36–50. (In Polish.)

KUSTOV, Y. I. (1988) [Trends in the development of raptor populations in the Minusinsk lowlands.] Pp.130–134 in V. G. Shvetsov, ed. [Rare land vertebrates of Siberia.] Novosibirsk: Nauka. (In Russian.)

KUTZENBERGER, H. (1991) [Changes of the Ortlan Bunting population (Emberiza hortulana) and the landscape of the Weinvierrtels (Niederösterreich) since 1960.] Vienna: Universität für Bodenkultur. (In German.)

KUZNETSOV, A. V. (1994) [Birds of prey of the Kostroma lowland.] Pp.86–93 in E. N. Kurochkin, ed. [Modern ornithology.] Moscow: Nauka. (In Russian.)

LACK, D. (1944) Correlation between beak and food in the Crossbill, Loxia curvirostra Linnaeus. Ibis 86: 552–553.

LACK, D. AND SOUTHERN, H. N. (1949) Birds on Tenerife. Ibis 91: 607–626.

LACK, P. (1986) The atlas of wintering birds in Britain and Ireland. Calton, U.K.: T. and A. D. Poyser.

LAMARCHE, B. (1980) [List of birds of Mali.] Malimbus 2: 121–158. (In French.)

LAMBERTINI, M., GUSTIN, M., FARALLI, U. AND TALLONE, G. (1991) [Important Bird Area-Italy: areas of European importance for wild birds in Italy.] Parma: Lega Italiana Protezione Uccelli. (In Italian.)

LANG, M., BANDORF, H., DORNBERGER, W., KLEIN, H. AND MATTERN, U. (1990) [Breeding distribution, population development and ecology of the Ortolan (Emberiza hortulana) in Franconia.] Ökol. Vögel 12: 97–126. (In German.)

LANGEVELD, M. (1991) Important Bird Areas in the European Community. A shadow list of special protection areas. Cambridge, U.K.: International Council for Bird Preservation.

LARKINS, D. (1984) Little terns breeding colony on artificial sites at Port Botany, New South Wales. Corella 8: 1–10.

LARSSON, K., FORSLUND, P., GUSTAFSSON, L. AND EBBINGE, B. (1988) From the high Arctic to the Baltic: the successful establishment of a Barnacle Goose Branta leucopsis population on Gotland, Sweden. Ornis Scand. 19: 182–189.

LASKE, V., NOTTMEYER-LINDEN, K. AND CONRADS, K. (1991) [The birds of Bielefeld.] Bielefeld: Ilex-Bücher Natur. (In German.)

LAURSEN, K. (1989) Estimates of sea duck wintering populations of the western Palearctic. Dan. Rev. Game Biol. 13: 1–22.

LAURSEN, K., PIHL, S. AND KOMDEUR, J. (1992) New figures of seaduck winter populations in the western Palearctic. IWRB Seaduck Bull. 1: 6–8.

LAURSEN, K., PIHL, S., DURINCK, J., FRIKKE, J., SKOV, H., HANSEN, M. AND DANIELSEN, F. (in prep.) Numbers and distribution of waterfowl in Denmark, 1987–1989. Dan. Rev. Game Biol.

LEBEDEVA, M. I. (1990) [History of storks investigation in the U.S.S.R..] Pp.17–35 in B. P. Savickij and E. G. Samusienko, eds. [Storks: distribution, ecology, conservation.] Minsk: Nauka i Tekhnika. (In Russian.)

LEBRERO, F. (1991) [Character of the ornithological communities of the Cadiz lagoons in an annual cycle.] Pp.73–96 in [Management plan for the use of the Cadiz lagune nature reserves.]

LECONTE, M. (1985) Present status of the Griffon Vulture on the northern slopes of the western Pyrenees. Pp.117–128 in I. Newton and R. D. Chancellor, eds. Conservation studies on raptors. Cambridge, U.K.: International Council for Bird Preservation (Techn. Publ. 5).

LEDANT, J. AND JACOB, J. (1980) [Status and conservation of the Woodlark in Belgium.] Gerfaut 70: 95–103. (In Flemish.)

LEFRANC, N. (1973) [Notes on the recent history of the Red-backed Shrike Lanius collurio in western Europe.] Alauda 3: 239–252. (In French.)

LEFRANC, N. (1978) [The Lesser Grey Shrike Lanius minor in France.] Alauda 46: 193–208. (In French.)

LEFRANC, N. (1979) [Contribution to the ecology of the Red-backed Shrike (Lanius collurio L.) in the middle Vosges.] Oiseau et R.F.O. 49: 245–298. (In French.)

LEFRANC, N. (1980) [Biology and population fluctuations of shrikes in western Europe.] *Oiseau et R.F.O.* 50: 89–116. (In French.)

LEFRANC, N. (1993) [*The shrikes of Europe, Northern Africa and the Middle East.*] Paris: Delachaux et Niestlé. (In French.)

LEFRANC, N. (in press) General biology, changes in the breeding distribution and present status of the Lesser Grey Shrike *Lanius minor* in western Europe. International Shrike Symposium, Florida (January 1992).

LE GRAND, G. (1981) Report on survey in Madeira in 1981 (unpublished report).

LE GRAND, G., EMMERSON, K. AND MARTIN, A. (1984) The status and conservation of seabirds in the Macaronesian Islands. Pp.377–391 in J. P. Croxall, P. G. H. Evans and R. W. Schreiber, eds. *Status and conservation of the world's seabirds.* Cambridge, U.K.: International Council for Bird Preservation (Techn. Publ. 2).

LESCOURRET, F. AND ELLISON, L. (1989) [Distribution and habitat of natural populations of Grey Partridge *Perdix perdix* in mountains in France.] Pp.101–112 in *Actes du Colloque Galliformes de Montagne, Grenoble 1987.* Paris: Office National de la Chasse. (In French.)

LESHEM, Y. (1990) Raptor migration over Israel. Pp.166–167 in I. Newton, ed. *Birds of prey.* Australia: Weldon Owen.

LESTAN, S. (1992) [The White Stork in Lorraine: history and population development.] Pp.59–66 in J.-L. Mériaux, A. Schierer, C. Tombal and J.-C. Tombal, eds. [*The storks of Europe.*] Metz: Institut Européen d'Ecologie/ AMBE. (In French.)

LEVEQUE, R. (1956) [A Gull-billed Tern colony in the Camargue.] *Nos Oiseaux* 23: 233–246. (In French.)

LEVER, C. (1977) *The naturalized animals of the British Isles.* London: Hutchinson.

LEVER, C. (1987) *Naturalized birds of the world.* Harlow, U.K.: Longman.

LIBBERT, W. (1936) [Migration of the Common Crane (*Grus grus*).] *J. Orn.* 84: 297–337. (In German.)

LINDEMAN, G. V. (1983a) [Nest construction by the Steppe Eagle between the Volga and Ural rivers.] Pp.136–138 in V. E. Flint, ed. [*Conservation of raptors.*] Moscow: Nauka. (In Russian.)

LINDEMAN, G. V. (1983b) [The Long-legged Buzzard in semi-deserts east of the Volga river.] Pp.76–78 in V. M. Galushin, ed. [*Ecology of raptors.*] Moscow: Nauka. (In Russian.)

LINDÉN, M., MØLLER, A. P., SOLER, M. AND MORENO, J. (in prep.) Selection and micro-evolution in nest-site choice in a cavity nesting bird, the Black Wheater *Oenanthe leucura.*

LINDGREN, F. (1975) [Observations concerning the Siberian Jay (*Perisoreus infaustus*): in particular its breeding biology.] *Fauna och Flora* 70: 198–210. (In Swedish.)

LINDSTRÖM, E. R., ANDRÉN, H., ANGELSTAM, P., CEDERLUND, G., HÖRNFELDT, B., JÄDERBERG, L., LEMNELL, P.-A., MARTINSSON, B., SKÖLD, K. AND SWENSON, J. E. (in press) Disease reveals the predator—sarcoptic mange, red fox predation and prey populations in south-central Scandinavia. *Ecology.*

LIPKOVICH, A. D. (1985) [Notes on the biology of the Caucasian Black Grouse, Great Rosefinch and Güldenstädt's Redstart in highlands of northern Ossetia.] Pp.102–105 in V. E. Sokolov and T. B. Sablina, eds.

[*Studies and conservation of rare and vanishing animal species of the U.S.S.R. fauna.*] Moscow: Nauka. (In Russian.)

LIPPENS, L. AND WILLÉ, H. (1972) [*Atlas of the birds of Belgium and western Europe.*] Tielt: Lannoo. (In French.)

LIPU (1991) [Report from the Raptor Rehabilitation Centre.] Parma: Lega Italiana Protezione Uccelli (unpublished report). (In Italian.)

LITVINENKO, N. M. AND NEUFELDT, I. A. (1988) [*The Palearctic Cranes.*] Vladivostok: Academy of Sciences of the U.S.S.R., Amur-Ussuri Branch (Collection of Scientific Papers). (In Russian.)

LLANDRES, C. AND URDIALES, C. (1990) [*The birds of Doñana.*] Barcelona: Lynx. (In Spanish.)

LLOYD, C. S., TASKER, M. L. AND PARTRIDGE, K. E. (1991) *The status of seabirds in Britain and Ireland.* London: T. and A. D. Poyser.

LOBACHEV, V. S. (1961) [Data on the Long-legged Buzzard in semi-deserts east of the Volga river.] *Biological Sciences, Scientific Papers in Higher Education* 1: 37–43. (In Russian.)

LOCKIE, J. D. (1955) The breeding habits and food of Short-eared Owls after a vole plague. *Bird Study* 2: 53–69.

LØFALDLI, L., KALAS, J.-A. AND FISKE, P. (1992) Habitat selection and diet of Great Snipe *Gallinago media* during breeding. *Ibis* 134: 35–43.

LÖHRL, H. (1960) [Comparative studies of the breeding biology and behaviour of the nuthatches *Sitta whiteheadi* Sharpe and *Sitta canadensis*.] *J. Orn.* 101: 245–264. (In German.)

LÖHRL, H. (1961) [Comparative studies of the breeding biology and behaviour of the nuthatches *Sitta whiteheadi* Sharpe and *Sitta canadensis*.] *J. Orn.* 102: 111–132. (In German.)

LOPUSHKOV, V. A. (1988) [Loss of eagles.] *Hunting and game management* 12: 29. (In Russian.)

LORENZ, T. (1887) [Contribution to the knowledge of avifauna on the northern side of the Caucasus.] Moscow: Liessner und Roman. (In German.)

LORENZO, J. A. AND GONZÁLEZ, J. (1993) [*Birds of El Médano, Tenerife, Canary Islands.*] Santa Cruz de Tenerife: Asociación Tinerfeña de Amigos de la Naturaleza. (In Spanish.)

LOSHKAREV, G. A. (1976) Population dynamics of partridge in the foothills of the Northern Caucasus. *Ekologiya* 3: 275–276.

LOSKE, K.-H. AND LEDERER, W. (1987) [Population development and fluctuation in four trans-Saharan migrants in Westphalia: *Riparia riparia, Hirundo rustica, Anthus trivialis* and *Muscicapa striata*.] *Charadrius* 23: 101–127. (In German.)

LOSKOT, V. M. (1983) Life history of the eastern Black-eared Wheatear *Oenanthe hispanica melanoleuca* (Güid), in the U.S.S.R. *Acad. Sci. U.S.S.R.* 116: 79–107.

LOSKOT, V. M. (1988) [New data on the distribution and life history of the Radde's Accentor (*Prunella ocularis* Radde).] *Proc. Zool. Inst., Leningrad* 182: 89–115. (In Russian.)

LOSKOT, V. M. (1991) [Distribution and life history of the Caucasian Great Rosefinch *Carpodacus rubicilla rubicilla* (Güld.).] *Proc. Zool. Inst., Leningrad* 231: 43–116. (In Russian.)

LOVARI, S. (1974) The feeding habits of four raptors in

central Italy. *Raptor Res.* 8: 45–47.

LOVATY, F. (1991) [Distribution and abundance of the Ortolan Bunting (*E. hortulana*) in the Mende region (Department of Lozère, south of the Massif central, France).] *Nos Oiseaux* 41: 99–106. (In French.)

LOVE, J. A. (1983) *The return of the Sea Eagle.* Cambridge, U.K.: Cambridge University Press.

LØVENSKIOLD, H. L. (1964) Avifauna of Svalbard with a discussion on the geographical distribution of the birds in Spitsbergen and adjacent islands.*Norsk Polarinst. Skrifter* 129: 1–460.

LUCIO, A. J. AND PURROY, F. J. (1992) Red-legged Partridge (*Alectoris rufa*) habitat selection in northwest Spain. *Gibier Faune Sauvage* 9: 417–429.

LÜGGER, U. (1992) [The influence of the habitat quality on the breeding progress of the Red-backed Shrike and related energetic costs in the adults.] *J. Orn.* 133: 322. (In German.)

LÜPS, P. (1981) [Is the Rock Partridge disappearing from the Alps?.] *Naturforschende Gesellschaft und Rheinaubund, Schaffhauesen, Flugbatt* (Ser. II) 16: 1–22. (In German.)

LYAYSTER, A. T. AND SOSNIN, G. V. (1942) [*Birds of Armenia.*] Erevan: Armen. Filiala Akademii Sci. U.S.S.R. (In Russian.)

LYSENKO, V. I. (1980) [Conservation of waders in the Zaporozhe region.] Pp.67–68 in V. E. Flint, ed. [*A novelty in the studies of wader biology and distribution.*] Moscow: Nauka. (In Russian.)

LYSENKO, V. J. (1992) [*Fauna of the Ukraine: Birds, 5: Anseriformes.*] Kiev: Naukova Dumka. (In Russian.)

MACDONALD, S. D. AND MACPHERSON, A. H. (1962) Breeding places of the Ivory Gull in Arctic Canada. *Nat. Mus. Can. Bull. Ottawa* 183: 111–117.

MACKOWICZ, R. (1970) Biology of the Woodlark *Lullula arborea* in the Rezpin forest (western Poland). *Acta Zool. Cracov.* 15: 61–160.

MADGE, S. AND BURN, H. (1988) *Wildfowl.* London: Christopher Helm.

MADSEN, F. J. (1954) On the food habits of the diving ducks in Denmark. *Dan. Rev. Game Biol.* 2: 157–266.

MADSEN, J. (1984) Study of the possible impact of oil exploration on goose populations in Jameson Land, East Greenland: a progress report. *Nor. Polarinst. Skr.* 181: 141–151.

MADSEN, J. (1991) Status and trends of goose populations in the western Palearctic in the 1980s.*Ardea* 79: 113–122.

MADSEN, J., BREGNBALLE, T. AND MEHLUM, F. (1989) Study of the breeding ecology and behaviour of the Svalbard population of Light-bellied Brent Goose *Branta bernicla hrota. Polar Res.* 7: 1–21.

MADSEN, J., BREGNBALLE, T. AND HASTRUP, A. (1992) Impact of the Arctic Fox *Alopex lagopus* on nesting success of geese in south-east Svalbard, 1989. *Polar Res.* 11: 35–39.

MADSEN, J., KOMDEUR, J. AND CRACKNELL, G. (1993) International action for the Lesser White-fronted Goose*Anser erythropus.* Proc. 7th Nordic Ornithological Congress.

MAFF (1992) *Arable area payments explanatory booklet.* London: MAFF.

MAGDALENO, G. AND MUÑOZ-COBO, J. (1993) Territoriality and reproductive biology of the Woodchat Shrike in southern Spain. Proceedings International Shrike Symposium, Lake Pacid, Florida.

MAGEE, J. D. (1965) The breeding distribution of the Stonechat in Britain and the causes of its decline. *Bird Study* 12: 83–89.

MAGNIN, G. (1987) *An account of the illegal catching and shooting of birds in Cyprus during 1986.* Cambridge, U.K.: International Council for Bird Preservation (Study Rep. 21).

MAGNIN, G. (1988) *Falconry and hunting in Turkey during 1987.* Cambridge, U.K.: International Council for Bird Preservation (Study Rep. 34).

MAGNIN, G. (1991) Hunting and persecution of migratory birds in the Mediterranean region. Pp.63–75 in T. Salathé, ed. *Conserving migratory birds.* Cambridge, U.K.: International Council for Bird Preservation (Techn. Publ. 12).

MAKATSCH, W. (1962) [Some observations at the breeding grounds of the Spur-winged Plover (*Hoplopterus spinosus*).] *J. Orn.* 103: 219–228. (In German.)

MAKATSCH, W. (1968) [Observations at a breeding site of Audouin's Gull (*Larus audouinii*).] *J. Orn.* 109: 43–56. (In German.)

MAKATSCH, W. (1969) [The Spur-winged Plover, one of the most recent additions to Europe's breeding avifauna.] *Natur and Museum* 99: 379–385. (In German.)

MAKATSCH, W. (1981) [*The birds of the German Democratic Republic.*] Leipzig-Radebeul: Neumann-Verlag. (In German.)

MALAKOU, M., JERRENTRUP, H., KYRIAZI, A., HATZANTONIS, D. AND PAPAYANNAKIS, E. (1988) Integrated management of coastal wetlands of the Mediterranean type in northern Greece. Unpublished report to EC-DG XI.

MALCHEVSKIY, A. S. AND PUKINSKIY, Y. B. (1983) [*Birds of Leningrad region and adjacent territories.*] Leningrad: Leningrad University. (In Russian.)

MANRIQUE, J. (1993) [*The birds of Almería.*] Almería: Instituto de Estudios Almerienses, Exma. Diputación Provincial. (In Spanish.)

MANRIQUE, J. AND DE JUANA, E. (1991) Land-use changes and the conservation of dry grassland birds in Spain: a case study of Almena Province. Pp.49–58 in P. D. Goriup, L. A. Batten and J.-A. Norton, eds. *The conservation of lowland dry grassland birds in Europe.* Newbury, Berkshire: Joint Nature Conservation Committee.

MANRIQUE, J. AND MIRALLES, J. M. (1988) [The Trumpeter Finch.] *Quercus* 32: 34–36. (In Spanish.)

MANRIQUE, J., SUÁREZ, F. AND GARZA, V. (1990) [The Dupont's Lark in Spain.] *Quercus* 57: 6–11. (In Spanish.)

MÁÑEZ, M. (1981) [The food of the Little Owl (*Athene noctua*) in Spain.] Madrid: Universidad Complutense de Madrid (Master thesis). (In Spanish.)

MÁÑEZ, M. (1987) [Owls (Strigiformes).] Pp.103–136 in Federacíon de Amigos de la Tierra, ed. [*Annual Ornithology: Raptors.*] Madrid: Editorial Miraguano. (In Spanish.)

MÁÑEZ, M. (1991) [Status of bird species in the Doñana National Park including those listed in the Spanish Red data list as Endangered and Vulnerable.] Pp.41–49 in Andalus, ed. [*Workshop on wetlands of Andalucia.*] Málaga: Asoc. Andalus, Fund. Bios and Finca el Retiro. (In Spanish.)

MARCHANT, J. H., HUDSON, R., CARTER, S. P. AND WHITTINGTON, P. (1990) *Population trends in British breeding birds.* Tring, U.K.: British Trust for Ornithology.

MARCO, J. AND GARCIA FERRÉ, D. (1983) [*Pterocles orientalis.*] Pp.122–123 in J. Muntaner, X. Ferrer and A. Martínez-Vilalta, eds. [*The atlas of breeding birds in Catalonia and Andorra.*] Barcelona: Ketres. (In Catalán.)

MARCSTRÖM, V., KENWARD, R. AND ENGREN, E. (1988) The impact of predation on boreal tetraonids during vole cycles: an experimental study. *J. Anim. Ecol.* 53: 859–872.

MARÉCHAL, P. (1993) [On the external factors influencing the habitat quality of the Red-backed Shrike.] *Vogeljaar* 41: 34–48. (In German.)

MARINKOVIC, S., SUSIC, G., GRUBAC, B., SOTI, J. P. AND SIMONOV, N. (1985) The Griffon Vulture in Yugoslavia. Pp.131–135 in I. Newton and R. D. Chancellor, eds. *Conservation studies on raptors.* Cambridge, U.K.: International Council for Bird Preservation (Techn. Publ. 5).

MARJAKANGAS, A. (1982) Poor breeding success in the Spotted Flycatcher *Muscicapa striata* in 1981 due to bad weather. *Ornis Fenn.* 59: 36–37.

MARQUISS, M., RATCLIFFE, D. A. AND ROXBURGH, R. (1985) The numbers, breeding success and diet of Golden Eagles in southern Scotland in relation to changes in land-use. *Biol. Conserv.* 33: 1–17.

MARTÍN, A. (1979) [Contribution to the study of the Canarian avifauna: the biology of the Blue Chaffinch (*Fringilla teydea teydea* Moquin-Tandon).] Tenerife: La Laguna University (thesis). (In Spanish.)

MARTÍN, A. (1987) [*Atlas of the breeding birds of the island of Tenerife.*] Santa Cruz de Tenerife: Instituto de Estudios Canarios (Monogr. 32). (In Spanish.)

MARTÍN, A., HERNÁNDEZ, E., DELGADO, G. AND QUILIS, V. (1984) [Nesting of the Madeiran Storm-petrel *Oceanodroma castro* (Harcourt, 1851) in the Canary Islands.] *Doñana Acta Vert.* 11: 337–341. (In Spanish.)

MARTÍN, A., DELGADO, G., NOGALES, M., QUILIS, V., TRUJILLO, O., HERNANDES, E. AND SANTANA, F. (1989) [First records of nesting of the Manx Shearwater *Puffinus puffinus*, the White-faced Petrel *Pelagodroma marina* and the Roseate Tern *Sterna dougallii* on the Canary Islands.] *Oiseau et R.F.O.* 59: 73–83.

MARTÍN, A., HERNÁNDEZ, E., NOGALES, M., QUILIS, V., TRUJILLO, O. AND DELGADO, G. (1990) [*The Red Book of terrestrial vertebrates of the Canaries.*] Santa Cruz de Tenerife: Servicio de publicaciones de la Caja General de Ahorros de Canarias. (In Spanish.)

MARTÍN, A., HERNÁNDEZ, M. A. AND RODRIGUEZ, F. (1993) [The first breeding of the Bolle's Pigeon on the island of Hierro (Canary Islands).] *Alauda* 61: 148. (In Spanish.)

MARTÍNEZ, C. (1991) Patterns of distribution and habitat selection of a Great Bustard *Otis tarda* populations in north-western Spain. *Ardeola* 38: 137–146.

MARTÍNEZ, I. AND CARRERA, E. (1983) [New colony of Audouin's Gull *Larus audouinii* Payr in Spain.] *Butll. Inst. Catalana Hist. Nat.* 49: 159–161. (In Spanish.)

MARTÍNEZ VILTATA, A. (1992) [New observations on the Ebro delta.] *GIAM* 16: 7. (In Spanish.)

MARTÍN-NOVELLA, C., CRIADO, J. AND NAVESO, M. A. (1993) [The mark of the new Common Agricultural Policy: nature conservation and water management.] *Ecosistemas* 5: 24–27. (In Spanish.)

MARTINS, R. P. (1989) Turkey: Bird Report 1982–86. *Sandgrouse* 11: 1–41.

MASSA, B. (1985) [Atlas of the fauna of Sicily: birds 1979–1983.] *Naturalista Sicil.* 9 (Suppl.). (In Italian.)

MASSA, B., LO VALVO, F., SIRACUSA, M. AND CIACCIO, A. (1991) [The Lanner (*Falco biarmicus feldeggii* Schiegel) in Italy: status, biology and taxonomy.] *Naturalista Sicil.* 15: 27–63. (In Italian.)

MASSOLI-NOVELLI, R. (1987) [Contribution to the knowledge of the migration of Great Snipe *Gallinago media.*] *Riv. Ital. Orn. Milano* 57: 14–20. (In Italian.)

MATTHYSEN, E. AND ADRIENSEN, F. S. P. (1989) [Winter territoriality and social behaviour in the Corsican Nuthatch *Sitta whiteheadi* Sharpe.] *Alauda* 57: 155–168. (In French.)

MAYAUD, N. (1956) [Study of the migration and winter quarters of *Sterna caspia* from Eurasia.] *Alauda* 24: 206–218. (In French.)

MAYAUD, N. (1966) [Contribution to the knowledge of Red-crested Pochard *Netta rufina* (Pallas) in western Europe.] *Alauda* 34: 191–199. (In French.)

MAYHEW, P. (1988) The daily energy intake of the European Wigeon in winter. *Ornis Scand.* 19: 217–223.

MAYOL, J. (1977) [Contribution to the study of the Black Vulture in Mallorca.] *Bol. Soc. Hist. Nat. Baleares* 22: 150–178. (In Spanish.)

MAYOL, J. (1986) Human impact on seabirds in the Balearic Islands. Pp.379–396 in MEDMARAVIS and X. Monbailliu, eds. *Mediterranean marine avifauna.* Berlin and Heidelberg: Springer-Verlag (NATO ASI Ser. G. 12).

McCRACKEN, D. I., FOSTER, G. N., BIGNAL, E. M. AND BIGNAL, S. (1992) An assessment of Chough *Pyrrhocorax pyrrhocorax* diet using multivariate analysis techniques. *Avocetta* 16: 19–29.

McCULLOCH, M. N., TUCKER, G. M. AND BAILLIE, S. R. (1992) The hunting of migratory birds in Europe: a ringing recovery analysis. *Ibis* 134 (Suppl. 1): 55–65.

McGREGOR, P. AND BYLE, P. A. F. (1992) Individually distinctive Bittern booms—a possible censusing tool. *Bioacoustics* 4: 93–109.

McNICHOLL, M. K. (1975) Larid site tenacity and group adherence in relation to habitat. *Auk* 92: 98–104.

McVEAN, D. N. R. AND RATCLIFFE, D. A. (1962) *Plant communities of the Scottish Highlands.* London: Her Majesty's Stationery Office (Nature Conservancy Monogr. 1).

MEAD, C. (1979) Mortality and causes of death in British Sand Martins. *Bird Study* 26: 107–112.

MEAD, C. J. AND WILSON, J. D. (1993) Skylarks to ascend in 1994? *BTO News* 188: 1.

MEADOWS, B. S. (1972) Kingfisher numbers and stream pollution. *Ibis* 110: 443.

MEBS, T. (1959) [A study of the biology of the Lanner.] *Vogelwelt* 80: 142–149. (In German.)

MEES, G. F. (1979) [Distribution and numbers of the Whiskered Tern in Europe and northern Africa.] *Zool. Bijdr.* 26: 1–63. (In Dutch.)

MEHLUM, F. (1984) [Concentrations of seabirds near glaciers in Svalbard.] *Fauna* 37: 156–160. (In Swedish.)

MEHLUM, F. (1989) Summer distribution of seabirds in the northern Greenland and Barents Seas. *Norsk Polarinst. Skrifter* 191: 1–56.

MEHLUM, F. (1990) Seabird distribution in the northern Barents Sea marginal ice-zone during late summer. *Polar Res.* 8: 61–65.

MEHLUM, F. AND FJELD, P. E. (1987) Catalogue of seabird colonies in Svalbard. *Norsk Polarinst. Rapp.* 35.

MEIER-PEITHMANN, W. (1992) [Abundance and population development of the Ortolan Bunting *Emberiza hortulana* in the Hannoversches Wendland.] In [*Symposium on the Ortolan Bunting, Vienna 4–6 July 1992.*] Vienna: Universität für Bodenkultur. (In German.)

MEININGER, P. L. (1986) [The Avocet *Recurvirostra avosetta*, plovers *Charadrius* and terns *Sterna* as breeding birds in the delta area in 1975–1985.] *Limosa* 59: 1–14. (In Dutch.)

MEININGER, P. L. AND MULLIÉ, W. C. (1981) Egyptian wetlands as threatened wintering areas for waterbirds. *Sandgrouse* 3: 62–77.

MEININGER, P. L., BERREVOETS, C. M. AND STRUCKER, R. C. W. (1992) [*Coastal breeding birds in the delta area including an overview of 13 years of monitoring, 1979–1991.*] Middelburg, Netherlands: Rijkswaterstaat Dienst Getijdewateren. (Rapport DGW 92.024). (In Dutch.)

MEISSNER, W. AND KOSAKIEWICZ, M. (1992) Aerial survey along Polish Baltic coast in January 1991. *IWRB Seaduck Bull.* 1: 21–22.

MEKLENBURTSEV, R. N. (1954) [Black-throated Accentor *Prunella atrogularis*.] Pp.632–638 in G. P. Dementiev and N. A. Gladkov, eds. [*Birds of the Soviet Union,* 5.] Moscow: Sovetskaya Nauka. (In Russian.)

MELTOFTE, H. (1985) Populations and breeding schedules of waders, Charadrii, in high-Arctic Greenland. *Medd. om Grønland, Bioscience* 16: 1–43.

MELTOFTE, H. (1986) Hunting as a possible factor in the decline of the Fennoscandian population of Curlews *Numenius arquata. Vår Fågelv.* 11: 135–140.

MELTOFTE, H. (1993) [Wader migration through Denmark: populations, non-breeding phenology and migratory strategies.] *Dansk Ornit. Foren. Tidsskr.* 87: 1–180. (In Danish.)

MELTOFTE, H. AND LYNGS, P. (1981) [Spring migration of waders Charadrii near Blåvandshuk 1964–1977.] *Dansk Ornit. Foren. Tidsskr.* 75: 23–30. (In Danish.)

MENDELSSOHN, H. (1972) The impact of pesticides on bird life in Israel. *Internatn. Counc. Bird Preserv. Bull.* 11: 75–104.

MENDELSSOHN, H. (1975a) The White Stork in Israel. *Vogelwarte* 28: 123–131.

MENDELSSOHN, H. (1975b) Report on the status of some bird species in Israel in 1974. *Internatn. Counc. Bird Preserv. Bull.* 12: 265–270.

MENDELSSOHN, H., MARDER, U. AND YOM-TOW, T. (1969) On the decline of migrant Quail (*Coturnix c. coturnix*) populations in Israel and Sinai. *Israel J. Zool.* 18: 317–323.

MENZEL, H. (1962) [*The Wryneck* Jynx torquilla.] Wittenberg Lutherstadt: Ziemsen Verlag. (In German.)

MENZEL, H. (1984) [*The Redstart* Phoenicurus phoenicurus.] Wittenberg Lutherstadt: Ziemsen Verlag. (In German.)

MESTRE, P., PERIS, S., SANTOS, T., SUÁREZ, F. AND SOLER, B. (1987) The decrease of the Black-eared Wheatear *Oenanthe hispanica* on the Iberian peninsula. *Bird Study* 34: 239–243.

MEWES, W. (1980) [The stock of cranes, *Grus grus* (L. 1758) in the three northern districts of the G.D.R.] *Arch. Natursch. Landesforsch.* 20: 213–234. (In German.)

MEWES, W. (1989) [Summering Cranes.] Pp.115–118 in H. Prange, ed. *Der Graue Kranich.* Wittenberg Lutherstadt: Ziemsen Verlag. (In German.)

MICHEV, T. (1990) [*The atlas of breeding birds in Bulgaria.*] Tulcea: Repro. (In Bulgarian.)

MICHEYEV, A. V. (1952) [Caucasian Black Grouse.] Pp.78–83 in G. P. Dementiev and N. A. Gladkov, eds. [*The birds of the Soviet Union,* 4.] Moscow: Sovetskaya Nauka. (In Russian.)

MIHELSONS, H. A. (1982) [The Steppe Eagle (*Aquila nipalensis* Hodgs).] Pp.92–96 in [*Bird migration in east Europe and north Asia. Raptors-Cranes.*] Moscow: Nauka. (In Russian.)

MIKKOLA, H. (1983) *Owls of Europe.* Calton, U.K.: T. and A. D. Poyser.

MIKUSKA, T. (1992) [Heron populations in Croatia.] Zagreb: Zagreb University (Diploma). (In Yugoslavian.)

MILDENBERGER, H. (1950) [Contributions to the ecology and breeding biology of the Stonechat.] *Bonn. Zool. Beitr.* 1: 11–20. (In German.)

MILDENBERGER, H., ED. (1984) [*The birds of the Rheinland,* 2.] Düsseldorf: Kilda Verlag. (In German.)

MINEYEV, Y. N. (1991) Distribution and numbers of Bewick's Swans, *Cygnus bewickii* in the European northeast of the U.S.S.R. Pp.52–67 in J. Sears and P. J. Bacon, eds. *Third IWRB International Swan Symposium, Oxford 1989.* Wildfowl (Suppl. 1).

MINORANSKIY, V. A. (1967) [Influence of hail on breeding of birds.] *Ornitologiya* 8: 374. (In Russian.)

MISHCHENKO, A. L. (1988) [Additions to the new edition of the Red Data Book of Russia.] Pp.32–37 in V. I. Il'yashenko, ed. [*Rare animals in the Russian Federation.*] Moscow: TSNIL Glavokhota RSFSR. (In Russian.)

MITCHELL, J. R., MOSER, M. E. AND KIRBY, J. S. (1988) Declines in midwinter counts of waders roosting on the Dee estuary. *Bird Study* 35: 191–198.

MOCCI DEMARTIS, A. (1992) [Barbary Partridge *Alectoris barbara* (Bonnaterre 1790).] Pp.787–791 in P. Brichetti, P. de Francesci and N. Baccetti, eds. *Fauna d'Italia, Aves I. Gaviidae–Phasionidae.* Bologna: Calderini. (In Italian.)

MOCCI DEMARTIS, A. AND MASSOLI-NOVELLI, R. (1978) [Distribution characteristics and feasibility of releases of the Barbary Partridge *Alectoris barbara* (Bonnaterre).] *Boll. Soc. Sarda Sci. Nat.* 17: 71–107. (In Italian.)

MOISEEV, A. P. (1980) [Nesting biology of the Black Lark in central and northern Kazakhstan.] Pp.120–126 in [*Biology of birds in the Naurzum Reserve.*] Alma-Ata: Kainar. (In Russian.)

MOLAMUSOV, K. T. (1967) [*Birds of the central Northern Caucasus.*] Nalchik: Kabardino-Balkar (In Russian.)

MOLL, K. H. (1956) [Crane observations at the Lake Müritz area.] *Beitr. Vogelkunde* 8: 221–253, 368–388, 412–439. (In German.)

MOLL, K. H. (1962) [*The Osprey* Pandion haliaetus.] Wittenberg Lutherstadt: Ziemsen Verlag. (In German.)

MØLLER, A. P. (1978) [Distribution, population size and changes in gulls Larinae breeding in Denmark, with a review of the situations in other parts of Europe.] *Dansk Ornit. Foren. Tidsskr.* 72: 15–39. (In Danish.)

MØLLER, A. P. (1977) [Food composition of the Gull-billed Tern *Gelochelidon n. nilotica* Gmel. during breeding in north Jutland, Denmark, and Camargue, France, with a review of food items in other areas.] *Dansk Ornit. Foren. Tidsskr.* 71: 103–111. (In Danish.)

MØLLER, A. P. (1978) [Distribution, population size and changes in gulls Larinae breeding in Denmark, with a review of the situations in other parts of Europe.] *Dansk Ornit. Foren. Tidsskr.* 72: 15–39. (In Danish.)

MØLLER, A. P. (1981) Migration of European Sandwich Tern, *Sterna sandvicensis* I. *Die Vogelwarte* 31: 74–94.

MØLLER, A. P. (1983) Changes in Danish farmland habitats and their population of breeding birds. *Holarctic Ecol.* 6: 95–100.

MØLLER, A. P. (1985) Breeding habitat selection in the Swallow *Hirundo rustica*. *Bird Study* 30: 134–142.

MØLLER, A. P. (1989) Population dynamics of a declining Swallow *Hirundo rustica* population. *J. Anim. Ecol.* 58: 1051–1063.

MOLODAN, G. N. (1980) [The breeding of the Pratincole in north-east Priazovye.] *Vestnik Zool.* 4: 96–97. (In Russian.)

MOLODAN, G. N. (1988) [Black-winged Pratincole.] Pp.117–118 in M. A. Voinstvenskiy, ed. [*Colonial waterbirds of south Ukraine: the waders.*] Kiev: Naukova Dumka. (In Russian.)

MOLODAN, G. N. AND POZHIDAYEVA, S. I. (1991) [The state of the Black-winged Pratincole population in the Ukraine and the methods for its preservation.] Pp.85–86 in V. M. Galushin, ed. [*Abstracts 10th U.S.S.R. Ornithological Conference, part 2.*] Vitebsk, Minsk: Nauka i Tekhnika. (In Russian.)

MONK, J. F. (1963) The past and present status of the Wryneck in the British Isles. *Bird Study* 10: 112–132.

MONTEVECCHI, W. A. (1993) Birds as indicators of changes in marine prey stocks. Pp.217–266 in R. W. Furness and J. D. D. Greenwood, eds. *Birds as monitors of environmental change*. London: Chapman and Hall.

MONVAL, J.-Y. AND PIROT, J.-Y. (1989) *Results of the IWRB International Waterfowl Census 1967–86*. Slimbridge, U.K.: International Waterfowl and Wetlands Research Bureau (Spec. Publ. 8).

MOPT (1992) [*Project guidelines of hydrological catchment plans.*] Madrid: Ministerio de Obras Públicas y Transportes. (In Spanish.)

MOPTMA (1994) [*National Hydrological Plan: analysis of scenarios.*] Madrid: Dirección General de Obras Hidráulicas, Ministerio de Obras Públicas, Transportes y Medio Ambiente. (In Spanish.)

MOREAU, R. E. (1972) *The Palaearctic–African bird migration systems*. London and New York: Academic Press.

MOREL, M. Y. (1987) [The Turtle Dove *Streptopelia turtur* in West Africa: migratory movements and food composition.] *Malimbus* 9: 23–42. (In French.)

MORENO, A. C. (1991) [Distribution, biology and essential habitat requirements of Blue Chaffinch on Gran Canaria.] Gran Canaria: Gobierno de Canarias, Viceconsejería de Medio Ambiente (unpublished). (In Spanish.)

MORENO, J., SOLER, M., MØLLER, A. P. AND LINDÉN, M. (in press) The function of stone carrying in the Black Wheater *Oenanthe leucura*. *Anim. Behav.*

MORGAN, R. AND GLUE, D. (1977) Breeding, mortality and movements of Kingfishers. *Bird Study* 24: 15–24.

MOROZOV, V. V. (1990) [Rare breeding waders of the Moscow and Klyasma rivers.] Pp.144–149 in V. T. Butjev, ed. [*Rare bird species of the central European Russia.*] Moscow: U.S.S.R. Ornithological Society, Moscow Division. (In Russian.)

MORRIS, A. (1993) The 1992 Nightjar survey: a light at the end of the tunnel for this threatened species? *BTO News* 185: 8–9.

MORRISON, R. I. G. AND DAVIDSON, N. C. (1990) Migration, body condition and behaviour of shorebirds during spring migration at Alert, Ellesmere Island, N.W.T. Pp.544–567 in C. R. Harington, ed. *Canada's missing dimension. Science and history in the Canadian Arctic islands*. Ottawa: Canadian Museum of Nature.

MOSEIKIN, V. N. (1991) [Rare nesting birds of prey between the Volga and Ural rivers.] Pp.93–94 in A. P. Shkljarov, ed. [*Abstracts 10th U.S.S.R. Ornithological Conference, part 2.*] Vitebsk, Minsk: Nauka i Tekhnika. (In Russian.)

MOSEILIN, V. N. (1992) Ecology and protection of the Little Bustard in the Saratov region. *Bustard Studies* 5: 78–91.

MOSER, M. (1983) Purple Heron in the Camargue. Pp.104–113 in P. R. Evans, H. Hafner and P. L'Hermite, eds. *Shorebirds and large waterbirds conservation*. Brussels: Commission of the European Communities.

MOSER, M. (1984) Resource partitioning in colonial herons with particular reference to the Grey Heron *Ardea cinerea* L. and the Purple Heron *Ardea purpurea* L. in the Camargue, south France. Durham, U.K.: Durham University (Ph.D. thesis).

MOUGIN, J.-L. (1988) [On the nesting and the rearing of young in White-faced Petrel *Pelagodroma marina hypoleuca* on Selvagem Grande.] *Cyanopica* 4: 167–184. (In French.)

MOUGIN, J.-L. (1989) [Evaluation of the energy expenditure and food consumption in Bulwer's Petrel *Bulweria bulwerii*, in relation to weight loss during periods of fasting.] *Bul. Mus. Mun. Funchal* 41: 25–39. (In French.)

MOUGIN, J.-L., JOUANIN, C. AND ROUX, F. (1988) [Migration of Cory's Shearwater *Calonectris diomedea*.] *Oiseau et R.F.O.* 58: 113–119. (In French.)

MOUGIN, J.-L., JOUANIN, C. AND ROUX, F. (1992) [Breeding chronology of Little Shearwater *Puffinus assimilis* Gould and Audubon's Shearwater *P. lherminieri* Lesson.] *Oiseau et R.F.O.* 62: 247–277. (In French.)

MOUNTFORT, G. (1957) *Portrait of a wilderness: the story of the Coto Doñana expeditions*. London: Hutchinson.

MUDGE, G. P. AND TALBOT, T. R. (1993) The breeding biology and causes of nest failure of Scottish Black-throated Divers *Gavia arctica*. *Ibis* 135: 113–120.

MÜLLER, C. Y. (1983) [The significance of old reed beds for Spoonbills and herons in the Neusiedler See area.] *Egretta* 26: 43–46. (In German.)

MÜLLER, C. Y. (1984) [Population and migration of the Spoonbills *Platalea leucorodia* L. in the Austrian-Hungarian area.] *Egretta* 27: 45–67. (In German.)

MULLIÉ, W. C., VERWEY, P. J., BERENDS, A. G., EVERTS, J. W., SÈNE, F. AND KOEMAN, J. H. (1991) The impact of pesticides on Palearctic migratory birds in the western Sahel region. Pp.37–61 in T. Salathé, ed. *Conserving migratory birds*. Cambridge, U.K.: International Council for Bird Preservation (Techn. Publ. 12).

MUNDY, P. J. (1985) The biology of the vultures: a summary of the workshop proceedings. Pp.457–482 in I. Newton and R. D. Chancellor, eds. *Conservation studies on raptors*. Cambridge, U.K.: International Council for Bird Preservation (Techn. Publ. 5).

MUNTANER, J. (1981) [Status of breeding diurnal raptors of Balearic islands.] Pp.62–65 in G. Cheylan and G. C. Thibault, eds. [*Mediterranean raptors I*]. Aix-en-Provence, France: Parc Naturel Régional de la Corse/Centre de Recherche Ornithologique de Provence. (In French.)

MUNTANER, J., FERRER, X. AND MARTÍNEZ-VILLALTA, A. (1983) [*Atlas of the breeding birds of Cataluña and Andorra.*] Barcelona: Ketres. (In Catalan.)

MUNTEANU, D. (1992) National report from Romania. Pp.167–170 in M. van Roomen and J. Madsen, eds. *Waterfowl and agriculture: review and future perspective of the crop damage conflict in Europe.* Slimbridge, U.K.: International Waterfowl and Wetlands Research Bureau (Spec. Publ. 21).

MUNTEANU, D., WEBER, P., SZABÓ, J., GOGU-BOGDAN, M. AND MARINOV, M. (1991) A note on the present status of geese in Romania. *Ardea* 79: 165–166.

MUNTJANU, A. I. (1977) [Nesting of the Steppe Eagle in eastern parts of the Rostov region.] Pp.236–237 in [*7th U.S.S.R. Ornithological Conference, Abstracts,* 2.] Kiev. (In Russian.)

MUÑOZ-COBO, J. (1984) [Hunting of birds and thrushes in Jaén.] Madrid and Cambridge: Sociedad Española de Ornitología and International Council for Bird Preservation (unpublished manuscript). (In Spanish.)

MUÑOZ-COBO, J. (1987) [Bird communities of Jaen olives groves.] Madrid: Universidad Complutense de Madrid (Ph.D. thesis). (In Spanish.)

MUÑOZ-COBO, J. (1990) [Dynamics of breeding birds in the old olive trees of Jaen.] *Revta Científica de ANSE* 1: 99–117. (In Spanish.)

MUÑOZ-COBO, J. (1992) Breeding bird communities in the olive tree plantations of southern Spain: the role of the age of trees. *Alauda* 60: 118–122.

MURTON, R. K. (1968) Breeding, migration and survival of Turtle Doves. *Brit. Birds* 61: 193–212.

NADLER, T. (1976) [*Little Tern* Sterna albifrons.] Wittenberg Lutherstadt: Ziemsen Verlag. (In German.)

NANKINOV, D. N. (1982) [The Steppe Eagle (*Aquila nipalensis* Cabanis) in south-east Europe.] *Ornitologiya* 7: 137–142. (In Russian.)

NANKINOV, D., STOYANOV, G., KOUZMANOV, G. AND TODOROV, R. (1991) Information on the situation of diurnal raptors in Bulgaria. *Birds of Prey Bull.* 4: 293–302.

NASRULLAEV, N. I. (1990) [Birds of the eastern highlands of Bogoss range.] *Ornitologiya* 24: 154–156. (In Russian.)

DE NAUROIS, R. (1969) [Brief notes on the avifauna of the Cape Verde archipelago: fauna, endemism, ecology.] *Bull. Inst. Fond. Afr. Noire* (Sér. A) 31: 143–218. (In French.)

NAVARRO MEDINA, J. D. AND ROBLEDANO AYMERICH, F. (1992) Marbled Teal in southern Alicante (Comunidad Valenciana, eastern Spain). *IWRB Threatened Waterfowl Res. Group Newsl.* 2.

NAVESO, M. A. (1992a) *Proposal to declare the steppeland of Madrigal-Peñaranda as an Environmentally Sensitive Area.* Madrid: Spanish Ornithological Society.

NAVESO, M. A. (1992b) *Proposal to declare the steppeland of Villafáfila as an Environmentally Sensitive Area.* Madrid: Spanish Ornithological Society.

NAVESO, M. A. AND GROVES-RAINES, S. (1992) *Proposal to declare the steppeland of Tierra de Campos as an Environmentally Sensitive Area.* Madrid: Spanish Ornithological Society.

NEATH, C. D. AND HUTCHINSON, B. (1978) Little Gulls in Britain and Ireland. *Brit. Birds* 71: 563–582.

NEGRO, J. J., DE LA RIVA, M. AND BUSTAMANTE, J. (1991)

Patterns of winter distribution and abundance of Lesser Kestrels (*Falco naumanni*) in Spain. *J. Raptor Res.* 25: 30–35.

NEHLS, H. W. (1973) [Common Gull.] *Falke* 20: 380–387.

NELSON, J. B. (1978) *The Gannet.* Berkhamsted, U.K.: T. and A. D. Poyser.

NERUCHEV, V. V. AND MAKAROV, V. I. (1982) [Data on nesting bird fauna and populations of the lower Emba river.] *Ornitologiya* 17: 125–129. (In Russian.)

NETHERSOLE-THOMPSON, D. (1975) *Pine Crossbills: a Scottish contribution.* Berkhamsted, U.K.: T. and A. D. Poyser.

NETTLESHIP, D. N. AND BIRKHEAD, T. R., EDS. (1985) *The Atlantic Alcidae: the evolution, distribution and biology of the auks inhabiting the Atlantic Ocean and adjacent water areas.* Orlando: Academic Press.

NEUFELDT, I. A., ED. (1982) [*Cranes in the U.S.S.R.*] Leningrad: Academy of Sciences of the U.S.S.R. (In Russian.)

NEUFELDT, I. A. (1986) [Results of an ornithological expedition to the south-eastern Altai.] *Proc. Zool. Inst. Acad. Sci. USSR.* 150: 7–43. (In Russian.)

NEUFELDT, I. A. AND KESKPAIK, J., EDS. (1987) [*Crane study in the U.S.S.R.*] Tartu: Academy of Sciences of the Estonian S.S.R. (Communications of the Baltic Commission for the Study of Bird Migration No. 19). (In Russian.)

NEUFELDT, I. A. AND KESKPAIK, J., EDS. (1989) [*Common Crane researches in the U.S.S.R.*] Tartu: Academy of Sciences of the U.S.S.R. (Communications of the Baltic Commission for the Study of Bird Migration No. 21). (In Russian.)

NEUFELDT, I. A. AND VON VIETINGHOFF-SCHEEL, E. (1984) *Phoenicurus erythrogaster.* In H. Dathe and I. A. Neufeldt, eds. [*Atlas of the distribution of birds of the Palearctic,* 12.] Berlin: Akademische Verlag. (In German.)

DEL NEVO, A. J., DUNN, E. K., MEDEIROS, F. M., LE GRAND, G., AKERS, P. AND MONTEIRO, L. R. (1990) Status, distribution and conservation of Garajau Rosado *Sterna dougallii* and Garajau Comum *Sterna hirundo* in the Azores. Sandy, U.K.: Royal Society for the Protection of Birds (preliminary report).

DEL NEVO, A. J., DUNN, E. K., MEDEIROS, F. M., LE GRAND, G., AKERS, P., AVERY, M. I. AND MONTEIRO, L. R. (1993) The status of Roseate Terns *Sterna dougallii* and Common Terns *Sterna hirundo* in the Azores. *Seabird* 15: 30–37.

NEWTON, I. (1979) *Population ecology of raptors.* Berkhamsted, U.K.: T. and A. D. Poyser.

NEWTON, I. AND GALBRAITH, E. A. (1991) Organochlorines and mercury in the eggs of Golden Eagles *Aquila chrysaetos* from Scotland. *Ibis* 133: 115–120.

NEWTON, I., BOGAN, J. A. AND HAAS, M. B. (1988) Organochlorines and mercury in the eggs of British Peregrines *Falco peregrinus. Ibis* 131: 355–376.

NEWTON, I., WYLLIE, I. AND FREESTONE, P. (1990) Rodenticides in British Barn Owls. *Environ. Pollut.* 68: 101–117.

NEWTON, I., WYLLIE, I. AND ASHER, A. (1991) Mortality causes in British Barn Owls *Tyto alba* with a discussion of aldrin and dieldrin poisoning. *Ibis* 133: 162–169.

NEWTON, I., WILLIE, I. AND ASHER, A. (1994) Pollutants in Great Britain. *Brit. Birds* 87: 22–25.

NIEHUIS, M. (1990) [The Lesser Grey Shrike *Lanius minor* (Gmelin, 1788).] *Mainzer Naturwiss. Arch., Beih.* 13:

169–185. (In German.)

NIELSEN, C. O. AND DIETZ, R. (1989) Heavy metals in Greenland seabirds. *Medd. om Grønland, Bioscience* 29.

NIELSEN, O. K. AND CADE, T. J. (1990) Seasonal changes in food habits of Gyrfalcons in NE-Iceland. *Ornis Scand.* 21: 202–211.

NIETHAMMER, G. (1955) [The identification of *Galerida cristata* and *G. theklae*.] *J. Orn.* 96: 411–417. (In German.)

NIEWOLD, F. J. J. (1982) Hypotheses on the cause of the decline in the Black Grouse populations in the Netherlands. Pp.107–116 in T. W. I. Lovel, ed. *Proceedings of the second international symposium on grouse*. Suffolk: World Pheasant Association.

NIEWOLD, F. J. J. AND NIJLAND, H. (1982) [The outlook for the West European moor- and heathland Black Grouse.] *Zeits. für Jagdwiss.* 33: 227–241. (In German.)

NIKIFOROV, L. P. AND HYBET, L. A. (1981) [Regulation of numbers and distribution of Great Snipe in natural and anthropogenic habitats.] Pp.147–150 in H. A. Mikhelson, ed. [*Abstracts 10th Baltic Ornithological Conference*, 2.] Riga: Institute of Biology, Latvian Academy of Sciences. (In Russian.)

NIKIFOROV, M. E. (1992) Size and mobility of grey partridge (*Perdix perdix*) winter coveys in Belorussia. *Gibier Faune Sauvage* 9: 447–453.

NIKIFOROV, M. E., YAMINSKY, B. V. AND SHKLIAROV, L. P. (1989) [*Birds of Byelorussia: handbook to nests and eggs*.] Minsk: Vysheishaya Shkola Publ. (In Russian.)

NIKOLAUS, G. (1987) *Distribution atlas of Sudan's birds with notes on habitat and status*. Bonn: Zoologisches Forschungs Institut/Museum Alexander Koenig (Bonner Zoologische Monographien 25).

NILSSON, L. (1969) Food consumption of diving ducks wintering at the coast of south Sweden. *Oikos* 20: 128–135.

NILSSON, S. G. (1977) Adult survival rate of the Black-throated Diver *Gavia arctica*. *Ornis Scand.* 8: 193–195.

NOGALES, M. (1985) [Contribution to the study of the flora and fauna of the Pajonales, Ojeda and Inagua mountains (Gran Canaria).] Tenerife: La Laguna University (thesis). (In Spanish.)

NORDERHAUG, A. AND NORDERHAUG, M. (1984) Status of the Lesser White-fronted Goose *Anser erythropus*, in Fennoscandia. *Swedish Wildl. Res.* 13: 171–185.

NORTON, W. J. E. (1958) Notes on birds in the Elburz Mountains of North Persia. *Ibis* 100: 179–189.

NOTTORF, A. (1978) [Methods and successes in the protection of the Black Stork *Ciconia nigra* in Lower Saxony.] *Ber. Dtsch. Sekt. int. Rat Vogelschutz* 18: 36–40. (In German.)

NOVAL, A. (1975) [*The book of Iberian fauna: birds*, 4.] Oviedo: Naranco. (In Spanish.)

NTIAMOA-BAIDU, Y. (1991) Species protection as a strategy for conservation action in Africa: the case of the Roseate Tern in Ghana. Pp.169–175 in T. Salathé, ed. *Conserving migratory birds*. Cambridge, U.K.: International Council for Bird Preservation (Techn. Publ. 12).

NYGÅRD *ET AL.* (in prep.) The wintering population of the Steller's Eider *Polysticta stelleri* in Europe and its possible breeding area.

O'BRIAIN, M. AND HEALY, B. (1991) Winter distribution of light-bellied brent geese *Branta bernicla hrota* in Ireland. *Ardea* 79: 317–326.

O'CONNOR, R. J. AND SHRUBB, M. (1986) *Farming and birds*. Cambridge, U.K.: Cambridge University Press.

ODSJÖ, T. AND SONDELL, J. (1976) Reproductive success in Ospreys *Pandion haliaetus* in southern and central Sweden, 1971–1973. *Ornis Scand.* 7: 71–84.

OEHME, G. (1987) [On the phenomenon of eggshell thinning as exemplified by the case of the White-tailed Eagle *Haliaeetus albicilla* in the DDR.] Pp.159–170 in M. Stubbe, ed. [*Population ecology of birds of prey and owls*.] Halle, Germany: Wis. Beitr. Univ. Halle (Saale). (In German.)

OGILVIE, M. A. (1983) The number of Greenland Barnacle Geese in Britain and Ireland. *Wildfowl* 34: 77–88.

OGILVIE GRANT, W. R. (1896) On the birds observed on the Salvage Islands. *Ibis* 41–55.

ØIEN, I. J. AND AARVAK, T. (1993) [*Status of Lesser White-fronted Goose Anser erythropus in Fennoscandia*.] Trondheim: Norwegian Ornithological Society. (In Norwegian.)

OKULEWICZ, J. AND WITKOWSKI, J. (1979) [Jack Snipe *Lymnocryptes minimus* (Brünn., 1764), again a breeding bird in Poland.] *Przeglad Zoologiczny* 23: 255–257. (In Polish.)

D'OLIVEIRA, M. P. (1896) [*Birds of the Iberian peninsula and especially of Portugal*.] Coimbra: Imprensa da Universidade. (In Portuguese.)

OLIVEIRA, P. AND JONES, M. J. (in press) Population numbers, habitat preferences and the impact of the Long-toed Laurel Pigeon on agricultural fields: prospectives for future management. Symposium on flora and fauna of the Atlantic islands, Madeira, October 1993.

OLSSON, V. (in press) Status and trends of *Lanius excubitor* and *Lanius collurio* in Sweden. In R. Yosef and F. E. Lohrer, eds. Proceedings of the 1st International Shrike Symposium.

VAN OORDT, G. J. (1929) The recent breeding places of the Avocet (*Recurvirostra avosetta*) L. in north-west Europe. *Verh. Int. Orn. Kongr.* 6: 223–226.

ORIA, J. AND CABALLERO, J. (1992a) [Monitoring and conservation of Spanish Imperial Eagle in central Spain.] Madrid: Instituto Nacional para la Conservación de la Naturaleza (unpublished). (In Spanish.)

ORIA, J. AND CABALLERO, J. (1992b) [Population and threats to the Black Vulture in central Spain.] Madrid: Instituto Nacional para la Conservación de la Naturaleza (unpublished). (In Spanish.)

ORMEROD, S. J. AND TYLER, S. J. (1993) Birds as indicators of changes in water quality. Pp.179–216 in R. W. Furness and J. D. D. Greenwood, eds. *Birds as monitors of environmental change*. London: Chapman and Hall.

ORR, C. D. AND PARSONS, J. L. (1982) Ivory Gulls *Pagophila eburnea*, and ice-edges in Davis Strait and the Labrador Sea. *Can. Field-Nat.* 96: 323–328.

OSBORNE, P. E. (1986) *Survey of the birds of Fuerteventura, Canary Islands, with special reference to the status of the Canarian Houbara Bustard Chlamydotis undulata*. Cambridge, U.K.: International Council for Bird Preservation (Study Rep. 10).

OSIECK, E. R. AND HUSTINGS, F. (1994) [*Red data and important birds in the Netherlands*.] Zeist: Vogelbescherming Nederland (Techn. Rep. 12). (In Dutch.)

OSMOLOVSKAYA, V. I. (1949) [Ecology of steppe birds of prey in Northern Kazakhstan.] *Proc. Naurzum Nat. Re-*

serve 2: 117–152. (In Russian.)

VAN OSTENBRUGGE, R., STOLK, P. AND VAN ROOMEN, M. (1992) Waterfowl and agriculture: review and future perspective of the crop damage conflict in Europe. Pp.151–158 in M. van Roomen and J. Madsen, eds. *National report from the Netherlands.* Slimbridge, U.K.: International Waterfowl and Wetlands Research Bureau (Spec. Publ. 21).

ÖSTERLÖF, S. (1977) Migration, wintering areas and site tenacity of European Osprey *Pandion h. haliaetus* (L.). *Ornis Scand.* 8: 61–79.

OWEN, M. (1984) Dynamics and age structure of an increasing goose population—the Svalbard Barnacle Goose *Branta leucopsis. Nor. Polarinst. Skr.* 181: 37–47.

OWEN, M. (1992) National report from United Kingdom. Pp.167–170 in M. van Roomen and J. Madsen, eds. *Waterfowl and agriculture: review and future perspective of the crop damage conflict in Europe.* Slimbridge, U.K.: International Waterfowl and Wetlands Research Bureau (Spec. Publ. 21).

OWEN, M. AND PIENKOWSKI, M. W., EDS. (1991) *Goose damage and management workshop, April 1990.* Martin Mere, U.K.: Joint Nature Conservation Committee.

PAKARINEN, R. (1989) [A survey of the population size of the Black-throated Diver in 1985–1986 in Finland.] *Lintumies* 24: 2–11. (In Finnish with English summary.)

PAKARINEN, R. AND JÄRVINEN, O. (1984) [The Red-throated Diver *Gavia stellata* in Finland: a ecological population analysis of its status and population trends.] *Lintumies* 19: 46–54. (In Finnish with English summary.)

PALMA, L. (1985) The present situation of birds of prey in Portugal. Pp.3–14 in I. Newton and R. D. Chancellor, eds. *Conservation studies on raptors.* Cambridge, U.K.: International Council for Bird Preservation (Techn. Publ. 5).

PALMER, R. S. (1976) *Handbook of North American birds,* 3. New Haven: Yale University Press.

PALUDAN, K. (1938) [On the birds of the Zagros mountains.] *J. Orn.* 86: 562–638. (In German.)

PALUDAN, K. (1959) On the birds of Afghanistan. *Vidensk. Medd. Dansk. Naturh. For.* 122: 1–332.

PANEK, M. (1992) Mechanisms of determining population levels and density regulation in Polish grey partridges. *Gibier Faune Sauvage* 9: 325–335.

PANOW, E. N. (1974) [*The wheatears of the northern Palearctic.*] Wittenberg Lutherstadt: Ziemsen Verlag.

PANOW, E. N. (1983) [*Shrikes of the Palearctic.*] Wittenberg Lutherstadt: Ziemsen Verlag. (In German.)

PANTELIS, V. S. (1980) The Cyprian Chukars (*Alectoris chukar cypriotes*). Pp.18–24 in C. L. Coles, M. Reydellet, G. van Tuyll, L. van Maltzahn and J. Bugalho, eds. *Partridges of the* Alectoris *genus.* Paris: International Council for Game and Wildlife Conservation.

PAPAEVANGELOU, E. (1980) General situation of the partridge species in Greece. Pp.71–77 in C. L. Coles, M. Reydellet, G. van Tuyll, L. van Maltzahn and J. Bugalho, eds. *Partridges of the Alectoris genus.* Paris: International Council for Game and Wildlife Conservation.

PARRA, F. AND LEVASSOR, C. (1982) [Winter food of the Pin-tailed Sandgrouse in La Mancha.] *Bol. Est. Cent. Ecol.* 19: 99–108. (In Spanish.)

PARSLOW, J. L. F. (1967a) Changes in status among breeding birds in Britain and Ireland. *Brit. Birds* 60: 97–123.

PARSLOW, J. L. F. (1967b) Changes in status among breeding birds in Britain and Ireland. *Brit. Birds* 60: 177–202.

PARSLOW, J. L. F. AND EVERETT, M. J. (1981) *Birds in need of special protection in Europe.* Strasbourg: Council of Europe (Nature and Environment Series 24). (In French.)

PARSLOW, J. L. F. AND JEFFERIES, D. J. (1977) Gannets and toxic chemicals. *Brit. Birds* 70: 366–372.

PASPALEVA-ANTONOVA, M. (1964) [A contribution to the bird fauna of the Liulin Mountain.] *Bull. Inst. Zool. and Museum* 16: 35–59. (In Bulgarian with German summary.)

PASZKOWSKI, W. (1977) [*Catalogue of the avifauna of Brunswick: non-Passeriformes.*] Clausthal-Zellerfeld. (In German.)

PATERSON, A. M., MARTÍNEZ-VILALTA, A. AND DIES, J. I. (1992) Partial breeding failure of Audouin's Gull in two Spanish colonies in 1991. *Brit. Birds* 85: 97–100.

PÄTZOLD, R. (1971) [*Woodlark and Crested Lark* Lullula arborea *L. and* Galerida cristata *L.*] Wittenberg Lutherstadt: Ziemsen Verlag. (In German.)

PEAKALL, D. B. (1962) The past and present status of the Red-backed Shrike in Great Britain. *Bird Study* 9: 198–216.

PEAKALL, D. B. AND BOYD, H. (1987) Birds as bio-indicators of environmental conditions. Pp.113–118 in A. W. Diamond and F. L. Filion, eds. *The value of birds.* Cambridge, U.K.: International Council for Bird Preservation (Techn. Publ. 6).

PEAL, R. E. F. (1968) The distribution of the Wryneck in the British Isles 1964–1966. *Bird Study* 15: 111–126.

PEDERSEN, M. B. (1989a) [Wintering strategy of the Jack Snipe in Denmark.] *Dansk Ornit. Foren. Tidsskr.* 83: 69–73.

PEDERSEN, M. B. (1989b) [Changes in the occurrence of the roosting and moulting Snipes and Jack Snipes on inland habitats in Denmark.] *Dansk Ornit. Foren. Tidsskr.* 83: 75–82.

PEDERSEN, M. B. (1990) [Project Jack Snipe.] *Vår Fågelv.* 49: 485–487. (In Swedish.)

PEDERSEN, M. B. (1991) Winter population estimates of Jack Snipe and Common Snipe in Denmark. *Dansk Ornit. Foren. Tidsskr.* 85: 173–174.

PEDERSEN, M. B. (1992) Breeding status of the Jack Snipe in south Baltic: a preliminary study in Lithuania. WWF Sweden (unpublished report).

PEDERSEN, M. B. (in press) 'Tenant pendling' and weather dependent habitat shifts in the Jack Snipe *Lymnocryptes minimus*—a case of how to winter in southern Scandinavia. *Wader Study Group Bull.*

PEITZMEIER, J. (1951) [Observations on changes in some bird species in north-west Germany related to climate.] Pp.477–483 in *Proc. X. Internat. Orn. Congress, Uppsala.* Uppsala: Almquist abd Wiksell. (In German.)

PEKLO, A. M. (1987) [*Flycatchers of the U.S.S.R. fauna.*] Kiev. (In Russian.)

PERCIVAL, S. M. (1991) The population structure of Greenland Barnacle Geese *Branta leucopsis* on the wintering grounds on Islay. *Ibis* 133: 357–364.

PERCIVAL, S. M. (1993) The effects of reseeding, fertilizer application and disturbance on the use of grasslands by Barnacle Geese, and the implications for refuge management. *J. Appl. Ecol.* 30: 437–443.

PERCY, LORD W. (1951) *Three studies in bird character.* Tavistock: Country Life.

PEREA, J. L., MORALES, M. AND VELASCO, J. (1990) [*The*

Egyptian Vulture in Spain.] Madrid: Instituto Nacional para la Conservación de la Naturaleza. (In Spanish.)

PERENNOU, C. (1991) [*International waterfowl census in tropical Africa.*] Slimbridge, U.K.: International Waterfowl and Wetlands Research Bureau (Spec. Publ. 15). (In French.)

PERENNOU, C. AND MUNDKUR, T. (1991) *Asian waterfowl census 1991.* Slimbridge, U.K.: International Waterfowl and Wetlands Research Bureau.

PERERVA, V. I. AND GRAZHDANKIN, A. V. (1983) [Ecological and behavioral adaptations of the Steppe Eagle to electric powerlines.] Pp.42–45 in [*Ecology of raptors.*] Moscow. (In Russian.)

PÉREZ PADRÓN, F. (1983) [*The birds of the Canaries.*] Cabildo Insular de Tenerife: Aula de Cultura del Excmo. (In Spanish.)

PERSSON, C. (1987) Sand Martin *Riparia riparia* populations in south-west Scandia. Sweden 1964–86. *J. Zool., Lond. (B)* 1.

PERSSON, K. (1978) [Bird observations in the county of Norrbottens 1977–78.] *Norrbottens Natur* 34: 20–24. (In Swedish.)

PETERSEN, Æ. (1976) Size variables in puffins *Fratercula arctica* from Iceland and bill features as criteria of age. *Ornis Scand.* 7: 185–192.

PETERSEN, Æ. (1977) [Icelandic Black Guillemots (*Cepphus grylle islandicus*) recovered in Greenland and Mandt's Guillemot (*C. g. mandtii*) recovered in Iceland.] *Náttúrufraedingurinn* 47: 149–153. (In Icelandic with English summary.)

PETERSEN, Æ. (1979) [The breeding birds of Flatey and some adjoining islets, in Breidafjordur, north-west Iceland.] *Náttúrufraedingurinn* 49: 229–256. (In Icelandic with English summary.)

PETERSEN, Æ. (1981) Breeding biology and feeding ecology of Black Guillemots. Oxford: Oxford University (Ph.D. thesis).

PETERSEN, Æ. AND SKÍRNISSON, K. (1980) [The mink in Iceland.] *Rit Landverndar* 7: 80–94. (In Icelandic.)

PETERSEN, C. (1945) [The Green Woodpecker (*Picus viridis*) in Denmark.] *Dansk Ornit. Foren. Tidsskr.* 39: 133–186. (In Danish.)

PETERSON, R. T. (1984) Least terns find sandy salvation on man-made beach. *Smithsonian* 15: 68–74.

PETRETI, A. AND PETRETI, F. (1980) [Status and conservation of the Short-toed Eagle, *Circaetus gallicus*, in Italy: first data.] Pp.108–110 in [*Mediterranean raptors.*] Ajaccio: Parc Naturel Régional de la Corse/Centre de Recherche Ornithologique de Provence. (In French.)

PETRETI, F. (1988) Notes on the behaviour and ecology of the Short-toed Eagle in Italy. *Gerfaut* 78: 261–286.

PETROV, P. A. (1964) [Food of the Long-legged Buzzard (*Buteo rufinus*) Cretzschm. in the Lower Kuma river.] *Zool. Zh.* 43: 1412–1414. (In Russian.)

PICOZZI, N. AND HEWSON, R. (1970) Kestrels, Short-eared Owls and field voles in Eskdalemuir in 1970. *Scott. Birds* 6: 185–190.

PIENKOWSKI, M. W. (1991) Recommendations. *Wader Study Group Bull.* 61 (Suppl.): 87–88.

PIENKOWSKI, M. W., STROUD, D. A. AND REED, T. M. (1987) Problems in maintaining breeding habitat, with particular reference to peatland waders. *Wader Study Group Bull.* 49 (Suppl.): 95–101.

PIERSMA, T. AND DAVIDSON, N. (1992) The migration of knots. *Wader Study Group Bull.* 64 (Suppl.): 209.

PIERSMA, T. AND JUKEMA, J. (1990) Budgeting the flight of a long-distance migrant: changes in nutrient reserve levels of Bar-tailed Godwits at successive spring staging sites. *Ardea* 78: 315–337.

PIERSMA, T., PROKOSCH, P. AND BREDIN, D. (1992) The migration system of Afro-Siberian Knots *Calidris canutus canutus. Wader Study Group Bull.* 64 (Suppl.): 52–63.

PIHL, S. AND LAURSEN, K. (1993) *Baltic Task Force.* Slimbridge, U.K.: International Waterfowl and Wetland Research Bureau (News 9).

PIKULA, J., BEKLOVA, M. AND KUBIK, V. (1984) [The breeding biology of *Tyto alba.*] *Prirodoved Pr. Ustavu Cesk. Akad. Ved. Brne* 18: 1–56. (In Czech.)

PIMM, S. L. (1991) *The balance of nature?: ecological issues in the conservation of species and communities.* Chicago: Chicago University Press.

PLEGUEZUELOS, J. (1991) [*Historical evolution of the nesting avifauna in the south-east Iberian peninsula (1850–1985).*] Sevilla: Consejería de Cultura y Medio Ambiente, Junta de Andalucía.

PLEGUEZUELOS, J. M. (1992) [*Breeding birds in the East Béticas mountains and the depressions of Guadix, Baza and Granada.*] Granada: Granada University. (In Spanish.)

PLEGUEZUELOS, J. AND MANRIQUE, J. (1987) [Distribution and status of steppic birds breeding in south-east Spain.] Pp.349–358 in [*I International Congress on Steppic Birds.*] León: Junta de Castilla y León. (In Spanish.)

POKROVSKAYA, I. W. (1963) [Ecology of the Wryneck.] *Leningr. gos. pedag. Inst., Utsh. zap.* 230: 19–32. (In Russian.)

POOLE, A. F. (1989) Regulation of Osprey *Pandion haliaetus* populations: the role of nest site availability. Pp.227–234 in B.-U. Meyburg and R. D. Chancellor, eds. *Raptors in the modern world: proceedings of the III World conference on birds of prey and owls. Eilat, Israel 22–27 March 1987.* Berlin and London: World Working Group on Birds of Prey and Owls.

POORTER, E. P. R. (1990) [*Stopover sites of Dutch Spoonbills within their European flyway.*] Zeist, Netherlands: Vogelbescherming (Tech. Rap. 6). (In Dutch.)

PORTELLI, P. (1992) Numbers and facts about bird killing in Malta. In B.-U. Meyburg, ed. *Abstracts IV World Conference on Birds of Prey, Berlin.* Berlin: B.-U. Meyburg World Working Group on Birds of Prey and Owls.

PORTENKO, L. A. (1937) [*The bird fauna of the Extra-Polar part of the north Ural.*] Moscow/Leningrad: Acad. Sci. USRR. (In Russian.)

PORTENKO, L. A. AND VON VIETINGHOFF-SCHEEL, E. (1976) [Black-throated Accentor.] In H. Dathe, ed. [*Atlas of the distribution of Palearctic birds,* 5.] Berlin: Academisches Verlag. (In German.)

POSLAWSKI, A. N. (1969) [Migration and moult of the Curlew at the north shore of the Caspian Sea and adjacent deserts.] *Falke* 16: 184–188. (In German.)

POSTELNYKH, A. V. (1986) [Changes in numbers of birds of prey in the Oka Nature Reserve.] Pp.162–163 in V. D. Ilyichev, ed. [*Abstracts 9th U.S.S.R. Ornithological Conference,* 2.] Leningrad: Zoological Institute, U.S.S.R. Academy of Sciences. (In Russian.)

POTAPOV, R. L. (1984a) [Caspian Snowcock.] Pp.135–136

585

in A. M. Borodin, ed. [*Red data book of the U.S.S.R.*, 1.] Moscow: Department of Nature Conservation. (In Russian.)

POTAPOV, R. L. (1984b) [Caucasian Black Grouse.] In A. M. Borodin, ed. [*Red data book of the U.S.S.R.,* 1.] Moscow: Department of Nature Conservation. (In Russian.)

POTAPOV, R. L. (1985) [*Fauna of the U.S.S.R.: Family Tetraonidae.*] Leningrad: Nauka. (In Russian.)

POTAPOV, R. L. (1987) [Order Galliformes.] Pp.248–260 in R. L. Beme, N. P. Grachev, I. A. Isakov, A. I. Koshelev, E. N. Kurochkin, R. L. Potapov, A. K. Rustamov and V. E. Flint, eds. [*Birds of the U.S.S.R.: Galliformes and Gruiformes.*] St Petersburg: Nauka (Science). (In Russian.)

POTTS, G. R. (1980) The effects of modern agriculture, nest predation and game management on the population ecology of partridges (*Perdix perdix* and *Alectoris rufa*). *Adv. Ecol. Res.* 11: 2–79.

POTTS, G. R. (1985) The partridge situation in Italy: a view from Britain. Pp.9–13 in F. Dessi-Fulgheri and T. Mingozzi, eds. *Atti Sem. Biologia Galliformi.* Arcavacata: Calabria University.

POTTS, G. R. (1986) *The Partridge: pesticides, predation and conservation.* London: Collins.

POTTS, G. R. (1988) The impact of releasing hybrid partridges on wild Red-legged populations. *Game Conserv. Rev.* 20: 81–85.

POTTS, G. R. (1990) Causes of the decline in partridge populations and effect of the insecticide dimethoate on chick mortality. Pp.62–71 in J. T. Lumeij and Y. R. Hoogeveen, eds. *The future of wild Galliformes in the Netherlands.* The Hague: Gegevens Koninklijke Bibliotheek.

POTTS, G. R. (1991) The introduction of the Chukar. *Brit. Birds* 84: 289.

POULSEN, J. G. (1993) Comparative ecology of Skylarks (*Alauda arvensis* L.) on arable farmland. (Thesis.)

PRANGE, H. (1986–1987) Staging and migration of cranes in the G.D.R. *Aquila* 93/94: 75–90.

PRANGE, H., ED. (1989) [*The Common Crane.*] Wittenberg Lutherstadt: Ziemsen Verlag. (In German.)

PRANGE, H. (1991) [Migration and resting of the Common Crane (*Grus grus*) in East Germany in 1988.] *Vogelwarte* 36: 35–47. (In German.)

PRANGE, H. (in press) [Conservation of the Common Crane in Europe.] *Naturschutz heute.* (In German.)

PRANGE, H. AND MEWES, W. (1987) The Common Crane in the German Democratic Republic. Pp.263–269 in *Proceedings 1987 International Crane Workshop Qiqihar, China.* Baraboo, W.I.: International Crane Foundation.

PRANGE, H. AND MEWES, W. (1989) [The situation of the Common Crane (*Grus grus*) in central Europe.] *Beitr. Vogelkunde* 15: 1–32. (In German.)

PRATER, A. J. (1972) The ecology of Morecombe Bay. III: the food and feeding habits of Knot (*Calidris canutus* L.) in Morecambe Bay. *J. Appl. Ecol.* 9: 179–194.

PRATER, A. J. (1981) *Estuary birds of Britain and Ireland.* Calton, U.K.: T. and A. D. Poyser.

PRIEDNIEKS, J., STRAZDS, M., PETRINS, A. AND STRAZDS, A. (1989) [*Latvian breeding bird atlas 1980–1984.*] Riga, Latvia: Zinatne Publishing House.

PRINS, H. H. T. AND YDENBERG, R. C. (1985) Vegetation growth and a seasonal habitat shift in the Barnacle Goose. *Oecologia* 66: 122–125.

PRODON, R. (1985) [Introduction to the breeding biology of the Black Wheatear *Oenanthe leucura* in France.] *Alauda* 53: 295–305. (In French.)

PRODON, R., FONS, R. AND PETER, A. M. (1994) [The impact of fire on the vegetation, birds and small mammals in the east Mediterranean Pyrenees preliminary results.] *Rev. Ecol. (Terre Vie)* 39: 129–158. (In French.)

PROKOSCH, P. (1988) [The Schleswig-Holsteinische Wadden Sea as a spring stopover site for Arctic wader populations, with Grey Plover (*Pluvialis squatarola*, L. 1758), Knot (*Calidris canutus*, L. 1758) and Bar-tailed Godwit (*Limosa lapponica*, L. 1758) as examples.] *Corax* 12: 273–442. (In German.)

PROKOSCH, P. (1991) Present status and recent changes in numbers and feeding sites of *Branta* species on the coasts of the Federal Republic of Germany during the 1980s. *Ardea* 79: 135–140.

PROP, J., VAN EERDEN, M. R. AND DRENT, R. H. (1984) Reproductive success of the Barnacle Goose *Branta leucopsis* in relation to food exploitation on the breeding grounds, western Spitsbergen. *Nor. Polarinst. Skr.* 181: 87–117.

PSILOVIKOS, A. (1992) Changes in Greek wetlands during the twentieth century: the case of the Macedonian inland waters and of the river deltas of the Aegean and Ionian coasts. Pp.175–196 in P. A. Gerakis, ed. *Conservation and management of Greek wetlands.* Gland, Switzerland: International Union for Conservation of Nature and Natural Resources.

PTUSHENKO, E. S. AND INOZEMTSEV, A. A. (1968) [*Biology and practical value of the birds in the Moscow oblast and adjacent territories.*] Moscow: Moscow University. (In Russian.)

RABAÇA, J. E. (1983) [Contribution to the study of the avifauna of cork oak forest *Quercus suber*.] Lisbon: Lisbon University (B.Sc. thesis). (In Portuguese.)

RAMOS, J. A. (1989) [Ecology and conservation of *Porphyrio porphyrio*, with special reference to Ludo, Parque Natural da Ria Formosa.] Algarve University (unpublished). (In Spanish.)

RAMSAR CONVENTION BUREAU (1990) *Proceedings of the fourth meeting of the Conference of the Contracting Parties (Montreux, Switzerland).* Gland, Switzerland: Ramsar Convention Bureau.

RATCLIFFE, D. A. (1962) Breeding density in the Peregrine *Falco peregrinus* and Raven *Corvus corax. Ibis* 104: 13–39.

RATCLIFFE, D. (1990) *Birdlife of mountain and upland.* Cambridge, U.K.: Cambridge University Press.

RATCLIFFE, D. A. (1993) *The Peregrine Falcon.* Second edition. London: T. and A. D. Poyser.

RATZKE, B. AND SCHRECK, W. (1993) [Spontaneous recolonization and high breeding concentrations of the Red-backed Shrike after habitat improvements on the former waste-deposit of Berlin.] *Berliner Orn. Ber.* 2: 32–37. (In German.)

RAVENSCROFT, N. O. M. (1989) The status and habitat of the nightjar *Caprimulgus europaeus* in coastal Suffolk. *Bird Study* 36: 161–169.

RAZIN, M. AND URCUN, J.-P. (1992) [*Migration study camp at Pointe de Grave (Gironde), Spring 1992.*] Rochefort: Ligue pour la Protection des Oiseaux. (In French.)

REAL, J. (1991) [Bonelli's Eagle in Catalonia: status, feeding ecology, breeding biology and demography.] Barcelona:

Barcelona University (Ph.D. thesis). (In Spanish.)

REAL, J. AND MAÑOSA, S. (1992) [*The conservation of Bonelli's Eagle in Catalonia.*] Barcelona: Memoria Barcelona University/Miguel TORRES SA. (In Spanish.)

REAL, J., MAÑOSA, S., DEL AMO, R., SANCHEZ, J. A., SANCHEZ, M. A., CARMONA, D. AND MARTINEZ, J. E. (1991) [The decline of the Bonelli's Eagle: a question of demography.] *Quercus* 70: 6–12. (In Spanish.)

REAL, J., MAÑOSA, S., CHEYLAN, G., BAYLE, P., CUGNASSE, J. M., SANCHEZ-ZAPATA, J. A., SANCHEZ, M. A., CARMONA, D., MARTINEZ, J. E., RICO, L., CODINA, J., DEL AMO, R. AND EGUIA, S. (1992) A preliminary demographic approach to the Bonelli's Eagle population decrease in Spain and France. In B.-U. Meyburg, ed. *Abstracts IV World Conference on Birds of Prey, Berlin*. Berlin: World Working Group on Birds of Prey and Owls.

REE, V. (1986) [Concentrations of seabirds along Austfonna glacier in Svalbard.] *Vår Fuglefauna* 9: 177–185. (In Swedish.)

REED, A. AND BOURGET, A. (1977) Distribution and abundance of waterfowl wintering in southern Quebec. *Canadian Field-Nat.* 91: 1–7.

REES, E. C., BOWLER, J. M. AND BUTLER, L. (1990) Bewick's and Whooper Swans: the 1989–90 season. *Wildfowl* 41: 176–181.

REES, E. C., BOWLER, J. M., BEEKMAN, J. H., ANDERSEN-HARILD, P., MINEYEV, Y. N., SCHADILOV, Y. M. L., BELOUSOVA, A. V., MOROZOV, Y. V., POOT, M., PEBERDY, K. J. AND SCOTT, D. K. (in press) International collaboration study of Bewick's Swans nesting in the European northeast of Russia. *Russian Orn. J.*

REICHHOLF, J. (1983) [Outbreaks of duck botulism in the summer of 1982 in Bavaria.] *Anz Orn. Ges. Bayern* 22: 37–56. (In German.)

REICHHOLF, J. (1989) [Why did the Gull-billed Tern *Gelochelidon nilotica* and Stone Curlew *Burhinus oedicnemus* vanish from Bayern?.] *Anz Orn. Ges. Bayern* 28: 8–14.

REINKE, E. (1991) Breeding waders on wet grasslands (inland sites) in West Germany: examples for conservation programmes. *Wader Study Group Bull.* 61 (Suppl.): 25–27.

RENAUD, W. E. AND MACLAREN, P. L. (1982) Ivory Gull (*Pagophila eburnea*) distribution in late summer and autumn in eastern Lancaster Sound and western Baffin Bay. *Arctic* 35: 141–148.

RENDON, M., VARGAS, J. M. AND RAMIREZ, J. M. (1991) [*Seasonal dynamics and reproduction of the Common Flamingo* (Phoenicopterus ruber roseus) *in the Laguna de Fuente de Piedra (southern Spain). Technical meeting on the status and problems of the flamingo* (Phoenicopterus ruber roseus) *in the western Mediterranean and north-west Africa.*] Sevilla: Junta de Andalucía. (In Spanish.)

RENZONI, A. (1974) The decline of the Grey Partridge in Italy. *Biol. Conserv.* 6: 213–215.

REYNOLDS, J. C., ANGELSTAM, P. AND REDPATH, S. M. (1988) Predators, their ecology and impact on gamebird populations. Pp.107–116 in P. J. Hudson and M. R. W. Rands, eds. *Ecology and management of gamebirds*. Oxford: Blackwell Scientific Publications.

RHEINWALD, G. (1989) [Attempt at an overall analysis.] Pp.221–227 in G. Rheinwald, J. Ogden and H. Schulz,

eds. [*White stork: status and conservation proceedings of the first international stork conservation symposium, Walsrode 14–19 October 1985.*] Braunschweig: Dachverband Deutscher Avifaunisten (Schriftenreihe 10). (In German.)

RHEINWALD, G., OGDEN, J. AND SCHULZ, H., EDS. (1989) [*White stork: status and conservation proceedings of the first international stork conservation symposium, Walsrode 14–19 October 1985.*] Braunschweig: Dachverband Deutscher Avifaunisten (Schriftenreihe 10). (In German.)

RIABOV, V. F. (1982) [*Steppe avifauna of northern Kazakhstan.*] Moscow: Nauka. (In Russian.)

RINNE, J. (1986–1987) Crane (*Grus grus*) migration in Finland. *Aquila* 93/94: 149–151.

RIOLS, C. (1986–1987) Wintering of Common Crane in France. *Aquila* 93/94: 123–135.

RISTOW, D. AND WINK, M. (1985) Breeding success of Eleonora's Falcon and conservation management. Pp.147–152 in I. Newton and R. D. Chancellor, eds. *Conservation studies on raptors*. Cambridge, U.K.: International Council for Bird Preservation (Techn. Publ. 5).

RISTOW, D. AND WINK, M. (in press) Distribution of non-breeding Eleonora's Falcon.

RISTOW, D., CONRAD, B., WINK, C. AND WINK, M. (1980) Pesticide residues of failed eggs of Eleonora's Falcon from an Aegean colony. *Ibis* 122: 74–76.

RISTOW, D., WINK, C. AND WINK, M. (1983) [Biology of *Falco eleonorae*. 12: Adaptations of hunting behaviour to wind-dependent migrant abundances.] *Vogelwarte* 32: 7–13. (In German.)

RISTOW, D., WINK, C. AND WINK, M. (1986) Assessment of Mediterranean autumn migration by prey analysis of Eleonora's Falcon. First conference on birds wintering in the Mediterranean region. *Ric. Biol. Selv.* 10 (Suppl.): 285–295.

RISTOW, D., RISTOW, T. AND WINK, M. (1988) Use of nest boxes by Eleonora's Falcon (*Falco eleonorae*). *Hellenic Orn. Soc. Newsl.* 4: 22–24.

RISTOW, D., FELDMANN, F., SCHARLAU, W., WINK, C. AND WINK, M. (1991) Population dynamics of Cory's Shearwater (*Calonectris diomedea*) and Eleonora's Falcon (*Falco eleonorae*) in the eastern Mediterranean. Pp.199–212 in A. Seitz and V. Loeschke, eds. *Species conservation: a population-biological approach*. Basel: Birkhäuser Verlag.

RITTINGHAUS, H. (1961) [*The Kentish Plover.*] Wittenburg-Lutherstadt: Ziensen Verlag (New Brehm Library 282). (In German.)

RIZZO, M. C., MIGLIORE, L. AND MUSA, B. (1993) Insects, small mammals and breeding performance of farmland populations of the Common Kestrel in Sicily. Pp.11–18 in M. K. Nicholls and R. Clarke, eds. *Biology and conservation of small falcons*. London: The Hawk and Owl Trust.

ROBEL, D. (1991) [The last breeding attempt of the Roller *Coracias garrulus* unsuccessful in Germany.] *Vogelwelt* 112: 148–149. (In German with English summary.)

ROBERTS, P. J. (1982) Foods of the Chough on Bardsey Island, Wales. *Bird Study* 29: 155–161.

ROBINSON, P. J. (1989) The legal status of diurnal birds of prey in Africa. Pp.577–590 in B.-U. Meyburg and R. D. Chancellor, eds. *Raptors in the modern World: proceed-*

ings of the *III World conference on birds of prey and owls. Eilat, Israel 22–27 March 1987*. Berlin and London: World Working Group on Birds of Prey and Owls.

ROCAMORA, G. (in prep.) [The Corsican Nuthatch in the cluster pine *Pinus pinaster* forests of southern Corsica.] *Alauda*. (In French.)

RODRÍGUEZ, F. AND MORENO, A. C. (1993) [Conservation programme of Blue Chaffinch *Fringilla teydea polatzeki* (Harter 1905) on Gran Canaria 1991–1993. 1: populations, reproduction, habitat characteristics and predation.] Gran Canaria: Gobierno de Canarias, Viceconsejería de Medio Ambiente (unpublished). (In Spanish.)

RODRÍGUEZ, F., DÍAZ, G., ALMEIDA, R. S. AND NOGALES, I. (1987) [Ornithological news: Cream-coloured Coursor (*Cursorius cursor*)]. *Ardeola* 34: 284. (In Spanish.)

RODRÍGUEZ, R. AND HIRALDO, F. (1975) [Dietary requirements of *Porphyrio porphyrio* in the Guadalquivir marshes.] *Doñana Acta Vertebrata* 2: 201–213. (In Spanish.)

RODRIGUEZ-TEIJEIRO, J. D., PUIGCERVER, M. AND GALLEGO, S. (1992) Mating strategy in the European Quail (*Coturnix c. coturnix*) revealed by male population density and sex ratio in Catalonia (Spain). *Gibier Faune Sauvage* 9: 377–386.

ROELOFS, J. G. M., BOXMAN, A. W. AND VAN DIJK, H. F. G. (1989) [Effects of airborne ammonium on natural vegetation and forests.] Pp.38–41 in H. Ellenberg, A. Rüger and G. Vauk, eds. [*Eutrophication: the most serious threat in nature conservation*.] Norddeutsche Naturschutzakademie (Berichte 2). (In German.)

ROGACHEVA, H. (1992) *The birds of central Siberia*. Husun.

ROSE, P. M. AND SCOTT, D. A. (1994) *Waterfowl population estimates*. Slimbridge, U.K.: International Waterfowl and Wetlands Research Bureau (Spec. Publ. 29).

ROUX, F. (1973) Censuses of Anatidae in the central delta of the Niger and the Senegal delta, January 1972. *Wildfowl* 24: 63–80.

ROUX, F., JARRY, G. AND LAMARCHE, B. (1979) [Research on the Anatidae wintering in the inner Niger delta, January–March 1970.] (Rapport CRBPO/ONC). (In French.)

RSPB AND NCC (1991) *Death by design: the persecution of birds of prey and owls in the U.K. 1979–1989*. Sandy and Peterborough, U.K.: Royal Society for the Protection of Birds/Nature Conservation Committee.

RUFINO, R., ED. (1989) [*Atlas of breeding birds of continental Portugal*.] Lisbon: CEMPRA/SNPRCN. (In Portuguese.)

RÜGER, A., PRENTICE, C. AND OWEN, M. (1986) *Results of the IWRB International Waterfowl Census 1967–1983*. Slimbridge, U.K.: International Waterfowl and Wetlands Research Bureau (Spec. Publ. 6).

RUIZ, X. (1985) An analysis of the diet of Cattle Egrets in the Ebro delta, Spain. *Ardea* 73: 49–60.

RUTSCHKE, E. (1989) [*Ducks of Europe*.] Berlin: VEB Deutscher Landwirtschaftsverlag. (In German.)

RUWET, J.-C. (1982) [Status and development, in a European context, of the Black Grouse (*Tetrao tetrix*) in the Belgian Ardenne mountains. *Cathiers d'Éthologie Appliquée* 2: 81–104. (In French.)

SACK, R. (1961) [On wintering Jack Snipe.] *Falke* 8: 183–187. (In German.)

SACKL, P. (1985) [The Black Stork *Ciconia nigra* in Austria: expansion, population dynamics and distribution.] *Vogelwelt* 106: 121–141. (In German.)

SALATHÉ, T. AND YARAR, M. (1992) Towards a management plan for Lake Burdur. Dogal Hayati Koruma Dernegi and Tour du Valat (unpublished report).

SALMON, D. G. (1988) The numbers and distribution of Scaup *Aythya marila* in Britain and Ireland. *Biol. Conserv.* 43: 267–278.

SALOMONSEN, F. (1950–1951) [*The birds of Greenland*.] Copenhagen: Ejnar Munksgaard. (In Danish.)

SALOMONSEN, F. (1961) [Ivory Gulls (*Pagophila eburnea* Phipps) breeding in Greenland.] *Dansk Ornit. Foren. Tidsskr.* 55: 177–180. (In Danish.)

SALVI, A. (1986–1987) Crane (*Grus grus*) migration over France from autumn 1981 to spring 1984. *Aquila* 93/94: 107–113.

SAMORODOV, Z. A. (1982) [Birds of the Volga old tributary–Sarpa river and adjacent territories to the northwest of the Caspian Sea.] Pp.47–101 in A. I. Fomichov, ed. [*The animal world of Kalmykia, its preservation and rational use*.] Elista: Kalmyk State University. (In Russian.)

SAMWALD, O. (1989) [Drastic population decrease of Roller *Coracias garrulus* in Austrian Styria.] *Acrocephalus* 10: 38–40. (In Czech with English summary.)

SAMWALD, O. AND SAMWALD, F. (1989) [Population numbers, phenology, breeding biology and decline of the Roller *Coracias garrulus* in Styria, Austria.] *Egretta* 32: 37–57. (In German.)

SÁNCHEZ, A. (1989) [Seasonal changes in the altitudinal distribution of birds in the Sierra de Gredos (Sistema Central mountains, Spain).] *Acta Biol. Mont.* 9: 77–84. (In Spanish.)

SÁNCHEZ, A. (1991) [Structure and seasonality of birds communities in the Sierra de Gredos (Avila, Spain).] *Ardeola* 38: 207–232. (In Spanish.)

SÁNCHEZ, A. AND RODRÍGUEZ, A. (1992) [*Evolution of the Black Vulture in Extremadura (1988–1992)*.] Mérida Bádajoz: Consejería de Obras Públicas y Medio Ambiente. (In Spanish.)

SÁNCHEZ, J. F., MARTÍNEZ, J. M., MUÑOZ, F., TRUJILLO, D. AND BARONE, R. (1991) [Ornithological news.] *Ardeola* 38: 350. (In Spanish.)

SÁNCHEZ GUZMÁN, J. M., SÁNCHEZ GARCÍA, A., FERNÁNDEZ GARCÍA, A. AND MUÑOZ DEL VIEJO, A. (1993) [*The Common Crane (Grus grus) in Extremadura: its status and relationship with land used for farming*.] Badajóz: Area de Biología Animal, Badajóz University. (In Spanish.)

SÁNCHEZ-LAFUENTE, A. M., MUÑOZ-COBO, J., VALERA, F. AND REY, P. (1987) [On the new nucleus of Crested Coot (*Porphyrio porphyrio* L.) in Jaen province.] In [*Proceedings of the IX Spanish Ornithological Congress*.] Madrid: Sociedad Española de Ornitología. (In Spanish.)

SAN SEGUNDO, C. (1993) The Black Stork in Spain: a review. Abstracts of 1st International Black Stork Conservation and Ecology Symposium.

SANTOS, T. AND ALVAREZ, J. (1990) [Effects of eucalypt plantations on forest bird communities in a Mediterranean maquis (Toledo mountains, west-central Spain).] *Ardeola* 37: 319–324. (In Spanish.)

SARA, M. (1988) [Notes on the distribution of *Alectoris graeca whitakeri* in western Sicily.] Pp.207–216 in M. Spagnesi and S. Tosa, eds. *Atti I Conv. Naz. Biol. Selvaggina (Suppl. Ric. Biol. Selvaggina, XIV)*. Bologna: Instituto nazionale di biologia. (In Italian.)

SATUNIN, K. A. (1907) [Contributions to the knowledge of

the birds of Caucasian area.] *Zapiski Kavkaz. Otd. Russ. Geogr. Ob-stva* 26: 1–144. (In Russian.)

SAUROLA, P. (1985) [Finnish birds of prey: status and population changes.] *Ornis Fenn.* 62: 64–72. (In Finnish.)

SAVARD, J.-P. L. (1986) Territorial behaviour, nesting success and brood survival in Barrow's Goldeneye and its congeners. British Columbia: British Columbia University (Ph.D. thesis).

SCHANDY, T. (1984) [Occurrence and habitat choice of the Great Snipe *Gallinago media* on Hardangervidda, southern Norway.] *Vår Fuglefauna* 7: 205–208. (In Norwegian.)

SCHENK, S., ARESU, H. M. AND SERRA, G. (1987) [Conservation and ecology of the Griffon Vulture (*Gyps fulvus*)in the Sardegna Nord-Occidentale (1971–1984).] Pp.217–234 in Istituto Nazionale de Biologia della Salvaggina, ed. [*Mediterranean raptors III*.] Bologna.

SCHERZINGER, W. (1982) [Woodpeckers in the Bavarian Forest National Park.] *Wiss. Schriftr. Bayer. Staatsmin. ELF* 9: 119. (In German.)

SCHERZINGER, W. (1991) [The mosaic-cycle concept in view of zoological species conservation.] *Laufener seminartbeitr.* 5: 30–42. (In German.)

SCHIERER, A. (1992) [Population of the White Stork in Alsace.] Pp.53–58 in J.-L. Mériaux, A. Schierer, C. Tombal and J.-C. Tombal, eds. [*The storks of Europe*.] Metz: Institut Européen d'Ecologie/AMBE. (In French.)

SCHIFFERLI, A. (1967) [On the migration of Swiss and German Black Kites according to ringing recoveries.] *Orn. Beob.* 64: 34–51. (In German.)

SCHIFFERLI, A., GEROUDET, P. AND NINKLER, R. (1980) [*The atlas of breeding birds in Switzerland*.] Sempach, Switzerland: Station Ornithologique Suisse de Sempach. (In German and French.)

SCHIFFERLI, L. (1993) [Birds in agricultural lands of Switzerland.] *Rev. Suisse Zool.* 100: 501–518.

SCHLÄPFER, A. (1988) [Population studies of the Skylark *Alauda arvensis* in an area of intensive agriculture.] *Orn. Beob.* 85: 309–371. (In German.)

SCHMID, H. (1993) [Status of Green, Grey-headed and Lesser Spotted Woodpeckers (*Picus viridis*, *P. canus* and *Dendrocopos minor* in Switzerland.] *Orn. Beob.* 90: 201–212. (In German.)

SCHMIDT, E. AND FARKAS, T. (1974) [*The Rock Thrush*.] Wittenberg Lutherstadt: Ziemsen-Verlag. (In German.)

SCHMITZ, E. (1905) [Daily observations from Madeira.] *Orn. Jahrb.* 16: 219–226. (In German.)

SCHNEIDER, M. (1988) [Periodically flooded permanent grassland allows optimum breeding success of the White Stork (*Ciconia ciconia*) in the Save-Lowlands (Croatia/ Yugoslavia).] *Vogelwarte* 34: 164–173. (In German.)

SCHRÖDER, P. AND BURMEISTER, G. (1974) [*The Black Stork*.] Wittenberg Lutherstadt.

SCHULZ, H. (1985) A review of the world status and breeding distribution of the Little Bustard. *Bustard Studies* 2: 131–152.

SCHULZ, H. (1988) [*White Stork migration: ecology, threats for and conservation of the White Stork in Africa and the Middle East*.] Weikersheim: Verlag Josef Margraf. (In German.)

SCHULZ, H. (1989) [The migration of the White Stork (*Ciconia ciconia*): results of a WWF-research project.] *Schriftenreihe Bayer. landesamt für Umweltschutz* 92: 77–85. (In German.)

SCHULZ, H. (in press) [On the population status of the White Stork *Ciconia ciconia*: new perspective on the 'Bird of the Year' 1994?.] *Ber. Vogelschutz.*

SCHULZ, R. AND STOCK, M. (1991) Kentish Plovers and tourists. *Wadden Sea Newsl.* 1: 20–24.

SCHULZE-HAGEN, K. (1991) [Aquatic Warbler.] Pp.252–291 in U. N. Glutz von Blotzheim and K. Bauer, eds. [*Handbook of the birds of central Europe, 12*.] Wiesbaden: AULA-Verlag. (In German.)

SCHULZE-HAGEN, K., FLINKS, H. AND DYRCZ, A. (1989) [Prey selection by the Aquatic Warbler *Acrocephalus paludicola* in the breeding season.]*J. Orn.* 130: 251–255. (In German.)

SCHÜZ, E. (1953) [The migration divide of the White Stork: results from ringing recoveries.] *Bonn. Zool. Beitr.* 4: 31–72. (In German.)

SECONA (1992) [*Recovery programme for the Black Vulture in Mallorca*.] Palma de Mallorca: Consejería de Agricultura y Pesca. (In Spanish.)

SELLIN, D. (1989) [Comparative investigation of habitat structure in the Aquatic Warbler.] *Vogelwelt* 110: 198–208. (In German.)

SEMAGO, L. (1985) [The Levant Sparrowhawk.] *Nauka i Zhizn* 7: 159–160. (In Russian.)

SEO (1992) Proposals to declare Madrigal-Peñaranda, Villafáfila and Tierra de Campos as Environmentally Sensitive Areas. Madrid: Sociedad Española de Ornitología (unpublished reports).

SEO (1993) Conservation status and habitat requirements of the Little Bustard. Madrid: Sociedad Española de Ornitología (unpublished report).

SEREZ, M. (1992) Status and conservation of Phasianidae in Turkey. *Gibier Faune Sauvage* 9: 523–526.

SÉRIOT, J. AND ROCAMORA, G. (1992) [*Raptors and aerial electric power-line network in France: analysis of mortality and solutions*.] Rochefort: Electricité de France/ Ligue pour la Protection des Oiseaux. (In French.)

SERRE, D., BIRKAN, M., PELARD, E. AND SKIBNIEWSKI, S. (1989) [Mortality, nesting and breeding success of Partridges (*Perdix perdix belesiae*) in agricultural habitats of the Beauce.]*Gibier Faune Sauvage* 6: 97–124. (In French.)

SHARROCK, J. T. R., ED. (1976) *The atlas of breeding birds in Britain and Ireland*. Calton, U.K.: T. and A. D. Poyser.

SHARROCK, J. T. R. AND RARE BIRDS BREEDING PANEL (1982) Rare breeding birds in the U.K. in 1980. *Brit. Birds* 75: 154–178.

SHAW, G. AND DOWELL, A. (1990) Barn Owl conservation in forests. *Forestry Commission Bull.* 90.

SHAWYER, C. R. (1985) *Rodenticides: a review and assessment of the potential hazard to non-target wildlife with special reference to the Barn Owl* Tyto alba. London: The Hawk Trust.

SHAWYER, C. R. (1987) *The Barn Owl in the British Isles: its past, present and future*. London: The Hawk Trust.

SHAWYER, C. R. (1989) *Habitat requirements of Barn Owls: the future of Barn Owl conservation in Britain*. Symposium Proceedings. London: The Hawk Trust.

SHAWYER, C. (1994) *The Barn Owl*. London: Hamlyn.

SHEPEL, A. I. (1992) [*Birds of prey and owls in the Perm region*.] Irkutsk: Irkutsk University Press. (In Russian.)

SHEVCHENKO, V. L. (1976) [Loss of Steppe Eagles.]*Nature* 8: 144. (In Russian.)

SHEVCHENKO, V. L. AND DEBELO, P. V. (1991) [Sociable Plover in the northern Cis-Caspian.] Pp.165–166 in A. F. Kovshar, ed. [*Rare birds and mammals of Kazakhstan.*] Alma-Ata: Gylym. (In Russian.)

SHIRIHAI, H. AND CHRISTIE, O. A. (1992) Raptor migration at Eilat. *Brit. Birds* 85: 141–186.

SHIRIHAI, H. AND YEKUTIEL, D. (1991) Raptor migration at Eliat, spring 1988. Pp.2–12 in D. Yekutiel, ed. *Raptors in Israel: passage and wintering populations.* Eilat: International Birdwatching Center, Eilat.

SHNITNIKOV, A. V. (1957) [Variability in the general humidity of the northern Hemisphere continents.] *Zapiski Geogr. Obsh. SSSR* 16: 1–336. (In Russian.)

SHORTEN, M. (1974) *The European Woodcock (*Scolopax rusticola*).* Fordingbridge, U.K.: The Game Conservancy (Rep. 21).

SHRUBB, M. (1980) Farming influences on the food and hunting of the Kestrel. *Bird Study* 30: 201–206.

SHRUBB, M. (1993) *The Kestrel.* London: Hamlyn (Hamlyn Species Guides 2).

SIBLEY, C. G. AND MONROE, B. L. (1990) *Distribution and taxonomy of birds of the world.* New Haven: Yale University Press.

SIBLEY, C. G. AND MONROE, B. L. (1993) *A supplement to distribution and taxonomy of birds of the world.* New Haven: Yale University Press.

SIEGFRIED, W. R. AND SKEAD, D. M. (1971) Status of the Lesser Kestrel in South Africa. *Ostrich* 42: 1–4.

SIGG, H. (1991) *Bird conservation priorities in North Cyprus.* Cambridge, U.K.: International Council for Bird Preservation (Study Rep. 42).

SIIVONEN, L. (1935) [On the Redstart's, *Phoenicurus ph. phoenicurus,* pristine nesting habitats.] *Ornis Fenn.* 12: 89–99. (In German.)

SIMEONOV, S. D. AND PETROV, T. H. (1980) Studies on the food of the Imperial Eagle *Aquila heliaca,* the Buzzard *Buteo buteo* and the Rough-legged Buzzard *Buteo lagopus. Ecology* 7: 22–30.

SIMEONOV, S. D., MITCHEV, T. M. AND NANKINOV, D. N. (1990) [*Fauna of Bulgaria, 20: Birds, 1.*] Sofia. (In Bulgarian.)

SIMMS, E. (1985) *British warblers.* London: Collins.

SIOKHIN, V. D. (1988) [*Colonial waterbirds of southern Ukraine.*] Kiev: Naukova Dumka. (In Russian.)

SIRENKO, V. A. (1980) [Influence of anthropogenic factors on wader numbers on the lagoons of Belosarayskoy and Krivoy spits in 1978.] Pp.75–76 in V. E. Flint, ed. [*A novelty in the studies of wader biology and distribution.*] Moscow: Nauka. (In Russian.)

SITTERS, H. P. (1986) Woodlarks in Britain, 1968–83. *Brit. Birds* 79: 105–116.

SKINNER, J. (1987) [Additional information on the Turtle Dove in the Niger flood zone in Mali.] *Malimbus* 9: 133–134. (In French.)

SLUYS, R. AND VAN DEN BERG, M. (1982) On the specific status of the Cyprus Pied Wheatear *Oenanthe cypriaca. Ornis Scand.* 13: 123–128.

SMIT, C. J. AND PIERSMA, T. (1989) Numbers, midwinter distribution, and migration of wader populations using the East Atlantic flyway. Pp.24–63 in H. Boyd and J.-Y. Pirot, eds. *Flyways and reserve networks for waterbirds.* Slimbridge: International Waterfowl and Wetlands Research Bureau (Spec. Publ. 9).

SMIT, C. J. AND WOLFF, W. J., EDS. (1981) *Birds of the Wadden Sea.* Rotterdam: A. A. Baltiema.

SMIT, C. J., LAMBECK, R. H. D. AND WOLFF, W. J. (1987) Threats to coastal wintering and staging areas for waders. *Wader Study Group Bull.* 49 (Suppl.): 105–113.

SMITH, M. E. (1969) The Kingfisher in Wales: effects of severe weather. *Nature in Wales* 11: 109–115.

SMITH, P. C. AND EVANS, P. R. (1973) Studies of shorebirds at Lindisfarne, Northumberland. 1: feeding ecology and behaviour of the Bar-tailed Godwit. *Wildfowl* 24: 135–139.

SMITH, P. H. (1975) The changing status of Little Gulls *Larus minutus* in north Merseyside, England. *Seabird* 10: 12–21.

SNOW, D. W. (1964) Movements and mortality of British Kestrels. *Bird Study* 15: 65–83.

SOF (1990) [*Swedish birds.*] Second revised edition. Stockholm: Sveriges Ornitologiska Förening. (In Swedish.)

SOIKKELI, M. (1990) Breeding success of the common gull in a Finnish population in 1979–87. *Baltic Birds* 5: 159–162.

SOLER, M., ZUÑIGA, J. AND CAMACHO, I. (1983) [Feeding and breeding biology of some bird species in the Hoya de Guadix area (south Spain).] *Trab. Monogr. Dep. Zool. Univ. Granada (N.S.)* 6: 27–100. (In Spanish.)

SOLHEIM, R. (1989) Snowy Owl found breeding in Finnmark. *Vår Fuglefauna* 12: 175–177.

SOLOMATIN, A. O. (1973a) [Biology of the Sociable Plover.] Pp.93–94 in V. E. Flint, ed. [*Fauna and ecology of waders.*] Moscow: Moscow State University. (In Russian.)

SOLOMATIN, A. O. (1973b) [Colonial nesting of waders in the Naurzum zapovednik.] Pp.141–143 in V. E. Flint, ed. [*Fauna and ecology of waders.*]. Moscow: Moscow State University. (In Russian.)

SOLOMATIN, A. O. (1984) [Nesting of harriers in the Pavlodar Priirtyshje.] Pp.155–157 in N. M. Chernova, ed. [*Problems of Regional Ecology, abstracts,* 1: *Third All-Union Conference of Zoologists from Pedagogical Institutes.*] Vitebsk: Vitebsk State Pedagogical Institute. (In Russian.)

SOLONEN, T. (1985) [*Birds of Finland.*] Helsinki: Linnutieto. (In Finnish.)

SOULÉ, M. E., ED. (1986) *Conservation biology.* Michigan: Michigan University.

SOULÉ, M. E., ED. (1987) *Viable populations for conservation.* Cambridge, U.K.: Cambridge University Press.

SOUTHWOOD, T. R. E. AND CROSS, D. J. (1969) The ecology of the partridge 3. Breeding success and the abundance of insects in natural habitats. *J. Anim. Ecol.* 38: 497–509.

SOVON (1987) [*Atlas of the birds of the Netherlands.*] Arnhem: Samenwerkende Organisaties Vogelonderzoek Nederland. (In Dutch.)

SOVON (1988) [New estimates of breeding bird numbers in the Netherlands.] *Limosa* 61: 155–162. (In Dutch.)

SPANGENBERG, E. P. AND LEONOVICH, V. V. (1958) [New data on the geographical distribution and biology of birds on the eastern coast of the White Sea.] Pp.194–202 in D. I. Shcherbakov, ed. [*Problems of the north,* 2.] Moscow: Akademii Nauk SSSR. (In Russian.)

SPIERENBURG, T. J., ZOUN, P. E. F. AND SMIT, T. (1990) Poisoning of wild birds by pesticides. In *Wild bird mortality in the Netherlands 1975–1989.* Working Group on Wild Bird Mortality, NSPB.

SPITZENBERGER, F. (1988) [*Protection of species in Austria,*

8.] Vienna: Ministry for the environment, young people and families (Green Series). (In German.)

SPITZNAGEL, A. (1990) The influence of forest management on woodpecker density and habitat use in floodplain forests of the Upper Rhine Valley. Pp.147–164 in A. Carlson and G. Aulén, eds. *Conservation and management of woodpecker populations.* Uppsala: Swedish University of Agricultural Sciences, Dept. of Wildlife Ecology (Rep. 17).

STAAV, R. (1979) Dispersal of Caspian Terns in the Baltic. *Ornis Fenn.* 56: 13–17.

STASTNY, K., RANDÍK, A. AND HUDEC, K. (1987) [*Atlas of the breeding distribution of birds in Czechoslovakia 1973–1977.*] Prague: Academia. (In Czech.)

STEINER, H. M. AND HÜNI-LUFT, I. (1971) [Distribution and ecology of the Ortlan Bunting (*Emberiza hortulana*) in the Weinviertel.] *Egretta* 14: 44–52. (In German.)

STENBERG, I. (1990) [Preliminary results of a study on woodpeckers in Møre and Romsdal county, western Norway.] Pp.67–79 in A. Carlson and G. Aulén, eds. *Conservation and management of woodpecker populations.* Uppsala: Swedish University of Agricultural Sciences, Dept. of Wildlife Ecology (Rep. 17). (In Swedish.)

STEPANIAN, L. S. (1990) [*Survey of the avifauna of the U.S.S.R..*] Moscow: Nauka. (In Russian.)

STERBETZ, I. (1968) [The migration of the Lesser White-fronted Goose of the Hungarian Puszta.] *Ardea* 56: 259–266. (In German.)

STERBETZ, I. (1974) [*The pratincole.*] Wittenberg Lutherstadt: Ziemsen Verlag. (In German.)

STERBETZ, I. (1982) Migration of *Anser erythropus* and *Branta ruficollis* in Hungary 1971–1980. *Aquila* 89: 107–114.

STEWART, P. F. AND CHRISTENSEN, S. J. (1971) *A check list of the birds of Cyprus.* London: British Ornithologists' Union.

STIEFEL, A. AND SCHLEUFLER, H. (1984) [*The Redshank.*] Wittenberg Lutherstadt: Ziemsen Verlag. (In German.)

STJERNBERG, T., ED. (1981) [*Project Sea Eagle in Finland and Sweden.*] Helsinki: Jord- och Skogbruksministeriet. (In Finnish.)

STOLT, B.-O. (1974) [The occurrence of the Yellowhammer, *Emberiza citrinella* and Ortolan Bunting, *Emberiza hortulana*, at Uppsala during the 1960s.] *Vår Fågelv.* 33: 210–217. (In Swedish.)

STØRKERSEN, Ø. (1992) Norwegian Red list. Directorate for Nature Management (DN-report 1992–6).

STOWE, T. J. AND BECKER, D. (1989) Status and conservation of Corncrakes *Crex crex* outside the breeding grounds. *Tauraco* 2: 1–23.

STOWE, T. J. AND HUDSON, A. (1991a) Radio telemetry studies of Corncrake in Great Britain. *Vogelwelt* 112: 10–16.

STOWE, T. J. AND HUDSON, A. (1991b) Corncrakes outside the breeding grounds, and ideas for a conservation strategy. *Vogelwelt* 112: 103–107.

STOWE, T. J., NEWTON, A. V., GREEN, R. E. AND MAYES, E. (1993) The decline of the Corncrake *Crex crex* in Britain and Ireland in relation to habitat. *J. Appl. Ecol.* 30: 53–62.

STRAZDS, M. (1983) [Great Snipe.] Pp.95–96 in A. Viksne, ed. *Birds of Latvia.* Riga: Zinatne. (In Russian.)

STRAZDS, M. (1993) Distribution and status of the Black Stork within the former U.S.S.R. Abstracts of 1st International Black Stork Conservation and Ecology Symposium.

STRAZDS, M., LIPSBERGS, J. AND PETRINS, A. (1990) Black Stork in Latvia: numbers, distribution and ecology. *Baltic Birds* 5: 174–179.

STRIGUNOV, V. I. (1982) [Nesting of the Long-legged Buzzard in the Ukraine.] *News in Zoology* 4: 71–74. (In Russian.)

STRIGUNOV, V. I. (1984) [Populations and distribution of birds of prey over a forest-steppe zone in Ukraine.] Pp.161–162 in N. M. Chernova, ed. [*Problems of Regional Ecology, abstracts,* 1: *Third All-Union Conference of Zoologists from Pedagogical Institutes.*] Vitebsk: Vitebsk State Pedagogical Institute. (In Russian.)

STROUD, D., REED, T. M., PIENKOWSKI, M. W. AND LINDSAY, R. A. (1987) *Birds, bogs and forestry: the peatlands of Caithness and Sutherland.* Peterborough, U.K.: Nature Conservancy Council.

STROUD, D. A., MUDGE, G. P. AND PIENKOWSKI, M. W. (1990) *Protecting internationally important bird sites. A review of the EEC Special Protection Area network in Great Britain.* Peterborough, U.K.: Nature Conservancy Council.

STRUWE, B. AND NEHLS, H. W. (1992) [Results of international waterbird counts in January 1990 on the German Baltic coast.] *Seevögel* 13: 17–28. (In German.)

SUÁREZ, F. (1980) [Reproduction of *Oenanthe hispanica*.] *Ardeola* 23: 64–79.

SUÁREZ, F. (1987) [Nestling food of two symbiotopic steppe species in the Iberian peninsula: Black-eared and Common Wheatears.] Pp.193–208 in Consejeria de Agricultura, ed. [*First International Congress of Steppic Birds.*] León, Spain: Junta de Castilla y Léon. (In Spanish.)

SUÁREZ, F. (1988) [Natural history of *Oenanthe hispanica* in the breeding season.] Madrid: Universidad Complutense de Madrid (Ph.D. thesis).

SUÁREZ, F. AND GARZA, V. (1989) [Wintering of Dupont's Lark, *Chersophilus duponti*, in the Iberian peninsula.] *Ardeola* 36: 107–110. (In Spanish.)

SUÁREZ, F. AND MANRIQUE, J. (1992) Low breeding success in Mediterranean shrubsteppe passerines. Note on the Thekla Lark *Galerida theklae*, Lesser Short-toed Lark *Calandrella rufescens*, and Black-eared Wheatear *Oenanthe hispanica. Ornis Scand.* 23: 24–28.

SUÁREZ, F., SANTOS, T. AND TELLERÍA, J. L. (1982) The status of Dupont's Lark, *Chersophilus duponti*, in the Iberian peninsula. *Gerfaut* 72: 231–235. (In Spanish.)

SUÁREZ, F., FERNÁNDEZ, A. AND DE LOPE, M. J. (1989) [A note on the effects of aridity on the structure and composition of the passerine community in the high plateau of alpha (*Stipa tenacissima*) in Morocco.] *Bull. Inst. Scientifique* 10: 185–192. (In Spanish.)

SUÁREZ, F., SAINZ, H., SANTOS, T. AND GONZÁLEZ, F. (1991) [*The Iberian peninsula.*] Madrid: Centro de Publicaciones Ministerio de Obras Públicas y Transportes. (In Spanish.)

SUÁREZ, F., YANES, M., HERRANZ, J. AND MANRIQUE, J. (1993) Nature reserves and the conservation of Iberian shrub-steppe passerines: the paradox of nest predation. *Biol. Conserv.* 63: 77–81.

SÜDBECK, P. (1993) [On the territories of the Grey-headed Woodpecker *Picus canus*.] *Beih. Veröff. Naturschutz Landschaftspflege* 67: 143–156. (In German.)

SUETENS, W. (1989) *Raptors of Europe.* Alleur, Belgium:

591

Editions du Perron.

SULLIVAN, M. A. (1985) Common Gulls nesting successfully on a roof in Aberdeen. *Scott. Birds* 13: 229.

SULTANA, J. AND GAUCI, C. (1982) *A new guide to the birds of Malta.* Valetta: Maltese Ornithological Society.

SUMMERS, R. W. AND UNDERHILL, L. G. (1991) The growth of the population of Dark-bellied Brent Geese *Branta b. bernicla* between 1955 and 1988. *J. Appl. Ecol.* 28: 574–585.

SUMMERS, R. W., UNDERHILL, L. G., PEARSON, D. J. AND SCOTT, D. A. (1987) Wader migration systems in southern and eastern Africa and western Asia. *Wader Study Group Bull.* 49 (Suppl.): 15–34.

SUNYER, C. (1992) [Post fledging period.] Pp.47–63 in R. Heredia and B. Heredia, eds. [*The Bearded Vulture* (Gypaetus barbatus) *in the Pyrenees: ecological characteristics and biological conservation.*] Madrid: Instituto Nacional para la Conservación de la Naturaleza. (In Spanish.)

SURVILLO, A. V. (1983) [Ecology of the Steppe Eagle in Kalmykia and eastern parts of the Rostov region.] Pp.56–60 in [*Species and their productivity within the ranges.*] Moscow: Nauka. (In Russian.)

SUSHKIN, P. P. (1914) [On the avifauna of Caucasus.] *Orn. Vestnik* 5: 1–43. (In Russian.)

SUTHERLAND, W. J. AND CROCKFORD, N. J. (1993) Factors affecting the feeding distribution of Red-breasted Geese *Branta ruficollis* wintering in Romania. *Biol. Conserv.* 63: 61–65.

SVAZAS, S. (1992) The threat of an ever increasing oil and industrial activity in Lithuanian coastal waters for the waterfowl areas of international importance. *IWRB Seaduck Bull.* 1: 43–44.

SVAZAS, S. AND PAREIGIS, V. (1992) The significance of Lithuanian Baltic coastal waters for the wintering population of the Velvet Scoter. *IWRB Seaduck Bull.* 1 (Abstract): 41–42.

SVENSSON, S., OLSSON, O. AND SVENSSON, M. (1992) [Changes in the bird fauna. Forecasts of population trends and required research: a literature review.] Solna: Naturvårdsverket.

SWANBERG, P. O. (1965) Studies of less familiar birds, 138: Great Snipe. *Brit. Birds* 58: 504–508.

SWANBERG, P. O. (1986–1987) Migration routes of Swedish Cranes (*Grus grus*): present knowledge. *Aquila* 93/94: 63–72.

SWATSCHEK, I., RISTOW, D., SCHARLAU, W., WINK, C. AND WINK, M. (1993) [Population genetics and pedigree analysis in *Falco eleonorae*.] *J. Orn.* 134: 137–143. (In German.)

SYTNIK, R. M. (1988) [*Rare and endangered plants and animals in Ukraine.*] Kiev: Naukova Dumka. (In Russian.)

SZABÓ, L. V. (1975) Nesting of the Black-winged Pratincole in Hortobágy. *Aquila* 80–81: 55–72.

SZEDERKENYI, N., FAUST, R., VARGA, G., TARNOKY, E., DEKANY, D. AND KOLTAY, P. (1956) [Damage to bees by Bee-eaters.] *Meheszet, Budapest* 3: 125–126. (In Hungarian.)

SZEKELY, T. (1991) Status and breeding biology of Kentish Plovers *Charadrius alexandrinus* in Hungary: a progress report. *Wader Study Group Bull.* 62: 17–23.

TAIT, W. (1924) *The birds of Portugal.* London: H. F. and G. Witherby.

TAPPER, S. C. (1992) *Game heritage: an ecological review from shooting and gamekeeping records.* Fordingbridge,
U.K.: Game Conservancy.

TASKER, M. L., JONES, P. H., BLAKE, B. F. AND DIXON, T. J. (1985) The marine distribution of the Gannet *Sula bassana* in the North Sea. *Bird Study* 32: 82–90.

TASKER, M. L., WEBB, A., HALL, A. J., PIENKOWSKI, M. W. AND LANGSLOW, D. R. (1987) *Seabirds in the North Sea.* Peterborough, U.K: Nature Conservancy Council.

TASKER, M. L., WEBB, A. AND MATTHEWS, J. M. (1991) A census of the large inland Common Gull colonies of Grampian. *Scott. Birds* 16: 106–112.

TEIXEIRA, A. M. AND MOORE, C. C. (1983) The breeding of the Madeiran Petrel *Oceanodroma castro* on Farilhao Grande, Portugal. *Ibis* 125: 382–384.

TEIXEIRA, R. M., ED. (1979) [*Atlas of Dutch breeding birds.*] Deventer: Vereniging tot Behoud Natuurmonumenten in Nederland/Stichting Ornithologisch Veldonderzoek Nederland. (In Dutch.)

TELLERÍA, J. L. (1981) [*Bird migration on the Gibraltar Strait,* 2.] Madrid: Universidad Complutense de Madrid. (In Spanish.)

TELLERÍA, J. L. AND GALARZA, A. (1990) [Avifauna and landscape in northern Spain: effects of exotic tree reforestations.] *Ardeola* 37: 229–245. (In Spanish.)

TELLERÍA, J. L. AND POTTI, J. (1984) [Distribution of warblers (G. *Sylvia* Cl. *Aves*) in the Sistema Central mountains (Spain).] *Doñana Acta Vert.* 11: 93–103. (In Spanish.)

TELLERÍA, J. L., SANTOS, T., ALVAREZ, G. AND SÁEZ-ROYUELA, G. (1988a) [Avifauna of the cereal cultivations in the interior of Spain.] Pp.173–317 in F. Bernís, ed. [*Birds of urban and agricultural areas.*] Madrid: Sociedad Española de Ornitología (Monogr. 2). (In Spanish.)

TELLERÍA, J. L., SUÁREZ, F. AND SANTOS, T. (1988b) Bird communities of the Iberian shrubsteppes: seasonality and structure along a climatic gradient. *Holarctic Ecol.* 11: 171–177.

TELLERÍA, J. L., SANTOS, T. AND DÍAZ, M. (in press) Effects of agricultural practices on bird populations in the Mediterranean region: the case of Spain. In W. Hagemeijer and T. Verstrael, eds. *Bird Numbers 1992. Distribution, Monitoring and Ecological Aspects. Proceedings of the 12th International Conference of IOAC and EOAC.* Voorburg: Samenwerkende Organisaties Vogelonderzoek Nederland/CBS.

TERRASSE, J. F. (1989) [The Black Vulture (*Aegypius monachus*) is still part of the French fauna.] *Alauda* 57: 231–232.

TERRASSE, J. F. (1991) [The Bearded Vulture in the French Pyrenees.] Pp.127–136 in R. Heredia and B. Heredia, eds. [*The Bearded Vulture* (Gypaetus barbatus) *in the Pyrenees: ecological characteristics and biological conservation.*] Madrid: Instituto Nacional para la Conservación de la Naturaleza. (In Spanish.)

TERRASSE, J.-F. AND TERRASSE, M. (1977) [The Osprey *Pandion haliaetus* (L.) in the western Mediterranean.] *Nos Oiseaux* 34: 111–127. (In French.)

TEWES, E. (1992) Food supply of the Black Vulture in Mallorca and other factors relating to its reproduction (unpublished report).

VON THANNER, R. (1905) [A collecting trip on Fuerteventura.] *Orn. Jahrb.* 16: 50–66.

VON THANNER, R. (1910) [Contributions to Gran Canarian

ornithology.] *Orn. Jahrb.* 21: 81–101. (In German.)

THAURONT, M. AND DUQUET, M. (1992) [Distribution and wintering conditions of the White Stork *Ciconia ciconia* in Mali.] Pp.288–296 in J.-L. Mériaux, A. Schierer, C. Tombal and J.-C. Tombal, eds. [*The storks of Europe.*] Metz: Institut Européen d'Ecologie/AMBE. (In French.)

THÉVENOT, M. (1989) [Wintering of Slender-billed Curlew in Morocco.] *Alauda* 57: 47–59. (In French.)

THIBAULT, J. C. (1983) [*The birds of Corsica.*] Ajaccio: Parc Naturel Régional de la Corse. (In French.)

THIBAULT, J. C. (1993) Breeding distribution and numbers of Cory's Shearwater (*Calonectris diomedea*) in the Mediterranean. Pp.25–35 in J. S. Aguilar, X. Monbailliu and A. M. Paterson, eds. *Status and conservation of seabirds: ecogeography and Mediterranean Action Plan. Proceedings II Mediterranean Seabird Symposium, Mallorca, 1989.* Madrid: Sociedad Española de Ornitología/BirdLife/MEDMARAVIS.

THIOLLAY, J. M. (1968a) [Essay on raptors in southern France: distributional ecology.] *Alauda* 36: 179–189. (In French.)

THIOLLAY, J. M. (1968b) [The feeding habits of our raptors: some French findings.] *Nos Oiseaux* 29: 251–269. (In French.)

THIOLLAY, J. M. (1968c) [Notes on the diurnal raptors of Corsica.] *Oiseaux* 38: 187–208. (In French.)

THIOLLAY, J.-M. (1989) Distribution and ecology of Palearctic birds of prey wintering in West and central Africa. Pp.95–109 in B.-U. Meyburg and R. D. Chancellor, eds. *Raptors in the modern World: proceedings of the III World conference on birds of prey and owls. Eilat, Israel 22–27 March 1987.* Berlin and London: World Working Group on Birds of Prey and Owls.

THIRGOOD, S. J. AND HEATH, M. F. (1994) Global patterns of endemism and the conservation of biodiversity. Pp.207–227 in P. L. Forey, C. J. Humphries and R. I. Vane-Wright, eds. *Systematics and conservation evaluation.* Oxford: Clarendon Press.

THOMPSON, K. R. (1987) The ecology of the Manx Shearwater *Puffinus puffinus* on Rum, West Scotland. Glasgow, Scotland: Glasgow University (Ph.D. thesis).

TIAINEN, Y. (1987) [Great Snipe.] *Suomen Luonto* 46: 22–23. (In Finnish.)

TIMMERMAN, A. (1962) [Red-crested Pochard in the Netherlands.] *Limosa* 35: 28–39. (In Dutch.)

TIMOFEEV, A. N. (1990) [Notes on some rare and little known mountain birds of Balkariya.] Pp.234–235 in A. N. Khokhlov, ed. [*Poorly known birds of the northern Caucasus.*] Stavropol: Gos. Pedag. Institut. (In Russian.)

TINARELLI, R. (1993) The Kentish Plover Project in Italy: report for 1992. *Wader Study Group Kentish Plover Project Newsl.* 2: 15–18.

TJALLINGII, S. T. (1970) [Census of breeding Avocets in the Netherlands in 1969.] *Levende Nat.* 73: 222–229, 251–255. (In Dutch.)

TJERNBERG, M. (1981) Diet of the Golden Eagle *Aquila chrysaetos* during the breeding season in Sweden. *Holarctic Ecol.* 4: 12–19.

TKATSHENKO, V. I. (1966) [Ecology of the Gallinaceous birds in the north-west Caucasus Highlands.] *Proc. Teberda State Reservation, Stavropol* 6: 5–144. (In Russian.)

TODD, W. E. C. (1963) *Birds of the Labrador peninsula and adjacent areas.* Toronto: Toronto Press University.

TOMBAL, C. AND TOMBAL, J. C. (1986) [The Gull-billed Tern *Gelochelidon nilotica* in the Ebro delta, Catalogna, during the post-breeding season.] Unpublished. (In French.)

TOMIALOJC, L. (1976) [*Birds of Poland.*] Warsaw: Panstwowe Wydawnictwo Naukowe. (In Polish.)

TOMIALOJC, L. (1990) [*The birds of Poland: their distribution and abundance.*] Warsaw: Panstwowe Wydawnictwo Naukowe. (In Polish.)

TOMIALOJC, L. (1992) [Lesser Grey Shrike *Lanius minor.*] Pp.218–220 in Z. Glowacinski, ed. [*Polish red data book for animals.*] Warsaw: Panstwowe Wydawnictwo Rolniczei i Lesne. (In Polish.)

TOMIALOJC, L. AND WESOLOWSKI, T. (in prep.) [Bird community stability in a primeval forest: 15-year data from Bialowieza National Park (Poland).] *Orn. Beob.* (In German.)

TOMKOVICH, P. S. (1984) [Birds on Franz Josef Land.] *Ornitologiya* 20: 3–17. (In Russian.)

TOMKOVICH, P. S. (1992) Breeding range and population changes of waders in the former Soviet Union. *Brit. Birds* 85: 344–365.

TÖMMERAAS, P. (1978) [Artificial nests for Gyrfalcon *Falco rusticolus* and Peregrine Falcon *Falco peregrinus.*] *Vår Fuglefauna* 1: 142–151. (In Swedish.)

TÖMMERAAS, P. J. (1993) The status of the Gyrfalcon *Falco rusticolus* research in northern Fennoscandia 1992. *Fauna Norvegica, Ser. C. Cinclus* 2: 75–82.

TOROPOV, K. V. (1983) [The birds of prey and owls of the northern Kulunda.] Pp.102–105 in A. P. Kuchin, ed. [*Birds of Siberia, abstracts. Second Siberian Ornithological Conference.*] Gorno-Altaisk: Gorno-Altaisk State Pegagogical Institute. (In Russian.)

TORRES, J. A., ARENAS, R. AND AYALA, J. M. (1986) [Historic evolution of the Spanish population of the White-headed Duck (*Oxyura leucocephala*).] *Oxyura* 3: 5–19. (In Spanish.)

VON TREUENFELS, C.-A. (1989) [*Cranes: birds of luck.*] Hamburg: Rasch und Röhring Verlag. (In German.)

TRIPLET, P. (1981) [Crested Lark *Galerida cristata* in the Somme.] *Oiseau et R.F.O.* 51: 323–328. (In French.)

TRUKHIN, A. M. AND KOSYGIN, G. M. (1987) Distribution of seabirds in ice of the western part of Bering and Chukotsk Seas. Pp.6–21 in N. M. Litvinenko, ed. *Distribution and biology of seabirds of the Far East.* Vladivostok: Academy of Sciences of the U.S.S.R., Far East Branch.

TSIMBOS, T. (1988) Structured development and integrated management. Committee on Nature and Man, Panorama, Athens. (Report to EC-DG XI).

TSOVEL, A. (1990) Autumn migration of soaring birds in the northern valleys, 1988–1989. *Torgos* 17: 47–53.

TUCK, L. M. (1972) *The snipes.* Ottawa: Canadian Wildlife Service (Monogr. 5).

TUCKER, G. M. (1991) The status of lowland dry grassland birds in Europe. Pp.37–48 in P. D. Goriup, L. A. Batten and J. A. Norton, eds. *The conservation of lowland dry grassland birds in Europe.* Peterborough, U.K.: Joint Nature Conservation Committee.

TUCKER, G. M. (1993) Effects of agricultural practices on field use by invertebrate-feeding birds in winter. *J. Appl. Ecol.* 29: 779–790.

TURNER, E. L. (1924) *Broadland birds.* Tavistock, U.K.:

Country Life.

TYE, A. AND TYE, H. (1987) The importance of Sierra Leone for wintering waders. *Wader Study Group Bull.* 49 (Suppl.): 71–75.

UEA KAÇKAR EXPEDITION (1993) Preliminary report.

U.K. RUDDY DUCK WORKING GROUP (1993) News release.

ULFSTRAND, S. AND HÖGSTEDT, G. (1976) [How many birds breed in Sweden?.] *Anser* 15: 1–32. (In Swedish.)

ULLRICH, B. (1971) [Studies on the ethology and ecology of Woodchat Shrike (*L. excubitor*), Lesser Grey Shrike (*L. minor*) and Red-backed Shrike (*L. collurio*).] *Vogelwarte* 26: 1–77. (In German.)

ULLRICH, B. (1987) [Orchards.] Pp.551–570 in J. Hölzinger, ed. [*Birds of Baden-Württemberg, 1: threats and conservation.*] Karlsruhe: E. Ulmer Verlag. (In German.)

UNDERHILL, L. G., PRYS-JONES, R. P., SUROECHKOVSKI, E. E., GOREN, N. M., KARPOV, V., LAPPOR, H. G., VAN ROOMEN, M. W. J., RYBKIN, A., SCHEKKERMAN, H., SPIEKMAN, H. AND SUMMERS, R. W. (1993) Breeding of waders (Charadrii) and Brent Goose *Branta bernicla bernicla* at Pronchisheheva Lake, north-eastern Taimyr, Russia, in a peak and decreasing lemming year. *Ibis* 135: 277–292.

URBAN, E. K. AND BROWN, L. H. (1971) *A checklist of the birds of Ethiopia.* Addis Ababa, Ethiopia: Haile Sellassie I University Press.

URBAN, E. K., FRY, C. H. AND KEITH, S. (1986) *The birds of Africa,* 2. London: Academic Press.

URCUN, J.-P. (1993) [*Study of the spring migration at Pointe de Grave (Gironde), spring 1993.*] Rochefort: Ligue pour la Protection des Oiseaux. (In French.)

URDIALES, C. (1993) [Prospective study for the initiation of a management plan for the Andalusian Hemipode in the Doñana National Park: final report.] Instituto Nacional para la Conservación de la Naturaleza, Parque Nacional de Doñana (unpublished). (In Spanish.)

URDIALES, C. AND PEREIRA, P. (1994) [*Identification key of O. jamaicensis, O. leucocephala and their hybrids.*] Madrid: Instituto Nacional para la Conservación de la Naturaleza. (In Spanish.)

URIOS, V., ESCOBAR, J. V., PARDO, R. AND GÓMEZ, J. A. (1991) [*Atlas of breeding birds in Valencia.*] Valencia: Generalitat Valenciana, Consellería d'Agricultura i Pesca. (In Spanish.)

USHAKOV, V. E. (1916) [Nest and eggs of *Numenius tenuirostris,* Vieill.] *Orn. Vestnik* 3: 185–187. (In Russian.)

USHAKOV, V. E. (1925) [Colonial nesting of the Slender-billed Curlew in Tara district of Omsk government.] *Ural'skiy okhotnik* 2: 32–35. (In Russian.)

VADER, W., ANKER-NILSSEN, T., BAKKEN, V., BARRETT, R. AND STRANN, K.-B. (1989) Regional and temporal differences in breeding success and population development of fish-eating seabirds in Norway after collapses of herring and capelin stocks. Pp.143–150 in S. Myrberget, ed. *Trans 19th IUGB Congress, Trondheim.* Trondheim: Norwegian Institute for Nature Research.

VÄISÄNEN, R. A., JÄRVINEN, O. AND RAUHALA, P. (1986) How are extensive, human-caused habitat alterations expressed on the scale of local bird populations in boreal forests? *Ornis Scand.* 17: 282–292.

VALVERDE, J. A. (1960) [Vertebrates of the Guadalquivir marshes.] *Arch. Inst. Aclim. Almería* 9: 1–168. (In Spanish.)

VALVERDE, J. (1964) [Data on the Marbled Teal in the Marismas.] *Ardeola* 9: 121–132. (In Spanish.)

VALVERDE, J. A. (1967) [*Structure of a community of terrestrial invertebrates.*] Madrid: CSIC (Monogr. 1).

VAN BERKEL, J. B. J. M. (1993) [The Red-backed Shrike in Bargerveen 1978–1990.] *Vogeljaar* 41: 26–33.

VANGELUWE, D. AND STASSIN, P. (1991) [Wintering of the Red-breasted Goose *Branta ruficollis* in northern Dobrogea, Romania, and a review of the species' wintering status.] *Gerfaut* 81: 65–99. (In French.)

VAN NIEUWENHUYSE, D. AND VANDEKERKHOVE, K. (1989) [Population increase of the Red-backed Shrike in the South of the Gaume (Belgium) from 1979–1988.] *Oriolus* 55: 60–65. (In Belgian.)

VARSHAVSKI, S. N., VARSHAVSKI, B. S., GARBUZOV, V. K., KAMNEV, P. I., POPOV, A. V., SHILOV, M. N. AND SHCHEPOTIEV, N. V. (1983) [Peculiar features of distribution and numbers of the Steppe Eagle in the western part of its range in connection with numbers of Little Suslik.] Pp.48–53 in [*Species and their productivity within their ranges.*] Moscow: Nauka. (In Russian.)

VASIC, V., GRUBAC, B., SUSIC, G. AND MARINKOVIC, S. (1985) The status of birds of prey in Yugoslavia with particular reference to Macedonia. Pp.45–53 in I. Newton and R. D. Chancellor, eds. *Conservation studies on raptors.* Cambridge, U.K.: International Council for Bird Preservation (Techn. Publ. 5).

VASILIU, G. D. (1968) [Check-list of Romanian birds.] *Alauda* (Suppl): 1–120. (In French.)

VASSILAKIS, K. AND VASSILAKOPOULOU, R. (1993) *Dam construction at the Nestos River.* Athens: Hellenic Ornithological Society.

VAURIE, C. (1959) *Birds of the Palearctic fauna: passeriformes.* London: H. F. and G. Witherby.

VEEN, J. (1977) Functional and causal aspects of nest distribution in colonies of Sandwich Tern (*Sterna sandvicensis* Lath). *Behaviour (Suppl.).*

VEIGA, J. P. (1985) [*Ecology of raptors in a Mediterranean mountain ecosystem: approach to its community structure.*] Madrid: Universidad Complutense de Madrid. (In Spanish.)

VELASCO, T. (1992) Waders along inland rivers in Spain. *Wader Study Group Bull.* 64: 41–44.

VELASCO, T. AND ALBERTO, L. J. (1993) Numbers, their localities and distribution maps of waders wintering in Spain. *Wader Study Group Bull.* 70: 33–41.

VELIZHANIN, G. A. (1928) [Additions to the avifauna of the Barnaul district.] *Uragus* 1: 12–20. (In Russian.)

VAN DER VEN, J. A. (1986–1987) Results of the first meeting of ICF's Working Group on European Cranes. *Aquila* 93/94: 241–243.

VERNER, W. (1909) *My life among the wild birds in Spain.* London: John Bale, Sons and Danielsson.

VEROMAN, H. (1987) [The population of the White Stork in Estonia in 1984.] *Falke* 5: 138–140. (In German.)

VETROV, V. V. (1991) [White-tailed Sea-Eagle and Imperial Eagle as nesting birds in the Lugansk region, eastern Ukraine.] Pp.109–111 in [*Proceedings 10th U.S.S.R. Ornithological Conference, part 2.*] Minsk. (In Russian.)

VETROV, V. V. (1992) [Nesting of the Pallid Harrier in Volgograd and Rostov regions.] Pp.262–263 in E. N. Nurochkin, ed. [*Modern ornithology 1991.*] Moscow: Nauka. (In Russian.)

VIELLIARD, J. (1970) [The distribution of Ruddy Shelduck *Tadorna ferruginea.*] *Alauda* 38: 87–125. (In French.)

VIKSNE, J. AND ED. (1983) [*Birds of Latvia: territorial dis-*

tribution and numbers.] Riga, Latvia: Zinatne Publishing House. (In Latvian.)

VILLAGE, A. (1989) Factors limiting European Kestrel *Falco tinnunculus* numbers in different habitats. Pp.193–202 in B.-U. Meyburg and R. D. Chancellor, eds. *Raptors in the modern World: proceedings of the III World conference on birds of prey and owls. Eilat, Israel 22–27 March 1987.* Berlin and London: World Working Group on Birds of Prey and Owls.

VILLAGE, A. (1990) *The Kestrel.* London: T. and A. D. Poyser.

VINOGRADOV, V. (1990) *Anser erythropus* in the U.S.S.R. Pp.199–203 in G. V. T. Matthews, ed. *Managing waterfowl populations. Proc. IWRB Symp., Astrakhan, 1989.* Slimbridge, U.K.: International Waterfowl and Wetlands Research Bureau (Spec. Publ. 12).

VIÑUELA, J. (1992) [Reproductive ecology of Black Kite in Doñana National Park.] Madrid: Universidad Complutense de Madrid (Ph.D. thesis). (In Spanish.)

VITOVICH, O. A. (1977) [Reestablishment of Caucasian Black Grouse density in areas after the cessation of grazing.] In [Theses of VIII Ornithological Conference of the U.S.S.R.] Kiev. (In Russian.)

VOINSTVENSKY, M. A. (1950) [Nesting record of the Long-legged Buzzard in the Black Forest, Kirovograd region.] Pp.162–163 in A. B. Kistyakovsky, ed. [*Collection of papers,* 2.] Kiev: Zoological Museum, Kiev State University. (In Russian.)

VOISIN, C. (1991) *The herons of Europe.* London: T. and A. D. Poyser.

VOLSØE, H. (1951) The breeding birds of the Canary Islands, 1. Introduction and synopsis. *Vidensk. Medd. fra Dansk naturh. Foren.* 113: 1–153.

VOOUS, K. H. (1960) *Atlas of European birds.* London: Nelson.

VOOUS, K. H. (1977) *List of recent Holarctic bird species.* London: British Ornithologists' Union.

VOOUS, K. H. (1978) The Scottish Crossbill: *Loxia scotica. Brit. Birds* 71: 3–10.

VOOUS, K. H. (1988) *Owls of the northern hemisphere.* London: Collins.

WADLEY, N. J. P. (1951) Notes on the birds of central Anatolia. *Ibis* 93: 63–89.

WAGNER, T. (1993) [Seasonal changes in the prey composition of the Red-backed Shrike.] *J. Orn.* 134: 1–11. (In German.)

WALLACE, D. I. M. (1969) Observations on Audouin's Gulls in Majorca. *Brit. Birds* 62: 223–229.

WALLIN, K., JÅRÅS, T., LEVIN, M., STRANDVIK, P. AND WALLIN, M. (1983) Reduced adult survival and increased reproduction in Swedish Kestrels. *Oecologia* 60: 302–305.

WALMSLEY, J. G. (1989) Control of breeding Herring Gulls (*Larus cachinnans*). In *Annual Report (1988–1989) of the Biological Station Tour du Valat.* Arles: Biological Station Tour du Valat.

WALTER, H. (1979) *Eleonora's Falcon: adaptation to prey and habitat in a social raptor.* Chicago: Chicago University Press.

WARHAM, J. (1990) *The petrels: their ecology and breeding systems.* London: Academic Press.

WARNES, J. M. AND STROUD, D. A. (1989) Habitat use and food of Choughs on the island of Islay, Scotland. Pp.46–51 in E. Bignal and D. J. Curtis, eds. *Proceedings of an international workshop on the conservation of the Chough* Pyrrhocorax pyrrhocorax *in the EC, 11–14 November 1988.* Tarbento, U.K.: Scottish Chough Study Group.

WATSON, A. (1957) The behaviour, breeding and food-ecology of the Snowy Owl *Nyctea scandiaca. Ibis* 99: 419–462.

WATSON, D. (1977) *The Hen Harrier.* Berkhamsted, U.K.: T. and A. D. Poyser.

WATSON, G. E. (1962) Three sibling species of *Alectoris* partridge. *Ibis* 104: 353–367.

WATSON, J. (1992) Status of the Golden Eagle *Aquila chrysaetos* in Europe. *Bird Conserv. Internatn.* 2: 175–183.

WATSON, J. AND DENNIS, R. (1992) Nest site selection by Golden Eagles in Scotland. *Brit. Birds* 85: 469–481.

WATSON, J., RAE, S. R. AND STILLMAN, R. (1992) Nesting density and breeding success of Golden Eagles in relation to food supply in Scotland. *J. Anim. Ecol.* 61: 543–550.

WAWRZYNIAK, H. AND SOHNS, G. (1977) [*The Aquatic Warbler.*] Wittenberg Lutherstadt: Ziemsen Verlag. (In German.)

WEBB, A., HARRISON, N. M., LEAPER, G. M., STEELE, R. D., TASKER, M. L. AND PIENKOWSKI, M. W. (1990) *Seabird distribution west of Britain.* Peterborough, U.K.: Nature Conservancy Council.

WEBER, P. AND MUNTEANU, D. (1994) [*The atlas of breeding birds of Romania.*] Bucuresti: Sor. (In Romanian.)

WELSH, D. A. (1987) Birds as indicators of forest stand condition in boreal forests of eastern Canada. Pp.259–267 in A. W. Diamond and F. L. Filion, eds. *The value of birds.* Cambridge, U.K.: International Council for Bird Preservation (Techn. Publ. 6).

WESOLOWSKI, T. AND TOMIALOJC, L. (1986) The breeding ecology of woodpeckers in a temperate primaeval forest—preliminary data. *Acta Orn.* 22: 1–21.

WESOLOWSKI, T., GLAZEWSKA, E., GLAZEWSKI, L., NAWROCKA, B., NAWROCKI, P. AND OKONSKA, K. (1985) Size, habitat distribution and site turnover of gull and tern colonies on the middle Vistula. *Acta Orn.* 21: 45–67.

WIDÉN, P., ANDRÉN, H., ANGELSTAM, P. AND LINDSTRÖM, E. (1987) The effect of prey vulnerability: Goshawk predation and population fluctuations of small game. *Oikos* 49: 233–235.

WIETFELD, J. (1981) Bird communities of Greek olive plantations in the breeding season. Pp.127–128 in F. J. Purroy, ed. [*Bird census in the Mediterranean.*] León: León University.

WIKLUND, C. G. AND STIGH, J. (1983) Nest defence and evolution of reversed sexual size dimorphism in Snowy Owls *Nyctea scandiaca. Ornis Scand.* 14: 58–62.

WIKLUND, C. G. AND STIGH, J. (1986) Breeding density of Snowy Owls *Nyctea scandiaca* in relation to food, nest sites and weather. *Ornis Scand.* 17: 268–274.

WILLEBRAND, T. (1988) Demography and ecology of a black grouse Tetrao tetrix population. Uppsala: Uppsala University (Ph.D. thesis).

WILLGOHS, J. F. (1961) The White-tailed Eagle in Norway. *Acta Univ. Bergensis Ser. Math. Rer. Nat.* 12.

WILLIAMSON, K. (1967) The bird community of farmland. *Bird Study* 14: 210–226.

WILSON, J. D. (1993) The BTO birds and organic farming project—one year on. *BTO News* 185: 10–12.

WILSON, J. D. AND BROWNE, J. J. (1993) *Habitat selection and breeding success of Skylarks* Alauda arvensis *on organic and conventional farmland*. Thetford, U.K.: British Trust for Ornithology (BTO Research Rep. No. 129).

WINK, M., WINK, C. AND RISTOW, D. (1980) [Biology of *Falco eleonorae*, 8: clutch size in relation to food supply, hunting success and weight of adult birds.] *J. Orn.* 121: 387–390. (In German.)

WINK, M., WINK, C. AND RISTOW, D. (1982) [Biology of *Falco eleonorae*. 10: the influence of nest-site orientation on breeding success.] *J. Orn.* 123: 401–408. (In German.)

WINK, M., WINK, C., SCHARLAU, W. AND RISTOW, D. (1987) [Philopatry and gene flow in island birds: *Falco eleonorae* and *Calonectris diomedea*.] *J. Orn.* 128: 485–488. (In German.)

WINKLER, R. (1987) [Avifauna of Switzerland, an annotated species list: II non-Passeriformes.] *Orn. Beob.* 6 (Suppl). (In German.)

WINSTANLEY, D. R., SPENCER, R. AND WILLIAMSON, K. (1974) Where have all the Whitethroats gone? *Bird Study* 21: 1–14.

WITT, H.-H. (1977) [On the biology of Audouin's Gull *Larus audouinii*: reproduction and diet.] *J. Orn.* 118: 134–155. (In German.)

WITT, H.-H. (1982) [Diet and breeding distribution of Audouin's Gull *Larus audouinii* in comparison with Yellow-legged Gull *Larus argentatus michahellis*.] *Seevögel* 3: 87–91. (In German.)

WITT, H.-H., CRESPO, J., DE JUANA, E. AND VARELA, J. (1981) Comparative feeding ecology of Audouin's Gull *Larus audouinii* and the Herring Gull *Larus argentatus* in the Mediterranean. *Ibis* 123: 519–526.

WOLDHEK, S. (1979) *Bird killing in the Mediteranean.* Zeist, Netherlands: European Committee for Prevention of Mass Destruction of migratory Birds.

WOOD, N. A. (1975) Habitat preference and behaviour of Crested Coot in winter. *Brit. Birds* 68: 118.

WRI/IUCN/UNEP (1992) *Global biodiversity strategy: guidelines for action to save, study and use earth's biotic wealth sustainably and equitably.* World Resources Institute/International Union for Conservation of Nature and Natural Resources/United Nations Environment Program.

WRIGHT, N. J. R. AND MATTHEWS, D. W. (1980) New nesting colonies of the Ivory Gull *Pagophila eburnea* in southern East Greenland. *Dansk Ornit. Foren. Tidsskr.* 74: 59–64.

WÜST, W. (1986) [*Avifauna of Bavaria,* 2.] München: Orn. Ges. Bayern. (In German.)

YAKUBANIS, V. N. AND LITVAK, M. D. (1962) [Feeding of the Bee-eater in the Dniester area, Moldova.] Pp.49–55 in I. M. Ganja, ed. [*Collected essays of problems in ecology of practical significance regarding the birds of Moldova.*] Kishinev: Stinitsa. (In Russian.)

YALDEN, D. W. AND WARBURTON, A. B. (1979) The diet of the Kestrel in the Lake District. *Bird Study* 26: 163–170.

YANES, M. (in press) The importance of land management in steppe bird conservation in peninsular Spain. In *Proceedings of the III European Forum 'Ecology, Economy and Prospects in Agropastoral Systems'.* Peterborough, U.K.: Joint Nature Conservation Committee.

YEATES, G. K. (1946) *Bird life in two deltas: diaries of a birds' photographer in the estuaries of the Guadalquivir and the Rhone and their neighbourhoods.* Faber and Faber.

YEATMAN, L. (1976) [*Atlas of breeding birds of France.*] Paris: Société Ornithologique de France. (In French.)

YEATMAN-BERTHELOT, D. (1991) [*Atlas of wintering birds in France.*] Paris: Société Ornithologique de France. (In French.)

YEATMAN-BERTHELOT, D. AND JARRY, G. (in press) [*New atlas of breeding birds of France (1985–1989).*] Paris: Société Ornithologique de France. (In French.)

YLIMAUNU, O., YLIMAUNU, J., HEMMINKI, O. AND LIEHU, H. (1987) [Breeding ecology and size of the breeding Curlew *Numenius arquata* population in Finland.] *Lintumies* 22: 98–103. (In Finnish.)

ZANG, H. AND HECKENROTH, H. (1986) [*The birds of Niedersachen.*] Niedersachs: Natursch. (Landschaftspfl. B, H. 2.7). (In German.)

ZARUDNY, N. A. (1888) [Avifauna of the Orenburg territory.] *Zapiski Akad. Nauk.* 1: 1–338. (In Russian.)

ZASTROV, M. (1946) [On the distribution and the biology of the Golden Eagle (*Aquila chrysaetos*) in Estonia.] *Vår Fågelv.* 5: 64–80. (In Swedish.)

ZAWADZKA, D., OLECH, B. AND ZAWADZKI, J. (1990) [Population density, reproduction and food of the Black Stork in the Kampinoski National Park in the years 1979–1987.] *Nottatki Orn.* 31: 5–20. (In Polish.)

ZBINDEN, N. (1984) [Distribution, density and food of the Rock Partridge *Alectoris graeca* in autumn/winter in Tessin.] *Orn. Beob.* 81: 45–52. (In German.)

ZBINDEN, N. (1989) [Critical examination of the situation of the avifauna of Switzerland in the 1980s: Red List of threatened and vulnerable bird species in Switzerland.] *Orn. Beob.* 86: 235–241. (In German.)

ZIMMERMANN, R. (1931) [Biology of the Bittern.] *J. Orn.* 79: 324–332. (In German.)

ZINO, F. J. A. (1992) Cat amongst the Freiras. *Oryx* 26: 174.

ZINO, F. AND BISCOITO, M. (1994) Breeding seabirds in the Madeira archipelago. Pp.172–185 in D. N. Nettleship, J. Burger and M. Gochfeld, eds. *Seabirds on islands: threats, case studies, and action plans.* Cambridge, U.K.: BirdLife International (BirdLife Conservation Series no. 1).

ZINO, F. J. A. AND BISCOITO, M. J. (in press) The interrelation between food availability and reproduction in *Columba trocaz.* Symposium on flora and fauna of the Atlantic islands, Madeira, October 1993.

ZINO, F. J. A. AND ZINO, P. A. (1986) An account of the habitat, feeding habits, density, breeding and need of protection of the Long-toed Wood-pigeon *Columba trocaz. Bocagiana* 97: 1–16.

ZINO, P. A. (1969) [Observation on *Columba trocaz.*] *Oiseau et R.F.O.* 39: 261–264. (In French.)

ZINO, P. A. AND ZINO, F. (1986) Contribution to the study of the petrels of the genus *Pterodroma* in the archipelago of Madeira. *Bol. Mus. Mun. Funchal* 38: 141–165.

ZUBAROVSKI, V. M. (1977) [*Fauna Ukraine,* 5: *birds,* 2.] Kiev: Naukova Dumka. (In Ukrainian.)

ZUCKERBROT, Y. D., SAFRIEL, U. N. AND PAZ, U. (1980) Autumn migration of Quail *Coturnix coturnix* at the north coast of the Sinai peninsula. *Ibis* 122: 1–14.

INDEX OF SPECIES

This index covers only the individual species accounts.